Cost Accounting

Text, Problems and Cases

Sixth Edition

Cost Accounting

Text, Problems and Cases

Sixth Edition

Jawahar Lal
Ex-Head, Department of Commerce
Ex-Dean, Faculty of Commerce and Business
Delhi School of Economics
University of Delhi

Seema Srivastava
Assistant Professor, Department of Commerce
Moti Lal Nehru College (Day)
University of Delhi

Manisha Singh
Dean, Academics
ICFAI Business School, Bengaluru

McGraw Hill Education (India) Private Limited

Published by McGraw Hill Education (India) Private Limited,
Registered Office: Anjana Complex No: 5/90 A, Butt Road, St. Thomas Mount, Chennai – 600016, Tamil Nadu, India.

Cost Accounting, 6/e

First reprint 2023

Print Edition
ISBN-13: 978-93-5316-838-4
ISBN-10: 93-5316-838-4

E-Book Edition
ISBN-13: 978-93-5316-839-1
ISBN-10: 93-5316-839-2

02 03 04 05 06 RAJ 27 26 25 24 23

Managing Director: *Lalit Singh*
Head—Higher Education Portfolio: *Hemant K. Jha*
Project Manager—Production Services: *Atul Gupta*
Head—Production: *Pankaj Manohar*
Manager—Production: *Reji Kumar*

Typeset at Phi Business Solutions Limited, #98-99, Sub-City Centre, Sector 34-A, Chandigrah and printed and bound in India at Rajkamal Electric Press, Kundli, Haryana.

Cover Designer: Creative Designer
Cover Image Source: zhangyang13576997233/Shutterstock
Cover Printer: Rajkamal Electric Press

Visit us at: www.mheducation.co.in
Toll free in India: 1800 103 5875
Write to us at: info.india@mheducation.com
CIN: U80302TN2010PTC111532

Preface to the Sixth Edition

Business is witnessing changes in the environment due to global competition and technological innovations. This change is also visible in the use of accounting and non-accounting information in organisations. Changes in business environment are driven by the business needs to create and sustain a competitive advantage.

The new environment demands more relevant cost and performance information about a business firm's products and activities. To improve their operational activities, business firms require accurate, timely and detailed information. To accomplish this and to sustain the competitive advantage, the study of Cost Accounting is required.

The Sixth edition of Cost Accounting is a continued attempt to deal with the subject of cost accounting in a practical manner. This is to ensure that it becomes a practical guide for business firms to increase their profitability and performance. The fact that the previous editions of the book have been appreciated by the students and the academic community, has inspired us to make the revised edition a highly valuable and user-friendly text. The text provides an update on different aspects of cost accounting in a more logical, lucid and comprehensive manner.

Structure of the Book

The text is structured into five parts.

Part One 'Conceptual Framework' discusses Financial Accounting, Cost Accounting and Management Accounting; Cost: Concepts and Classifications.

Part Two 'Elements of Cost' covers the topics of Materials Control; Materials Costing; Labour Cost: Accounting and Control; Factory Overheads: Distribution; Administrative, Selling and Distribution Overheads; Activity-Based Costing (ABC).

Part Three 'Costing Methods and Accounting of Costs' deals with Single or Output Costing; Job, Contract and Batch Costing; Process Costing; Service Costing; Cost Control Accounts; Integrated Accounting System; Reconciliation of Cost and Financial Accounts.

Part Four 'Cost Analysis for Decision Making and Control' discusses Marginal (Variable) Costing; Alternative Choices Decisions; Pricing Decisions; Standard Costing; Budgeting; Responsibility Accounting and Divisional Performance Measurement.

Part Five 'Specialised Topics' focuses on topics such as Uniform Costing and Inter-firm Comparison; Cost Audit.

Chapter Organisation

All the chapters in the book have been carefully and logically organised to enable students to understand concepts and theories underlying cost accounting. Each chapter has the following components:

- Comprehensive and updated coverage - The book presents latest updated materials on cost accounting concepts, techniques and use of information for planning, control and decision-making.
- Learning objectives - All the chapters in the book begin with learning objectives to provide an overview of chapter contents, and serve as a framework for learning and understanding.
- Solved numerical problems - Solved numerical problems based on real world situations have been included in the chapters for better understanding of cost accounting concepts and techniques.
- Theory questions - Thought provoking theoretical questions are given at the end of each chapter to enable students test their understanding of discussion presented in the chapter.
- Self evaluation questions - These questions given at the end of chapters help students in reviewing the important ideas and explanations presented in the chapters.
- Practical problems - Unsolved numerical problems with answers, with varying difficulty levels, have been given in the relevant chapters.
- Managerial cases - Almost all chapters in the book have managerial cases which would help students to extend their thought process to new situations and to shift from class room to the business world to enhance their analytical power and to use multiple concepts to solve them.

Changes and New Features in the Revised Edition

1. 19 new cases on the topics such as Value-Chain Analysis, Cost Reduction Alternatives, Cost Concept, Material Purchase Control, ABC costing, Contract costing, Decision making, etc. have been included so that readers can relate better.
2. Excel Templates – Chapter-wise additional material accessible via QR code, including Excel Spreadsheets, for the Solved Problems and other Practice Questions that illustrate the application of accounting concepts.
3. All the chapters have been improved and updated in various ways. However, the following chapters have been significantly improved:

   Chapter 1 Financial Accounting, Cost Accounting and Management Accounting
   Chapter 2 Cost: Concepts and Classifications
   Chapter 8 Activity-Based Costing (ABC)
   Chapter 16 Marginal (Variable) Costing
4. Inclusion of additional practical problems - Each chapter now contains new solved and unsolved numerical problems.
5. Adapted problems - Numerical problems, solved and unsolved, have been adapted and included from the examination papers of the following courses:
   - B Com (Hons)/ B Com of Indian Universities
   - Institute of Chartered Accountants of India
   - Institute of Cost Accountants of India
   - CIMA (UK)

Online Supplements

The web supplements contains the following material:

For Instructors: (download from https://connect.mheducation.com)

Solutions Manual, Test Bank, PowerPoint Lecture slides, Solutions to case studies, Excel Templates.

For Students: (download from www.mheducation.co.in)

Test Bank, Solutions to case studies, Excel Templates

Target Market

The sixth edition of the book fits well with the course contents of the following:

(i) MBA, PGDBM, BBA, short term courses & MDPs in Cost Accounting/Management Accounting.
(ii) B. Com (Hons) / B. Com of University of Delhi for the two papers – (1) Cost Accounting, and (2) Management Accounting.
(iii) B. Com and M. Com courses of other Indian universities having these papers.
(iv) C.A. and I.C.W.A. examinations.
(v) M.F.C., MIB, MHRD, C.S., C.F.A. and other professional examinations having a course on Cost Accounting.

It is our strong conviction that this edition would prove highly relevant and useful text to the students pursuing these courses.

ACKNOWLEDGEMENTS

Many people, including our colleagues and friends at different universities and institutes, have helped us in writing this book. We appreciate their assistance and constructive suggestions. To students at University of Delhi, other Indian universities, management institutes and professional institutes who have been using this text and inspiring us, we owe special thanks.

We have been continuously getting all support and encouragement from our family in completing this project. We sincerely acknowledge and appreciate their valuable cooperation.

We would welcome suggestions and opinions from the readers to further improve the quality of the book.

Publisher and the authors would also like to thank the following reviewers for providing their valuable suggestions and comments:

Shankar Jyoti Doley *Delhi School of Economics, Delhi*
Megha Aggarwal *Banasthali University, Vanasthali, Rajasthan*
Madhur Tandon *Jagran Institute of Management, Kanpur, Uttar Pradesh*
Ashu Jain *Amity International Business School, Amity University, Noida, Uttar Pradesh*
Nitin Gupta *Lovely Professional Institution, Phagwara, Punjab*
Sumita Shroff Goyal *Nirma University Institute of Commerce, Ahmedabad, Gujarat*
M Ajoy Kumar *Siddaganga Institute Of Technology, Tumakuru, Karnataka*

Jawahar Lal
Seema Srivastava
Manisha Singh

Preface to the First Edition

This book has been written to serve as a text and provides a vigorous and interesting coverage of the topics in a simple manner. It is designed to help students understand the role of cost accounting, a subject of considerable interest and utility, in accomplishing three broad objectives: (i) cost ascertainment; (ii) cost analysis and cost control; and (iii) managerial decision-making. To achieve these objectives, the contents of the text have been divided into five parts. Part I explains the objectives and role of cost accounting, and basic cost concepts. Part II emphasises the basic elements of cost and Part III discusses cost accumulation and costing making. Part IV is devoted to a discussion on the foundations of managerial planning, control and decision-making. Part V discusses some independent topics which are important in cost accounting.

Part I consists of two chapters which covers the basic concepts and techniques in depth, before a student is exposed to the more vital areas of cost accounting.

Chapter 1 deals with cost accounting, financial accounting, objectives of cost accounting and the cost accounting department.

Chapter 2 provides a survey of basic cost concepts, such as fixed cost, variable cost, semi-variable cost, direct cost, indirect cost, product cost, period cost, opportunity cost, sunk cost, differential cost, joint cost, common cost, and other cost concepts.

Part II is devoted to the basic elements of cost.

Chapters 3, 4, 5, 6 and 7 discuss in detail, each of the components making up the cost of goods manufactured—materials, labour, overhead costs, and expenses.

Part III explains the approaches to product cost accounting, i.e. the basic cost methods. It also stresses methods of accounting systems—integrated and non-integrated.

Chapters 8, 9, 10, 11 describe in great detail cost accumulation methods, such as single costing, job costing, process costing, and operating costing respectively.

Chapters 12, 13, 14 and 15 are devoted to cost control accounts, reconciliation of cost and financial accounts, integrated accounts, and uniform costing and inter-firm comparison.

Part IV consists of four chapters whose principal emphasis is on the internal uses of cost accounting data for managerial planning, control and decision-making.

Chapter 16, 17, 18 and 19 cover and make an in-depth study of budgeting, standard costing and variance analyses, variable costing, and decision-making problems.

Part V comprises four independent chapters which cover a few but important areas in cost accounting.

Chapters 20, 21, 22 and 23 explain responsibility accounting and cost control, marketing cost analyses and decisions, mechanised accounting, cost audit and costing requirements.

I strongly believe that cost accounting books available at present in India and used by the students, both university and professional, have not responded adequately and satisfactorily to their changing requirements and objectives. Most such books lack relevant, up-to-date and adequate material, logical presentation, practical problems, and satisfactory explanation of basic cost accounting concepts, cost analysis, and managerial uses of cost accounting data.

The present book not only avoids the limitation of these presently available books, but also has several features to help students adequately in their academic and professional courses. Basically, it aims at achieving the following important objectives:

- Detailed coverage of all topics and related subject matter in cost accounting.
- Adequate flexibility to fulfil the needs of different university and professional courses in cost accounting which vary in terms of coverage and emphasis.
- Simple, clear and logical presentation, and an integrated approach to the study of cost accounting, making the subject appear as one comprehensive unit.
- A wide range of illustrations beginning with simple ones and subsequently presenting complex problems. This will help create confidence among students and encourage them to accept challenges later.
- A wide range of thought-provoking questions and problems varying in content, length and difficulty. Most problems are new and have been taken from university and professional examinations, such as B Com (Hons), B Com, M Com, CA, ICWA, ICMA and CIMA (UK), CMA and CPA (USA).
- Coordination between the questions and problems at the end of each chapter and the discussions and explanations presented in the body of the chapter. This facilitates the learning process among students and increases understanding of the subject.

The present book will be very useful for the following courses:

- B Com (Hons), B Com and M Com examinations
- The Institute of Chartered Accountants of India examinations (Intermediate)
- The Institute of Cost and Works Accountants of India examinations (Intermediate)
- Company Secretaries examination
- Master of Business Administration (MBA) examination
- The Institute of Chartered Financial Analysts of India
- Other professional examinations

I am grateful to numerous persons and friends who have given valuable suggestions in the course of writing this text. The materials found in an existing source and used in the book have been duly acknowledged. I appreciate the permissions given by various publishers to use the published materials in this text.

To my wife Pratibha, and our children Sanjay, Seema and Rajnish, I acknowledge a special debt. Their constant support, encouragement and patience have greatly eased my burden and made this project possible.

I sincerely welcome criticisms, views and suggestions from readers for improvement of this text.

July 1985 **Jawahar Lal**

List of Abbreviations

SCFP	Statements of changes in Financial Position
GAAP	Generally Accepted Accounting Principles
ICMA	The Institute of Cost and Management Accountants
JIT	Just-In-Time
CIMA	Charted Institute of Management Accountants
WIP	Work-In-Process or Progress
ABC	Activity Based Costing
ABM	Activity Based Management
EOQ	Economic Order Quantity
ROQ	Reorder Quantity
ROL	Recorder Level
TQM	Total Quality Management
AQL	Acceptable Quality Level
FIFO	First-in, First-out
LIFO	Last-in, First-out
HIFO	Highest-in, First-out
WN	Working Note
CVP	Cost-Volume-Profit
BEP	Break-even Point
DMV	Direct Material Variances
DMCV	Direct Material Cost Variance
DMPV	Direct Material Price Variance
DMUV	Direct Material Usage Variance
DLCV	Direct Labour Cost Variance
DLRV	Direct Labour Rate Variance
DLRTV	Direct Labour Rate Time Variance
DLITV	Direct Labour Idle Time Variance
LCV	Labour Cost Variance
LEV	Labour Efficiency Variance
LYV	Labour Yield Variance
LRV	Labour Rate Variance
ITV	Idle Time Variance
LMV	Labour Mix Variance
ZBB	Zero Base Budgeting
PPBS	Planning, Programming and Budgeting System
ROI	Return On Investment
RI	Residual Income

Brief Contents

Detailed Contents

PART 1

Conceptual Framework

The first part of this book discusses the basic nature of financial accounting, cost accounting and management accounting and different cost concepts and classifications. The distinctive features and scope of financial, cost and management accounting alongwith their similarities, dissimilarities and roles have been discussed in the first chapter. The second chapter focuses on different cost classifications for different purposes, cost control, cost reduction and preparation of cost sheet.

- *Financial Accounting, Cost Accounting and Management Accounting*
- *Cost: Concepts and Classifications*

Chapter 1

Financial Accounting, Cost Accounting and Management Accounting

Learning Objectives

After reading this chapter, you should be able to:

1. understand financial accounting, its scope, nature and limitations;
2. describe cost accounting, its objectives, advantages and its importance in management;
3. discuss management accounting, its inter-relationships and dissimilarities with cost accounting and financial accounting;
4. explain costing, its types, methods and techniques;
5. understand the role of cost accounting department in a manufacturing concern;
6. define throughput and backflush costing, cost centres, cost objects, cost drivers and cost units;
7. explain cost accounting system, factors influencing it, its features, difficulties in its installation and arguments against it; and
8. understand the role of management accountant.

Modern business needs continuous information regarding costs of business activities to plan accurately for the future, to control business results, and to make a proper appraisal of the performances of persons working in an organisation. The fulfilment of these goals requires details about the costs incurred and benefits (revenues) obtained which are provided by what are known as "cost accounting", and "management accounting". In comparison, financial accounting does not provide management with detailed cost and revenue information relevant to its needs. Before examining the nature and contribution of cost accounting it would be appropriate to discuss the nature of financial accounting and its limitations in greater detail.

FINANCIAL ACCOUNTING

Financial accounting is concerned with providing information to external users such as shareholders (existing and potential), creditors, financial analysts, labour unions, government authorities, and the likes. Financial accounting is oriented towards the preparation of financial statements which summarise the results of operations for selected periods of time and show the financial position of the business at particular dates. The following points are important to understand the scope and nature of financial accounting:

Objectives

The basic objective of financial accounting is to provide useful information, through preparing general purpose reports, to investors, creditors and other users in making sound investment and economic decisions. These general purpose reports provide information on management performance to judge its effectiveness in utilising the resources and running the enterprise.

Contents

The end product of the financial accounting process is the financial statements that communicate useful information to decision-makers such as profit and loss account, balance sheet and cash flow statement.

Accounting System

Journals, ledgers and other accounting techniques used in financial accounting depend upon the concept of the double-entry system. Financial accounting also uses Generally Accepted Accounting Principles (GAAP)[1] to record, classify and summarise business transactions and to prepare financial statements.

Measurement Unit

Financial accounting measures business transactions, economic resources and economic obligations and changes in them in terms of monetary units of a society in which it operates. For example, the common denominator or yardstick used for accounting measurement is the rupee in India and dollar in U.S.A.

Users of Financial Accounting Information

As stated earlier, financial accounting information is intended primarily to serve external users. Examples of such users are owners, creditors, potential owners, suppliers, management, tax authorities, employees, customers, financial analysts and advisers, stock exchanges, financial press and reporting agencies, trade associations, labour unions, general public etc.

LIMITATIONS OF FINANCIAL ACCOUNTING

Financial accounting is significant for managements as it helps them to direct and control the firm's activities and functions and to determine appropriate managerial policies in different areas, such as production, sales, administration and finance. However, financial accounting suffers from the following limitations which have been responsible for the emergence of cost accounting:

---

1. Generally Accepted Accounting Principles (GAAP) encompass the conventions, rules and procedures necessary to define accepted accounting practice at a particular time.

1. Financial accounting does not provide detailed cost information for different departments, processes, products, jobs, different services and functions.
2. Financial accounting does not set up a proper system of controlling materials and supplies which leads to losses on account of misappropriation, misutilisation, scrap, defectives, etc.
3. The recording and accounting for wages and labour are not done for different jobs, processes, products and departments. This creates problems in analysing the cost associated with different activities and rewarding workers and employees for the above-average performance.
4. It is difficult to know the behaviour of costs in financial accounting as expenses are not classified into fixed and variable, direct and indirect costs.
5. Financial accounting does not possess an adequate system of standards to evaluate the performance of departments and employees working in the departments.
6. Financial accounting contains historical cost information which is accumulated at the end of the accounting period. The historical cost is not a reliable basis for predicting future earnings, solvency, or overall managerial effectiveness.
7. Financial accounting does not provide necessary information to management in taking important decisions about expansion of business, dropping of a product line, starting a new product, alternative methods of production, improvement in product etc.
8. Financial accounting does not provide cost data to determine the price of the product being manufactured or the service being rendered to the consumers.

In spite of the above limitations, financial accounting has utility and will continue to serve management in the future also. Because of growing business requirements, the scope of financial accounting is changing and can be expected to continue to change.

COST ACCOUNTING

Cost accounting, as a tool of management, provides management with detailed records of the costs relating to products, operations or functions. Cost accounting refers to the process of determining and accumulating the cost of some particular product or activity. It also covers classification, analysis and interpretation of costs. The costs so determined and accumulated may be the estimated future costs for planning purposes, or actual (historical) costs for evaluating performance. The Institute of Cost and Management Accountants (ICMA), London, defines cost accounting as "the process of accounting for cost from the point at which expenditure is incurred or committed to the establishment of its ultimate relationship with cost centres and cost units. In its widest usage, it embraces the preparation of statistical data, the application of cost control methods and the ascertainment of the profitability of activities carried out or planned".

COST ACCOUNTANCY

Cost accounting has been differentiated from cost accountancy. The Institute of Cost and Management Accountants, London has defined cost accountancy as the "application of costing and cost accounting principles, methods and techniques to the science, art and practice of cost control and ascertainment of profitability as well as presentation of information for the purpose of managerial decision-making". According to this definition, the term "cost accountancy" includes costing, cost accounting, budgetary control, cost control and cost audit. Although literature in the U.K. in the area of cost accounting tends to differentiate between cost accounting and cost accountancy, U.S. literature does not appear to point out any basic difference between these two terms.

COSTING

Costing is defined as "the technique and process of ascertaining costs".

According to CIMA, "An organisation costing system is the foundation of the internal financial information system for managers. It provides the information that management needs to plan and control the organisation's activities and to make decisions about the future."

COST ACCOUNTING AND MANAGEMENT

Management requires adequate, systematic and useful cost data and reports to manage a business enterprise and to achieve business objectives. The useful information provided by cost records and reports in cost accounting assists management in performing the following important tasks:

1. Cost accounting helps in determination and analysis of cost of departments, processes, jobs, products, sales territories, sales order etc. This advantage is not available to manufacturing companies alone. In fact, the analysis of cost and income can be made in almost all types of organisation—profit or non-profit.

   The example given below points out how cost accounting by products, may reveal facts and data which cannot be developed in financial accounting. Cost statements produced at regular, short intervals, which are not prepared in financial accounting, would have enabled the firm to take prompt action to overcome the problems of producing and selling Product C.

   The analysis (based on cost statements) points out that the contribution of firm products to total net profit (15%) vary significantly among products. Product C does not cover its prime costs, and causes a net loss to the firm of ₹8,000 in the year; its selling and distribution costs are also particularly more compared to the other products.

   The firm may decide to discontinue Product C, but before deciding this, an enquiry may be made of the cost structure to find out whether or not more efficient manufacturing, selling and distribution are possible. At the same time, attention must be paid to pricing policy. It should be investigated as to whether the selling price of this product can be increased to a profitable level.

Table 1.1 Cost Statements

Particulars	*A*	*B*	*C*	*D*	*Total*
Sales	₹60,000	₹60,000	₹40,000	₹40,000	₹2,00,000
Materials	30,000	22,000	26,000	24,000	1,02,000
Wages	12,000	8,000	12,000	8,000	40,000
Direct Exp.	2,000	2,000	3,000	1,000	8,000
Prime Cost	44,000	32,000	41,000	33,000	1,50,000
Work Exp.	1,600	2,000	500	200	
Selling Exp.	400	1,600	2,000	400	

(Contd.)

Particulars	*A*	*B*	*C*	*D*	*Total*
Distribution Exp.	1,000	400	3,500	200	
General Adm. Exp.	1,000	4,000	1,000	200	
Overhead costs	4,000	8,000	7,000	1,000	20,000
Total Cost	48,000	40,000	48,000	34,000	1,70,000
Profit	12,000	20,000	–(8000)	6,000	30,000
Percentage Profit/Loss	20%	$33\frac{1}{3}\%$	(–)20%	15%	15%

2. Cost accounting helps management in controlling cost which is probably the most important objective of every business firm. Cost accounting facilitates this task through accumulation and utilisation of cost data regarding different products, activities or functions. Each cost should be examined in the light of service or benefit obtained so that management can keep the cost at the lowest possible point.
3. One of the important uses (perhaps the most important) of cost information is in helping to make revenue decisions. Revenue decisions can be divided into the following three categories:
   (i) Pricing—Cost data are vital in pricing new products, and to make a decision as to whether to lower or raise a price.
   (ii) Product mix—Management generally has to make short-term and long-term product mix decisions. For short-term cost, data are used to determine which product to push in the market. Similarly, in the long-run the questions of increasing and decreasing capacity can be solved with the help of relevant cost information.
   (iii) Profit-volume decisions—Profit is mainly the result of a combination of three factors, namely cost, volume and selling price. Decisions like reducing price and having additional sales, maintaining *status quo* and accepting a lower income, increasing quality of the product and having extra volume of sales, increasing selling price and improving the turnover, are significant.

   Cost data assists managements in making sound decisions in all these important areas.
4. Cost accounting helps in making special cost studies and investigations which are vital to management in formulating policies and plans directed towards profitable operations. Such special studies include pricing of a new product or new services, elimination of seasonal conditions, expansion or contraction programmes, replacement of machinery and equipment, dropping a product, changes in methods of distributing products and changes in production methods.
5. Cost accounting assists and participates in the formulation and execution of budgets and standards. Cost information for managerial decision-making and planning is the most important justification of a sound cost accounting system.

OBJECTIVES OF COST ACCOUNTING

There is a direct relationship among information needs of management, cost accounting objectives, and techniques and tools used for analyses in cost accounting. Cost accounting has the following three important objectives:

1. To determine product costs.
2. To facilitate planning and control of regular business activities.
3. To supply information for short- and long-run decisions.

Product Costing

The objective of determining the cost of products is of prime importance in cost accounting. The total product cost and cost per unit of product are important in making inventory valuation, deciding price of the product, and managerial decision-making. Product costing covers the entire cycle of accumulating manufacturing and other costs and subsequently assigning them to work-in-progress and finished goods.

Planning and Control

Another important objective of cost accounting is the creation of useful cost data and information for the purposes of planning and control by management. The different alternative plans are evaluated in terms of respective cost and associated benefits.

The management control over business operations aims to establish balance between actual and budgeted performances. A properly designed cost accounting system includes the following steps in the control process:

1. Comparing actual business performances with budgets and standards.
2. Analysing the variance between budget and standards and actuals by causes, and management responsibility so that corrective action may be taken.
3. Providing managers with data and reports about their individual performances and performance of subordinates.

Information for Decisions

An important purpose of the cost accounting system is to provide data and special analyses for short- and long-run decisions of a non-recurring nature. Appropriate cost information must be accumulated to make a wide variety of short- and long-run decisions.

According to Henke and Spoede,[2] the following are the objectives of cost information developed in cost accounting:

1. As a basis for valuing manufactured inventories and cost of goods sold in externally presented financial reports.
2. In controlling operations through the evaluation of operating results and the placement of responsibilities for the uses of organisational resources on the shoulders of specifically identifiable persons within the organisation.
3. In planning operations through the establishment of cost and budgetary goals.
4. In making day-to-day operating decisions (a part of controlling operations).

[2] Emerson O. Henke and Charlene W. Spoede, *Cost Accounting: Managerial Use of Accounting Data,* PWS-KENT Publishing Company, Boston, 1991, p. 5.

COST ACCOUNTING VS. FINANCIAL ACCOUNTING

Financial accounting is that branch of accounting which accumulates and presents data primarily for use by investors, creditors and other external parties. Financial accounting is designed to meet external information needs and to comply with generally accepted accounting principles.

Cost accounting focuses primarily on accounting for the flows of costs and is concerned with the development of systems for relating costs to the products or services produced by an organisation.

Financial accounting and cost accounting differ in the following respects:

1. *Nature* Basically, financial accounting classifies, records, presents and interprets, in terms of money, transactions and events that are of a financial character, and provides management with the facts and figures necessary for the preparation of the periodic financial statements—the balance sheet, the income statement and the cash flow statement. Financial accounting provides information about the business in a general way. In contrast to financial accounting, cost accounting classifies, records, presents and interprets, in a significant manner, the material, labour and overhead costs involved in manufacturing and selling each product, or each job or rendering a service.
2. *Primary users of information* The users of financial accounting statements are mainly external to the business enterprise such as shareholders, creditors, financial analysts, government authorities, stock exchange, labour unions, etc.

   The information generated under the cost accounting system is used by members of management at different levels. Thus, different sets of information could be developed under cost accounting and supplied to different persons responsible for activities in the organisation. Cost accounting provides information to the management for proper planning, operation, control and decision-making.
3. *Accounting system* Financial accounting strictly follows the double-entry system for recording, classifying and summarising business transactions. Cost accounting may not be based on the double-entry system. The data under cost accounting may be gathered for small or large segments or activities of an organisation, and monetary as well as other measures can be used for different activities in the firm.
4. *Accounting principles* Financial accounting data is primarily meant for external users. The "generally accepted accounting principles" are important in financial accounting and are used extensively while recording, classifying, summarising and reporting business transactions.

   On the contrary, cost accounting is not bound to use "the generally accepted accounting principles". It can use any accounting technique or practice which generates useful information.
5. *Analysis of profit* Financial accounts in financial accounting give the accounts of the whole business and disclose the net profit or loss of the business as a whole. However, cost accounting discloses profit or loss of each product, job, service or division. In financial accounting, costs are reported in aggregate while costs are broken down on a unit basis in cost accounting.
6. *Scope of transactions* Financial accounting relates to all commercial transactions of a business and includes all expenses in preparing financial accounts. However, cost accounting and cost accounts relate to transactions connected with the manufacture of goods and services and include only those expenses which enter into the production.

Financial accounts are concerned with external transactions, that is, transactions between the business concern on one side and third parties on the other. These transactions form the basis for payment or receipt of cash. Cost accounts are concerned with internal transactions which do not form the basis of payment or receipt of cash.

7. *Unit of measurement* All information under financial accounting is in terms of money. That is, transactions measured in terms of money have already occurred. In comparison, cost accounting applies any measurement unit that is useful in a particular situation. Besides the monetary unit, the cost accountant may find it necessary to use such measures as labour hours, machine hours and product units for the purpose of analysis and decision-making. Financial accounts deal mainly with historical actual facts and figures whereas cost accounts deal partly with historical facts and figures and partly with future estimates and projections.
8. *Time span* Financial accounting data and statements are developed for a definite period, usually yearly, half yearly, quarterly. It requires financial statements to be developed and presented at regular time-intervals. Cost accounting reports and statements are prepared whenever needed. Reports may be prepared on a monthly, weekly or even daily basis. Frequency of reports is determined by particular planning and controlling needs, objectives of cost control and cost determination.

Inspite of the above differences, both financial and cost accounting are in agreement regarding actual cost data and product costing analyses. Closing inventory values and cost of goods manufactured and sold are the main examples. For the preparation of the income statement, financial accountant receives the necessary data from the cost accountant.

MANAGEMENT ACCOUNTING

Management accounting deals with providing information including financial accounting information to managers for their use in planning, decision-making, performance evaluation, control, management of costs and cost determination for financial reporting. Management accounting contains reports prepared to fulfil the needs of managements.

The National Association of Accountants (USA), in Statement No. 1A (Statements on Management Accounting, 1982), has defined management accounting as:

> "...the process of identification, measurement, accumulation, analysis, preparation and communication of financial information used by management to plan, evaluate, and control within the organisation and to assure appropriate use and accountability for its resources."

The CIMA (UK) defines the term, "management accounting" in the following manner:

> "Management accounting is an integral part of management concerned with identifying, presenting and interpreting information used for:
>
> 1. formulating strategy;
> 2. planning and controlling activities;
> 3. decision taking;
> 4. optimising the use of resources;
> 5. disclosure to shareholders and others external to the entity;
> 6. disclosure to employees; and
> 7. safeguarding assets."

Thus, management accounting is concerned with data collection from internal and external sources, analysing, processing, interpreting and communicating the information for use within the organisation so that management can more effectively plan, make decisions, and control operations.

Management accounting is not only confined to the area of product costing, cost and price data. In management accounting, the objective is to have a data pool which will include any and all information that management may need. For example, if management decides to depend on long-terms debt for expansion of business, it may be investigated as to what effect this decision will have upon the earnings per share? Should debt in the equity structure be too large or small? Similarly, management may be interested in knowing the adequacy of cash flow receipts to pay current obligations or the effect of inflation on business decisions and performances. Thus, this field of accounting helps management in the total situation. In achieving this goal, management accounting makes use of information that is drawn from financial accounting and other disciplines, such as economics, finance, statistics, operational research and the like.

The term "management" includes the activities and functions of all individuals who are working at different positions in an organisation such as

- Executive directors with management responsibilities
- Senior managers
- Middle-level managers
- Lower-level managers
- Supervisors/inspectors/foremen and other personnel in a supervisory position
- Employees and workers (who are not in the position of managers) such as operating workers; production line workers; employees, workers and clerks working in different departments; salespersons.

Management accounting, in future, may include many areas of managerial and operating activities to help managers in their tasks and business firms to achieve its objectives and vision. Further, it is likely that management accounting may discard some of its activities currently within its scope and include some new activities as mainstream management accounting activities to cope with changing complex business environment. The following table summarises some of the areas considered to be part of management accounting:

Table 1.2 Some Areas of Activity Considered to be Part of Management Accounting

- Budgeting, planning and forecasting
- Calculating the profitability of products, services and operations
- Measuring organisational, divisional and departmental performance
- Comparing results and performance within and between organisations
- Assisting in the performance of increasing effectiveness and efficiency
- Assessing the performance of past and future capital investments
- Advising on decisions about product mix, markets to be served and selling prices
- Advising on decisions on whether to outsource products, components, activities and services
- Advising on decisions involving the investment of scarce funds between a range of possible alternatives
- Assisting in the making of a wide range of strategic decisions.

Source: Hugh Coombs, David Hobbs and Ellis Jenkins, *Management Accounting*, Sage Publications, New Delhi, 2007, p.7.

COST ACCOUNTING AND MANAGEMENT ACCOUNTING

Although over the years, the subject matter of cost accounting has broadened, it is concerned mainly with the techniques of product costing and deals with only cost and price data. It is limited to product costing procedures and related information processing. It helps management in planning and controlling costs relating to both production and distribution activities.

Management accounting may be defined as the application of accounting techniques for providing information designed to help all levels of management in planning and controlling the activities of a business enterprise and in decision-making. In management accounting, the objective is to have an information system which may provide all information that management may need for planning, control and decision-making. For example, if management decides to depend on equity capital for expansion of business, it may be investigated as to what effect this decision will have upon the company's share prices. Similarly, management may be interested in knowing the adequacy of cash inflows to pay liabilities on the due date or the effect of growing competition and use of latest technology on business decisions and performances. Thus, management accounting helps management in the total situation and in accomplishing all managerial functions.

Some points of distinction between cost accounting and management accounting are as follows (Table 1.3):

Table 1.3 Differences between Cost Accounting and Management Accounting

Cost Accounting	*Management Accounting*
1. Cost accounting is primarily concerned with cost ascertainment and supplying cost information to managers and others involved in planning, control and decision-making.	1. Management accounting deals with the total situation and aims to provide all relevant information including financial accounting, cost accounting to persons working at different levels in an organisation.
2. It focuses on cost control and cost reduction to maximise profit.	2. Management accounting deals with planning, controlling and decision-making.
3. It can be established and can function without management accounting.	3. Management accounting cannot operate without first installing cost accounting system in an organisation.
4. Maintenance of cost accounts is compulsory in certain specified industries as per the Companies Act.	4. Management accounting is optional and need not be compulsorily installed in organisations.
5. It uses techniques like, marginal costing, breakeven analysis, standard costing, uniform costing, inter firm comparison for cost analysis and cost control.	5. Management accounting may use techniques available in cost accounting, financial accounting and other techniques available in other disciplines such as operational research, economics, etc.
6. Cost accountants help in the functions of cost ascertainment, cost analysis and cost control.	6. Management accountants provide essential services to management and actively participate in planning, controlling, and decision-making as well.

In spite of the differing parameters of cost accounting and management accounting cost, accounting is generally indistinguishable from what is known as management or managerial accounting. Both these accounting systems are closely linked as they use common basic data and reports to a significant degree. Much of the information used to prepare accounting statements and reports in cost accounting is also used in management accounting reports. Management accounting utilises the same (and also additional) data to prepare budgets, performance reports, control reports, and data analyses for decision-making, planning and control purposes.

DIFFERENCES BETWEEN MANAGEMENT ACCOUNTING AND FINANCIAL ACCOUNTING

The differences between cost accounting and financial accounting are also the points of difference between management accounting and financial accounting. As stated earlier, financial accounting implies the preparation of a set of financial statements, for each accounting period, in accordance with laws, rules, regulations and accounting standards and is concerned with shareholders, governmental authorities and other parties outside the business enterprise. Management accounting is not governed by any statute and is an internal function which aims to provide information to management.

Financial accounting takes an overall view of a business enterprise by totalling the results of its divisions and departments into a single summarised financial statement. Management accounting focuses attention at the lowest levels of production or any other activity in the organisation for providing help in planning, controlling and decision-making.

Financial accounting records past historical information. However, management accounting primarily uses present and future information. The past information in management accounting acts only as a guide in predicting the future.

COST ACCOUNTING, FINANCIAL ACCOUNTING AND MANAGEMENT ACCOUNTING

The discussion in the preceding paragraphs has tried to bring out differences as well as interdependency between cost accounting, financial accounting and management accounting. It is significant to note that all accounting information tends to rely on the same basic data system and set of accounts. Although an organisation can have different accounting systems designed for different purposes, some companies still depend on a single system to provide the basic accounting information. The single system typically focuses on providing information for financial accounting purposes, but its informational output can be adopted to meet most internal management requirements.

Barfield, Raiborn and Kinney[3] observe:

> "Cost accounting creates an overlap between financial accounting and management accounting. Cost accounting integrates with financial accounting by providing product costing information for financial statements and with management accounting by providing some of the quantitative, cost-based information managers need to perform their tasks.
>
> The cost accounting overlaps cause the financial and management accounting systems to articulate or be joined together to form an informational network. As these two systems articulate, accountants must understand how cost accounting provides cost information for financial statements and supports management

3. Jesset T. Barfield, Cecily A. Raiborn and Michael R. Kinney, Cost Accounting, Traditions and Innovations, 5th Edition, Thomson South Western, 2003, p.7.

information needs. Organisations that do not manufacture products may not require elaborate cost accounting systems. However, even service companies need to understand how much their services cost so that they can determine whether it is cost-effective to be engaged in particular business activities or not."

There is no realistic dividing line between cost accounting and management accounting particularly with regard to the provision of information for planning and control. Cost accounting is at a more basic level than management accounting and in many organisations is primarily concerned with the ascertainment of product costs. But the cost accounting system is also an important source of data for management accounting purposes.[4]

ROLE OF MANAGEMENT ACCOUNTANT

A management accountant is an accountant who participates in all accounting work within the organisation, including maintaining the accounting records, preparing financial statements, preparing many specialised managerial reports and statements, generating information for different levels of management, coordinating budgeting, accounting and reporting functions. Management accountant plays a vital role in helping managers in performing management functions such as planning, organising, coordination, control, decision-making etc. However, the management accountant is a part of the management and not just a service arm to management. He acts as a manager and decision-maker and exercises managerial influence and, of course, is responsible for the management of the entire accounting, reporting and budgeting functions.

ADVANTAGES OF COST ACCOUNTING

Business enterprises can derive many advantages from the cost accounting system. Some advantages are listed below:

1. The cost accounting system provides data about profitable and unprofitable products and activities. After investigating the causes of low profitability and unprofitability, management can take suitable corrective measures which may lead to higher profit.
2. All items of costs can be analysed to minimise the losses and wastage emerging from the manufacturing process and reduce the costs associated with different activities.
3. Production/manufacturing methods may be improved or changed so that costs can be controlled and profit increased.
4. Cost data can be obtained and compared with standard cost within the firm or industry.
5. Cost accounting helps management in avoiding losses arising due to many factors, such as low demand, competitive conditions, change in technology, seasonal demand for the product and the like.
6. Cost accounting also provides cost data and information to determine the price of the product. The cost of the product is perhaps the most important determinant of product pricing.
7. Negotiations with government and labour unions can easily be made with the information provided by the cost accounting system.

---

4. T. Lucey, Management Accounting, ELBS, London, 1996, p. 2.

8. Cost accounting helps management in knowing the costs of different alternatives and selecting the most advantageous course of action. Decisions like make or buy, continue or drop a product, buy or lease, sell or process further, operate or shut down and other short-term decisions are easily solved with the help of cost accounting data.
9. More accurate and reliable financial accounts can be prepared promptly for use of management.
10. An adequate cost accounting system ensures maximum utilisation of physical and human resources, checks fraud and manipulations, and helps employees as well as the employers in their basic goals of getting higher earnings and maximising the profit of the concern.

METHODS OF COSTING

As stated earlier, the term "costing" refers to the techniques and processes of determining costs of a product manufactured or a service rendered. Different methods are applied in business enterprises to ascertain costs depending upon the nature of the product, production method and specific business conditions. For example, in a textile or steel company, raw material passes through different stages (processes) and production is done continuously. In some other industries, production is done at different customers' specific orders and each job is obviously different from the other jobs. In service industries like transport, hospital, banks etc., all activities and costs incurred relate mainly to performing certain services (or activities). There are two methods of costing:

(A) Job Costing
(B) Process Costing

All other methods of costing are only variants of the above two methods of costing. All possible variations of job and process costing are as follows:

(A) Job Costing	**(B) Process Costing**
(i) Batch Costing	(i) Unit or Single Output Costing
(ii) Contract or Terminal Costing	(ii) Operating (Service) Costing
(iii) Multiple or Composite Costing	(iii) Operation Costing

Job Costing

Job costing is used in those business concerns where production is carried out as per specific order and customers specifications. Each job (or product) is separate and distinct from the other jobs or products. The method is popular in enterprises engaged in house-building, ship-building, machinery production and repair. Job costing has the following variants:

(i) Batch Costing

Batch costing is used to determine the cost of a group of identical or similar products. The batch consisting of similar products is the unit and not the single item within the batch. This method can be usefully applied for the production of nuts and bolts, medicines, components and other items which are manufactured in distinct batches.

(ii) Contract or Terminal Costing

This method of costing, based on the principle of job costing, is used by house builders and civil contractors. The contract becomes the cost unit for which relevant costs are accumulated.

(iii) Multiple or Composite Costing

This costing method is used in those industries where the nature of the product is complex, such as motor cars, aeroplanes, etc. In such cases, costs are accumulated for different components making the final product and then totalled to ascertain the total cost of the product.

Process Costing

This costing method is used in those industries where production is done continuously, such as chemicals, oil, gas, paper, etc. It is difficult to trace the costs to specific units and the total cost is averaged for the number of units manufactured. Sometimes, total cost and per unit cost is calculated at each stage of production for control purposes. Process costing has the following variants:

(i) Unit or Single Output Costing

This method is used where a single item is produced and the final production is composed of homogeneous units. The per-unit cost is obtained by dividing the total cost by the total number of units manufactured.

(ii) Operating (Service) Costing

Operating costing method is used by those organisations which render services and do not manufacture any physical item, such as transport, power house, hospital etc. The cost units differ among these service organisations depending upon the nature of service being rendered. But usually, the units are passenger-mile, tonne-mile, a bed in hospital, and per student in a college.

(iii) Operation Costing

This costing method aims at ascertaining the costs of each operation rather than the process. In this method, the assumption is that the output is achieved through a number of different operations. In the industries where process consists of distinct operations, the operation costing method is applied. It offers better control and facilitates the computation of unit operation cost at the end of each operation.

Besides the above variations of job costing and process costing, the different techniques or types of costing (discussed below) can be found in these two methods of costing and can be used to determine costs therein.

TECHNIQUES (TYPES) OF COSTING

The terms "techniques" or "types" refer to the manner of ascertaining costs of a product, job or activity. But these terms (techniques or types) also necessarily indicate what types of costs are being ascertained such as historical cost, standard cost, absorption (full) cost, marginal cost etc. It is clear that the term "Methods of Costing" itself signifies only the method(s), job costing or process costing, that is being used to determine costs without indicating the types of costs (historical, standard, full or marginal) which are ascertained under the two methods of costing (Job or Process Costing). The following are generally the techniques of costing:

Historical Costing

Historical costing is the system of costing under which costs are determined after they have been incurred.

Standard Costing

Under standard costing, standard costs are determined and used, and then compared with the actual costs to determine the extent of variances so that remedial action can be taken. Standard costs are the pre-determined costs in conformity with the most efficient operation and use of the resources within the film.

Absorption or Full Costing

Under this costing method, all manufacturing costs, fixed and variable, are charged to products, jobs, processes, etc. and are included in total cost.

Variable or Marginal Costing

Variable costing method charges only variable production costs to products or jobs, and thus the cost of the products or jobs consists of only variable production and not fixed production costs. The fixed production, administration, selling and distribution costs, both fixed and variable, are written off against profits in the periods in which they arise.

Uniform Costing

Truly speaking, uniform costing is not a technique of costing, but is an attempt by several undertakings and organisations to use similar costing principles and/or practices.

COSTING SYSTEM

The term "costing system" refers to an accounting system followed to accumulate costs, to ascertain costs of products or jobs, to prepare cost information using some procedures and principles for recording of cost data. Since there are two basic methods of costing—Job Costing and Process Costing, to ascertain costs, the costing system followed by business enterprises are also divided into two categories:

1. Job Order Costing System
2. Process Costing System

It should be understood that within these two costing systems, further, business enterprises may follow different techniques of costing such as historical cost, standard cost, full cost, marginal cost etc., which have been discussed earlier.

THROUGHPUT COSTING

Throughput costing is also known as super-variable costing. This costing technique considers only direct materials as true variable cost and other remaining costs as period costs to be charged in the period in which they are incurred. Thus, in throughput costing, inventory is valued in terms of only direct material costs. In this costing, contribution is equal to revenue minus all variable direct materials cost of goods sold. GAAP in India and in other countries of the world do not permit use of this method for valuation of inventories. This costing is not used for external reporting because it gives significant different net income figures than those revealed by absorption costing. In this costing, inventory figures are very low. Throughput costing has not achieved widespread use even for internal reporting purposes.

In throughput accounting, return is defined as sales less material costs in contrast to contribution which is sales less all variable costs (material, labour and variable overheads). The assumption is that all costs, except materials, are fixed in relation to throughput in the short run.

Throughput accounting is beneficial in a Just-In-Time (JIT) situation. It helps to direct attention to bottlenecks and forces management to concentrate on the key elements in making profits namely, inventory reduction and reducing the response time to customer demand.[5]

BACKFLUSH COSTING

CIMA (UK) defines backflush costing as:

> "A cost accounting system which focuses on the output of the organisation and then works backwards to allocate costs between cost of goods sold and inventory."

Backflush is a simple and clear book-keeping system created to reflect key aspects of JIT systems which imply little or no work-in-progress and demand pull. There are many variants of backflush accounting, a more popular among them is creating a single account "Raw and In-Process Account" in place of separate Raw Materials and Work-In-Process (WIP) accounts. When goods are sold, the standard cost of the materials in the finished goods would be credited, that is, backflushed to Raw and In-Process Account. All conversion costs, that is, labour and material is transferred to the cost of finished goods production and not to WIP account.

The following example illustrates the applications of backflush accounting.

EXAMPLE 1.1

A firm has the following transactions for the month of January 2020.

	(₹)
Raw materials purchase	8,50,000
Conversion costs	6,86,000
	Units
Production	4,900
Sales	4,850

There are no opening inventory of raw materials, WIP and finished goods. The standard cost per unit is ₹310 (₹170 for materials + ₹140 conversion cost). There was no closing WIP at the end of the period.

Required: Make journal entries for a backflush accounting system using a Raw Materials and In-Progress account.

5. T. Lucy, *Management Accounting*, Ibid, p. 483.

☞ Solution

	₹	₹
Raw materials and In-Progress A/c Dr.	8,50,000	
To creditors		8,50,000
(Purchase of raw materials on credit)		
Finished goods A/c Dr.	15,19,000	
Raw materials and In Progress A/c		8,33,000
Conversion cost control A/c		6,86,000
(Cost of goods produced 4,900 units)		
Cost of sales A/c Dr.	15,03,500	
To finished goods stock		15,03,500
(Cost of goods sold, 4,850 units × ₹310)		

At the end of January 2020, there will be two separate stock balances:

Raw materials and In-Progress A/c = ₹8,50,000 – 8,33,000
= ₹1,70,00

Finished goods (50 units @ ₹310) = ₹15,500

Notes: 1. Raw materials and In-Progress A/c amount is calculated as follows:
4,900 units × ₹170 = ₹8,33,000
2. All the entries shown above are at standard cost.
3. Figures have been chosen as such to avoid variances.

Backflush is an easy method. There is no separate account for WIP. Materials are not tracked through the production process as is found in traditional cost accounting. Accounting entries are very few; supporting vouchers and work flow documents are less required. Backflush accounting does not provide any incentives to managers for producing the stock.

INSTALLATION OF A COST ACCOUNTING SYSTEM

A cost accounting system is a system that accumulates costs, assigns them to cost objects, that is, products, jobs, processes, etc. and reports cost information. In addition to this, a proper cost accounting system assists management in the planning and control of business operations, in analysing product profitability, and in accomplishing business objectives through optimum utilisation of available resources. The underlying principles, procedures and objects of all costing system are the same, but the application of these principles and methods may vary with the circumstances. Basically, two main questions are involved in installing a cost accounting system: (i) factors influencing cost accounting system, and (ii) features of cost accounting systems.

Factors Influencing the Cost Accounting System

The following factors should be considered before designing the cost accounting system:

1. *Size of the firm* The complexity and outline of the cost accounting system depends on the size of the business enterprise and management requirements. As the size of the firm and business grow, management requirements for cost data and information increase. A large firm has to develop a large volume of cost data regarding the activities of various departments of the business enterprise.

2. *Manufacturing process or methods* The manufacturing process includes production layout and arrangement, production scheduling, production control methods, plant and equipment capacities, inspection and testing of materials, degree of complexity in the production procedure and factory layout of the particular business firm for which it is designed. Methods of wage payment (piece-rate, time-rate, incentive schemes), methods of collecting hours worked, inventory system, overhead recovery, and other problems related with the factory are the factors vital in designing a cost accounting system.
3. *Nature and number of products* If a single product is manufactured, all costs of direct material, direct labour and other factory expenses can be directly allocated to that product. But in the case of more than one product being produced, some costs of production relating to two or more products are to be equitably apportioned among them. In this situation, the process of developing cost data is more complex, which, in turn, influences the designing of the cost system.
4. *Management control needs* The designing of the cost accounting system in a business firm is guided by the management control requirement. The costing system should supply data to persons at different levels in the organisation to take suitable action in their respective areas.
5. *Raw materials* The nature of raw materials and the degree of waste therein influence the designing of the cost accounting system in a manufacturing concern. There are some materials which have a high degree of spoilage. The issuing of materials, methods of pricing and control over spoilage are accordingly adopted as to suit the specific type of materials.
6. *Staff efficiency* The working and formulation of the cost accounting system depends, to a great extent, on the efficiency of personnel and staff engaged in it.
7. *Comparability* A business enterprise follows cost accounting systems prevailing in other business firms within the same industry. This is necessary to facilitate comparison of its own cost data with data produced for the industry.
8. *Organisational structure* The cost accounting system must correspond to the organisational division or authority so that individual foremen, supervisors, department heads, or executives can be held accountable for the costs incurred in their respective departments.
9. *External factors* The adoption of a costing system depends mainly on internal factors and situations within the firm. However, external factors may influence scope of the costing system to be applied by a business firm. For example, Cost Accounting Rules are applicable to manufacturing companies in India which require certain cost information to be developed and submitted to government authorities.

Features of Cost Accounting System

The cost accounting system may be used by all types of business organisations—manufacturing and non-manufacturing. The cost accounting system should be practical, that is, it must be helpful to the business. There must be no attempt to make the business suit the system. The following are the essential features of a cost accounting system:

1. *Basis for accumulating costs* A fundamental feature of any system is the method of accumulating manufacturing costs. Costs may be accumulated by individual jobs (job order cost system) or by manufacturing departments or processes (process cost system).

   A job order cost system has the unique feature of accumulating manufacturing costs separately for each batch or job. Within a process cost system, costs are accumulated by process or department.

Cost of production reports are prepared for each process in the factory. A process cost system is best suited for standard products that are manufactured continuously for mass production.

2. *Relationship with financial accounting* Most cost accounting systems are complementary/supplemental in their relation to financial accounting. In this role, cost accounting systems imply physical inventory counts to determine quantities of materials, work-in-process and finished goods. Inventory quantities must be counted and unit costs determined before periodic financial statements can be prepared. An integrated system removes the need of coordination between financial accounting and cost accounting. Integrated systems are comparatively more sophisticated, costly and conducive to cost control than supplemental system.
3. *Basis of product costs* In many cost accounting systems, cost estimates are desirable in addition to actual or historical costs. Actual costs incurred for a period are used to compute product costs. A system using actual material cost, actual labour cost and estimated overhead rate is called a normal cost system. In contrast, standard costs may be developed for the purpose of product costing. Standard costs are carefully pre-determined estimates of what material, labour and overhead costs should be on a per-unit basis, given product specifications and desired operating efficiency.
4. *Full (absorption) costing or marginal (variable) costing* Another important question relating to the cost accounting system is whether all manufacturing costs are to be accumulated and attached to products. The traditional opinion is that all manufacturing costs—variable and fixed—should be charged to products. This method is known as full costing or absorption costing, because fixed manufacturing costs are absorbed by units produced. An alternative viewpoint is that only variable manufacturing costs should be attached to products. In this method, fixed manufacturing costs are recorded as expenses of the accounting period.

Difficulties in Installation of a Costing System

The installation of costing system in business organisations is not an easy task. There are many difficulties, as listed below, which are faced by organisations while setting up costing system.

(1) Opposition from the Existing Staff

The existing staff, likely to oppose the introduction of costing system, may resent the additional work and may not provide cooperation which is necessary for the success of cost accounting system.

(2) Shortage of Trained Manpower

Installation of cost accounting system requires trained staff to operate the system effectively which organisations may not have, thus, affecting adversely the better application of the system.

(3) Error in Measuring Requirements

The organisations, big and small, have varying requirements as to the costing system. Organisations may not know their specific requirements accurately. Consequently, the installation of costing system either will not meet their requirements or will provide unnecessary sophistication and dose of accounting procedures.

(4) Non-cooperation from Management

Resistance is noticed not only from the lower and middle staff but also from the members of top management. Managers may not support the Managing Director in his efforts to minimise costs and control activities as these might be looked upon as an interference in their managerial authorities.

ARGUMENTS AGAINST COST ACCOUNTING

Cost accounting undoubtedly helps managements in managing the affairs of business efficiently and in accomplishing business goals. However, some organisations do not look with favour the installation of cost accounting system. Some arguments which are advanced against adopting cost accounting are as follows:

(1) The system of cost accounting may prove costly and small organisations may not find it profitable. The collection, analysis, allocation and maintenance of cost data are a time-consuming and difficult task which requires efficient manpower.

(2) All business organisations are required to prepare financial accounts to determine profit and financial position. Installation of cost accounting system along with financial accounting system increases work load.

(3) Cost accounting system itself is not an end but only a means to achieve certain objectives. The system itself will not improve efficiency, control costs and avoid wastage. Sometimes management personnel become inactive with the mere installation of the cost accounting system.

However, all the above arguments are not valid. Keeping in view the advantages and contributions of cost accounting to management, as explained earlier, it can be rightly said that cost accounting is a necessity for all business organisations. For manufacturing firms, cost accounting is vital necessity to reduce cost, to avoid waste, to improve efficiency and to provide cost data to management for planning, control and decision-making.

COST CENTRE

CIMA defines cost centre as "a production or services, function, activity or item of equipment whose costs may be attributed to cost units. A cost centre is the smallest organisational sub-unit for which separate cost allocation is attempted". A cost centre is an individual activity or group of similar activities for which cost are accumulated. For example, in production department, a machine or group of machines within a department or a work group is considered as cost centre. Any part of an enterprise to which costs can be charged is called as "Cost Centre". The following are the types of cost centres usually found in a manufacturing company.

Impersonal Cost Centre

A cost centre which consists of a location or item of equipment (or a group of these).

Personal Cost Centre

A cost centre which consists of a person or group of persons.

Operation Cost Centre

A cost centre which consists of the machines and/or persons carrying out similar operations.

Process Cost Centre

A cost centre which consists of a specific process or a continuous sequence of operations.

Cost Centre in a manufacturing concern:
Two main types of a cost centre are found in a manufacturing concern.

- ***Production Cost Centre:*** It is a cost centre where raw material is handled for conversion into finished product. Here, both direct and indirect expenses are incurred. Machine shops, welding shops and assembly shops etc. are examples of a production cost centre.
- ***Service Cost Centre:*** It is a cost centre which serves as an ancillary unit to a production cost centre. Payroll processing department, HRD, power house, gas production shop, material service centres, plant maintenance centres etc. are examples of a service cost centre.

COST OBJECTS

Cost object is anything for which a separate measurement of cost is required. Cost object may be a product, a service, a project, a customer, a brand category, an activity, a department or a programme etc.

Examples of Cost Objects are as follows:

- **Product** — *Smart Phone, Tablet Computer, SUV Car, Book etc.*
- **Services** — *An Airline Flight from Delhi to Mumbai, Concurrent Audit Assignment, Utility Bill Payment Facility etc.*
- **Project** — *Metro Rail Project of DMRC, Road Projects of NHAI etc.*
- **Activity** — *Quality Inspection of Materials, Placing of Orders etc.*
- **Process** — *Refinement of Crudes in Oil Refineries, Melting of Billets or Ingots in Rolling Mills etc.*
- **Department** — *Production Department. Finance & Accounts, Safety etc.*

COST DRIVERS

A cost driver is a factor or variable which affects level of cost. Generally, it is an activity which is responsible for cost incurrence. Level of activity or volume of production is the example of a cost driver. An activity may be an event, task, or unit of work etc.

CIMA official terminology defines cost driver as "the factor influencing the level of cost. Often used in the context of ABC to denote the factor which links activity resource consumption to product outputs, for example the number of purchase orders would be a cost driver for procurement cost."

Examples of a cost drivers are number of machines setting ups, number of purchase orders, hours spent on product inspection, number of tests performed etc.

COST UNIT

CIMA defines cost unit as "a quantity/unit of a product or service in relation to which costs are ascertained." A cost unit is a unit of product or unit of service to which costs are ascertained by means of allocation, apportionment and absorption. It is a unit of quantity of product, service or time or a combination of these in relation to which costs are expressed or ascertained. The cost units which pass through the cost centre, the direct and indirect costs of the cost centre are charged to the units of production by means of an absorption rate. The unit of output in relation to which cost incurred by a cost centre is expressed is called Cost Unit. Cost units can be developed for all kinds of organisations whether manufacturing, commercial or public utility services.

In the job costing method, cost unit is a single specific order; in batch costing it consists of a group of similar articles; and in contract costing, it consists of a single product (contract). The cost units used in different industries cannot be uniform. The cost units and centres should be those which suit the business and which are readily understood and accepted by all concerned.

Table 1.4 gives examples of cost units (that is, unit of cost activity) and method of costing used in different industries.

Table 1.4 Cost Unit and Method of Costing

Industry/Enterprise	*Cost Unit*	*Method of Costing*
1. Building	House or square foot of area	Job Costing, Contract Costing
2. Chemical	Tonne, pound or kilogram	Process Costing
3. Cement	Tonne	Process Costing
4. Automobile	Number	Process Costing
5. Steel	Tonne	Process Costing
6. Transport	Tonne kilometre, Passenger kilometre	Operating Costing
7. Cable	Metre	Process Costing
8. Gas	Cubic foot or cubic metre	Process Costing
9. Nuts and bolts	Gross or some measure of standard weight	Job Costing
10. Power	Per kilowatt hour or per unit of electricity generated	Process Costing or Operating Costing
11. Paper	Ream	Process Costing
12. Timber	Cubic foot	Process Costing
13. Brewery	Per dozen bottles or per gallon of draught brew	Process Costing
14. Biscuits	Per (WT)	Process Costing
15. Hospital	Per bed occupied/out-patient visit	Operating Costing
16. Case-making	Per case	Job Costing
17. Road contractors	Per mile	Job Costing
18. Ice cream	Per gallon	Process Costing
19. Knitted textiles	Per pound/kg of fabric	Process Costing
20. Canned fruit	Per dozen cans or per gross cans	Process Costing
21. Soft drinks	Cases of 24 bottles each	Process Costing
22. Oil extraction, petrochemicals, refinery	Gallons, litres, tonnes, barrel	Process Costing
23. Pharmaceuticals	1,000 nos. tablets, ampulses	Process Costing
24. Machine building	Numbers	Job Costing
25. Readymade garments	Numbers, a batch of clothing	Batch Costing
26. Aircraft	Numbers	Job Costing

(Contd.)

Industry/Enterprise	*Cost Unit*	*Method of Costing*
27. Sugar	Tonnes, kilograms	Process Costing
28. Furnishing	Each article by numbers	Job Costing
29. Confectionary	Per kg	Process Costing
30. Clothing (automatic process)	Per dozen articles	Process Costing
31. Bicycle manufacturing	Number	Multiple Costing
32. Textiles	Metres, yards, per lb. of cloths	Process Costing
33. Flour	Tonnes	Process Costing
34. Parts manufacturing	Nos. of articles in tens, hundreds, thousands	Job Costing
35. Brickworks	Per 1,000 bricks made	Unit Costing
36. Goods transportation	Per tonne km	Operating Costing
37. Ship building	Each contract	Contract Costing
38. Canteen	A meal	Operating Costing

COST ACCOUNTING DEPARTMENT

The organisation of business enterprises differ widely in their nature and structure. Also, the accounting information is required to be provided to various persons within the organisation for decision-making. These factors greatly influence the designing of an organisational structure and the cost accounting department. In a typical manufacturing company, the Chief Accounting Officer is the controller or head of the accounting division (Fig. 1.1). The controller performs other functions besides determining the cost of product, such as budgeting, general (financial) accounting, systems and procedures, data processing, taxes and reports, internal auditing. Figure 1.2 depicts the different functions of the accounting department within the purview of the Chief Accounting Officer.

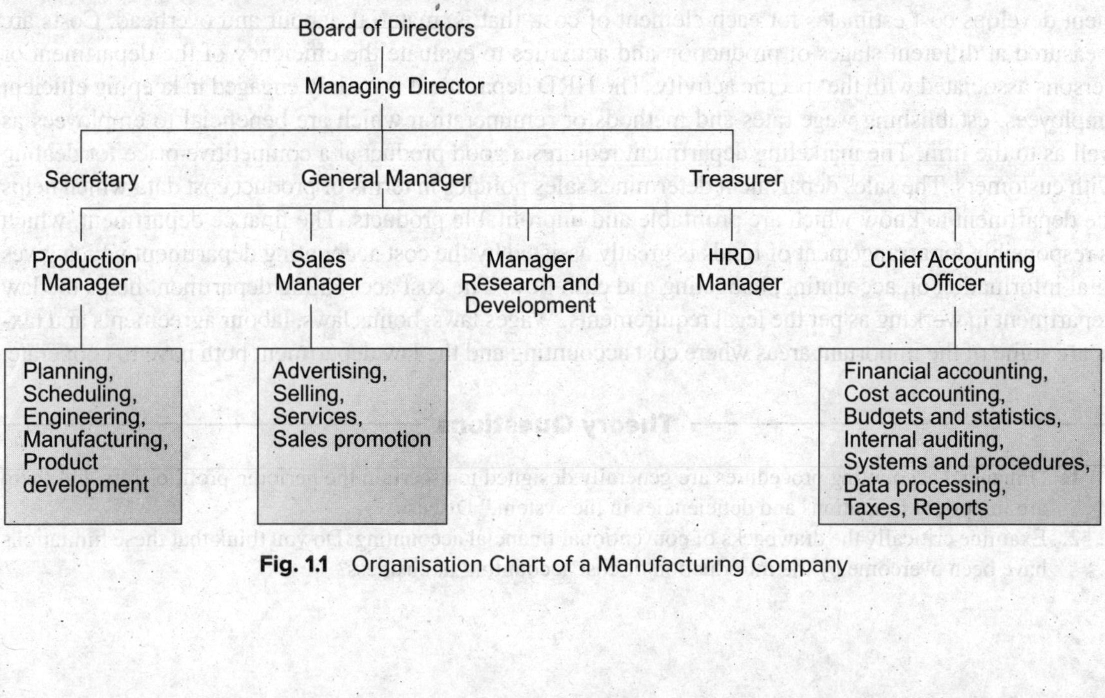

Fig. 1.1 Organisation Chart of a Manufacturing Company

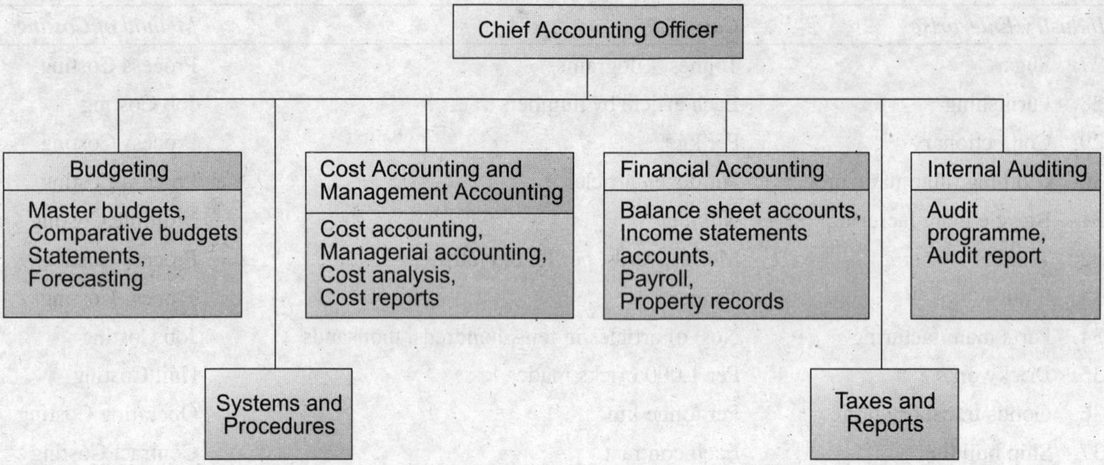

Fig. 1.2 Organisation of the Department of the Chief Accounting Officer

The cost accounting department discharges many important functions in a manufacturing concern. It keeps full records about material, labour and overhead. After accumulating all different costs, it analyses them so that they can be used by management for planning, control and decision-making.

The cost accounting department, further, divides its responsibilities into different components to get prompt and timely reports. Coordination is needed among these functions (or departments) within the cost accounting department. Generally, these functional units are under the supervision of the Chief Accounts Officer (Fig. 1.2).

The cost accounting department and its activities are closely connected with other departments and their activities in the organisation. For example, the production department is responsible for designing, planning and producing products upto the finished product stage. The research and development department develops cost estimates for each element of cost, that is, material, labour and overhead. Costs are measured at different stages of production and activities to evaluate the efficiency of the department or persons associated with the specific activity. The HRD department is mainly engaged in keeping efficient employees, establishing wage rates and methods or remuneration which are beneficial to employees as well as to the firm. The marketing department requires a good product at a competitive price for dealing with customers. The sales department determines sales policies in terms of product cost data which helps the department to know which are profitable and unprofitable products. The finance department, which is responsible for arrangement of funds is greatly assisted by the cost accounting department which gives vital information on accounting, budgeting and cash flow. The cost accounting department helps the law department in working as per the legal requirements. Wages laws, bonus laws, labour agreements and taxes are some of the important areas where cost accounting and the law department both have to cooperate.

Theory Questions

1. "Financial accounting procedures are generally designed to ascertain the periodic profit or loss, but there are important limitations and deficiencies in the system." Discuss.
2. Examine critically the drawbacks of conventional financial accounting. Do you think that these limitations have been overcome by the introduction of cost accounting in business?

3. What is cost accounting? What are its objectives? How do cost accounting records help in the planning and control of operations of a business enterprise?
4. What is meant by cost accounting? In what essential respects does cost accounting differ from financial accounting?
5. Explain fully the concept of cost. How does cost accounting contribute to the effective and efficient management of an industrial establishment?
6. What is the function of a costing department in a manufacturing concern? How is the costing department useful to other departments in a manufacturing concern?
7. SV Ltd. is a manufacturing company which has a sound system of financial accounting. The management of the company, therefore, feels that there is no need for the installation of a cost accounting system. Prepare a report for management, bringing out the distinction between cost and financial accounting systems and the need for the introduction of a sound cost accounting system.
8. "A cost keeping system, that simply records costs for the purpose of fixing sale prices, has accomplished only a small part of its mission." What are the other functions of costing?
9. "Cost accounting is an unnecessary luxury for business establishments." Do you agree with the statement? Discuss.
10. Explain the important objectives of cost accounting.
11. What is cost accounting? Discuss briefly its important functions in a business firm.
12. "Cost accounting has come to be an essential tool of the management." Comment.
13. "Cost accounting is a system of foresight and not a postmortem examination; it turns losses into profits, speeds up activities and eliminates waste." Discuss.
14. State the primary objectives of installation of a costing system. Apart from technical costing problems, what practical difficulties would you meet and how would you overcome them?
15. (a) State and explain the main differences between financial accounting and cost accounting.
    (b) What is a cost centre and how does it differ from a department of a factory?
16. How far is cost information helpful for the following purposes?
    (a) Fixation of selling prices
    (b) Control of costs
    (c) Management decisions
17. "Limitations of financial accounting have made the management to realise the importance of cost accounting." Comment.
18. What are the advantages of introduction of costing system in an industrial organisation?
19. Mention the factors which should be considered in installing a costing system in an organisation.
20. What is meant by cost accounting? Explain the difference between financial accounting and cost accounting.
21. What purposes do cost centres serve? Are cost centres and cost units related to each other?
22. "Cost accounting is becoming more and more relevant in the emerging economic scenario in India". Comment.
23. Discuss the essentials of good cost accounting system.
24. You have been asked to install a costing system in a manufacturing company. What practical difficulties will you expect and how will you propose to overcome the same?
25. What is meant by management accounting? Discuss its objectives.
26. What are the objectives of cost accounting?
27. "Cost accounting system is neither unnecessary nor expensive; rather it is profitable investment." Comment.
28. Explain the importance of cost accounting as a managerial tool.
29. Define the term "Cost" and "Cost Accounting". Explain the objectives of cost accounting.
30. "Cost accounting is a tool of managerial planning and control." Explain.
31. (a) State briefly the advantages of cost accounting.
    (b) Distinguish between financial accounting and cost accounting.

32. Define cost unit. How does it differ from cost centre?
33. Explain the points of distinction between management accounting and cost accounting.
34. What is management accounting? How does management accounting differ from cost accounting and financial accounting?
35. State the objectives and limitations of management accounting.
36. "Evolution of cost accounting is the outcome of deficiencies in the financial accounting system." Discuss.
37. You are working with a firm of cost consultants. A client having a large manufacturing FMCG Co. comes to you for advice for installing a cost accounting system in his organisation. What are the basic considerations you would keep in mind in designing a cost accounting system for your client? What are the practical difficulties you perceive on its implementation by your client and how do you propose to overcome the same?
38. "Management accounting is the presentation of accounting information in such a way as to assist the management in the creation of policy and in the day-to-day operations of an undertaking." Elucidate.
39. What is a cost centre? State briefly the different types of cost centres.
40. A cost accounting system that simply records costs for the purpose of fixing sale prices has accomplished only a small part of its mission." Explain.

Self-Evaluation Questions

1. *List A* gives you different methods of costing which can be used in one or more industries or organisations given in *List B*. Mention the correct costing method of the industries in *List B*.

List A Process, Operating, Single Output, Job, Contract, Multiple

List B

(i) Chemical works	(ii) Road transport company
(iii) Coal	(iv) Nursing home
(v) Paint	(vi) Construction industries
(vii) Cement manufacturing	(viii) Soap manufacturing
(ix) Railways	(x) Ship builders
(xi) Bicycle manufacturing	(xii) Readymade garments
(xiii) Telephone	(xiv) Cotton textiles
(xv) Aluminum	(xvi) Paper mill
(xvii Furniture manufacture	(xviii) Meat packing
(xix) Sugar	(xx) Steel
(xxi) Paper boxes	(xxii) Air conditioners
(xxiii) Locomotive	(xxiv) Tyres and tubes
(xxv) Leather	(xxvi) Pianos
(xxvii) Toys and novelties	(xxviii) Oil refinery
(xxix) Baby food	(xxx) Radio receivers

☞ ***Answer***

(i) Process (ii) Operating (iii) Single (iv) Operating (v) Process (vi) Contract (vii) Process (viii) Process (ix) Operating (x) Contract (xi) Multiple (xii) Batch (xiii) Operating (xiv) Process (xv) Process (xvi) Process (xvii) Job (xviii) Process (xix) Process (xx) Process (xxi) Process (xxii) Multiple (xxiii) Multiple (xxiv) Process (xxv) Process (xxvi) Batch (xxvii) Batch (xxviii) Process (xxix) Batch (xxx) Multiple

2. State the method of costing that would be most suitable for
(a) Oil refinery
(b) Bicycle manufacturing
(c) Interior decoration
(d) Airlines company
(e) Printing

Answer

	Industry	Method of Costing
(a)	Oil Refinery	Process Costing
(b)	Bicycle Manufacturing	Multiple Costing
(c)	Interior decoration	Job Costing
(d)	Airlines	Operating Costing
(e)	Printing	Job Costing (Cost Unit-Order/jobs)

3. Indicate whether the following statements are True or False:

(i) The rental of a car which includes a fixed daily rate plus an extra fee for each kilometre driven is an example of a step cost.

(ii) Assuming inflation, if a company wants to maximise net income, it would select FIFO as the method of pricing raw materials.

(iii) Overtime premium paid to all factory workers is usually considered direct labour.

(iv) Period costs are invariable and are expensed out as and when the inventory is sold.

(v) Idle facility and idle time are the same.

Answer

(i) False (ii) True (iii) False (iv) True (v) False

CASE STUDY

Value-Chain Analysis – A Case of Spectron Dilemma

Spectron Ltd., based in Bangalore, was dealing in assembling and trading of computers. It purchased computer parts from various suppliers and sold them to its distributors across south India region. The company assembled computers based on demand and followed JIT for most of its parts. Lately, because of most of the established companies reducing the prices for their computers, Spectron was facing major competition and reduction in the demand for its product.

To tackle the situation, Spectron MD, R. Raghavan hired a consultant Mr. Krishnan to analyse the situation and suggest changes in the cost and pricing of the products. Krishnan, after a week of studying the various costs related to assembling of the computers couldn't find any way of cost reduction. He then proceeded to look at the vendors for various parts. He started with the Fan (heat sink) and Sound cards and identified the vendors for it. Spectron submitted to him the following details related to the two vendors Norton Electronics and Sintara Electronics supplying these parts:

	Norton Electronics		*Sintara Electronics*	
	Fan	*Sound card*	*Fan*	*Sound card*
Purchase price per unit (₹)	11	26	12	28
No. of units purchased	40,000	20,000	5,000	5,000

Krishnan realised that Spectron used to purchase these parts majorly from Norton Electronics for the obvious reasons of lesser price. At the same time, the company did not want to depend on a single vendor and therefore also procured these parts in small numbers from Sintara Electronics.

Upon further analysis, Krishnan could also identify some more costs related to these parts. They were costs related to repair of defective pieces of these fans and sound cards which amounted to

₹2,00,000 and also overtime paid to compensate for late delivery amounting to ₹50,000. He found that fan and sound cards, although brought at a cheaper price, were not always 100% defect-free. Krishnan got hold of the detail that out of 40,000 fans purchased from Norton, 800 were defective and also that out of 20,000 sound cards purchased, 190 needed repairs. The number of defective fans and sound cards from Sintara out of 5,000 pieces purchased each were 6 and 4 respectively.

Krishnan discovered that Sintara Electronics followed the JIT policy religiously and not once did it delivered the consignment late. Norton, on the other hand, delayed the delivery of fans to Spectron 30 times in the year and 20 times was responsible for the late shipment of sound cards.

Based on his discovery and analysis thereon, Krishnan submitted his report to Spectron Computers. The report suggested that the company should change its policy of buying majorly from Norton and instead purchase maximum number of parts from Sintara. Spectron MD—Raghavan was surprised to read the report as he could not understand the basis of this suggestion.

QUESTION FOR DISCUSSION:

Why do you think Krishnan gave the suggestion to purchase the computer parts—fan and sound cards from Sintara instead of Norton? Show your answer through calculating the costs related to purchase of fan and sound cards from both the suppliers.

Chapter 2

Cost: Concepts and Classifications

Learning Objectives

After reading this chapter, you should be able to:

1. explain costs and its different classification, natural classification of costs, different costs for decision-making, planning and control;
2. explain expenses, loss, fixed cost, variable cost, mixed cost, direct and indirect cost, capital and revenue cost;
3. explain cost control, cost reduction, cost management and difference between cost control and cost reduction;
4. identify costs for control—controllable and uncontrollable costs, standard costs;
5. understand cost reduction techniques and cost reduction areas; and
6. define cost sheet, and explain its preparation.

The three important areas in cost accounting are cost ascertainment, cost analysis and cost control. For cost accounting to be useful in these areas, costs must be accumulated, classified and grouped in such a manner that (i) total costs and units costs can be determined; (ii) trends in costs behaviour can be observed; (iii) cost can be controlled; and (iv) useful analysis can be made based on past as well as future costs for planning, control and decision-making. These requirements call for an understanding of the concept of cost and of its appropriate classifications. The purpose of this chapter is to explain the concept of cost and different cost classifications.

COST

Cost is the amount of expenditure, actual (incurred) or notional (attributable), relating to a specific thing or activity. The specific thing or activity may be a product, job, service, process or any other activity.

Cost is the amount of resources given up in exchange for some goods or services. The resources given up are generally in terms of money or, if not in terms of money, they are always expressed in monetary terms. The term "cost" itself is without any significant meaning and, therefore, it is always advisable to use it with an adjective or phrase that will convey the meaning intended, such as prime, direct, indirect, fixed, variable, controllable, opportunity, imputed, sunk, differential, marginal, replacement and the like. Each such adjective or description implies a certain attribute or characteristic which is important in computing, measuring and analysing the cost.

Basically, when a cost is incurred, it could be in the form of deferred cost (asset) or expired cost (expense). Deferred costs are unexpired costs, capitalised costs, which provide benefits in the future periods and known as assets and hence appear on the balance sheet. Examples of deferred or unexpired costs are plant, equipment, building, inventory, prepaid rent and insurance. When these deferred costs (assets) are used up, to the extent used, they become expenses and appear on the income statement and are deducted from revenues. Expired costs are costs which have been used up totally in generating revenue. They are not capitalised but only shown as expenses on income statement.

EXPENSES

Expenses are expired costs, incurred and totally used up in generation of revenue. Examples of expired costs are costs of goods sold expense, selling and administrative expenses. Expenses need not necessarily have to be paid in cash immediately; even a promise to pay could be made for the benefits obtained. The manufacturing costs are capitalised in the form of finished goods inventory and when a sale is made, they expire (becoming expenses). The cost of unsold inventory which was an asset earlier, now becomes expenses (costs of goods sold) as it has contributed to the generation of revenue.

Factory (or manufacturing) overhead is treated as cost (an asset) because this is included in the cost of finished goods inventory which is an asset unless sale is made. Selling and administrative expenses, when not included in the cost of finished goods inventory, are treated only as expenses and not cost (asset). Factory overheads are assets because they are supposed to add utility to the goods manufactured. For example, depreciation of a factory machine increases the utility of the goods manufactured which are therefore included in work-in-progress and finished goods inventory. But selling and distribution overheads do not add to the utility of goods manufactured and are treated merely as expenses and are deducted from revenues whenever incurred. Similarly, depreciation of a factory building is a cost, but depreciation of an office building is an expense.

LOSS

Loss is lost cost. The term "loss" is used to describe mainly two accounting events. In traditional financial accounting, it is used to denote a situation where expenses exceed revenues for an accounting period, that is, the opposite of net income (earnings) for the accounting period. Secondly, a loss arises due to the cost of an asset being more than the sale proceeds when the asset is sold. This unfavourable event does not arise from a normal business activity but from non-operating transactions or events. This definition of loss is used to identify the opposite of gain. That is, if no benefit is received from the cost incurred or it becomes definite that no benefit will accrue, the cost becomes a lost cost, that is, loss.

Loss is unrelated to revenue generation and is only offset against revenue of the period in which the loss occurred. Examples of loss are loss on sale of fixed asset and loss of a stock due to fire.

CLASSIFICATION OF COSTS

The achievement of the objectives of cost accounting requires that cost should be ascertained, classified and grouped. Cost classification may be defined as the process of grouping costs according to their common characteristics. There are many objectives of cost classifications depending on the requirements of management. However, the following objectives are considered very useful and significant:

(i) Determining product costs for stock valuation and profit measurement
(ii) Planning
(iii) Decision-making
(iv) Control
(v) Cost management

The different cost classifications are as follows:

1. Natural Classifications of Costs
   (i) Direct material
   (ii) Direct labour
   (iii) Direct expenses
   (iv) Factory overhead
   (v) Selling and distribution and administrative overheads
2. Cost behaviour (in relation to changes in output, activity or volume)
   (i) Fixed cost
   (ii) Variable cost
   (iii) Mixed cost (semi-variable and semi-fixed cost)
3. Degree of Traceability to the Product
   (i) Direct cost
   (ii) Indirect cost
4. Degree of Association with the Product
   (i) Product cost
   (ii) Period cost
5. Functional Classification of Costs
   (i) Manufacturing cost
   (ii) Selling and distribution cost
   (iii) Administrative cost
6. Relationship with the Accounting Period
   (i) Capital cost
   (ii) Revenue cost
7. Costs for Decision-making and Planning
   (i) Opportunity cost
   (ii) Sunk cost
   (iii) Relevant cost
   (iv) Differential cost
   (v) Imputed cost
   (vi) Out-of-pocket cost

(vii) Fixed, variable and mixed cost
(viii) Shutdown cost
8. Costs for Control
(i) Controllable and uncontrollable cost
(ii) Standard cost
(iii) Fixed, variable and mixed cost
9. Other Costs
(i) Joint cost
(ii) Common cost

NATURAL CLASSIFICATION OF COSTS

The term "natural classification" refers to the basic physical characteristics of the cost. In a manufacturing concern, generally, the following costs are incurred:

1. *Direct material* Direct materials refer to the cost of materials which are conveniently and economically traceable to specific units of output. The term "direct materials" is denoted by certain other names also, such as process material, prime cost material, production material, stores material and construction materials. Some examples of direct materials are raw cotton in textiles, crude oil to make diesel, steel to make automobile bodies etc. The following groups of materials fall within the definition of direct materials:

(a) All materials specially purchased for a particular job, order, process or product.
(b) All materials (including primary materials and raw materials) acquired and subsequently requisitioned from the stores for production.
(c) Components or parts purchased or produced and requisitioned from the storeroom.
(d) Material passing from one process to another process.
(e) Primary packing materials, for example, wrappings, cardboard boxes, etc.

Items, such as import duties, dock charges, transport cost of materials, storing of materials, cost of purchasing and receiving materials are properly added to their invoiced price, and thus, the materials are charged out at this increased cost.

Chapters 3 and 4 discuss in detail direct materials and materials cost.

2. *Direct labour* Direct labour is defined as the labour of those workers who are engaged in the production process. It is the labour expended directly upon the materials comprising the finished product. Other terms for the direct labour are process labour, productive labour and operating labour. Examples are the labour of machine operators and assemblers. However, a worker may be performing direct labour for a certain number of hours but as an indirect worker for the balance of the day. For example, manufacturing concerns frequently have workers who may be working on an assembly line or operating a machine as direct workers for three or four hours, but later in the day may help in repairing machinery or in doing other work as indirect workers.

Chapter 5 explains direct labour and accounting and control of direct labour cost in detail.

3. *Direct expenses (Chargeable expenses)* These include any expenditure other than direct material and direct labour directly incurred on a specific product or job. Such special necessary expenses can be identified with product or job and are charged directly to the product as part of the prime cost. Examples of direct expenses are:

(a) Cost of hiring special machinery or plant.
(b) Cost of special moulds, designs and patterns.
(c) Experimental costs and expenditure on model and pilot schemes.
(d) Fees paid to architects, surveyors and other consultants.
(e) Cost of transport and conveyance to the site of job or operations.
(f) Inward carriage and freight charges on special materials.
(g) Cost of patents and royalties.
(h) Cost of defective work, for example, where several trials are necessary before an appropriate one is obtained. The cost of such trials is taken as direct expense.
(i) Licence fees.
(j) Hire charges for plants and equipments for a specific product or job.
(k) Components and parts processed for a special job.
(l) Insurance charges on special materials chargeable to a job.

Other things remaining the same, the term "direct expenses" (chargeable expenses), whenever used in costing, refers to a specific product or job. That is, whether some expenses are direct or not, cost is decided in terms of specific job or product as product or job is considered the cost unit. However, some expenses which cannot be directly identified with product or job (and hence are not direct expenses), can sometimes be identified with a department, function, territory, customer, division etc. For example, salary of branch office manager, depreciation of plant, rent and rates, heating and lighting, insurance expenses etc. are direct in relation to some department or activity but become indirect with regard to a product or job because these expenses are incurred for more than one product or job.

The total of the above three elements of costs—(i) direct materials, (ii) direct labour and (iii) direct expenses—is prime cost. According to Official Terminology of Chartered Institute of Management Accountants (CIMA) (London), prime cost is the total cost of direct material and direct labour. Thus, direct expenses are not included in prime cost as per CIMA Terminology. The CIMA defines direct cost as the expenditure which can be economically identified with a specific saleable cost unit.

4. *Factory overhead* Factory overhead, also called manufacturing overhead or factory burden, may be defined as the cost of indirect materials, indirect labour and indirect expenses. The term "indirect materials" refers to materials that are needed for the completion of the product but whose consumption with regard to the product is either so small or so complex that it would not be appropriate to treat it as a direct materials item. They are production supplies and other materials that cannot conveniently or economically be charged to a specific unit of output. Examples of such items are lubricants, cotton waste, handtools, works stationery etc.

The term "indirect labour" is the labour cost of production-related activities that cannot be associated with or conveniently and economically traced to specific products via physical observation. Some examples of indirect labour are foremen, shop clerks, general helpers, cleaners, material handlers, plant-guards, employees engaged in maintenance work or other service work.

The term "indirect expenses" covers all indirect expenditure incurred by the manufacturing enterprise from the time when production has started to its completion and its transfer to the finished goods store. Any expenses not classified as direct expenses are known as indirect expenses. The Institute of Cost and Management Accountants (UK) defines indirect expenses as the "expenses which cannot be allocated but which can be apportioned to or absorbed by cost centres or cost units." They are incurred for the benefit of more than one product, job or activity and must be apportioned by appropriate bases to the various functions. Expenses of this type include items such as heat, light, maintenance, factory managers' salary etc.

The total of two elements—(i) prime cost, and (ii) factory overheads—is known as "Factory cost". Direct labour and factory overhead together are known as Conversion Costs because they are the costs of converting raw materials into finished products.

Chapter 6 explains in detail the nature and accounting of overhead costs.

5. *Selling, distribution and administrative overheads* Selling and distribution overheads usually begin when the factory costs end. Such expenses are generally incurred when the product is in saleable condition. It covers the cost of making sales and delivering/despatching products. These costs include advertising, salesmen salaries and commissions, packing, storage, transportation, and sales administrative costs.

Administrative overhead includes costs of planning and controlling the general policies and operations of a business enterprise. Usually, all costs which cannot be charged either to the production or sales division are considered as administrative costs. Typical of such items are fees of the board of directors, the chairman's salary, the rent for general offices and costs of the general accounting and other departments. Sometimes, some such expenses such as manager's salary are often allocated to manufacturing and included in factory overhead.

The sum of (i) prime cost, (ii) factory overhead, and (iii) selling and distribution and administrative overhead is the total cost, that is, the cost "to make and sell".

Chapter 7 discusses selling and distribution and administrative overhead costs.

Figure 2.1 presents the natural classification of costs as discussed above.

Direct Material + Direct Labour + Direct Expenses = Indirect Materials + Indirect Labour + Indirect Expenses =			(1) Prime Cost + Factory Overhead
Threads, lubricants, glue, other factory supplies.	Supervision, Inspection, superintendence, salary of factory clerks, experimental work, general helpers, cleaners, employees engaged in maintenance work.	Rent, insurance —fire and liability, taxes, depreciation, maintenance and repair, power, light, heat, misc., factory overhead, small tools, hire of machinery.	(2) Factory cost
Selling and Distribution Overhead + Administrative Overhead =			+
Advertising, samples, salesmen's salaries, depreciation of sales equipment, rent of branches, telephone, telegraph, supplies, stationery and printing, freight and carriage out, sales promotion, sales accounting, misc. expenses.	Office salaries, rent, executive salaries, depreciation of equipment, telephone and telegraph, travel, property taxes, auditing expenses, stationery and printing, postage, other administrative expenses.		Selling and Distribution, and Administrative overhead. (3) Total cost

Fig. 2.1 Natural Classification of Costs in a Manufacturing Concern

COST BEHAVIOUR (IN RELATION TO CHANGES IN OUTPUT OR ACTIVITY OR VOLUME)

Costs can be classified into (i) fixed, (ii) variable and (iii) mixed costs in terms of their variability or changes in cost behaviour in relation to change in output, or activity or volume. Activity may be indicated in any forms such as units of output, hours worked, sales, etc.

Fixed Cost

Fixed cost is a cost which does not change in total for a given time period despite wide fluctuations in output or volume of activity. These costs are also known as standby costs, capacity costs or period costs. Examples of fixed costs are rent, property taxes, supervising salaries, depreciation on office facilities, advertising, insurance, etc. They accrue or are incurred with the passage of time and not with the production of the product or the job. This is the reason why fixed costs are expressed in terms of time, such as per day, per month or per year and not in terms of unit. It is totally illogical to say that a supervisor's salary is so much per unit. But it can be said that supervisor's salary is so much per month.

Any fixed cost can be represented by a constant (See Fig. 2.2).

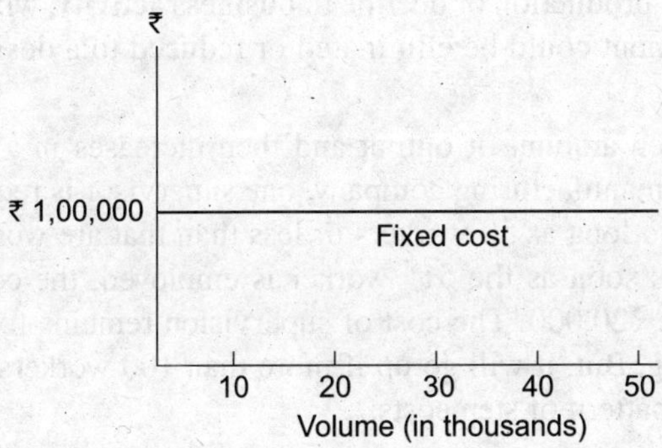

Fig. 2.2 Fixed Cost

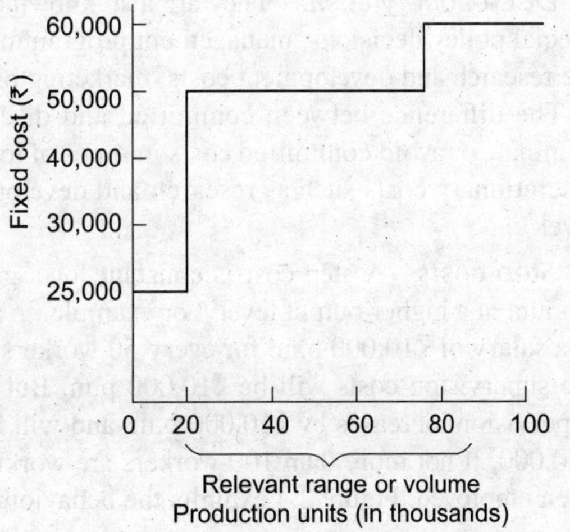

Fig. 2.3 Total Fixed Cost at Different Levels of Production

However, it should be improper to say that fixed costs never change in amount. The basic concept is that the term "fixed" refers to fixity (non-variability) related to specific volume (or relevant range); the term does not imply that there will be no changes in fixed cost. This characteristic of fixed cost has been shown in Fig. 2.3. According to Fig. 2.3, the following are the fixed costs at different levels of production:

1. ₹50,000 fixed cost between 20,000 and 80,000 units of production.
2. ₹60,000 fixed cost in excess of 80,000 units. This assumes that increase in production after a certain level (80,000 units) requires increase in fixed expenses which have been fixed earlier, for example, additional supervision, increase in quality control costs etc.
3. ₹25,000 fixed cost from zero units (shut down) to 20,000 units. This explains that if the level of activity comes to less than 20,000 units, some fixed costs may not be incurred. For example, if the plant is shut down or production is reduced, many of the fixed costs, such as costs on accounting functions, supplies, staff, will not be incurred.

However, if laying off of staff and personnel etc. is not possible, then the fixed cost will remain at ₹50,000.

Fixed costs can be classified in the following categories for the purpose of analysis:

1. *Committed costs* Such costs are primarily incurred to maintain the company's facilities and physical existence, and over which management has little or no discretion. Plant and equipment depreciation, taxes, insurance premium rate and rent charges are examples of committed costs.

2. *Managed costs* Managed costs are related to current operations which must continue to be paid to ensure the continued operating existence of the company, for example, management and staff salaries.

3. *Discretionary costs* They are also known as programmed costs. Discretionary costs result from special policy decisions, management programmes, new researches, etc. Some examples of such costs are research and development costs, marketing programmes, new system development costs.

The difference between committed and discretionary costs lies in the fact that it is difficult to eliminate or avoid committed costs in times of low production or decline in business activity, whereas discretionary costs such as research and development could be eliminated or reduced to a desirable level.

4. *Step costs* A step cost is constant for a given amount of output and then increases in a fixed amount at a higher output level. For example, in a manufacturing company, one supervisor is required at a salary of ₹10,000 p.m. for every 50 workers So long as 50 workers or less than that are working, the supervision costs will be ₹10,000 p.m. But as soon as the 51st worker is employed, the cost of supervision increases by ₹10,000 p.m. and will be ₹20,000. The cost of supervision remains fixed at ₹20,000, if not more than 100 workers are working. But, it will go up if more than 100 workers have been employed. Figure 2.4 exhibits the behaviour pattern of step costs.

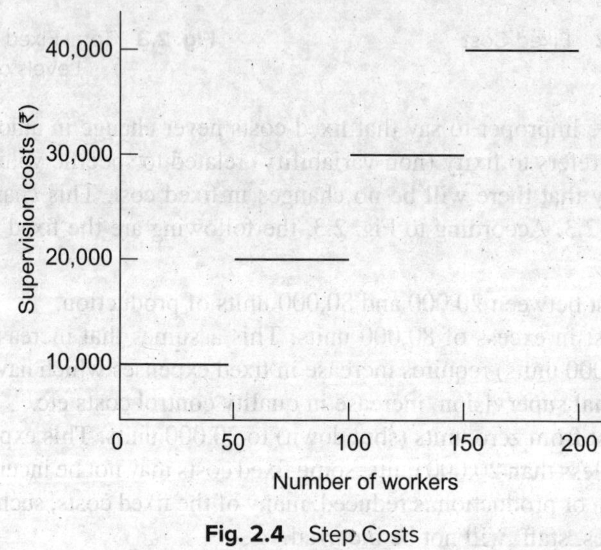

Fig. 2.4 Step Costs

Variable Cost

Variable costs are those costs that vary directly and proportionately with the output. There is a constant ratio between the change in the cost and change in the level of output. Direct materials cost and direct labour cost are the costs which are generally variable costs. For example, if direct material cost is ₹50 per unit, then for producing each additional unit, a direct material cost of ₹50 per unit will be incurred. That is, the total direct material cost increases in direct proportion to increase in units manufactured. However, it should be noted that it is only the total variable costs that change as more units are produced; the per unit variable cost remains constant.

Variable overheads like factory supplies, indirect materials, sales commission, office supplies, are some other examples of variable costs. If the factory is shut down, variable costs are eliminated. Variable cost is always expressed in terms of units or percentage of volume; it cannot be stated in terms of time. Variable cost is depicted in Fig. 2.5. The figure shows graphically the behaviour pattern of direct material cost. For every increase in the units produced, there is a proportionate increase in the cost. When production increases to 3,000 units from a level of 2,000 units, the cost of direct materials increases in direct proportion at the constant rate of ₹50 per unit. The variable cost line in Fig. 2.5 has been shown as linear rather than curvilinear. That is, on a graph paper this variable cost line appears as an unbroken straight line in place of a curve.

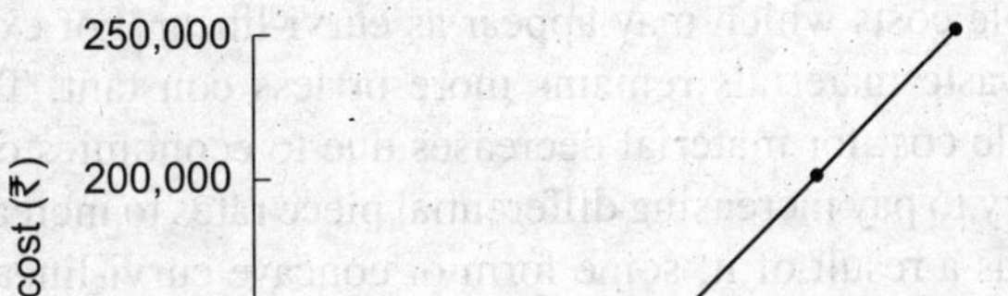

Fig. 2.5 Behaviour of Variable Costs (Direct Materials Cost)

However, the above pattern of variable cost line is the simplest possible and represents only those costs which vary in direct proportion to the level of activity. A completely linear variable costs over all levels of production or activity levels, as shown in Fig. 2.5 is very unlikely. In reality, a variable cost may be linear only over the normal range of activity levels and beyond the normal range of activity; variable cost per unit may show non-linear or curvi-linear line as displayed in Fig. 2.6. It implies that variable costs as displayed in Fig. 2.6 are not varying in direct proportion to output or activity changes.

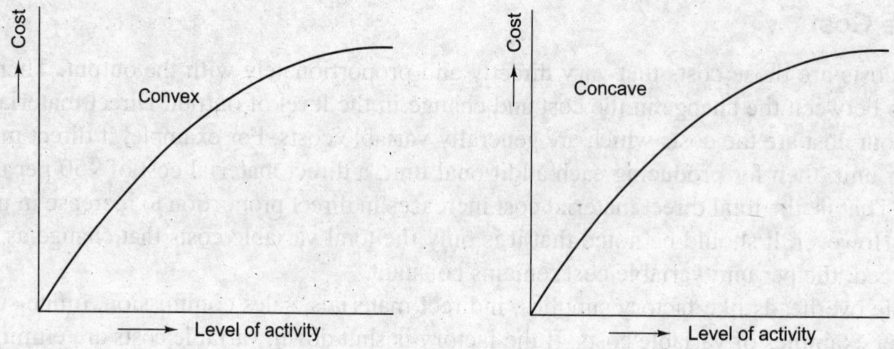

Fig. 2.6 Curvi-Linear Variable Costs

Convex — where each extra unit of output causes a less than proportionate increase in cost, that is, economies of scale operate.

Concave — where each extra unit of output causes a more than proportionate increase in cost, that is, diminishing returns operate.

There are some variable costs which may appear as curvi-linear. For example, in some production process the amount of waste materials remains more or less constant. Therefore, when production increases, the unit variable cost for material decreases due to economies of scale. On the other hand, when it becomes necessary to pay increasing differential piece rates to increase production, diminishing returns will operate and as a result of it, some form of concave curvi-linear relationship will emerge. That is, unit variable cost for labour will increase due to diminishing returns operating in this situation.

It can be concluded, therefore, that the classification of fixed and variable costs made in relation to one factor, that is, production volume is simplistic and is, at best, only a crude approximation of reality. In other words, it is known that the underlying variable cost relationship and function are curvi-linear, yet a linear approximation is assumed frequently.

Mixed Cost

Mixed costs are costs made up of fixed and variable elements. They are a combination of semi-variable costs and semi-fixed costs. Because of the variable component, they fluctuate with volume; because of the fixed component, they do not change in direct proportion to output. Semi-fixed costs are those costs which remain constant upto a certain level of output after which they become variable as shown in Fig. 2.7. Semi-variable cost is the cost which is basically variable but whose slope may change abruptly when a certain output level is reached as shown in Fig. 2.8.

An example of a mixed cost is the earnings of a worker who is paid a salary of ₹1500 per week (Fixed) plus a bonus of ₹1 for each unit completed (variable). If he increases his weekly output from 1,000 units to 1,500 units, his earnings increase from ₹2,500 to ₹3,000.

Earnings	*Units produced*	
	1,000	1,500
Fixed component	₹1,500	₹1,500
Variable component	1000	1,500
Total	₹2,500	₹3,000

An increase of 50% in output brings only a 20% increase in his earnings. Mathematically, mixed costs can be expressed as follows:

Total mixed cost = Total fixed cost + (Units × Variable cost per unit)

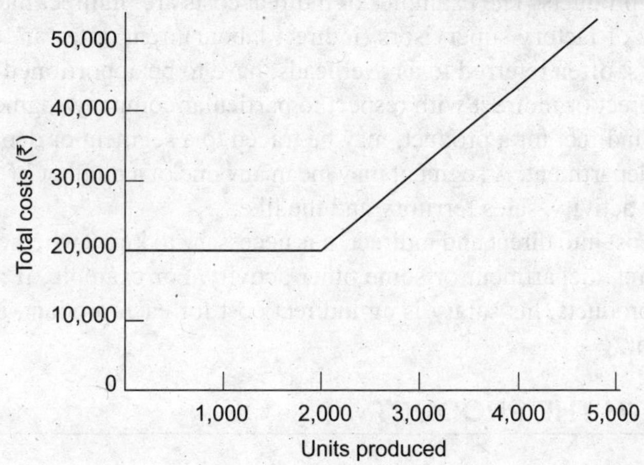

Fig. 2.7 Semi-fixed Cost

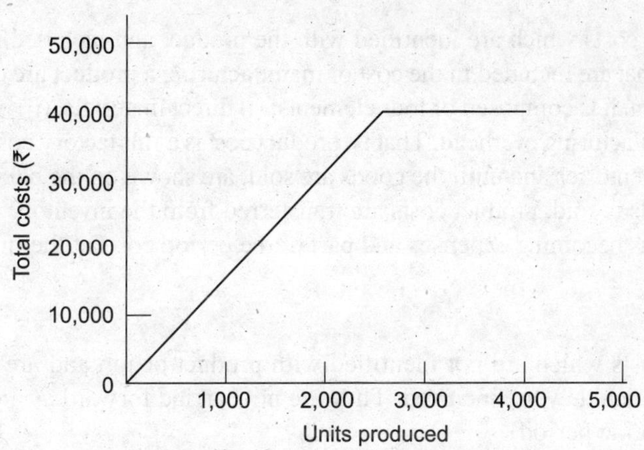

Fig. 2.8 Semi-variable Cost

DEGREE OF TRACEABILITY TO THE PRODUCT

Cost is divided into direct and indirect cost in terms of degree of traceability to the product.

Direct Cost

Costs which are easily traceable or identifiable with a product are called direct costs. If output units are the objects of costing, then direct costs represent costs and resources that can be traced to or identified with the finished product.

Direct materials, direct labour and direct expenses are examples of direct costs.

Indirect Cost

Indirect costs are those costs which cannot be identified with, or traced to a single product because they are incurred for several products. The examples of indirect costs are: indirect materials (lubricants and scrap materials), salary of factory supervisors (indirect labour), rent, rates and depreciation (indirect expenses). Indirect costs, often referred to as overheads, have to be apportioned to different products.

Costs also may be direct or indirect with respect to particular company segments or divisions. That is some cost which are indirect for a product, may be traced to a segment or department and thus, will be direct costs for that department. A segment may mean any one of a number of things, namely department, division, specific activity, sales territory and the like.

Before dividing the cost into direct and indirect, it is necessary to know whether it is being associated with a product, sales area, department or some other activity. For example, if a salesman simultaneously handles several products, his salary is an indirect cost for each product, but a direct cost to his sales area or department.

ASSOCIATION WITH THE PRODUCT

Cost is classified into product costs and period costs in terms of association with the product.

Product Cost

Product costs are those costs which are identified with the product and included in inventory values. In other words, the costs that are included in the cost of manufacturing a product are called product costs. In a manufacturing concern, it is composed of four elements: (i) direct materials, (ii) direct labour, (iii) direct expenses, and (iv) manufacturing overhead. That is, product cost is a full factory cost. Prior to sale, product costs are deferred as inventories and until the goods are sold, are shown on the balance sheet as assets. As finished inventory goods is sold, product costs are transferred from the inventory accounts to the cost of goods sold account, thus becoming expenses and part of the period costs at the time revenue is realised.

Period Cost

Period costs are the costs which are not identified with product or job and are deducted as expenses during the period in which they are incurred. They are not carried forward as a part of value of inventory to the next accounting period.

These costs are necessary to generate revenues, but they cannot be directly associated with units of product. Difference of opinion exists regarding whether certain costs should be considered as product or period costs. It is generally accepted that selling and administrative expenses should be treated as period costs for the following reasons:

(i) It is difficult to select equitable bases to apportion these costs to products. On the other hand, product costs can be assigned to specific products through objective and direct measurements and some by allocation.

(ii) The majority of these expenses are fixed regardless of the change in production or activity.

(iii) It is difficult, if not impossible, to determine the relationship between the incurrence of these costs and the production of individual units of output.

(iv) It is difficult to get evidence as to any future benefits that would be obtained from these expenses at the end of the accounting period. Such is the case with clerical salaries, used postage, office supplies, rent, advertising, sales promotion, consulting fees which may be expected to provide future benefits, but they are usually expensed when incurred. Even if it is argued that there will be future benefits, it is difficult to make accurate measurements of such benefits.

Effect of Product Costs and Period Costs

The net income of a business enterprise is influenced by the amount of product costs and period costs. Therefore, the manner in which some costs are divided as product or period will have a bearing on the reported net income of a business firm. Product costs, in the first instance, influence the value of inventory as such costs by nature should be included in the cost of product. Product costs affect net income in the period in which products representing the product costs have been sold. This event of influencing net income may take place in the current accounting period or subsequent accounting period. In other words, products costs do not reach the income statement and will not influence net income of a business enterprise until the product is sold. However, period costs appear directly on the income statement in the month or the period in which they are incurred.

FUNCTIONAL CLASSIFICATION OF COSTS

Functional classification of costs refers to how the cost was used (manufacturing, administration or selling). A functional classification implies that the business performs many functions for which costs are incurred. In measuring net income, expenses are usually classified by function and grouped under the headings of manufacturing, selling and administrative costs. Manufacturing costs are all production costs incurred to manufacture the products and to bring them to a saleable condition, including direct materials, direct labour and indirect manufacturing (or factory overhead) costs. Selling and administrative charges may be treated as expenses when incurred or charged to prepaid expense accounts such as prepaid insurance. Functional classification is also important because it provides an opportunity to the management to evaluate the efficiency of departments performing different functions in the organisation.

RELATIONSHIP WITH ACCOUNTING PERIOD

Capital Cost and Revenue Cost

Costs can also be divided into two broad classes on the basis of the accounting period to which they relate: (i) capital expenditures, and (ii) revenue expenditures. A capital expenditure provides benefit to future periods and is classified as an asset; a revenue expenditure is assumed to benefit the current period and is classified as an expense. A capital expenditure will flow into the cost stream as an expense when the asset is used up or written off.

The distinction between capital and revenue expenditures is vital to the proper matching of costs and revenue and to the accurate measurement of periodic net income.

COSTS FOR DECISION MAKING AND PLANNING

Opportunity Cost

Opportunity cost is the cost of opportunity lost. It is the cost of selecting one course of action in terms of the opportunities which are given up to carry out that course of action. Opportunity cost is the benefit lost by rejecting the best competing alternative to the one chosen. The benefit lost is usually the net earnings or profits that might have been earned from the rejected alternative. For example, assume that a manufacturer can sell a semi-finished product to a customer for ₹5,00,000. He decides, however, to keep it and finish it. The opportunity cost of the semi-finished product is ₹5,00,000 because this is the amount of economic resources foregone by the manufacturer to complete the product. Similarly, capital which is invested in plant and inventories cannot now be invested in shares and debentures that will earn interest and dividends. The loss of interest and dividend that would be earned is the opportunity cost. Other examples of opportunity cost are when the owner of a business foregoes the opportunity to employ himself elsewhere; or a machine used to make Product A is said to have an opportunity cost if the machine can be sold or if it can also make Product B.

Opportunity costs are important in decision-making and evaluating alternatives. Decision-making is selecting the best alternative which is facilitated by the help of opportunity costs. But opportunity costs are not recorded in an accounting system as they relate to opportunities lost.

Sunk Cost

A sunk cost is the cost that has already been incurred. Generally known as unavoidable cost, it refers to all past costs since these amounts cannot be changed once the cost is incurred. They are the costs which have been created by a decision in the past and cannot be changed or avoided by any decision that is made in the future. Examples of sunk costs are the book values of existing assets, such as plant and equipment, inventory, investment in securities, etc. Except the possible gains or losses on sales of any of such assets, the book value is not relevant for decisions regarding whether to use them or dispose them off.

Some argue that the total cost of a fixed asset is not the sunk cost, but sunk cost is the difference between the purchase price of a fixed asset and the net amount that could be realised from its sale. For example, if a plant has a book value of ₹10,00,000 and a scrap value of ₹50,000, then the sunk cost is ₹9,50,000 (₹10,00,000 – ₹50000) and not ₹10,00,000. That is, the sunk cost is the difference between book value and scrap value.

Relevant Cost

Relevant costs are those future costs which differ between alternatives. Relevant costs may also be defined as the cost which are affected and changed by a decision. On the contrary, irrelevant costs are those costs which remain the same and not affected by the decision whatever alternative is chosen. Relevant costs have the following two features:

(i) Relevant costs are only future costs, that is, those costs which are expected to be incurred in future. Relevant costs therefore, are not historic (sunk) costs which have already been incurred and cannot be changed by a decision.

(ii) Relevant costs are only incremental (additional) or avoidable costs. Incremental costs refer to an increase in cost between two alternatives. Avoidable costs are those which are not incurred from one alternative to another.

To take an example, assume a business firm purchased a plant for ₹10,00,000 and has now a book value of ₹1,00,000. The plant had become obsolete and cannot be sold in its present condition. However, the plant can be sold for ₹1,50,000 if some modification is done on it which will cost ₹60,000. In this example, ₹60,000 (modification cost) and ₹1,50,000 (sales value), both are relevant as they reflect future—incremental costs and future revenues respectively. The firm will have incremental benefit of ₹90,000 (₹1,50,000 – ₹60,000) on sale of the plant.

₹10,00,000 has already been incurred and being a sunk cost is not relevant to the decision, that is, whether modification should be done. Similarly, the book value of ₹1,00,000, which has to be written off, whatever alternative future action is chosen, is also not relevant because it cannot be changed by any future decision.

EXAMPLE 2.1

Welgrow Ltd is a manufacturer of garden seed compost. At the moment, it makes six different types and is considering adding a new basic compost to its range. Initially, it will make a batch of 10,000 kg and has listed the following costs involved.

1. Exclusive use of the company's mixing machine will be needed for one week. The depreciation of this machine is included as a production overhead at ₹52,000 per year.
2. The trial batch will need 7,000 kg of vermiculite. Welgrow does not use this material and does not have any of it in stock at present; its market price is ₹100 per kg.
3. Several years ago, Welgrow bought a large quantity of black sand at ₹10 per kg for a special project. A left-over surplus of 3,000 kg is currently in stock as it has proved impossible to resell. Welgrow has no alternative use for this surplus other than as an ingredient in the new compost.
4. To ensure successful marketing of this new product at the right time, a contract for advertising space with a total cost of ₹50,000 has been signed. A deposit of 20% has been paid and the balance is due one month before launch next spring.
5. An aluminium storage bin, which was due to have been offered for sale at the realistic price of ₹10,000, will be used for the new compost.

Consider each item and state why you think it is relevant or not. Calculate the relevant cost to Welgrow of the decision to go ahead. Also, calculate the breakeven selling price of the new compost.

Solution

Item	*Avoidable*	*Future*	*Cash*	*Note*	*Amount*	*Relevant (₹)*
1. Mixing machine		X		1		
2. Vermiculite	X	X	X	2	7,000 @ ₹100	7,00,000
3. Black sand				3		–
4. Advertising space			X	4		–
5. Storage bin	X	X	X	5		10,000
					Relevant cost	7,10,000

For the batch of 10,000 kg, the breakeven selling price is ₹71 per kg.

Note:

1. Depreciation is a non-cash expense.
2. Vermiculite needs to be bought in at replacement cost.
3. Sunk cost with no alternative use.
4. The 20% deposit is sunk and the 80% remainder is committed.
5. Opportunity cost.

Differential Cost

Differential cost is the difference in total costs between any two alternatives. Differential costs are equal to the additional variable expenses incurred in respect of the additional output, plus the increase in fixed costs, if any. This cost may be calculated by taking the total cost of production without the additional contemplated output and comparing it with the total costs incurred if the extra output is undertaken.

Differential costs are also known as incremental costs, although technically an incremental cost should refer only to an increase in cost from one alternative to another; decrease in cost should be referred to as decremental cost. Differential cost is a broader term, encompassing both cost increases (incremental costs) and cost decreases (decremental costs) between alternatives.

For example, assume that a company has normal capacity to manufacture 50,000 units of a product; production beyond that point would require the installation of additional plant and equipment that would increase the amount of fixed costs. Normal utilisation of available capacity ranges between 40,000 and 50,000 units. Fixed costs for the range of output and expanded capacity have been estimated as follows:

	Normal Capacity	*Expanded Capacity*
Number of units	40,000 to 50,000	50,000 to 60,000
Fixed costs	₹2,00,000	₹2,50,000

Now, assume that the variable cost is ₹4 per unit. A statement comparing manufacturing costs at three different production levels would be as follows:

	Number of Units		
	40,000	*50,000*	*60,000*
Variable costs	₹1,60,000	₹2,00,000	₹2,40,000
Fixed costs	₹2,00,000	2,00,000	2,50,000
Total manufacturing cost	3,60,000	4,00,000	4,90,000
Average cost per unit	₹9.00	₹8.00	₹8.17
Incremental costs	—	40,000	90,000
Additional output (units)	—	10,000	10,000
Incremental cost per unit	—	₹4.00	₹9.00

The additional capacity which would be required to expand operations to 60,000 units would increase the fixed costs by ₹50,000. The incremental cost of an additional 10,000 units would be total of ₹90,000 or ₹9.00 per unit. The average cost of the 60,000 units would be ₹8.17 per unit.

The concept of differential costing is vital in planning and decision-making. It is an important tool in evaluating the profitability of alternative choice decisions and helping management in choosing the best alternative. The differential cost analysis can assist management in knowing the additional profit that would be earned if idle or unused capacity is used for extra production or if some additional investments are made by the firm.

Imputed Cost

Imputed costs are costs not actually incurred in some transaction but which are relevant to the decision as they pertain to a particular situation. These costs do not enter into traditional accounting system. Interests on internally generated funds, rental value of company-owned property and salaries of owners of a single proprietorship or partnership are some examples of imputed costs. Costs paid or incurred are not imputed costs. For example, if ₹5,00,000 is paid for purchase of raw materials, it is an outlay cost but not an imputed cost, because it would enter into ordinary accounting systems. When a company uses internally generated funds, no actual interest payment is required. But, if the internally generated funds are invested in some projects, interest would have been earned. The revenue foregone (loss of interest) represents an opportunity cost, and thus, imputed costs are opportunity costs.

Out-of-Pocket Cost

While imputed costs do not involve cash outlays, out-of-pocket costs signify the cash cost incurred on an activity. Non-cash costs such as depreciation are not included in out-of-pocket costs. This cost concept is significant for management in deciding whether or not a particular project will at least return the cash expenditures associated with the project selected by management. Similarly, acceptance of a special order for production may necessitate the consideration of out-of-pocket costs that need not be incurred if the special order proposal is not accepted. Depreciation on plant and equipment is not relevant in decision-making because no cash goes outside the business.

Fixed, Variable and Mixed Costs

Fixed, variable and mixed costs have been explained in the preceding sections.

Shut Down Cost

Shut down costs are those costs which have to be incurred under all situations in the case of stopping manufacture of a product or closing down a department or a division. Shut down costs are always fixed costs. If the manufacture of a product is stopped, variable costs like direct materials, direct labour, direct expenses and variable factory overhead will not be incurred. However, a part of fixed costs (if not total fixed costs) associated with the product will be incurred, such as rent, watchman's salary, property taxes etc. Such fixed costs are unavoidable. Some fixed costs associated with the product become avoidable and need not be incurred in case production is stopped, such as supervisor's salary, factory manager's salary, lighting, etc. Shutdown costs, thus, refer to minimum fixed costs which are incurred in the event of closure of a department or division.

COSTS FOR CONTROL

Controllable and Uncontrollable Cost

The concept of controllable cost is very important in cost accounting and contributes to the achievement of the objectives of cost control and responsibility accounting. The ICMA (UK) defines controllable cost as "a cost which can be influenced by the action of a specified member of an undertaking" and a non-controllable cost as "a cost which cannot be influenced by the action of a specified member of an undertaking". Basically, a controllable cost is the cost over which a manager has direct and complete decision authority. That is, controllable costs can be controlled (reduced) by a manager at a given organisational level. Some examples of controllable costs are indirect labour, lubricants, cutting tools, and power costs incurred in the machining department.

Controllable costs do not imply that they are 100% controllable. Some costs are partly controllable by a responsibility centre manager. For example, the cost of raw materials is controlled by the production managers as well as purchase managers. The production manager controls at quantity level, and the purchase manager at the price level. Such costs are reported to both of them, but one responsible manager should be held accountable for those costs which he can control.

The term "controllable cost" should not be confused with the terms "variable cost" and "direct cost". These terms are not synonymous. Variable costs vary with the output but are not necessarily controllable. For example, factory supplies used for servicing plant and equipment may vary with the output in the production department, but the production manager cannot control them.

It is contended that two factors: (i) the time period factor, and (ii) the decision-making authority, can make a cost controllable or uncontrollable. If the time period is long enough, all costs can be controllable and curtailed. Similarly, the decision-making authority influences the cost. If a manager has been delegated the authority to spend the cost, he can control it. But all costs can be said to be controllable by somebody in the organisation. The managing director of a company is responsible for all costs. But practically, the responsibility and authority of controlling costs is delegated to different levels in the organisation.

Standard Cost

Standard costs are those costs which are planned or pre-determined cost estimates for a unit of output in order to provide a basis for comparison with actual costs. Standard costs are used to prepare budgets. Standard cost is a unit concept and indicates standard cost per unit of output, per labour hour etc. On the contrary, the term "Budgeted Cost" is a total concept and indicates total budgeted cost of an item at some activity level or output level such as budgeted cost of material is ₹8,00,000 if 8000 units are manufactured.

Fixed, Variable and Mixed Costs

Fixed, variable and mixed costs have been discussed earlier in this chapter.

OTHER COSTS

Joint Cost

Joint costs arise where the processing of a single raw material or production resources results in two or more different products simultaneously. Joint costs relate to two or more products produced from a common production process or element-material, labour, or overhead or any combination thereof, or so locked together that one cannot be produced without producing the other(s).

Thus, joint cost is the cost of two or more products that are not identifiable as individual types of products until a certain stage of production known as the split-off point (point of separation) is reached. For example, kerosene, fuel oil, petrol and other oil products are derived from crude oil. Joint costs are total costs incurred upto the point of separation. Joint costs can be apportioned to different products only by means of some suitable bases of apportionment.

Common Cost

Common costs are those which are incurred for more than one product, job, territory or any other specific costing object. Common costs are not easily identifiable with individual products and, therefore, are generally apportioned.

Common costs are not only common to products, but they may be common to processes, functions, responsibilities, customers, sales territories, periods of time and similar costing units. For example, the salary of a manager of a production department, which is manufacturing three products, is an example of common cost with respect to the products. But his salary is direct cost to the departments located in the factory. The basic point is that a particular (common) cost may be direct to one object and common as far as other objects are concerned.

Although both the terms, "common costs" and "joint costs" are sometime used interchangeably, they differ from each other. Joint costs emerge when multiple products are manufactured in a common process and when common inputs are used. The multiple products have a definite quantitative relationship to each other and the production of one product influences the output of the other product, though in a lesser proportion. Common costs are not the result of any manufacturing compulsion or the use of any single raw material. Besides, common costs do not have much difficulty. But the apportionment of joint cost involves many difficulties in cost accounting.

COST CONTROL, COST REDUCTION AND COST MANAGEMENT

Cost Control

Cost control refers to management actions to keep the costs within standards and/or budget. Cost control can be defined as the comparative analysis of actual costs with appropriate standards or budgets to facilitate performance evaluation and formulation of corrective measures. It aims at accomplishing conformity between actual result and standards or budgets, keeping expenditures within prescribed limits. Cost control has the following features:

1. Creation of responsibility centres with defined authority and responsibility for cost incurrence.
2. Formulation of standards and budgets that incorporate objectives and goals to be achieved.
3. Timely cost control reports (responsibility reporting) describing the variances between budgets and standards and actual performance.
4. Formulation of corrective measures to eliminate and reduce unfavourable variances.
5. A systematic and fair plan of motivation to encourage workers to accomplish budgetary goals.
6. Follow-up to ensure that corrective measures are being effectively applied.

Cost control does not necessarily mean reducing the cost but its aim is to have the maximum utility of the cost incurred. In other words, the objective of cost control is the performance of the same job at a lower cost or a better performance for the same cost.

Cost Reduction

Meaning

Cost reduction may be defined as a planned, positive approach to bring costs down. It implies real and permanent reduction in the unit cost of goods manufactured or services rendered without impairing their (product or goods) quality or suitability for the use intended that is, without reducing their value in terms of utility or satisfaction to the customers. The goal of cost reduction is achieved in two ways: (i) by reducing the cost per unit, and (ii) by increasing productivity. The steps for cost reduction include elimination of waste, improving operations, increasing productivity, search for cheaper materials, improved standards of quality, and finding other means to reduce unit costs.

Cost reduction has to be achieved using internal factors within the organisation. Reduction of costs due to external factors, such as reduction in taxes, government subsidies, grant etc., does not come under the concept of cost reduction. It should not be the result of wind falls.

With the globalisation of the Indian economy, it is necessary to reduce costs so that prices of our goods are really competitive in the world markets. This requires a massive effort on cost reduction in Indian industries.

Thus, cost reduction techniques occupy a prominent position in any organisation aiming to maximise profits.

Management should always attempt to remove difficulties generally found in cost reduction programmes. Some such difficulties are as follows:

(i) Workers and employees may not welcome cost reduction programmes and may resist their implementation.
(ii) Cost reduction programmes are generally carried out on an *ad hoc* basis.
(iii) The schemes may be applied in some areas but it should cover all activities.
(iv) Cost reduction programmes may be implemented hurriedly, whereas, they should be carried out after careful thought and in a planned manner.

Difference between Cost Control and Cost Reduction

Cost reduction is a much wider concept than cost control. As stated earlier, cost control aims at controlling costs within prescribed limits with the help of budgets and standards. The following are the differences between the two:

Cost Control	*Cost Reduction*
1. Cost control process involves (a) setting targets and standards, (b) ascertaining actual performance, (c) comparing actual performance with targets, (d) investigating the variances, and (e) taking corrective action. In cost control, standards form benchmarks for evaluating actual performance.	1. Cost reduction is not concerned with setting targets and standards, and maintaining performance according to standards. It involves critical examination of the various products, processes, methods etc. with a view to reduce costs and improve efficiency and effectiveness.
2. It aims at adherence to and achieving standards, that is, cost targets. It assumes existence of standards and these standards are not challenged over the period.	2. It aims at real and permanent reduction in costs. Thus, it aims at improving the standards. It challenges standards and assumes existence of concealed potential savings in the standards.
3. It lacks a dynamic approach as the only objective is not to exceed the standards.	3. It is continuous, dynamic and innovative in nature, looking always for measures and alternative to reduce costs.
4. It is a preventive function.	4. It is a never ending corrective function.
5. In cost control, costs are optimised before they are incurred. Being a routine exercise it is operation-oriented.	5. In cost reduction, there is always assumed a scope for reducing the incurred costs under controlled conditions. It is research-oriented, always trying to reduce costs through planned research.
6. It is generally applicable to items which have standards	6. This is applicable to every activity of the business.

(Contd.)

Cost Control	Cost Reduction
7. It contains guidelines and directive of management as to how to do a thing.	7. It adds thinking and analysis to action at all levels of management.
8. It requires close monitoring and timely corrective actions.	8. It demands creativity.
9. Budgetary control and standard costing are important tools of cost control.	9. It uses techniques like value engineering, value analysis, work study, operation research, ABC analysis, simplification and standardisation etc.

Both cost control and cost reduction are continuous processes in an enterprise. In all organisations, there should be planned, dynamic programme for cost reduction so that cost standards required for cost control may be improved continuously. However, cost reduction programme is neither a substitute nor it can replace a cost control system which emphasises prompt investigation into variances and taking immediate corrective actions.

Techniques of Cost Reduction

Generally speaking, the following tools and techniques are used for the purpose of cost reduction:

1. Value analysis or value engineering
2. Work study
3. Job evaluation and merit rating
4. Production planning and control
5. Organisation and method study
6. Operations and method study, work study
7. Rationalisation
8. Quality control
9. Economic order quantity
10. Use of better technology
11. Mechanisation and automation
12. Standardisation
13. Simplification
14. ABC analysis
15. Budgetary control and standard costing
16. Programme Evaluation and Review Technique (PERT) analysis
17. Cost-benefit analysis
18. Improvement in the design of a product, design analysis
19. Market research
20. Inventory management and control

Cost Reduction Areas

Some of the important cost reduction areas are as follows:

1. Product improvement Product improvement and the level of efficiency determine the costs incurred. Important factors in product improvement are:

(a) Quality of the product.
(b) Unnecessary weight, materials content, machine or labour operations.

(c) Waste and losses to be eliminated.
(d) Proper designing of the product.

2. Production planning and control The area of production methods and organisation is important for the purpose of cost reduction. There are many vital activities relating to production and production planning where a cost reduction programme may be applied, for example, materials control, labour control, production layout, system analysis, time and motion study, work measurements, standardisation of methods, designing of tools, equipment and machinery, modernisation of plant and equipment, use of incentive schemes, etc.

3. Marketing areas In marketing, the following are the cost reduction areas: channels of distribution, sales promotion schemes, marketing research plan, territorial responsibilities, methods of remunerating salesmen, advertising methods, after-sales service costs, packaging methods, materials handling, transport arrangement, etc.

4. Administrative areas Administrative functions include personnel, purchase and general administration.

The goal of cost reduction requires efficiency administration, effective purchasing procedure and a fair personnel policy and schemes. Some of the important areas are investment planning, cash discount policy, mechanised system of accounting, labour relations, labour welfare measure, and availability of servicing facilities.

5. Factory organisation and methods A considerable cost reduction can be affected by studying factory organisation and various methods being used in the factory.

(i) Factory management must ensure correct assignment of authority and responsibility.
(ii) There should be well-defined channels of communication to avoid ambiguity, misunderstanding and differences of opinion.
(iii) Overlapping of responsibility should be clearly avoided.
(iv) Delegation of responsibility should be encouraged.
(v) Cooperation and close-relationship between the various executives should be encouraged.

6. Utility services Utility services include power, water, steam, repair and maintenance, transport and clerical services, etc.

The following points should be considered:

(i) Supply of utilities at economical costs or scope for any further increase in utilisation.
(ii) Proper system for preventive and curative maintenance.
(iii) Wastage and other losses in distribution to be kept to minimum.
(iv) Use of up-to-date equipment and the mechanisation of the routine as far as possible.
(v) Due attention to work flow and loading factor.

7. Finance The following points are important in this connection:

(i) Methods of funding capital expenditure to be cost effective.
(ii) Procuring capital at economical cost.
(iii) Employing capital in a manner so as to give the maximum return.

Cost Management

Cost management is a wider term than cost control and cost reduction. It considers both cost control and cost reduction in its perspective. In cost management, the objective is to increase productivity of resources and factors of production and to relate them to enhance profitability. It continuously looks for and identifies opportunities to have higher return on investment by studying customer needs, bringing improvement in the existing products or services, smoothening process and layout of manufacturing goods or services with a view to supply them to the customers and to ensure customer's satisfaction so as to maximise margins and earn higher profits. In this way, cost management achieves its goals by creating and sustaining linkages among revenue, cost, products manufactured or services rendered and the use of resources and infrastructure of an organisation.

Cost management identifies, collects, measures, classifies and reports information that is useful to managers and other internal users in cost ascertainment, planning, controlling and decision-making.

Horngreen, Datar and Foster[1] are of the opinion that the term cost management has no uniform definition. Therefore, these authors use cost management to describe the approaches and activities of managers in short- and long-run planning and control decisions that increase value for customers and lower the costs of products and services. For example, managers make decisions regarding the amounts and kinds of materials being used, changes in plant processes and changes in product designs. Information from accounting systems helps managers to manage costs, but the information and the accounting systems themselves are not cost management.

Developing information within cost management requires that one should be aware about the cost structure of a business enterprise. Managers should know how to ascertain costs of different activities, processes, customers, goods, services and any other costing objects. Financial accounting does not deal with these costs and these costs are not found on the financial statements. However, knowledge about these costs is essential to help managers in productivity enhancement, strategic planning and management, total quality management, management control. By nature cost management includes both management accounting information system as well as cost accounting.

EXAMPLE 2.2

A company manufactures and retails clothing. You are required to group the costs which are listed below and numbered 1 to 20 into the following classification: (Each cost is intended to belong to only one classification).

(a) Direct Materials
(b) Direct Labour
(c) Direct Expenses
(d) Indirect Production Overhead
(e) Selling and Distribution Costs
(f) Research and Development Costs
(g) Finance Cost
(h) Administration Costs

1. Charles T. Horngree, Srikant M. Datar and George Foster, *Cost Accounting, A Managerial Emphasis*, Pearson Education, 2008, p. 3.

1. Telephone rental plus metered calls
2. Wages of security guards for factory
3. Parcels sent to customers
4. Wages of operatives in cutting department
5. Developing a new product in the laboratory
6. Wage of fork lift truck drivers who handle raw materials
7. Wages of storekeepers in materials store
8. Chief accountant's salary
9. Cost of painting advertising slogans in delivery vans
10. Auditor's fee
11. Cost of advertising on television
12. Lubricants for sewing machines
13. Floppy disks for general office computer
14. Maintenance contract for office photo copying machine
15. Interest on bank overdraft
16. Market research undertaken prior to new product launch
17. Carriage on purchase of raw materials
18. Royalty paid on number of units of a particular product produced
19. Road licences for delivery vehicles
20. Amount payable to a company for broadcasting music throughout the factory

☞ ***Solution***

Cost Element	*Numbers*
Direct materials	17
Direct labour	4
Direct expenses	18
Finance cost	15
Research and development expenses	5
Selling and distribution cost	3, 9, 11, 16, 19
Administration cost	1, 8, 10, 13, 14
Indirect production costs	2, 6, 7, 12, 20

COST STATEMENT OR COST SHEET

Cost statement is a statement which is prepared usually to present the detailed costs of total production during the period in question. It provides information relating to cost per unit at different stages of the total cost of production or at different stages of completion of the product. Sometimes, standard cost data are also provided to facilitate comparison with the actual cost incurred. The preparation of the cost sheet requires understanding of the treatment of the following items:

1. Stock of raw materials The cost statement requires the determination of the value of raw materials consumed for the output produced. If the opening stock of raw materials, purchase of raw materials during the period and closing stock of raw materials are given, then the value of raw materials consumed is computed as follows:

	₹
Opening stock of raw materials	
Add: Purchase of raw materials	
Total	
Less: Closing stock of raw materials	
Value of raw materials consumed	

2. Stock of work-in-progress Work-in-progress represents the accumulated costs on goods that have not yet been completed. As such these goods are not yet available for sale. The degree of completion of work-in-progress is usually expressed as a fraction or as a percentage, such as 2/5 complete for materials or 50% complete for labour.

Work-in-progress is valued on a prime-cost or factory-cost basis. In case it is to be valued on a factory cost basis, the following procedure would be followed:

	₹
Prime cost	
Add: Factory overhead	
Add: Work-in-progress (beginning)	
Total	
Less: Work-in-progress (closing)	
Factory cost	

3. Stock of finished goods Finished goods inventory covers the products on which all factory work has been completed. It carries the cost of completed production. Nothing more is to be done to finished goods at the factory and no further costs are added to finished goods. If opening and closing stock of finished goods are given, then they would be adjusted as under:

	₹
Cost of production	
Add: Finished goods (beginning)	
Total	
Less: Finished goods (closing)	
Cost of goods sold	

As stated earlier, cost sheet gives details about the cost of manufacturing a product or completing an activity. A cost sheet discloses:

(1) Prime Cost
(2) Factory Cost (also known as Works Cost)
(3) Cost of Production
(4) Total Cost (or Cost of Sales)

A cost sheet shows total cost and cost per unit. Cost per unit is obtained by dividing total cost by the number of units produced. A cost sheet will have separate columns for the total and the unit cost of each element of cost. Cost sheet can be prepared on weekly, monthly or other time period basis as desired by management. Specimen of a cost sheet is given below:

Specimen of Cost Sheet
Cost Sheet for the Period ____________
Production ____________ Units

	Total Cost (₹)	*Cost Per Unit (₹)*
Direct materials:		
Opening stock		
Purchases		
Carriage inwards		
Less: Closing stock		
Less: Scrap		
Direct materials consumed		
Direct wages		
Direct expenses		
I. *Prime Cost*		
Add: Factory Overheads:		
Indirect materials		
Loose tools		
Indirect wages		
Rent and rates (factory)		
Lighting and heating (factory)		
Power and fuel		
Repairs and maintenance		
Cleaning		
Drawing office expenses		
Cost of research and experiments		
Depreciation of factory plant		
Works stationery		
Welfare service expenses		
Insurance—Fixed assets etc.		
—Stock and finished goods		
Works Managers' salaries		
II. *Factory or Works Cost*		
Add: Office and Administrative Overheads:		
Rent and rates (office)		
Salaries (office)		

(Contd.)

	Total Cost (₹)	Cost Per Unit (₹)
Lighting and heating		
Insurance of office building and equipments etc.		
Telephone and postages		
Printing and stationery		
Depreciation of furniture and office equipments and buildings		
Legal expenses		
Audit fees		
Bank charges		
III. *Cost of Production*		
Add: Selling and Distribution Overheads:		
Showroom rent and rates		
Lighting and heating		
Salesmen's salaries		
Commissions		
Travelling expenses of salesmen		
Sales printing and stationery		
Advertising		
Bad debts		
Postage		
Depreciation and expenses of delivery van		
Debt collection expenses		
Carriage freight outwards		
Samples and other free gifts		
IV. *Cost of Sales*		
Net profit (or loss)		
Sales		

Note: Items of expenses which are an appropriation of profit should not form a part of the costs of a product. Examples of such expenses are: (i) Income tax; (ii) Dividends to shareholders; (iii) Commission (out of profit) to managing directors or partners; (iv) Capital loss, that is, loss arising out of sale of assets; (v) Interest on loan; (vi) Donations; (vii) Capital expenditure; (viii) Discount on shares and debentures; (ix) Underwriting commission; (x) Writing off goodwill.

EXAMPLE 2.3

Vijay Industries manufactures a product X. On 1st January 2020, there were 5000 units of finished product in stock. Other stocks on 1st January 2020 were as follows:

Works-in-progress	₹57,400
Raw materials	₹1,16,200

The information available from cost records for the year ended 31st December 2020 was as follows:

	₹
Direct materials	9,06,900
Direct labour	3,26,400
Freight on raw materials purchased	55,700
Indirect labour	1,21,600
Other factory overheads	3,17,300
Stock of raw materials on 31.12.2020	96,400
Work in progress on 31.12.2020	78,207
Sales (1,50,000 units)	30,00,000
Indirect materials	2,13,900

There are 15000 units of finished stock in hand on 31st December 2020. You are required to prepare:

A statement of cost and profit assuming that opening stock of finished goods is to be valued at the same cost per unit as the finished stock at the end of the period.

Solution

Statement of Cost and Profit of Product X

Particulars	*Amount* (₹)	*Amount* (₹)
Opening stock of raw materials	1,16,200	
Add: Direct materials	9,06,900	
Add: Freight on raw materials purchased	55,700	
	10,78,800	
Less: Closing stock of raw materials	96,400	
Value of Raw Materials Consumed		9,82,400
Add: Direct wages		3,26,400
Prime cost		13,08,800
Add: Factory overheads:		
Indirect materials	2,13,900	
Indirect labour	1,21,600	
Other factory overheads	3,17,300	
	6,52,800	
Add: Opening work-in-progress	57,400	
	7,10,200	
Less: Closing work-in-progress	78,200	6,32,000
Works Cost of Goods Manufactured		19,40,800
Add: Opening stock of finished goods 5,000 units @ ₹12.13		60,650
		20,01,450
Less: Closing stock of finished goods 15,000 units @ ₹12.13		1,81,950
Cost of Goods Sold		18,19,500
Profit		11,80,500
Sales		30,00,000

WORKING NOTES:

Units produced during the year are not given and therefore have been computed as follows:

$$\text{Sales} = \text{Opening stock} + \text{Units produced} \quad \text{Closing stock}$$

$$1{,}50{,}000 = 5{,}000 + X - 15{,}000$$

$$-X = 5{,}000 - 15{,}000 - 1{,}50{,}000$$

$$\text{Hence} \quad X = 1{,}60{,}000 \text{ units}$$

$$\text{Value of closing stock} = \frac{\text{Total cost}}{\text{Units produced}} = \frac{₹19{,}40{,}800}{1{,}60{,}000} = ₹12.13 \text{ per unit}$$

$$= 15{,}000 \text{ units} \times ₹12.13 = ₹1{,}81{,}950$$

Value of opening stock of 5,000 units × ₹12.13 = ₹60,650

EXAMPLE 2.4

The following particulars relating to the year 2020 have been taken from the books of a chemical works manufacturing and selling a chemical mixture:

Stock on January 1, 2020	*kg*	₹
Raw materials	2,000	2,000
Finished mixture	500	1,750
Factory stores		7,250
Purchases:		
Raw materials	1,60,000	1,80,000
Factory stores		24,250
Sales:		
Finished mixture	1,53,050	9,18,000
Factory scrap		8,170
Factory wages		1,78,650
Power		30,400
Depreciation of machinery		18,000
Salaries:		
Factory		72,220
Office		37,220
Selling		41,500
Expenses:		
Direct		18,500
Office		18,200
Selling		18,000

(Contd.)

Stock on December 31, 2020	*kg*	₹
Raw materials	1,200	
Finished mixture	450	
Factory stores		5,550

The stock of finished mixture at the end of 2020 is to be valued at the factory cost of the mixture for that year. The purchase of raw materials remained unchanged throughout 2020.

Prepare a statement giving the maximum possible information about cost and its break-up for the year 2020.

Solution

Statement of Cost for the Year 2020

		Quantity (*kg*)	*Amount* (₹)
Raw materials consumed:			
Opening stock		2,000	2,000
Add: Purchases		1,60,000	1,80,000
		1,62,000	1,82,000
Less: Closing stock of raw materials at current prices		1,200	1,350
Cost of raw materials consumed		1,60,800	1,80,650
Factory wages			1,78,650
Direct expenses			18,500
Prime cost		1,60,800	3,77,800
Add: Factory overheads (factory stores)			
Opening stock	7,250		
Add: Purchases	24,250		
	31,500		
Less: Closing stock	5,550		
Factory stores consumed	25,950		
Power	30,400		
Depreciation	18,000		
Salaries	72,220		1,46,570
			5,24,370
Less: Sale of scrap		7,800	8,170
Factory cost		1,53,000	5,16,200

(Contd.)

		Quantity (kg)	Amount (₹)
Add: Opening stock of finished mixture		500	1,750
		1,53,500	5,17,950
Less: Closing stock of finished mixture (valued at factory cost of current year production)		450	1,518
		1,53,050	5,16,432
Add: Office overheads:			
Salaries	37,220		
Expenses	18,200		55,420
Cost of production of finished mixture sold			5,71,852
Add: Selling and distribution overhead:			
Salaries	41,500		
Expenses	18,000		59,500
Cost of goods sold or cost of sales:			6,31,352
Profit			2,86,648
Sales		1,53,050 kg	9,18,000

✍ WORKING NOTES:

1. Value of closing stock of raw materials $\left(\dfrac{₹1,80,000}{₹1,60,000} \times 1,200\text{kg}\right) = ₹1,350$
2. Value of factory scrap given in the question is ₹8,170. Hence, quantity of factory scrap will be:

	(kg)
Sales	1,53,050
Add: Closing stock	450
	1,53,500
Less: Opening stock	500
Produced during the year	1,53,000
Inputs introduced	1,60,800
Scrap	7,800

✍ EXAMPLE 2.5

The following figures are extracted from the trial balance of Gogetter Co. on 30th September, 2020:

Inventories:	₹	₹
Finished stock	80,000	
Raw materials	1,40,000	
Work-in-process	2,00,000	
Office appliances	17,400	
Plant and machinery	4,60,500	

(Contd.)

Inventories:	₹	₹
Buildings	2,00,000	
Sales		7,68,000
Sales return and rebates	14,000	
Materials purchases	3,20,000	
Freight incurred on materials	16,000	
Purchases returns		4,800
Direct labour	1,60,000	
Indirect labour	18,000	
Factory supervision	10,000	
Repairs and upkeep factory	14,000	
Heat, light and power	65,000	
Rates and taxes	6,300	
Miscellaneous factory expenses	18,700	
Sales commission	33,600	
Sales travelling	11,000	
Sales promotion	22,500	
Distribution deptt. sales and expenses	18,000	
Office salaries and expenses	8,600	
Interest on borrowed funds	2,000	

Further details are available as follows:

(i) Closing inventories:

Finished goods	1,15,000
Raw materials	1,80,000
Work-in-process	1,92,000

(ii) Accrued expenses on:

Direct labour	8,000
Indirect labour	1,200
Interest on borrowed funds	2,000

(iii) Depreciation to be provided on:

Office appliance	5%
Plant and machinery	10%
Buildings	4%

(iv) Distribution of the following costs:

Heat, light and power to factory, office and selling in the ratio 8:1:1.

Rates and taxes two-thirds to factory and one-third to office. Depreciation on buildings to factory, office and selling in the ratio 8:1:1.

(Contd.)

With the help of the above information, you are required to prepare a condensed profit and loss statement of Gogetter Co. for the year ended 30th September, 2020 along with supporting schedules:

(a) Cost of sales.
(b) Selling and distribution expenses.
(c) Administration expense.

☞ ***Solution***

Gogetter Company Profit and Loss Statement
For the Year Ended 30th September, 2020

Gross Sales	₹7,68,000	₹
Less: Returns	14,000	7,54,000
Less: Cost of sales (Schedule 1)		7,14,020
Net Operating Profit		39,980
Less: Interest on borrowed funds		4,000
Net Profit		35,980

(i) Schedule 1: Cost of Sales

Raw Material:	₹	₹
Opening Balance		1,40,000
Add: Material purchased	3,20,000	
Add: Freight on material	16,000	
Less: Purchased returns	(4,800)	3,31,200
Cost of materials available		4,71,200
Less: Closing stock		1,80,000
Raw materials consumed		2,91,200
Direct labour		1,68,000
Prime cost		4,59,200
Factory Overheads:		
Indirect labour	19,200	
Factory supervision	10,000	
Repairs and factory upkeep	14,000	
Heat, light and power	52,000	
Rates and taxes	4,200	
Miscellaneous factory expenses	18,700	
Depreciation of plant	46,050	
Depreciation of buildings	6,400	1,70,550
Gross Works Cost		6,29,750

(Contd.)

	₹
Add: Opening work-in-process	2,00,000
	8,29,750
Less: Closing work-in-process	1,92,000
Works cost	6,37,750
Add: Administration expenses (Schedule 3)	18,870
Cost of production	6,56,620
Add: Opening stock of finished goods	80,000
	7,36,620
Less: Closing stock of finished goods	1,15,000
Cost of production of goods sold	6,21,620
Add: Selling and distribution overheads (Schedule 2)	92,400
Cost of sales	7,14,020

(ii) Schedule 2: Selling and Distribution Overheads (Expenses)

Sales commission	33,600
Sales travelling	11,000
Sales promotion	22,500
Distribution deptt: Salaries and expenses	18,000
Heat, light and power	6,500
Depreciation of buildings	800
	92,400

(iii) Schedule 3: Administrative Overheads (Expenses)

Office salaries and expenses	8,600
Depreciation of office appliances	870
Depreciation of buildings	800
Heat, light and power	6,500
Rates and taxes	2,100
	18,870

EXAMPLE 2.6

X Ltd. manufactures four brands of toys—*A, B, C* and *D*. If the company limits the manufacture to just one brand, the monthly production will be:

A—50000 units
B—100000 units
C—150000 units
D—300000 units

You are given the following set of information from which you are requested to find out the profit or loss made on each brand showing clearly the following elements—

(a) Direct Cost
(b) Works Cost
(c) Total Cost

	A	*B*	*C*	*D*
Actual production (units)	6750	18000	40500	94500
Direct wages (₹)	15000	27500	37500	105000
Direct materials cost (₹)	50000	92500	127500	380000
Selling price per unit (₹)	20	15	10	8

Factory overhead expenditure for the month was ₹1,62,000. Selling and distribution cost should be assumed @ 20% of works cost. Factory overhead expenses should be allocated to each brand on the basis of units which could have been produced in a month when single-brand production was in operation.

☞ Solution

The relative ratios of each brand of products are as follows:

1 Unit of *A* = 2 units of *B* = 3 units of *C* = 6 units of *D*. Therefore, the overhead ratio in the inverse order should be 1 : 2 : 3 : 6. In case of *D*, the overhead expense rate will be

$$\frac{₹1,62,000}{6750 \times 6 + 18000 \times 3 + 40500 \times 2 + 94500}$$

$$= ₹\frac{162000}{270000}$$

$$= ₹0.60$$

The overhead expense rate for the various brands are:

A — ₹6 × 0.60 = ₹3.60
B — ₹3 × 0.60 = ₹1.80
C — ₹2 × 0.60 = ₹1.20
D — ₹1 × 0.60 = ₹0.60

This follows the logic that the rate should be highest in case of brand which will be produced in least number when single brand production is in operation.

Statement of Profitability of Brands

	A ₹	*B* ₹	*C* ₹	*D* ₹	*Total* ₹
Direct materials	50,000	92,500	1,27,500	3,80,000	6,50,000
Direct wages	15,000	27,500	37,500	1,05,000	1,85,000
Prime cost	65,000	1,20,000	1,65,000	4,85,000	8,35,000
Factory overhead	24,300	32,400	48,600	56,700	1,62,000
Works cost	89,300	1,52,400	2,13,600	5,41,700	9,97,000

(Contd.)

	A ₹	B ₹	C ₹	D ₹	Total ₹
Selling and distribution cost (20% of works cost)	17,860	30,480	42,720	1,08,340	1,99,400
Total Cost	1,07,160	1,82,880	2,56,320	6,50,040	11,96,400
Sales	1,35,000	2,70,000	4,05,000	7,56,000	15,66,000
Profit	27,840	87,120	1,48,680	1,05,960	3,69,600

EXAMPLE 2.7

On June 30, 2020, a flash flood damaged the warehouse and factory of ABC Corporation completely destroying the work-in-progress inventory. There was no damage to either the raw materials or finished goods inventories. A physical verification taken after the flood revealed the following valuations:

Raw materials	₹	62,000
Work-in-progress		0
Finished goods	₹	1,19,000

The inventory on Jan. 1, 2020, consisted of the following:

Raw materials	₹	30,000
Work-in-progress	₹	1,00,000
Finished goods	₹	1,40,000
		2,70,000

A review of the books and records disclosed that the gross profit margin historically approximated 25% of sales. The sales for the first six months of 2020 were ₹3,40,000. Raw material purchases were ₹1,15,000, direct Labour costs for this period were ₹80,000, and manufacturing overhead has historically been 50% of direct labour. Compute the cost of work-in-progress inventory lost at June 30, 2020 by preparing a statement of cost and profit.

Solution

Computation of Work-in-Progress Inventory Lost on June 30, 2020

	₹
Sales	3,40,000
Less: Gross Profit @ 25%	85,000
Cost of goods sold	2,55,000
Add: Closing stock of finished goods	1,19,000
	3,74,000
Less: Opening stock of finished goods	1,40.000
Cost of finished goods produced (1)	2,34,000

(Contd.)

		₹
Less: Raw materials consumed:		
purchases	1,15,000	
Add: Opening stock	30,000	
	1,45,000	
Less: Closing stock	62,000	
	83,000	
Add: Wages	80,000	
Manufacturing overhead	40,000	
Opening stock of work-in-progress	1,00,000	
		3,03,000
Closing stock of work-in-progress		69,000

This can be verified as follows:

	₹
Raw materials consumed	83,000
Direct wages	80,000
Manufacturing overhead	40,000
Work-in-progress	1,00,000
	3,03,000
Less: Closing stock of work-in-progress	69,000
Work costs	2,34,000
Add: Opening stock of finished goods	1,40,000
	3,74,000
Less: Closing stock of finished goods	1,19,000
Cost of goods sold	2,55,000
Add: Gross profit @ 25%	85,000
Sales	3,40,000

EXAMPLE 2.8

The particulars obtained from the records of M/s. Jeevan Industries for the year 2019 are given below:

for excel template, scan

	₹
Opening stock	
Raw materials	1,40,000
Finished goods (1,000 units)	20,000
Purchases	2,10,000
Factory wages	3,80,000
Factory overheads	70,000
Office overheads	40,000
Selling overheads	9,600
Sales (3,200 units)	9,28,000

Closing stock

Raw materials	19,600
Finished goods (900 units)	1,64,080

Prepare a cost sheet showing prime cost, factory cost, cost of production, total cost and sales per unit.

During 2020, the industry expects to receive an order for 5000 units. It is estimated that

(i) the prices of raw materials and factory wages will rise by 15% and 10% respectively.

(ii) there will be no change in the total factory overheads and office overheads.

(iii) selling overheads per unit will remain the same.

Prepare an estimated cost sheet. The factory intends to earn the same rate of profit on cost.

☞ *Solution*

Cost Sheet for 2019

Output: 3,100

		Amount ₹	*Amount Per Unit ₹*
Opening stock of raw material	1,40,000		
+ Purchases	2,10,000		
	3,50,000		
– Closing stock of raw material	19,600		
Cost of raw material consumed		3,30,400	106.58
Factory wages		3,80,000	122.58
Prime Cost		7,10,400	229.16
+ Factory overhead		70,000	22.58
Work Cost		7,80,400	251.74
+ Office overhead		40,000	12.90
Cost of Production		8,20,400	264.64
+ Opening stock of finished goods		20,000	
		8,40,400	264.64
– Closing stock of finished goods		1,64,080	52.93
Cost of Goods Sold		6,76,320	211.71
+ Selling overhead		9,600	3.00
Cost of Sales		6,85,920	214.71
Profit		2,42,080	75.29
Sales		9,28,000	290.00

$$\% \text{ of Profit on sales} = \frac{2,42,080}{9,28,000} \times 100 = 26.08$$

$$\% \text{ of Profit on cost} = \frac{2,42,080}{6,85,920} \times 100 = 35.29\%$$

Estimated Cost Sheet for 2020

		Amount ₹	Amount for Unit ₹
Material consumed (5,000 × 106.58)	5,32,900		
+ 15% Increase in price	79,935		
Material		6,12,835	122.567
Factory wages (5,000 × 122.58)	6,12,900		
+ 10% increase in price	61,290	6,74,190	134.838
Prime Cost		12,87,025	257.405
+ Factory overhead		70,000	14.00
Work Cost		13,57,025	271.405
+ Office overhead		40,000	8.00
Cost of Production		13,97,025	279.405
+ Selling overhead (5,000 × 3.00)		15,000	3.00
Cost of Sales		14,12,025	282.405
+ Profit (35.29% of cost) *i.e.* 35.29% of 14,12,025		4,98,462	99.692
Sales		19,10,487	382.097

EXAMPLE 2.9

Popeye Company is a metal and wood cutting manufacturer, selling products to the home construction market. Consider the following data for the month of October, 2020.

	₹
Sandpaper	5,000
Material-handling costs	1,75,000
Lubricants and coolants	12,500
Miscellaneous indirect manufacturing labour	1,00,000
Direct manufacturing labour	7,50,000
Direct materials, October 1, 2020	1,00,000
Direct materials, October 31, 2020	1,25,000
Finished goods, October 1, 2020	2,50,000
Finished goods, October 31, 2020	3,75,000
Work-in-process, October 1, 2020	25,000
Work-in-process, October 31, 2020	35,000
Plant-leasing costs	1,35,000
Depreciation-plant equipment	90,000

(Contd.)

Property taxes on plant equipment	10,000
Fire insurance on plant equipment	7,500
Direct materials purchased	11,50,000
Sales revenues	34,00,000
Marketing promotions	1,50,000
Marketing salaries	2,50,000
Distribution costs	1,75,000
Customer-service costs	2,50,000

Required

(i) Prepare an income statement with a separate supporting schedule of cost of goods manufactured.

(ii) For all manufacturing items, indicate by *V* or *F* whether each is basically a variable cost or a fixed cost (where the cost object is a product unit).

☞ ***Solution***

Popeye Company 'Schedule for Cost of Goods Manufactured' for the Month Ending October, 2020

Direct Materials	₹	₹
Beginning inventory	1,00,000	
Purchase of direct materials	11,50,000	
Cost of direct materials available for use	12,50,000	
Ending inventory	1,25,000	
Direct materials used		11,25,000(V)
Direct manufacturing labour		7,50,000(V)
Indirect Manufacturing Costs		
Sand paper	5,000(V)	
Material-handling cost	1,75,000(V)	
Lubricants and coolants	12,500(V)	
Misc. indirect manufacturing labour	1,00,000(V)	
Plant leasing cost	1,35,000(F)	
Depreciation-plant and equipment	90,000(F)	
Property tax-plant and equipment	10,000(F)	
Fire insurance-plant and equipment	7,500(F)	5,35,000
Manufacturing cost incurred during the month of October, 2020		24,10,000
Add: Op. Work-in-progress		25,000
		24,35,000
Less: Cl. Work-in-progress		35,000
Cost of goods manufactured (to income statement)		24,00,000

Popeye Company: Income Statement for the Month Ending October 31, 2020

Revenues	₹	₹
		34,00,000
Cost of goods sold:		
Beginning finished goods	2,50,000	
Cost of goods manufactured	24,00,000	
Cost of goods available for sale	26,50,000	
Ending finished goods	3,75,000	22,75,000
Gross margin		11,25,000
Marketing, Distribution and Customer Service Costs:		
Marketing promotions	1,50,000	
Marketing salaries	2,50,000	
Distribution costs	1,75,000	
Customer service cost	2,50,000	8,25,000
Operating income		3,00,000

EXAMPLE 2.10

A fire occurred in the factory premises on October 31, 2020. The accounting records have been destroyed. Certain accounting records were kept in another building. They reveal the following for the period September 1, 2020 to October 31, 2020.

(i)	Direct materials purchased	₹ 2,50,000
(ii)	Work-in-process inventory, 1.9. 2020	₹ 40,000
(iii)	Direct materials inventory, 1.9. 2020	₹ 20,000
(iv)	Finished goods inventory, 1.9. 2020	₹ 37,750
(v)	Indirect manufacturing costs	40% of conversion cost
(vi)	Sales revenues	₹ 7,50,000
(vii)	Direct manufacturing labour	₹ 2,22,250
(viii)	Prime costs	₹ 3,97,750
(ix)	Gross margin percentage based on revenues	30%
(x)	Cost of goods available for sale	₹ 5,55,775

The loss is fully covered by insurance company. The insurance company wants to know the historical cost of the inventories as a basis for negotiating a settlement, although the settlement is actually to be based on replacement cost, not historical cost.

Required

(i) Finished goods inventory, 31.10. 2020
(ii) Work-in-process inventory, 31.10. 2020
(iii) Direct materials inventory, 31.10. 2020

Solution

WORKING NOTES

1. *Direct Material Inventory Cost (used during the month):*
   = Prime cost – Direct manufacturing labour cost
   = ₹3,97,750 – ₹2,22,250 = ₹1,75,500
2. *Conversion and Indirect Manufacturing Cost:*

Conversion cost	= (Direct manufacturing cost + Indirect manufacturing cost)
But indirect manufacturing cost	= 40% of conversion cost
or conversion cost	= Direct manufacturing cost + 40% of conversion cost
or 0.60 conversion cost	= Direct manufacturing cost
or conversion cost	$= \dfrac{\text{Direct manufacturing cost}}{0.60}$
	$= \dfrac{₹\,2,22,250}{0.60} = ₹3,70,417$
or Indirect manufacturing cost	= 40% × ₹3,70,417
	= ₹1,48,167

3. *Cost of Goods Manufactured*

	₹
Cost of goods available for sale	5,55,775
Less: Finished goods 1.9.2020	37,750
Cost of goods manufactured	5,18,025

(i) Finished Goods Inventory, 31.10. 2020

	₹
Sales revenue	7,50,000
Less: Gross margin (30% of revenue)	2,25,000
Cost of goods sold: (a)	5,25,000
Cost of goods available for sale: (b)	5,55,775
Finished goods inventory, 31.10.2020: {(b) – (a)}	30,775

(ii) Work-in-process inventory, 31.10.2020:

	₹
Prime cost	3,97,750
Add: Indirect manufacturing cost	1,48,167
(Refer to working note 2)	
Add: Opening work-in-process, 1.9.2020	40,000
Manufacturing cost to account for	5,85,917
Less: Cost of goods manufactured	5,18,025
Work-in-process inventory, 31.10.2020	67,892

(iii) Direct Material Inventory, 31.10.2020

	₹
Direct materials inventory, 1.9.2020	20,000
Add: Direct material purchased	2,50,000
	2,70,000

Less: Direct material inventory (used during the month) (*Refer to working note 1*)	1,75,500
Direct material inventory, 31.10.2020	94,500

EXAMPLE 2.11

A company manufactures radios, which are sold at ₹1,600 per unit. The total cost is composed of 30% for direct materials, 40% for direct wages and 30% for overheads. An increase in material price by 30% and in wage rates by 10% is expected in the forthcoming year, as a result of which the profit at current selling price may decrease by 40% of the present profit per unit. You are required to prepare a statement showing current and future profits at present selling price.

How much selling price should be increased to maintain the present rate of profit?

Solution

Let X be the cost, Y be the profit and ₹1,600 selling price per unit of radio manufactured by a company. Hence

$$X + Y = 1{,}600 \quad \text{(i)}$$

Statement of Present and Future Costs of a Radio

Particulars	*Present Cost* (₹) (*a*)	*Increase in Cost* ₹ (*b*)	*Anticipated Future Cost* (₹) (*c*) = (*a*) + (*b*)
Direct material	0.3 X	0.09 X	0.39 X
Direct labour	0.4 X	0.04 X	0.44 X
Overheads	0.3 X		0.30 X
Total	X	0.13 X	1.13 X

An increase in material price and wage rates resulted into a decrease in current profit by 40 percent at present selling price; therefore, we have:

$$1.13\,X + 0.6\,Y = 1{,}600 \quad \text{(ii)}$$

On solving (i) and (ii) we get:

$$X = ₹1{,}207.55$$

$$Y = ₹392.45$$

Current profit ₹392.45 or 32.5% of cost
Future profit ₹235.47

Statement of Revised Selling Price to Maintain the Present Rate of Profit

	₹
Direct material cost (*0.39 × ₹1,207.55*)	470.94

(*Contd.*)

	₹
Direct labour cost *(0.44 × ₹1,207.55)*	531.32
Overheads *(0.30 × ₹1,207.55)*	362.27
Total cost	1,364.53
Profit *(32.5% of total cost)*	443.47
Revised selling price	1,808.00

EXAMPLE 2.12

A factory incurred the following expenditure during the year 2019:

		₹
Direct material consumed		12,00,000
Manufacturing wages		7,00,000
Manufacturing overhead:		
Fixed	3,60,000	
Variable	2,50,000	6,10,000
		25,10,000

In the year 2020, following changes are expected in production and cost of production.

(i) Production will increase due to recruitment of 60% more workers in the factory.
(ii) Overall efficiency will decline by 10% on account of recruitment of new workers.
(iii) There will be an increase of 20% in fixed overhead and 60% in variable overhead.
(iv) The cost of direct material will decrease by 6%.
(v) The company desires to earn a profit of 10% on selling price.

Ascertain the cost of production and selling price.

Solution

Budgeted Cost Sheet for the Year 2020

Particulars		*Amount* ₹
Direct material consumed	12,00,000	
Add: 44% due to increased output	5,28,000	
	17,28,000	
Less: 6% for decline in price	1,03,680	16,24,320
Direct wages (manufacturing)	7,00,000	
Add: 60% increase	4,20,000	11,20,000

(Contd.)

Prime Cost			27,44,320
Manufactured Overhead:			
Fixed	3,60,000		
Add: 20% increase	72,000		
		4,32,000	
Variable	2,50,000		
Add: 60% increase	1,50,000		
		4,00,000	8,32,000
Cost of Production			35,76,320
Add: 1/9th of Cost or 10% on selling price			3,97,368.88
Selling Price			39,73,688.88

Production will increase by 60% but efficiency will decline by 10%

160 – 10% of 160 = 144%

So increase by 44%

Note: If we consider that variable overhead once will change because of increase in production (from 2,50,000 to 4,00,000), then with efficiency declining by 10%, it shall be 3,60,000. Then again, as mentioned in point no. (iii) of this question, it will increase by 60%. Then variable overhead shall be ₹3,60,000 × 160% = 5,76,000. Hence, total costs shall be ₹37,52,320 and profit shall be 1/9th of ₹37,52,320 = 4,16,924. Thus, selling price shall be 41,69,244.

☞ *Alternative Solution*

Students may use a combined factor to arrive at the figures in respect of materials and variable overheads as under:

2019 production	100
Increase in 2020:	60% = 160%
Efficiency decline 10%	160 × 90% = 144%
Materials	12,00,000 × 144% = ₹17,28,000
Variable overheads	2,50,000 × 144% = ₹3,60,000

Note: Variable overhead is a product cost, and consequently, if the output increases by 44%, the variable overheads will also go up proportionately with the increase in output. The other 60% increase given in the question is the increase in expense or rate or price of the overhead items like increase in tariff and increase in the price of consumables

✎ EXAMPLE 2.13

The following are the costing records for the year 2019 of a manufacturer:

(i) Production 1,000 units; Cost of Raw Materials ₹20,000; Labour Cost ₹12,000; Factory Overheads ₹8,000; Office Overheads ₹4,000; Selling Expenses ₹1,000; Rate of Profit 25% on the Selling Price.

(ii) The manufacturer decided to produce 1,500 units in 2020. It is estimated that the cost of raw materials will increase by 20%, the labour cost will increase by 10%, 50% of the overhead charges are fixed and the other 50% are variable. The selling expenses per unit will be reduced by 20%. The rate of profit will remain the same.

Prepare a cost statement for the year 2020 showing the total profit and selling price per unit.

☞ Solution

Statement of Cost

(Output 1000 Units)

	Cost per Unit (in ₹)	*Total Cost (in ₹)*
Raw materials	20	20,000
Labour	12	12,000
Prime Cost	32	32,000
Add: Factory overhead	8	8,000
Works Cost	40	40,000
Add: Office overhead	4	4,000
Cost of Production	44	44,000
Add: Selling expenses	1	1,000
Cost of Sales	45	45,000
Add: Profit (25% on selling price or 33.33% on cost of sales)	15	15,000
Selling Price	60	60,000

Cost Sheet for Manufacturing 1,500 Units

(Output: 1,500 Units)

	Cost Per Unit (in ₹)	*Total Cost (in ₹)*
Raw material (₹20 × 120% × 1,500)	24.00	36,000
Labour (₹12 × 110% × 1,500)	13.20	19,800
Prime Cost	37.20	55,800
Add: Factory overhead (₹8,000 × 50% + ₹4 × 1500)	6.67	10,000
Work Cost	43.87	65,800
Add: Office overhead (₹4,000 × 50% + ₹2 × 1500)	3.33	5.000
Cost of Production	47.20	70.800
Add: Selling expenses (₹1 × 80% × 1500)	0.80	1,200
Cost of Sales	48.00	72,000
Add: Profit (25% on selling price or 33.33% on cost of sales)	16.00	24,000
Selling Price	64.00	96.000

Theory Questions

1. Define the term "cost". How is it different from expense?
2. What is meant by "differential cost"?
3. What is the meaning of the term incremental cost? Does incremental cost mean the same thing as variable cost?
4. Explain the nature of product and period cost. How do they affect net income of a business enterprise?
5. "Product cost is a general term that denotes different costs allocated to products for different purposes." Describe three purposes. Explain the composition of "product cost" for the purpose of external financial reporting along with its rationale.
6. Distinguish between
   (a) Expired cost and unexpired cost
   (b) Direct and indirect costs
7. (a) Distinguish between fixed cost and variable costs.
   (b) Explain the significance of "decision-making cost".
   (c) Elucidate the meaning and formulation of "product cost" for the purpose of income measurement and determination of financial position.
8. Distinguish between
   (a) Prime cost and conversion cost.
   (b) Controllable and uncontrollable cost.
9. Bring out clearly the significance of the following costs for management:
   (a) Opportunity cost (b) Sunk cost
   (c) Imputed costs (d) Out-of-pocket costs
10. Discuss the various costs used in decision-making and explain their characteristics.
11. Distinguish between period costs and product costs. Why this distinction is considered important?
12. Distinguish between the following:
    (i) Controllable cost and non-controllable cost; and
    (ii) Direct material and indirect material.
13. (a) Distinguish between out-of-pocket cost and opportunity cost.
    (b) Explain and illustrate the distinction between "direct cost" and "indirect cost", specially from the point-of-view of decision-making.
14. Explain whether you agree with each of the following statements:
    (a) "All direct costs are variable."
    (b) "Variable costs are controllable and fixed costs are not."
    (c) "Sunk costs are irrelevant when providing decision-making information."
15. Lists two costs which are used in decision-making but not entered in the accounting system under that designation.
16. Name a cost which is reflected in the accounting system but not used in decision-making?
17. Explain briefly the following concepts:
    (a) Sunk cost (b) Differential cost
    (c) Variance analysis (d) Key factor
    (e) Cost reduction
18. Enumerate the basic principles of cost control.
19. Explain the meaning of relevant costs in managerial decisions. Give examples.
20. What do you mean by cost reduction? How is it different from cost control?

21. "The term cost must be qualified according to its context." Comment.
22. "Direct costs and variable costs are not necessarily the same." Comment.
23. Explain the following with the suitable examples:
    (a) Imputed cost
    (b) Sunk cost
24. Distinguish between:
    (a) Controllable cost and non-controllable cost
    (b) Variable cost and fixed cost
    (c) Costing and cost accounting
    (d) Explicit and implicit cost.
25. Explain the significance of cost reduction in the present global economy. Mention some important techniques used for cost reduction. Also, mention the important areas in a manufacturing company to be subjected to cost reduction drives.
26. Explain the following:
    (i) Explicit and implicit costs
    (ii) Period costs and discretionary costs
27. Discuss cost classifications based on variability and controllability.
28. Distinguish between cost reduction and cost control.
29. Explain the nature and scope of cost control and cost reduction. Which of the two is superior?
30. Explain "cost management".
31. Distinguish between
    (i) Cost control and cost reduction
    (ii) Controllable cost and uncontrollable cost
    (iii) Direct and indirect labour costs
32. Explain the term cost, expense and loss.
33. Distinguish between
    (i) Product cost and period cost
    (ii) Imputed cost and out-of-pocket cost
    (iii) Prime cost and conversion cost
34. Distinguish between controllable and uncontrollable cost.
35. Explain the distinction between cost control and cost reduction. Enumerate some of the important tools/techniques of cost reduction and cost control.
36. Define the terms cost control, cost reduction and cost management. How are they different from each other?
37. "Product design provides the greatest scope for cost reduction." Discuss.
38. Explain components of total cost.
39. Explain the following with a suitable example.
    (i) Imputed cost
    (ii) Cost unit
    (iii) Cost centre
40. Distinguish between direct cost and indirect cost.
41. Explain cost object.
42. What is a cost centre? State briefly the different types of cost centres.
43. How is cost control different from cost reduction?
44. What is the difference between relevant costs and irrelevant costs? Explain.
45. State the essential feature of relevant cost?

Self-Evaluation Questions

1. Match the items in Column 1 with the best choice in Column 2

Column 1	*Column 2*
1. Total fixed costs	A Costs incurred during a period
2. Incurred costs	B Total amount remains constant
3. Cost of goods manufactured	C Expired costs
4. Total manufacturing costs	D Direct materials and direct labour
5. Unit variable cost	E Costs of completed production after adjustment for work-in-progress inventory
6. Prime costs	F Direct labour and factory overhead
7. Expenses that are matched against revenue	G Added cost of a new product
8. Materials, labour and factory overhead	H Remains constant per unit
9. Conversion costs	I Direct materials, direct labour and factory overhead
10. Cost of goods sold	J Cost of goods manufactured, adjusted for changes in finished goods stock

2. Classify each of the following costs using the following classifications:
(a) Direct materials
(b) Direct labour
(c) Manufacturing overhead
(d) Non-manufacturing expense
   (i) Managing Director's salary
   (ii) Oil for a milling machine
   (iii) Salary of the milling machine operator
   (iv) Salary of the supervisor of assembly department for products A, B and C
   (v) Depreciation on the factory building
   (vi) Income tax expense
   (vii) Depreciation on direct materials warehouse
   (viii) Depreciation on the administrative office building
   (ix) Rent on the finished goods warehouse
   (x) Rent on the sales office
   (xi) Insurance on the truck used for delivery of finished goods sold
   (xii) Petrol for the truck used for transfer of work in process from one department to another
   (xiii) Contribution to Earthquake Relief Fund paid
   (xiv) Interest on borrowed money

3. Classify each of the following manufacturing costs using the following classifications:
(a) Fixed
(b) Variable
(c) Mixed
   (i) Rent on the factory building
   (ii) Salary of the supervisor of the casting department
   (iii) Wages of machine operators
   (iv) Overtime premium for machine operators
   (v) Fire insurance on the factory equipment

(vi) Cost of water used to cool production machinery
(vii) Depreciation on production machinery
(viii) Cost of paint used on products
(ix) Cost of electricity used to operate production machinery
(x) Lubricants used for production machinery.

4. Classify each of the following costs of a manufacturing company using the following classifications:
A – Production overhead
B – Selling and distribution overhead
C – Administration overhead
D – Research and development overhead
(i) Depreciation of factory plant and equipment
(ii) Trade discount given to customers
(iii) Cost of oils used to lubricate production machinery
(iv) Motor vehicles licenses for lorries
(v) Cost of chemicals used in laboratory
(vi) Commission paid to sales representative
(vii) Salary of the secretary to the Finance Director
(viii) Holiday pay of machine operators
(ix) Salary of the security guard in raw materials warehouse
(x) Fees to advertising agency
(xi) Rent of finished goods warehouse
(xii) Insurance of the company's premises
(xiii) Salary of scientist in laboratory
(xiv) Salary of supervisor working in the factory
(xv) Cost of typewriter ribbons in the general office
(xvi) Protective clothing for machine operatives.

5. Choose the correct answer for the following multiple-choice questions:
(i) For a manufacturing company, which of the following is an example of a period rather than a product cost?
(a) depreciation on factory equipment
(b) wages of sales people
(c) wages of machine operators
(d) insurance on factory equipment
(ii) Prime costs and conversion costs share which common element of total cost?
(a) variable overhead
(b) fixed overhead
(c) direct materials
(d) direct labour
(iii) Indirect materials are
(a) a prime cost
(b) a fixed cost
(c) an irrelevant cost
(d) a factory overhead cost
(iv) Factory overhead
(a) is a prime cost
(b) can be a variable cost or a fixed cost
(c) can only be a fixed cost
(d) includes all factory labour

(v) Fixed cost per unit increases when
  (a) production increases
  (b) production decreases
  (c) variable cost per unit decreases
  (d) prime cost per unit decreases

(vi) Factory supplies for a manufacturing plant are generally
  (a) prime cost
  (b) period costs
  (c) variable costs
  (d) excluded from product costs

(vii) Costs that increase as the volume of activity decreases within the relevant range are:
  (a) average cost per unit
  (b) average variable cost per unit
  (c) total fixed costs
  (d) total variable costs

6. Macframe Ltd makes photograph frames and sells them to national retail chains. The following costs are incurred in connection with its manufacturing process. Decide whether each cost is direct or indirect and give reasons.

1. Picture frame moulding.
2. Pay of assembly department's supervisor.
3. Heating oil used for cutting department.
4. Pay of employees' assembly frames.
5. Dab of glue put in each corner joint of frame.

Answer:

1. Picture frame moulding is a direct cost—identifiable and measurable.
2. Pay of assembly department's supervisor is an indirect cost—not specifically identifiable in product.
3. Heating oil used for cutting department is an indirect cost—not specifically identifiable in product.
4. Pay of employees' assembly frames is direct cost—identifiable and measurable.
5. Dab of glue put in each corner joint of frame is, in theory, a direct cost as it is identifiable and measurable. However, in practice, this would be treated as an indirect cost as the cost of measuring and valuing the dab of glue would be far greater than the value of the information gained. Accounting activities should always be carried out in a commercially sensible manner.

Problems

1. From the following particulars, prepare a cost sheet for the year ended 31.12.2020:

	₹
Stock of finished goods (1.1.2020)	6,000
Stock of raw materials (1.1.2020)	40,000
Work-in-progress (1.1.2020)	15,000
Purchase of raw materials	4,75,000
Carriage inwards	12,500
Factory rent, taxes	7,250

Other production expenses	43,000
Stock of goods (31.12.2020)	15,000
Wages	1,75,000
Work manager's salary	30,000
Factory employees salary	60,000
Power expenses	9,500
General expenses	32,500
Sales for the year	8,60,000
Stock of raw materials	50,000
Work-in-progress (31.12.2020)	10,000

Answer:

Prime cost ₹6,52,500; Factory cost ₹8,07,250;
Total cost ₹8,39,750,
Profit ₹29,250, Total sales ₹8,60,000.

for excel template, scan

2. A manufacturing company has shown ₹3,23,80,000 as "Establishment Expenses" which include the following expenses:

		(’000) ₹
1.	Warehouse wages	3,600
2.	Office salaries	2,260
3.	Office lighting	140
4.	Directors remuneration	2,800
5.	Rent, rates and insurance of warehouses	620
6.	Warehouse lighting	540
7.	Trade magazine	140
8.	Bank charges	200
9.	Bad debts	340
10.	Agents commission	11,500
11.	Warehouse repair	1,020
12.	Travelling expenses	1,520
13.	Rent, rates and insurance of office	460
14.	Printing and stationery	3,000
15.	Donation	300
16.	Discount allowed	3,940

From the above information, find out the total of (i) selling expenses, (ii) distribution expenses, (iii) administration expenses, and (iv) expenses which will not be considered in determining total costs.

Answer:

(i) Selling expenses ₹1,33,60,000; (ii) Distribution expenses ₹57,80,000 (iii) Administrative expenses ₹90,00,000; and (iv) Expenses not to be considered ₹42,40,000.

3. The books of Adarsh Manufacturing Company present the following data for the month of April 2020:
Direct labour cost ₹17,500 being 175% of works overheads
Cost of goods sold excluding administrative expenses ₹56,000.
Inventory accounts showed the following opening and closing balances:

	April 1	*April 30*
Raw materials	₹8,000	₹10,600
Work-in-progress	10,500	14,500

Finished goods	17,600	19,000

Other data are:

Selling expenses	₹3,500
General and administrative expenses	2,500
Sales for the month	75,000

You are required to:

(i) Compute the value of materials purchased

(ii) Prepare a cost statement showing the various elements of cost and also the profit earned.

Answer:

(i) Value of materials purchased ₹36,500

(ii) Cost of production of goods sold ₹56,000, Cost of sales ₹62,000.

Profit ₹13,000.

4. The following particulars relate to a company for a period of three months:

Raw materials 1.1.2020	55,000
Raw materials 31.3.2020	35,000
Factory wages	80,000
Materials purchased	60,000
Sales	1,54,000
Indirect expenses	10,000
Stock of finished goods (1.1.2020)	Nil
Stock of finished goods (31.3.2020)	30,000
No. of units produced during the period was	2,000

Prepare a statement of cost for the period and compute the price to be quoted for 500 units in order to realise the same % of profit as for the period under review, assuming no alteration in wages and cost of materials.

Answer:

Price to be quoted ₹46,750.

5. The Vardhman Ltd. manufactures one product. A summary of its activities for the year 2020 is given below:

	Units	₹
Sales	80,000	8,00,000
Material inventory 1-1-2020		40,000
Material inventory 31-12-2020		32,000
W.I.P. 1-1-2020		55,000
W.I.P. 31-12-2020		72,000
Finished goods 1-1-2020	16,000	64,000
Finished goods 31-12-2020	34,000	1,51,265
Material purchases		1,52,000
Direct labour		1,45,000
Manufacturing overhead		1,08,000
Selling expenses		50,000
General expenses		40,000

Prepare a cost sheet.

Answer

Cost of sales ₹3,98,735; profit ₹4,01,265.

6. From the understated particulars, you are required to prepare a monthly cost sheet of Soap Manufacturers Ltd. showing therein:
   (i) Prime cost;
   (ii) Works cost;
   (iii) Cost of production;
   (iv) Cost of sales; and
   (v) Profit per unit.

	₹
Opening Inventory (1-1-2020):	
Raw materials	6,000
Work-in-progress	9,620
Finished goods (1,000 units)	13,680
Closing inventory (31-12-2020):	
Raw materials	7,000
Work-in-progress	8,020
Finished goods	?
Donations to home for destitute	2,100
Raw materials purchased	72,000
Import duty on raw materials purchased	14,400
Productive wages	18,000
Machine hours worked	21,600 hours
Machine hour rate	₹1.50
Chargeable expenses	₹2,000
Office and administration expenses	₹1 per unit
Selling expenses	₹0.90 per unit
Units sold	8,000 units
Units produced	8,200 units
Profit on sale	10%

Answer

Prime cost ₹105,400; Works cost ₹1,39,400; Cost of production ₹1,47,600; Cost of sales ₹1,46,880; Profit per unit ₹2.04.

7. The particulars obtained from the records of M/s Jain Industries for the year 2020 are given below, from which you are required to prepare a cost sheet and a statement showing estimated cost for 1,000 units in future:

	₹
Opening Stock:	
Raw materials	1,40,000
Finished products	20,000
Purchases	2,10,000
Factory wages	3,80,000
Factory overheads	70,000
Office overheads	40,000

Closing stock:	
Raw materials	600
Finished goods	1,60,000
Sales	7,50,000

At the end of the year, the number of units produced, including the closing stock and the number of units sold, was 4,000.

On the basis of the above, the company wanted to supply 1,000 units in future. It is estimated that the prices of raw materials and labour may rise by 15% and 10% respectively. Assume that the same percentage of profits on sales will be made.

☞ ***Answer***

Total cost ₹6,80,400;
Selling price for 1,000 units ₹2,52,211.)

8. The books of JP Industries reveal the following information for the year ended 31st March, 2019:

	(₹)
Direct material	1,20,000
Direct wages	2,00,000
Overheads (Fixed 6% and Variable 40%)	1,00,000

(i) Output will be raised by employing 50% more workers;
(ii) Overall efficiency will fall by 10% because of new workers;
(iii) Material price will decrease by 5%;
(iv) Variable overheads will vary with the number of workers;
(v) Fixed expenses will increase by 20%;
(vi) Assume that there will be no opening and closing stocks of any type.

Required

(a) Calculate the cost of material and labour for the year 2019–20.
(b) Ascertain the selling price of the output for the year 2019–20 to earn a profit of 20% on the selling price.

☞ ***Answer***

Total cost ₹5,85,900;
Selling price ₹7,32,375

CASE STUDIES

1. Cost Reduction Alternatives—Case of Spic & Span

Spic & Span, a soap manufacturing company, was facing a huge competition from Rinx-it, a new entrant in the market. Rinx-it was offering its product—washing soap (100 gm bar) at ₹16 where-as the same quality (weight and size) soap manufactured by Spic & Span was priced at ₹17. In two months of entering the market, Rinx-it with its lower price and savvy advertisement, had already eaten 20% market share of Spic & Span.

On discussing the issue with the marketing manager—Rehan Dixit and the HR manager—Anurag Sharma, the General Manager – Sales—Amitabh Saraff was given two alternatives to tackle the issue. The first one by Anurag was to replace 50% of the permanent labour force with contractual labour to decrease the human resource costs. Rehan submitted a marketing plan with more emphasis on advertising including the celebrity endorsement.

Amitabh knew that replacing full-time workers with the contractual labour would indeed decrease the cost in the short run, however, he was not sure if the quality and production consistency could be maintained and whether in the long run the arrangement would remain profitable. Similarly, although Rehan's plan indicated an increase in sales and therefore market share but it also meant increase in the cost because of celebrity endorsement and new advertisement. This meant further decrease in the already meagre profit margin.

He discussed his dilemma with his Operations Manager—Raghav. Raghav, after couple of days of deliberations, suggested two alternatives to Amitabh. First one was to use slimmer soap cover (paper case) to decrease the expense on paper quality by 80 paisa per soap and take a cut of remaining 20 paisa on profit margin. The other alternative was to cut down on the packing cost by using a bigger carton which would fit 150 soaps instead of 100 soaps. This method could reduce the packing cost by 50 paisa per soap.

Amitabh, although liking both the ideas, was not sure which one would work better. Should he go for any one of these four suggestions or opt for a mix of these?

QUESTIONS FOR DISCUSSION:

1. Which of the four methods of cost reduction suggested to Amitabh looks better compared to others? Discuss the merits and demerits of each alternative suggested.
2. Should Amitabh go for either of these or a mix of the methods suggested? Identify the two cost reduction methods which will work the best.
3. What is the difference between cost reduction and cost control? Do you think that instead of opting for any or more of these alternative suggested, Amitabh should concentrate on controlling his cost of production?

2. Cost Concept and Cost Sheet—Case of Sitcom Technology

Sitcom Technology was founded by two IIT graduates—Rehan and Nixit in the year 2016 with an objective of providing IT solution to various companies. They launched their FinTech start-up after getting funded ₹25,00,000 by Business Ventures, one of the FinTech Angel investors. This was in the form of a loan at 12% rate of interest.

Rehan utilised his unused two-bedrooms flat in Bannerghatta, Karnataka worth ₹60,00,000 for the office. Although he could get ₹20,000 per month as rent for the same in the market, he rented it out to his start-up at ₹15,000 per month and also decided to waive off the security deposit of ₹10,00,000 (going rate).

The other assets bought for their enterprise were four computers and a server (₹2,00,000), two printers cum scanner (₹18,000), two cordless phones & four mobiles (₹62,000), modem for WiFi and other Internet accessories (₹6,000) and office furniture (₹1,70,000). In addition to these, they also invested ₹40,000 in purchasing annual licenses for lot of software.

Nixit picked up two of his juniors as Programmer and Visualiser cum Graphic Designer after negotiating heavily on their hourly remuneration of 1,000 per hour on freelancing basis. Depending on the number of hours invested in development of a particular software/ERP/IT Solution, they were paid. In the month of April 2019, Sitcom Technology paid them ₹84,000 for 42 hours of work put in by each one of them.

In addition to these two, a telephone operator and a data entry staff were also hired at ₹13,000 and ₹17,000 per month respectively. The monthly expenses of Sitcom Technology in April 2019 were:

Expenses	*Amount (₹)*
Salaries	30,000
Rent	15,000
Wages (peon)	10,000
Electricity	5,000
Telephone & internet charges	12,000
Office stationery	4,000
Trade magazines	500
Conveyances	8,000
Advertising charges	1000
Tours & Travel	16,000
Snacks	6,000
Miscellaneous	5,000

In April 2019, Sitcom Technology received two project orders from leading banks and one small programme development work outsourced by a leading IT company in Electronic City. The work was completed in the same month with all four of them putting in lot of hours. The revenue generated from these three projects was ₹4,10,000.

QUESTIONS FOR DISCUSSION:

1. Identify different types of costs discussed in the case and provide one more example of each. Is there an example of opportunity cost or sunk cost in the case?
2. Rehan and Nixit are exploring the option of purchasing a vehicle for the daily commute of their staff members. Till now, they had been doing a car pool (Nixit's car) with everyone paying ₹2,000 to Nixit and claiming the same as conveyance expense from Sitcom Technology. Given this scenario, what costs can be considered as relevant or irrelevant cost?
3. Classify the costs discussed in the case as fixed or variable, product or period costs, controllable and uncontrollable costs.
4. Prepare the cost sheet for April 2019 and calculate the profit generated assuming the depreciation on fixed assets to be 10%.

PART 2

Elements of Cost

Cost ascertainment is basic prerequisite for cost analysis, cost control and cost management by the management of an organisation. Therefore, knowledge of different elements of costs constituting a product or job is necessary to understand their significance, nature and behaviour in relation to change in output or activity. The different chapters in Part 2 discuss material costs, labour costs, factory overhead, administrative and selling and distribution overheads and issues relating to these costs for proper attention by the managers and accountants. Activity-based costing and some emerging concepts in cost accounting have also been explained in Part 2.

- *Materials Control*
- *Materials Costing*
- *Labour Costs: Accounting and Control*
- *Factory Overheads: Distribution*
- *Administrative and Selling and Distribution Overheads*
- *Activity-Based Costing*

Chapter 3

Materials Control

Learning Objectives

After reading this chapter, you should be able to:

1. explain what material is and the concept and objectives of material control;
2. discuss purchasing and receiving procedure;
3. discuss significant issues in materials procurement;
4. explain stores organisation, storage layout, issue of materials returned to storeroom and supplier;
5. discuss inventory system, its methods, nature of inventory, concept and different techniques of inventory control; and
6. identify different material losses and their accounting treatment.

MATERIALS

The term "materials", generally used in manufacturing concerns, refers to raw materials used for production, sub-assemblies and fabricated parts. The terms "materials" and "stores" are sometimes used interchangeably. However, both the terms differ. "Stores" is wider in meaning and comprises many other items besides raw materials, such as tools, equipments, maintenance and repair items, factory supplies, components, jigs, fixtures. Sometimes, finished goods and partly finished goods are also included within the scope of this term.

CONCEPT AND OBJECTIVES OF MATERIALS CONTROL

Materials cost constitutes a prime part of the total cost of production of manufacturing firms. Proper accounting, therefore, for and control over materials purchase, consumptions, and inventories is important for effective management of a business firm. Materials control basically aims at efficient purchasing of materials, their efficient storing and efficient use or consumption.

Materials control consists of controls at two levels: (i) quantity controls, and (ii) financial controls. For instance, the production department in a manufacturing company aims at quantity controls, i.e., lesser and lesser units should be used in the production department. Although lesser units would result in lower investments on purchase of materials, yet the user (production) department normally does not think in terms of expenditure. In contrast, the finance manager is interested in keeping the investments on materials at the lowest point. In materials control, balance has to be maintained between two opposing needs, that is, (i) maintenance of sufficient inventory for efficient production and (ii) maintenance of investment in inventory at the lowest level. In detail, the following are the objectives in a good system of materials control:

1. Materials of the desired quality will be available when needed for efficient and uninterrupted production.
2. Material will be purchased only when need exists and in economic quantities.
3. The investment in materials will be maintained at the lowest level consistent with operating requirements.
4. Purchase of materials will be made at the most favourable prices under the best possible terms.
5. Materials are protected against loss by fire, theft, handling with the help of proper physical controls.
6. Materials should be stored in such a way that they can provide minimum of handling time and cost.
7. Vouchers will be approved for payment only if the material has been received and is available for issue.
8. Issues of material are properly authorised and properly accounted for.
9. Materials are, at all times, charged as the responsibility of some individual.

PURCHASING AND RECEIVING PROCEDURE

Purchasing procedures vary with different business firms, but all of them follow a general pattern in the purchases and receipt of materials and payment of obligations. The important steps may be listed as follows:

1. Purchase requisition A form known as a purchase requisition is commonly used as a formal request to the purchasing department to order goods or services. The purchase requisition serves three general purposes:

(i) It automatically starts the purchasing process and informs the purchasing department of the need for the purchase of materials.
(ii) It fixes the responsibility of the department/personnel making the purchase requisition.
(iii) It can be used for future reference.

Usually, purchase requisitions are prepared by the storekeepers for regular store items which are below or approaching the minimum level of stock or to replace stock of materials and parts in stores. The production control department can also give requisitions for the purchase of specialised materials. A typical purchase requisition contains details, such as number, date, department, quantity, description, specification, signature of the person initiating the requisition, and signature of one or more officers approving the purchase (see Fig. 3.1). Copies of the purchase requisition are sent to the purchasing department and accounting department.

2. Purchase order After the requisition is received duly approved, the purchasing department places an order with a supplier, offering to buy certain materials at stated prices and terms. The purchase order is a formal contract for the supply of materials. The order should clearly state the materials required and the price; and provide information, such as delivery period and the department for whom the materials are purchased (Fig. 3.2). Copies of the purchase order are sent to the department concerned, the sender of the purchase requisition, and the stores department advising them to expect the materials as specified and where to send them upon receipt. Copies of the purchase requisition and the purchase order are sent to accounting department, to be used in checking the supplier's invoice when a voucher is being prepared for payment.

3. Receiving materials The receiving department performs the function of unloading and unpacking materials which are received by an organisation. This will need an inspection report which is sometimes incorporated in the receiving report, indicating the items accepted and rejected, with reason.

ABC Company Limited
Purchase Requisition

Purchase Requisition No. ____________

Purchase Order No. ____________

Date ____________

Department ____________

Delivery Required ____________

Item No.	*Quantity*	*Particulars of Articles*	*Grade or Quality*	*Remarks*

Requested by ________ Checked by ________ Approved by

Fig. 3.1 Purchase Requisition

ABC Company Limited Purchase Order

Date ____________ Purchase Order No. ____________

Supplier ____________ Requisition No. ____________

Department No. ____________

Date Required ____________

Please supply the following items on the terms and conditions mentioned herewith:

Item no.	*Quantity*	*Particulars about Items*	*Rate Per Unit*	*Total Cost*	*Remarks*

Purchase Manager

(Contd.)

Terms and Conditions:

____

____

____

____

____

Fig. 3.2 Purchase Order

Several copies of the receiving report or goods received note (Fig. 3.3) are prepared, one going to each department interested in the arrival of materials, including stores, buying and accounts departments.

ABC Company Limited
Materials Receiving Report

Purchase Order No. ________________

Date ____________________________

Received from ________________

(Vendor's Name and Address)

____

____

____

____

Items no.	*Quantity Received*	*Particulars*	*Weight, If Any*	*Remarks*

Counted by __________ Approved by ____________

Inspected by __________

Fig. 3.3 Materials Receiving Report

4. Approval of invoices Invoice approval indicates that goods according to the purchase order have been received and payment can now be made. However, if the goods or equipment received are not of the type ordered, or are not in accordance with specifications, or are damaged, the purchasing department issues a return order indicating that the goods are to be returned to the supplier.

5. Marking payment After the purchase invoice total is approved, the process of making payment begins. Payment depends on the terms agreed upon on any particular order, and any terms which differ from normal practice should be considered individually. When it is found that items written on the invoice qualify for payment, a remittance advice is prepared after providing for deduction on discounts, if any.

Creating a Purchase Department

It is useful to set up a separate purchase department to perform purchasing activities relating to purchase of materials and other stores. The organisation of the purchase department depends on the size of the organisation and the quantum of purchases it is likely to make. A purchase department generally performs the following functions:

(i) Purchasing materials and stores after receiving requisitions from the stores department for regular or routine items or from the departmental head, works manager or planning department for the purchase of special items, if any.
(ii) Purchasing materials of right quality.
(iii) Determining the quantity, quality, items, price, time to buy and the supplier from whom purchases are to be made.
(iv) Possessing knowledge about possible sources of supply, prices of materials and supplies prevailing in the market, terms and conditions relating to purchases, market trends, usual lead time taken by the suppliers.
(v) Having expertise in drafting of purchase agreements and contracts.
(vi) Avoiding the purchase of obsolete, deteriorated and surplus materials.
(vii) Purchasing at the most favourable terms and conditions, at the lowest rates and from the best market and the most reliable suppliers.
(viii) Ensuring timely delivery of purchased items.
(ix) Comparing the invoice received from the suppliers with the purchase order to ensure that materials received are of right quality, in right quantity and at right prices.
(x) Knowing the defaulters suppliers.
(xi) Having information about consumption and usage pattern of materials of production and other departments and stock levels maintained by them and the stores department.
(xii) Preparing a latest list of approved suppliers along with brief particulars about their dealing terms.
(xiii) Possessing details about materials and stores received, on order, and outstanding.

Qualities of Purchase Manager

A purchase manager or a purchaser should possess the following qualities:

(i) Having information and knowledge about all aspects of materials to be purchased such as quantity, specifications, quality, price, purchasing procedures, etc.
(ii) Having knowledge about the sources of supply, market conditions, terms of delivery, qualities and dealings of different suppliers.
(iii) Knowing the policy of management, funds position, requirements of manufacturing units and stores departments.
(iv) Having good information base such as price lists, business journals and periodicals, catalogues, industrial directories to enable him to find the best market for the purchase of materials.
(v) Having knowledge about government policies, taxes on purchase of such materials, import and export restrictions thereon.
(vi) Having fair knowledge about the legal provisions and rules relating to making of agreement and contract.
(vii) Having expertise and skill to organise and manage his department efficiently and in coordination and cooperation with other departments of the organisation.

SOME ISSUES IN MATERIALS PROCUREMENT

It is generally accepted that quantities be bought in economic size so that there may not be over-stocking. If a company purchases in large quantities, the cost of carrying the inventory would be high because of the high investment involved. Working capital which could have been used for other productive purposes has to be diverted. Over-stocking requires more storage space which, in turn, means increase in insurance expenses, storage costs and deterioration in quality and depreciation in quantity. In contrast, if purchases are made in small quantities (under-stocking), frequent orders would have to be placed for the purchase of materials. There will be danger of "stock outs" also. Because of under-stocking, production is likely to suffer; materials have to be purchased immediately at high prices; low output would increase cost and decrease profit; and the other department's work may be adversely affected.

Economic Order Quantity (*EOQ*) (Re-order Quantity)

The *EOQ* is the optimum or the most favourable quantity which should be purchased each time the purchases are to be made. The *EOQ* is one where the cost of carrying inventory is equal or almost equal to the cost of not carrying inventory (cost of placing orders). Also at *EOQ* level, the total of these two costs is minimum.

The cost of carrying the inventory is the real out-of-pocket cost associated with having inventory on hand, such as warehouse charges, insurance, heat, light, and losses due to spoilage, breakage, pilferage. Another opportunity cost, which is not the out-of-pocket cost, is important and should be considered, that is, cost incurred (capital used) in purchasing the inventory. If funds have been borrowed to finance the inventory purchase, interest payments on borrowed funds will be the direct cost. Carrying or holding costs of inventory are explicit as well as implicit. That is, some costs are readily ascertained from accounting records while others require extensive study to estimate them because they are not expressly stated. Insurance on inventory is an explicit cost while the cost of funds invested in inventory is implicit cost. Generally, inventory carrying costs are considered to be proportional to the value of inventory carried.

The costs of not carrying adequate inventory arise because of frequent placing of order at short intervals. This includes costs, such as extra purchasing, handling and transportation costs, higher price due to small order quantities, frequent stock-outs resulting in disruption of production schedules, overtime and extra set-up time, loss of sales and customer goodwill, etc.

The costs of carrying the inventory and ordering costs change in the reverse order. The costs of placing the order decrease as the size of the order increases since with a bigger size of order, the number of the order will be lower. However, simultaneously the costs of carrying the inventory will go up because purchases have been made in large quantities. It may be possible to have a point which provides the lowest total cost and this point (ideal size) is known as the *EOQ*. This equilibrium can be determined mathematically as follows:

$$EOQ = \sqrt{\frac{2 \times U \times O}{IC}}$$

where U = Annual usage in units

O = Cost of placing an order

I = Per cent cost of carrying inventory

C = Cost per unit of material

Assume

Annual usage units	= 6,000
Cost of placing an order	= ₹30
Carrying cost as a per cent of inventory	= 20%
Cost per unit of material	= ₹5

Then,

$$EOQ = \sqrt{\frac{2 \times 6,000 \times 30}{5 \times 20\%}}$$

$$= \sqrt{3,60,000}$$

$$= 600 \text{ units}$$

In the above example, the *EOQ* is 600 units. That is, ten orders per year are needed. At the level of 600 units, the ordering costs and the carrying costs are equal and also the total cost is at minimum as it is clear from Table 3.1.

Table 3.1 Table Showing Economic Order Quantity

Annual Usage	*Orders Per Year*	*Units Per Order*	*Average Inventory (Units)*	*Value Per Order (₹)*	*Average Inventory Amount (₹)*	*Order Cost (₹)*	*Carrying Cost (20%)*	*Total cost (₹)*
6,000	1	6,000	3,000	30,000	15,000	30	3,000	3,030
units	2	3,000	1,500	15,000	7,500	60	1,500	1,560
	3	2,000	1,000	10,000	5,000	90	1,000	1,090
	4	1,500	750	7,500	3,750	120	750	870
	5	1,200	600	6,000	3,000	150	600	750
	6	1,000	500	5,000	2,500	180	500	680
	7	857	429	4,285	2,142	210	428	638
	8	750	375	3,750	1,875	240	376	616
	9	667	334	3,335	1,668	270	334	604
	10	600	300	3,000	1,500	300	300	600
	11	545	273	2,725	1,363	330	272	602
	12	500	250	2,500	1,250	360	250	610

Table 3.1 shows that quantities of other orders resulting in more or less than ten orders per year are not so economical as they involve higher total costs.

The *EOQ* formula is sometimes expressed in the following manner which is not in any way different from the formula explained earlier.

$$EOQ = \sqrt{\frac{2U \times P}{S}}$$

where U = Annual demand or consumption or purchased quantity (in units)

P = Cost of placing an order

S = Annual cost of carrying inventory per unit (storage and interest)

Similarly, *EOQ* formula may be expressed in any other manner with the same answer of economic order quantity.

The ordering costs, holding costs, total costs and *EOQ* can be shown graphically also as displayed in Fig. 3.4.

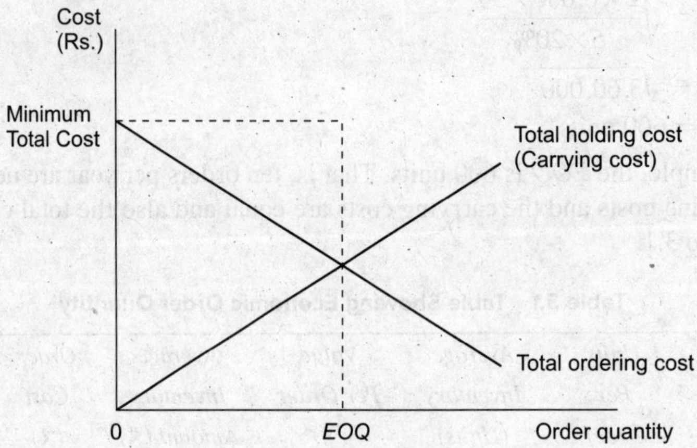

Fig. 3.4 Behaviour of Carrying Costs, Ordering Costs, Minimum Total Costs and Economic Order Quantity

When to Order (Re-order Level)

The *EOQ* determines how much to buy at a particular time. But the question "when to buy" is equally important for business firms. This question is easy to answer only if we know the lead time—the time interval between placing an order and receiving delivery—and know the *EOQ*, and are certain of the consumption pattern during lead time. The order point or re-order level is a point or quantity level at which if materials in stores reach, the order for supply of materials must be placed. This point automatically initiates a new order. The order point is calculated from three factors:

1. The expected usage.
2. The time interval between initiating an order and its receipt, referred to as the lead time.
3. The minimum inventory, or safety stock.

Some business firms fix re-order level taking into account maximum usage and maximum lead time so that the stock will not reach the zero level.

The formula for computing re-order level is:

(1) Re-order level = Safety stock + (Average usage × Average re-order period or lead time)

In terms of maximum usage and maximum lead time, the formula for re-order level is as follows:

(2) Re-order level = Maximum re-order period × Maximum usage

It is advisable to use the first formula given above to calculate re-order level. However, when adequate information is not given about the factors of this formula, the second formula can be used if information is available about the factors of this formula.

For example, if daily usage is 400 units of material which have a lead time of 20 days and the safety (minimum) stock is 500 units, the order point will be calculated as follows:

Daily consumption × Lead time = 400 × 20	= 8,000 units
Add safety stock	= 500 units
Order point units	8,500 units

The order point is determined after considering the worst possible expected conditions. This only ensures that the minimum stock will always remain in the inventory and will not be used atleast in the short run. However, situations may arise where there will be stock-out and thus, the order point may not be an absolutely accurate forecasting.

Determination of Safety or Minimum Stock Level

It is advisable to carry a reserve or safety stock to prevent stock-out. The safety stock should be used only in abnormal circumstances, and the working stock in ideal or normal conditions. Therefore, for normal working conditions, the stock should not be allowed to fall below the safety limit, kept only for emergencies. If the usage pattern is known with certainty, and the lead time is also known accurately, then no safety stock would be needed. However, if either usage or lead time is subject to variation then it is necessary for a business firm to maintain safety stock levels equal to the difference between the expected usage over lead time and the maximum usage over lead time that the firm feels is necessary for cost minimisation. The safety stock level can be computed by using the following formula:

Safety or minimum stock level = Ordering level – (Average rate of consumption × Re-order period)

Maximum Stock Level

The maximum level ensures that the stocks will not exceed this limit although there may be low demand for materials or quick delivery from the suppliers. Maximum stock level can be computed as follows:

Maximum stock level = Re-order level + *EOQ* – (Minimum consumption × Minimum re-order period)

Some factors to be considered in deciding the maximum stock level are as follows:

(i) Holding or carrying cost of inventory
(ii) Availability of storage facility
(iii) Seasonal nature of some products such as agricultural products
(iv) Availability of funds
(v) Future price trends of raw materials or components
(vi) Government policies or restrictions
(vii) Properties of some raw materials such as explosive, chemical, inflammable
(viii) Availability of raw materials in the international market.

Danger Level

Generally, the danger level of stock is indicated below the safety or minimum stock level. Sometimes, depending on the practices of the firm and circumstances prevailing, the danger level is determined between re-order level and minimum level. In the second case (danger level being between re-order level and minimum level), the firm can only take steps to ensure that materials ordered will arrive in time.

Average Stock Level

Average stock level is computed in the following manner:

$$= \frac{\text{Minimum + Maximum stock}}{2}$$

or

$$= \frac{\text{Minimum level + Re-order quantity}}{2}$$

The following example further illustrates the different stock levels.

Maximum usage (units)	650 per day
Minimum usage (units)	300 per day
Normal usage (units)	500 per day
Economic order quantity (units)	75,000
Re-order period—lead time	25 to 30 days
Minimum level (units) (10 days at normal usage)	5,000

The different stock levels will be as follows:

Re-order level = Normal usage × Normal lead time + Minimum level

= (500 × 30) + 5,000

= 20,000 units

Maximum level = Re-order level + *EOQ* – Minimum quantity used in re-order period

= 20,000 + 75,000 – (300 × 25)

= 87,500 units

$$\text{Average level} = \frac{\text{Maximum} + \text{Minimum}}{2}$$

$$= \frac{87{,}500 + 5{,}000}{2}$$

= 46,250 units

After placing an order, if usage goes above average or if the lead time is longer than expected, then the stock will fall below minimum. However, stock will not be exhausted, so long as the maximum usage and maximum re-order periods are not exceeded. In the above example, maximum usage during the lead time would cause an extra 4,500 units (30 days × 150 units) to be consumed. Therefore, in this situation, the purchasing officer should try to chase supplies to ensure that delivery promises are kept.

The different stock levels, as found in the above example, are displayed in Fig. 3.5.

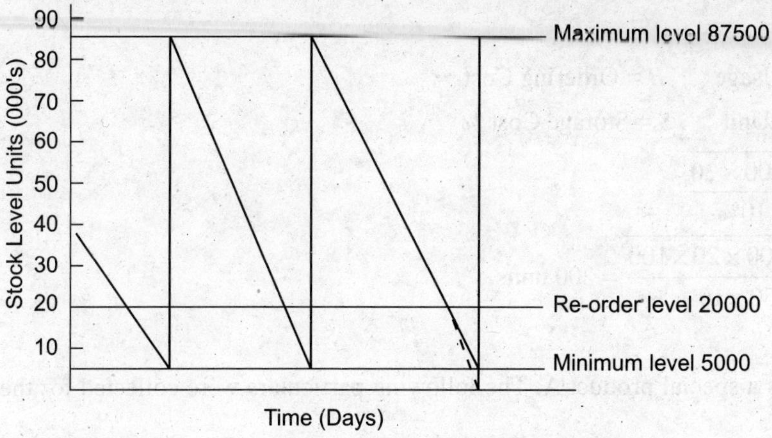

Fig. 3.5 Stock Levels

EXAMPLE 3.1

Z Ltd. provides the following information in respect of material *R*.

Supply period	: 5 to 15 days
Rate of Consumption	
Average	: 15 units per day
Maximum	: 20 units per day
Yearly	: 5000 units

Ordering costs are ₹20 per order
Purchase price per unit is ₹50
Storage costs are 10% of unit value
Compute:

(i) Re-order Level
(ii) Minimum Level
(iii) Maximum Level

Solution

(i) Re-order Level = Maximum consumption × Maximum supply period
= 20 × 15 = **300 units**

(ii) Minimum Level = Re-order level – (Normal consumption × Normal supply period)
= 300 – (15 × 10) = **150 units**

(iii) Maximum Level = Re-order level + Re-order quantity*
– (Minimum consumption × Minimum supply period)
= 300 + 200 – (10 × 5) = **450 units**

Working Notes:

$$\text{* Re-order quantity} = \sqrt{\frac{2AB}{CS}}$$

where, A = Annual Usage B = Ordering Cost

C = Cost Per Unit S = Storage Cost %

$$= \sqrt{\frac{2 \times 5{,}000 \times 20}{50 \times 10\%}}$$

$$= \sqrt{\frac{2 \times 5{,}000 \times 20 \times 100}{50 \times 10}} = 200 \text{ units}$$

EXAMPLE 3.2

Medical Aids Co. manufactures a special product A. The following particulars were collected for the year 2020:

Cost of placing an order	₹100
Annual carrying cost per unit	₹15
Normal usage	50 units per week
Minimum usage	25 units per week
Maximum usage	75 units per week
Re-order period	4 to 6 weeks

Compute from the above: (i) Re-order quantity; (ii) Re-order level; (iii) Minimum level; (iv) Maximum level; (v) Average stock level. (Weeks in a year 52).

Solution

(i) Re-order quantity $= \sqrt{\frac{2U \times P}{S}}$

Where U = Annual demand for input units

P = Cost of placing an order

S = Annual carrying cost per unit

$$= \sqrt{\frac{2 \times 2{,}600{*} \times ₹100}{15}}$$

= 186 units (approx)

*Annual demand for input units

= 52 weeks × Normal usage of input units per week

= 52 × 50 = 2,600 units

(ii) Re-order level = Maximum re-order period × Maximum usage

= 6 weeks × 75 units = 450 units

(iii) Minimum level = Re-order level – (Normal usage × Average re-order period)

= 450 units – (50 units × 5 weeks)

= 450 units – 250 units = 200 units

(iv) Maximum level = Re-order level – (Minimum usage × Minimum re-order period) + Re-order quantity.

= 450 units – (25 units × 4 weeks) + 186 units

= 450 units – 100 units + 186 units

= 536 units

(v) Average stock level = $\frac{1}{2}$ (Minimum stock level + Maximum stock level)

= $\frac{1}{2}$ (200 units + 536 units)

= 368 units

EXAMPLE 3.3

A company manufactures a special product which requires a component "Alpha". The following particulars are available for 2020:

Annual demand	8,000 units
Cost of placing an order	₹200 per order
Cost per unit of "Alpha"	₹400
Carrying cost % p.a.	20%

The company has been offered a discount of 4% on the purchase of "Alpha" provided the order size is 4,000 components at a time.

Required:

(i) Calculate Economic order quantity.

(ii) Advise whether the discount offer can be accepted.

Solution

$$EOQ = \sqrt{\frac{2 \times A \times B}{C}} \text{ or } \sqrt{\frac{2 \times U \times P}{S}}$$

$$EOQ = \sqrt{\frac{2 \times 8{,}000 \times 200}{400 \times 0.2}}$$

$$EOQ = \sqrt{4000}$$

= 200 units

Where $U = A$ = Annual demand

$P = B$ = Cost of placing an order

$S = C$ = Carrying cost per unit per annum

Inventory cost = Cost of purchase + Ordering cost + Carrying cost.

Inventory cost (including purchase price) at *EOQ*

$$= (8000 \times 400) + \left(\frac{8000}{200}\right)200 + \left(\frac{200}{2}\right)(400 \times 0.2)$$

$\Rightarrow$ 32,00,000 + 8,000 + 8,000 ⇒ ₹32,16,000

If order size = 4,000 units

Price = 400 × 0.96 = 384

S = 384 (0.2) = 76.80

Inventory cost (including purchase price) at order size of 4000 units

$$= (8000 \times 384) + \left(\frac{8000}{4000}\right)200 + \left(\frac{4000}{2}\right)(384 \times 0.2)$$

= 30,72,000 + 400 + 1,53,600

= ₹32,26,000

Alternatively, discount offer to be rejected

S = 400 × 0.2 instead of 384 (0.2)

Inventory cost in the case = $(8000 \times 384) + \left(\frac{8000}{4000}\right)200 + \left(\frac{4000}{2}\right)(400 \times 0.2)$

= 30,72,000 + 400 + 1,60,000 = 32,32,400

Comparing it with 32,16,000 → discount offer is rejected

Example 3.4

A. S. Ltd. produces a product "RED" using two components *X* and *Y*. Each unit of "RED" requires 0.4 kg of *X* and 0.6 kg of *Y*. Weekly production varies from 350 units to 450 units averaging 400 units. Delivery period for both the components is 1 to 3 weeks. The economic order quantity for *X* is 600 kg and *Y* is 1000 kg. Calculate–

(i) Re-order level of *X*;
(ii) Maximum level of *X*;
(iii) Minimum level of *Y*.

Solution

	Kg/Unit	*Max Consumption*	*Min Consumption*	*Re-order Period*	*EOQ*
X	0.4	450 × 0.4 = 180	350 × 0.4 = 140	1 – 3	600
Y	0.6	450 × 0.6 = 270	350 × 0.6 = 210	1 – 3	1,000

(i) Re-order level of *X* = Maximum consumption × Maximum re-order period

= 180 × 3 = 540 kg

(ii) Maximum level of X = Re-order level + Re-order quantity – Minimum consumption × Minimum re-order period

$$= 540 + 600 - (140 \times 1)$$
$$= 1140 - 140 = 1000 \text{ kg.}$$

(iii) Minimum level of Y = Re-order level – (Average consumption × Average re-order period)

$$= 270 \times 3 - (400 \times 0.6 \times 2)$$
$$= 810 - 480$$
$$= 330$$

✍ EXAMPLE 3.5

ABC Co. buys in lots of 125 boxes which is a three-month's supply. The cost per box is ₹125 and the ordering cost is ₹250 per order. The inventory carrying cost is estimated at 20% of unit value per annum. You are required to ascertain–

(i) The total annual cost of existing inventory policy.
(ii) How much money would be saved by employing the economic order quantity?

☞ Solution

(i) Total annual cost of existing inventory policy.

Total cost = Number of units × Cost per box + Ordering cost + Carrying cost

$$= (125 \times 4)\ 125 + (250 \times 4) + \left(\frac{125}{2} \times 125 \times \frac{20}{100}\right) = 65{,}062.50$$

(ii) $$EOQ = \sqrt{\frac{2 \times U \times P}{S}}$$

where U = Annual usage
P = Cost of placing an order
S = Cost of storage per unit per annum

$$= \sqrt{\frac{2 \times (125 \times 4) \times 250}{125 \times \frac{20}{100}}} = 100 \text{ units}$$

$$\text{Total cost} = 500 \times 125 + \left(\frac{100}{2} \times 125 \times \frac{20}{100}\right) + 5 \times 250$$
$$= 65{,}000$$
$$\text{Total saving} = 65{,}000 - 65{,}062.50$$
$$= 62.50$$

✍ EXAMPLE 3.6

Re-order quantity of material "X" is 5,000 kg; Maximum level of 8,000 kg; Minimum usage 50 kg. per hour; minimum re-order period 4 days; daily working hours in the factory is 8 hours. You are required to calculate the re-order level of material "X".

Solution

Re-order level = Maximum level – [Re-order quantity – (Minimum usage per day × Minimum re-order period)

= 8,000 kg. – [5,000 kg. – (400 kg* × 4)]

= 8,000 kg. – 3,400 kg. = 4,600 kg

Hence, re-order level is 4,600 kg.

*Minimum usage per day = 50 kg. × 8 = 400 kg.

EXAMPLE 3.7

ZED company supplies plastic crockery to fast food restaurants in metropolitan city. One of its products is a special bowl, disposable after initial use, for serving soups to its customers. Bowls are sold in pack 10 pieces at a price of ₹50 per pack.

The demand for plastic bowl has been forecasted at a fairly steady rate of 40,000 packs every year. The company purchases the bowl direct from manufacturer at ₹40 per pack within a three days lead time. The ordering and related cost is ₹8 per order. The storage cost is 10% per cent per annum of average inventory investment.

Required:

(i) Calculate economic order quantity.

(ii) Calculate number of orders needed every year.

(iii) Calculate the total cost of ordering and storage bowls for the year.

(iv) Determine when the next order should be placed. (Assuming that the company does maintain a safety stock and that the present inventory level is 333 packs with a year of 360 working days.)

Solution

(i) Economic order quantity

$$EOQ = \sqrt{\frac{2 \times C \times O}{UI}}$$

$$= \sqrt{\frac{2 \times 40{,}000 \times 8}{4}}$$

$$= \sqrt{1{,}60{,}000} = 400 \text{ packs.}$$

(ii) Number of orders per year

$$\frac{\text{Annual requirements}}{\text{Economic order quantity}}$$

$$\frac{40{,}000}{400} = 100 \text{ order per year}$$

(iii) Ordering and storage costs

	₹
Ordering costs: 100 orders × ₹8.00	800
Storage cost: (400/2) × (10% of 40)	800
Total cost of ordering & storage	1,600

(iv) Timing of next order

(a) Day's requirement served by each order.

$$\text{Number of days requirements} = \frac{\text{No. of working days}}{\text{No. of orders in a year}} = \frac{360}{100} = 3.6 \text{ days supply}$$

This implies that each order of 400 packs supplies for requirements of 3.6 days only.

(b) Days requirement covered by inventory

$$= \frac{\text{Units in inventory}}{\text{Economic order qunantity}} \times (\text{Day requirement served by an order})$$

$$\therefore \frac{333}{400} \times 3.6 \text{ days} = 3 \text{ days requirement}$$

(c) Time interval for placing next order

Inventory left for day's requirement – Lead time of delivery

3 days' requirements – 3 days lead time = 0

This means that next order for the replenishment of supplies has to be placed immediately.

EXAMPLE 3.8

Average usage is 50 units per week; Minimum re-order period is 4 weeks; Maximum usage is 75 units per week; Average re-order period is 5 weeks; and Average stock level is 375 units. Calculate Re-order quantity.

Solution

Step-1 Average usage = (Minimum usage + Maximum usage)/2

50 units = (Minimum usage + 75 units)/2

Minimum usage = (50 × 2) – 75 units = 25 units

Step-2 Average re-order period = (Minimum re-order period + Maximum re-order period)/2

5 week = (4 weeks + Maximum re-order period)/2

10 weeks = 4 weeks + Maximum re-order period

Maximum re-order = 10 week – 4 weeks = 6 weeks period

Step-3 Re-order level = Maximum rate of consumption × Maximum re-order period

= 75 units × 6 weeks = 450 units

Step-4 Minimum level = Re-order level – (Normal rate of consumption × normal re-order period)

= 450 units – (50 units × 5 weeks) = 200 units

Step-5 Average stock level = ½ (Minimum level + Maximum level)

375 units = ½ (200 units + Max. level)

Max. level = 750 – 200 = 550 units

Step-6 Max. level = Re-order level + Re-order quantity – (Minimum rate of consumption × Minimum re-order period)

550 units = 450 units + re-order quantity – (25 units × 4 weeks)

Re-order quantity = 550 units – 450 units + 100 units = 200 units.

Alternatively, Average stock level = Minimum level + ½ Re-order quantity

375 units = 200 units + ½ Re-order quantity

Re-order quantity = 750 units – 400 units = 350 units

✍ EXAMPLE 3.9

Shagoon India Ltd. provides the following information in respect of material *X*

Supply period	: 5 to 15 days
Rate of Consumption	:
Average	: 15 units per day
Maximum	: 20 units per day
Yearly	: 5,000 units

Ordering costs are ₹20 per order.

Purchase price per unit is ₹50.

Storage costs are 10% of unit value.

Compute:

(i) Re-order Level
(ii) Minimum Level
(iii) Maximum Level

☞ *Solution*

(i) Re-ordering Level = Maximum usage per period × Maximum re-order per period
= 20 units per day × 15 days
= 300 units

(ii) Maximum Level = *ROL* + *ROQ* – (Min. rate of consumption × Min. re-order period)
= 300 units + 200 units – (10 units per day × 5 days)
= 450 units

(iii) Minimum Level = *ROL* – (Average rate of consumption × Average re-order period)
= 300 units – (15 units per day × 10 days)
= 150 units

Working Notes:

1. $ROQ = \sqrt{\dfrac{2U \times P}{S}} = \sqrt{\dfrac{2 \times 5000 \text{ units} \times ₹20}{₹5}} = 200 \text{ units}$

where *ROQ* = Re-order quantity
U = Annual consumption

P = Cost per order

S = Storage cost per unit

2. Average rate of consumption

$$= \frac{\text{Minimum rate of consumption } (x) + \text{Maximum rate of consumption}}{2}$$

$$15 \text{ units per day} = \frac{x + 20 \text{ units per day}}{2}$$

or $x = 10$ units per day.

✍ EXAMPLE 3.10

From the following data, calculate the economic order quantity and the re-order point for Part Z:

Working days in a year	200
Safety stock	400 units
Lead time	10 days
Order costs	₹300 per order
Holding cost	15% of cost
Annual consumption	10,000 units
Cost per unit	₹10

for excel template, scan

☞ *Solution*

$$EOQ = \sqrt{\frac{2U \times P}{S}}$$

$$\sqrt{\frac{2 \times 10{,}000 \times ₹300}{15\% \times 10}} = \sqrt{\frac{6{,}000{,}000}{1.5}} = \sqrt{4000000} = 2000 \text{ units}$$

Trial and error calculation to arrive at the above answer:

Times ordered	4	5	6
Order size (units)	2,500	2,000	1,666
Average stock (units)	1,250	1,000	833
Holding costs (₹)	1,875	1,500	1,250
Order costs (₹)	1,200	1,500	1,800
Holding cost has been calculated as follows:	₹3,075	₹3,000	₹3,050

Average stock units × Cost per unit × 15%

Economic order quantity: 2,000 units, order 5 times per annum.

Re-order point:

Daily consumption × Lead time (10,000 ÷ 200) × 10	= 500
Add safety stock	400
Re-order point	900 units

Holding cost has been calculated as follows:
Average stock units × Cost per unit × 15%

✍ EXAMPLE 3.11

Eats Ltd. supplies a number of products to bakers and confectioners. One of their products consists of packets of cake decorations. The cake decorations are sold in packets of twelve decorations for ₹20 per packet. The demand for the cake decorations is very constant and has over a long period of time been at the rate of 2,000 packets per month. The packets cost Eats Ltd. ₹10 each from the manufacturer and a lead time of four days is required from date of order to date of delivery. Ordering costs are ₹1.20 per order and the holding or carrying cost is 10 per cent per annum.

(a) Calculate the following:
  (i) the economic order quantity
  (ii) the number of orders to be placed per annum
  (iii) the total cost of buying and carrying cake decorations per annum.
(b) Assume that the present stock level is 200 packets and that no buffer stocks are kept. When must the next order be given to the supplier? (For purposes of your calculation, one year consists of 360 days).
(c) There are certain major difficulties often experienced by firms in seeking to use the *EOQ* formula. List them briefly.

☞ *Solution*

(a) (i) $EOQ = \sqrt{\frac{2U \times P}{S}}$

$$\sqrt{\frac{2 \times 24{,}000 \times 1.20}{0.10 \times 10}} = \sqrt{\frac{57{,}600}{1}} = 240 \text{ units}$$

(ii) Number of orders to be placed per annum

$$\frac{\text{Annual usage}}{EOQ} = \frac{24{,}000}{240} = 100 \text{ orders}$$

(iii) Cost of buying 100 orders × ₹1.20	₹120
Cost of holding = average stock × holding cost per unit = 120 units × ₹1	₹120
Total cost of buying and holding cake decorations per annum	₹240

(b) $\frac{200}{2{,}000} = \frac{1}{10}$ th of a month or 3 days supply.

With a lead time of four days the order must be placed tomorrow without fail.

(c) Difficulties often experienced by firms in seeking to use the *EOQ* formula are difficulty of estimating, with accuracy, such items as the annual demand for stock items, the cost of ordering and the cost of carrying. Also the *EOQ* formula makes the assumption that stock is used at a constant rate throughout the year. This may not be so.

✍ EXAMPLE 3.12

A company uses three raw materials *A*, *B* and *C* for a particular product for which the following data apply:

Raw Material	Usage Per Unit of Product kg	Re-order Quantity (kg)	Price Per kg	Delivery (in weeks) Min.	Av.	Max.	Re-order Level (kg)	Minimum Level (kg)
A	10	10,000	0.10	1	2	3	8,000	
B	4	5,000	0.30	3	4	5	4,750	
C	6	10,000	0.15	2	3	4		2,000

Weekly production varies from 175 to 225 units, averaging 200 units of the said product. What would be the following quantities:

(i) Minimum stock of *A*?
(ii) Maximum stock of *B*?
(iii) Re-order level of *C*?
(iv) Average stock level of *A*?

☞ **Solution**

(i) *Minimum stock of A*

Re-order level – (Average rate of consumption × Average time required to obtain fresh delivery)

= 8,000 – (2,000 × 2) = 4,000 kg

(ii) *Maximum stock of B*

Re-order level – (Minimum consumption × Minimum re-order period + Re-order quantity)

= 4,750 – (4 × 175 × 3) + 5,000

= 9,750 – 2,100 = 7,650 kg

(iii) *Re-order level of C*

Maximum re-order period × Maximum usage = 4 × 1,350 = 5,400 kg

or

Re-order level of *C* = Minimum stock of *C* + (Average rate of consumption × Average time required to obtain fresh delivery)

= 2,000 + [200 × 6 × 3] kg = 5,600 kg

(iv) *Average stock level of A*

$$= \frac{\text{Minimum stock + maximum stock}}{2} = \frac{4,000 + 16,250}{2}$$

= 10,125 kg

Working Note:

Maximum stock of *A* = *ROL* + *ROQ* – (Min. consumption × Min. re-order period)

= 8,000 kg + 10,000 – [(175 × 10) × 1]

= 16,250 kg

✍ EXAMPLE 3.13

A manufacturer requires 9,600 units of a certain component annually. This is currently purchased from a regular supplier at ₹50 per unit. The cost of placing an order is ₹60 per order and the annual carrying cost is ₹5 per piece. What is the economic order quantity (*EOQ*) for placing order?

Recently, the supplier has expressed his willingness to reduce the price to ₹48, if the total requirements are obtained from him in two equal orders and to ₹47, if the entire quantity required is purchased in one lot. Analyse the cost of the three options and recommend the best course.
What other factors should also be considered before the decision is taken?

Solution

Economic Order Quantity (*EOQ*)

$$= \sqrt{\frac{2 \times \text{Annual consumption} \times \text{Cost of placing an order}}{\text{Cost of carrying one unit inventory for one year}}}$$

$$= \sqrt{\frac{2 \times 9600 \times 60}{5}} = \sqrt{230400} = 480 \text{ units}$$

Analysis of costs of three options

No. of order (options)	20	2	1
Size of order (units)	480	4,800	9,600
Price per unit of components (₹)	50	48	47
Average stock (units)	240	2,400	4,800
Total ordering cost (₹) @ ₹60	1,200	120	60
Total carrying cost (₹) @ ₹5	1,200	12,000	24,000
Total cost of components (₹)	4,80,000	4,60,800	4,51,200
Grand total cost (annual)	4,82,400	4,72,920	4,75,260

Recommendation: From the above analysis it reveals that the most economical order quantity is 4,800 units of components. Therefore placing two orders is marginally best.
Other factors to be considered are as follows:

- Availability of sufficient storage space.
- Possible deterioration in quality due to long storage.
- Opportunity cost of funds required for investment in the inventory.

Total cost of components = No. of orders × Size of order (units) × Price per unit of component (₹)

EXAMPLE 3.14

RST Limited has received an offer of quantity discount on its order of materials as under:

Price Per Tonne	*Tonnes Number*
₹9,600	Less than 50
₹9,360	50 and less than 100
₹9,120	100 and less than 200
₹8,880	200 and less than 300
₹8,640	300 and above

The annual requirement for the material is 500 tonnes. The ordering cost per order is ₹12,500 and the stock holding cost is estimated at 25% of the material cost per annum.

Required:

(i) Compute the most economical purchase level.

(ii) Computer EOQ if there are no quantity discounts and the price per tonne is ₹10,500.

☞ ***Solution***

(i)

Order Size	*No. of Orders*	*Cost of Purchase*	*Ordering Cost*	*Carrying Cost*	*Total Cost*
(Q Units)		*(AQ × Per unit cost)*	*No. of Orders × ₹12,500*	*2 × C × 25%*	*(3 + 4 + 5)*
(1)	*(2)*	*(3)*	*(4)*	*(5)*	*(6)*
40	12.5	48,00,000 (500 × 9,600)	1,56,250	48,000 $\left(\frac{40}{2} \times 9{,}600 \times 0.25\right)$	50,04,250
50	10	46,80,000 (500 × 9,360)	1,25,000	58,500 $\left(\frac{50}{2} \times 9{,}360 \times 0.25\right)$	48,63,500
100	5	45,60,000 (500 × 9,120)	62,500	1,14,000 $\left(\frac{100}{2} \times 9{,}120 \times 0.25\right)$	47,36,500
200	2.5	44,40,000 (500 × 8,880)	31,250 (2.5 × 12,500)	2,22,000 $\left(\frac{200}{2} \times 8{,}880 \times 0.25\right)$	46,93,250
300	1.67	43,20,000 (500 × 8,640)	20,875 (1.67 × 12,500)	3,24,000 $\left(\frac{300}{2} \times 8{,}640 \times 0.25\right)$	46,64,875

The above table shows that the total cost of 500 units including ordering and carrying cost is minimum (₹46,64,875) where the order size is 300 units. Hence, the most economical purchase level is 300 units.

(ii) $EOQ = \sqrt{\frac{2AO}{c \times i}} = \sqrt{\frac{2 \times 500 \times 12500}{10500 \times 25\%}} = 69$ tonnes.

✍ EXAMPLE 3.15

IPL Limited uses a small casting in one of its finished products. The castings are purchased from a foundry. IPL Limited purchases 54,000 castings per year at a cost of ₹800 per casting.

The castings are used evenly throughout the year in the production process on a 360-day-per-year basis. The company estimates that it costs ₹9,000 to place a single purchase order and about ₹300 to carry one casting in inventory for a year. The high carrying costs result from the need to keep the castings in carefully controlled temperature and humidity conditions, and from the high cost of insurance.

Delivery from the foundry generally takes 6 days, but it can take as much as 10 days. The days of delivery time and percentage of their occurrence are shown in the following tabulation:

Delivery time (days)	:	6	7	8	9	10
Percentage of occurrence	:	75	10	5	5	5

Required:

(i) Compute the economic order quantity (*EOQ*).

(ii) Assume the company is willing to assume a 15% risk of being out of stock. What would be the safety stock and the re-order point?

(iii) Assume the company is willing to assume a 5% risk of being out of stock. What would be the safety stock and the re-order point?

(iv) Assume 5% stock-out risk. What would be the total cost of ordering and carrying inventory for one year?

(v) Refer to the original data. Assume that using process re-engineering the company reduces its cost of placing a purchase order to only ₹600. In addition, company estimates that when the waste and inefficiency caused by inventories are considered, the true cost of carrying a unit in stock is ₹720 per year.

(a) Compute the new *EOQ*.

(b) How frequently would the company be placing an order, as compared to the old purchasing policy?

☞ ***Solution***

(i) *Computation of economic order quantity (EOQ)*

(A) Annual requirement	= 54,000 castings
(B) Cost per casting	= ₹800
(O) Ordering cost	= ₹9,000/order
($c \times i$) Carrying cost per casting p.a	= ₹300

$$EOQ = \sqrt{\frac{2AO}{c \times i}} = \sqrt{\frac{2 \times 54000 \times 9000}{300}} = 1800 \text{ casting}$$

(ii) *Safety stock*

(Assuming a 15% risk of being out of stock)

Safety stock for one day = 54,000/360 days = 150 castings

Re-order point = Minimum stock level + Average lead time × Average consumption

= 150 + 6 × 150 = 1,050 castings.

(iii) *Safety stock*

(Assuming a 5% risk of being out of stock)

	Safety stock for three days	= 150 × 3 days	= 450 castings
	Re-order point	= 450 casting + 900 castings	= 1,350 castings
(iv)	Total cost of ordering	= (54,000/1,800) × ₹9,000	= ₹2,27,000
	Total cost of carrying	= (450 + 1/2 × 1,800) × ₹300	= ₹4,05,000

(v) (a) Computation of new *EOQ*:

$$EOQ = \sqrt{\frac{2 \times 54{,}000 \times 600}{720}} = 300 \text{ castings}$$

(b) Total number of orders to be placed in a year is 180. Each other is to be placed after 2 days (1 year = 360 days). Under old purchasing policy, each order is placed after 12 days.

EXAMPLE 3.16

The Complete Gardener is deciding on the economic order quantity for two brands of lawn fertiliser: Super Grow and Nature's Own. The following information is collected.

	Fertiliser	
	Super Grow	*Nature's Own*
Annual Demand	2,000 Bags	1,280 Bags
Relevant ordering cost per purchase order	₹1,200	₹1,400
Annual relevant carrying cost per bag	₹480	₹650

Required:

(i) Compute *EOQ* for Super Grow and Nature's Own.

(ii) For the *EOQ*, what is the sum of the total annual relevant ordering costs and total annual relevant costs for Super Grow and Nature's Own?

(iii) For the *EOQ*, compute the number of deliveries per year for Super Grow and Nature's Own.

Solution

(i) $$EOQ = \sqrt{\frac{2SC_0^*}{iC_1}}$$

*Here S = Annual demand of fertiliser bags.

C_1 = Cost per bag.

C = Relevant ordering cost per purchase order

iC_1 = Annual relevant carrying cost per bag

EOQ for Super Grow Fertiliser

$$\sqrt{\frac{2 \times 2{,}000 \text{ bags} \times ₹1{,}200}{₹480}} = 100 \text{ bags.}$$

EOQ for Nature's Own Fertiliser

$$\sqrt{\frac{2 \times 1{,}280 \text{ bags} \times ₹1{,}400}{₹560}} = 80 \text{ bags.}$$

(ii) *Total annual relevant costs for Super Grow Fertiliser*

= Total annual relevant ordering costs + Total annual relevant carrying costs

$$= \frac{S}{EOQ} C_0 + \frac{1}{2} EOQ \times iC_1$$

$$= \frac{2{,}000 \text{ bags}}{100 \text{ bags}} ₹1{,}200 + \frac{1}{2} \; 100 \text{ bags} \times ₹480$$

$$= ₹24{,}000 + ₹24{,}000 = ₹48{,}000$$

Total annual relevant costs for Nature's Own Fertiliser

$$= \frac{1{,}280 \text{ bags}}{80 \text{ bags}} \times ₹1{,}400 + \frac{1}{2} \; 80 \text{ bags} \times ₹560$$

$$= ₹22{,}400 + ₹22{,}400 = ₹44{,}800$$

(iii) *Number of deliveries for Super Grow Fertiliser per year.*

$$= \frac{S}{EOQ} \text{ (annual demand of fertiliser bags)}$$

$$= \frac{2{,}000 \text{ bags}}{100 \text{ bags}} = 20 \text{ orders}$$

Numbers of deliveries for Nature's Own Fertilisers per year.

$$= \frac{1{,}280 \text{ bags}}{80 \text{ bags}} = 16 \text{ orders}$$

✍ EXAMPLE 3.17

A company manufactures 5,000 units of a product per month. The cost of placing an order is ₹100. The purchase price of the raw material is ₹10 per kg. The re-order period is 4 to 8 weeks. The consumption of raw materials varies from 100 kg to 450 kg per week; the average consumption being 275 kg. The carrying cost of inventory is 20% per annum. You are required to calculate re-order quantity, maximum level, minimum level and average level.

☞ Solution

$$\text{Re-order quantity} = \sqrt{\frac{2 \times U \times P}{S}}$$

where U = Annual usage

P = Cost of placing an order

S = Cost of storage one unit per annum

$U = 5{,}000 \times 12 = 60{,}000$; $P = 100$; $S = 20\%$ of $10 = 2$

$$\therefore \quad \text{Re-order quantity} = \sqrt{\frac{2 \times 60{,}000 \times 100}{2}}$$

$$= 2449.48 \text{ or } 2450 \text{ (approx)}$$

Re-order level: Maximum usage × Maximum re-order period

$$= 450 \times 8 = 3{,}600$$

Maximum level = Re-order level + Re-order quantity – (Minimum usage × Minimum re-order period)

= 3,600 + 2,450 – (100 × 4) = 5,650

Minimum level = Re order level – (Average usage × Average re-order period)

= 3,600 – (275 × 6) = 1,950

$$\text{Average level} = \frac{\text{Maximum level} + \text{Minimum level}}{2}$$

$$= \frac{5650 + 1950}{2} = 3,800$$

or

Average level = Minimum level + 1/2 Re-order quantity

= 1,950 + 1/2 × 2,450 = 3,175

✍ EXAMPLE 3.18

The quarterly production of a company's product which has a steady market is 20,000 units. Each unit of a product requires 0.5 kg of raw material. The cost of placing one order for raw material is ₹100 and the inventory carrying cost is ₹2 per annum. The lead time for procurement of raw material is 36 days and a safety stock of 1,000 kg of raw materials is maintained by the company. The company has been able to negotiate the following discount structure with the raw material supplier.

Order Quantity	*Discount*
kg.	₹
Upto 6,000	Nil
6,000 – 8,000	400
8,000 – 16,000	2,000
16,000 – 30,000	3,200
30,000 – 45,000	4,000

You are required to

(i) Calculate the re-order point taking 30 days in a month.

(ii) Prepare a statement showing the total cost of procurement and storage of raw material after considering the discount of the company elects to place one, two, four or six orders in the year.

(iii) State the number of orders which the company should place to minimise the costs after taking *EOQ* also into consideration.

☞ *Solutions*

1. Annul production (units) 80,000
   (20,000 units per quarter × 4 quarters)
2. Raw material required for 80,000 units in kg 40,000
   (80,000 units × 0.5 kg)

3. $EOQ = \sqrt{\dfrac{2 \times 40{,}000 \text{ kg} \times ₹100}{₹2}} = 2{,}000 \text{ kg}$

4. Total cost of procurement and storage when the order size is equal to *EOQ* or 2,000 kg

No. of orders (40,000 kg/2,000 kg)	20
Ordering cost (₹) (20 orders × ₹100)	2,000
Carrying cost (₹) (1/2 × 2,000 kg × ₹2)	2,000
Total cost	4,000

(i) Re-order point = Lead time consumption + Safety stock
= 4,000 kg + 1,000 kg = 5,000 kg
(40,000 kg/360 days) × 36 days.

(ii)

Statement Showing the Total Cost of Procurement and Storage of Raw Materials

(After Considering the Discount)

Order Size	*No. of Orders*	*Total Cost of Procurement*	*Average Stock*	*Total Cost of Storage of Raw Materials*	*Discount*	*Total Cost*
kg		₹	*kg*	₹	₹	₹
(1)	(2)	(3) = (2) × ₹100	(4) = 1/2 (1)	(5) = (4) × ₹2	(6)	(7) = [(3) + (5)] – (6)
40,000	1	100	20,000	40,000	4,000	36,100
20,000	2	200	10,000	20,000	3,200	17,000
10,000	4	400	5,000	10,000	2,000	8,400
6,666.66	6	600	3,333	6,666	400	6,866

(iii) Number of orders which the company should place to minimise the costs after taking *EOQ* also into consideration is 20 orders, each of size 2,000 kg. The total cost of procurement and storage in this case comes to ₹4,000, which is minimum.

STORES ORGANISATION

Efficient storing—after efficient purchasing—is another important step in materials control system.

The storekeeper and persons working in stores are primarily responsible for safeguarding the materials and keeping materials and supplies in proper places until required in production. It is difficult to list out all the functions performed by stores in different organisations. But usually they perform the following functions:

1. Acting as a buffer or protection against the consequences of non-availability.
2. Acting as a link between bulk purchases and the breaking down into units of need.
3. Providing security.
4. Avoiding damage and deterioration.

5. Establishing a proper system for ensuring control over usage, through a discipline of authority for withdrawals, formalised rationing of materials issued, recording of data for control, etc.
6. Marshalling during the course of manufacture.
7. Performing checking function on work done.
8. Serving as a means of reducing cost in movement of materials through systematic location, economy of handling, etc.
9. Forming a basis for good housekeeping, discipline and control.
   Storage brings a sense of tidiness and good arrangements and help to emphasise the importance of responsibility and accountability.

Storage Layout

Storage layout, i.e. careful design and arrangement of storerooms is desirable for savings in cost. Materials can be stored according to: (i) account number specially given for different types of materials; (ii) the frequency of use of the item; (iii) the production area where the item is used; or (iv) the nature, size and shape of the item. Practically, no single one of these factors could be the sole basis for deciding the storing arrangement, but shape and size of the materials significantly influence storeroom arrangement.

The basic accounting records of any inventory system are the documents required to authorise and record materials movement into or out of the stores. These are the goods received note, materials requisition and materials return note. Stores ledger cards—stock ledger cards or materials ledger cards—may show quantities on order, expected delivery dates and quantities reserved or required for work due to be processed (Fig. 3.6).

ABC Company Limited
Stores Ledger Card

Description__________ Code

Unit __________ Location __________

Maximum __________ Minimum __________

Re-order Level __________ Re-order Quantity __________

Receipt	*Issues*	*Physical Balance*	*Reserved*	*Ordered*	*Free Balance*
Date Ref. Qty.	*Date Ref. Qty.*		*Date Ref. Cum Qty.*	*Date Ref. Cum Qty*	

Fig. 3.6 Stores Ledger Card

Bin card Bin cards usually show quantities of each type of material received, issued and on hand. The bin card is placed in the bin or shelf or is hung over the almirah or the rack otherwise known as bin. Separate bin cards are prepared for each item of stores and if two different materials are kept in one almirah, two bin cards, one of each, are prepared, treating the almirah as two bins. A physical bin card is presented in Fig. 3.7.

ABC Company Limited
Bin Card

Description ______________ Bin No. ______________
Store Ledger No. ______________ Code No. ______________
Minimum Level ______________ Unit No. ______________

	Received		Issue		Balance	
Date	*Ref.*	*Qty.*	*Ref.*	*Qty.*	*Quantity*	*Check*
May 1, 2008					500	
May 15, 2008		200			700	
May 30, 2008				300	400	
June 7, 2008		150			550	
June 25, 2008				400	150	

Fig. 3.7 Bin Card with Sample Data

Classification and Codification of Materials

Classification and codification of materials facilitates prompt identification of the materials in storage or when they are being issued to production departments. All items in the stores department should be properly classified and codified. Codification implies giving some symbols through letters or figures under a proper codification system. Codification provides certain benefits: (i) Simplicity in identifying and tracing the stores. (ii) Full particulars need not be given and thus clerical labour and time are saved. (iii) Secrecy is maintained about the details of the stores and all employees may not know them. (iv) Codification is necessary to adopt a mechanical system of accounting.

Issue of Materials

It is the quality of every good system of materials control that no materials can be issued from storerooms except on properly prepared and approved materials requisitions or stores requisitions. The materials requisition is a written order to the storekeeper to deliver materials or supplies to the place and the department designated or to give the materials to the person presenting a properly executed requisition. The materials requisition note (see Fig. 3.8) includes date, requisition number, department charged, name of stock ledger account to be credited, description of materials, quantity, unit price, total value, delivery point, signature of the person requisitioning the material and signature of the department executive approving the request for material. The requisitions are prepared in triplicate, one copy is retained by the preparer and two are sent to the storekeeper.

Department having standard materials requirements or a comparatively fixed list of materials or supplies generally use a special form of materials requisition called the "bill of materials". The bill of materials is a printed or duplicated form listing all the materials and part necessary for a typical job or production (see Fig. 3.9). In preparing such a requisition, it is necessary only to indicate the quantity in the blank space in front of the name or symbol of the material required.

ABC Company Limited
Materials Requisition Note

Job No. ____________ Serial No. ____________

Date ____________

Code No.	*Description*	*Qty or Weight*	*Rate*	*Unit*	*Amount*	*Cost Office Stores Ledger*

Authorised by ____________ Storekeeper ____________

Prices entered by ____________ Received by ____________

Bin Card entered ____________ Calculation checked ____________

Fig. 3.8 Materials Requisition Note

ABC Company Limited
Bill of Material

Job/Work Order No. ____________ No. ____________

Description of Job ____________ Date ____________

Details of Issues

S. No.	*Description*	*Code No.*	*Date*	*Rate (₹)*	*Amount (₹)*	*Remarks*

Prepared by ____________ Stores Department Cost Department

Checked by ____________

Fig. 3.9 Bill of Material

Materials Returned to the Storeroom

Materials requisitioned from a storeroom and not needed or found to be defective are returned to the storeroom, where a returned material report is prepared either by the person returning the materials or by the storekeeper upon receipt of the materials. Two copies of the report are usually prepared; the original is used as a basis for crediting the accounts charged while the duplicate is retained in the files of the department returning the materials to the storeroom (Fig. 3.10).

Some departments may prefer to use the excess materials on the next job instead of returning them to the storeroom. But, it is always advisable to prepare a returned materials report, otherwise one job will be charged unnecessarily with too much materials cost and the other job with too little. A materials transfer note (see Fig. 3.11) is prepared to transfer costs from one original job to the new job and also the transfer is noted in the stock records.

ABC Company Limited
Material Return Note

Issuing Department ______________ No. ______________
Job No. ______________ Date ______________

S.No.	*Description*	*Code No.*	*Quantity*	*Rate (₹)*	*Amount (₹)*

Signature of
Works Manager/Foreman

Fig. 3.10 Material Return Note

ABC Company Limited
Materials Transfer Note

Serial No. ______________
Date ______________

The following materials have been transferred:

From Job No. ______________ To Job No. ______________

Code	*Description*	*Quantity*	*Cost Office*		
			Rate	*Unit*	*Amount*

Authorised	Delivered	Received	Priced

Fig. 3.11 Materials Transfer Note

Materials Returned to Supplier

It may be necessary to return any rejected, specified excess, damaged or unsatisfactory materials to the supplier. Since goods are returned after having been received in storerooms and entered in the stock ledger accounts, some correcting entries are required. From the reject/despatch note issued by the purchasing department, information regarding the quantity and value may be entered in the Received Section of the stock ledger accounts in red ink. Alternatively, an entry can be made in the Issued Section with a special notation or symbol to indicate that the goods were returned to the supplier and not issued to departments or jobs or processes.

INVENTORY SYSTEMS

There are two principal ways of accounting for inventories:

Perpetual Inventory System

The perpetual inventory method requires a continuous record of additions to or reductions in materials, work-in-progress, and cost of goods sold on a day-to-day basis. Physical inventory counts are usually taken atleast once a year in order to check on the validity of the accounting records. The Institute of Cost and Management Accountant (U.K.) has defined perpetual inventory as:

A system of records maintained by the controlling department which reflects the physical movement of stocks and their current balance... A perpetual inventory is usually checked by a programme of continuous stocktaking, and the two terms are sometimes loosely considered synonymous. Perpetual inventory means the system of records, whereas continuous stocktaking means the physical checking of those records with actual stocks.

The perpetual inventory method has the following advantages:

1. The stock-taking task which is long and costly is avoided under this method.
2. The inventory of different items of materials in accordance with the stores ledger can be promptly prepared for the preparation of the income statement and balance sheet at interim periods if required without a physical inventory being taken.
3. Management may be informed daily of the number of units and the value of each kind of material on hand—information which tends to eliminate delays and stoppage in production.
4. The investment in materials and supplies may be kept at the lowest point in conformity with operating requirements.
5. A system of internal check is always in operation and the activities of different departments, such as purchasing, stores and production are continuously checked against each other.
6. It is not necessary to stop production so as to carry out a complete physical stock-taking.
7. Discrepancies and errors are promptly discovered and localised and remedial action can be taken to avoid their occurrence in the future.
8. This method has a moral effect on the staff, makes them disciplined and careful and acts as a check against dishonest actions.
9. The disadvantages of excessive stock are avoided, such as loss of interest on capital invested in stock, loss through deterioration and risk of obsolescence.

Periodic Inventory System

Under the periodic method, the entire book inventory is verified at a given date by an actual count of materials on hand. This physical inventory is usually taken near the end of the accounting period. This method provides for the recording of purchases, purchase returns and purchase allowances on a daily basis but does not provide for a continuous inventory or for a daily computation of the cost of goods sold. At the end of each accounting period, a physical count is made of the quantity of goods on hand and the value of the inventory is determined by using an inventory pricing method (FIFO, LIFO or Average Cost) and attaching cost to units counted. The cost of goods sold is computed by deducting closing inventory from the sum of opening inventory and purchases made during the current period. It is assumed that goods not on hand at the end of accounting period have been sold. There is no system and accounting for shrinkage, losses, theft and waste throughout the accounting period and they can be discovered only after the end of the period.

It can be concluded that perpetual inventory assists management in planning future purchases, reduces possibilities of stock shortages and aids in the reduction of waste, spoilage, etc., associated with the storage of inventory. But, it is also more costly of the two procedures. The periodic inventory procedure is simple in concept and application. Yet it normally requires the shutdown of operation while it is carried out; it is error-prone due to inexperience of inventory takers; it cannot pinpoint shortages resulting from theft or waste.

Difference between Perpetual Inventory System and Periodic Inventory System

The following are the differences between perpetual inventory system and periodic inventory system.

Perpetual Inventory System	*Periodic Inventory System*
1. In this system, records are maintained continuously which reflects the physical movements of stock and current balance after every receipt and issue.	1. In this system, stock taking is done only at the end of a specified period, generally at the end of an accounting year. Therefore, data about current balance, issue and receipts of materials can be known only at the end of accounting period.
2. Production is not stopped for stock taking	2. Production is suspended for a few days to facilitate stock taking.
3. It is relatively an expensive method.	3. It is a less costly method.
4. This inventory system is appropriate for large enterprises.	4. This system is suitable for small organisations.

INVENTORY SHORTAGES (LOSSES) AND OVERAGES

Under the perpetual inventory system, inventory accounts are maintained up-to-date in a stores ledger. It is, however, necessary to make physical counts of the materials at regular intervals to compare with the stores ledger records. It is possible that physical counting of materials may not agree with the stores ledger. The difference may be because of the following reasons:

A. Unavoidable

1. Evaporation
2. Absorption, moisture
3. Temperature changes affecting the volume of stock
4. Shrinkage
5. Deterioration of quality in stores, for example, through rust
6. Loss due to breaking bulk or cutting up.

B. Avoidable

1. Pilferage
2. Unsuitable storage
3. Careless handling
4. Under and over issues
5. Materials unused but not returned to stores

INVENTORY CONTROL

Nature of Inventory

Inventory is a store of goods and stocks. The Institute of Chartered Accountants of India (Accounting Standards 2) defines inventories as:

"Tangible property held (i) for the sale in the ordinary course of business, or (ii) in the process of production for such sale, or (iii) for consumption in the production of goods or service for sale, including maintenance supplies and consumables other than machinery spares."

In other words, in manufacturing organisations, inventories include (a) raw-materials, (b) work-in-progress, (c) finished produced goods, and (d) manufacturing supplies. In trading concerns, inventories consist of (a) merchandise held for sale, and (b) office, packing and other supplies.

Meaning of Inventory Control

Inventory control is the technique of maintaining inventory items (raw materials, work-in-progress, finished products, factory supplies) at desired levels. Manufacturing firms face several inventory control problems as compared to service-oriented organisations. In manufacturing organisations, production is of some tangible physical product. Therefore, emphasis is given to control of all inventory items. In service organisations, the focus is on service, and therefore, there is very little emphasis on inventory control. In such service firms, services are used (consumed) as they are generated and not stocked for future consumption. However, there are some service organisations, such as hospitals, military organisations, educational institutions which have to maintain inventories of items related to their nature of work.

Importance of Inventory Control

Inventory control is of great significance in almost all types of business enterprises. If inventories pile up due to over-production or slow demand, capital is tied up and which cannot be used for other productive purposes. Alternatively, production is likely to suffer because of inadequate inventory on hand. As stated earlier in this chapter, the basic objective of inventory control is identical to materials control, that is, maintaining inventory of adequate size for uninterrupted production and lowest investment on the inventory in conformity with production requirements.

Inventory control is also necessary because of the following significant factors:

1. *Demand fluctuations* There are likely to be fluctuations in demand pattern. To cope with the changing consumers' demand, it is necessary that adequate inventory should be maintained.
2. *Uncertainty about lead time* Sometimes, the supplier may take more time in supplying the raw materials than expected. During this additional time, inventory has to be maintained so that the production does not suffer.
3. *Avoiding over-stocking and under-stocking* Over-stocking and under-stocking both are undesirable and should be avoided.

Inventory Control Techniques

Different business concerns may apply different inventory control techniques to meet specific requirements and circumstances. However, the following techniques are commonly used by firms for inventory control:

1. Two-bin system—bag and tag system.
2. Order cycling system.
3. Determination of inventory levels.
4. Statistical control system.
5. Control ratios.
6. Reservation system.
7. Budgetary control system.
8. ABC classification and control method (Pareto Analysis)
9. Perpetual inventory system.
10. Just-in-Time-Method

Pareto or ABC Analysis

In a large manufacturing company, where stocks of direct materials and component parts consist of many thousands of different items, companies find it useful to divide materials, parts, supplies and finished goods into sub-classifications for purposes of inventory control. Many business firms introduce a system of analysing stocks by value categories known as "ABC or Pareto Analysis". Under this method, inventory items are ranked according to investments in each item in the inventory. The large value items are grouped together into one class for inventory control purposes. The lowest value items are grouped into another class and those items which are of intermediate value are grouped into a "middle" classification. High value items are labelled "Class A", middle value items, "Class B", and low value items, "Class C". All items in stock are listed in order of descending values showing quantity held and the corresponding value of the materials (see Table 3.3).

The percentage given in Table 3.3 are only guidelines and are subject to change according to prevailing circumstances and choice of management. Table 3.2 shows that only 20% of the items represent 72% of the total costs .

Table 3.3 Stock Analysis under ABC

	Items		*Investment*	
Class	*No. of Items*	*Per cent of Total Items*	*Total Cost*	*Per cent of Total*
A	20,000	20%	2,88,000	72%
B	30,000	30%	76,000	19%
C	50,000	50%	36,000	9%
	100,000	100%	4,00,000	100%

The items under Class *A* are subject to greater continuous control and planning than are the items under other categories. The Class *A* items account for high annual consumption costs and correspondingly high investment in inventories. Because of high investments in Class *A* items, there would be frequent ordering and low safety stocks. This also assumes that the cost of placing and following up orders is relatively low in comparison with the costs of carrying excess inventories. A number of things can be done to reduce inventory of "*A*" items. For example, *A* items can generally be ordered for specific runs, the economic order quantity could be applied; local suppliers could be asked to stock supplies so that delivery time can be shortened. On the other hand, where the total annual purchase cost is relatively low as in the case of Class *C* items, there will be less frequent ordering and higher safety stocks. Items in Class *C* receive the least amount of control and should be under simple physical controls such as the two-bin system with safety stocks.

A graph can be prepared to show quantity and amount of items in different categories in descending order of value (Fig. 3.12).

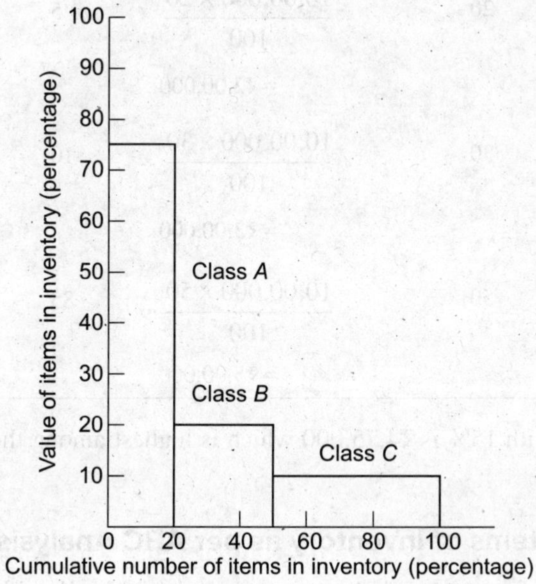

Fig. 3.12 ABC (Pareto) Method of Inventory Classifications

EXAMPLE 3.19

A factory uses 4,000 varieties of inventory. In terms of inventory holding and inventory usage, the following information is compiled:

No. of Varieties of Inventory	*%*	*% Value of Inventory Holding (Average)*	*% of Inventory Usage (in end product)*
3,875	96.875	20	5
110	2.75	30	10
15	0.375	50	85
	100.00	100	100

Classify the items of inventory as per ABC analysis with reasons.

Solution

Assume ₹10,00,000 as value of inventory of 4,000 varieties in this factory.

No. of Varieties of Inventory (Items)	% of Varieties	% Value of Inventory Holding (Average)	Value of Inventory Holding (Average)	% of Inventory Usage (in end product)	Value of Inventory Usage (in end product)
3,875	96.875	20	$\frac{10,00,000 \times 20}{100}$ = ₹2,00,000	5	$\frac{20,00,000 \times 5}{100}$ = ₹10,000
110	2.750	30	$\frac{10,00,000 \times 30}{100}$ = ₹3,00,000	10	$\frac{3,00,000 \times 10}{100}$ = ₹30,000
15	0.375	50	$\frac{10,00,000 \times 50}{100}$ = ₹5,00,000	85	$\frac{5,00,000 \times 85}{100}$ ₹4,75,000

Value of inventory items with 15% is ₹4,75,000 which is highest among the three varieties of inventory items.

Classification of the Items of Inventory as per ABC Analysis

Category A: 15 number of varieties of inventory items should be classified as those of *A* category because of the following reasons:

(i) They constitute 0.375% of total number of varieties of inventory items handled by stores of factory. This is the minimum as per the given classification in the table.
(ii) The total usage of these items is 50% of total use value of inventory holding (average) which is maximum according to the given table.
(iii) The consumption of these items is about 85% of usage in end product.

Category B: 110 number of inventory items should be classified as those of *B* category because of the following reasons:

(i) They constitute 2.750% of total number of varieties of inventory items handled by the stores of the factory.
(ii) They require moderate investment of about 30% of total use value of inventory holding (average).
(iii) Their consumption is moderate about 10% of inventory usage in the end-product.

Category C: 3,875 number of varieties of inventory items should be classified as those of category *C* because of the following reasons:

(i) They constitute 96.875% of total varieties of inventory items handled by stores of factory.
(ii) They require investment of 20% of total use value of average inventory holding.
(iii) Their consumption is minimum, that is, just 5% of inventory usage in end product.

Kanban

Kanban is a Japanese term which means display on instruction card. In a manufacturing or factory organisation, Kanban contains many information such as re-order point, lead time, delivery location, source of supply, part number, quantity of parts that should be possessed etc. It is a system of markers which authorises production and movement to the process which requires the parts.

Business firms can use Kanban or any other similar technique as a production control tool. The employees in the production department manufacture parts as per the details mentioned on the Kanban which is used like production card. If in a factory, there is no Kanban card, production may not be done and transfer of materials may not take place.

Kanban is highly useful if used with JIT. The JIT pull system means that components are not made until requested by the next process. This is normally done by monitoring parts consumption at each stage and using a system of Kanban. Kanban, therefore, will reduce inventory, decrease lead or supply time and finally will increase productivity through integrating different processes.

Just-In-Time (JIT) Method

Just-In-Time (JIT) is a purchasing and inventory control method in which materials are obtained just in time for production to provide finished goods just in time for sale. There are two aspects of JIT: (i) Just-In-Time (JIT) Production, and (ii) Just-In-Time (JIT) purchasing. JIT with regard to production means producing only what is needed, when it is needed, in the quantity just needed. A JIT manufacturing system requires making goods or services only when the customer, internal or external, requires it. According to CIMA Official Terminology:

> "JIT is a technique for the organisation of work flows, to allow rapid, high quality, flexible production whilst minimising manufacturing waste and stock level." Further, CIMA defines JIT production as "a system which is driven by demand for finished products, whereby each component on a production line is produced only when needed for the next stage."

JIT purchasing requires better coordination with suppliers so that materials arrive immediately prior to their use. Firms using JIT purchasing enter into long-term contracts with them to enable vendors to plan their annual production. Under JIT purchasing, *EOQ* is much lower as compared to *EOQ* under conventional purchasing. JIT purchasing provides significant savings in cost.

JIT aims to achieve the following objectives:

(i) Zero inventory
(ii) Zero breakdown
(iii) 100% on-time delivery service
(iv) elimination of non-value added activities
(v) Zero defects.

JIT is a demand-pull system. Demand for customer output (not plans for using input resources) triggers production. Production activities are "pulled" not "pushed" into action. The major differences between JIT manufacturing and traditional manufacturing are as follows:

JIT	*Traditional*
1. Pull system	1. Push system
2. Insignificant or Zero inventories	2. Significant inventories

(Contd.)

JIT	Traditional
3. Manufacturing cells (work centres)	3. Process structure
4. Multifunction labour	4. Specialised labour
5. Total quality management (TQM)	5. Acceptable quality level (AQL)
6. Simple cost accounting	6. Complex cost accounting

JIT production and JIT purchasing reduces or eliminates inventory and the costs associated with carrying the inventory. JIT emphasises that workers immediately correct the system making defective units because they have no inventory. With no inventory to draw from for delivery to customers, just-in-time relies on high-quality materials and production. It is required that the companies that use just-in-time manufacturing must eliminate all the sources of failure in the system. Production people must be better trained so that they can carry out their works without errors. Suppliers must be able to produce and deliver defect-free materials or components just when they are required, and equipment must be maintained so that machine failures are eliminated.

JIT applies to raw materials inventory as well as to work-in-process inventory. The goals are that both raw materials and work in progress inventory are held to absolute minimums. JIT is used to complement other materials planning and control tools, such as *EOQ* and safety stock levels. In JIT system, production of an item does not commence until the organisation receives an order. When an order is received for a finished product, productions people give orders for raw materials. As soon as production is complete to fill the order, production ends. In theory, in JIT, there is no need for inventories because no production takes place until the organisation knows that it will sell them. In practice, however, companies using just-in-time inventory generally have a backlog of orders or stable demand for their products to assure continued production.

The fundamental objective of JIT is to produce and deliver what is needed, when it is needed, at all stages of the production process—just in time to be fabricated, sub-assembled, assembled, and despatched to the customer. Although in practice there are no such perfect plans, JIT is an ideal, and therefore, a worthy goal. The benefits are low inventory, high-manufacturing cycle rates, high output per employee, minimum floor space requirements, minimum indirect labour, and perfect in-process control. An associated requirement of a successful JIT operation is the pursuit of perfect quality in order to reduce, to an absolute minimum, delays caused by defective product units.[1]

INVENTORY TURNOVER

Business enterprises can analyse the turnover of different items of stock to find out which stocks are slow-moving. Inventory turnover ratio enables the management to avoid capital being locked up in undesirable stocks. This ratio indicates the efficiency or inefficiency with which inventories are maintained. Inventory turnover ratio is calculated as follows:

$$\frac{\text{Cost of materials consumed}}{\text{Cost of average stock held during the period}}$$

The cost of average stock here is taken as the average of opening and closing stock.

1. Milton F. Usry and Lawrence H. Hammer, *Cost Accounting, Planning and Control*, Cincinnati: South Western Publishing Co., 1999, p. 257.

The stock turnover can also be calculated in days as below:

$$\frac{\text{Days during the period}}{\text{Inventory turnover ratio}}$$

Detection of Slow-Moving and Non-Moving or Obsolete Materials

It is essential for a business firm to detect slow-moving and non-moving or obsolete materials. Obsolete materials become useless or obsolete due to change in product, process, design or method of production. Obsolete materials are different from slow-moving materials. Slow-moving stocks move at a slow rate. In case of slow and non-moving materials, capital remains locked unnecessarily and also cost of storing continue to be incurred if these materials are stored in excess of the requirements. Management should make proper investigation into slow-moving and obsolete materials and take steps to minimise losses arising therefrom. Management should prepare regular reports to examine the situations relating to these stocks so that useless stocks could be disposed of or used in some profitable work and effective steps could be taken to increase the movement of slow-moving stocks.

FSND Analysis

FSND analysis shows the duration of inventory in an organisation analysing their moving position. "F" stands for fast-moving items being consumed in a short period of time, "S" stands for slow-moving items. "N" indicates normal-moving items and "D" indicates dead stock having no further demand.

To conduct this analysis, the last date of receipt or the last date of issue, whichever is later, is taken into account and the period, usually in terms of number of months, that has elapsed since the last movement is recorded.

Such an analysis helps to identify:

(i) active items which require to be reviewed regularly;
(ii) surplus items whose stocks are higher than their rate of consumption; and
(iii) non-moving items which are not being consumed.

The following steps are needed in conducting the FSN analysis.

(i) Calculation of average stay and the consumption rate of the material in warehouse. (ii) FSN Classification of materials based on average stay in the inventory. (iii) FSN Classification of the material based on consumption rate; (iv) and finally classifying inventory based on above FSND analysis.

EXAMPLE 3.20

The following data are available in respect of material *X* for the year ended 31st March, 2020:

	₹
Opening stock	90,000
Purchases during the year	2,70,000
Closing stock	1,10,000

Calculate:

(i) Inventory turnover ratio, and
(ii) The number of days for which the average inventory is held.

Solution

$$\text{Inventory turnover ratio} = \frac{\text{Cost of goods sold}}{\text{Average stock}}$$

$$\text{Cost of goods sold} = \text{Opening stock} + \text{Purchases} - \text{Closing stock}$$

$$= 90{,}000 + 270{,}000 - 1{,}10{,}000 = 2{,}50{,}000$$

$$\text{Average stock} = \frac{\text{Opening stock} + \text{closing stock}}{2}$$

$$\text{Average stock} = \frac{90{,}000 + 1{,}10{,}000}{2} = 1{,}00{,}000$$

$$\frac{2{,}50{,}000}{1{,}00{,}000} = 2.5 \text{ times}$$

$$\text{No. of days for inventory held} = \frac{\text{No. of days in a year}}{\text{Inventory turnover ratio}}$$

$$= \frac{365}{2.5} = 146 \text{ days}$$

EXAMPLE 3.21

From the following data, calculate stock holding period for sugar and milk. Which is fast-moving item?

	Sugar	*Milk*
	₹	₹
Opening stock	20,000	10,000
Purchases	1,60,000	2,00,000
Closing stock	10,000	10,000

Assume 1 year = 365 days

Solution

	Sugar	*Milk*
Value of Inventory Consumed:		
1. Opening stock	20,000	10,000
2. Purchase	1,60,000	2,00,000
3. Closing stock	(–) 10,000	(–) 10,000
	1,70,000	2,00,000
Average Inventory:		
Opening stock	20,000	10,000
Closing stock	10,000	10,000
	30,000	20,000

(Contd.)

	Sugar	Milk
Average Stock	15,000	10,000
Inventory Turnover Ratio =	1,70,000	2,00,000
	15,000	10,000
	11.33	20.00
Inventory Holding Period:	365/11.33	365/20
	32.21 Days	18.25 Days

Hence, milk is the fast-moving item.

EXAMPLE 3.22

Compute the materials turnover ratio for materials A and B and comment upon the results.

	Materials A (₹)	Materials B (₹)
Opening stock	10,000	35,000
Purchase during the year	76,000	50,000
Closing stock	6,000	25,000

for excel template, scan

Solution

Cost of Materials Consumed	*Materials A*	*Materials B*
Opening stock	10,000	35,000
Add: Purchases	76,000	50,000
	86,000	85,000
Less: Closing stock	6,000	25,000
Cost of materials consumed	80,000	60,000

Average Stock held	*Materials A*	*Materials B*
Opening stock	10,000	35,000
Closing stock	6,000	25,000
	16,000	60,000
	16,000 ÷ 2	60,000 ÷ 2
Average stock	8,000	30,000

Material turnover ratio

$$= \frac{\text{Cost of materials consumed}}{\text{Cost of stock held}}$$

$$\text{Materials } A = \frac{80,000}{8,000} = 10 : 1 \text{ or } 10$$

$$\text{Materials } B = \frac{60{,}000}{30{,}000} = 2 : 1 \text{ or } 2$$

Materials turnover in days

$$= \frac{\text{Days during the year}}{\text{Materials turnover ratio}}$$

$$\text{Materials } A = \frac{365}{10} = 36.5 \text{ days}$$

$$\text{Materials } B = \frac{365}{2} = 182.2 \text{ days}$$

From the above results, it can be said that materials *A* are very fast-moving materials, while materials *B* are very slow-moving when compared with materials *A*. Since, the normal standard inventory turnover ratio should be 2 : 1, the materials *B* turnover ratio can be said to be normal. Materials *A* turnover ratio is 36.5 days which shows that an average stock is being kept for 36.5 days. In contrast, materials *B* average stock is being kept for 182.5 days. Therefore, materials *B* are slow-moving materials.

ACCOUNTING FOR MATERIAL LOSSES

Some materials losses are bound to occur during manufacturing operations because of the nature of the raw materials or other factors which reduce the expected production. These losses may be waste, scrap, spoilage, or defective.

Scrap

Scrap is residue from manufacturing operations that has measurable but relatively minor recovery value. Scrap is saleable material resulting from the primary manufacturing operations. Scrap results from: (i) the processing of materials, (ii) defective and broken parts, (iii) obsolete stock, revisions or abandonment of experimental projects, and scrapping of worn out or obsolete machinery. In some cases, scrap can be sold and should therefore be collected and placed in storage so that it can be sold to scrap dealers. Scrap should be accounted for in some manner not only from the point of view of efficiency, but because scrap is often a tempting source of theft.

Treatment of Scrap

Scrap may be treated in the cost accounts in the following ways:

1. Where the value of scrap is very insignificant, it is not considered in the cost accounts. That is, the cost of scrap is charged to good units and income from the sale of scrap is treated as other income.
2. If the value of scrap is significant, the net sale proceeds of scrap (sales value of scrap—cost of selling the scrap) is deducted from the material cost. That is, the amount (net) realised from the sale is treated as a reduction in the materials cost that has been charged to the individual job or product.

3. The scrap may be sold in a period different from that in which it was created and if the scrap has a low sales value, only a quantity record of the scrap should be maintained. It is not valued and does not appear on the balance sheet.

Scrap Report

It is advisable to prepare a daily or weekly scrap report to account for scrap and to compare it with pre-determined norms or standards which, in turn, can reveal unexpected items and unusual amounts. A specimen of scrap report is given in Fig. 3.13.

Production Department					*Scrap Report*	
		For the Week Ending April 10, 2008				
No.	*Description*	*Units Used*	*Units Scrapped*	*% Scrap*	*Cost*	*Reasons*
	Total for week					

Fig. 3.13 A Specimen of Scrap Report

Spoilage

Spoilage can be defined as the materials which in the process of manufacture are badly damaged or have developed some imperfection which cannot economically be corrected, and thus the goods ought to be sold as seconds. Spoiled units fail to reach the required standard of quality specifications. The cost of spoiled goods may be treated by either of the following methods:

1. The loss due to spoilage may be charged to a specific product or job on which the spoilage occurred, if it is clearly traceable to the work done on that order.
2. The normal spoilage loss may be charged to factory overhead and thus spread over the cost of all jobs/products.
3. The cost of abnormal spoilage (that is, due to causes not inherent in the manufacturing process) is transferred to the Costing Profit and Loss Account. Abnormal loss is unexpected and should have been avoided by management. It is considered controllable by management.

Spoilage Report

A spoilage report should be prepared detailing the spoiled units and cost of spoiled units and other relevant information (Fig. 3.14). To control spoilage, allowance for a normal spoilage should be determined in advance and actual spoilage should be compared with the standard (allowed) spoilage. A spoilage report may enable managements to provide overall control over the spoilage costs. If all or many departments are involved, spoilage costs are then treated as a factory overhead. Sometimes, spoilage can be controlled by the individual machine operators. This requires daily or weekly spoilage reports which can reveal the spoiled work occurred, the reason for its occurrence and the cost of correcting the defects.

Spoilage Report

Units/Deptt No.____________ Date____________
Production Order No. ____________

Units Produced	Units Spoiled	Normal Spoilage		Abnormal Spoilage		Cost of Abnormal Spoilage (₹)	Reason for Spoilage	Action taken
		Qty	%	Qty	%			

Fig. 3.14 A Spoilage Report

Defectives

Defective products are such semi-finished or finished products which in the process of manufacturing have developed some imperfection, but which, unlike spoiled materials, can by the expenditure of additional labour and possibly materials, be made into perfect finished articles. In the manufacturing process, imperfections may arise because of sub-standard materials, bad workmanship, careless planning, laxity in inspection, etc. If the unit can be reprocessed in one or more stages and made into a standard saleable product, it is often profitable to rework the defective unit. Defective work is to be distinguished from spoiled work. Defective work is work in which there is some imperfection which can be reworked or reconditioned by the application of additional materials, labour and/or processing and brought to the point of standard. However, the spoiled units cannot be reconditioned and the units must be sold either as scrap or as second or third-grade products.

The accounting treatment for defective work is similar to that relating to spoiled goods. The cost of defectives can be treated in the following manner:

1. Normal defectives, that is, those defectives which are inherent in the manufacturing process and are identified as normal, can be treated in the following manner:
   (a) Charged to good products—The loss (the additional cost of defectives) is absorbed by good units produced.
   (b) Charged to general factory overheads—If defective units occur irregularly, the added cost of reworking and perfecting the defective goods is properly charged to factory overheads and apportioned as a part of that factory overhead.
   (c) Charged to the department overhead—If the department responsible for defective goods can be identified, the additional cost of perfection is charged to that department.
2. If the defective units are clearly identifiable with a specific job or production order and the defects are peculiar to the job, the cost to complete the defective units can be charged to that job.
3. If defectives are abnormal and as due to reasons beyond the control of the business firm, the rework cost is charged to the Costing Profit and Loss Account.

Defectives Report

Inspectors scrutinise work-in-process at the completion of each stage of production in order to separate defective and spoiled products from those which equal the standard of perfection required of all finished production.

After inspection if it is found that it is necessary to recondition work found defective, a defective work report (see Fig. 3.15) is prepared and attached to the production order representing the defective work. The defective work report contains the number of the production order, a description of the nature of the defective work, the number of units involved, and additional cost of material, labour and applied factory overheads necessary to bring the products upto standard.

Waste (or Wastage)

The terms "spoilage" and "waste" are sometimes used synonymously. However, wastage generally refers to that portion of raw material which is lost in storing, handling and in manufacturing processes. It does not possess any recovery or realisable value. Waste for the purpose of accounting treatment is classified in two categories: Normal waste and Abnormal waste; (i) Normal waste is expected (unavoidable) and uncontrollable. It is treated as a part of the cost of the product, that is, the cost of normal waste unit is borne by the good remaining units. (ii) Abnormal waste is unexpected (avoidable) and controllable. It is valued like good output. Its cost is transferred to the Costing Profit and Loss Account. In case of normal waste, cost-per-unit of the finished output is relatively inflated, but in abnormal waste, cost per unit remains the same for abnormal units as well as good finished units.

Defective Work Report

Production Order No. ____________ No. ____________

No. of Units ____________ Date ____________

Department Responsible for Spoilage ____________

Nature of Defects ____________

Department (Job No.)	*Description of Additional Work Required*	*Rework Costs*			*Total Costs*
		Materials Cost	*Labour Cost*	*Applied Factory Overhead*	

Fig. 3.15 Defective Work Report

Theory Questions

1. Describe the meaning, objectives and basic principles of materials control system.
2. What are the important requirements of a materials control system?
3. Distinguish between bill of material and stores requisition.
4. Explain *ABC* system of inventory control.
5. Explain Just-In-Time purchases.
6. What do you understand by "inventory control"? State its objects.
7. What are the objectives of inventory control? How is inventory control affected through *ABC* analysis of stores?
8. Define waste, scrap, defectives and spoilage with examples. Discuss the respective treatment in cost accounts and set out a procedure for their control.
9. "The Perpetual Inventory System is an integral part of materials control." Discuss this statement by bringing out briefly the salient features and advantages of the system.
10. In ABC Company Ltd. waste, scrap, spoilage and defectives are very high. Suggest and explain various methods for accounting of wastage and scrap and also treatment of costs incurred on spoilage and defective work.
11. Distinguish between spoilage and defectives in a manufacturing company. Discuss their treatment in cost accounts and suggest a procedure for their control.
12. In a meeting of the department heads of a company, the purchase procedure and materials accounting were strongly criticised and blamed for high cost of materials. The Managing Director of the company authorises

you to investigate and suggest improvements. Give your suggestions indicating the assumptions on which they are based.

13. Distinguish between Bin Card and Stores Ledger.
14. Enumerate the various factors to be considered in fixing the re-order level of raw material item.
15. Explain the concept of *ABC* analysis as a technique of material control.
16. What do you mean by inventory control? What are its techniques? Discuss briefly *ABC* system of inventory control.
17. Describe the procedure for the efficient system of physical control of materials till it reaches the stores.
18. Distinguish between periodic and perpetual inventory system. Explain their comparative advantages and disadvantages.
19. What are the causes of discrepancies in stock records? How would you treat these discrepancies?
20. Under what circumstances is it essential to use continuous stock taking for control over materials? State its advantages.
21. Write short notes on the following:
    (i) Re-order quantity
    (ii) Re-order level
    (iii) Maximum stock level
    (iv) Minimum stock level
22. Discuss *ABC* analysis as a system of inventory control.
23. Discuss the accounting treatment of spoilage and defectives in cost accounting.
24. Write detailed explanatory notes on the following:
    (i) JIT manufacturing (ii) Kanban
25. Distinguish between JIT and traditional manufacturing.
26. What is JIT? Discuss the advantages of JIT manufacturing system.
27. Distinguish between purchase requisition and purchase order with their specimen.
28. What are the requirements of an efficient system of material control?
29. "Perpetual inventory system is an integral part of material control." Comment.
30. Explain briefly
    (a) *ABC* Analysis as a technique of inventory control.
    (b) Objectives of Material Control
31. Explain the concept of material control. State briefly its objectives.
32. What is re-order level? What are the factors affecting re-order level?
33. What is a "Bin Card"? Give a specimen form of Bin Card and discuss its utility.
34. Explain what is meant by "Minimum Level", "Maximum Level", and "Ordering Level" with regards to maintenance of stocks. How these levels are determined?
35. Differentiate between Periodic and Perpetual Inventory System.
36. Explain Economic Order Quantity.

Self-Evaluation Questions

Select the correct answer for the following multiple-choice questions:

1. Which one of the following items is not included in the annual carrying costs of inventory?
    (a) Cost of capital
    (b) Insurance on inventory
    (c) Annual warehouse depreciation
    (d) Taxes on inventory
    (e) Inventory breakage on stored inventory
2. Economic order quantity (*EOQ*) model is used by a business to
    (a) Minimise the cost of placing orders

(b) Minimise the unit purchase price of inventory
(c) Minimise the number of orders placed during a year
(d) Minimise the required amount of safety stock
(e) Minimise the combined costs of placing orders and carrying inventory

3. The calculation of inventory re-order point in units requires the
(a) Purchase price per month
(b) Annual demand for units
(c) Daily demand for units
(d) Storage cost per unit
(e) Warehouse capacity

4. Materials control system would be most useful to a
(a) Manufacturer (b) Wholesaler
(c) Hospital (d) Retailer

5. Which of the following items would most likely be included in the calculation of economic order quality?
(a) Price (b) Cost
(c) Demand (d) Supply

6. Given the following information, identify the correct calculation for the economic order quantity (*EOQ*)

Cost per purchase order	₹	40
Annual cost of carrying one unit in stock for one year	₹	1.20
Annual consumption units		20,000

(a) $\sqrt{\dfrac{2(20000 \times ₹40)}{₹1.20}}$ (c) $\sqrt{\dfrac{2 \times 20{,}000 \times ₹1.20}{₹20}}$

(b) $\sqrt{\dfrac{20000 \times ₹40}{₹1.20}}$ (d) $\sqrt{\dfrac{20{,}000 \times ₹1.20}{₹20}}$

Problems

1. Calculate the *EOQ* from the following information:

Monthly requirement	= 1000 units
Ordering cost	= ₹60 per order
Price per unit	= ₹100
Inventory carrying cost	= 15% on average inventory

Ans: *EOQ* 309.84 units

2. P. Ltd. is engaged in the manufacture of industrial pumps of a standard description. The company uses about 75,000 valves per year for its production and the usage is fairly constant at 6,250 valves per month. The valves cost ₹1.50 per unit when brought in quantities and the carrying cost is estimated to be 20% of average inventory investment on the annual basis. The cost to place an order and process the delivery is ₹18. It takes 45 days to receive delivery from the date of an order and a safety stock of 3,200 valves is desired.
You are required to determine:
(i) the most economical order quantity; and
(ii) the re-order point.

Ans: (i) *EOQ* 3000 units
(ii) 12,575 units

3. A producer has estimated annual purchase requirement of 30,000 units of a material. Unit price of material is ₹50. Annual cost of carrying inventory is 20%. Ordering cost for an order is ₹60. Find out Economic Order Quantity (*EOQ*).

Ans: *EOQ* 600 units

4. Annual requirement of a particular item of inventory is 10,000 units. Inventory carrying cost per unit per year is 20% and ordering cost is ₹40 per order. The price quoted by the supplier is ₹4/unit. However, the supplier is ready to give a discount of 5% for orders of 1,500 units or more. Is it worthwhile to avail of the discount offer?

Ans: Offer should be accepted for making an order of 1,500 units

5. If the minimum stock level and average stock level of raw-material *A* are 4,000 and 9,000 units respectively, find out its "Re-order quantity".

Ans: 10,000 units

6. A company manufactures a product having a monthly demand of 2,000 units. For one unit of finished product 2 kg of a particular raw material item is needed. The purchase price of the materials is ₹20 per kg. The ordering cost is ₹120 per order and the holding cost is 10% per annum. Calculate:
   (i) Economic order quantity
   (ii) Annual cost of purchasing and storage of raw materials at that quantity.

Ans: *EOQ* (in kg) 2,400 kg
Annual cost of purchasing and storage ₹9,67,200.

7. From the details given below, calculate:
   (i) Re-ordering Level
   (ii) Maximum Level
   (iii) Minimum Level
   (iv) Danger Level

   Cost of placing a purchase order is ₹20.
   Number of units to be purchased during the year is 5,000.
   Purchase price per unit inclusive of transportation cost is ₹50.
   Annual cost of storage per unit is ₹5.
   Details of lead time: Average 10 days; Maximum 15 days; Minimum 6 days; For emergency purchases 4 days.
   Rate of Consumption Average: 15 units per day, Maximum: 20 units

Ans: Re-ordering level 300 units
Maximum level 440 units
Minimum level 150 units
Danger level 60 units

8. G. Ltd. produces a product which has a monthly demand of 4,000 units. The product requires a component *X* which is purchased at ₹20. For every finished product, one unit of component is required. The ordering cost is ₹120 per order and the holding cost is 10% p.a.
   You are required to calculate:
   (i) Economic order quantity.
   (ii) If the minimum lot size to be supplied is 4,000 units, what is the extra cost the company has to incur?
   (iii) What is the minimum carrying cost the company has to incur?

Ans: (i) *EOQ* 2400 units
(ii) Extra cost ₹640
(iii) ₹2,400

9. ZEE is product manufactured out of three raw materials *M*, *N* and *Q*. Each unit of ZEE requires 10 kg, 8 kg, and 6 kg of *M*, *N* and *Q* respectively. The re-order levels of *M* and *N* are 15,000 kg and 10,000 kg respectively while the minimum level of *Q* is 2,500 kg. The weekly production of ZEE varies from 300 to 500 units, while the weekly average production is 400 units.
   You are required to compute
   (i) the minimum stock level of *M*,

(ii) the maximum stock level of *N*, and
(iii) the re-order level of *Q*.
The following additional data are given:

	M	*N*	*Q*
Re-order quantity (in kg)	*20,000*	*15,000*	*20,000*
Delivery (in weeks)			
Minimum	2	4	3
Average	3	5	4
Maximum	4	6	5

Ans: Minimum stock level of *M* is 3,000 kg
Maximum stock level of *N* is 15,400 kg
Re-order level of *Q* is 15,000 kg

10. Materials *X* and *Y* are used as follows:
Minimum usage – 50 units each per week
Maximum usage – 150 units each per week
Normal usage – 100 units each per week
Ordering quantities $X = 600$ units
$Y = 1000$ units
Delivery period $X = 4$ to 6 weeks
$Y = 2$ to 4 weeks
Calculate for each material: (a) Minimum level; (b) Maximum level; and (c) Order level.

Ans.	*Material X*	*Material Y*
Minimum level	400 units	300 units
Maximum level	1300 units	1500 units
Order level	900 units	600 units

11. XYZ Company buys in lots of 500 boxes which is a 3 months' supply. The cost per box is ₹125 and the ordering cost is ₹150. The inventory carrying cost is estimated at 20% of unit value. What is the total annual cost of the existing inventory policy? How much could be saved by employing the economic order quantity?

Ans: Total annual cost of existing inventory ₹6,850
EOQ 155 units
Saving in annual cost if *EOQ* is adopted ₹2,962.50

12. The following information in an inventory problem is available:

Annual demand	2,400 units
Unit price (₹)	2.40
Ordering cost (₹)	4.00
Storage cost (₹)	2% per year
Interest rate	10% p.a.
Lead time	1/2 month

Calculate *EOQ*, re-order level and total annual inventory cost. How much does the total inventory cost vary if the unit price is changed to ₹5?

Ans: *EOQ* 258 units, Re-order level 100 units, Total annual inventory cost ₹5837.15.
Difference in total inventory cost ₹6272.55

13. Calculate the material turnover ratio for the year 2012 from the following information:

	Material X (₹)	*Material Y* (₹)
Opening Stock	25,000	87,500
Closing Stock	15,000	62,500
Purchases	1,90,000	1,25,000

Determine the fast-moving material

Ans: Turnover ratio
Material *X*-10
Material *Y*-2
Material *X* is the fast-moving material.

14. A company's monthly requirement of an inventory item is 1,800 units. The cost of processing an order is ₹5 and the carrying cost per unit is 20 paise. The company supplier agrees to offer the following quantity discounts:

	Upto				*Above*
Lot size (in units)	400	401–600	601–800	801–1,000	1,000
Discount (in ₹)	Nil	6	10	15	20

Lead time is 2 days and the company wishes to keep a safety equal to 50% of the usage in the lead time.

(a) Find the economic ordering quantity (*EOQ*) without considering the offer of discount.
(b) Calculate the re-order point taking 30 working days in a month.
(c) Tabulate different types of cost as also effect of discount on different order sizes taking 1, 2, 3..., 7 orders a month and indicate the *EOQ*.

Ans: (a) 1039 units
(b) 180 units
(c) 450 units

15. JP Limited manufacturers of a special product, follows the policy of *EOQ* (Economic Order Quantity) for one of its components. The component's details are as follows:

Purchase price for component ₹200
Cost of an order ₹100
Annual cost of carrying one unit in inventory: 10% of purchase price.
Total cost of inventory and ordering per annum: ₹4,000.
The company has been offered a discount of 2% on the price of the component, provided the lot size is 2,000 components at a time.

You are required to:

(a) Compute the *EOQ*
(b) Advise whether the quantity discount offer can be accepted.
(Assume that the inventory carrying cost does not vary according to discount policy.)
(c) Would your advice differ if the company is offered 5% discount on a single order?

Ans: (a) *EOQ* 200 units
(b) Discount should be accepted because the total inventory cost will be lower by ₹3,900 as compared to the total cost under *EOQ* policy.

CASE STUDY

A Case of Materials Purchase Control in Apex Endura Pvt. Ltd.

Apex Endura Pvt Ltd. dealt in cement manufacturing with plants in Bommanhalli, Bangalore, and Bellary in Karnataka. Cement in its factory was made from limestone (₹200 per ton) and clay. These raw materials were extracted from the quarry which was crushed to a very fine powder and then blended in the correct proportions. This blended raw material, known as the 'raw feed', was heated in a rotary kiln in temperature of about 1400°C to 1500°C. The raw feed was then cooled down and then passed directly to the cement mill where it was processed further to produce the finishes goods, i.e., cement. They sold their final product at ₹325 per bag of 50 kg. They were able to sell between 1,20,000 to 1,50,000 cement bags per year.

The raw materials were purchased from some of the regular suppliers in Bidar and Bijapur in Karnataka. For the year 2019–20 too, the company had invited tenders for the limestone blocks of 100 kg each. The quotations were received as under:

Particulars	*Supplier 1*	*Supplier 2*
Rate	₹20 per unit (100 kg block)	₹18 (up to 1000 units—each unit being 100-kg block)
Trade discount	10%	₹16.5 (for orders above 1,000 units)
Cash discount	5% discount if the bills are paid within 2 weeks after issue of receipts	6% interest per annum will be added if bills are not paid within 2 weeks
Transport charges	₹10 per 100 units	₹30 per 100 units

The quality and the other conditions of the suppliers were the same. The company paid 50% of its total monthly bills every fortnight.

It costed the company ₹50 for processing each purchase. The cost of carrying the inventory (50% on an average) in the storehouse was ₹1 per unit.

Ravish, the Purchase Manager of Apex Endura, although tempted by lower prices quoted by the second supplier, was feeling little apprehensive about the transport charges and the late payment condition. The price of the raw material in the previous year was ₹18 per unit without any discount and excluding the transport charges of ₹20 per 100 units of limestone blocks. This year, just like the previous year, the total requirement month-wise for the limestone blocks was 5,000 units.

Unable to decide on his own, Ravish called his Cost Accountant, Hemanth to look at the quotations and give his recommendations.

✍ QUESTIONS FOR DISCUSSION:

1. Assume that you are the Cost Accountant—Hemanth. What would be your recommendation?
2. Would your decision change if the company's policy of paying its monthly bills within 15 days changes to one month?
3. What was the difference in price of the recommended supplier with the previous year's price?
4. Calculate the EOQ for the company and compare it with the recommended quotation. Should the company change to EOQ quantity?

Chapter 4

Materials Costing

Learning Objectives

After reading this chapter, you should be able to:

1. explain meaning and treatment of different items in determining the cost of materials received;
2. discuss different methods of costing materials issued;
3. explain pricing of materials returned to vendor and storerooms; and
4. identify the factors to be considered in selecting a material pricing method.

COSTING MATERIALS RECEIVED

The invoice received from the supplier is the basic document providing a base figure for determining the cost of materials to be entered in the accounting books. This figure, however, is subject to adjustment and some other items may affect the cost of materials received. These items are as follows:

Discounts

Discounts may be trade discount, cash discount and quantity discount.

Trade discount is allowed when a supplier sells the materials to a retailer who, in turn, resells the materials. Trade discount is deducted from the purchase price to determine the cost of materials purchased.

Cash discount is also known as purchase discount. Cash discount arises after the materials have been purchased and is offered by the supplier to his customer, provided payment is made at once or within an agreed stipulated time. There are two methods of treating such purchase or cash discounts.

1. The cash discount received while purchasing materials should be deducted from the invoice price of the materials. Thus, the materials cost price will be relatively reduced.
2. Alternatively, it may be treated as an item of financial nature (as additional income) and therefore be kept outside the purview of cost accounting. The full invoice price should be charged to the materials account crediting the suppliers with the net invoice price, and the discount earned account with the amount of cash discount received. It can be argued, however, that there is little justification for recording income on purchase; one can only earn income by selling or holding assets. Income is not produced by buying.

Quantity discount is a reduction in price given by a supplier to all large users of his product. This discount is deducted from the purchase price in arriving at the materials cost price. Also, this discount varies according to the size of the order for the purchase of materials.

Carriage Inwards on Raw Materials

It represents the expenditure incurred in bringing raw materials to the factory from outside and include sea, land and air freight, insurance, duties, dock charges, etc.

There is a difference of opinion as to treatment of carriage inwards. Accounting theory suggests that such charges are proper additions to the costs of materials purchased, since these costs are incurred in bringing the materials to the factory. But what is sound in theory is not always practicable, and deviations from theory are common. Where such costs are immaterial (small), or it is difficult to trace or even allocate such charges to specific items of materials (the cost to allocate such expenses to individual products outweighs the benefits to be obtained from such allocation), then these charges should be treated as an indirect manufacturing cost (factory overhead) which should be apportioned to product indirectly.

Material Handling Charges

The term "material handling costs" refers to the expense involved in receiving, storing, issuing and handling materials. Generally, such costs are part of the cost of materials and should be treated as a direct cost. But, in practice, such costs are most often treated as indirect costs. There is a practical difficulty in apportioning this cost to various materials items. The costs of operating the service departments involved in materials handling become a part of indirect manufacturing cost which is apportioned among the producing departments and then they are charged to product on labour hours, labour cost, machine hours, weight or any other appropriate basis.

EXAMPLE 4.1

A consignment consisted of two chemicals *A* and *B*. The invoice gave the following data:

		₹
Chemical *A*	4 tonnes at ₹5.00 per kg	20,000
Chemical *B*	2 tonnes at ₹2.00 per kg	4,000
Sales tax		1,200
Freight		900
Total		26,100

A shortage of 2 quintals in *A* and 1 quintal in *B* was noticed and it was considered normal. What rate per kg would you adopt for pricing issues assuming provision of 20% towards further deterioration?

Solution

	Chemical A	*Chemical B*
Quantity	4,000 kg	2,000 kg
Less shortage	200 kg	100 kg
Net quantity	3,800 kg	1,900 kg

(Contd.)

	Chemical A	*Chemical B*
Provision for deterioration (20%)	760 kg	380 kg
Net issuable quantity	3,040 kg	1,520 kg
Cost	₹20,000	₹4,000
Sales tax (on values) 5%	1,000	200
Freight on weight (₹150 per tonne)	600	300
	21,600	4,500
Issue price per kg	₹21,600 ÷ 3,040 kg	₹4,500 ÷ 1,520 kg
	₹7.105	₹2.96

EXAMPLE 4.2

A foundry is melting pig iron for producing castings. Coke and limestone are used to melt the metal. 150 kg of coke and 50 kg of limestone are required to melt one tonne of pig iron. The loss in melting is 5% and the rejection amounts to 10% of the casting made. Cost of pig iron is ₹895 per tonne. Cost of coke is ₹650 per tonne. Cost of limestone is ₹100 per tonne. Rejections fetch a return of 60 paise per kg. Find the cost of raw material per kg of saleable castings.

Solution

Cost of Material	*Amount (₹)*
Pig iron 1,000 kg	895.00
Coke 150 kg @ ₹0.650	97.50
Limestone 50 kg @ ₹0.100	5.00
	997.50
Normal rejections 95 kg @ ₹0.60	(57.00)
Net total cost	940.50
Quantity of saleable cost iron: Input	1,000 kg
Loss in melting @ 5% of 1,000 kg	(50 kg)
Output	950 kg
Normal rejections @ 10% of 950 kg	(95 kg)
Saleable output	855 kg

$$\text{Raw material cost per kg of saleable casting} = \frac{₹940.50}{855 \text{ kg}} = ₹1.10$$

Notes:

1. Normal rejection: 10% of (input – melting loss), that is, 10% of (1000 – 50).
2. Cost of normal loss is borne by good units which are in good condition. This principle is used extensively in process costing method.

EXAMPLE 4.3

From the following particulars, workout the issue rate per 1,000 each of first class and second class bricks.

(a) Paid for supply at the kiln site for 30 lakh first class bricks @ ₹30 per 1,000.
(b) Paid for supply at the kiln site for 60 lakh second class bricks @ ₹25 per 1,000.
(c) Paid carriage charges for carrying all bricks from kiln to store yard @ ₹1.50 per 1,000.
(d) Paid unloading charges ₹90 (lump sum).
(e) Paid for stacking in the store yard ₹180 (lump sum).
(f) Breakage in handling: 1% for first class bricks, 2% for second class bricks.

Solution

	Total Cost (₹) First Class Bricks	*Total Cost (₹)* Second Class Bricks
Amount paid towards the cost of bricks:	90,000	1,50,000
Carriage charges @ ₹1.50 per 1,000	4,500	9,000
Unloading charges (apportioned in the ratio of quantity, that is, 30 : 60)	30	60
Paid for stacking in the store yard (apportioned in the ratio of quantity, that is, 30 : 60)	60	120
	94,590	1,59,180

$$\text{Cost per 1,000} = \frac{\text{Total cost}}{(\text{Total number in '000} - \text{Normal loss})}$$

First class brick — *Second class brick*

$$= \frac{₹94,590}{(3,000 - 1\% \text{ of } 3,000)} \qquad \frac{₹1,59,180}{(6,000 - 2\% \text{ of } 6,000)}$$

$$= ₹31,8485 \qquad ₹27.0714$$

Thus, (a) Issue rate per 1,000 of first class bricks ₹31.8485
(b) Issue rate per 1,000 of second class bricks ₹27.0714.

Notes: In this case, cost-unit has been taken as 1,000 bricks.

EXAMPLE 4.4

The particulars relating to 1,200 kg of a certain raw material purchased by a company during June were as follows:

(a) Lot prices quoted by supplier and accepted by the company for placing the purchase order:
Lot up to 1,000 kg @ ₹22 per kg
Between 1,000 – 1,500 kg @ ₹20 per kg
Between 1,500 – 2,000 kg @ ₹18 per kg
Prices are F.O.R. supplier's factory
(b) Trade discount 20%

(c) Additional charge for container @ ₹10 per drum of 25 kg
(d) Credit allowed on return of containers @ ₹8 per drum
(e) Sales tax @ 10% on raw material and 5% on drum
(f) Total freight paid by the purchaser ₹240
(g) Insurance at 2.5% (on net invoice value) paid by the purchaser
(h) Stores overhead applied at 5% on total purchase cost of material

The entire quantity was received and issued to production. The containers were returned in due course. Draw up a suitable statement to show:

(i) Total cost of material purchased
(ii) Unit cost of material issued to production

☞ Solution

	Amount ₹	Cost Per Unit ₹
Raw material 1,200 kg @ ₹20	24,000.00	20.00
Trade discount @ 20%	(4,800.00)	(4.00)
	19,200.00	16.00
Charge for containers 48 @ ₹10	480.00	0.40
	19,680.00	16.40
Sales tax: Raw material @ 10% on ₹19,200	19,20.00	1.60
Containers @ 5% on ₹480	24.00	0.02
Net invoice value	21,624.00	18.02
Freight paid	240.00	0.20
Insurance @ 2.5% on ₹21,624	540.60	0.45
	22,404.00	18.67
Credit for containers 48 @ ₹8	(384.00)	(0.32)
	22,020.60	18.35
Stores overhead applied 5% on ₹22,020.60	1,101.03	0.92
	23,121.03	19.27
(i) Total cost of material purchased	₹23,121.63	
(ii) Unit cost of material issued to production	₹19.27	

Notes:

1. Drums required = $\frac{\text{Total quantity}}{\text{Quantity per drum}} = \frac{1{,}200 \text{ kg}}{25 \text{ kg}}$ = 48 numbers
2. If excise duty is to be charged separately, the amount is to be calculated on basic price, that is, on ₹24,000. The discount of 20% is to be calculated on basic price. Sales tax is to be calculated on (Basic price + Excise duty – Trade discount). Amount against other items is to be charged accordingly. Excise is to be deducted if Modvat/Cenvat Credit is available along with credit for container.
3. Sales tax refund is not available on ₹8 being the amount refunded on return of containers.
4. Usually, stores overheads are included in factory overheads and are not applied to materials as indicated in the given illustration.

COSTING MATERIALS ISSUED

Where materials have been purchased for a specific product or specific job, the cost of materials received is wholly debited (charged) to that job. But most often, materials are purchased for several products or jobs. If all purchases were made at the same price, there would be no problem in costing materials issued and in inventory valuation. However, purchases made at different times usually carry different prices and the stores ledger card shows not one but several prices for the same kind of materials. Therefore, it becomes essential to consider the price at which it should be charged to production. Several methods are in use concerning the pricing of materials issued from the storeroom. They may be listed as follows:

A. Cost Price Methods
   1. First-In, First-Out (FIFO)
   2. Last-In, First-Out (LIFO)
   3. Highest-In, First-Out (HIFO)
   4. Base Stock Price

B. Average Price Methods
   1. Simple average
   2. Weighted average
   3. Periodic simple average
   4. Periodic weighted average
   5. Moving simple average method
   6. Moving weighted average method

C. Normal Price Methods
   1. Standard price
   2. Inflated price
   3. Replacement or market price

First-In, First-Out (FIFO)

The FIFO method follows the principle that materials received first are issued first. After the first lot or batch of materials purchased is exhausted, the next lot is taken up for supply. It does not suggest, however, that the same lot will be issued from stores. Sometimes, all materials are tagged with their arrival date and issued in date order especially with stocks that deteriorate. The inventory is priced at the latest costs.

Advantages

A good system of inventory management requires that oldest units should be sold or used first and inventory should consist of the latest purchases. This is found in the FIFO method of costing. Under the FIFO method, management has little or no control over the selection of units in order to influence recorded profits. Valuation of inventory and cost of goods manufactured are consistent and realistic. Besides, the FIFO method is easy to understand and operate.

Disadvantages

The objective of matching current cost with current revenues is not achieved under the FIFO method. If the prices of materials are rising rapidly, the current production cost may be understated. If the sales price is fixed, then sales revenue may not produce enough income to cover the purchase of raw materials. The valuation of inventory in terms of current cost depends on the frequency of price changes and the stock turnover. In case stocks turnover rapidly, the inventory valuations will reflect current prices. There are other limitations under the FIFO method. FIFO costing is improper if many lots are purchased during the period at different prices. This method overstates profit especially with high inflation. It does not consider the cost of replacing used materials, a situation created by high inflation.

The FIFO method is suitable where (i) the size and cost of raw materials units are large, (ii) materials are easily identified as belonging to a particular purchased lot, and (iii) not more than two or three different receipts of the materials are on hand at one time.

Example 4.5 explains the FIFO method of costing.

EXAMPLE 4.5

The following is a summary of the receipts and issue of materials in a factory during January.

January

1 Opening balance 500 units @ ₹25 per unit
3 Issue 70 units
4 Issue 100 units
8 Issue 80 units
13 Received from supplier 200 units @ ₹24.50 per unit
14 Returned to store 15 units @ ₹24 per unit
16 Issue 180 units
20 Received from supplier 240 units @ ₹24.75 per unit
24 Issue 304 units
25 Received from supplier 320 units @ ₹24.50 per unit
26 Issue 112 units
27 Returned to store 12 units @ ₹24.50 per unit
28 Received from supplier 100 units @ ₹25 per unit

Work out on the basis of First-In, First-Out. This revealed that on the 15th there was a shortage of five units and another on the 27th of eight units.

Solution

Stores Ledger Account (FIFO)

	Receipts			*Issue*			*Stock*		
Date	*Qty*	*Rate*	*Amt*	*Qty*	*Rate*	*Amt*	*Qty*	*Rate*	*Amt*
Jan.									
1	—	—	—	—	—	—	500	25.00	12,500
3	—	—	—	70	25	1,750	430	—	10,750
4	—	—	—	100	25	2,500	330	—	8,250
8	—	—	—	80	25	2,000	250	—	6,250
13	200	24.50	4,900	—	—		250	25.00	6,250
	Refund						200	24.50	4,900

(Contd.)

	Receipts			Issue			Stock		
Date	*Qty*	*Rate*	*Amt*	*Qty*	*Rate*	*Amt*	*Qty*	*Rate*	*Amt*
Jan.									
14	15	24.00	360	—	—	—	250	25.00	6,250
							200	24.50	4,900
							15	24.00	360
15	—	—	Shortage	5	25	125	245	25.00	6,125
							200	24.50	4,900
							15	24.00	360
16	–	–	–	180	25	4,500	65	25.00	1,625
							200	24.50	4,900
							15	24.50	360
20	240	24.75	5,940	–	–	–	65	25.00	1,625
							200	24.50	4,900
							15	24.00	360
							240	24.75	5,940
24	–	–		65	25.00	1,625			
				200	24.50	4,900			
				15	24.00	360			
				24	24.75	594	216	24.75	5,346
25	320	24.50	7.680	–	–	–	216	24.75	5,346
							320	24.50	7,680
26	–	–	–	112	24.75	2,772	104	24.75	2,574
							320	24.00	7,680
27	12	24.50	294	–	–	–	104	24.75	2,574
							320	24.00	7,680
							12	24.50	294
27	–	–	Shortage	8	24.75	198	96	24.75	12,376
							320	24.00	7,680
							12	24.50	294
28	100	2,500	2,500	–	–	–	96	24.75	2,376
							320	24.00	7,680
							12	24.50	294
							100	25.00	2,500

Closing stock 528 units = ₹12,750

Last-In, First-Out (LIFO)

The LIFO method of costing and inventory valuation is based on the principle that materials entering production are the most recently purchased. The method assumes that the most recent cost, generally the replacement cost is the most significant in matching cost with revenue in the income determination. The cost of the last lot of materials received is used to price materials issued until the lot is exhausted, then the next lot pricing is used, and so on through successive lots. The inventory is priced at the oldest costs.

Advantages

1. It provides a better matching of current costs with current revenues.
2. It results in real income in times of rising prices, by maintaining net income at a lower level than other costing methods.
3. In industries subject to sharp materials price fluctuations, the method minimises unrealised inventory gains and losses and tends to stabilise reported operating profits. Income is reported only when it is available for distribution as dividends or for other purposes.
4. Probably the most important arguments in favour of LIFO is its role in tax saving. It is generally considered a cheap form of tax avoidance by business firms. By valuing inventory at beginning-of-period prices and calculating cost of sales at the current prices, the firm creates secret reserves which are not taxed. As long as prices and inventory levels do not decline, this benefit remains and in this case the tax saving is permanent. However, if the tax rates go up in the meantime, the so-called tax saving will be eliminated by higher tax rates.
5. LIFO produces an income statement which shows correct profit or losses and financial position. It correlates current cost and sales, and income statements show the result of operation, excluding profits or losses due to changing price levels.

Disadvantages

The following are the limitations of the LIFO method of costing:

1. Inventory valuations do not reflect the current prices and therefore are useless in the context of current conditions.
2. The argument that LIFO should be used for matching current costs with current revenue is not sound. The most recent purchase costs are matched against the revenues of the current period. However, unless both purchases and sales occur regularly in even quantities, the revenues will not be matched with the current costs at the time of sale. When purchases are irregular and unrelated to the timing of sales, the matching is illogical and unsystematic, particularly if prices and costs are changing rapidly.
3. The profit of a firm can be manipulated with the LIFO method in operation. By timing purchases, a company can cause higher or lower costs to flow into the income statement, thus increasing or decreasing reported net income at will.
4. Another limitation which also results from LIFO's lowering of the earnings figure is the effect it will have on existing bonus and profit sharing plans. Employees and managers who are interested in the growth of these plans may have difficulty in understanding a drop in the benefits which were created wholly or partially by an accounting change.

During a period of rising costs, LIFO produces the desirable effect of reducing taxable income and tax liability; thereby conserving cash. On the other hand, it also affects the profit reported in the financial statements.

EXAMPLE 4.6

Prepare a stores ledger account from the following transactions under the LIFO method.

Jan.	1	Received 1,000 units @	₹1.00 per unit
	10	Received 260 units @	₹1.05 per unit
	20	Issued 700 units	
Feb.	4	Received 400 units @	₹1.15 per unit
	21	Received 300 units @	₹1.25 per unit
March	16	Issued 620 units	
April	12	Issued 240 units	
May	10	Received 500 units @	₹1.10 per unit
	25	Issued 380 units	

☞ ***Solution***

Stores Ledger Account (FIFO)

	Receipts			*Issue*			*Stock*		
Date	*Qty*	*Rate*	*Amt.*	*Qty*	*Rate*	*Amt.*	*Qty*	*Rate*	*Amt.*
1	2	3	4	5	6	7	8	9	10
January									
1	1,000	1.00	1,000	–	–	–	1,000	1.00	1,000
10	260	1.05	273	–	–	–	1,260		1,273
20	–	–	–	260	1.05	273	560		560
				440	1.00	440			
February									
4	400	1.15	460	–	–	–	960		1,020
21	300	1.25	375	–	–	–	1,260		1,395
March									
16	–	–	–	300	1.25	375	640		652
				320	1.15	368			
April									
12	–	–	–	80	1.15	92	400		400
				160	1.00	160			
May									
10	500	1.10	550	–	–	–	900		950
25	–	–	–	380	1.10	418	520		532

The Closing Stock consists of

120 units at ₹1.10 = 132

400 units at ₹1.00 = 400

₹532

Highest-In, First-Out (HIFO)

This method is based on the principle that materials received at the highest price in the stock are issued first. This will have the effect of pricing materials issued at the highest price and inventory valuation being made at the lowest possible prices. If the prices fluctuate widely, the highest cost will always be entering into the cost of goods sold. For instance, suppose on a particular date the stock ledger shows stock representing 500 units at the rate of ₹20,700 units at the rate of ₹12, and 300 units at the rate of ₹25. If materials are issued, then out of the above three lots, first of all 300 units would be issued. After this lot is over, then the second lot of 500 units, which becomes the highest priced stock after dispatches of 300 units, would be taken up for transmission to production departments. Like other methods, this method also requires detailed records on the stores ledger.

Base Stock Price

Under this method, it is assumed that the minimum stock of a commodity which must always be carried is in the nature of a fixed asset and is never realised while the business continues. This minimum stock is carried at original cost. The stock in excess of this figure would be treated in accordance with one of the other methods, that is, FIFO or LIFO. The limitation of this method is that while measuring the return on capital employed in the business, the stock value may be under-valued and therefore the resulting business results will not be reliable.

EXAMPLE 4.7

From the following information, prepare a stores ledger account assuming 100 units as base stock following the FIFO method:

Rate		*Rate Per Unit (₹)*
January 1, 2020	Received 500 units	20
January 10	Received 300 units	24
January 15	Issued 700 units	—
January 20	Received 400 units	28
January 25	Issued 300 units	—
January 27	Received 500 units	22
January 31	Issued 200 units	—

Solution

Stores Ledger Account
Base Stock Price with FIFO (minimum stock 100 units)

	Receipts			*Issue*			*Stock*		
Date	*Qty*	*Rate*	*Amt*	*Qty*	*Rate*	*Amt*	*Qty*	*Rate*	*Amt*
2020									
Jan. 1	500	20	10,000	–	–	–	500	20	10,000
Jan. 10	300	24	7,200				500	20	10,000
							300	24	7,200

(Contd.)

Date	Receipts Qty	Rate	Amt	Issue Qty	Rate	Amt	Stock Qty	Rate	Amt
Jan. 15	–	–	–	400	20	8,000	100	20	2,000
				300	24	7,200			
Jan. 20	400	28	11,200	–	–	–	400	28	11,200
Jan. 25	–	–	–	300	28	8,400	100	20	2,000
							100	28	2,800
Jan. 27, 2020	500	22	1100				500	22	11,000
Jan. 31	–	–	–	100	28	2,800	100	20	2,000
				100	22	2,200	400	22	8,800

Simple Average

This method is based on the principle that materials issued should be priced on an average price and not on exact cost price. The simple average is an average of prices without having regard to the quantities involved. It should be used when prices do not fluctuate very much and the stock value is small. The average under this method is calculated by dividing the total of rates of materials in the store room by the number of rates of prices. This method is easy to operate.

✍ EXAMPLE 4.8

Prepare a stores ledger account by following the simple average method on the basis of information given in Example 4.6.

☞ *Solution*

Stores Ledger Account
(Simple Average Price Method)

Date	Receipts Qty	Rate	Amt	Issue Qty	Rate	Amt	Stock Qty	Rate	Amt
2020									
Jan. 1	500	20	10,000	–	–	–	500	20	10,000
Jan. 10	300	24	7,200	–	–	–	500	20	10,000
							300	24	7,200
Jan. 15	–	–	–	700	22	15,400	100		1,800
Jan. 20	400	28	11,200	–	–	–	500		13,000
Jan. 25	–	–	–	300	26	7,800	200		5,200
Jan. 27	500	22	11,000	–	–	–	700		16,200
Jan. 31	–	–	–	200	25	5,000	500		11,200

Average price for different issues has been calculated as follows:

Jan. 15 700 units = 20 + 24/2 = ₹22 per unit

Jan. 25 300 units = 24 + 28/2 = ₹26 per unit

Jan. 31 200 units = 28 + 22/2 = ₹25 per unit

Weighted Average

Under this method, issue of materials is priced at the average cost price of the materials in hand, a new average being computed whenever materials are received. In this method, total quantities and total costs are considered while computing the average price and not the total of rates divided by total number of rates as in simple average. The weighted average is calculated each time a purchase is made. The quantity bought is added to the stock in hand, and the revised balance is then divided into the new cash value of the stock. The effect of early price is thus eliminated. This method avoids fluctuations in price and reduces the number of calculations to be made, as each issue is charged at the same price until a fresh purchase necessitates the computation of a new average. It gives an acceptable figure for stock values.

Advantages

The following are the advantages of the weighted average method:

1. The method is logical and consistent as it absorbs cost while determining the average for pricing material issues.
2. The changes in the prices of materials do not much affect the materials issues and stock.
3. The method follows the concept of total stock and total valuation.
4. Both cost of materials issued and in stock tend to reflect actual costs.

Disadvantages

However, the weighted average method also has the following disadvantages:

1. Simplicity and convenience are lost when there is too much change in the prices of materials.
2. An average price is not based on actual price incurred, and therefore is not realistic. It follows only arithmetical convenience.

EXAMPLE 4.9

Prepare a store ledger account on the basis of information given in Example 4.6 by following the weighted average method.

Solution

	Receipts			*Issue*			*Stock*		
Date	*Qty*	*Rate*	*Amt*	*Qty*	*Rate*	*Amt*	*Qty*	*Rate*	*Amt*
2020									
Jan. 1	500	20	10,000	–	–	–	500	20	10,000
Jan. 10	300	24	7,200	–	–	–	800	21.50	17,200
Jan. 15	–	–	–	700	21.50	15,050	100		2,150
Jan. 20	400	28	11,200	–	–	–	500	26.70	13,350
Jan. 25	–	–	–	300	26.70	8,010	200		5,340
Jan. 27	500	22	11,000	–	–	–	700	23.34	16,340
Jan. 31	–	–	–	200	23.34	4,668	500		11,672

Periodic Simple Average

In cost accounting, where job costs may be prepared infrequently, say monthly, or bimonthly, it may be necessary to price materials issued by taking the average price ruling during that period. If it is calculated monthly, the average of the unit prices of all the receipts during the month is adopted as the rate for pricing issues during the month. Only a simple calculation has to be done at the end of the accounting period. The opening stock is not considered for computing periodic simple average because it has not been purchased during the current period and would have been included in the previous year's calculations. However, purchases made during the current year and closing stock are taken into account while computing this average. Basically, this method follows the principle of simple average price, but a period is set for which the average is calculated. Taking the above example, the total receipts and issue of the materials would be shown as follows:

Receipts			*Issues*		
Qty	*Rate*	*Amt*	*Qty*	*Rate*	*Amt*
1,700	94	39,400	1,200	23.50	28,200

$$\text{The periodic simple average} = \frac{\text{Total prices of the materials}}{\text{Total no. of prices}}$$

$$= \frac{94}{4}\ ₹23.50$$

Closing stock = Units 1700 – 1200 = 500
= ₹39,400 – 28,200 = ₹11,200.

The above rate, that is, ₹23.50 per unit will be used for pricing the materials issued during the period.

Periodic Weighted Average

This method is quite similar to the weighted average price method with only one difference that in this method average price is not calculated at the time of every new receipt of materials but only periodically. Periodic weighted average is calculated by dividing the total value of the materials purchased during a given period, by the total quantity purchased during the same period. Opening stock—its value and quantity —both are not considered while computing this average. In the above example, the periodic weighted average will be computed as follows:

	Receipts			*Issues*		
	Qty	*Rate*	*Amt*	*Qty*	*Rate*	*Amt*
Total	1,700	23.18	39,400	1200	23.18	27,816

Closing stock quantity = 500
Amount = ₹11,584

Periodic weighted average

$$= \frac{\text{Total cost of materials purchased}}{\text{Total quantity purchased}}$$

$$= \frac{39{,}400}{1{,}700}$$

$$= 23.18$$

Moving Simple Average

Under this method, periodic simple average prices are further averaged. In this way, moving average is obtained by dividing periodic average prices of different periods by the number of periods taken. The periods chosen cover the period in which the material is issued. The following example explains this method.

Months	*Periodic Average Price* (₹)	*Moving Average Price* (₹)
January	2.55	
February	2.65	
March	2.72	
April	2.95	
May	3.15	
June	3.25	2.88
July	3.40	3.02
August	3.50	3.16
September	3.68	3.32
October	3.80	3.46
November	3.90	3.59
December	4.15	3.74

In the above example, moving average has been obtained for a six-month period.

The moving simple average method will give prices to be used for materials issues which are below the periodic average prices. This will be true when prices are showing an upward trend. In periods of falling prices, the resulting issue prices under the moving average method will be greater than the periodic average prices. This influences the value of closing stock which may be under-valued or over-valued.

Moving Weighted Average

This method finds the materials issues price by dividing the total of the periodic weighted average prices for a number of periods by the total number of such periods. This is similar to the moving simple average method.

Standard Price

This method charges materials issued into the factory at a pre-determined budgeted or estimated price reflecting a normal or an expected future price. A standard price is fixed for each class of materials in advance after making proper investigations. Receipts and issues of materials are recorded in quantities only on the materials ledgers, thereby simplifying the record-keeping. The difference between actual price and standard price is transferred to a purchase price variance which reveals to what extent actual costs are different from standard materials cost. Materials are charged into cost of goods sold at the standard price avoiding inconsistencies in different actual cost methods.

This method helps in knowing the purchase efficiency. If the total actual cost is less than the standard price, there will be favourable purchasing efficiency and vice versa. This method is simple to operate and provides stability in costing system. However, standard price does not often reflect actual or expected cost, but only a generalised target. The stock value need not show actual cost incurrence and therefore does not necessarily conform to acceptable principles of stock valuation.

Inflated Price

This price includes carrying costs, cost of contingencies and also the losses arising out of evaporation, shrinkage, etc. This method aims to cover/recover the full cost of materials purchased.

Replacement Price or Market Price

Under this method, materials issues are priced at replacement price on the date the issue is made. The replacement cost (market price) is the cost of securing the same type of material at the current moment in time. This method has the following advantages:

Advantages

1. The replacement cost approach matches current revenue against current cost and is therefore useful in measuring the operating results of a business firm correctly and accurately.
2. The use of replacement cost brings out clearly the difference between holding gains and operating gains and financial statement users will have a better understanding of the financial statement. If replacement cost is not used, the profit resulting due to holding of materials and inventory is taxed and therefore, impairs the capital of a business firm.
3. The replacement price, if used, will disclose good or bad buying made by the purchase department of the firm.
4. The replacement cost approach helps in determining a selling price for the product which is competitive and realistic.
5. In case the prices of materials have decreased, the materials should be charged to the production at the current replacement price and the resulting loss should be taken into consideration in the accounts of the firm.

Disadvantages

However, this method has certain disadvantages. Firstly, the objectivity is lost in accepting the replacement cost as the basis of materials pricing. The "replacement" concept is a relative one and in the absence of market for the materials, no equitable replacement price is determinable. This increases the subjectivity in selection of a current replacement price. Secondly, this is not based on actual cost, that is, cost incurred, and therefore may add confusion and complications in cost accounting. Thirdly, this method is workable only when market prices are available and reflect current cost of replacing the materials.

EXAMPLE 4.10

From the records of an oil distributing company, the following summarised information is available for the month of March 2020.

Sales of the month: ₹19,25,000

Opening Stock as on 1.3. 2020: 1.25,000 litres @ ₹6.50 per litre

Purchases (including freight and insurance):
March 5 1,50,000 litres @ ₹7.10 per litre
March 27 1,00,000 litres @ ₹7.00 per litre
Closing stock as on 31.3. 2020: 1,30,000 litres.
General administrative expenses for the month: ₹45,000

On the basis of the above information, work out the following using FIFO and LIFO methods of inventory valuation assuming that pricing of issues is being done at the end of the month after all receipts during the month:

(a) Value of closing stock as on 31.3. 2020
(b) Cost of goods sold during March 2020
(c) Profit or loss for March 2020

☞ ***Solution***

(A) FIFO Method of Pricing Issues

Stores Ledger

Date	Particulars	Receipts Qty Litre	Receipts Rate ₹ Per Litre	Receipts Value ₹	Issues Qty Litres	Issues Rate ₹ Per Litre	Issues Value ₹	Balance Qty Litres	Balance Rate ₹ Per Litre	Balance Value ₹
1.3.2020	Balance b/d							1,25,000	6.50	8,12,500
5.3.2020	Purchases	1,50,000	7.10	10,65,000				2,75,000		18,77,500
27.3.2020	Purchases	1,00,000	7.00	7,00,000				3,75,000		25,77,500
	Issues				1,25,000	6.50	8,12,500	2,50,000		17,65,000
	(3,75,000 – 1,30,000 = 2,45,000 units)				1,20,000	7.10	8,52,000	1,30,000		9,13,000
		2,50,000		17,65,000	2,45,000		16,64,500			

(B) LIFO Method of Pricing Issues

Stores Ledger

Date	Particulars	Receipts Qty Litres	Receipts Rate Per Litre ₹	Receipts Value ₹	Issues Qty Litres	Issues Rate Per Litre ₹	Issues Value ₹	Balance Qty Litres	Balance Rate Per Litre ₹	Balance Value ₹
1.3.2020	Balance b/d							1,25,000	6.50	8,12,500
5.3.2020	Purchases	1,50,000	7.10	10,65,000				2,75,000		18,77,500
27.3.2020	Purchases	1,00,000	7.00	7,00,000				3,75,000		25,77,500
	Issues				1,00,000	7.00	7,00,000			
					1,45,000	7.10	10,29,500	1,30,000		8,48,000
		2,50,000		17,65,000	2,45,000		17,29,500			

Closing stock, cost of goods sold, profit under FIFO

	(a) Value of closing stock		₹ 9,13,000
	(b) Cost of goods sold (8,12,500 + 8,52,000)		₹ 16,64,500
	(c) Profit		
	Sales		₹ 19,25,000
Less:	Cost of goods sold		₹(16,64,500)
	General administration expenses		₹ (45,000)
	Profit		₹ 2,15,500

Closing stock, cost of goods sold, profit under LIFO

	(a) Value of closing stock		₹ 8,48,000
	(b) Cost of goods sold (7,00,000 + 10,29,500)		₹ 17,29,500
	(c) Profit:		
	Sales		₹ 19,25,000
Less:	Cost of goods sold	17,29,500	
	General administration expenses	45,000	17,74,500
	Profit		₹ 1,50,500

EXAMPLE 4.11

Show how the items given ahead relating to purchases and issue of raw material item will appear in the stores ledger card, using weighted average method for issue pricing:

		Units	*Prices Per Units* ₹
Jan. 1	Opening balance	300	20
Jan. 5	Purchases	200	22
Jan. 11	Issue	150	?
Jan. 22	Purchases	200	23
Jan. 24	Issue	150	?
Jan. 28	Issue	200	?

Solution

Store Ledger Account

	Receipt			*Issue*			*Balance*	
Date	*Qty.*	*Rate*	*Amt.*	*Qty.*	*Rate*	*Amount*	*Qty.*	*Amt.*
Jan 1	—	—	—	—	—	—	300	6,000
Jan 5	200	22	4,400	—	—	—	500	10,400
Jan 11	—	—	—	150	20.80	3,120	350	7,280
Jan 22	200	23	4,600	—	—	—	550	11,880
Jan 24	—	—	—	150	21.60	3,240	400	8,640
Jan 28	—	—	—	200	21,60	4,320	200	4,320

Issue Prices:

$$\text{Jan 11} = \frac{10{,}400}{500}$$
$$= ₹20.80 \text{ per unit}$$

$$\text{Jan 24} = \frac{11{,}880}{550} = ₹21.60 \text{ per unit}$$

$$\text{Jan 28} = \frac{8{,}640}{400} = ₹21.60 \text{ per unit}$$

EXAMPLE 4.12

The Stock Ledger Account for Material *X* in a manufacturing concern reveals the following data for the quarter ended Sept. 30, 2020.

			Receipts		*Issues*	
			Quantity Units	*Price ₹*	*Quantity Units*	*Price ₹*
July	1	Balance b/d	1,600	2.00		—
July	9		3,000	2.20	—	—
July	13		—	—	1,200	2,556
Aug.	5		—	—	900	1,917
Aug.	17		3,600	2.40	—	
Aug.	24		—	—	1,800	4,122
Sept.	11		2,500	2.50	—	—
Sept.	27		—	—	2,100	4,971
Sept.	29		—	—	700	1,656

Physical verification on Sept. 30, 2020 revealed an actual stock of 3,800 units.

You are required to:

(a) Indicate the method of pricing employed above.

(b) Complete the above account by making entries you would consider necessary including adjustments, if any, and giving explanations for such adjustments.

Solution

(a) The verification of the value of issues applied in the problem shows that Weighted Average Method of pricing has been followed. For example, the issue price of 1,200 units of July 13 will be ₹2.13 $\left(\frac{₹2{,}556}{1{,}200 \text{ units}}\right)$ which is the weighted average price of purchases made on July 9 and July 1 opening stock, calculated as follows:

$$\text{Weighted average price} = \frac{(1{,}600 \text{ units} \times ₹2) + (3{,}000 \text{ units} \times ₹2.20)}{1{,}600 \text{ units} + 3{,}000 \text{ units}}$$

$$= \frac{₹9{,}800}{4{,}600 \text{ units}}$$

$$= ₹2.13$$

(b) The complete Stores Ledger account giving the transactions as stated in the problem together with the necessary adjustments is given below:

Stores Ledger Account (Weighted Average Method)

Date		*Receipts*			*Issues*			*Balance*		
		Qty ₹	*Rate* ₹	*Amount* ₹	*Qty* ₹	*Rate* ₹	*Amount* ₹	*Qty*	*Rate*	*Amount*
July	1	1,600	2.00	3,200				1,600	2.00	3,200
	9	3,000	2.20	6.600				4,600	2.13	9,800
	13				1,200	2.13	2,556	3,400	2.13	7,244
Aug.	5				900	2.13	1,917	2,500	2.13	5,327
	17	3,600	2.40	8,640				6,100	2.29	13,967
	24				1,800	2.29	4,122	4,300	2.29	9,845
Sept.	11	2,500	2.50	6,250				6,800	2.37	16,095
	27				2,100	2.37	4,971	4,700	2.37	11,124
	29				700	2.37	1,656	4,000	2.37	9,468
	30				200*	2.37	473	3,800	2.37	8,995

Closing Stock: 3,800 units, value of closing stock = ₹8,995

* Shortage of 200 units has been charged at the weighted average price of the goods in stock.

Closing stock 3,800 units × ₹2.37 = ₹9,006. Since the figures of issue prices have been taken directly as given in the question, there is a minor difference in the value of closing stock.

✍ EXAMPLE 4.13

for excel template, scan

Show how the items given ahead relating to purchase and issue of a raw material item will appcar in the Stores Ledger using LIFO, FIFO and Weighted Average Methods of pricing the materials issue:

2020		*Units*	*Price Per Unit* ₹
Feb. 1	Opening balance	300	20
Feb. 5	Purchase	200	22
Feb. 11	Issue	150	?
Feb. 22	Purchases	200	23
Feb. 24	Issue	150	?
Feb. 28	Issue	200	?
	Shortage	5	?

Stores Ledger FIFO Method

Date	*Particulars*	*Receipt*			*Issue*			*Balance*	
		Qty	*Rate*	*Amount*	*Qty*	*Rate*	*Amount*	*Qty*	*Amount*
Feb. 1	Opening balance	—	—	—	—	—	—	300	6,000
Feb. 5	Purchases	200	22	4,400				500	10,400
Feb. 11	Issue				150	20	3,000	350	7,400
Feb. 22	Purchase	200	23	4,600				550	12,000
Feb. 24	Issue				150	20	3,000	400	9,000
Feb. 28	Issue				200	22	4,400	200	4,600
Feb. 28	Shortage				5	23	115	195	4,485

Note: Value of Cl. stock is 195 units @ ₹23 per unit = ₹4,485.

Stores Ledger LIFO Method

Date	*Particulars*	*Receipt*			*Issue*			*Balance*	
		Qty	*Rate*	*Amount*	*Qty*	*Rate*	*Amount*	*Qty*	*Amount*
Feb. 1	Opening balance	—	—	—	—	—	—	300	6,000
Feb. 5	Purchases	200	22	4,400				500	10,400
Feb. 11	Issue				150	22	3,300	350	7,100
Feb. 22	Purchase	200	23	4,600	—	—	—	550	11,700
Feb. 24	Issue				150	23	3,450	400	8,250
Feb. 28	Issue				50 [200]	23	1,150 [4250]		
					50	22	1,100		
					100	20	2,000	200	4,000
Feb. 28	Shortage				5	20	100	195	3,900

Note: Value of closing stock is 195 units @ ₹20 each = ₹3,900.

Stores Ledger Weighted Average Method

Date	*Particulars*	*Receipt*			*Issue*			*Balance*	
		Qty	*Rate*	*Amount*	*Qty*	*Rate*	*Amount*	*Qty*	*Amount*
Feb. 1	Opening balance							300	6,000
Feb. 5	Purchase	200	22	4,400				500	10,400
Feb. 11	Issue				150	$\frac{10,400}{500}$ = 20.8	3,120	350	7,280
Feb. 22	Purchase	200	23	4,600	—	—	—	550	11,880
Feb. 24	Issue				150	$\frac{11,880}{550}$ = 21.6	3,240	400	8,640
Feb. 28	Issue				200		4,320	200	4,320
Feb. 28	Shortage				5	21.6	108	195	4,212

EXAMPLE 4.14

The following are the details of receipts and issues of a material of stores in a manufacturing company for the period of three months ending 30th June, 2020:

Receipts:

Date	*Quantity (Kg)*	*Rate (Kg)*
April 10	1,600	5
April 20	2,400	4.90
May 5	1,000	5.10
May 17	1,100	5.20
May 25	800	5.25
June 11	900	5.40
June 24	1,400	5.50

There was 1,500 kg in stock at April 1, 2020 which was valued at ₹4.80 per kg.
Issues:

Date	*Quantity (Kg)*
April 4	1,100
April 24	1,600
May 10	1,500
May 26	1,700
June 15	1,500
June 21	1,200

Issues are to be priced on the basis of weighted average method. The stock verifier of the company reported a shortage of 80 kg on 31st May, 2020 and 60 kg on 30th June, 2020. The shortage is treated as inflating the price of remaining material on account of shortage.

You are required to prepare a Stores Ledger Account.

Solution

Stores Ledger Account for the Three Months Ending 30th June, 2020
(Weighted Average Method)

	Receipts				*Issues*				*Balance*		
Date	*GRN No. MRR No.*	*Qty. (Kg)*	*Rates (₹)*	*Amounts*	*Requisition. No.*	*Qty. (Kg)*	*Rates (₹)*	*Amount (₹)*	*Qty. (Kg)*	*Amount (₹)*	*Rate for Further Issue (₹)*
2020											
April 1									1,500	7,200	4.80
April 4						1,100	4.80	5,280	400	1,920	4.80

(Contd.)

Date	Receipts				Issues				Balance		
	GRN No. MRR No.	Qty. (Kg)	Rates (₹)	Amounts	Requisition. No.	Qty. (Kg)	Rates (₹)	Amount (₹)	Qty. (Kg)	Amount (₹)	Rate for Further Issue (₹)
April 10		1,600	5.00	8,000					2,000	9,920	$\frac{9,920}{2,000} = 4.96$
April 20		2,400	4.90	11,760					4,400	21,680	$\frac{21,680}{4,440} = 4.93$
April 24						1,600	4.93	7,888	2,800	13,792	$\frac{13,792}{2,800} = 4.93$
May 5		1,000	5.10	5,100					3,800	18,892	$\frac{18,892}{3,800} = 4.97$
May 10						1,500	4.97	7,455	2,300	11,437	$\frac{11,437}{2,300} = 4.97$
May 17		1,100	5.20	5,720					3,400	17,157	$\frac{17,157}{3,400} = 5.05$
May 25		800	5.25	4,200					4,200	21,357	$\frac{21,357}{4,200} = 5.09$
May 26						1,700	5.09	8,653	2,500	12,704	$\frac{12,704}{2,500} = 5.09$
May 31					Shortage	80			2,420	12,704	$\frac{12,704}{2,420} = 5.25$
June 11		900	5.40	4,860					3,320	17,564	$\frac{17,564}{3,320} = 5.29$
June 15						1,500	5.29	7,935	1,820	9,629	$\frac{9,629}{1,820} = 5.29$
June 21						1,200	5.29	6,348	620	3,281	$\frac{3,281}{620} = 5.29$
June 24		1,400	5.50	7,700					2,020	10,981	$\frac{10,981}{2,020} = 5.40$
June 30					Shortage	60			1,960	10,981	$\frac{10,981}{1,960} = 5.60$

EXAMPLE 4.15

The following transactions in respect of material *Y* occurred during the six months ended 30th June, 2020.

Month	*Purchase (Units)*	*Price Per Unit (₹)*	*Issued (Units)*
January	200	25	Nil
February	300	24	250
March	425	26	300
April	475	23	550
May	500	25	800
June	600	20	400

Required:

The chief accountant argues that the value of closing stock remains the same, no matter which method of pricing of material issues is used. Do you agree? Why or why not? Detailed stores ledgers are not required.

Solution

In the given problem, the total number of units purchased from January to May 2020 is 1,900 and the same have also been issued during this period. Thus, there was no stock at the end of May, 2020 which could become opening stock for the next month. In June, 2020; only a single purchase and a single issue of material was made. The closing stock is of 200 units. In this situation, stock of 200 units at the end of June, 2020 will be valued at ₹20 per unit irrespective of the pricing method of material issues. Hence, one would agree with the argument of the Chief Accountant.

However, this will not be true with the value of closing stock at the end of each month. Moreover, the value of closing stock at the end of June, 2005 would have been different under different pricing methods if there were several purchases at different prices and several issues during the month.

EXAMPLE 4.16

ABC Limited provides you the following information. Calculate the cost of goods sold and ending inventory, applying the LIFO method of pricing raw materials under the Perpetual and Periodical Inventory Control Systems.

Date		*Particulars*	*Units*	*Per Unit Cost (₹)*
January	1	Opening stock	200	10
	10	Purchases	400	12
	12	Withdrawals	500	–
	16	Purchases	300	11
	19	Issues	200	–
	30	Receipts	100	15

Also explain in brief the reasons for a difference in profit, if any.

☞ Solution

Computation of Cost of Goods Sold and Ending Inventory

Particulars	Under Perpetual Inventory Method Units × Rate = Amount ₹	Under Periodic Inventory Method Units × Rate = Amount ₹
(i) Cost of Goods sold/withdrawn or issued:		
On 12th Jan.	400 × 12 = 4,800	100 × 15 = 1,500
	100 × 10 = 1,000	300 × 11 = 3,300
		300 × 12 = 3,600
	5,800	700 ₹ 8,400
On 19th Jan.	200 × 11 = 2.200	
	Total ₹ 8,000	
(ii) Ending inventory	100 × 10 = 1,000	100 × 12 = 1,200
	100 × 11 = 1,100	200 × 10 = 2,000
	100 × 15 = 1,500	
	300 ₹ 3,600	300 ₹ 3,200

Reasons for Difference in Profits. The cost of goods sold/issued/withdrawn is more under Periodic Inventory System as compared to Perpetual Inventory System. Hence, the profit under the former will be less as compared to the later. Alternatively, it can be so said that less the amount of ending inventory, less will be the profits.

✍ EXAMPLE 4.17

The following are the particulars regarding receipts and issues of certain material:

Opening stock	1,000 kg @ ₹9.00 per kg
Purchased	5,000 kg @ ₹8.50 per kg
Issued	600 kg
Issued	3,750 kg
Issued	650 kg
Purchased	2,500 kg @ ₹8 per kg

The credit balance of price variance account, before transfer to costing profit and loss account, was ₹500.

Calculate the standard rate at which the above issues should be made, and determine the value of closing stock.

☞ **Solution**

The standard price at which the materials were issued in the last period was ₹9. This gave a profit of ₹500.

Therefore, this time, materials should be valued at a lower standard price as compared to last period. The standard price for this period should therefore be:

$$\frac{₹9,000 - ₹500}{1,000} = \frac{₹8,500}{1,000} = ₹8.50 \text{ per kg}$$

Value of the Closing Stocks:

Opening stock	1,000	per kg @ ₹9	₹9,000
Purchases	5,000	kg @ ₹8.50	42,500
Purchases	2,500	kg @ ₹8	20,000
	8,500		71,500
Less: Issues	5,000	@ ₹8.50	42,500
Balance	3,500 units		₹29,000

The value of stock at standard price is ₹29,750 (3500 × 8.50). The stock therefore will be valued at ₹29,750 and ₹750 will be debited to the price variance account.

EXAMPLE 4.18

The annual accounts of a trading company are to be made up to December 31 but it was not possible to carry out a stock-taking until January 5 at which date the stock was valued at cost at ₹68,567.

The following transactions took place between 1st and 5th January:

	₹
Goods received	4,600
Goods returned	200
Sales	10,500
Returns by customers	625

The rate of gross profit is 25% of cost.

Prepare a statement to show the valuation of stock as at 31st December.

☞ **Solution**

Statement Showing the Valuation of Stock

		₹	₹
Stock as at 5th January			68,567
Add:	Goods returned		200
	Cost of goods sold:		
	Sales	10,500	

(Contd.)

		₹	₹
Less:	Gross profit $\left(\frac{25}{125} \times 10{,}500\right)$	2,100	
			8,400
			77,167
Less:	Goods received	4,600	
	Returns by customers	625	
			5,225
	Valuation of stock on 31st December		71,942

PRICING OF MATERIALS RETURNED TO VENDOR

A business firm may return materials to a supplier. In the financial books, purchase returns are valued at the price at which they are purchased. In cost accounting, the following rules are generally applicable as to the valuation of such purchase returns.

1. In case the firm is following the FIFO method, the materials returned to the supplier would be valued at the price of the oldest goods in stock on the date on which the materials are returned.
2. The materials returned would be valued at the price of the latest units received and still in stock, if the firm is following the LIFO method.
3. Purchase returns would be valued at average price if the firm is following the average price method. The quantity and value of materials returned are shown generally in the issues column. Alternatively, they may be shown in the receipts column in red ink.

Example

200 units were received from *A* @ ₹4 per unit.
200 units were received from *B* @ ₹5 per unit
50 units received from *A* were returned to him.

In the first situation (when the firm is following FIFO method), assume 300 units were issued to production. In this, 50 units will be valued @ ₹5 per unit. However, if only 100 units were issued to production, then 50 units will be valued @ ₹4 per unit under FIFO method.

In the second situation (LIFO method), if 300 units have already been issued to production, 50 units will be valued @ ₹4 per unit. However, if only 100 units have been issued to production, then 50 units returned to A will be valued @ ₹5 per unit.

In the third situation, when the firm is following average price method, units returned will be valued in terms of average price (simple or weighted average as the case may be). Simple average or weighted average price will be calculated in the manner as explained earlier in this chapter.

PRICING OF MATERIALS RETURNED TO STOREROOM

When materials are returned from requisitioning departments to the storeroom for credit, the problem arises as to the proper method of handling such returns in stock ledger sheets. The following rules apply in this regard.

1. In case the firm is following the LIFO or FIFO method, the returned materials should be recorded at a price at which they have been originally issued and those units will be issued at the old price on the next requisition which is received. Alternatively, they may be treated as new purchases and retaining the original pricing, they can be given a position after the last purchase received.
2. If the firm is following the average price method, the returned materials should be recorded at the price originally issued, but a new average cost should be computed as if the goods returned were a new purchase.
3. Materials returned can be recorded at the current issue price also. That is, materials returned are priced at a price at which materials have been issued on the date of returns from the stores department. In this way, in this method, the issue price of materials (on the date of returns) is used to price materials returned to storeroom. In this method, there is no need to search original issue price of the materials returned and thus, this method saves time and clerical work.

The quantity and value of materials returned to the storeroom should be shown in the Issues column in red ink or alternatively they may be shown in the Receipts column.

SELECTION OF A MATERIALS PRICING METHOD

The various methods which are in use have advantages and disadvantages from the viewpoint of both convenience and accounting aspects. The factors which should be taken into consideration while deciding materials pricing methods are as follows:

1. Customs and practices within the industry or group of companies: This produces more comparable figures.
2. Frequency of price fluctuations and frequency of materials purchases.
3. Relative value of materials cost to total cost of products or jobs manufactured.
4. Range of price fluctuations.
5. Relative rate of stock turnover.
6. Quantities of materials to be purchased at any one time.
7. The effect of the different pricing methods on tax liability.
8. The accuracy with which materials issues can be computed.
9. Cost of clerical work involved in maintaining records.
10. The possibility of using different methods for various classes of items in the inventory.
11. The relationship of selling prices to the costs that are matched with those prices.

Costing materials present important, often complex and sometimes highly controversial questions concerning the valuation of materials used in production and the value of inventory remaining to be consumed at a future period. The different methods of materials pricing are difficult to compare adequately; this is a complex task. Some industries prefer the use of market prices for charging materials into production; market prices are the prices prevailing at the time the materials are used. These are the prices which would have to be paid if the materials were purchased at the time. This approach to materials costing has been gaining popularity over the recent years. This method reflects the current position, the current cost and the efficiency of purchasing done by a firm. In periods of rising prices, lowest material cost will flow into production under FIFO, highest materials cost under LIFO, and average costing will produce a material cost figure which is between FIFO and LIFO figures. In a period of falling prices, the reverse situation will be found i.e., FIFO will show the highest cost of materials used, LIFO the lowest cost of materials used, and average costing will show a cost figure between FIFO and LIFO figures.

It is true that no one best method can be suggested, which is applicable to all situations; pricing methods may vary within the same company. It must be emphasised that whatever method is adopted, it must be consistently used from period to period. The most appropriate method is the one which produces accurate and meaningful cost figures for purposes of control and analysis and matching costs against revenue produced in order to determine the net operating income.

Theory Questions

1. What are the methods of pricing materials issues? When do you advocate pricing the issues at cost price based on last-in, first-out?
2. State the various methods of pricing the issue of materials or stores. State the method to be adopted for the issue of materials for an industry where their cost is fluctuating constantly
3. Explain the following two methods of pricing issue of materials and also the circumstance under which these methods are used.
   (i) FIFO
   (ii) LIFO
4. Describe the following methods of valuing materials issued to production and discuss the advantage and disadvantage of each?
   (i) First-In, First-Out; (ii) Weighted Average; (iii) Replacement Price.
5. Explain the FIFO methods of valuation of materials issues. Discuss the effects of rising prices and falling prices on these two methods of pricing of materials issues.
6. What factors have to be considered for adopting a method for the pricing of materials? In the light of these and relevant factors, give a comparative description of LIFO and FIFO.
7. What are the conditions that favour the adoption of the Last-In, First-Out system of materials pricing? Explain its working and indicate its advantages and limitations.
8. Give the advantages and disadvantages of the actual cost basis of pricing of material issues.
9. Explain FIFO and LIFO methods of pricing of material issues. Which of these should be preferred in rising and falling prices and why?
10. Under conditions of rising prices, which of the following two methods of pricing material issues would you recommend and why?
    (i) FIFO
    (ii) LIFO
11. Briefly contrast the effects of using First-In, First-Out with the Last-In, First-Out methods of pricing material issues from stores.
12. Write short notes on:
    (i) LIFO vs FIFO
    (ii) Bill of Materials
    (iii) Perpetual Inventory System.
13. Differentiate between FIFO and LIFO methods of material issue under inflationary conditions.
14. Briefly contrast the effect of using FIFO with the LIFO methods of pricing material issues from stores.
15. Distinguish between simple and weighted average methods of pricing of issue of materials.
16. Distinguish between LIFO and FIFO methods of pricing the issues of materials. Which one do you think is better and why in case of inflationary conditions?
17. Differentiate between LIFO and FIFO methods of pricing material issues.

Self-Evaluation Questions

1. Which method of materials pricing best approximates specific identification of the actual flow of costs and units in most manufacturing situations?
   (a) Average cost (b) FIFO
   (c) LIFO (d) Base stock
2. Alpha company was using FIFO (and not LIFO) for materials pricing and its value of inventory was found lower. Assuming no opening inventory, what direction did the purchase prices move during the period?
   (a) Up (b) Down
   (c) Steady (d) Cannot be determined
3. A materials pricing method in which the oldest cost incurred rarely has an effect on the closing inventory valuation is
   (a) FIFO (b) LIFO
   (c) Simple average (d) Weighted average
4. Alpha company has been using LIFO method of materials pricing for 15 years. Its 2020 closing inventory was ₹ 15,000 but it would have been ₹ 26,000 if FIFO had been used. Thus, if FIFO had been used, this company's net income before taxes would have been
   (a) ₹ 11,000 less over 15-year period (b) ₹ 11,000 greater over 15-year period
   (c) ₹ 11,000 greater in 2020 (d) ₹ 11,000 less in 2020

Problems

1. The particulars relating to the import of sealing ring invoiced by AB and Co., during December 2020 are given below:
   (a) Sealing ring 1,000 pieces @ $2.00 CIF Mumbai Port.
   (b) Customs duty was paid @ 100% on invoice value (which was converted to Indian currency by adopting an exchange rate of ₹ 17.20 per $).
   (c) Clearing charges ₹ 1,800 for the entire consignment.
   (d) Freight charges ₹ 1,400 for transporting the consignment from Mumbai port to factory premises.

   It was found on inspection that 100 pieces of the above material were broken, and therefore, rejected. There is no scrap value for the rejected part. Also, no refund for the broken material would be admissible as per the terms of the contract. The management decided to treat 60 pieces as normal loss and the rest 40 pieces as abnormal loss. The entire quantity of 900 pieces was issued to production.

   Calculate:
   (a) Total cost of material.
   (b) Unit cost of material issued to production.

   Also state briefly how the value of 100 pieces rejected in inspection will be treated in costs.

   Ans: (a) ₹ 72,000 (b) ₹ 76.59 per piece
2. From the following details of stores receipts and issues of material "EXA" in a manufacturing unit, prepare the Stock Ledger using "Weighted Average" method of valuing the issues:

   Nov. 1 Opening stock 2,000 units @ ₹ 5 each.
   Nov. 3 Issued 1,500 units to Production.
   Nov. 4 Received 4,500 units @ ₹ 6.00 each.
   Nov. 8 Issued 1,600 units to Production.
   Nov. 9 Returned to stores 100 units by Production Department (from the issues of November 3).

Nov.	16	Received 2,400 units @ ₹ 6.50 each.
Nov.	19	Returned to the supplier 200 units out of the quantity received on November 4.
Nov.	20	Received 1,000 units @ ₹ 7.00 each.
Nov.	24	Issued to Production 2,100 units.
Nov.	27	Received 1,200 units @ ₹ 7.50 each.
Nov.	29	Issued to Production 2,800 units.

(use rates upto two decimal places).

Ans: Cost of issued materials ₹18,256
Closing stock ₹19,558

3. You are presented with the following information by Sphix Engineering Co. relating to the first week of September, 2020.

Materials—The transactions in connection with the materials are as follows:

	Receipts		*Issues*
Days	*Units*	*Rate Per Unit (₹)*	*Units*
1st	40	15.00	
2nd	20	16.50	
3rd			30
4th	50	14.30	
5th			20
6th			40

Calculate the cost of materials issued under FIFO method and Weighted Average Method of issue of materials.

Ans:

	Cost of Materials Issued		*Stock*	
	Units	*Amt* ₹	*Units*	*Amt.* ₹
FIFO	90	1,359	20	286
Weighted Average	90	1,350	20.	295

for excel template, scan

4. Show the stores ledger entries as they would appear when using
(a) the weighted average method
(b) the LIFO method of pricing issues, in connection with the following transactions:

April		Unit	Value
1	Balance in hand	300	600
2	Purchased	200	440
4	Issued	150	
6	Purchased	200	460
11	Issued	150	
19	Issued	200	

	April	Unit	Value
20	Purchased	200	480
27	Issued	250	

In a period of rising prices such as above what are the effects of each method?

Ans: (a) 150 units ₹342; (b) 150 units ₹300.

5. On January 1, Mr. G started a small business buying and selling a special yarn. He invested his savings of ₹4,00,000 in the business and during the next six months, the following transactions occurred:

Yarn Purchase				*Yarn Sales*			
Date of Receipt		*Quantity Boxes*	*Total Cost (₹)*	*Date of Despatch*		*Quantity Boxes*	*Total Value (₹)*
January	13	200	7,200	February	10	500	25,000
February	8	400	15,200	April	20	600	27,000
March	11	600	24,000	June	25	400	15,200
April	12	400	14,000				
June	15	500	14,000				

The yarn is stored in premises Mr G. has rented and the closing stock of yarn counted on 30th June was 500 boxes.

Other expenses incurred and paid in cash during the six-months period amounted to ₹2,300.

Required:

(a) Calculate the value of the material issues during the six-month period and the value of closing stock at the end of June, using the following methods of pricing:
  (i) FIFO
  (ii) LIFO, and
  (iii) Weighted average

(b) Calculate and discuss the effect each of the three methods of material pricing will have on the reported profit of the business, and examine the performance of the business during the first six month period.

Ans:

	Closing Stock	*Cost of Sales*	*Profit*
FIFO	₹14,000	₹19,600	4,500
LIFO	₹19,600	₹54,800	10,100
Weighted Average	₹16,486	₹57,914	6,986

6. A consignment consisted of two chemicals *A* and *B*. The invoices gave the following data:

Chemical *A*—4,000 lb @ ₹ 2.50 per lb...	₹	10,000
Chemical *B*—3,200 lb @ ₹ 3.25 per lb...	₹	10,400
Sales tax	₹	816
Railway freight	₹	384
Total cost	₹	21,600

A shortage of 200 lb in *A* and 128 lb in *B* was noticed due to breakage. What stock rate would you adopt for pricing issues assuming a provision of 5% towards further deterioration?

Ans: Material *A* ₹ 2.94
Material *B* ₹ 3.76

7. The Directors of Quality Machineries Ltd. requests you to ascertain the amount at which the inventory should be included in the financial statement for the year 2019–20. The value of inventory as shown in the books is ₹ 12,50,000.

   To determine the net realisable value of the inventory (on test check basis), you had selected several items whose books value was ₹3,50,000.

   You ascertain that except for items (a) to (c) below, the cost was in excess of the realisable value by ₹29,532. The following items require special treatment:

   (a) One machine (cost ₹1,30,000) can now fetch ₹1,15,000. It was priced at ₹70,000 and was written down to the same figure at the end of 2019–20.

   (b) A pump (cost ₹50,000) was expected to realise ₹35,000. A special commission of 15% would have to be paid to the broker.

   (c) 6 units of product no. 15,710 were in stock and each valued at ₹5,520; the selling price was ₹4,500 per unit; selling expenses are 10% of the selling price.

   Taking into consideration only the above mentioned items requiring special treatment, compute the value of their inventory as at 31st March, 2020, you would consider reasonable.

   Ans: Value of all the items of inventory ₹ 11,01,398.

Chapter 5

Labour Costs: Accounting and Control

Learning Objectives

After reading this chapter, you should be able to:

1. explain direct and indirect labour, their nature;
2. discuss the importance of various organisational departments in exercising control over labour costs;
3. explain straight time and piece work methods of wage system, different incentive wage plans;
4. describe method study, time and motion study, work measurement, merit rating and various job evaluation methods, difference between job evaluation and merit rating;
5. discuss labour turnover, its causes and costs; and
6. explain treatment of labour-cost related items such as overtime premium, idle time, fringe benefits etc.

INTRODUCTION

Proper control and accounting for labour costs is one of the most important objectives of all business firms. Cost accounting for labour has three primary objectives:

1. Determining labour costs in the cost of product or service.
2. Reporting labour costs for planning and control.
3. Reporting labour costs for decision-making.

For a manufacturing business firm engaged in producing a specific product, labour costs are accumulated and charged to the product as they are produced. Similarly, in a service (not-for-profit) organisation, total cost as well as the cost of different functions (services) are to be determined. This helps the organisation to know what it costs them to provide a service or perform some activities.

The second objective is to provide management with labour cost information for effective planning of the labour force in the organisation and for adequate control of labour costs. The control process of labour cost involves a comparison of actual labour costs with standard labour cost. The differences between the two are then analysed and possible reasons are determined so that management can take suitable action to control the labour cost expenditure in future periods.

Labour cost information is used for decision-making purposes also. Many managerial decisions, such as pricing decisions, expansion of business, dropping a product line, replacement of plant and equipment, entering into a new market, etc. require information about current actual labour costs and emerging trends therein.

DIRECT LABOUR AND INDIRECT LABOUR

Direct Labour

Direct labour consists of the wages paid to labour which convert raw materials into some form of finished output. Direct labour cost comprises the wages which can be identified with, and allocated to cost units. Examples of some direct labour functions in a manufacturing enterprise would be assembly line workers, moulders, operators, samplers and finishers.

Indirect Labour

Indirect labour is the labour which is not engaged in converting raw materials into finished output. The indirect labour cost is the cost which "cannot be allocated[1] but which can be apportioned to, or absorbed by, cost centres or cost units". Indirect labour includes, among others, foremen, inspectors, watchmen, supervisors, factory clerks, store-keepers and time-keepers. In fact, after charging to departments and to products, all labour costs which can, as a practical matter, be charged directly, the indirect labour costs remain.

ORGANISATION FOR LABOUR CONTROL

The significant portion of labour costs in the total cost of production points out its importance and need for effective control over labour and labour-related costs. The following departments/functions contribute to the efficient utilisation of labour and adequate control over labour costs.

1. Personnel Department
2. Engineering Department
3. Time-keeping Department
4. Payroll Department
5. Cost Accounting Department

Personnel Department

The main function of the personnel department is to provide an efficient labour force. The personnel manager/director, with the help of department heads, is responsible for the execution of the policies formulated by board of directors regarding employment, discharge, classification of employees, wages and wage systems. Hiring of employees may be for replacement or for expansion. Replacement hiring starts when a department head or a foreman sends an employee requisition (see Fig. 5.1) to the personnel department.

---

[1] The term "allocation" means the allotment of whole items of cost to cost centres or cost units.

The personnel department prepares an Employee's Record Card on engaging a new worker. This will show full personal details of the employee, particulars of previous employment, medical category and wage rate. Normally, spaces are also provided for subsequent recording of transfers and promotions, wage rate revisions, details of attendance, merit and conduct reports, sickness and accidents and the date and reason for leaving (see Fig. 5.2).

Engineering Department

The engineering department maintains control over working conditions and production methods for each job and department or process by performing the following functions:

1. Preparation of plans and specifications for each job scheduled for production.
2. Supervision of production activities with production departments.

Employee Requisition

Requisition No. ________

Date ________

Department ________

Report to
(Supervisor or Foreman's Name)

on ________

Number of employees requested	Job Specification Description No.

Requisitioned by ________ Approved by ________

Fig. 5.1 Employee Requisition

Front

Particulars			*Employment Record*	
Home address	Date	Department	Grade	Employment
Date employed				
Date of birth				
Married/Single				
Height				
Weight				
General physique				
(Category)				

Previous Employment	Date	Rate	Particulars	Date (Wage Rate Record)	Rate	Particulars
References:						
Notes:						

Fig. 5.2 a Employee's Record Card (Front Side)

Back								
Time-keeping and Merit					*Training, Progress and Conduct*			
Year	Days Lost		Overtime	Lost Time	Merit and	Date	Particulars	
	Sickness	Others	Hours	Hours	Notes			

Date left:

Reason for leaving:

General remarks:

Fig. 5.2 b Employee's Record Card (Back Side)

3. Inspection of parts and jobs at successive stages of production and at the completion of production.
4. Initiation and supervision of research and experiment work.
5. Safety and efficient working conditions.

Time-keeping Department

The first step in accounting for labour cost is to prepare an accurate record of the time spent by each employee. Time-keeping in labour costing and control is important because of the following reasons:

1. It accumulates the total number of hours worked by each employee so that his earnings can be calculated.
2. Absence of a time-keeping arrangement will create frustration among those employees who are punctual or bound by the attendance rules.
3. Certain benefits like pension and gratuity, leave with pay, provident fund, salary and promotion are linked with continuity of service of employees. Attendance records, in this regard, can be helpful and useful to employees.
4. Overhead costs being indirect costs are apportioned to different products on some equitable basis. Time-keeping is necessary if apportionment is to be done on the basis of labour hours.
5. Time-keeping records and attendance details may be used by the firm for analysis proposes and by researchers, government authorities, etc.

Clock Card

The most common form of attendance record is the clock card on which the employee punches the time at which he comes in and leaves the factory. Each week, a new card is prepared for each employee on the payroll. At the end of the week, the cards are collected and transferred to the payroll department for calculation of gross earnings.

Daily Time Report

No. ______________________

Name ______________________

Nature of Work ______________________

(Contd.)

Job No.	Time On		Time Off		Time Worked	
	Hours	*Minutes*	*Hours*	*Minutes*	*Hours*	*Minutes*
561	8	00	12	00	4	00
357	12	30	1	30	1	00
816	1	30	2	15	0	45
548	2	15	3	00	0	45
751	3	00	4	30	1	30
Foreman						

Fig. 5.3 Daily Time Report

Clock cards provide a record of the total hours, employees were available on jobs. However, this card does not reveal as to how employees spend their time which is an important question to be solved before entries can be made in the cost records. This information is supplied by time tickets or daily labour summaries (see Fig. 5.3) on which time-keepers record the daily activities of direct labour; time spent on specific orders, time spent on indirect labour operations such as machine maintenance, or idle time waiting for reassignment or machine set-up.

Disc Method

A second method of recording time is by using a metal disc which contains an identification number for each employee. A board containing hooks to which employees' discs are attached is kept near the entrance to the plant. On arrival, the employee removes his disc and places it in a box, or alternatively hooks it on a second board against his number. The box is removed at starting time, and the time-keeper becomes aware of late arrivals by requiring the workers concerned to report to him before starting. The time-keeper will record in an Attendance Register any late arrivals and workers leaving early. He will also detail the absentees each day.

Attendance Records

The simplest form of attendance records is a manual register which each employee signs into on arrival and departure, noting his times in and out. This type of time-keeping record is subject to limitations and many abuses by employees. In a business firm where a large number of workers are employed, and if the worker records his own time, it provides very little check upon late arrivals. The disadvantages of manual registers and time registers are the hold-ups that occur when each worker has to sign his name in turn, and the amount of clerical work involved in the posting of entries to individual attendance records.

Time-booking

Time-booking like time-keeping is equally important. Time-booking means recording the time spent by a worker on each job, process or operation. Time-booking fulfils the following purposes:

1. To determine amount of labour cost which can be obtained through time-booking record.
2. To determine the quantity and value of work done.
3. To determine earnings like wages, bonus which depend on the time taken by a worker in performing job or jobs in a factory.

Recording work time can be done by any one of the following methods:

Job Ticket

Job tickets are given to all workers where time for commencing the job is recorded as well as the time when the job has been completed. After completing one job, the worker is given another job ticket for the next job to be completed by him.

Labour Cost Card

This card is meant for a job which involves many operations or stages of completion. Instead of giving one card to each worker, only one card is passed on to all workers and time taken on the job is recorded by each one of them. This card discloses the aggregate labour cost of the job or the product.

Weekly Time Sheets

A sheet is given to each worker to record time on a weekly basis. However, weekly time sheets should be filled up without much delay on each day failing which some inaccuracies are bound to occur on the time sheets.

Daily Time Sheets

Each worker records the time spent by him on the work during the day for which a sheet is provided to each worker. Since time is recorded on a daily basis, accuracy is built up on the time sheets. However, daily time sheets are generally not used. This could be used for maintenance and repairmen who have to do different jobs in different departments.

Time and Job Card

This card records the attendance time of workers and work time of a worker on a single sheet.

Payroll Department

Preparation of the payroll from clock cards, job or time tickets, or time sheets is done by the payroll department. The payroll department (tabulation) is an intermediate function between the time-keeping (accumulation) and the cost accounting (analysis) department. The following are the functions of the payroll department:

1. To compute employee wages.
2. To pay employees and for prompt and accurate reporting of wages and salaries to employees.
3. To prepare departmental payroll summaries.
4. To maintain individual employee payroll records.
5. To calculate payroll taxes, deductions and other related payroll liabilities.
6. Compilation of labour statistics for management.

The responsibilities of the payroll department in controlling and accounting for labour costs are as follows:

1. To maintain a record of the job classification, department and wage rate for each employee.
2. To verify and to summarise the time of each worker as shown on the daily time cards.
3. To compute the wages earned by each worker.
4. To prepare the payroll for each department showing the total amount earned for the period by each employee.

5. To compute the payroll deductions under the Acts.
6. To compute the payroll deductions authorised by the employee for union dues, charitable donation, saving bonds, and health and accidental insurance.
7. To maintain a permanent payroll record for each employee.
8. To distribute salary and wage payments.

Cost Accounting Department

The cost accounting department is responsible for the accumulation and classification of all cost data of which labour costs are one of the most important elements. On the basis of the labour summary or the time or job cards, the cost department records direct labour cost on the appropriate cost sheets or production reports and indirect costs on the departmental expense sheets.

WAGE SYSTEMS

An important aspect of labour cost control is a wage system designed primarily for exercising management control over labour. The following objectives should be considered in the selection of a wage system:

1. Acceptance by employees to avert slowdowns and work stoppages.
2. Provision for flexibility.
3. Provision for economy in administration.
4. Supplying of labour statistics for use in industrial relations and for trade associations, government agencies, and competitors.
5. Stabilisation of labour turnover.
6. Minimising of absenteeism.
7. Provision for incentive plans.

Basically, there are two wage systems to pay for labour: (i) straight time which is by hour, day, or week, and (ii) piece work, which is by the unit of product.

Straight Time

Under the time basis, the worker is paid at an hourly, daily or weekly rate and his remuneration depends upon the time for which he is employed and not upon his production. If a worker works for an overtime, the wage agreement usually provides that all hours worked in excess of an agreed number are paid for at a higher rate. The time-basis wage system for direct labour is found in those industries where:

1. The speed of production cannot be influenced by the energy or dexterity of the worker.
2. The quality of work is of paramount importance.
3. It is difficult to measure the work done by the employee.

From the point of view of the worker, the straight time method has both advantages and disadvantages. Workers have feelings of security and certainty which appeal to them. They can depend upon a definite wage or salary regardless of the amount of work completed or the efficiency of their work, provided it is above the minimum requirements. However, this wage system does not give proper recognition or reward to efficient workers whose productivity is above the average of the other workers. There is little incentive to achieve better or superior performance.

From the employer's view-point, time wage systems are easy to compute and understand and provide economy in time-keeping and payroll recording. But on the other hand, constant supervision is required, otherwise considerable wasted time may be paid for. Among the workers, the inefficient workers receive the same wages as the efficient workers, thus tending to cause dissatisfaction and frustration among the workers and increasing the labour cost per unit produced.

The time basis is still the most popular wage system for workers, such as clerks, accountants, stenographers, factory helpers, members of the supervisory staff and officers whose work cannot be standardised and measured satisfactorily. This is preferred by skilled and efficient workers with whom the quality of work is a more important factor than volume of production.

Piece Work

Under this method, a fixed rate is paid for each unit produced, job performed or number of operations completed, and the worker's wages thus depend upon his output and not upon the time he spends in the factory.

Piece-rates are of advantage to management in the following respects:

1. Managerial supervision is not much needed for production, since each worker assumes responsibility for his own time output.
2. Higher production reduces overhead costs per unit of output.
3. Labour costs can be computed in advance of production with the aid of fixed-rate unit or job.
4. Labour control becomes easier by isolating workers whose work is inefficient and below the minimum standard requirements.

Piece work has some limitations too. It attaches more premium to the quantity than the quality of work. It has the tendency of increasing imperfections, spoiled work, and detectives and higher depreciation costs result because of considerable wear and tear of plant and machinery. Also, this system does not maintain a regular wage for the employee.

To avoid the limitations of straight or simple piece work system, a guarantee is normally provided in the system that the employee's wages shall not fall below a certain minimum figure. This is known as "piece-rates with guaranteed day rate". Under this method, the worker receives a straight piece-rate for the number of pieces produced, provided that his total wage is greater than his earnings on a time-rate basis. When the piece-rate earnings fall below this level, the time-rate earnings are paid instead. An alternative form of the methods is the guaranteed time rate (per hour, day or week), plus a piece-rate payment for output above a stated minimum. Labour cost per piece decreases with increasing production until piece-rate earnings exceed the guarantee, therefore, the labour cost per piece remains constant.

INCENTIVE WAGE PLANS

The basic purpose of an incentive wage is to induce a worker to produce more so that he can earn a higher wage and, at the same time, unit costs can be reduced. Incentive wage plans aim to ensure greater output, to help control over labour costs by minimisation of total cost for a given volume of production and to have a basis for reward from hours served to work accomplished.

Incentive wage scheme has the following objectives:

1. Uninterrupted and higher production without any dispute between the labour and management.
2. Stability in labour turnover.

3. Reducing labour absenteeism.
4. Developing cooperation, mutual trust, attitude of team work among workers and between workers and supervisory staff.
5. Control of labour cost and reduction in labour cost unit of output.
6. Improving administrative efficiency.
7. Accurate budgeting through reliable labour cost information.
8. Generating workers' satisfaction by avoiding work stoppages, slow down, and by providing incentive schemes.

The following are the essentials (desirable characteristics) of a successful incentive wage plan:

1. A wage incentive system should be based upon standards of performance—time and motion studies, job evaluation, and merit rating.
2. The incentive plan should be understood by all employees before installation (or hiring).
3. All direct labour tasks should be on an incentive basis.
4. Only standard or acceptable quality production should be considered while determining the bonus.
5. Once the standard is set, it should not be changed unless the method changes.
6. The incentive programme must be fairly and intelligently administered.
7. It is highly desirable that indirect personnel participate in the incentive plan.
8. A high reward should be paid for performance above standard.
9. Individual incentives should be used wherever it is possible to do so.
10. Minimum wage should be guaranteed to every worker.
11. The views of both employers and employees should be considered while designing incentive schemes.
12. The cost of establishing and operating the incentive plans should be reasonable.
13. The incentive plans should help in standard cost and budgetary control programmes.

Incentive wage plans involve wage rates based upon various combinations of output and time and are known as "differential piece-rates" and "bonus plans" as well. Generally, the following types of incentive plans are used:

1. Taylor Differential Piece-rate System
2. Merrick Differential Piece-rate System
3. Gantt Task Bonus Plan
4. Premium Bonus Plans (Halsey, Halsey-Weir, Rowan, Bedaux, Emerson, etc.)

Taylor Differential Piece-rate System

Under this system, there are two wage rates, a low one for output below standard and a higher one for above standard performance. The system aims to discourage below average workers by providing no guaranteed hourly wage and by setting low piece-rates for low-level production, and a high-rate resulting in high earnings if an efficient level of production is attained. For example, in a factory, workers earn ₹240 per eight hour day and that production averages 12 units per hour per worker or ₹2.50 per unit. The Taylor system might suggest a pay of ₹2 per unit if the worker averaged 14 units or less per hour, but ₹3 per unit to workers averaging 15 units or more per hour. The main advantages of the Taylor system are that it provides a strong incentive to the efficient worker, and is simple to understand and operate. But the incentive level may be set so high that it cannot attract most workers.

Merrick Differential Piece-rate System

This is an improvement over the Taylor system and depends on using three rates instead of two as in the Taylor system. Normal piece-rates are paid on output, when it does not exceed 83% of the standard output. 110% of normal piece-rate are paid when the output is between 83% and 100%, and 120% of the normal piece-rate is paid if the output is above 100%.

The Merrick system is useful to highly-efficient workers as it provides incentives for higher production. Similarly, it takes into account the less-efficient worker who can at least achieve 83% of the standard output. This minimum output is probably achievable by all workers.

Gantt Task and Bonus Plan

This system combines a guaranteed time-rate with a bonus and piece-rate plan using the differential piece-rate principle. Remuneration under the plan is computed as follows:

Output	*Payment*
1. Output below standard (high task)	Time-rate (guaranteed)
2. Output at standard	Bonus @ 20% on the time-rate
3. Output above standard	High piece-rate on worker's whole output

This plan provides incentives and opportunities to those who reach high-level production. At the same time, it provides security and encouragement to less-skilled workers. It is simple to understand and workers are also satisfied in which they receive the total reward for their efforts. A limitation of the plan is the tendency on the part of trade unions to demand a high fixed guaranteed time-rate. But the incentive element of the plan would be lost in case too high a rate is fixed.

Premium Bonus Plans

Under the time-rates basis, any additional production above normal levels benefits the employer, whereas with the piece-rates system the benefit goes to the employee (apart from indirect benefits to the employer). Bonus plans have been developed to produce a compromise, in which any savings are shared between employer and employee. The following are the principal schemes under premium bonus plans.

Halsey Premium Plan

The principle of the Halsey scheme is that the worker receives a fixed proportion of any time which he can save by completing the job in less than the allowed time. The most common fixed proportion is 50%, but this can be varied. This plan ensures that the employee receives time wages until he produces in less than standard time. For above standard production, savings are shared with the employer with the result that the rate of increase happens to be lower for the employee. The cost per unit decreases when production exceeds standard.

Halsey-Weir Plan

This plan is also known as the Wier Premium Scheme and is based on a $33\frac{1}{2} : 66\frac{2}{3}$ sharing plan. Under this scheme, the total emoluments of a worker are the aggregate of guaranteed hourly wages for actual time worked, plus the amount of bonus at the rate of $33\frac{1}{3}$% of the time saved. Bonus is allowed at the same hourly rate at which he shall be paid for actual time worked.

Rowan Plan

This scheme is similar to the Halsey plan in which a standard time is fixed for the completion of a job and the bonus is paid in respect of the time saved. But a ceiling is applied to the size of the bonus. The bonus hours are calculated as a proportion of the time taken which the time saved bears to the time allowed, and is paid for at time-work rates. The bonus may be computed as follows:

$$\text{Bonus} = \frac{\text{Times taken}}{\text{Time allowed}} \times \text{Time saved} \times \text{Time rate}$$

Bedaux Point Plan

Under the Bedaux point plan, a guaranteed hourly rate is paid until standard production is attained, and a premium or additional wage is paid for units in excess of standard. Instead of being paid as piece-rate, an hour's work is converted to points by dividing a standard hour's production in units into 60 minutes. In other words, if 10 units are standard, then each unit is 6 points and if 15 units are standard then each units is 4 points. At standard performance, the worker produces a point per minute and for the first 60 points produced in an hour, the worker receives the hourly rate. For excess production, it is common practice to pay the worker 75% of the rate, and the foremen, supervisors and other indirect labour personnel receive 25% of the rate.

Emerson Efficiency Plan

Under the Emerson plan, a minimum daily wage is guaranteed and a standard time is determined for each job or operation. During each payroll period, a record is kept of the hours worked and the units produced, and the efficiency of each employee is then determined by dividing actual hours into the standard time for the units produced. For example, if the standard is 10 units per hour and a worker produces 320 units in an 80-hour week, the standard time for his output is 32 hours and he has worked at 80% efficiency. Below 67% efficiency, the worker is paid his hourly rate, and from 67% up to 100% efficiency, step bonus rates apply. Above 100% efficiency, an additional bonus of 1% of the hourly rate is paid for each 1% increase in efficiency.

Groups Bonus Schemes

Where a group of workers is collectively responsible for manufacturing a product, it may not be possible to adopt individual incentive schemes. The production of the workers as a whole is measured, and the total bonus determined by one of the individual incentive schemes is capable of group application. The computed bonus can then be shared equally, or between workers of different skills in differing specified proportions. A group bonus scheme has the following objectives:

1. Developing collective interest and team spirit among all workers and employees.
2. Developing interest among foremen and supervisors to improve performance.
3. Reducing spoilage in materials consumption.
4. Reducing idle time.
5. Achieving maximum production at minimum cost.
6. Motivating workers to produce more to get bonus on the basis of team performance.

Group bonus schemes may be employed:

1. where individual output cannot be measured, but that of a group of worker can, for example, on a production line.

2. where output depends less upon the efforts of particular individuals, and more upon the combined efforts of a group, department, or even of the whole undertaking; or
3. where the management wishes to encourage a team spirit.

The following types of group bonus schemes are in common use:

Budgeted Expenditure Bonus

In this scheme, the value of bonus depends upon savings in actual expenditure as compared with the budget. This scheme can be applied to indirect workers and staff besides direct workers.

Cost Efficiency Bonus

This bonus is allowed for savings in specific costs, for example, labour cost or materials cost.

Priestman System

This is a system used in foundries in which a production standard is fixed every month for the entire work. Where production exceeds the standard, workers receive during the following month additional pay equal to the percentage in output over standard. Where production does not exceed standard, no bonus is paid though time rates are guaranteed.

Towne Gain-sharing System

This method, introduced by H.R. Towne in the USA, is based on the principle that bonus consists of half the reduction in labour cost below standard. The bonus is divided between foremen and operatives, but as it is generally paid half-yearly; it tends to be ineffectual as an incentive to individual effort. The payment to foremen and supervisory staff, however, encourages them to reduce labour costs.

In India, payment of bonus, under the Payment of Bonus Act 1965, is compulsory, although the amount of bonus may vary from company to company. A minimum bonus of 8.33% is payable whether a company has earned profit or not. The amount of minimum bonus is generally treated as an item of direct labour cost. However, the amount exceeding the minimum bonus is an appropriation of profit. Bonus linked with productivity is treated as an item of overhead cost.

Profit Sharing and Co-partnership

Profit sharing schemes are schemes in which there is an agreement between the employer and his workers whereby he pays them in addition to wages, a pre-determined share of the profits of undertaking. Co-partnership or co-ownership confers upon employees the opportunity to share in the capital of the business and to receive that part of the profits that accrue to their share of ownership. Both profit sharing and co-partnership schemes recognise the contribution of employees in the profit of the business firm.

These schemes, however, suffer from the following limitations:

1. Lazy and inefficient workers share equally with hard-working and efficient workers.
2. When the share is paid to the workers in cash they tend to regard it merely as a bonus, and not as a share of the result achieved jointly by themselves and their employers.
3. It is difficult to determine the share of profits to be given to each worker and there may be a certain amount of distrust about declared profits also.
4. The additional earnings under these plans are relatively small and may appear to the workers totally insignificant.

5. The share of profits to be paid to workers may be reduced by bad management.
6. Distribution of the benefit under schemes is done normally once in a year. Therefore, employees do not have much interest in it.
7. Sometimes, this scheme is restricted to employees who have a specified number of years of service in the factory. Thus, this creates dissatisfaction among the newer and younger employees who also have contributed to the profits of the year.
8. The workers share in the good years, but do not bear their share of losses incurred in other years.

Bonus Schemes for Indirect Workers

Indirect work cannot be measured as accurately as the direct work. If only direct workers are paid on incentive scheme, this may create considerable disappointment among indirect workers. Therefore, incentive schemes may be introduced for indirect workers as well, either to increase the efficiency of the services they provide to direct labour or to induce foremen and supervisory staff to increase department efficiency and to reduce costs.

WORK STUDY

The successful operation of incentive wage schemes depends on making a proper work study. Work study is the study of job, methods and equipment to ensure that the best way to do the job has been followed by a worker. Work study consists of two complementary techniques or methods: (i) methods study, and (ii) work measurement.

Method Study

Method study is done to improve methods of production and to achieve the most effective use of materials, manpower and plant. The following stages are involved in methods study:

1. First of all, work for the purpose of methods study should be selected. Generally, methods study is done in jobs which involve complexity and costly operations.
2. After selecting a particular job or work, details about the work should be gathered, such as purpose, location, sequence, relationship with the other work, methods of working, operators and facilities, etc.
3. After studying the relevant details of a work, an improved method should be developed for effectiveness, efficiency and operational simplicity. Unnecessary operations and activities should be avoided. An improved method might change the location and sequence of work, production methods and layout.
4. The method so developed should be used for the job or work for which it has been designed.
5. Follow-up is necessary to enquire as to whether the improved method is being implemented in practice and to find out deviations, if any.

Methods study ensures efficient and maximum use of resources like material, labour, plant facilities; it improves the production methods by reducing/eliminating the work content and unnecessary methods; and it attains the maximum production which is good for the firm as well as the workers.

Work Measurement

Work measurement aims at determining the effective time required to perform the work. The ineffective, wasteful or avoidable time is separated from effective required time to complete the work. The effective time so established in work measurement can be used for the following purposes:

1. Incentive wage schemes which require time taken for completing a work.
2. Improving utilisation of men, machines and materials.
3. Assisting in production control.
4. Setting labour standards.
5. Achieving the objectives of cost control and cost reduction.

The following stages are involved in work measurement:

1. Selection of the work.
2. Measuring the actual time taken in the work done.
3. The total time so established for a job should be adjusted for fatigue, time taken in setting the tools, idleness involved in the work itself, etc.

The standard time is further considered to know the time saved under incentive schemes and to determine the wage rate at the incentive level. This is explained with the help of the following example:

	Minutes Per Job
Time before incentive schemes	50
Allowances 10%	5
Basic or standard time	55
Time saved under incentive conditions (20%)	11
Time under incentive conditions	44

JOB EVALUATION AND MERIT RATING

Job Evaluation

Job evaluation is the technique of analysis and assessment of jobs to determine their relative value within the firm so that a fair wage and salary structure can be established for the various job positions. In other words, job evaluation aims at providing a rational and equitable basis for differential salaries and wages for different classes of workers. Following are the objectives (or benefits) of job evaluation:

1. It aims at developing a systematic and rational wage structure as well as job structure.
2. It aims at establishing consistency between the wage and salary structure adopted within the firm and that of other firms within the industry or geographical area.
3. Controversies and disputes relating to salary between the employers and employees can be settled by designing job evaluation techniques within the firm which can satisfy employers and employees both.
4. Wage and salary structure established on the basis of job evaluation will be fair, reliable and satisfying to the employees. Employees' skills, efforts and competence are properly considered in determining wage rates.
5. Stability and fairness in the wage and salary structure are very useful for the administration which can formulate business policies and plans as workers cooperation is fully ensured.

6. Job evaluation discloses characteristics and conditions relating to different jobs and these job requirements are very helpful at the time of recruiting the workers. The employment department can appoint only those workers who are found suitable in terms of such job requirements.

Methods of Job Evaluation

Methods of job evaluation can be listed as follows:

Point Ranking Method

Under this method, each job is analysed in terms of job factors. Job factors may consist of elements like skill, effort, working conditions, hazards, responsibility etc.. However, different job factors may emerge in different jobs. After specifying job factors, each of them is assigned weightage or points depending on its value for the job. For example, in a particular job, education may be given the higher point as compared to supervision, if the job requires a high degree of education. Finally, the jobs are ranked in the order of points or weights secured by them. Grades are further developed for these different weightages so that wage rates or wage structure can be suitably designed for them. For example, the following wage scales can be worked-out depending on the weights grade.

Weights or Points	*Grade*	*Salary Scale (₹)*
50–100	I	10,000–15,000
151–200	II	15,000–20,000
201–250	III	20,000–30,000
251–300	IV	30,000–40,000
301–350	V	40,000–50,000
351–400	VI	50,000–60,000
401–450	VII	60,000–80,000
451–500	VIII	80,000–1,00,000

This method is theoretically sound and objective, but it is difficult to operatc. The relative weights and points of different job factors need to be developed very carefully and in an objective manner.

Ranking Method

The ranking method only requires that different jobs in an organisation should be rearranged in an order which can be done either from the lowest to the highest or in the reverse. Before doing ordering of jobs, all jobs should be properly studied in terms of job requirements, worker's qualification, responsibilities, working conditions, etc. Finally, wage scales are determined in terms of ranks.

This method is very simple to operate, less costly and easy to understand. However, this method may be useful for small organisations only, where jobs are few and well-defined. But in a large organisation where jobs are complex and highly involved, this method cannot be beneficial.

Grading Method

This method is an improvement over the ranking method. Under this method, a hypothetical scale or standard of job values is determined, and each job after being analysed in terms of a pre-determined grade, is given a grade or class. Pre-determined grades or yardsticks are formulated after examining existing jobs in the enterprise. The grades or the class should be established after making an investigation of job factors, such as complexity in the job, supervision, responsibility, education, etc.

This method is simple, less costly and administratively feasible. It attempts at applying a rational basis for grading jobs.

Merit Rating

Merit rating is the comparative evaluation and analysis of the individual merits of the employees. It analyses the differences in performance between employees who are working on similar jobs and would therefore earn the same wages. In this task, merit rating accomplishes more than job evaluation. Merit rating has the following objectives:

1. To evaluate the merit of an employee for the purpose of promotion, increment, reward and other benefits.
2. To establish and develop a wage system and incentive scheme.
3. To determine the suitability of an employee for a particular job.
4. To analyse the merits (or demerits) of a worker and help him in developing his capability and competence for the job.

The characteristics and factors that are considered in merit appraisal of the workers are the following:

1. Cooperation
2. Quality of work done
3. Attendance and regularity
4. Education, skill and experience
5. Character and integrity
6. Initiative

Merit rating is beneficial to the business enterprise and the workers. It increases the output, improves labour-management relations, and encourages workers to have fair competition among themselves. However, merit rating has the following drawbacks;

1. The rating of employees may be subjective and this creates dissatisfaction among them.
2. Evaluators or raters tend to give much premium to past ratings of an employee who might have improved himself in the course of time.
3. Rates may be influenced by raters' own attitudes and self-made rating factors which are not consistent with the merit rating process. Incentives schemes may not be introduced advantageously if merit rating is inaccurate, unreliable and subjective.

Differences Between Job Evaluation and Merit Rating

Job evaluation and merit rating differ on the following counts:

1. Job evaluation is the assessment of the relative worth of jobs within a business enterprise and merit rating is the assessment of the relative worth of an employee with respect to a job. In other words, job evaluation rates the jobs, but merit rating rates employees on their jobs.
2. Job evaluation helps in establishing a rational wage and salary structure. But merit rating helps in fixing fair wages for each worker in terms of his competence and performance.
3. Job evaluation brings uniformity in wage and salary rates. But merit rating aims at providing a fair rate of pay for different workers on the basis of their performances.

TIME AND MOTION STUDY

Time study determines the time spent on each element of a job. The total time taken by all elements (stages) of a job is called the standard time. This standard time is the time which should be taken by an average employee to complete a job under standard (normal) working conditions.

Motion study implies dividing the work into fundamental elements or basic operations of a job or a process for the purpose of eliminating unnecessary (defective) elements or operations in a job. After investigating all movements in a job, process, or operation, it finds out the most scientific and systematic method of performing the operation or completing the job. Thus, time study fixes the standard time for a job or process, and motion study eliminates wasteful motions or the movement of a worker on the job. Both are complementary to each other.

Objectives

Following are the objectives of time and motion study:

1. Eliminating unnecessary motions, fatigue and improving human efforts.
2. Improving method, procedure, techniques and process relating to a job.
3. Utilising effectively materials, machines, human resources and other facilities.
4. Improving working environment, layout and design of plant and equipment.

Benefits

Time and motion study is quite beneficial to the management in the following respects:

1. Proper and fuller utilisations of materials, plant, labour and other resources.
2. Help in assessment of labour requirements.
3. Setting of labour cost standards and control of the labour cost.
4. Determination of fair-wage rates and effective wage incentive schemes.
5. Preparation of labour budgets.
6. Standardising jobs, equipments and methods by determining the best method of operating in the time set.
7. Improvement in work methods by comparing the time taken to complete the same type of work under different possible methods.
8. Proper planning and effective cost control.

LABOUR TURNOVER

Labour turnover is the rate at which employees leave employment at a factory and is normally measured as the ratio of the number of persons leaving in a period to the average number on the payroll. For example, if 100 persons leave a company in a year and the average number on the payroll is 500, labour turnover is expressed as 20% p.a. In this calculation, all persons who leave must be included, whether they leave voluntarily or are dismissed and irrespective of whether they are replaced. There are three methods of calculating of labour turnover.

1. Separation Method = $\dfrac{\text{No. of employees leaving during the year}}{\text{Average number of employees on roll during the period}} \times 100$

2. Replacement Method = $\dfrac{\text{No. of employees replaced}}{\text{Average number of employees on roll during the period}} \times 100$

3. Flux Method = $\dfrac{\text{No. of employee leaving + No. of employees replaced i.e. new employees}}{\text{Average number of employees on roll during the period}} \times 100$

or

Flux Method (with new recruitment) =

$$\frac{\text{No. of separation + No. of replacement + No. of new recruitments}}{\text{Average number of workers}} \times 100$$

Among the three methods, the first method is to be preferred, as it is more appropriately a long-term indicator. This formula is more satisfactory as management is primarily concerned with the loss of labour, after money has been spent on training. The effects of a high- or low-turnover rate should then be analysed, e.g., on training costs, on production efficiency and employee morale.

Causes of Labour Turnover

Labour turnover is caused by many factors which may be listed as follows:

Avoidable Causes

These causes may be eliminated by taking suitable measures by the business firm. Avoidable causes are the following:

1. Low wages and earnings.
2. Unsatisfactory working conditions.
3. Bad relations among workers and between workers and supervisor.
4. Existence of rival trade unions in the organisation.
5. Unsuitability of job.
6. Lack of conveyance, accommodation, medical, educational facilities, recreational amenities, etc.

Unavoidable Causes

Sometimes, workers have to leave the organisation because of management requirements and actions. These are known as unavoidable causes and may be described as follows:

1. Termination of service due to misbehaviour, indiscipline, etc.
2. Retrenchment or lay off due to shortage of resources, low demand, seasonal nature of business.

Personal Causes

Sometimes, workers leave the organisation at their own will and management can do nothing in this regard. These are known as personal factors which are the following:

1. Change for better job
2. Death
3. Retirement due to old age and ill health
4. Family troubles and constraints
5. Change for a better place or environment.

Cost of Labour Turnover

The cost of labour turnover consists of two elements:

1. Preventive costs
2. Replacement costs

Preventive Costs

Preventive costs include all those costs which are incurred to prevent workers from leaving the organisation and keeping them satisfied. Preventive costs may broadly be of the following types:

1. *Personnel administration* A part of personnel administration costs may be incurred to establish a good relationship between the management and the employees and to remove workers' grievances. These costs are known as preventive costs.
2. *Medical and health care* The costs incurred for providing medical benefits to the workers and their families are included in the labour turnover costs.
3. *Welfare measures* Welfare measures include facilities like sports, educational facilities, transport, housing, cooperative stores, canteens. The availability of those facilities prevents workers from leaving the organisation and keeps them satisfied.
4. *Wage and retirement benefits* These include facilities like pension, provident fund, gratuity, bonus, incentive schemes etc. If an organisation has provided these benefits, the rate of labour turnover will be appreciably reduced.

Replacement Costs

Replacement costs include the costs which are incurred for the recruitment and training of new workers. Also, they cover costs which arise as a result of wastages, losses, lower production because of less competent and inexperienced new employees. Broadly, they include the following items:

1. *Personnel department expenses* The personnel department has to recruit new workers in case of high labour turnover, and therefore, the costs of the personnel department goes up.
2. *Cost of training of new workers* New workers are first to be given necessary trainings before they are given regular jobs. Also, production time is lost during the training of the workers.
3. *Inefficiency of new workers* New employees are comparatively less efficient, and therefore, production is adversely affected.
4. *Delay in getting new workers* It takes times to find new workers who will be suitable for the jobs. In the meantime, existing employees may be given overtime which is again a burden on the organisation.
5. *Cost of breakages of tools and equipments* New workers, being inexperienced, break more tools than the old experienced workers. Sometimes, machine break-down may occur and hamper production.
6. *Costs of spoilage and defectives* More spoilage and defectives are likely to occur due to mishandling and carelessness of the new workers. The greater the spoilage and defectives, the larger will be the cost of production.

Measures to Reduce Labour Turnover

Turnover can rarely be traced to one single cause and is usually the result of a combination of a number of causes. The management after knowing the reasons for labour turnover should frame suitable policies and take action to reduce the turnover rate. An appropriate Labour Turnover Accounting can be adopted to manage labour turnover efficiently and effectively. Labour turnover accounting implies the identification, measurement and monitoring of labour turnover data. More specifically, this would include the regular cost measurement of labour turnover and the implementation of a labour turnover cost control programme. Knowledge about the true costs of labour turnover will stimulate management to take appropriate action to reduce its cost.

Job enrichment, "human relations" training for managers, and effective communication throughout the company are vital in reducing labour turnover. Job enrichment means that jobs should, wherever possible, be restructured so that employees have opportunities to increase their skill, use their initiative, and assume more responsibility for their work.

Managers should be given training in "human relations" and "management". Any improvement in personnel relations between management and employees will not only bring out improvement in industrial relations within the company but will also reduce the rate of labour turnover.

Furthermore, effective communication throughout the business firm will help control the high rate of labour turnover. There is great need to provide people with information on the affairs of the enterprise where they are working and on matters affecting their working conditions and future employment prospects.

TREATMENT OF LABOUR COST-RELATED ITEMS

Overtime

Overtime is the time put in by employees and work done by them beyond normal hours of work. According to the Factories Act 1948, every worker is to be paid overtime at a higher rate, generally at double the normal wage rate, if he is required to work for more than 8 hours a day. In case the Factories Act is not applicable in some situations, it is the practice to pay to workers for overtime work at higher rate. The excess over normal wage rate is called overtime premium. In cost accounting, the overtime premium is separated from regular earnings and consideration must be given to the reasons for the overtime payment to decide as to how they should be treated in cost accounts.

Treatment of Overtime Premium

The treatment of overtime premium is decided in terms of factors and reasons which have caused overtime work. They are explained as follows:

1. Accepting rush orders which cannot be finished in regular working hours, and therefore, overtime work becomes necessary. In this case, since the overtime work is due to one particular order, the overtime premium should be charged to that particular order or job. Also, payment for such overtime work should be recovered from the customer who has given such an order. That is, the contract price for the job would include the overtime premium factor.
2. Scheduling more production than the production which can be completed in normal working hours. For example, a company with a normal capacity of 8,000 units to be completed in 800 labour hours decides to produce 10,000 units which require 1,000 labour hours, 200 overtime hours are necessary. Such overtime work may be caused due to temporary higher demand, higher seasonal demand or due to company's own decision for additional production. In this case, the overtime premium will be charged to each of 10,000 units completed during the period. Overtime

premium cannot be charged to only 2,000 units that have to be completed after regular working hours.

3. Overtime work may become necessary because of abnormal circumstances, that is, factors which are beyond the control of management, such as fire, flood, etc. In this case, the overtime premium is transferred to the Costing Profit and Loss Account and is not charged to the units or jobs completed.
4. Overtime work may be caused due to fault or delay of another department in the organisation. In this case, the overtime premium is charged to the department which is at fault or is responsible for the delay.

Overtime payments made to workers engaged in direct labour are treated as direct labour cost and charged to the jobs or units completed. Overtime payments made to indirect labour are the part of factory overheads, overtime payments made to the staff of administrative departments are treated as administrative overheads and overtime payments made to the staff of selling and distribution departments are treated as selling and distribution overheads.

Idle Time

Where workers are remunerated on a time basis, some difference between the time for which they are paid and that which they actually spend upon production is bound to arise. This difference is known as idle time, and represents the time for which the employer must pay but from which he obtains no direct advantage. Idle time does not include holidays, leave, etc. Idle time may be normal or abnormal.

Normal Idle Time

Normal idle time is that idle time which is unavoidable, of normal nature, and inherent in a production or work environment. Normal idle time is caused by factors such as:

1. Time lost in moving from one job to another.
2. Time lost in waiting for materials or instructions.
3. Time taken in getting from the gate of the factory to the department in which the worker is engaged and the reverse journey at the end of the day.
4. Temporary absence from duty because of minor accidents, personal needs, tea-breaks, etc.

The wastage of time due to the above factors cannot be avoided, and therefore, idle time must be accepted as implied in production. Under the above situations, idle time will be of normal variety and constitute a legitimate charge to factory overhead. Thus, payment made for idle time is part of the cost of a product or job.

Abnormal Idle Time

Abnormal idle time is that time which is not caused by or connected with the usual routine of manufacture. The time wasted may represent abnormal idle time. The loss (or expenses) incurred and caused by abnormal conditions, cannot be regarded as part of the cost of the product and should be transferred to the Costing Profit and Loss Account. Examples of abnormal idle time would be:

1. Time lost through the breakdown of machinery due to the inefficiency of the work engineers or to the failure of the power supply.
2. Time lost through lack of materials occasioned by the slackness of the store-keeper in notifying the buying department of his requirements.

3. Bottlenecks in production, resulting in a temporary absence of parts for further processing.
4. Strike, lock-out, fire, wind, water damage, etc.

Fringe Benefits

An employee's salary or wage normally consists of basic wages, dearness allowance, house rent allowance, city compensatory allowance, etc. Besides the salary, workers are provided some indirect cash or fringe benefits, such as vacation and holiday pay, workmen's compensation insurance, pension costs, hospitalisation benefits, group insurance, sick pay, overtime and night shift premium, profit sharing bonus. These indirect benefits constitute fringe benefits. They tend to improve employee morale, loyalty and stability. The cost of these benefits is treated as a direct charge to production by using a supplemental wage rate. Alternatively, they are treated as factory overhead.

Shift Premium

Payment of higher hourly rates for evening and night shifts is a common feature. Treatment of shift premium follows the same reasoning as overtime premium. Where shift premium is needed to meet the requirements of a particular order or job, the additional cost should be charged to the job concerned and is accordingly excluded from production overhead. When shift premium is incurred in order to increase the output as a whole, the premium element should be separated from direct wages and treated as a production overhead. In this case, similar operations should carry the same cost, regardless of when they were performed. and should be spread over all units manufactured.

Holiday and Vacation Pay

Most employees are entitled to statutory holidays or compulsory holiday such as Independence Day, Republic Day, etc. Payments which are made to an employee while he is absent on vacation and holidays, are accrued monthly and spread out over the year's production. The total amount is charged to the full year's overhead expense. In this way, no single period is forced to carry the whole burden. This should not be treated otherwise because the number of holidays varies from month to month. If the expenses are apportioned monthly on the month's production, the cost of production in a particular month would be too heavy as compared with the costs in other months, when there are no holidays.

Alternatively, an inflated rate of direct wages can be used to absorb both the normal weekly wages and the appropriate part of holidays.

Learners' or Apprentices' Wages

In many plants, new workers receive some preliminary training before they can become economically productive. Apprentices generally take more time than skilled workers to perform a given task and they are likely to cause more scrap. On the other hand, they are paid a lower rate per hour. The wages of workers under training, who cannot normally make any real contribution to production, should be treated as production overhead and should be charged to the annual output through inclusion in the factory overhead rates.

In case of unusual training programmes due to the opening of a new plant or the activities of a second or third shift, a case can be made for treating the training cost as development or starting load cost and deferring a portion of the cost over a considerable period of time or over the life of the contract.

Attendance Bonuses

Sometimes, workers who perform the full number of shifts in a working week, or who lose no time over a stated period, are entitled to an attendance bonus. Such bonuses are part of wages and sometimes are treated as direct wages and charged by means of an inflated direct wages rate. Alternatively, they may be treated as a production overhead. In process or contracting industries, they may properly be charged direct to the process concerned.

Leave with Pay

In a factory, workers are entitled to annual leave with full pay for some days in a year. Besides, medical leave, casual leave, earned leave, special leave, etc. are also available. It is not generally treated as a direct charge to a product or job but as factory overhead and recovered through departmental overhead rates. Alternatively, an inflated rate of direct wages cost can be applied to absorb both normal wages and an appropriate portion of leave with pay.

Employer's Contribution to Insurance

The employer's share of insurance for the employees engaged in manufacturing is treated as production overhead. When a contractor's employees tend to remain on one job for many weeks at a time, it is possible to treat the contributions as a direct charge to the contract concerned. In the case of process workers too, it is frequently possible to charge insurance contributions direct to the process. Also, an inflated direct labour rate can be employed so as to absorb the contributions, but this practice is rarely followed.

Casual Workers

Casual workers should be issued clock cards to show the number of hours worked. If casual workers are engaged on specific production or jobs, they should be treated as direct charge to the specific production. If these workers are performing indirect work, it should be treated as overhead expense. Due care should be exercised by the wage department in making payment to casual workers. The clock cards should be properly signed by the foremen and forwarded to the wages department for payment.

Out-Workers

In some trades, for example, in knit wear and in manufacturing lampshades certain work is performed by workers in their own homes. In such cases, there is no need to maintain time records as the workers are paid according to the work they complete. However, control should be exercised over out-workers in the following respects.

1. Issue of materials to out-workers and its comparison with the finished output.
2. Inspection of the output and rejection of the defective work.
3. Return of the output within the agreed time so as to fulfil customer's orders and contracts.

Outside Workers

Outside workers are employees working outside the factory on building sites or moving from place to place on small installations or repair work. If these employees report to the factory first for instructions, their arrival times can be recorded. But if they go direct to the site, it may be necessary for them to complete their own time sheets with some supervision or check on the times. For example, a foreman may travel from site to site or the customer may be asked to sign the time sheet which will form the basis of a charge to him. Where a large number of workers are engaged upon a site for a long period, for example, on a civil engineering contract, it is usual for time recording clocks to be installed at the site. When casual workers are engaged for outside work, a head office clerk should attend to pay these workers. Alternatively, the foreman may be issued a petty cash fund from which to make the payments.

Example 5.1

The three workers—Govind, Ram and Shyam—produced 80, 100 and 120 pieces of a product X respectively on a particular day in May, 2020 in a factory. The time allowed for 10 units of Product X is 1 hour and their hourly rate is ₹4.

Calculate for each of these three workers the following:

(i) Earnings for the day

(ii) Effective rate of earnings per hour under:

(a) Straight piece-rate plan

(b) Halsey premium bonus plan (50% sharing)

(c) Rowan premium bonus plan of labour remuneration.

Solution

Standard production per hour	= 10 units
Hourly rate	= ₹4
Piece rate per unit	= ₹0.40
Normal Production per day of 8 hours	= 8 × 10 units = 80 units

(i) Earning per day under time wage system = 8 hrs × ₹4 per hour = ₹32

(ii) Effective rate of earning per hour

(a) Straight piece-rate plan:

	Earning Per Day	*Effective Earning per Hour (8 Hours Per Day)*
	Total	*Per Hour*
Govind = 80 units × Per hour 0.40	₹32	₹4/-
Ram = 100 units × Per hour 0.40	₹40	₹5/-
Shyam = 120 units × Per hour 0.40	₹48	₹6/-

(b) Halsey premium bonus plan (50% sharing)

Earning = Actual Time Taken × Rate Per Hour + (Std Time – Actual Time)	*× Rate per hour*	*× 50%*
Govind = 8 × 4 + (8 hrs – 8 hrs) × 4 × 50%	₹32	₹4/-
Ram = 8 × 4 + (10 hrs – 8 hrs) × 4 × 50% = (32 + 4)	₹36	₹4.5/-
Shyam = 8 × 4 + (12 hrs –8 hrs) × 4 × 50% = (32 + 8)	₹40	₹5/-

(c) Rowan plan: Time taken × Hourly rate + Bonus

$$\text{Bonus} = \frac{\text{Time saved}}{\text{Standard time}} \times \text{Actual time taken} \times \text{Hourly rate}$$

Govind's Earning	$= 8 \times 4 + \frac{0}{8} \times 8 \times 4 = 32 + 0$	₹32	₹4
Ram	$= 8 \times 4 + \frac{2}{10} \times 8 \times 4 = 32 + 6.4$	₹38.4	₹4.8
Shyam	$= 8 \times 4 + \frac{4}{12} \times 8 \times 4 = 32 + 10.67$	₹42.67	₹5.33

Example 5.2

Standard output in 10 hours is 240 units; actual output in 10 hours is 264 units. Wages rate is ₹10 per hour. Calculate the amount of bonus and total wages under Emerson Plan.

Solution

$$\text{Efficiency percentage} = \frac{264}{240} \times 100 = 110\%$$

As per Emerson plan, in case of above 100% efficiency, bonus of 20% of basic wages plus 1% for each 1% increase in efficiency is admissible.

So, new bonus percentage = 20 + (110 – 100) = 30

$$\text{Total Bonus} = \frac{30}{100}\ (\text{hours worked} \times \text{rate per hour})$$

$$= \frac{30}{100} \times 10 \times 10 = ₹30$$

Total wages = ₹(10 × 10) + 30 = ₹130.

Example 5.3

Standard time for a job is 90 hours. The hourly rate of guaranteed wages is ₹50. Because of the saving in time, a worker A gets an effective hourly rate of wages of ₹60 under Rowan premium bonus system. For the same saving in time, calculate the hourly rate of wages a worker B will get under Halsey premium bonus system assuring 40% to worker.

Solution

Increase in hourly rate of wages (Rowan plan) is (₹60 – ₹50) = ₹10

This is equal to

$$\frac{\text{Time saved}}{\text{Standard time}} \times \text{Hourly rate}$$

$$\text{Or } 10 = \frac{\text{Time saved}}{\text{Standard time}} \times 50$$

$$\text{Or } \frac{\text{Time saved}}{90} \times 50 = 10$$

$$\text{Time saved} = \frac{900}{50} = 18 \text{ Hours}$$

Time taken = (90 – 18) = 72 hours

Effective hourly rate under Halsey system:

Time saved = 18 hours

Bonus @ 40% = 18 × 40% × 50 = ₹360

Total wages = (50 × 72 + 360) = 3,960

Effective hourly rate = 3,960 ÷ 72 Hours = ₹55

EXAMPLE 5.4

A factory has a piece-rate system. Production fixed for a day is 50 units. Remuneration payable to workers is as follows:

(i) Wages ₹5 per piece, subject to a minimum of ₹200 per day
(ii) Dearness allowance – ₹60 per day
(iii) Incentive bonus – up to 80% efficiency – Nil
Above 80% efficiency – ₹40
For every 1% increase in efficiency above 80%
Calculate the earnings of Mr. Amal and Mr. Kamal whose performance for the month of April, 2009 is as under:
Amal worked for 20 days – output 60 units
Kamal works for 24 days – output 1,080 units

Solution

Calculation of Earnings of Mr. Amal and Mr. Kamal

Name	*Days Worked*	*Std Output*	*Actual Output*	*Efficiency*	*Pc. Rate*	*Min. guaranteed*	*Basic*	*D.A*	*Incentive*	*Total (₹)*
Amal	20	1,000	60	0 6%	300	4,000	4,000	1,200		5200
Kamal	24	1,200	1,080	90%	5,400	4,800	5,400	1,440	400	7240

Kamal's incentive 10% increase by ₹40 × 10 hrs. = ₹400

EXAMPLE 5.5

Which is better plan out of Halsey (50% sharing) bonus scheme and Rowan bonus scheme for an efficient worker? In which situation the worker gets same bonus in both schemes?

Solution

Rowan bonus scheme pays more bonus if the time saved is below the 50 per cent of time allowed; and if the time saved is more than 50 per cent of time allowed, then Halsey bonus scheme pays more bonus. Generally, time saved by a worker is not more than 50 per cent of time allowed. So, the Rowan bonus scheme is better for an efficient worker. When the time saved is equal to 50 per cent of time allowed then both plans pays same bonus to a worker.

Bonus under Halsey Plan

$$= \text{Standard wage rate} \times 50/100 \times \text{Time saved} \qquad \text{(i)}$$

Bonus under Rowan Plan

$$= \text{Standard wage rate} \times \frac{\text{Time taken}}{\text{Time allowed}} \times \text{Time taken} \qquad \text{(ii)}$$

Bonus under Halsey plan will be equal to the bonus under Rowan plan when the following condition holds good

$$= \text{Standard wage rate} \times 50/100 \times \text{Time saved}$$

$$= \text{Standard wage rate} \times \frac{\text{Time taken}}{\text{Time allowed}} \times \text{Time saved}$$

or $\frac{1}{2} = \frac{\text{Time taken}}{\text{Time allowed}}$

or Time taken = $\frac{1}{2}$ of time allowed.

Hence, when the time taken is 50% of the time allowed, the bonus under Halsey and Rowan plans is equal.

EXAMPLE 5.6

'X', an employee of ABC Co. gets the following emoluments and benefits:

(i) Basic pay	₹1,000 p.m.
(ii) Dearness allowance	₹200 p.m.
(iii) Bonus	20% of salary and D.A.
(iv) Other allowances	₹250 p.m.
(v) Employee's contribution to P.F.	10% of salary and D.A.

'X' works for 2,400 hours per annum, out of which 400 hours are non-productive and treated as normal idle time.

Find out the effective hourly cost of employee 'X'.

Solution

Statement of Monthly Earnings

Basic pay	1,000
Dearness allowance	200
	1,200
Bonus (20% of salary and D.A)	240
Other allowances	250
	1,690
Provident fund (10% of Basic + DA)	120
	1,810

Yearly salary = 1,810 × 12
= 21,720
Effective hours = 2,400 – 400
= 2,000
Effective hourly cost = 21,720 ÷ 2,000
= ₹10.86 per hour.

If P.F. is not included

Yearly salary = 1,690 × 12
= 20,280
Effective hourly cost = 20,280 ÷ 2,000
= ₹10.14 per hour.

EXAMPLE 5.7

Two workers '*A*' and '*B*' produce the same product using the same material. Their normal wage rate is also the same. '*A*' is paid bonus according to Rowan scheme while '*B*' is paid bonus according to Halsey scheme. The time allowed to make the product is 50 hours. '*A*' takes 30 hours while '*B*' takes 40 hours to complete the product. The factory overhead rate is ₹5 per person-hour actually worked. The factory cost of product manufactured by '*A*' is ₹3,490; and the factory cost for product manufactured by '*B*' is ₹3,600.

Required:

(i) Compute the normal rate of wages.
(ii) Compute the material cost.
(iii) Prepare a statement comparing the factory cost of the product as made by two workers.

Solution

Let *x* be the cost of material and y be the normal rate of wage/hour

	Worker A	*Worker B*
	₹	₹
Material cost	x	x
Labour wages	$30y$	$40y$
Bonus	Rowan system	Halsey system
	$\frac{\text{Time saved}}{\text{Time allowed}} \times \text{hours worked} \times \text{rate}$	Hours saved × 50% × rate
	$= \frac{20}{50} \times 30 \times y = 12y$	$= 10 \times \frac{1}{2} \times y = 5y$
Overheads	30 × 5 = 150	40 × 5 = 200
Factory cost	$x + 42y + 150 = 3{,}490$	$x + 45y + 200 = 3{,}600$
	$\therefore x + 42y = 3{,}340 \text{ – (1)}$	$\therefore x + 45y = 3{,}400 \text{ – (2)}$

Solving (1) and (2), we get
$x = 2{,}500$ and $y = 20$

(i) Normal rate of wages is ₹20 per hour.
(ii) Cost of materials = ₹2,500
(iii) **Comparative Statement of Factory Cost**

	Worker A	*Worker B*
	₹	₹
Material cost	2,500	2,500
Wages	30 × 20 = 600	40 × 20 = 800
Bonus	$\left(\frac{20}{50}\times 30\times 20\right)=240$	$\left(10\times\frac{1}{2}\times 20\right)=100$
Overheads	30 × 5 = 150	40 × 5 = 200
Factory cost	3,490	3,600

EXAMPLE 5.8

The employees in a factory are paid wages at the rate of ₹7 per hour for an eight-hour shift. Each employee produces 5 units per hour. The overhead is ₹10 per direct labour hour. Employees and the management are considering the following piece-rate wage proposal:

Up to 45 units per day of 8 hours	₹1.30 per unit
From 46 units to 50 units	₹1.60 per unit
From 51 units to 55 units	₹1.65 per unit
From 56 units to 60 units	₹1.70 per unit
Above 60 units	₹1.75 per unit

The working hours are restricted to 8 hours per day. Overhead rate does not change with increased production.

Prepare a statement indicating advantages to employees as well as to management of production levels of 40, 45, 55 and 60 units.

for excel template, scan

Solution

Present cost of manufacture:

Wages per hour		₹7
Overhead per hour		₹10
Conversion cost per hour		₹17
Conversion cost per unit	17/5 =	₹3.40

Statement Showing Advantage to Employees

Output	*Time Wages Per Day*	*Piece Wages Per Unit.*	*Per Day*	*Benefit to Employees*
	₹	₹	₹	₹
40	56.00	1.30	52.00	– 4.00
45	56.00	1.30	58.50	+ 2.50
55	56.00	1.65	90.75	+34.75
60	56.00	1.70	102.00	+46.00

Statement Showing Advantage to Management

Output	*Proposed Piece Rate*	*Piece Wages*	*Overhead*	*Proposed Total Cost*	*Total Cost as Per Existing Scheme @ 3.40*	*Savings*
	₹	₹	₹	₹	₹	₹
40	1.30	52.00	80.00	132.00	136.00	+ 4.00
45	1.30	58.50	80.00	138.50	153.00	+ 14.50
55	1.65	90.75	80.00	170.75	187.00	+ 16.25
60	1.70	102.00	80.00	182.00	204.00	+ 22.00

✎ EXAMPLE 5.9

A worker produced 200 units in a week's time. The guaranteed weekly wage payment for 45 hours is ₹81. The expected time to produce one unit is 15 minutes which is raised further by 20% under the incentive scheme. What will be the earnings per hour of that worker under Halsey (50% sharing) and Rowan bonus schemes?

☞ *Solution*

Earning Per Hour under Halsey (50% sharing) Bonus Scheme

$$\text{Time allowed for actual weekly production} = \frac{200 \text{ units} \times 18 \text{ minutes}}{60 \text{ minutes}}$$

$$= 60 \text{ hours}$$

Time saved = Time allowed – Actual time taken

= 60 hours – 45 hours = 15 hours

Earning = (Hours worked × Rate per hour) + 1/2 (Time saved) × Rate per hour

= 45 hours × ₹1.80 + 1/2 × 15 hour × ₹1.80

= ₹81 + ₹13.50 = ₹94.50

$$\text{Earnings (per hour)} = \frac{₹94.50}{45 \text{ hours}} = ₹2.10 \text{ per hour}$$

Earnings Per Hour under Rowan Bonus Scheme

$$\text{Earnings} = \text{Hours worked} \times \text{Rate per hour} + \frac{\text{Time saved}}{\text{Time allowed}} \times \text{Time taken} \times \text{Rate per hour}$$

$$= 45 \text{ hours} \times ₹1.80 + \frac{15 \text{ hours}}{60 \text{ hours}} \times 45 \text{ hours} \times ₹1.80$$

$$\text{Earnings per hour} = \frac{₹101.25}{45 \text{ hour}} = ₹2.25 \text{ per hour}$$

Working Notes:

1. Expected time to produce one unit under incentive scheme = 15 + 20%
 = 18 minutes
2. Wage rate per hour (₹81/45 hours) = ₹1.80

✍ EXAMPLE 5.10

A skilled worker in XYZ Ltd. is paid a guaranteed wage rate of ₹30 per hour. The standard time per unit for a particular product is 4 hours. *P*, a machineman, has been paid wages under the Rowan Incentive Plan and he had earned an effective hourly rate of ₹37.50 on the manufacture of that particular product.

What could have been his total earnings and effective hourly rate, had he been put on Halsey Incentive Scheme (50%)?

☞ *Solution*

Let, *T* hours be the total time worked in hours by the skilled worker (machineman *P*); ₹30 is the rate per hour; standard time is 4 hours per unit and effective hourly-earning rate is ₹37.50, then

$$\text{Earning} = \text{Hours worked} \times \text{Rate per hour} + \frac{\text{Time saved}}{\text{Time allowed}} \times \text{Time taken} \times \text{Rate per hour}$$

(Under Rowan Incentive Plan)

$$₹37.5T = T \times ₹30 + \frac{(4-T)}{4} \times T \times ₹30 = ₹105$$

$$₹37.5 = ₹30 + (4 - T) \times ₹7.5$$

or $₹7.5\,T = ₹22.5$

or $T = 3$ hours

Total Earnings and Effective Hourly Rate of Skilled Worker (machineman *P*) under Halsey Incentive Scheme (50%)

Total earnings = Hours worked × Rate per hour + 1/2 Time saved × Rate per hour

(Under 50% Halsey Incentive Scheme)

= 3 hours × ₹30 + 1/2 × 1 hour × ₹30

$$\text{Effective hourly rate} = \frac{\text{Total earnings}}{\text{Hours taken}} = \frac{₹105}{3 \text{ hours}} = ₹35$$

✍ EXAMPLE 5.11

The finishing shop of a company employs 60 direct workers. Each worker is paid ₹400 as wages per week of 40 hours. When necessary, overtime is worked up to a maximum of 15 hours per week per worker at time rate plus one-half as premium. The current output on an average is 6 units per man hour which may be regarded as standard output. If bonus scheme is introduced, it is expected that the output will increase to 8 units per man hour. The workers will, if necessary, continue to work overtime up to the specified limit although no premium on incentives will be paid.

The company is considering introduction of either Halsey Scheme or Rowan Scheme of Wage Incentive System. The budgeted weekly output is 19,200 units. The selling price is ₹11 per unit and the direct material cost is ₹8 per unit. The variable overheads amount to ₹0.50 per direct labour hour and the fixed overhead is ₹9,000 per week.

Prepare a statement to show the effect on the company's weekly profit of the proposal to introduce (a) Halsey Scheme, and (b) Rowan Scheme.

☞ ***Solution***

Working Notes:

1. Total available hours per week (60 workers × 40 hours) — 2,400
2. Total standard hours required to produce 19,200 units (19,200 units/6 units per hour) — 3,200
3. Total labour hours required after the introduction of bonus scheme to produce 19,200 units (19,200 units/8 units per man hour) — 2,400
4. Time saved in hours (3,200 hours – 2,400 hours) — 800
5. Wage rate per hour (₹) (₹400/40 hours) — 10
6. Bonus:

(i) Halsey Scheme $= \frac{1}{2} \times$ Time saved × Wage rate per hour

$$= \frac{1}{2} \times 800 \text{ hours} \times ₹10 = ₹4{,}000$$

(ii) Rowan Scheme $= \frac{\text{Time saved}}{\text{Time allowed}} \times$ Time taken × Wage rate per hour

$$= \frac{800 \text{ hours}}{3{,}200 \text{ hours}} \times 2{,}400 \text{ hours} \times ₹10$$

$$= ₹6{,}000$$

Statement Showing the Effect on the Company's Weekly Present Profit by the Introduction of Halsey and Rowan Schemes

	Present (₹)	*Halsey* (₹)	*Rowan* (₹)
Sales revenue: (A) (19,200 units × ₹11)	2,11,200	2,11,200	2,11,200
Direct material cost (19,200 units × ₹8)	1,53,600	1,53,600	1,53,600
Direct wages *(Refer to working notes 2 and 3)*	32,000 (3,200 hrs. × ₹10)	24,000 (2,400 hrs. × ₹10)	24,000 (2,400 hrs. × ₹10)
Overtime premium	4,000 (800 hrs. × ₹5)		

(Contd.)

	Present (₹)	*Halsey* (₹)	*Rowan* (₹)
Bonus	–	4,000	6,000
(Refer to working notes 6)			
(i) and (ii) Variable overheads	1,600	1,200	1,200
	(3,200 hrs. × 0.50 P)	(2,400 hrs. × 0.50 P)	(2,400 hrs. × 0.50 P)
Fixed overheads	9,000	9,000	9,000
Total cost: (*B*)	2,00,200	1,91,800	1,93,800
Profit: {(*A*) – (*B*)}	11,000	19,400	17,400

EXAMPLE 5.12

In a factory, Ram and Sham produce the same product using the same input of same material and at the same normal wage rate.

Bonus is paid to both of them in the form of normal time wage rate adjusted by the proportion which time saved bears to the standard time for the completion of the product. The time allotted to the product is fifty hours. Ram takes thirty hours and Sham takes forty hours to produce the product. The factory cost of the product for Ram is ₹3,100 and for Sham ₹3,280. The factory overhead rate is ₹12 per man hour.

Calculate (i) Normal wage rate; (ii) Cost of material used for the product; and (iii) the Input of material if the unit material cost is ₹16.

Solution

Let x be the cost of material and y be the normal rate of wages per hour

Factory Cost of Workman Ram

	₹
Material	x
Wages	$30y$
Bonus ($30y \times 20/50$)	$12y$
Overheads	360
Factory cost	$x + 42y$ + ₹360

Factory Cost of Workman Sham

Material	x
Wages	$40y$
Bonus ($40y \times 10/50$)	$8y$
Overheads	480
	$x + 48y + 480$

The following two equations can be made

$$x + 42y + 360 = ₹3{,}100 \quad \text{(i)}$$

$$x + 48y + 480 = ₹3{,}280 \quad \text{(ii)}$$

On subtracting Eq. (i) from Eq. (ii)

$$6y + 120 = 180$$

or $$6y = 180 - 120$$

$$y = 60/6 = 10$$

On substituting the value of y in Eq. (i)

$$x + 420 + 360 = 3{,}100$$

or $$x = 3{,}100 - 780$$

or $$x = 2{,}320$$

Thus:

(i) Normal wage rate is ₹10 per hour.
(ii) Cost of material used for the product is ₹2,320.
(iii) Input of material is 2,320/16 = 145 units.

EXAMPLE 5.13

A company has its factories at two locations. Rowan plan is in use at location *A* and Halsey plan at location *B*. Standard time and basic rate of wages are same for a job which is similar and is carried out on similar machinery. Time allowed is 60 hours.

Job at location *A* is completed in 36 hours while at *B*, it has taken 48 hours. Conversion costs at respective places are ₹1,224 and ₹1,500. Overheads account for ₹20 per hour.

Required:

(a) To find out the normal wage rate; and
(b) To compare respective conversion costs.

Solution

Let ₹ x per hour be the normal wage rate

∴ Wages at location *A* will be ₹36 x and ₹48 x for location *B*.

Time allowed is 60 hours

Hence, for time saved, bonus will be payable as under

Location A

$$\text{Bonus under Rowan Scheme} = \frac{\text{Time saved}}{\text{Time allowed}} \times \text{hrs worked} \times \text{Rate}$$

$$= \frac{24}{60} \times 36 \times x = ₹14.4x$$

Total wages ₹36 x + ₹14.4 x = ₹50.4 x

Overheads @ ₹20 per hour worked ₹720

Hence, total conversion cost is $50.4\,x + 720$ = ₹1,224 (given)

or $x = 10.$

Location B

Bonus under Halsey plan	=	50% of Time saved × Rate per hour
	=	50% of $12 \times x$ = ₹6 x
Total wages	=	$48\,x$ + ₹6 x = ₹54 x
Overheads ₹20 per hour	=	₹960
Total conversion cost is $54\,x + 960$	=	₹1,500
or x	=	₹10.

Comparative Conversion Cost

Particulars	*A (Rowan)*	*B (Halsey)*
Wages @ ₹10 per hour	₹360	₹480
Bonus	₹144	₹60
Overheads	₹720	₹960
	₹1,224	₹1,500

✎ EXAMPLE 5.14

Following are the particulars for April, 2020 relating to four employees working in Department "*M*" of a factory, exclusively for Job. No. 120.

Name	*Designation*	*Wages (₹)*	*Per*
A	Foreman	8000	month
B	Mechanic	150	day
C	Machine operator	120	day
D	Workman	100	day

The normal working hours per week of six days are 48, or 8 hours per day. Sundays are paid holidays. (There were no other holidays during the month).

Provident Fund contribution was 8% of monthly wages by employee.

Provident Fund contribution was 8% of monthly wages by employer.

Employee State Insurance Contribution was 3% of monthly wages by employee and 5% of monthly wages by employer.

From the foregoing data, calculate:

(a) Net wages payable by the employer for the month;
(b) The total amount of Provident Fund contribution to be deposited by employer;
(c) Employee State Insurance contribution to be deposited by employer;
(d) Total labour cost to the employer for the month of April, chargeable to the job; and
(e) The total cost of the job requiring materials is valued at ₹60,000 and overheads at 50% of prime cost.

☞ ***Solution***

(a) Calculation of Net Wages Payable for the Month

Gross wages for April, 2020	₹	
A Foreman (a) ₹8000 p.m.	8,000	
B Mechanic (a) ₹150 per day × 30 days	4,500	
C Machine Operator @ ₹120 per day × 30 days	3,600	
D Workman (a) ₹100 per day × 30 days	3,000	
		19,100.00
Less: Deductions		
(i) Provident Fund Contribution @ 8% of ₹19100 by employees	1,528	
(ii) ESI Contribution @ 3% of ₹19100 by employees	573	
		2,101.00
Net Wages Payable		16,999.00

(b)	Employer's share of Provident Fund (8% of ₹19,100)	₹1,528
	Employee's share of Provident Fund (8% of ₹19,100)	1,528
	Total amount of Provident Fund contribution to be deposited by employer (both contributions)	3,056
(c)	Employer's share of ESI (5% of ₹19,100)	955
	Employee's share of ESI (3% of ₹19,100)	573
	ESI contribution to be deposited by employer (both contributions)	1,528
(d)	Total labour cost to employer	
	Total gross wage	19,100
	Add: Employer's contribution towards P.F.	1,528
	Employer's contribution towards ESI	955
		21,583
(e)	Total cost of job	
	Material	₹60,000
	Labour cost as per (d) above	21,583
	Prime cost	81,583
	Overheads at 50% of Prime cost	40,791
	Total cost of the job	1,22,374

EXAMPLE 5.15

The Cost Accountant of Tirupati Electronics Ltd. has computed labour turnover rates for the quarter ending 31st March, 2020 as 10%, 5% and 3% respectively under "Flux Method", "Replacement

Method", and "Separation Method". If the number of workers replaced during that quarter is 30, find out the number of (a) workers recruited and joined, and (b) workers left and discharged.

Solution

Computation of Labour Turnover Rate

1. Replacement Method = $\dfrac{\text{Number of replacements}}{\text{Average number of workers}}$

= Putting the values in formula

$$\frac{5}{100} = \frac{30}{\text{Average Number of workers}}$$

Hence, average number of workers = $\dfrac{30 \times 100}{5} = 600$

2. Separation Method $\dfrac{\text{No. of separations}}{\text{Average number of workers}}$

or $= \dfrac{3}{100} = \dfrac{X}{600}$

$X = 18$

3. Flux Method $= \dfrac{\text{Number of separations + Number of additions}}{\text{Average number of workers}}$

$= \dfrac{10}{100} = \dfrac{18 + \text{No. of additions}}{600}$

$= \text{No. of additions} = \dfrac{600 - 1{,}800}{100} = \dfrac{4{,}200}{100}$

$= 42$

Hence, the number of Additions = 42

From the above, the following information as desired by the question can be computed.

(a) Workers recruited and joined = 42
(b) Workers left and discharged = 18

EXAMPLE 5.16

The following information relates to work force in a factory during the year 2019–20:

Number of workers on April 1, 2019	2,350
Number of workers on March 31, 2020	2,850
Number of workers who quit on their own	200
Number of workers who availed golden handshake opportunity	100
Number of workers employed during 2019–20 including those employed due to expansion	800

Calculate annual labour turnover rate and equivalent monthly turnover rate under different methods.

☞ Solution

1. According to Separation Method:
Annual Labour Turnover Ratio

$$= \frac{\text{No. of separations during the year}}{\text{Average No. of workers}} \times 100$$

$$= \frac{200 + 100}{\frac{2{,}350 + 2{,}850}{2}} \times 100 = 11.54\%$$

$$\text{Equivalent monthly rate} = \frac{\text{Annual Labour Turnover Rate}}{12}$$

$$\frac{11.54}{12} = .96\%$$

2. According to Replacement Method:
Annual Labour Turnover Ratio

$$= \frac{\text{Actual No. of replacements}}{\text{Average No. of workers}} \times 100$$

$$= \frac{100}{2{,}600} \times 100 = \frac{100}{26} = 3.85\%$$

$$\text{Equivalent monthly turnover rate} = \frac{\text{Annual labour turnover rate}}{12}$$

$$= \frac{3.85}{12} = .32\%$$

3. According to Flux Method:
Annual Labour Turnover Rate

$$= \frac{\text{No. of separations + No. of replacements}}{\text{Average No. of workers}}$$

$$= \frac{400}{2{,}600} \times 100 = 15.39\%$$

$$\text{Equivalent monthly labour turnover rate} = \frac{15.39}{12} = 1.28\%$$

✍ EXAMPLE 5.17

The following information is collected from the personnel department of ST Limited for the year ending 31st March, 2020:

Number of workers at the beginning of the year	8,000
Number of workers at the end of the year	9,600
Number of workers left the company during the year	500
Number of workers discharged during the year	100
Number of workers replaced due to leaving and discharges	700
Additional workers employed for expansion during the year	1,500

You are required to calculate labour turnover rate by using separation method, replacement method and flux method.

Solution

Calculation of labour turnover rate:

1. Separation method:

$$\text{Labour turnover rate} = \frac{\text{Number of workers separated during the year}}{\text{Average number of workers on rolls during the year}} \times 100$$

$$= \frac{600}{8,800} \times 100$$

$$= 6.82\%$$

Average number of workers separated during the year = Number of workers left the company during the year + Number of workers discharged during the year
= 500 + 100 = 600

$$\text{Average number of workers on rolls during the year} = \frac{8,000 + 9,600}{2} = 8,800$$

2. Replacement Method:

$$\text{Labour turnover rate} = \frac{\text{Number of workers replaced during the year}}{\text{Average number of workers on rolls during the year}} \times 100$$

$$= \frac{700}{8,800} \times 100$$

$$= 7.95\%$$

3. Flux Method:

$$\text{Labour turnover rate} = \frac{\text{Number of workers separated + Number of workers replaced}}{\text{Average number of workers on rolls during the year}} \times 100$$

$$= \frac{600 + 700}{8,800} \times 100$$

= 14.77% = ₹288

EXAMPLE 5.18

The cost accountant of Y Ltd. has computed labour turnover rates for the quarter ended 31st March, 2020 as 10%, 5% and 3% respectively under "Flux Method", "Replacement Method" and "Separation Method". If the number of workers replaced during the quarter is 30, find out the number of (a) workers left and discharged and (b) workers recruited and joined.

Solution

Step-1 Calculation of average number of workers on roll

Labour turnover Rate (Replacement method) – (No. of Replacements/Average No. or Workers) × 100

or, 5 = (30/Average Number of workers) × 100

or, Average number of workers on roll = 600

Step-2 Calculation number of workers left and discharged

Labour Turnover Rate (Separation Method) = (No. of Separations/Average No. of Workers) × 100

3 = (No. of Separations/600) × 100

No. of Separations = 18

Hence, number of workers left and discharged comes to 18.

Step-3 Calculation number of workers recruited and joined

$$\text{Labour Turnover Rate (Flux method)} = \frac{(\text{No. of Separations(S)} + \text{No. of Accessions(A)})}{\text{Average No. of workers}} \times 100$$

or, $10 = (18 + A) \times 100$

or, $A = (60 - 18) = 42$

No. of workers recruited and joined = 42

EXAMPLE 5.19

The management of Sunshine Ltd. wants to have an idea of the profit lost/foregone as a result of labour turnover last year.

Last year, sales amounted to ₹66,00,000 and the P/V Ratio was 20%. The total number of actual hours worked by the direct labour force was 3.45 lakhs. As a result of the delays by the personnel department in filling vacancies due to labour turnover, 75,000 potentially productive hours were lost. The actual direct labour hours included 30,000 hours attributable to training new recruits, out of which half of the hours were unproductive. The costs incurred consequent on labour turnover revealed an analysis of the following:

	₹
Settlement cost due to leaving	27,420
Recruitment costs	18,725
Selection costs	12,750
Training costs	16,105

Assuming that the potential production lost due to labour turnover could have been sold at prevailing prices, ascertain the profit foregone/lost last year on account of labour turnover.

Solution

Basic Calculations

(i) Actual productive hours = Actual hrs. Worked – Unproductive training hrs.
= 3,45,000 hrs. – 15,000 hrs. = 3,30,000

(ii) Sales per productive hour = Total sales/Actual productive hrs.
= ₹66,00,000/3,30,000 hrs. = ₹20

(Contd.)

(iii)	Potential productive hours lost	= 75,000 hrs.
(iv)	Sales foregone	= 75,000 hrs. × ₹20 = ₹15,00,000
(v)	Contribution foregone	= Sales foregone × P/V Ratio
		= ₹15,00,000 × 20% = ₹3,00,000

M/s Sunshine Ltd.
Statement of Profit Foregone as a Result of Labour Turnover

		₹
Contribution Foregone *(See note (v) above)*		3,00,000
Add: Settlement cost due to leaving	27,420	
Recruitment costs	18,725	
Selection costs	12,750	
Training costs	16,105	
		75,000
Total profit foregone		3,75,000

EXAMPLE 5.20

The capacity usage ratio and the capacity utilisation ratio in respect of a machine for a particular month is 80% and 90% respectively. The available working hours in a month is 200 hours.

The break-up of idle-time is as follows:

Waiting for job	5 hours
Breakdown	4 hours
Waiting for tools	3 hours

Calculate the idle-time cost and present the same in a tabular form when the hourly fixed cost of running the machine is ₹8.00.

for excel template, scan

Solution

Total available working hours		200 hours
Standard capacity usage	0.80 × 200	160 hours
Normal (unavoidable) idle-time	(200 – 160)	40 hours
Actual hours worked	0.90 × 160	144 hours
Abnormal idle capacity	(160 – 144)	16 hours
Available idle-time	(16 – 12)	4 hours

Idle-time Report

Particulars	*Hours*		*Amount*		
Normal idle-time	40		₹8 × 40		₹320
Abnormal idle-time:					
Waiting for job	5		₹8 × 5	₹40	
Breakdown	4		₹8 × 4	32	
Waiting for tools	3		₹8 × 3	24	
Avoidable	4	16	₹8 × 4	32	₹128
Total		56			₹448

EXAMPLE 5.21

The profitability position of TARGET LTD. for the year ending 31.03.2020 is as follows:

	(₹ in Lakhs)	(₹ in Lakhs)
Annual turnover		200
Variable costs:		
Direct material	60	
Direct labour	40	
Variable overheads	50	150
Marginal contribution		50
Fixed overheads		10
Profit		40

The profit for the year did not match with company's expectation and works management attributed it to labour turnover.

Analysis of the data revealed the following:

Permanent workmen worked during the year	960,000 Direct labour hours
Apprentice workmen worked	80,000 Direct labour hours
	1,040,000 Direct labour hours

The effectiveness of direct labour hours put in by apprentice workmen was 50% and delay in replacing against separations during the year resulted in loss of 20,000 Direct labour hours.

You are required to calculate the loss of profit on account of loss of production from labour turnover.

Solution

Effective direct labour hours:	
Permanent workmen	9,60,000 hours
Apprentice workmen 50% of 80,000 hrs	40,000 hours
Total	10,00,000 hours

Sales per direct labour hour = ₹200 lakhs ÷ 100,00,000

= ₹20

Loss of production hours:

For replacement		20,000 hours
For apprentices		40,000 hours
	Total	60,000 hours
= 60,000 hrs × ₹20		= ₹12,00,000
= ₹(200 + 12) lakhs		= ₹212 lakhs
= (₹40 lakhs/10,40,000 hrs) × 20,000		= ₹76,923

Materials and Variable OH for extra 12 lakhs of Sales:

₹(110 lakhs/200 lakhs) ×12 lakhs = ₹6,60,000

Potential Profit with no Labour Turnover		₹
Sales		2,12,00,000
Less variable costs:		
Direct labour ₹(40,00,000) + 76,923)		40,76,923
Direct materials and variable OHs ₹(1,10,00,000 + 6,60,000)		1,16,60,000
	Total	1,57,36,923
Contribution		54,63,077
Less: Fixed costs		10,00,000
Potential profit		44,63,077
Actual profit		40,00,000
Loss of profit due to labour turnover		4,63,077
Alternatively:		₹
Loss of potential sales		12,00,000
Less: Variable costs		
Direct labour costs	76,923	
Materials and variable overheads	6,60,000	7,36,923
Contribution loss for labour turnover:		4,63,077

Theory Questions

1. Describe the various methods of recording time.
2. What are the merits and demerits of time-rate and piece-rate systems of wage payment? State the situations in which each system is effective and useful.
3. What are the reasons for booking workers on idle time in a factory? How is idle time controlled and treated in cost accounts?
4. Discuss individual bonus systems, group bonus systems and bonus systems for indirect workers.
5. List the characteristics desirable in any Incentive Wages Plan.
6. Distinguish between systems of wage payments known as Taylor's Differential Piece-Rate and Emerson's Efficiency system.
7. What is labour turnover? How will you measure it? What are its causes and effects on labour costs?

8. What is idle time? Indicate the different categories into which idle time can be classified and state which of them can be effectively controlled and how?
9. A company is considering installing a workers' profit sharing scheme in lieu of an individual bonus scheme. You are required to specify the disadvantages of the former.
10. (a) Describe the treatment of payments to labour for overtime work and in respect of holiday with pay in cost accounts.
    (b) Distinguish between Taylor's differential piece-rate and the Emerson Efficiency Plan system of incentive wage payments.
11. For each of the pay roll costs given below, state the accounting treatment that you would recommend, giving your reason:
    (a) Idle time in the finishing department because the assembly department delayed its production.
    (b) Overtime resulting from a customer saying "I want this job done in a week, and if you have to work overtime, I do not mind".
    (c) Labour time involved in reworking 5 units out of a batch of 50, on a process where 10% of the completed units are expected to be defective.
12. Discuss labour turnover and different methods of measuring it.
13. What do you mean by labour turnover? What are the costs associated with it? How would you treat these costs in cost accounting?
14. Under the Rowan Premium Bonus system, a less efficient worker can obtain same bonus as a highly-efficient worker. Discuss with suitable example.
15. Discuss the effect of overtime payment on productivity.
16. Explain the purpose of time-keeping and time-booking and state what detailed records are normally maintained under each. Do you feel any need for reconciliation of these two? What is the benefit you expect if such reconciliation is carried out?
17. Write a short essay on "Time and Motion Study", stating the benefits to be derived by management from such study.
18. How are payments to workers in respect of overtime work and set-up time treated in cost accounts?
19. What is idle time? Explain the causes leading to idle time and its treatment in cost accounts.
20. Explain the nature and significance of "Labour Turnover".
21. What are the effects of labour turnover on cost of production?
22. Enumerate the causes of labour turnover. What is the impact of high-labour turnover on the cost of production?
23. "High wages do not necessarily mean high labour cost". Elucidate.
24. How is payroll accounting function organised in a manufacturing establishment?
25. Explain what is meant by group bonus and state the objectives of introducing a group bonus schemes.
26. What do you understand by overtime premium? What is the effect of overtime payment on productivity and cost? Discuss the treatment of overtime premium in cost accounts and suggest a procedure for control of overtime.
27. What do you understand by time and motion study? Explain how standard time is set under time study. State how time and motion study is useful to management.
28. Define job evaluation and distinguish it from merit rating. Explain the method and objectives of job evaluation.
29. What do you understand by "idle time"? Distinguish between "Normal" and "Abnormal' idle time. How would you deal with each one of them in cost accounts? Give a suitable example to clarify your answer.
30. How will you treat the following in cost accounts?
    (i) Interest on capital
    (ii) Leave wages
    (iii) Research and development cost
    (iv) Audit fees

31. State the circumstances in which time-rate system of wage payment can be preferred in a factory.

32. Discuss briefly how you will deal with casual workers and workers employed on outdoor work in cost accounts.

33. Explain direct labour and indirect labour.

34. Distinguish between:

(i) Payment by time and payment by result.

(ii) Separation method and replacement method of labour turnover.

35. What is meant by labour turnover? Discuss its causes.

36. (a) Explain meaning, causes and effects of "labour turnover".

(b) Describe the role of Pay-roll department and Cost Accounting department in control over labour costs.

37. Describe the causes of labour turnover. What measures do you suggest to keep the rate of labour turnover at a low level? Discuss.

38. Explain "Job Card" and "Time Card".

39. What is meant by labour turnover? State any three causes of labour turnover. How is it measured? State any three methods to reduce labour turnover.

40. Explain the costs associated with labour turnover.

41. Distinguish between casual and outworkers.

42. Explain the effects of labour turnover. What are the costs involved in labour turnover? How can we reduce the impact of labour turnover?

43. What is labour turnover? How does it affect cost of production? How is it measured and how will you treat its cost in cost accounts?

44. Distinguish between time-keeping and time-booking. What are the various methods of time-keeping and time-booking ? Discuss briefly.

Problems

1. There are two piece-workers, Rakhal and Upendra, who are paid ₹5 for each piece work executed, which costs ₹15 per piece in materials.

In a working day of 8 hours, Rakhal can complete 4 pieces and Upendra only 3. If the overhead charges are ₹1.50 per hour, show that which of the two piece-workers is more useful to the factory.

Ans: Rakhal's cost of production is ₹23 per unit. Upendra's cost of production is ₹24 per unit. Rakhal's employment will be useful as his cost is lesser than that of Upendra's cost.

2. The standard hours of job *X* is 100 hours. The job has been completed by Amar in 60 hours, Akbar in 70 hours and Anthony in 95 hours. The bonus system applicable to the job is as follows:

Percentage of time saved to time allowed	*Bonus*
Saving up to 10%	10% of time saved
From 11% to 20%	15% of time saved
From 21% to 40%	20% of time saved
From 41% to 100%	25% of time saved

The rate of pay is ₹10 per hour. Calculate the total earnings of each worker and also the rate of earnings per hour.

Ans: Amar ₹11.33, Akbar ₹10.857, Anthony ₹10.052

3. Calculate total monthly remuneration of three workers *A*, *B* and *C* from the following data:

(a) Standard production per month per worker is 1,000 units. Actual production during months *A, B and C is* 850 units, 750 units and 950 units respectively.

(b) Piecework rate is ₹10 per unit (actual production).

(c) Additional production bonus is ₹10 for each percentage or actual production exceeding 80%.

(d) Dearness pay is fixed as ₹50 per month.

Ans: *A*–₹8,600; *B*–₹7,550; *C*–₹9,700.

4. From the following particulars, find the amount of cash required for payment of wages in a factory for a particular month:

	₹
1. Wages for normal hours worked	40,000
2. Overtime wages	10,500
3. Leave wages	5,000
4. Contribution to Provident Fund:	
Employee's share	4,000
Employer's share	3,500
5. House rent to be recovered from	
10 employees @ ₹200 per month.	

Ans: Cash required ₹49,500

5. A worker is paid ₹50 per hour and the 5 days working week contains 42 hours. The daily allowance for approved absence from his place of work, maintenance of machine etc. is 12 minutes and his job card shows that his time chargeable during the week to various jobs is as follows:

Job No.	305	20 hrs.
Job No.	310	10 hrs.
Job No.	320	8 hrs.

The unaccounted time is caused by a power failure. Show how his wages for the week would be dealt within cost accounts.

6. *XYZ* Co. employs its workers for a single shift of 8 hours per day for 25 days in a month. The company has recently fixed the standard output of 40 units per day per worker for a mass production item and introduced an incentive scheme to boost output. Details of wages payable to the workers are as follows:

(i) Basic wages	: ₹3 per unit subject to a guaranteed minimum wages of ₹80 per day worked.
(ii) Dearness allowance	: ₹40 per day worked.
(iii) Incentive bonus	:
Up to 80% efficiency	: Nil
For efficiency above 80%	: ₹50 for every 1% increase above 80%.

The details of performance of 2 workers for a particular month are as follows:

Workers	No. of Days Worked	Output (Units)
A	25	820
B	18	500

Calculate the total earnings of both the workers for the month.

Ans: *A*, ₹3560; *B* ₹2220

7. A factory has a piece-work scheme for mass production of a certain component for a T.V. manufacturer. The standard production fixed for a day of 8 hours is 40 units. The piece work rate is ₹4 per piece. The details of remuneration payable to the workers are as follows:

Production	*Wages*	*Dearness Allowance*	*Incentive Bonus*
Up to 80% efficiency	Per week wages @ ₹4 per piece subject to guaranteed minimum wages of ₹100/day	₹60/ day	Nil
Above 80%	-do-	-do-	₹40/- for every 1% increase in efficiency above 80%

Three workers Ram, Salim and Tom gave the following performance for May 2007:

Name of the Worker	*No. of Days Worked*	*Output (Units)*
Ram	20	480
Salim	24	864
Tom	25	1,100

Calculate their total earnings.

Ans: Ram ₹3200; Salin ₹5296; Tom ₹7100.

8. The standard labour time required for the production of a certain component has been fixed as 4 hours. An incentive scheme was introduced recently to raise labour productivity. The relevant details of the scheme are as follows:

Efficiency	*Incentive as a Percentage of Basic Wages*
Below 100%	No incentive
100% (that is, 4 hrs/unit)	10%
Above 100%	1% additional incentive for every 1% increase in efficiency above 100% fractions excluded.

Four workers *A*, *B*, *C* and *D* produced 16, 12, 14 and 10 units respectively in a particular week of 48 hours. The basic wages of all the workers is ₹15 per hour.

Calculate the efficiency, incentive bonus, total earnings and labour cost per unit in respect of each of the above four workers.

Ans:	*Total Earnings*	*Labour Cost Per Unit*
A	₹1029.60	₹64.35
B	792.00	66.00
C	907.20	64.80
D	720.00	72.00

9. From the following particulars, you are required to work out the earnings of a worker for a week under

(i) Straight Piece Rate;
(ii) Differential Piece Rate;
(iii) Halsey Premium Scheme (50% sharing); and
(iv) Rowan Premium Scheme.

Weekly working hours	48
Hourly wage rate (₹)	7.50
Piece rate per unit (₹)	3.00
Normal time taken per piece	24 minutes
Normal output per week	120 pieces
Actual output for the week	150 pieces

Differential piece rate	80% of piece rate when output is below normal and 120% of piece rate when output above normal.

Ans: Straight Piece Rate ₹ 450; Differential Piece rate ₹540; Halsey Scheme ₹405; Rowan Scheme ₹432.

10. Following particulars have been extracted from the books of Supreme Engineers Limited:

Time allowed for the job	15 hrs	15 hrs	15 hrs
Time taken	15 hrs	12 hrs	9 hrs

Bonus ratio for Halsey 50%
Rate per hour ₹2

(a) You are required to compute the quantum of wages under Halsey Scheme and Rowan Scheme. Which of these schemes would you like to introduce in this company if the time taken to complete the job is likely to reduce to 6 hours after three months?

(b) An alternative method of payment by result is by a straight piece work rate for completion of the job in 7 hours is feasible. Would you like to switch over to this method of payment given further that hourly rate would be reckoned at ₹1.50 for fixation of the piece rate? Please give reasons for your advice.

Ans:

Time Taken	*Wages Halsey*	*Wages Rowan*
	₹	₹
15	30	30
12	27	28.80
9	24	25.20
6	21	19.20

11. The management of Bina and Rina Ltd. is worried about its increasing labour turnover in the factory, and before analysing the causes and taking remedial steps, it wants to have an idea of the profit foregone as a result of labour turnover in the last year.

Last year sales amounted to ₹83,03,300 and P/V ratio was 20 per cent. The total number of actual hours worked by the direct labour force was 4.45 lakhs. As a result of the delays by the personnel department in filling vacancies due to labour turnover, 1,00,000 potentially productive hours were lost. The actual direct labour hours included 30,000 hours attributable to training new recruits, out of which half of the hours were unproductive.

The cost incurred consequent on labour turnover revealed, on analysis, the following:

Settlement cost due to leaving	₹43,820
Recruitment costs	₹26,740
Selection costs	₹12,750
Training costs	₹30,490

Assuming that the potential production lost as a consequence of labour turnover could have been sold at prevailing prices, find the profit foregone last year on account of labour turnover.

Ans: Profit foregone ₹5,00,000.

12. A company's basic wage rate is ₹3.00 per hour and its overtime rates are:

Evenings	Time and one-third
Weekends	Double time

During the previous year the following hours were worked:

	Hours
Normal time	2,20,000
Time plus one-third	20,000
Double time	10,000

The following times have been worked on these jobs:

	Job-A Clock Hours	Job-B Clock Hours	Job-C Clock Hours
Normal time	3,000	5,000	4,000
Evening overtime	300	600	1,050
Weekend overtime	100	50	300
Total	3,400	5,650	5,350

You are required to calculate the labour cost chargeable to each job where overtime is worked regularly throughout the year as the company policy due to labour shortage.

Ans: Job *A* ₹10,880; Job *B* ₹18080; Job *C* ₹17,120.

13. Both direct and indirect labours of a department in a factory are entitled to production bonus in accordance with a group incentive scheme, the outline of which is as follows:

(a) For any production in excess of the standard rate fixed at 10,000 units per month (of 25 days) a general incentive of ₹10 per unit is paid in aggregate. The total amount payable to each separate group is determined on the basis of an assumed percentage of such excess production being contributed by it, namely @ 70% by direct labour, @ 10% by inspection staff, @ 12% by maintenance staff and @ 8% by supervisory staff.

(b) Moreover, if the excess production is more than 20 per cent above the standard, direct labours also get a special bonus @ ₹5 per unit for all production in excess of 120% of standard.

(c) Inspection staff are penalised @ ₹20 per unit for rejection by customer in excess of 1% of production.

(d) Maintenance staff are also penalised @ ₹20 per hour of breakdown.

From the following particulars for a month, work out the production bonus earned by each group:

(a) Actual working days: 20

(b) Production: 11,000 units

(c) Rejection by customer: 200 units

(d) Machine breakdown: 40 hours.

Ans: Direct labour ₹28,000; Inspection staff ₹1,200; Maintenance staff ₹2,800; Supervisory staff ₹2,400.

14. In a unit, 10 men work as a group. When the production of the group exceeds the standard output of 200 pieces per hour, each man is paid an incentive for the excess production in addition to his wages at hourly rates. The incentive is at half of the percentage of the excess production over the standard production. Each man is paid incentive at the rate of this percentage of wage rate of ₹2 per hour. There is no relation between the individual workman's hourly rate and the bonus rate.

In a week, the hours worked are 500 and the total production is 1,20,000 pieces.

(a) Compute the total amount of the bonus for the week.

(b) Calculate the total earnings of two workers *A* and *B* of the group:

A worked 44 hours and his basic rate per hour was ₹2.20.

B worked 48 hours and his basic rate per hour was ₹1.90.

Ans: Total earnings *A* ₹105, *B* ₹100.80

15. The time taken for a particular operation for Operator *X* in the process division of a manufacturing concern on three different counts was 24, 22 and 27 minutes while that of Operator *Y* was 20, 23 and 26 minutes. It has been ascertained that the rating of *X* is 70/60 and that of *Y* is 55/60. Allowances for fatigue, and personal needs are assumed at 15%. Calculate, using the above information as a base for that particular operation,

(i) the standard time;

(ii) the time allowed under an incentive allowance of 30% of standard time.

Ans: Standard time 28.448 minutes
Time allowed 36.982 minutes.

CASE STUDY

A Case of Bhivani Industries

Amitesh had joined Bhiwani Industries Ltd. recently on April 15, 2019 in place of their regular Cost Accountant Siddhartha. The first job that Amitesh was given was to read the company's HR manual and to understand the wages payment systems. The next responsibility was to prepare the earning statements of two types of workers i.e., full-time and fixed-time labourers in the factory and allocate the same to various types of jobs in the company.

Bhiwani Industries based in Electronic City, Bangalore, manufactured Uni Booster parts for brake application and sold them to their regular clients like Tyco Electricals, Mazda and Volvo. The company employed full-time (regular), part-time, fixed-time, contractual and daily-wage labourers. Only the full-time and fixed-time workers were eligible for the Dearness Allowance and Provident Funds. The remaining workers were given a lump sum amount per month based on the contract.

The basic wages of both full-time and fixed-time workers were ₹10,000 per month. The difference was in Dearness Allowance. While the full-time labourers got DA @ 60% of their basic wages, the fixed-time workers got 50% DA. Provident Funds at the rate of 8% on basic wages remained the same for both. Even the Employee's State Insurance was same at the rate of 2% on basic wages for both sets of workers.

The normal working hours for the month were 200 hours. Overtime was paid at double the normal wages plus Dearness Allowance. The company contributed equal amount to Provident Fund and Employee's State Insurance scheme to that of employees. There were 25 working days in a month and one paid holiday.

These two set of workers were engaged on different job of manufacturing Disc brakes (A), Drum brakes (B), and Disc pads (C) during the year. They were employed on jobs A, B & C during the month April 2019 in the following proportion in terms of number of hours on an average:

Jobs	*A*	*B*	*C*
Full Time	100	40	60
Fixed Time	80	60	60

Overtime of 10 hours (average) was done on job **B** by fixed-time workers. During the month, the full-time workers on an average did 8 hours of leave/idle time.

Amitesh was not able to prepare the earning statements based on the information collected. He decided to contact Siddhartha to get some pointers.

✍ QUESTIONS FOR DISCUSSION:

Imagine that you are Siddhartha, the previous Cost Accountant with the company and answer the following:

1. Calculate normal wage rate per hour and overtime rate.
2. Calculate net wages payable per labourer per month to both types of workers.
3. Show the allocation of the labour cost to different jobs.

Chapter 6

Factory Overheads: Distribution

Learning Objectives

After reading this chapter, you should be able to:

1. explain factory overheads—concepts, its classification, nature, its collection and codification, its allocation and apportionment, its accounting and distribution;
2. discuss different methods of absorption of factory overheads; merits and demerits of apportionment and absorption of overheads; and
3. explain actual overhead rate, pre-determined overhead rate, under- or over-absorption of overhead.

FACTORY OVERHEAD—CONCEPT

Factory overhead costs are operating costs of a business enterprise which cannot be traced directly to a particular unit of output, that is, product or jobs. Factory overhead is the aggregate of indirect materials, indirect wages and indirect expenses. The term "overhead" is used interchangeably with such terms as "burden", "supplementary costs", "indirect expense", "factory expense". The word "overhead" is more appropriate than burden and supplementary costs because the latter terms imply an unnecessary charge, an extra cost or an element of cost resulting from inefficiency. The term "overhead" is preferable to manufacturing expenses, because manufacturing expenses often refer to all manufacturing costs, both direct and indirect. Overhead may be used for all types of business enterprises while manufacturing expense is restricted in its use to manufacturing concerns.

FACTORY OVERHEAD—FIXED, SEMI-VARIABLE AND VARIABLE

Factory overhead costs can be divided into fixed, semi-variable and variable costs. Fixed overhead costs are commonly described as those that do not vary in total amount with increases or decreases in productive activity or volume of output for a given period of time, usually, a year. Management salaries, building depreciation, rent, property taxes and amortisation of leaseholds are some examples of fixed overhead. Fixed costs are constant in total amount, but vary per unit as production activity changes.

Semi-variable or semi-fixed are those which remain fixed in total amount over a relatively short range of variation in output and then are abruptly changed to a new level, where they remain fixed in total amount for another short range of output. For example, if a third shift is added without increasing plant facilities, normally fixed costs, such as supervision salaries may increase because of the necessity of night supervision, insurance premiums may be raised because of additional fire, theft, and accident risk, and some equipment rentals may be accelerated.

Variable costs include repairs, powers, workmen's compensation, supplies and indirect labour which are typical of cost varying in total amount, with changes in productive activity. The increase or decrease in variable overhead costs need not be in the same proportion to the change in output. However, in many cases there is a directly proportional relationship. Variable costs per unit remain relatively constant with changes in production. Thus, variable costs fluctuate in total amount but tend to remain constant per unit as production activity changes. Variable overheads are generally considered controllable as they directly relate to the volume of output and by reducing the level of activity they can be reduced/avoided. Also, by comparing the actual variable overheads with budgeted variable overheads, such overheads can be controlled and kept within targets and tolerance limits.

FACTORY OVERHEADS—ACCOUNTING AND DISTRIBUTION

Factory overheads by nature cannot be identified or associated directly with specific products or jobs. However, they should be included in total cost of products or jobs. The following steps are important in distribution of overhead costs among products or jobs.

1. Collection and codification
2. Allocation and apportionment
3. Absorption

COLLECTION AND CODIFICATION OF FACTORY OVERHEADS

The first step in distribution of factory overhead costs is their collection and codification under proper headings. Similar overhead cost items should be grouped together. The grouping of overhead costs is done through a technique known as "codification". Codification is a method of identifying and describing various overhead expenses in numbers or letters or in a combination of both so that cost data can easily be collected. Codification of the entire items is done through a proper coding system. Following are briefly the objectives of codification:

1. To collect overhead items of similar nature.
2. To help in the allocation and apportionment of overhead costs to different departments or cost centres.
3. To make an analysis of overhead cost items for planning and control purposes.
4. To help in adopting a mechanised system of accounting.
5. To maintain a reasonable number of accounts which could be economical and useful.

Methods of Codification

Generally, the codification follows Standing Order Number or Cost Accounting Number. Standing Order Number covers production overhead items and Cost Accounting Number includes administration, selling and distribution overhead items. However, both follow the same principle of accumulating overhead cost items. Some important methods of codification are the following:

Serial Numbering System

Under this method, each item is allotted a fixed number in serial order, for example,

01 Factory supplies
02 Indirect labour
03 Insurance
04 Factory rent

Number Blocks

Under this method, a block number is assigned to cover items of expenditure, for example, 0–10 for maintenance expenses, 11–20 for supervision expenses, etc.

Combination of Alphabets and Numbers

Under this method, a code is used which combines the number as well as the alphabets, for example,

M_1 = Maintenance of plant
M_2 = Maintenance of tools
M_3 = Maintenance of factory building
M_4 = Maintenance of office building

In the above example, M stands for maintenance and different numbers for different types of maintenance expenses.

Numerical Codes

Under this system, a code number usually consisting of nine digits is used. The first two digits signify whether the cost is fixed or variable, the next three indicate head of expense, the next two the analysis of expense for further subdivision, and the last two digits indicate the cost centre which incurs the expenditure, for example,

10/121/05/08 Fixed/salary/officers/production.

Mnemonic Method

Under this method, the letters/alphabets are used to indicate an item such as D.P.T. for depreciation on plant and tools.

Among the above methods, the numerical code method is more suitable than the others for a large organisation. This method is easy to operate where a mechanical system of accounting is used. A large number of items could be covered under this method.

Sources of Overhead Collection

Different sources are available in an organisation to collect overhead expenses such as:

1. Store requisitions for items like indirect materials.
2. Financial accounts—A large number of items may be taken from the financial accounts of the business enterprise.
3. Wages book—Most indirect wages and labour-related costs.
4. Cash book—For indirect expenses.

5. Registers and reports—Plant and machinery register for depreciation; scrap, waste, spoilage can be discovered through investigation.

ALLOCATION AND APPORTIONMENT OF FACTORY OVERHEADS

Difference between Allocation and Apportionment

The following are the differences between allocation and apportionment.

1. Allocation implies that costs are directly allocated to cost centre. Overhead that cannot be directly allocated are apportioned on some suitable basis.
2. Allocation allots whole amount of cost to cost centre or cost unit whereas apportionment allots part of cost to cost centre or cost unit.
3. No basis is required for allocation. Apportionment is made on the basis of area, assets value, number of workers, etc.

Departmentalisation of Overhead

Departmentalisation of factory overhead means dividing the company into segments called departments or cost centres where expenses are incurred. In a manufacturing concern, there are mainly two types of cost centres—producing departments and service departments. A production department represents a subunit of the company where manufacturing activity takes place. Some typical examples of producing departments include assembly finishing, blending, painting and grinding departments. Service departments represent cost centres which provide support for the producing departments. Materials handling, personnel, plant maintenance, inspection, storage, purchasing, receiving, shipping, medical and other similar activities which are not directly involved in production are considered to be service activities.

Benefits of Departmentalisation

Departmentalisation serves two purposes: (i) closer control of factory overhead costs, and (ii) more accurate costing of jobs and products. Closer control is possible because departmentalisation makes the incurrence of costs in a department or cost centre, the responsibility of someone who heads the department or the cost centre.

More accurate costing of jobs and products is possible, if products are passed through more than one department. A job or product going through a department is charged with factory overhead for work done on that product in that department. Therefore, jobs or products are charged with different amounts of factory overhead depending on the number of departments through which they pass. This process results in accurate and reliable cost figures for the products or job.

Primary Distribution

Some factory overheads can be directly identified with a particular department or cost centre as having been incurred for that cost centre. Examples of such factory overheads are repairs and maintenance expenses incurred in specific departments, supervision, indirect labour, overtime, indirect materials and factory supplies, equipment depreciation.

Expenses such as power, light, rent, depreciation of factory building, expenses shared by all departments, cannot be charged directly to a department, be it producing or service. These expenses do not originate in any specific department. They are incurred for all and must, therefore, be apportioned or prorated to any or all departments using such items. Cost apportionment is the process of charging expenses in an equitable proportion to the various cost centres or departments. The Institute of Cost and Management Accountants (U.K.) defines cost apportionment, "as the allotment of proportions of items of cost to cost centres or cost units." The apportionment should be done on some rational and equitable bases. In cost accounting, this is known as primary distribution of factory overhead.

It would be difficult to give a comprehensive list of the bases of apportionment, but the following bases are in common use:

1. Floor area occupied—Overheads such as lighting and heating, rent and rates, depreciation on building, building repairs, caretaking, watching and patrolling.
2. Capital values—Depreciation on plant and machinery, insurance on building, and plant and machinery, maintenance of plant and machinery.
3. Direct labour hours and/or machine hours—Insurance on jigs, tools and fixtures, power, works management remuneration, repairs and maintenance cost.
4. Number of workers employed—Canteen, accident insurance, medical, dental and first aid, pensions, personnel department expenses, profit sharing payments, recreation, supervision, time office, wages department.
5. Technical estimate—Fire prevention, oil and grease, steam, water without meter.

Example 6.1

The Modern Company has four departments. *A*, *B* and *C* are the production departments and *D* is a servicing department. The actual costs for a period are as follows:

			₹('000)
Indirect Materials			
	Production department	*A*	950
		B	1,200
		C	200
	Servicing department		1,500
Indirect Wages			
	Production department	*A*	900
		B	1,100
		C	300
	Servicing department		1,000
	Rent		2,000
	Repair		1,200
	Depreciation		900
	Light		200

(Contd.)

Indirect Materials	₹('000)
Supervision	3,000
Insurance	1,000
Employee's insurance (employer's liability)	300
Power	1,800

The following data are also available in respect of four departments:

	Departments			
	A	*B*	*C*	*D*
Area (sq. ft)	150	110	90	50
No. of workers	24	16	12	8
Total wages ('000)	₹ 8,000	₹ 6,000	₹ 4,000	₹2,000
Value of plant ('000)	₹24,000	₹18,000	₹ 12,000	₹6,000
Value of stock ('000)	₹15,000	₹ 9,000	₹ 6,000	—

Apportion the above costs to the various departments on the most equitable method.

Solution

Departmental Distribution Summary **(₹'000)**

			Production Departments		*Servicing Departments*	
Items	*Basis*	*Total*	*A*	*B*	*C*	*D*
Indirect material	Allocation	3,850	950	1,200	200	1,500
Indirect wages	Allocation	3,300	900	1,100	300	1,000
Rent	Area	2,000	750	550	450	250
Repairs	Plant value	1,200	480	360	240	120
Depreciation	Plant value	900	360	270	180	90
Light	Area	200	75	55	45	25
Supervision	No of workers	3,000	1,200	800	600	400
Insurance	Value of stock	1,000	500	300	200	—
Employees insurance	Wages	300	120	90	60	30
Power	Plant value	1,800	720	540	360	180
	Total	17,550	6,055	5,265	2,635	3,595

Notes: (i) It has been assumed that insurance has been taken for stock.

(ii) Power expenses have been apportioned on the basis of value of plant because no other information has been given.

✍ EXAMPLE 6.2

Selfhelp Ltd. has gensets and produces its own power. Data for power costs are as follows:

Horse Power Hours	Production Deptts.		Service Deptts.	
	A	*B*	*X*	*Y*
Needed capacity production	10,000	20,000	12,000	8,000
Used during the month of May	8,000	13,000	7,000	6,000

During the month of May, costs for generating power amounted to ₹9,30,000; of this ₹2,50,000 was considered to be fixed cost. Service Deptt *X* renders service to *A*, *B* and *Y* in the ratio 13:6:1, while *Y* renders service to *A* and *B* in the ratio 31:3. Given that the direct labour hours in Deptts *A* and *B* are 1,650 hours and 2,175 hours respectively, find the power cost per labour hour in each of these two Deptts.

☞ ***Solution***

Selfhelp Ltd. Overheads Distribution Summary

Particulars	*Basis of Charge*	*Total ₹*	*Production Deptts*		*Service Deptts.*	
			A	*B*	*X*	*Y*
			₹	₹	₹	₹
(1)	*(2)*	*(3)*	*(4)*	*(5)*	*(6)*	*(7)*
Fixed cost	H.P. hours needed at capacity production (5:10:6:4)	2,50,000	50,000	1,00,000	60,000	40,000
Variable cost	H.P. hours used (8:13:7:6)	6,80,000	1,60,000	2,60,000	1,40,000	1,20,000
Total overheads		9,30,000	2,10,000	3,60,000	2,00,000	1,60,000
Service Deptt. *X* overheads apportioned to *A*, *B* and *Y* (13:6:1)			1,30,000	60,000	– 2,00,000	10,000
Service Deptt. *Y* overheads apportioned to *A* and *B* (31:3)			1,55,000	15000		–1,70,000
Total overheads of production deptts.			4,95,000	4,35,000	—	—
Labour hours worked			1,650	2,175		
Power cost per labour hour			300	200		

APPORTIONMENT OF SERVICE DEPARTMENTS OVERHEADS TO PRODUCING DEPARTMENTS

Secondary Distribution

The primary distribution of factory overhead apportions all overhead costs to the different departments or cost centres—production and service departments both. However, it is necessary that overhead costs of service departments (accumulated through direct allocation or primary distribution) should be further assigned to producing departments. This is due to the reason that service departments do not themselves manufacture anything and it is the production departments or cost centres which are involved in manufacturing activities. The reassignment or reapportionment of service departments overhead to producing departments or centres is termed as secondary distribution. Secondary distribution is useful in the following manner:

1. It helps in determining the cost of products or jobs sold and value of inventory.
2. It helps in determining the effect of various managerial decisions and actions on the total cost of the business firm. For example, decisions as to add or to drop a product line require information about its cost effect, which can be estimated after secondary distribution has been made.
3. It helps subsequently in determining the price of the product or job. In case of contracts based on cost in place of market price, secondary distribution helps in fixing a selling price which is advantageous to the parties concerned.
4. It promotes motivation among employees of the producing departments to take up service department activities.

Bases for Secondary Distribution

It is difficult to suggest a sample list of service departments and equitable bases of distribution of overhead costs. The general basis for apportioning service departments' overheads to producing departments are the following:

1. *Services rendered (benefits obtained)* This is perhaps the most popular method of apportioning service department costs. The services rendered to different departments, that is, benefits obtained by them can be a suitable basis. If a producing department has received large benefits, it must be charged for a share of overhead costs incurred to provide that quantity of benefits. This method is simple and economical.
2. *Ability to pay* This method suggests that a large share of servicing departments overhead costs should be assigned to those producing departments whose product contributes the most to the income of a business enterprise. However, it is difficult to measure the "ability to pay" of different departments and this method is also not based on equity.
3. *Survey or analysis* This method is applied where a suitable base is difficult to find or it would be too costly to select a method which is considered suitable. For example, the postage cost could be apportioned on a survey of postage used during a year.
4. *Efficiency or incentives* This method uses standards and budgets and apportions the overhead costs on the basis of a present budget or standard. Sometimes, this method is used along with the bases of services rendered or ability to pay method.

In selecting a suitable base for apportioning service department overheads, considerations should be given to practicability, simplicity, economy, theoretical soundness and assistance in accurate costing and cost control.

The following list gives a few service departments and bases commonly used to apportion the respective overhead costs:

Service Department	*Apportionment Base*
Personnel	Number of employees, labour hours, labour cost.
Purchasing	Number of orders, cost of materials.
Receiving	Cost of materials, number of units, number of orders.
Stores	Cost of materials, number of requisitions filled, number of units handled.
Factory Office	Number of employees, labour hours, labour cost.
Machine Maintenance and Repair	Machine hours, labour hours, labour cost, services rendered.
Engineering	Machine hours, labour hours, service rendered.
Payroll or Time-keeping Department	Total labour or machine hours or number of employees in each department
Welfare, Canteen, Recreation, Medical	Number of employees in each department.
Building Service Department	Relative area of each department.
Internal Transport Service	Weight, value, graded products, weight and distance.

Inter-departmental Services

While apportioning service departments overhead, one may notice two situations: (i) The entire amount of a servicing department is to be distributed to only the producing departments. This does not involve any practical difficulty and provides the simplest and quickest method for apportioning costs of the servicing department. (ii) Services provided by some servicing departments are used partly by other servicing departments. That is, many service departments serve each other. For example, the payroll department in a firm prepares payroll for the entire organisation, but it depends on the building maintenance department for repair and maintenance services. Similarly, the building maintenance department provides services for all departments using the building, but it gets service from departments like stores, factory office and personnel. This second situation is known as inter-departmental services.

Methods

There are mainly two methods of dealing with inter-departmental service:

A. *Continuous apportionment* In this method, the process of apportioning service departments overhead is continued until the figures become immaterial or totally exhausted. The following steps are involved in this method:

   (a) Use the given percentages to apportion the original total of the first service department. This closes the account of the first service department and transfers prorated amounts to other departments.

(b) Use the given percentages of second service department whose total is made up of original amount plus prorated amount of service department first. This closes the account of second service department and assigns prorated amounts to the other departments including service department first also.
(c) Follow the same procedure to all other service departments.
(d) Repeat a second cycle of apportionment starting with the service department first, whose total consists, at present, only of amounts prorated from other service departments. In this way, the service department totals become less and less with each cycle of apportionment because each time a substantial amount is apportioned to the producing departments.
(e) Stop the above cycle at any point where it is found that the remaining figures (to be apportioned) are too small to be of any consequence or when the figures are totally exhausted.

EXAMPLE 6.3

The overhead of a manufacturing company has been analysed to the point of primary distribution as given below.

		₹
Production departments:	Machine	10,00,000
	Assembly	4,00,000
Service departments:	Canteen	2,00,000
	Powerhouse	3,00,000

The canteen is to be apportioned on the basis of employees:

	Employees	*%*
Machine	240	60
Assembly	140	35
Powerhouse	20	5
	400	100

The powerhouse is to be apportioned on the basis of electricity used:

	Thousand Kilowatts	*%*
Machine	270	75
Assembly	36	10
Canteen	54	15
	360	100

Solution

The apportionment would be done in the following manner:

	Machine	*Assembly*	*Canteen*	*Powerhouse*
Primary apportionment	10,00,000	4,00,000	2,00,000	3,00,000

(Contd.)

	Machine	Assembly	Canteen	Powerhouse
Apportion: Canteen	1,20,000	70,000	– 2,00,000	10,000
Powerhouse	2,32,500	31,000	46,500	– 3,10,000
Canteen	27,900	16,300	– 46,500	2,300
Powerhouse	1,800	200	300	– 2,300
Canteen	200	100	– 300	
Total Service Deptts.	3,82,400	1,17,600		
Total Production Overhead	13,82,400	5,17,600		

B. *Algebraic method or simultaneous equation* **This method helps in finding out the amount of overhead of each servicing department by solving simultaneous equations. The total expenses of service departments can be directly transferred to production departments.**

EXAMPLE 6.4

A company has three production departments, *A*, *B* and *C* and two service departments, *P* and *Q*. The following figures are available as per departmental distribution summary:

		₹
Production departments	*A*	3,150
	B	3,700
	C	1,400
Service departments	*P*	2,250
	Q	1,000

The expenses of the service departments are to be apportioned on a percentage basis as follows:

		A	B	C	P	Q
Service deptt.	*P*	40%	30%	20%		10%
Service deptt.	*Q*	30%	30%	20%	20%	—

Solution

Let X = total overhead of deptt. P

Y = total overhead of deptt. Q

Therefore $$X = 2,250 + \frac{20}{100} Y \quad (1)$$

$$Y = 1,000 + \frac{10}{100} X \quad (2)$$

$$10X = 22,500 + 2Y \quad (3)$$

$$10Y = 10,000 + 1X \quad (4)$$

Multiplying Eq. (3) by 5

$$50X - 10Y = 1,12,500 \qquad (5)$$

$$-X + 10Y = 10,000 \qquad (6)$$

Adding $\quad 49X = 1,22,500$

$$X = 2,500$$

and $\quad Y = 1,250$

Secondary Distribution Summary

	Total	*Production Department*			*Servicing Deptt.*	
	₹	*A*	*B*	*C*	*P*	*Q*
		₹	₹	₹	₹	₹
As per summary	11,500	3,150	3,700	1,400	2,250	1,000
Service deptt. *P*		1,000	750	500	– 2,250	250
	11,500	4,150	4,450	1,900		– 1,250
Service deptt. *Q*		375	375	250	250	– 1,250
	11,500	4,525	4,825	2,150	—	—

Service departments' overheads represent the sum of the service department cost plus the costs apportioned from other service departments. After obtaining total overhead cost of servicing departments, the total of each service department is apportioned to producing departments on the basis of percentage or proportion (for the services rendered) of the specific producing departments.

EXAMPLE 6.5

A factory is having three production departments *A*, *B* and *C* and two service departments—Boiler-house and Pump-room. The boiler-house has to depend upon the pump-room for supply of water and pump-room in its turn is dependent on the boiler-house for supply of driving the pump. The expenses incurred by the production departments during a period are *A*, ₹8,00,000; *B*, ₹7,00,000; and *C*, ₹5,00,000. The expenses for boiler-house are ₹2,34,000 and the pump-room are ₹3,00,000.

The expenses of the boiler-house and pump-room are apportioned to the production departments on the following basis:

	A	*B*	*C*	*B.H.*	*P.R.*
Expenses of boiler-house	30%	40%	30%	—	10%
Expenses of pump-room	40%	20%	20%	20%	—

Show clearly as to how the expenses of boiler-house and pump-room would be apportioned to *A*, *B* and *C* departments. Use algebraical equation.

Solution

Let X be the overhead of boiler-house and Y be the total overhead of pump-room.

$$X = 2{,}34{,}000 + .2Y$$

$$Y = 3{,}00{,}000 + .1X$$

$$10X - 2Y = 23{,}40{,}000 \quad \text{(i)}$$

$$-X + 10Y = 30{,}00{,}000 \quad \text{(ii)}$$

On multiplying Eq. (i) by 5 and adding it to Eq. (ii)

$$50X - 10Y = 1{,}17{,}00{,}000$$

$$-X + 10Y = 30{,}00{,}000$$

$$49X = 1{,}47{,}00{,}000$$

$$X = 3{,}00{,}000$$

On substituting this value in Eq. (ii)

$$-3{,}00{,}000 + 10Y = 30{,}00{,}000$$

$$10Y = 33{,}00{,}000$$

$$Y = 3{,}30{,}000$$

Distribution of Overheads

	Total	Departments		
		A	B	C
	₹	₹	₹	₹
Amount for the departments	20,00,000	8,00,000	7,00,000	5,00,000
Boiler-house	2,70,000*	60,000	1,20,000	90,000
Pump-room	2,64,000**	1,32,000	66,000	66,000
	25,34,000	9,92,000	8,86,000	6,56,000

* ₹3,00,000 less 1/10 for the Pump-room
** ₹3,30,000 less 1/5 for the Boiler-house

EXAMPLE 6.6

A company has three production departments and two service departments. The departmental distribution summary for a particular period has the following totals. You are required to compute the total share of overheads of the service departments to be distributed to production departments:

	Total
Production Department:	
(P_1—₹800; P_2—₹700; P_3—₹500)	₹2,000
Service departments:	
(S_1—₹234; S_2—₹300)	₹534

The expenses of service departments are charged out on a percentage basis as follows:

	P_1	P_2	P_3	S_1	S_2
S_1	20%	40%	30%	—	10%
S_2	40%	20%	20%	20%	—

☞ ***Solution***

Overhead Apportionment Summary (using Repeated Distribution Method)

Details	*Production Department*			*Service Department*	
	P_1	P_2	P_3	S_1	S_2
Allocated expenses	800	700	500	234	300
Apportion expenses of S_1 to all other departments in 2 : 4 : 3 : 1	46.80	97.60	70.20	– 234	23.40
	846.80	797.60	570.20	0	323.40
Apportioning expenses of S_2 to all other departments in the ratio of 4 : 2 : 2 : 2	129.36	64.68	64.88	64.88	– 323.40
	976.16	862.28	634.88	64.68	0
Apportioning expenses of S_1 to other departments in the ratio of 2 : 4 : 3 : 1	12.94	25.88	19.40	– 64.68	6.46
	989.10	888.16	654.28	0	6.46
Apportioning expenses of S_2 to other departments in the ratio of 4 : 2 : 2 : 2	2.59	1.29	1.29	1.29	– 6.64
	991.69	889.45	655.57	1.29	0
Apportioning expenses of S_1 to other departments in the ratio of 2 : 4 : 3 : 1	0.29	0.57	0.43	– 1.29	0.12
	991.98	890.02	656.00	0	0.12
					Negligible
Total overhead of Production departments are	992	890	656 (Rounded off)		

Simultaneous Equation Method

Let x be the total overhead of service department S_1 and y be the total overhead of service department S_2

$$\therefore \quad x = 234 + 20\%\ y = x = 234 + \frac{1}{5}y \qquad \text{(i)}$$

$$y = 300 + 10\%\ x = y = 300 + 1/10x \qquad \text{(ii)}$$

Multiply Eq. (i) by 5 and (ii) by 10

$$5x = 1170 + y \qquad \text{(i)}$$

$$10y = 3000 + x \qquad \text{(ii)}$$

or

$$5x - y = 1170 \qquad \text{(i)}$$

$$-x + 10y = 3000 \qquad \text{(ii)}$$

Multiply Eq. (i) by 10

$$50x - 10y = 11700$$

$$-x + 10y = 3000$$

$$49x = 14700$$

$$x = \frac{14700}{49} ₹300$$

Putting the value of x in Eq. (ii)

$$10y = 3000 + 300$$

$$10y = 3300$$

$$y = \frac{330\not{0}}{\not{1}0} = 300$$

Secondary Distribution Summary

		P_1	P_2	P_3
(i)	Primary distribution	₹800	700	500
(ii)	90% of S_1 expenses distributed in production departments in the ratio of 2 : 4 : 3	60	120	90
(iii)	80% of S_2 expenses distributed in production departments in the ratio of 4: 2: 2	132	66	66
	Total overhead of P_1, P_2, P_3	992	886	656

EXAMPLE 6.7

A factory has three production departments A, B and C and also two service departments X and Y. The primary distribution of the estimated overheads in the factory has just been completed. These details and the quantum of service rendered by the service departments, to the other departments are given below:

Departments	A	B	C	X	Y
Primary distribution (₹)	2,40,000	2,10,000	2,50,000	1,40,000	96,000
Service rendered by					
Deptt. 'X'	30%	20%	35%	—	15%
Deptt. 'Y'	25%	40%	25%	10%	—

Prepare a statement showing the distribution of service department overheads to the production departments by the simultaneous equation method.

☞ ***Solution***

Let P and N be the total overheads of the service departments X and Y respectively.
Then,

$$P = 1{,}40{,}000 + 0.10\,N \text{ that is, } 10P - N = 1{,}40{,}000$$

$$N = 96{,}000 + 0.15P \text{ and } -0.15P + N = 96{,}000$$

$$\text{(By adding)} \qquad 9.85P = 14{,}96{,}000$$

$$P = \frac{14{,}96{,}000}{9.85} = ₹1{,}51{,}878$$

By substitution, $N = 96{,}000 + 0.15 \times 1{,}51{,}878$

$$= 96{,}000 + 22{,}782 = ₹1{,}18{,}782$$

Statement Showing the Distribution of Service Departments Overheads to the Production Departments

	Production Departments			
Distribution of Overheads of	*A (₹)*	*B (₹)*	*C (₹)*	*Total (₹)*
Deptt X (85% of ₹1,51,878)	45,563	30,376	53,157	1,29,096
Deptt Y (90% of ₹1,18,782)	29,696	47,513	29,695	1,06,904
Total	75,259	77,889	82,852	2,36,000

✍ EXAMPLE 6.8

The following cost information for a period is available for a small engineering unit:

(a) Allocated expenditure

		Allocated			
	Total (₹)	*Production Departments*		*Service Departments*	
		Machine Shop	*Assembly*	*General Plant Services*	*Stores and Misc.*
Indirect wages	29,300	8,000	6,000	4,000	11,300
Stores consumed	6,700	2,200	1,700	1,100	1,700
Supervisory salaries	14,000	—	—	14,000	—
Other salaries	10,000	—	—	10,000	—

(b) Expenditure to be apportioned

Power and fuel	₹ 15,000
Rent	15,000
Insurance	3,000
Depreciation	1,00,000

(c) Additional information available:

	Floor Area (Sq. ft.)	*H.P. Hrs.* —	*No. of Employees*	*Investment (₹)*
Machine shop	2,000	3,500	30	6,40,000
Assembly	1,000	500	15	2,00,000
General plant	500	—	5	10,000
Stores and maintenance	1,500	1,000	10	1,50,000

(d) Basis of distribution of service department costs:

	Machine Shop	*Assembly*	*General Plant Services*	*Stores and Misc.*
Stores and maintenance	50%	20%	30%	—
General plant and service	In proportion to the number of employees			

You are required to prepare an overhead distribution statement in detail. Service department costs are to be distributed by continued distribution. Carry through three cycles. Calculations are to be shown to the nearest rupee.

Solution

Small Engineering Unit
Departmental Primary Distribution Summary

₹

	Basis of Allocation	*Total*	*Production Departments*		*Service Departments*	
			Machine Shop	*Assembly*	*General Plant Services*	*Stores and Misc.*
(A) Allocated expenditure (₹)						
Indirect wages	Direct	29,300	8,000	6,000	4,000	11,300
Stores consumed	Direct	6,700	2,200	1,700	1,100	1,700
Supervisory salaries	Direct	14,000	—	—	14,000	—
Other salaries	Direct	10,000	—	—	10,000	—
(B) Apportioned expenditure (₹)						
Power and fuel	H.P. × hrs	15,000	10,500	1,500	—	3,000

(Contd.)

	Basis of Allocation	Total	Production Departments: Machine Shop	Production Departments: Assembly	Service Departments: General Plant Services	Service Departments: Stores and Misc.
Rent	Floor area (sq. ft)	15,000	6,000	3,000	1,500	4,500
Insurance	Investment	3,000	1,920	600	30	450
Depreciation	Investment	1,00,000	64.000	20,000	1,000	15,000
		1,93,000	92,620	32,800	31,630	35,950

Secondary Distribution Summary

₹

Particulars	Total	Production Departments: Machine Shop	Production Departments: Assembly	Service Departments: General Plant	Service Departments: Stores and Misc.
As per primary distribution	1,93,000	92,620	32,800	31,630	35,950
Re-distribution of stores & misc. (50%, 20%, 30%)		17,975	7,190	10,785	(35,950)
		1,10,595	39,990	42,415	—
Re-distribution of general plant (30 : 15 : 10)		23,135	11,568	(42,415)	7,712
		1,33,730	51,558	—	7,712
Re-distribution of stores & misc. (50%, 20%, 30%)		3,856	1,542	2,314	(7,712)
		1,37,586	53,100	2,314	—
Re-distribution of general plant (30 : 15 : 10)		1,262	631	(2,314)	421
		1,38,848	53,731	—	421
Re-distribution of stores & misc. (50%, 20%, 30%)		211	84	126	(421)
		1,39,059	53,815	126	—
Re-distribution of general plant (30 :15 : 10)		69	34	(126)	23
		1,39,128	53,540	—	23
Distribution of stores & misc. (50%, 20%, 30%)		16	7	—	(23)
	1,93,000	1,39,144	53,856	—	—

EXAMPLE 6.9

for excel template, scan

MM Ltd. has three production departments *X*, *Y*, *Z* and two service departments *S* and *C*. The following details are extracted from the books of accounts in respect of indirect expenses incurred during April, 2020:

Indirect Cost:	*Amount (₹)*
Indirect wages	9,000
Lighting and heating	1,200
Rent and rates	12,000
Electric power	6,000
Depreciation	24,000
Sundry expenses	7,800
	60,000

Following further details are collected for distribution of the above costs:

Particulars	*Departments*				
	X	*Y*	*Z*	*S*	*C*
Value of machinery (in ₹'000)	60	50	80	10	–
Horse power of machines	40	45	60	5	–
Light points (nos.)	20	30	40	20	10
Floor space (sq. metres)	150	200	250	100	50
Direct wages (in ₹'000)	30	20	40	4	6
Machine hours worked	4,250	3,380	7,120		

The costs of the service departments are apportioned percentagewise as follows:

Departments	*X*	*Y*	*Z*	*S*	*C*
S	20	30	40	–	10
C	40	20	30	10	–

Calculate:

(a) Overhead recovery rates showing the basis of apportionment.

(b) Total cost of job 321 (with element-wise and department-wise cost break down), the job card of which contain the following details:

Particulars	*Deptt. X*	*Deptt. Y*	*Deptt. Z*
Direct materials used	₹268	₹131	₹102
Direct wages	₹300	₹250	₹300
Machine hours worked	10	12	12

☞ Solution

(a) Overhead recovery rates:

Departmental Overhead Distribution Summary
(Repeated Distribution Method)

₹

Items	*Basis of Apportionment*	*Total*	*Production Department*			*Service Department*	
			X	*Y*	*Z*	*S*	*C*
Indirect wages	Direct wages	9,000	2,700	1,800	3,600	360	540
Lighting and heating	No. of light points	1,200	200	300	400	200	100
Rent and rates	Floor space	12,000	2,400	3,200	4,000	1,600	800
Electric power	H.P. of machines	6,000	1,600	1,800	2,400	200	
Depreciation	Value of machines	24,000	7,200	6,000	9,600	1,200	
Sundry expenses	Direct wages	7,800	2,340	1,560	3,120	312	468
Direct wages	As given	10,000	–	–	–	4,000	6,000
Total		**70,000**	**16,440**	**14,660**	**23,120**	**7,872**	**7,908**
Service Deptt. *S*	Given (20%, 30%, 40%, 10%)		1,574	2,362	3,149	(7,872)	787
Service Deptt. *C*	(40%, 20%, 30%, 10%)		3,478	1,739	2,609	869	(8,695)
Service Deptt *S*	(20%, 30%, 40%, 10%)		174	261	347	(869)	87
Service Deptt. *C*	(40%, 20%, 30%, 10%)		35	17	26	9	(87)
Service Deptt. *S*	(20%, 30%, 40%)		2	3	4	(9)	–
Total			**21,703**	**19,042**	**29,255**	–	–
Machine hours worked	Hrs.		4,250	3,380	7,120		
Overhead recovery Rate (₹) (Overhead/machine hr.)			5.11	5.63	4.11		

(b) Computation of total cost of job-321

Particulars	*Deptt. X*	*Deptt. Y*	*Deptt. Z*	*Total*
Machine hours worked	10	12	12	
	₹	₹	₹	₹
Direct material used	268	131	102	501
Direct wages	300	250	300	850
Overhead cost	51	68	49	168
Total	**619**	**449**	**451**	**1,519**

ABSORPTION OF FACTORY OVERHEADS

Meaning of Absorption

After all service departments overhead have been apportioned to producing departments, the next step is to spread factory overhead to different products or jobs produced. This is termed as "overhead absorption" in cost accounting. The Institute of Cost and Management Accountants (U.K.) defined overhead absorption as "the allotment of overhead to cost units". Known by different names, such as recovery, overhead application, overhead costing, levy, burden rate, etc. the term "absorption" implies that expenses pertaining to a producing department or cost centre are, finally charged to or absorbed in the cost of products, jobs, etc. passing through it. As a result of absorption, the cost of each unit of product of the producing departments includes an equitable share of the total overhead of that department.

Methods of Absorption

Some method of overhead absorption has to be applied to absorb factory overhead to individual products or jobs, etc. on some equitable basis. The rate which is used to charge overhead cost to the products or jobs is known as absorption rate. The following are the generally recognised methods of absorption or absorption rates.

Percentage on Direct Materials

An absorption rate based on materials cost is obtained by dividing total estimated factory overhead by total direct materials cost expected to be used in the manufacturing process. If factory overhead is ₹3,00,000 and materials cost is ₹2,50,000, the absorption rate will be:

$$\frac{3,00,000}{2,50,000} \times 100 = 120\%$$

Each job or product would be charged on the basis of 120% absorption rate. For example, if the materials cost of product is ₹50,000, the factory overhead to be charged for their product would be ₹60,000 (50,000 × 120%).

Advantages The "percentage on direct material cost" method is simple and easy to understand and apply. This method will give correct overhead cost figure where the prices of raw materials do not differ significantly, where quantity and cost of materials in each product are uniform, and where processing for the different products is also uniform. It is useful in very simple types of small business firms.

Disadvantages This method has the following disadvantages:

1. There is no logical relationship between material cost of a product and factory overhead used in production.
2. Materials prices are subject to fluctuations quite often and this phenomenon leads to high or low overhead costs, even though overhead figures remain unchanged.
3. Most of the overhead expenses vary with time. For example, a product or job using cheap materials but a longer period of processing should bear more for overhead as compared to a job or product which uses expensive materials but a shorter period of processing. But the use of direct material cost totally ignores the time factor which is an important factor in allocation/apportionment of overhead costs.

4. This method is not proper where part of the materials passes through all processes, and part through only some processes.
5. The mere fact that a job consumes material of a very expensive nature does not imply that the overhead incurred on that job will also be heavier. If the materials cost basis is used to charge overhead, the product using expensive materials will, in this case, be charged with more than its share of overhead.

Percentage on Direct Wages

Percentage on direct wages is computed in the following manner:

$$\frac{\text{Factory overhead}}{\text{Direct labour cost}} \times 100$$

If factory overhead is ₹2,00,000 and the direct labour cost is also ₹2,00,000, then absorption rate based on direct wages will be 100%.

A job or a product with a direct labour cost of ₹30,000 would be charged with ₹30,000 for factory overhead.

Advantages This method has the following advantages:

1. It is simple to operate and understand.
2. It considers the time factor, as labour cost is computed by multiplying number of hours spent on work by an hourly labour rate. The more hours worked, the higher the labour-cost and the greater the use and therefore the charge for factory overhead.
3. Labour rates fluctuate, but less frequently than that of prices of materials.

Disadvantages The disadvantages are the following:

1. It depends on cost of direct labour which may not reflect accurately the contribution of factory overhead in the cost of product. Many expenses such as taxes, property insurance and depreciation are functions of time.
2. It does not take into account variations, if any, in the rates of remuneration for different types of labour and therefore, the wages incurred on different jobs are not necessarily in the same ratio as the hours spent. This fact would be clear where workers are paid on a piece-rate basis as in this system wages depend on output and not upon time. This limitation is clear from the following example.

	Job A *(16 Hr)*	*Job B* *(20 Hr)*
Direct materials	600	600
Direct labour	400	400
Prime cost	1,000	1,000
Factory overhead (75% on direct wages)	300	300
Factory cost	1,300	1,300

As job *B* has taken 25% extra time to complete work than *A*, the job carried out by *B* must have occupied the factory for a longer period than *A*'s, but as is clear from the above statement, the charge for factory overhead is the same in each case.

3. Total direct labour cost represents the sum of high- and low-wage production workers. By applying overhead on the basis of direct labour cost, a job or product is charged with more overhead when a high-rate operator performs work instead of a low-rate worker leading to incorrect distribution of factory overhead.

Prime Cost Percentage

The prime cost basis combines the total of direct materials cost and direct labour cost and uses this total as a basis for charging overhead. The formula used in determining the rate is:

$$\frac{\text{Factory overhead}}{\text{Prime cost}} \times 100$$

If in a case the factory overhead is ₹4,56,000 and prime cost is ₹6,00,000, then prime cost percentage rate will be

$$\frac{4,56,000}{6,00,000} \times 100 = 76\% \text{ of prime cost}$$

Advantages This method is simple to operate. It considers both materials and labour in charging overhead to each job or product. The prime cost data is easily available without any additional problem of accumulation.

Disadvantages The disadvantages are:

1. Two items, that is, materials and labour both of which possess many disadvantages influence the charging of factory overhead to jobs and products.
2. Where the cost of materials is a larger part of the prime cost, the time factor (direct labour costs) will be ignored which is more related to the factory overhead.
3. It ignores time factor in absorbing factory overhead.
4. It can be useful to only a few departments where the type of labour and value of materials used are constant.

The following example illustrates the demerits of this method.

	Job A	*Job B*
Direct materials	₹30,000	₹4,000
Direct wages (Job *A* 50 hours @ ₹4 per hour		
and job *B* 200 hours @ ₹4 per hour)	200	800
Prime cost	₹30,200	₹4,800
Factory overhead (50% on prime cost)	15,100	2,400
Factory cost	45,300	7,200

The above example indicates that the labour expended on job *B* is four times than that of job *A*. But this fact is not reflected in the factory overhead charged to these two jobs.

Unit of Production Basis

The unit of production method is the simplest and most direct method of charging factory overhead. The unit might be a kilo, foot, a machine, a hundred pieces or whatever unit of measure is used for the product. As a formula, the computation is as follows:

$$\frac{\text{Factory overhead}}{\text{Units of production}}$$

If factory overhead is ₹3,00,000 and the company intends to produce 2,50,000 units during the next period, each unit completed would be charged with ₹1.20 (₹3,00,000 ÷ 2,50,000 units) as its share of factory overhead. Thus, an order with 1,000 completed units would be charged ₹1,200 (1,000 units × ₹1.20) for factory overhead.

The usefulness of this method is limited normally to those situations where only one product is produced. It is used most satisfactorily in small manufacturing concerns having relatively simple manufacturing processes or in large concerns manufacturing few articles in large quantities. If several products manufactured are alike or closely-related, absorption of factory overhead can be made on a weight or a point basis, such as in the following example:

Points value of product *A*	5 points
Points value of product *B*	7 points

Production units *A* 4000, *B* 5000.

Overhead to be absorbed ₹5,50,000

$$\text{Rate per unit} = \frac{5{,}50{,}000}{(4000 \times 5) + (5{,}000 \times 7)} = ₹10$$

Rate per unit of *A* = 5 × ₹10 = ₹50

Rate per unit of *B* = 7 × ₹10 = ₹70

Labour Hour/Production Hour Rate

One of the most widely used methods for overhead application is the labour hour basis. Since many companies require direct labour workers to record their time spent on each job, or in each department of a process cost factory, the data for absorption of overhead on this basis is readily available. The equation for determining the overhead rate under this method is:

$$\frac{\text{Factory overhead}}{\text{Direct labour hours}}$$

If factory overhead is ₹4,00,000 and direct labour hours are 2,00,000, then overhead rate based on direct labour hours would be ₹2 per hour of direct labour (₹4,00,000 ÷ 2,00,000 hours). A product that requires 5,000 direct labour hours would be charged with ₹10,000 (5,000 hours × ₹2) for factory overhead.

Advantages The following are the advantages:

1. As long as direct labour is the chief factor in manufacturing processes, the direct labour hour method is useful as the most equitable basis for charging overhead.
2. This method uses the time factor and production taking the same time is charged with the same amount of overhead, though the direct labourer may be getting different wage rates.

Disadvantages The disadvantages are:

1. The method requires accumulation of direct labour hours by job, product or department. Time-keeping should be adequate to provide this information.
2. This method cannot be used where machines are used extensively for production.

Machine Hour Rate

The machine hour rate is used where the work is performed primarily on machines. The formula used in computing the rate is:

$$\frac{\text{Factory overhead}}{\text{Machine hours}}$$

If factory overhead is ₹3,00,000 and total machine hours are 1,50,000, the machine hour rate is ₹2 per machine hour (₹3,00,000 ÷ 1,50,000 hours).

Advantages This method can be used advantageously where the machine is the major factor in production. In capital-intensive industries, plans and machines are used in large quantities and one operator may attend to several machines or several operators may attend to a single machine. By making the machine the basis, overhead costs can be equitably absorbed among different products.

Disadvantages The disadvantages are:

1. Machine hour data has to be collected, and therefore, it requires additional clerical work. The cost of collection and accounting activities goes up and therefore, is not workable for small business firms.
2. The method cannot be used universally by all business concerns. It can be used where production is mainly through machines.

Types of Machine Hour Rate

Two types of machine hour rate may be calculated such as:

1. *Ordinary machine hour rate* This rate takes into account only those overhead expenses which are directly attributed to the running of a machine. Such expenses are power, fuel, repair, maintenance and depreciation. The total of all these expenses is divided by the total machine hours.
2. *Composite machine hour rate* This method takes into account not only expenses directly connected with the machine as mentioned above, but also other expenses which are known as standing or fixed charges. Such expenses are rent and rates, supervisory, labour, lighting and heating, etc. These expenses being fixed in nature are determined for a particular period and then apportioned among different departments on some equitable bases. The overhead expenses thus apportioned to each department are further apportioned among the machines (machine cost centres) in that department, on an equitable basis. Generally, composite machine hour rate is calculated.

The following are bases used for the apportionment of expenses for computing machine hour rate.

Overhead Expenses	*Basis*
1. Standing Charges	
(i) Supervision	Estimated time devoted to each machine
(ii) Rent and rates	Floor area occupied by each machine
(iii) Heating and lighting	Number of points or floor occupied by each machine
(iv) Lubricating oil and consumable stores	Capital values, machine hours or past experience
(v) Insurance	Insured value of each machine
(vi) Miscellaneous expenses	Equitable basis depending on facts

(Contd.)

Overhead Expenses	Basis
2. *Machine or Variable Expenses*	
(i) Depreciation	Machine hours
(ii) Repairs	Machine hours or capital values or cost of repairs spread over the working life of machine
(iii) Power	Horse power of machines or machine hours or meter readings

SELECTING AN ABSORPTION RATE

The above absorption rates have their own merits and demerits. The method to be used depends on the factors and circumstances prevailing in a manufacturing firm. Whatever method is selected by a firm, it must achieve the following objectives:

1. The basic objective is to select an absorption rate which helps in determining the accurate amount of factory overhead to be charged to individual products, jobs, processes, etc.
2. A secondary objective in selecting a method of absorption is to minimise clerical effort and cost. When two or more absorption rates tend to charge the same amount of overhead, the simplest base could be used.
3. The selection of an absorption rate is also influenced by other factors, such as type of industry, legal requirements, if any, policy of management, etc. in addition to the suitability of a method under specific circumstances.

Arguments in Favour of Apportionment and Absorption of Overheads

The following are the arguments generally advanced in favour of apportionment and absorption of overheads:

1. *Product costing* The process of apportionment and absorption helps in determining the total or full cost of a product and in turn assists in making product profitability analysis by comparing selling prices of different products with related full costs. Also, product cost can be used as a floor when fixing the price of a product.
2. *Stock valuation* Apportionment and absorption facilitates inclusion of productions overhead in the valuation of work-in-progress and closing stock. For work-in-progress, the amount of production overhead included indicates the degrees of completion of the products. Closing stock also rightly bears a share of manufacturing overhead. It is also clear that a proportion of manufacturing overhead is transferred to the next accounting period via work-in-progress and closing stock. Valuation of closing stock and work in progress in terms of full cost including production overhead is accepted for the purpose of financial reporting and by taxation and other regulatory authorities.
3. *Production overheads as product costs* Apportionment and absorption of overheads achieves the objectives of recognising production overheads as product costs. It ensures the rationality that manufacturing of product requires incurrence of production overheads, and if manufacturing overhead is not incurred, production is not possible.
4. *Cost control* Apportionment and absorption of overhead makes the centres or department managers aware about the costs they are considered to be accountable. Therefore, it develops a sense of responsibility among the production and service cost centre managers. These managers

can relook at these costs which are being charged to their departments through budgeting process. Consequently, managers can take steps to control costs assigned to their departments.

5. *Full costs used for government projects and activities* In all government projects and govt-funded activities, full costs are considered including manufacturing overhead. Governments and development agencies also provide grants to cover the full costs. Audit process to verify full costs implies apportionment and absorption of overheads.

Limitations of Apportionment and Absorption

Apportionment and absorption of overheads are criticised on the following grounds:

1. Different methods of apportionment and absorption tend to charge varying amounts of manufacturing overheads to products and thus making the resulting product costs doubtful. Also, distribution of overheads based on different methods leads to inconsistencies and arbitrariness.
2. Since product costs themselves become unreliable and inaccurate, due to more or less arbitrary cost apportionment process, it cannot be used to set product price.
3. Those business firms which use one overall rate or a single plant wide rate instead of multiple rates of absorption may not find product cost data useful for planning, control and decision-making.
4. Apportionment and absorption of overheads due to their underlying arbitrary methods may give product undercosting or product overcosting. In undercosting, a product uses relatively a larger quantity of resources but is found to have a relatively low total cost. On the other hand, overcosting implies that a product consumes smaller quantity of resources but is shown to have higher costs.

Blanket and Departmental Overhead Rate

Blanket overhead rate refers to the computation of one single overhead rate for the entire factory. This is also known as plantwide or the single overhead rate for the entire factory. It is determined as follows:

$$\text{Blanket overhead rate} = \frac{\text{Overhead cost for the entire factory for the period}}{\text{Base for the period (Labour hours, Machine hours)}}$$

It is useful in companies producing the main product in continuous process, e.g. chemical plant, glass plant, etc.

When separate overhead rates are computed for each department, cost centre or product line, they are called departmental rates. Generally, separate rates for separate departments are suitable for absorption of overheads.

Blanket rate is simple to calculate and involves minimal clerical work and cost. Computation of departmental rates involves more clerical work but these are more reliable and correct for absorption of overhead costs.

✎ EXAMPLE 6.10

Calculate machine hour rate from the following details provided by a production Department of ABC Ltd.

(i) Bought machinery of ₹4,50,000
(ii) Installation charges ₹50,000
(iii) Life of machine 5 years
(iv) Working hours per year 2,500
(v) Repair charges 75% of depreciation

(vi) Electric power consumed: 10 units per hour @ ₹3
(vii) Lubricating oil ₹40 per day of 8 hours
(viii) Consumable stores @ ₹80 per day of 8 hours
(ix) Wages of machine operator @ ₹200 per day of 8 hours

☞ **Solution**

Calculation of Machine Hour Rate

		Rate Per Hour (₹)
(A) Standing Charges:	NIL	
(B) Operating Expenses:		
(i) Depreciation	$= \frac{₹4,50,000 + 50,000}{5 \text{ years}}$	
Hourly rate	$= \frac{₹1,00,000}{2500 \text{ hrs}}$	= 40.00
(ii) Repair charges (75% of depreciation)	= ₹75,000	
	Hourly rate $= \frac{75,000}{2500 \text{ hrs}}$	= 30.00
(iii) Electric power (10 units × ₹3)		= 30.00
(iv) Lubricating oil (₹40/8 hrs)		= 5.00
(v) Consumable stores (₹80/8 hrs)		= 10.00
(vi) Wages of machine operator (₹200/8hrs)		= 25.00
Machine hour rate		140.00

EXAMPLE 6.11

The following information is made available from the costing records of a factory:

(i) The original cost of the machine	₹1,00,000
Estimated life	10 years
Residual value	₹5,000

Factory operates for 48 hours per week—52 weeks in a year. Allow 15% towards machine maintenance downtime. 5% may be allowed as setting up time.

(ii) Electricity used by the machine is 10 units per hour at a cost of 50 paise per unit.
(iii) Repairs and maintenance cost is ₹500 per month.
(iv) Two operators attend the machine during operation along with two other machines. Their total wages, including fringe benefits, amount to ₹5,000 per month.
(v) Other overheads attributable to the machine are ₹10,431 per year.

Using the above data, calculate machine hour rate.

Solution

Calculation of Machine Hour Rate.

			₹
Annual working hours 48 × 52		=	2,496
Less: Machine maintenance and setting up time. (15% + 5%) = 20%		=	499
Normal working hours per annum		=	1,997
Standing charges per annum:			
Two operators wages along with two other machines = $\frac{5000 \times 12 \times 1}{3}$	20,000		
Other overheads	10,431		
Total standing charges	30,431		
Hourly rate of standing charges ₹30431/1997			15.238
Variable expenses per hour:			
Depreciation: $\frac{1{,}00{,}000 - 5{,}000}{10 \times 1997}$			4.757
Repairs and maintenance = $\frac{500 \times 12}{1997}$			3.004
Power 10 unit × .50			5.000
Machine hour rate			27.999

Example 6.12

From the following particulars, calculate machine hour rate:

(i) Cost of machine ₹1,00,000
Estimated life 10 years
Scrap value ₹ 10,000

(ii) Estimated working time 50 weeks of 44 hours each. It includes the following:
Time taken up in maintenance 200 hrs.
Setting up time 100 hrs.
However, setting up time is regarded as productive time.

(iii) Power used during production is 16 units per hour @ 9 paise per unit. No current is taken during maintenance or setting up time.

(iv) The machine requires a chemical solution which is replaced at the end of each week at a cost of ₹20 each time.

(v) Cost of maintenance ₹1,200 per annum.

(vi) Two attendants control the operation of this machine together with five other identical machines. Their combined weekly wages amount to ₹120.

(vii) General work overheads allocated to this machine for the year amount to ₹2,000.

Solution

Working Note:

Effective Machine Hours	*Hrs.*
Actual working hours 50 weeks × 44 hrs	2,200
Less: Time required for maintenance	200
Effective machine hours	2000

Computation of Machine Hour Rate

Standing Charges	₹
Overhead allocated to machine	2,000
Wages of attendants $\frac{120 \times 50}{6}$	1,000
Total standing charges	3,000
Hourly rate of standing charges $\frac{3000}{2000}$	1.50
Machine Expenses	
Depreciation $\frac{1,00,000 - 10,000}{10 \times 2000}$	4.50
Repair and maintenance $\left(\frac{1200}{2000}\right)$	0.60
Chemical $\left(\frac{20 \times 50}{2000}\right)$	0.50
Power $\left(\frac{1900 \times 16 \times 0.09}{2000}\right)$	1.37
Machine hour rate	8.47

Example 6.13

A machine shop in a factory has five machines of exactly similar type and specification. One operator is employed on each machine at ₹20 per hour. The factory works a 40-hour week which includes four hours for set-up time for each machine. The operators are paid fully for 40 hours. Costs are reported for the machine shop on the basis of thirteen four-weekly periods.

The following details applicable to the cost centre/machine are available:

1. Set up time is unproductive and no power is consumed during the set up time.
2. Original cost of machine is ₹1,30,000.
3. Depreciation on machine is to be provided at 10% per annum on original cost.
4. Maintenance and repairs per work per machine amounts to ₹25.
5. Consumable stores per week per machine amount to ₹27.
6. Power consumed is 10 units per hour per machine at 80 paise per unit.
7. Wages paid to the operators are considered as indirect.

8. Overheads apportioned to the cost centre are:

Rent	₹3,000 p.a.
Heat and light	₹4,000 p.a.
Misc. expenses	₹6,000 p.a.

You are required to calculate:

(i) Cost of running one machine for a four-week period; and

(ii) The machine hour rate.

Solution

Calculations of Cost of Running One Machine for a Four-week period.

Standing Charges:	₹
1. Rent	3,000
2. Heat and light	4,000
3. Sundry expenses	6,000
Total expenses of 5 machines	13,000

Total expenses for one machine for 4-week period

$= \frac{13{,}000}{5} \times \frac{4}{13}$	800
4. Wages of operator (40 × 4 × ₹20)	3,200
(i) Total Standing Charges (i)	4,000
Machine Expenses:	
1. Depreciation $\left(1{,}30{,}000 \frac{10}{100}\right) \times \frac{4}{13}$	4,000
2. Repairs and maintenance (25 × 4)	100
3. Power (36 × 10 × .80)	288
Total machine expenses (ii)	4,496
Total machine expenses (i + ii)	8,496

(ii) Machine hour rate:

= Total cost ÷ Total productive time

= ₹8,496 ÷ 36 hrs × 4

= ₹59 per effective productive hour

EXAMPLE 6.14

From the following data of textile factory machine room, compute an hourly machine rate, assuming that the machine room will work on 90% capacity throughout the year and that a breakdown of 10% is reasonable. There are three days holiday at Deepawali, two days at Holi and two days at Christmas exclusive of Sundays. The factory works 8 hours a day and 4 hours on Saturday. Number of machines (each of the same type) is 40.

Expenses Per Annum:

	₹
Power	3,12,000
Light	64,000
Salaries to foremen	1,20,000
Lubricating oil	6,600
Repairs to machines	1,44,600
Depreciation	78,560

☞ ***Solution***

Computation of Machine Hour Rate

Standing Charges	₹	₹ *Per Hour* (80,640 hrs)
Light	64,000	
Salaries to foremen	1,20,000	
Lubrication oil (assumed fixed)	6,600	
	1,90,600	2.364
Running Charges	(3,12,000/80640)	3.869
Repair	(144600/80640)	1.793
Depreciation	(78,560/80,640)	0.974
Machine hour rate		9.000

Working Note: *Calculation of Effective Machine Hours*

		(Hrs.)
Total hours 365 × 8	=	2920
Less: Saturday only 4 hours work (52 × 4)	208	
Sundays holiday (52 × 8)	416	
Holiday on Deepawali, Holi and Christmas (3 + 2 + 2) × 8	56	680
Machine hours worked		2,240
Less: 10% breakdown (normal)		224
Effective machine hour per machine		2,016

Total machine hours = Effective machine hours per machine × Number of machines

= 2,016 × 40 = 80,640 hrs.

EXAMPLE 6.15

The following data relate to a manufacturing department for a period:

	Budgeted Data (₹)	*Actual Data* (₹)
Direct material	1,00,000	1,40,000
Direct labour	2,00,000	2,50,000
Production overhead	2,00,000	2,30,000
Direct labour hours	50,000	62,500
Machine hours	40,000	50,000

Job *ZX* was one of the jobs worked on during the period. The actual data relating to this job were direct material ₹6,000; direct labour ₹3,000; direct labour hours 750; and machine hours 750.

Required:

(i) Calculate the production overhead absorption rate pre-determined for the period based on:
   (1) % direct material cost (2) Machine hours

(ii) Calculate the production overhead cost to be charged to job *ZX* based on the rates calculated under (i) above.

(iii) Assuming that a machine hour rate of absorption is used, calculate the under/over absorption for the period and state the appropriate treatment on the accounts.

Solution

(i) (1) Direct material cost rate $= \dfrac{\text{Production overhead}}{\text{Direct material cost}}$

$$= \left(\frac{2,00,000}{1,00,000}\right) \times 100 = 200\%$$

(2) Machine hour rate $= \dfrac{\text{Production overhead}}{\text{Machine hours}}$

$$\frac{2,00,000}{40,000} = ₹5$$

(ii) Production overhead charged to job *ZX*
On the basis of direct material cost rate = 200% of 6,000 = ₹12,000
On the basis of machine hour rate = 750 hr. × ₹5 = ₹3,750

(iii) If machine hour rate of absorption is used, then:
Overhead absorbed = Machine hours × Rate = 50,000 × 5 = ₹2,50,000
Actual overhead = ₹2,30,000
∴ Over absorption of overhead = ₹20,000

Treatment of over-absorption of overhead Over- or under-absorption of overhead can be shown in cost accounts in following three ways:

1. In case of seasonal factory or a new project over- or under-absorption may be carry forward to next accounting year.

2. Over- and under-absorption may be adjusted by applying supplementary rate. The rate may be calculated as

$$\text{Supplementary rate} = \frac{\text{Amount of over or under absorbed overhead}}{\text{Actual base}}$$

$$\text{In this case, supplementary rate will be} = \frac{20{,}000}{50{,}000}\left[\frac{\text{(Over absorbed overhead)}}{\text{Machine hour}}\right]$$

$$= ₹0.40 \text{ (negative)}$$

The cost of job or product is decreased by deducting the extra amount or overhead charged by applying a negative supplementary rate.

3. If the difference between actual and absorbed overhead is not very large or the difference is due to abnormal circumstances such difference should be transferred to costing profit and loss account at the end of the accounting year.
In this over-absorption is ₹20,000 which is not very small or not due to abnormal reason and neither our business is seasonal in nature, hence, using supplementary rate is the best option.

EXAMPLE 6.16

The cost of a machine is ₹66,000, and it has an estimated scrap value of ₹6,000 at the end of its estimated effective life of 10 years. Annually the machine works on all the 365 days at a rate of 8 hours a day of which 120 hours p.a. are consumed by maintenance. About 1/7th of the total productive time is consumed in setting the machines. Various costs relating to the working of the machine are as follows:

(i) Two units of power are consumed every hour at the rate of ₹1.40 per unit.
(ii) Monthly cleaning and oiling expenses for the machine are ₹280.
(iii) Annual maintenance of machine amounts to ₹2,800.
(iv) Three operators combined together control operation of ten identical machines and each of them gets a monthly salary of ₹2,100.
(v) Annual departmental overheads apportioned to the machine are: fixed: ₹5,480; variable: ₹12,600.
Compute the machine hour rate in each of the following cases:
(a) Setting up time is regarded productive but power is not consumed during setting up time.
(b) Setting up time is not regarded productive but power is consumed during setting up time.

Solution

	Setting Up Time is Productive Time	*Setting Up Time is Non-productive Time*
	(2,800 Hrs)	(2,400 Hrs)
Annual Standing Charges		
Cleaning & oiling (280 × 12)	3,360	3,360
Operator's salary $\left(2100 \times \frac{3}{10} \times 12\right)$	7,560	7,560
Departmental overhead (fixed)	5,480	5,480
	16,400	16,400

(Contd.)

	Setting Up Time is Productive Time	*Setting Up Time is Non-productive Time*
Annual standing charges per hour	$\frac{16400}{2800} = 5.86$	$\frac{16400}{2400} = 6.83$
Machine Charges		
Depreciation $\left(\frac{66000 - 6000}{10}\right)$	2.14	2.50
Departmental overhead fixed 12,600	4.50	5.25
Power $\left(2 \times 1.40 \times \frac{2400}{2800}\right); \left(2 \times 1.40 \times \frac{2800}{2400}\right)$	2.40	3.27
Maintenance $\frac{2800}{2800}, \frac{2800}{2400}$	1.00	1.17
	15.90	19.02

Notes:

Annual working hours 365 days @ 8 hours every day = 2920 hours
Less maintenance hours = 120 hours
Effective hours = 2,800 hours
1/7th of productive time is setting up time i.e. 400 hours
If setting up time is not productive then effective working hours shall be = 2,800 – 400 hours = 2,400 hours

EXAMPLE 6.17

A manufacturing unit has added a new machine to its fleet of five existing machines. The total cost of purchase and installation of the machine is ₹7,50,000. The machine has an estimated life of 15 years and is expected to realise ₹30,000 as scrap at the end of its working life.

Other relevant data are as follows:

(i) Budgeted working hours are 2,400 based on 8 hours per day for 300 days. This includes 400 hours for plant-maintenance.

(ii) Electricity used by the machine is 15 units per hour at a cost of ₹2.00 per unit. No current is drawn during maintenance.

(iii) Estimated cost of maintenance of the machine is ₹500 per week of 6 working days.

(iv) The machine requires special oil for heating which is replaced once every month at a cost of ₹2,500.

(v) Three operators control the operations of the entire battery of 6 machines and the average wages per person amounts to ₹450 per week plus 40% fringe benefits.

(vi) Departmental and general work overheads allocated to the operation of 5 machines during the last year were ₹60,000.

During the current year, it is estimated that there will be an increase of 12.5% of this amount. No incremental overhead is envisaged for the installation of the new machine.

Compute the machine-hour rate for the recovery of machine expenses.

Solution

Effective Machine Hours	
Number of working days per annum	300
Total number of working hours @ 8 hours per day (300 × 8)	2,400
Less: Time spent in maintenance	400
Effective machine hours	2,000

Computation of Machine Hour Rate

Standing Charges	
Operator's wages 450 × 3 × 50	67,500
40% Fringe benefits	27,000
Departmental and general work overheads (60,000 + 12.5% of 60,000)	67,500
Standing Charges for 6 Machines	1,62,000
Standing charges for one machine	27,000
Standing charges per machine per hour $\frac{27,000}{2,000} =$	13.50
Machine Charges	
Depreciation $\frac{7,50,000 - 30,000}{2,000 \times 15}$	24.00
Electricity (15 units @ ₹2)	30.00
Special oil $\left(\frac{2,500 \times 12}{2,000}\right)$	15.00
Maintenance $\frac{500 \times 300}{6 \times 2,000}$	12.50
Machine Hour Rate	95.00

EXAMPLE 6.18

A machine shop cost centre contains three machines of equal capacities. Three operators are employed on each machine, who are paid ₹20 per hour each. The factory works for forty-eight hours in a week which includes 4-hours set-up time. The work is jointly done by operators. The operators are paid fully for the forty-eight hours. In addition, they are paid a bonus of 10 per cent of productive time. Costs are reported for this company on the basis of thirteen four-weekly period.

The company for the purpose of computing machine hour rate includes the direct wages of the operator and also recoups the factory overheads allocated to the machines. The following details of factory overheads applicable to the cost centre are available:

- Depreciation is 10% per annum on original cost of the machine. Original cost of the each machine is ₹52,000.

- Maintenance and repairs per week per machine is ₹60.
- Consumable stores per week per machine are ₹75.
- Power: 20 units per hour per machine at the rate of 80 paise per unit.
- Apportionment to the cost centre: Rent per annum ₹5,400; heat and light per annum ₹9,720; and foreman's salary per annum ₹12,960.

Required:

(i) Calculate the cost of running one machine for a four-week period.

(ii) Calculate machine hour rate.

☞ ***Solution***

Computation of Cost of Running One Machine for a Four-week Period

	₹
Standing Charges	*Per Annum*
Rent	5,400
Heat and light	9,720
Forman's salary	12,960
	28,080
	₹
Total expenses for one machine for four-week period = $\frac{28,080 \times 4}{3 \times 13}$	2,880
Wages: Hours per week = 48 hours for 4 weeks = 48 × 4 = 192	
Wages 192 × 20	3,840
Bonus (192–16) = 176 × 20 × .10	352
(i) Total standing charges	7,072

Machine Expenses

	₹
Depreciation = $\left(52,000 \times 10\% \times \frac{4}{13}\right)$	1,600
Repairs and maintenance = (60 × 4)	240
Consumable stores (75 × 4)	300
Power (192 – 16) = 176 × 20 × .80	2,816
(ii) Total machine expense	4,956
Total expenses (i) + (ii)	12,028

$$\text{Machine hour rate} = \frac{12,028}{176} = 68.34$$

✍ **EXAMPLE 6.19**

Calculate machine hour rate for recovery of overheads for a machine from the following information:

Cost of machine is ₹25,00,000 and estimated salvage value is ₹1,00,000. Estimated working life of the machine is 10 years. Annual working hours are 3,000 in the factory. The machine is required 400 hours per annum for repairs and maintenance. Setting-up time of the machine is 156 hours per annum to be treated as productive time. Cost of repairs and maintenance for whole working life of the machine is ₹3,50,000. Power used 15 units per hour at a cost of ₹5 per unit. No power is consumed during maintenance and setting-up time. A chemical required for operating the machine is ₹9,880 per annum. Wages of an operator is ₹4,000 per month. The operator, devoted one-third of his time to the machine. Annual insurance charges 2 per cent of cost of machine.

Light charges for the department are ₹2,500 per month, having 48 points in all, out of which only 8 points are used at this machine. Other indirect expenses are chargeable to the machine are ₹6,500 per month.

Solution

Computation of Machine Hour Rate
Running Hours (3,000 – 400) = 2,600 Per Annum

Particulars	*Total Amount* (₹)	*Rate Per Hour* (₹)
Fixed Charges (Standing Charges)		
Operator's wages: $\frac{₹4{,}000 \times 12}{3}$	16,000	
Insurance: 2% of ₹25,00,000	50,000	
Light charges: $\frac{₹2{,}500 \times 12 \times 8}{48}$	5,000	
Other indirect expenses: ₹6,500 × 12	78,000	
Total standing charges	1,49,000	
Hourly rate for fixed charges: $\frac{₹1{,}49{,}000}{2{,}600}$		57.31
Variable Expenses (Machine Expenses) Per Hour		
Depreciation : $\frac{₹25{,}00{,}000 - ₹1{,}00{,}000}{10 \times 2{,}600}$		92.31
Repairs and maintenance : $\frac{₹3{,}50{,}000}{10 \times 2{,}600}$		13.46
Power: $\frac{₹5 \times 15 \times 2{,}444}{2{,}600}$		70.50
Chemical: $\frac{₹9{,}880}{2{,}600}$		3.80
Machine hour rate		237.38

✍ EXAMPLE 6.20

The budgeted working conditions for cost centre are as follows:

Normal working per week	42 hours
Number of machines	14
Normal weekly loss of hours on maintenance	5 hours per machine
Number of weeks works per year	48
Estimated annual overheads	₹1,24,320
Actual results in respect of a 4-week period are:	
Overhead incurred	₹10,200
Machine hours produced	2,000

On the basis of the above information you are required to calculate:

(i) The machine hour rate.

(ii) The amount of under- or over-absorption of overhead.

☞ ***Solution***

(i)	Normal working hours per annum –	
	14 machines × 42 hrs. per week × 48 weeks =	28,224 hrs.
	Normal loss of hours per year due to maintenance 14 × 5 × 48 hrs.	3,360 hrs.
	Effective hours per year 28,224 – 3,360	24,864 hours
	Estimated annual overhead	₹1,24,320

$$\textbf{Machine Hour Rate } \frac{1{,}24{,}320}{24{,}864} = ₹5$$

(ii)	Overhead absorbed 2000 hrs × ₹5 =	₹10,000
	Overhead incurred =	₹10,200
	Overhead under absorbed =	₹ 200

✍ EXAMPLE 6.21

A machine shop of Avon Ltd. has six identical machines manned by 6 operators. The machines cannot be worked without an operator wholly engaged on it. The cost of all these 6 machines including installation charges works out to ₹12 lakh and these machines are deemed to have a scrap value of 10% at the end of its effective life (9 years). These particulars are furnished for a six-month period.

Normal available hours per month	218
Absenteeism (without pay) hours	18
Leave (with pay) – hours	20
Stoppage for repairs and maintenance etc. hours	20
Average rate of wages per day of 8 hours	₹80
Production bonus estimated	15% on wages
Value of power consumed	₹24,150

(Contd.)

Supervision and indirect labour	₹9,900
Lighting and electricity	₹4,800
These particulars are for a year:	
Repairs and maintenance including consumables	₹36,000
Insurance	₹60,000
Other sundry works expenses	₹36,000
General management expenses allocated	₹1,09,040

You are required to work out a comprehensive machine hour rate for the machine shop.

Solution

AVON LTD.

(1) **Computation of total machine hours utilised:**

Normal available hours p.m. per operator:		218 hours
Less: Unutilised hours due to:		
Absenteeism	18 hours	
Leave	20	
Stoppage for repairs and maintenance etc.	20	58
Total hours utilised p.m. per operator		160
Total hours utilised for 6 months for 6 operators: 160 × 6 × 6		= 5,760 hours

It is given in the question that the machine cannot work without an operator wholly engaged on it. Therefore, hours utilised for six operators that is, 5,760 hours represent the total machine hours.

(2) **Total wage to 6 operators for six months:**

Average rate of wages per hour = ₹80/8 = ₹10

Normal hours for which wages are to be paid: 218 – 18 = 200 hours.

Wages for 6 months for 6 operators @ ₹10 = 200 × 6 × 6 × 10 = ₹72,000.

Computation of Comprehensive Machine Hour Rate for the Machine Shop

		₹
Operator wages (Ref: W-2)	(for six months)	72,000
Production bonus (15% of wages)	,,	10,800
Power consumed	,,	24,150
Supervision and indirect labour	,,	9,900
Lighting and electricity	,,	4,800
Repair and maintenance (36,000/2)	,,	18,000
Insurance (60,000/2)	,,	30,000
Depreciation for 6 months		
[(12 lakhs – 1.20 lakhs)/9]/2	(for six months)	60,000

(Contd.)

	₹
Other sundry works expenses for 6 months	18,000
General management expenses for 6 months	54,520
Total overheads for six months	3,02,170
Comprehensive machine hour rate	
(3,02,170/5,760)	52.46

EXAMPLE 6.22

Calculate the comprehensive machine hour rate of a machine from the following:

(i) Cost of the machine ₹25 lakhs, having a scrap value of ₹1 lakh after 10 years.

(ii) The machine will be operated for three shifts of 7 hrs. each for 300 working days in a year of which 300 hrs. will be utilised for minor repairs and maintenance.

(iii) Wages payable: ₹8,000 p.m. for an operator; ₹3,000 p.m. for a helper for every shift; and ₹16,000 per month to one supervisor per shift for the department accommodating four machines including the above machine.

(iv) Other details :

Power consumption	: 25 units (kWh @ ₹4.80 per unit)
Repairs and maintenance	: ₹30,000 per annum
General lighting and heating	: ₹4,000 p.m. for the whole department having the four machines
Insurance	: ₹18,000 per machine per annum
Rent, rates and taxes	: ₹3,000 p.m. for the department
Factory overhead	: ₹36,000 per annum for the department

Solution

Computation of Comprehensive Machine Hour Rate

	Annual working hours (300 × 7 × 3)	6,300
Cost: ₹25,00,000	*Less*: for minor repair and maintenance	300
Life: 10 years, scrap value: ₹1,00,000	Net working hours	s6,000

Depreciation: ₹2,40,000 p.a.

(i) *Running Expenses:*

	Per Annum	Per Hour (based on 6000 hours)

	(₹)	(₹)
Wages to operators: 3 × ₹8,000 × 12	2,88,000	48
Wages to helper: 3 × ₹3,000 × 12	1,08,000	18
Power: 6,000 × 25 × ₹4.80	7,20,000	120
Repairs and maintenance	30,000	5
	11,46,000	191
(ii) *Fixed Expenses:*		
Supervisor's Salary: ₹ $\frac{16,000 \times 12 \times 3}{4}$	1,44,000	24
General lighting and heating ₹ $\frac{4000 \times 12}{4}$	12,000	2
Insurance	18,000	3
Rent, rates and taxes ₹ $\frac{3000 \times 12}{4}$	9,000	1.50
Factory overhead ₹ $\frac{3600}{4}$	9,000	1.50
Depreciation	2,40,000	40
	4,32,000	72
Total	**15,78,000**	**263**

Comprehensive Machine Hour Rate: ₹263

Example 6.23

In a factory, a machine is considered to work for 208 hours in a month. It includes maintenance time of 8 hours and set-up time of 20 hours.

The expense data relating to the machine are as under:

– Cost of the machine is ₹5,00,000. Life 10 years. Estimated scrap value at the end of life is ₹20,000.

	₹
– Repairs and maintenance per annum	60,480
– Consumable stores per annum	47,520
– Rent of building per annum (The machine under reference occupies 1/6 of the area)	72,000
– Supervisor's salary per month (Common to three machines)	6,000
– Wages of operator per month per machine	2,500
– General lighting charges per month allocated to the machine	1,000
– Power 25 units per hour at ₹2 per unit	

Power is required for productive purposes only. Set-up time, though productive, does not require power. The Supervisor and Operator are permanent. Repairs and maintenance and consumable stores vary with the running of the machine.

Required:

Calculate a two-tier machine hour rate for (a) set-up time; and (b) running time.

☞ ***Solution***

Computation of Machine Hour Rate

✍ **WORKING NOTES:**

(i) Effective hours for standing charges (208 hours – 8 hours)	200
(ii) Effective hours for variable costs (208 hours – 28 hours)	180

1. *Standing Charges Per Hour*

	Per Month ₹	Per Hour ₹
Supervisor's salary (₹6,000/3 machines)	2,000	
General lighting	1,000	
Rent (₹72,000/6 × 12)	1,000	
Total standing charges	4,000	
Standing charges per hour (₹4,000/200 hours)		20

2. *Machine Expenses Per Hour*

	Per Month ₹	Per Hour ₹
Depreciation (₹5,00,000 – ₹20,000)/ (10 years × 12 months)	4,000	20 (₹4,000/200 hours)
Repairs and maintenance (₹60,480/12 months)	5,040	28 (₹5,040/180 hours)
Consumable stores (₹47,520/12 months)	3,960	22 (₹3,960/180 hours)
Power (25 units × ₹2 × 180 hours)	9,000	50 (₹9,000/180 hours)
Wages	2,500	12.50 (₹2,500/200 hours)
Total machine expenses	24,500	132.50

Computation of Two-tier machine hour rate

	Set-up Time Rate Per Machine Hour ₹	Running Time Rate Per Machine Hour ₹
Standing charges *(Refer to Working Note 2)*	20.00	20.00
Machine expenses *(Refer to Working Note 3)*		
Depreciation	20.00	20.00
Repair and maintenance	–	28.00
Consumable stores	–	22.00
Power	–	50.00
Machine hour rate of overheads	40.00	140.00
Wages	12.50	12.50
Comprehensive machine hour rate	52.50	152.50

EXAMPLE 6.24

In a manufacturing company, factory overheads are charged as fixed percentage basis on direct labour, and office overheads are charged on the basis of percentage of factory cost. The following information are available related to the year ending 31st March, 2020:

	Product A	*Product B*
Direct materials	₹19,000	₹15,000
Direct labour	₹15,000	₹25,000
Sales	₹60,000	₹80,000
Profit	25% on cost	25% on sales price

You are required to find out:

(i) The percentage of factory overheads on direct labour.
(ii) The percentage of office overheads on factory cost

Solution

Let, the percentage of factory overheads on direct labour is "x" and percentage of office overheads on factory cost is "y" than the total cost of product A and product B will be as follows:

	Product A (₹)	*Product B* (₹)
Direct materials	19,000	15,000
Direct labour	15,000	25,000
Prime cost	34,000	40,000
Factory overheads (Direct labour × x)	$150x$	$250x$
Factory cost (i)	$34{,}000 + 150x$	$40{,}000 + 250x$
Office overheads (Factory cost × y) (ii)	$340y + 1.5xy$	$400y + 2.5xy$
Total cost [(i) + (ii)]	$34{,}000 + 150x + 340y + 1.5xy$	$40{,}000 + 250x + 400y + 2.5xy$

Total cost on the basis of sales is:

	Product A (₹)	Product B (₹)
Sales	60,000	80,000
Less: Profit		
Product A – 25% on cost or 20% on sales	12,000	
Product B – 25% on sales		20,000
Total cost	48,000	60,000

Thus,

Total cost of *A* is $34,000 + 150x + 340y + 1.5\,xy = 48,000$

or $150x + 340y + 1.5\,xy = 14,000$ (i)

Total cost of *B* is $40,000 + 250x + 400y + 2.5xy = 60,000$

or $250x + 400y + 2.5\,xy = 20,000$ (ii)

Equation (ii) multiplied by 0.6 and after deducting from equation (i), we get

$$150x + 340y + 1.5xy = 14,000 \quad \text{(i)}$$
$$\_150x \pm 240y \pm 1.5\,xy = \_12,000 \quad \text{(ii)}$$
$$100y = 2,000$$
$$\text{or } y = 20$$

Putting value of *y* in equation (i), we get

$150x + 340 \times 20 + 1.5x \times 20 = 14,000$

or $150x + 30x = 14,000 - 6,800$

or $180x = 7,200$

or $x = 40.$

Hence, (i) the percentage of factory overheads on direct labour = 40 and

(ii) the percentage of office overheads on factory cost = 20.

EXAMPLE 6.25

Lewington Ltd makes a variety of kitchen fittings and equipment. It uses a three-stage process involving cutting, assembly and finishing. The following figures are extracted from its budget for the current year:

	Cutting	Assembly	Finishing
Production overheads (₹000)	1,600	2,000	1,400
Machine hours	40,000	25,000	14,000
Direct labour hours	10,000	40,000	20,000

The company uses an absorption costing system for calculating its costs.

A batch of 300 "DX" workstations has just been produced using ₹3,300 of materials, ₹4,500 of direct labour and the following quantities of time:

	Cutting	Assembly	Finishing
Machine hours	50	25	10
Direct labour hours	20	45	20

Required:
Calculate the unit production cost and the total production cost of the batch of "DX" workstations using the following three alternative bases:

1. All overhead absorption rates are calculated on a machine-hour basis.
2. All overhead absorption rates are calculated on a direct labour-hour basis.
3. The cutting overhead absorption rate is calculated on a machine-hour basis but the assembly and finishing rates are calculated on a direct-labour hour basis.

Comment on your findings.

Solution

WORKINGS

	Cutting	Assembly	Finishing
OAR/mh	$\frac{16,00,000}{40,000}$	$\frac{20,00,000}{25,000}$	$\frac{14,00,000}{14,000}$
	=₹40/mh	=₹80/mh	=₹100/mh
OAR/dlh	$\frac{16,00,000}{10,000}$	$\frac{20,00,000}{40,000}$	$\frac{14,00,000}{20,000}$
	=₹160/dlh	=₹50/dlh	=₹70/dlh

1 Machine Hour Rates

		₹	
Direct materials		3,300	
Direct labour		4,500	
Prime cost		7,800	
Production overheads:			
Cutting	50 mh × ₹40/mh = 2,000		
Assembly	25 mh × ₹80/mh = 2,000		
Finishing	10 mh × ₹100/mh = 1,000		
		5,000	
Production cost		12,800	**Cost/unit ₹42.67**

2 Direct Labour Hour Rates

		₹	
Direct materials		3,300	
Direct labour		4,500	
Prime cost		7,800	
Production overheads:			
Cutting	20 dlh × ₹160/dlh = 3,200		
Assembly	45 dlh × ₹50/dlh = 2,250		
Finishing	20 dlh × ₹70/dlh = 1,400		
		6,850	
Production cost		14,650	**Cost/unit ₹48.83**

3 Mixed Rates		₹
Direct materials		3,300
Direct labour		4,500
Prime cost		7,800
Production overheads:		
Cutting	50 mh × ₹40/mh =2,000	
Assembly	45 dlh × ₹50/dlh = 2,250	
Finishing	20 dlh × ₹70/dlh = 1,400	
		5,650
Production cost		13,450 **Cost/unit ₹44.83**

Comment: The choice of OAR makes a significant difference to the production cost (over 10% in this case). This illustrates the approximate nature of absorption costing.

OVERHEAD RATES: ACTUAL VS PREDETERMINED (STANDARD)

The basic purpose of overhead absorption rates is to absorb total factory overhead in products or jobs manufactured. This objective can be achieved through actual overhead rate or predetermined overhead rate.

Actual Overhead Rate

When the absorption is based on actual overhead, it is known as actual absorption rate. This can be calculated only after the end of the accounting period when all cost and production figures have been collected. This method has the following disadvantages:

1. Product cost cannot be determined until some considerable time after the end of the accounting period. This may not help in controlling cost and in fixing selling prices.
2. There are likely to be variations in the overhead incurred because of the seasonal nature of some overhead costs, change in the volume of production and efficiency of the factory for different periods.
3. Some overhead costs are of fixed nature, such as depreciation, supervision, property taxes, etc. These overhead costs being constant give a different per unit cost when divided by differing production volumes. Also, some overheads like fire insurance premium are paid in advance but this should be charged to all work done/products manufactured during the year. How should the absorption be done? It creates an inequitable situation.

Pre-determined Overhead Rate or Standard Rate

Because of the limitations of the actual overhead rate stated above, a pre-determined or standard overhead rate is generally used by companies. This is a rate calculated in advance of the period in which it is to be used, by dividing the estimated period overhead to be absorbed by the estimated period production. Production may be measured on any of the absorption bases, such as prime cost, labour hours, etc.

The primary objective of pre-determined overhead rate is to provide a reasonably constant unit cost and to avoid unit cost fluctuations caused by seasonal overhead cost fluctuations, changes in volume, or accounting methods.

Secondly, pre-determined overhead rates also make possible the immediate costing of job or products completed during the month. When a job is finished, the absorption rate is multiplied by the absorption base to find out the total amount to be charged to the product or job. Under a process of costing system, pre-determined overhead rate is used to charge overhead to the output of the process in question.

Thirdly, pre-determined rates contribute effectively to standard costing and budgetary control programmes as these programmes use estimated costs and standard cost to measure production activities.

Under- or Over-Absorption of Overhead

The use of a pre-determined or standard rate may, therefore, result in under-absorption or over-absorption. When the amount absorbed is less than the actual overhead, there is under-absorption. Over-absorption arises when the amount absorbed is more than the actual overhead. Since actual overheads are not recorded in cost accounts, under-absorption and over-absorption can be treated in any one of the following ways:

Automatic Counterbalancing

In a seasonal business firm, the balance (due to under or over-absorption) may be carried forward to the subsequent period with the expectation that it will be counterbalanced at the end of accounting period. This is clear from the following example.

Months	*Production Units*	*Overhead Absorbed ₹2 Per Unit*	*Actual Overhead*	*Under or Over-Absorption*
July	1000	2000	3,000	– 1,000
August	1500	3000	4,200	– 1,200
September	3000	6000	3,800	+ 2,200

Use of Supplementary Rate

1. A supplementary rate can be used to adjust the amount of under- or over-absorption. The supplementary rate is determined by dividing the amount of under-or over-absorption by the actual absorption base. Under-absorption is adjusted by using a plus supplementary rate while a minus supplementary rate is used to correct over-absorption. For instance, in the above example, a plus supplementary rate of ₹1 per unit (₹1000/1000 units) can be used to increase the recorded overhead by ₹1,000 for the month of July. Similarly, a minus supplementary rate of ₹0.733 $\left(\frac{2200}{3000}\right)$ can be used to decrease the recorded overhead by ₹2,200. When the amount of under-absorbed and over-absorbed overhead is significant or large, because of difference due to wrong estimation, then the cost of product needs to be adjusted by using supplementary rates to avoid misleading impression.
2. **Writing off to costing P & L A/c:** Small difference between the actual and absorbed amount should simply be transferred to costing P & L A/c. However, if difference is large then investigate the causes and after that abnormal loss shall be transferred to costing P & L A/c.

EXAMPLE 6.26

X Ltd. which absorbs overheads at a pre-determined rate provides you the following information:

Overheads actually incurred	₹1,50,000
Overheads absorbed	₹1,00,000
Goods sold	12,000 units
Stock of finished goods	11,000 units
Stock of work-in progress	(20% complete)

Unabsorbed overheads were due to rising price levels.

Required: How would under-absorbed overheads be treated in Cost Accounts?

Solution

Step 1: Under-absorbed overheads = Actual overheads – Absorbed overheads
= ₹1,50,000 – ₹1,00,000 = ₹50,000.

Step 2: Total equivalent units
= 12,000 + 11,000 + 20% of 10,000 = 25,000 units

Step 3: Supplementary rate

$$= \frac{\text{Amount of under absorbed overheads}}{\text{Total equivalent units}}$$

$$= \frac{₹50{,}000}{25{,}000} = ₹2 \text{ per unit}$$

Step 4: Charging by supplementary rate:

Cost of sales (12,000 units × ₹2)	= ₹ 24,000
Stock of finished goods (11,000 units × ₹2)	= ₹ 22,000
Stock of work-in-progress (200 units × ₹2)	= ₹ 4,000
	= ₹ 50,0000

Step 5: Journal Entry

Cost of sales A/c	Dr. ₹24,000	
Finished goods ledger control A/c	Dr. ₹22,000	
Work-in progress ledger control A/c	Dr. ₹ 4,000	
To overheads control A/c		₹50,000

EXAMPLE 6.27

The budgeted working conditions for a cost centre are as follows:

Normal working hours per week	42 hours
Number of machines	14
Normal weekly loss of hours on maintenance etc.	5 hours per machine
No. of weeks worked per year	48
Estimated annual overheads	₹1,24,320
Estimated direct wage rate	₹4 per hour

Actual results in respect of a 4-week period are:

Wages incurred	₹ 9,000
Overhead incurred	₹10,200
Machine hours worked	2,000 hours

You are required to calculate:

(a) The overhead rate per machine hour, and

(b) The amount of under/over absorption of wages and overheads.

Solution

Normal working hours for the year = 48 weeks × 42 hours per week × 14 machines
= 28,224 hours

Loss in hours due to maintenance : 48 weeks × 5 hours × 14 = 3,360 hours

Net effective hours p.a. = 28,224 – 3,360 = 24,864 hours

Estimated annual overheads = ₹1;24,320

Overhead rate per machine = 1,24,320/ 24,864 hours = ₹5

Wages absorbed = 4 weeks × 42 hours × 14 machines × ₹4 = 9,408

Wages incurred = 9,000

Over-absorbed wages = 408

Overheads absorbed = 2,000 hours × ₹5 per hour = ₹10,000

Overheads incurred = 10,200

Under absorbed overheads = ₹200

EXAMPLE 6.28

The actual total expenditure of a light engineering factory was ₹6,75,912. Overheads were recorded at the rate of ₹2 per hour at normal capacity of the factory. Out of 10,000 units produced, only 8,000 units were sold. 500 units were in work-in-progress. Actual hours worked were 2,84,756. Sixty per cent of the difference between the actual and applied overheads was due to fluctuations in material prices and labour rates. There was a fire in the factory during this accounting period and the company lost ₹50,000 of which the buildings accounted for ₹30,000 and the balance represented loss of materials stored in the godown. A sum of ₹10,000 was paid as wages to workmen during the strike period. The balance amount represented the difference between the actual and applied overheads due to operational efficiency or inefficiency.

Required:

Calculate the under/over absorption of production overheads for the period and state the appropriate treatment in cost accounts.

Solution

Unabsorbed Overheads

Overheads recovered from production 2,84,756 × 2 =	5,69,512
Actual overheads	6,75,912
Under recovery	1,06,400

Out of the total amount of unabsorbed overheads ₹1,06,400, 60% was due to fluctuations in the prices of material and labour rates. The amount of ₹63,840 (that is, 60% of ₹1,06,400) should therefore be charged to units produced by means of supplementary rate.

$$\text{Supplementary rate} = \left(\frac{63,840}{10,500}\right) = ₹6.08$$

Apportionment of Overheads

The amount of ₹63,840 will be apportioned between cost of sales, finished goods and work-in-progress as follows:

			₹
Cost of Sales Account	(8,000 × 6.08)	=	48,640
Finished Goods Account	(2,000 × 6.08)	=	12,160
Work-in-progress Account	(500 × 6.08)	=	3,040
			63,840

The balance of ₹42,560 (40% of ₹1,06,400) which represents unabsorbed overheads on account of abnormal factors such as strike, operational inefficiency etc. should be charged to Costing Profit & Loss Account.

EXAMPLE 6.29

Sweet Dreams Ltd. uses a historical cost system and absorbs overhead on the basis of predetermined rate. The following data are available for the year ended 31st March, 2020:

	₹
Manufacturing overheads:	
Amount actually spent	1,70,000
Amount absorbed	1,50,000
Cost of goods sold	3,36,000
Stock of finished goods	96,000
Works-in-progress	48,000

Using two methods of disposal of under-absorbed overheads show the implication on the profits of the company under each method.

Solution

The following are the two methods for disposal of under-absorbed overheads:

The total unabsorbed overhead of ₹20,000 can be written off in Costing Profit and Loss Account. In case of this method, the profits of the concern will get reduced by ₹20,000 for the period.

Supplementary: A supplementary rate may be used to adjust the overhead cost of each cost unit. The total under-absorbed amount may, at the end of accounting period, be apportioned on proportionate basis over cost of goods sold; stock of finished goods and work-in-progress. This can be done as shown below:

Apportionment of Under-Absorbed Overhead

	₹	₹	₹
Cost of goods sold (WN 1)	3,36,000	14,000	3,50,000
Stock of finished goods (WN 2)	96,000	4,000	1,00,000
Work-in-progress (WN 3)	48,000	2,000	50,000
	4,80,000	20,000	5,00,000

✍ Working Notes:

(1) Under-absorbed overheads absorbed by cost of goods sold $= \frac{₹3,36,000}{₹4,80,000} \times ₹20,000 = ₹14,000$

(2) Under-absorbed overheads absorbed by stock of finished goods $= \frac{₹96,000}{₹4,80,000} \times ₹20,000 = ₹4,000$

(3) Under-absorbed overhead absorbed by WIP $= \frac{₹48,000}{₹4,80,000} \times ₹20,000 = ₹2,000$

✍ Example 6.30

In a manufacturing unit, overhead was recovered at a pre-determined rate of ₹20 per labour-hour. The total factory overhead incurred and the labour-hours actually worked were ₹45,00,000 and 2,00,000 labour-hours respectively. During this period, 30,000 units were sold. At the end of the period, 5,000 units were held in stock while there was no opening stock of finished goods. Similarly, though there was no stock of uncompleted units at the beginning of the period, at the end of the period there were 10,000 uncompleted units which may be reckoned at 50% complete.

On analysing the reasons, it was found that 60% of the unabsorbed overheads were due to defective planning and rest were attributable to increase in overhead costs.

How would unabsorbed overheads be treated in cost accounts?

☞ Solution

Computation of Unabsorbed Overheads

Labour hours actually worked	2,00,000
Overhead rate per hour	₹20
Overheads absorbed at ₹20 per labour hour (*A*)	40,00,000
(20,00,000 hours × ₹20)	
Overheads actually incurred (*B*)	45,00,000
Unabsorbed overheads (*B*) – (*A*)	5,00,000
Unabsorbed overheads	
(a) due to defective planning (that is, 60% of ₹5,00,000)	3,00,000
(b) Balance of unabsorbed overheads due to increase in overhead costs	2,00,000
	5,00,000

Disposition of Unabsorbed Overhead

(i) The unabsorbed overheads of ₹3,00,000 due to defective planning may be treated as abnormal and should therefore be charged to Costing Profit and Loss Account.

(ii) Balance of unabsorbed overheads of ₹2,00,000 may be treated as normal and, therefore, should be charged by a supplementary overhead absorption rate computed as under:

Total production during the year:

Units produced	35,000
Add: Equivalent units of work-in-progress 10,000 units, 50% complete	5,000
Total units	40,000

Supplementary overhead absorption rate comes to:

$$= \left(\frac{₹2,00,000}{40,000}\right) = ₹5 \text{ per unit}$$

Disposition of Normal Unabsorbed Overheads of ₹2,00,000

		₹
(i)	Charged to Costing Profit & Loss Account (as part of cost of units sold 30,000 units × ₹5)	1,50,000
(ii)	Charged to Closing Stock of Finished Goods: 5,000 finished goods in stock @ ₹5 per unit	25,000
(iii)	Charged to Work-in-Progress: 10,000 units, 50% complete, that is, 5,000 equivalent units @ ₹5 per unit	25,000
	Total	2,00,000

EXAMPLE 6.31

A company absorbs production overheads on the basis of pre-determined machine hour rate. For the month of March 2020, the budgeted machine hours were 8,500. During the month, the actual machine hours worked were 7,928; actual overheads were ₹1,46,200; and there was under absorption of ₹7,460.

Required:

Ascertain the budgeted level of overheads for the month.

Solution

Budgeted machine hours		8,500
Actual machine hours worked		7,928
Over-absorption of machine hour		572
Actual overhead	₹	1,46,200
Less under-absorption	₹	7,460
Budgeted overhead for month of March	₹	1,38,740

✍ EXAMPLE 6.32

The following particulars are available in respect of a department of a concern for a month.

Actual overhead expenses ₹1,00,000 (including ₹20,000 paid one time on account of an old claim).

Actual machine hours worked 10,000 hrs.

Pre-determined overhead recovery rate— ₹6 machine hour.

On analysis of under-absorbed overheads, it was noted that 70% of under-absorption is due to defective planning and 30% is due to increase in expenditure. The department produced 20,000 units in the month, out of which 15,000 units were sold and 5,000 units remained in stock.

You are required to show treatment of under- or over-absorbed overheads in cost accounts.

☞ Solution

	₹
Actual overhead (1,00,000 – 20,000)	80,000
Pre-determined overhead (10,000 × ₹6)	60,000
Under-absorption of overhead	20,000

Reasons for under-absorption of overhead:

$$\text{Defective planning } \left(20{,}000 \times \frac{70}{100}\right) = ₹14{,}000$$

$$\text{Increase in expenditure } \left(20{,}000 \times \frac{30}{100}\right) = ₹6{,}000$$

- Under recovery of ₹14,000 is due to defective planning being abnormal should be transferred to costing profit and loss A/c.
- Under recovery of ₹6,000 is due to increase in expenditure will be recovered from cost of sales account and finished goods stock account in the ratio of 15,000 : 5000 that is, 3 : 1.

$$\text{So, amount charged to cost of sales} = 6{,}000 \times \frac{15{,}000}{20{,}000} = ₹4{,}500$$

$$\text{Finished goods stock A/c} = 6{,}000 \times \frac{5{,}000}{20{,}000} = ₹1{,}500$$

✍ EXAMPLE 6.33

Jones Ltd. has a budgeted activity level of 50,000 direct labour hours and budgeted production overheads of ₹100,000. You are required to calculate the under-absorbed and over-absorbed overheads, giving reasons, if,

(a) 50,000 direct labour hours are worked and the actual overheads were ₹94,000.
(b) 43,000 direct labour hours are worked and the actual overheads were ₹100,000.
(c) 43,000 direct labour hours are worked and the actual overheads were ₹94,000.

☞ Solution

$$\text{Recovery rate} = \frac{₹100{,}000}{50{,}000 \text{ hours}} = ₹2/\text{hour}$$

(a) Recovered overheads (50,000 hours × ₹2) ₹100,000
Actual overheads incurred; ₹ 94,000
Over-absorbed ₹ 6,000

The reason for this over-absorption is expenditure, that is, actual costs are less than anticipated.

(b) Recovered overheads (43,000 hours × ₹2) ₹ 86,000
Actual overheads incurred: ₹100,000
Under-absorbed ₹ 14,000

The reason for this under-absorption is a production volume variance, that is, 7,000 less hours were worked than expected at ₹2/hour = ₹14,000.

(c) Recovered overheads (43,000 hours × ₹2) ₹86,000
Actual overheads incurred: ₹94,000
Under-absorbed ₹ 8,000

The reason for this under-absorption is two-fold:

(i) production volume variance of (50,000 hours – 43,000 hours) × ₹2/hour = ₹14,000 adverse
(ii) expenditure variance of (₹100,000 – ₹94,000) = ₹6,000 favourable. In total ₹8000 is adverse (under-absorbed)

Over-absorbed and under-absorbed overheads are charged to the profit and loss account via an under-absorbed/over-absorbed overhead account. Over-absorbed overheads will be credited to the profit and loss account, and under-absorbed overheads will be debited to it.

EXAMPLE 6.34

The total overhead expenses of a factory are ₹4,46,380. Taking into account the normal working of the factory, overhead was recovered in production at ₹1.25 per hour. The actual hours worked were 2,93,104. How would you proceed to close the books of accounts, assuming that besides 7,800 units produced of which 7,000 were sold, there were 200 equivalent units in work-in-progress?

On investigation, it was found that 50% of the unabsorbed overhead was on account of increase in the cost of indirect materials and indirect labour and the remaining 50% was due to factory inefficiency. Also give the profit implication of the method suggested.

Solution

	₹
Actual factory overhead expenses incurred	4,46,380
Less: Overheads recovered from production (2,93,104 hours × ₹1.25)	3,66,380
Unabsorbed overheads	80,000

Reasons for Unabsorbed Overheads

(i) 50% of the unabsorbed overhead was on account of increase in the cost of indirect materials and indirect labour.	40,000
(ii) 50% of the unabsorbed overhead was due to factory inefficiency.	40,000

Treatment of Unabsorbed Overheads in Cost Accounting

1. Unabsorbed overhead amount of ₹40,000, which was due to increase in the cost of indirect material and labour should be charged to units produced by using a supplementary rate.

$$\text{Supplementary rate} = \frac{₹40{,}000}{(7{,}800 + 200)\text{ units}} = ₹5 \text{ per unit}$$

The sum of ₹40,000 (unabsorbed overhead) should be distributed by using a supplementary rate among cost of sales, finished goods and work-in-progress as below:

	₹
Cost of sales (7,000 units × ₹5)	35,000
Finished goods (800 units × ₹5)	4,000
Work-in-progress (200 units × ₹5)	1,000
	40,000

The use of cost of sales figure would reduce the profit for the period by ₹35,000 and will increase the value of stock of finished goods and work-in-progress by ₹4,000 and ₹1,000 respectively.

2. The balance amount of unabsorbed overheads, that is, ₹40,000 due to factory inefficiency should be charged to costing profit and loss account, as this is an abnormal loss.

EXAMPLE 6.35

PQR manufacturers—a small scale enterprise—produces a single product and has adopted a policy to recover the production overheads of the factory by adopting a single-blanket rate based on machine hours. The budgeted production overheads of the factory are ₹10,08,000 and budgeted machine hours are 96,000.

For a period of first six months of the financial year 2019–20, following information were extracted from the books:

Actual production overheads	₹6,79,000
Amount included in the production overheads:	
Paid as per court's order	₹ 45,000
Expenses of previous year booked in current year	₹ 10,000
Paid to workers for strike period under an award	₹ 42,000
Obsolete stores written off	₹ 18,000

Production and sales data of the concern for the first six months are as follows:

Production:	
Finished goods	22,000 units
Works-in-progress (50% complete in every respect)	16,000 units
Sale:	
Finished goods	18,000 units

The actual machine hours worked during the period were 48,000 hours. It is revealed from the analysis of information that 1/4 of the under-absorption was due to defective production policies and the balance was attributable to increase in costs.

You are required:

(i) To determine the amount of under-absorption of production overheads for the period,
(ii) To show the accounting treatment of under-absorption of production overheads, and
(iii) To apportion the unabsorbed overheads over the items.

☞ ***Solution***

(i) **Amount of under-absorption of production overheads during the period of first six months of the year 2019–20:**

		Amount (₹)
Total production overheads actually incurred during the period		6,79,000
Less: Amount paid to workers as per court order	45,000	
Expenses of previous year booked	10,000	
Wages paid for the strike period	42,000	
Obsolete material written off	18,000	1,15,000
		5,64,000
Less: Production overheads absorbed	(48,000 hours * × ₹10.50)	5,04,000
Amount of under-absorbed production overheads		60,000

$$\text{Budgeted machine hour rate} = \frac{₹10,08,000}{96,000 \text{ hours}} = ₹10.50 \text{ per hour}$$

(ii) **Accounting treatment of under-absorbed production overheads:**
As, one/fourth of the under-absorbed overheads were due to defective production policies, this being abnormal, hence should be debited to Profit and Loss Account.
Amount to be debited to Profit and Loss Account = (60,000 × 1/4) ₹15,000.
Balance of under-absorbed production overheads should be distributed over works-in-progress, finished goods and cost of sales by applying supplementary rate*.
Amount to be distributed = (60,000 × 3/4) ₹45,000

$$\text{Supplementary rate} = \frac{₹45,000}{30,000 \text{ units}} = ₹1.50 \text{ per unit}$$

(iii) **Apportionment of under-absorbed production overheads over WIP, finished goods and cost of sales:**

	Equivalent Completed Units	*Amount (in ₹)*
Work-in-progress (16,000 units × 50% × 1.50)	8,000	12,000
Finished goods (4,000 units × 1.50)	4,000	6,000
Cost of sales (18,000 units × 1.50)	18,000	27,000
Total	30,000	45,000

Theory Questions

1. Explain the general principles to be kept in mind while considering whether item of expenditure is to be treated as overhead.
2. Differentiate between apportionment and absorption of overhead.
3. What is the importance of machine hour as a basis for the absorption of factory overheads?
4. Explain briefly various methods of absorption of factory overheads.
5. What do you mean by over-absorption and under-absorption of overheads? How would you treat such over- and under-absorbed factory-overheads in cost accounts?
6. Distinguish between allocation, apportionment and absorption of overheads.
7. What are the requisites of a good method of absorption of factory overhead?
8. Explain how you would treat under/over-absorption of overheads in cost accounts.
9. Discuss the secondary distribution of overheads.
10. Describe the different bases on which factory expenses can be apportioned. Describe the merits and suitability of each of them.
11. Write a detailed critical note on the direct labour cost method of absorption of factory overheads.
12. What information is necessary to calculate a machine hour rate for overhead absorption? State the conditions in which the method is most effective.
13. Explain the concept of absorption of factory overheads.
14. What do you understand by classification, allocation and apportionment in relation to overhead expenses? Explain fully.
15. Briefly describe two ways of dealing with apportioning service department costs among departments which, in addition to doing work for the main operation departments, also serve one another.
16. Discuss the statement that the impact of overheads under varying conditions of production and sales is of greater interest to the management than its method of apportionment and allocation.
17. Overhead costs are usually classified according to variability. What are the necessities for such classification and what purpose do such classifications serve?
18. State in short the reasons for the use of pre-determined rates for factory overhead absorption.
19. Describe the "prime cost" method of absorption of factory overheads. Explain fully and illustrate the basic conditions necessary for its application.
20. Why do you consider departmentalisation of overheads necessary?
21. Factory *A* has a lower rate of overhead absorption than Factory *B*. Both factories produce the same type of goods. Discuss whether this can be taken as a sign that Factory *A* is more efficient than Factory *B*.
22. Explain the different methods for apportionment of Service Department's cost over Production Departments.
23. Explain why pre-determined overhead absorption rates are preferred to overhead absorption rates calculated from factual information after the end of a financial period.
24. What are the causes of under/over absorption of factory overheads? How will you deal with them in cost accounts?
25. Explain the steps involved in the process of distribution of factory overheads.
26. Distinguish between allocation and apportionment of overheads.
27. Explain blanket and departmental overhead rate.
28. What is meant by under-absorption and over-absorption overheads? How will you deal with them in cost accounts?
29. What is meant by under-absorption and over-absorption of overhead? What are its causes?
30. Differentiate between:
    (i) Cost apportionment and cost absorption.
    (ii) Actual and pre-determined overhead rate of absorption.
31. What are the methods of secondary distribution of overheads for dealing with reciprocal services?

32. What is Machine Hour Rate? What procedure is followed for computation of machine hour rate?
33. Define overhead. How are under- and over-absorbed overheads treated in cost accounts?
34. What do you mean by overheads? How will you classify the overheads?
35. What do you mean by over-absorption and under-absorption overheads? How would you treat such over- and under-absorbed factory overheads in cost accounts?
36. Distinguish between actual and pre-determined overhead rate of absorption.
37. Explain Percentage Methods and Hourly Rate Methods of Absorption of factory overheads.

Self-Evaluation Questions

Select the correct answer for the following multiple choice questions:

1. Factory overhead includes
(a) All manufacturing costs
(b) All manufacturing costs except direct materials and direct labour
(c) Indirect materials but not indirect labour
(d) Indirect labour but not indirect materials

2. In order to identify costs that relate to a specific product, an allocation base should be chosen that
(a) does not have a cause and effect relationship
(b) has a cause and effect relationship
(c) considers variable costs but not fixed costs
(d) considers direct materials and direct labour but not factory overhead.

3. Which method of inventory pricing best approximates specific identification of the actual flow of costs and units in most manufacturing situations?
(a) Average cost
(b) First-in, First-out
(c) Last-in, First-out
(d) Base stock

4. Prime cost means
(a) Direct materials
(b) Direct labour
(c) Direct materials and direct labour
(d) Factory overhead and direct materials

5. Added cost of a new product will be
(a) Materials and labour
(b) Materials, labour and factory overhead
(c) Materials, labour, factory and administrative overhead
(d) Materials, labour and administrative overhead.

6. The budgeted fixed overheads amounted to ₹84,000. The budgeted and actual production amounted to 20,000 units and 24,000 units respectively. This means that there will be:
(a) an under-absorption of ₹16,800
(b) an under-absorption of ₹14,000
(c) an over-absorption of ₹16,800
(d) an over-absorption of ₹14,000

7. The rent of business premises should be shared out between cost centres according to:
(a) Floor area or cubic capacity
(b) The number of employees
(c) The replacement value of machinery and equipment
(d) The number of kilowatt hours

8. The insurance of buildings is best apportioned to cost centres using:
   (a) Floor area or cubic capacity
   (b) The number of employees
   (c) The replacement value of machinery and equipment
   (d) The number of kilowatt hours
9. The canteen expenses should be apportioned to cost centres by:
   (a) Floor area or cubic capacity
   (b) The number of employees
   (c) The replacement value of machinery and equipment
   (d) The number of kilowatt hours
10. In the absence of more realistic information, supervision should be split up according to:
   (a) Floor area or cubic capacity
   (b) The number of employees
   (c) The replacement value of machinery and equipment
   (d) The number of kilowatt hours
11. Which of the following bases of apportionment is most suited to sharing up the lighting costs between departments and cost centres?
   (a) Floor area or cubic capacity
   (b) The number of employees
   (c) The replacement value of machinery and equipment
   (d) The number of kilowatt hours
12. Indirect costs can also be described as:
   (a) Overhead costs
   (b) Prime costs
   (c) Variable costs
   (d) Total costs
13. Indirect costs which cannot be identified with a particular cost centre are shared out between cost centres using:
   (a) A recovery rate
   (b) An absorption rate
   (c) A method of apportionment
   (d) A method of allocation
14. Which of the following is not an indirect cost?
   (a) Wages of production department machine operator
   (b) Wages of a production department cleaner
   (c) Materials used for machine maintenance in the production department
   (d) Materials used to clean the production department floor

Problems

1. A manufacturing company has two production departments—*X* and *Y* and three service departments—Time keeping, Stores and Maintenance. The departmental summary showed the following expenses for October 2020.

Production Departments:	₹	₹
X	16,000	
Y	10,000	26,000

Service Departments:

Time-keeping	4,000	
Stores	5,000	
Maintenance	3,000	12,000
		38,000

The other information are as follows:

Particulars	*Production Departments*		*Service Departments*		
	X	Y	Time-keeping	Stores	Maintenance
No. of employees	40	30	20	16	10
No. of stores requisitions	24	20	–	–	6
Machine-hours	2,400	16,000	–	–	–

You are required to make departmental allocation of expenses.

Ans: Total overhead costs
Deptt. *X* ₹22,845
Deptt. *Y* ₹15,155

2. Deccan Manufacturing Ltd. has three departments which are regarded as production departments. Service department's costs are distributed to these production departments using the "Step Ladder Method" of distribution. Estimates of factory overhead costs to be incurred by each department in the forthcoming year are as follows. Data required for distribution is also shown against each department:

Department	*Factory Overhead* ₹	*Direct Labour Hours*	*No. of Employees*	*Area in Sq. m.*
Production:				
X	1,93,000	4,000	100	3,000
Y	64,000	3,000	125	1,500
Z	83,000	4,000	85	1,500
Service:				
P	45,000	1,000	10	500
Q	75,000	5,000	50	1,500
R	1,05,000	6,000	40	1,000
S	30,000	3,000	50	1,000

The overhead costs of the four service departments are distributed in the same order, viz., *P*, *Q*, *R*, and *S* respectively on the following basis:

Department	*Basis*
P	Number of employees
Q	Direct labour hours
R	Area in square metres
S	Direct labour hours

Required:

(a) Prepare a schedule showing the distribution of overhead costs of the four service departments to the three production departments; and

(b) Calculate the overhead recovery rate per direct labour hour for each of the three production departments.

Ans: (a) Total overheads: Production Departments *X* ₹3,00,000, *Y* ₹1,35,000, *Z* ₹1,60,000
(b) Recovery rate: *X* ₹75, *Y* ₹45, *Z* ₹40.

3. Modern Manufacturers Ltd. has three Production Departments P_1, P_2, P_3 and two Service Departments S_1 and S_2, the details pertaining to which are as under:

	P_1	P_2	P_3	S_1	S_2
Direct wages (₹)	3,000	2,000	3,000	1,500	195
Working hours	3,070	4,475	2,419	—	—
Value of machines (₹)	60,000	80,000	1,00,000	5,000	5,000
H.P. of machines	60	30	50	10	—
Light points	10	15	20	10	5
Floor space (sq. ft)	2,000	2,500	3,000	2,000	500

The following figures extracted from accounting records are relevant:

Rent and rates	₹5,000
General lighting	600
Indirect wages	1,939
Power	1,500
Depreciation on machines	10,000
Sundries	9,695

The expenses of the Service Departments are allocated as under:

	P_1	P_2	P_3	S_1	S_2
S_1	20%	30%	40%	–	10%
S_2	40%	20%	30%	10%	–

Find out the total cost of product *X* which is processed for manufacture in Departments P_1 P_2 and P_3 for 4, 5 and 3 hours respectively, given that its direct material cost is ₹50 and direct labour cost ₹30.

Ans: Total Cost of Product *X* ₹117.25.

4. You are supplied with the following information and required to work out the production hour rate of recovery of overheads in Departments *A*, *B* and *C*.

Particulars	*Total*	*Production Departments*			*Service Departments*	
		A	*B*	*C*	*P*	*Q*
Rent	12,000	2,400	4,800	2,000	2,000	800
Electricity	4,000	800	2,000	500	400	300
Indirect labour	6,000	1,200	2,000	1,000	800	1,000
Depreciation of machinery	5,000	2,500	1,600	200	500	200
Sundries	4,500	910	2,143	847	300	300
Working hour	–	1,000	2,500	1,400	–	–

Expenses of Service Departments P and Q are apportioned as under:

	A	B	C	P	Q
P	30%	40%	20%	–	10%
Q	10%	20%	50%	20%	–

Ans: Deptts. *A* ₹9.50; *B* ₹6; *C* ₹5.

5. Modern Machines Ltd. has three Production Departments (*A*, *B* and *C*) and two Service Departments (*D* and *E*). From the following figures extracted from the records of the company, calculate the overhead rate per labour hour:

	₹
Indirect materials	15,000
Indirect wages	10,000
Depreciation on machinery	25,000
Depreciation on building	5,000
Rent, rates and taxes	10,000
Electric power for machinery	15,000
Electric power for lighting	500
General expenses	15,000
Total	95,500

Items	*Total*	*A*	*B*	*C*	*D*	*E*
Direct materials	60,000	20,000	10,000	19,000	6,000	5,000
Direct wages	40,000	15,000	15,000	4,000	2,000	4,000
Value of machinery	2,50,000	60,000	1,00,000	40,000	25,000	25,000
Floor area (sq. ft)	50,000	15,000	10,000	10,000	5,000	10,000
Horse power of machines	150	50	60	30	5	5
No. of light points	50	15	10	10	5	10
Labour hours	15,000	5,000	5,000	2,000	1,000	2,000

The expenses of Service Departments D and E are to be apportioned as follows:

	A	B	C	D	E
D	40	20	30	–	10
E	30	30	40	–	–

Ans: Overhead rate per direct labour hour
Deptt. *A* ₹8.38
Deptt. *B* ₹7.95
Deptt. *C* ₹15.44

6. ABC Ltd. has three production departments P_1, P_2 and P_3 and two service departments S_1 and S_2. The following data are extracted from the records of the company for the month of October, 2020:

	₹
Rent and rates	62,500
General lighting	7,500
Indirect wages	18,750
Power	25,000
Depreciation on machinery	50,000
Insurance of machinery	20,000

Other information

	P_1	P_2	P_3	S_1	S_2
Direct wages (₹)	37,500	25,000	37,500	18,750	6,250
Horse Power of machines used	60	30	50	10	
Cost of machinery (₹)	3,00,000	4,00,000	5,00,000	25,000	25,000
Floor space (sq. ft)	2,000	2,500	3,000	2,000	500
Number of light points	10	15	20	10	5
Production hours worked	6,225	4,050	4,100		

Expenses of the service departments S_1 and S_2 are reapportioned as below:

	P_1	P_2	P_3	S_1	S_2
S_1	20%	30%	40%	–	10%
S_2	40%	20%	30%	10%	–

Required:

(i) Compute overhead absorption rate per production hour of each production department.

(ii) Determine the total cost of product X which is processed for manufacture in department P_1 P_2 and P_3 for 5 hours, 3 hours and 4 hours respectively, given that its direct material cost is ₹625 and direct labour cost is ₹375.

Ans: (i) Rate per hour, P_1, 8.60, P_2 13.93; P_3, 18.01

(ii) Total cost ₹1157

7. The production department of a factory furnishes the following information for the month of October:

Materials used	₹54,000	
Direct wages	₹45,000	
Overhead	₹36,000	
Labour hours worked		36,000
Hours of machine operation		30,000

For an order executed by the department during the period, the relevant information was as follows:

Materials used	₹6,00,000	
Direct wages	₹3,20,000	
Labour hours worked		3,200
Hours of machine operation		2,400

Required:

Calculate the overhead charges chargeable to the job by the following methods:

(i) Direct materials cost percentage rate;

(ii) Labour hour rate; and
(iii) Machine hour rate.

Ans: (i) ₹4,00,000 (ii) ₹3,200 (iii) ₹2880

8. Meerut Manufacturing Company makes several product lines which are processed through three production departments—*X*, *Y* and *Z*.

The information concerning the relevant data for a year is as follows:

	Factory Overhead (Including Share of Service Department)	*Direct Labour Hours*	*Direct Labour Cost*
	₹		₹
Department *X*	1,24,000	80,000	1,60,000
Department *Y*	2,30,000	1,15,000	2,41,500
Department *Z*	5,46,000	1,05,000	1,99,500

Production records at the end of the year indicated the following for the product line "Krish":

Unit produced		20,000	
	Deptt. *X*	Deptt. *Y*	Deptt. *Z*
	₹	₹	₹
Prime cost	45,000	10,500	59,500
Direct labour hours	10,000	5,000	30,000

You are required to:

(a) Calculate the departmental and plant-wide, overhead rate based on direct labour hours;
(b) Compute the cost of "Krish" line for the year by using (i) plant-wide rate; (ii) departmental rates; and
(c) Comment on the results.

Ans: (a) Deptt. rate, Deptt *X* = ₹1.55, Deptt. *Y* ₹2.00, Deptt. *Z* ₹5.20 Plant wide rate ₹3
(b) Cost plantwide ₹2,50,000; Deptt. rates *X*, ₹60,500; *Y*, ₹20,500; *Z* ₹2,15,500.

9. A company has three production centres—*A*, *B* and *C* and two service cost centres—*X* and *Y*. Costs allocated to service centres are required to be apportioned to the production centres to find out cost of production of different products. It is found that benefit of service cost centres is also received by each other along with the production cost centres.

Overhead costs as allocated to the five cost centres and estimates of benefit of service cost centres received by each of them are as follows:

Cost Centres	*Overhead Costs as Allocated*	*Estimates of Benefits Received from Service Centres (%)*	
	(₹)	X	Y
A	80,000	20	20
B	40,000	30	25
C	20,000	40	50
X	20,000	–	5
Y	10,000	10	–

Required: Work out final overhead costs of each of the production departments including reapportioned cost of service centres using

(a) Continuous distribution method; and
(b) Simultaneous equation method.

Ans: Total overhead costs, Deptt. *A* ₹86,533, Deptt. *B* ₹49,196, Deptt *C* ₹34271.

10. Atlas Engineering Ltd. accepts a variety of jobs which require both manual and machine operations. The budgeted Profit and Loss Account for the period 2019–20 is as follows:

	(₹ *in Lakhs)*	
Sales		75
Less: Cost of sales		
Direct materials	10	
Direct labour	5	
Prime Cost	15	
Production overhead	30	
Production Cost	45	
Administrative, selling and distribution overhead	15	60
Profit		15
Other Budgeted Data		
Labour hours for the period	2,500	
Machine hours for the period	1,500	
No. of jobs for the period	300	

An enquiry has been received recently from a customer and the production department has prepared the following estimate of the prime cost required for the job:

	₹
Direct material	2,500
Direct labour	2,000
Prime cost	4,500
Labour hours required	= 80
Machine hours required	= 50

Required:

(a) Calculate by different methods, six overhead absorption rates for absorption of production overhead and comment on the suitability of each.
(b) Calculate the production overhead cost of the order based on each of the above rates.
(c) Give your recommendation to the company.

Ans: Production overhead cost for the job

Direct labour hour rate	₹ 9,600
Machine hour rate	₹ 10,000
Direct material cost percentage	₹ 7,500
Direct labour cost percentage	₹ 12,000
Prime cost percentage	₹ 9,000
Job rate	₹ 10,000

11. An engineering company, engaged in the manufacture of various heavy engineering products, has installed one Pegard Numerical Control Horizontal Borer for specialised manufacturing operations. Calculate the machine hour rate on the basis of the following particulars:

(i) F.O.B. cost of machine, ₹24 lakhs. (ii) Customs duty, insurance, freight, etc. ₹11 lakhs. (iii) Installation expenses ₹3 lakhs. (iv) Cost of tools adequate for 2 years only ₹4 lakhs. (v) Cost of machine room ₹3 lakhs. (vi) Cost of air-conditioning for machine room ₹2 lakhs. (vii) Rate of interest on term loan to finance the above capital expenditure 12% per annum. (viii) Salaries, etc. for operators and supervisory staff ₹2 lakhs per year. (ix) Cost of electricity ₹11 per hour. (x) Consumption of stores ₹5,000 per month. (xi) Other expenses ₹5 lakhs per annum. (xii) Assume rate of depreciation as 10% per annum on fixed assets. (xiii) Total working hour in the machine room is 200 hours in a month. (xiv) Loading and unloading time is 10% of machine time. (xv) You can make suitable assumptions, if necessary, for the purpose of your computation.

Ans: ₹915.66

12. Compute the machine hour rate from the following data:

(i)	Total machine cost to be depreciated	₹2,30,000
(ii)	Life 10 years.	
(iii)	Depreciation on straight line	
(iv)	Departmental overheads (annual)	
	Rent	₹ 50,000
	Heat and lighting	₹ 20,000
	Supervision	₹1,30,000
(v)	Department area	70,000 sq ft
	Machine area	2,500 sq ft
(vi)	26 machines in the department	
(vii)	Annual cost of reserve equipment for the machines	1,500
(viii)	Hours run on production	1,800
(ix)	Hours for setting and adjusting	200
(x)	Power cost ₹0.50 per hour of running time	
(xi)	Labour (a) when setting and adjusting, full time attention; (b) when machine is producing; one man can look after 3 machines.	
(xii)	Labour rate ₹6 per hour	

Ans: Machine hour rate ₹20.14

13. In a light engineering factory, the machine shop consists of three cost centres (*A*, *B* and *C*) each having three distinct sets of machines. The following are the details of estimates for the year 2020:

	Total	*A*	*B*	*C*
1. No. of workers	800	200	200	400
2. No. of machine hours	1,00,000	30,000	30,000	40,000
3. % of horse power	100	40	25	35
		(Amount in lakhs of ₹)		
4. Value of assets	40.00	10.00	16.00	14.00
5. Direct wages	30.00	8.00	10.00	12.00
6. Depreciation	4.00			
7. Indirect labour	9.00			
8. Insurance charges	2.00			

(Contd.)

	Total	A	B	C
9. Electricity	3.00			
10. Supervisory salaries	1.60			
11. Staff welfare expenses	3.00			
12. Other expenses	6.00			

Required:

Work out a composite machine hour rate for each of the three cost centres and indicate clearly the basis of apportionment of expenses between the cost centres.

Ans: Machine hour rate:
Deptt. *A* = ₹53.50; *B* = 63.67; *C* = ₹58.63.

14. (a) Calculate the machine hour rate of a machine with information given below:

Operating Date:

Total number of weeks per quarter	=	13
Total number of hours per week	=	48
Stoppage due to maintenance	=	8 hrs. p.m.
Time taken for set-up	=	2 hrs/week
Cost Details:		
Cost of machine	=	₹2,00,000
Repair and maintenance	=	₹24,000 p.a.
Consumable stores	=	₹30,000 p.a.
Rent, rates and taxes	=	₹8,000 per quarter
Operator's wages	=	₹3,000 p.m.
Supervisor's salary	=	₹5,000 p.m.
Cost of power	=	15 units per hour at ₹3 per unit

Notes:

(i) Life of the machine is 10 years. Depreciation is provided on straight line basis and is treated as variable cost.

(ii) Repairs and maintenance and consumable stores are variable costs.

(iii) Power is consumed for production runs only and for set-up maintenance. But cost of power is to be borne by the total time excluding maintenance stoppages.

(iv) The supervisor is supervising work on five identical machines including the one now considered.

(b) The company hires out excess capacity in the machine shop for outside jobs. Assuming that hire charges are fixed at variable cost plus 20% what rate should be quoted by the company?

Ans: (a) ₹109.16
(b) Rate ₹91.00

15. A machine was purchased on 1st January 2020 for ₹5 lakhs. The total cost of all machinery inclusive of the new machine was ₹75 lakhs. The following further particulars are available:

Expected life of the machine 10 years.
Scrap value at the end of 10 years ₹5,000.
Repairs and maintenance for the machine during the year ₹2,000.
Expected number of working hours of the machine per year 4,000 hours.
Insurance premium annually for all machines ₹4,500.
Power consumption for the machine per hour @ 75 paise per unit – 25 units.
Area occupied by the machine 100 sq. ft.
Area occupied by other machines 1,500 sq. ft.
Rent per month of the department ₹800.

Lighting charges for 20 points for the whole department out of which three points are for the new machine—₹120 per month.

Compute the machine hour rate for the new machine.

Ans: ₹31.904

16. During the year ended 31st March 2020, the factory overhead costs of three production departments of an organisation are as under:

Department *X*	₹48,950
Y	₹89,200
Z	₹64,500

The basis of apportionment of overhead is given below:

Department *X*	₹5.00 per machine hour for 10,000 hours
Y	75% of direct labour cost of ₹1,20,000
Z	₹4.00 per piece for 15,000 pieces

Calculate department-wise under- or over-absorption of overheads and present the data in a tabular form.)

Ans: Deptt. *X* ₹1050 (Over), Deptt. *Y*, ₹800 (Over), Deptt. *Z* ₹4,500 (under)

17. In a factory, overheads of a particular department are recovered on the basis of ₹5 per machine hour. The total expenses incurred and the actual machine hours for the department for the month of August were ₹80,000 and 10,000 hours, respectively. Of the amount of ₹80,000, ₹15,000 became payable due to an award of the labour court ₹5,000 was in respect of expenses of the previous year booked in the current month (August). Actual production was 40,000 units, of which 30,000 units were sold. On analysing the reasons, it was found that 60 per cent of the under-absorbed overhead was due to defective planning and the rest was attributed to normal cost increase. How would you treat the under-absorbed overhead in the cost accounts?

Ans: ₹6000 (under-absorption) should be transferred to costing profit and loss A/c as it is abnormal in nature. The other ₹4,000 will be treated as: Cost of sales ₹3,000; Finished goods ₹1,000.

18. The Pipe Company manufactures two products—*A* and *B* during the first year of its operations. For the purpose of product costing, an overhead rate of application of ₹1.70 per direct labour was used, based on budgeted factory overhead of ₹3,40,000 and budgeted direct-labour hours of 2,00,000 as follows:

	Budgeted Overhead	*Budgeted Hours*
Department 1	₹2,40,000	₹1,00,000
Department 2	1,00,000	1,00,000
Total	₹3,40,000	₹2,00,000

The number of labour-hours required to manufacture each of these products was:

	Product A	*Product B*
Department 1	4	1
Department 2	1	4
	5	5

At the end of the year, there was no work in process. There were, however, 2,000 and 6,000 finished units, respectively, of products *A* and *B* on hand. Assume that budgeted activity was attained.

(a) What was the effect on the company's income of using a plant-wise overhead rate instead of departmental overheads rates?

(b) Assume that material and labour costs per unit of product *A* were ₹10 and that the selling price was established by adding 40 per cent to cover profit and selling and administrative expenses. What difference in selling price would result from the use of departmental against plant-wise overhead rates?

Ans: (a) Overstatement of company's income by ₹8,400
(b) Difference in selling price ₹2.94

19. You are given the following data:

Budgeted labour hours	8,500
Budgeted overheads	₹1,48,750
Actual labour hours	7,928
Actual overheads	₹1,46,200

Compute:
(i) Overhead absorption rate and
(ii) The amount of under- or over-absorption of overhead.

Also briefly state how under- or over-absorption of overheads are treated in cost accounts?

Ans: Under-absorption ₹7460

CASE STUDY

A Case of Crasim Springs Industries Ltd.

Crasim Spring Industries Ltd. was located in Bommasandra, Bangalore in Karnataka. It manufactured stock & custom springs, and formed metal parts & related products for a wide range of industries. The company offered stock springs, plus spare capacities to produce more custom springs, wire-forms, stampings and four-slide parts. Reyansh had joined the company recently in April 2019 as its Cost Accountant with a responsibility to ascertain various costs and prepare cost-sheet.

The company used two identical large machines and four identical small machines. The larger machines costed ₹2,00,000 each with a scrap value of ₹40,000 per machine whereas each of the smaller ones was acquired at ₹40,000 with a scrap value of ₹1,000 each. Both the large machines occupied half of the factory space together and the four small ones occupied the remaining half. Each large machine employed three workers permanently and the small machines engaged two full-time workers each. The labourers were paid by piece work. The total wages paid to these workers for each month were ₹1,80,000. The raw material consumed per month on an average was ₹1,20,000 per large machine and ₹60,000 per smaller machine.

The working life of large machines was 12,000 hours and that of smaller ones was 9,000 hours. Crasim Spring Industries engaged each of its machines for 120 hours per month. The larger machines consumed 20 units of power each per hour and the smaller machines consumed 2 units per hour each. The power consumption costed 50 paisa per unit. The other expenses with respect to the machines, like repairs & maintenance, were estimated to be ₹40,000 for each large machine and ₹12,000 for each smaller one during its working life.

The other expenses of the factory were as follows:

Particulars	*Amount (₹) Per Year*
Production Manager's Salary (devoted half of his time to factory which was equally utilised for the six machines therein)	48,000
Factory rent and rates	64,000

Particulars	*Amount (₹) Per Year*
Electricity (to be apportioned in the ratio of workers employed)	18,200
Insurance of machines (to be apportioned on the basis of insurable value of each machine)	28,000
Lubricating oil and consumable stores	32,000

The company prepared its cost-sheet every quarter. To do that, Reyansh was asked to determine the machine hour rate for large machine and small machine separately.

QUESTIONS FOR DISCUSSION:

1. Taking a period of three months as basis, calculate the machine hour rate for large and small machine respectively.
2. Calculate total machine cost for all six machines put together for each month and for the quarter April–June 2019.
3. Calculate the prime cost for Crasim Springs Ltd. quarter ending June 2019.

Chapter 7

Administrative, Selling and Distribution Overheads

Learning Objectives

After reading this chapter, you should be able to:

1. describe administrative overheads—meaning, items and distribution;
2. describe selling and distribution overheads—meaning, items and apportionment; and
3. explain the treatment of some items of expenses such as interest on capital, depreciation.

Chapter 6 has discussed factory overhead and its distribution among products and jobs. This chapter focuses on administrative overheads, selling and distribution overheads and treatment of some items of expenses in cost accounting.

ADMINISTRATIVE OVERHEADS

Administrative overheads are those expenses which are incurred for formulating the policy, directing the organisation and controlling the operations of an undertaking. In other words, administrative overheads are incurred for general management and control of the organisation. Administrative overheads include the following items of overheads:

A. *Indirect material:*
   1. Printing and stationery used in the office.
   2. Cost of brushes, dusters and other office supplies.

B. *Indirect labour*
   1. Salaries, allowances, fees of board of directors, managing director, chairman, board staff, cost accountant, accounts manager and his staff, secretary and his staff, treasurer and his staff.
   2. Salaries, allowances, fees of legal adviser and his staff, public relations officer and his staff, remuneration of internal auditors and statutory auditors.

C. *Indirect expenses:*

1. Office rent, rates and insurance
2. Office lighting, heating and cleaning
3. Depreciation and repairs of office buildings, furniture and fittings
4. Legal charges
5. Bank charges
6. Trade subscriptions and donations
7. Miscellaneous office expenses

There is lesser fluctuation in the amounts of administrative overheads as compared to factory overheads which may change largely in relation to changes in output.

Distribution of Administrative Overheads

The method of distributing administrative overheads is more or less the same as in the case of factory overheads. All items of administrative overheads are collected and grouped under proper classification heads. The overheads are then apportioned among the various administrative departments (cost centres). Some examples of administrative departments are office department, accounts department, personnel department, secretarial department, law department etc.. Those administrative overheads which can be identified with specific departments are directly allocated to them. The remaining administrative overheads are apportioned among those administrative departments for which they have been incurred, on an equitable basis.

A single rate for the total administrative overheads may be obtained without going into details of these overheads incurred for various departments. The Administrative Overhead Rate may be computed using any one of the following basis:

1. As a percentage of Factory Cost; $\frac{\text{Total Administrative Overhead}}{\text{Total Factory Cost}} \times 100$
2. As a percentage of Factory Overheads; $\frac{\text{Total Administrative Overhead}}{\text{Total Factory Overhead}} \times 100$
3. As a percentage of Sales; $\frac{\text{Total Administrative Overhead}}{\text{Total Sales}} \times 100$
4. As a percentage of Gross Profit; $\frac{\text{Total Administrative Overhead}}{\text{Gross Profit}} \times 100$
5. As a percentage of Conversion Costs. $\frac{\text{Total Administrative Overhead}}{\text{Total Conversion Costs}} \times 100$

Conversion cost includes the cost of direct labour, direct expanses and factory overheads.

The above treatment, that is, calculating an administrative overhead rate for charging administrative overheads, is based on the assumption that administrative overheads are an additional and separate element of cost of a product or job.

Besides the above treatment, the following two procedures are also suggested to deal with the administrative overheads:

1. *Apportionment between production and selling divisions* Under this method, administrative overheads are divided between production and selling divisions on some suitable basis. After

such distribution, administrative overheads lose their identity. This method follows the logic that an organisation has only two functions to perform, namely production and selling.

2. *Transfer to costing profit and loss account* Under this method, administrative overheads are transferred to Costing Profit and Loss Account. This method is based on the assumption that administrative overheads are not directly concerned with the production function of the organisation and therefore should not be included in the cost of production. This method reduces the cost of product or job.

SELLING AND DISTRIBUTION OVERHEADS

Selling overheads include the costs incurred in promoting sales and retaining customers. Distribution overheads include the costs of the process which begins with making the packed product available for despatch and ends with making the reconditioned returned empty packages available for reuse. Distribution overheads strictly begin when an order has been obtained and generally ends when goods are to be despatched.

Broadly, selling overheads include the following items.

(a) *Indirect materials* They include cost of printing and stationery, mailing literature, catalogue, price lists etc.

(b) *Indirect labour* This includes salaries, commission, allowances etc. of salesman, representative, sales manager, marketing manager etc.

(c) *Indirect expenses* Advertising, bad debts, rent of showroom, insurance of showroom, collection charges, travelling and entertainment expenses, expenses of branch establishment, sales office expenses, fees of directors who devote time to sales function, are some examples of indirect expenses.

Broadly, distribution overheads include the following items:

(a) *Indirect materials* Cost of packing cases; oil, grease, spare parts used in maintenance of delivery vehicles.

(b) *Indirect labour* Wages of packers, van drivers, despatch clerks, etc.

(c) *Indirect expenses* Godown expenses including rent, insurance, freight, carriage outwards and other transport charges, depreciation and running expenses of delivery vans.

Apportionment of Selling and Distribution Overheads

Although, selling and distribution overheads differ in nature with each other, for the purpose of apportionment and absorption, both the overheads can be taken together. Selling and distribution overheads should be classified into two groups in order to charge them finally to products:

(a) *Direct overheads* Direct overheads are the overheads which can be directly identified with a particular product or products. For example, sales promotion expenses or transport charges incurred for a product should be charged directly to that product only.

(b) *Indirect overheads* These are such selling and distribution overheads which cannot be identified with particular product or products. Such indirect overheads are apportioned using the following steps:

(1) *Collection and classification of overheads*—All selling and distribution overheads should be collected and classified according to their nature into certain groups such as advertising,

exhibition, bad debts, depreciation of vehicles used for sale, discount, freight, heating, insurance, lighting, packing, postage, commission, rent, repairs, etc.

(2) *Apportionment of overheads*—After collecting and classifying overheads, they should be further allocated to one or more cost centres or departments or functions to which they relate. If any item (items) of overheads cannot be totally transferred to a particular department or functions it should be apportioned among the departments or functions on an equitable basis for which they have been incurred. Some examples of apportionment of overheads in terms of functions (or departments) are the following:

(i) *Direct selling*—This includes overheads such as expenses incurred on sales executive, sales staff, sales office expenses, etc.

(ii) *Advertisement and sales promotion*—This includes expenses incurred on exhibition, posters, cinema slides, distribution of samples, etc.

(iii) *Credit and collection*—This includes costs incurred on debt collection, bad debts, legal costs.

(iv) *Transportation*—Costs such as insurance for goods in transit, demurrage, maintenance staff and depreciation of transport vehicles are included in this group.

(v) *Warehousing and storage costs*—This includes expenses incurred on secondary packing for storage, warehouse rent, internal transport, insurance, etc.

(vi) *General administration*—This includes costs such as royalty on sales, sales invoicing, maintenance of accounts, cost of investment in stocks, etc..

The above costs which belong to different cost centres are subsequently apportioned to various areas or territories or zones on an equitable basis as shown in Table 7.1.

Table 7.1 Costs Apportioned to Various Areas or Territories

Function	*Basis of Apportionment*	*Total.* ₹	*Territories* I *East Zone*	II *West Zone*	III *North Zone*	IV *South Zone*
1. Direct selling	Allocation					
2. Advertising and sales promotion	Sales value					
3. Credit & Collection	No. of orders or Cash collected					
4. Transportation	Sales value					
5. Warehousing	Sales value					
6. General administration	No. of orders or No. of invoices or Sales value					

(3) *Absorption of overheads* After apportionment of overheads, selling and distribution overheads of each territory, or zone or area are charged to different products sold in that area or territory on a suitable basis. This may be done by one or more of the following methods:

(i) *Rate per article*—If this method is adopted, the overhead costs are divided by the number of products sold in that territory during a certain period.

(ii) *A percentage of sales*—This is suitable for apportionment of direct selling costs, general administration, finance costs, etc. If selling overhead of a sales zone is ₹50,000 and the sales of that zone are ₹2,00,000, an addition should be made to the cost of products by 25% of the selling price of that product.

(iii) *A percentage of works cost*—Where selling overheads are small, this method can be adopted, even though various articles are produced, as little advantage would be gained by using a more complicated system.

(iv) *A percentage of cash collected*—This method may be used for apportionment of credit and collection costs such as bad debts, legal expenses, etc.

EXAMPLE 7.1

Following data is available relating to a company for a certain month:

	Territory		
	I	*II*	*III*
Selling expenses	₹7,600	₹4,200	₹6,240
Distribution costs	₹4,000	₹1,800	₹2,000
No. of units sold	16,000	6,000	10,000
Sales	₹76,000	₹28,000	₹52,000

Required:

The company adopts sales basis and quantity basis for application of selling and distribution costs, respectively.

(a) Compute the territory-wise overhead recovery rates separately for selling and distribution costs.

(b) Compute the amounts of selling and distribution costs chargeable to a consignment of 2,000 units of a product, sold in each territory at ₹4.50 per unit.

Solution

(a) Computation of Overhead Recovery Rates

1. Selling Cost Recovery Rate = $\dfrac{\text{Selling Expenses}}{\text{Sales}} \times 100$

2. Distribution Cost Recovery Rate = $\dfrac{\text{Distribution Costs}}{\text{No. of Units Sold}}$

Territory	*Selling Cost Recovery Rate*	*Distribution Cost Recovery Rate*
I	$\dfrac{₹7{,}600}{₹76{,}000} \times 100$ = 10% on sales	₹$\dfrac{4{,}000}{16{,}000}$ = 25 paise per unit

(Contd.)

Territory	Selling Cost Recovery Rate	Distribution Cost Recovery Rate
II	$\frac{₹\,4{,}200}{₹\,28{,}000} \times 100 = 15\%$ on sales	$₹\,\frac{1{,}800}{6{,}000} = 30$ paise per unit
III	$\frac{₹\,6{,}240}{₹\,52{,}000} \times 100 = 12\%$ on sales	$₹\,\frac{2{,}000}{10{,}000} = 20$ paise per unit

(b) Computation of Selling and Distribution Costs Chargeable to Consignment

Territory	*I*	*II*	*III*
No. of units sold	2,000	2,000	2,000
Sales at ₹4.50 per unit	₹ *9,000*	₹ 9,000	₹ 9,000
Selling cost chargeable	₹ *900.00*	₹ 1,350.00	₹ 1,080.00
Distribution cost chargeable	₹ 500.00	₹ 600.00	₹ 400.00
Total	₹ 1,400.00	₹ 1,950.00	₹ 1,480.00

EXAMPLE 7.2

XYZ Ltd., a manufacturing company, having an extensive marketing network throughout the country, sells its products throughout four-zone sales offices, viz., *A*, *B*, *C* and *D*. The budgeted expenditures for January 2020 are given below:

			₹
Sales Manager's salary			1,20,000
Expenses relating to sales manager's office			80,000
Travelling salesman's salaries			3,20,000
Travelling expenses			36,000
Advertisements			30,000
Godown rent: Zone	*A*	15,000	
	B	25,200	
	C	9,800	
	D	18,000	68,000
Insurance on inventories			20,000
Commission on sales @ 5% on sales			6,00,000

The following further particulars are also available:

Zone	*Sales in ₹ Lakhs*	*No. of Salesmen*	*Total Mileage Covered*	*Allocation of Advertisement*	*Average Stock in ₹ Lakhs*
A	36	5	6,000	30%	6
B	48	6	14,000	30%	8
C	16	2	4,500	20%	4
D	20	3	5,500	20%	2

Based on the above details, compute the zone-wise selling overheads as a percentage to sales.

☞ Solution

Books of XYZ Ltd.
Computation of Zone-wise Selling Overhead Rates

Items of Expense	*Basis of Charge*	*Total* ₹	*Zones* A ₹	B ₹	C ₹	D ₹
Sales manager's salary	Sales	1,20,000	36,000	48,000	16,000	20,000
Sales manager's office expenditure	Sales	80,000	24,000	32,000	10,667	13,333
Salesmen's salaries	No. of salesmen	3,20,000	1,00,000	1,20,000	40,000	60,000
Travelling expenses	Mileage covered	36,000	7,200	16,800	5,400	6,600
Advertisement	Budgeted ratio	30,000	9,000	9,000	6,000	6,000
Godown rent	Actuals	68,000	15,000	25,200	9,800	18,000
Insurance	Average inventory	20,000	6,000	8,000	4,000	2,000
Commission on sales	Sales	6,00,000	1,80,000	2,40,000	80,000	1,00,000
Total overheads		12,74,400	3,77,200	4,99,000	1,71,867	2,25,933
Amount of sales		1,20,00,000	36,00,000	48,00,000	16,00,000	20,00,000
Overheads as a percentage of sales = $\frac{\text{Overhead}}{\text{Sales}} \times 100$		10.62%	10.48%	10.40%	10.74%	11.30%

✎ EXAMPLE 7.3

A company manufacturing a sole product sells it through three salesmen, *A*, *B* and *C* stationed in three regions. Besides, sales are also affected through a sales depot situated at the company's headquarters. The following information is obtained from the books of the company for December 2020.

Sales		₹4 lakhs
Cost of sales		2.50 lakhs
Gross profit		1.50 lakhs, 37.5% of sales
Selling expenses:		
Salesmen's salaries	₹3,500	
Commission	22,000	
Travelling expenses	9,000	
Advertisement expenses	60,000	
Other selling expenses	35,500	
	₹1,30,000	
Net profit	₹20,000,	5% of sales

The management is not satisfied with the net profit and asks you to investigate. You find that salesmen *B* and *C* are paid salaries at ₹1,500 and ₹2,000 per month respectively besides a commission of 5% on sales. The salesman *A*, however, receives a commission of 10% on sales but no salary. Travelling expenses paid were ₹2,000, ₹4,000 and ₹3,000 respectively for *A*, *B* and *C*. Advertising expenses were apportioned equally to *A*, *B* and *C*, after deducting a sum of ₹3,000 spent in headquarters. Other selling expenses for headquarters amounted to ₹17,500, the rest being apportioned to *A*, *B* and *C*, on the basis of sales. The break-up of the sales was as follows:

Headquarters		₹40,000
Salesmen	*A*	80,000
	B	1,20,000
	C	1,60,000

Prepare a statement showing the individual profit or loss from each salesman. Comment on the results indicating your suggestions for improving the position

Solution

Statement of Profit and Loss

Items	*Total*	*Headquarters*	*Salesman*		
			A	B	C
Sales	₹4,00,000	₹40,000	₹80,000	₹1,20,000	₹1,60,000
Less: Cost of sales (62.5% of sales)	2,50,000	25,000	50,000	75,000	1,00,000
Gross profit	1,50,000	15,000	30,000	45,000	60,000
Salaries	3,500	—	—	1,500	2,000
Commission	22,000	—	8,000	6,000	8,000
Travelling	9,000	—	2,000	4,000	3,000
Advertising	60,000	3,000	19,000	19,000	19,000
Other selling expenses	35,500	17,500	4,000	6,000	8,000
	1,30,000	20,500	33,000	36,500	40,000
Net profit	20,000	– 5,500	– 3,000	8,500	20,000

According to the statement, the headquarters and the salesman *A* are showing a net loss of ₹5,500 and ₹3,000 respectively. In the case of headquarters, for a gross profit of ₹15,000 the selling expenses are ₹20,500, besides the sales being only ₹40,000. In spite of ₹19,000 being spent on advertisement, the sales of the salesman *A* are only ₹80,000. The existing state of affairs at the headquarters may be corrected by cutting down selling costs or stopping it from selling anything at all. In the case of the salesman *A*, attempt should be made to push up or change the salesman himself. If possible, the sales territory in charge of *A* may be closed down and attempts may be made to push up the sales of the other two territories.

EXAMPLE 7.4

A company is supplying its products to the ultimate consumers through the wholesalers to retailers. The Managing Director thinks that if they sell through the retailers or to the consumers direct, they can increase their sales, earn better prices, and make more profit. As a cost accountant of the company, you are required to advise the Managing Director in selecting the channels of distribution from the following information:

Channels of Distribution	*1*	*2*	*3*
	To Consumer Direct	*To Retailer Direct*	*To Wholesaler*
Sale price per unit (₹)	9.50	8.50	7.25
Estimated sales per year (Nos.)	6,00,000	5,70,000	5,40,000
Selling and distribution cost per unit (₹)	3	1.60	0.90+
Cost of product:			
Variable cost @ ₹4 per unit			
Fixed cost ₹5,00,000			

In selecting the channels of distribution, what factor besides cost would you consider?

Solution

Profit and Loss Statement

	Channels of Distribution		
	1	*2*	*3*
	To Consumer	*To Retailer*	*To Wholesaler*
Cost of production:	₹	₹	₹
Variable	4.00	4.00	4.00
Fixed	0.83	0.88	0.93
	4.83	4.88	4.93
Selling and distribution cost:	3.00	1.60	0.90
Cost of sales	7.83	6.48	5.83
Sales	9.50	8.50	7.25
Net profit	1.67	2.02	1.42

Channel 2 gives the highest profit. In selecting the channels, besides cost, factors such as, the nature of the product, the demand for it, the type of customers and the possibility for expansion, etc. should also be considered.

EXAMPLE 7.5

A company is making a study of the relative profitability of the two products—*A* and *B*. In addition to direct costs, indirect selling and distribution costs to be allocated between the two products are as under:

Particulars	₹
Insurance charges for inventory (finished)	78,000
Storage costs	1,40,000
Packing and forwarding charges	7,20,000
Salesmen salaries	8,50,000
Invoicing costs	4,50,000

Other details are:

Particulars		Product A	Product B
Selling price per unit	(₹)	500	1,000
Cost per unit (exclusive of indirect selling and distribution costs)	(₹)	300	600
Annual sales in units		10,000	8,000
Average inventory	(Units)	1,000	800
Number of invoices		2,500	2,000

One unit of product *A* requires a storage space twice as much as product *B*. The cost of packing and forwarding one unit is the same for both the products. Salesmen are paid salary plus commission @ 5% on sales and equal amount of efforts are put forth on the sales of each of the products.

Required:

(i) Set up a schedule showing the apportionment of the indirect selling and distribution costs between the two products.

(ii) Prepare a statement showing the relative profitability of the two products.

For excel template, scan

☞ ***Solution***

(i) Statement of Apportionment of Indirect Selling and Distribution Costs

Items	Basis of Apportionment	Total	Products	
			A	B
		₹	₹	₹
Insurance charges	Average Inventory Value (1,000 × ₹500) : (800 × ₹100)	78,000	30,000	48,000
Storage cost	Average Inventory Storage Space (1000 × 2) : (800 × 1)	1,40,000	1,00,000	40,000
Packing & forwarding charges	Annual Sales in units (10 : 8)	7,20,000	4,00,000	3,20,000
Salesmen salaries	Efforts of salesmen (1 : 1)	8,50,000	4,25,000	4,25,000
Salesmen commission	(Annual Sales Value) (5 : 8)	6,50,000	2,50,000	4,00,000
Invoicing costs	No. of Invoices (25 : 20)	4,50,000	2,50,000	2,00,000
		28,88,000	14,55,000	14,33,000

(ii) Statement Showing the Relative Profitability of the Products

Products	*A*	*B*
	₹	₹
Annual sales value	50,00,000	80,00,000
	(10,000 units × ₹500)	(8,000 units × ₹1,000)
Less: Cost of sales	30,00,000	48,00,000
	(10,000 units × ₹300)	(8,000 units × ₹600)
Gross profit:	20,00,000	32,00,000
Less: Indirect selling & distribution cost	14,55,000	14,33,000
[*Refer to* (i) *above*]		
Profit	5,45,000	17,67,000
Profitability as percentage of sales	10.9%	22.8%
	$\left(\frac{₹5,45,000}{₹50,00,000} \times 100\right)$	$\left(\frac{₹17,67,000}{₹80,00,000} \times 100\right)$

TREATMENT OF SOME ITEMS OF EXPENSES

Interest on Capital

There is a difference of opinion as to whether interest on capital employed in manufacture should be treated as an item of cost.

The following arguments are advanced in support of treating interest as an item of costs:

1. Interest is the reward of capital just as wages are the reward of labour. Profit, in the true sense, cannot be computed without considering interest.
2. The comparison of operations, different processes, etc. without due consideration of the interest factor, may lead to unreliable conclusions.
3. Interest considers time factors as it is computed on the basis of time and time is regarded as an important factor in production.
4. The inclusion of interest is of particular importance where articles of different values are produced and the capital invested in each product line differs considerably.
5. The cost of carrying inventory cannot be determined without giving due recognition to the interest on capital employed in it.

The following arguments are against including interest in the cost accounts:

1. Cost accounting considers only actual expenditures and can include only interest paid.
2. The interest factor is in no way connected with cost of manufacture. Whatever may be the method of raising finances—owned capital, loans, debentures, etc—does not affect manufacturing cost. It only affects the profits of the period.
3. Inclusion of interest in product costing will inflate the values of inventory and work-in-progress and therefore will tend to increase the profit unreasonably.

4. Interest is calculated on capital and the term "capital" has many concepts such as total capital employed in business, both equity capital and borrowed capital.
5. A reliable and correct rate of interest is difficult to determine and is likely to be influenced by naked fluctuations.
6. The cost accounting and product costing systems get complicated unnecessarily by inclusion of interest on capital and financial statements also become misleading.

There is one point upon which opinion is not divided. If interest is to be considered at all, it must not be confined merely to such interest as may actually have been paid by the business. In other words, interest should be ignored entirely or else included in respect of the whole capital employed, whether such capital requires the payment of interest or not. Therefore, if it is decided to exclude interest from the cost accounts, interest which has been paid, must also be ignored.

Of late, cost accountants in India tend to agree that interest on capital or funds borrowed from outside and paid or to be paid in cash should be included in product cost. This has been supported on the grounds that it implies cash outflow and affects the operating results of a business firm. The Bureau of Industrial Costs and Prices in India includes actual interest on borrowed funds as an element of cost in cost price studies. However, the Bureau does not consider the notional type of interest (interest on owned capital) as an element of cost.

Depreciation

Depreciation is the diminution in the value of fixed assets due to use and/or the lapse of time. The following are the methods of depreciation.

1. *Straight line method* This method provides for depreciation by means of equal periodic charges over the life of the asset. For example, suppose the cost of a plant is ₹1,00,000 and its life is 10 years. Then, the charge of depreciation per annum will be ₹10,000.
2. *Diminishing balance method* This method tends to write-off higher amounts in the beginning and comparatively lower amounts in subsequent parts of the life of an asset. The amount of depreciation is calculated at a constant rate at the balance of the value of the asset after deducting the amounts of depreciation previously provided. For example, taking the above illustration, the amounts of depreciation at the rate of 10% p.a. would be ₹10,000 for the first year, ₹9,000 for the second year, ₹8,100 for the third year, and so on.
3. *Production unit method* This method charges the amount of depreciation by means of fixed rate per unit of production calculated by dividing the value of the asset by the estimated number of units to be produced during its life. The formula for calculating depreciation under this method is as follows:

$$\text{Depreciation (per unit)} = \frac{\text{Original cost-residual value}}{\text{Estimated output during its life}}$$

4. *Annuity method* This method assumes that the capital used in the purchase of plant should have earned interest if invested somewhere else. The amount of depreciation in this method is calculated by dividing the aggregate of the cost of the asset depreciated and interest at a given rate, at a constant rate, on the written down value of the asset.
5. *Sinking fund method* Under the annuity method, expected interest on the investment (equivalent to the cost of the asset) is assumed. However, no actual investment is made. But under the sinking fund method, the amount of depreciation written off every year is invested in some securities,

which would accumulate at compound interest to provide, at the end of the life of the asset, a sum equal to its cost. This method provides for depreciation of fixed periodic charges.

6. *Endowment policy method* This method is similar to the sinking fund method. It provides for depreciation by means of fixed periodic charges equivalent to the premium on an endowment policy for the amount required to provide, at the end of the life of the asset, a sum equal to its cost. The amount of depreciation is equivalent to the premium payable on the policy.
7. *Production hour method* This method provides for depreciation by means of a fixed rate per hour of production by using the following formula:

$$\text{Depreciation (per unit)} = \frac{\text{Cost of the asset}}{\text{Estimated number of working hours of its life}}$$

8. *Sum-of-the-year digits method* This method provides for depreciation by means of differing periodic rates computed according to the following formula. If n is the estimated life of the asset, the rate is calculated for each period as a fraction in which the denominator is always the sum of the series 1, 2, 3,…n and the numerator for the first period is n, for the second period is $n - 1$, and so on.

Rent

The rent payable by a manufacturer or businessman who does not have his own building is undoubtedly an expense which must be charged to production. In many cases, however, the premises are owned by the businessman and no rent is paid. In such circumstances, a charge in lieu of rent should be made in the cost accounts in order that the true cost of production may be ascertained.

Capacity

The term "capacity" signifies volume capacity of a business enterprise.

Capacity costs are those fixed expenses which are incurred by a business enterprise in order to sustain its ability to conduct business. A firm has to incur these expenses irrespective of volume of its business or operations.

Capacity costs generally do not vary with output level. Such expenses can be reduced or avoided only by closing down business or outsourcing.

Example of capacity costs are expenses such as rent or lease payment, depreciation on equipment or machinery, property taxes, insurance and basic utilities such as heating. These type of expenses need to be incurred in order to provide a functional office or facilitate conduct of business.

Capacity of firm can be measured in the following manner:

1. *Maximum theoretical capacity* It is that capacity of a plant or department which will be achieved under 100% operating time. It assumes round-the-clock operation of all plants with no allowance for machine downtime, waits and delays or holidays. It cannot be achieved in reality.
2. *Practical capacity* The practical capacity of a plant is the theoretical maximum capacity less normal and unavoidable operating interruption, such as repairs, wait, breaks, machine failure, etc.
3. *Normal activity or capacity* Normal capacity involves consideration of both the ability to produce and the ability to sell. For this, a sales budget is prepared which determines normal activity. This is a long-term measure that represents the practical plant capacity less the estimated idle capacity.

4. *Expected activity or capacity* This capacity indicates the activity budgeted for the current year. It can be more or less than the normal activity level, but will never be more than the practical capacity. It is similar to normal capacity but for a short period of time.

The normal capacity concept is generally the most suitable for product cost determinations which further help in determining selling prices and valuation of inventories for purposes of financial statements. Expected capacity level tends to increase product unit costs when lower output than normal capacity output is achieved.

Idle Capacity

Idle capacity denotes that plant, machinery and equipments are available for manufacturing or other purposes, but are not being used totally. The Institute of Cost and Management Accountants (U.K.) defines idle capacity cost as "the cost of abnormal idleness of fixed assets or available services." Idle capacity is the difference between the normal capacity and capacity utilised based on expected sales. For example, if the normal capacity of a plant is to produce 50,000 units a month, but the plant is being used to manufacture only 40,000 units per month due to some reason (say, a low market demand of the product), then, in such a situation 10,000 units will be treated as the idle capacity of the plant. The idle capacity may arise due to lack of product demand, non-availability of raw materials, shortage of skilled labour, absenteeism, shortage of power, fuel or supplies, seasonal nature of the product, etc.

Idle capacity costs are mostly fixed in nature and are to be incurred because of unused capacity. Such costs consist of depreciation, maintenance, insurance premium, rent, property taxes, certain utilities, management and supervisory salaries and similar annual expenses. These costs remain unabsorbed or unrecovered due to under-utilisation of plant capacity. Idle capacity cost can be computed in the following manner:

$$\text{Idle capacity cost} = \text{Idle capacity} \times \frac{\text{Total overhead related to a plant}}{\text{Normal plant capacity}}$$

Treatment of Idle Capacity Cost

(a) If idle capacity is due to unavoidable reasons such as repairs & maintenance, changes over of job, etc., a supplementary overhead rate may be used to recover the idle capacity cost. In this case, the costs are charged to production capacity utilised.

(b) If idle capacity cost is due to avoidable reasons such as faulty planning, power failure etc, the cost should be charged to Profit/Loss Accounts.

(c) If idle capacity is due to seasonal factors, then the cost should be charged to cost of production by inflating overhead rates.

Idle capacity cost can be divided into normal and abnormal idle capacity costs. Under normal circumstances such as servicing of a machine, intermittent use of plant during the processing might cause idle capacity; such costs are treated as an overhead expense. If the idle capacity costs have occurred due to abnormal circumstances such as lack of work or jobs, such costs would be transferred to the costing profit and loss account and hence would not be included in the factory overheads. If the idle capacity cost is due to seasonal normal factors, then the cost would be charged to units produced by inflating overhead rates.

Idle Facilities

In a firm, idle facilities may be caused due to not using the facilities provided by fixed assets (such as plant, equipment, building, space etc.) and service functions (such as personnel services, productions services, material services etc.). The term idle facility is, therefore, broader and includes many factors causing idle facility besides including the factors responsible for idle capacity. The term "idle facility" is considered different from "idle capacity" in the sense that the idle capacity generally refers to under-utilisation of production or plant capacity and idle capacity costs are mostly fixed in nature and cannot be absorbed or recovered due to under-utilisation of plant capacity. If a part of total facilities is not being utilised due to any reason such as lack of power, lack of demand, non-availability of raw material, fuel etc., it is known as idle facilities. Idle facilities are different from idle time and in an organisation idle time may not be found although there exist idle facilities. The treatment of cost of idle facilities is similar to that of idle capacity cost.

Set-up Time

Often, machinery and support equipment must be adjusted before a particular operation or job can be started. The time involved in getting the equipment ready for production is usually traceable to a specific operation or job and therefore, would be regarded as part of the direct cost of the job. Alternatively, setting-up cost can be normally treated as a factory overhead and charged to all products, jobs, etc.

Packing Expenses

In almost all business firms manufacturing some product, expenses are incurred on packing materials which are known as packing expenses. Packing materials usually include items such as wrapping paper, bags, boxes, wood, twine, hoops, iron, cartons, glue, etc.

Packing expenses are treated in cost accounts in the following manner:

1. Prime packing materials, i.e., materials which are necessary for the product are charged to the cost of the product as an element of prime cost, e.g., paper required for wrapping in the manufacture of cigarettes.
2. Secondary packing materials are needed while delivering/transporting the products and such expenses are treated as distribution overhead.
3. Special packing material expenses, if required by the customer, are charged directly to the job or product.
4. Fancy packing expenses to attract customers are selling overhead.
5. The overhead costs of the packing department should be apportioned to different products on some suitable basis such as labour cost, sale value of the product, if they cannot be charged directly to the product.

Research and Development

The cost of research specifically undertaken for a job or product may be regarded as a direct cost of that job and charged thereto. If costs on research and development are incurred for the general advantage, they may be charged to production overhead. Research directed towards the improvement of methods and current products may be treated as production overhead and should be charged to production generally. But costs incurred for the search of new products, discovery or development of new methods, products or processes are not connected with current production and should be charged directly to the profit and loss account.

Cost of unsuccessful research is treated as factory overhead, provided the expenditure is normal and is provided in the budget. If it is not budgeted, it is written off to the profit and loss account. If the research is extended for long time, some failure cost is spread over to successful research.

Bad Debts

From past experience, the average bad debts incurred may be determined. This figure should be expressed as a percentage of the credit sales of the business and the resulting figure included in the distribution overhead.

Catalogues and Price Lists

The production of catalogues is often costly and takes place at intervals of several years. For costing purposes, the expenditure incurred including the cost of staff engaged in collecting the necessary information, is charged to a suspense account and a proportion of the costs is allocated to selling and distribution every year. In such a way, the full cost of the publication is recovered from sales by the time a new edition is brought out. In financial accounts the cost of catalogues is usually written off in the year in which it is incurred.

Tools

In most manufacturing concerns, tools are used in the manufacture of articles. Tools include drills, reamers, plugs and dies, go and no-go gauges and general cutting tools for lathes, milling machines, shapers and the like. The accounting treatment of tools is as follows:

1. Tools are treated as indirect materials if they are used for more than one product. The cost associated with such tools would be equitably apportioned among different products.
2. Sometimes, tools are requisitioned and acquired for a specific job or product to ensure better quality and lowest cost for the product. When the expenditures can be measured and traced to the product which will receive the exclusive benefit from the use of tool, they are charged directly to the product. In such a case, tools are treated as direct expense.
3. Tools received with machines and equipment are capitalised as capital expenditure but tools purchased subsequently are only revenue expenditures.
4. In computing the machine hour rate (for absorption of overhead) the cost of tools, depreciation, repair and maintenance are taken into account.

Patterns

Patterns are used in foundry work, where molten metal, usually cast iron, is poured into moulds. Patterns are generally permanent. Basically, there are two possibilities. First, a foundry may design its own product which may be useful to buyers. Second, the foundry (often) makes castings to a particular design of requirement for its customers. In both the cases, the cost of the patterns is treated as direct expenses like special tools.

Designs

In a company engaged in the manufacture of some complete articles, the design function includes the following functions:

1. Originating and developing new products.
2. Improving and developing the current product lines according to changes in technology and customer's habits.
3. Specifying and communicating the standards of quality.
4. Interpreting the product in the form of product specifications and/or materials and parts lists.
5. Preparing drawings and plans to define and interpret each component for manufacture.

The cost of a design may be charged totally to a specific order from a customer or alternatively, the cost of design may be apportioned over a number of years as part of research and development expenses. In this way, it can be treated as a deferred, revenue expenditure.

Blue Prints

A drawing office in a manufacturing company prepares drawings and blue prints with respect to products or customer's orders. Blue prints are copies of drawings prepared for immediate use. The following accounting treatments are in practice:

1. The cost of blue prints for immediate use is charged direct to the specific product or customer's order.
2. The cost of drawings for specific products or jobs is charged directly to the specific products or jobs.
3. The cost of drawings for standard and regular products is depreciated over the period of their life and therefore only depreciated value is considered for the year ending.

Advertising

Normal advertising in trade journals, periodicals and newspapers, by posters, radio or television and the cost of publicity literature and samples are treated as selling and distribution overhead at the time they are incurred and apportioned over the various products. Expenditure on advertising of a more permanent nature without regard to any specific product or article such as extensive campaigning required to launch a new product must be considered as a whole and is apportioned in a more or less arbitrary manner. Alternatively, such advertising costs can be capitalised and written off over a short period of years in the profit and loss account. In such a case, advertising depends upon policy and not upon output.

Carriage & Freight

If these are incurred for incoming material, it is included in the material cost whether direct or indirect material.

It is treated as distribution cost for transportation of finished goods.

Royalties

Royalties of general nature may be treated as part of selling overhead but those paid for the use of patents or the right to market particular products are normally charged direct.

EXAMPLE 7.6

Explain how to deal with the following in the cost accounts. Each answer should be in two or three sentences only, showing also the appropriate journal entry, wherever necessary:

(a) A shortage of 10 kg of a store item (book value ₹150) was noticed during physical verification. Investigations revealed that it was due to natural causes.

(b) An abnormal gain of ₹42,500 was noticed in process A of a chemical factory at the end of a month.

(c) A sum of ₹15,000 was realised by sale of saw dust and useless scantlings in a furniture-making business.

(d) In a factory, using historical cost system, there was an under-recovery of fixed factory overheads amounting to ₹24,000 at the end of the accounting period.

(e) A company spent ₹15 lakhs on advertisement in the national television network before launching a new product.

(f) A sum of ₹20,000 was incurred on printing and stationery in connection with the issue of non-convertible debentures by a company.

(g) A sum of ₹7,500 was paid as wages to workers in a factory when there was no work due to power failure.

(h) Overtime wages amounting to ₹500 was incurred to meet an urgent order of a customer who wanted the delivery date to be advanced.

Solution

The action to be taken is briefly explained as follows:

(a) The loss is due to natural causes; hence, the loss incurred may be debited to "Factory Overhead" or "Stores Overheads" and credited to the "Stores Control Account". Simultaneously corrections may be carried out in the Bin Card and stores ledger.

(b) Abnormal gain may be credited to costing profit and loss account and debited to process account.

(c) The amount should be credited to "Miscellaneous Income Account". It should not affect cost of the products.

(d) The amount under recovered as fixed overheads should be transferred by debiting the costing profit and loss account and crediting to overheads control account.

(e) The impact of the advertisement cost on the sales for each year should be carefully estimated and only the proportionate amount of advertisement should be charged to costs each year. The balance should be treated as a deferred revenue expenditure.

(f) This item is of pure finance and therefore should not be included in cost account.

(g) The idle time wages, if abnormal, should be debited to costing profit and loss account direct, as an extra ordinary expense. In case the power failure is frequent and such costs are incurred often, it may be debited to idle time wages under "factory overheads" as a normal cost.

(h) The overtime wages have to be borne by the customer, since work is rushed at his specific request. The concerned job and WIP will be directly debited by crediting the wages control account.

EXAMPLE 7.7

A machine was purchased from a manufacture who claimed that his machine could produce 36.5 tonnes in a year consisting of 365 days. Holidays, break-down, etc., were normally allowed in the factory for

65 days. Sales were expected to be 25 tonnes during the year and the plant actually produced 25.2 tonnes during the year. You are required to state the following figures:

(a) Rated capacity
(b) Practical capacity
(c) Normal capacity
(d) Actual capacity

☞ **Solution**

(a) Rated capacity — 36.5 tonnes
(Refers to the capacity of a machine or a plant as indicated by its manufacturer)

(b) Practical capacity — 30 tonnes
(Defined as actually utilised capacity of a plant)

i.e. $\frac{36.5}{365} \times (365 - 65)$ tonnes

(c) Normal capacity — 25 tonnes
(It is the capacity of a plant utilised based on sales expectancy)

(d) Actual capacity — 25.2 tonnes
(Refers to the capacity actually achieved)

Theory Questions

1. Explain the nature of administrative overheads. How are they apportioned to products?
2. Discuss the methods of absorption of selling and distribution overheads.
3. What problems are faced in applying administrative costs partly to the manufacturing and partly to the selling departments of a concern? How will you control administrative overhead of a concern?
4. Set out the main arguments for and against inclusion of interest on capital in cost accounts.
5. How do you deal with the following in cost accounts?
   (a) Advertising
   (b) Research and development cost
   (c) Bad debts
   (d) Rent of factory buildings
6. "Interest is a factor which cannot be disregarded by management." Comment on this statement.
7. The level of production activity fluctuates widely in your company from month to month. Because of this the incidence of depreciation on unit cost varies considerably. The management decides that you find out a suitable method to correct this.
8. In a manufacturing company where costing is done with a view to fix prices, state whether and, if so, to what extent the following items are included in cost.
   (i) Interest on borrowings
   (ii) Bonus and gratuity
   (iii) Depreciation on plant and machinery
9. Discuss the treatment of the following items in cost accounts:
   (i) Capacity cost
   (ii) Set-up time
   (iii) Packing expenses
   (iv) Blue print and design
10. State the meaning and treatment of overtime premium in cost accounts.
11. How would you treat the following in costing-
    (i) Interest on capital
    (ii) Bad debts
    (iii) Packing expenses

12. Explain treatment of cost of idle time in cost accounts.
13. Explain the treatment of overtime in cost accounts.
14. Explain idle time and idle capacity.
15. Write short notes on capacity cost concepts.
16. What is idle time? Explain normal and abnormal idle time along with treatment in cost accounts.
17. What are the arguments for and against inclusion of interest on capital in cost accounts?
18. What is idle time? Give reasons for idle time? How do you treat idle time in cost accounts?

Problems

1. A company is producing three types of products, *A*, *B*, *C*. The sales territory of the company is divided into three areas, *X*, *Y* and *Z*. The estimated sales for the year are as under:

	Territories		
Product	*X* (₹)	*Y* (₹)	*Z* (₹)
A	50,000	20,000	—
B	30,000	—	80,000
C	—	70,000	40,000

Budgeted advertising cost is as under:

	Territories			*Total*
	X	*Y*	*Z*	₹
Local cost	3,200	4,500	4,200	11,900
General	—	—	—	5,800

You are required to find the advertising cost per cent on sales for each product and the territory showing how you will present the statement to management.

Ans:

	Products		
	A	*B*	*C*
Advertising as a percentage of sales	6.28%	5.64%	6.45%

2. A match factory sells its goods in four district zones—South, North, East and West. You have been given the particulars for January 2020 in respect of each zone mentioned as follows:

Zones	*Net Sales (in Lakhs)*	*No. of Salesmen*	*Average Mileage Covered*	*Advertising Budget*	*Stock Held in a Time (in Lakhs)*	*Transportation Charges*
South	500	30	3,000	25%	2.00	25%
North	13.50	50	4,500	30%	5.00	50%
East	3.50	20	2,700	25%	1.50	15%
West	3.00	25	2,400	20%	1.50	10%

The following are the expenses of the previous month:

Sales manager and his establishment		₹62,000
Travelling representatives' salaries		36,000
Travelling representatives' travelling allowance		12,000
Advertising		24,000
Godown rent at out-stations:	₹	
South zone	7,500	
North zone	10,500	
East zone	4,800	
West zone	3,600	26,400
Insurance on inventories at out-stations		12,200
Commission on sales @ 2 1/4%		62,500
Transportation charges outward		36,000
You are required to compute selling overhead rates as a percentage of sales.		2,71,100

Ans: Overhead as per cent of sales
South zone 12.2%, North zone 9.6%, East zone 12.2%, West zone 12.5%.

Chapter 8

Activity-Based Costing (ABC)

Learning Objectives

After reading this chapter, you should be able to:

1. explain Activity-Based Costing (ABC)—definition, its stages and flow of costs, its advantages and disadvantages and its utility in service organisations;
2. discuss the classification of activities in manufacturing organisations for ABC; and
3. discuss the concepts of cost driver, target costing, Kaizen costing, Life cycle costing, Activity-Based Management (ABM) and the differences between traditional costing system and activity-based costing system.

MEANING OF ACTIVITY-BASED COSTING (ABC)

Activity-Based Costing (ABC) is that costing in which costs are first traced to activities and then to products. The ABC is a costing system which focuses on activities performed to produce products. Activities become the focal points for cost accumulation. This costing system assumes that activities are responsible for the incurrence of costs and products create the demands for activities. Costs are charged to products based on individual product's use of each activity. In traditional product costing system, costs are, first, traced not to activities but to an organisational unit, such as department or plant and then to products. It means that under both ABC and traditional costing system, the second and final stage consists of tracing costs to the product. By emphasising activities, ABC tries to ascertain the factors that cause each major activity, cost of such activities and the relationship between activities and products produced. The relationship between activities and products has been shown in the Figure 8.1.

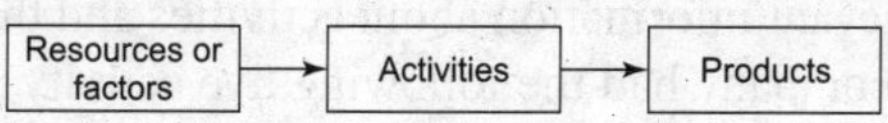

Fig. 8.1 ABC Process

STEPS IN ABC (STAGES AND FLOW OF COSTS IN ABC)

There are two primary stages in ABC—first tracing costs to activities; and second, tracing activities to products. The different steps in the two stages of ABC are as follows:

Step 1: Identify Activities

An activity is a unit of work. If you go to a restaurant for lunch/dinner, a waiter or waiters might perform the following units of work:

- Seat customer and offer menu
- Take your order
- Send orders to kitchen
- Bring food
- Replenish beverages
- Determine and bring bill
- Collect money and give change
- Clear table

Each of these is an activity and the performance of each activity consumes resources that cost money.

The first step in developing activity-based product costs is to identify the activities performed in the organisation. Think of activities as "verbs" that answer the question "What do you do?". If you had to answer the question, what might be some of your responses? "I study, I sleep, I eat." Asking this question of employees is one way to determine the activities they perform; another is to observe what they do. Either way, this step is the most time-consuming part of implementing an activity-based costing system and the one that can generate the greatest error.

In addition to identifying the activities, you need to determine how much time the employees spend in performing each activity. Let's go back to your answer to the question "What do I do?". While you might find it easy to list what you do, saying how much time you spend on each activity might be harder. For instance, the amount of time you spend studying probably varies each week, depending on what class tests you have. The same is true for many employees; the time they spend on certain tasks varies from one month to the next. Nevertheless, employees must take such an estimate so that the resources consumed by the activities (that is, their salaries and other costs) can be calculated.

As activities are identified, the time spent on that activity and the resources consumed by that activity must be tracked.

Step 2: Develop Activity Cost Pools

After all the activities have been identified and the appropriate level of details has been selected, the activities are combined into activity cost pools based on their cost drivers. For example, Apollo Sports Co.'s managers determined that "moving materials from the storeroom to the cutting room" and "packing finished products" were both batch activities. Because pants, jerseys and jackets are produced in batches, the number of batches produced determines the frequency of these warehousing and packaging activities and the resources consumed. Therefore, managers combined those two activities into one pool. After gathering all the relevant information about activities and their drivers, Apollo Sports Co.'s managers determined that the company had the following five activity pools:

Activity Pool	**Activity Driver**
Product design	Number of product lines
Warehousing/packaging	Number of batches
Cutting	Number of cuts
Sewing	Direct labour hours
General	Not assigned to products

Once the activity pools have been determined, manufacturing overhead costs can be assigned to them. This is referred to as a first-stage allocation because costs are assigned first to the activity pools before being assigned to cost objects. Figure 8.2 shows the first-stage allocation of manufacturing overhead resources for Apollo Sports. These allocations were based on employee estimates of time spent and the resources used to complete the activities. Notice that the ₹13,26,000 that relates to the machine is not included in the costs allocated to the activity pools, since those costs are traceable directly to the jackets. All the remaining manufacturing overhead costs are allocated to the activity pools.

	Machine Costs Traceable to Jackets	Product Design	Warehouse/ Packaging	Cutting	Sewing	General	Total
Indirect labour	₹25,140	₹4,00,000	₹4,00,000	₹75,000	₹1,50,000	₹10,59,860	₹21,10,000
Depreciation	₹40,920		₹73,960		₹3,46, 960		₹4,61,840
Indirect materials	₹12,59,940	₹3,75,120	₹11,08,690	₹13,58,610	₹10,10,640		₹51,13,000
Rent						₹11,00,000	₹11,00,000
Utilities					₹4,13,300	₹1,70,000	₹5,83,300
Insurance						₹ 5,50,000	₹5,50,000
Other		₹63,770	₹1,22,970	₹37,470	₹1,47,300	₹ 42,850	₹ 4,14,360
Total	₹13,26,000	₹8,38,890	₹17,05,620	₹14,71,080	₹20,68,200	₹29,22,710	₹1,03,32,500

Fig. 8.2 Step 2: Allocation of manufacturing overhead costs to activity pools.

Step 3: Calculate Activity Cost Pool Rates

After the manufacturing overhead costs have been assigned to activity cost pools, the next step in developing activity-based product costs is to calculate an activity rate for each cost pool. Activity rate is calculated as follows:

$$\text{Activity Rate} = \frac{\text{Total activity cost pool resources}}{\text{Total activity driver volume}}$$

Figure 8.3 shows the calculation of the four activity rates for Apollo Sports. Let's review the calculations. For product design, the activity cost totals ₹8,38,890 (see Figure 8.2). Since the number of product lines is the cost driver and Apollo has three product lines (pants, jerseys and jackets), the denominator is 3 product lines. The calculation of the activity rate is:

$$\frac{₹8{,}38{,}890}{3\,\text{product lines}} = ₹2{,}79{,}630 \text{ per product line}$$

	Total Cost (A)	Total Activity (B)	Activity Rate (A)/(B)
Product design	₹8,38,890	3 product lines	₹2,79,630 per product line
Warehousing/packaging	₹17,05,620	9,170 batches	₹186 per batch
Cutting	₹14,71,080	56,580 cuts	₹26 per cut
Sewing	₹20,68,200	86,175 direct labour hours	₹24 per direct labour hour

Fig. 8.3 Step 3: Calculation of activity rates.

For warehousing/packaging, the activity cost totals ₹17,05,620. The number of batches produced is the cost driver for this activity pool. It is calculated as follows:

	Budgeted Production		Units Per Batch		Number of Batches
Pants	1,83,500	÷	50	=	3,670
Jerseys	66,500	÷	35	=	1,900
Jackets	18,000	÷	5	=	3,600
Total					9,170

Given this number of batches, the activity rate for this pool is calculated as:

$$\frac{₹17,05,620}{9,170\text{ batches}} = ₹186\text{ per batch}$$

For cutting, the activity cost totals ₹14,71,080. The number of cuts is the cost driver for this activity pool; it is calculated as follows:

	Batches		Cuts Per Batch		Total Cuts
Pants	3,670	×	4	=	14,680
Jerseys	1,900	×	5	=	9,500
Jackets	3,600	×	9	=	32,400
Total					56,580

Given this number of cuts, the activity rate is calculated as:

$$\frac{₹14,71,080}{56,580\text{ cuts}} = ₹26\text{ per cut}$$

Finally, for sewing, the activity cost totals ₹20,68,200. Direct labour hours are the cost driver for this activity pool, and it is calculated as follows:

	Budgeted Production	Direct Labour Hours Per Unit		Total Direct Labour Hours
Pants	1,83,500	0.25 hours	=	45,875
Jerseys	66,500	0.20 hours	=	13,300
Jackets	18,000	1.50 hours	=	27,000
Total				86,175

Given this number of direct labour hours, the activity rate is calculated as:

$$\frac{₹20,68,200}{86,175\text{ direct labour hours}} = ₹24\text{ per direct labour hour}$$

Step 4: Allocate Costs to Products or Services

With the activity rates calculated, one can allocate the costs to products or services. The following formula can be used to allocate costs to products or services.

Allocated Cost = Activity rate ×Activity driver consumption

Figure 8.4 shows the cost allocations to the three products. Notice that each product has four allocations, one for each of the activity pools. Notice, too, that the activity rate column for each product is the same, since the activity rates are constant, regardless of the product that is consuming the resource. However, each product uses the activities to different degree, and those differences in usage drive the differences in allocated costs. For example, the cutting cost allocated to pants is ₹26 × 14,680 cuts = ₹3,81,680; to jackets, it is ₹8,42,400—why? The answer is that jackets require many more cuts than pants, even though the company makes fewer jackets than pants. Let's reconcile how the overhead costs from the first-stage allocation (see Figure 8.2) were allocated to the three products:

		Overhead Costs
Pants		₹24,44,930
Jerseys		11,99,230
Jackets		
ABC allocation	₹24,39,630	
Machine costs	₹13,26,000	37,65,630
Total costs allocated		₹74,09,790
General costs not allocated		29,22,710
Total overhead costs		₹1,03,32,500

All the overhead costs have been accounted for. When the overhead cost allocated to the jackets is added to the machine costs traced to the jackets, the total overhead cost of the jackets becomes ₹37,65,630. Notice that this amount is more than the overhead cost allocated to pants. Even though budgeted production called for only 18,000 jackets as compared to 1,83,500 pants, jacket production requires many more activities than pants production.

Pants	Activity Rate		Activity		ABC Cost
Product design	₹2,79,630 per product line	×	1 line	=	₹2,79,630
Warehousing/packaging	₹186 per batch	×	3,670 batches	=	6,82,620
Cutting	₹26 per cut	×	14,680 cuts	=	3,81,680
Sewing	₹24 per direct labour hour	×	45,875 direct labour hours	=	11,01,000
					₹24,44,930

Jerseys	Activity Rate		Activity		ABC Cost
Product design	₹2,79,630 per product line	×	1 line	=	₹2,79,630
Warehousing/packaging	₹186 per batch	×	1,900 batches	=	3,53,400
Cutting	₹26 per cut	×	9,500 cuts	=	2,47,000
Sewing	₹24 per direct labour hour	×	13,300 direct labour hours	=	3,19,200
					₹11,99,230

Jackets	Activity Rate		Activity		ABC Cost
Product design	₹2,79,630 per product line	×	1 line	=	₹2,79,630
Warehousing/packaging	₹186 per batch	×	3,600 batches	=	6,69,600
Cutting	₹26 per cut	×	32,400 cuts	=	8,42,400
Sewing	₹24 per direct labour hour	×	27,000 direct labour hours	=	6,48,000
					₹24,39,630

Fig. 8.4 Step 4: Allocating activity costs to products.

Step 5: Calculate Unit Product Costs

The last step in the preparation of activity-based costing data is to calculate the unit product cost. In Step 4, we calculated the total overhead allocated to each product. For decision-making purposes, we need to convert that amount to a unit cost by dividing the total overhead cost by the total number of units produced. For example, the overhead cost for a pair of pants would be Rs. 13.3 (rounded), calculated as

$$\frac{₹24{,}44{,}930}{1{,}83{,}500 \text{ pants}} = ₹13.3 \text{ per pair of pants}$$

To calculate the total product cost per unit, we need to add the direct materials and direct labour costs to this overhead cost. The total activity-based cost for a pair of pants would be

Direct materials	₹44.7
Direct labour	24.0
Overhead	13.3
Total product cost per unit	₹82.0

Figure 8.5 shows the calculation of the total product costs and unit costs for all three products based on the budgeted production for 2020.

	Pants	Jerseys	Jackets	Total Costs
Traceable overhead			₹13,26,000	₹13,26,000
Allocated overhead	₹24,44,930	₹11,99,230	₹24,39,630	₹60,83,790
Total overhead cost	₹24,44,930	₹11,99,230	₹37,65,630	₹74,09,790
Unit produced	÷ 1,83,500	÷ 66,500	÷ 18,000	
Overhead per unit	₹13.3	₹18.0	₹209.2	
Direct materials	44.7	68.5	447.2	
Direct labour	24.0	19.2	144.0	
	₹82	₹105.7	₹800.4	

Fig. 8.5 Step 5: Calculating unit product costs.

Let us compare the activity-based overhead allocation to Apollo's original allocation, based on direct labour cost. Figure 8.6 shows the manufacturing overhead costs allocated to each of the products under the two methods. Notice that the total amount of manufacturing overhead allocated to the products differ between the two methods—₹1,03,32,500 under the traditional approach and ₹74,09,790 under the activity-based approach. The difference between the amount of manufacturing overhead allocated under the two methods is the ₹29,22,710 general overhead cost pool that was not allocated to products under activity-based costing.

	Pants	Jerseys	Jackets	Total
Traditional				
Direct labour cost	₹44,00,000	₹12,74,000	₹25,92,000	₹82,66,000
Overhead rate	125%	125%	125%	125%
= Allocated overhead	₹55,00,000	₹15,92,500	₹32,40,000	₹1,03,32,500
% of total overhead	53.23%	15.41%	31.36%	
ABC				
Traceable			₹13,26,000	₹13,26,000
+ Product design	₹2,79,630	₹2,79,630	₹2,79,630	₹8,38,890
+ Warehousing/packaging	6,82,620	3,53,400	6,69,600	17,05,620
+ Cutting	3,81,680	2,47,000	8,42,400	14,71,080
+ Sewing	11,01,000	3,19,200	6,48,000	20,68,200
= Allocated overhead	₹24,44,930	₹11,99,230	₹37,65,630	₹74,09,790
% of allocated overhead	33.00%	16.18%	50.82%	
+Organisational-level				
Overhead (not allocated)				29,22,710
= Total overhead				₹1,03,32,500

Fig. 8.6 Comparison of traditional and activity-based costing.

Although the total amount of allocated overhead differs between the two methods, we can still compare the percentage of overhead allocated to each product. Notice that where the big differences occur in Figure 8.6. Under the traditional costing method, pants were allocated 53.23% of manufacturing overhead, yet under activity-based costing, pants received just 33% of manufacturing overhead. The other major difference between the two methods was for Jackets, which were allocated 31.36% of total overhead under the traditional method and 50.82% under activity-based costing. What caused the differences in the relative amount of manufacturing overhead allocated under the two methods to pants, a high-volume product, and jackets, a low-volume product? One obvious cause is the costs associated with the machine. Under traditional costing, these costs were shared by all three products. However, under activity-based costing, these costs are traced directly to jackets, reducing the amount of overhead allocated to pants and increasing the amount of overhead allocated to jackets.

A second cause of the difference in costs results from the cutting operation. Jacket production required more cutting than pant production, even though Apollo produced only one-tenth the numbers of jackets as pants. This shift in cost from a high-volume to a low-volume product is quite common in newly implemented activity-based costing systems. This is because low-volume products, like jackets, tend to use as many product-level activities as other products, while generating as many or more batch-level activities.

ACTIVITY COST DRIVERS

Like a resource driver that is used to trace resource to activities, an activity cost driver is used to trace activity costs to cost objects. Activity driver is defined as a measure of the frequency and intensity of the demands placed on activities by cost objects. An activity driver is used to assign costs to cost objects.

A cost driver is an activity which generates cost. A cost driver is a factor, such as the level of activity or volume, that causally affects costs (over a given time span). That is, a cause-and-effect relationship exists between a change in the level of activity or volume and a change in the level of the total costs of that cost objects. Thus, cost drivers signify factors, forces or events that determine the costs of activities. Based on activity usage (consumption), activity costs are traced to cost objects.

In a manufacturing organisation, the following are examples of some activity cost drivers (see Figure 8.7).

Some Examples of Activity Cost Drivers

1. Number of receiving orders for the receiving department.
2. Number of purchase order for the cost of operating the purchase department.
3. Number of dispatch orders for the dispatch department.
4. Number of units.
5. Number of setups.
6. Amount of labour cost incurred.
7. Value of materials in a product.
8. Number of materials handling hours.
9. Number of inspections.
10. Number of schedule changes.
11. Number of parts received per month.
12. Number of machine hours used on a product.
13. Number of set up hours.
14. Number of direct labour hours.
15. Number of sub-assemblies.
16. Number of vendors.
17. Number of purchasing and ordering-hours.
18. Number of units scrapped.
19. Number of labour transactions.
20. Number of customer orders processed.
21. Number of parts.
22. Number of employees.

Fig. 8.7 Activity Cost Drivers

It should be understood that direct costs do not need cost drivers as they can be traced directly to a product. Direct costs are themselves cost drivers. However, all other factory or manufacturing costs need cost drivers. The cost driver of variable costs is the level of activity or volume whose change causes the variable costs to change proportionately.

Costs that are fixed in the short run have no cost driver in the short run but may have cost drivers in the long run. For instance, costs of testing personal computers (which comprise costs of testing department equipment and staff costs) may not change with changes in the volume of production. Therefore, these costs would be fixed in the short run. In the long run, however, an organisation may need to increase/decrease testing department's equipment and staff to the levels needed to support future production volumes. So, in the long run, volume of production or activity becomes cost drivers of these testing and staff costs.

SELECTION OF ACTIVITY COST DRIVERS

In traditional product costing, the numbers of cost drivers used are few such as direct labour hours, machine hours, direct labour cost, units produced. But, ABC may use a multitude of cost drivers that relate costs more closely to the resources consumed and activities occurring. There are difficulties in choosing realistic cost drivers. There are no simple rules that pertain to the selection of cost drivers. The best approach is to identify the resources that constitute a significant proportion of the product costs and to determine their cost behaviour. When identifying and selecting activity drivers, match the activity to the activity level, which is defined as a description of how an activity is used by a cost object (product/service) or activity. Some activity levels describe the cost object that uses the activity and nature of its use.

According to Hilton[1], the following three factors are important in selecting appropriate cost drivers.

1. *Degree of correlation*—The central concept of an activity-based costing system is to assign the costs of each activity to product lines on the basis of how each product line consumes the cost driver identified for that activity. The idea is to infer how each product line consumes the activity by observing how each product line consumes the cost driver. Therefore, the accuracy of the resulting cost assignment depends on the degree of correlation between consumption of the activity and consumption of the cost driver.
2. *Cost of measurement*—Designing any information system entails cost-benefit trade-offs. The more activity cost pools there are in an activity-based costing system, the greater will be the accuracy of the cost assignments. However, more activity cost pools also entail more cost drivers, which results in greater costs of implementing and maintaining the system. Similarly, the higher the correlation between a cost driver and the actual consumption of the associated activity, the greater the accuracy of the cost assignments. However, it may also be more costly to measure the more highly-correlated cost driver.
3. *Behavioural effects*—Information systems have the potential not only to facilitate decisions but also to influence the behaviour or decision maker. This can be good or bad, depending on the behavioural effects. In identifying cost drivers, an ABC analyst should consider the possible behavioural consequences. For example, in a JIT production environment, a key goal is to reduce inventories and material handling activities to the absolute minimum level possible. The number of material moves may be the most accurate measure of the consumption of the material handling activity for cost assignment purpose. It may also have a desirable behavioural effect of motivating managers to reduce the number of times materials are moved, thereby reducing material.

Dysfunctional behavioural effects are also possible. For example, the number of vendor contacts may be a cost driver for the purchasing activity of vendor selection. This could induce purchasing managers to contact fewer vendors, which could result in the failure to identify the lowest-cost or highest-quality vendor.

---

[1] Ronald W. Hilton, *Managerial Accounting*, McGraw Hill, pp. 182–183.

ABC focuses on the drivers which cause overheads and traces overheads to products in terms of usage of cost drivers. Therefore, under ABC, a large proportion of overheads are product related. In traditional costing systems, however, most support overheads are assigned to products in general arbitrary manner and therefore cannot be related to products. ABC by identify appropriate cost drivers and cost pools makes the product costs more accurate and reliable. Further, ABC, in this way, helps in better cost management and cost control by managing the activities which cause costs.

Miller[2] observes that tips for identifying activity drivers include the following:

- Pick activity drivers that correlate with the actual consumption of the activity.
- Minimise the number of unique drivers. Cost and complexity are directly correlated with the number of drivers.
- Pick activity drivers that encourage improved performance.
- Pick activity drivers that are already available and/or have a low cost of collection.

Classification of Activities in Manufacturing Organisations

In manufacturing organisations, activities are identified and classified into different categories or segments of the production process. The grouping of activities is preferably done using the different levels at which activities are performed. Broadly, activities are classified into one of four activity categories:

1. Unit-level Activities.
2. Batch-level Activities.
3. Product-level Activities.
4. Facility-level Activities.

Unit level activities are those activities which are performed each time a unit is produced. They are repetitive activities. For example, direct labour hours, machine hours, and power are used each time a unit is produced. Direct materials and direct labour activities are also unit level activities, although they are not overhead costs. Costs of unit level activities vary with the number of units produced.

Batch level activities are those activities which are performed each time a batch of goods or products is produced. The costs of batch level activities vary with the number of batches but are fixed with respect to the number of units in each batch. Machine setups, inspections, production scheduling, materials handling are examples of batch level activities which are related to batches but not to individual products.

Product level activities are those activities which are performed to support the production of each different type of product. Maintenance of equipment, engineering charges, testing routines, maintaining bills of materials, handling materials are some examples of product-level activities.

Facility-level activities are those which are needed to sustain a factory's general manufacturing process. These activities are common to a variety of products and are most difficult to link to product specific activities. Examples of facility-level activities are factory management, maintenance, security and plant depreciation.

In ABC system, facility level activities and costs are treated as period cost as they are found difficult to assign to different products. The costs associated with the first three categories—unit level, batch

[2] John A. Miller, *Implementing Activity-Based Management in Daily Operations*, John Wiley and Sons, 1996, p. 54.

level and product level—are assigned to products, using cost drivers that reflect the cause and effect relationship between activity consumption and cost.

Several additional examples of the costs driven by activities at each above level are presented in Fig. 8.8.

Activity Level	*Reason for Activity*	*Examples of Activity Cost*
1. Unit level	Performed for each unit of product produced or sold	• Cost of raw materials • Cost of inserting a component • Utilities cost of operating equipment • Some costs of packaging • Sales commissions
2. Batch level	Performed for each batch of product produced or sold	• Cost of processing sales order • Cost of issuing and tracking work order • Cost of equipment setup • Cost of moving batch between workstations • Cost of inspection (assuming same number of units inspected in each batch)
3. Product level	Performed to support each different product that can be produced	• Cost of product development • Cost of product marketing such as advertising • Cost of specialised equipment • Cost of maintaining specialised equipment
4. Facility level	Performed to maintain general manufacturing capabilities	• Cost of maintaining general facilities such as buildings and grounds • Cost of nonspecialised equipment • Cost of maintaining nonspecialised equipment • Cost of real property taxes • Cost of general advertising • Cost of general administration such as the plant manager's salary

Fig. 8.8 Activity Levels and Associated Activity Costs

Source: Wayne J. Morse, James R. Davis, Al. L. Hartgraves, *Management accounting: A Strategic Approach*, South Western College Publishing, 2000, p. 54.

Comparing ABC with Traditional Costing System

In traditional costing system, overhead costs are assumed to be influenced by only units produced. It means, in traditional costing system, costs of batch level, product level and facility level activities are fixed costs, that is, costs of these do not vary as production volume changes. Unit-based cost systems apportion fixed overhead to individual products and variable overhead are directly assigned to products using the base of number of units produced.

When fixed overheads are apportioned on the basis of units made, as in traditional costing, such apportionment is likely to be arbitrary and also may not reflect activities and cost actually consumed by the products. ABC improves product costing procedure (as compared to traditional costing) because it recognises that many so-called fixed overhead costs vary in proportional to changes other than production units. It means, under ABC, the other two level activities—batch level and product level—are assumed to influence fixed overhead costs and batch level and product level, thus, are accepted as non-unit-based cost drivers. By establishing the link between these cost drivers and fixed overhead costs, they are finally traced to individual products. Figure 8.9 presents an overview of product cost determination under traditional costing and ABC system.

Traditional Costing and Activity-based Costing System

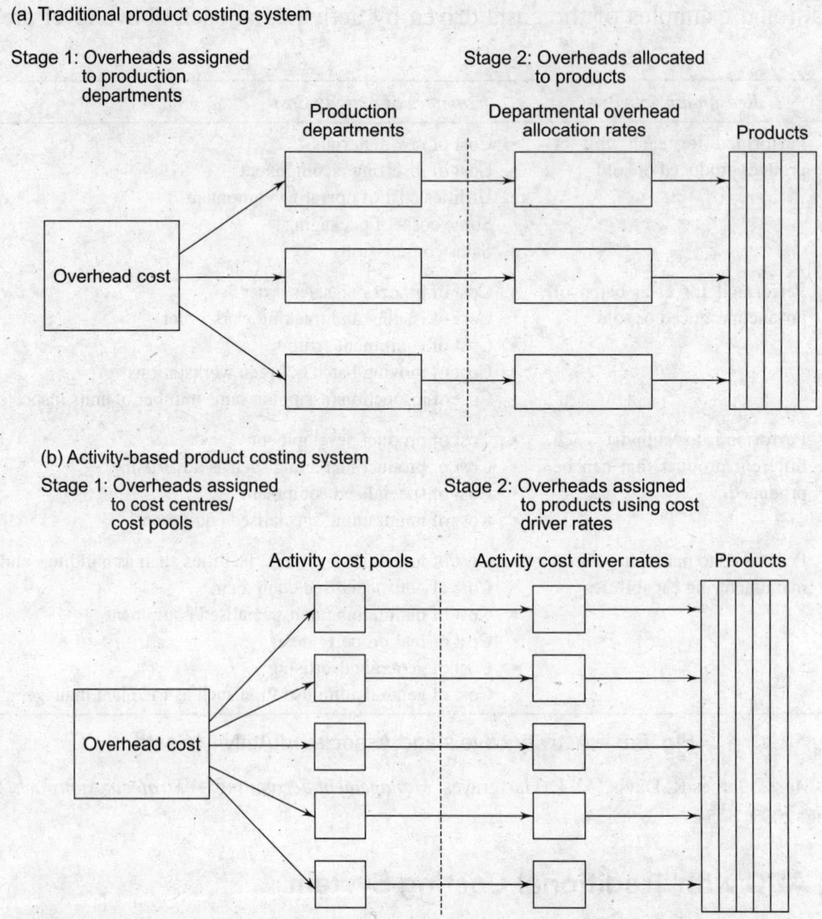

Fig. 8.9 Comparison of Traditional and Activity-based Costing System

Source: J. Innes and F. Mitchell, *Activity-Based Costing: A Review with Case Studies*, 1990, CIMA, U.K.

Figure 8.9 displays that both the costing systems follow a two-stage allocation procedure. In traditional costing, in the first stage, overhead costs are allocated to production departments. But, in ABC, in the first stage, overhead costs are assigned to each major activity and not to departments. In traditional costing, overheads are pooled/collected department-wise. But, in ABC, many activity-based cost pools or cost centres are created. In traditional costing, overhead costs of service departments are allocated/reapportioned to production department and therefore in this costing system finally only fewer cost pools exist. But, ABC creates separate cost pools for service activities as well and overhead costs of these service activities (service departments) are assigned directly to specific products through applying cost driver rates. Thus, in ABC, there is no need to allocate/reapportion overheads of service departments.

The fundamental differences in the conventional and ABC cost system are summarised in Fig. 8.10.

	Traditional	ABC
• Cost pools	• One or a limited number	• Many, to reflect different activities
• Applied rate	• Volume-based, financial	• Activity-based, non-financial
• Suited for	• Labour-intensive, Low-overhead companies	• Capital-intensive, product-diverse, high-overhead companies
• Benefits	• Simple, inexpensive	• Accurate product costing, possible elimination of non-value-added activities

Fig. 8.10 Traditional and ABC System

Advantages of ABC

The following are the advantages of ABC.

1. ABC brings accuracy and reliability in product cost-determination by focussing on cause and effect relationship in the cost incurrence. It recognises that it is activities which cause costs, not products, and it is product which consumes activities.
2. In advanced manufacturing environment and technology where support functions overheads constitute a large share of total costs, ABC provides more realistic product costs.
3. ABC identifies the real nature of cost behaviour and helps in reducing costs and identifying activities which do not add value to the product. With ABC, managers are able to control many fixed overhead costs by exercising more control over the activities which have caused these fixed overhead costs. This is possible since behaviour of many fixed overhead costs in relation to activities now become more visible and clear.
4. ABC uses multiple cost drivers, many of which are transaction-based rather than product volume. Further, ABC is concerned with all activities within and beyond the factory to trace more overheads to the products.
5. ABC traces costs to areas of managerial responsibility, processes, customers, departments besides the product costs.
6. ABC improves greatly the manager's decision-making as they can use more reliable product cost data. ABC helps usefully in fixing selling prices of products as more correct data of product cost is now readily available.
7. ABC produces reliable and correct product cost data in case of greater diversity among the products manufactured such as low-volume products, high-volume products. Traditional costing system is likely to bring errors and approximation in product cost determination due to using arbitrary apportionment and absorption methods.
8. ABC provides cost driver rates and information on transaction volumes which are very useful to management for cost management and performance appraisal of responsibility centres. Cost driver rates can be used advantageously for the design of new products or existing products as they indicate overhead costs that are likely to be applied in costing the product.

Colin Drury[3] observes:

> "ABC provides not only a base for calculating more accurate product costs but also a mechanism for managing costs. An ABC system focuses management attention on the underlying causes of costs. It assumes that

[3] Colin Drury, *Management and Cost Accounting*, Thomas Learning, 2000, p. 285.

resource-consuming activities cause costs and that products incur costs through the activities they require for designing, engineering, manufacturing, marketing, delivery, invoicing and servicing. By collecting and reporting on the significant activities in which a business engages, it is possible to understand and manage costs more effectively.

With an ABC system, costs are managed in the long run by controlling the activities that drive them. In other words, the aim is to manage the activities rather than costs. By managing the forces that cause the activities (that is, cost drivers), costs will be managed in the long-term. The application of activity-based systems may have the greatest potential for contributing to cost management, budgeting, control and performance evaluation."

Demerits of ABC

The following are the limitations of ABC.

1. Activity-based costing is a complex system and requires lot of records and tedious calculations.
2. For small organisations, traditional cost accounting system may be more beneficial than activity-based costing due to the simplicity of operation of the former.
3. Sometimes, it is difficult to attribute costs to single activities as some costs support several activities.
4. ABC has numerous cost pools and multiple cost drivers and therefore can be more complex than traditional product costing systems.
5. Some difficulties emerge in the implementation of ABC system, such as selection of cost drivers, assignment of common costs, varying cost driver rates etc.
6. ABC has different levels of utility for different organisations such as large manufacturing firm can use it more usefully than the smaller firms. Also, it is likely that firms depending on cost-plus pricing can take advantages from ABC as it gives accurate product cost. But, those firms who use market-based prices may not favour ABC. The level of technology and manufacturing environment prevailing in different firms also affect the application of ABC.
7. It can prove costly to manage ABC system.
8. ABC system can only be successful if there is a total support from top management.

The decision to use ABC is comparing costs and benefits relating to this system. The advantages to a company of ABC system depends on many factors such as level of competition, number of products manufactured and product diversity. It can be claimed that those companies who operate in a more competitive environment, are in dire need of correct product cost data for taking sound decisions with regard to determination of selling prices and taking better cost management measures. Whether a company manufactures and sells smaller number or large number of products, it influences the operation of ABC system and the degree of sophistication in the system.

ABC in Service Organisations

The discussion of ABC so far has focussed on manufacturing companies where important cost components like direct material and direct labour can be traced to individual products. Therefore, indirect costs are likely to be a much smaller proportional of total costs in such manufacturing companies. In service organisations, most of the costs are treated fixed and indirect, and therefore irrelevant for most decisions. No attempt is made to make profitability analysis in service organisations. There is a greater need of using ABC in service companies. Kaplan and Cooper[4] suggest that service companies are ideal

4. R.S. Kaplan and R. Cooker, *Cost and Effect: Using Integrated Systems to Drive Profitability and Performance*, Harvard Business School Press, 1998.

candidates for ABC, even more than manufacturing companies. Earlier, service organisations were government-owned or operated in highly regulated, protected and non-competitive environment. Thus, service organisations were not under any pressure to improve profitability by eliminating non-value added or non-profit activities. The prices of services were simply increased to cover cost increases. No effort was made to design a cost system that accurately measures the costs and profitability of individual services.

However, due to privatisation, deregulation and increasing competition, the service organisations need to have cost and management accounting systems which can help them to accurately measure cost and resulting profitability for their services, customers and markets. Therefore, ABC would prove advantageous to service organisations to understand their cost base and to make decisions on value-added/non-value added activities.

TARGET COSTING

Target costing implies developing product cost in terms of what the market will pay for a product with specific characteristics.

Target costing is a systematic approach to establishing product cost goals based on market driven standards. It is a strategic management process for reducing costs at the early stages of product planning and design. Target costing begins with identifying customer needs and calculating an acceptable target sales price for the product. Working backward from the sales price, companies establish an acceptable target profit and calculate the target cost as follows:

Target Cost = Target Price – Target Profit

Target costing is different from standard costing. While target costs are determined by market driven standards (target sales price – target profit = target cost), standard costs are determined by design – driven standards with less emphasis on what the market will pay (engineered costs + desired markup = desired sales price).

Since the early 1970s, target costing has been used by some companies, especially Japanese companies which aim to ascertain cost in a different manner. Target costing is a common practice where markets are extremely competitive. The market determines the price of products and there is a little opportunity for the individual organisations to set prices. Therefore, controlling cost is extremely important.

KAIZEN COSTING

Kaizen Costing, also referred as continuous improvement costing, is a mechanism for reducing and managing costs. Kaizen is the Japanese term for making continuous improvements in relatively small activities rather than major innovative improvement. The major difference between target and Kaizen costing is that target costing is applied during the design stage whereas Kaizen costing is applied during the manufacturing stage of the product life cycle.

The objective of Kaizen costing is to reduce actual costs to manufacture a product below the standard cost. Standard cost system generally aim to achieve the cost standards set by management while Kaizen costing systems are more concerned with reducing actual costs below standard costs. The potential cost reductions are smaller with Kaizen costing because the products are already in the manufacturing stage of their life cycles and a significant proportional of costs will have become locked-in.

Barfield, Raiborn and Kinney[5] have stated the following differences between target costing and Kaizen costing.

	Target Costing	*Kaizen Costing*
What?	A procedural approach to determining a maximum allowable cost for an identifiable, proposed product assuming a given target profit margin	A mandate to reduce costs, increase product quality, and/or improve production processes through continuous improvement efforts
Used for?	New products	Existing products
When?	Development stage (includes design)	Primary production stages (introduction and growth; possibly, but not probably, maturity)
How?	Works best through aiming at a specified cost reduction objective; used to get original production standards	Works best through aiming at a specified cost reduction objective; reductions are integrated into original production standards to sustain improvements and provide new challenges
Why?	Extremely large potential for cost reduction because 80% to 90% of a product's lifelong costs are embedded in the product during the design and development stages	Limited potential for reducing cost of existing products, but may provide useful information for future target costing efforts
Focus?	All product inputs (material, labour, and overhead elements) as well as production processes and supplier components	Depends on where efforts will be most effective in reducing production costs; generally begins with the most costly component and (in the more mature companies) ends with overhead components

LIFE-CYCLE COSTING

Life-cycle costs are all the costs associated with the product for its entire life cycle. They include development (planning, design and testing), production (conversion activities), and logistics support (advertising, distribution, warranty and so on). Identifying costs during the different phases of a product's life cycle helps to develop understanding of costs and subsequently in managing the costs incurred throughout its life cycle. Life-cycle costs provide important information for pricing.

ACTIVITY-BASED MANAGEMENT (ABM)

As stated earlier in this chapter, Activity-Based Costing (ABC) is concerned with ascertainment of costs. In ABC, resources are assigned to activities based upon consumption and activities are assigned to cost objects (products, jobs, services) based on consumption. ABC assumes and gives due importance to causal relationship of cost drivers to activities.

Activity-Based Management (ABM) emphasises on management of activities with the objectives of improving the value received by the customer and the profit achieved by business enterprise by

5. Jesset T. Barfield, Cecily A. Raiborn and Michael R. Kinney, *Cost Accounting, Traditions and Innovations,* 5th Ed; Thomson, 2003, p.721.

providing this value. It includes cost driver analysis, activity analysis and performance measurement and depends on ABC for its major source of data. Holst and Savage[6] observe:

> "ABC is used to answer the question 'What do things cost?' while ABM, employing a process view, is concerned with what factors cause costs to occur. Using ABC data, ABM focuses on how to redirect and improve the use of resources to increase the value created for customers and other stakeholders".

Through focusing on activity analysis, cost driver analysis and activity-based costing, ABM helps companies to produce more efficiently, determine costs more accurately and control and evaluate performance more effectively. ABM through activity analysis analyses activities, classifies them into value-added and non-value added activities and finally develops means and methods of minimising or eliminating non-value added activities.

EXAMPLE 8.1

A company manufactures two products, *A* and *B*, using common facilities. The following cost data for a month are presented to you:

	A	*B*
Units produced	1,000	2,000
Direct labour hours per unit	2	3
Machine hours per unit	6	1.5
Set-up of machines	15	50
Orders	18	70
Machine activity expenses		₹3,00,000
Set-up related expenses		₹30,000
Expenses relating to orders		₹35,000

Calculate the overheads per unit absorbed using activity-based costing approach.

Solution

Calculation of Rate per Cost Driver

Activity	*Activity Cost (₹)*	*Cost Driver*	*Rate per Cost Driver (₹)*
(i) Machine related	3,00,000	Machine hours (1,000 × 6 + 2,000 × 1.5)	3,00,000/9,000 = 33.3333
(ii) Set up related	30,000	No. of set ups (15 + 50)	30,000/65 = 461.538
(iii) Orders related	35,000	No. of orders (18 + 70)	35,000/88 = 397.73

6. Randolf Holst and Robert J., *Savage, Tools and Techniques for Implementing Activity-Based Management* in Steve Player et al (Eds.) Arthur Anderson's *Global Lesions on Activity-Based Management*, John Wiley and Sons, New York, 1999, p 4.

Product	*A*		*B*	
Output unit	1,000		2,000	
Activity	*Cost (₹)*	*Rate p.u. (₹)*	*Cost (₹)*	*Rate p.u. (₹)*
(i) Machine related	600 × 33.33 = 2,00,000	200.000	3,000 × 33.3333 = 1,00,000	50.000
(ii) Set up related	15 × 461.538 = 6923	6.923	50 × 461.538 = 23,076.90	11.538
(iii) Orders related	18 × 397.73 = 7,159	7.159	70 × 397.73 = 27,841.10	13.921
	2,14,082	214.082	1,50,918	75.458

EXAMPLE 8.2

ABC Manufacturing Co. has been using a cost system that allocates all factory overhead costs to products based on 350 per cent of direct labour cost. The company has just decided to use Activity-Based Cost (ABC) system that traces indirect costs to products based on consumption of major activities as indicated below.

Activity	*Annual Cost Driver Quantity*	*Cost (₹)*	*Product' Cost Driver Consumption*
Labour	₹3,00,000	30,000	₹10,000
Machining	20,000 hours	5,00,000	800 hours
Setup	10,000 hours	1,00,000	100 hours
Production order	2,000 orders	2,00,000	12 orders
Material handling	1,000 requisitions	20,000	5 requisitions
Parts administration	12,000 parts	4,80,000	18 parts

Required:

Compare the total annual costs of the product using both the traditional volume-based and new ABC system.

Solution

Cost system	*Pool Rate*	*Cost Driver Consumption*	*Cost Assignment (₹)*
Traditional cost system	*350%*	*₹10,000*	*₹35,000*
ABC System:			
(i) Labour	10%	₹10,000	₹1,000
(ii) Machining	₹25 per hour	800 hours	20,000
(iii) Set up	₹10 per hour	100 hours	1,000
(iv) Production order	₹100 per order	12 orders	1,200
(v) Material handling	₹20 per requisition	5 requisitions	100
(vi) Parts administration	₹40 per part	18 parts	720
			₹24,020

Conclusion: The total cost of product under ABC is ₹24,020 whereas under traditional cost system it is ₹35,000.

EXAMPLE 8.3

ABC manufacturing company has three accounts clerks responsible for processing purchase invoices. Each clerk is paid a salary of ₹3,00,000 p.a. and is capable of processing 5000 invoices per year (working efficiently). In addition to the salary, the company spends ₹90,000 per year for forms, postage etc. (assuming that 15,000 invoices are processed). During the year, 12,500 invoices were processed.

Required:

1. Calculate the activity rate for the purchase order activity. Break the activity into fixed and variable components.
2. Compute the total activity availability and break this into activity usage and unused activity.
3. Calculate the total cost of resources supplied and break this into activity usage and unused activity.

Solution

1. Activity rate	= [(3 × ₹3,00,000) + ₹90,000]/15,000
	= ₹66 per invoice
Fixed activity rate	= ₹9,00,000/15,000
	= ₹60 per invoice
Variable activity rate	= ₹90,000/15,000
	= ₹6 per invoice
2. Activity availability	= Activity usage + Unused activity
15,000 invoices	= 12,500 invoices + 2,500 invoices
3. Cost of resources supplied	= Cost of activity used + Cost of unused activity
₹9,00,000 + (₹6 × 12,500)	= (₹66 × 12,500) + (₹60 × 2500)
₹9,75,000	= ₹8,25,000 + 1,50,000

EXAMPLE 8.4

for excel template, scan

A company manufacturing two products furnishes the following data for a year:

Product	*Annual Output (Units)*	*Total Machine Hours*	*Total Number of Purchase Orders*	*Total Number of Set-ups*
A	5,000	20,000	160	20
B	60,000	1,20,000	384	44

The annual overheads are as under:

	₹
Volume related activity costs:	5,50,000
Set-up related costs	8,20,000
Purchase related costs	6,18,000

You are required to calculate the cost per unit of each product *A* and *B* based on:

(a) Traditional method of charging overheads.
(b) Activity-based costing method

Solution

(a) **Traditional method of charging overheads:**

		₹
Volume related activity costs		5,50,000
Set-up related costs		8,20,000
Purchase related costs		6,18,000
Total costs		₹19,88,000
Total machine hours (20,000 + 1,20,000)	=	1,40,000
Total cost per hour (₹19,88,000/1,40,000)	=	₹14.20
Cost per unit of A = (20,000 × ₹14.20)/5,000	=	₹56.80
Cost per unit of B = (1,20,000 × ₹14.20)/60,000	=	₹28.40

(b) **Activity-based costing method of charging overheads:**

Volume-related activity cost per machine hour: ₹5,50,000/1,40,000	=	₹3.9286
Set-up costs per set-up: ₹8,20,000/64	=	₹12,812.50
Purchase related costs per purchase order: ₹6,18,000/544	=	₹1136.029

Cost Per Unit of Product

Particulars	*Cost Driver*	*A*	*B*
Volume-related costs	Machine hours	₹78,572	₹4,71,432
Set-up costs	Number of set-ups	2,56,240	5,63,728
Purchase related costs	Number of purchase orders	1,81,765	4,36,235
	Total costs	₹5,16,577	₹14,71,395
Cost per unit		₹103.32	₹24.52

EXAMPLE 8.5

A company manufacturing two products L and M, furnishes the ahead data for the year —

Product	*Annual Output (Units)*	*Machine Hours (Per Unit)*	*Direct Labour Hours (Per Unit)*	*Total number of Orders Handled*	*Total Number of Setups*
L	5,000	3	1	15	10
M	7,000	1	2	60	40

Annual overhead costs:	₹
Relating to machine activity	2,20,000
Relating to production run set-ups	20,000
Relating to handling of orders	45,000
	2,85,000

Required

Calculate the production overhead to be absorbed by one unit of each of the products L and M using the following costing methods.

(i) A traditional costing approach using a direct labour hour rate to absorb overheads.

(ii) An activity-based costing approach, using suitable cost drivers to trace overheads to products.

Solution

(i) **Traditional Costing Method**

$$\text{Direct labour hour rate} = \frac{\text{Total cost}}{\text{Direct labour hours}}$$

$$= \frac{2,85,000}{5,000 \times 1 + 7,000 \times 2} = ₹15 \text{ per labour hour}$$

Cost Per Unit

	Labour Hours	*Rate Per Hour*	*Total Cost*	*Per Unit*
L	5,000 × 1	15	75,000	15 per unit
M	7,000 × 2	15	2,10,000	30 per unit
			2,85,000	

(ii)

$$\text{Cost per setup} = \frac{\text{Set ups cost}}{\text{Number of set ups}} = \frac{20,000}{50} = 400 \text{ per set up}$$

$$\text{Machine hour rate} = \frac{2,20,000}{5,000 \times 3 + 7,000 \times 1} = \frac{2,20,000}{15,000 + 7,000} = ₹10.$$

$$\text{Cost per order} = \frac{\text{Cost related to order}}{\text{Number of orders}} = \frac{45,000}{75} = ₹600 \text{ per order}$$

Activity-Based Costing

	Output	*Machine Hour Rate*	*Order Cost*	*Setups*	*Total*	*Cost Per Unit*
L	5,000	5,000 × 3 × 10 = 1,50,000	15 × 600 = 9,000	10 × 400 = 4,000	1,63,000	1,63,000 / 5,000 = 32.60
M	7,000	7,000 × 1 × 10 = 70,000	60 × 600 = 36,000	40 × 400 = 16,000	1,22,000	1,22,000 / 7,000 = 17.43
		2,20,000	45,000	20,000	2,85,000	

EXAMPLE 8.6

A company manufacturing two products furnishes the following data for a year:

Product	*Annual Output (Units)*	*Total Machine Hours*	*Total Number of Purchase Orders*	*Total Number of Set-ups*
A	5,000	20,000	160	20
B	60,000	1,20,000	384	44

The annual overheads are as under:	₹
Volume-related activity costs	5,50,000
Set-up-related costs	8,20,000
Purchase-related costs	6,18,000

You are required to calculate the cost per unit of each product *A* and *B* based on:

(i) Traditional method of costing using machine hour rate method; and
(ii) Activity-based costing method; and comment on the result.

☞ *Solution*

Traditional Method

(i) Machine hour rate $= \dfrac{\text{Total cost}}{\text{Total machine hours}}$

$$= \frac{5,50,000 + 8,20,000 + 6,18,000}{20,000 + 1,20,000}$$

$$= \frac{1,98,000}{14,000} = ₹14.20 \text{ per hr.}$$

Traditional Costing Statement

Product	*Output*	*Overhead*	*Machine Hours*	*Cost Allocated*	*Overhead Cost Per Unit*
A	5,000	14.20	20,000	20,000 × 14.2 = 2,84,000	28,400 ÷ 5,000 = 56.80
B	60,000	14.20	1,20,000	1,20,000 × 14.20 = 17,04,400	17,04,000 ÷ 60,000 = 28.40
				19,88,000	

(ii) Activity-based Costing

Calculating of Activity Cost-Rates

Type of Cost	*Amount (₹)*	*No. of Events*	*Cost Per Activity*
Volume	5,50,000	1,40,000 machine hour	3.9285 per hour
Set-up related	8,20,000	64 set-ups	12,812.50 per set-up
Purchase Related	6,18,000	160 + 384 = 544 Purchase orders	1,136.029 per purchase

Statement of Overhead per Unit under ABC

1	*2*	*3*	*4*	*5*	*6 = 3 + 4+ 5*	*7 = 6 ÷ 2*
Product	*Units*	*Volume Related Cost*	*Set-up Related Cost*	*Purchase Order Related Cost*	*Total Cost*	*Cost Per Unit*
A	5,000	20,000 × 3.93 = 78,600	12,812.50 × 20 = 2,56,250	1,136.03 × 160 = 1,81,764.80	5,16,614.80	103.22 (App.)
B	60,000	1,20,000 × 3.94 = 4,71,600	12,812.50 × 44 = 5,63,750	1,136.03 × 384 = 4,36,235.52	14,71,585.52	24.53 (App.)

Comparative Statement of Overhead Cost per Unit

Product	*Overhead Cost Per Unit Under Traditional Costing*	*Cost Per Unit Under Activity-based Costing*
A	56.80	103.32
B	28.40	24.53

Traditional costing results in under costing of the low-volume product and over costing of the high-volume product

Low-volume product A

A firm following traditional costing will keep selling price low (as cost is low) → this will lead to high sales and yet increasing losses in the books of account.

High-volume product B

There will be overcosting of high-volume product in case of a firm following traditional costing. So, a higher selling price will be fixed → leading to lower sales volume and hence piling investories.

The more accurate alternative is ABC.

✍ EXAMPLE 8.7

ABC Ltd. is following Activity-Based Costing. Budgeted overheads and cost driver volumes are as follows:

for excel template, scan

Cost Pool	*Budgeted/Overheads (₹)*	*Cost Driver*	*Budgeted Volume*
Material procurement	11.60 lakh	No. of orders	2,200
Material handling	5.00 lakh	No. of movement	1,360
Maintenance	19.40 lakh	Maintenance hours	16,800
Set-up	8.30 lakh	No. of set-ups	1,040
Quality Control	3.52 lakh	No. of inspection	1,800
Machinery	14.40 lakhs	No. of machine hours	48,000

The company has produced a batch of 5,200 components, its material cost was ₹2.60 lakhs and labour cost ₹4.90 lakh. Usage activities of the said batch are as follows:

Material orders – 52, Material movements – 36, Maintenance hours – 1,380, Set-ups – 50, Quality Control inspection – 56 and Machine hours – 3,600

Calculate:

(i) Cost driver rates that are used for tracing appropriate amount of overheads to the said batch.
(ii) The cost of batch of component.

☞ *Solution*

(i) Cost driver rates are calculated as under:

Material procurement	₹	11,60,000 ÷ 2,200	= ₹527
Material handling	₹	5,00,000 ÷ 1,360	= ₹368
Set-up	₹	8,30,000 ÷ 1,040	= ₹798
Maintenance	₹	19,40,000 ÷ 16,800	= ₹115
Quality control	₹	3,52,000 ÷ 18,00	= ₹195
Machinery	₹	14,40,000 ÷ 48,000	= ₹ 30

(ii) Calculation of price cost of a batch of 5,200 components

Direct material =	₹2,60,000
Direct labour =	₹4,90,000
	₹7,50,000

(iii) Overhead are charged to the batch as below:

			₹
Material procurement	52 × 527	=	27,404
Material handling	36 × 368	=	13,248
Set-up	50 × 798	=	39,900
Maintenance	1,380 × 115	=	1,58,700
Quality control	56 × 195	=	10,920
Machines	3,600 × 30	=	1,08,000
Total overhead absorbed		=	3,58,172

Total cost of production of the batch of 5,200 components:

	₹
Prime cost	7,50,000
Overhead as per activity based costing	.3,58,172
	11,08,172

Example 8.8

The Caesar Company manufactures picnic tables. The company's southeastern plant has changed from a labour-intensive operation to a robotics environment. As a result, management is considering changing from a direct-labour-based overhead rate to an activity-based cost method. The controller has chosen the following activity cost pools and cost drivers for the factory overhead:

	Expected		
	Overhead Cost	*Cost Driver*	*Annual Cost Driver*
Purchase orders	₹200,000	Number of orders	10,000 orders
Set-up costs	₹ 25,000	Number of set-ups	5,000 set-ups
Testing costs	₹ 48,000	Number of tests	6,000 tests
Machine maintenance	₹2,50,000	Machine hours	10,000 hours

Required:

(a) Compute the overhead rate for each cost driver.

(b) An order for 10 large picnic tables had the following requirements:

Number of purchase orders	6
Number of set-ups	25
Number of product tests	8
Machine hours	150

How much overhead would be assigned to this order?

(c) What could management do to reduce the overhead costs assigned to these tables? What would be the impact on company net income of reducing overhead assigned to the tables?

Solution

(a) Purchasing orders:
₹2,00,000/10,000 = ₹20 per order
Set-up costs:
₹25,000/5,000 = ₹5 per set-up
Product testing:
₹48,000/6,000 = ₹8 per product test
Machine costs:
₹2,50,000/10,000 = ₹25 per machine hour

(b)

Purchasing costs (6 orders × ₹20 per order)	₹120
Set-up costs (25 set-ups × ₹5 per set-up)	125
Product testing (8 tests × ₹8 per test)	64
Machine costs (150 hours × 25 per machine hr)	₹3,750
Total overhead assigned using ABC	₹4,059

(c) Since machine costs are the most significant components of the overhead costs, management could design the product to reduce the number of machine hours assigned to this product. Alternatively, management could reduce the costs associated with the machine. It would have no effect on the total net income; the cost reduction on one product will be shifted to another product or to period costs.

EXAMPLE 8.9

FOAMSTAR LTD. makes three main products using broadly the same production method and equipment for each. A conventional product costing system is used at present although an ABC, system is being considered. Details of the three products for a typical period are:

	Hours Per Unit		*Material Per Unit*	*Volume Units*
	Labour Hours	*Machine Hours*	₹	
Product *P*	0.50	1.50	20	750
Product *Q*	1.50	1.00	12	1,250
Product *R*	1.00	3.00	25	7,000

Direct labour costs ₹6 per hour and production overheads are absorbed on a machine hour basis. The rate for the period is ₹28 per machine hour.

Further analysis shows that the total of production overheads can be divided as follows:

	%
Cost relating to set-ups	35
Cost relating to machinery	20
Cost relating to materials handling	15
Cost relating to inspection	30
Total production overhead	100

The following activity volumes are associated with the product line for the period as a whole. Total activities for the period:

	Number of Set-ups	Number of Movements of Materials	Number of Inspection
Product *P*	75	12	150
Product *Q*	115	21	180
Product *R*	480	87	670
	670	120	1,000

Required:

(i) Calculate the cost per unit for each product using conventional methods.
(ii) Calculate the cost per unit for each product using ABC principles.
(iii) Comment on the reasons for any differences in the costs in your answers to (i) and (ii):

☞ ***Solution***

FOAMSTAR LTD.

(i) Statement showing product cost per unit (conventional method):

	Product *P*	Product *Q*	Product *R*
Direct labour @ ₹6	3.00	9.00	6.00
Material	20.00	12.00	25.00
Production overhead @ ₹28	42.00	28.00	84.00
(Machine hours – 1.5, 1, 3)	65.00	49.00	115.00

(ii) ABC Principles – Total production overhead based on machine hours weightage
(750 × 1.50 + 1,250 × 1 + 7,000 × 3) ₹28 = ₹6,54,500

		₹
Set-up costs	35%	2,29,075
Machining	20%	1,30,900
Material handling	15%	98,175
Inspection	30%	1,96,350
		6,54,500

	Total ₹	*Product P* ₹	*Product Q* ₹	*Product R* ₹
Set-ups (75 : 115 : 480)	2,29,075	25,643	39,319	1,64,113
Machining (1,125 : 1250 : 21,000)	1,30,900	6,300	7,000	1,17,600
Materials handling (12 : 21 : 87)	98,175	9,817	17,181	71,177
Inspection (150 : 180 : 670)	1,96,350	29,452	35,343	1,31,555
	6,54,500	71,212	98,843	4,84,445
Number of units		750	1250	7000
Production overhead per unit (rounded)		95	79	69

Product Cost per Unit—ABC Principles

	Product P	*Product Q*	*Product R*
	₹	₹	₹
Direct labour	3.00	9.00	6.00
Materials	20.00	12.00	25.00
Production overhead	95.00	79.00	69.00
	118.00	100.00	100.00

(iii) Reasons for difference:

- Set-up cost has been distributed based on number of set-ups, it is more logical than conventional approach.
- Material handling cost is logically distributed based on number of movements of materials.
- Inspection cost is also based on inspection activity.

Hence, Product *P* and Product *Q* have received proportionally more production overhead under ABC principle than conventional product costing methods.

WORKING NOTES:

Costs of machining have been split in proportion to the total machine hours per product.

Product – *P*	750 × 1.50	=	₹ 1,125
Product – *Q*	1250 × 1.00	=	₹ 1,250
Product – *R*	7000 × 3.00	=	₹21,000
			₹23,375

EXAMPLE 8.10

Hinj Ltd manufactures and sells four products: arms, brackets, clips and D-rings. This year, for the first time, it is operating an activity-based costing system in parallel with its long-standing absorption costing system (which absorbs overheads on a machine hour basis).

The planned production activity cost pools and cost driver activity levels for all the output for the year are as follows:

Activity	**Cost Pool (₹)**	**Activity Level**
Purchasing materials	41,500	1,000 purchase orders
Storing materials	41,600	650 issue notes
Setting up machinery	26,400	200 set-ups
Running machinery	73,000	7,300 machine hours
Total production overheads	1,82,500	

An analysis of actual annual production output for two of the products is as follows:

	Arms	Brackets
Units produced	1,000	500
Purchase orders	190	325
Stores issue notes	105	200
Set-ups	35	60
Machine hours	2,600	1,275
Direct materials	₹8,250	₹3,750
Direct labour	₹46,000	₹7,600

Required:

1. Calculate the production cost per unit for arms and brackets using the machine hour overhead absorption rate.
2. Calculate the production cost per unit for arms and brackets using the activity-based costing system.
3. Comment on your findings.

☞ ***Solution***

1. Absorption costing

$$\text{OAR} = \frac{\text{Total overheads}}{\text{Total machine hours}} = \frac{1,82,500}{7,300} = ₹25\,\text{mh}$$

		Arms		Brackets
Direct materials		8,250		3,750
Direct labour		46,000		7,600
Overheads	(2,600 @ ₹25)	65,000	(1,275 @ ₹25)	31,875
		₹1,19,250		₹43,225
Per unit	**[1,000]**	**₹119.25**	**[500]**	**₹86.45**

2 Activity-based costing

	Cost Pool (₹)	Activity Level	Cost Driver Rate
Purchasing	41,500	1,000 purch. orders	₹41.50/order
Stores	41,600	650 issue notes	₹64.00/issue
Set-ups	26,400	200 set-ups	₹132.00/set-up
Machine running costs	73,000	7,300 machine hours	₹10.00/mh

		Arms		Brackets
Direct materials		8,250		3,750
Direct labour		46,000		7,600
Purchasing	(190 × ₹41.5)	7,885	(325 × ₹41.5)	13,487.5
Stores	(105 × ₹64)	6,720	(200 × ₹64)	12,800
Set-ups	(35 × ₹132)	4,620	(60 × ₹132)	7,920
Machining	(2,600 × ₹10)	26,000	(1,275 × ₹10)	12,750
		₹99,475		₹58,307.5
Per unit	**[1000]**	**₹99.47**	**[500]**	**₹116.61**

3 *Comment*: The above shows that, under absorption costing, "Arms" have been overcosted and "Brackets" undercosted. One possible effect of this cross-subsidy is that "Arms" have been overpriced and "Brackets" underpriced. This, in turn, will affect their sales volumes in the market place.

EXAMPLE 8.11

Wilcock & Co. is a firm of solicitors which currently operates an absorption costing system but is experimenting with an activity-based costing system. The current annual budget shows the following:

	₹000	₹000
Sales revenue		2,422
Direct labour	1,384	
Overhead costs	346	
		1,730
Operating profit		692

Wilcock & Co. absorbs overheads as a percentage of the total cost of direct labour and its standard profit margin is 40% of total cost.

As part of the investigation into ABC, the solicitors wish to compare the two systems on a recently completed fraud case. The cost of solicitors' time used directly on this case is ₹15,000.

Their experimental ABC system is based on the following annual analysis:

Activity	*Cost Driver*	*Annual Cost Pool* (₹)	*Annual Use of Cost Drivers*
Clerical support	Clerical hours	1,56,000	26,000 hours
General administration	Administration hours	60,000	3,000 hours
Photocopying	Number of photocopies	25,000	5,00,000 copies
Telephone	Telephone calls	1,05,000	70,000 calls
	Total	3,46,000	

The fraud case caused the following activities to happen:

Activity	*Cost Driver*	*Use of Cost Drivers*
Clerical support	Clerical hours	500 hours
General administration	Administration hours	70 hours
Photocopying	Number of photocopies	1,500 copies
Telephone	Telephone calls	400 calls

Required:

For the fraud case:

1. Calculate the absorption cost and selling price.
2. Calculate the activity-based cost and selling price.
3. Compare your findings and comment on them.

☞ Solution

1. Overhead absorption rate = $\frac{3,46,000}{13,84,000}$ = 25% of direct labour cost

Absorption costing of fraud cause:	₹
Direct labour	15,000
Overheads (₹15,000 × 25%)	3,750
Absorption cost	**18,750**
Profit margin (40% × ₹18,750)	7,500
Price charged to customer	**26,250**

2. Activity-based costing of fraud case:

Activity	*Cost Driver*	*Annual Cost Pool (₹)*	*Annual Use of Cost Drivers*	*Cost Driver Rates*
Clerical support	Clerical hours	1,56,000	26,000 hours	₹6.00/clerical hour
General administration	Admin. hours	60,000	3,000 hours	₹20.00/admin hours
Photocopying	Number of copies	25,000	5,00,000 copies	₹0.05/copy
Telephone	Telephone calls	1,05,000	70,000 calls	₹1.50/call
		3,46,000		

Activity	*Cost Driver*	*Contract's Use of Cost Drivers*	*Cost Driver Rates*	*Overhead Attached (₹)*
Clerical support	Clerical hours	500 hours	₹6.00/clerical hour	3,000
General administration	Admin. hours	70 hours	₹20.00/admin hour	1,400
Photocopying	Number of copies	1,500 copies	₹0.05/copy	75
Telephone	Telephone calls	400 calls	₹1.50/call	600
			Total overhead	5,075
			Direct cost	15,000
			AB cost	**20,075**
			Profit (@ 40%)	8,030
			Selling price	**28,105**

3. **Comparison:**

	Cost	**Selling Price**
Absorption cost	18,750	26,250
Activity-based cost	20,075	28,105
Difference	(1,325)	(1,855)

The current absorption costing system is undercosting this case by ₹1,325, which results in a shortfall in sales revenue of ₹1,855. This case is being subsidised by other cases, which will be overcosted and overpriced.

Theory Questions

1. What is Activity-Based Costing? Why is it needed?
2. What is a cost driver? What is the role of cost driver in tracing costs to products?
3. Explain the steps in applying Activity-Based Costing (ABC) in a manufacturing company.
4. How are activities grouped in a manufacturing company?
5. Distinguish between activity-based costing and traditional costing system.
6. What are the benefits of Activity-Based Costing?
7. Define unit level activities, batch level activities, product level activities and facility level activities.
8. "Overhead costs are source of product cost distortion." Do you agree? Explain.
9. Explain the concept of Activity-Based Costing and Cost Drivers.
10. Explain briefly each of the following categories in Activity-Based Costing (ABC) by giving at least two examples:
    (i) Unit-level activities (ii) Batch-level activities
    (iii) Product-level activities (iv) Facility-level activities
11. Discuss the different stages in Activity-Based Costing.
12. Distinguish between target costing and Kaizen costing.
13. What is life cycle costing?
14. Write short notes on:
    (i) Target costing (ii) Kaizen costing
15. Define Activity-Based Management (ABM). What is its importance?
16. Distinguish between Activity-Based Costing (ABC) and Activity-Based Management (ABM).
17. Write a short note on "Acting-Based Costing".
18. Explain the following terms in relation to Activity-Based Costing:
    (a) Cost object (b) Cost primer (c) Cost pool

Self-Evaluation Questions

Mr. Ashok Kumar owns a large department store in Delhi. For 10 years, the accountant has applied overheads to the various departments—produce, meat, dairy, canned foods, bakery and floral—based on the basis of employee hours worked. Mr. Ashok Kumar's son who is a commerce student in University of Delhi has suggested his father should consider Activity-Based Costing (ABC): In an attempt to implement ABC, Mr. Ashok Kumar and his son have identified the following activities. They need your help in determining a cost driver for each of the activities.

Cost pool

(a) Placing orders
(b) Checking out customers
(c) Bagging groceries
(d) Delivering groceries
(e) Stocking shelves
(f) Janitorial and Maintenance

(g) Training employees
(h) Administrative
(i) Advertising and Marketing
(j) Accounting and legal service.

Ans: Cost drivers are

(a) Number of orders
(b) Number of customers, sales volume.
(c) Number of customers, sales volume
(d) Number of delivery orders
(e) Hours worked stocking
(f) Square feet occupied
(g) Total number of employees, number of new employees
(h) Sales volume
(i) Number of advertisement campaigns
(j) Sales volume.

Problems

1. ABC Company produces two types of stereo units. Activity data follows:

Activity Usage Measures	*Product-Costing Data*		
	Deluxe	*Regular*	*Total*
Units produced per year	5,000	50,000	55,000
Prime costs (₹)	39,000	3,69,000	4,08,000
Direct labour hours	5,000	45,000	50,000
Machine hours	10,000	90,000	100,000
Production runs	10	5	15
Number of moves	120	60	180

Activity Cost Data (Overhead Activities)

Activity	*Activity Cost (₹)*
Setting up equipment	60,000
Material handling	30,000
Using power	50,000
Testing	40,000
Total	180,000

Required:

(i) Calculate the consumption ratios for each activity.
(ii) Group activities based on the consumption ratios and activity level.
(iii) Calculate a rate for each pooled group of activities.
(iv) Using the pool rates, calculate unit product costs.

Ans: (i) *Consumption Ratios*

	Deluxe	*Regular*
Set-ups	0.67	0.33
Material handling	0.67	0.33
Power	0.10	0.90
Testing	0.10	0.90

(ii) Batch level: set-ups and material handling
Unit level: Power and testing

(iii) Batch level pool ₹6,000 per run
Unit level ₹0.90 per machine hour

(iv) Unit costs: ABC
Deluxe ₹21.60
Regular ₹9.60

2. ABC Company has been incurring two types of overhead costs-material handling and quality inspection. The costs expected for these categories for the coming year are as follows:

Material handling	₹10,00,000
Quality inspection	₹30,00,000

The company currently charges overhead using direct labour hours and expected actual capacity. This figure is 50,000 direct labour hours.

The factory manager has been asked to submit a bid and has assembled the following data concerning proposed job.

	Job
Direct materials	₹37,000
Direct labour (1,000 hours)	₹70,000
Number of material moves	10
Number of inspections	5

The manager has been informed that many competitors use an ABC approach to assign overhead to jobs. Before submitting his bid for the proposed job, he wants to assess the effects of this alternative approach. He estimates that the expected number of material moves for all jobs during the year is 1,000. He also expects 5,000 quality inspections to be performed.

Required:

(a) Compute the total cost of the proposed job using direct labour hours to assign overhead. Assume the bid price is full manufacturing cost plus 25%, what would be the manager's bid?

(b) Compute the total cost of the job using the number of material moves to allocate material-handling costs and the number of inspections to allocate the quality inspections costs. Assume bid price is full manufacturing costs plus 25%. What should be his bid using this approach?

(c) Which approach do you think best reflects the actual cost of the job? Explain.

Ans: (a) Bid price ₹2,33,750
(b) Bid price ₹1,50,000
(c) ABC best reflects the actual cost of the proposed job.

3. S. Chand and Co., a leading publisher, publishes two versions of a text book. One is paperback and the other is hard bound. Management is considering publishing only the higher-quality book. The firm assigns its ₹5,00,000 of overhead to the two types of books. The overhead is composed of ₹2,00,000 of utilities and ₹3,00,000 of quality control inspectors' salaries. Some additional data follow:

	Paperback	Hard Bound
Revenues	₹16,00,000	₹14,00,000
Direct costs	₹12,50,000	₹6,00,000
Production (units)	5,00,000	3,50,000
Machine hours	42,500	7,500
Inspections	2,500	12,500

Required:

(a) Compute the overhead cost that should be allocated to each type of text book using cost drivers appropriate for each type of overhead cost.

(b) The firm has used machine hours to allocate overhead in the past. Should the publisher stop producing the paperback books? Explain why management was considering this action and what its decision should be.

Ans: (a) Paperback ₹2,20,000; Hard bound ₹2,80,000
(b) The publisher should not stop producing the paperback books

4. Statusline and Company is a manufacturer of a range of white goods. Cost structure of its different products is as follows:

Standard Cost of the Products

Particulars	*Product P*	*Product Q*	*Product R*
Direct materials	25.00	20.00	20.00
Direct labour @ ₹5 per hour	15.00	20.00	25.00
Production overheads	15.00	20.00	25.00
	55.00	60.00	70.00
Quantity produced (units)	10,000	20,000	30,000

Production overhead is absorbed on the basis of Direct Labour Hours. Statusline and Company wishes to introduce Activity-Based Costing (ABC) system and has identified four major cost pools for production overhead and their associated cost drivers. Information on these activity cost pools and their drivers is given below:

Activity Cost Pool	*Cost Driver*	*Cost Associated with Activity Cost Pool (₹)*
Stores receiving	Purchase requisition	1,48,000
Inspection/Quality control	Number of production runs	4,47,000
Material handling and dispatch	Orders executed	1,05,000
Production scheduling/Machine set-ups	Number of set-ups	6,00,000

Further relevant information on the three products is also given below:

Particulars	*Product P*	*Product Q*	*Product R*
No. of purchase requisitions	300	450	500
No. of production runs	750	1,050	1,200
No. of orders executed	180	270	300
No. of set-ups	360	390	450

Required:

(i) Calculate the activity-based production cost of all the three products.
(ii) Comment on the differences between the original traditionally calculated Costs and Activity-Based Costs (ABC) you calculated.

Ans:

	Products		
	P	*Q*	*R*
(i) Total production costs (ABC)	₹75.25	62.12	61.83

(ii) Product *R* is significantly overcosted in traditional system than in ABC while *P* is greatly under-costed. Product *R* is a high-volume product with a high direct labour content, while *P* is a low-volume product with a low direct labour content.

5. Motorola Corporation manufactures cell phones and pagers in a particular factory. Assume that overhead costs are currently allocated using direct labour hours, but the controller has recommended an activity-based costing system using the following data:

Activity	*Cost Driver*	*Activity Level*		
		Cost	*Cell Phones*	*Pagers*
Production set-up	Number of set-ups	₹1,00,000	12	8
Material handling and requisition	Number of parts	20,000	70	30
Packaging and despatching	Number of units despatched	1,60,000	1,20,000	40,000
Total overhead		₹2,80,000		

(a) Compute the amount of overhead allocated to each of the products under activity-based costing.
(b) Compute the amount of overhead to be allocated to each product using labour hours as the allocation base. Assume 60,000 labour hours were used to assemble cell phones and 20,000 labour hours were used to assemble pagers.
(c) Should the company adopt an ABC system?

Ans: (a) Cell phones ₹1,94,000; Pagers ₹86,000
(b) Cell phones ₹2,10,000; Pagers ₹70,000
(c) The company should adopt ABC system.

CASE STUDY

Case of ABC Costing at Edgewood Corporation

Edgewood Corporation manufactured office furniture—a fire-resistant commercial office almirah—that it sold to various distributers in Karnataka and bordering states at ₹6,000 per unit. The cost of direct material and direct labour were ₹1,800 and ₹500 respectively. Edgewood had two overhead departments—D1 for taking care of manufacturing and D2 for pertaining to administration and selling. The total overhead costs for the year 2018 had been ₹60,00,000 for 1,000 almirahs produced and sold. This cost included the costs related to both the departments as listed below:

D1—Manufacturing overhead	₹40,00,000
D2—Selling and administrative overhead	₹20,00,000

The company had a simple activity-based costing system in place that it used for internal decision-making like determining price or deciding quantity to be produced in a particular financial year. The company's activity based costing system had the following activity cost pools and activity measures:

Sr. No.	*Activity Cost Pool*	*Activity Measures*
1	Assembling and fitting units	Number of units assembled
2	Processing orders for material	Number of orders made
3	Customers support	Number of customers catered to
4	Others*	Not applicable

Note: * Costs assigned to the "others" activity cost pool had no activity measure; they consisted of the costs of unused capacity and organisation-sustaining costs—neither of which was assigned to products, orders or customers.

Edgewood Corporation followed the system of distributing the costs of manufacturing overhead and of selling and administrative overhead to the activity cost pools based on supervisor's record of number of labour hours in each department, the results of which were reported below:

Distribution of Overheads Across Activity Cost Pools

	Assembling & Fitting	*Processing Orders*	*Customers Support*	*Other*	*Total*
Manufacturing overhead	50%	35%	5%	10%	100%
Selling and administrative overhead	10%	45%	25%	20%	100%
Total activity	1,000 units	250 orders	100 customers	–	–

One of the distributors, "Smart Homes" had placed an order of total 125 office almirahs put together at four different times in the year 2018. However, before this could be recorded and billed, the cost accountant of Edgewood Corporation has resigned and left the organisation. The distributer had already sent two reminders to send the invoice as March 2019 was just a week away. The owner Soham Tyagi had asked the accountant to prepare the cost summary and then the invoice for this transaction. The summary submitted by the accountant was as follows:

Cost Summary

Particulars	*Amount (₹)*
Sales (₹6000 × 125 units)	7,50,000
Less: Costs	
Direct materials (₹1800 per unit × 125 units)	2,25,000
Direct labour (₹500 per unit × 125 units)	62,500
Overheads (₹60,00,000 × 125/1000)	7,50,000
Profit/Loss	(2,87,500)

Soham Tyagi was worried after this summary. He wondered if the price quoted was less. However, in all these previous years, he had been getting a satisfactory profit at the given sales price. So, what had changed?

QUESTIONS FOR DISCUSSION:

1. Is the cost summary prepared by the accountant correct as per ABC?
2. Perform the first-stage allocation of overhead costs to the activity cost pools.
3. Compute activity rates for the activity cost pools.
4. Construct a table showing the overhead costs of the 125 units through four orders made by Smart Home distributer.

PART 3

Costing Methods and Accounting of Costs

Different industries need to follow a method of product costing for determining unit cost and total cost. Part 3 is devoted to discussion of product costing methods—Job Costing and Process Costing and their variants. Cost accounting system and its reconciliation with financial accounting has also been covered in this part.

- *Single or Output Costing*
- *Job, Contract and Batch Costing*
- *Process Costing*
- *Service Costing*
- *Cost Control Accounts*
- *Integrated Accounting System*
- *Reconciliation of Cost and Financial Accounts*

Chapter 9

Single or Output Costing

Learning Objectives

After reading this chapter, you should be able to:

1. explain nature of single or output costing;
2. describe nature of production statement;
3. understand operation costing; and
4. explain the nature of estimated cost sheet.

NATURE

The term "single or output costing" is applied where a single product or only a few grades of similar articles are manufactured, for example, paper, cement, brick, coal, wine, etc. The total cost per unit is obtained by dividing the total cost of production by the number of units manufactured. The total cost of the product is determined in a cost sheet format (as discussed in Chapter 2). Since only one product is usually produced involving a single process, all costs are directly charged to that product. There is no problem of apportionment as to the products. Where several grades of the product are manufactured, it may be necessary to apportion the overhead costs relating to more than one variety of the product.

PRODUCTION STATEMENT

The production or output statement shows sales, stocks and profit besides the cost in a statement format. The difference between a cost sheet and production statement is that a cost sheet merely records the costs incurred during the period, whereas a production statement records sales, stocks and profit in addition to the costs incurred. Figure 9.1 gives the specimen of a production account.

OPERATION COSTING

Operation costing is a costing method which determines the unit product cost by each operation constituting the production process. It is different from process costing in the sense that each operation is considered as separate cost centre and unit product cost is determined for each operation and not for each process as in process costing. All costs of direct material, direct labour, direct expenses are collected for each operation through direct measurement, and overhead is apportioned equitably among different operations.

Operation costing is generally used in those industries where repetitive manufacturing is done, that is, where production includes large production runs or batches of common processes and/or materials.

Production Account **Output ______**

Particulars	*Amount* ₹	*P*	*Particulars*	*Amount* ₹	*P*
To direct material			By prime cost c/d		
To direct labour					
To direct expenses					
To prime cost b/d			By factory cost c/d		
To factory overheads					
To factory cost b/d			By cost of production c/d		
To office and administrative overheads					
To opening stock of finished goods			By closing stock of finished goods		
To cost of production b/d			By cost of goods sold c/d		
To cost of goods sold b/d			By sales		
To selling and distribution exp.					
To profit					

Fig. 9.1 Specimen of a Production Account

ESTIMATED COST SHEET

An estimated cost sheet is prepared before the production is commenced. These estimated costs are subsequently compared with actual costs so that costs can be controlled and be kept within prescribed limits. Besides, the estimated costs can be used by management for fixing selling prices and taking decisions regarding profit planning, production, administration and marketing. Estimation of costs is done on the basis of current situations and future circumstances are likely to have impact on different elements of costs. Estimated costs are always needed for submitting tenders or quotations for a specific order. The price to be quoted in a tender includes a reasonable percentage of profit. Care should be exercised while quoting price of a tender because the tender quoting the lowest price is accepted by the customer.

The treatment of stock of raw material, work-in-progress and finished goods is the same as explained in Chapter 2 while discussing preparation of Cost Sheet (Statement).

EXAMPLE 9.1

A company presently sells an equipment for ₹35,000. Increase in prices of labour and material cost is anticipated to the extent of 15% and 10% respectively in the coming year. Material cost represents 40% of cost of sales and labour cost 30% of cost of sales. The remaining relate to overheads. If the existing selling price is retained, despite the increase in labour and material prices, the company would face a 20% decrease in the existing amount of profit on the equipment.

You are required to arrive at a selling price so as to give the same percentage of profit on increased cost of sales, as before. Prepare a statement of profit/loss per unit, showing the new selling price and cost per unit in support of your answer.

Solution

Selling price = ₹35,000

Let us assume present total cost of sales as x.

Particulars	*Present Condition*	*Anticipated Condition*
Direct material	$0.4x$	$0.46x$
Labour	$0.3x$	$0.33x$
Overhead	$0.3x$	$0.30x$
	x	$1.09x$
Profit	₹35,000 – x	₹35,000 – $1.09x$

From the above, the following equation can be made:

$$(35{,}000 - x) - (35{,}000 - 1.09x) = 20\% \text{ of } (35{,}000 - x)$$

or $$-x + 1.09x = 7{,}000 - .2x$$

or $$.29x = 7{,}000$$

or $$x = ₹24{,}137$$

Hence, the present total cost of sales is ₹24,137.

Statement of Profit (Loss)

Particulars		*Present* ₹	*Anticipated* ₹
Material:			
Present	24,137 × .4	9,654.80	
Anticipated	24,137 × .46		11,103.02
Labour:			
Present	24,137 × .3	7,241.1	
Anticipated	24,137 × .33		7,965.21
Overheads	24,137 × .3	7,241.1	7,241.10
Total cost of sales		24,137.00	26,309.33
Profit (45% of cost of sales)		10,863.00	11,839.20
Selling price		35,000.00	38,148.53

For the present condition, total cost is ₹24,137, and sales (as given) are ₹35,000. Therefore, profit (balancing figure) would be ₹10,863 (₹35,000 – 24,137). This profit of ₹10,863 amounts to 45% of cost of sales. Applying 45% for the anticipated condition, the profit comes to ₹11,839.20.

Hence, new selling price of the equipment should be (say) ₹38,150.

EXAMPLE 9.2

The following balances have been obtained from the books of Rivatex Limited for the year ending December 31, 2020.

	₹('000)
Stock on 1st January, 2020:	
Manufactured goods	974
Raw materials	300
Depreciation of plant	1,300
Discount allowed	374
Printing and stationery	93
Purchases:	
Manufactured goods	1,274
Raw materials	8,726
Repairs to plant	250
Office rent and rates	650
Coal	579
Carriage inwards	391
Office salaries	940
Carriage outwards	233
General expenses	317
Factory rent and rates	2,271
Manufacturing wages and salaries	11,029
Travelling expenses	279
Sales	29,942

(Contd.)

Stocks on 31st December, 2020

Manufactured goods	2,794
Raw materials	200

Goods manufactured are to be debited to the sales department at current market prices, namely ₹2,71,50,000.

You are required to prepare accounts in such a form as to disclose: (i) Cost of raw materials consumed, (ii) Prime cost, (iii) Factory cost, (iv) Gross profit on manufacture, (v) Cost of manufactured goods, (vi) Gross profit on sales, and (vii) Net profit that may be considered rational from the accounting point of view.

☞ ***Solution***

Production Account

		(₹ '000)		(₹ '000)
To opening stock of raw materials		300	By closing stock of raw materials	200
To purchases of raw materials		8,726	By cost of raw materials consumed	9,217
To carriage inwards		391		
		9,417		9,417
To cost of raw materials consumed		9,217	By prime cost c/d	20,246
To manufacturing wages and salaries		11,029		
		20,246		20,246
To prime cost b/d		20,246	By factory cost c/d	24,646
To factory overheads:				
Depreciation on plant		1,300		
Repairs to plant		250		
Coal		579		
Factory rent and rates		2,271		
		24,646		24,646
To factory cost b/d		24,646	By sales value	27,150
To office overheads:				
Printing and stationery	93			
Office rent and rates	650			
Office salaries	940			
General expenses	317	2,020		
Cost of production		26,646		
To gross profit on manufacture		504		
		27,150		27,150

(Contd.)

	(₹ '000)		(₹ '000)
To opening stock of goods manufactured	974	By closing stock of mfd. goods	2,794
To goods transferred from mfg. deptt.	27,150	By cost of goods mfd.	25,330
	28,124		28,124
To cost of goods mfd.	25,330	By sales	29,942
To purchase of manufactured goods	1,274		
To gross profit	3,338		
	29,942		29,942
To selling and distribution:		By gross profit	3,338
Travelling expenses 279			
Discount allowed 374			
Carriage outward 233			
	886		
To net profit	2,452		
	3,338		3,338

General Profit and Loss Account

	(₹'000)		(₹'000)
To stock reserve (for unrealised profit on increase in stock of ₹1,820)	34	By gross profit on manufacture	504
		By net profit	2,452
To net profit	2,922		
	2,956		2,956

Notes:

1. It has been presumed that:
   (i) Stock of manufactured goods consists of only those goods which have been manufactured in the factory and they are at current market price.
   (ii) Office overheads have been incurred only in respect of goods manufactured in the factory.
   (iii) Selling overheads have been incurred for sale of both the types of goods, that is, those manufactured in the factory as well as those purchased from outside.
2. Stock reserve has been calculated as follows:

$$\frac{504}{27,150} \times 1,820 = 33.78 \text{ or ₹}34.$$

EXAMPLE 9.3

For excel template, scan

A factory can produce 60,000 units per annum at its optimum (100%) capacity.

The estimated costs of production are as follows:

Direct material	₹3 per unit
Direct labour	₹2 per unit
Indirect expenses:	
Fixed	₹1,50,000 per annum
Variable	₹5 per unit
Semi-variable	₹50,000 per annum up to 50% capacity and an extra expense of ₹10,000 for every 25% increase in capacity or part thereof.

The factory produces only against orders (and not for own stock).

If the production programme of the factory is as indicated below and the management desires to ensure a profit of ₹1,00,000 for the year, work out the average selling price at which each unit should be quoted:

First 3 months of the year: 50% of capacity; remaining 9 months 80% of capacity.

Ignore selling, distribution and administration overheads.

Solution

Statement of Cost

	First 3 Months *7,500 Units*	*Remaining 9 Months* *36,000 Units*	*Total* *43,500 Units*
Direct material @ ₹3 per unit	₹22,500	₹1,08,000	₹1,30,500
Direct labour @ ₹2 per unit	₹15,000	₹72,000	₹87,000
Prime cost	37,500	1,80,000	2,17,500
Add: Indirect expenses:			
Fixed (1:3)	37,500	1,12,500	1,50,000
Variable @ ₹5 per unit	37,500	1,80,000	2,17,500
Semi-variable			
for first 3 months @			
₹50,000 per annum	12,500		
For remaining 9 months			
@ ₹70,000 per annum		52,500	65,000
Total cost	1,25,000	5,25,000	6,50,000
Profit	—	—	1,00,000
Sales	—	—	7,50,000

EXAMPLE 9.4

With Foot Cold Limited manufactured and sold 1,000 refrigerators in the year ending 31st March, 2020. The summarised Trading, Profit and Loss Account is set out below:

Particulars	₹	*Particulars*	₹
To costs of materials	80,000	By sales	4,00,000
To direct wages	1,20,000		
To manufacturing expenses	50,000		
To gross profit c/d	1,50,000		
	4,00,000		4,00,000
To management and staff salaries	60,000	By gross profit b/d	1,50,000
To rent, rates, insurance	10,000		
To selling expenses	30,000		
To general expenses	20,000		
To net profit	30,000		
	1,50,000		1,50,000

For the year ending 31st March, 2021 it is estimated that:

(1) Output and sale will be 1,200 refrigerators.
(2) Prices of raw materials will rise by 20% on the previous year's level.
(3) Wages rates will rise by 5%.
(4) Manufacturing cost will rise in proportion to the combined cost of materials and wages.
(5) Selling cost per unit will remain unchanged.
(6) Other expenses will remain unaffected by the rise in output.

You are required to submit a statement for the Board of Directors showing the price at which the refrigerator should be marketed so as to show a profit of 10% on selling price.

Solution

Statement showing the price at which refrigerator should be marketed in 2020–21 is as follows:

Particulars	₹	₹
Materials [₹80,000/100]	80	
Add: 20% increase $\left(\frac{20}{100} \times ₹80\right)$	16	96.00
Direct wages [₹1,20,000/1000]	120	
Add: 5% increase $\frac{5}{100} \times ₹120$	6	126.00

(Contd.)

Particulars	₹	₹
Prime Cost		222.00
Manufacturing expenses (note)		55.50
Work Cost		277.50
Management and staff salaries (₹60000/1200)		50.00
Rent, Rates and Insurance (₹10000/12000)		8.33
General expenses (₹20000/1200)		16.67
Cost of Production		352.50
Selling expenses (₹30000/1000)		30.00
Cost of Sales		382.50
[Profit 10% on selling price or 1/9 on cost]		42.50
Selling Price		425.00

Note: During the year ending on 31st March, 2021 the combined cost of materials and wages per unit will be:

	₹
Materials consumed	96
Direct wages	126
	222

During the year ending on 31st March, 2020, the combined cost of materials and wages was ₹200 per unit and manufacturing expenses were ₹50 per unit.

$$\therefore \quad \text{Manufacturing expenses in 2020–21 will be} = \frac{50 \times 222}{200} = ₹55.50$$

✎ EXAMPLE 9.5

An article passes through three successive operations from the raw materials stage to the finished product stage. The following data are available from the production records of a particular month:

Operation No.	*No. of Pcs. Input*	*No. of Pcs. Rejected*	*No. of Pcs. Output*
1	60,000	20,000	40,000
2	66,000	6,000	60,000
3	48,000	8,000	40,000

Required:

(i) Determine the input required to be introduced in the first operation in number of pieces in order to obtain finished output of 100 pieces after the last operation.

(ii) Calculate the cost of raw material required to produce one piece of finished product, given the following information:

Weight of the finished piece is 0.10 kg and the price of raw material is ₹20 per kg.

☞ Solution

(i) Statement of Production (for a Month)

Operation No.	*Input, Total No.*	*Rejections*		*Output, Total No.*
		Total No.	*% Rejection to Output*	
1	60,000	20,000	50%	40,000
2	66,000	6,000	10%	60,000
3	48,000	8,000	20%	40,000

Input required for final output of 100 units:

	No. of Pcs.
Output of process 3	100
Loss in process no. 3, 20%	20
Input to process 3 or output of process 2	120
Loss in process 2, 10%	12
Input to process 2 or output of process 1	132
Loss in process 1, 50%	66
Input to process 1	198

(ii) To produce 100 pieces of final output, 198 pieces of initial input are used. The weight of one piece of finished output is 0.10 kg. Thus, the weight of input to produce one piece of output is 0.198 kg. The rate being ₹20, the cost of materials for producing one piece is ₹3.96.

Theory Questions

1. Explain the nature of single costing.
2. Describe briefly the procedure of presenting costs under single costing. Explain giving an example.
3. Explain the nature of operation costing.

Problems

1. The following details have been obtained from the cost records of Comet Paints Limited:

	₹
Stock of raw materials on Sept. 1, 2020	75,000
Stock of raw materials on Sept. 30, 2020	91,500
Direct wages	52,500
Indirect wages	2,750
Sales	2,11,000

(Contd.)

	₹
Work-in-progress on Sept. 1, 2020	28,000
Work-in-progress on Sept. 30, 2020	35,000
Purchases of raw materials	66,000
Factory rent, rates and power	15,000
Depreciation of plant and machinery	3,500
Expenses on purchases	1,500
Carriage outwards	2,500
Advertising	3,500
Office rent and taxes	2,500
Travellers, wages and commission	6,500
Stock of finished goods on Sept. 1, 2020	54,000
Stock of finished goods on Sept. 30, 2020	31,000

Prepare a production account giving the maximum possible break-up of costs and profit.

Ans: Prime cost ₹1,03,500; Works cost ₹1,17,750; Cost of production ₹1,43,250; Cost of sales ₹1,55,750; Profit ₹55,250.

2. The Managing Director of a small manufacturing concern consults you as to the minimum price at which he can sell the output of one of the departments of the company which is intended for mass production in future. The company's records show the following particulars for this department for the past year:

Production and Sales	*100 Units*
	₹
Materials	13,000
Direct labour	7,000
Direct charges	1,000
	₹
Works overheads	7,000
Office overheads	2,800
Selling overheads	3,200
Profit	5,000
	39,000

You ascertain that 40% of the works overheads fluctuate directly with production and 70% of the selling overheads fluctuate with sales. It is anticipated that the department would produce 500 units per annum and that direct labour charges per unit will be reduced by 20%, while fixed works overheads charges will increase by ₹3,000. Office overheads and fixed selling overheads charges are expected to show an increase of 25% but otherwise no changes are anticipated.

Ans: Prime cost ₹98,000; Factory cost ₹1,19,200; Total cost 1,35,100; Profit ₹19867.60.

3. The following budgeted cost information is available from the records of a manufacturing concern:

		(₹ *Lakhs*)
Direct materials		61.20
Direct wages:		
Rolling shop (1,20,000 hours)	6.00	
Milling shop (2,40,000 hours)	14.40	20.40
Work overheads (allocation on labour hours):		
Rolling shop	9.60	
Milling shop	28.80	38.40
Administrative overheads		24.00
Selling overheads		28.80
Distribution overheads		14.40

The concern follows absorption method of costing. On the basis of above data, prepare a schedule of overhead rates. The Sales Division of the concern requires a cost estimate for a product for which following information are available:

Direct material	:	Material *X* 120 kg @ ₹30 per kg Material *Y* 72 kg @ ₹55 per kg
Direct labour	:	Rolling shop 40 hours @ ₹6 per hour. Milling shop 70 hours @ ₹5 per hour.

You are required to work out the cost estimate showing cost per unit using the above information and the overhead rates so computed.

Ans: Total cost of Job, ₹14,523.60

4. Baluja Shoe Company manufactures two types of shoes *A* and *B*. Production costs for the year ended 31st December 2020 were as follows:

Direct material	₹15,00,000
Direct wages	8,40,000
Production overhead	3,60,000
	27,00,000

There was no work-in-progress at the beginning or at the end of the year. It is ascertained that:

(i) The cost of direct materials in type *A* shoes is twice as much as that in type *B*.
(ii) The direct wages for type *B* shoes were 60% of those of type *A* shoes.
(iii) Production overhead was the same per pair of *A* and *B* type.
(iv) Administrative overhead for each type was 150% of direct wages.
(v) Selling cost was ₹1.50 per pair.
(vi) Production during the year:

Type *A* 40,000 pairs of which 36,000 were sold.
Type *B* 1,20,000 pairs of which 1,00,000 were sold.

(vii) Selling price was ₹44 for type *A* and ₹28 per pair for type *B*.

Prepare a statement showing cost and profit.

		Cost	*Profit*
Ans:	Type *A*	₹13,50,000	₹2,34,000
	Type *B*	₹22,50,000	₹5,50,000

5. Meera Industries Limited is a single product organisation having a manufacturing capacity of 6,000 units per week of 48 hours. The output data vis-à-vis different elements of cost for three consecutive weeks are as follows:

Units Produced	*Direct Material* (₹)	*Direct Labour* (₹)	*Total Factory Overheads (Variable and Fixed)* ₹
2,400	4,800	6,000	37,200
2,800	5,600	7,000	38,400
3,600	7,200	9,000	40,800

As a cost accountant, you are asked by the company management to work out the selling price assuming an activity level of 4,000 units per week and a profit of 20% on selling price.

Ans: Selling price per unit ₹18.75

Chapter 10

Job, Contract and Batch Costing

Learning Objectives

After reading this chapter, you should be able to:

1. describe job costing—nature and its advantages and disadvantages;
2. explain the nature of job cost sheet and contract costing as well;
3. explain sub-contract, work-in-progress in contract costing, cost-plus contract and batch costing and economic batch quantity;
4. describe how costs are recorded on jobs and on contract as well; and
5. explain the methods of determining profit on incomplete contracts and the procedure of ascertaining value and profit of contract.

NATURE OF JOB COSTING

Job costing is a costing method applied to determine the cost of specific jobs or lots of productions generally manufactured according to customers' specifications. The main feature of the job order costing system is that no two orders are necessarily alike and all orders do not pass through the same manufacturing process. Generally, the job order system is used by manufacturing concerns where an order is produced to a customer's specifications, such as building, contracting, machine tool manufacturing, furniture, foundries, job printing and general engineering. A job may be a product, unit, batch, sales order, project, contract, service, specific programme or any other cost objective that is clearly distinguishable and unique in terms of materials and other services used.

Advantages

Job costing has the following advantages:

1. More accurate costing is possible because all costs are compiled and specifically identified with a specific order or product.
2. It is simple as the recording of direct materials and direct labour hours is done by product or job.
3. Job cost sheets can be used to control efficiency and estimate future work.
4. It provides a basis for comparing one job cost to another or for comparing a job cost sheet to a cost estimate.

Disadvantages

Job costing has the following disadvantages:

1. It requires detailed record-keeping for different jobs.
2. The record-keeping for different jobs may prove complicated.
3. A job may be charged for inefficiencies (downtime) although it has not caused it.

JOB COST SHEET AND JOB LEDGER

The focal point of a job order cost system is the cost sheet on which charges for direct materials, direct labour, and indirect manufacturing costs can be accumulated as work on a job order progresses. It is in summary form and records the job number and other specifications and descriptive information as given in the production order. The design of the cost sheet and the number of columns to be used must be determined in terms of departmental and manufacturing characteristics of the business operations. Basically, the recorded costs are grouped under three major headings: material costs, labour costs and applied manufacturing overhead costs. Figure 10.1 presents a specimen of a job cost sheet. When a production order is started in process, a cost sheet identified by a job number is set up in the accounting department.

ABC Company
Job Order Cost Sheet

Customer Name ________ Date ________ Job Order No. ________
Product description ________
Selling price ________ Total cost ________
Cost per unit ________

	Department 1	*Department 2*	*Department 3*
Materials:			
Date(s)			
Requisition no.			
Amount			
Labour:			
Date(s)			
Job time card no.			
Amount			
Overhead:			
Rate/Basis			
Amount absorbed			

Cost Summary:	*Deptt. 1*	*Deptt. 2*	*Deptt. 3*	*Total*
Material	________	________	________	________
Labour				
Overhead	________	________	________	________
Total	________	________	________	________

Units completed ________ Date Completed ________

Fig. 10.1 Specimen of a Job Sheet

When the job order is finished/completed, the cost summary at the bottom of the form is completed and a unit cost for the job order is computed.

RECORDING COSTS ON JOBS

Materials Costs

Materials used in manufacturing and/or completing jobs are known as direct materials which become part of the finished product. Direct materials are directly charged to the job on which they are used and indirect materials or factory supplies are part of manufacturing overhead and are allocated to the various jobs.

Labour Costs

Direct labour costs can be identified with specific jobs with the help of "job time tickets". When a worker begins work on an order, the starting time is noted on the ticket; when the job order is finished, the stopping time is written in, and the time spent on a job is noted. Earnings (wages) are then computed using the employee's hourly rate.

Direct Expenses

Generally speaking, direct expenses are directly charged to individual jobs for which they are incurred. The invoices (of direct expenses) as documentary evidence can be marked with the number of the jobs to which the cost is to be allocated.

Overhead

Overhead costs are usually charged to work-in-progress by means of a pre-determined absorption rate calculated in advance of production. This is derived on the basis of budgeted figures.

RECORDING COMPLETED JOBS

When a job is finished, its cost is determined by totalling prime costs and absorbed overhead. The cost sheet is then marked "completed" and removed from the job ledger. An entry is made to the proper account in the finished goods ledger.

When no unit on a job order is completed, the total cost incurred on the job order so far becomes work-in-progress. Under job costing, the value of closing work-in-progress is obtained from the work-in-progress account. The work-in-progress at the end of an accounting period is carried forward to the subsequent accounting period as opening stock. The expenditure incurred on the job in this subsequent period is added to the opening stock.

EXAMPLE 10.1

The following information for the year ended 31st December, 2020 is obtained from the books and records of a factory:

	Completed Jobs	W.I.P.
	₹	₹
Raw materials supplied from stores	88,000	32,000
Wages	1,00,000	40,000
Chargeable expenses	10,000	4,000
Materials returned to stores	1,000	—

Factory overheads are 80% of wages. Office overheads are 25% of factory cost and selling distribution overheads are 10% of cost of production.

The complete jobs realised ₹4,10,000. Write up:

(i) Work-in-progress Ledger Control Account;
(ii) Completed Job Ledger Control Account; and
(iii) Cost of Sales Account.

☞ ***Solution***

Consolidated Work-in-Progress Account

Dr.	₹	*Cr.* ₹
To raw material consumed	32,000	
To wages	40,000	
To chargeable expenses	4,000	
To factory overheads (80% of wages)	32,000	
Factory cost	1,08,000	
To administrative overheads (25% of ₹1,08,000)	27,000	
	1,35,000	1,35,000

Note: Selling and distribution overhead has not been charged in work-in-progress account.

Consolidated Completed Job Account

Dr.		₹		*Cr.* ₹
To raw material consumed	88,000	87,000	By customer's account (Amt. of jobs completed)	
Less: Returned to store	(–) 1,000			4,10,000

(Contd.)

Dr.	₹		Cr. ₹
To wages	1,00,000		
To chargeable expenses	10,000		
To factory overheads (80% of ₹1,00,00 of wages	80,000		
Factory cost	2,77,000		
To admn. overheads (25% of ₹2,77,000)	69,250		
Cost of production	3,46,250		
To selling and distribution overhead	34,625		
To N.P. transferred to P and L A/c	29,125		
	4,10,000		4,10,000

Cost of Sales Account

Dr.	₹		Cr. ₹
To materials consumed	87,000	By balance c/d	3,80,875
To wages	1,00,000		
To direct charges	10,000		
To factory overhead (80% of wages)	80,000		
Factory cost	2,77,000		
To admn. overheads (25% of ₹2,77,000)	69,250		
	3,46,250		
To selling and distribution 10% of ₹3,46,250	34,625		
Cost of sales	3,80,875		3,80,875

EXAMPLE 10.2

Xavier company manufactures many products. Each product passes through two production departments, which have the following cost structures:

	Department A	*Department B*
Normal monthly volume (based for over-head rate)	5,000 direct labour hours	10,000 pounds of materials
Monthly fixed costs at normal volume	₹10,000	₹40,000
Monthly variable costs at normal volume	15,000	20,000

for excel template, scan

Two job orders that went through the factory last month had the following results:

	Job I (Product X)		*Job 2 (Product Y)*	
	Quantity	*Cost* (₹)	*Quantity*	*Cost* (₹)
Direct inputs:				
Direct materials	480 1bs	2,400	1,500 1bs	4,800
Direct labour:				
Department *A*	180 hrs	1,620	100 hrs	900
Department *B*	60 hrs	420	40 hrs	280
Output	600 units		1,000 units	

Required:

(a) Calculate the unit cost of each of these jobs on a full costing basis.
(b) Recalculate unit costs on a variable costing basis.
(c) Why are the relative variable costs of these two products so different from their relative full costs?

☞ ***Solution***

(a) Full-costing overhead rates:
Department *A*: ₹25,000/5,000 = ₹5 a direct labour-hour
Department *B*: ₹60,000/10,000 = ₹6 a pound
Job order costs:

	Job 1	*Job 2*
Direct materials	₹2,400	₹4,800
Direct labour:		
Department *A*	1,620	900
Department *B*	420	280
Overhead: Department *A* at ₹5	900	500
Department *B* at ₹6	2,880	9,000
Total	₹8,220	₹15,480
Unit cost Job 1, ₹8220/600 units, Job 2, ₹15480/1000 units	₹13.70	₹15.48

(b) Variable costing overhead rates:
Department *A*: ₹15,000/5,000 = ₹3 a direct labour-hour
Department *B*: ₹20,000/10,000 = ₹2 a pound

Job order costs:

	Job 1	Job 2
Direct materials	₹2,400	₹4,800
Direct labour:		
Department *A*	1,620	900
Department *B*	420	280
Overhead:		
Department *A* at ₹3	540	300
Department *B* at ₹2	960	3,000
	₹5,940	₹9,280
Unit cost	₹9.90	₹9.28

(c) Variable unit cost of job 2 is less than that of job 1; full cost was greater for job 2 than for job 1. The main reason is that job 2 used much more of department *B*'s capacity than job 1, and department *B* has a much higher proportion of fixed costs than department *A*. Total profit is thus much more sensitive to variations in sales of product *Y* (job 2) than to variations in sales of product *X*.

EXAMPLE 10.3

An advertising agency has received an enquiry for submission of quotation. Bill of materials prepared by the production department for the job states the following requirement of materials:

Paper 10 reams @ ₹1,800 per ream
Ink and other printing material ₹5,000
Binding material and other consumables ₹3,000

Some photography is required for the job. The agency does not have a photographer as an employee. It decides to hire one by paying ₹10,000 to him. Estimated job card prepared by production department specifies that service of following employees will be required for this job:
(1) Artist (₹12,000 per month) 80 hours; (2) Copywriter (₹10,000 per month) 75 hours; (3) Client servicing (₹9,000 per month) 30 hours.

The primary packing material will be required to the tune of ₹4,000. Production overheads 40% of direct cost while the selling and distribution overheads are likely to be 25% on production cost. The agency expected a profit of 20% on the quoted price. The agency works 25 days in a month and 6 hours a day.

You are required to determine the price to be quoted for the job.

Solution

Quotation for Printing Job

	Amount (₹)	Amount (₹)
Direct Material Required:		
Paper (1800 × 10)	18,000	
Ink and others printing material	5,000	

(Contd.)

	Amount (₹)	Amount (₹)
Binding material and consumables	3,000	
Primary packing materials	4,000	
		30,000
Direct Labour Spent:		
Artist (12000 × 80)/ (25 × 6)	6,400	
Copywriter (10000 × 75)/(25 × 6)	5,000	
Client Servicing (9000 × 30)/ (25 × 6)	1,800	
		13,200
Photographer's charge		10,000
Prime Cost		53,200
Factory overhead applied @ 40% on direct cost		21,280
Production Cost		74,480
Selling & Distribution overhead applied @ 25% on production cost		18,620
Total Cost		93,100
Profit (20% on price i.e. 25% on cost)		23,275
Price to be Quoted		**1,16,375**

EXAMPLE 10.4

Tilly Ltd has been approached by a customer who wants a special job done and is willing to pay ₹20,000 for it. The job would require the following materials:

Material	*Total Units Required*	*Units in Stock*	*Book Value of Units in Stock (₹/Unit)*	*Realisable Value (₹/Unit)*	*Replacement Cost (₹ /Unit)*
A	1,000	0	–	–	6
B	1,000	600	2	2.5	5
C	1,000	700	3	2.5	4
D	200	200	4	6	9
E	500	500	5	–	–

Material *B* is regularly used by Tilly Ltd in the manufacture of its standard products.

Material *C* and *D* are specialist materials, in stock due to previous overbuying. No other use can be found for material *C*. However, the stock of material *D* could be used in another job as a substitute for 300 units of material *M*. Tilly has no stock of material *M* at present but it can be purchased locally at ₹5 per unit.

Since the stock of material *E* was acquired, its sale has been banned by the government (although previously acquired stocks are allowed to be used up). It is a toxic chemical and Tilly is expecting to pay ₹500 in the near future for its safe disposal as it has no other use for it.

Required:
To help Tilly Ltd, decide whether or not to accept the job and calculate the relevant cost of materials needed.

☞ ***Solution***

Item	*Avoidable*	*Future*	*Cash*	*Note*	*Amount*	*Relevant*
Material *A*	X	X	X	1	1,000 × ₹6	6,000
Material *B*	X	X	X	2	1,000 × ₹5	5,000
Material *C*	X	X	X	3	700 × ₹2.50	1,750
Material *C*	X	X	X	4	300 × ₹4	1,200
Material *D* (200 units)	X	X	X	5	300 × ₹5	1,500
Material *E*	X	X	X	6	₹500	(500)
					Relevant cost	**₹14,950**

Notes:

1. All 1,000 units need buying in at replacement cost.
2. 600 units from stock need replacing and 400 units need buying at replacement cost.
3. Opportunity cost = resale value.
4. Remaining 300 units bought in at replacement cost.
5. Opportunity cost is greater of resale value of ₹1,200 (200 × ₹6) and saving the purchase of 300 units of M, ₹1,500 (300 × ₹5)
6. Opportunity benefit: using the stock of *E* in production avoids disposal costs of ₹500.

CONTRACT COSTING

Contract costing, sometimes known as terminal costing, follows the same principles as job costing, and is used by such concerns as firms of builders and public works contractors who undertake work on a contract basis.

Following are the special features of contract costing:

1. The contractor begins work on a small number of large contracts in the course of a year.
2. The contracts are completed away from the contractor's premises.
3. The contracts may continue over more than one accounting period.
4. Materials are purchased and delivered direct to the contract site and/or are drawn from the central stores.
5. The payroll is prepared at either the site or at a central administrative office.
6. Sub-contractors may be employed, for example, ventilation engineers, lift manufacturers, flooring specialists, etc.
7. Plant and equipment may be purchased, or hired for the duration of the contract from another business or from a central plant department.
8. Payment by the customer for various stages of the contract is made only on receipt of architect's certificate for the completed stage. A reduction called retention money is withheld by the customer until a specific period of time, agreed in the original contract, has passed.

9. The contract price is normally estimated in advance of the work. Additional work found necessary may be charged on a cost-plus basis. In addition, clauses may be inserted to allow the contractor to pass on to the customer additional costs incurred as a result of increase in material, labour and other costs.

RECORDING COSTS ON CONTRACT

Under contract costing, a contract is basically the cost unit and for the purpose of control, it can be regarded as a cost centre. Under contract costing, only allocation is required directly to the contract. Overhead costs are normally incurred at the head office and are sometimes known only as storage costs. Such overhead costs tend to be of a small figure and are often absorbed on some arbitrary basis such as a percentage on prime cost.

A separate account, the contract account, is opened for each individual contract for the purpose of determining the profit or loss on each contract. In the contract account the following costs are recorded:

Materials

Materials required for a specific contract are debited to the contract account. Materials returned under the materials returned note are credited with the contract.

Materials transferred from one contract to another are recorded in material transfer notes; the contract receiving the material is debited and the contract giving the material is credited. Materials not required for current use are sometimes sold at the site, and the amount received from sale of materials is credited to the contract account, and any profit or loss, being the difference between the cost and sale value, is transferred to the profit and loss account. This also applies not only to materials, but also to sale of plant, machinery, tools, etc. At the end of the accounting period, the value of materials remaining unutilised on site is carried forward as a charge against the next period. In the accounting year, the amount will be debited to the materials or stores at site account and credited to the contract account. Materials stolen or destroyed by fire are transferred to the profit and loss account and also shown on the credit side of the contract account.

The customer or contractee may supply certain materials from own stock to be utilised in construction work. Such materials should not be debited (charged) to the contract account; a separate memorandum record outside the account will be sufficient. Such materials do not affect the contract price.

Wages

Wages of all workers engaged on a particular contract are allocated direct to that contract, regardless of work they perform. Where workers move from one contract to another, time-sheets must be maintained and wages may be distributed on the basis of time spent under each contract. The wages of the head office and central stores are considered as overhead and are charged to contracts on an equitable basis. Wages accrued or outstanding at the end of the period should appear on the debit side of contract.

Expenses

All expenses other than material and wages are charged to individual contracts as and when they are incurred. Examples of such expenses are hire charge of plants obtained from outside, architects' and consultants' fees, electricity, insurance, etc.

Plant and Machinery

For use of plant and machinery in a particular contract, the depreciation may be charged in any one of the following ways:

1. When the plant has been specially purchased for a particular contract and will be exhausted at site, the total cost of the plant is debited to the contract in which it is used. When the contract is completed or the plant is no longer required, it may be sold at site and contract is credited with the sale proceeds. If it is not sold, the contract is credited with the depreciated (re-valued amount) value. Thus, the contract account stands debited with the amount of depreciation. This method has the drawback that the debit side is unnecessarily inflated with the plant value, and the cost of contract at first sight appears to be very high. In order to overcome this problem, the difference between the original cost at commencement and the depreciated value at the end of the period is obtained and charged to the contract account concerned as plant depreciation.
2. When the plant is sent to the contract site only for a short period, it is usual to charge the contract for the use on a daily or hourly basis. Depreciation is charged at an hourly rate for the hours the plant has worked. If the plant is taken on hire, only the hire charges are debited to the contract and not depreciation.

Sub-Contract

When a sub-contractor is engaged for a special work connected with the main contract, the work performed by the sub-contractor forms a direct charge to the main contract. The payments made to sub-contractors are charged in totals to the concerned contract account as direct expense and no detailed record, or break-up of the sub-contract amount is necessary for cost purposes.

Materials issued to the sub-contractor, free of charge, should be charged to the contract account. Heavy tools and equipment may be supplied to sub-contractor on a rental basis. The depreciation on these equipments should be charged to the contract account and the rental received is credited to it or shown as a deduction from the sub-contractor's bill.

VALUE AND PROFIT OF CONTRACT

As the contract work proceeds, the surveyor appointed by the contractee issues certificates to the effect that so much portion has been completed. The contractor will get money according to this certificate and a certain portion thereof shall be retained by the contractee. The money so retained is called retention money. For example, if a certificate has been issued for ₹2,00,000 and 70% has been paid, the following entries will be made:

First Method

1. Contractee's account	2,00,000	
To contract A/c		2,00,000
(being value of the work certified)		
2. Bank A/c Dr	1,40,000	
To contractee's A/c		1,40,000
(being amount of cash received)		

Second Method

The amount of work certified will be debited to the work-in-progress account and credited to the contract account. The work-in-progress account is shown as an asset in the balance sheet after deducting the amount received from the contractee. Until the contract is completed, the amount received from the contractee is advance payment and is deducted from work-in-progress in the balance sheet. When the contract is completed, the contractee account is debited with the contract price. In the next year, the work-in-progress account is transferred to the debit side of the contract account. On completion of the contract, the contractee's personal account is debited and the contract account credited. Taking the above example, the journal entries will be as follows:

1. Work-in-progress A/c	₹2,00,000	
To Contract A/c		₹2,00,000
(being work certified)		
2. Bank A/c Dr	₹1,40,000	
To Contractee's A/c		1,40,000
(being amount received)		

Balance Sheet

Asset Side

	(₹)
Work-in-progress	2,00,000
Less: Amount received	1,40,000
	60,000

Such work which has not been so far approved by the contractee's architect or surveyor is termed as "work uncertified". It is valued at cost and credited to the contract account and debited to the work-in-progress account, which will be transferred in the next year to the debit side of the contract account.

Work certified and work uncertified can be found in the following manner:

Cost of Work Certified:	*Cost of Work Uncertified:*
Cost of work to date	Total cost to date
Less: Cost of work uncertified	*Less*: Cost of work certified
Materials on hand	Materials on hand
Plant at site	Plant at site
= Cost of work certified	= Cost of work uncertified

WORK-IN-PROGRESS

Work-in-progress includes the amount of work certified (valued at contract price) and the amount of work uncertified. The work-in-progress account will appear on the asset side of the balance sheet. The amount of cash received from the contractee and reserve for contingencies (as discussed in the case of incomplete contracts) will be deducted out of this amount. The work-in-progress account appears as follows in the balance sheet.

1. When work certified has been treated according to the first method:

Balance sheet as on ________

Work-in-progress:
Balance in the contractee's A/c
Add: Work uncertified
Less: Reserve for unrealised profit

2. When work certified has been treated according to the second method:

Balance sheet as on ________

Work-in-progress:	
Value of work certified	________
Cost of work uncertified	________
Less: Reserve for unrealised profit	________
Less: Amount received from contractee	________

In contract accounts, the value of work-in-progress consists of: (i) the cost of work completed, both certified and uncertified, (ii) the cost of work not yet completed; and (iii) the amount of profit taken as credit. Taking these into account, the work-in-progress in the balance sheet can be shown as follows:

Balance sheet as on ________

Work-in-progress:	
Cost of work certified	________
Cost of work uncertified	________
Less: Amount received from contractee	________
Add: Profit taken as credit to Profit and Loss A/c	________

PROFIT ON INCOMPLETE CONTRACTS

Many contracts take more than one financial year to be completed. A problem arises whether profit on such a contract should be worked out only on its completion or whether some profits may be computed every year. The conservative method is to value work-in-progress only at cost and no credit is taken for profit till it is actually earned. This method, however, results in wide fluctuations in the net profit of the enterprise from year to year. If several contracts are completed in a year, the profit will be high while in extreme cases in some years, when not a single contract is fully completed, the profit will be nil. It becomes necessary, therefore, to compute profit on partly completed contracts and take credit for a part of it in the accounts at the year end.

The manner of computation of profit is largely dependent upon how for the contract has advanced, that is, the stage of completion it has reached.

1. Profit should be considered in respect of work certified only, work uncertified should always be valued at cost.
2. For contracts which have been completed less than one-fourth of the contract, no profit should be computed and credited to the profit and loss account.
3. In case of contracts which are completed by more than 25% but less than 50%, one-third of notional profit, reduced in the ratio of cash received to work-certified, is transferred to profit and loss A/c. The balance in the notional profit is carried forward in the same contract as profit in suspense as a provision against future losses, increase in costs and other contingencies. The following formula is used to determine the amount of profit to be transferred to profit and loss A/c.

$$\frac{1}{3} \times \text{Notional profit} \times \frac{\text{Cash received}}{\text{Work certified}}$$

Notional profit is the difference between the value of work certified and cost of work certified. It is determined in the following manner.

Notional profit = Value of work certified – (cost of work to date – cost of work not yet certified)

4. In case contracts are complete between 50% and 90% (more than 50% but less than 90%), two-third of notional profit, reduced by the proportion of cash received to work certified, is transferred to profit and loss A/c. The formula to be used for this purpose is:

$$\frac{2}{3} \times \text{Notional profit} \times \frac{\text{Cash received}}{\text{Work certified}}$$

5. In case contracts are complete by 90% or more than 90%, the contract is considered almost complete. In such contracts, the estimated total profit is first determined by deducting the total costs to date and additional expenditure necessary to complete the contract from the contract price. A portion of this estimated total profit is credited to profit and loss A/c, which can be determined by using any one of the following formulae:

(i) $\text{Estimated Profit} \times \frac{\text{Work certified}}{\text{Contract price}}$

(ii) $\text{Estimated Profit} \times \frac{\text{Work certified}}{\text{Contract price}} \times \frac{\text{Cash received}}{\text{Work certified}}$

or

$\text{Estimated Profit} \times \frac{\text{Cash received}}{\text{Work certified}}$

The second formula is preferable to first formula. In case estimated profit cannot be determined due to some reason, for example, if additional expenditure is not mentioned, then the amount of profit to be transferred to profit and loss A/c is determined using the following formula:

$$\text{Notional Profit} \times \frac{\text{Work certified}}{\text{Contract price}}$$

6. The total of loss, if any, should be transferred to the profit and loss account by crediting the contract account.

In contract accounting, the profit earned on contracts is reduced proportionately by the amount of cash received, otherwise the unrealised profit may stand for distribution as dividends. Also, the sound principle of conservatism requires that all future contingencies and possible losses should be accounted for before determining the profit on contract.

Retention Money in Contract Costing

A contractor does not receive the full payment of the work certified by the surveyor. Contractee retains some amount to be paid after some time, when it is ensured that there is no default in the work done by the contractor. If any deficiency or defect is noticed, it is to be rectified by the contractor before the release of the retention money. Thus, the retention money provides a safeguard against the default risk in the contracts.

COST-PLUS CONTRACT

A cost-plus contract is a contract in which the value of the contract is determined by adding a fixed margin of profit to the total cost of the contract. Such types of contracts are entered into when it is not possible to estimate the contract cost with reasonable accuracy due to unstable price of material, labour, services, etc. The contractee agrees to pay this inflated value of contract which includes a profit margin as per the agreement. Inclusion of such a clause in a contract is called an Escalation Clause. Both the parties determine in advance the possible costs that would be included in the cost of contract. The profit to be added to the cost of contract may be agreed as a percentage on cost or the capital employed. Cost-plus contracts are generally needed when the costs of contracts cannot be accurately determined due to unstable and fluctuating conditions of materials, labour and service, etc. The price of materials, labour and services usually tend to fluctuate over a long period. The contractor presents evidential proof of increased costs to the contractee to claim reimbursements. Under the escalator clause, the contract price is increased for a given increase in the prices of inputs. For instance, it may be agreed that if the prices of raw materials go up by 15%, the contract price will be increased by 2%.

Cost-plus contracts are useful to both the parties—contractor (manufacturer) and contractee (customer). The contractor is suitably protected against any fluctuations in the prices of materials, labour, and overhead which will be used in production or completion of the job. A cost-plus contract is beneficial to the contractee (customer) also. The contractee is protected against an uncertain market which may push up the cost of the contract. The price agreed to be paid by the contractee is based on actual cost. In this way, the contract price is not determined arbitrarily.

Costs plus contracts have the following advantages:

1. The contractor is assured of a fixed percentage of profit. There is no risk of incurring any loss on the contract.
2. It is useful especially when the work to be done is not definitely fixed at the time of making the estimate.
3. Contractee can ensure himself about "the cost of the contract", as he is empowered to examine the books and document of the contractor to ascertain the veracity of the cost of the contract.

EXAMPLE 10.5

A contract is estimated to be 80% complete in its first year of construction as certified. The contractee pays 75% of value of work certified, as and when certified and makes the final payment on the completion of contract. Following information is available for the first year:

	₹
Cost of work-in-progress uncertified	8,000
Profit transferred to Profit & Loss A/c at the end of year 1 on incomplete contract	60,000
Cost of work to date	88,000

Required:

Calculate the value of work-in-progress certified and amount of contract price.

Solution

As the contract is 80% complete, so 2/3rd of the notional profit on cash basis has been transferred to Profit & Loss A/c in the first year of contract.

$\therefore$ Amount transferred to Profit & Loss A/c = $\frac{2}{3}$ × Notional Profit × % of cost received

$$\text{or, } 60{,}000 = \frac{2}{3} \times \text{Notional Profit} \times \frac{75}{100}$$

$$\text{or, Notional Profit} = \frac{60{,}000 \times 3 \times 100}{2 \times 75}$$

$$= ₹\ 1{,}20{,}000$$

Computation of value of work certified

Cost of work to date	= ₹ 88,000
Add: Notional profit	= ₹1,20,000
	₹2,08,000
Less: Cost of work uncertified	= 8,000
Value of work certified	= ₹2,00,000

Since the value of work certified is 80% of the contract price, therefore

$$\text{Contract price} = \frac{\text{Value of work certified}}{80\%}$$

$$= \frac{₹2{,}00{,}000}{80\%}$$

$$= ₹2{,}50{,}000$$

✍ EXAMPLE 10.6

Compute a conservative estimate of profit on a contract (which has been 90% complete) from the following particulars. Illustrate four methods of computing the profit transferable to Profit & Loss Account.

	₹
Total expenditure to date	4,50,000
Estimated further expenditure to complete the contract (including contingencies)	25,000
Contract price	6,12,000
Work certified	5,50,800
Work uncertified	34,000
Cash received	4,40,640

☞ ***Solution***

(a) Notional Profit

Value of work certified	5,50,800

(Contd.)

Less: Cost of work certified (Total expenditure to date – work not certified) (4,50,000 – 34,000)	4,16,000
	1,34,800

Estimated Profit

Contract Price	6,12,000
–Total expenditure to date	– 4,50,000
–Estimated expenditure to be incurred	–25,000
	1,37,000

Profit Transferred to Profit & Loss A/c

Method I

$$\text{Notional profit} \times \frac{\text{Work certified}}{\text{Contract price}} = 1{,}34{,}800 \times \frac{5{,}50{,}800}{6{,}12{,}000} = 1{,}21{,}320$$

Method II

$$\text{Notional profit} \times \frac{2}{3} \times \frac{\text{Cash received}}{\text{Work certified}}$$

$$= 1{,}34{,}800 \times \frac{2}{3} \times \frac{4{,}40{,}640}{5{,}50{,}800} = 71{,}893.33$$

Method III

$$\text{Estimated profit} \times \frac{\text{Work certified}}{\text{Contract price}} \times \frac{\text{Cash received}}{\text{Work certified}}$$

$$= 1{,}37{,}000 \times \frac{5{,}50{,}800}{6{,}12{,}000} \times \frac{4{,}40{,}640}{5{,}50{,}800} = 1{,}09{,}600$$

Method IV

$$\text{Estimated profit} \times \frac{\text{Cost to date}}{\text{Estimated total cost of work}} \times \frac{\text{Cash received}}{\text{Work certified}}$$

$$= 1{,}37{,}000 \times \frac{4{,}50{,}000}{4{,}75{,}000} \times \frac{4{,}40{,}640}{5{,}50{,}800} = 1{,}03{,}831.20$$

EXAMPLE 10.7

The ABC Ltd. has undertaken the construction of a bridge over the River Yamuna for a Corporation. The value of the contract is ₹15,00,000 subject to retention of 20% until one year after certified completion of the contract, and final approval of the Corporation's Engineer. The following are the details as shown in the books on 30th June, 2020.

Labour on site	4,05,000	Materials on hand on June 30, 2009	6,300
Materials purchased	4,20,000	Wages, accrued on June 30, 2009	7,800
Materials sent from stores	81,200	Direct expenses accrued on June 30, 2009	1,600
Plant	12,100	Work not yet certified at cost	16,500
Direct expenses	23,000	Amount certified by the corporation's engineer	11,00,000
General overhead	37,100	Cash received on account	8,80,000
Allocated to the contract			

Prepare:

(a) Contract Account;
(b) Contractee's Account; and
(c) Show how it would appear in the Balance Sheet.

☞ ***Solution***

Contract Account

Particulars		₹	*Particulars*		₹
To materials :			By material in hand		6,300
Purchased	4,20,000		By work-in-progress		
Sent from stores	81,200	5,01,200	Work certified	11,00,000	
To labour on site	4,05,000		Work uncertified	16,500	11,16,500
Add: Wages accrued	7,800	4,12,800			
To Direct expenses	23,000				
Add: accured	1,600	24,600			
To plant		12,100			
To general overhead		37,100			
To profit c/d		1,35,000			
		11,22,800			11,22,800
To profit & loss account*		72,000	By profit b/d		1,35,000
To work-in-progress account		63,000			
		1,35,000			1,35,000

*The profit taken to Profit and Loss Account has been arrived at as follows:

$$₹135000 \times \frac{2}{3} \times \frac{80}{100} = ₹72,000$$

Contractee's Account

Particulars	₹	*Particulars*	₹
To balance c/d	8,80,000	By cash	8,80,000

ABC Ltd.
Extract from Balance Sheet
At 30th June, 2020

Liabilities	₹	*Assets*	₹	₹
Wages accrued	7800	Work-in-progress:	₹	
		Value of work certified	11,00,000	
Direct expenses accrued	1600	Add: Work uncertified	16,500	
			11,16,500	
		Less: Reserve	63,000	
			10,53,500	
		Less: Cash received	8,80,000	1,73,500
		Material in hand		6,300

EXAMPLE 10.8

Two contracts, commenced on 1st January and 1st July, 2020 respectively, were undertaken by a contractor and their accounts on 31st Dec., 2020 showed the following position:

	Contract 1 (₹)	*Contract 2* (₹)
Contract price	4,00,000	2,70,000
Expenditure:		
Materials	72,000	58,000
Wages paid	1,10,000	1,12,000
General charges	4,000	2,800
Plant installed	20,000	16,000
Materials on hand	4,000	4,000
Wages accrued	4,000	4,000
Work certified	2,00,000	1,60,000
Cash received in respect thereof	1,50,000	1,20,000
Work done but not certified (at cost)	6,000	8,000

The plant was installed on the date of commencement of each contract; depreciation thereon is to be taken at 10% per annum.

Prepare the Contract Accounts in the tabular form and ascertain the profit or loss to be taken to Profit and Loss Account.

☞ *Solution*

Contract I

Particulars	*Amount*	*Particulars*		*Amount*
To material	72,000	By material in hand		4,000
To wages (1,10,000 + 4,000)	1,14,000	By work-in-progress		
To gen. charges	4,000	Work certified	2,00,000	
To plant	20,000	Work uncertified	6,000	2,06,000
To notional profit	18,000	By plant (20,000 – 2,000)		18,000
	2,28,000			2,28,000
To P & L *(working note-1)*	9,000	By notional profit		18,000
To work-in-progress (reserve)	9,000			
	18,000			18,000

☞ *Working Note-1*

Percentage of completion is 50% i.e. $\left(\frac{2,00,000}{4,00,000}\right)$

So, amount transferred to Profit & Loss Account is

$$= \text{Notional profit} \times 2/3 \times \frac{\text{Cash Received}}{\text{Work Certified}}$$

$$= 18,000 \times 2/3 \times \frac{1,50,000}{2,00,000} = 9,000$$

Contract 2

Particulars	*Amount*	*Particulars*		*Amount*
To material	58,000	By material on hand		4,000
To wages (1,12,000 + 4,000)	1,16,000	By WIP		
To general charges	2,800	Work certified	1,16,000	
To plant	16,000	Work uncertified	8,000	1,68,000
		By plant	16,000	
		Less: Dep. @ 10% for 6 months	800	15,200
		By loss tr. to P & L A/c		5,600
	1,92,800			1,92,800

Since there is a loss the entire loss will be transferred to Profit & Loss A/c.

✍ Example 10.9

The following trial balance was extracted on 31st Dec., 2020 from the books of SR Ltd. (Contractors):

	Debit (₹)	Credit (₹)
(1) Share capital (shares of ₹10 each)	—	3,51,800
(2) P & L A/c on 1st Jan., 2020	—	25,000
(3) Provision for dep. on machinery	—	63,000
(4) Cash received on A/c (Contract No. 7)	—	12,80,000
(5) Creditors	—	81,200
(6) Land and building (cost)	74,000	—
(7) Machinery (cost)	52,000	—
(8) Bank	45,000	—
(9) *Contract No. 7*:		
Materials	6,00,000	—
Direct labour	8,30,000	—
Expenses	40,000	—
Machinery sent at site	1,60,000	—
	18,01,000	18,01,000

Contract No. 7 commences on 1st Jan., 2020. The contract price is ₹24,00,000 and the contractee has so far paid ₹12,80,000 being 80% of the work certified. The cost of work done since certification is estimated at ₹16,000.

On 31st Dec., 2020, after the above trial balance was extracted, the machinery costing ₹42,000 was returned to store and material then on site was valued at ₹27,000. Provision is to be made for direct labour which is outstanding and for depreciation on machinery at 12.5% on cost.

You are required to prepare the Contract A/c and the Balance Sheet of the company as on 31st Dec., 2020 assuming this was the only contract in hand during the period.

☞ **Solution**

Contract No. 7 A/c

	₹		₹
To material sent to site	6,00,000	By work-in-progress :	
To direct labour	8,30,000	Work certified	16,00,000
To expenses	40,000	Work uncertified	16,000
To machinery sent to site	1,60,000	By machinery returned to store	42,000
To provision for dep. on machinery	20,000	By material at site	27,000
To balance c/d (notional profit)	1,53,000	By machinery at site	1,18,000
	18,03,000		18,03,000
To Profit & Loss A/c	81,600	By balance b/d (notional profit)	1,53,000
To work-in-progress (reserve)	71,400		
	1,53,000		1,53,000

Working Notes:

Since more than $\frac{1}{2}$ of the work has been certified, profit to be transferred to P & L. A/c can be calculated as follows:

$$₹1,53,000 \times \frac{2}{3} \times \frac{80}{100} = ₹81,600$$

Provision for Depreciation on Machinery A/c

	₹		₹
To balance c/d	89,500	By balance b/d	63,000
		By Contract No. 7 (12.5 % on ₹1,60,000)	20,000
		By P. & L. A/c (12.5% on ₹52,000)	6,500
	89,500		89,500

Profit and Loss A/c

	₹		₹
To provision for dep. on machinery	6,500	By balance b/d	25,000
To balance c/d	1,00,100	By Contract No. 7	81,600
	1,06,600		1,06,600

Work-in-Progress A/c

	₹		₹
To Contract No. 7:		By reserve	71,400
Work certified	16,00,000	By balance c/d	15,44,600
Work uncertified	16,000		
	16,16,000		16,16,000

Balance Sheet as on 31st Dec 2020

Liabilities	(₹)	*Assets*		(₹)
Share capital	3,51,800	Land and building		74,000
Profit & Loss A/c	1,00,100	Machinery cost		94,000
Provision for dep. on machinery	89,500	Bank		45,000
Creditors	81,200	Contract No. 7:		
		Work certified	16,00,000	
		Work uncertified	16,000	
			16,16,000	
		Less: Reserve	71,400	
			15,44,600	
		Less: Cash received	12,80,000	2,64,600

(Contd.)

Liabilities	(₹)	*Assets*	(₹)
		Material at site	27,000
		Machinery at site	1,18,000
	6,22,600		6,22,600

EXAMPLE 10.10

ABC Ltd. began to trade on 1st January, 2020. During 2020 the company was engaged on only one contract of which the contract price was ₹5,00,000. Of the plant and materials charged to the contract, plant which cost ₹5,000 and materials which cost ₹4,000 were lost in an accident. On 31st December, 2020, plant which cost ₹5,000 was returned to the store, the cost of work done but uncertified was ₹2,000 and materials costing ₹4,000 were in hand on site. Charge 10% depreciation on plant. Prepare Contract A/c and the Balance Sheet from the following:

Trial Balance as on 31st December, 2020

	₹	₹
Share capital		1,20,000
Creditors		10,000
Cash recd.		
(80% of work certified)		2,00,000
Land and building	43,000	
Bank balance	25,000	
Charged to contract:		
Materials	90,000	
Plant	25,000	
Wages	1,40,000	
Expenses	7,000	
	3,30,000	3,30,000

Solution

Contract A/c

	₹		₹	₹
To material	90,000	By W.I.P		
To plant	25,000	Work certified	2,50,000	
		Work uncertified	2,000	2,52,000
To wages	1,40,000	By P and L A/c (Ab. Loss)		
To expenses	7,000	Material	4,000	
To balance c/d	21,000	Plant	5,000	9,000
		By plant returned to stores		4,500

(Contd.)

	₹		₹	₹
		(Cost less depreciation (5000 – 500))		
		By plant at site		13,500
		By material at site		4,000
	2,83,000			2,83,000
To P and L A/c	11,200	By balance b/d		21,000
To reserve	9,800			
	21,000			21,000

Balance Sheet of ABC Ltd. as on 31. Dec. 2020

Liabilities		*Amount*	*Assets*		*Amount*
Share capital		1,20,000	Land and building		43,000
P and L A/c	11,200		Plant in store		4,500
Less: Ab. Loss	9,000	2200	Plant at the site		13,500
			Material at site		4,000
Creditors		10,000	Work in progress		
			Work certified	2,50,000	
			Work uncertified	2,000	
				2,52,000	
			Less: Reserve	9800	
				2,42,200	
			Less: Cash received	2,00,000	42,200
			Bank		25,000
		1,32,000			1,32,000

EXAMPLE 10.11

Modern Construction Ltd. obtained a contract No. B-37 for ₹40 lakh. The following balances and information relate to the contract for the year ended 31st March, 2020:

	1.4.2019 (₹)	31.3.2020 (₹)
• Work-in-progress:		
• Work certified	9,40,000	30,00,000
• Work uncertified	11,200	32,000
• Materials at site	8,000	20,000
• Accrued wages	5,000	3,000

Additional information relating to the year 2019–20 are:

	₹
• Materials issued from store	4,00,000
• Materials directly purchased	1,50,000
• Wages paid	6,00,000
• Architect's fees	51,000
• Plant hire charges	50,000
• Indirect expenses	10,000
• Share of general overheads for B-37	18,000
• Materials returned to store	25,000
• Materials returned to supplier	15,000
• Fines and penalties paid	12,000

The contractee pays 80% of work certified in cash. You are required to prepare:

(i) Contract Account showing clearly the amount of profits transferred to Profit and Loss Account.

(ii) Contractee's Account.

(iii) Balance Sheet

☞ ***Solution***

Books of Modern Constructions Ltd.

Contract No. B-37 Account for the year ended 31st March, 2020

		₹				₹
To	WIP b/d (9,40,000 + 11,200)	9,51,200	By	wages accrued b/d		5,000
To	Stock (materials) b/d	8,000	By	materials returned to store		25,000
To	Materials issued	4,00,000	By	materials returned to suppliers		15,000
To	Materials purchased	1,50,000	By	WIP c/d-		
To	Wages paid	6,00,000		Work certified	30,00,000	
To	Wages accrued c/d	3,000		Uncertified work	32,000	30,32,000
To	Architect's fees	51,000	By	Materials stock c/d		20,000
To	Plant hire charges	50,000				
To	Indirect expenses	10,000				
To	General overheads	18,000				
To	Notional profit c/d	8,55,800				
		30,97,000				30,97,000
To	Profit and loss account $\left(\frac{2}{3}\times 8,55,800\times\frac{80}{100}\right)$	4,56,427	By	Notional Profit b/f		8,55,800

(Contd.)

	₹		₹
To WIP reserve c/d	3,99,373		
	8,55,800		8,55,800

Note:
Fines and penalties are not shown in contract accounts.

Contractee's Account

		₹			₹
To	Balance c/d	24,00,000	By	balance b/d (80% of 9,40,000)	7,52,000
			By	bank	16,48,000
		24,00,000			24,00,000

Balance Sheet (Extract) as on 31.3.2020

		₹			₹
Profit and loss account	4,56,427		Materials stock at site		20,000
Less: Fines	12,000	4,44,427	Materials stock in stock		25,000
Outstanding wages		3,000	WIP:		
			Work certified	30,00,000	
			Work uncertified	32,000	
				30,32,000	
			Less: Advance	24,00,000	
				6,32,000	
			Less: WIP		
			Reserve	3,99,373	2,32,627

EXAMPLE 10.12

A construction company undertook a contract at an estimated price of ₹108 lakh, which includes a budgeted profit of ₹18 lakh. The relevant data for the year ended 31.03.2020 are as under:

	(₹ '000)
Materials issued to site	5,000
Direct wages paid	3,800
Plant hired	700
Site office costs	270
Materials returned from site	100
Direct expenses	500

(Contd.)

	(₹ '000)
Work certified	10,000
Progress payment received	7,200

A special plant was purchased specifically for this contract at ₹8,00,000 and after use on this contract till the end of 31.02.2020, it was valued at ₹5,00,000. This cost of materials at site at the end of the year was estimated at ₹18,00,000. Direct wages accrued as on 31.03.2020 was ₹1,10,000.

Required:
Prepare the Contract Account for the year ended 31st March, 2020 and compute the profit to be taken to the Profit and Loss account.

☞ *Solution*

Contract Account for the Year Ended 31st March, 2020

Dr. Particulars	Amount (₹)		*Cr.* Amount (₹)
	₹'000		*₹'000*
To materials issued to site	5,000	By materials at site	1,800
To direct wages	3,800	By materials returned	100
To wages accrued	110	By cost of contract	8,780
To plant hire	700		
To site office costs	270		
To direct expenses	500		
To depreciation of special plant	300		
	10,680		10,680
To cost of contract	8,780	By work certified	10,000
To profit and poss account *(Refer to working note-2)*	1,200		
To work-in-progress c/d (profit in reserve)	20		
	10,000		10,000

WORKING NOTES:

1. Percentage of contract completion $= \dfrac{\text{Cost of work certified}}{\text{Value of the contract}} \times 100$

$$= \frac{100 \text{ lakh}}{108 \text{ lakh}} \times 100 = 92.59\%$$

2. Since the percentage of contract completion is more than 90%, therefore, the profit to be taken to Profit and Loss Account can be computed by using the following formula.
   Profit to be taken to P and L A/c

$$= \text{Budgeted/Estimated Profit} \times \frac{\text{Cash received}}{\text{Work certified}} \times \frac{\text{Work certified}}{\text{Contract price}}$$

$$= 1{,}800 \times \frac{7{,}200}{10{,}000} \times \frac{10{,}000}{10{,}800}$$

$$= 1{,}800 \times \frac{7{,}200}{10{,}800}$$

$$= ₹1{,}200$$

EXAMPLE 10.13

Surya Construction Ltd. with a paid up share capital of ₹50 lakhs undertook a contract to construct MIG apartments. The work commenced on the contract on 1st April 2019. The contract price was ₹60 lakh. Cash received on account of the contract upto 31st March, 2020 was ₹18 lakh (being 90% of the work certified). Work completed but not certified was estimated at ₹1,00,000. As on 31st March 2020 material at site was estimated at ₹30,000, machinery at site costing ₹2,00,000 was returned to stores and wages outstanding were ₹5,000. Plant and machinery at site is to be depreciated at 5%.

The following were the ledger balances (Dr.) as per trial balance as on 31st March 2020:

	₹
Land and building	23,00,000
Plant and machinery (60% at site)	25,00,000
Furniture	60,000
Materials	14,00,000
Fuel and power	1,25,000
Site expenses	5,000
Office expenses	12,000
Rates and taxes	15,000
Cash at bank	1,33,000
Wages	2,50,000

Required:
Prepare the Contract Account and Balance Sheet.

Solution

Contract Account

Dr.				*Cr.*
Particulars		₹	*Particulars*	₹
To materials	14,00,000		By work certified	
Less: Material at site	(–) 30,000	13,70,000	$\frac{18{,}00{,}000 \times 100}{90} = 20{,}00{,}000$	

(Contd.)

Dr. Particulars		₹	Particulars		₹ *Cr.*
To wages	2,50,000		By work uncertified	= 1,00,000	21,00,000
Add O/s	+ 5,000	2,55,000			
To fuel and power		1,25,000			
To site expenses		5,000			
To office expenses		12,000			
To rates & taxes		15,000			
To depreciation on machine at site $\left(\frac{25,00,000 \times 60 \times 5}{100 \times 100}\right)$		75,000			
To balance c/d		2,43,000			
		21,00,000			21,00,00
To profit and loss account $2,43,000 \times \frac{1}{3} \times \frac{90}{100}$		72,900	By balance b/d		2,43,000
To reserve transferred to W/P		1,70,100			
		2,43,000			2,43,000

WORKING NOTES. 1. WORK CERTIFIED

	₹
$\frac{18,00,000 \times 100}{90} =$	20,00,000
Less: Cash received =	18,00,000
	2,00,000
Less: Profit transferred to WIP	1,70,100
	29,900
Add: Work uncertified	1,00,000
Work-in-progress	1,29,900

2. No depreciation has been charged on land and building and furniture as the same have not been shown at site.
3. Machinery returned to stores ₹2,00,000 – 5% of ₹2,00,000
   = ₹2,00,000 – 10,000
   = ₹1,90,000

Balance Sheet
as on 31st March 2020

Liabilities	*Amt.*	*Assets*		*Amt.*
Authorised and subscribed		Work in progress (1)		1,29,900
capital	—	Land and building		23,00,000
Issued and paid up capital	50,00,000	Machinery		
		at site	15,00,000	
O/S Wages	5,000	(–) Depreciation	(–) 75,000	
Profit and loss account	72,900		14,25,000	
		(–) Returned	(–) 1,90,000	12,35,000
		Machinery at office	10,00,000	
		(+) Returned from site	+ 1,90,000	11,90,000
		Furniture		60,000
		Bank		1,33,000
		Materials at site		30,000
	50,77,900			50,77,900

EXAMPLE 10.14

A contractor, who prepares his account on 31st December each year, commenced a contract on 1st April, 2020. The costing records concerning the said contract reveal the following information on 31st December, 2020.

Materials charged to site	₹2,58,100
Labour engaged	5,60,500
Foremen's salary	79,300

Plants costing ₹2,60,000 had been on site for 146 days. Their working life is estimated at 7 years and their final scrap value at ₹15,000. A supervisor, who is paid ₹4,000 p.m., has devoted approximately three-fourths of his time to this contract. The administrative and other expenses amounts to ₹1,40,000. Materials in hand at site on 31st December, 2020 cost ₹25,400. Some of the material costing ₹4,500 was found unsuitable and was sold for ₹4,000 and a part of the plant costing ₹5,500 (on 31.12.2020) unsuited to the contract was sold at a profit of ₹1,000.

The contract price was ₹22,00,000 but it was accepted by the contractor for ₹20,00,000. On 31st December, 2020 two-thirds of the contract was completed. Architect's certificate had been issued covering 50% of the contract price and ₹7,50,000 has so far been paid on account. Prepare contract account and state how much profit or loss should be included in the financial accounts on 31st December, 2020. Workings should be clearly given. Depreciation is charged on time basis.

☞ Solution

Contract Account
(From April 1, Dec. 31 2020)

Particulars	₹	Particulars	₹
To materials	2,58,100	By materials at site	25,400
To labour engaged	5,60,500	By materials sold	4,000
To foremen's salary	79,300	By profit and loss account	500
To supervisor's salary (WN:1)	27,000	(Loss on sale of materials)	
To depreciation of plant (WN: 2)	14,000	By cost of work done c/d	10,49,000
To administrative and other expenses	1,40,000		
	10,78,900		10,78,900
To cost of work done b/d	10,49,000	By work-in-progress:	
To profit c/d	2,13,250	Work certified (WN: 3)	10,00,000
		Work uncertified (WN: 3)	2,62,250
	12,62,250		12,62,250
To profit and loss account	1,06,625	By profit b/d	2,13,250
(2,13,250 × 2/3 × 7,50,000/10,00,000)			
To work-in-progress A/c (reserve)	1,06,625		
	2,13,250		2,13,250

Contractee's Account

To balance c/d	₹7,50,000	By bank	₹7,50,000

Extracts from Balance Sheet as on 3lst December, 2020

Liabilities	₹	Assets		₹
Profits and loss A/c (WN: 4)	1,07,125	Work-in-progress:		
		Work certified	10,00,000	
		Work uncertified	2,62,250	
			12,62,250	
		Less: Reserve	1,06,625	
			11,55,625	
		Less: Cash received	7,50,000	4,05,625
		Material at site		25,400
		Plant at site (WN: 5)		2,40,500

WORKING NOTES:

1. Supervisor's salary: 3/4 (9 months × ₹4,000) = ₹27,000
2. Depreciation of plant: (₹2,60,000 – ₹15,000)/7 years × 146/365 = ₹14,000
3. Cost of work uncertified:

Cost of 2/3rd of the contract is ₹10,49,000
The estimated cost of the total contract will amount to ₹10,49,000 × 3/2 = ₹15,73,500
Cost of 50% of the contract, as certified by the architect would be ₹15,73,500/2 = ₹7,86,750.
Cost of work done but uncertified would, therefore, be ₹10,49,000 – ₹7,86,750 = ₹2,62,250.

Profit and Loss Account

To contract account	₹500	By contract account	₹1,06,625
(Loss on sale of materials)		(Profit transferred)	
To balance c/d	1,07,125	By profit on sale of plant	1,000
	1,07,625		1,07,625

Plant Account

To balance b/d	₹2,60,000	By contract account (depreciation)	₹14,000
To profit and loss account	1,000	By bank (sale)	6,500
(Profit on sale of plant)		By balance c/d	2,40,500
	2,61,000		2,61,000

EXAMPLE 10.15

The contract ledger of Alpha Co. revealed the following expenditure on account of contract on 31st December, 2020.

	₹
Materials	2,10,000
Plant	70,000
Wages	2,93,000
Expenses	15,000
Establishment charges	10,000

The contract was started on 1st Jan., 2020 and the contract price was ₹10,00,000. Cash received to date was ₹4,80,000 representing 80% of the work certified, the remaining 20% being retained until completion. The value of plant on 31st December, 2020 was ₹20,000 and the value of material on hand was ₹6,000. The cost of work finished but not certified on the said date was ₹50,000.

Some of the materials, costing ₹20,000 were found unsuitable and were sold for ₹16,000 and a part of the plant costing ₹5,000 unsuited to the contract was sold at a profit of ₹1,000.

In order to calculate the profit made on the contract to 31st December, 2020 the contractors estimated further expenditure that would be incurred in completing the contract and took to the credit of profit and loss account for the year that proportion of the estimated net profit to be realised on the contract which the value of work certified bore to the contract price.

The estimates were as follows:

(a) that the contract would be completed by 30th June 2021.
(b) that a further sum of ₹30,000 would have to be spent on plant and the residual value of the plant on the completion of the contract would be ₹12,000.

(c) the materials in addition to those on hand on 31st December, 2020 would cost ₹1,00,000 and that further sundry expenses of ₹7,000 would be incurred.
(d) that the wages on the contract for the six months to June, 2021 would amount to ₹1,69,900.
(e) that the establishment charges would cost the same amount per month as in the previous year.
(f) that ₹18,000 would be sufficient to meet the contingencies.

Prepare the contract account for the year ended 31st December, 2020 and show your calculations of the profit to be credited to profit and loss account of the year.

Solution

Contract Account
(For the Year Ended 31.12.2020)

	₹			₹
To materials	2,10,000	By materials sold		16,000
To wages	2,93,000	By P and L A/c		
To plant	70,000	(Loss on material sold)		4,000
To Sundry expenses	15,000	By plant sold		6,000
To establishment charges	10,000			
To P and L A/c (profit on plant sold)	1,000	By plant on site		20,000
To balance c/d	1,03,000	By material in hand		6,000
		By work-in-progress account :		
		Work certified	6,00,000	
		Work uncertified	50,000	6,50,000
	7,02,000			7,02,000
2000, Dec. 31		2000 Dec. 31		
To P and L A/c:		By Balance b/d		1,03,000
$\left(\text{Profit ₹}\frac{1,09,100 \times 6,00,000}{10,00,000}\right)$	65,460			
To work-in-progress (balance of profit)	37,540			
	1,03,000			1,03,000

Estimated Contract Account on Completion

	₹		₹
To materials (2,10,000 + 1,00,000)	3,10,000	By materials sold	16,000
		By P and L A/c (loss on materials sold)	4,000
To wages (2,93,000 + 1,69,000)	4,62,900	By plant sold	6,000
To plant (70,000 + 30,000)	1,00,000	By plant at the close	12,000

(Contd.)

	₹		₹
To P and L A/c: Plant sold	1,000	By contractee's account	
To Sundry exp. (15,000 + 7,000)	22,000	Contract price	10,00,000
To establishment charges (10,000 + 5,000)	15,000		
To contingencies	18,000		
To P and L A/c:			
Profit on completion estimated	1,09,100		
	10,38,000		10,38,000

EXAMPLE 10.16 (Escalation Clause)

Deluxe Limited undertook a contract for ₹5,00,000 on 1st July 2019. On 30th June 2020, when the accounts were closed, the following details about the contract were gathered:

	₹
Materials purchased	1,00,000
Wages paid	45,000
General expenses	10,000
Plant purchased	50,000
Materials on hand 30.6.2020	25,000
Wages accrued 30.6.2020	5,000
Work certified	2,00,000
Cash received	1,50,000
Work uncertified	15,000
Depreciation of plant	5,000

The above contract contained an escalation clause which reads as follows:

"In the event of prices of materials and rates of wages increase by more than 5% the contract price will be increased accordingly by 25% of the rise in the cost of materials and wages beyond 5% in each case".

It was found that since the date of signing the agreement the prices of materials and wage rates increased by 25%. The value of the work certified does not take into account the effect of the above clause.

Prepare the contract account. Workings should form part of the answer.

Solution

Contract Account

	₹		₹
To materials	1,00,000	By work-in-progress:	
To wages (45,000 + 5,000)	50,000	Work certified	2,00,000

(Contd.)

	₹		₹
To general expenses	10,000	Work uncertified	15,000
To depreciation on plant	5,000	Contract escalation	
To profit:		*(Working note-1)*	5,000
Transferred to P and L *(working note-2)*	20,000	By materials in hand	25,000
Taken to WIP	60,000		
	2,45,000		2,45,000

WORKING NOTES:

1. Escalation charges:

(a) Materials

	Total increase (₹)	Up to 5% (₹)	Beyond (₹)
Effect of increase in price of materials	75,000 × 25/125 = 15,000	75,000 × 5/125 = 3,000	= 12,000

(b) Wages

Effect of increase in wage rates	50,000 × 25/125 = 10,000	50,000 × 5/125 = 2,000	= 8,000
Total increase (a) + (b)	= 25,000	= 5,000	=20,000
Increase in contract Price (25% of increase beyond 5%)	20,000 × 25/100	= ₹5,000	

2. Computation of profit transferred to profit and loss account: Since more than 1/4th but less than 1/2 of the contract has been completed, 1/3 of the profit earned as reduced on cash basis has been transferred to profit and loss account.

$$80,000 \times \frac{1}{3} \times \frac{1,50,000}{2,00,000} = ₹20,000$$

EXAMPLE 10.17 (Escalation Clause)

SB Constructions Limited has entered into a big contract at an agreed price of ₹1,50,00,000 subject to an escalation clause for material and labour as spent out on the contract and corresponding actuals are as follows:

	Standard		*Actual*	
Material	*Quantity (Tonnes)*	*Rate Per Tonne*	*Quantity (Tonnes)*	*Rate Per Tonne*
		(₹)		(₹)
A	3,000	1,000	3,400	1,100
B	2,400	800	2,300	700
C	500	4,000	600	3,900
D	100	30,000	90	31,500

(Contd.)

Material	Standard		Actual	
	Quantity (Tonnes)	Rate Per Tonne	Quantity (Tonnes)	Rate Per Tonne
Labour:	Hours	Hourly Rate (₹)	Hours	Hourly Rate (₹)
L_1	60,000	15	56,000	18
L_2	40,000	30	38,000	35

You are required to:

(i) Give your analysis of admissible escalation claim and determine the final contract price payable.

(ii) Prepare the contract account, if the all expenses other than material and labour related to the contract are ₹13,45,000.

☞ Solution

Statement Showing Additional Claim due to Escalation Clause

Material	Std. Qty/Hours	Std. Rate	Actual Rate	Variation in Rate (₹)	Escalation Claim (₹)
	(a)	(b)	(c)	(d) = (c–b)	(e) = (a × d)
A	3000	1000	1100	+100	+3,00,000
B	2400	800	700	–100	–2,40,000
C	500	4000	3900	–100	–50000
D	100	30000	31500	+1500	+1,50,000
	Material escalation claim				1,60,000
Labour:					
L_1	60,000	15	18	+3	+1,80,000
L_2	40,000	30	35	+5	+2,00,000
	Labour escalation claim				3,80,000

Statement Showing Final Contract Price

	₹	₹
Agreed contract price		1,50,00,000
Add: Agreed escalation claim:		
Material cost	1,60,000	
Labour cost	3,80,000	5,40,000
Final Contract Price		1,55,40,000

Contract Account

Dr.	₹		Cr. ₹
To material:		By contractee's A/c	1,55,40,000
A–3,400 × ₹1,100			
B–2,300 × ₹700			
C–600 × ₹3,900			
D–90 × ₹31,500	1,05,25,000		
To Labour:			
L_1–56,000 × ₹18			
L_2 –38,000 × ₹35	23,38,000		
To other expenses	13,45,000		
To profit and loss account	13,32,000		
	1,55,40,000		1,55,40,000

BATCH COSTING

As stated earlier, a job order can be for an item or a number of items. In the case of the latter, the order is strictly a batch and the total batch cost must be divided by the quantity to give the cost per item. While job costing is concerned with the costing of jobs that are made to a customer's particular requirements, batch costing is used where articles are manufactured in definite batches and held in stock for sale to customers generally. When each order is finished/completed, the cost sheet is totalled and the total cost divided by the quantity produced to show the cost per article or per dozen, etc.

ECONOMIC BATCH QUANTITY

"What should be the optimum size of a batch?" is an important question. If the size is higher, the unit costs may tend to decline, but the units in inventory will go up. The size of the batch influences the clerical and other machine set-up costs also. Therefore, an economic batch quantity should be determined. Generally, the following formula is used which is similar in nature to economic order quantity.

$$E = \sqrt{\frac{2U.S}{C\left(1-\frac{U}{R}\right)}}$$

where E = Economic order quantity
U = Annual usage in units
S = Set-up and order processing costs
R = Annual rate of production
C = Cost of carrying one unit in inventory for one year

If the production of the batch is done over a short period, $\frac{U}{R}$ loses its significance and only then the following formula is applied:

$$E = \sqrt{\frac{2U.S}{C}}$$

EXAMPLE 10.18

A jobbing factory has undertaken to supply 200 pieces of a component per month for the ensuing six months. Every month a batch order is opened against which materials and labour hours are booked at actuals. Overheads are levied at a rate per labour hour. The selling price contracted for is ₹8 per piece. From the following data, present the cost and profit per piece of each batch order and overall position of the order for 1,200 pieces.

for excel template, scan

Month	*Batch Output*	*Material Cost* (₹)	*Direct Wages* (₹)	*Direct Labour* (hr)
Jan.	210	650	120	240
Feb.	200	640	140	280
March	220	680	150	280
April	180	630	140	270
May	200	700	150	300
June	220	720	160	320

The other details are:

Month	*Chargeable Expenses* (₹)	*Direct Labour* (hr)
Jan.	12,000	4,800
Feb.	10,560	4,400
March	12,000	5,000
April	10,580	4,600
May	13,000	5,000
June	12,000	4,800

Solution

Cost Sheet for Six Months Ending 30th June

(Output 1230 Units)

Month	*Jan.*	*Feb.*	*March*	*April*	*May*	*June*	*Total*
Batch output (in units)	210	200	220	180	200	220	1,230
Sales value (in ₹)	1,680	1,600	1,760	1440	1,600	1,760	9,840

(Contd.)

Month	*Jan.*	*Feb.*	*March*	*April*	*May*	*June*	*Total*
Cost of materials (in ₹)	650	640	680	630	700	720	4,020
Direct wages (in ₹)	120	140	150	140	150	160	860
Chargeable expenses (in ₹)	600	672	672	621	780	800	4,145
Total cost (in ₹)	1,370	1,452	1,502	1,391	1, 630	1, 680	9,025
Total cost per unit (in ₹)	6.52	7.26	6.83	7.73	8.15	7.64	7.34
Profit per batch (in ₹)	310	148	258	49	–30	80	815
Profit per unit (in ₹)	1.48	0.74	1.17	0.27	–0.15	0.36	0.66

Overall position of the order for 1,200 units:

Sales value of 1,200 units @ ₹8 per unit	₹9,600
Total cost for 1,200 units @ ₹7.34 per unit	₹8,808
Profit	₹792

Note: Chargeable expenses have been charged to different batches on the basis of direct labour hours for different months; for example

$$\text{For January } \frac{₹12{,}000}{4{,}800} \times 240 = 600$$

Example 10.19

A work order for 500 units of a commodity has to pass through four different machines of which the machines hour rates are

	₹
No. I	1.25
No. II	3.00
No. III	4.00
No. IV	2.50

The following expenses have been incurred on the work order. Materials ₹20,000 and wages ₹1,500.

Machine	I	Worked for	200 hours
Machine	II	Worked for	300 hours
Machine	III	Worked for	240 hours
Machine	IV	Worked for	100 hours

After the work order had been executed, materials worth ₹1,000 were returned to stores.

Office overheads are to be estimated @ 60% of works cost: 10% of the production is going to be discarded, being unsatisfactory for which 1/2 the amount can be realised from sale in the junk market. Find out the rate of selling price per unit if 20% profit on selling price is desired.

☞ ***Solution***

Statement Showing Cost and Selling Price for 500 Units

	₹	₹	₹
Material used	20,000		
— Less returned	1,000		19,000
Wages			1,500
Prime cost			20,500
Work overhead: Hours × Rate			
Machine No. I 200 × ₹1.25		250	
Machine No. II 300 × ₹3.00		900	
Machine No. III 240 × ₹4.00		960	
Machine No. IV 100 × ₹2.50		250	2,360
Work cost			22,860
Office overheads: 60% of works cost			13,716
			36,576
Less: Sale of discarded units			
10 % discarded	₹3,657.60		
Half to be realised	1,828.80		
Loss	1,828.80		1,828.80
Total cost			34,747.20
Profit 20% on selling price or 25% on cost			8,686.80
Sales			43,434.00

Selling price per unit

$$\frac{₹43,434}{500} = ₹86.86 \text{ approx.}$$

Note: It has been presumed that net resulted output is 500 units, that is, the quantum of work order, after the discarded units have been adjusted for.

Theory Questions

1. (i) What is the nature of job costing? How are the costs recorded on job orders?
   (ii) Explain the meaning of contract costing and batch costing.
2. Indicate how you would deal with the following items:
   (a) Plant and machinery purchased and used on contract work.
   (b) Amounts received from contractee.
   (c) Materials lying unused at site.
3. (i) Discuss the implications of cost-plus contracts from the viewpoint of:
   (a) Manufacturer
   (b) Customer
   (ii) What is the relevance of the escalation clause provided in a contract?

4. Describe briefly the nature of accounting problems associated with job costing.
5. How will you treat profit on incomplete contracts in cost accounts?
6. What do you understand by cost-plus contract and escalation clause in contract costing?
7. Distinguish between job costing and process costing.
8. Explain the following:
   (i) Notional profit in contract costing.
   (ii) Retention money in contract costing.
9. Discuss the process of estimating profit/loss on incomplete contracts.
10. Explain job costing and contract costing.
11. What is meant by retention money in context of contract costing? What is its objective?
12. Explain commonly accepted practice for computation of profit on incomplete contracts.

Self-Evaluation Questions

Choose the correct answer for the following multiple-choice questions:

1. Which of the following production activities would be most likely to employ job order costing?
   (a) Ship building (b) Candy manufacturing
   (c) Toy manufacturing (d) Crude oil refining
2. In job-order costing, the basic document to accumulate and ascertain the cost of each order is the
   (a) Purchase order (b) Requisition sheet
   (c) Invoice (d) Job cost sheet
3. Which of the following will not be used in job-order costing?
   (a) Standards
   (b) Marginal costing
   (c) Averaging of direct labour and material rates
   (d) Factory overhead allocation based on direct labour hours applied to the job.

Problems

Job Costing

1. The following information for the year ending December 31, 2020 is obtained from the books and records of a factory:

	Completed Jobs	*Work-in-Progress*
	₹	₹
Raw materials supplied from stores	90,000	30,000
Wages	1,00,000	40,000
Chargeable expenses	10,000	4,000
Materials transferred to work-in-progress	2,000	2,000
Materials returned to stores	1,000	

Factory overheads are 80% of wages and office overhead is 25% of factory cost.

The value of executed contracts during 2021 was ₹4,10,000. Prepare the:

(i) consolidated completed jobs account, and (ii) consolidated work-in-progress account.

Ans: (i) Profit ₹63,750
(ii) Balance c/d in WIP ₹1,35,000

2. A factory uses a job costing system. The following data are available from the books at the year ending 31st March 2020.

	₹
Direct material	9,00,000
Direct wages	7,50,000
Profit	6,09,000
Selling and distribution overhead	5,25,000
Administrative overhead	4,20,000
Factory overhead	4,50,000

Required:

(a) Prepare a cost sheet indicating the prime cost, works cost, production cost, cost of sales and sales value.

(b) In 2020–21, the factory has received an order for a number of jobs. It is estimated that the direct materials would be ₹12,00,000 and direct labour would cost ₹7,50,000. What would be the price for these jobs if the factory intends to earn the same rate of profit on sales, assuming that the selling and distribution overhead has gone up by 15%. The factory recovers factory overhead as a percentage of direct wages and administrative and selling and distribution overhead as a percentage of works cost, based on the cost rates prevalent in the previous year.

Ans: (a) Prime cost ₹16,50,000, Works cost ₹21,00,000, Production cost ₹25,20,000, Cost of sales ₹30,45,000, Sales value ₹36,54,000. (b) Sales value ₹42,84,000, Profit ₹7,14,000.

3. Honesty Engineering Works has a machining shop in which it manufactures two auto parts, *P1* and *P2* out of forging *F1* and *F2*. For the quarter ending December 2020, following cost data are available:

	₹
Consumption of raw materials: *F1*	1,50,000
: *F2*	2,00,000
Wages and salaries	1,53,000
Stores and spares	12,000
Repairs and maintenance	15,000
Power	16,000
Insurance	8,000
Depreciation	50,000
Factory overheads	68,000
Administration overhead	64,400
Distribution overheads	75,000
Total cost	8,11,400

You are given following further information:

(a) Production and sale of *P1* and *P2* were as under:

	P1	*P2*
Production (pieces)	6,000	4,000
Sales of above pieces (₹)	4,80,000	5,20,000

(b) Direct wages paid were ₹36,000 in case of *P1* and ₹32,000 for *P2*. This basis is used for apportioning wages and salaries and factory overheads. Following machine-hours were utilised in production of these products:

P1	550
P2	450

(c) Stores and spare, repairs and maintenance, power, insurance and depreciation are charged to cost of both the products on the basis of machine hours used.
Administrative overheads are apportioned on the basis of respective conversion costs while distribution overheads on the basis of their sales realisation.

(d) All the production was sold out:

Required:

Prepare cost sheets of both the products and work out profit earned on each of them.

Ans: Profit P1 ₹86,940, P2 ₹1,01,660

4. A manufacturing company has an installed capacity of 1,20,000 units per annum. The cost structure of the product manufactured is an under:

Variable cost (per unit)	
Material	₹8.00
Labour (subject to a minimum of ₹56,000 per month)	₹8.00
overheads	₹3.00
Fixed overheads	₹1,04,000 per annum
Semi-variable overheads	₹48,000 per annum at 60% capacity, which increase by ₹6,000 per annum for increase of every 10% of the capacity utilisation or any part thereof.

The capacity utilisation for the next year is estimated at 60% for 2 months, 75% for 6 months and 80% for the balance part of the year. If the company is planning to have a profit of 25% on the selling price, calculate the estimated selling price for each unit of production. Assume there is no opening or closing stock.

Ans: Selling Price per unit ₹28.

5. The expenses of a new machine for a particular month are as under:
(i) Power ₹50,000, (ii) maintenance and repairs ₹10,000, machine operator's wages ₹2,000, (iv) supervision ₹6,000 (v) Depreciation ₹40,000. Other particulars are given below:

Product	*Rate of Production (Units/hr.)*	*Production Units*
A	30	1,800
B	10	500
C	6	300
D	4	260

The entire production was offered to the Government on "cost-plus 20%" basis. Material cost per unit are: *A*: ₹40; *B*: ₹60; *C*: ₹100; and *D*: ₹300. Prepare a statement showing product wise "cost" and "offer price".

Ans:

	Products			
	A	*B*	*C*	*D*
Cost per unit (₹)	56	108	180	420
Offer price (₹)	67.20	129.60	216	504

6. In a manufacturing company, a product passes through five operations. The output of the fifth operation becomes the finished product. The output rejection, output, and labour and overheads of each operation for a period are as under:

Operation	*Input (Units)*	*Rejection (Units)*	*Output (Units)*	*Labour and Overhead (₹)*
1	21,600	5,400	16,200	1,94,400
2	20,250	1,350	18,900	1,41,750
3	18,900	1,350	17,550	2,45,700
4	23,400	1,800	21,600	1,40,400
5	17,280	2,880	14,440	86,400

You are required to:

(a) Determine the input required in each operation for one unit of the final output.

(b) Calculate the labour and overhead cost at each operation for one unit of the final output and the total labour and overhead cost of all operations for one unit of the final output.

Ans:

	Operations				
	1	2	3	4	5
(a) Input required (units)	2.00	1.50	1.40	1.30	1.20
(b) Labour and overhead per unit of output (₹)	18.00	10.50	18.20	7.80	6.00

Contract Costing

7. An expenditure of ₹1,94,000 has been incurred on a contract to the end of 31st March, 2020. The value of work certified is ₹2,20,000. The cost of work done but not yet certified is ₹6,000. It is estimated that the contract will be completed by 30th June, 2020 and an additional expenditure of ₹40,000 will have to be incurred to complete the contract. The total estimated expenditure on the contract is to include a provision of $2\frac{1}{2}$% for contingencies. The contract price is ₹2,80,000 and ₹2,00,000 has been realised in cash up to 31st March, 2020.

Calculate the proportion of profit to be taken to the Profit and Loss Account as on 31st March, 2000 under different methods.

Ans: Total notional profit ₹32,000;
Profit to be taken to P and L A/c
(a) ₹31,546.42 (b) using conservative method ₹28678.57

8. SV Construction Ltd. has obtained a contract for construction of a bridge. The value of the contract is ₹12 lakhs and the work commenced on 1st October, 2019. The following details are shown in their books for the year ending 30th September 2020.

	₹
Plant purchased	60,000
Wages paid	3,40,000
Material issued to site	3,36,000

(Contd.)

	₹
Direct expenses	8,000
General overheads apportioned	32,000
Wages accrued as on 30.9.2020	2,800
Materials at site as on 30.9.2020	4,000
Direct expenses accrued as on 30.9.2020	1,200
Work not certified at cost	14,000
Cash received being 80% of work certified	6,00,000

Life of plant purchased is 5 years and scrap value is nil.

1. Prepare the contract account for the year ending 30th September, 2020
2. Show the amount of profit which you consider might be fairly taken on the contract and how you have calculated it.

Ans: Profit taken to Profit and Loss A/c ₹19,200.

9. The following particulars relate to a contract account of Ajit Engineers.

	₹
Material sent to site	85,349
Labour	74,375
Plant	15,000
Direct expenses	3,167
Establishment charges	4,126
Material returned to store	549
Work certified	1,95,000
Work not certified	4,500
Material in hand at the end of the year	1,883
Wages accrued	2,400
Direct expenditure accrued	240
Value of plant at the end of the year	11,000
Contract price	2,50,000
Cash received	1,80,000

You are required to prepare:

(i) Contract account showing profit transferred to profit and loss account: and

(ii) Contractee account

Ans: Notional profit ₹28,275

10. An amount of ₹19,80,000 was incurred on a contract work up to 31.03.2020. Certificates have been received to date to the value of ₹24,00,000 against which ₹21,60,000 has been received in cash. The cost of work done but not certified amounted to ₹45,000. It is estimated that by spending an additional amount of ₹1,20,000 (including provision for contingencies) the work can be completed in all respects in another two months. The agreed contract price of the work is ₹25 lakhs. Compute a conservative estimate of the profit to be taken to the profit and loss account.

11. The following is the summarised information relating to contract accounts number 100:

	₹
Contract price	6,00,000
Wages	1,64,000
General expenses	8,600
Materials	1,20,000
Cash received (80% of certified work)	2,40,000
Materials at site	10,000
Plant	20,000

Included in the above information are wages ₹3,500, materials ₹4,000 and other expenses₹2,500 which were incurred since certification. Depreciate plant at 10%. Prepare contract A/c

Ans: Profit transferred to Profit and Loss A/c, ₹13,547

12. The following is the trial balance of Premier Construction Company engaged on the execution of Contract No. 1047 for the year 31st Dec., 2020:

		₹
Contractee's account (amount received)		3,00,000
Buildings	1,60,000	
Creditors		72,000
Bank balance	35,000	
Capital account		5,00,000
Materials	2,00,000	
Wages	1,80,000	
Expenses	47,000	
Plant	2,50,000	
	8,72,000	8,72,000

The work on contract 1047 was commenced on 1st January 2020. Material costing ₹1,70,000 were sent to the site of the contract but those of ₹6,000 were destroyed in an accident. Wages of ₹1,80,000 were paid during the year. Plant costing ₹50,000 was used on the contract all through the year. Plant with a cost of ₹2 lakhs was used from 1st January to 30th September and was then returned to stores. Materials of the cost of ₹4,000 were at site on 31st December, 2020.

The contract was for ₹6,00,000 and the contractee pays 75% of the work certified. Work certified was 80% of the total contract work at the end of 2020. Uncertified work was estimated at ₹15,000 on 31st December, 2020. Expenses are charged to contract at 25% of wages. Plant is to be depreciated at 10% p.a.

Prepare Contract No. 1047 account for the year 2020 and make out the Balance Sheet as on 31st December, 2020 in the books of Premier Construction Company.

Ans: Profit taken to Profit and Loss A/c, ₹45,000
B/s total `6,04,000

13. AKP Builders Ltd. commenced a contract on April 1, 2019. The total contract was for ₹5,00,000. Actual expenditure for the period April 1, 2019 to March 31, 2020 and estimated expenditure for April 1, 2020 to December 31, 2020 are given below:

	2019–20 (Actuals)	2019–20 (9 Months) (Estimated)
Material issued	90,000	85,750
Labour: paid	75,000	87,325
Outstanding at the end	6,250	8,300
Plant	25,000	–
Sundry expenses: Paid	7,250	6,875
Prepaid at the end	625	–
Establishment charges	14,625	

A part of the material was unsuitable and was sold for ₹18,125 (Cost being ₹15,000) and a part of plant was scrapped and disposed of for ₹2,875. The value of plant at site on 31 March, 2020 was ₹7,750 and the value of material at site was ₹4,250. Cash received on account to date was ₹1,75,000 representing 80% of the work certified. The cost of work uncertified was valued at ₹27,375.

The contractor estimated further expenditure that would be incurred in completion of the contract:

- The contract would be completed by 31st December, 2020.
- A further sum of ₹31,250 would have to be spent on the plant and the residual value of the plant on the completion of the contract would be ₹3,750.
- Establishment charges would cost the same amount per month as in the previous year.
- ₹10,800 would be sufficient to provide for contingencies.

Required:

Prepare contract account and calculate estimated total profit on this contract. Profit transferrable to the profit and loss account is to be calculated by reducing estimated profit in proportion of work certified and contract price.

Ans: Profit taken to Profit and Loss A/c, ₹29,960.55

14. Pioneer Construction Company Ltd. obtained a contract for the erection of a multi-storey building. Building operations started in July 2020. The contract price was ₹9,00,000. On 30th June 2021, the end of the financial year, the cash received on account was ₹3,60,000, being 80% of the amount on the surveyor's certificate.

The following additional information is given:

	₹
Materials issued to contract	1,80,000
Materials on hand at site as on 30th June 2021	7,500
Wages	2,46,600
Plant purchased specially for contract and to be depreciated at 10% per annum	30,000
Direct expenses incurred	12,900
General overhead allocated to contract	7,600
Work finished but not yet certified: cost	15,000

You are required to prepare the contract account and statement showing the profit on the contract to 30th June 2021, indicating what proportion of the profit the company would be justified in taking to the credit of the profit and loss account, and to show what entries in respect of the contract would appear in the balance sheet.

Ans:	Profit taken to P & L A/c	₹ 11,946
	Balance sheet	
	Plant	₹ 27,000
	WIP	₹1,02,046

15. The following information relates to a building contract for ₹10,00,000.

	2019	*2020*
	₹	₹
Materials issued	3,00,000	84,000
Direct wages	2,30,000	1,05,000
Direct expenses	22,000	10,000
Indirect expenses	6,000	1,400
Work certified	7,50,000	10,00,000
Work uncertified	8,000	—
Materials at site	5,000	7,000
Plant issued	14,000	2,000
Cash recd. from contractor	6,00,000	10,00,000

The value of plant at the end of 2019 and 2020 was ₹7,000 and ₹5,000 respectively.
Prepare: (i) the contract account, and (ii) contractee account for two years—2019 and 2020 taking into consideration such profit for transfer to the profit and loss account as you think proper.

Ans: Profit taken to Profit and Loss account 2019, ₹1,05,600; 2020, ₹1,32,000

16. Alcon Construction Company Ltd. commenced its business of construction on 1.1.2020. The trial balance as on 31.12.2020 showed the following balances:

	Dr. (₹)	*Cr.* (₹)
Paid up share capital		1,00,000
Cash received on account of contract (80% of work certified)		1,20,000
Land and buildings	30,000	
Machinery at cost (75% at site)	40,000	
Bank	4,000	
Materials at site	40,000	
Direct labour	55,000	
Expenses at site	2,000	
Lorries and vehicles	30,000	
Furniture	1,000	
Office equipment	10,000	
Postage and telegrams	500	

(Contd.)

	Dr. (₹)	Cr. (₹)
Office expenses	2,000	
Rates and taxes	3,000	
Fuel and power	2,500	
	2,20,000	2,20,000

The contract price is ₹3,00,000 and work certified is ₹1,50,000. The work completed "since certification" is estimated at ₹1,000 (at cost). Machinery costing ₹2,000 was returned to stores at the end of the year. Stock of materials at site on 31.12.2020 was of the value of ₹5,000. Wages outstanding were ₹200. Depreciation on machinery was at 10%.

You are required to calculate the profit from the contract and show how the work-in-progress will appear in the balance sheet as on 31.12.2020.

Ans: Profit taken to profit and loss account = ₹28,427
Amount shown in balance sheet = ₹6,127

17. The PQR Co. Ltd. undertakes to build a cooling tower at a contract price of ₹6,75,000. It is estimated that it will take two years to complete, and work is commenced on 1st May 2019. The company's year ended on 30th September, and on that date, in 2020 the position of the contract was as follows:

	Certificates to Sept. 15, 2020		₹4,75,000
Less:	10% retention		47,500
			4,27,500
Add: Extra work over contract as agreed		₹3,100	
	Last time	230	3,330
	This time		4,30,830
	Less: Cash paid on account		4,08,330
Amount now due (and paid Oct. 24, 2020)			₹22,500

Expenditure on the contract was as follows:

Materials sent by suppliers direct to site	₹2,12,000
Materials sent from plant and stores yard	₹1,500
Wages	₹1,05,000
Haulage of plant	2,400
Expenses incurred on contract	3,800
Establishment charges apportioned to contract	30,300

On 30th September 2020, it is estimated that materials on site amounted to ₹3,050.
During the contract, plant to the value of ₹35,000 was transferred from the site. The plant remaining on site at 30th September was valued at ₹32,000.

The amount of work done (at cost) between the date of the last certificate and the end of the financial year was estimated ₹10,250.

PQR Co. Ltd. is careful as to the amount of profit to be taken on uncompleted contracts, and as only a few months' work had been done at 30th September 2019 no profit at all was then taken.

(a) You are required, supposing the company were to take credit for profit on the contract, to:

(i) Calculate the amount that you consider may be fairly taken into the firm's accounts at 30th September 2020;

(ii) Calculate the work-in-progress figure. How would this new figure be shown in the balance sheet of PQR Co. Ltd.?

(b) Show the contract account in the firm's costing ledger to record the above facts.

Ans: Profit taken to profit and loss account = ₹65,240
Work-in-progress = ₹4,39,190

18. A contractor has entered into a long-term contract at an agreed price of ₹1,75,000 subject to an escalation clause for materials and wages as spelt out in the contract and corresponding actual are as follows:

Materials	*Standard*	*Actual*
A	5,000 kg. @ ₹5/-	5,050 kg. @ ₹4.80
B	3,500 kg. @ ₹8/-	3,450 kg. @ ₹7.90
C	2,500 lt. @ ₹6/-	2,600 lt. @ ₹6.60
Wages:		
P	2,000 hr. @ ₹7/-	2,100 hr. ₹@ 7.20
Q	2,500 hr. @ ₹7.50/-	2,450 hr. ₹@ 7.50
R	3,000 hr. @ ₹6.50/-	3,100 hr. ₹@ 6.60

Reckoning the full actual consumption of materials and wages, the company has claimed a final price of ₹1,77,360. Give your analysis of the admissible escalation claim and indicate the final price payable.

Ans: Final price payable ₹1,75,850

Batch Costing

19. Component SW-10X is made entirely in machine shop No. ASW II. Material cost is ₹20 per component. Each component takes 6 minutes to produce and the machine operator is paid ₹15 per hour. Machine-hour rate is ₹72 per hour. The setting up of the machine to produce the equipment takes 3 hours for the operator. You are required to prepare cost sheets cost sheets showing the setting-up costs and the production costs, both in total (that is, for the batch) and per component, assuming a batch size of (a) 100 components, (b) 150 components, and (c) 200 components.

Ans:

	Batch Size		
	100	150	200
Total cost (₹)	3,131	4,566	6,301

20. All Play and No. Work Ltd. is specialists in the manufacture of sports goods. They manufacture croquet mallets but purchase the wooden balls, iron arches and stakes required to complete a croquet set.

Mallets consist of a head and handle. The handle uses 1.5 board feet per handle at ₹40 per board foot. The spoilage loss is negligible for manufacture of handles. Heads frequently split and create considerable scrap. A head requires 0.20 board feet of high quality lumber costing ₹70 per board foot. Spoilage normally works out to 20% of the completed heads, 4% of the spoiled heads can be salvaged and sold as scrap at ₹10 per spoiled head.

In the department, machining and assembling the mallets, 12 men work 8 hours per day for 25 days in a month. Each worker can machine and assemble 15 mallets per uninterrupted 50 minutes time frame. In each 8-hour working day, 15 minutes are allowed for coffee-break, 8 minutes on an average for training, and 9 minutes for supervisory instructions. Besides, 10% of each day is booked as idle time to cover checking in and checking out, changing operations, getting material and other miscellaneous matters. Workers are paid at a comprehensive rate of ₹6 per hour.

The department is geared to produce 40,000 mallets per month and the normally expenses of the department are as under:

	₹
Finishing and painting the mallets	50,800
Lubricating oil for cutting machines	300
Depreciation for cutting machines	700
Repairs and maintenance	100
Power to run the machines	200
Plant manager's salary	2,700
Other overheads allocated to the department	1,20,000

As the mallets are machined and assembled in lots of 500, prepare a total cost sheet for one lot and advise the management on the selling price to be fixed per mallet in order to ensure a minimum of 20% margin on selling price.

Ans: Selling price to be fixed at ₹1,02,292

CASE STUDY

1. Contract Costing: Case of Almeria Construction

Almeria Construction Pvt. Ltd. was a renowned construction company in Bangalore. Since its incorporation in 2004 with a paid up capital of ₹2,50,00,000, it had completed many projects in and around the city like Almeria Infinite, Boulevard, Almeria Greens, and Almeria Landscape, Stone Park etc. Currently in the year 2018–19, it was working on three projects simultaneously–Almeria Emerald (₹ 3,00,000 contract price) in Banshankari; Almeria Villas (contract price—₹10,00,00,000) in Koramangala and Almeria Habitat (Contract price—₹6,00,00,000) in Whitefield.

The contractor and the owner—Ashwani Bhadoria used to depend on his chief accountant Manish Pandey for recording all the contract account work. Manish used to get the costs data from all the construction sites from the site engineers and junior accountants posted there. He had received the same for the year 2018–19 as well, as given below:

Particulars	*Emerald, Banshakari*	*Villas, Koramangala*	*Habitat, Whitefield*
Direct wages	10,25,000	16,00,000	42,00,000
Rates and taxes	70,000	85,233	98,250
Direct expenses	20,500	35,500	58,547

(Contd.)

Particulars	*Emerald, Banshakari*	*Villas, Koramangala*	*Habitat, Whitefield*
General overhead allocated	60,000	1,00,000	1,25,000
Fuel and power expenses	6,25,000	8,50,000	11,30,000
Materials issued	70,00,000	1,00,00,000	1,86,00,000
Cash received	90,00,000	2,04,00,000	2,56,00,000
Cash received as percentage of work certified	90%	85%	80%
Work not certified	5,00,000	12,00,000	20,00,000

As on 31st March, the wages outstanding were ₹25,000 and ₹10,000 for Banshankari and Koramangala site. The materials at site at the year-end was estimated at ₹150,000 for Emerald, ₹6,00,000 for Villas and ₹8,00,000 for Habitat. The plant and machinery of ₹1,25,00,000 had been in use for the entire year at these three sites for 3 months, 4 months and 5 months respectively and it was returned back only on the last day. The company had a policy of depreciating the plant and machinery at site at 10% p.a.

The other financial details with respect to Almeria Construction Pvt Ltd were as follows:

Cash and bank balances	26,81,000
Furniture	12,00,000
Land and building	3,65,00,000
Bank loan (@ 8% interest paid annually on 31st March	2,00,00,000
Transport vehicles	30,35,970

Just before Manish could prepare the contract accounts and the balance sheet, he contacted Dengue and was hospitalised. The contractor Ashwani was in the dilemma as to whom he can entrust this responsibility. He also wanted to know the progress of each project and which one was contributing maximum profit to his balance sheet so far.

QUESTION FOR DISCUSSION:

1. Evaluate the project completion stage of each project—Emerald, Villas and Habitat.
2. Prepare the contract account for each project and determine the profit to be transferred to the balance sheet as on 31st March 2019
3. Prepare the balance sheet for Almeria Construction Pvt. Ltd. as on 31st March 2019.

2. A Case of 'The Modern Muffler'

Seetharaman was employed in 'The Modern Muffler', a service station of a leading car company. The customers of this Service Station comprised of both individuals and transport agencies wanting the regular servicing or repair jobs for their car(s). The service station used job costing for calculating the cost of each servicing job and determining the price. Seetharaman was engaged in the business of executing jobs according to the customers' requirements and submitting the necessary cost details to his manager Boski Chatterjee.

The customers were billed for the service rendered on the basis of job cost plus additional margin for office & administrative and selling & distribution overheads. Further 10% to 20% (depending on the materials used and time spent) of job cost was added as profit margin. For the jobs not completed during the period, work-in-progress (WIP) account was prepared. The value of WIP inventory was calculated in this account by debiting all the cost incurred in the execution of the jobs and crediting the cost of completed jobs.

It was the last month of the financial year and Seetharaman was inspecting the details about two of the jobs under him during the month of March 2019. The statement looked as follows:

Particulars	*Job No. 7123*	*Job No. 7124*	*Total*
	₹	₹	₹
Opening balance of job in hand as on March 1, 2019:			
Direct material	1,600	8,400	10,000
Direct labour	3,000	9,000	12,000
Factory overheads absorbed	4,000	8,000	12,000
Total	**8,600**	**25,400**	**34,000**

The Service Supervisor—Rehman had handed him the material consumed for the month of March totalling to ₹18,500. He also discussed with him about the distribution of labour hours among the workers engaged in those jobs during the month. The statement given to him was as follows:

Jobs	*Material Required*	*Direct Labour Distribution*	
	₹	*Hours*	₹
Job No. 7123	2,400	400	12,000
Job No. 7124	5,600	200	9,000
Job No. 7125	4,500	300	13,500
Job No. 7126	6,000	100	4,500
Total	**18,500**	**1,000**	**39,000**

The Modern Muffler had a policy of applying overheads to jobs according to direct labour hour rate which was currently ₹20 per hour. For the month of March 2019, the factory overhead amounted to ₹42,000.

During the month, two of these jobs (7124 and 7125) were completed. Seetharaman was asked by Boski to prepare the bill for the customers at a price which included 15% of the billing price of the job for administration and selling expenses and additional 15% and 10% of the billing price respectively for Job 7124 & 7125 as profit margin. He was also required to prepare and submit the job cost sheet for these Jobs as well as statement showing the value of the work-in-progress inventory to Boski.

Seetharaman was perplexed. He knew how to calculate the percentages on the basis of costs; however, this was a different ball game all together. He decided to ask Boski for more clarity.

✍ QUESTIONS FOR DISCUSSION:

Imagine that you are Boski and help Seetharaman to prepare—

1. Job Cost-Sheet for Job No. 7124 and 7125.
2. Determine the price of these jobs for billing the customers.
3. Calculate the value of work in progress inventory.
4. Prepare an Income Statement for the month of March 2019 showing profit earned.

Chapter 11

Process Costing

Learning Objectives

After reading this chapter, you should be able to:

1. explain process costing—its nature, characteristics and its costing procedures; its differences with job costing;
2. explain preparation of process cost accounts under furnishes you the following information relating to Processarious situations;
3. understand waste, scrap, abnormal gain; equivalent production analysis; joint product and by-product; and
4. discuss the procedure of accounting for joint product and by-product as well.

NATURE OF PROCESS COSTING

Process costing is that form of operations costing which is used where standardised goods are produced in large volume with continuous production flow. This costing method is used in industries like chemicals, petroleum, textiles, steel, rubber, cement, plastic, shoes, sugar and coal. Those concerns which produce items such as screws, bolts and small electrical parts can also use this costing method. Process costing is also used in the assembly-type industry which manufactures items, such as typewriters, automobiles, aeroplanes and household electrical appliances such as washing machines, refrigerators, electrical irons, radios, television sets, etc. For example, an electronics manufacturing company may have the following process or cost centres: materials set-up, wiring, and soldering. Service industries, such as gas, water, electric power and heat may also follow process cost accounting.

Characteristics

A process costing method has the following distinctive characteristics:

1. *Cost collection* Manufacturing costs are accumulated for each production department or process.
2. *Time period assumption* Manufacturing costs are accumulated by department or process for specific time periods, say a month, and the process costing is designed to measure units produced during this time period.

3. *Averaging process* The most important point is that product costing under process costing is an averaging process. The unit cost is obtained by accumulating all manufacturing costs and dividing it by units produced or some measure of production.
4. *Separate ledger* Each process or department has its own account and records the processing costs incurred by the department.
5. *Homogeneous product* Under processing industries, the production is continuous and emphasis is on uniform or standardised product. It is difficult to identify a specific unit of output with the time of production.
6. *Transfer to finished goods* Completed units and their associated costs are transferred to next process if something is still to be done on those units. Completed units are transferred to finished goods if nothing is to be done.
7. *Cost of spoiled units* Cost of lost or spoiled units is added to the cost of good units completed, thus increasing the average cost per unit.

Process Costing and Job Costing

Process costing and job costing differ on the following counts:

1. *Applicability* Job costing is applicable in situations where the objective is to identify costs with specific products or jobs. Process costing, on the other hand, is used in case of mass production of similar units that continuously pass through different departments or processes.
2. *Cost collection* In job costing, manufacturing costs are accumulated for particular jobs or batches of product using job cost sheets. In process costing, manufacturing costs are accumulated for entire departments or processes and the cost of particular jobs or batches or products is not determinable.
3. *Time-period assumption* In job costing, costs are accumulated for a specific product or job without taking into account the production time which may be more than one accounting period. In process costing, costs are accumulated for specific departments/processes for a given time period (say a month). That is, production is measured for specific time periods in process costing.
4. *Purpose* In job costing, production is generally dependent on customers' orders and specifications. Under process costing, production is done for storing stock of goods and for future sale.
5. *Computation of unit costs* In job costing, unit cost is obtained by dividing the cost of the job order by units produced in the job order. Under process costing, unit costs are obtained by dividing departmental/process costs by process production.
6. *Work-in-progress* In job costing, one work-in-progress account is maintained. But, in process costing, individual work-in-progress accounts are prepared for each production/process department to ascertain manufacturing costs by process.

COSTING PROCEDURES UNDER PROCESS COSTING

In process costing, an account is maintained for each process to which all costs of material, labour, direct expenses and overhead are debited:

Materials

In process costing, all the materials required for production are issued to the first process, where after processing, they are passed on to the next process and so on; each process merely performs the same operation on the material which has been passed on from the first process. Alternatively, materials may pass from the first process to the second process, where extra or new raw materials are added; then more materials are added in the next process; this may continue until completion.

Labour

Labour costs incurred in a particular process are posted to the debit of the process account concerned. However, where workers are engaged in more than one process, the gross wages are distributed to each process on the basis of time spent on each process.

Direct Expenses

Items of expenditure which can be directly attributed to a process are debited to the relative process account. Examples of such expenses are cost of electricity, depreciation and hire charges of equipments.

Factory Overhead

Expenses which are not charged direct are apportioned on the basis of absorption rates. Also, overhead may be recovered at a pre-determined rate based on direct wages, prime cost, etc.

PREPARATION OF PROCESS COST ACCOUNTS

As stated earlier, for each process an individual process account is prepared. The method of preparing process accounts is discussed herewith on the basis of the following situations which may be found in a production situation:

1. Process costing having no process loss and no opening and closing work-in-progress.
2. Process costing having process losses or gains (normal loss, abnormal loss, abnormal gain).
3. Process costing having opening and closing work-in-progress at various stages of completion.
4. Process costing having opening and closing work-in-progress with process losses or gains.
5. Inter-process profits.

Process Costing Having No Process Loss/Gain and No Opening and Closing Work-in-Progress

The preparation of process accounts is very easy, if no loss or gain has arisen during the processing operation of the product. All costs of material, labour, direct expense, and apportioned overhead are debited to the process account. The total (accumulated) costs of the process are transferred to the second process as raw materials (input) for that process.

EXAMPLE 11.1

From the following figures, show the cost of three processes of manufacture. The production of each process is passed on to the next process immediately on completion.

	Process A	*Process B*	*Process C*
Wages and materials	₹30,400	₹12,000	₹29,250
Works overheads	5,600	5,250	6,000

(Contd.)

	Process A	*Process B*	*Process C*
Production in units	36,000	37,500	48,000
Stock (Units from preceding process—1st July, 2020)		4,000	16,500
Stock (Units from preceding process—31st July, 2020)		1,000	5,500

☞ ***Solution***

Process *A* Account

To wages and materials	₹30,400	By transfer to process *B*	
To works overheads	5,600	@ ₹1 per unit	₹36,000
	36,000		36,000

Process *B* Account

To stock: unit from preceding process @ ₹1 per unit	₹4,000	By stock: units from preceding process @ ₹1 per unit	₹1,000
To transfer from process *A*	36,000	By transfer to process *C* @ ₹ 1.50 per unit	56,250
To wages and material	12,000		
To works overheads	5,250		
	57,250		57,250

Process C Account

To stock: units from preceding process @ ₹1.50 per unit	₹24,750	By stock: units from preceding process @ ₹1.50 per unit	₹8,250
To transfer from process *B*	56,250	By transfer to finished goods account @ ₹2 per unit	₹1,08,000
To wages and materials	29,250		
To works overheads	6,000		
	1,16,250		₹1,16,250

✍ **EXAMPLE 11.2**

The Neodrug manufacturers process *A* product "plant food" through three distinct processes, the product of one process being transferred to the next process and so on to finished product intact.

Raw materials, labour and direct expenses incurred on each of the processes are given below:

Particulars	*Process A*	*Process B*	*Process C*
Raw materials	₹1,00,000	₹80,000	₹20,000
Labour	50,000	60,000	70,000
Direct expenses	15,000	25,000	50,000

The overhead expenses for the period amounted to ₹3,60,000 and is to be distributed to the processes on the basis of labour wages.

There were no stocks in any of the processes at the beginning or at the close of the period. Ignore wastages.

(a) Assuming that the output was 1,00,000 kilos, show the process accounts of *A*, *B* and *C* indicating also the unit cost per kilo under each element of cost and the output in each process.

(b) If 10% of the output is estimated to be lost in the course of sale and sampling, what should be the selling price per unit (correct to two decimal place) so as to provide for gross profit of $33\frac{1}{2}$% on selling price.

☞ ***Solution***

Process A

	Per kg	*Total*		*Per kg*	*Total*
To raw materials	1.00	1,00,000	By transfer to process *B*	2.65	2,65,000
To labour	0.50	50,000			
To direct expenses	0.15	15,000			
To overheads	1.00	1,00,000			
	2.65	2,65,000		2.65	2,65,000

Process B

	₹	₹		₹	₹
To transfer from process *A*	2.65	2,65,000	By transfer to process *C*	5.50	5,50,000
To raw materials	0.80	80,000			
To labour	0.60	60,000			
To direct expenses	0.25	25,000			
To overheads	1.20	1,20,000			
	5.50	5,50,000		5.50	5,50,000

Process C

	₹	₹		₹	₹
To transfer from process *B*	5.50	5,50,000	By transfer to finished goods a/c	8.30	8,30,000
To raw materials	0.20	20,000			
To labour	0.70	70,000			
To direct expenses	0.50	50,000			
To overheads	1.40	1,40,000			
	8.30	8,30,000		8.30	8,30,000

(b) Cost of finished goods		₹8,30,000
Profit ($33\frac{1}{3}$% on selling price)		4,15,000
	Sales	12,45,000

Gross output	1,00,000 kg
Less—wastage 10%	10,000
	90,000 kg

$$\text{Selling price per kg} = \frac{12,45,000}{90,000 \text{ kg}} = ₹13.83 \text{ per kg}$$

Process Costing Having Process Losses and/or Gains

All materials put into process are not likely to be good saleable products. Some loss, scrap and wastage are inevitable in process industries. Process loss can be divided into two categories: (i) Normal loss, (ii) Abnormal loss. Normal loss is the loss which is unavoidable, uncontrollable and expected in normal conditions. It may be inherent in the manufacturing process. Abnormal process loss is controllable and avoidable and generally caused by abnormal or unexpected conditions, such as bad designing, poor materials, accident and negligence, etc.

The treatment of normal and abnormal losses differs in process accounts. Normal losses are absorbed by good production. Assume, for example, that 25,000 units of a mixture were put into process and that during processing 5,000 units were lost through evaporation. This in an unavoidable loss. If the total cost recorded was ₹25,00,000, the remaining 20,000 units would be assigned a unit cost of ₹125.

$$\frac{\text{Cost of production}}{\text{Number of units completed}} = \frac{₹25,00,000}{20,000} = ₹125$$

Abnormal losses are valued as good units. The unit cost which is used to value good units is also applied for valuation of abnormal loss units. The cost of abnormal loss units computed in this manner is transferred to a separate abnormal loss account and credited to relevant process account. Subsequently, this loss is transferred to the costing profit and loss account and the abnormal loss account is thus closed.

Waste (Spoilage)

Waste is without any value. If waste is part of the normal process loss, the cost is absorbed by the good production. Alternatively, if waste represents abnormal process loss, the waste (abnormal loss) is valued like good units and treated as abnormal process loss.

Defectives:

Normal defectives can be recovered : charged to good production
: charged to general overhead
: charged to department.

If defectives are abnormal and are due to causes beyond the control of organisation then they should be charged to profit and loss account.

Scrap

Scrap means discarded material emerging from certain manufacturing operations. It has some but minor value. Where the normal loss is in the form of scrap and has some realisable value, the process account is credited with the amount which could be realised from sale of normal scrap. The abnormal loss, if represented by scrap may have a similar realisable value. The amount realised from sale of scrap representing abnormal loss is credited to the abnormal loss account and the balance in the abnormal loss account is transferred to the costing profit and loss account. The question of crediting the amount realised from sale of scrap representing abnormal loss in the relevant process account does not arise. The relevant process account is credited and the abnormal loss account is debited with the cost of abnormal loss valued as finished output. In case, there are normal loss, abnormal loss and scrap, the following procedure will help in the preparation of process accounts:

1. Normal loss should be computed on the basis of information given in the question.
2. The cost per unit of production after taking into account normal loss units should be determined assuming that abnormal loss does not exist. The cost per unit is calculated on the basis of the following information:
   (a) Normal production, i.e. inputs (units) minus normal loss units.
   (b) Normal cost of production, i.e. all costs incurred (appearing on the debit side of a process account) minus proceeds (if any) realised from the sale of normal loss units.

   Normal cost of production divided by normal production will give the cost per unit of output.
3. The cost per unit determined as above is used to value abnormal loss units and that would be the cost of abnormal loss.
4. The abnormal loss account is debited and the relevant process account credited with the amount and quantity of abnormal loss as calculated in (3) above.
5. The cost per unit as obtained in (3) will also be used to determine the cost of good production units produced by the process.
6. The proceeds realised from the sale of normal loss representing scrap is transferred to the relevant process account.
7. The proceeds realised from the sale of abnormal loss representing scrap is transferred to a separate abnormal loss account and not to the relevant process account.
8. The abnormal loss account is closed by transferring the total cost of abnormal loss units to the costing profit and loss account if there is no scrap. In case, abnormal loss represents scrap, only the net amount (total cost of abnormal loss units minus scrap) will be transferred to the costing profit and loss account.

Abnormal Gain (Effectives)

Abnormal gain arises when the actual loss is less than the normal loss expected. The abnormal gain is valued in the same manner as abnormal loss and is credited to a separate account known as the abnormal gain account. The abnormal gain account appears on the debit side of the relevant process account. The amount of scrap which would otherwise have been realised, had there been normal loss and no abnormal gain, is debited to the abnormal gain account and the balance is credited to the costing profit and loss account. Cost per unit of output computed (as mentioned above) is used to value the output transferred to the next process.

EXAMPLE 11.3

A raw material has to pass through three successive processes to reach the finished product stage. The loss of material expressed as percentage of input is: Process I: 10%; Process II: 20%; Process III: 25%.

Required:
Calculate the raw material introduced in Process I if the finished product transferred from Process III is 1,080 units.

Solution

Let input introduced in Process I = 100 units

Process	Input	Net Loss	Output
I	100	10	90
II	90	18	77
III	72	18	54

For 54 units output, input required = 100 units.

$$\therefore \quad \text{For 1080 units} = \frac{1{,}080 \times 100}{54} = 2{,}000 \text{ units}$$

EXAMPLE 11.4

PCT introduced 1,000 units in a process at a cost of ₹10 per unit. Wages and overheads incurred are ₹9,000 and ₹8,000 respectively. It is expected that 10% of total output is likely to be defective. Actual output of good units is 850. Cost of rectification of a defective unit is ₹5. There is no wastage or scrap of materials.

Required:
Calculate the cost per unit if:

(i) defectives are rectified;
(ii) defectives are not rectified but sold as "seconds" @ ₹9 each.

Solution

Particulars	*If Defectives are Rectified* ₹	*If Defectives are Not Rectified* ₹
Cost of materials (1,000 units @ ₹10)	10,000	10,000
Wages	9,000	9,000
Overheads	8,000	8,000
	27,000	27,000
Add: Cost of rectification of normal defectives (100 × ₹5)	500	

(Contd.)

Particulars	If Defectives are Rectified ₹	If Defectives are Not Rectified ₹
Less: Realisable value of normal defectives (100 × ₹9)	—	900
Cost of goods produced (*A*)	27,500	26,100
No. of units (*B*)	1,000	900
Cost per unit (*A* ÷ *B*)	₹27.50	29

Treatment of Abnormal Defectives:

(a) Cost of certification of abnormal defectives (i.e., 50 × 5 = ₹250) will be charged to costing Profit & Loss Account.

(b) Loss on sale of abnormal defectives (i.e., 50 × ₹29 – ₹9 = ₹1,000) will be charged to costing Profit & Loss Account.

Working notes:

Normal defective = 10% of 1,000 units = 100 units.
Abnormal Defective = 1000 – 100 – 850 = 50 units

EXAMPLE 11.5

D. Ltd. introduced 5,000 units in a process at a cost of ₹10,000. The wages and overheads incurred are ₹10,000 and ₹8,000 respectively. It is expected that 10% of the output is likely to be defective. Actual output of goods is 4,400 units.

The rectification of defective units costs ₹4 per unit.

Calculate the cost per unit and show how you will deal with the cost of rectification of abnormal defective units.

Solution

Process Account

	Units	Amt.		Units	Amt.
To units introduced	5,000	10,000	By abnormal loss*	100	600
To wages		10,000	By finished stock a/c @ ₹6	4900*	29,400
To overheads		8,000			
To cost of rectification$_1$* (500 units @ ₹4)	—	2,000			
	5,000	30,000		5,000	30,000

Working Notes:

1. Rectification of normal defective units is an item of factory overheads. Hence, 10% of 5,000 units, i.e., 500 units multiplied by ₹4, i.e., ₹2,000 has been added to the cost.

2. Total Output = Actual output + Rectified units = 4,400 + 500 = 4,900 units.
3. There is no normal loss.

$$\therefore \text{ Cost per unit} = \frac{\text{Normal cost}}{\text{Normal output}} = \frac{30,000}{5,000} = ₹6$$

$$\text{Normal cost} = \text{Total cost} - \text{Scrap value of normal loss}$$
$$= 30,000 - 0 = ₹30,000$$

$$\text{Normal output} = \text{Units introduced} - \text{Units of normal loss}$$
$$= 5,000 - 0 = 5,000$$

4. Units of abnormal loss = 5,000 – 4,900 = 100 units

Value of abnormal loss = Units of abnormal loss × Cost per unit
= 100 × 6 = ₹600

5. Cost of rectification of abnormal defective units is debited to the costing Profit & Loss Account.

EXAMPLE 11.6

The output of Process *X* was 5,000 units. Normal loss allowed was 10% of input. Abnormal loss was 400 units. The following further information is obtained:

Material @ ₹5 per unit
Labour ₹8,000
Overheads ₹6,700
Wastage realised ₹2.50 per unit

Prepare Process *X* account and Abnormal Loss account.

Solution

(a) Let the input be *x* units

$$\text{Normal loss} = 10\% \text{ of input}$$
$$= x \times \frac{10}{100} = \frac{x}{10} \text{ units}$$

Abnormal loss = 400 units

Output = 5,000 units

Now, Input = Output + Abnormal loss + Normal loss

$$x = 5,000 + 400 + \frac{x}{10}$$
$$x = 5,400 + \frac{x}{10}$$
$$10x = 54,000 + x$$
$$9x = 54,000$$
$$x = 6,000$$

∴ Units introduced = 6,000

Alternate Method:

$$\text{Input} = \frac{(\text{Output} + \text{Abnormal loss}) \times 100}{90}$$

$$= \frac{(5,000 + 400) \times 100}{90} = \frac{5,400 \times 100}{90}$$

$$= 6,000 \text{ units}$$

Process *X* Account

Particulars	*Units*	*Amount* ₹	*Particulars*	*Units*	*Amount* ₹
To materials @ ₹5 per unit	6,000	30,000	By normal loss @ ₹2.50 per unit	600	1,500
To labour		8,000	By abnormal loss @ ₹8 per unit	400	3,200
To overheads		6,700	By output transferred to process *Y* a/c @ ₹8 per unit	5,000	40,000
	6,000	44,700		6,000	44,700

Working Notes:

1. Normal loss = 10% of 6,000 = $\frac{10 \times 6000}{100}$
   = 600 units
2. Value of abnormal loss

$$= \frac{\text{Total cost} - \text{Value of normal loss}}{\text{Total input} - \text{Units of normal loss}} \times \text{Units of abnormal loss}$$

$$= \frac{44,700 - 1,500}{6,000 - 600} \times 400 = ₹3,200$$

Abnormal Loss Account

Particulars	*Units*	*Amount* ₹	*Particulars*	*Units*	*Amount* ₹
To process "X" account	400	3,200	By sale of scrap @ ₹2.50 per unit	400	1,000
			By costing profit & loss a/c	—	2,200
	400	3,200		400	3,200

EXAMPLE 11.7

for excel template, scan

The product of a manufacturing concern passes through two processes–*A* and *B*. The normal losses and abnormal losses are defective units having a scrap value of ₹2 and ₹5 per unit in processes *A* and *B* respectively. The following information relates to the month ending 31-3-2020:

	Process A	*Process B*
Raw materials issued @ ₹5	3,000 units	—
Normal loss	10% of input	5% of input
Output	2,800 units	2,600 units
Additional components	₹1,000	₹780
Direct wages	₹4,000	₹3,000
Direct expenses	₹10,000	₹14,000
Production overhead (as a percentage of direct wages)	75%	125%

There was no opening or closing work in progress but opening and closing stocks of finished goods were ₹20,000 and ₹23,000 respectively.

Prepare Process A/c, Finished Stock A/c, Normal Loss A/c, Abnormal Loss A/c and Abnormal Gain A/c.

Solution

Process *A*

Particulars	*Qty*	*Amount*	*Particulars*	*Qty*	*Amount*
To raw material	3,000	15,000	By normal loss	300	600
To additional input	–	1,000	(10% of input) (@ ₹2 per unit)		
To direct wages		4,000	By output to process *B*	2,800	33,600
To direct expenses		10,000	@ ₹12/- (W.N.1)		
To production overhead					
(75% of direct wages)		3,000			
To abnormal gain (WN-1)	100	1,200			
	3,100	34,200		3,100	34,200

$$\text{Normal cost per unit} = \frac{\text{Total cost of normal units}}{\text{Normal units}} = \frac{33{,}000 - 600}{3{,}000 - 300}$$

$$= \frac{32{,}400}{2{,}700} = ₹12/-$$

Cost of abnormal gain = 100 × 12.

Process *B*

Particulars	*Qty*	*Amount*	*Particulars*	*Qty*	*Amount*
To process *A* Trf	2,800	33,600	By normal loss (5% of 2,800)	140	700

(Contd.)

Particulars	Qty	Amount	Particulars	Qty	Amount
To additional input		780	By abnormal loss (W.N.2)	60	1,228
To direct wages		3,000	By transfer to finished stock	2,600	53,202
To direct expenses		14,000	@ 20.4623		
To production overhead		3,750			
(125% of direct wages)					
	2,800	55,130		2,800	55,130

Working Note 2.

$$\text{Normal cost per unit for process } B = \frac{\text{Total cost of normal units}}{\text{Normal units}}$$

$$= \frac{55{,}130 - 700}{2{,}800 - 140}$$

$$= \frac{54{,}430}{2{,}660} = 20.462$$

Cost of abnormal loss = 60 × 20.462 = 1,228 (Approx)

Finished Stock

Particulars	Amount	Particulars	Amount
To balance b/d	20,000	By cost of goods sold	50,202
To process *B*—transfer from process *B*	53,202	By balance c/d	23,000
	73,202		73,202

Normal Loss Account

Particulars	Qty	Amount	Particulars	Qty	Amount
To process *A*	300	600	By abnormal gain	100	200
To process *B*	140	700	By bank-sale of waste units	340	1,100
	440	1,300		440	1,300

Abnormal Loss Account

Particulars	Qty	Amount	Particulars	Qty	Amount
To process *B*	60	1,228	By bank-sale proceed @ ₹5	60	300
			By profit and loss a/c		928
	60	1,228		60	1,228

Abnormal Gain Account

Particulars	Qty	Amount	Particulars	Qty	Amount
To normal loss @ ₹2	100	200	By process *A*	100	1,200
To profit and loss A/c		1,000			
	100	1,200		100	1,200

EXAMPLE 11.8

for excel template, scan

At the end of process *A*, carried on in a factory during the week ending July 31st, 2020 the number of units produced was 850 excluding 50 units damaged at the very end of the process. The damaged units realised ₹3 per unit as scrap. A normal wastage of 10 per cent occurs during the process, the wastage realised was ₹2 per unit.

A unit of raw material costs ₹4. The other expenses for the week were:

	₹
Wages	500
Power	200
General expenses	450

40% of the output is sold so as to show a profit of $16\frac{2}{3}$ per cent on the selling price; the rest of the output is transferred to process *B*.

Prepare process *A* account.

Solution

Dr. **Process *A* Account** *Cr.*

Particulars	*Units*	₹	*Particulars*	*Units*	₹
To material @ ₹4			By normal wastage		
per unit	1,000	4,000	(@ ₹2 per unit)	100	200
To wages		500	By damaged units sold		
To power		200	(@ ₹3 per unit)	50	150
To general expenses		450	By sale (40% of production at		
To P & L A/c		384	profit of ($16\frac{2}{3}$% on S.P.)	340	2,304
			By transfer to process *B* (60% of production at cost price)	510	2,880
	1,000	5,534		1,000	5,534

Working Notes:

Material input = 1,000 units

1. Normal wastage = $\frac{1,000 \times 10}{100}$ = 100 units
   sold @ ₹2 per unit = 100 × 2 = ₹200
2. Damaged units = 50
   sold @ ₹3 per unit = 50 × 3 = ₹150
3. Cost of production of 850 units
   ₹4,000 + 500 + 200 + 450 – (₹200 + 150) = ₹4,800
4. Sale 40% of production at profit of $16\frac{2}{3}$% 16% on S.P. or 20% on C.P.

$$\frac{4,800 \times 40 \times 120}{100 \times 100} = ₹2,304$$

5 Remaining 60% of production transferred to process *B* at cost

$$= \frac{₹4,800 \times 60}{100} = ₹2,880$$

EXAMPLE 11.9

The product manufactured by the Standard Chemicals Ltd. passes through three processes I, II and III. The following costs have been incurred for the month of September, 2020:

Details		Process I (₹)	Process II (₹)	Process III (₹)
1. Material consumed		40,000	7,500	5,000
2. Direct wages		22,500	10,000	10,000
3. Direct expenses		20,500	2,250	2,505
Total		83,000	19,750	17,505
		(units)	(units)	(units)
4. Output		3,900	3,850	3,200
5. Finished process stock:				
(i) 01.9.2020		600	550	800
(ii) 30.9.2020		500	800	Nil
6. Stock valuation on 01.9.2020 (₹ per unit)		24.50	31.00	37.00
7. Percentage of wastage		2	5	10
8. Net realisable value of wastage per unit	(₹)	13.50	16.25	21.00

Four thousand units of raw materials were introduced in Process I at a cost of Rupees twenty thousand.

Stocks are valued and transferred to subsequent processes at weighted average cost. The percentage of wastage is computed on the number of units entering the process concerned.

Prepare: (i) Process Accounts; (ii) Process Stock Accounts; (iii) Normal Wastage Accounts; (iv) Abnormal Wastage/Effectives Account.

Solution

(i) and (ii)

Process I Account

Particulars	*Units*	₹	*Particulars*	*Units*	₹
To input	4,000	20,000	By normal wastage	80	1,080
To materials		40,000	By abnormal wastage	20	520
To direct wages		22,500	By process *I* stock a/c	3,900	1,01,400
To direct expenses		20,500			
	4,000	1,03,000		4,000	1,03,000

Process I Stock Account

Particulars	Units	₹	Particulars	Units	₹
To balance b/d	600	14,700	By process *II* a/c	4,000	1,03,200
(@ ₹24.5 per unit)	3,900	1,01,400	By balance c/d	500	12,900
To process *I* a/c	4,500	1,16,100	(@ ₹25.8 per unit)	4,500	1,16,100

Process II Account

Particulars	Units	₹	Particulars	Units	₹
To process I stock A/c			By normal wastage	200	3,250
(@ ₹25.8 per unit)	4,000	1,03,200	By process stock a/c		
To direct material		7,500	(@ ₹31.5 per unit)	3,850	1,21,275
To direct wages		10,000			
To direct expenses		2,250			
To abnormal effectives a/c	50	1,575			
	4,050	1,24,525		4,050	1,24,525

Process II Stock Account

Particulars	Units	₹	Particulars	Units	₹
To balance b/d	550	17,050	By process *III* a/c	3,600	1,13,175
(@ ₹31 per unit)			By balance c/d		
To process *II* a/c	3,850	1,21,275	(@ ₹31.44 per unit)	800	25,150
	4,400	1,38,325		4,400	1,38,325

Process III Account

Particulars	Units	₹	Particulars	Units	₹
To process II stock a/c	3,600	1,13,175	By normal wastage a/c	360	7,560
To materials		5,000	By abnormal wastage a/c	40	1,520
To direct wages		10,000	By process *III* stock a/c	3,200	1,21,600
To direct expenses		2,505			
	3,600	1,30,680		3,600	1,30,680

Process III Stock Account

Particulars	Units	₹	Particulars	Units	₹
To balance b/d	800	29,600	By finished goods		
(@ ₹37 per unit)			stock a/c	4,000	1,51,200
To process *III* A/c	3,200	1,21,600	(@ ₹37.8 per unit)		
	4,000	1,51,200		4,000	1,51,200

(iii) Normal Wastage Account

Particulars	Units	₹	Particulars	Units	₹
To process I a/c	800	1,080	By sale proceeds:		
To process II a/c	200	3,250	Process I	800	1,080
			Process II	150	2,438
			By abnormal effectives a/c	50	812
	1,000	4,330		1,000	4,330

(iv) Abnormal Wastage Account

Particulars	Units	₹	Particulars	Units	₹
To process I a/c	20	520	By sales proceeds:		
To process III a/c	40	1,520	Process I	20	270
			Process III	40	840
			By costing profit/loss a/c		930
	60	2,040		60	2,040

Abnormal Effectives Account

Particulars	Units	₹	Particulars	Units	₹
To normal wastage a/c	50	812	By process II a/c	50	1,575
To costing profit/loss a/c		763			
	50	1,575		50	1,575

Working Notes:

1. *Cost of Abnormal Wastage in Process I* $= \dfrac{\text{Normal cost}}{\text{Normal output}} \times$ Abnormal wastage in units

$$= \frac{1,03,000 - 1,080}{3,920} \times 20$$

$$= \frac{1,01,920}{3,920} \times 20 = ₹520$$

2. *Cost of Abnormal Effectives in Process II* $= \dfrac{\text{Normal cost}}{\text{Normal output}} \times$ Abnormal effectives in units

$$= \frac{1,22,950 - 3,250}{3,800} \times 50$$

$$= \frac{1,19,700}{3,800} \times 50 = ₹1,311$$

3. *Cost of Abnormal Wastage in Process III* $= \dfrac{\text{Normal cost}}{\text{Normal output}} \times$ Abnormal wastage in units

$$= \frac{1,30,680 - 7,560}{3,600 - 360} \times 40$$

$$= \frac{1,23,120}{3,240} \times 40 = ₹1,520$$

EXAMPLE 11.10

A product passes through two processes. The output of Process I becomes the input of Process II and the output of Process II is transferred to warehouse. The quantity of raw materials introduced into Process I is 20,000 kg. at ₹10 per kg. The cost and output data for the month under review are as under:

	Process I	*Process II*
Direct materials	₹60,000	₹40,000
Direct labour	₹40,000	₹30,000
Production overheads	₹39,000	₹40,250
Normal loss	8%	5%
Output	18,000	17,400
Loss realisation of ₹/Unit	2.00	3.00

The company's policy is to fix the selling price of end product is such a way as to yield a profit of 20% on selling price.

Required

(i) Prepare the Process Accounts

(ii) Determine the selling price per unit of the end product.

Solution

Process I Account

Dr. *Cr.*

Particulars	*Kg.*	*Rate / kg.* ₹	*Amount* ₹	*Particulars*	*Kg.*	*Rate / kg.* ₹	*Amount.* ₹
To raw material	20,000	10	2,00,000	By normal loss	1,600	2.00	3,200
To direct material			60,000	By abnormal loss (*Refer to Working Notes 1 and 2*)	400	18.25	7,300
To direct labour			40,000				
To production overheads			39,000	By transfer to process *II*	18,000	18.25	3,28,500
	20,000		3,39,000		20,000		3,39,000

Process II Amount

Dr. *Cr.*

Particulars	*Kg*	*Rate/ kg.* ₹	*Amount* ₹	*Particulars*	*Kg*	*Rate/ kg.* ₹	*Amount* ₹
To process *I* account	18,000	18.25	3,28,500	By normal loss	900	3.00	2,700
To direct materials			40,000	By transfer to warehouse	17,400	25.50	4,43,700
To direct labour			30,000				
To production overheads			40,250				
To abnormal gain	300	25.50	7,650				
	18,300		4,46,400		18,300		4,46,400

Working Notes:

1. **Abnormal Loss in Process I:**

Required production (20,000 kg. – 1,600 kg.)	18,400
Actual production (in kg.)	18,000
Abnormal loss (in kg.)	400

2. **Value of Abnormal Loss in Process I:**

$$= \left(\frac{\text{Normal cost of normal output}}{\text{Normal output}}\right) \times \text{Abnormal loss}$$

$$= \left(\frac{₹3,35,800}{18,400 \text{ kg.}}\right) \times 400 \text{ kg.} = ₹18.25 \times 400 \text{ kg.} \qquad = 7,300$$

3. **Abnormal Gain in Process II:**

Required production (18,000 kg. – 900 kg.)	17,100
Actual production	17,400
Abnormal gain (in kg.)	300

4. **Value of Abnormal Gain in Process I:**

$$= \left(\frac{₹4,36,050}{17,100 \text{ kgs}}\right) \times 300 \text{ kg} = ₹25.50 \times 3,000 \text{ kg} = ₹7,650.00$$

(ii) **Determination of Selling Price of the End Product:**

If the cost price of end product is ₹80 the unit sale price is ₹100.

If the cost price of end product is ₹1, the unit sale price is $\frac{100}{80}$.

If the cost price is ₹25.50, then the sale price of the end product is $\frac{100}{80} \times 25.50$

$= ₹31.875.$

EXAMPLE 11.11

A company manufactures its sole product by passing the raw material through the distinct processes in its factory. During the month of April 2020, the company purchased 96,000 kg of raw material at

₹5 per kg and introduced the same in Process I. Further particulars of manufacture for the month are given below:

	Process I	*Process II*	*Process III*
Material consumed	₹33,472	₹27,483	₹47,166
Direct labour	80,000	72,000	56,000
Overheads	1,20,000	1,08,000	84,000
Normal waste in process as % of input	3%	1%	1%
Sale value of waste (₹/kg)	2	3	5
Actual output during the month (kg)	93,000	92,200	91,500

Prepare the three process accounts and accounts relating to abnormal loss/gain, if any.

Solution

Process I Account

	Quantity (kg)	*Rate (₹)*	*Amount (₹)*		*Quantity (kg)*	*Rate (₹)*	*Amount (₹)*
To input of raw material	96,000	5.00	4,80,000	By Process-II A/c (transferred to)	93,000	7.60	7,06,800
To other materials			33,472	By normal waste Aa/c (3% of 96,000)	2,880	2.00	5,760
To direct labour			80,000	By Aabnormal loss a/c	120	7.60	912
To overheads			1,20,000				
	96,000		7,13,472		96,000		7,13,472

Process II Account

	Quantity (kg)	*Rate (₹)*	*Amount (₹)*		*Quantity (kg)*	*Rate (₹)*	*Amount (₹)*
To Process-I a/c (transferred from)	93,000	7.60	7,06,800	By Process-III a/c (transferred to)	92,200	9.90	12,780
To materials			27,483	By normal waste (1% of 93,000)	930	3.00	2,790
To direct labour			72,000				
To overheads			1,08,000				
To abnormal gain	130	9.90	1,287				
	93,130		9,15,570		93,130		9,15,570

Process-III Account

	Quantity (kg.)	*Rate (₹)*	*Amount (₹)*		*Quantity (kg.)*	*Rate (₹)*	*Amount (₹)*
To Process-II a/c (transferred from)	92,200	9.90	9,12,780	By finished good stock	91,500	12.00	10,98,000

(Contd.)

	Quantity (kg.)	Rate (₹)	Amount (₹)		Quantity (kg.)	Rate (₹)	Amount (₹)
To materials			47,166	By normal waste			
To direct labour			56,000	(1% of 92,200)	922	5.00	4,610
To overheads			84,000				
To abnormal	222	12.00	2,664				
	92,422		11,02,610		92,422		11,02,610

Abnormal Loss Account

	Quantity (kg)	Amount (₹)		Quantity (kg)	Amount (₹)
To Process-I account	120	912	By cash @ ₹2 (normal waste)	120	240
			By profit and loss account		672
	120	912		120	912

Abnormal Gain Account

	Quantity (kg)	Amount (₹)		Quantity (kg)	Amount (₹)
To Process-II a/c (normal waste) @ ₹3	130	390	By Process-II a/c	130	1,287
To Process-III a/c (normal waste) @ ₹5	222	1,110	By Process-III a/c	222	2,664
To profit and loss	—	2,451			
	352	3,951		352	3,951

Working Notes:

Valuation of Output, Abnormal Loss/Gain are worked out below:

$$\frac{\text{Total cost of input} - \text{Sale value of normal waste}}{(\text{Input quantity} - \text{Quantity of normal waste})}$$

Process I:

$$\frac{7,13,472-5,760}{96,000-2,880}=\frac{7,07,712}{93,120}=₹7.60$$

Process II:

$$\frac{9,14,283-2,790}{93,000-930}=\frac{9,11,493}{92,070}=₹9.90$$

Process III:

$$\frac{10,99,946-4,610}{92,200-922}=\frac{10,95,336}{91,278}=₹12.00$$

EXAMPLE 11.12

RST Limited processes product *Z* through two distinct process—Process I and Process II. On completion, it is transferred to finished stock. From the following information for the year 2019–20, prepare Process -I, Process -II and Finished Stock A/c:

Particulars	*Process I*	*Process II*
Raw materials used	7,500 units	—
Raw materials cost per unit	₹60	—
Transfer to next process/finished stock	7,050 units	6,525 units
Normal loss (on inputs)	5%	10%
Direct wages	₹1,35,750	₹1,29,250
Direct expenses	60% of direct wages	65% of direct wages
Manufacturing overheads	20% of direct wages	15% of direct wages
Realisable value of scrap per unit	₹12.50	₹37.50

6,000 units of finished goods were sold at a profit of 15% on cost. Assume that there was no opening or closing stock of work-in-progress.

Solution

Process-I Account

	Qty.	*Rate*	*Amount*		*Qty.*	*Rate*	*Amount*
To Raw material	7,500	60	4,50,000	By Normal loss (5% × 7,500)	375	12.50	4,688
To Direct wages			1,35,750	By Abnormal loss	75	96.79	7,260
To Direct expenses 60% of direct wages			81,450	By Process-II Account	7,050	96.79	6,82,402
To Manufacturing overheads (20% of direct wages)			27,150				
	7,500		6,94,350		7,500		6,94,350

Planned output – Process I = 7,500 –375 = 7,125 units

Actual output = 7,050 units

Abnormal loss = (7,125 units – 7,050 units) = 75 units.

$$\text{Cost per unit} = \frac{6,94,350 - 4,688}{7,125} = ₹96.7947. \qquad (96.80 \text{ approx.})$$

Process -II Account

		Qty.	Rate	Amount			Qty.	Rate	Amount
To	Process I	7,050	96.79	6,82,402	By	Normal loss (10%)	705	37.50	26,438
To	Direct wages			1,29,250	By	Finished Stock A/c	6,525	140.05	9,13,823
To	Direct expenses 65% of direct wages			84,013					
To	Manufacturing overheads (15% of direct wages)			19,387					
To	Abnormal gain	180	140.05	25.209					
		7,230		9,40,261			7,230		9,40,261

Planned output of Process II = 7,050 – 705 = 6,345 units

$$\text{Cost per unit} = \frac{9{,}15{,}052 - 26{,}438}{6{,}345} = ₹140.05$$

Abnormal gain = Actual output – Planned output

= 6,525 – 6,345

= 180 units.

Finished Stock Account

		Qty.	Rate	Amount			Qty.	Rate	Amount
To	Process II	6,525	140.05	9,13,823	By	Sales A/c	6,000	161.06	9,66,341
To	Profit and Loss Account			1,26,044	By	Balance c/d	525	140.05	73,526
		6,525		10,39,867			6,525		10,39,867

EXAMPLE 11.13

A company manufactures a chemical product by a series of operations in three processes. Raw material is fed into Process I and the finished chemical that comes out of Process III is transferred to the finished goods store. The following particulars relating to operations for April 2020 are given below:

	Process I	Process II	Process III
Raw materials issued 80,000 kg	₹9,60,000		
Direct wages	₹1,25,600	₹1,72,000	₹1,42,500
Overhead costs	₹1,68,000	₹1,77,280	₹1,24,690

(Contd.)

	Process I	Process II	Process III
Normal processing loss (% of input)	3%	2%	1%
Output transferred to next process	74,000 kg	69,400 kg	69,000 kg
Work-in-process (processed material awaiting transfer to next process)	3,000	2,400	–

Prepare the accounts of Processes I, II and III and also abnormal loss and abnormal gain accounts, if any.

Solution

If waste sold has nil value, process accounts would appear as follows:

Process-I Account

Particulars	*Quantity (kg)*	*Amount (₹)*	*Particulars*	*Quantity (kg)*	*Amount (₹)*
To materials issued	80,000	9,60,000	By normal loss	2,400	—
To direct wages		1,25,600	By abnormal loss	600	9,693
To overheads		1,68,000	By W.I.P. (Closing Balance)	3,000	48,464
			By process II	74,000	11,95,443
	80,000	12,53,600		80,000	12,53,600

$$\text{(Rate for valuation : } = \frac{\text{Actual Cost}}{\text{Normal Output}} = \frac{12,53,600}{80,000 - 2,400} = \frac{12,53,600}{77,600 \text{ kg}} = ₹16.1546)$$

Process-II Account

Particulars	*Quantity (kg)*	*Amount (₹)*	*Particulars*	*Quantity (kg)*	*Amount (₹)*
To Process I	74,000	11,95,443	By Normal loss	1,480	–
To Direct wages		1,72,000	By Abnormal loss	720	15,336
To Overheads		1,77,280	By W.I.P. (Closing Balance)	2,400	51,122
			By Process III	69,400	14,78,265
	74,000	15,44,723		74,000	15,44,723

$$\text{(Rate for valuation: } \frac{\text{Actual Cost}}{\text{Normal Output}} = \frac{15,44,723}{74,000 - 1,480} = \frac{15,44,723}{72,520 \text{ kg}} = ₹21.30)$$

Process III Account

Particulars	Quantity (kg)	Amount (₹)	Particulars	Quantity (kg)	Amount (₹)
To Process II	69,400	14,78,265	By normal loss	694	
To direct wages		1,42,500	By finished goods store	69,000	17,52,924
To overheads		1,24,690			
To abnormal gain	294	7,469			
	69,694	17,52,924		69,694	17,52,924

(Rate for valuation: $\frac{\text{Actual cost}}{\text{Normal output}} = \frac{17,45,455}{69,400 - 694} = \frac{17,45,455}{68,706}$ = ₹25.4047)

Abnormal Loss Account

Particulars	Quantity (kg)	Amount (₹)	Particulars	Quantity (kg)	Amount (₹)
To Process I	600	9,693	By profit and loss account	–	25,029
To Process II	720	15,336			
		25,029			25,029

Abnormal Gain Account

Particulars	Quantity (kg)	Amount (₹)	Particulars	Quantity (kg)	Amount (₹)
To profit and loss account	–	7,469	By Process III	294	7,469
		7,469			**7,469**

Process Costing Having Work-in-Progress at Different Stages of Completion

When a process consists of opening and closing stock fully completed, the cost unit is obtained by dividing the total cost including the cost of opening stock by the number of units completed. This unit cost is used to price the output transferred to the next process and to value the units which remain in inventory. The following example illustrates this situation:

Process I

Particulars	Units	₹	Particulars	Units	₹
To stock (opening)	2,000	3,500	By transfer to second process	9,000	27,000
To materials	10,000	20,050			
To wages		9,450	By stock	3,000	9,000
To Overhead		3,000			
	12,000	36,000		12,000	36,000

$$\text{Unit cost} = \frac{₹36{,}000}{12{,}000 \text{ units}} = ₹3 \text{ per unit}$$

The unit cost, ₹3 per unit, has been used to price the goods transferred to the second process as well as to the stock.

Closing Work-in-Progress

In most situations, process may consist of partially completed closing units at the end of an accounting period. It is apparent that a partially completed unit must carry a cost that is lower than a finished unit. It follows that where there are inventories of closing work-in-progress, units costs cannot be computed by simply dividing the total cost by the number of units processed. Units in work-in-process must be converted to a base that can be equated with finished production. This analysis is known as Equivalent Production Analysis.

CIMA defines Equivalent Units as "a notional quantity of completed units substituted for an actual quantity of incomplete physical units in progress, when the aggregate work content of the incomplete units is deemed to be equivalent to that of the substituted quantity of completed units e.g. 150 units 50 percent complete = 75 equivalent units".

When opening and closing stocks of work-in-process exist, unit costs cannot be computed by simply dividing the total cost by total number of units still in process. We can convert the work-in-process units into finished units called equivalent units so that the unit cost of these units can be obtained.

$$\text{Equivalent completed units} = \frac{\text{Actual number of units in the}}{\text{process of manufacture}} \times \frac{\text{Percentage of}}{\text{work completed}}$$

The two principal methods of calculating equivalent units are:

(i) Weighted average

(ii) First-In, First-Out.

Equivalent Production Analysis

Before unit costs can be computed, closing inventories of work-in-progress must be converted into finished equivalents (also called equivalent production). This is done by multiplying the actual number of units in process by their stage of completion measured in terms of cost. Thus, 2,000 units in an inventory estimated to be 50% complete are equal in cost to 1,000 units that have been completed:

Actual number of units × Stage of completion = Finished equivalent

2,000 × 50% = 1,000 units

The following four possibilities may exist with regard to work-in-progress or the question of equivalent production:

1. Closing work-in-progress without any process loss or gain.
2. Closing work-in-progress with process loss or gain.
3. Opening and closing work-in-progress with no process loss or gain.
4. Opening and closing work-in-progress along with process loss or gain.

Situation I (Only Closing Work-in-Progress)

In this case, equivalent production is determined in the case of closing work-in-progress by applying percentages of completion for each element of cost. After computing equivalent production, the cost per unit of equivalent production is found and this cost per unit is used to value the finished output transferred to the second process and also closing work-in-progress units. It should be noted that the cost per unit (for each element of cost) is applied to equivalent production of work-in-progress units and not to work-in-progress units directly.

Examples 11.14 to 11.15 explain the preparation of process accounts in this situation.

EXAMPLE 11.14

The product manufactured by a light engineering factory undergoes two operations. The following data are available relating to expenses incurred on production during November, 2020:

	Machining	*Finishing*
Units as input	90,000	60,000
Expenses incurred in process :	₹	₹
Direct material	2,70,000	Nil
Direct labour	1,28,000	45,000
Overheads	64,000	1,35,000

At the end of the month, there were 30,000 units lying incomplete in Machining Operation. While the full quantity of material has been consumed for the total production, the expenditure on Labour and Overheads was estimated to be $66\frac{2}{3}\%$ in respect of the incompleted products.

You are required to prepare a detailed Cost Statement showing the final cost per unit assuming:

(i) Completed units of Machining Operations are transferred to the Finishing Operation;

(ii) Finishing Operation has completed all the units received from the earlier operation during November 2020 leaving no work-in-progress at the end of the month.

Solution

(i) Statement of Equivalent Production

Machining Operation:		*Total Units*	*DM*	*DL*	*OV*
			Equivalent Units		
Completed units		60,000	60,000	60,000	60,000
Incompleted units		30,000	30,000	20,000	20,000
Total		90,000	90,000	80,000	80,000
Finishing operation : units					
Transfer from machining operation	60,000	60,000	60,000	60,000	60,000

(ii) **Statement of Cost Per Unit of Machining Operation**

	DM	DL	Overheads
Costs incurred	2,70,000	1,28,000	64,000
Output	90,000	80,000	80,000
Cost per unit	3.00	1.60	.80

Statement of Total Cost

		Total
Machining Operation Costs:		
Direct material		2,70,000
Direct labour		1,28,000
Overheads		64,000
		4,62,000
Less: Closing stock (30,000 units)		
DM 30,000 × 3	= 90,000	
DL 20,000 × 1.6	= 32,000	
OV 20,000 × .08	= 16,000	1,38,000
Cost of finished output from machining operation		3,24,000
Add: Finished operation costs:		
Direct labour		45,000
Overheads		1,35,000
Total cost after finishing operation		5,04,000
Total output		Units 60,000
Cost per unit		₹8.40

EXAMPLE 11.15

A manufacturing concern, engaged in mass production produces standardised electric motor in one of its departments. From the following particulars of a job of 50 motors, you are required to value the work-in-progress and finished goods.

(a) Costs incurred as per job card:

Direct material	₹75,000	Overheads	₹60,000
Direct labour	₹20,000		

(b) Selling price per motor: ₹4,500

(c) Selling and distribution expenses are at 30% of sales value.

(d) 25 motors are completed and transferred to finished goods.

(e) Completion stage of work-in-progress:

Direct material	100%	Direct labour and overhead 60%	

☞ Solution

Statement of Equivalent Production and Cost

Particulars	*Direct Material*		*Labour & Overhead*		
	%	*Qty*	*%*	*Qty*	*Total*
Transferred to finished goods	100	25	100	25	
Work-in-progress	100	25	60	15	
Equivalent units		50		40	
Total cost (₹)		75,000		80,000	1,55,000
Cost per equivalent unit (₹)		1,500		2,000	3,500

Actual Cost of Production Per Unit of Finished Goods

Direct material	₹1,500
Labour & overhead	₹2,000
Total	₹3,500

Market Value per Unit of Finished Goods

Selling price	₹4,500
Less: Selling and distribution overheads @ 30% of ₹4,500	₹1,350
	₹3,150

Stocks should be at the lower of the cost (that is, ₹3,500) or market value (that is, ₹3,150). Hence, basis of valuation will be market value in this case.

Value of Work-in-Progress

Direct material: ₹1,500 × 25 units	= ₹37,500
Labour & Overhead: ₹(3,150 – 1,500) × 15 units	= ₹24,750
	₹62,250

Value of Finished Goods Stock

25 units × ₹3,150	= ₹ 78,750
Total value of inventory = ₹78,750 + ₹62,250	= ₹1,41,000

Situation 2 (Closing Work-in-Progress and Process Loss or Gain)

Process loss may occur (i) early in a process or during a process; or (ii) at the final stages of a process. The point of occurrence of normal losses (spoiled units) has an important bearing on deciding which of the following two approaches should be used in process accounting:

1. *First Approach* — Cost of normal loss units should be spread over the entire production, that is, cost of normal loss units should be included in the cost of all units computed as equivalent production.
2. *Second Approach* — Cost of normal loss units should be included in the cost of all good units which have been completed and thus cost of normal loss units will not be charged to closing work-in-progress.

The first approach is followed when normal loss occurs at the beginning of or during a process. Since the normal loss occurs early in processing, it applies to both completed production and units that are left in process; all work (production) done in that period should be charged with the normal loss. This is achieved by using a value of zero as the finished equivalent of the units lost, thus forcing the good unit that remains to absorb the cost of the bad units. The normal loss units are completely ignored, the cost per unit is increased. Costs for the period are divided by a smaller number of equivalent units, thereby increasing the cost per unit. Cost apportionment to units completed and units still in process is computed using the higher unit cost. Thus, normal spoilage costs are automatically spread over all the equivalent good units (units completed and units in process).

The second approach is followed when normal process loss occurs at the end of a process (for example, loss discovered after final inspection). In this case, as mentioned above, cost of normal loss units is included in the cost of only completed units and not in closing work-in-progress units. If the lost units occur at the end of a process, they are usually regarded as belonging to the completed units and hence costs are charged to those units which have been finished. Since none of the units lost or spoiled (normal loss units) come from closing work-in-progress, no part of the cost of spoiled units should be charged to the units still in process; the cost of spoiled units must be absorbed by the good units completed. This is done by first treating the normal loss units as completed and charging them with the same cost that applies to good completed units. The cost charged to normal loss units is then added to the cost of the good completed units, thus excluding any of the cost of the normal loss units in cost of work-in-progress units.

In absence of specific information regarding occurrence of normal loss, it should be preferably assumed that normal loss has taken place during a process and not at the end of a process. Hence, in such a case, the first approach (as mentioned above) should be followed.

Examples 11.16 to 11.18 explain the above two approaches.

EXAMPLE 11.16

During the month of April 2020, 4,000 units were introduced into process *A* at the cost of ₹23,200. At the end of the month, 3,000 units were completed and transferred to process *B* account. 720 units were still in process and 280 units were scrapped. A normal wastage of 5% was expected. It was estimated that the incomplete units have reached a stage in production as follows:

Materials	75%
Labour and overheads	50%

The additional costs incurred were:

Materials	₹ 6,160
Wages	₹ 13,760
Overheads	₹ 6,880

Unit scrapped realised at ₹2 per unit.

Prepare:

1. A statement showing equivalent production
2. Statement of evaluation and process *A* account.

☞ Solution

1. **Statement of Equivalent Production**

Input (units)	*Output*	*Units*	*Equivalent Production*			
			Material		*Labour and Overhead*	
			Qty.	*%*	*Qty.*	*%*
4,000	Normal loss	200	–	–	–	–
	Abnormal loss	80	80	100	80	100
	Finished production	3,000	3,000	100	3,000	100
	Work-in-progress	720	540	75	360	50
4,000	Total	4,000	3,620		3,440	

2. Statement showing cost per unit

Statement of Cost

Elements of Cost	*Cost (₹)*	*Equivalent Production Unit*	*Cost Per Units (₹)*
Materials			
Cost of units introduced	23,200		
Direct materials	6,160		
	29,360		
Less: Scrap value of normal loss 200 units × 2	400		
	28,960	3,620	8
Wages	13,760	3,440	4
Overheads	6,880	3,440	2
Total	49,600		14

Statement of Evaluation

Particulars	*Element of Cost*	*Equivalent Production (Units)*	*Cost Per Unit ₹*	*Cost ₹*	*Total Cost ₹*
Abnormal	Material	80	8	640	
loss	Labour	80	4	320	
	Overheads	80	2	160	1,120
Finished					
Production	Material	3,000	8	24,000	
	Labour	3,000	4	12,000	
	Overheads	3,000	2	6,000	42,000

(Contd.)

Particulars	*Element of Cost*	*Equivalent Production (Units)*	*Cost Per Unit* ₹	*Cost* ₹	*Total Cost* ₹
Work-in-progress	Material	540	8	4,320	
	Labour	360	4	1,440	
	Overheads	360	2	720	6,480
					49,600

EXAMPLE 11.17

SBL LTD. furnishes you the following information relating to process *B* for the month of April, 2020:

(i) Opening work-in-progress—Nil
(ii) Units introduced—10,000 units @ ₹5 per unit
(iii) Expenses debited to the process *B*—₹5,000
(iv) 8,000 units of finished output were transferred to the next process during the month
(v) Normal loss in process—10% of input.
(vi) Closing work-in-progress—800 units.
(vii) Completion stage, closing work-in-progress material 100%, labour and overhead 50%, abnormal loss material 100%, labour and overhead 80%.
(viii) Scrap realisation: Normal loss—@ ₹2 per unit; abnormal loss—@ ₹4 per unit.

You are required to prepare:

(1) Statement of equivalent production.
(2) Statement of cost of each element.
(3) Statement of evaluation.
(4) Process *B* account.
(5) Abnormal loss account.

Solution

(1) Statement of equivalent production

SBL LTD.

Input Units	*Particulars*	*Output Units*	*Equivalent Production*			
			Material		*Labour and Overheads*	
			Units	*%*	*Units*	*%*
–	Opening WIP	–	–	–	–	–
10,000	Introduced during the month	–	–	–	–	–
	Finished output (transferred to next process)	8,000	8,000	100%	8,000	100%
	Normal loss	1,000	–	–	–	–

(Contd.)

Input Units	Particulars	Output Units	Equivalent Production			
			Material		Labour and Overheads	
			Units	%	Units	%
	Abnormal loss	200	200	100%	160	80%
	Closing WIP	800	800	100%	400	50%
10,000		10,000	9,000		8,560	

(2) Statement of cost of each element

Particulars	Materials ₹	Labour ₹	Overheads ₹	Total ₹
Units introduced	50,000			50,000
Processing material	24,600	10,400	5,000	40,000
	74,600	10,400	5,000	90,000
Loss: Scrap realisation for normal loss (1000 × 2)	2,000			2,000
Net cost	72,600	10,400	5,000	88,000
Equivalent production (units)	9,000	8,560	8,560	
Cost per unit (₹)	8.067	1.215	0.584	9.666

(3) Statement of evaluation

Items	Elements	Equivalent Unit	Cost Per Unit (₹)	Cost ₹	Total
Finished output transferred to next process	Materials Labour				
	Overheads	8,000	9.866	78,926	78,926
Abnormal loss	Materials	200	8.067	1,613	
	Labour	160	1.215	194	
	Overheads	160	0.584	93	1,900
Closing WIP	Materials	800	8.067	6,454	
	Labour	400	1.215	486	
	Overheads	400	0.584	234	7,174

(4) Process-*B* account for the month April 2020

Dr. *Cr.*

Particulars	Units	Amount ₹	Particulars	Units	Amount ₹
To Units introduced	10,000	50,000	By Finished output	8,000	78,926
Processing materials	–	24,600	Transferred		

(Contd.)

Particulars	Units	Amount ₹	Particulars	Units	Amount ₹
Direct labour		10,400	- Normal loss	1,000	2,000
Overheads		5,000	- Abnormal loss	200	1,900
			- Closing WIP	800	7,174
	10,000	90,000		10,000	90,000

(5) Abnormal loss account

Dr.					Cr.
Particulars	Units	Amount ₹	Particulars	Units	Amount ₹
To process-*B* account	200	1,900	By cash/bank (realisation of scrap @ ₹4/-	200	800
			By profit and loss account		1,100
	200	1,900		200	1,900

✍ EXAMPLE 11.18 *(NORMAL LOSS DURING A PROCESS)*

R.P. Ltd. furnishes you the following information relating to process *B* for the month of October 2020.

(i) Opening work-in-progress—Nil

(ii) Units introduced—10,000 units @ ₹3 per unit.

(iii) Expenses debited to the process:

Direct materials	₹14,650
Labour	₹21,148
Overheads	₹42,000

(iv) Normal loss in process—One per cent of input.

(v) Closing work-in-progress—350 units—Degree of completion

Material	100%
Labour and overheads	50%

(vi) Finished output 9,500 units

(vii) Degree of completion of abnormal loss:

Material	100%
Labour and overheads	80%

(viii) Units scrapped as normal loss were sold at ₹1 per unit.

(ix) All the units of abnormal loss were sold at ₹2.50 per unit.

Prepare:

1. Statement of equivalent production;
2. Statement of cost of finished goods, abnormal loss and closing work-in-progress.

☞ Solution

1. **Statement of Equivalent Production (Process *B*)**

	Total Units	Material Unit	Completion %	Labour Units	Completion %	Over-heads	Completion %
		Equivalent Production					
Finished output	9,500	9,500	100	9,500	100	9,500	100
Normal loss 1% of input of 10,000	100	—	—	—	—	—	—
Abnormal loss (balancing fig.)	50	50	100	40	80	40	80
Closing work-in-progress	350	350	100	175	50	175	50
	10,000	9,900		9,715		9,715	

Statement of Cost Per Equivalent Unit

	Material	Labour	Overhead
Units introduced 10,000 × 3	30,000	—	—
Add: Direct material	14,650		
	44,650		
Less: Sale of normal scrap 100 × 1	100		
	44,550	21,148	42,000
Cost per equivalent unit of production	₹44,550 / 9,900 = ₹4.50	₹21,148 / 9,715 = ₹2.18	₹42,000 / 9,715 = ₹4.32
Total cost per unit of production	= (4.50 + 2.18 + 4.32) = ₹11.00		

2. **Statement of Cost**

Finished goods	= 9,500 × 11			1,04,500
Abnormal loss:				
Material	= 50 × 4.50	=	225.0	
Labour	= 40 × 2.18	=	87.2	
Overheads	= 40 × 4.32	=	172.8	485
Closing WIP:				
Material	= 350 × 4.50	=	1,575	
Labour	= 175 × 2.18	=	382	
Overhead	= 175 × 4.32	=	756	2,713
		Total		1,07,698

3. **Process-*B* Account**

	Units	*Amount* (₹)		*Units*	*Amount* (₹)
The opening WIP	Nil	Nil	By normal loss	100	100
To units introduced	10,000	30,000	By abnormal loss	50	485
To direct materials		14,650	By finished output (₹11 per unit)	9,500	1,04,500
To labour		21,148	By closing WIP c/d	350	2,713
To overheads		42,000			
	10,000	1,07,798		10,000	1,07,798
To material	12,000	60,000	By spoilage	1,000	—
			By output transferred	10,000	1,10,000
To labour		33,600			
To overhead		22,400	By closing work-in-progress	1,000	6,000
	12,000	1,16,000		12,000	1,16,000

Note: As entire material is placed in the process at the beginning of the first process, it has been assumed that closing work-in-progress is complete 100% with regard to materials. Therefore, percentage of completion of 20% has been applied only in case of labour and overhead.

Situation 3 (Opening and Closing Work-in-Progress without Process Loss or Gain)

A process account may have opening work-in-progress as well as closing work-in-progress. The treatment of closing work-in-progress is the same with regard to equivalent production and determining its cost. In case of opening work-in-progress, the production or finished units completed during the period will comprise two lots: (i) the first lot will be of opening work-in-progress which is partially incomplete and which will be completed during the period; (ii) the second lot of production will be of those units which are introduced into the process during the current period and have been completed during the period.

Since costs tend to vary from period to period, each lot may carry different unit costs. The procedure of calculating equivalent production for opening work-in-progress units depends on which method of costing (cost flow assumption) has been used. If standard costing is not used, generally accepted accounting practices permit use of any one of the following three cost flow assumptions:

1. First-In, First-Out (FIFO)
2. Weighted Average Costing
3. Last-In, First-Out (LIFO)

FIFO The FIFO method of costing is based on the assumption that opening work-in-progress units are the first to be completed, the first costs incurred in the period should be attached to units in opening work-in-progress. After opening work-in-progress units have been completed, new units are taken up during the current period. Equivalent production of opening work-in-progress can be calculated as follows:

Equivalent production = Units in opening W.I.P × Percentage of work needed to finish the units. Costs associated with the opening inventory in process are separated from costs of units started and completed during the period, and the costs of the two periods are not combined before final transfer of completed units out of process. No unit of opening work-in-progress is automatically found in closing work-in-progress.

Weighted Average Costing Under average costing, opening work-in-progress units and costs both are combined with new production started in current period (both unit and cost) and weighted average cost per unit is determined by dividing the total cost (opening work-in-progress cost + current cost) by equivalent production. Costs attached with the opening inventory lose their identity because of this merger. The opening inventory cost is treated as if it were current period cost. No distinction is made between completed units from opening inventory and completed units from the new production. In fact, all units finished during the current accounting period are treated as if they were started and finished during that period. Therefore, equivalent production (of opening work-in-progress) will be all units of opening work-in-progress. There is only one final unit cost for all completed units—a weighted average unit cost.

FIFO and average costing, although based on different costing concepts, do not necessarily produce significantly different unit costs. The differences in unit costs between the two costing methods may exist only under the following conditions:

1. Opening work-in-progress units are large, relative to the number of units started during the current period. The lesser number of units in opening inventory will have little influence on the average cost.
2. The stage of completion of the opening work-in-progress units is quite advanced. In absence of this, previous period costs of opening inventory will not have any impact on the average cost.
3. Previous period costs are substantially different from current period costs.

Average costing under normal conditions (if the above conditions do not exist) is the most appropriate, accurate and simple. However, if the above conditions prevail, the average cost may not be helpful in efficiency measurement and cost control.

LIFO In LIFO method, the assumption is that the units entering into the process in the last are the first to be completed. This method influences differently the costs of complete units and the closing work-in-progress. The cost of opening work-in-progress is charged to the closing work-in-progress and thus the closing work-in-progress appears at the cost of opening work-in-progress. The completed units appear at their current costs.

Examples 11.19 to 11.24 present FIFO, Average Costing and LIFO methods in process accounts.

EXAMPLE 11.19 (FIFO)

From the following details prepare statement of equivalent production and statement of cost by using FIFO:

Opening work-in-process	2,000 units
Materials (100% complete)	₹7,500
Labour (60% complete)	₹3,000
Overhead (60% complete)	₹1,500
Introduced into the process	8,000 units

There are 2,000 units in closing work-in-progress and the stage of completion is estimated to be: Materials 100%, labour 50%, overhead 50%, 8,000 units are transferred to next process.

The process cost for the period are:

Material	₹1,00,000
Labour	₹78,000
Overhead	₹39,000

Solution

Statement of Equivalent Units

Particulars	*Units*	*Materials*		*Labour*		*Overheads*	
		%	*Unit*	%	*Unit*	%	*Unit*
Opening work-in-progress	2,000	–	–	40%	800	40%	800
Finished stock introduced and completed	6,000	100%	6,000	100%	6,000	100%	6,000
Closing work-in-progress	2,000	100%	2,000	50%	1,000	50%	1,000
			8,000		7,800		7,800

Statement of Cost

Particulars	*Materials*	*Labour*	*Overhead*
Cost	1,00,000	78,000	39,000
Equivalent units	8,000	7,800	7,800
	12.50/-	10/-	5/-

Statement of Evaluation

Particulars		
Cost of opening WIP	800 × 10 + 800 × 5	12,000
Cost of units introduced and completed during the year	6,000 × 12.5 + 6,000 × 10 + 6,000 × 5	1,65,000
Closing in W.I.P.	2,000 × 12.5 + 1,000 × 10 + 1,000 × 5	40,000

✍ EXAMPLE 11.20 (FIFO)

Following information is available regarding process *A* for the month of October 2020:

Production Record:

(i) Opening work-in-progress — 40,000 units
(Material: 100% complete, 25% complete for labour & overheads)

(ii) Units introduced — 1,80,000 units

(iii) Units completed — 1,50,000 units

(iv) Units in-process on 31.10.2020 — 70,000 units
(Material: 100% complete, 50% complete for labour & overheads)

Cost Record:

Opening work-in-progress:

Material	₹1,00,000
Labour	₹25,000
Overheads	₹45,000

Cost incurred during the month:

Material	₹6,60,000
Labour	₹5,55,000
Overheads	₹9,25,000

Assume that FIFO method is used for W.I.P. inventory valuation.

Required:

(i) Statement of equivalent production
(ii) Statement showing cost for each element
(iii) Statement of apportionment of cost
(iv) Process-*A* account

☞ Solution

Statement of Equivalent Production (FIFO Method)

Particulars				*Equivalent Production*			
				Material		*Labour & Overheads*	
Input (Units)		*Output*	*Units*	*% Completion*	*Qty.*	*% Completion*	*Qty.*
Opening WIP	40,000	Transfer to Process II					
Introduced	1,80,000	Opening WIP completed	40,000	—	—	75%	30,000
		Introduced & completed	1,10,000	100%	1,10,000	100%	1,10,000
		Closing WIP	70,000	100%	70,000	50%	35,000
	2,20,000		2,20,000		1,80,000		1,75,000

Statement Showing Cost for Each Element

Item of Cost	*Equivalent Production*	*Cost Incurred*	*Cost Per Unit*
Material	1,80,000	6,60,000	3.66667
Labour and overheads	1,75,000	14,80,000	8.45714
			12.12381

Statement of Evaluation

Transfer to Process II		
Opening WIP completed		
Cost incurred already	1,70,000	
Cost incurred during the month		
Labour & overheads	2,53,714	4,23,714
(30,000 × 8.45714)		
Introduced and completed 1,10,000 × 12.12381		13,33,619
		17,57,333
Closing WIP		
Material 70,000 × 3.6667	2,56,667	
Labour and overheads 35,000 × 8.45714	2,96,000	5,52,667

Process-*A* Account

Particulars	*Units*	*Amount*	*Particulars*	*Units*	*Amount*
To opening WIP	40,000	1,70,000	By Process-II Account	1,50,000	17,57,333
To materials	1,80,000	6,60,000			
To labour		5,55,000	By closing WIP	7,000	5,52,667
To overheads		9,25,000			
	2,20,000	23,10,000		2,20,000	23,10,000

✍ EXAMPLE 11.21 (FIFO)

The Vega Manufacturing Co. uses FIFO method of inventory valuation in process costing. The following data relate to Process I for the month of April, 2020:

(i) Beginning work-in-process:
- Quantity : 1,500 units
- Value : ₹4,500

(ii) Introduced during the month : 5,000 units
(iii) Transferred to Process II : 5,500 units
(iv) Ending work-in-process : 1,000 units
(v) Degree of completion:

	Beginning W.I.P	Ending W.I.P
Materials	100%	100%
Conversion	80%	60%

(vi) Cost added during the month:
- Materials : ₹10,000
- Labour : ₹9,800
- Overheads : ₹4,900

You are required to:

(i) Prepare a statement of equivalent production;

(ii) Prepare Process-I account.

☞ ***Solution***

Statement of Equivalent Production

Production	*Units*	*Material*		*Labour*	*Overhead*
		% of Completion	*Equ. Pro.*	*% of Completion*	*Equ. Pro.*
Opening WIP	1,500	–	–	20	300
Completely processed during the period (5,500 – 1,000)	4,500	100	4,500	100	4,500
Closing WIP	1,000	100	1,000	60	600
Total	7,000		5,500		5,400

Statement of Cost

Element of Cost	*Cost Incurred During the Year (₹)*	*Equivalent Production Units*	*Cost Per Units (₹)*
Materials	10,000	5,500	1.818
Labour	9,800	5,400	1.815
Overhead	4,900	5,400	0.907
	24,700		4.540

Statement of Evaluation

	₹	₹
Opening work-in-progress (current cost):		
Material		
Labour: 300 units @ 1.815	545	
Overhead: 300 units @ .907	273	818
Closing WIP:		
Material: 1,000 units @ 1.818	1,818	
Labour: 600 units @ 1.815	1,089	
Overhead: 600 units @ .907	545	3,452
Units completely processed during the year (4,500 @ ₹4.540)		20,430
		24,700

Process Account

Particulars	Units	₹	Particulars	Units	₹
To opening WIP	1,500	4,500	By finished stock to next		
To material	5,000	1,000	process (₹4,500 + 818 +		
To labour		9,800	₹20,430)	5,500	25,748
To overhead		4,900	By closing WIP	1,000	3,452
	6,500	29,200		6,500	29,200

EXAMPLE 11.22 (LIFO)

From the following information prepare: (a) Statement of equivalent production; (b) Statement of cost for each element; (c) Statement of apportionment of cost; and (d) Process account for process *A* using the LIFO method of inventory costing for the month of December 2020.

Units in process, Dec. 2020	10,000
(All material used, 50% completed regarding labour and overhead)	
New units introduced	20,000
Total units	30,000
Production report reveals the following information:	
Units completed	15,000
Units in process on December 31, 2020	
(All material used, 50% complete regarding labour and overhead)	15,000
Loss in process	Nil

Cost Record

Work-in-process as on December 1, 2020

	₹	₹
Material		3,600
Labour		3,900
Overhead		3,900
Cost for December, 2020	₹	
Material	14,400	
Labour	31,150	
Overhead	31,150	
Total Cost	88,100	

Solution

Process *A* (LIFO Method)
Statement of Equivalent Production

Input		Output		Equivalent Production					
Particulars	Units	Particulars	Units	Material		Labour		Overhead	
				Units	%	Units	%	Units	%
Opening stock	10,000	Unit completed	15,000	15,000	100	15,000	100	15,000	100

(Contd.)

Input		Output		Equivalent Production					
Particulars	Units	Particulars	Units	Material		Labour		Overhead	
				Units	%	Units	%	Units	%
New units		Closing inventory							
introduced	20,000	(a) Work on O/WIP	10,000*	—		—		—	
		(b) New units	5,000	5,000	100	2,500	50	2,500	50
	30,000		30,000	20,000		17,500		17,500	

*No work has been done on units which represented opening work-in-process.

Statement of Cost of Each Element

Elements of Cost	Cost in Process ₹	Equivalent Production Units	Cost Per Unit ₹
Material	14,400	20,000	0.72
Labour	31,150	17,500	1.78
Overhead	31,150	17,500	1.78
	76,700		

Statement of Apportionment of Cost

Item	Elements	Equivalent Production Units	Cost Per Unit ₹	Cost ₹	Total ₹
Units completed	Material	15,000	0.72	10,800	
	Labour	15,000	1.78	26,700	
	Overhead	15,000	1.78	26,700	64,200
Closing Inventory					
Opening WIP	Material	—	0.72	—	
	Labour	—	1.78	—	
	Overhead	—	1.78	—	
New units	Material	5,000	0.72	3,600	
	Labour	2,500	1.78	4,450	
	Overhead	2,500	1.78	4,450	12,500
					76,700

Process-A Account

Particulars	Units	Amount ₹	Particulars	Units	Amount ₹
To opening			By units		
WIP	10,000	11,400	completed	15,000	64,200
Units introduced	20,000		By closing stock	15,000	23,900

(Contd.)

Particulars	Units	Amount ₹	Particulars	Units	Amount ₹
Material		14,400			
Labour		31,150			
Overhead		31,150			
	30,000	88,100		30,000	88,100

Note: Process A/c has been credited with an amount of ₹23,900 being the cost of closing stock, determined as follows:

	₹
Costs of Opening WIP:	
Material	3,600
Labour	3,900
Overhead	3,900
	11,400
Add: Cost of work done on opening WIP	Nil
Add: Costs of newly introduced units	12,500
	23,900

EXAMPLE 11.23 (FIFO)

Vinal Ltd. produces Article *B* from a material which passes through two processes namely *P* and *Q*. The details relating to a month are as under:

	Process P	Process Q
Materials introduced (units)	10,000	
Transferred to next process (units)	9,000	
Work-in-progress:		
At the beginning of the month (units)	—	600
At the end of the month (units)	1,000	400
Expenses:		
Work-in-process at the beginning of the month	—	9,400
Materials introduced at the beginning of the process	1,20,000	
Labour and overheads	27,600	18,200

Stage of completion of work-in-process:

Process *P*: Closing W.I.P. 20% complete in respect of labour and overheads.

Process *Q*: Opening W.I.P. $33\frac{1}{3}\%$ complete in respect of labour and overheads.

Closing W.I.P. 25% complete in respect of labour and overheads.

The finished output *B* emerging out of Process *Q* is sold at ₹20 per unit.

The management is considering an alternative by which the finished output *B* could be further treated by installing a new machine at a capital cost of ₹8 lakhs. In such an event, the final product known as article *N* produced by this operation could be sold at ₹25 per unit. The operating expenses of the aforesaid further treatment are estimated at ₹23,000. The company desires a return on investment of 25%.

Required:

(a) Prepare the process cost accounts for processes *P* and *Q*.
(Show the working of equivalent units and cost per equivalent unit in each process).
(b) Prepare a statement of profitability of product *B* as it emerges from process *Q*.
(c) Advise the management whether further treatment of product *B* by installing the new machine should be taken up or not.

☞ ***Solution***

(a) Process Cost Accounts

Equivalent Units—Process *P*

Input units		*Materials*		*Labour & Overhead*	
		Units	*Completion (%)*	*Units*	*Completion (%)*
9,000	Units completed	9,000	100	9,000	100
1,000	Closing stock	1,000	100	200	20
	Equivalent units	10,000		9,200	
	Expenses	₹1,20,000		₹27,600	
	Cost per equivalent unit ₹	12		₹3	

Cost of closing stock = 1,000 × ₹12 + 200 × ₹3 = ₹12,600
Cost of completed units = ₹1,20,000 + ₹27,600 – ₹12,600 – ₹1,35,000

Equivalent Units—Process *Q*

Input		*Materials*		*Labour & Overhead*	
		Units	*Completion %*	*Units*	*Completion %*
600	Opening stock (work completed in current period)	—		400	$66\frac{2}{3}$
8,600	Units completed (units started less closing stock; 9,000 – 400)	8,600	100	8,600	100
400	Closing stock (work done in current period)	400	100	100	25
	Equivalent units	9,000		9,100	

(Contd.)

Input	Materials		Labour & Overhead	
	Units	Completion %	Units	Completion %
Expenses	₹1,35,000		₹18,200	
Cost per equivalent unit	₹15		₹2	

Cost of closing stock = 400 × ₹15 + 100 × ₹2 = ₹6,200

Cost of finished stock (Product *B*) = ₹9,400 + ₹1,35,000 + ₹18,200 – ₹6,200

= ₹1,56,400

Process-*P* Account

	Units	₹		Units	₹
To materials	10,000	1,20,000	By transfer to process *Q*	9,000	1,35,000
To labour and overhead		27,600	By closing stock	1,000	12,600
	10,000	1,47,600		10,000	1,47,600

Process-*Q* Account

	Units	₹		Units	₹
To opening stock	600	9,400	By transfer to finished stock (Product *B*)	9,200	1,56,400
To process *P*	9,000	1,35,000			
To labour and overhead		18,200			
			By closing stock	400	6,200
	9,600	1,62,600		9,600	1,62,600

(b) Profitability of product *B*

Sales (9,200 units at ₹20 per unit)	₹1,84,000
Cost of production	₹1,56,400
Profit per month	₹ 27,600

	₹	₹
(c) Further processing of product *B* to final product *N*		
Sales (9,200 units of *N* @ ₹25)		₹2,30,000
Cost of production:		
Upto product *B* stage	₹1,56,400	
Further processing	₹ 23,000	₹1,79,400
Profit per month		₹ 50,600
Profit without further processing		₹ 27,600
Additional profit by further processing		₹ 23,000 per month

Desired return on fresh investment	= 25% on ₹8,00,000
	= 2,00,000 per year
	= ₹16,667 per month

Further processing results in:

Additional profit per month of ₹23,000 which works out to a return of 34.5% $\frac{23,000 \times 12 \times 100}{8,00,000}$ on investment as against the desired return of 25%.

Therefore, subject to the consideration of other non-cost factor, if any, the proposal for further processing is recommended for acceptance.

Example 11.24 (Average Costing)

Following information is available regarding process *A* for the month of February, 2020:

Production Record

Units in process as on 1.2.2020	4,000
(All materials used, 25% complete for labour and overhead)	
New units introduced	16,000
Units completed	14,000
Units in process as on 28.2.2020	6,000
(All materials used, $33\frac{1}{3}$% complete for labour and overhead)	

Cost Records

Work-in-process as on 1.2.2020	₹
Materials	6,000
Labour	1,000
Overhead	1,000
	8,000
Cost during the month:	
Materials	25,600
Labour	15,000
Overhead	15,000
	55,600

Presuming that average method of inventory is used, prepare:

(i) Statement of equivalent production.
(ii) Statement showing cost for each element.
(iii) Statement of apportionment of cost.
(iv) Process cost account for process *A*.

☞ Solution

(i) Statement of Equivalent Production (Average Cost Method)

Particulars			Materials		Labour		Overhead	
Input (Units)	*Output*	*Units*	*% Completion*	*Equivalent Units*	*% Completion*	*Equivalent Units*	*% Completion*	*Equivalent Units*
20,000	Completed	14,000	100	14,000	100	14,000	100	14,000
	WIP	6,000	100	6,000	$33\frac{1}{3}$	2,000	$33\frac{1}{3}$	2,000
20,000		20,000		20,000		16,000		16,000

(ii) Statement of Cost

Particulars	Materials	Labour	Overhead	Total
Cost of opening work-in-progress (₹)	6,000	1,000	1,000	8,000
Cost incurred during the month (₹)	25,600	15,000	15,000	55,600
Total cost (₹): (i)	31,600	16,000	16,000	63,600
Equivalent units: (ii)	20,000	16,000	16,000	
Cost per equivalent unit (₹) (iii) = (i)/(ii)	1.58	1	1	3.58

(iii) Statement of Cost Apportionment

			₹	₹
Cost of output transferred: (i)	14,000 units @	₹3.58		50,120
Cost of closing work-in-progress: (ii)				
Materials	6,000 units @	₹1.58	9,480	
Labour	2,000 units @	₹1	2,000	
Overhead	2,000 units @	₹1	2,000	13,480
Total Cost: (i) + (ii)				63,600

Dr. **(iv) Process-*A* Account** Cr.

Particulars	Units	₹	Particulars	Units	₹
To opening WIP	4,000	8,000	By completed units	14,000	50,120
To materials	16,000	25,600	By closing WIP	6,000	13,480
To labour		15,000			
To overhead		15,000			
	20,000	63,600		20,000	63,600

Situation 4 (Opening and Closing Work-in-Progress with Process Losses or Gains)

In this situation, due adjustments are made for normal loss, abnormal loss, and abnormal gain in calculation of equivalent production. However, there is no change in the treatment of normal loss, abnormal loss and abnormal gain. Normal spoilage cost is borne by the good units produced; proceeds realised from the sale of normal loss scrap are credited to the relevant process account. These proceeds (sale of scrap) are also taken into account while calculating cost per unit of equivalent production. Abnormal loss units are valued like good units.

Examples 11.25 to 11.30 display the preparation of Process Accounts in this situation.

EXAMPLE 11.25

The following data are available in respect of Process I for March, 2020:

(i) Opening stock of work-in-progress: 800 units at a cost of ₹4,000.

(ii) The degree of completion of opening W.I.P.:

Materials	100%
Labour	60%
Overhead	60%

(iii) Input of materials at a total cost of ₹36,800 for 9,200 units.

(iv) Direct wages incurred ₹16,740.

(v) Production overheads ₹8,370.

(vi) Units scrapped 1,200 units. The stage of completion of these units was:

Materials	100%
Labour	80%
Overhead	80%

(vii) Closing work-in-progress: 900 units. The stage of completion of these units was:

Materials	100%
Labour	70%
Overhead	70%

(viii) 7,900 units were completed and transferred to the next process.

(ix) Normal loss is 8% of the total input (opening stock plus units put into the process).

(x) Scrap value is ₹4 per unit.

You are required to:

(a) Compute equivalent production.

(b) Calculate cost per equivalent unit.

(c) Calculate the cost of abnormal loss (or gain), closing work-in-progress and units transferred to the next process using FIFO method.

(d) Show the Process Account for March, 2020.

Solution

Statement of Equivalent Output (FIFO Method)

Input	*Particulars*	*Unit*	*Material*		*Labour and Overhead*	
			%	Unit	%	Unit
	Opening stock	800	–	–	40%	320

(Contd.)

Input	Particulars	Unit	Material %	Material Unit	Labour and Overhead %	Labour and Overhead Unit
	Normal loss					
	(8% of total input)	800	–	–	–	–
	Abnormal loss					
	(1200 – 800)	400	100%	400	80%	320
	Finished goods	7,100	100%	7,100	100%	7,100
	Closing W.I.P.	900	100%	900	70%	630
	Equivalent output	10,000		8,400		8,370

Cost Per Equivalent Unit

Particulars	Amount ₹	Eq. unit	Per Unit
Material	36,800		
Less: Scrap (800 × 4)	3,200		
	33,600	8,400	4
Labour and Overhead			
(16,740 + 8,370)	25,110	8,370	3
Cost per equivalent unit			7
W.N. Cost of Abnormal Loss			
Material (400 × 4)			1,600
Labour and Overhead (320 × 3)			960
			2,560
Cost of Closing W.I.P.			3,600
Material (900 × 4)			1,890
Labour and overhead (630 × 3)			5,490

Process Account

Particulars	Unit	Amount ₹	Particulars	Unit	Amount
To opening W.I.P.	800	4,000	By normal loss	800	3,200
To material	9,200	36,800	By abnormal loss	400	2,560
To labour		16,740	By finished goods*	7,900	54,660
To overhead		8,370	By closing W.I.P.	900	5,490
	10,000	65,910		10,000	65,910

Cost of Finished Goods

Cost of completing op. stock (4,000 + 320 × 3)	4,960
Cost of completing next 7,100 units (7,100 × 7)	49,700
	54,660

EXAMPLE 11.26

From the following information prepare:

(a) Statement of equivalent production;
(b) Statement of element of cost/unit;
(c) Statement of apportionment of cost;
(d) Process-II account under FIFO method.

(i) Opening stock—800 units costing ₹6,038 (transferred in cost ₹1,200, material ₹1,578, labour ₹1,710, overheads ₹1,550)
(ii) Transferred from previous Process I—12,000 units costing ₹16,350.
(iii) Cost incurred in Process II:

Material	₹11,600
Labour	₹20,760
Overheads	₹15,570

(iv) Normal loss in Process II—10%
(v) Scrap realised @ ₹10/10 units
(vi) Closing stock—1800 units
(vii) Transfer to next process—9,700 units
(viii) Degree of completion:

	Op. Stock (%)	*Cl. Stock (%)*	*Scrapped Units (%)*
Material	60	60	100
Labour	40	51	41
Overheads	40	51	41

Solution

Statement of Equivalent Production

			Material		*Labour and Overhead*	
Input	*Particulars*	*Output*	*%*	*Unit*	*%*	*Unit*
800	Opening W.I.P. finished	800	40%	320	60%	480
12,000	Input introduced					
	Units introduced and finished	8,900	100%	8,900	100%	8,900
	Normal loss	1,200	—	—	—	—
	Abnormal loss	100	100%	100	41%	41
	Closing stock	1,800	60%	1,080	51%	918
12,800		12,800		10,400		10,339

Statement of Cost per Unit

Particulars	*Material I*	*Material II*	*Labour*	*Overhead*
Cost	16,350	11,600	20,760	15,570
Less: Sale of Scrap	—	1,200	—	—

(Contd.)

Particulars	Material I	Material II	Labour	Overhead
	16,350	10,400	20,760	15,570
Equivalent production	10,400	10,400	10,339	10,339
Per unit cost	1.5721	1	2.0079	1.5059

Statement of Apportionment of Cost

Particulars	*Item*	*Equivalent Units*	*Rate Per Unit*	*Total*
Cost of Completed Units				
Opening cost of 800 units				6,038
further cost on opening stock	Material I	320	1.5721	
	Material II	320	1.0000	
	Labour	480	2.0074	
	Overhead	480	1.5059	2,510
Cost of Units Introduced and Finished During the Year				
Cost of 8,900 completed units	Material I	8,900	1.5721	
	Material II	8,900	1.0000	
	Labour	8,900	2.0079	
	Overhead	8,900	1.5059	54,165
Total cost of finished goods				62,713
Cost of Abnormal Loss	Material I	100	1.5721	
100 units Abnormal Loss	Material II	100	1.0000	
	Labour	41	2.0079	
	Overhead	41	1.5059	401
Closing Work in Progress				
1,800 units of closing W.I.P.	Material I	1,080	1.5721	
	Material II	1,080	1.0000	
	Labour	918	2.0079	
	Overhead	918	1.5059	6,004

Process-II Account

Particulars	*Unit*	*Amount*	*Particulars*	*Unit*	*Amount*
To opening stock	800	6,038	By normal loss	1,200	1,200
To units received from			@ ₹1 per unit		
Process II	12,000	16,350	By abnormal loss	100	401
To material		11,600	By transfer to finished	9,700	62,713
To labour		20,760	products		

(Contd.)

Particulars	Unit	Amount	Particulars	Unit	Amount
To overhead		15,570	By closing W.I.P.	1,800	6,004
	12,800	70,318		12,800	70,318

EXAMPLE 11.27

From the following information relating to Process I of a factory for the month of March, 2020, prepare the statement of equivalent production, statement of cost, statement of evaluation and process account using average cost method:

(i) Opening work-in-progress: 500 units

Materials	₹27,000
Labour	₹8,000
Overheads	₹12,500
	₹47,500

(ii) Cost incurred during March, 2020

Input of materials (14,000 units)	₹5,74,750
Labour	₹1,19,300
Overheads	₹1,78,450

(iii) Process loss:
Normal loss: 10% of opening W/P and input
Value of scrapped unit: ₹10 each
Actual loss during March, 2020: 1,500 units
Degree of completion: Material 100%, Labour and Overheads 60%

(iv) Closing work-in-progress: 1,000 units
Degree of completion : Materials 100%, Labour and Overheads 70%

(v) Processed units transferred to Process II: 12,000 units during March, 2020.

Solution

Statement of Equivalent Production and Cost (Average Cost Method)

Particulars		Equivalent Production					
		Material		Labour		Overheads	
		Completion (%)	Units	Completion (%)	Units	Completion (%)	Units
Units finished during the period	12,000	100	12,000	100	12,000	100	12,000
Normal loss (10% of 14,500)	1,450	–	–	–	–	–	–
Abnormal loss (1500 – 1450)	50	100	50	60	30	60	30
Cl. WIP	1,000	100	1,000	70	700	70	700
	14,500						
Equivalent prod. (units)			13,050		12,730		12,730
Cost:	₹		₹		₹		₹
Opening balance	47,500		27,000		8,000		12,500

(Contd.)

Incurred during the period	8,72,500	5,74,750	1,19,300	1,78,450
	9,20,000	6,01,750	1,27,300	1,90,950
Less value of normal loss realised (1450 × 10)	14,500	14,500		
Total cost	9,05,500	5,87,250	1,27,300	1,90,950
Equivalent production units		13,050	12,730	12,730
Cost p.u. of equivalent production		45	10	15

Statement of Evaluation

(1) Cost of output transferred to Process II 12,000 × ₹70 = ₹8,40,000

(2) Value of abnormal loss

Material	50 × 45 =	2,250
Labour	30 × 10 =	300
Overheads	30 × 15 =	450
		3,000

(3) Closing WIP

Material	1,000 × 45 =	45,000
Labour	700 × 10 =	7,000
Overheads	700 × 15 =	10,500
		62,500

Process-I Account

Particulars	*Units*	*Amt (₹)*	*Particulars*	*Units*	*Amt (₹)*
Op. WIP	500	47,500	By normal loss	1,450	14,500
Material introduced	14,000	5,74,750	Abnormal loss	50	3,000
Labour		1,19,300	Transfer to Process II	12,000	8,40,000
Overheads		1,78,450	Cl. WIP	1,000	62,500
	14,500	9,20,000		14,500	9,20,000

✍ EXAMPLE 11.28

The following details are related to the work done in process "*A*" of XYZ Company during the month of March, 2020:

Opening work-in-progress (2,000 units)	
Materials	₹80,000
Labour	₹15,000
Overheads	₹45,000
Materials introduced in process "*A*" (38,000 units)	₹14,80,000
Direct labour	₹3,59,000
Overheads	₹10,77,000

Units scrapped: 3,000 units

Degree of completion :

Materials	100%
Labour and overheads	80%

Closing work-in-progress: 2,000 units

Degree of completion:

Materials	100%
Labour and overheads	80%

Units finished and transferred to Process "*B*": 35,000 units

Normal loss:

5% of total input including opening work-in-progress

Scrapped units fetch ₹20 per piece.

You are required to prepare:

(i) State of equivalent production
(ii) Statement of cost per equivalent unit
(iii) Statement of valuation, and
(iv) Process "*A*" Account, Normal Wastage Account and Abnormal Wastage/Effectives Account.

☞ ***Solution***

Average method has been used.

Statement of Equivalent Production

Input	*Units*	*Output*	*Units*	Equivalent units			
				Material		*Labour and Overheads*	
				%	*Units*	*%*	*Units*
Opening WIP	2,000	Normal wastage	2,000	—	—	—	—
Introduced	38,000	Abnormal wastage	1,000	100%	1,000	80%	800
		Closing WIP	2,000	100%	2,000	80%	1,600
		Finished units	35,000	100%	35,000	100%	35,000
	40,000		40,000		38,000		37,400

Statement of Cost per Equivalent unit

Category	*Total Cost*	*Eq. Unit*	*Cost Per Eq. unit*
Material	(80,000 + 14,80,000) – (2,000 × 20) = 15,20,000	38,000	40
Labour	(15,000 + 3,59,000) = 3,74,000	37,400	10
Overheads	(45,000 + 10,77,000) = 11,22,000	37,400	30
		Total cost per equivalent unit	80

Statement of Valuation

Abnormal wastage = (1,000 × 40) + 800 (10 + 30) = 72,000
Closing WIP = (2,000 × 40) + 1,600 (10 + 30) = 1,44,000
Finished units = 35,000 (80) = 28,00,000

Process Account

Particulars	*Units*	*Amount*	*Particulars*	*Units*	*Amount*
To opening WIP	2,000	1,40,000	By normal wastage @ 20%	2,000	40,000
(80,000 + 15,000 + 45,000)			By abnormal wastage	1,000	72,000
To material	38,000	14,80,000	By closing WIP	2,000	1,44,000
To labour		3,59,000	By finished units	35,000	28,00,000
To overheads		10,77,000	@ ₹80 per unit		
	40,000	30,56,000		40,000	30,56,000

Normal Wastage Account

Particulars	*Units*	*Amount*	*Particulars*	*Units*	*Amount*
To process	2,000	40,000	By sale proceeds	2,000	40,000

Abnormal Wastage Account

Particulars	*Units*	*Amount*	*Particulars*	*Units*	*Amount*
To proceeds account	1000	72,000	By sale @ × 20	1,000	20,000
			By costing P & L A/c		52,000
	1,000	72,000		1,000	72,000

EXAMPLE 11.29

The following data relate to process Q –

(i) Opening work-in-progress 4000 units
Degree of completion –

Materials	100%	₹24,000
Labour	60%	₹14,400
Overheads	60%	₹ 7,200

(ii) Received during the month of April from process P —
40,000 units ₹1,71,000

(iii) Expenses incurred in process Q during the month –

Materials	₹ 79,000
Labour	₹1,38,230
Overheads	₹ 69,120

(iv) Closing work-in-progress 3,000 units
Degree of completion —

Materials 100%
Labour and overheads 50%

(v) Units scrapped — 4000 units
Degree of completion –
Material 100%, labour and overheads 80%

(vi) Normal loss : 5% of current input.

(vii) Spoiled goods realised ₹1.50 each on sale.

(viii) Completed units are transferred to warehouse.

Prepare, using FIFO method –

(a) Statement of equivalent production;
(b) Statement of cost per equivalent unit;
(c) Statement of evaluation;
(d) Process *Q* account;
(e) Abnormal loss account.

☞ *Solution*

Statement of Equivalent Production

Input	*Particulars*	*Output*	*Material* %	*Material* Unit	*Labour* %	*Labour* Unit	*Overheads* %	*Overheads* Unit
4,000	Opening W.I.P.	4,000	–	–	40	1,600	40	1,600
40,000	Units completed & transferred to warehouse	33,000	100	33,000	100	33,000	100	33,000
	Normal loss	2,000	–	–	–	–	–	–
	Abnormal loss	2,000	100	2,000	80	1,600	80	1,600
	Closing W.I.P	3,000	100	3,000	50	1,500	50	1,500
44,000		44,000		38,000		37,700		37,700

Statement of Cost per Equivalent Units

	Cost	*Equivalent Units*	*Cost Per Equivalent Unit*	
Material I	1,71,000	38,000	4.50	
Material II	79,000			
Recovery of Spoilage	–3,000			
	76,000	38,000	2.00	
Labour	1,38,230	37,700	3.67	5.50
Overhead	69,120	37,700	1.83	
Total			12	

Statement of Evaluation

Particulars	Element of Cost	Equivalent Unit	Cost/Unit	Cost
Opening W.I.P	Material I	–	–	–
	Material II	–	–	–
	Labour	1,600	3.67	5,872
	Overheads	1,600	1.83	2,928
				8,800
Units introduces & completed during the year	Material I Material II Labour Overhead	33,000	12	3,96,000
Closing W.I.P.	Material I	3,000	4.50	13,500
	Material II	3,000	2.0	6,000
	Labour	1,500	3 .67 ⎤ 5.50	
	Overhead	1,500	1.83 ⎦	8,200
				27,750
Abnormal Loss	Material I	2,000	4.50	9,000
	Material II	2,000	2.00	4,000
	Labour	1,600	3 .67 ⎤ 5.50	
	Overhead	1,600	1.83 ⎦	8,800
				21,800

Process A/c

Particulars	Unit	Amount	Particulars	Unit	Amount
To opening W.I.P	4,000	45,600	By normal loss	2,000	3,000
To material I	40,000	1,71,000	By cost of finished Goods	37,000	4,50,400
To material II		79,000	By abnormal loss	2,000	21,800
To labour		1,38,230	By closing W.I.P.	3,000	27,750
To overhead		69,120			
	44,000	5,02,950		44,000	5,02,950

Abnormal Loss Account

Particulars	Unit	Amount	Particulars	Unit	Amount
To proces account	2,000	21,800	By sale	2,000	3,000
			By costing P & L A/c	–	18,800
	2,000	21,800		2,000	21,800

EXAMPLE 11.30

ABC Limited manufactures a product "ZX" by using the process namely RT. For the month of May, 2020, the following data are available:

	Process RT
Material introduced (units)	16,000
Transfer to next process (units)	14,400
Work-in-process:	
At the beginning of the month (units)	4,000
(4/5 completed)	
At the end of month (units)	3,000
(2/3 completed)	
Cost records:	
Work in process at the beginning of the month	
Material	₹ 30,000
Conversion cost	₹ 29,200
Cost during the month : materials	₹1,20,000
Conversion cost	₹1,60,800

Normal spoiled units are 10% of goods finished output transferred to next process. Defects in these units are identified in their finished state. Material for the product is put in the process at the beginning of the cycle of operation, whereas labour and other indirect cost flow evenly over the year. It has no realisable value for spoiled units.

Required:

(i) Statement of equivalent production (average cost method);
(ii) Statement of cost and distribution of cost; and
(iii) Process accounts.

Solution

Statement of Equivalent Production of Process *RT*

Input units	*Details*	*Output Units*	*Equivalent Production*			
			Material % Units	*%*	*Conversion Cost Units*	
4,000	Opening WIP					
16,000	Introduced completed and transfer to next	14,400	14,400	100%	14,400	100%
	Normal spoilage	1440	1,440	100%	1,440	100%
	Abnormal spoilage	1,160	1,160	100%	1,160	100%
	Closing WIP	3,000	3,000	100%	2,000	66.67%
20,000		20,000	20,000		19,000	

Statement Showing Cost of Each Element

	Opening (₹)	*Cost in Process* (₹)	*Total* (₹)	*Equivalent Units*	*Cost Per Units*
Materials	30,000	1,20,000	1,50,000	20,000	7.50
Conversion cost	29,200	1,60,800	1,90,000	19,000	10.00

Statement of Apportionment of Cost

Units completed	Material	14,400	7.50	
	Conversion cost	14,400	10.00	2,52,000
	Normal spoilage (10%)			25,200
Closing stock	Material	3,000	7.50	
	Conversion cost	2,000	10.00	42,500
Abnormal stock	Material	1,160	7.50	
	Conversion cost	1,160	10.00	20,300

Process Account

	₹		₹
To opening WIP	59,200	By profit and loss account (abnormal)	20,300
To material	1,20,000	By transfer to next process	2,77,200
To conversion cost	1,60,800	By closing WIP	42,500
	3,40,000		3,40,000

INTER-PROCESS PROFITS

In processing industries, sometimes, the output of each process transferred to the next process is charged at an inflated cost or market value instead of only at actual cost. That is, each process is charged with its input at current prices. Truly speaking, the efficiency of each process should be determined in terms of current prices and not on the basis of a price relating to the previous period. In the manner, profit or loss determined will be realistic and remedial action may be taken where the profit on any process is insufficient. The profit or loss made by the transferor process is thus revealed in the process account.

Inter-process profits accounting tends to make the costing records more complicated. Also such profits will inflate the value of stock and work-in-progress in excess of the actual costs. For financial accounting purposes, such inflated stocks are to be brought down at the lower cost or market value. Thus, for balance sheet purposes, the values of stocks computed under inter-process profits are not useful. Stock adjustment is needed purely for reasons of prudence and to conform to generally accepted accounting principle. But, for individual process accounts, the inclusion of departmental process profits may be necessary.

EXAMPLE 11.31

The following are the details in respect of processes *X* and *Y* of a processing factory:

	Process X	Process Y
	₹	₹
Material	10,000	—
Labour	10,000	14,000
Overhead	4,000	10,000

The output of process *X* is transferred to process *Y* at a price calculated to give a profit of 20% on the transfer price and the output of process *Y* is charged to finished stock at a profit of 25% on the transfer price. The finished department realised ₹1,00,000 for the finished goods received from process *Y*. You are asked to show process accounts and total profits, assuming there was no opening and no closing work-in-progress.

Solution

Process-*X* Account

	₹		₹
To material	10,000	By transfer to process *Y*	30,000
To labour	10,000		
To overhead	4,000		
To profit (20% of transfer price)	6,000		
	30,000		30,000

Process-*Y* Account

	₹		₹
To transfer from process *X*	30,000	By transfer to finished stock a/c	72,000
To labour	14,000		
To overhead	10,000		
To profit (25% of the transfer period)	18,000		
	72,000		72,000

Profit and Loss Account

	₹		₹
To cost of sale	72,000	By sales	1,00,000
To profit c/d	28,000		
	1,00,000		1,00,000
To total profit	₹52,000	By profit b/d	₹28,000
		By profit on process *X*	6,000
		By profit on process *Y*	18,000
	52,000		52,000

EXAMPLE 11.32

Pharma Limited produces product "Glucodin" which passes through two processes before it is completed and transferred to finished stock. The following data relates to March, 2020:

	Process I	Process II	Finished Stock
	₹	₹	₹
Opening stock	1,50,000	1,80,000	4,50,000
Direct materials	3,00,000	3,15,000	
Direct wages	2,24,000	2,25,000	
Factory overheads	2,10,000	90,000	
Closing stock	74,000	90,000	2,25,000
Inter process profit included in opening stock	NIL	30,000	1,65,000

Output of Process I is transferred to Process II at 25 percent profit on the transfer price, whereas output of Process II is transferred to finished stock at 20 percent on transfer price. Stock in processes are valued at prime cost. Finished stock is valued at the price at which it is received from Process II. Sales for the month is ₹28,00,000.

You are required to prepare Process-I A/c, Process-II A/c, and Finished Stock A/c showing the profit element at each stage.

Solution

Process-I Account

	Particulars	Total (₹)	Cost (₹)	Profit (₹)	Particulars	Total (₹)	Cost (₹)	Profit (₹)
To	Opening balance	1,50,000	1,50,000	–	By Transfer to Process-II A/c	10,80,000	8,10,000	2,70,000
To	Direct material	3,00,000	3,00,000	–				
To	Direct wages	2,24,000	2,24,000	–				
		6,74,000	6,74,000	–				
Less:	Closing stock	74,000	74,000	–				
	Prime cost	6,00,000	6,00,000	–				
To	Factory overhead	2,10,000	2,10,000	–				
	Total cost:	8,10,000	8,10,000	–				
	Profit 25% on transfer price i.e. $33\frac{1}{3}$ on total cost	2,70,000	–	2,70,000				
		10,80,000	8,10,000	2,70,000		10,80,000	8,10,000	2,70,000

Process-II A/c

Particulars	Total (₹)	Cost (₹)	Profit (₹)	Particulars	Total (₹)	Cost (₹)	Profit (₹)
To Opening stock	1,80,000	1,50,000	30,000	By Transfer to Process-II A/c	22,50,000	15,15,000	7,35,000
To Direct material	3,15,000	3,15,000	–				
To Direct wages	2,25,000	2,25,000	–				
To Transfer from Process-I A/c	10,80,000	8,10,000	2,70,000				
	18,00,000	15,00,000	3,00,000				
Less: Closing stock	90,000	75,000	15,000				
Prime cost	17,10,000	14,25,000	2,85,000				
To Factory overhead	90,000	90,000					
Total cost:	18,00,000	15,15,000	2,85,000				
Profit 20% on transfer price i.e. 25% on cost	4,50,000	–	4,50,000				
	22,50,000	15,15,000	7,35,000		22,50,000	15,15,000	7,35,000

Working Note: Profit element in closing stock = $\frac{3,00,000}{18,00,000} \times 90,000 = 15,000$

Finished Stock Account

Particulars	Total (₹)	Cost (₹)	Profit (₹)	Particulars	Total (₹)	Cost (₹)	Profit (₹)
To Opening stock	4,50,000	2,85,000	1,65,000	By sales	28,00,000	16,50,000	11,50,000
To Transfer from Process II	22,50,000	15,15,000	7,35,000				
	27,00,000	18,00,000	9,00,000				
Less: Closing stock	2,25,000	1,50,000	75,000				
Total cost	24,75,000	16,50,000	8,25,000				
Profit (balancing figure)	3,25,000	3,25,000					
	28,00,000	16,50,000	11,50,000		28,00,000	16,50,000	11,50,000

Working Note: Profit element in closing finished stock = $\frac{9,00,000}{27,00,000} \times 2,25,000 = 75,000$

Calculation of Profit on Sale

Process	*Apparent Profit*	*Add Unrealised Profit in Opening Stock*	*Less Unrealised Profit in Closing Stock*	*Actual Profit*
	₹	₹	₹	₹
Process I	2,70,000			2,70,000
Process II	4,50,000	30,000	15,000	4,65,000
Finished stock	3,25,000	1,65,000	75,000	4,15,000
				11,50,000

JOINT PRODUCT AND BY-PRODUCT

Joint Product

Joint products may be defined as distinctly different major products that are inevitably produced simultaneously from common inputs or by common processing. The quantity and sales value of each joint product are such that none of them may be designated as minor products; all joint products are major products.

Many industries, such as chemicals, oil refining, mining, meat packing and similar industries are involved in such joint production processes and manufacture two or more products from the same raw material. In oil refining, for example, fuel, oil, gasoline, kerosene, lubricating oils are but a few of the many products that emerge.

An increase in the output of one product will bring about an increase in the quantity of others, or vice versa, but not necessarily in the same proportion. At the same phase of production, two or more separately identifiable products will result from the joint production process. This phase or point is referred to as the split-off point.

Joint products have the following characteristics:

1. Joint products are the primary objectives of manufacturing operations.
2. The sales value of each of the joint products are relatively high and none of the joint products are significantly greater in value than other joint products.
3. The joint products may require further processing or may be sold directly after the split-off point.
4. Joint products require simultaneous common processing.
5. The manufacturer has little or no control over the relative quantities of the various products that will result.

By-Product

The term "by-product" is often used synonymously with the term "minor products". It refers to those multiple products that have insignificant sales values relative to those of major products. Otherwise, by-products are the same as joint products. By-products are those products that result incidentally from the manufacture of the main product or products. Processing is not aimed in their direction.

ACCOUNTING FOR JOINT PRODUCT COST

When two or more products are classified as joint products, each individual product must be charged with a proportionate share of the total cost of the joint products. Prior to the point of split-off, products are not subject to identification and costs are joint; after separation, product identification is possible and costs become separable. Thus, joint cost is a cost incurred prior to the point at which separately identifiable products emerge from the same process.

Accounting for joint product costs achieve the following objectives:

1. Allocating joint product costs incurred prior to the split-off point.
2. Identifying the production costs incurred after the split-off point to process joint products.

If a product is sold immediately after split-off, its unit costs consist totally of allocated joint costs. If a joint product is processed further after split-off, its unit cost will contain allocated joint costs plus the material, labour and overhead costs of additional processing. The following are apportionment bases usually found in practice for apportionment of joint costs:

1. Physical quantity method.
2. Relative market or sales value method.
3. Average unit cost method.
4. Weighted average cost method.
5. Contribution margin method.
6. Net realisable method.

Physical Quantity Method

Under the quantity method, cost allocation is a simple apportionment of cost in proportion to volume. These physical measures may be units, pounds, kilograms, tonnes, gallons, etc.

The following example illustrates this method.

Product	*Kg.*	*Proportion to Total*	*Cost Allocated (₹)*	*Cost Per Kg (₹)*
A	30,000	1/2	1,80,000	6
B	20,000	1/3	1,20,000	6
C	10,000	1/6	60,000	6
	60,000		3,60,000	6

Relative Market or Sales Value Method

The relative sales value method is often used to apportion joint product costs at the split-off point. The result is a percentage of cost to sales value for the output of the joint process. The sales value of each of the joint products is then multiplied by this percentage to arrive at the apportioned cost for that joint product.

The data given in the above example is being used herewith to explain the sales value method.

Product	*Quantity Produced*	*Unit Sales Price*	*Sales Value of Production*		*Cost Apportioned*	
		₹	*Amount*	*%*	*Total*	*Per Unit*
A	30,000	4	1,20,000	20	72,000	2.4
B	20,000	9	1,80,000	30	1,08,000	5.4
C	10,000	30	3,00,000	50	1,80,000	18.0
	60,000		6,00,0000	100	3,60,000	

Cost can be allocated in the following two ways:

1. Ratio of cost to sales value $= \dfrac{₹3,60,000}{₹6,00,000} = 60\%$

Product *A*	60% of ₹1,20,000	=	₹ 72,000
Product *B*	60% of ₹1,80,000	=	₹1,08,000
Product *C*	60% of ₹3,00,000	=	₹1,80,000

2. Ratio of sales value of product to total sales value applied to total cost:

Product *A*	20% of ₹3,60,000	=	₹ 72,000
Product *B*	30% of ₹3,60,000	=	₹1,08,000
Product *C*	50% of ₹3,60,000	=	₹1,80,000

Profits Under the Sales Value Method Move As the Sales Price

Product	*Cost* (₹)	*Selling Price* (₹)	*Profit* *Amount* (₹)	%
A	72,000	1,20,000	48,000	40%
B	1,08,000	1,80,000	72,000	40%
C	1,80,000	3,00,000	1,20,000	40%

Average Unit Cost Method

This method apportions total manufacturing costs to the various products by using an average unit cost obtained by dividing the total number of units produced into the total manufacturing cost. If all units produced are measured in terms of the same unit and do not differ greatly, this method can be used without much disadvantage. But, when the units manufactured are not measured in similar terms, this method cannot be applied.

The average cost is computed by using the following formula:

$$\frac{\text{Total manufacturing cost}}{\text{Total number of units produced}}$$

Weighted Average Cost Method

Under this method, weight factors are often assigned to each unit based upon size of the unit, difficulty of manufacture, time used in making the units, difference in type of labour employed, amount of material used, etc. Finished production of every kind is multiplied by weight factors to apportion total costs to individual units. This method is also known as the survey method.

Contribution Margin Method Under this method, joint costs are segregated into two parts—variable and fixed. The variable costs are apportioned over the joint products on the basis of units produced (average method) or physical quantities. If the products are further processed, then all variable cost incurred be added to the variable cost determined earlier. Then, contribution is calculated by deducting variable cost from their respective sales values. The fixed costs are then apportioned over the joint products on the basis of contribution ratios.

Net Realisable Value Method In this method, joint cost is apportioned on the basis of net realisable value of the joint products,

Net Realisable Value = Sale value of joint products (at finished stage)
(–) estimated profit margin
(–) selling & distribution expenses, if any
(–) post split-off cost

ACCOUNTING FOR BY-PRODUCTS

By-products can be classified into two categories according to their marketable condition at the split-off point: (i) those sold in their original form without need for any further processing; (ii) those which require further processing in order to be saleable. Because of wide variations in the nature of by-products, different accounting treatments are found in practice, such as the following:

1. *Sales of by-product as other income* If the value of the by-product is comparatively small, many manufacturers treat the by-product like scrap material, and sell it. The sale proceeds of by-product are treated as other income.
2. *Sales of by-products as a reduction in the cost of joint products* This method can be followed by reducing the cost of the main product by the total estimated income from the by-product less the selling expense incurred in effecting the sale of the by-product.
   By-products which are not sold, are kept in stock at nil value.
3. *Treating by-products having no cost at the time of separation but charging them with all costs after separation* In such a case, costs incurred after separation should be deducted from the saleable value of the by-product and the balance should be credited to the profit and loss account or the relevant process account.
4. *Recording costs of by-products* This method is applied when the by-products are of relatively high value and also require additional processing after separation from the main product. This requires apportionment of joint costs of the product upto the split-off point. The cost of further processing the by-product is debited to the by-product account. This by-product account is credited with the sale proceeds of the by-products, and any profit or loss is transferred to the costing profit and loss account.
5. *Replacement cost method* The replacement cost method is used in those industries where by-products resulting from the manufacturing process are used within the company. The cost assigned to the by-product is the purchase or replacement cost existing in the market.
6. *Market value (reversal cost) method* This method reduces the manufacturing cost of the main product, not by the actual revenue received, but by an estimated market value of the by-product prevailing at the time the by-product is recovered or sold.

EXAMPLE 11.33

Work out the estimated pre-separation cost per tonne of by-products *Y* and *Z* from the following data:

Cost of manufacture before separation ₹25,60,000.

Main product is *X*. There are two by-products *Y* and *Z* whose selling prices are as under :

Sale price of *Y*: ₹500 per tonne, and

Sale price of *Z*: ₹800 per tonne.

Selling and distribution expenses have been estimated to be 25% of selling price and net profit is expected to be 10% of selling price. Cost of manufacture each tonne after separation from the main products are:

₹95 for by-product *Y*: ₹145 for by-product *Z*. Assume equal weight for *Y* and *Z*.

Solution

Statement of Estimated Pre-Separation Cost Per Tonne of By-Product

	By-Product	
	Y	Z
	₹ Per Tonne	₹ Per Tonne
Sales price	500	800
Less profit (10% of selling price)	–50	–80
Total cost	450	720
Less selling & distribution expenses 25% of sales price	–125	–200
	325	520
Less cost after separation	–95	–145
Pre-separation cost per tonne of by-product	230	375

EXAMPLE 11.34

A factory is engaged in the production of a chemical *X* and in the course of its manufacture a by-product *Y* is produced, which after a separate process has a commercial value. For the month of March 2020 the following are summarised cost data:

	Joint Expenses	Separate Expenses	
	X	X	Y
	₹	₹	₹
Materials	19,200	7,360	780
Labour	11,700	7,680	2,642
Overheads	3,450	1,500	544

The output of the month was 142 kg of *X* and 49 kg of *Y*. The selling price of *Y* averaged ₹280 per kg. Assuming the profit on *Y* is estimated at 50% of selling price, calculate the cost of *X* per tonne.

Solution

Statement Showing Y's Share in Joint Expenses

		₹
Selling price (49 × 280)		13,720
Less:	Profit (50%)	6,860
	Total cost	6,860
Less:	Subsequent cost after separation (780 + 2642 + 544)	3,966
	Share of joint expense of *Y*	2,894
Total Joint Expenses (19,200 + 11,700 + 3,450)		34,350

(Contd.)

			₹
Less:	Share of joint expenses of *Y*		2,894
	Share of joint expenses of *X*		31,456

Total Cost of *X*

			₹
	Share of joint expense of *X*		31,456
Add:	Further cost after separation		
	Material	7,360	
	Labour	7,680	
	Overhead	1,500	16,540
	Total cost of *X*		47,996

Cost per kg of $X = \frac{47,996}{142} = ₹338$ per kg.

EXAMPLE 11.35

In the course of manufacture of the main product *P*, by-products *A* and *B* also emerge. The joint expenses of manufacture amount to ₹1,19,550. All the products are processed further after separation and sold as per details given below:

	Main Product	By-product	
	P	*A*	*B*
	(₹)	(₹)	(₹)
Sales	90,000	60,000	40,000
Cost beyond split-off stage	6,000	5,000	4,000
Profit as percentage of sales	25%	20%	15%

Selling and administration overheads are absorbed as percentage of cost of sales. Prepare a statement showing the apportionment of joint cost to the main product and by-products. Also prepare main product-*P* account.

Solution

Statement Showing the Apportionment of Joint Costs

		Main Product	*By-Product*		*Total*
		P	*A*	*B*	
		₹	₹	₹	₹
Sales		90,000	60,000	40,000	1,90,000
Less:	Profit (that is 25%, 20% and 15% respectively from *P*, *A* and *B*)	22,500	12,000	6,000	40,500

(Contd.)

		Main Product	By-Product		Total
		P	A	B	
	Cost of sales	67,500	48,000	34,000	1,49,500
Less:	Selling expenses (675 : 480 : 340) ₹1,49,500 – ₹1,19,550 – 14,000 = ₹14,950	6,750	4,800	3,400	14,950
	Cost of production	60,750	43,200	30,600	1,34,550
Less:	Cost after separation	6,000	5,000	4,000	15,000
	Value at split-off point	54,750	38,200	26,600	1,19,550

P (Main Product) Account

To joint expenses of manufacture	1,19,550	By transfer of share in Joint expenses	
To separate expenses	6,000	By product A	38,200
		By product B	26,600
	1,25,550	By cost of product P	60,750
To cost of product P	60,750		1,25,550
To selling and admn. exp.	6,750	By sales	90,000
To profit	22,500		
	90,000		90,000

✍ EXAMPLE 11.36

A company produces two joint products *P* and *Q* in 70 : 30 ratio from basic raw materials in department *A*. The input output ratio of department *A* is 100 : 85. Product *P* can be sold at the split of stage or can be processed further at department *B* and sold as product *AR*. The input output ratio is 100 : 90 of department *B*. The department *B* is created to process product *A* only and to make it product *AR*.
The selling prices per kg. are as under:
Product *P* ₹85; Product *Q* ₹290; and Product *AR* ₹115
The production will be taken up in the next month.
Raw materials 8,00,000 kg.
Purchase price ₹80 per kg.

	Deptt. A ₹Lakh	Deptt. B ₹Lakh
Direct materials	35.00	5.00
Direct labour	30.00	9.00
Variable overheads	45.00	18.00
Fixed overheads	40.00	32.00
Total	150.00	64.00

Selling expenses:

	₹*in Lakh*
Product *P*	24.60
Product *Q*	21.60
Product *AR*	16.80

Required:

(i) Prepare a statement showing the apportionment of joint costs.
(ii) State whether it is advisable to produce product *AR* or not.

☞ ***Solution***

Input in Deptt. "A" 80,000 kg.
Yield 85%
Therefore output = 85% of 8,00,000 = 6,80,000 kg.
Ratio of output for *P* and *Q* = 70 : 30.
Product of *P* = 70% of 6,80,000 = 4,76,000 kg.
Product of *Q* = 30% of 6,80,000 = 2,04,000 kg.
Statement showing apportionment of joint cost

	P	*Q*	*Total*
Product kg.	4,76,000	2,04,000	
Selling price per kg.	₹85.00	290.00	
	₹lakhs	₹lakhs	₹lakhs
Sales	404.60	591.60	996.20
Less: Selling expenses	24.60	21.60	46.20
Net sales	380	570	950
Ratio	40%	60%	100%

	₹lakhs
Raw materials (8,00,000 kg. × ₹80)	640
Process cost of department "*A*"	150
	790

Apportionment of Joint Cost
(In the ratio of net sales i.e. *P* : *Q*., 40% : 60%.
Joint cost of "*P*" = ₹316 lakhs
Joint cost of "*Q*" = ₹474 lakhs

Statement Showing the Profitability of Further Processing of Product "P" and Converted into Product "AR"

Product "AR"

Output = 90% of 4,76,000 kg. = 4,28,400 kg

	₹*lakhs*
Joint costs	316.00
Cost of department *B*	64.00
Selling expenses	16.80
	396.80
Sales value (₹115 × 4,28,400)	492.66
Profit (492.66 – 396.80)	95.86

If "*P*" is not processed, profitability is as under.

	₹*lakhs*
Sales	380.00
Less: Joint expense	316.00
Profit	64.00

Further processing of product "*P*" and converting into product "*AR*" is beneficial to the company because the profit increased by ₹31.86 lakhs (95.86 – 64.00).

EXAMPLE 11.37

A factory is engaged in the production of a chemical BOMEX and in the course of its manufacture, a by-product BRUCIL is produced, which after further processing has a commercial value. For the month of April, 2020, the following are the summarised cost data:

	Joint Expenses	*Separate Expenses*	
		BOMEX	*BRUCIL*
	₹	₹	₹
Materials	1,00,000	6,000	4,000
Labour	50,000	20,000	18,000
Overheads	30,000	10,000	6,000
Selling price per unit		98	34
Estimated profit per unit on sale of BRUCIL			4
		Units	Units
No. of units produced		2,000	2,000

The factory uses reverse cost method of accounting for by-products whereby the sales value of by-products after deduction of the estimated profit, post separation costs and selling and distribution expenses relating to the by-products is credited to the joint process cost account.

You are required to prepare statement showing:

(i) the joint cost allocable to BOMEX.
(ii) the product-wise and overall profitability of the factory for April, 2020.

☞ Solution

(i) Statement of Joint Cost Allocable to BOMEX

Total Joint Expenses	₹	₹
Materials	1,00,000	
Labour	50,000	
Overheads	30,000	
		1,80,000
Less: Joint cost allocable to the production of 2,000 units of BRUCIL at the split-off point *(See Working Note)*		32,000
Cost of production of 2,000 units of BOMEX		1,48,000

(ii) Productwise and Overall Profitability Statement for the Month of April 2020

Particulars	*Products*				*Total*
		BOMEX		*BRUCIL*	₹
Sales (units)		2,000		2,000	
Selling price per unit (₹)		98		34	
Total sales (₹)		1,96,000		68,000	
Less: Cost of production at the split-off point	1,48,000		32,000		
Post separation cost	36,000		28,000		
		1,84,000		60,000	
Profit (₹)		12,000		8,000	20,000

Working Note:

Computation of the Joint Expenses Chargeable to the By-product BRUCIL

Units produced	2,000
Selling price unit (₹)	34
Total sales: (2,000 × ₹34)	(₹) 68,000
Less: Profit (2,000 × ₹4)	(₹) 8,000
Cost of sales	60,000
Less: Selling and distribution expenses	Nil
Less: Expenses after separation (₹4,000 + ₹18,000 + ₹6,000)	28,000
Cost of production at the split-off point	32,000

EXAMPLE 11.38

Raw materials AXE costing ₹150 per kg. and BXE costing ₹90 per kg. are mixed in equal properties for making product *A*. The loss of material in processing works out to 25% of the product. The production expenses are allocated at 40% of direct material cost. The end product is priced with a margin of 20% over the total cost.

Material BXE is not easily available and substitute raw material CXE has been found for BXE costing ₹75 per kg. It is required to keep the proportion of this substitute material in the mixture as low as possible and at the same time maintain the selling price of the end product at existing level and ensure the same quantum of profit as at present.

You are required to compute the ratio of the mix of the raw materials AXE and CXE.

Solution

Working Notes:

(i) Computation of material mix ratio:

Let 1 kg. of product *A* requires 1.25 kg. of input of materials AXE and BXE

Raw materials are mixed in equal proportions.

Then, raw material AXE = $\frac{1.25}{2}$ = .625 kg.

Then, raw material BXE = $\frac{1.25}{2}$ = .625 kg.

(ii) Computation of selling price/kg. of product *A*

	₹
Raw material AXE .625 kg. × 150 = ₹93.75	
Raw material BXE .625 kg. × 90 = ₹56.25	150.00
Production expenses (40% of material cost)	60.00
Total cost	210.00
Add: Profit 20% of total cost	42.00
Selling price	252.00

(iii) Computation of proportions of materials AXE and CXE in *A*

Let material CXE required in product *A* be *m* kg.

Then, for purchasing 1 kg of product *A*, material AXE requirement = (1.25 – *m*) kg.

To maintain same level of profit and selling price as per *Working Note (ii)*, it is required that the total cost of material in 1 kg. of product *A* should not exceed ₹150.

That is, *m* kg. × ₹75 + (1.25 – *m*) kg. × 150 = ₹150

or 75 *m* + 187.5 – 150 *m* = 150

or 75 *m* = 37.5

or *m* = 0.5 kg.

Raw material AXE requirement in product *A* = 1.25 – 5 = 0.75 kg.

So, proportion of materials AXE and CXE

= 0.75 : 50

that is 3 : 2.

EXAMPLE 11.39

In a chemical plant four different products viz. *AB, BC, CD* and *DD* emerge from the input of crude oil. Product *AB* can be sold immediately, but the remaining three products require further processing before they can be marketed.

In a month, 40,000 litres of crude oil were procured at a cost of ₹30 per litre and processed at a cost of ₹3 lakhs. The details of output obtained, further processing cost, selling price per unit etc. are given below.

Product	*Output kg*	*Further Processing Cost (₹)*	*Selling Price at the Point of Sale*
AB	8,000 kg		₹45/kg
BC	10,000 kg	80,000	₹60/kg
CD	12,000 kg	120,000	₹70/kg
DD	5,000 litres	60,000	₹80/litre

Prepare:

(i) Statement showing apportionment of joint cost on suitable basis and product-wise profitability statement.

(ii) If the company finds a market for *CD* at ₹63/kg without further processing, will it be advisable to accept it?

Solution

Joint cost of manufacture:

(i) Cost of 40,000 litre of crude oil @ ₹30 litre	=	₹12,00,000
Processing cost	=	₹ 3,00,000
	Total	₹15,00,000

Apportionment of joint cost is done at net sales value at split-off point as follows:

(In Thousand of Rupees)

Product	*Output/ Sales*	*Selling Price Per Unit*	*Sales*	*Further Processing Cost*	*Net Sales Value*	*Apportionment of Joint Cost*	*Total Cost*	*Net Profit*
(1)	*(2)*	*(3)*	*(4)*	*(5)*	*(6)* (4 – 5)	*(7)*	*(8)* (5 + 7)	*(9)* (4 – 8)
AB	8,000 kg	₹45	360	–	360	278	278	82
BC	10,000 kg	60	600	80	520	402	482	118
CD	12,000 kg	70	840	120	720	557	677	163
DD	5,000 litres	80	400	60	340	263	323	77
			2,200	260	1,940	1,500	1,760	440

(ii) If the company is able to get market for *CD* at ₹63/kg. It is worth selling at the split-off point, instead of processing further and selling as it is clear from the following details:

Sales value after further processing	₹8,40,000.00
Sales value at split-off point at ₹63/kg. 1,20,000 kg. × ₹63	₹7,56,000.00

Incremental sales value	₹84,000.00
Further processing cost required, if sold @ ₹70/kg.	₹1,20,000.00

Further, processing cost is more than the incremental revenuc by ₹36,000. Hence, in this case, it is better to sell at split-off point without further processing.

Theory Questions

1. Discuss the distinguishing features of a process cost system?
2. Compare the cost accumulation and summarising procedures of a job order cost system and a process cost system.
3. What is equivalent production? What is its effect on computed unit cost?
4. Discuss the possible effects on a department's unit costs when materials are added to work-in-progress.
5. How is opening work-in-progress handled in average costing?
6. What are some of the disadvantages of the FIFO costing method?
7. What is the meaning of the term "split-off"? What is its significance in product costing?
8. What are joint costs? What problems are created by joint costs?
9. Explain the difference between a main product and a by-product.
10. How can the income from the sale of by-products be shown on the income statement?
11. Does the showing of income from by-products on the income statement influence the unit cost of the main product?
12. What is the difference between physical quantity method and sales value method?
13. Define and explain the terms "joint products" and "by-products". Enumerate the method which may be employed in costing "joint product".
14. Define joint products and by-products. Explain the various bases available for apportionment of joint costs to joint products.
15. Explain with an example the concept of "equivalent production" for valuation of work-in-progress.
16. (i) What are the three most common methods of allocating joint product cost? Write a brief explanatory note on each.
    (ii) Explain the procedure of accounting for by-products.
17. Distinguish between normal and abnormal wastage of materials with specific reference to their accounting treatment and control.
18. What are equivalent units of production? Mention two principal methods of calculating equivalent units.
19. Explain briefly the procedure for the valuation of work-in-progress.
20. Mention the different methods of by-product cost accounting.
21. Distinguish between joint products and by-products.
22. (a) Distinguish between scrap and wastage and their treatment in cost accounts.
    (b) What is the meaning of joints products and by-products
23. What do you mean by scrap? How will you treat it in cost accounts?
24. Explain Spoilage and Defectives.
25. Define normal loss, abnormal loss and abnormal gain. How are these treated in cost accounts.
26. Explain waste and scrap.
27. Differentiate between joint product and by-product.
28. Distinguish between normal loss and abnormal loss.

Self-Evaluation Questions

Choose the correct answer for the following multiple choice questions:

(i) When should process costing method be used in assigning costs of products?
   (a) If the product is manufactured on the basis of each order received.
   (b) When production is only partially completed during the accounting period.
   (c) If the product is composed of mass-produced homogeneous units.
   (d) In situations in which standard costing techniques should not be used.

(ii) Which of the following characteristics applies to process costing but not to job-order costing?
   (a) Identifiable batches of production
   (b) Equivalent units of production
   (c) Averaging process
   (d) Use of standard costs

(iii) Which is the best cost accumulation procedure to use when there is a continuous mass production of like units?
   (a) Actual (b) Standard
   (c) Job order (d) Process

(iv) Which of the following is a characteristic of a process costing method?
   (a) Work-in-progress inventory restated in terms of completed units.
   (b) Costs are accumulated by order.
   (c) It is used by a company manufacturing on customers' orders.
   (d) Standard costs are not applicable.

(v) Normal wastage and abnormal wastage should be classified as:

	Normal	*Abnormal*
(a)	Period cost	Period cost
(b)	Product cost	Period cost
(c)	Period cost	Product cost
(d)	Product cost	Product cost

(vi) Normal wastage is properly classified as:
   (a) An extraordinary item (b) Period cost
   (c) Product cost (d) Deferred charge

(vii) If the amount of wastage in a manufacturing process is abnormal, it should be classified as:
   (a) Deferred charge (b) Joint cost
   (c) Period cost (d) Product cost

(viii) The type of wastage that should not affect the recorded costs of closing inventories is:
   (a) Abnormal wastage (b) Normal wastage
   (c) Seasonal wastage (d) Standard wastage

(ix) Each of the following is a method by which to allocate joint costs except
   (a) Relative sales value (b) Relative profitability
   (c) Relative weight, volume (d) Average unit cost

(x) When two products are produced during a common process, what is the factor that determines whether the products are joint products or one principal product and a by-product?
   (a) Potential marketability for each product
   (b) Amount of work expended in the production of each product
   (c) Relative total sales value
   (d) Management policy

(xi) Joint costs are most frequently allocated based upon relative:
   (a) Profitability (b) Conversion costs
   (c) Sales value (d) Prime costs

(xii) In order to compute equivalent units of production using FIFO method of process costing, work for the period must be broken down to units.
 (a) Completed during the period and units in ending inventory.
 (b) Completed from the beginning inventory, started and completed during the month and units in closing inventory.
 (c) Started during the period and units transferred out during the period.
 (d) Processed during the period and units completed during the period.

(xiii) From the industries listed below, choose the one most likely to use process costing in accounting for production costs:
 (a) Road builders (b) Electrical contractor
 (c) Newspaper publisher (d) Automobile repair shop

(xiv) What are transferred-in costs as used in a process cost accounting system?
 (a) Labour that is transferred from another department within the same plant instead of hiring temporary workers from the outside.
 (b) Cost of the production of a previous internal process that is subsequently used in a succeeding internal process
 (c) Supervisory salaries that are transferred from an overhead-cost centre to a production-cost centre
 (d) Ending work-in-process inventory of a previous process that will be used in a succeeding process

(xv) Purchased materials added in the second department of a three-department process that do not increase the number of units produced in the second department would
 (a) not change the amount transferred to the next department.
 (b) decrease total work-in-process inventory.
 (c) increase the factory overhead portion of the ending work-in-process inventory.
 (d) increase total unit cost.

(xvi) The units transferred-in from the first department to the second department should be included in the computation of the equivalent-units divisor for the second department for which of the following methods of process costing?

	First-In, First-Out	*Weighted Average*
(a)	yes	yes
(b)	yes	no
(c)	no	yes
(d)	no	no

(xvii) Purchased materials added in the second department of a three-department process that increase the number of units produced in the second department would always
 (a) change the direct labour cost percentage in the ending work-in-process inventory.
 (b) cause no adjustment to the unit cost transferred in from the first department.
 (c) increase total unit costs.
 (d) decrease total ending work-in-process inventory.

(xviii) The percentage of completion of the beginning work-in-process inventory should be included in the computation of the equivalent units of production for which of the following methods of process costing?

	First-In, First-Out	*Weighted Average*
(a)	yes	no
(b)	yes	yes
(c)	no	yes
(d)	no	no

(xix) In the computation of manufacturing cost per equivalent unit, the weighted-average method of process costing considers
 (a) current costs only.
 (b) current costs plus cost of ending work-in-process inventory.

(c) current costs less cost of beginning work-in-process inventory.
(d) current costs plus cost of beginning work-in-process inventory.

(xx) In a given process-costing system, the equivalent-units divisor is computed for the weighted-average method. With respect to conversion costs, the percentage of completion for the current period only is included in the calculation of the

	Beginning Work-in-Process Inventory	*Ending Work-in-Process Inventory*
(a)	no	no
(b)	no	yes
(c)	yes	no
(d)	yes	yes

(xxi) The first-in, first-out method of process costing differs from the weighted-average method in that the first-in, first-out method
(a) considers the stage of completion of beginning work-in-process inventory in computing equivalent units of production, whereas the weighted-average method does not.
(b) does not consider the stage of completion of beginning work-in-process inventory in computing equivalent units of production, whereas the weighted-average method does.
(c) is applicable only to those companies using the first-in, first-out inventory pricing method, whereas the weighted-average method may be used with any inventory pricing method.
(d) allocates costs based on whole units, whereas the weighted-average method uses equivalent units.

Problems

Process costing having no process loss and no opening and closing work-in-progress

1. Prepare process cost accounts from the following data:

₹

Items	*Total*	*Process I*	*Process II*	*Process III*
Direct material	4,40,000	3,60,000	60,000	20,000
Direct wages	80,000	20,000	40,000	20,000
Direct expenses	1,00,000	60,000	—	40,000

Production overhead incurred is ₹1,60,000 and is recovered on 200% of direct wages. Production during the period was 20,000 units. There was no opening or closing work-in-progress.

Ans:	*Cost Per Unit (₹)*	*Amt. (₹)*
Process-I A/c	24.00	4,80,000
Process II A/c	33.00	6,60,000
Process-III A/c	39.00	7,80,000

2. From the following figures, prepare process accounts indicating the cost of process and the total cost. The production was 480 articles per week.

	Process I	*Process II*	*Process III*
Materials	₹3,000	₹1,000	₹400
Labour	1,600	4,000	1,200
Factory overheads	520	1,440	500

Office overheads amounting to ₹1,700 should be apportioned on the basis of wages. Ignore stock-in-hand and work-in-progress at the beginning and end of the work.

Ans: Process I—Transfer to Process II ₹5,520.
Process II—Transfer to Process III ₹12,960.
Process III—Transfer to finished stock ₹15,360

Process Costing Having Process Losses or Gains (Normal Loss, Abnormal Loss, Abnormal Gain)

3. In a certain process, material is mixed and cooked in batches of 1,000 lbs each. Cooking results in 10 per cent loss of weight of the mixture. Since the cooking requires considerable skill and constant watching, there is generally a further loss for spoilage which is not discovered until processing has been completed. Also, past experience shows that normally two batches out of every ten started in the process are spoiled in this way.

In a given month, the production records show:

(i) Production started in the process—50 batches of 1,000 lbs each.
(ii) Production completed and transferred to finished goods is 34,200 lbs.
(iii) There is no inventory of work-in-process at the beginning or end of the month.

Costs recorded during the month amounted to ₹45,000. Prepare the process account for the month and determine the cost per pound of finished product.

Ans: Finished stock A/c, ₹43,971

4. The finished product of a manufacturing company passes through three processes, viz., I, II and III. The normal wastage in each process is 5%, 7% and 10% for the Processes I, II and III respectively (calculated with reference to the number of units fed into each process). The scrap generated out of wastage has a sale value of 70 paise per unit, 80 paise per unit and ₹1 per unit in the Process I, II and III respectively. The output of each process is transferred to the next process and the finished output emerges from the Process III and transferred to stock. There was no stock of work-in-progress in any process in a particular month. The details of cost data for the month are given below:

Particulars	*Processes*		
	I	*II*	*III*
Materials used (₹)	1,20,000	40,000	40,000
Direct labour cost (₹)	80,000	60,000	60,000
Production expenses (₹)	40,000	40,000	28,000
Output in units (actuals)	38,000	34,600	32,000

Process I was fed with 40,000 units of raw input at cost of ₹3,20,000.
Prepare the process accounts.

Ans: Process-I A/c, Transfer to Process II, Units 38,000, ₹5,58,600.
Process-II A/c, Transfer to Process III, Units 34,600, ₹6,81,888.
Process-III—transfer to finished stock A/c, Units 32,000, ₹8,28,700.

5. A product passes through three processes—*P*, *Q*, and *R*. The details of expenses incurred on three processes during the year 2020 were as under:

Particulars	*P*	*Q*	*R*
Units issued	10,000		
Cost per unit	100		

(Contd.)

Particulars		*P*	*Q*	*R*
Sundry materials	₹	10,000	15,000	5,000
Labour	₹	30,000	80,000	65,000
Direct expenses	₹	6,000	18,150	27,200
Sale price of output per unit	₹	120	165	250

Management expenses during the year amounted to ₹80,000 and selling expenses were ₹50,000. Both these are not allocable to the processes.
Actual output of the three processes was as under:
Process *P*—9,300 units; Process *Q*—5,400 units; Process *R*—2,100 units.
Two-thirds of the output of process *P* and one half of the output of process *Q* was passed on to the next process and the balance was sold. The entire output of process *R* was sold.
The normal wastage of the three processes calculated on the input of every process was:
Process *P*—5 per cent; Process *Q*—15 per cent; Process *R*—20 per cent.
The wastage of process *P* was sold at ₹2 per unit, that of process *Q* at ₹5 per unit and that of process *R* at ₹10 per unit.
Prepare the three Process Accounts and a Statement of Income for 2012 showing fully the accounting treatment of Process Wastage.

Ans: Income statement, Net loss ₹32,450.

6. A product passes through two distinct processes *A* and *B* and then to finished stock. The output of *A* passes direct to *B* and that of *B* passes to finished product. From the following information you are required to prepare the process account.

	Process A ₹	*Process B* ₹
Material consumed.	12,000	6,000
Direct labour	14,000	8,000
Manufacturing expenses	4,000	4,000
Input in process *A* (units)	10,000 units	
Input in process *A* (value)	10,000	
Output (units)	9,400 units	8,300 units
Normal wastage (percentage of input)	5%	10%
Value of normal wastage (per 100 units)	8	10

No opening or closing stock is held in process.

Ans: Process *A* output transferred to process *B*, 9400 units; ₹39,539
Process *B*, 8300 units; ₹56359

7. In a manufacturing unit, raw material passes through four processes—I, II, III and IV and the output of each process is the input of the subsequent process. The loss in the four processes—I, II, III and IV—are respectively 25%, 20%, 20% and $16\frac{2}{3}\%$ of the input. If the end, product at the end of Process IV is 40,000 kg, what is the quantity of raw material required to be fed at the beginning of Process I and the cost of the same at ₹5 per kg?

Find out also the effect of increase or decrease in the material cost of the end product for variation of every rupee in the cost of the raw material.

Ans: Decrease in cost from ₹12.50 to ₹10 per kg.

8. Ayush Ltd. produces a Herbal Shampoo which is made by subjecting certain crude herbs to two successive processes: *A* and *B*. The following data in respect of processing have been obtained from the accounting records of the company for a cost period:

Particulars	*Process A*	*Process B*
Inputs (units)	50,000	46,000
Normal loss	10%	?
Costs incurred:	₹	₹
Materials (Herbs)	9,00,000	1,96,000
Direct labour	4,26,000	2,47,000
Production overhead	2,84,000	1,78,000
Realisable scrap value/unit	7	20

The output of process *A* is transferred direct to process *B*. The output of process *B* was 43,200 units, which were sold at ₹60 per unit showing a profit of 20% on cost.

You are required to prepare the Process Cost Accounts assuming that there was no closing stock of W.I.P. and finished goods.

Ans: Process *A* 45000 units, ₹15,75,000
Process *B* 43,200 units, ₹21,60,000
Profit ₹4,32,000.

9. An article passes through three successive operations from the raw material to the finished product stage. The following data are available from the production records of a particular month:

Operation No.	*No. of Pieces Input*	*No. of Pieces Rejected*	*No. of Pieces Output*
1	60,000	20,000	40,000
2	66,000	6,000	60,000
3	48,000	8,000	40,000

(a) Determine the input required to be introduced in the first operation in number of pieces in order to obtain finished output of 100 pieces after the last operation.

(b) Calculate the cost of raw material required to produce one piece of finished product, given the following:

- Weight of the finished piece is 0.10 kg and
- The price of raw material is ₹20 per kg.

Ans: (a) 19.80 kg (b) ₹3.96

10. Department I of Coromandel Chemicals conducts a process which requires mixing of materials and cooking of the mixture in batches of 1,000 lbs each. Cooking results in 10 per cent loss of weight of the mixture. Also, past experience shows that two batches out of every ten started in the process are spoiled.
The production records for May, 2020 show the following:

(i) Production started in the process: 50 batches of 1,000 lbs each.
(ii) Production completed and transferred to finished goods: 34,200 lbs.
(iii) There is no inventory of work-in-process at the beginning or at the end of the month.

Costs recorded during the month totalled ₹45,000. Prepare the account of the process conducted by Department I.

Ans: Abnormal loss 800 lbs, ₹1,029.
Finished goods 34,200 lbs, ₹43,971

11. Product *Z* is obtained after it passes through three distinct processes. The following information is obtained from the accounts for the month ending December 31, 2020.

₹

Items	*Total*	*Process*		
		I	*II*	*III*
Direct material	7,542	2,600	1,980	2,962
Direct wages	9,000	2,000	3,000	4,000
Production overhead	9,000			

1,000 units at ₹3 each were introduced to Process I. There was no stock, material or work-in-progress at the beginning or end of the period. The output of each process passes direct to the next process and finally to finished stores. Production overhead is recovered at 100% of direct wages. The following additional data are obtained:

Process	*Output During the Month*	*Percentage of Normal Loss to Input*	*Value of Scrap Per Unit*
Process I	950	5%	₹2
Process II	840	10%	4
Process III	750	15%	5

Prepare the process cost accounts and abnormal gain or loss accounts.

Ans: Process I 950 units ₹9,500 II 840 units ₹16,800 III 750 units ₹28,500
Abnormal loss Process II–15 units ₹300
Abnormal gain Process III–36 units, ₹1,368

12. The finished product of a factory has to pass through three processes—*A*, *B* and *C*. The normal wastage of each process is 2% in *A*, 5% in *B* and 10% in *C*. The percentage of waste is computed on the number of units entering each process.

The scrap value of wastage of processes *A*, *B* and *C* are ₹10, ₹40, ₹20 per 100 units respectively.

The output of each process is transferred to the next process and the finished products are transferred from process *C* into stock. The following further information is obtained:

	Processes		
	A	*B*	*C*
	₹	₹	₹
Materials consumed	12,000	4,000	4,000
Direct labour	8,000	6,000	6,000
Manufacturing expenses	2,000	4,000	2,000

2,000 units were put into the process *A* at a cost of ₹16,000. The output of each process has been *A*—19,600 units, *B*—18,400 units and *C*—16,700 units.

There was no stock of work-in-progress in any process.

Prepare the process accounts.

Ans: Process *A*, units 19,600 ₹37,960 Process *B*, units 18,400 ₹50,959, Abnormal loss (Process *B*) 220 units, ₹609 Process *C*, finished goods units 16,700 ₹63,120 Abnormal Gain Process *C* 140 units ₹529

13. Product *ZENU* is made by three sequential processes I, II, III. In Process III, a by-product arises and after further processing in process *XY*, at a cost of ₹2 per unit, by-product *XYZ* is produced. Selling and distribution expenses of ₹1 per unit are incurred in marketing *XYZ* at a selling price of ₹9 per unit.

	Process I	*Process II*	*Process III*
Standards provided for:			
Normal loss in process of input, of	10%	5%	10%
Loss in process, having a scrap value per unit, of	₹1	₹3	₹5

For the month of April 2020, the following data are given:

	Process I	*Process II*	*Process III*	*Process XY*
Output (in units)	8,800	8,400	7,000 of *ZENU*	420 of *XYZ*
Costs:				Total
Direct Materials:				
Introduced (10,000 units)	₹20,000			20,000
Direct materials added	6,000	₹12,640	₹23,200	41,840
Direct wages	5,000	6,000	10,000	21,000
Direct expenses	4,000	6,200	4,080	14,280

Budgeted production overhead for the month was ₹84,000.
Absorption is based on a percentage of direct wages.
There are no stocks at the beginning or end of the month. You are required, using the information given, to prepare accounts for:
(a) each of Process I, II and III; and (b) Process *XY*.

Ans:
Process I—Transfer to Process II, 8800 units, ₹52,800
Process II—Transfer to Process III, 8400 units, ₹1,00,800
Process III—Net sales value, 420 units, ₹2,520.
XY-Process A/c, Finished goods stock A/c, units 420, ₹3780.

14. A product, which uses 100 tonnes as input per month passes through two processes. The details of cost in Process 1 for April 2020 are:

Process 1	*Cost Per Tonne*
Direct material cost	₹26,100
Direct labour cost	7,800
Overhead	13,500

The total loss in Process 1 is 2% of input, and the scrap is 8% of input with a value of ₹12,000 per tonne. The material to Process 2 is transferred at cost. The process direct labour cost at Process 2 is ₹9,000 per tonne of input. The overhead is 60% of direct labour cost. The scrap at Process 2 is 20% of input with a value of ₹12,000 per tonne. Draw up a cost sheet to present the manufacturing cost of the product showing clearly the cost of scrap and waste at each stage of manufacturing.

Ans:	*Process 1*	*Process 2*
Loss	2 tonne	—
Scrap	8 tonne, ₹96,000	18 tonne, ₹2,16,000

for excel template, scan

15. The product of a manufacturing concern passes through two processes *A* and *B* and then to finished stock. It is ascertained that in each process 5% of the total weight is lost and 10% is scrap, which from processes *A* and *B* realises ₹80 per kg and ₹200 per kg respectively. The following are the figures relating to both the processes:

	Process A	*Process B*
Materials kg	1,000	70
Cost of materials (₹ per kg)	125	200
Wages (₹)	28,000	10,000
Manufacturing expenses (₹)	8,000	5,250
Output (kg)	830	780

Prepare the process cost account showing cost per kg of each process. There was no stock or work-in-process in any process.

Ans:	*Process A*	*Process B*
Abnormal loss	20 kg, ₹3,600	—
Abnormal gain	—	15 kg, ₹3,150
Transfer to process *B*	830 kg, ₹1,49,400	—
Transfer to finished stock	—	780 kg, ₹1,63,800

16. XYZ Ltd. manufactures and sells three chemicals produced by consecutive processes known as *X*, *Y* and *Z*. In each process, 2% of the total weight put in is lost and 10% is scrap, which from processes *X* and *Y* realised ₹100 a unit and from *Z* ₹200 a unit. The products of the three processes are dealt with as follows:

	X	*Y*	*Z*
Sent to warehouse for sale	25%	—	100%
Passed on to next process	75%	100%	—

The following particulars relate to the month of March:

Materials used (units)	100	140	1,348
Cost per unit of materials (₹)	120	200	80
Manufacturing expenses (₹)	30,800	25,760	1,810

Prepare an account of each process, showing the cost per unit of each process.

Ans:	*X*	*Y*	*Z*
Cost of production (₹)	₹41,800	83,050	1,62,114.40

17. A product passes through three processes. Figure relating to production for the 6 months of 2020 are as follows:

	Process I	*Process II*	*Process III*
Raw materials used	1,000 kg.		
Cost per kg.	₹200		
Manufacturing wages and expenses	₹72,500	₹40,800	₹10,710
Weight lost	5%	10%	20%
Scrap-sold at ₹50 per kg	50 kg	30 kg	51 units
Sales price per kg	₹350	₹500	₹800

Management expenses were ₹17,500, selling expenses were ₹10,000 and interest on borrowed capital were ₹4,000.

Two thirds of Process I and one-half of Process II are passed on to the next process and the balances are sold.

You are required to prepare process cost accounts in a form suitable for presentation to the directors at their next board meeting when the production policy of the company will be discussed.

Ans: Net profit ₹5,940.

Process Costing Having Opening and Closing Work-in-Progress With or Without Normal Loss, Abnormal Loss and Abnormal Gain

18. (Normal loss at beginning of or during a process)
AB Ltd. is engaged in the process engineering industry. During the month of April 2020, 2,000 units were introduced in Process *X*. The normal loss was estimated at 5% of input. At the end of the month, 1,400 units had been produced and transferred to Process *Y*, 460 units were incomplete units and 140 units during the process had to be scrapped. The incomplete units had reached the following stage of completion:

Material	75%	Completed
Labour	50%	"
Overhead	50%	"

Following is further information in Process *X*:

	₹
Cost of the 2,000 units	58,000
Additional direct material	14,400
Direct labour	33,400
Direct overhead	16,700
Units scrapped realised ₹10 each	

Prepare a statement of equivalent production, statement of cost, statement of evaluation and the Process *X* account.

Ans: Apportionment of cost, Abnormal loss ₹2,800, Finished production ₹98,000, Work-in-progress ₹20,700, Cost per unit ₹70.

19. (Normal loss at the end of a process)
The finished products of a factory pass through two processes, the entire material being placed in process at the beginning of the first process. From the following production and cost data relating to the first process, prepare a statement of equivalent production, statement of cost, and process account. Spoilage of 1,000 units occur at the end of the first process.

Process Costs	₹
Materials	60,000
Labour	33,600
Overhead	22,400
Units put into Process I	12,000
Transferred to Process II	10,000
Closing inventory (20% complete)	1,000

Ans: Cost per unit ₹10, Completed units transferred ₹1,10,000, Work-in-progress ₹6,000

20. (FIFO)

The accountant of a chemical company provides you the following data:

	Units	*Amount (₹)*
Work-in-process, beginning of period	2,000	
Direct materials		4,200
Direct labour and manufacturing overhead		1,950
Addition to work-in-process in April	4,000	
Direct materials		9,000
Direct labour and manufacturing overhead		7,500
Total		22,650
Work-in-process, end of period	1,500	

Further, work-in-process at the beginning of the period is complete to the extent: materials 100% and labour and manufacturing overhead 75%. Work-in-process at the end of the period is complete to the extent: materials 100% and direct labour and manufacturing overhead only 50%.

You are required to:

(i) Calculate the number of units of product transferred to finished-goods stock during the period. Assume no units are lost in process.
(ii) Calculate the number of equivalent whole units of work completed during the period.
(iii) Calculate the unit cost for materials during the month of April using First-In, First-Out method of inventory issue.

Ans: (i) 4,500 (ii) 3750 (iii) ₹2.25

21. (Average Costing)

Prepare a statement of equivalent production, statement of cost, process account from the following information using the average method:

Opening Stock	20,000	units
Material	₹ 10,000	
Labour	₹ 4,000	
Overhead	₹ 5,000	
Units Introduced	₹ 80,000	units

(Contd.)

Material	₹ 40,000
Wages	₹ 31,000
Overhead	₹ 30,000

During the period, 60,000 units were completed and transferred to Process II.
Closing stock 40,000 units, degree of completion.

Material	100%
Wages and overhead	25%

Ans: Equivalent production 70,000 units, Cost per unit of equivalent production ₹1.50, Units completed and transferred ₹90,000, Closing work-in-progress ₹30,000

22. (Average Costing)
The beginning inventory in Process No. 2 at the beginning of a period was valued at ₹2,950 made up of ₹1,400 towards materials, ₹1,000 towards labour and ₹550 towards overheads for 100 units. The value added during the period was ₹53,600 towards an introduction of 4,100 units from the previous process besides ₹40,800 towards labour and ₹19,400 towards overheads. Out of 3,600 units completed, 3,300 units were transferred to the next process leaving the balance in stock. 400 units were held back in process with half completion towards labour and overheads while 200 units were loss in processing considered normal and hence should be borne by the entire inventory. Prepare a cost of production statement using average cost basis.

Ans: Cost of units transferred ₹99,000; Cost of units held in stock ₹9,000; Cost of WIP ₹8,75; Cost per unit Material ₹13.75, Labour ₹11.00; Overheads ₹5.25.

23. Roy and Johnson (P) Ltd. gives the following particulars relating to Process *A* in its plant for the month of December2020:

			Cost	₹
Work-in-progress (opening balance) on 1.12.2020—500 units:				
			Material	4,800
			Labour	3,200
			Overheads	6,400
				14,400
Units introduced during the month			19,500	
Processing costs incurred during the month:				
	Materials	₹1,86,200		
	Labour	72,000		
	Overheads	1,06,400	₹3,64,600	
Output: Units transferred to Process *B*		18,200		
Units scrapped (completely processed)		1,400		
Work-in-process (closing balance)		400		

[Degree of completion: Materials 100%
Labour and overhead 50%]
Normal loss in processing is 5% of total input and normal scrapped units fetch ₹1 each.
Prepare the following statements for process *A* for December 2020:

(a) Statement of Equivalent Production;
(b) Statement of Cost;
(c) Statement of Evaluation;
(d) Process-*A* Account.

Ans: Output completed and transferred ₹3,64,000; Abnormal loss ₹8,000; Closing work-in-progress ₹6,000; Cost per unit, material ₹10; Labour ₹4, Overhead ₹6.

24. XP Ltd. furnishes you the following information relating to Process II.

(i) Opening work-in-progress—NIL
(ii) Units introduced 42,000 units @ ₹12
(iii) Expenses debited to the process:

		₹
Direct material	=	61,530
Labour	=	88,820
Overhead	=	1,76,400

(iv) Normal loss in the process = 2% of input.
(v) Closing work-in-progress—1200 units

Degree of completion —	Materials	100%
	Labour	50%
	Overhead	40%

(vi) Finished output—39,500 units
(vii) Degree of completion of abnormal loss:

Material	100%
Labour	80%
Overhead	60%

(viii) Units scraped as normal loss were sold at ₹4.50 per unit.
(ix) All the units of abnormal loss were sold at ₹9 per unit.

Prepare:
(a) Statement of equivalent production.
(b) Statement showing the cost of finished goods, abnormal loss and closing work-in-progress.
(c) Process-II account and abnormal loss account.

Ans: Normal loss 840 units, ₹3,780
Abnormal loss 460 units, ₹8,275
Finished goods 39,500 units, ₹7,98,877
Closing WIP 1,200 units, ₹19,798

25. The following information is given in respect of Process No. 3 for the month of January, 2020.
Opening stock—2,000 units made-up of:

Direct material I	₹12,350
Direct material II	₹13,200
Direct labour	₹17,500
Overheads	₹11,000

Transferred from Process No. 2: 20,000 units @ ₹6.00 per unit.
Transferred to Process No. 4: 17,000 units

Expenditure incurred in Process No. 3:

Direct materials	₹30,000
Direct labour	₹60,000
Overheads	₹60,000

Scrap: 1,000 units—Direct Materials 100%, Direct Labour 60%, Overheads 40%. Normal Loss 10% of production.

Scrapped units realised ₹4 per unit.

Closing Stock: 4,000 units—Degree of completion: Direct Materials 80%, Direct Labour 60% and Overheads 40%.

Prepare Process No. 3 Account using average price method, alongwith necessary supporting statements.

Ans : Process 3 A/c
Normal loss 1,800 units ₹7,200, finished goods 17,000 units ₹2,81,822,
Closing balance 4,000 units, ₹48,290
Abnormal gain 800 units, ₹13,262

26. The following data relate to Process *Q*:

(i) Opening work-in-process 4,000 units

Degree of completion:

Materials	100%	₹	24,000
Labour	60%	₹	14,400
Overheads	60%	₹	7,200

(ii) Received during the month of April, 2020 from Process *P*

40,000 units	₹	1,71,000

(iii) Expenses incurred in Process *Q* during the month

Materials	₹	79,000
Labour	₹	1,38,230
Overheads	₹	69,120

(iv) Closing work-in-process: 3,000 units

Degree of completion:

Materials	100%
Labour & Overheads	50%

(v) Units scrapped 4,000 units

Degree of completion:

Materials	100%
Labour and Overheads	80%

(vi) Normal loss: 5% of current input

(vii) Spoiled goods realised ₹1.50 each on sale.

(viii) Completed units are transferred to warehouse.

***Required:* Prepare:**

(i) Equivalent units statement.

(ii) Statement of cost per equivalent unit and total costs.

(iii) Process-*Q* Account.

(iv) Any other account necessary.

Ans: Process-*Q* A/c
Normal loss 2,000 units, ₹3,000
Completed units 37,000; ₹4,50,400
CWP 3,000 units, ₹27,750
Abnormal loss 2,000 units, ₹21,800

27. The following data pertains to Process 1 for March 2020 of Beta Ltd.:

Opening work-in-progress	1,500 units at	₹15,000
Degree of completion:		
Material 100%; Labour and Overheads $33\frac{1}{3}\%$		
Input of materials	18,500 units at	₹52,000
Direct labour		₹14,000
Overheads		₹28,000
Closing work-in-progress	5,000 units	

Degree of completion: Material 90% and Labour and Overhead 30%

Normal process loss is 10% of total input

(Opening work-in-progress units + Units put in)

Scrap value ₹2.00 per unit.

Units transferred to the next process: 15,000 units.

You are required to:

(a) Compute equivalent units of production.
(b) Compute cost per equivalent unit for each cost element, that is, materials, labour and overheads.
(c) Compute the cost of finished output and closing work-in-progress.
(d) Prepare the process and other accounts.

Assume: (i) FIFO method is used by the company.

(ii) The cost of opening work-in-progress is fully transferred to the next process.

Ans: Cost per equivalent unit ₹6, Cost of 15,000 units of finished output ₹99,000; Cost of closing WIP ₹18,000

28. (Average Costing)

From the following details prepare statement of equivalent production, statement of cost and find the value of

(a) Output transferred, and
(b) Closing work-in-progress applying average method of valuation of process stock and FIFO method.

Opening work-in-progress	2,000units
Materials (100% complete)	₹7,500
Labour (60% complete)	3,000
Overheads (60% complete)	1,500
Units introduced into this process	8,000

There are 2,000 units in process and the state of completion is estimated to be:

Materials	100%
Labour	50%
Overheads	50%

8,000 units are transferred to next process.

The process costs for the period are:

Materials	₹1,00,000
Labour	78,000
Overhead	39,000

Ans: Equivalent units: Materials 10,000, labour and overheads 9,000 each: (a) ₹1,99,784, (b) ₹35,723

29. The following details relate to an intermediary process in a factory:

	% Degree of Completion	No. of Units	Cost ₹
Opening work-in-progress:		300	12,300
(a) Materials	50%		
(b) Labour	80%		
(c) Overheads	80%		
Transfer from previous process	100%	3,800	1,36,800
Process material added			7,900
Direct wages			37,400
Overheads			14,960
Transfer to next progress (finished)	100%	3,500	
Closing work-in-progress:		600	
(a) Material	100%		
(b) Labour	80%		
(c) Overheads	80%		

Prepare:

(a) Process cost accounts for the intermediary process.
(b) Statement of equivalent units (on FIFO basis).
(c) Statement of distribution of cost on the basis of equivalent units.

Ans: Transfer to next process 3,500 units ₹1,79,840; Closing stock 600 units ₹29,520

30. (Average Cost Method)

The following details are given in respect of a manufacturing unit for the month of April 2020:

(i) Opening work-in-progress 5,000 units

	₹
(a) Materials (100% complete)	18,750
(b) Labour (60% complete)	7,500
(c) Overheads (60% complete)	3,750

(ii) Units introduced into the process 17,500 units
(iii) 17,500 units are transferred to the next process
(iv) Process cost for the period are

Material	₹2,50,000
Labour	₹1,95,000
Overheads	₹ 97,500

(v) The stage of completion of units in closing WIP are estimated to be: Material 100%, Labour 50% and Overheads 50%.

You are required to prepare a statement of equivalent unit of production, statement of cost. Also find the value of

(i) Output transferred
(ii) Closing work-in-progress, using average cost method.

Ans: Average cost per equivalent unit ₹27.132, value of output transferred ₹4,74,810, value of closing WIP ₹97,690

31. (Average Cost Method)

Process 2 receives units from Process 1 and after carrying out work on the units transfers them to Process 3.

For the accounting period the relevant data were as follows:

Opening WIP 200 units (25% complete) valued at	₹5,000
800 units received from Process I valued at	₹8,600
840 units were transferred to Process 3	
Closing WIP 160 units (50% complete)	

The costs of the period were ₹33,160 and no units were scrapped.

Required:

Prepare the Process Account for Process 2 using the Average Cost Method of valuation.

Ans: Average cost per complete unit ₹50.826
cost of production
840 complete units ₹42,694
160 WIP units ₹ 4,066

32. (Opening and Closing Work-in-Progress)

The following data relate to process *Y* for accounting period 2.

At the beginning of period 2, there were 800 units partly completed which had the following values:

	Value (₹)	*Percentage Complete*
Input material (from Process *X*)	8,200	100
Material introduced	5,600	55
Labour	3,200	60
Overheads	2,400	45

During the period, 4,300 units were transferred from process *X* at a value of ₹46,500 and other costs were:

	₹
Material introduced	24,000
Labour	19,500
Overhead	18,200

At the end of the period, the closing WIP was 600 units which were at the following stage of completion:

Input material	100% complete
Material introduced	50% complete
Labour	45% complete
Overheads	40% complete

The balance of 4,500 units was transferred to finished goods.

Calculate the value of units transferred to finished goods and the value of WIP and prepare the process account using

(i) the FIFO method, and
(ii) the average cost method.

Inter Process Profit

33. The manufacturing operations of JK Ltd. involve three distinct processes in connection with the same unit. The output of process *P* is charged to process *Q* at a profit of 25% on cost, and the output of process *Q* is charged to process *R* on similar basis. The completed product is transferred into stock at a price which gives process *R* a profit of 25% on transfer price. From the following particulars prepare the process cost accounts and finished goods account. Stock in each process has been valued at prime cost.

Process	*P*	*Q*	*R*
Materials consumed	₹14,000	₹21,000	₹7,000
Labour	21,000	14,000	28,000
Closing stock	7,000	14,000	21,000
Sales ₹1,26,000.			

Closing stock of finished products amount to ₹14,000. Show also the actual realised profit to be taken to the credit of the Profit and Loss Account.

Ans: Profit, Process *P* ₹7,000, Process *Q* ₹14,000, Process *R* ₹28,000, Finished stock A/c ₹28,000, Actual realised profit ₹66,220, cost of closing stock: Process *Q* ₹12,600, Process *R* ₹17,080, Finished stock ₹8,540.

34. Cheap Sweets Ltd. has divided its manufacture into two processes—*A* and *B*. After leaving process *B*, the product is passed into finished stock.
The output of process *A* is transferred to process *B* at a price which gives process *A* a profit of 25% thereon, and the output of process *B* is transferred to finished goods at a price which gives process *B* a profit of 20% thereon.
The following information is provided in respect of the year ended 31st December, 2020:

	Process A	*Process B*
Stock on Ist January, 2020	₹3,200	2,000
Materials used	6,400	2,700
Direct labour	12,500	8,500
Overheads	2,500	1,700
Stock on 31st December, 2020	2,100	900

Process stocks consist of products which have passed through the process completely and are valued at prime cost to the process concerned.
Finished goods were in stock on Ist January, 2020 to the value of ₹10,200 and on 31st December, 2020 to the value of ₹6,200. Both the opening and closing stocks were valued at the price at which they were transferred from process *B*.
Sales amounting to ₹68,400 were effected during the year and included all the goods in stock at the beginning of the year.
The reserves on Ist January, 2020 for unrealised profit included in stock valuation were: Process *B*—₹350; Finished goods—₹3,430.
Prepare the Process Accounts, Finished Goods Account and Trading Account for the year ended 31st December, 2020.

Ans: Profit Process *A* ₹7,500, Process *B* ₹11,000, Finished goods stock A/c ₹9,400, Trading A/c Profit ₹29,413.

Joint Product and By-Products

35. Calculate the estimated cost of production of by-products *X* and *Y* at the point of separation from the main product.

	By-Product *X*	*By-Product* *Y*
Selling price per unit	₹12	₹24

(Contd.)

	By-Product X	By-Product Y
Cost per unit after separation from the main product	₹3	₹5
Units produced	500	200

Selling expenses amount to 25% of total works cost, that is, including both pre-separation and post-separation work cost.

Selling prices are arrived at by adding 20% of total cost, that is, the sum of works cost and selling expenses.

Ans: Total cost By-product *X* ₹2500, By-product *Y* ₹2,200, Cost per unit *X* ₹5, *Y* ₹11

36. In an oil mill, four products emerge from a refining process. The total cost of input during the quarter ending March 2020 is ₹1,48,000. The output, sales and additional processing costs are as under:

Product	*Output in Litres*	*Additional Processing Cost After Split-Off Point (₹)*	*Sales Value ₹*
AOXE	8,000	43,000	1,72,500
BOXE	4,000	9,000	15,000
COXE	2,000		6,000
DOXE	4,000	1,500	45,000

In case, these products were disposed off at the split-off points, that is, before further processing, the selling price would have been:

AOXE ₹15.00; *BOXE* ₹6.00; *COXE* ₹3.00; *DOXE* ₹7.50.

Prepare a statement of profitability based on the following facts:

1. If the products are sold after further processing is carried out in the mills.
2. If they are sold at the split-off point.

Ans: 1. Profit *AOXE* ₹30,833, *BOXE* ₹13,733 Loss, *COXE* ₹1,067, *DOXE* ₹18,833. 2. Profit *AOXE* ₹21,333, *BOXE* ₹4,267, *COXE* ₹1,067, *DOXE* ₹5,333.

37. B Ltd. manufactures product *A* which yield two by-products *B* and *C*. The actual joint expenses of manufacture for a period were ₹8,00,000.

It was estimated that the profits on each product as a percentage of sales would be 30%, 25% and 15% respectively. Subsequent expenses were:

	A	*B*	*C*
Materials	₹10,000	₹7,500	₹2,500
Direct wages	20,000	12,500	5,000
Overheads	15,000	12,500	7,500
	45,000	32,500	15,000
Sales were	₹6,00,000	₹4,00,000	₹2,50,000

Prepare a statement showing the apportionment of the joint expenses of manufacture over the different products.

Ans:

	A	*B*	*C*
Share of joint costs (₹)	3,55,800	2,54,700	1,89,500

38. Two products P and Q are obtained in a crude form and require further processing at a cost of ₹5 for P and ₹4 for Q per unit before sale. Assuming a net margin of 25 per cent on cost, their sale prices are fixed at ₹13.75 and ₹8.75 per unit respectively. During the period, the joint cost was ₹88,000 and the outputs were:

P 8,000 units
Q 6,000 units

Ascertain the joint cost per unit.

Ans:	*P*	*Q*
Joint cost per unit (₹)	8	4

39. Bright Chemicals Ltd. electrolyses common salt to obtain three joint products—caustic soda, chlorine and hydrogen. During a costing period, the expenditure relating to the inputs for the common process amounted to ₹3,50,000. After separation, expenses amounting to ₹1,60,000, ₹75,000, and ₹10,000 were incurred for caustic soda, chlorine and hydrogen respectively. The entire production was sold and ₹3,75,000; ₹2,50,000; and 60,000 were realised for caustic soda, chlorine and hydrogen respectively. The selling expenses were estimated at 5% of realisations from sale. The management expected profits @ 15%; 10% and 5% of realisations from sale of caustic soda, chlorine and hydrogen respectively.

Draw a columnar statement showing the apportionment of joint costs and the profitability of each product.

Ans:	Caustic soda	Chlorine	Hydrogen
Profit (₹)	44,000	12,700	Loss (950)

40. In manufacturing, the main product A, a company processes the resulting waste material into two by-products M_1 and M_2. Using the method of working back from sales value to an estimated cost, you are required to prepare a comparative profit and loss statement of the three products from the following data:

(i) Total cost upto separation point was ₹1,36,000.

	A	*M1*	*M2*
(ii) Sale (all production)	₹3,28,000	₹32,000	₹48,000
(iii) Cost after separation	–	₹ 9,600	₹14,400
(iv) Estimated net profit percentage to sale value	–	20%	30%
(v) Estimated selling expenses as percentage of sale value	20%	20%	20%

Ans:	Main Product	By-Products	
	A	*M1*	*M2*
Net profit (₹)	1,45,600	6,400	14,400

41. In a concern engaged in process industry, four products emerge from a particular process of operation. The total cost of input for the period ended 30th September, 2020 is ₹2,53,500. The details of output, additional cost after "split-off point" and sales value of the products are given below.

Product	*Output*	*Additional Processing Cost After Split-Off Point*	*Sales Value*
	kg	₹	₹
A	8,000	60,000	1,68,000
B	5,000	10,000	1,10,000
C	3,000	–	60,000
D	4,000	20,000	90,000

If the products are sold at "split-off point" without further processing, the sales value would have been

	₹
A	1,15,000
B	90,000
C	55,000
D	80,000

You are required to prepare a statement of profitability based on the products being sold:
(i) after further processing, and
(ii) at the split-off point.

Ans:	A	B	C	D
Profit after further processing	(₹) 27,000	25,000	15,000	17,500
Profit at the split-off point	(₹) 29,257	22,897	13,993	20,353

42. A company manufactures products *A*, *B*, and *C* from a joint process. Additional data are as follows:

	Product			
	A	*B*	*C*	*Total*
Units produced	8,000	4,000	2,000	14,000
Joint costs	₹72,000	*a*	*b*	₹1,20,000
Sales value at split-off	*c*	*d*	₹30,000	2,00,000
Additional costs to process further	14,000	10,000	6,000	30,000
Sales value if processed further	1,40,000	60,000	40,000	2,40,000

Derive the values for the lettered spaces.

Ans: (a) ₹30,000; (b) ₹18,000; (c) ₹1,20,000; (d) ₹50,000

43. JB Limited produces four joint products, *A*, *B*, *C* and *D*, all of which emerge from the processing of one raw material. The following are the relevant data:
Production for the period:

Joint Product	*Number of Units*	*Selling Price Per Unit (₹)*
A	500	18.00
B	900	8.00
C	400	4.00
D	200	11.00

The company budgets for a profit of 10% on sales value. The other estimated costs are:

	₹
Carriage inwards	1,000
Direct wages	3,000
Manufacturing overhead	2,000
Administration overhead	10% of the sales value

You are required to:

(a) Calculate the maximum price that may be paid for the raw material.

(b) Prepare a comprehensive cost statement for each of the products allocating the materials and other costs based upon.

(i) Number of units

(ii) Sales value

Ans: (a) ₹10,000

(b) (i) Total cost *A*, ₹4,500; *B*, ₹8,100; *C*, ₹3000; *D*, ₹1,800

(ii) Total cost *A*, ₹8,100; *B*, ₹6,480; *C*, ₹1,440; *D*, ₹1,980 .

44. A company processes a raw material in its Department 1 to produce three products, viz, *A*, *B* and *X* at the same split-off stage. During a period, 1,80,000 kg of raw materials were processed in Department 1 at a total cost of ₹12,88,000 and the resultant output of *A*, *B* and *X* were 18,000 kg, 10,000 kg. and 54,000 kg respectively. *A* and *B* were further processed in Department 2 at a cost of ₹1,80,000 and ₹1,50,000 respectively.

X was further processed in Department 2 at a cost of ₹1,80,000. There is no waste in further processing. The details of sales effected during the period were as under:

Particulars		*A*	*B*	*X*
Quantity Sold	(kg)	17,000	5,000	44,000
Sales value	(₹)	12,24,000	2,50,000	7,92,000

There were no opening stocks. If these products were sold at split-off stage, the selling prices of *A*, *B* and *X* would have been ₹50, ₹40 and ₹10 per kg respectively.

Required:

(i) Prepare a statement showing the apportionment of joint costs to *A*, *B* and *X*.

(ii) Present a statement showing the cost per kg of each product indicating joint cost, further processing cost and total cost separately.

(iii) Prepare a statement showing the product wise and total profit for the period.

(iv) State with supporting calculations as to whether any or all the products should be further processed or not.

Ans:

	A	B	C
(i) Apportionment of joint costs (₹)	6,30,000	2,80,000	3,78,000
(ii) Total cost per kg (₹)	45	43	9
(iii) Profit (₹)	4,59,000	35,000	3,96,000

(iv) Product *B* should not be further processed.

45. A company purchases raw materials worth ₹11.04 lakhs and processes them into four products *P*, *Q*, *R* and *S*, which have a unit sale value of ₹3, ₹9, ₹16 and ₹60 respectively at split-off point, as they could be sold as such to other processors. However, during a year, the company decided to further process and sell products *P*, *Q* and *S*, while *R* was not to be processed further but sold at split-off point to other processors. The processing of raw materials into the four products cost ₹28 lakhs to the company. The other data for the year were as under:

Product	*Output (Units)*	*Sales (₹in Lakhs)*	*Additional Processing Cost After Split-Off (All Variable Costs) (₹ in Lakhs)*
P	10,00,000	46.00	12.00
Q	20,000	4.00	2.40
R	10,000	1.60	–
S	18,000	12.000	0.40

You are required to work out the following information for managerial decision-making:

(a) If the joint costs are allocated amongst the four products on the basis of "Net realisable Value" at split-off point, what would be the company's annual income?

(b) If the company had sold off all the other three products at split-off stage, identify the increase/decrease in the company's annual income as compared to (a) above.

(c) What sales strategy could the company have planned to maximise its profit in the year?

(d) Identify the net increase in income if the strategy at (c) is adopted, as compared to (a) above.

Ans: (a) ₹9.76 lakhs (b) Annual income will decline by ₹4.60 lakhs (d) Overall income will increase by ₹0.20 lakhs.

CASE STUDY

A Case of Ambika Spinning Mills and Export Ltd.

Ambika Mills was established in the year 1998 as textile manufacturing concern in Ahmedabad, Gujarat. The company was using process costing for its three-stage production process of converting the fibre into yarn and then yarn into fabric. These processes were *Spinning*, *Weaving* or *Knitting* and *Finishing* comprising of *dyeing* and *printing*. The output of each of these processes was charged to the next process at a price calculated to give profit of 20% on transfer price which also meant 25% of the cost price. The output of the third process i.e., the final product (fabric) was charged to finished stock-account on a similar basis of 20% profit.

The company was running on profit since its inception year and this year 2018–19 too seemed no difference. The method of valuation of the company's stock was at prime cost. Although, having sold all the finished products previous year (2017–18) as well as no work-in-progress at the beginning of the year, the company did not have any type of opening stock. However, there were some stocks left at the end of the current year (2018–19).

The primary raw material i.e. 150 cotton bale of 180 kg each this year was purchased for the first process i.e., *spinning*, from Gintex Industries at ₹18 per kg. The other raw material costed ₹1,14,000. The direct wages paid to the first process workers to produce the cotton yarn/thread amounted to ₹4,00,000.

₹4,00,000 were spent on raw material for the second process i.e., *weaving*. The wages paid to the weavers amounted to ₹6,00,000 for producing the fabric. In the third process, these fabrics were then dyed and printed for which the raw material worth ₹2,00,000 was purchased. The workers for this process were paid direct wages of ₹8,00,000.

The company's Cost Accountant—Rehan was presented with the following closing data at the end of the current year on March 31, 2019:

Costs	*Spinning*	*Weaving*	*Printing*	*Closing Stock*
Stock as on March 31, 2019	2,00,000	4,00,000	6,00,000	3,00,000

Sales during the year 2019 amounted to ₹36,00,000.

Rehan had the task of preparing the Process Cost Accounts for all three processes showing the profit element at each stage and also calculate the actual realised profits. He also had to determine the value of closing stock to be transferred to balance-sheet at the end. However, he was puzzled about the overheads of ₹9,00,000. Ambika Spinning Mills had a policy of charging overheads directly to Profit and Loss Account where as Rehan was of the opinion that it should be charged to the Process Account. He decided to do it both the way this time and let his management take a call.

QUESTIONS FOR DISCUSSION:

1. Prepare the following ignoring the overheads:
   (a) Process Accounts showing the profit component at each stage.
   (b) Actual Profit realised.
   (c) Value of stock to be transferred to the Balance-Sheet.
   (d) Process Account taking overheads into account (assignment).

Chapter 12

Service Costing

Learning Objectives

After reading this chapter, you should be able to:

1. understand service costing;
2. explain transport costing—its nature and composition of costs involved; and
3. describe the nature of power house costing and canteen costing.

SERVICE COSTING

Service costing, also known as operating costing, is especially used where services are rendered and articles are not produced. According to the Institute of Cost and Management Accountants (UK), "operating costing is that form of operation costing which applies where standardised services are provided either by an undertaking or by a service cost centre within an undertaking". Service costing is particularly suitable for the costing of road and rail transport services, electricity undertakings and hospitals, etc. The following cost units are usually applied in different service undertakings:

Nature of Business	*Cost Unit*
Public carriers, trucks, goods trains	Per tonne km or per km
Electricity supply	Per kilowatt hour
Passenger buses and trains	Per km
Hospitals	Per patient day
	Per bed, per operation
Road maintenance	Per km of road
Hotels	Per room
Road lighting	Per lamp
Canteen	Per meal

NATURE OF SERVICE COSTING

Service costs are usually collected under the following headings:

1. Fixed or standing charges;
2. Semi-fixed or maintenance charges; and
3. Variable or running charges.

An important feature of service costing is that mostly such costs are fixed in nature. For example, the costs of operating a theatre are usually not influenced by the size of the audience.

TRANSPORT COSTING

In transport undertakings, the cost unit is normally the tonne-mile or passenger-mile but the organisation of transport undertakings varies according to the nature of the undertakings. For example, rail transport is more complicated than road transport as provision has to be made not only for the vehicles but also for the maintenance of the permanent way, the station, signalling facilities, yards, engines, wagons, etc. For the railway, separate cost centres need to be established.

Composition of Costs

In transport operating costing, the total costs consist of: (i) standing charges, (ii) running (variable) charges, and (iii) maintenance charges.

Standing Charges

In motor transport costing, the following are commonly the standing charges:

1. Licence duty and insurance
2. Garage costs and administrative expenses
3. Drivers' wages
4. Depreciation
5. Tax

Running (Variable) Costs

The following variable costs are found in motor transport costing:

1. Petrol
2. Oil
3. Grease

Maintenance Charges

1. Repairs and maintenance
2. Tyres
3. Garage charges

Cost Units

In transport costing, passenger-kilometre or tonne-kilometre is generally the cost unit. After collecting total cost, the cost per unit (per passenger-km or tonne-km) is determined. The cost per unit is calculated as follows:

No. of vehicles × Capacity × Distance travelled × Days × Passenger/Weight actually carried.

Ascertainment of Costs

Accumulation and control of costs in transport costing are achieved through a daily log-sheet and operating cost-sheet. A daily log-report is a document which contains information regarding each journey, for example, passenger or weight carried, starting and returning time, distance covered, oil or petrol used. Figure 12.1 gives a proforma of a Daily Log Sheet.

Daily Log Sheet

Vehicle No. ____________	Date ____________
Driver's Name ____________	Starting time ____________
Licence No. ____________	Returning time ____________

Particulars of Journey

Trip No.	*Starting*		*Arriving*		*Goods Carried*	
Place	*Time*		*Place*	*Time*	*Out Collected en route*	*Distance*

Petrol consumption:	Time lost:	Worker's time
At start ____________	Loading ____________	Driver ____________
Recd./purchased during the journey ____________	Unloading Traffic ____________	Mechanic ____________
At finish ____________		
Total consumption ____________	Accident ____________	Cleaner ____________
Oil ____________		
Grease ____________		

Fig. 12.1 Daily Log Sheet

The operating cost-sheet or cost-statement is also known as the performance statement for each vehicle. Such cost-sheets (Fig. 12.2) accumulate relevant costs regarding a vehicle from different sources, such as daily log -sheet, wage book, purchase register or summary, repairs details, etc. Operating costs on a cost-sheet are usually divided into three headings:

1. Running (variable) charges
2. Standing (fixed) charges
3. Maintenance charges

The operating cost-sheet acts as a cost control device. The total and per unit cost calculated can be compared with past figures and performance can be evaluated.

(ABC Transport Company)
Cost-Sheet (Monthly)

Vehicle No. ______________________ Month ______________________

Registration No. ______________________ Days operated ______________________

	Charges		Amount ₹
(A)	Running Charges:		
	Petrol		
	Oil		
	Grease		
	Total		
(B)	Standing Charges:		
	Depreciation		
	Insurance		
	Interest		
	Tax		
	Licence fees		
	Driver's salary		
	Total		
(C)	Maintenance Charges:		
	Repairs		
	Tyres		
	Spares		
	Garage charges		
	Total		
	Total charges	₹ ______________	
	Total tonne-km/passenger	km ______________	
	Cost per tonne-km/passenger	km ______________	

Fig. 12.2 Cost-Sheet

Power House Costing

Power house costing is applied in those undertakings which are engaged in the production of steam and generation of electricity. In large firms, a power house (boiler house) is generally a service department assisting the production department. Operating cost-statement in this case can be prepared after collecting data about the costs of producing the steam and costs of generating the electricity. The unit of cost for production of steam may be "Per 1b" and for generation of electricity "per kilowatt". A composite unit of cost may be used, that is, the kilowatt-hour. A proforma of a power house operating cost-sheet is given in Fig. 12.3. This operating cost-sheet shows also different elements of cost of steam production and generation of electricity.

Power House Cost-Sheet

Month ____________ Total steam consumption ____________

Total steam produced ____________ Electricity generated ____________

	Items	*Cost Per Unit (Cost Per 1,000 lb)*	*Total Cost*
(A)	Fixed Overheads:		
	Rent, rates, etc.		
	Depreciation of plant		
	Depreciation of building		
	Insurance		
(B)	Maintenance Charges:		
	Meters		
	Furnace		
	Service materials		
	Tools and accessories		
(C)	Labour Charges:		
	Coal handlers		
	Ash removers		
(D)	Fuel:		
	Fuel		
	Power		
(E)	Water Charges:		
	Water purchased		
	Water softening		
(F)	Supervision and Other Charges:		
	Foremen		
	Engineers		
	General labourer		
	Cleaners		
	Total		

Fig. 12.3 Power House Cost-Sheet

CANTEEN COSTING

In most organisations, canteen facilities are provided at subsidy so that food and other items can be provided at minimum price. The costs are accumulated on a cost-sheet which gives the total cost incurred. From the total cost the subsidy is deducted to arrive at the net cost of operating the canteen. After comparing the net cost with the sales proceeds, profit/loss is calculated. A specimen of canteen cost-sheet is given in Fig. 12.4.

Canteen Cost-Sheet

Month ______________________

Items		Total Costs		Cost Per Meal
		Current Month (₹)	Previous Month (₹)	
(A)	Provisions:			
	Bread			
	Biscuits			
	Cakes			
	Eggs			
	Meat			
	Fish			
	Vegetables			
	Milk			
	Fruit			
	Others			
(B)	Labour and Supervision:			
	Supervisor			
	Cooks			
	Helpers			
	Counter clerks			
	Cleaners			
	Sweepers			
(C)	Maintenance:			
	Crockery			
	Glassware			
	Towels			
	Rent			
	Light			
	Gas			
	Insurance			
	Consumable stores			
	Total cost			
Less:	Subsidy			
	Net cost			
	Sales			
	Profit/Loss			

Fig. 12.4 Canteen Cost-Sheet

EXAMPLE 12.1

A truck starts with a load of 10 tonnes of goods from station *P*. It unloads 4 tonnes at station *Q* and rest of the goods at station *R*. It reaches back directly to station *P* after getting reloaded with 8 tonnes of goods at station *R*. The distances between *P* to *Q*, *Q* to *R* and then from *R* to *P* are 40 km, 60 km and 80 km respectively. Compute absolute tonne-km and commercial tonne-km.

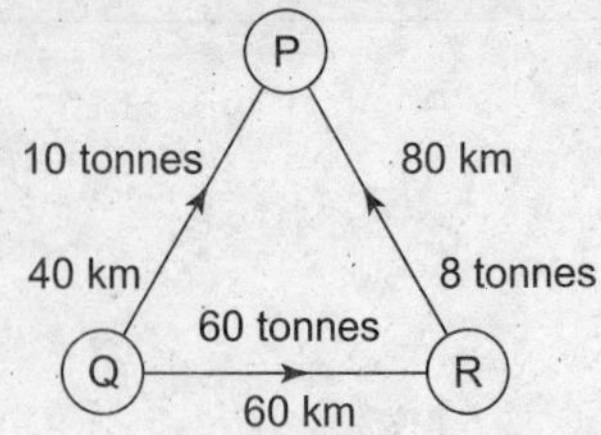

Solution

Absolute tonnes km:
10 tonnes × 40 km + 6 tonnes × 60 km = 400 + 360 = 760 tonnes km
Return Journey: 8 tonnes × 80 km = 640 tonnes km
Total absolute ton km = 760 + 640 = 1,400 tonne km.

EXAMPLE 12.2

Keerti Transport Ltd. operates a fleet of lorries. The records for lorry: L—14 reveal the following information for September, 2020:

Days maintained	:	30
Days operated	:	25
Days idle	:	5
Total hours operated	:	300
Total km covered	:	2,500
Total tonnage carried	:	200 (4 tonnes load per trip, return journey empty)
Total cost for the month	:	₹2,70,000

Prepare a performance statement showing:

(i) Cost per day operated
(ii) Cost per kilometre r
(iii) Cost per hour
(iv) Cost per round-trip
(v) Cost per commercial tonne-km.

Solution

Total cost for the month ₹2,70,000

(i) Cost per day operated ₹2,70,000/25 days = ₹10,800

(ii) Cost per km = $\frac{₹2,70,000}{2,500 \text{ kms}}$ = ₹108

(iii) Cost per hour = $\frac{₹2,70,000}{300 \text{ hrs}}$ = ₹900

(iv) Cost per round-trip = $\frac{₹2,70,000}{50}$ = ₹5,400

(v) Cost per commercial tonne-km = $\frac{₹2,70,000}{5,000}$ = ₹54

Tonne km = $\frac{2,500 \text{ km}}{50}$ = 500 tonne km

EXAMPLE 12.3

Calculate total passenger kilometres from the following information:
Number of buses 6, number of days operating in a month 25, trips made by each bus per day 8, distance covered 20 kilometres (one side), capacity of bus 40 passengers, normally 80% of capacity utilisation.

Solution

Calculation of passenger kilometres:
6 × 25 × 8 × 2 × 20 × 40 × 80% = 15,36,000 passenger km.

EXAMPLE 12.4

A lorry starts with a load of 24 tonnes of goods from station A. It unloads 10 tonnes at station B and rest of goods at station C. It reaches back directly to station A after getting reloaded with 18 tonnes of goods at station C. The distance between A to B, B to C and then from C to A are 270 km, 150 km and 325 km respectively. Compute "Absolute tonnes kms" and "Commercial tonnes-kms".

Solution

Absolute tonnes-km

= Tonnes (unit of weight) × Km (unit of distance)

= 24 tonnes × 270 km + 14 tonnes × 150 km + 18 tonnes × 325 km

= 6,480 +2,100 + 5,850

= 14,430 tonnes km

Commercial tonnes km

= Average load × total km travelled

$= \left(\frac{24+14+18}{3}\right)$ tonnes × 745 km

= 13,906.67 tonnes-km

EXAMPLE 12.5

A City Municipality arranges for the removal of its garbage by means of motor vehicle transport. The following vehicles are maintained:

No. of Vehicles	Specification
20	5 tonne lorries
30	4 tonne lorries
50	3 tonne lorries
40	2 tonne lorries

On an average, each lorry makes six trips a day and in each trip covers an average distance of five km. Each lorry carries garbage of 60% its capacity. On an annual average, 20% of the lorries are laid up for repairs. The conservancy work is carried out daily. Calculate tonne-km utilised for removal of garage per month.

Solution

Calculation of Tonne-Km

No. of Vehicles	Specification	Total Capacity
20	5	100
30	4	120
50	3	150
40	2	80
		450

Tonne-Km

Total Capacity × Trip per day × Distance × Capacity utilisation × Effective use × No. of days in a month.

$$450 \times 6 \times 5 \times \frac{60}{100} \times \frac{80}{100} \times 30 = 1{,}94{,}400 \text{ tonne-km}$$

EXAMPLE 12.6

A bus started from Delhi for Mussoorie with 50 passengers on board. 20 passengers got off at Dehradun and the bus proceeded with the remaining passengers. In the evening, the same bus left Mussoorie with 50 passengers, 10 passengers got off at Dehradun and the bus resumed its journey with remaining passengers for Delhi. The distance between Delhi and Dehradun is 280 km and between Dehradun to Mussoorie it is 20 km.

Compute the cost per passenger km, if the total cost of running the bus comes out to be ₹5,000.

Solution

Total passengers kilometres covered:

(i)	Delhi to Dehradun = 50 passengers × 280 km	14,000
(ii)	Dehradun to Mussoorie = 30 passengers × 20 km (20 passengers got off at Dehradun)	600

Back journey in the evening

(i) From Mussoorie = 50 passengers × 20 km	1,000
(ii) From Dehradun to Delhi = 40 passengers × 280 km	11,200
(10 passengers got off at Dehradun)	26,800

Total cost of running the bus = ₹5,000

Total passenger kilometres covered = 26,800 km

$$\text{Cost per passenger km.} = \frac{₹5{,}000}{26{,}800 \text{ km}}$$

$$= ₹0.186$$

EXAMPLE 12.7

From the following information, calculate the bus fare to be charged from each passenger for the journeys:

(a) Delhi to Agra;
(b) Delhi to Bhiwani;
(c) Delhi to Chandigarh:

(i) Delhi to Agra	200 km
Delhi to Bhiwani	120 km
Delhi to Chandigarh	250 km
(ii) Effective passenger-km	3,72,000

(iii) Total operating costs (excluding conductor's commission @15% and passenger tax @ 5% of total takings) ₹1,48,800.

(iv) Desired profit—30% on total takings.

Solution

Effective passenger-km = 3,72,000

Total operating cost (excluding Conductor's Commission and Passenger Tax) 1,48,800

Conductor's Commission

(15% of total takings, that is, ₹2,97,600) = 44,640

Passenger Tax (Working Note (ii))

(5% of total takings that is, ₹2,97,600) = 14,880 (*Working Note (iii)*)

Desired Profit (30% of total takings that is, 2,97,600) = 89,280 (*Working Note (iv)*)

Total takings = 2,97,600

Effective passenger-km = 3,72,000

$$\text{Rate per passenger-km} = \frac{2{,}97{,}600}{3{,}72{,}000} \times 100 = ₹0.80$$

Proposed fare to be charged per passenger-km.

Delhi to Agra = ₹0.80 × 200 km

= ₹160

$$\text{Delhi to Bhiwani} = ₹0.80 \times 120 \text{ km} = ₹96$$

$$\text{Delhi to Chandigarh} = ₹0.80 \times 250 \text{ km} = ₹200$$

Working Notes:

(i) Conductor's Commission = 15% of Total takings

Passenger's Tax = 5% of Total takings

Desired Profit = 30% of Total takings

Commission + Passenger Tax + Profit = 50% of Total takings

Cost (Balance)	50%	Operating Cost	= 1,48,800
Total Takings	100%	100% of this	= 1,48,800
			2,97,600

(ii) $$\text{Conductor's, Commission} = \frac{2{,}97{,}600 \times 15}{100} = ₹44{,}640$$

(iii) $$\text{Passenger Tax} = \frac{2{,}97{,}600 \times 5}{100} = ₹14{,}880$$

(iv) $$\text{Profit} = \frac{2{,}97{,}600 \times 30}{100}$$

$$\text{Total} = ₹89{,}280$$

EXAMPLE 12.8

Mr. Singh started transport business with a fleet of 10 taxis. Expenses of operating the fleet are given below:

(i) Cost of each taxi	₹3,80,000
(ii) Salary of office and garage staff	₹38,000 p.m.
(iii) Rent of garage	₹12,000 p.m.
(iv) Driver's salary per taxi	₹4,000 p.m.
(v) Insurance, tax and sundry expenses per taxi	₹55,200 per yr.

The life of a taxi is 3,00,000 km at the end of which it is estimated to be sold at ₹20,000. A taxi is expected to run on an average 4,000 km per month. Petrol consumption is 12 km per litre of petrol costing ₹30 per litre. You are required to:

(i) Calculate the cost of running taxi per km by preparing a statement of operating cost; and

(ii) Find out the profit Mr. Singh may expect to earn during the first month of operations if the hire charge is ₹10 per km. Assume that during the month each taxi runs on an average 4,000 km of which 800 km it runs empty.

Solution

(i) Calculation of cost of running a taxi per km

Total Running = 4,000 km

Effective Running = 4,000 km – 800 km = 3,200 km.

	Amt. p.m. (each taxi)	₹
Standing Charges:		
Salary of office and garage staff (38,000 ÷ 10) =	3,800	
Rent of garages (12,000 ÷ 10) =	1,200	
Driver's salary	4,000	
Insurance, Tax and Sundry Exp. (55,200 ÷ 12)	4,600	
	13,600	
Fixed charges per taxi per km 13600 ÷ 3200		4.25
Variable Expenses:		
Depreciation = $\frac{3,80,000 - 20,000}{3,00,000} \times 4,000 =$	4,800	
Petrol cost = $\frac{400 \times 30}{12}$	10,000	
	14,800	
Variable cost per taxi per km.	14,800 ÷ 3,200	4.625
Total cost per km per taxi		**8.875**

(ii) Profit v the month

	₹
Hire charges per km	10.00
Less: Total cost per km	8.875
Profit per km	1.125

Total profit per taxi = 1.125 × 3,200 km = ₹3,600

Total profit for 10 taxis = 3,600 × 10 = ₹36,000 p.m.

EXAMPLE 12.9

A transport company is running four buses between Delhi and Alwar, covering a distance of 100 km. The seating capacity of each bus is 40 passengers. The following particulars are obtained from its books for the month of October 2020:

for excel template, scan

	₹
Wages of drivers, conductors	9,600
Salaries of office staff	3,000
Honorarium of accountant	1,000
Diesel, oil etc	16,000
Repairs and maintenance	3,200
Road tax and insurance	6,400
Depreciation	10,400
Interest and other charges	8,000

Actual passengers carried were 75% of the seating capacity. All the buses ran for 30 days. Each bus made one round trip per day.

Find out the fare the company should charge per passenger/km if it wants a profit of 20% on the taking.

Solution

Cost-Statement

Period: October, 2020
Passenger km = 7,20,000

		₹	Total ₹
(a)	Standing Charges:		
	Salaries of office staff	3,000	
	Honorarium of Accountant	1,000	
	Road tax and insurance	6,400	
	Depreciation	10,400	
	Interest and other charges	8,000	
	Total (a)		28,800
(b)	Maintenance Charges		
	Repairs	3,200	
	Total (b)		3,200
(c)	Running Charges		
	Wages of drivers and conductors	9,600	
	Diesel oil etc.	16,000	
	Total (c)		25,600
	Total of (a + b + c) ₹		57,600
(d)	Total passenger km for the month (km)	7,20,000	
(e)	Cost per passenger km. ₹(57,600 ÷ 7,20,000 km)	0.08	
	Passenger km.		
	100 × kms. × 2 ways × 4 buses × 30 days × 40 passengers =		9,60,000
	Less: 25% empty (or 75% capacity) =		2,40,000
			7,20,000
	Total cost	₹57,600	
	Profit to be added		
	20% of taking or 25% of cost	₹14,400	
	Expected Revenue	72,000	
	Total no. of passengers in a month:		
	40 passengers × 2 ways × 4 buses × 30 days =		9,600
	Less: 25% empty or 75% capacity		2,400
			7,200
	Fare per passenger per trip		
	₹72,000 ÷ 7,200 = ₹10		

EXAMPLE 12.10

Hira Singh owns a taxi, a bus and a truck. The bus is 50-seater. The maximum capacity of the truck is 10 tonnes. The taxi runs on an average 3,000 km. in a month out of which 20% is normal running without fare. Variable cost of running the taxi is ₹8 per kilometre.

The bus and the truck run between Delhi and Jaipur, one way distance being 300 km. The bus makes 25 round-trips in a month and is generally 90% occupied. Variable cost of running a bus is ₹13.50 per kilometre. The truck makes 20 round-trips in a month and is fully loaded on outward journey but only 90% loaded on return. Variable cost of running a truck is ₹9.50 per kilometre.

You are required to calculate:

(i) Total variable cost per month and variable cost per effective kilometre for the taxi;
(ii) Total variable cost per month and variable cost per effective passenger-kilometre for the bus; and
(iii) Total variable cost per month and variable cost per effective tonne-kilometre for the truck.

Solution

Computation of total variable cost per month and variable cost per effective km for the taxi:

(A) *Total variable cost per month:*

$$= ₹3{,}000 \times 8$$
$$= ₹24{,}000 \text{ per month.}$$

(B) *Variable cost per effective km:*

$$= \frac{\text{Total variable cost}}{\text{Average kg in a month with fare}}$$
$$= \frac{24{,}000}{1{,}800}$$
$$= ₹13.33 \text{ per effective km}$$

(ii) Computation of total variable cost per month and variable cost per effective passenger km for bus:

(A) **Total variable cost per month:**

$$= \text{Total km of 25 trips} \times \text{Rate of VC}$$
$$= (300 \times 2 \times 25) \times 13.50$$
$$= ₹2{,}02{,}500.$$

(B) **Variable cost per effective passenger km**

$$\text{Passenger km} = (300 \times 2 \times 25) \times 50 \times 90\%$$
$$= 15{,}000 \times 50 \times \frac{90}{100}$$
$$= 6{,}75{,}000 \text{ passenger km}$$

$$\text{Variable cost per effective passenger km} = \frac{2{,}02{,}500}{6{,}75{,}000} = 0.30 \text{ per passenger p. km.}$$

(iii) Total variable cost per month of the truck:

$$= (300 \times 2 \times 20) \times 9.50$$
$$= ₹1{,}14{,}000$$

(C) **Variable cost per effective tonne-kilometre:**

Effective tonne-kilometre

$$= (300 \times 1 \times 20 \times 10)\ 100\% + (300 \times 1 \times 20 \times 10) \times 90\%$$

$$= (60{,}000) \times \frac{100}{100} + 60{,}000 \times \frac{90}{100}$$

$$= 60{,}000 + 54{,}000$$

$$= 1{,}14{,}000 \text{ tonnes kilometres.}$$

$$\text{Rate} = \frac{\text{VC}}{\text{tonne km}} = \frac{1{,}14{,}000}{1{,}14{,}000} = ₹1 \text{ per tonne km}$$

EXAMPLE 12.11

Global Transport Ltd. charges ₹90 per tonne for its 6 tonne truck lorry load from city A to city B. The charges for the return journey are ₹84 per tonne. No concession or reduction in these rates is made for any delivery of goods at intermediate station C. In January, 2020, the truck made 12 outward journeys for city B with full load out of which 2 tonne were unloaded twice in the way at city C. The truck carried a load of 8 tonnes in its return journey for 5 times but was once caught by police and ₹1,200 were paid as fine. For the remaining trips the truck carried full load out of which all the goods on load were unloaded once at city C. The distance from city A to city C and city B are 140 km and 300 km respectively.

Annual fixed costs and maintenance charges are ₹60,000 and ₹12,000 respectively. Running charges spent during January, 2020 are ₹2,944.

You are required to find out the cost per absolute tonne-kilometre and the profit for January, 2020.

Solution

Global Transport Ltd.
Operating Cost and Profit Statement During January, 2020

	Amount ₹
Fixed costs (₹60,000/12)	5,000
Maintenance charges (₹12,000/12)	1,000
Running costs	2,944
Total operating cost	8,944
Cost per absolute tonne-km	0.20
(₹8,944/44, 720 absolute tonne km)	
Net revenue received (Working Note 4)	12,168
Less: Total operating costs (as given above)	8,944
Profit	3,224

Working Notes:

1. *Absolute tonne-km for outward journeys:*
   (i) From city *A* to city *B*:
   10 journeys × 300 km × 6 tonne = 18,000 tonne-km
   (ii) From city *A* to city *C*:
   2 journeys × 140 km × 6 tonne = 1,680 tonne-km

(iii) From city *C* to city *B*:

2 journeys × 160 km × 4 tonne	=	1,280 tonne-km
Total:		20,960 tonne-km

2. *Absolute km for return journeys:*

(i) From city *B* to city *A*:

5 journeys × 300 km × 8 tonne	=	12,000 tonne-km
6 journeys × 300 km × 6 tonne	=	10,800 tonne-km

(ii) From city *B* to city *C*:

1 journey × 160 km × 6 tonne	=	960 tonne-km
Total:		23,760 tonne-km

3. *Total absolute tonne-km of outward and return journeys:*
= 20,960 tonne-km + 23,760 tonne-km = 44,720 tonne-km.

4. *Net revenue received during January, 2020:*

	₹
12 trucks × 6 tonne × ₹90 (from city *A* to city *B*)	6,480
5 trucks × 8 tonne × ₹84 (from city *B* to city *A*)	3,360
6 trucks × 6 tonne × ₹84 (from city *B* to city *A*)	3,024
1 truck × 6 tonne × ₹84 (from city *B* to city *C*)	504
Total revenue:	13,368
Less: Fine paid	1,200
Net revenue received	12,168

EXAMPLE 12.12

A transport company is running 4 buses between Delhi and Meerut covering a distance of 100 km. The seating capacity of each bus is 40 passengers. The following particulars are obtained from the books for the month of March, 2020:

	₹
Wages of drivers and conductors	19,200
Salaries of office staff	6,000
Honorarium to accountant	2,000
Diesel, oil, etc.	32,000
Repairs and maintenance	6,400
Road tax and insurance	12,800
Depreciation	20,800
Interest and other charges	16,000

Actual passengers carried were 75% of the seating capacity. All the buses ran for 30 days. Each bus made one round-trip per day. Find out the cost per passenger-km.

Solution

Total passenger-km
100 km × 2 ways × 4 buses × 30 days × 40 passengers × 75% capacity = 7,20,000 passenger-km

Cost-Statement for March 2020

Standing Charges		
Salaries of office staff	6,000	
Honorarium of accountant	2,000	
Road tax and insurance	12,800	
Interest and other charges	16,000	
		36,800
Running Charges		
Wages of drivers and conductors	19,200	
Diesel, oil, etc	32,000	
Repair and maintenance	6,400	
Depreciation	20,800	78,400
Total charges		1,15,200
Cost per passenger km 1,15,200/7,20,000 = ₹0.16 passenger km		

EXAMPLE 12.13

A Transport Co. charges ₹120 per tonne for a 5-tonne lorry load from station A to station B. The charges for return trip are ₹110 per tonne. In the month of July, 2020, a truck has made 10 outward journeys with full-load out of which 3 tonnes were unloaded twice at C station on the way. It returned without any load once only from station C to station A. The expenses incurred were:

Annual fixed charges	₹38,400
Annual maintenance	₹19,200
Monthly running charges	₹2,404

You are required to find the cost per tonne-kilometre (absolute) and the profit for the month of July, 2020, assuming that no concession is made for delivery at the intermediate stations.

Distance from station A to station B is 210 km, and from station A to station C 120 km. The truck carried a load of 8 tonnes 5 times in the month while returning from station B but was once caught by the police and was fined ₹2,000.

Solution

Distance 210 kms

Station *A* ———— Station *C* ———— Station *B*

—— Distance 120 kms —— Distance 90 kms ——

Calculation of Tonne-kilometre Absolute

Station		
A to *B*	8 times × 5 tons × 210 km	8,400
C to *B*	2 times × 2 tons × 90 km	360
A to *C*	2 times × 5 tons × 120 km	1,200
C to *A*	1 time × nil tons × 120 km	–
B to *A*	5 times × 8 tons × 210 km	8,400
B to *A*	4 times × 5 tons × 210 km	4,200
B to *C*	1 time × 5 tons × 90 km	450
		23,010

Calculation of Cost Per Tonne-kilometre

Expenses	*Yearly*	*Monthly*
Annual fixed	38,400	3,200
Annual maintenance	19,200	1,600
Running charges		2,404
Total (A)		7,204
Monthly ton-kilometre (B)		23,010
Cost per ton-kilometre (A / B)		.313 approx.

$$\text{Cost per tonne kilometre (absolute if fine charges also included)} = \frac{7,204 + 2,000}{23,010} = 0.40$$

Profit for the month of July, 2020:

Revenue	
Station A to Station B = 10 times × 5 tons × ₹120 per ton	₹6,000
Station B to Station A = 5 times × 8 tons × ₹110 per ton	₹4,400
Station B to Station A = 5 times × 5 tons × ₹110 per ton	₹2,750
	₹13,150
Less: Total cost	₹–7,204
Less: Fines paid	₹–2,000
Profit	₹3,946

✍ EXAMPLE 12.14

A transport company has been given a 40-kilometre-long route to run 5 buses. The cost of each bus is ₹6,50,000. The buses will make 3 round-trips per day carrying on an average of 80 percent passengers of their seating-capacity. The seating-capacity of each bus is 40 passengers. The buses will run on an average 25 days in a month. The other information for the year 2019–20 is given below:

Garage rent	₹4,000 per month
Annual repair and maintenance	₹22,500 each bus
Salaries of 5 drivers	₹3,000 each per month
Wages of 5 conductors	₹1,200 each per month
Manager's salary	₹7,500 per month
Road tax, permit fee, etc.	₹5,000 for a quarter
Office expenses	₹2,000 per month
Cost of diesel per litre	₹33
Kilometre run per litre for each bus	6 kilometres
Annual depreciation	15% of cost
Annual insurance	3% of cost

You are required to calculate the bus fare to be charged from each passenger per kilometre, if the company wants to earn profits of $33\frac{1}{3}$ percent on taking (total receipts from passengers).

☞ ***Solution***

Operating Cost-Sheet for the Year 2019–20

(Total Passenger-Km = 1,15,20,000)

Particulars	*Total Cost* (₹)	*Cost Per Passenger-km* (₹)
A. Fixed Charges:		
Garage rent (4,000 × 12)	48,000	
Salary of drivers (3,000 × 5 × 12)	1,80,000	
Wages of conductors (1200 × 5 × 12)	72,000	
Manager's salary (7,500 × 12)	90,000	
Road tax, permit fee, etc. (5,000 × 4)	20,000	
Office expenses (2,000 × 12)	24,000	
Insurance $\left(6,50,000 \times \frac{3}{100} \times 5\right)$	97,500	
Total A	5,31,500	0.046
B. Variable Charges:		
Repairs and maintenance (22,500 × 5)	1,12,500	0.010
Depreciation $\left(6,50,000 \times \frac{15}{100} \times 5\right)$	4,87,500	0.042
Diesel: $\frac{3,60,000}{6} \times ₹33$	19,80,000	0.172

(Contd.)

Particulars	*Total Cost (₹)*	*Cost Per Passenger-km (₹)*
Total B	25,80,000	0.224
Total Cost (A + B)	31,11,500	0.270
Add: $33\frac{1}{3}$ per cent profit on takings or 50% on cost	15,55,750	0.135
Bus fare to be charged from each passenger per km	46,67,250	0.405

Working Notes:

(i) Total kilometres to be run during the year 2019–20
$= 40 \times 2 \times 3 \times 25 \times 12 \times 5 = 3,60,000$ kilometres

(ii) Total passenger kilometres
$= 3,60,000 \times 40 \times \frac{80}{100} = 1,15,20,000$ passenger km

✍ EXAMPLE 12.15

Zenith Transport Company has been given a route of 40-kilometre-long to run bus. The bus costs the company a sum of ₹1,00,000. It has been insured at 3% p.a. and the annual tax will amount to ₹2,000. Garage rent is ₹200 per month. Annual repairs will be ₹2,000 and the bus is likely to last for 5 years. The driver's salary will be ₹300 per month and the conductor's salary will be ₹200 per month in addition to 10% of takings as commission (to be shared by the driver and the conductor equally).

Cost of stationery will be ₹100 per month. Manager-cum-accountant's salary is ₹700 per month. Petrol and oil will be ₹50 per 100 kilometre. The bus will make 3 up-and-down trips carrying on an average 40 passengers on each trip.

Assuming 15% profit on takings, calculate the bus fare to be charged from each passenger. The bus will run an average 25 days in a month.

☞ Solution

Statement Showing Fare to be Charged

Particulars	*Amount/ Annum (₹)*	*Amount/ Month (₹)*
(A) *Standing Charges*		
* Insurance @ 3% on ₹1,00,000	3,000	
* Tax	2,000	
* Garage rent @ ₹200/-month	2,400	
* Driver's salary @ ₹300/- month	3,600	
* Conductor's salary @ ₹200/- month	2,400	
* Stationery @ ₹100/- month	1,200	
* Manager-cum-accountant's salary @ ₹700 month	8,400	

(Contd.)

Particulars	Amount/ Annum (₹)	Amount/ Month (₹)
* Total standing charges	23,000	1,916.67
(B) *Running Expenses*		
* Depreciation ₹1,00,000/5	20,000	1,666.67
* Repairs	2,000	166.66
* Petrol & oil ₹0.50 × [40 km × 2 × 3 × 25]		3,000.00
* Commission		900.00
* Profit		1,350.00
Total taking		9,000.00
Fare per passenger kilometre (₹9,000/2,40,000)	0.0375	0.0375
Fare/Passenger (₹9,000/6,000)		₹1.50

* Computation of commission and profit.
Less: Total taking be x
Commission @ 10% = $\frac{x}{10}$, Profit is 15% of taking.

* Hence, profit = $\frac{15x}{100} = \frac{3x}{20}$

* Total cost without commission = ₹6,750 (Standing charges + Running charges)

* Hence, x = ₹6,750 + $\frac{x}{10} = \frac{3x}{20}$

Solving the equation for x, we get x = ₹9,000, which is total takings.

* Therefore, commission will be 10% of total taking = ₹900

* Profit @ 15% of total taking = ₹1,350

\# Total passenger kilometres as computed is shown below:
40 km. × 2 (up + down) × 3 trips × 25 days × 40 passengers
= 2,40,000 passengers km/month.

EXAMPLE 12.16

EPS is a Public School having 25 buses each plying in different directions for the transport of its school students. In view of large number of students availing of the bus service, the buses work two shifts daily both in the morning and in the afternoon. The buses are garaged in the school. The workload of the students has been so arranged that in the morning, the first trip picks up senior students and the second trip plying an hour later picks up junior students. Similarly, in the afternoon, the first trip takes the junior students and an hour later the second trip takes the senior students home.

The distance travelled by each bus, one way is 16 km. The school works 24 days in a month and remains closed for vacation in May and June. The bus fee, however, is payable by the students for all the 12 months in a year.

The details of expenses for the year 2019–2020 are as under:

Driver's salary—payable for all in 12 months	₹5,000 per month per driver.
Cleaner's salary payable for all the 12 months (one cleaner has been employed for every five buses).	₹3,000 per month per cleaner
Licence fees, taxes etc.	₹2,300 per bus per annum
Insurance premium	₹15,600 per bus per annum

Repairs and maintenance	₹16,400 per bus per annum
Purchase price of the bus	₹16,50,000 each
Life of the bus	16 years
Scrap value	₹1,50,000
Diesel cost	₹18.50 per litre

Each bus gives an average of 10 km per litre of diesel. The seating capacity of each bus is 60 students. The seating capacity is fully occupied during the whole year.

The school follows differential bus fees based on distance travelled as under:

Students Picked Up and Dropped Within the Range of Distance from the School	*Bus Fee*	*Percentage of Students Availing this Facility*
4 km	25% of Full	15%
8 km	50% of Full	30%
16 km	Full	55%

Ignore interest. Since the bus fees have to be based on average cost, you are required to

(i) Prepare a statement showing the expenses of operating a single bus and the fleet of 25 buses for a year; and

(ii) Work out average cost per student per month in respect of:

(a) Students coming from a distance of upto 4 km from the school.

(b) Students coming from a distance of upto 8 km from the school; and

(c) Students coming from a distance of upto 16 km from the school.

☞ Solution

(a) (i) EPS Public School Statement Showing the Expenses of Operating a Single Bus and the Fleet of 25 Buses for a Year

Particulars	*Per Bus Per Annum (₹)*	*Fleet of 25 Buses Per Annum (₹)*
Running costs: (*A*)		
Diesel	56,832	14,20,800
(Refer to Working Note 1)		
Repairs and maintenance costs: (*B*)	16,400	4,10,000
Fixed charges:		
Driver's salary	60,000	15,00,000
Cleaner's salary	7,200	1,80,000
Licence fee, taxes etc.	2,300	57,500
Insurance	15,600	3,90,000
Depreciation	93,750	23,43,750
Total fixed charges: (*C*)	1,78,850	44,71,250
Total expenses: (*A* + *B* + *C*)	2,52,082	63,02,050

(ii) Average cost per student per month in respect of students coming from a distance of:

(a) 4 km from the school (₹2,52,082/354 students × 12 months) (Refer to Working Note 2)	₹59.34
(b) 8 km from the school (₹59.34 × 2)	₹118.68
(c) 16 km from the school (₹59.34 × 4)	₹237.36

Working Notes:

1. *Calculation of diesel cost per bus:*

No. of trips made by a bus each day	4
Distance travelled in one trip both ways (16 km × 2 trips)	32 km
Distance travelled per day by a bus (32 km × 4 shifts)	128 km
Distance travelled during a month (128 km × 24 days)	3,072 km
Distance travelled per year (3,072 km × 10 months)	30,720 km
No. of litres of diesel required per bus per year (30,720 km/10 km)	3,072 litres
Cost of diesel per bus per year (3,072 litres × ₹18.50)	₹56.832

2. *Calculation of number of students per bus:*

Bus capacity of 2 trips	120 students
1/4th-fare-students (15% × 120 students)	18 students
$\frac{1}{2}$-fare 30% students (equivalent to 1/4th-fare-students)	72 students
Full fare 55% students (equivalent to 1/4th-fare-students)	264 students
Total 1/4th-fare-students	354 students

EXAMPLE 12.17

A company runs a holiday home. For this purpose, it has hired a building at rent of ₹10,000 per month alongwith 5% of total takings. It has three types of suites for its customers, viz., single room, double room and triple room.

Following information is given:

Type of Suite	*Number*	*Occupancy Percentage*
Single room	100	100%
Double room	50	80%
Triple room	30	60%

The rent of double-room suite is to be fixed at 2.5 times of the single-room suite and that of triple-room suite as twice of the double-room suite.

The other expenses for the year 2020 are as follows:

	₹
Staff salaries	14,25,000
Room attendant's wages	4,50,000
Lighting, heating and power	2,15,000
Repairs and renovation	1,23,500
Laundry charges	80,500
Interior decoration	74,000
Sundries	1,53,000

Provide profit @ 20% on total taking and assume 360 days in a year.

You are required to calculate the rent to be charged for each type of suite.

☞ ***Solution***

(i) Total Equivalent Single-Room Suites

Nature of Suite	*Occupancy*	*Equivalent Single Room suites*
Single-room suites	100 × 360 × 100% = 36,000	36,000 × 1 = 36,000
Double-room suites	50 × 360 × 80% = 14,400	14,400 × 2.5 = 36,000
Triple-room suites	30 × 360 × 60% = 6,480	6,480 × 5 = 32,400
		Total 1,04,400

(ii) Statement of Total Cost

	₹
Staff salaries	14,25,000
Room attendant's wages	4,50,000
Lighting, heating and power	2,15,000
Repairs and renovation	1,23,500
Laundry charges	80,500
Interior decoration	74,000
Sundries	1,53,000
	25,21,000
Building rent 10,000 × 12 + 5% on total takings	1,20,000
	+ 5% on takings
Total cost	26,41,000 + 5% on total takings

Profit is 20% of total takings

∴ Total takings = ₹26,41,000 + 25% of total takings

Let x be rent for single-room suite

Then $1,04,400\ x = 26,41,000 + 25\%$ of $(1,04,400\ x)$

or $1,04,400\ x = 26,41,000 + 26,100\ x$

or $78,300\ x = 26,41,000$

or $x = 33.73$

(ii) Rent to be charged for single-room suite = ₹33.73
Rent for double-room suites ₹33.73 × 2.5 = ₹84.325
Rent for triple-room suites ₹33.73 × 5 = ₹168.65

EXAMPLE 12.18

A club runs a library for its members. As part of club policy, an annual subsidy of upto ₹5 per member including cost of books may be given from the general funds of the club. The management of the club has provided the following figures for its library department.

Number of club members	5,000
Number of library members	1,000
Library fee per member per month	₹100
Fine for late return of books	₹1 per book per day
Average no. of books returned later per month	500
Average no. of days each book is returned late	5 days
Number of available old books	50,000 books
Cost of new books	₹300 per book
Number of books purchased per year	1,200 books
Cost of maintenance per old book per year	₹10

Staff details	No.	Per Employee Salary Per Month (₹)
Librarian	01	10,000
Assistant Librarian	03	7,000
Clerk	01	4,000

You are required to calculate:

(i) The cost of maintaining the library per year excluding the cost of new books;
(ii) The cost incurred per member per month on the library excluding cost of new books; and
(iii) The net income from the library per year.

If the club follows a policy that all new books must be purchased out of library revenue:

(a) What is the maximum number of books that can be purchased per year?
(b) How many excess books are being purchased by the library per year?

Also, comment on the subsidy policy of the club.

Solution

Computation of Total Revenue

No. of library members		1,000
Library fees per month	₹	1,00,000

Late fees per month (500 × 5 × 1)		₹	2,500
Total revenue per month		₹	1,02,500
Total revenue per annum (1,02,500 × 12)		₹	12,30,000

Computation of Total Cost

Staff Details	No.	Salary Per Month ₹	Total Cost ₹
Librarian	1	10,000	10,000
Assistant Librarian	3	7,000	21,000
Clerk	1	4,000	4,000
Total staff cost per month			35,000
Total staff cost per year (35,000 × 12)			4,20,000
	No.	**Cost Per Book**	
Books maintenance cost	50,000	₹10	5,00,000
Total maintenance cost per annum excluding cost of new books (4,20,000 + 5,00,000)			9,20,000
Cost incurred per library member per annum (₹9,20,000/1,000)		₹	920
Cost incurred per member per month on the library excluding cost of new books (920/12)		₹	76.67
Cost incurred per club member per annum (9,20,000/5,000)		₹	184
Cost incurred per club member per month (184/12)		₹	15.33
Net income from the library per annum (12,30,000 – 9,20,000)		₹	3,10,000
Cost per new book		₹	300
Maximum number of new books per annum (3,10,000/300)			1033.333
Present number of books purchased			1,200
Excess books purchased (1200 – 1033.333)			166.6667
Subsidy being given per annum		₹	50,000
Subsidy per library member per annum (50,000/1,000)		₹	50
Subsidy per club member per annum (50,000/5,000)		₹	10

Comment: The club is exceeding its subsidy target to members by ₹45 (₹50 – 5) per library member and ₹5 (₹10 – 5) per club member.

for excel template, scan

EXAMPLE 12.19

PQ Limited plans to start a lodging house at a tourist centre with a capacity of 32 single occupancy rooms. Cost per day per room has been estimated as under:

	Cost per day per room (₹)
(A) When occupied:	
(a) Electricity and utilities	4
(b) Linen, laundry and sanitary supplies	9
When unoccupied:	
(c) Dusting, sweeping and cleaning	2
	15

(B) Over and above these costs, the following expenses represent the estimate of fixed charges per annum that is 365 days)

Staff expenses	₹3,20,000
Other office expenses	64,000
Taxes, insurance, maintenance and depreciation	42,320
	₹4,26,320

PQ Limited defines 100% occupancy to mean all the 32 rooms to fetch revenue for all the 365 days. You are required to answer the following, using a planning period of one year:

(a) What should be the tariff per day per room in order to reach break-even at an occupancy level of 50%?

(b) What would be the profits, if the occupancy level reaches (a) 60%; (b) 70%; and (c) 80% respectively?

(c) What would be the profits, if the tariff per day is reduced by 10% from the answer in (a) above and the occupancy level is 100%?

Solution

(a) 100% occupancy = 32 × 365 days = 11,680 room-days
50% occupancy = 0.5 × 11,680 = 5,840 room-days
60% occupancy = 0.6 × 11,680 = 7,008 room-days
70% occupancy = 0.7 × 11,680 = 8,176 room-days
80% occupancy = 0.8 × 11,680 = 9,344 room-days

(i) *Tariff to break-even at 50% occupancy level*

Fixed cost	₹4,26,320
Expenses when unoccupied ₹2 × 11,680	23,360
Expenses when occupied ₹13 × 5,840	75,920
	5,25,600

Tariff per day to break-even: ₹5,25,600/5,840 = ₹90

(ii) *Profit at various occupancy levels*

Contribution margin = (₹90 – ₹13) = ₹77

Profit = (Man days occupied – BEP man-days) × Contribution margin

Therefore,

Profit at 60% occupancy level = (7,008 – 5,840) × ₹77 = ₹89,936

Profit at 70% occupancy level = (8,176 – 5,840) × ₹77 = ₹1,79,872

Profit at 80% occupancy level = (9,344 – 5,840) × ₹77 = ₹2,69,808

(iii) *Contribution margin at reduced tariff* = (0.90 × ₹90 – 13) = ₹68

Profit at 100% occupancy level = Contribution – Fixed costs

= ₹11,680 × ₹0.68 – ₹4,26,320 – ₹23,360 = ₹3,44,560

Theory Questions

1. What do you understand by operating costing? In what industries is this costing applied?

2. Write notes on (i) Transport-costing (ii) Power house costing and (iii) Canteen costing.

3. Distinguish between operating costing and operation costing.

4. Write a short note on the "transport costing".

Problems

1. A truck starts with a load of 10 tonnes of goods from station *P*. It unloads 4 tonnes at station *Q* and rest of the goods at station *R*. It reaches back directly to station *P* after getting reloaded with 8 tonnes of goods at station *R*. The distances between *P* to *Q*, *Q* to *R* and then from *R* to *P* are 40 km, 60 km and 80 km respectively. Compute absolute tonne-km and commercial tonne-km.

Ans: Absolute tonne-km 1,400
Commercial tonne-km 1,440

2. A transport company maintains a fleet of lorries for carrying goods from Delhi to Panipat, 100 km off. Each lorry, which operates 25 days on an average in a month, starts every day from Delhi with a load of 4 tonne and returns from Panipat with a load of 2 tonnes. Calculate the total commercial tonne-km and cost per commercial tonne-km when the total monthly charges for a lorry are ₹27,000. What rate per tonne should the company charge if it plans to earn a gross profit of 20% on the freightage?

Ans: Rate per tonne-km ₹2.25

3. A Transport Service Company is running 4 buses between two towns which are 50 miles apart. Seating capacity of each bus is 40 passengers. The following particulars were obtained from their books for April 2020.

	₹
Wages of drivers, conductors and cleaners	2,40,000
Salaries of office and supervisory staff	1,00,000
Diesel oil and other oils	4,00,000
Repairs and maintenance	80,000
Taxation, insurance etc.	1,60,000
Depreciation	2,60,000
Interest and other charges	2,00,000

Actual passengers carried 75% of the seating capacity. All the four buses run on 30 days of the month. Each bus made 1 round-trip per day. Find out the cost per passenger mile.

Ans: ₹4.00

4. The Madras Transport Company which keeps a fleet of lorries, shows the following information: Kilometres run for April 2020—30,000 km.

	₹
Wages for April 2020	2,00,000
Petrol, oil, etc, for April 2020	4,00,000
Original cost of vehicles	1,00,00,000
Repairs for April 2020	6,00,000
Garage rent etc. for April 2020	1,00,000
Licence, insurance etc for the year	6,00,000

Depreciation is to be allowed @ 25% per annum on original cost. Prepare a statement for April 2020 showing the cost per running kilometre.

Ans: ₹52.00

5. A transport service company is running five buses between two towns which are 50 km apart. Seating capacity of each bus is 50 passengers. The following particulars were obtained from their books for April, 2020:

	₹
Wages of drivers, conductors and cleaners	24,00,000
Salaries of office staff	10,00,000
Diesel oil and other oil	35,00,000
Repairs and maintenance	8,00,000
Taxation, insurance etc.	16,00,000
Depreciation	26,00,000
Interest and other expenses	20,00,000
	1,39,00,000

Actual passengers carried were 75 per cent of seating capacity. All buses ran on all days of the month. Each bus made one round trip per day.
Find out the cost per passenger-km.

Ans: Cost per passenger-km ₹24.71

6. Anami Transport Company has given a route 40-km-long to run bus. The bus costs the company a sum of ₹1,00,000. It has been insured at 3% p.a and the annual tax will amount to ₹2,000. Garage rent is ₹200 p.m. Annual repairs will be ₹2,000 and the bus is likely to last for 5 years. The driver's salary will be ₹300 p.m. and the conductor's salary will be ₹200 p.m. in addition to 10% of takings as commission (to be shared by the driver and the conductor equally).
Cost of stationery will be ₹100 p.m. Manager-cum-Accountant's salary is ₹700 p.m. Petrol and oil will be ₹50 per 100 km. The bus will make three up-and-down trips carrying, on an average, 40 passengers on each trip. Assuming 15% profit on takings, calculate the bus fare to be charged from each passenger. The bus will run on an average 25 days in a month.

Ans: Fare per passenger ₹1.50

7. The Kangaroo Transport Ltd. operates a fleet of lorries. The records for lorry L-14 reveal the following information for September 2020:

Days maintained	30	
Days operated	25	
Days idle	5	
Total hours operated	300	
Total km covered	2,500	
Total tonnage carried	200	(4 tonne-load per trip, return journey empty)

The following further information is made available:

(a) Operating costs for the month: petrol ₹40,000, oil ₹17,000, grease ₹9,000, wages to driver ₹55,000, wages to khalasi ₹35,000.

(b) Maintenance costs for the month: repairs ₹17,000, overhaul ₹6,000, tyres ₹15,000, garage charges ₹10,000.

(c) Fixed cost for the month based on the estimates for the year; insurance ₹5,000, licence, tax etc., ₹8,000, interest ₹4,000, other overhead ₹19,000.

(d) Capital costs: cost of acquisition ₹54,00,000; residual value at the end of 5 years life is ₹36,00,000.

Prepare a cost-sheet and performance statement showing:

(a) Cost per day maintained;
(b) Cost per day operated;
(c) Cost per kilometre;
(d) Cost per hour;
(e) Cost per commercial tonne-km.

Ans: (a) ₹9,000 (b) ₹10,800 (c) ₹108 (d) ₹900 (e) ₹54

8. Elegant Hotel has a capacity of 100 single rooms and 20 double rooms. It has a sport centre with a swimming pool, which is also used by persons other than residents of the hotel. The hotel has a shopping area at the basement and restaurant at the roof top. The following information is available:

(i) Average occupancy: 75% for 365 days of the year

(ii) Current costs are:

	Variable cost rupees per day	Fixed cost rupees per day
Single room	400	200
Double rooms	500	250

(iii) Average sales per day of restaurant ₹1,00,000; contribution is at 30%. Fixed cost ₹10,00,000 per annum.

(iv) The sports centre swimming pool is likely to be used by 50 non-residents daily; average contribution per day non-resident is estimated at ₹50; fixed cost is ₹5,00,000 per annum.

(v) Average contribution per month from the shopping arcade is ₹50,000; fixed cost is ₹6,00,000 per annum.

You are required to find out:

(a) Rent chargeable for single and double room per day, so that there is a margin of safety of 20 per cent on hire of rooms and that the rent for a double room should be kept at 120% of a single room.

(b) Evaluate the profitability of restaurant, sports centre and shopping area separately.

Ans: (a) Rent per day for single room ₹756

Rent per day for double room ₹907

(b) Profit–Nil

9. Mr Harry is a travelling inspector for the Environment Protection Agency. He uses his own car and the agency reimburses him at ₹18 per kilometre. Mr Harry claims he needs to be paid ₹22 per kilometre just to break even. A scrutiny of his expenses by the agency reveals the following:

	₹
Oil charge every 4,800 km	1,200
Maintenance (other than oil) every 9,600 km	18,000
Yearly insurance (comprehensive with accident benefits)	40,000
Cost of car, with an average residual value of ₹6,00,000 and with a useful life of 3 years.	10,80,000

Petrol is ₹50 a litre and Harry gets 8 km per litre for his car. When Harry is on the road, he averages 192 kilometres a day. He works 5 days a week, has 10 days vacation in a year besides 6 holidays and spends 15 working days a month in the office.

You are required to determine:

(a) An equitable rate of reimbursement on the basis of the schedule he presently follows and

(b) the number of kilometres a year he would have to travel, to break-even at the current rate of re-imbursement.

Ans: (a) ₹24.4 (b) 20,780 kms.

10. *SMC* is a public school having five buses each plying in different directions for the transportation of its students. In view of a large number of students availing of the bus service, the buses work two shifts daily both in the morning and in the afternoon. The buses are garaged in the school. The workload of the students has been so arranged that in the morning the first trip picks up senior students and the second trip plying an hour later picks up the junior students.

Similarly, in the afternoon the first trip drops the junior students and an hour later the second trip takes the senior students home.

The distance travelled by each bus one way is 8 km. The school works 25 days in a month and remains closed for vacation in May, June and December. Bus fee, however, is payable by students for all the 12 months in a year.

The details of expenses for a year are as under:

	₹	
Driver's salary	450	per month
Cleaner's salary	350	per month
(Salary payable for all 12 months)		
(One cleaner employed for all the five buses)		
Licence fee, taxes, etc.	860	per bus p.a.
Insurance	1,000	per bus p.a
Repairs and maintenance	3,500	per bus p.a
Purchase price of the bus	1,50,000	each
Life 12 years		
Scrap value	30,000	
Diesel cost	2.00	per litre

Each bus gives an average mileage of 4 km per litre of diesel.

Seating capacity of each bus is 50 students.

The seating capacity is fully occupied during the whole year.

Students picked up and dropped within a range of upto 4 km of distance from the school are charged half fare and 50% of the students travelling in each trip are in this category. Ignore interest. Since the charges are to be based on average cost you are required to:

(i) Prepare a statement showing the expenses of operating a single bus and a fleet of five buses for a year.

(ii) Work out the average cost per student per month in respect of:

(a) Students coming from a distance of upto 4 km from the school, and

(b) Students coming from a distance beyond 4 km from the school.

	Per bus	fleet of buses
Ans: Cost per month	₹2,400	₹12,000

11. A lodging home is being run in a small hill station with 50 single rooms. The home offers concessional rates during six off-season months in a year. During this period, half of the full-room rent is charged. The management's profit margin is targeted at 20% of the room rent. The following are the cost estimates and other details for the year ending 31st March, 2020 (assume a month to be of 30 days):

(a) Occupancy during the season is 80%, while in the off season is 40% only;

(b) Expenses:

	₹
(i) Staff salary (excluding room attendants)	2,75,000
(ii) Repairs to buildings	1,30,500
(iii) Laundry and linen	40,000
(iv) Interior and tapestry	87,500
(v) Sundry expenses	95,400

(c) Annual depreciation is to be provided for buildings at 5% and on furniture and equipments at 15% on straight line basis:

(d) Room attendants are paid ₹5 per room/day on the basis of occupancy of the rooms in a month;

(e) Monthly lighting charges are ₹120 per room, except in four months of winter when it is ₹30 per room and this cost is on the basis of full occupancy for a month; and

(f) Total investments in the home is ₹100 lakhs of which ₹80 lakhs relate to buildings and balance for furniture and equipments.

You are required to work out the room rent chargeable per day for both during the season and the off-season months, on the basis of the foregoing information.

Ans: Room rent during season ₹197, during off season ₹98.50

CASE STUDY

A Case of DBRS Engineering Works

DBRS Engineering Works was situated in Karnataka with its power plant located in Hosur. The company had appointed Parul Jain as the Cost Accountant with the responsibility of maintaining the account books and also to determine the electricity cost per unit per month. Parul joined in the last week of the month of July in the year 2019, so the first thing that she did was to collect data for the respective month.

The following cost data extracted from the account books of the DBRS Engineering Works was submitted to her on July 31, 2019:

Variable costs: 1,200 tonnes of coal at the rate of ₹220 per tonne and 500 tonnes of coke at the rate of ₹300 per tonne were used during the month. The charges related to transporting, storing etc. of the fuel amounted to ₹10 per tonne. After the process, the cost of removing the ash was ₹5 per tonne. During the month, 160 tonnes of ash was removed. The water pumped from the Sipcot Lake in Hosur for the process was 160 thousand gallons. The cost of water pumping amounted to ₹7.50 paisa per thousand gallons. The cost of 50 gallons of lubricating oil used for the process in the power plant amounted to ₹80 per gallons.

Parul also collected the details related to the human resource cost at DBRS. She was told that the company employed one supervisor, two foremen, four mechanics and one porter. Their salaries and wages were as follows:

- Supervisor—₹8,000 per month
- Foreman—₹2,500 per month
- Mechanic—₹1,500 per month
- Porter—₹50 per day for 30 days

The total monthly technical supervision charges were ₹78,800. 25% of the same was for the production process. The cost of depreciation with respect to capital equipment was as follows:

Boiler (costing ₹4,00,000) was to be charged depreciation at the rate of 6% per annum; generator and other electrical assets costing ₹24,00,000 was to be depreciated at the rate of 4% per annum and factory premise (w.d.v. costing ₹2,40,000) was to be charged at the rate of 1% depreciation per annum.

Parul also got additional information related to electricity generated in units and related expenses. She was told that the total gross unit of electricity generated during the month of July 2019 was 97,000 units. There were some losses too during the month due to the leakage in the course of generation. These losses were 1,000 units due to some defective assets.

The Marketing Manager, Harini informed Parul about some of the incomes generated during the month. Income due to sale of 280 tonnes of fly ashes at the rate of ₹5 per tonne to a cement manufacturer amounted to ₹1,400. The price received from steam supplied to the manufacturing shops for 30,000 thermal units at the rate of ₹200 per 1,000 thermal units amounted to ₹6,000.

Parul was given the task of preparing the cost sheet for the month of July 2019. She was told that during the last month, per-unit cost of electricity generated was ₹4.95 and she was to ensure that the monthly increase in the cost, if any, should not be more than 1%. She decided to check with the previous Cost Accountant about the format before working on the same.

QUESTIONS FOR DISCUSSION:

1. Prepare cost sheet of DBRS Engineering Works Ltd. for the month of July 2019.
2. Was there any increase in the per-unit cost of electricity generated? If yes, what was the percentage increase?
3. What steps Parul can take to ensure cost control in the next month?

Chapter 13

Cost Control Accounts

Learning Objectives

After reading this chapter, you should be able to:

1. explain non-integrated system;
2. describe the procedure of accounting for cost items; and
3. discuss different journal entries for various transactions in cost control accounts.

NON-INTEGRATED SYSTEM

In cost accounting, the cost books are basically maintained under the following two systems:

1. Non-integral or non-integrated cost accounting.
2. Integral or integrated cost accounting.

The system is called non-integral when cost and financial transactions are kept separately. On the contrary, when cost and financial transactions are integrated, the accounting system is known as integrated or integral. Under the system of non-integral accounting, separate ledgers are maintained for cost and financial transaction. The financial accountants look after financial transactions and the cost accountants are responsible for cost accounting transactions. The financial accounting department maintains the following financial ledgers:

1. *General ledger* It contains all real, nominal and personal accounts except trade debtors and creditors account.
2. *Debtors ledger* It has personal accounts of trade debtors.
3. *Creditors ledger* It has personal accounts of trade creditors.

The cost accounting department maintains the following cost ledgers:

1. *Stores ledger* This ledger contains all stores accounts.
2. *Work-in-progress ledger* All costs of material, wages and overhead for each job or manufacturing in progress are posted to the respective job accounts in this ledger.
3. *Finished goods/stock ledger* This ledger records details of finished goods and jobs.

4. *Cost ledger* This is main ledger and records impersonal accounts, that is, accounts relating to income and expenditure. The following accounts are maintained in cost ledger.

(i) Cost Control Accounts—These accounts are maintained to exercise control over the three subsidiary ledgers discussed above and also to complete double entry in cost accounts. They summarise all detailed information contained in the subsidiary ledgers and also help in reconciliation of cost and financial accounts.

The important cost control accounts are as follows:

(a) Stores ledger control account—The purpose of stores ledger is to maintain item-wise record of raw materials and other stores. In cost ledger, a Stores Ledger Control Account is prepared relating to this subsidiary ledger. The total materials received in stores (which can be found in Purchases Journal also) is shown on the debit side of Stores Ledger Control Account and the total materials issued out of Stores (which can be found in Materials Abstract) is credited in the Account. The balance of this account shall tally with the total of the balances of the individual stores account in the Stores Ledger. Sometimes, separate ledgers are kept for raw materials and other stores. In that case, there will be two separate control account namely Materials Ledger Control Account and Stores Ledger Control Account.

(b) Work-in-progress ledger control account—For every job, product or process, materials, labour and factory expenses are incurred. All such costs are debited in different accounts relating to different jobs or products. These accounts are kept in a job or work-in-progress ledger. A work-in-progress ledger control account is prepared in the cost ledger. The cost of production of completed jobs will be credited to this account and the total expenses incurred on all the jobs will be debited so as to show the total work-in-progress at any time. The balance of this account must be equal to the total of individual balances of job or process accounts in the job ledger. The work-in-progress ledger control account is referred to as work-in-progress account also.

(c) Finished goods ledger control account—In finished goods ledger, a separate account is opened for recording the quantity and price of each finished product manufactured or job completed. In cost ledger, a finished goods ledger control account is maintained. It is also known as stock ledger control account. It gives the total value of finished goods in stock at a particular time.

(d) General ledger adjustment account—In cost ledger a general ledger adjustment account is opened to record all items of income and expenditure. This account is also referred to as cost ledger control account (in costing books). Personal accounts are shown in financial accounts and not in cost accounts. The general ledger adjustment account completes the double entry in the cost ledger and hence all such accounts which pertain to fixed assets or cash or outsiders are posted to this account. All expenditures are shown on the credit side of this account; and the result (benefits) of such expenditure in the form of sale is shown on the debit side of this account. The balance represents the value of stores, stock-in-hand and the amount of work-in-progress.

Cost ledger control account (in financial books)—Since the Costing Department does not act in isolation from the Financial Department and all the purchases and sales are recorded through financial books, a Cost Ledger Control Account must be opened in the financial books. This is only a memorandum account. In this account, all the items of revenue and expenditure affecting cost accounts are recorded. This account is just the reverse or contrast of the general ledger adjustment account in the cost ledger and, therefore, the balance of this account should tally with the balance of its counterpart in the cost ledger.

(ii) Other accounts—They include all other impersonal accounts (real as well as nominal) which effect costs, for example, wages control account, factory overhead account, administration overhead account, selling and distribution overhead account, cost of sales account, etc. Sometimes, following additional accounts are also opened:

(a) Overheads suspense account—Sometimes while valuing semi-finished jobs, factory overheads are not included. Similarly while valuing closing stock of finished goods, office and administrative overheads are not included. In such cases, normally at the end of an accounting period, the estimated amount of such overheads is debited to Works or Office Overheads Suspense Account and credited to Works or Office Overheads Account, as the case may be. In the beginning of next accounting period, the entries are reversed to close the suspense accounts.

(b) Capital orders—For each item of capital nature work to be performed in the factory itself, for example, producing tools and equipments, certain expenditures shall be incurred in the form of materials, wages and other expenses. Such expenditures should be recorded in Capital Order Account and later on capitalised.

(c) Service orders—If repairs and maintenance work is done in the factory, the cost is debited to Repairs and Maintenance Account and later transferred to various overheads account, because the expenditure might have been incurred on production, administration and selling and distribution departments.

No separate account is maintained for direct expenses since they are directly charged to work-in-progress account.

When the finished goods are sold, they are transferred to cost of sales account. In the last, a costing profit and loss account can be prepared with the help of all the above accounts.

ACCOUNTING FOR COST ITEMS

Materials

Some transactions relating to materials, such as purchase of materials and purchase returns influence both financial and cost ledgers. Some transactions namely, issues of materials from stores, transfer of materials from one job to another, return of excess material to stores, influence cost ledgers only.

Labour Cost

All wages are recorded in the cost accounting books through the wages control account and the general ledger adjustment account.

Overhead

The overhead—production, administration and selling and distribution—are absorbed to products or jobs on some equitable basis. Production overhead is absorbed on the basis of direct materials cost, direct labour cost, labour hours, machine hours or rate per unit. The production overhead account is credited with the amount of overhead absorbed and the work-in-progress account is debited. The administration overhead account is credited and the finished goods account is debited to recover administrative overhead for the production. Alternatively, administrative overhead is directly transferred to the profit and loss account and is not charged to production. Similarly, selling and distribution overhead may be charged to production by crediting selling and distribution overhead and debiting the cost of sales account.

The amount of under-absorption and over-absorption is transferred to the costing profit and loss account. Alternatively, it may be carried forward to the next accounting period.

JOURNAL ENTRIES

The use of double entry system in costing records will help in the preparation of trial balance for the costing transactions. The entries for various transactions which can be made with the help of control accounts are mentioned below:

(1) Receipts of materials into stores (cash and credit purchases)

In Cost Books

Cost Ledger: Stores Ledger Control Account Dr.

To General Ledger Adjustment A/c

Stores Ledger: Individual stores accounts shall be debited.

In Financial Books

For credit purchases:

Purchases A/c Dr.

Cost Ledger Control A/c (memorandum)

To Creditors A/c

For cash purchases:

Purchases A/c Dr.

Cost Ledger Control A/c (memorandum)

To Cash A/c

(2) Returns to suppliers

In Cost Books

Cost Ledger: General Ledger Adjustment A/c Dr.

To Stores Ledger Control A/c

Stores Ledger: Individual Stores accounts shall be credited.

In Financial Books

Creditors A/c Dr.

To Purchase Returns A/c

To Cost Ledger Control A/c (memorandum)

(3) Receipt of materials for direct issue

In Cost Books

Cost Ledger: Work-in-progress Ledger Control A/c Dr.

To General Ledger Adjustment A/c

Job Ledger: Debit individual jobs for which materials have been received.

In Financial Books

Purchase A/c Dr.

Cost Ledger Control A/c (memorandum)

To Cash or Suppliers A/c

(4) Wages/Salaries paid
In Cost Books Dr.
Cost Ledger: Wages Control A/c
To General Ledger adjustment A/c
In Financial Books
Wages/Salaries A/c Dr.
Cost Ledger Control A/c (memorandum)
To Cash

(5) For payment of works, office and selling and distribution expenses
In Cost Books
Cost ledger:
Works Overheads A/c Dr.
Office Overheads A/c Dr.
Selling & Distribution Overheads A/c Dr.
To General Ledger Adjustment A/c
Overheads Ledger: Individual expenses accounts (if maintained) to be debited.
In Financial Books:
Expenses A/c Dr.
Cost Ledger Control A/c (memorandum)
To Cash

The following entries are made in cost books only and the financial account shall not be affected. The entries are merely for the transactions or transfers in Cost Ledger.

(6) For issue of direct material
In Cost Ledger:
Work-in-progress Ledger Control A/c Dr.
To Stores Ledger Control A/c
(Total as per materials abstract)
In Job and Stores Ledgers: Individual jobs for which materials have been received shall be debited and individual stores accounts in stores ledger shall be credited.

(7) For issue of indirect materials charging of indirect wages
In Cost Ledger: Dr.
Works/Office/Selling and Distribution Overheads A/c
To Stores Ledger Control A/c/Wages Control A/c
In Stores Ledger: Credit the individual Stores Accounts.

(8) For returns of materials from production to stores
In Cost Ledger: Dr.
Stores Ledger Control A/c
To Work-in-progress Ledger Control A/c
In Stores Ledger: Debit individual stores accounts.
In Job Ledger: Credit individual job accounts.

(9) Allocation of direct wages to production
In Cost ledger: Dr.
Work-in-progress Ledger Control A/c
To Wages Control A/c

(As per wages abstract)

In Job Ledger: Individual job accounts will be debited.

(10) Materials transferred from job No. 1 to job No. 2

In Job or Work-in-progress Ledger:

Job No. 2 A/c Dr.

To Job No. 1 A/c

(No entry is required in Work-in-progress Control A/c or Stores Ledger Control A/c)

(11) Allocation of overheads to jobs

(a) Works Overheads:

In Cost Ledger:

Work-in-progress Ledger Control A/c Dr.

To Works Overheads A/c

In Job Ledger:

Individual Job accounts to be debited.

(b) Office overheads:

In Cost ledger:

Finished Goods Ledger Control A/c

To Office Overheads A/c Dr.

In Finished Goods Ledger:

Individual Job/product accounts to be debited.

(12) For normal wastage of stores and normal idle time wages

In Cost Ledger:

Work Overheads A/c Dr.

To Stores Ledger Control A/c

To Wages Control A/c

In Overheads Ledger: Individual expense accounts (if maintained) to be debited.

In Stores Ledger: Individual stores accounts to be credited.

(13) For abnormal loss of material and abnormal idle time

In Cost Ledger:

Costing Profit and Loss A/c Dr.

To Stores Ledger Control A/c

To Wages Control A/c

In stores Ledger: Individual stores accounts to be credited.

(14) For cost of production of finished articles

In Cost Ledger:

Finished Goods Ledger Control A/c Dr.

To Work-in-progress Ledger Control A/c

In Finished Goods Ledger: Individual product accounts to be debited.

In Job Ledger: Individual job accounts to be credited.

(15) For cost of goods sold

In Cost Ledger:

Cost of Sales A/c Dr.

To Finished Goods Ledger Control A/c

In Finished Goods Ledger: Credit individual product accounts.

Following entries shall be made only in the Cost Ledger:

(16) For allocation of selling and distribution overheads
Cost of Sales A/c Dr.
To Selling Overheads A/c

(17) For sales
General Ledger Adjustment A/c Dr.
To Cost of Sales A/c

(18) For overhead on incomplete jobs
Works Overheads Suspense A/c Dr.
Office Overheads Suspense A/c Dr.
To Works Overheads A/c
To Office Overheads A/c.
(or alternatively the balances of works or office overheads may be carried forward)

(19) For transfer of profit
Cost of Sales A/c Dr.
To Costing Profit & Loss A/c

(20) For over-charge of overheads (say, office)
Office Overheads A/c Dr.
To Costing Profit and Loss A/c
(or alternatively, the balance may be carried forward)
However, if it is desired to charge a supplementary rate (negative), the following entry will be passed:
Office Overheads A/c
To Finished Goods Ledger Control A/c
To Cost of Sales A/c
(the two accounts will be credited in proportion to the value of finished goods in hand and cost of goods sold)

(21) For under-charge of overheads (say, works)
Costing Profit and Loss A/c Dr.
To Works Overheads A/c
(or alternatively the balance may be carried forward or treated as in case of Entry 20)

(22) For transfer of net profit
Costing Profit and Loss A/c
To General Ledger Adjustment A/c Dr.

EXAMPLE 13.1

Pass journal entries in the cost books (non-integrated system) for the following transactions:

(i) Materials worth ₹25,000 returned to stores from job.

(ii) Gross total wages paid ₹48,000. Employer's contribution to PF and State Insurance amount to ₹2,000. Wages analysis book detailed ₹20,000 direct labour, ₹12,000 towards indirect factory labour, ₹10,000 towards salaries to office staff and ₹8,000 for salaries to selling and distribution staff.

Solution

Journal Entries

Particulars		Dr. ₹	Cr. ₹
(i) Stores Ledger Control A/c	Dr.	25,000	
To WIP, Control A/c			25,000
(Being material returned from stores)			
(ii) Wages Control A/c	Dr.	50,000	
To General Ledger and Adjustment A/c			48,000
To Provident Fund and Employees' State Insurance Account			2,000
(Being gross total wages paid)			
Work-in-Progress Control A/c	Dr.	20,000	
Factory Overheads Control A/c	Dr.	12,000	
Office Overheads Control A/c	Dr.	10,000	
Selling Overheads Control A/c	Dr.	8,000	
To Wages Control A/c			50,000
(Being wages allocated)			

EXAMPLE 13.2

Pass journal entries in the cost books, maintained on non-integrated system, for the following:

(i) Issue of materials: Direct ₹5,50,000; Indirect ₹1,50,000
(ii) Allocation of wages: Direct ₹2,00,000; Indirect ₹40,000
(iii) Under/Over absorbed overheads: Factory (over) ₹20,000; Administration (under) ₹10,000

Solution

Journal Entries in Cost Books Maintained on Non-integrated System

		₹	₹
(i) Work-in-progress ledger control account	Dr.	5,50,000	
Factory overhead control account	Dr.	1,50,000	
To stores ledger control account			7,00,000
(Being issue of materials)			
(ii) Work-in-progress ledger control account	Dr.	2,00,000	
Factory overhead control account	Dr.	40,000	

(Contd.)

			₹	₹
	To wages control account			2,40,000
	(Being allocation of wages and salaries)			
(iii)	Factory overhead control account	Dr.	20,000	
	To costing profit & loss account			20,000
	(Being transfer of over absorption of overhead)			
	Costing profit & loss account	Dr.	10,000	
	To administration overhead control account			10,000
	(Being transfer of under absorption of overhead)			

EXAMPLE 13.3

The profit and loss account as shown in the financial books of a company for the year ended, 30.9.2020 together with a statement of reconciliation between the profit as per financial and cost accounts is given below:

for excel template, scan

Profit & Loss Account for the Year Ended 30.9.2020

	₹	₹		₹	₹
Opening stock:			Sales		15,00,000
Raw material	90,000		Closing stock:		
Work-in-progress	50,000		Raw material	98,000	
Finished goods	70,000	2,10,000	Work-in-progress	53,000	
Raw material purchases		5,00,000	Finished goods	72,000	
Direct wages		2,00,000			2,23,000
Factory overheads		2,00,000	Miscellaneous receipts		45,000
Administration expenses		1,70,000			
Selling and distribution expenses		2,20,000			
Preliminary expenses written off		75,000			
Debenture interest		30,000			
Net profit		1,63,000			
		17,68,000			17,68,000

Statement of Reconciliation of Profit as per Financial and Cost Account

		₹	₹
	Profit as per financial accounts		
(a)	Difference in valuation of stock		1,63,000
	Add: Raw materials-closing stock	1,200	
	Work in progress-opening stock	1,300	
	Finished goods-opening stock	2,000	
	Closing stock	1,000	
	Total (A)	5,500	
	Less: Raw materials-opening stock	1,650	
	Work in progress-closing stock	750	
	Total (B)	2,400	
	(A)–(B)		3,100
(b)	Other items		
	Add: Preliminary expenses written off	75,000	
	Debenture interest	30,000	
		1,05,000	
	Less: Miscellaneous receipts	45,000	60,000
	Profit as per cost accounts		2,26,100

You are required to prepare the following accounts as they would appear in the costing ledger:

(i) Raw material control account
(ii) Work-in-progress control account
(iii) Finished goods control account
(iv) Cost of sales account
(v) Costing profit & loss account

☞ ***Solution***

Basic Calculations
Computation of Items as Per Cost Accounts

Particulars	*As Per Financial Accounts ₹*	*Valuation Difference ₹*	*As Per Cost Accounts ₹*
Raw Materials			
Opening stock	90,000	+ 1,650	91,650
Closing stock	98,000	+ 1,200	99,200
Work-in-Progress			
Opening stock	50,000	– 1,300	48,700

(Contd.)

Particulars	*As Per Financial Accounts* ₹	*Valuation Difference* ₹	*As Per Cost Accounts* ₹
Closing stock	53,000	750	52,250
Finished Goods			
Opening stock	70,000	– 2,000	68,000
Closing stock	72,000	+ 1,000	73,000

Raw Material Control Account

To balance b/d	91,650	WIP control account (balancing figure)	4,92,450
To G.L. Adj. A/c	5,00,000		
		By balance c/d	99,200
	5,91,650		5,91,650

WIP Control Account

To balance b/d	48,700	By finished goods control account (balancing figure)	8,88,900
To raw material control account	4,92,450		
To wages control account	2,00,000		
To factory overhead control account	2,00,000	By balance c/d	52,250
	9,41,150		9,41,150

Finished Good Control Account

	₹		₹
To balance b/d	68,000	By cost of sales account (balancing figure)	10,53,900
To WIP control account	8,88,900		
To admn. overheads control account	1,70,000	By balance c/d	73,000
	11,26,900		11,26,900

Cost of Sales Account

	₹		₹
To finished good control account	10,53,990	By general ledger adjustment account	15,00,000
To selling and distribution control account	2,20,000		
To profit taken to costing P & L A/c	2,26,100		
	15,00,000		15,00,000

Costing Profit & Loss Account

	₹		₹
To balance transferred to general ledger adjustment account	2,26,100	By cost of sales account	2,26,100
	2,26,100		2,26,100

EXAMPLE 13.4

A company operates on historic job cost accounting system, which is not integrated with the financial accounts. At the beginning of a month, the operating balances in cost ledger were:

Particulars		₹ *(in Lakhs)*
Stores ledger control account		80
Work-in-progress control account		20
Finished goods control account		430
Building construction account		10
Cost ledger control account		540
During the month, the following transactions took place:		
Materials	— Purchased	40
	Issued to production	50
	Issued to general maintenance	6
	Issued to building construction	4
Wages	— Gross wages paid	150
	Indirect wages	40
	For building construction	10
Work overheads	— Actual amount incurred (excluding items shown above)	160
	Absorbed in building construction	20
	Under absorbed	8
Royalty paid		5
Selling distribution and administration overheads		25
Sales		450

At the end of the month, the stock of raw material and work-in-progress was ₹55 lakhs and ₹25 lakhs respectively. The loss arising in the raw material account is treated as factory overheads. The building under construction was completed during the month. Company's gross profit margin is 20% on sales.

Prepare the relevant control accounts to record the above transactions in the cost ledger of the company.

☞ Solution

Cost Ledger Control Account (₹in Lakhs)

Particulars	₹	Particulars	₹
To costing profit and loss account	450	By balance b/d	540
To building construction account	44	By stores ledger control account	40
To balance c/d	483	By wages control account	150
		By works overhead control account	160
		By royalty account	5
		By selling, distribution and administration overheads account	25
		By costing profit and loss account	57
	977		977

Stores Ledger Control Account

Particulars	₹	Particulars	₹
To balance b/d	80	By WIP control account	50
To cost ledger control account	40	By works overhead control account	6
		By building const. account	4
		By works overhead control account (loss)	5
		By balance c/d	55
	120		120

Work-in-Progress Control Account

Particulars	₹	Particulars	₹
To balance b/d	20	By finished goods control account	333
To stores ledger control account	50	By balance c/d	25
To wages control account	100		
To works overhead control account	183		
To royalty account	5		
	358		358

Finished Goods Control Account

Particulars	₹	Particulars	₹
To balance b/d	430	By cost of goods sold account *(See working note)*	360
To WIP control account	333	By balance c/d	403
	763		763

Cost of Sales Account

Particulars	₹	*Particulars*	₹
To cost of goods sold account	360	By costing profit and loss account	385
To selling, distribution and administration overheads account	25		
	385		385

Costing Profit & Loss Account

Particulars	₹	*Particulars*	₹
To cost of sales account	385	By cost ledger control account	450
To works overhead control account	8		
To cost ledger control account (profit)	57		
	450		450

Building Construction Account

Particulars	₹	*Particulars*	₹
To balance b/d	10	By cost ledger control account	44
To stores ledger control account	4		
To wages control account	10		
To works overhead control account	20		
	44		44

Works Overhead Control Account

Particulars	₹	*Particulars*	₹
To stores ledger control account	6	By building construction account	20
To wages control account	40	By WIP control account	183
To cost ledger control account	160	By costing profit and loss account	8
To stores ledger control account (loss)	5		
	211		211

Wages Control Account

Particulars	₹	*Particulars*	₹
To cost ledger control account	150	By works overhead control account	40
		By building const. account	10
		By WIP control account	100
	150		150

Royalty Account

Particulars	₹	Particulars	₹
To cost ledger control account	5	By WIP control account	5
	5		5

Cost of Goods Sold Account

Particulars	₹	Particulars	₹
To finished goods control account	360	By cost of sales account	360
	360		360

Selling, Distribution and Administration Overheads Account

Particulars	₹	Particulars	₹
To cost ledger control account	25	By cost of sales account	25
	25		25

Trial Balance

(₹in lakhs)

Particulars	Dr.	Cr.
Stores Ledger Control Account	55	
WIP control account	25	
Finished goods control account	403	
Cost ledger control account		483
	483	483

Working Note:

If selling price is ₹100, cost price is = ₹80

If selling price is ₹450, cost price will be = ₹$\frac{80}{100}$ × ₹450 = ₹360 lakhs

✍ Example 13.5

How will you transact the following in the material account and the stores ledger?

(a) Material ledger shows 120 units at an average cost of ₹10 while the physical count is 110 units, difference due to non-recording of a material requisition note.

(b) Physical units show 200 while the ledger balance shows a shortage due to non-receipt of an invoice for 20 units for a total cost of ₹100.

(c) Ledger balance indicates an excess of 50 units over the physical balance affected by atmospheric changes which are normal. The issue rate is ₹3.00 per unit.

(d) Physical balance shows a shortage, compared to the ledger balance of 10 units traced to having an effect of excess issue of material to production job. The issue price is ₹2.50 per unit.

Solution

(a) The material-requisition note will be recorded in the issue column of the particular material account in the stores ledger. The following will be the entry in the cost ledger:

Work-in-progress control account	Dr	₹100	
To stores ledger control account	Cr		₹100

The particular job account in the work-in-progress ledger will be debited.

(b) The invoice for 20 units will be posted in the receipt column of the particular material account in the stores ledger. The following will be the entry in the cost ledger.

Stores-ledger control account	Dr	₹100	
To general ledger adjustment account	Cr		₹100

(c) This is a normal loss, hence to be treated as factory overhead. The balance in the particular material account in the stores ledger will be corrected by entering the normal loss of 50 units in the issue column. The following will be the entry in the cost ledger.

Factory overhead control account	Dr.	₹150	
To stores ledger control account	Cr.		₹150

(d) The 10 units issued in excess of the quantity shown in the materials-issue document should be taken back in the stores. No accounting entry will be required.

However, if the material cannot be traced on the shop floor, the value of the material will be charged to the particular job. The excess issue will be entered in the issue column of the particular materials account in the stores ledger. The following will be the entry in the cost ledger:

Work-in-progress control account	Dr.	₹25	
To stores ledger control account	Cr.		₹25

The particular job account in the work-in-progress ledger will be debited.

EXAMPLE 13.6

As of 31st March, 2020, the following balances existed in a firm's cost ledger, which is maintained separately on a double entry basis:

	Debit	*Credit*
	₹	₹
Stores ledger control account	3,00,000.	—
Work-in-progress control account	1,50,000	—
Finished goods control account	2,50,000	—
Manufacturing overhead control account		15,000
Cost ledger control account		6,85,000
	7,00,000	7,00,000

During the next quarter, the following items arose:

	₹
Finished product (at cost)	2,25,000
Manufacturing overhead incurred	85,000

(Contd.)

	Debit ₹	Credit ₹
Raw material purchased		1,25,000
Factory wages		40,000
Indirect labour		20,000
Cost of sales		1,75,000
Materials issued to production		1,35,000
Sales returned (at cost)		9,000
Materials returned to suppliers		13,000
Manufacturing overhead charged to production		85,000

You are required to prepare the cost ledger control account, stores ledger control account, work-in-progress control account, finished stock ledger control account, manufacturing overhead control account wages control account, cost of sales account and the trial balance at the end of the quarter.

Solution

Cost Ledger Control Account

Dr.			*Cr.*
	₹		₹
To store ledger control account	13,000	By Opening balance	6,85,000
To Balance c/d	**9,42,000**	By Store Ledger Control account	1,25,000
		By Manufacturing Overhead Control account	85,000
		By Wages Control account	60,000
	9,55,000		9,55,000

Stores Ledger Control Account

Dr.			*Cr.*
	₹		₹
To opening balance	3,00,000	By WIP Control account	1,35,000
To cost ledger control account	1,25,000	By cost ledger control account (returns)	13,000
		By balance c/d	**2,77,000**
	4,25,000		4,25,000

WIP Control Account

Dr.	₹	Cr.	₹
To opening balance	1,50,000	By finished stock ledger control account	2,25,000
To wages control account	40,000	By balance c/d	1,85,000
To stores ledger control account	1,35,000		
To manufacturing overhead control account	85,000		
	4,10,000		4,10,000

Finished Stock Ledger Control Account

Dr.	₹	Cr.	₹
To opening balance	2,50,000	By cost of sales	1,75,000
To WIP control account	2,25,000	By balance c/d	3,09,000
To cost of sales account (sales return)	9,000		
	4,84,000		4,84,000

Manufacturing Overhead Control Account

Dr.	₹	Cr.	₹
To cost ledger control account	85,000	By opening balance	15,000
To wages control account	20,000	By WIP control account	85,000
		By under recovery c/d	5,000
	1,05,000		1,05,000

Wages Control Account

Dr.	₹	Cr.	₹
To transfer to cost ledger control account	60,000	By WIP control account	40,000
		By manufacturing overhead control account	20,000
	60,000		60,000

Cost of Sales Account

Dr.			*Cr.*
	₹		₹
To finished stock ledger control account	1,75,000	By finished stock ledger control account (sales return)	9,000
		By balance c/d	1,66,000
	1,75,000		1,75,000

Trial Balance

	₹		₹
Stores ledger control account	2,77,000	Cost ledger control account	9,42,000
WIP control account	1,85,000		
Finished stock ledger control account	3,09,000		
Manufacturing overhead control account	5,000		
Cost of sales account	1,66,000		
	9,42,000		9,42,000

Theory Questions

1. What is non-integral accounting system?
2. What are cost control accounts? Describe their advantages.
3. Mention the principal ledgers maintained in financial accounts and cost accounts.

Problems

1. During June 2020, the following transactions took place in *XYZ* Co. Ltd.

	₹
(i) Materials purchased:	
(a) Credit purchases	18,000
(b) Credit purchases for special job 800	
(c) Cash purchases	2,000
(ii) Returns to suppliers	1,000
(iii) Direct materials issued to production	12,000
(iv) Indirect materials issued	1,200
(v) Materials returned from production to stores	200
(vi) Materials transferred from Job No. 20 to Job No. 21	400

You are required to enter the transactions in the financial and cost books.

2. The following figures have been extracted from the cost records of a manufacturing unit:

	₹
Stores: Opening balance	30,000
Purchases	1,60,000
Transfers from work-in-progress	80,000
Issues to work-in-progress	1,60,000

Issues to repairs and maintenance	20,000
Deficiencies found in stock taking	6,000
Work-in-progress:	
Opening balance	60,000
Direct wages applied	60,000
Overheads applied	2,40,000
Closing balance	40,000

Finished products: Entire output is sold at a profit of 10% on actual cost from work-in-progress.

Other wages incurred ₹70,000; overhead incurred ₹2,50,000.

Items not included in cost records: Income from investments ₹10,000; Loss on sale of capital assets ₹20,000.

Draw up stores control account, work-in-progress control account, costing profit and loss account, profit and loss account and reconciliation statement.

3. As at 31st March, the following balances existed in a company's cost ledger:

	Dr.	*Cr.*
Raw materials control account	₹60,287	
Work-in-progress control account	24,473	
Finished stock control account	50,389	
Factory overhead control account	—	₹2,105
Cost ledger control account	—	1,33,044
	₹1,35,149	₹1,35,149

During the next three months the following items arose:

		₹
Finished output (at cost)		42,167
Factory overhead incurred		18,302
Raw materials purchased	₹	24,600
Direct wages payments	10,106	
Indirect labour (salaries)	4,333	14,439
Cost of sales		37,178
Materials issued to production		25,463
Sales returns (at cost)		1,076
Materials returned to and credited by suppliers		580
Factory overhead allocated to production		15,440

You are required to write up the accounts and schedule the closing balances, stating what each balance represents.

4. The following balance were extracted from a company's ledger as on 31st December, 2020:

	₹	₹
Raw materials control account	48,836	
Work-in-progress control account	14,745	
Finished stock control account	21,980	
Nominal ledger control account		85,561
	85,561	85,561

Further transactions took place during the following quarter as follows:

(Contd.)

	₹
Factory overhead—allocated to WIP	11,786
Goods finished—at cost	36,834
Raw materials purchased	22,422
Direct wages—allocated to WIP	18,370
Cost of goods sold	42,000
Raw materials—issued to production	17,000
Raw materials—credited by suppliers	1,000
Inventory audit—raw material losses	1,300
WIP rejected (with no scrap value)	1,800
Customer's returns (at cost) of finished goods	3,000

Prepare all the ledger accounts in cost ledger.

5. The cost ledger of Motors Ltd. showed the following balances as on 1st July, 2020:

	₹	₹
Stores ledger account	5,250	
Work-in-progress account	3,920	
Finished goods account	2,790	
Works overheads account		50
Administration overheads account	30	
General ledger adjustment account		11,940
	11,990	11,990

Further balances resulting from the operations for the year ended 30th June, 2020 were:

Stores purchases	₹18,000
Stores issued to production orders	19,650
Stored issued to repairs	750
Wages	30,750
Productive labour	29,500
Unproductive labour	1,250
Works overhead allocated to production orders	8,950
Carriage inwards	300
Works expenses	7,000
Administration expenses	900
Administration overheads allocated to production orders	920
Goods finished during the year	58,600
Finished goods sold	60,000
Sales expenses	670

Record the entries in the cost ledger accounts for the year ended 30th June, 2020 and prepare a schedule of balances as at that date, explaining what each balance represents.

6. In the course of physical verification of stores as on 31st March 2020, following differences are revealed in case of AB Ltd.

Material	*Unit*	*Rate (₹)*	*Physical Balance*	*Ledger Balance*	*Remarks*
A	Nos	7.00	600	680	Wrong counting
B	Litres	12.00	1,100	1,155	Normal evaporation loss
C	Nos	6.00	350	400	Material issues not accounted for
D	Kg	22.00	900	930	Shortage due to pilferage and theft
E	Nos	15.00	1,475	1,325	150 nos. received but not entered in ledger
F	Metres	10.00	291	291	Obsolete materials. Realised sales value ₹1,650 awaiting despatch.

Prepare journal entries in the cost ledger to give effect to the above adjustments as called for.

Chapter 14

Integrated Accounting System

Learning Objectives

After reading this chapter, you should be able to:

1. discuss the meaning and features of integrated accounting system;
2. describe the principal accounts in integral system;
3. explain different journal entries recorded in integral and non-integral accounting system; and
4. distinguish between interlocking and integration of cost and financial accounts.

MEANING AND FEATURES OF INTEGRATED ACCOUNTING SYSTEM

In integrated accounting system, the concept of a separate profit and loss account for financial and costing purposes is discarded in favour of a unified account which will serve both financial and costing purposes. It is such a system of accounting whereby cost and financial accounts are kept in the same set of books. Obviously, then there will be no separate set of books for costing and financial records. Integrated accounts provide or meet out fully the information requirements for costing as well as financial accounts. Such a system of accounting is referred to as the "integrated" or "integral" cost accounting system. A single book-keeping system which contains both financial and cost accounts is known as an integral accounting system. An integrated accounting system has the following advantages:

1. There is no problem of reconciliation as there will only be one profit amount.
2. This system is economical and easy to understand. Duplication of work and labour are avoided.
3. Cost data can be presented promptly and regularly.
4. All cost data and accounts are automatically checked and thus cost figures are accurate.

Essential prerequisites for integrated accounts:

(a) The management should take decisions about the extent of integration of the two sets of books.

(b) A suitable coding system must be made available so as to serve the accounting purposes of financial and cost accounts.

(c) An agreed routine, with regard to the treatment of provision for accruals, prepaid expenses, other adjustment necessary for preparation of interim accounts.

(d) Perfect coordination should exist between the staff responsible for the financial and cost accounts and an efficient processing of accounting document should be ensured.

The following factors should be considered before establishing an integrated cost accounting system:

1. *Degree of integration* The degree of integration should be determined. Some business firms may integrate up to the stage of prime cost or factory cost. On the other hand, many undertakings integrate the whole of the records.
2. *Control accounts* In place of classifying expenditure according to its nature, control accounts may be prepared for each of the elements of cost, such as:

   Material Control Account
   Direct Labour Control Account
   Factory Overhead Control Account
   Administrative Overhead Control Account
   Selling and Distribution Overhead Control Account.

   Some of the above control accounts could be separated into fixed and variable depending on the circumstances.
3. *Cost accumulation purposes* Full details about the cost data are provided to the cost accounting department so as to achieve the following objectives;
   (a) To provide the necessary costing data.
   (b) To form the basis of journal entries so that the control accounts can be cleared to suitable revenue accounts resulting into a cost of sales account.
4. Provisions for accrued expenses, prepayments and stocks should be dealt with by transfers to suitable suspense accounts, so that the balance remaining in each control account represents the charges for the period.

PRINCIPAL ACCOUNTS

Under integrated accounting, the following accounts are mainly kept:

Stock Control Account

This account is prepared for each of the following cost items:

(i) *Raw material* This account has opening stock and purchases on the debit side and material issues on credit side.
(ii) *Work-in-progress* This account is debited with opening stock and factory overhead and credited with cost of goods finished. The closing stock, if any, will be carried forward to the next year.
(iii) *Finished stock* This account is known as the finished goods account also. It is debited with goods finished and credited with the cost of sales.

The above stock accounts are usually used in place of the stock and purchase account which is maintained in the financial books.

Cost of Sales Account

The cost of goods sold is debited to this account and the finished goods account is credited.

Assets Account

Separate accounts are kept for different assets possessed by the firm, such as plant, furniture, building, etc. These individual assets accounts are prepared in the usual way. Any capital expenditure incurred is debited.

Debtors and Creditors Control Account

The creditors account mentions the transactions and their amounts with creditors and suppliers. The balance in creditors account should tally with the balance in the purchase ledger. Similarly, the debtors control account should tally with the sales ledger.

Prepayments Account and Outstanding Account

An expense account will show the prepaid amount made, if any. The prepaid amount is debited to the prepaid account and credited to overhead control accounts. Thus, the expense which is related to the period is charged to the work-in-progress account. In case of an expense due but not paid, the expense due account is credited and the overhead control account is debited. When the amount is actually paid, the expense due account is debited and cash account is credited or it can be adjusted through the overhead control account.

Direct Wages and Overhead Costs Control Account

When these costs are incurred, the appropriate control account is debited and the cash account credited. For example, the total direct wages paid will be debited to the direct labour control account. At the end of a period, they are transferred to work-in-progress accounts by crediting the appropriate control accounts and debiting the work-in-progress account. It is possible that actual payments for a period may not tally with the expenditure to be charged for the period and, therefore, adjustments should be made.

Departmental or Cost Centre Account

Under integrated account, an account is kept for each department or cost centre. This helps in knowing the cost of a department and controlling costs associated with different departments.

Cash Account

In this account, all cash receipts are debited and cash disbursements are credited.

JOURNAL ENTRIES

Journal entries which are recorded in integral and non-integral accounting systems are given in the following pages:

Journal Entries to be Recorded under Non-integral and Integral System

	Items	Non-integral System: Financial books	Non-integral System: Cost books	Integral System
1.	Purchase of materials on credit	Purchases A/c Dr. To Bought Ledger To Bought Ledger Control (or creditors) A/c	Stores Ledger Control A/c Dr. To General Ledger Adjustment A/c	Stores Ledger Control A/c Dr. (or creditors) A/c To Creditors A/c
2.	Issue of materials for production	No entry	Work-in-progress Ledger Control A/c Dr. To Stores Ledger Control A/c	Work-in-progress A/c Dr. To Stores Ledger Control A/c
3.	Payment of wages	Wages A/c Dr. To Cash To Insurance To Tax	Wages A/c (or Wages Control A/c) Dr. To General Ledger Adjustment A/c	Wages A/c (wages control A/c) Dr. To Cash A/c
4.	Analysis and distribution of wages	No entry	Work-in-progress A/c Dr. (for direct labour) Factory Ov. Control A/c Dr. (for factory indirect labour) Adm. Overhead Control A/c Dr. (for office indirect labour) S & D Overhead Control A/c Dr. (for selling and distribution indirect labour) To Wages Control A/c	Work-in-progress Control A/c Dr. Factory Overhead A/c Dr. Administration Overhead A/c Dr. S & D Overhead A/c Dr. To Wages Control A/c
5.	Payment for indirect expenses, for example power, repairs,etc.	Expenses A/c Dr. To Cash To Creditors	Factory/Adm./Selling & Dis. Overhead A/c Dr. To General Ledger adj. A/c	Factory/Office/Selling & Distribution Overhead A/c Dr. To Cash To Creditors
6.	Recording of factory overheads at predetermined rates	No entry	Work-in-progress Control A/c Dr. To Factory Overheads Control A/c	Work-in-progress Control A/c Dr. To Factory Overhead Control A/c

(Contd.)

7.	Factory overheads over-absorbed	No entry	Factory Overhead Control A/c Dr. To Costing P&L A/c (or alternatively the balance may be carried forward)	Factory Overhead A/c Dr. To P&L A/c
8.	Jobs completed	No entry	Stock Ledger Control A/c Dr. To Work-in-progress Ledger Control A/c	Stock Ledger Control A/c Dr. To Work-in-progress Ledger Control A/c
9.	Interest paid	Interest A/c Dr. To Cash	No entry	Interest A/c Dr. To Cash
10.	Rent of own premises	No entry	Works Overhead A/c Dr. To General Ledger Adjustment A/c	Works Overheads A/c Dr. To Rent (notional) A/c
11.	Abnormal idle time	No entry	Costing P&L A/c Dr To Wages A/c (or alternatively the balance may be carried forward)	Profit & Loss A/c Dr. To Wages A/c
12.	Sales (credit)	Sales Ledger Control (or Debtors) A/c Dr. To Sales A/c	General Ledger Adjustment A/c Dr. To Cost of Sales A/c	Sales Ledger Control A/c (Debtors) A/c To Sales

Distinction between "Interlocking" and "Integration" of Cost and Financial Accounts

When independent sets of books are maintained for cost and financial accounts, they are "interlocked" by control accounts maintained in the two sets of books. Cost ledger control account is maintained in the financial books and a general ledger adjustment account in the costing books. Thus, a link is established between the two sets of books. In costing books, all entries pertaining to fixed assets, cash, or outsiders are posted in general ledger adjustment account. In case it is desired to integrate the two trial balances into one, the cost ledger control account and general ledger adjustment account can be omitted because they are "contra" accounts.

Integration requires the maintenance of only one set of books in which all transactions are recorded. By eliminating cost ledger, all the control accounts are maintained in general ledger.

Integration is preferable to interlocking from the point of view of economy but sometimes due to practical difficulties, the maintenance of "interlocking" system is essential. Although integration (maintaining one set of accounts) offers better scope for economy and efficiency in accounting, sometimes it is desirable to have separate sets of accounts because of organisational problems involved in the maintenance of one set of books. Cost accounting has assumed considerable significance in the planning and control of business operations, and hence, the need for a separate costing department is felt by the management. Therefore, generally, "integral" system can be employed, with advantages, only in small units.

Example 14.1

Give journal entries for the following transactions under the integrated accounting:

(i) Materials purchased on credit;
(ii) Payment to creditors;
(iii) Issue of direct material for production;
(iv) Payment of wages; and
(v) Charging wages for production.

Solution

Journal entries under Integrated Accounting

(i) Material purchased on credit:

Stores ledger control account Dr.
    To creditors account
(For material purchased on credit)

(ii) Payment to creditors:

Sundry creditors account Dr.
    To bank account
(Amount paid to creditors)

(iii) Issue of direct materials for production:

Work-in-progress control account Dr.
    To stores control account
(Direct material issued to production)

(iv) Payment of wages:
To wages control account — Dr.
To cash account
(For wages paid)

(v) Charging wages for production:
Work-in-progress control account — Dr.
To wages control account
(For wages charged to production)

EXAMPLE 14.2

The following transactions are extracted from the books of *XYZ* Ltd. You are required to pass journal entries under integrated accounts system:

		₹
(i)	Purchase of raw materials on credit	4,00,000
(ii)	Carriage inward	3,000
(iii)	Paid to creditors	3,00,000
(iv)	Stores issued	2,50,000
(v)	Productive waged paid	2,00,000
(vi)	Unproductive wages paid	70,000
(vii)	Works overheads incurred	3,60,000
(viii)	Materials issued for repairs	2,000
(ix)	Selling expenses paid	10,000
(x)	Office expenses paid	4,000
(xi)	Works overhead absorbed	4,10,000
(xii)	Cost of completed jobs	8,60,000

Solution

(i)	Stores ledger control account	Dr	4,00,000	
	To creditors account			4,00,000
	(being raw material purchased on credit)			
(ii)	Stores ledger control account	Dr	3,000	
	To cash account			3,000
	(being carriage inward paid)			
(iii)	Creditors account		3,00,000	
	To cash account			3,00,000
	(being cash paid to creditors)			
(iv)	Work-in-progress control account	Dr	2,50,000	
	To stores ledger control account			2,50,000
	(being material issued to production)			
(v)	Wages control account	Dr	2,00,000	
	To cash account			2,00,000
	(being direct wages paid)			

(Contd.)

(vi)	Works overhead control account To cash (being unproductive wages paid)	Dr	70,000	70,000
(vii)	Works overhead control account To cash (being work expenses incurred)	Dr	3,60,000	3,60,000
(viii)	Works overhead control account To stores ledger control account (being material issued for repair)	Dr	2,000	2,000
(ix)	Selling and distribution overhead control account To cash (being selling exp. paid)	Dr	10,000	10,000
(x)	Office overhead control account To cash (being office expenses)	Dr	4,000	4,000
(xi)	Work in progress control account To work overhead control account (being works overhead absorbed)	Dr	4,10,000	4,10,000
(xii)	Finished stock control account To WIP control account (being cost of completion transfer to finished stock)	Dr	8,60,000	8,60,000

EXAMPLE 14.3

Journalise the following transactions in the integrated books of accounts:

(a)	Credit purchase	₹ 12,00,000
(b)	Production wages paid	7,00,000
(c)	Stocks issued to production orders	8,00,000
(d)	Work expenses charged to production	4,50,000
(e)	Finished goods transferred from production orders	18,00,000
(f)	Administration expenses charged to production	1,50,000
(g)	Work expenses outstanding	1,20,000
(h)	Work expenses paid	4,60,000

Solution

Journal Entries under Integral System of Accounting

	Particulars		*Dr. (₹)*	*Cr. (₹)*
(a)	Stores ledger control account To sundry creditors account (being purchases of goods on credit)	Dr.	12,00,000	12,00,000
(b)	Wages control account To cash/bank account (being wages paid in cash/cheque)	Dr.	7,00,000	7,00,000

(Contd.)

	Particulars		Dr. (₹)	Cr. (₹)
(c)	Work-in-progress control account	Dr.	8,00,000	
	To stores ledger control account			8,00,000
	(being stores issued against production order)			
(d)	Work-in-progress control account	Dr.	4,50,000	
	To production overhead account (being the work expenses allocated to production/jobs)			4,50,000
(e)	Finished goods ledger control account	Dr.	1,80,000	
	To work-in-progress ledger control account			1,80,000
	(being goods finished during the year transferred)			
(f)	Work-in-progress control account	Dr.	1,50,000	
	To administration overhead control account			1,50,000
	(being administration expenses charged to production)			
(g)	Production overhead control account	Dr.	1,20,000	
	To outstanding works overhead account (being works expenses incurred during the period but still unpaid)			1,20,000
(h)	Overhead control account	Dr.	4,60,000	
	To cash/bank account			4,60,000
	(being works expenses paid in cash/bank during the period)			

EXAMPLE 14.4

Record the following transactions in the ledger under the integral system and prepare the trial balance. Trial balance at the beginning of the period is as follows:

	Dr.	Cr.
Bank balance	₹ 1,500	
Stock:		
Finished goods	2,000	
Work-in-progress	3,250	
Raw materials	3,000	
Creditors		1,000
Debtors	500	
Fixed assets	51,000	
Depreciation provision		1,250
Capital account		55,000
Profit and loss account		4,000
	61,250	61,250

(Contd.)

Transactions during the year were:

	₹	₹
Materials purchased on credit		5,000
Materials issued to production:		
Direct	3,500	
Indirect	500	4,000
Payment to creditors		3,000
Wages paid:		
Direct	5,000	
Indirect	1,000	6,000
Finished goods produced		15,000
Cost of finished goods sold		16,000
Sales value		20,000
Receipt from debtors		17,500
Overhead incurred:		
Factory	3,000	
Office	500	
Selling and distribution	500	4,000
Depreciation (in addition to overheads)		250

☞ ***Solution***

Bank Account

	₹		₹
To balance b/d	1,500	By purchases ledger control account	3,000
To sales ledger control account	17,500	By wages control account	6,000
		By factory overheads	3,000
		By office overheads	500
		By selling and distribution overheads	500
		By balance c/d	6,000
	19,000		19,000

Finished Goods Ledger Control Account

	₹		₹
To balance b/d	2,000	By cost of sales account	16,000
To work-in-progress account	15,000	By balance	1,500
To office overheads account	500		
	17,500		17,500

Work-in-Progress Ledger Control Account

	₹		₹
To balance b/d	3,250	By finished goods ledger	
To stores ledger account	3,500	control account	15,000
To wages control account	5,000	By balance c/d	1,500
To factory overheads account	4,750		
	16,500		16,500

Stores Ledger Control Account

	₹		₹
To balance b/d	3,000	By W.I.P. ledger control Account	3,500
		By factory overheads account	500
To purchases ledger control account	5,000	By balance c/d	4,000
	8,000		8,000

Purchases Ledger Control Account
(Creditors account)

	₹		₹
To bank	3,000	By balance b/d	1,000
To balance b/d	3,000	By stores ledger control account	5,000
	6,000		6,000

Sales Ledger Control Account
(Debtors Account)

	₹		₹
To balance b/d	500	By bank	17,500
To cost of sales account	20,000	By balance c/d	3,000
	20,500		20,500

Factory Overheads Account

	₹		₹
To stores ledger control account	500	By W.I.P. ledger account	4,750
To wages control account	1,000		
To bank	3,000		
To depreciation provision	250		
	4,750		4,750

Wages Control Account

	₹		₹
To Bank	6,000	By work-in-progress account	5,000
		By factory overheads	1,000
	6,000		6,000

Cost of Sales Account

	₹		₹
To finished goods ledger control account	16,000	By sales ledger control account	20,000
To Profit and loss account	4,000		
	20,000		20,000

Office Overheads Account

To bank	₹ 500	By finished goods ledger control account	₹ 500

Selling and Distribution Overhead Account

To bank	₹ 500	By profit and loss account	₹ 500

Provision for Depreciation Account

To balance c/d	₹ 1,500	By balance b/d	₹ 1,250
		By factory overheads	250
	1,500		1,500

Profit and Loss Account

To selling and distribution overhead account	₹ 500	By cost of sales account	4,000
To net profit	3,500		
	4,000		4,000

Profit and Loss Appropriation Account

To balance c/d	₹ 7,500	By balance b/d	₹ 4,000
		By profit and loss account (profit for the year)	3,500
	7,500		7,500

Share Capital Account

To balance c/d	₹ 55,000	By balance b/d	₹ 55,000

Fixed Assets Account

To balance b/d	₹ 51,000	By balance c/d	₹ 51,000

Trial Balance

	Dr.	Cr.
Purchase ledger control account		3,000
Sales ledger control account	3,000	
Provision for depreciation		1,500
Bank	6,000	
Finished goods ledger control account	1,500	
Work-in-progress ledger control account	1,500	
Stores ledger control account	4,000	
Profit and loss account		7,500
Share capital		55,000
Fixed assets	51,000	
	67,000	67,000

EXAMPLE 14.5

BPR Limited keeps books on integrated accounting system. The following balance appears in the books as on April 1, 2019.

	Dr. (₹)	Cr. (₹)
Stores control account	40,950	–
Work-in-progress account	38,675	–
Finished goods account	52,325	–
Bank account	22,750	–
Creditors account		18,200
Fixed assets account	1,47,875	–
Debtors account	27,300	–
Share capital account	–	1,82,000
Provision for depreciation account	–	11,375
Provision for doubtful debts account	–	3,725
Factory overheads outstanding account	–	6,250
Pre-paid administration overheads account	9,975	–
Profit and Loss account	–	72,800
	3,17,100	3,17,100

The transactions for the year ended March 31, 2020, were as given below:

	₹	₹
Direct wages	1,97,925	–
Indirect wages	11,375	2,09,300

(Contd.)

Purchase of materials (on credit)	2,27,500
Materials issued to production	2,50,250
Material issued for repairs	4,550
Goods finished during the year (at cost)	4,89,125
Credit sales	6,82,500
	₹
Cost of goods sold	5,00,500
Production overheads absorbed	1,09,200
Production overheads paid during the year	91,000
Production overheads outstanding at the end of year	7,775
Administration overheads paid during the year	27,300
Selling overheads incurred	31,850
Payment to creditors	2,29,775
Payment received from debtors	6,59,750
Depreciation of machinery	14,789
Administration overheads outstanding at the end of year	2,225
Provision for doubtful debts at the end of the year	4,590

Required:
Write up accounts in the integrated ledger of BPR Limited and prepare a trial balance.

☞ ***Solution***

Stores Control Account

Dr.			*Cr.*
	₹		₹
To balance b/d	40,950	By WIP account	2,50,250
To creditors account	2,27,500	By production overheads account	4,550
		By balance c/d	13,650
	2,68,450		2,68,450

Wages Control Account

Dr.			*Cr.*
	₹		₹
To bank	1,97,925	By work-in-progress account	1,97,925
To bank	11,375	By production overheads account	11,375
	2,09,300		2,09,300

Work-in-Progress Account

Dr.			*Cr.*
	₹		₹
To balance b/d	38,675	By finish goods account	4,89,125
To wages control account	1,97,925	By balance c/d	1,06,925
To stores control account	2,50,250		
To production overheads account	1,09,200		
	5,96,050		5,96,050

Production Overheads Account

Dr.			*Cr.*
	₹		₹
To wages control account	11,375	By WIP account	1,09,200
To stores control account	4,550	By profit and loss account	14,039
To bank (91,000–6,250)	84,750	(Under-absorbed overheads written off)	
To production overheads outstanding	7,775		
To provision for depreciation	14,789		
	1,23,239		1,23,239

Finished Goods Account

Dr.			*Cr.*
	₹		₹
To balance b/d	52,325	By cost of sales account	5,00,500
To work-in-progress account	4,89,125	By balance c/d	80,450
To admn. overheads account	39,500		
	5,80,950		5,80,950

Administration Overheads Account

Dr.			*Cr.*
	₹		₹
To pre-paid admn. overheads account	9,975	By finished goods account	39,500
To bank	27,300		
To admn. overheads outstanding	2,225		
	39,500		39,500

Cost of Sales Account

Dr.			Cr.
	₹		₹
To finished goods account	5,00,500	To sales account	5,32,350
To selling overheads	31,850		
	5,32,350		5,32,350

Sales Account

Dr.			Cr.
	₹		₹
To cost of sales account	5,32,350	By Debtors account	6,82,500
To profit and loss account	1,50,150		
	6,82,500		6,82,500

Factory Overheads/Production Overheads Outstanding Account

Dr.			Cr.
	₹		₹
To bank	6,250	By balance b/d	6,250
To balance c/d	7,775	By production overheads	7,775
	14,025		14,025

Prepaid Administration Overheads Account

Dr.			Cr.
	₹		₹
To balance b/d	9,975	By Admn. overheads account	9,975
	9,975		9,975

Provision for depreciation Account

Dr.			Cr.
	₹		₹
To balance c/d	26,164	By balance b/d	11,375
		By production overheads account	14,789
	26,164		26,164

Provision for doubtful debts Account

Dr.			Cr.
	₹		₹
To balance c/d	4,590	By balance b/d	3,725
		By profit and loss account	865
	4,590		4,590

Profit and Loss Account

Dr.	₹		*Cr.* ₹
To provision for doubtful debts	865	By balance b/d	72,800
To production overheads	14,039	By sales account	1,50,150
To balance c/d	2,08,046		
	2,22,950		2,22,950

Debtors Account

Dr.	₹		*Cr.* ₹
To balance b/d	27,300	By bank account	6,59,750
To sales account	6,82,500	By balance c/d	50,050
	7,09,800		7,09,800

Creditors Account

Dr.	₹		*Cr.* ₹
To bank	2,29,775	By balance b/d	18,200
To balance c/d	15,925	By stores control account	2,27,500
	2,45,700		2,45,700

Fixed Assets Account

Dr.	₹		*Cr.* ₹
To balance b/d	1,47,875	By balance c/d	1,47,875
	1,47,875		1,47,875

Bank Account

Dr.	₹		*Cr.* ₹
To debtors	6,59,750	By balance b/d	22,750
		By direct wages	1,97,925
		By indirect wages	11,375
		By production overheads (₹ 84,750 + ₹ 6,250)	91,000
		By admn. overheads account	27,300
		By selling overheads account	31,850
		By creditors account	2,29,775
		By balance c/d	47,775
	6,59,750		6,59,750

Trial Balance
As on March 31, 2020

	Dr.	*Cr.*
	₹	₹
Stores control account	13,650	
Work-in-progress account	1,06,925	
Finished goods account	80,450	
Bank account	47,775	
Creditors account		15,925
Fixed assets account	1,47,875	
Debtors account	50,050	
Share capital account		1,82,000
Provision for depreciation account		26,164
Profit and Loss account		2,08,046
Production overheads outstanding account		7,775
Outstanding administrative overheads account		2,225
Provision for doubtful debt		4,590
	4,46,725	4,46,725

Theory Questions

1. What do you understand by "integrated accounts", and what are the principles involved? State the advantages of "integrated accounts".
2. What is an integrated accounting? State its advantages.
3. What do you understand by the integrated accounting system? State its advantages and prerequisites.
4. Distinguish between interlocking and integration system of cost and financial accounts?
5. Explain the accounts kept in integrated accounting system.
6. State the advantages of integrated cost and financial accounts.
7. Explain the basic requirements of an integrated system of accounting.
8. What is integrated accounting? Briefly describe the merits of integration.
9. Define integrated accounting system. Distinguish it with non-integrated accounting system.
10. What are the advantages of integrated accounts?
11. Distinguish between integral and non-integral system of accounting.

Problems

1. Journalise the following transactions assuming cost and financial accounts are integrated:

	(₹)
Raw materials purchases	40,000
Direct materials issued to production	30,000
Wages paid (30% indirect)	24,000
Direct wages charged to production	16,800
Manufacturing expenses incurred	19,000

Manufacturing overhead charged to production	18,400
Selling and distribution costs	4,000
Finished products (at cost)	40,000
Sales	58,000
Closing stock	NIL
Receipt from debtors	13,800
Payment to creditors	22,000

2. From the following particulars pass the journal entries in an integral accounting system:
   (a) Issued materials ₹3,00,000/- of which ₹2,80,000 (standard ₹2,40,000) is direct material.
   (b) Net wages paid ₹70,000/-, Deductions being ₹ 12,000/- (standard ₹75,000/-)
   (c) Gross salaries payable for the period is ₹26,000/- (standard ₹25,000/-), Deductions ₹ 2,000/-
   (d) Sales (credit) ₹8,00,000/-
   (e) Discount allowed ₹5,000/-
   (f) Salaries and wages allocation: ₹60,000/- direct (standard ₹ 62,000/-) and out of the balance, 50% production, 30% admn., and 20% selling and distribution overheads.

3. In the absence of the Chief Accountant, you have been asked to prepare a month's cost accounts for a company which operate a batch costing system fully integrated with the financial accounts. The following relevant information is provided to you:

		₹
Balances at the beginning of the month:		
Stores ledger control account		25,000
Work-in-progress control account		20,000
Finished goods control account		35,000
Prepaid production overheads brought forward from previous month		3,000
Transactions during the month:		
Materials purchased		75,000
Materials issued:		
To production	30,000	
To factory maintenance	4,000	34,000
Materials transferred between batches		5,000
Total wages paid:		
To direct workers	25,000	
To indirect workers	5,000	30,000
Direct wages charged to batches		20,000
Recorded non-productive time of direct worker		5,000
Selling and distribution overheads incurred		6,000
Other production overheads incurred		12,000
Sales		1,00,000
Cost of finished goods sold		80,000

(Contd.)

Cost of goods completed and transferred into finished goods during the month	65,000
Physical value of work-in-progress at the end of the month	40,000
The production overhead absorption rate is 150% of direct wages charged to work-in-progress.	

Required:

Prepare the following accounts for the month:

(a) Stores Ledger Control Account
(b) Work-in-Progress Control Account
(c) Finished Goods Control Account
(d) Production Overhead Control Account
(e) Profit and Loss Account

4. Dutta Enterprises operates an integral system of accounting. You are required to pass the journal entries for the following transactions that took place for the year ended 30.6.2020.
(Narrations are not required)

	₹
Raw materials purchased (50% on credit)	6,00,000
Materials issued to production	4,00,000
Wages paid (50% direct)	2,00,000
Wages charged to production	1,00,000
Factory overheads incurred	80,000
Factory overheads charged to production	1,00,000
Selling and distribution overheads incurred	40,000
Finished goods at cost	50,00,000
Sales (50% credit)	7,50,000
Closing stock	Nil
Receipts from debtors	2,00,000
Payments to creditors	2,00,000

Chapter 15

Reconciliation of Cost and Financial Accounts

Learning Objectives

After reading this chapter, you should be able to:

1. describe the need for reconciliation;
2. explain the reasons for differences in profit; and
3. discuss the reconciliation procedure.

NEED FOR RECONCILIATION

When a manufacturing firm uses an integrated accounting system, i.e., no separate cost and financial accounts, the question of reconciliation does not arise. Integration means that the same set of accounts fulfill the requirements of both i.e. Cost and Financial Accounts. But in many manufacturing concerns, cost and financial accounts are maintained separately and independently of each other. In such a case, profit disclosed by one accounting system tends to differ from that of the other accounting system. This creates problems and the need arises of reconciling the two accounting systems to arrive at one profit figure.

REASONS FOR DIFFERENCES IN PROFIT

Differences in the profits presented in cost and financial books may be due to the following reasons:

Items Appropriated or Charged to Profit but Not Found in Cost Accounts

1. Income tax.
2. Transfer to general reserve or any other fund to accumulated profits, for example, dividend equalisation reserve.
3. Dividend paid on the share capital.
4. Additional provisions for depreciation on plant, etc. and for bad debts.

5. Amounts written off as goodwill, preliminary expenses, underwriting commissions, debenture discount, capital issue expenses.
6. Appropriation for the purpose of repayment of loans or debentures.

Purely Financial Matters Not Found in Cost Accounts

1. Interest received on bank deposits,
2. Interest, dividends, etc. received on investments.
3. Rents received.
4. Losses on the sale of investments, machinery, buildings, etc.
5. Profits on the sale of fixed assets.
6. Transfer fees received.
7. Interest on bank loans, mortgages, debentures and other borrowed money.
8. Interest on proprietor's capital.
9. Damages payable.
10. Penalties payable.
11. Pension
12. Bonus of employees
13. Gratuity

Items included in Cost Accounting only

(i) Opportunity cost or notional rent of building owned.
(ii) Interest on capital employed in production
(iii) Salary of proprietor.
(iv) Under/over absorbed overheads in cost accounting
(v) Differences due to varying basis of valuation of inventory.
(vi) Differences due to different methods of calculating depreciation

Treatment of Items in Cost Books and Financial Books

In cost accounts, overheads are recovered on the basis of a pre-determined rate. In this way recovered overhead may not agree with the actual overhead incurred. Profit in cost books may be comparatively (as to financial books) higher or lower depending on the under-absorption or over-absorption of overhead. Reconciliation is necessary to eliminate differences in profits. If the amount of over- or under-absorption is transferred to the costing and profit and loss accounts, then financial profit will tally with the costing profit.

Differences in the Valuation of Stock and Work-in-Progress

In financial books, stock is valued at cost or market price whichever is lower. In cost accounting different methods of valuation of stock are in practice such as FIFO, LIFO, Average Costing, Weighted Average Costing, etc. Besides, work-in-progress in cost accounts is often valued on a prime cost basis and sometimes variable manufacturing overhead is included therein. In financial accounting, work-in-progress may be valued after taking into account administrative expenses also. Similarly, finished goods in financial accounting are valued at cost or market price whichever is lower. On the contrary, in cost accounting, finished stock is generally valued at total cost of production. Since the value of stocks (raw material, work-in-progress, finished goods) in the financial accounts and cost accounts differs, the profits also differ from financial to cost accounting.

Depreciation

In financial accounts, depreciation may be calculated on straight line method or diminishing balance method. But, in cost accounting, depreciation can be calculated in terms of machine hour or any other base.

Abnormal Losses and Gains

Abnormal losses and gains (discussed earlier) may be transferred to costing profit and loss account or alternatively may not be considered and excluded totally from cost accounts. In the first situation (transfer to costing and profit and loss account), there will be no difference between financial profit and costing profit. But in the second situation (exclusion from cost accounts) financial profit (losses) will differ from costing profit (loss) and adjustments will be required.

RECONCILIATION PROCEDURE

Reconciliation of cost and financial accounts is done on the principle of bank reconciliation statement. One may begin with profit as per the financial books or cost books and thereafter items causing differences in profit may be added or deducted depending on the circumstances. After all such items have been considered, profit as per other books may be arrived at. This reconciliation may be achieved through a mere statement (Reconciliation Statement) or preparing a Memorandum Reconciliation Account. Both these approaches are discussed below:

1. Reconciliation Statement The following steps are required to be completed to prepare a Reconciliation Statement:

(i) Profit as per any set of books (cost or financial) may be taken as a starting point. This profit plus making all suitable adjustments (in terms of causes of difference in profit) will finally result into profit figure as per the other set of books.
(ii) The effect of a particular cause of difference should be determined on the profits shown by the other set of books.
(iii) In case, the cause (causing the difference in profit) has given as increase in profit shown by the other set of books, the amount of such increase should be added to the profit as per the former set of books which has been taken as a starting point.
(iv) In case, the cause has decreased the profit shown by other set of books, the amount of such decrease should be deducted from the profit as per the former set of books which has been taken as the starting point.

Completion of the above steps will give the profit as per the other set of books.

2. Memorandum Reconciliation Account This reconciliation procedure is in the form of an account. The debit side (Dr.) of the Memorandum Reconciliation Account shows items to be deducted from the profit as per any set of books taken as a starting point. The credit side of this account shows profit figure accepted as a starting point as well as items to be added to this profit figure. The difference between the credit side and debit side will give profit as per the other set of books. A proforma of Memorandum Reconciliation Account is shown in Fig. 15.1.

Memorandum Reconciliation Account

Dr.			*Cr.*
Particulars	*Amt (₹)*	*Particulars*	*Amt (₹)*
To ________	—	By Profits as per cost accounts	—
To ________	—	By ________	—
To ________	—	By ________	—
To ________	—	By ________	—
To profit as per financial accounts	—		
Total	—	Total	—

Fig. 15.1

EXAMPLE 15.1

The following information is made available to you from the financial books of S.V. Ltd. for the year ended December 31, 2020:

	₹		₹
To direct materials used	3,00,000	By sales	
To direct wages	2,00,000	(2,00,000 units)	7,50,000
To factory expenses	1,20,000		
To office expenses	40,000		
To selling and distribution expenses	80,000		
To net profit	10,000		
	7,50,000		7,50,000

Normal output of the factory is 2,50,000 units. Factory overheads are fixed up to ₹60,000 and office expenses are fixed for all practical purposes. Selling and distribution expenses are fixed to the extent of ₹50,000; the rest are variable.

Prepare a statement reconciling the profits as per cost and financial accounts assuming that indirect expenses are absorbed on the basis of normal production capacity in cost accounts.

Solution

Statement of Cost and Profit

		₹
Direct material used		3,00,000
Direct wages		2,00,000
	Prime cost	5,00,000

(Contd.)

		₹
Factory expenses		
	$\frac{4}{5}$ th of fixed overhead 60,000 × $\frac{4}{5}$ = 48,000	
	Variable overhead (1,20,000 – 60,000) = 60,000	1,08,000
	Works cost for factory cost	6,08,000
Office expenses		
	$\frac{4}{5}$ th of fixed expenses 40,000 × $\frac{4}{5}$ = 32,000	32,000
	Cost of production	6,40,000
Selling and distribution expenses		
	$\frac{4}{5}$ th of fixed expenses 50,000 ₹ $\frac{4}{5}$ = 40,000	
	Variable overheads (80,000 – 50,000) = 30,000	70,000
	Cost of sales	7,10,000
	Profit	40,000
	Sales	7,50,000

Reconciliation Statement

		₹
Profit as per cost accounts		40,000
Less: Unabsorbed factory expenses	12,000	
Unabsorbed office expense	8,000	
Unabsorbed selling and distribution expenses	10,000	
		30,000
Profit as per financial accounts		10,000

Out of total factory overhead, ₹60,000 are fixed. The fixed factory overhead rate in financial accounts must have been determined on the basis of normal output i.e. 2,50,000 units Therefore, fixed factory overheads recovered in cost accounts must be ₹48,000 (i.e. $\frac{4}{5}$ th of 60,000) and 40,000 (i.e. $\frac{4}{5}$ th of ₹50,000) respectively.

EXAMPLE 15.2

The following figures are available from financial accounts for the year ended 31st March, 2020:

	₹
Direct material consumption	2,50,000
Direct wages	1,00,000

(Contd.)

Factory overheads	3,80,000
Administration overheads	2,50,000
Selling and distribution overheads	4,80,000
Bad debts	20,000
Preliminary expenses (written off)	10,000
Legal charges	5,000
Dividend received	50,000
Interest on deposit received	10,000
Sales 1,20,000 units	7,00,000
Closing stock :	
Finished stock – 40,000 units	1,20,000
Work-in-progress	80,000

The cost accounts reveal:
Direct material consumption : ₹2,80,000.
Factory overhead recovered at 20% on prime cost.
Administration overhead at ₹3 per unit of production.
Selling and distribution overhead at ₹4 per unit sold.

Required: Prepare

(i) Cost sheet;
(ii) Financial profit and loss account; and
(iii) Statement reconciling the profits disclosed by the costing profit and loss account and financial profit and loss account.

☞ ***Solution***

Cost Sheet

Particulars	₹
Direct material consumption	2,80,000
Direct wages	1,00,000
Prime Cost	3,80,000
+ Factory overheads [20% of ₹3,80,000]	76,000
	4,56,000
– Stock of W.I.P.	80,000
Work Cost/Factory Cost	3,76,000
+ Office and administration overheads (1,60,000* × ₹3)	4,80,000
Cost of Production	8,56,000
– Closing stock of finished goods	
$\left[\frac{8,56,000}{1,60,000} \times 40,000\right]$	2,14,000

(Contd.)

Particulars	₹
Cost of Goods Sold	6,42,000
+ Selling and distribution overhead (1,20,000 × ₹4)	4,80,000
Cost of Sales	11,22,000
Loss *(balancing figure)*	4,22,000
Sales	7,00,000

*Units product = No. of units sold + No. of units in closing stock

= 1,20,000 + 40,000 = 1,60,000 units

Dr. **Trading and Profit and Loss Account** *Cr.*

Particulars	₹	*Particulars*	₹
Direct material used	2,50,000	Sales	7,00,000
Direct wages	1,00,000	Closing stock	
Factory overheads	3,80,000	Finished stock	1,20,000
Administration overheads	2,50,000	– 40000 units	
Selling and distribution		Work-in-progress	80,000
overheads	4,80,000	Dividend received	50,000
Bad debts	20,000	Interest on deposit received	10,000
Preliminary expenses		Net loss *(balancing figure)*	5,35,000
(written off)	10,000		
Legal charges	5,000		
	14,95,000		14,95,000

Reconciliation Statement

Particulars	*+ (Plus)*	*– (Minus)*
Net loss as per cost accounts		4,22,000
Overvaluation of material used	30,000	
Under recovery of factory overheads		3,04,000
Over recovery of administration overheads	2,30,000	
Bad debts		20,000
Preliminary expenses W/o		10,000
Legal charges		5,000
Dividend received	50,000	
Interest on deposit received	10,000	
Overvaluation of closing stock		94,000
Net loss as per financial accounts	5,35,000	
	8,55,000	8,55,000

for excel template, scan

EXAMPLE 15.3

The following is the trading and profit & loss account of Omega Ltd.

Particulars	₹	Particulars		₹
To material consumed	23,01,000	By sales (30,000 units)		48,75,000
To direct wages	12,05,750	By finished goods stock (1000 units)		1,30,000
To production overheads	6,92,250			
To administration overheads	3,10,375	By work-in-progress:		
To selling and distribution overheads	3,68,875	Materials	55,250	
		Wages	26,000	
To bad debts written off	22,750	Production		
To goodwill written off	45,500	overheads	16,250	97,500
To fines	3,250	By dividends received		3,90,000
To interest on mortgage	13,000	By interest on bank deposits		65,000
To loss on sale of machine	16,500			
To taxation	1,95,000			
To net profit	3,83,000			
	55,57,500			55,57,500

The cost accounting records of Omega Ltd. which manufactures a standard unit show the following:

(i) Production overheads have been charged at 20% of prime cost.
(ii) Administration overheads have been recorded at ₹9.75 per finished unit.
(iii) Selling and distribution overheads have been recorded at ₹13 per unit sold.

Required:

(i) Prepare a costing profit and loss account, indicating net profit.
(ii) Prepare a statement reconciling the profit disclosed by cost records with the profit shown in financial accounts.

Solution

Costing Profit & Loss Account

Particulars	₹	Particulars	₹
Materials	23,01,000	Sales	48,75,000
Direct wages	12,05,750		
Prime Cost	35,06,750		
Production overheads (20% of ₹35,06,750)	7,01,350		
	42,08,100		
Less: Closing WIP	97,500		
Works Cost	41,10,600		

(Contd.)

Particulars	₹	*Particulars*	₹
Administration overheads (31,000 × 9.75)	3,02,250		
Cost of Production	44,12,850		
Less: Finished stock*	1,42,350		
Cost of Goods Sold	42,70,500		
Add: Selling & distribution overheads (30,000 × 13)	3,90,000		
Total cost	46,60,500		
Profit	2,14,500		
	48,75,000		48,75,000

$$\text{Value of finished stock} = \frac{\text{Cost of production}}{\text{Total units}}$$

$$= \frac{₹44{,}12{,}850}{31{,}000 \text{ units}} \times 1{,}000 = ₹1{,}42{,}350$$

Reconciliation Statement

Particulars	₹	₹
Profit as per cost accounts		2,14,500
Add: 1. Production overheads over-absorbed (₹7,01,350 – ₹6,92,250)	9,100	
2. Selling and distribution overheads over-absorbed (₹3,90,000 – ₹3,68,875)	21,125	
3. Dividends received	3,90,000	
4. Interest on bank deposits	65,000	4,85,225
		6,99,725
Less: 1. Administration overheads under-absorbed	8,125	
2. Bad debts	22,750	
3. Goodwill written off	45,500	
4. Fines	3,250	
5. Interest on mortgage	13,000	
6. Loss on sale of machine	16,250	
7. Taxation	1,95,000	
8. Difference in stock value ₹(1,42,350 – 1,30,000)	12,350	3,16,225
Profit as per financial accounts		3,83,500

EXAMPLE 15.4

A manufacturing company disclosed a net loss of ₹3,47,000 as per their cost accounts for the year ending March 31, 2020. The financial accounts, however, disclosed a net loss of ₹5,10,000 for the same period. The following information was revealed as a result of scrutiny of the figures of both the sets of accounts:

	₹
1 Factory overheads under-absorbed	40,000
2 Administration overheads over absorbed	60,000
3 Depreciation charged in financial accounts	3,25,000
4 Depreciation charged in cost accounts	2,75,000
5 Interest on investment not included in cost accounts	96,000
6 Income tax provided	54,000
7 Interest on loan funds in financial accounts	2,45,000
8 Transfer fees (credit in financial books)	24,000
9 Stores adjustment (credit in financial books)	14,000
10 Dividend received	32,000

Prepare a Reconciliation Statement.

Solution

Reconciliation Statement

	₹	₹
Net Loss As Per Cost Accounts		3,47,000
Add: Factory overheads under absorbed	40,000	
Income tax provided	54,000	
Depreciation under charged (₹3,25,000 – ₹2,75,000)	50,000	
Interest on loan funds in financial accounts	2,45,000	3,89,000
		7,36,000
Less: Administration overheads over-absorbed	60,000	
Interest on investment not included in cost accounts	96,000	
Transfer fee (credit in financial books)	24,000	
Store adjustment (credit in financial books)	14,000	
Dividend received	32,000	2,26,000
Net Loss As Per Financial Accounts		**5,10,000**

EXAMPLE 15.5

The cost accountant of a company has arrived at a profit of ₹73,24,150 based on cost accounting records for the year ended 31-3-2020. As cost auditor, you find the following differences between financial accounts and cost accounts.

(a)	Decrease in value of WIP and finished goods as per F/A	₹1,28,21,995
	As per cost accounts	₹1,31,04,220
(b)	Profit on sale of fixed assets	₹61,500

(c)	Loss on sale of investments	₹11,200
(d)	Voluntary retirement compensation included in salaries and wages in F/A	₹16,75,000
(e)	Donation paid	₹25,000
(f)	Major repairs and maintenance written off in F/A	₹13,26,000
	Amount in cost accounts	6,08,420
(g)	Insurance claim relating to previous year received during the year	₹14,29,000
(h)	Profit from retail trading activity	₹7,12,300

You are required to prepare a reconciliation statement between the profit figures as per costing and financial accounts. Calculate the profit as per financial books.

Solution

Reconciliation Statement

	(₹)
Profit as per cost account	73,24,150
Add: Decrease in value of WIP : 1,28,21,995 – 1,31,04,220	2,82,225
Add: Profit on sale of fixed asset	61,500
Less: Loss on sale of investments	11,200
Less: Voluntary Retirement Compensation	16,75,000
Less: Donations Paid	25,000
Less: Repairs and Maintenance 13,26,000 – 6,08,420	7,17,580
Add: Insurance claim	14,29,000
Add: Profit	7,12,300
Profit as per Financial Accounts	73,80,395

EXAMPLE 15.6

The audited financial accounts of a company showed a profit of ₹59,660, whereas the profit, as per the cost accounts, was ₹26,725. From the following information provided, you are required to prepare a reconciliation statement clearly bringing out the reasons for the difference between the two figures:

for excel template, scan

Profit and Loss Account for the Year Ended 31st March, 2020

Dr.	(₹)	*Cr.*	(₹)
Opening stock	24,70,000	Sales	34,65,000
Purchases	8,20,000	Closing stock	7,50,000
Direct wages	2,30,000		
Factory overheads	4,05,500		
Gross profit (c/d)	2,89,500		
	34,65,000		34,65,000
Administrative overheads	98,000	Gross profit (b/d)	2,89,500

(Contd.)

Dr.	(₹)	Cr.	(₹)
Selling overheads	1,34,340	Dividend received	2,500
Net profit	59,660		
	2,92,000		2,92,000

The cost records show:

(i) Closing stock balance of ₹7,95,400.
(ii) Direct wages absorbed during the year ₹2,18,800.
(iii) Factory overheads absorbed ₹4,65,000.
(iv) Administrative overheads absorbed @ 2.5% on sales.
(v) Selling overheads charged @ 5% of the value of sales.

☞ Solution

Reconciliation Statement

Profit as per financial account			=	₹59,660
Add: Difference in closing stock valuation	(₹7,95,400 – 7,50,000)		=	₹45,400
Add: Under absorption of wages	[₹230000 – 2,18,800]		=	₹11,200
Add: Under absorption admn. overheads	[98000 – 86625]		=	₹11,375
				₹1,27,635
Less: Over absorption of factory overheads	(4,65,000 – 4,05,500)	59,500		
Over absorption of selling overheads	(1,73,250 – 1,34,340)	38,910		
Less Dividend income		2,500		
				1,00,910
Profit as per cost accounts				₹26,725

✍ EXAMPLE 15.7

A manufacturing company has disclosed a net loss of ₹8,75,000 as per their cost accounting records for the year ended March 31, 2020. However, their financial accounting records disclosed a net loss of ₹7,19,250 for the same period. A scrutiny of the data of both the sets of books of accounts revealed the following information:

	₹
(i) Factory overheads over-absorbed	47,500
(ii) Administration overheads under-absorbed	32,750
(iii) Depreciation charged in financial accounts	2,25,000
(iv) Depreciation charged in cost accounts	2,42,250
(v) Interest on investments not included in cost accounts	62,750

(vi) Income Tax provided in financial accounts	7,250
(vii) Transfer fees (credit in financial accounts)	12,500
(viii) Preliminary expenses written off	27,500
(ix) Under-valuation of opening stock in cost accounts	6,250
(x) Under valuations of closing stock in cost accounts	17,500

Required:

Prepare a Memorandum Reconciliation account

Solution

Memorandum Reconciliation Account

Dr. *Cr.*

Particulars	₹	*Particulars*	₹
To net loss as per cost accounting records	8,75,000	By factory overheads over-absorbed	47,500
To administrative overheadsunder-absorbed	32,750	By excess charge of depreciation in cost accounts (2,42,250 – 2,25,000)	17,250
To income tax provided in financial accounts	7,250	By transfer fee	12,500
To preliminary expenses written off	27,500	By interest on investment not included in cost accounts	62,750
Under valuation of opening stock in cost accounts	6,250	Under valuation of closing stock in cost accounts	17,500
		By net loss as per financial records	7,91,250
	9,48,750		9,48,750

EXAMPLE 15.8

From the following data prepare a "Reconciliation Statement":

	₹
Profit as per cost accounts	1,45,500
Works overheads under-recovered	9,500
Administrative overheads under-recovered	22,750
Selling overheads over-recovered	19,500
Overvaluation of opening stock in cost accounts	15,000
Overvaluation of closing stock in cost accounts	7,500
Interest earned during the year	3,750
Rent received during the year	27,000
Bad debts written off during the year	9,000
Preliminary expenses written off during the year	18,000

☞ Solution

Reconciliation Statement

	₹ (+)	₹ (–)
Profit as per cost accounts	1,45,500	
Add: Over-recovery of selling overheads in cost account	19,500	
Over-valuation of opening stock in cost accounts	15,000	
Income excluded from cost accounts:		
Interest earned	3,750	
Rent received	27,000	
Less: Under-recovery of works overhead in cost accounts		9,500
Under-recovery of administration overhead in cost accounts		22,750
Over-valuation of closing stock in cost accounts		7,500
Expenses excluded from cost accounts:		
Bad debts		9,000
Preliminary expenses		18,000
	2,10,750	66,750
Profit as per financial accounts	1,44,000	

✍ EXAMPLE 15.9

The following information is available from the financial books of a company having a normal production capacity of 60,000 units for the year ended 31st March, 2020.

(i) Sales ₹10,00,000 (50,000 units).
(ii) There was no opening and closing stock of finished units.
(iii) Direct material and direct wages cost were ₹5,00,000 and ₹2,50,000 respectively.
(iv) Actual factory expenses were ₹1,50,000 of which 60% are fixed.
(v) Actual administrative expenses were ₹45,000 which are completely fixed.
(vi) Actual selling and distribution expenses were ₹30,000 of which 40% are fixed.
(vii) Interest and dividends received ₹15,000.

You are required to:

(a) Find out profit as per financial books for the year ended 31st March, 2020;
(b) Prepare the cost sheet and ascertain the profit as per cost accounts for the year ended 31st March, 2020 assuming that the indirect expenses are absorbed on the basis of normal production capacity; and
(c) Prepare a statement reconciling profits shown by financial and cost books.

☞ ***Solution***

(a) **Computation of Profit As Per Financial Books**
Profit and Loss Account
(For the Year Ended 31st March, 2020)

Particulars	₹	*Particulars*	₹
To direct material	5,00,000	By sales (50000 units)	10,00,000
To direct wages	2,50,000	By interest and dividends	15,000
To factory expenses	1,50,000		
To administrative expenses	45,000		
To selling and distribution expenses	30,000		
To profit	40,000		
	10,15,000		10,15,000

(b) **Cost Sheet (For the Year Ended 31st March, 2020)**

	₹	₹
Direct material		5,00,000
Direct wages		2,50,000
Prime Cost		7,50,000
Factory overheads:		
Variable	60,000	
Fixed ₹90,000 × 5/6	75,000	1,35,000
Works Cost		8,85,000
Administrative expenses ₹45,000 × 5/6		37,500
Cost of Production		9,22,500
Selling and distribution overheads:		
Variable	18,000	
Fixed ₹12,000 × 5/6	10,000	28,000
Cost of Sales		9,50,500
Profit		49,500
Sales		10,00,000

(c) **Statement of Reconciliation**
(Reconciling Profit Shown by Financial and Cost Accounts)

	₹(+)	₹(–)
Profit as per Cost Accounts	49,500	
Add: Income from interest and dividends excluded in cost accounts	15,000	
Less: Factory overheads undercharged in cost accounts		15,000
Administrative overheads undercharged in cost accounts		7,500

(Contd.)

	₹(+)	₹(–)
Selling and distribution overheads undercharged in cost accounts (₹30,000 – ₹28,000)		2,000
Profit as per financial accounts		40,000
	64,500	64,500

EXAMPLE 15.10

The financial records of Modern Manufacturers Ltd. reveals the following for the year ended 30.6.2020:

		(₹ *in Thousands*)
Sales (20000 units)		4,000
Materials		1,600
Wages		800
Factory overheads		720
Office and administrative overheads		416
Selling and distribution overheads		288
Finished goods (1230 units)		240
Work-in-progress: Materials	48	
Labour	32	
Overheads (factory)	32	112
Goodwill written off		320
Interest on capital		32

In the costing records, factory overhead is charged at 100% of wages, administration overhead at 10% of factory cost and selling and distribution overhead at the rate of ₹16 per unit sold.

Prepare a statement reconciling the profit as per cost records with the profit as per financial records of the company.

Solution

(a) Profit and Loss Account for the Year Ended 30th June, 2020 (₹'000)

To materials	1,600	By sales	4,000
To wages	800	By closing stock:	
To factory overheads	720	Finished goods	240
To office and administration overheads	416	Work-in-progress	112
To selling and distribution overheads	288		
To goodwill written off	320		
To interest on capital	32		
To net profit	176		
	4,352		4,352

(b) Profit As Per Cost Account (₹ '000)

Materials	1,600.00
Wages	800.00
Prime cost	2400.00
Factory overhead (100% of wages)	800.00
Factory cost (gross)	3,200.00
Closing W.I.P.	112.00
Factory cost (net)	3,088.00
Office and administration overheads (10% of factory cost)	308.80
Total cost of production	3,396.80
Closing stock of finished goods	(196.80)
Cost of production of unit sold	3,200.00
Selling and distribution overhead (₹16 × 20000)	320.00
Cost of sales	3,520.00
Profit (balancing figure)	480.00
Sales	4,000.00

Note: Value of closing stock of finished goods:

Number of units sold	20,000
Closing stock of finished goods	1,230
Number of units produced	21,230
Total cost of production	3,396.80

Value of closing stock of finished goods

$₹\frac{3396.80}{21,230} \times 1,230 = ₹196.80$

(c) Statement Reconciling the Profit As Per Cost Accounts with the Profit As Per Financial Accounts

	₹'000	*₹'000*
Profit as per cost accounts		480.00
Over-absorbed overhead: Factory overhead (800 – 720)	80.00	
Selling and distribution overhead (320 – 288)	32.00	112.00
Over-valuation of closing stock in financial accounts (240.00 – 196.80)		43.20
Under-absorbed overhead: Office and administration (416.00 – 308.80)		(107.20)
Goodwill written off in financial accounts		(320.00)
Interest on capital in financial accounts		(32.00)
Profit as per financial accounts		176.00

EXAMPLE 15.11

In reconciliation between cost and financial accounts, one of the areas of differences is for different methods of stock valuation. State with reasons, whether costing profit will be higher or lower than that of the financial profit in each of the following circumstances?

Items of Stock	Cost Valuation ₹	Financial Valuation ₹
Raw material (opening)	50,000	60,000
Work-in-progress (closing)	60,000	50,000
Finished stock (closing)	50,000	60,000
Finished stock (opening)	60,000	50,000

Solution

In the reconciliation, it does not matter in which form the stock is kept, that is, raw material, work-in-progress or finished stocks. The basic principle is that if the opening stock is larger, profit is lower, whereas if the closing stock is larger, profit is higher and vice versa. On the basis of this principle, the following conclusions on the four propositions can be drawn:

1. Raw material (opening) is lower in cost accounts and the costing profit will be higher by ₹10,000.
2. Work-in-progress (closing) is higher in cost accounts and costing profit will be higher by ₹10,000.
3. Finished stock (closing) is lower in cost accounts and costing profit will be lower by ₹10,000.
4. Finished Stock (opening) is higher by ₹10,000 in cost accounts and costing profit will, therefore, be lower by ₹10,000.

EXAMPLE 15.12

The financial books of a company reveal the following data for the year ended 31st March, 2020:

Opening Stock:	₹
Finished goods 875 units	74,375
Work-in-process	32,000
Raw materials consumed	7,80,000
Direct labour	4,50,000
Factory overheads	3,00,000
Goodwill	1,00,000
Administration overheads	2,95,000
Dividend paid	85,000
Bad debts	12,000
Selling and distribution overheads	61,000
Interest received	45,000
Rent received	18,000
Sales 14,500 units	20,80,000
Closing stock: Finished goods 375 units	41,250
Work-in-process	38,667

The cost records provide as under:

- Factory overheads are absorbed at 60% of direct wages.
- Administration overheads are recovered at 20% of factory cost.
- Selling and distribution overheads are charged at ₹4 per unit sold.
- Opening stock of finished goods is valued at ₹104 per unit.
- The company values work-in-progress at factory cost for both financial and cost profit reporting.

Required:

(i) Prepare statements for the year ended 31st March, 2020 show
- the profit as per financial records
- the profit as per costing records.

(ii) Present a statement reconciling the profit as per costing records with the profit as per financial records.

Solution

(i) Statement of Profit As Per Financial Records

OR

Profit and Loss Account of the Company

(For the Year Ended March 31, 2020)

	₹		₹
To opening stock of finished goods	74,375	By sales	20,80,000
To work-in-process	32,000	By closing stock of finished goods	41,250
To raw materials consumed	7,80,000	By work-in-process	38,667
To direct labour	4,50,000	By rent received	18,000
To factory overheads	3,00,000	By interest received	45,000
To goodwill	1,00,000		
To administration overhead	2,95,000		
To selling and distribution overheads	61,000		
To dividend paid	85,000		
To bad debts	12,000		
To profit	33,542		
	22,22,197		22,22,917

Statement of Profit As Per Costing Records

(For the Year Ended March 31, 2020)

	₹
Sales revenue (A)	20,80,000
(14,500 units)	
Cost of sales:	
Opening stock (875 units × ₹104)	91,000

(Contd.)

	₹
Add: Cost of production of 14,000 units *(Refer to working note-2)*	17,92,000
Less: Closing stock $\left(\frac{₹17.92,000 \times 375 \text{ units}}{14,000 \text{ units}}\right)$	48,000
Production cost of goods sold (14,500 units)	18,35,000
Selling and distribution overheads (14500 units × ₹4)	58,000
Cost of sales: (B)	18,93,000
Profit: {(A) – (B)}	1,87,000

(ii) Statement of Reconciliation

(Reconciling the Profit As Per Costing Records with the Profit As Per Financial Records)

	₹	₹
Profit as per cost accounts		1,87,000
Add: Administration overheads over absorbed (₹2,98,667 – ₹2,95,000)	3,667	
Opening stock overvalued (₹91,000 – ₹74,375)	16,625	
Interest received	45,000	
Rent received	18,000	83,292
		2,70,292
Less: Factory overheads under recovery (₹3,00,000 – ₹2,70,000)	30,000	
Selling and distribution overheads under recovery (₹61,000 – ₹58,000)	3,000	
Closing stock overvalued (₹48,000 – ₹41,250)	6,750	
Goodwill	1,00,000	
Dividend	85,000	
Bad debts	12,000	2,36,750
Profit as per financial accounts		33,542

Working Notes:

1. Number of units produced

	Units
Sales	14500
Add: Closing stock	375
Total	14875

Less: Opening stock	875
Number of unit produced	14000

2. Cost Sheet

	₹
Raw materials consumed	7,80,000
Direct labour	4,50,000
Prime cost	12,30,000
Factory overheads (*60% of direct wages*)	2,70,000
Factory cost	15,00,000
Add: Opening work-in-process	32,000
Less: Closing work-in-process	(38,667)
Factory cost of goods produced	14,93,333
Administration overheads (*20% of factory cost*)	2,98,667
Cost of production of 14000 units (*Refer to working note-1*)	17,92,000

Cost of production per unit:

$$= \frac{\text{Total cost of production}}{\text{No. of units produced}} = \frac{₹17,92,000}{14000 \text{ Units}} = ₹128$$

EXAMPLE 15.13

The following figures have been taken from the financial accounts of a manufacturing firm for the year of its operation:

	₹
Direct material consumption	50,00,000
Direct wages	30,00,000
Factory overheads	16,00,000
Administrative overheads	7,00,000
Selling and distribution overheads	9,60,000
Bad debts	80,000
Preliminary expenses written off	40,000
Legal charges	10,000
Dividends received	1,00,000
Interest on deposit received	20,000
Sales—120000 units	1,20,00,000
Closing stock:	
Finished stock—4000 units	3,20,000
Work-in-progress	2,40,000

The cost accounts for the same period reveal that the direct material consumption was ₹56,00,000; factory overhead is recovered at 20% on prime cost; administration overhead is recovered @ ₹6 per unit of production; and selling and distribution overheads are recovered at ₹8 per unit sold.

You are required to prepare costing and financial profit and loss accounts and reconcile the difference in the profit as arrived at in the two sets of accounts by preparing a "Reconciliation Statement".

☞ Solution

Costing Profit and Loss Account

		₹		₹
To	direct material consumed	56,00,000	By sales	1,20,00,000
To	direct wages	30,00,000		
	Prime cost	86,00,000		
To	factory overheads			
	(20% on prime cost)	17,20,000		
		1,03,20,000		
Less:	Work-in-progress	2,40,000		
	Works cost	1,00,80,000		
To	Administrative overheads			
	(₹6 per unit produced)	7,44,000		
	Cost of production (124000 units)	1,08,24,000		
Less:	Closing stock (4000 units)	3,49,161		
	Cost of production of goods sold	1,04,74,839		
	To selling & distribution overheads (8 × 1,20,000)	9,60,000		
	To net profit	5,65,161		
		1,20,00,000		1,20,00,000

Financial Profit and Loss Account

	₹		₹
To direct materials consumed	50,00,000	By sales	1,20,00,000
		By dividends	1,00,000
To direct wages	30,00,000	By interest on deposits	20,000
To factory overheads	16,00,000	By Closing Stock:	
To admn. overheads	7,00,000	Finished stock	3,20,000
To selling & distribution	9,60,000	Work-in-progress	2,40,000
To bad debts	80,000		
To pre-expenses	40,000		
To legal charges	10,000		
To net profit	12,90,000		
	1,26,80,000		1,26,80,000

Reconciliation Statement

		₹ (+)	₹ (–)
	Profit as shown by financial books	12,90,000	
Less:	Direct materials overcharged in costs		6,00,000
	Factory overheads over-absorbed in costs		1,20,000
	Administrative overheads undercharged in cost		44,000
Add:	Closing stock of finished goods overvalued in costs	29,161	
	Bad debts not recovered in costs	80,000	
	Preliminary expenses not charged in costs	40,000	
	Legal charges not charged in cost	10,000	
Less:	Dividends not included in costs		1,00,000
	Interest on deposits not included in costs		20,000
		14,49,161	8,84,000
Profit as per cost accounts			5,65,161
		14,49,161	14,49,161

EXAMPLE 15.14

The cost accountant of a company has arrived at a profit of ₹73,24,150 based on cost accounting records for the year ended 31.3.2020. As Cost Auditor, you find the following differences between the financial accounts and cost accounts (figures are in rupees):

			₹
(a)	Decrease in value of WIP and finished goods inventory		
	as per F/A	1,28,21,995	
	as per cost account	1,31,04,220	
(b)	Profit on sale of fixed assets		61,500
(c)	Loss on sale of investments		11,200
(d)	Voluntary retirement compensation included in salaries and wages in F/A		16,75,000
(e)	Donation paid		25,000
(f)	Major repairs and maintenance written off in F/A (Amount reckoned in cost accounts ₹6,08,420 for this job)		13,26,000
(g)	Insurance claim relating to previous year received during the year		14,29,000
(h)	Profit from retail trading activity		7,12,300

You are required to prepare a reconciliation statement between the profit figures as per costing and financial accounts. (Calculate the profit as per financial books).

Solution

Reconciliation of profit between cost accounts and financial accounts for the year ended 31.3.2020

	₹	₹	₹
Profit as per cost accounts			73,24,150
Add: (a) Difference in valuation of stock:			
Decrease in inventory as per cost accounts	₹1,31,04,220		
Decrease in inventory as per financial accounts	₹1,28,21,995		
Hence, valuation in financial books is higher by		2,82,225	
(b) Profit on sales of assets not included in cost accounts		61,500	
(c) Receipts of insurance claim relating to previous year		14,29,000	
(d) Profit from trading activity		7,12,300	24,85,025
			98,09,175
Less: (a) Loss on sale of investments		11,200	
(b) Voluntary retirement compensation not included in cost		16,75,000	
(c) Donation paid		25,000	
(d) Part of repairs and maintenance costs excluded in cost accounts (13,26,000 – 6,08,420)		7,17,580	24,28,780
Profit as per financial accounts			73,80,395

Theory Questions

1. Explain the need for reconciliation of cost and financial accounts.
2. It has been stated that the results worked out from the costing records and those worked out from the financial accounts may not necessarily agree. Why?
3. Give reasons as to why it is necessary to reconcile cost accounts and financial accounts. What is the accounting procedure to be adopted for their reconciliation?
4. Indicate the reasons why it is necessary for the cost and financial accounts of an organisation to be reconciled and explain the main sources of difference which would enter into such reconciliation.
5. Discuss the main sources of difference between profit shown by financial accounts and profit shown by cost accounts.
6. Describe in brief the conditions which necessitate reconciliation of financial and cost records.
7. What is a reconciliation statement? Give reasons for the difference in profit as per cost accounts and financial accounts.
8. Why is reconciliation of cost and financial accounts necessary? State the possible reasons for difference between profits shown by both the accounts.
9. Enumerate any five causes of difference between profit shown by cost and financial records.
10. List out eight items, either debit or credit, which appear in financial accounts but do not appear in cost accounts.

Problems

1. The following transactions have been extracted from the financial books of a company:

		₹	*Units*
Sales		2,50,000	20,000
Materials		1,00,000	
Wages		50,000	
Factory overheads		45,000	
Office and administration overheads		26,000	
Selling and distribution overheads		18,000	
Closing stock;			
Finished goods		15,000	1,230
Work-in-progress:			
Materials	3,000		
Wages	2,000		
Factory overheads	2,000	7,000	
Goodwill written off		20,000	
Interest on capital		2,000	

In costing books factory overhead is charged at 100% on wages, administration overhead at 10% of factory cost and selling and distribution at the rate of ₹1 per unit sold. Prepare a statement reconciling the profit as per cost and financial accounts.

Ans: Profit as per cost accounts ₹30,000
Profit as per financial accounts ₹11,000

2. The following figures are available from financial accounts for the year ending 31st March, 2020:

	₹
Direct material consumption	2,50,000
Direct wages	1,00,000
Factory overheads	3,80,000
Administration overheads	2,50,000
Selling and distribution overheads	4,80,000
Bad debts	20,000
Preliminary expenses (written off)	10,000
Legal charges	5,000
Dividend received	50,000
Interest on deposit received	10,000
Sales 1,20,000 units	7,00,000
Closing stock:	
Finished stock = 40,000 units	1,20,000
Work-in-progress	80,000

The cost accounts reveal:

Direct material consumption—₹2,80,000

Factory overhead recovered at 20% on prime cost.

Administration overhead at ₹3 per unit of production.

Selling and distribution overhead at ₹4 per unit sold.

Prepare:

(a) Costing profit and loss account.
(b) Financial profit and loss account.
(c) Statement reconciling the profits disclosed by the costing profit and loss account and financial profit and loss account.

Ans: Loss as per Cost A/c ₹4,22,000
Loss as per Financial Books ₹5,35,000

3. During the year a company's profits have been estimated from the costing system to be ₹46,126, whereas the financial accounts audited by the auditors disclose a profit of ₹33,248. Given the following information, you are required to prepare a reconciliation statement showing clearly the reasons for the difference:

To opening stock	₹4,94,358		By sales	₹6,93,000
To purchases	1,64,308			
	6,58,666			
Less: Closing Stock	1,50,242	5,08,424		
To direct wages		46,266		
To factory overhead		41,652		
To gross profit c/d		96,658		
		6,93,000		6,93,000
To administration expenses		19,690	By gross profit b/d	99,658
To selling expenses		44,352	By sundry income	632
To net profit		33,248		
		97,290		97,290

(a) Stock ledger closing balance is ₹1,56,394;
(b) Credit balance in wages control account is ₹49,734;
(c) Credit balance in factory overhead control account is ₹39,428;
(d) Administration expenses are charged to sales at 3% of selling price in cost accounts;
(e) Selling price includes 5% (on sales) provision for selling expenses;
(f) Sundry income is not considered in cost accounts.

4. From the information given below, prepare
(i) a statement showing costing profit and loss; and
(ii) another statement reconciling the costing profits with those shown by financial accounts:

Profit and Loss Account for the Year Ending 31st March, 2020

	₹		₹
To materials consumed	1,05,000	By sales (1,50,000 units)	2,00,000
To direct wages	45,000		
To indirect factory expenses	30,000		
To office expenses	9,000		
To selling and distribution expenses	6,000		
To net profit	5,000		
	2,00,000		2,00,000

The normal output of the factory is 1,00,000 units. Factory expenses of a fixed nature are ₹18,000. Office expenses are for all practical purposes constant. Selling and distribution expenses are constant to the extent of ₹3,000 and the balance varies with sales.

Ans: Loss as per cost accounts, ₹10.000

5. Prepare a "Reconciliation Account" from the following details:

Profit as per cost accounts were of ₹59,700 while the profits as per financial accounts were of ₹60,000. The values of opening and closing stock as shown in cost accounts and financial accounts were as under:

	Financial Accounts	*Cost Accounts*
Raw materials:		
Opening	25,000	25,300
Closing	30,000	29,600
W.I.P		
Opening	16,000	15,500
Closing	20,000	19,900

6. From the following figures prepare reconciliation statement:

	₹
Profit as per costing records	5,000
Factory overheads under-recovered in costing	3,000
Selling and administration overheads over-recovered in costing	2,000
Bank interest credited in financial books	500
Preliminary expenses written off in financial books	6,500
Opening stock value:	
in cost books	5,000
in financial books	4,000
Closing stock value:	
in cost books	12,000
in financial books	10,000

Ans: Loss as per Financial Accounts = ₹3000

7. From the following information, reconcile the profit as per cost accounts with financial accounts:

	Cost Account	Financial Account
	₹	₹
Profit	86,250	
Opening stock:		
Material	10,500	10,300
Work-in-progress	8,500	8,000
Closing stock:		
Material	14,200	15,000
Work-in-progress	6,000	5,600

Dividend and interest received ₹600.
Loss on sale of investments ₹1,000.
Interest charged by the bank not considered in financial accounts and cost accounts ₹1,500.
Goodwill written off during the year ₹2,500.
Preliminary expenses written off ₹3,000.
Overhead incurred ₹40,000.
Overhead absorbed in cost accounts ₹38,500.
Find out profit as per financial accounts.

Ans: Profit as per financial accounts ₹79,950

8. From the following figure, prepare a reconciliation statement:

	Cost Books	*Financial Books*
	₹	₹
Profit	50,000	?
Marketing overheads	8,000	8,000
Provision for bad debts	—	5,000
Factory overheads	8,500	7,000
Director's fees	—	2,000
Income tax paid	—	15,000
Rent of owned premises	6,000	—
Depreciation	11,250	12,000
Share transfer fee (Cr.)	—	1,000
Administrative overheads	5,000	8,000

Ans: Profit as per financial books ₹32,750

9. From the following profit and loss account, draw up a Memorandum Reconciliation Account, showing the profit as per cost accounts:

Profit & Loss Account (as at 31.12.2020)

	₹		₹
To Office salaries	11,282	By gross profits	54,648
To Office expenses	6,514	By dividend received	400
To Salesmen's salaries	4,922	By interest on bank deposits	150
To Sales expenses	9,304		
To Distribution expenses	2,990		
To Loss on sale of machinery	1,950		
To Fines	200		
To Discount on debentures	100		
To Net profit	17,936		
	55,198		55,198
To Income tax	8,000	Net profit	17,936
To Reserve	1,000		
To Dividend	4,000		
To Balance c/d	4,936		
	17,936		17,936

The cost accountant of the company has ascertained a profit of ₹19,636 as per his books.

10. M/s Modern Company Limited furnished the summary of the trading, and profit and loss account for the year ending 31st December, 2020.

	₹			₹
To raw materials	1,39,600	By sales (12000 units)		4,80,000
To direct wages	76,200	By finished stock (200 units)		8,000
To production overheads	42,600			
To selling and distribution overheads	42,700	By work-in-progress:		
		Materials	28,200	
To administration overheads	39,100	Wages	11,796	
To preliminary expenses: written off	2,200	Production overhead	7,999	
				47,995
To goodwill written off	2,501	By interest on securities (gross)		6,000
To dividend (net)	3,000			
To income tax	4,100			
To net profit	1,89,994			
	5,41,995			5,41,995

The company manufactures a standard unit. Scrutiny of cost records for the same period shows that:

(i) Factory overheads have been allocated to the production at 20% on prime cost.

(ii) Administration overheads have been charged at ₹3 per unit on units produced.

(iii) Selling and distribution expenses have been charged at ₹4 per unit on units sold.

You are required to prepare a statement of cost and work out profit as per cost accounts and to reconcile the same with that shown in the financial accounts.

Ans: Profit as per Cost Accounts ₹1,88,493

11. The profit as per cost accounts is ₹1,65,300. The following details are ascertained on comparison of the cost and financial accounts.

	Cost Accounts	*Financial Accounts*
	₹	₹
(a) Opening Stocks:		
Materials	32,600	33,000
Work-in-progress	20,000	21,000
(b) Closing Stocks:		
Materials	36,000	34,400
Work-in-progress	16,000	15,200
Finished goods	8,000	9,000

(c) Directors' fees paid ₹1,000, interest paid ₹800; reserve for bad debts ₹500, transfer fees collected ₹300, and dividends received ₹200 are exclusively taken in financial accounts, but ignored in cost accounts.

(d) Rent charged in costing but not in financial accounts ₹6,000.

(e) Preliminary expenses written off ₹13,000, but not charged in costing.

(f) Overheads charged in financial books ₹1,21,200, but recovered in costing ₹1,26,200.

Find out profit as per financial accounts and draw up a "Reconciliation Statement".

Ans: Profit as per Financial Accounts, ₹1,58,700

12. A Company's trading, and profit and loss account was as follows:

Dr.			*Cr.*
			₹
To purchase	25,210	By sales: 50000 units	
Less: Closing stock	4,080	@ ₹1.50 each	75,000
	21,130	By discount received	260
To direct wages	10,500	By profit on sale of land	2,340
To work expenses	12,130		
To selling expenses	7,100		
To administration expenses	5,340		
To depreciation	1,100		
To net profit	20,300		
	77,600		77,600

The profit as per cost accounts was only ₹19,770. Reconcile the financial and cost profits using the following information:

(a) Cost accounts valued closing stock at ₹4,280.
(b) The work expenses in the cost accounts were taken at 100% of direct wages.
(c) Selling and administration expenses were charged in the cost accounts at 10% of sales and ₹0.10 per unit respectively.
(d) Depreciation in the cost accounts was ₹800.

13. The following is the trading, and profit & loss account of M/s Time and Tide Limited for the year ending 31st December, 2020.

	₹			₹
To materials consumed	7,08,000	By sales 30,000 units		15,00,000
To direct wages	3,71,000	By finished stock		
To works overheads	2,13,000	1000 units		40,000
To administration overheads	95,500	By work-in-progress:		
To selling and distribution		Material	17,000	
overheads	1,13,500	Wages	8,000	
To net profit for the year	69,000	Works overhead	5,000	30,000
	15,70,000			15,70,000

In manufacturing a standard unit, the company's cost records show that:

(i) Work overhead has been charged to work-in-progress at 20% on prime cost.
(ii) Administration overheads have been recovered as ₹3 per finished unit.
(iii) Selling and distribution overheads have been recovered as ₹4 per unit sold.
(iv) The under- or over-absorbed overheads have not been adjusted into the costing profit & loss account.

Prepare:

(i) A costing profit and loss account indicating net profit.
(ii) A statement reconciling the profit as disclosed by the cost accounts and that shown in the financial accounts.

Ans: Profit as per Cost Account ₹66,000

14. From the accounts of M/s Shankar & Co. Ltd. the trading, and profit & loss accounts are reproduced as follows:

	₹		₹
To raw materials:		By work-in-progress:	
Opening stock	29,500	Materials	4,000
Purchase	1,86,500	Wages	5,500
To wages	2,98,000	Work expenses	3,300
To work expenses	1,90,750	By cost of goods manufactured	6,59,950
		By closing stock of raw materials	32,000
	7,04,750		7,04,750
To cost of goods sold	6,59,950	By sales (7600 units)	9,12,000
To administrative expenses	1,22,500	By finished stock (1400 units)	1,17,600
		By interest on investment	6,800

	₹		₹
To selling and distribution expenses	1,64,000		
To bad debts written off	17,500		
To net profit transferred			
to appropriation A/c	72,450		
	10,36,400		10,36,400

The following information is also available:

1. Accrued wages of ₹17,000 included in wages.
2. Works expenses are allocated to production at 60 per cent of direct labour cost.
3. Administrative expenses are allocated at ₹12 per unit of production.
4. Selling and distribution expenses are allocated so as to work out 20% of selling price.

   Prepare the costing profit and loss account and statement of reconciliation between the two accounts (cost and financial).

Ans: Profit as per Cost Account ₹91,200

PART 4

Cost Analysis for Decision Making and Control

Part 4 explains the procedure of making cost analysis for managerial decision making, control and planning. Managers need to understand behaviour of costs for better planning, effective control and sound decision making. The topics covered in this part are variable costing, alternative choices decisions, pricing decisions, standard costing, budgeting, responsibility accounting and divisional performance measurement.

- *Marginal (Variable) Costing*
- *Alternative Choices Decisions*
- *Pricing Decisions*
- *Standard Costing*
- *Budgeting*
- *Responsibility Accounting and Divisional Performance Measurement*

Chapter 16

Marginal (Variable) Costing

Learning Objectives

After reading this chapter, you should be able to:

1. explain concepts of marginal cost, marginal and absorption costing;
2. distinguish between absorption costing and marginal costing, advantages and limitations of marginal costing;
3. describe the preparation of income statement under absorption costing and marginal costing;
4. discuss methods of determining cost behaviour, cost-volume-profit (CVP) analysis and its limitations, curvilinear break-even analysis; and
5. understand cost indifference point.

CONCEPT OF MARGINAL COST AND MARGINAL COSTING

Marginal cost, in cost accounting, means variable production costs, that is, the costs which tend to vary in direct proportion to the changes in the production level. If an extra unit of output is produced, the costs which could be incurred for producing this extra unit will only be marginal (variable) costs since fixed costs remain constant.

Marginal costing is a costing technique in which only variable manufacturing costs are considered and used while valuing inventories and determining cost of goods sold. That is, only variable manufacturing costs are considered product costs and are allocated to products manufactured. These costs include direct materials, direct labour and variable factory overhead. Fixed factory (manufacturing) overheads are not considered product costs and are not used to value inventories and determine the cost of goods sold and are excluded from the cost of product. Fixed manufacturing costs are treated as period costs in marginal costing, that is, costs which are a function of a time rather than of production. In marginal costing, fixed manufacturing overheads are written off to the profit and loss account in the period in which they are incurred.

Absorption Costing

Absorption costing, also known as full costing, is a costing technique in which all manufacturing costs, variable and fixed, are considered as costs of production and are used in determining the cost of goods manufactured and inventories. All manufacturing costs are fully absorbed into finished goods.

As stated above, absorption costing treats fixed production overheads as production costs and variable costing treats them as period costs. A production cost is the total direct cost (prime cost) plus absorbed production overhead (see Fig. 16.1a). A period cost is one which relates to a time period rather than to the output of products or services (see Fig. 16.1b).

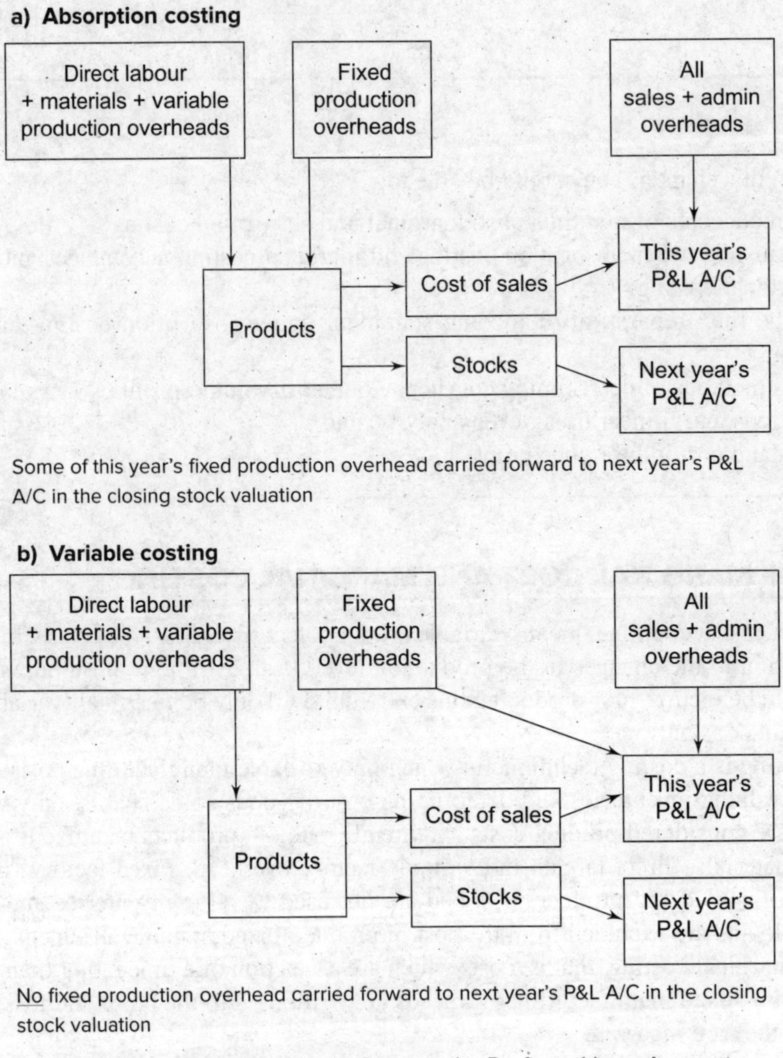

Fig. 16.1 Tracing Overhead Costs to the Profit and Loss Account

DIFFERENCE BETWEEN MARGINAL COSTING AND ABSORPTION COSTING

Marginal costing and absorption costing differ from each other in the following respects:

1. *Cost element in product cost* Marginal costing and absorption costing differ only in the treatment of fixed factory (manufacturing) overheads in the accounting records and financial statement. In both the costing techniques, it is agreed that selling and administrative expenses, whether variable or fixed, are period costs and these costs are not treated as product costs with the result that selling and administrative expenses are not included in the costs of inventories, and costs of goods sold. Similarly, it is also agreed that variable manufacturing costs are products costs, i.e., costs to be charged to the product. The disagreement between the two is only in regard to the treatment of fixed manufacturing costs.
The way the product cost is determined in absorption costing is illustrated in Fig. 16.2. Figure 16.2 shows the product cost as well as the total of direct costs (prime cost) and the production overheads.

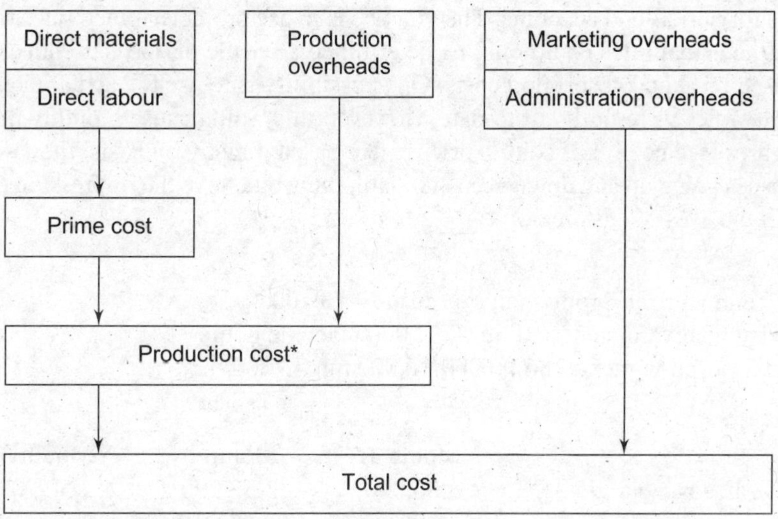

* This is used to value production and stock.
So, Production cost = Direct production cost + Indirect production cost.

Fig. 16.2 Outline of the Absorption Costing System

2. *Inventory values* Marginal costing and absorption costing do influence inventory values differently. The value of inventories under marginal costing is relatively at a lower figure as inventories are determined in terms of only variable production costs. In absorption costing, the value of inventories is comparatively at a higher figure because it considers fixed factory overhead also besides the variable production costs.

3. *Difference in net income* The treatment of fixed factory overhead brings differences in the net income figures in the two costing techniques. The magnitude of any difference in net income is a function of fixed manufacturing costs per unit and the change in inventory levels.

The question of difference in net income has been further explained in the following pages while discussing income statement under absorption costing and marginal costing.

INCOME STATEMENTS UNDER ABSORPTION COSTING AND MARGINAL COSTING

Income Statement under Absorption Costing

Under absorption costing, all costs are divided into three categories: manufacturing, selling, and administrative costs. In the income statement, all manufacturing costs (variable and fixed) are subtracted from the sales revenue to get a gross margin/gross profit on sales; and selling and administrative expenses (fixed and variable) are deducted from gross margin to arrive at the net income.

Chapter 6 showed how overhead absorption rates (OARs) are calculated via allocation, apportionment and an appropriate choice of the base. These OARs are used to determine the production cost and stock valuations for period-end accounts. The practice is to use pre-determined rates rather than actual rates. After all, the actual rates could only be determined after the period has ended, so selling price could not be based on actual absorption costs. One possibility is to use the actual rates of the last-but-one month so that rates were fairly up-to-date. However, this would cause monthly fluctuations in the product cost figures (see below). If selling prices were based directly on costs, they would be changed every month. Prices going up and down at each month-end would give the impression of instability and incompetence in the eyes of customers.

Annual Basis:

Estimated annual fixed-production overheads = ₹36,00,000
Estimated annual volume of activity = 12,000 machine hours
Overhead absorption rate = ₹36,00,000/12,000 mh = ₹300/mh

Monthly Basis:

	Month 1	Month 2	Month 3
Actual overheads incurred	3,00,000	3,52,000	2,50,000
Actual machine hours	1,000	1,100	909
Monthly actual OAR	₹300/mh	₹320/mh	₹275/mh

For these reasons, it is normal to calculate the OAR at the start of the year and apply it throughout. This means that the current year's production overhead cost and volume of activity used in the calculation are estimates rather than actual amounts. The major consequence of this is that the total amount of production overheads absorbed into product costs during the year is almost certainly going to be different from the amount of production overheads actually incurred. However, the profit and loss account must use the actual rather than the estimated figure. So, an adjustment is necessary to change the overheads in the profit and loss account from estimated to actual amounts.

It should be clearly understood that fixed manufacturing overheads are charged to units produced on the basis of per unit fixed manufacturing overhead rate obtained by dividing the standard fixed manufacturing overhead by normal output level as follows:

$$\frac{\text{Standard fixed manufacturing overhead}}{\text{Normal output (Capacity)}}$$

UNDER- AND OVER-ABSORPTION OF OVERHEADS

The first thing to note is that the overheads are absorbed by production and are in no way affected by sales volumes. Thus, if actual production volumes differ from planned volumes, either too much or too little, overhead will end up in the profit and loss account. (The greater the volume of production, the greater the amount of production overheads absorbed.) If actual sales volumes differ from planned volumes, no change will be caused to the amount of production overheads in the profit and loss account.

Pre-determined overhead absorption rate:

Estimated annual fixed production overheads = ₹5,00,000
Estimated annual volume of activity = 1,00,000 direct labour hours
Overhead absorption rate = ₹5,00,000/1,00,000 dlh = ₹5.00/dlh

If either of these estimates is incorrect (as they almost certainly will be), the amount of production overheads in the profit and loss account will be inaccurate.

i) Actual annual fixed production overheads = ₹5,25,000
   Actual annual volume of activity = 1,00,000 direct labour hours
   Overhead absorbed by production = 1,00,000 × ₹5.00
   = ₹5,00,000
   Underabsorption of overheads = ₹25,000 (5,00,000 – 5,25,000)
   Unless this adjustment is made, profit will be overstated by ₹25,000.
ii) Actual annual fixed production overheads = ₹5,00,000
   Actual annual volume of activity = 1,12,000 direct labour hours
   Overhead absorbed by production = 1,12,000 × ₹5.00
   = ₹5,60,000
   Over-absorption of overheads = ₹60,000 (5,60,000 – 5,00,000)
   Unless this adjustment is made, profit will be understated by ₹60,000.

If production is above or below the normal or standard output, adjustments are made for volume (capacity) variances. If the volume (capacity) variance is favourable, i.e., over-absorption (actual production being higher than normal capacity production), the amount of over-absorption is deducted from the total cost of goods manufactured and sold. If the volume (capacity) variance is unfavourable, i.e., under-absorption (actual production being lesser than normal capacity production), the amount of under-absorption is added to the cost of goods manufactured and sold. A proforma of income statement prepared under absorption costing is given in Fig. 16.3.

Income Statement (Absorption Costing)

		Amount ₹
Sales		
Less:	Manufacturing costs:	
	(1) Variable production costs:	
	Direct material cost	
	Direct labour cost	
	Variable manufacturing overhead	
	(2) Fixed factory (manufacturing) overhead	
	Cost of goods manufactured	
Add:	Beginning inventory	
	Cost of goods available for sale	
Less:	Closing inventory	
	Cost of goods sold	
	Over- or under-applied factory (manufacturing) overhead (Over-absorption to be deducted and under-absorption to be added)	
	Cost of goods sold at actual	
	Gross profit on sales	
Less:	Fixed selling and administrative expenses	
	Variable selling and administrative expenses	
	Net Income	

Fig. 16.3 Income Statement Proforma (Absorption Costing)

Income Statement under Marginal Costing

Under marginal costing, only variable costs of production (direct material, direct labour and variable manufacturing) are subtracted from sales revenue to determine a balance which is known by different names, such as marginal contribution, marginal income (profit), marginal revenue, marginal balance, profit pick-up, etc. All fixed costs, and variable selling, distribution and administrative costs are deducted from this balance to arrive at the net income. Since fixed manufacturing costs are not charged to products under marginal costing, there can be no volume (capacity) variance. Marginal contribution/marginal income under marginal costing is greater than the gross profit/gross margin under absorption costing. Figure 16.4 depicts a proforma of income statement prepared under marginal costing.

Under marginal costing, fixed manufacturing overheads are excluded, and therefore, inventory values are lower than inventory value computed under absorption costing. Income may be higher or lower depending upon whether inventories are built up or liquidated. That is, the income statement under absorption costing may reflect higher profit if the production is more than the normal capacity production and also lower sales has been made. This happens because above normal capacity production has over-absorbed its actual fixed manufacturing overhead.

Absorption/full costing and marginal costing influence differently gross profit, net profit, and inventory values of different month/periods. The following data and income statement prepared under both costing techniques explain this situation.

Income Statement (Marginal Costing)

		Amount (₹)
Sales		______
Less:	Variable production costs:	
	Direct material costs	______
	Direct labour cost	______
	Variable manufacturing (factory) overhead	______
	Cost of goods manufactured	______
Add:	Beginning inventory	______
	Cost of goods available for sale	______
Less:	Closing inventory	______
	Cost of goods sold	______
	Marginal contribution	______
Less:	Fixed manufacturing overhead	______
	Variable selling and administrative expenses	______
	Fixed selling and administrative expenses	______
	Net Income	______

Fig. 16.4 Income Statement Proforma (Marginal Costing)

Data:

Normal capacity is 20,000 units per month

Variable costs (direct materials, direct labour and variable factory overhead) per unit are ₹6.

Fixed factory overhead is ₹25,000 per month or ₹1.25 per unit at normal capacity.

Fixed selling and administrative expenses are ₹5,000 p.m.

Variable selling and administrative expenses are ₹1.00 per unit sold.

Sales price per unit is ₹10.

Actual production, sales and inventories in units are:

	First Month	Second Month	Third Month	Fourth Month
Units in beginning inventory	—	—	3,000	1,000
Units produced	17,500	21,000	19,000	20,000
Units sold	17,500	18,000	21,000	16,500
Units in closing inventory	—	3,000	1,000	4,500

Solution

Income Statement (Absorption Costing)

	First Month	Second Month	Third Month	Fourth Month
Sales	₹1,75,000	1,80,000	2,10,000	1,65,000
Variable cost per unit ₹6	1,05,000	1,26,000	1,14,000	1,20,000
Fixed factory overhead @ ₹1.25	21,875	26,250	23,750	25,000
Cost of goods manufactured	1,26,875	1,52,250	1,37,750	1,45,000
Add: Beginning inventory	—	—	21,750	7,250
Cost of goods available for sales	1,26,875	1,52,250	1,59,500	1,52,250
Less: Ending inventory	—	21,750	7,250	32,625
Cost of goods sold	1,26,875	1,30,500	1,52,250	1,19,625
Over- or under-applied factory overhead	3,125	(1,250)	1,250	—
Cost of goods sold at actual	1,30,000	1,29,250	1,53,500	1,19,625
Gross profit on sales	45,000	50,750	56,500	45,375
Selling and administrative expenses (fixed and variable)	22,500	23,000	26,000	21,500
Net income for the month	22,500	27,750	30,500.	23,875

NOTE:

In absorption costing income statement, fixed factory expenses are included in the unit cost and also in the inventory values.

(i) Ending inventory: Second month $\frac{3,000}{21,000} \times 1,52,250 = ₹21,750$

Third month $\frac{1,000}{22,000} \times 1,59,500 = ₹7,250$

$$\text{Fourth month } \frac{4,500}{21,000} \times 1,52,250 = ₹32,625$$

(ii) In first month, ₹3,125 is under-absorbed factory overhead due to production less than normal capacity and should be added to the cost of goods sold.

(iii) In the second month, ₹1,250 is over-absorbed factory overhead due to higher production and has therefore been subtracted.

(iv) In the third month, ₹1,250 is under-absorbed factory overhead and has been added back to cost of goods sold.

(v) In the fourth month, production is at normal capacity and there is no under- or over-absorption.

Income Statement (Marginal Costing)

	First month	*Second month*	*Third month*	*Fourth month*
Sales (₹)	1,75,000	1,80,000	2,10,000	1,65,000
Variable production cost:				
Variable manufacturing costs ₹6 per unit	1,05,000	1,26,000	1,14,000	1,20,000
Cost of goods manufactured	1,05,000	1,26,000	1,14,000	1,20,000
Add: Beginning inventory	—	—	18,000	6,000
Cost of goods available for sale	1,05,000	1,26,000	1,32,000	1,26,000
Less: Closing inventory	—	18,000	6,000	27,000
Cost of goods sold	1,05,000	1,08,000	1,26,000	99,000
Contribution	70,000	72,000	84,000	66,000
Less: Fixed factory overhead	25,000	25,000	25,000	25,000
Fixed selling and administrative expenses	5,000	5,000	5,000	5,000
Variable selling and administrative expenses	17,500	18,000	21,000	16,500
Total fixed costs and non-manufacturing variable costs	47,500	48,000	51,000	46,500
Net income for the month	22,500	24,000	33,000	19,500

NOTE:

Under marginal costing, fixed factory (manufacturing) overhead costs are not included in the product unit costs and costs of inventories.

(i) Valuation of closing inventory

Second month = 3,000 × ₹6 = ₹18,000

Third month = 1,000 × ₹6 = ₹ 6,000

Fourth month = 4,500 × ₹6 = ₹27,000

(ii) The question of under- or over-absorption of factory overhead does not arise under marginal costing.

A comparison of the income statements leads to the following conclusions:

1. Under variable costing, the closing inventory is costed at a smaller figure because only variable production costs are charged to the product.
2. Both costing methods report the same amount of profit in periods in which production and sales are equal and there is no inventory change (first month). This is because the amount of fixed factory overhead costs charged to the period was the same in each case. Under marginal costing, ₹25,000 was deducted from sales as period costs. Under absorption costing, ₹25,000 was charged to the sales in two parts; (a) ₹21,875 as part of the cost of sales (17,500 units × ₹1.25); and (b) ₹3,125 as unfavourable volume (capacity) variance.
3. When inventory of manufactured goods fluctuates from period to period, net income will differ somewhat under the two methods because absorption costing requires that part of the period costs be included in inventory, whereas marginal costing excludes period costs. Therefore:
   (i) When production exceeds sales (the inventory is increased), the net income reported under absorption costing is higher than that reported under variable costing. This follows because under absorption costing, a portion of the fixed costs budgeted for the period is shifted to the following period in the closing inventories whereas under marginal costing the total fixed costs are charged against income. This is clear from comparing the net income of the second and fourth month.
   (ii) When sale exceeds production (the inventories are decreased), marginal costing shows a higher profit because only current period costs are being charged against current revenues, whereas under absorption costing the period costs previously included in inventory are now being charged against current revenues. This situation is illustrated by the income of the third month.
4. Under marginal costing, profits always move in the same direction as sales volume. They cannot, of course, increase or decrease in direct proportion because unit fixed costs do not remain constant. Profit reported under absorption costing behave irregularly and sometimes in the opposite direction from sales. For example, sales of the fourth month are lower than the sales of the first month, yet the net income reported for the fourth month is higher than the net income for the first month.
5. The above income statements are prepared on the assumption that selling prices remained constant and that there were no changes in either the manufacturing costs or the selling and administrative expenses. Further, it has been assumed that overheads costs are absorbed at predetermined rates based on normal capacity.
6. The aggregate net income (of different months or periods taken together) will be the same under both costing methods provided production and sales, in total, are equal. In the above example, total production is 77,500 units and total sales are 73,000 units. Since production and sales are unequal, the combined net income is not the same.

Reconciliation of Net Income

The differences in the net income between absorption costing and marginal costing are due to: (i) amount of fixed factory overhead charged to inventory, (ii) Over- or under-absorbed fixed factory overhead having been deferred in absorption costing. The entire difference in net income can be explained by the amount of fixed factory overhead that is included in the beginning and closing inventories.

Reconciliation of Differences between Absorption and Marginal Costing Income

	Second Month (₹)	Third Month (₹)	Fourth Month (₹)
Marginal costing income	24,000	33,000	19,500
Absorption costing income	27,750	30,500	23,875
Difference to be explained	(3,750)	2,500	(4,375)
1. Differences in the value of opening and closing inventories:			
(a) Second month:			
Opening	0	—	—
Closing 18,000–21,750	(3,750)		
(b) Third month:			
Opening 18,000–21,750	—	3,750	
Closing 6,000–7,250	—	(1,250)	—
(c) Fourth month:			
Opening 6,000–7,250	—	—	(1,250)
Closing 27,000–32,625	—	—	(5,625)
	(3,750)	2,500	(4,375)

Inventory Values

Differences between the net incomes reported under absorption costing and marginal costing are also reflected in inventory values. As stated earlier, inventories under absorption costing absorb a part of the fixed manufacturing costs of a period, whereas inventories under marginal costing include only the variable manufacturing costs. Closing inventories calculated from the data given above would be as follows:

Closing Inventories

	First Month	Second Month	Third Month	Fourth Month
Absorption costing @ ₹7.25 per unit	—	21,750	7,250	32,625
Marginal costing @ ₹6.00 per unit	—	18,000	6,000	27,000

The following summarises the differences between marginal costing and absorption costing with regard to effect on net income:

1. If production = sales; absorption profit = marginal costing profit.
2. If production > sales; absorption profit > marginal costing profit.
3. If production < sales; absorption profit < marginal costing profit.
4. If production fluctuates and sales are constant; absorption profit fluctuates and marginal costing profit is constant.
5. If production is constant and sales fluctuates; both profits vary in the direction of sales.

APPLICATIONS (ADVANTAGES) OF MARGINAL COSTING

The marginal costing has great potentialities for management in different managerial tasks and decision-making processes. Marginal costing is particularly useful to management in (i) profit planning, (ii) product pricing decisions, (iii) cost control, (iv) managerial decision-making, and (v) the impact of fixed costs.

Profit Planning

Profit planning, generally known as budget or plan of operations, may be defined as the planning of future operations to attain a defined profit goal. Under marginal costing, the cost data needed for profit planning and decision-making are readily available from the accounting records and statements. It facilitates the analysis of cost-volume-profit relationships by separating fixed and variable costs on the income statement. Marginal costing helps management in planning and evaluating the profit resulting from a change in volume, in the sales-mix, in make or buy situations, in the selection of the most profitable products, customers, territories, and other segments of the entire business.

Product Pricing Decisions

Marginal costing provides more useful information to management for pricing than absorption costing. Marginal costing serves as the basis of product pricing in many cases. Under marginal costing, management has the data to determine when it is advisable to accept orders if other than normal conditions exist. In some cases, a sales order can be accepted even if it contributes partly to fixed costs. However, the full cost and not only the variable cost should be the basis of product pricing in the long run. The full cost is the cost which includes variable manufacturing cost and fixed manufacturing cost incurred in the production process.

Cost Control

Marginal costing provides continuing opportunities to review period costs in relation to the level of sales and net income. Separation of variable and period costs supports the use of standards, budgets, and responsibilities reporting to aid management in controlling costs. Marginal costing helps in preparing reports for all departments or responsibility centres based on standard costs, flexible budgets, and a division of all costs into their fixed and variable components. All managers can examine and interpret their reports with respect to the cost variances originating in their respective areas of responsibility. Reports prepared on the marginal costing basis and accompanied by additional information become valuable planning and control tools.

Impact of Fixed Costs

Marginal costing evaluates the impact of fixed costs on profits because the total amount of fixed costs for the period appears in the income statement. It is argued that managerial decisions can be easily made if fixed expenses are separated and are not mixed, in controlling operating costs.

Managerial Decision Making

The identification and classification of costs, as either fixed or variable, provide a framework for the accumulation and analysis of costs. This also provides a basis for the study of contemplated changes in production levels or proposed actions concerning new markets, plant expansion or contraction, or special promotional activities. The marginal income figure is useful figure to management because it can be readily projected to measure increments in net income which accompany increments in sales.

LIMITATIONS OF MARGINAL COSTING

The limitations of marginal costing are listed below:

1. The marginal costing method requires that all costs should be divided into fixed and variable components. It cannot be true under all circumstances. Examples of factors that might affect this assumption include quantity discounts on materials, and labour efficiency variances.
2. Complete product cost does not depend only on variable costs. Fixed costs should be considered in determining the product cost, for long-range pricing and other long-run policy decisions.
3. Income figure obtained under marginal costing has to be used carefully if management decides to expand business or drop a product line. Management has to consider other factors also before deciding to drop a product line such as customer goodwill.

COST BEHAVIOUR

Cost behaviour can be defined as the manner in which costs changes due to changes in volume or activity. In relation to cost behaviour analysis, fixed and variable cost classifications are generally found. A proper analysis of cost behaviour patterns is the basis of all profit planning and cost control. The separation of costs into fixed, variable and semi-variable is necessary in order to determine, analyse, control, measure or evaluate the following:

1. Departmental expenses allowed at various levels of production.
2. Operating efficiency of a department.
3. Use of variable costing method.
4. Utilisation of facilities.
5. Break-even point.
6. Relative profitability of territories, departments and customers.
7. Company profit position.
8. Cost-volume-profit analysis.
9. Marginal or differential cost for various decision-making purposes.
10. Effect of proposed capital expenditures.
11. Effect of alternative courses of action.

METHODS OF DETERMINING COST BEHAVIOUR

Several methods are used for segregating semi-variable costs into fixed and variable. There are four major techniques that are found in practice and they may be listed as follows:

1. High and low points method
2. Scattergraph method

3. Least squares regression method
4. Accounting or analytical approach.

High and Low Points Method

This approach considers the difference in total cost between two different volumes, and divides the incremental cost by the volume. As the words "high" and "low" imply the two levels of volume chosen are the highest and the lowest for the period under review. The result of this division is the estimated variable cost per unit. Then, the average activity level is computed together with the average cost for the periods in the data base. The fixed cost is estimated by taking the total average cost and subtracting the variable cost for the average activity level. The variable cost is computed by multiplying the average activity level by the variable cost per unit as determined above.

As a simple illustration, assume that a company incurred the following costs in two periods (high and low) in which 5,000 units and 10,000 units were produced:

	Cost Incurred	
	5,000 units	10,000 units
Insurance on factory building	₹30,000	₹30,000
Indirect material	₹45,000	₹70,000

Since insurance remained constant at the two volumes, there is no variable component. Indirect materials contain both a fixed and variable components.

Separation is made as follows:

Variable components:		
Indirect material cost of 10,000 units		₹70,000
Indirect material cost of 5,000 units		₹45,000
Cost of production of additional 5,000 units		₹25,000
Variable cost per unit ₹25,000 ÷ 5000 units		₹5
Fixed components:	5,000 units	10,000 units
Total indirect material cost	₹45,000	₹70,000
Variable components @ ₹5 per unit	₹25,000	₹50,000
Fixed costs for period	₹20,000	₹20,000

Scattergraph Method

In this method, various costs are plotted on a vertical line, the *y*-axis, and measurement figures (activity levels such as direct labour hours, units of output, percentage of capacity or direct labour cost) are plotted along a horizontal line, the *x*-axis. A straight line is fitted to this scatter of points by visual approximation. The slope of the line is used to estimate the variable costs and the intercept of the line with the vertical axis is considered as the estimated fixed cost.

Least Squares Regression Method

The method of least squares uses the equation for a straight line:

$Y = a + bx$, with a as the fixed element, and b as the degree of variability. For many accounting applications, regression provides an accurate estimate of fixed and variable costs.

Accounting or Analytical Approach

This approach to cost behaviour analysis is a close scrutiny of the chart of accounts and a classification of costs into their fixed and variable components according to their basic characteristics determined by the accountant using good judgement, knowledge, and experience. This approach is simple and inexpensive but in its simplicity lies its inherent weakness. The results obtained are not accurate and may happen to be mere guesses.

EXAMPLE 16.1

The following are the maintenance costs incurred in a machine shop for six months with corresponding machine hours:

Month	*Machine Hours*	*Maintenance Costs*
		₹
January	2,000	30,000
February	2,200	32,000
March	1,700	27,000
April	2,400	34,000
May	1,800	28,000
June	1,900	29,000
Total:	12,000	1,80,000

Analyse the maintenance cost which is semi-variable into fixed and variable element.

Solution

Computation of variable cost and fixed cost has been done according to range method.

	Machine Hours	*Maintenance Costs*
		₹
Highest point, April	2,400	34,000
Lowest point, March	1,700	17,000
	700	7,000

$$\text{Variable cost per machine hour} = \frac{\text{Change in maintenance costs}}{\text{Change in hours}}$$

$$= 7,000 \div 700 = ₹10$$

Total variable cost for 2,400 machine hours will be 2,400 × ₹10 = ₹24,000

Hence, fixed cost is (₹34,000 – ₹24,000) = ₹10,000

Analysis of Maintenance Cost into Fixed and Variable Element

	Machine Hours	*Maintenance Cost (₹)*	*Fixed Cost (₹)*	*Variable Cost (₹)*
January	2,000	30,000	10,000	20,000
February	2,200	32,000	10,000	22,000
March	1,700	27,000	10,000	17,000
April	2,400	34,000	10,000	24,000
May	1,800	28,000	10,000	18,000
June	1,900	29,000	10,000	19,000

COST-VOLUME-PROFIT (CVP) ANALYSIS

Profits of business firms are the result of many factors such as: (i) selling prices, (ii) volume of sales, (iii) unit variable costs, (iv) total fixed costs and (v) combinations in which the various product lines are sold, etc. To do an effective job in planning, management must have analyses which allow reasonably correct predictions of how profits will be affected by a change in any one of these factors. A cost-volume-profit (CVP) analysis is useful to management in knowing how profit is influenced by sales volume, sales price, variable expenses and fixed expenses.

Broadly, CVP analysis uses the techniques of (i) Break-even analysis and (ii) Profit-volume (P/V) analysis.

Break-even Analysis

A break-even analysis indicates at what level cost and revenue are equal and there is no profit and no loss. It is a simple and easily understandable method of presenting to management the effect of changes in volume on profits. Detailed analysis of break-even data will reveal to management the effect of alternative decisions which reduce or increase costs and which increase sales volume and income. It is a device which portrays the effects of any type of future planning by evaluating alternative courses of action.

Break-even Point

The break-even point can be defined as the point or sales level at which profit is zero and there is no loss. That is, break-even point is that point at which total costs are equal to total sales revenue. At the break-even point profit being zero, contribution (sales-variable cost) is equal to the fixed cost. If the actual volume of sales is higher than the break-even volume, there will be a profit. Beyond the break-even point, all the marginal contribution represents income.

Assume that a company manufactures and sells a single product as follows:

Selling price per unit = ₹20

Variable cost per unit = ₹10

Total fixed cost = ₹1,00,000

The break-even sales to cover fixed costs will be 10,000 units,

$$\text{Selling price per unit} = ₹20$$

$$\text{Variable cost per unit} = ₹10$$

$$\text{Contribution} = ₹10$$

$$\text{Break-even volume} = \frac{₹1,00,000 \text{ fixed cost}}{₹10 \text{ contribution margin}}$$

$$= 10,000 \text{ units.}$$

If the company can sell more than 10,000 units, it will earn profits because fixed costs remain constant. If less than 10,000 units are sold, a loss will be incurred. The profits will be equal to the number of units sold in excess of 10,000 units multiplied by the unit contribution margin. For example, if 25,000 units are sold, the company will be operating at 15,000 units above its break-even point and will earn a profit of ₹1,50,000 (15,000 units × ₹10 contribution margin).

Break-even Formula

The break-even point can be obtained directly by a mathematical formula. The basic formula to find out the break-even point is:

$$\text{Break-even sales (units)} = \frac{\text{Fixed cost}}{\text{Contribution margin per unit}}$$

$$\text{Break-even sales (volume)} = \frac{\text{Fixed cost}}{\text{C/S ratio (also known as P/V ratio*)}}$$

$$\text{Break-even sales volume} = \frac{\text{Total fixed expenses}}{1 - \text{Total variable expenses/Total sales volume}}$$

$$\text{Cash break-even point (units)} = \frac{\text{Cash fixed cost}}{\text{Cash contribution per unit}}$$

* C/S ratio is popularly known as P/V ratio because after fixed costs are fully recovered, that is, after break-even point, all contributions (sales-variable costs) become profit. However, before break-even point all contributions will not become profit since fixed costs are yet to be recovered.

Break-even Chart

Total revenues and total costs at different sales volume can be estimated and plotted on a break-even chart. This chart is constructed as follows:

1. A horizontal base line, the *x*-axis, is drawn and spaced into equal distances representing either plant capacity, or sales volume, or number of units.
2. A vertical line, the *y*-axis is drawn on the left side of the chart and also spaced into equal parts. This line indicates sales revenue and also costs.
3. A line parallel to the horizontal line (*x*-axis) is drawn for fixed costs.
4. A total cost line is drawn starting at the *y*-axis fixed cost point and moving to the right. This total cost line represents the total of all items of cost, fixed and variable.
5. The sales line is drawn starting at the zero point on the vertical axis and ending at the top on the right side.

6. The total cost line intersects the sales line at a point which is known as the break-even point.
7. The area to the left of the break-even point between the total cost line and the sales line is the loss area; the profit area lies to the right of the break-even point above the total cost line.

The data from the previous example are presented on the break-even chart (see Fig. 16.5).

From Fig. 16.5, it can be observed that the break-even point occurs when sales are 10,000 units at ₹2,00,000.

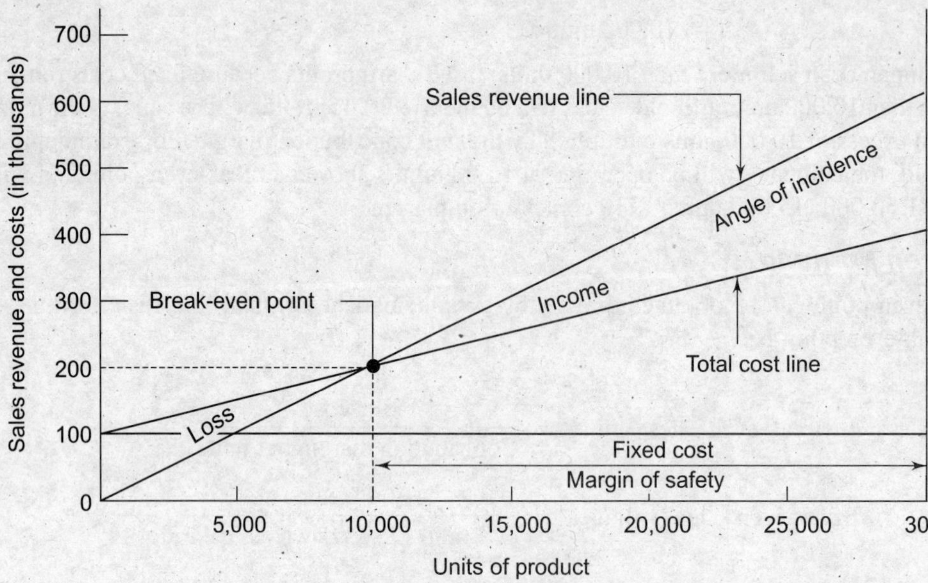

Fig. 16.5 Break-even Chart

Cash Break-even Point

If a firm has a minimum of available cash or the opportunity cost of holding excess cash is high, management may want to know the volume of sales that will cover all cash expenses, during a period. This is known as the cash break-even point.

Not all fixed operating costs involve cash payments. For example, depreciation expense is a non-cash charge. To find the cash break-even point, the non-cash charges must be subtracted from total fixed operating costs. Therefore, the cash break-even point is lower than the usual break-even point. The formula is:

$$\text{BEP} = \frac{FC - d}{P - V}$$

where P is selling price per unit

V is unit variable cost

FC is fixed operating costs

d is depreciation expenses

Thus, cash break-even point indicates break-even sales to cover only the fixed costs involving cash payments and to break-even.

This is illustrated below:

Let sales 20,000 units at ₹10 per unit

Variable costs, ₹4 per unit

Fixed cost ₹50,000 including depreciation, ₹10,000

Preference divided to be paid ₹20,000

Taxed to be paid ₹25,000

Assume that there are no lags in payment.

Break-even point (in units) will be 6667 units as displayed in Fig. 16.6.

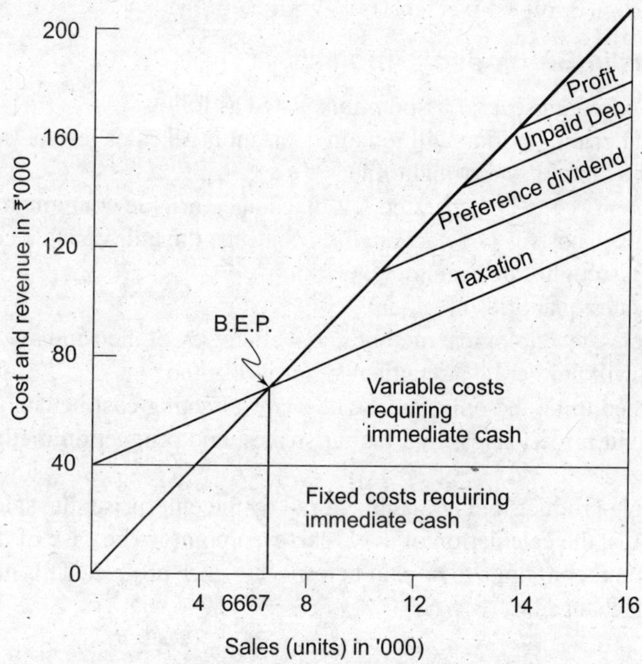

Fig. 16.6 Break-even Chart

Margin of Safety

This is the difference between sales and the break-even point. If the distance is relatively short, it indicates that a small drop in production or sales will reduce profits considerably. If the distance is long, it means that the business can still make profits even after a serious drop in production. It is important that there should be a reasonable margin of safety; otherwise a reduced level of production may prove dangerous. The margin of safety can be found by using the following formula:

$$\text{Margin of safety} = \text{Profit} \div \text{P/V ratio}$$

or

$$\text{Margin of safety} = \frac{\text{Profit} \times \text{Sales}}{\text{Sales} - \text{Variable cost}}$$

Angle of Incidence

This is the angle at which the sales line cuts the total cost line. Management's aim will be to have as large an angle of incidence as possible because a large angle of incidence shows a high rate of profit. A narrow angle would show that even fixed overheads are absorbed and profit accrues at a relatively low rate of return, indicating that variable costs form a large part of cost of sales.

Sales Formula

Often, it is necessary to know what level of sales is required to achieve a desired level of profit. The desired sales can be expressed in various ways:

Sales = Fixed cost + Variable cost + Profit

Sales = (Profit + Fixed cost) / P/V ratio

Basic Assumptions in Break-even Analysis

Break-even analysis is based on several assumptions listed as follows:

1. Selling prices and pricing policy will remain constant at all sales levels. If this is not true, sales revenue cannot be plotted as a straight line.
2. All costs and expenses can be separated into fixed and variable components.
3. The total of the fixed costs is constant at all sales levels; the unit variable costs remain the same. If this is not true, straight lines cannot be drawn.
4. Production and sales quantities are equal.
5. Managerial policies, technological methods, and efficiency of men and machines will not change and cost control will neither be strengthened nor weakened.
6. Volume is assumed to be the only important factor affecting cost behaviour. Other influencing factors such as unit prices, sales-mix, labour strikes, and production methodology remain constant.
7. In case of multiple products being manufactured by the enterprise, the sales-mix should remain unchanged. That is, the calculation of the break-even point in the case of multiple products predetermines the number of units to be sold in respect of each product. This multiproduct sales-mix should remain unchanged.

Curvilinear Break-even Analysis

Break-even analysis is based on the assumption that total sales line and total cost line are straight lines and have linear relationship between them. However, in reality, this may not be true and there may be no linear relationship between total sales line and total cost line. This may be due to the following reasons:

First, sales value may decline after demand level has reached at the saturation point.

Second, average variable cost per unit may decrease if a firm gets discount on the bulk purchase of raw materials when output increases.

In another situation, when the plant is being operated at higher capacity to have higher production, there is likely to be breakdowns and bottle-necks making variable cost per unit to increase. Therefore, after a particular level of output, variable cost per unit may increase.

In such cases, the contribution will not increase in linear proportion, that is, the total cost line will not be straight, as assumed but will be of curvilinear shape. This situation will give rise to two break-even points. The optimum profit is earned at the point where the distance between sales and total cost is the greatest. This is displayed in Fig. 16.7.

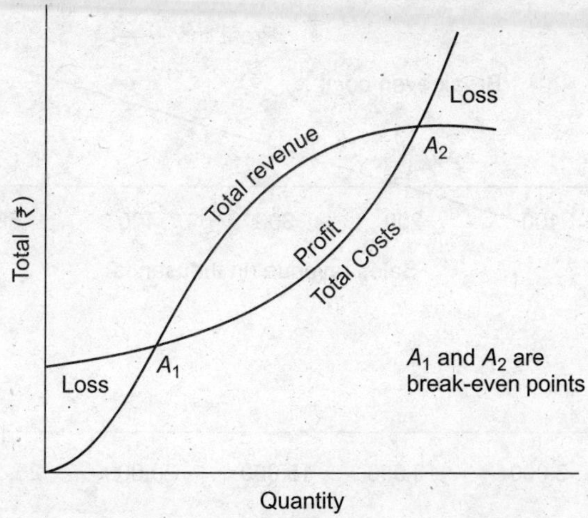

Fig. 16.7 Curvilinear Break-even Chart

Profit/Volume (P/V) Analysis

A P/V graph is sometimes used in place of or along with a break-even chart. Profits and losses are given on a vertical scale; and units of products, sales revenue or percentage of activity are given on a horizontal line. The horizontal line is drawn on the graph to separate profits from losses. The profits and losses at various sales levels are plotted and connected by the profit line. The break-even point is measured at the point where the profit line intersects the horizontal line. The P/V graph may be preferred to the break-even chart because profit and losses at any point can be read directly from the vertical scale; but the P/V graph does not clearly show how costs vary with activity.

Data used earlier to prepare the break-even chart are also used in preparing the P/V graph (see Fig. 16.8).

A cost-volume profit analysis can be used to measure the effect of factor changes and management decision alternatives on profits. These factors include possible changes in selling prices, changes in variable or fixed cost, expansion or contraction of sales volume, or other changes in operating methods or policies. Cost-volume profit analysis is also useful for problems of product pricing, sales-mix, adding or deleting product lines, and accepting special orders.

Changes in Selling Prices

The CVP graph is frequently used to illustrate the potential profit effects of contemplated price changes. Effects on the profit pattern are as follows:

1. *Increase in selling price* If the selling price is increased, it increases the P/V ratio, and the rate of fixed costs recovery is increased. The break-even point (break-even volume) declines, profit beyond the break-even point increases, losses below the break-even point decreases.

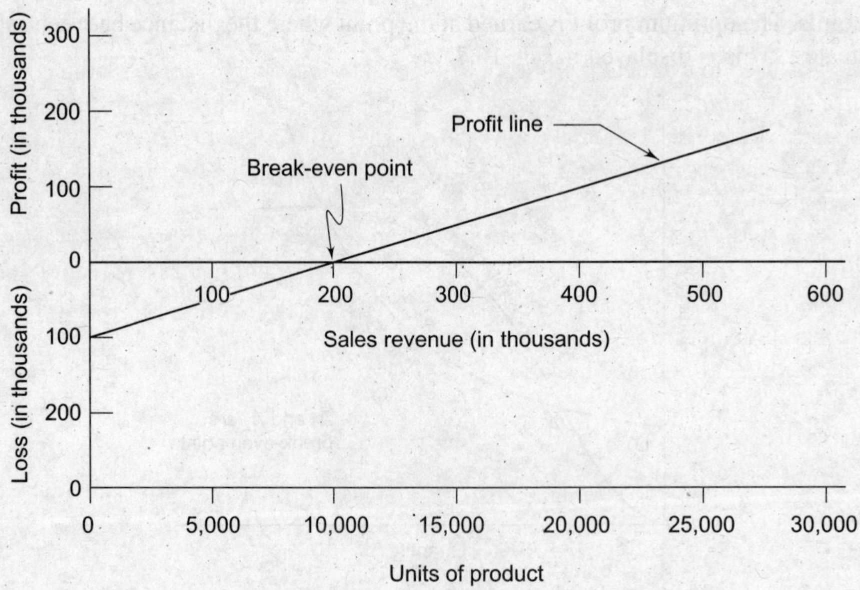

Fig. 16.8 Profit Volume (P/V) Graph

2. *Decrease in selling price* If the selling price decreases, it decreases the P/V ratio and the rate of fixed cost recovery declines. The break-even point increases.

Assume, for example, that a company produces a product with a selling price of ₹10 per unit and a variable cost of ₹4 per unit. Fixed costs are ₹36,000 per year. The effect of a 20% increase and 20% decrease in the present selling price is given below:

	Selling Price		
	Present	*20% Increase*	*20% Decrease*
Selling price per unit	₹10.00	₹12.00	₹8.00
Variable cost per unit	4.00	4.00	4.00
Marginal contribution per unit	6.00	8.00	4.00
P/V ratio	60%	$66\frac{2}{3}\%$	50%
Fixed costs	36,000	36,000	36,000
Break-even point in units	6,000	4,500	9,000
In volume	60,000	54,000	72,000
Changes in break-even point	–	–	–
In units	0%	– 25%	+ 50%
In sales volume	0%	– 10%	+ 20%

Changes in Variable Costs

The CVP graph is used to evaluate the impact of increases and decreases in variable costs per unit.

1. *Increase in variable costs* An increase in variable costs has the same effect as a decrease in the selling price. It decreases the P/V ratio and the rate of fixed cost recovery is slower. The break-even point moves to higher level; profits after the break-even point decreases; losses before the break-even point increases.
2. *Decrease in variable costs* A decrease in variable costs has the same effect as an increase in the selling price. A higher P/V ratio is achieved and the rate of fixed costs recovery is increased. The break-even point declines, profits beyond the break-even point are higher; losses before the break-even point are lower.

To illustrate the effect of change in variable costs, assume a company is selling a product for ₹40 a unit and has a variable cost of ₹20 per unit. Fixed costs total ₹48,000 per year. The effects of a 20% increase and a 20% decrease in variable cost are given in the following table:

	Present Variable Cost (₹)	*20% Increase* (₹)	*20% Decrease* (₹)
Unit selling price	40.00	40.00	40.00
Variable cost per unit	20.00	24.00	16.00
Marginal contribution	20.00	16.00	24.00
P/V ratio	50%	40%	60%
Fixed costs	48,000	48,000	48,000
Break-even point:			
Sales volume	96,000	1,20,000	80,000
Units	2,400	3,000	2,000

Changes in Fixed Cost

Increases and decreases in the fixed cost do not have any impact on the P/V ratio but they change the break-even point. With the same P/V ratio, the rate of the fixed costs recovery remains the same.

1. *Increase in fixed costs* If fixed costs are increased, the break-even point (break-even-volume) is higher. Profits above the break-even point are lower by the amount of the increase in fixed costs; below the break-even point losses increase by the amount of increase.
2. *Decrease in fixed costs* If fixed costs are decreased, it lowers the break-even point. The profits are greater by the amount of the decrease, and losses are smaller by the amount of the decrease in fixed costs.

Assume that a company has a P/V ratio of 40% and present fixed costs of ₹50,000. The effects of change in the fixed costs by ₹10,000 are as follows:

	Present Fixed Cost	*Increase By* ₹10,000	*Decrease By* ₹10,000
Fixed costs	₹50,000	₹60,000	₹40,000
P/V ratio	40%	40%	40%
Break-even point (₹)	1,25,000	1,50,000	1,00,000
Decrease	0	+25,000	– 25,000

From the above example, it is clear that the P/V ratio is the same in each situation and break-even point can be determined by dividing the amount of the change by the P/V ratio:

$$\frac{\text{Change in fixed costs}}{\text{P/V ratio}}$$

$$= \frac{₹10{,}000}{40\,\%} = ₹25{,}000$$

DESIRED OR TARGET PROFIT

Sometimes, management faces two decisions: (i) to increase sales volume through reduction in selling prices, and (ii) to increase selling prices in case the P/V ratio is low, with the expectation that a higher profit will be earned. These decisions should be taken carefully after studying the profit pattern and other factors; otherwise the results can be harmful particularly for those companies whose P/V ratios are already low. Also, if reduction in selling prices does not increase the sales volume, the price reduction will result only in lower profits. Price cuts, like increase in variable unit costs, decrease the contribution margin. On a unit basis, price decreases may appear to be insignificant, but when the unit differential is multiplied by thousands of units, the total effect may be significant. Perhaps, many more units will have to be sold to make up the loss in profit or to earn a target profit.

Assume that Company A hopes to increase its profits by selling more units; and to sell more, it plans to reduce its prices by 10%. The present price and cost structure and the desired one are given below:

	Present Price and Cost	*Desired Price and Cost*
Selling price	₹50	₹45
Variable cost	25	25
Contribution margin	25	20
Contribution margin (%)	50%	44.4%

At present, the contribution margin being 50%, Company A will break-even when sales are twice the fixed costs. This means that if fixed costs are ₹1,00,000, 4,000 units must be sold to earn a revenue of ₹2,00,000. But when the price is reduced to recover ₹1,00,000 in fixed costs, sales revenue must amount to ₹2,25,000. Not only must the revenue be higher but with a lower price per unit, more units must be sold to obtain that revenue; 5,000 units must be sold just to break-even. To overcome the effect of the cut in price, sales volume in physical units must be increased by 25%.

5,000 units to be sold at a lower price to break-even.
4,000 units to be sold at present price to break-even.
1,000 Increase in number of units.

$$\frac{1{,}000}{4{,}000} = 25\%$$

Sales revenue must be increased by $12\frac{1}{2}\%$.

₹2,25,000 sales revenue at new break-even point.
₹2,00,000 sales revenue at present break-even point.
₹25,000 increase in sales revenue.

$$\frac{25,000}{2,00,000} = \frac{1}{8} = 12\frac{1}{2}\%$$

The increase in sales volume required to overcome the effect of a price reduction is relatively greater when the rate of the contribution margin per unit is relatively low. If a product makes only a small contribution, then a reduction in selling price makes it all the more difficult to recover the fixed costs and to earn profits.

Similarly, a business firm may think of increasing the selling price if the P/V ratio is low. However, increase in selling price may reduce the sales volume.

Suppose, a company has the following present and proposed costs and selling price structure:

	Present	*Proposed*
Selling price per unit	₹100	₹120
Variable cost per unit	70	70
Contribution per unit	30	50
P/V Ratio	30%	41.67%
Increase in contribution	–	20

Decrease in the present sales volume without effecting the present $= \frac{20}{50} = 40\%$

If there is a 20% increase in the selling price, the sales volume should not decline by more than 40%. If decline in sales volume is less than 40% the profit position would be improved. Thus, any company with a P/V ratio of 30% can raise its selling price by 20% and absorbed a 40% reduction in sales volume without reduction in net income regardless of the amount of fixed costs involved.

MULTI-PRODUCT SITUATIONS

When there are multiple products with different contribution margins, the mix of the product has a direct effect on the fixed costs recovery and total profits of the firm. Different products have different P/V ratios because of different selling prices and variable costs. Some products make larger contributions to fixed cost recovery and profit than others. The total profits depend to some extent upon the proportions in which the products are sold.

For example, assume that a company with fixed costs of ₹25,000 per year manufactures two products A and B with P/V ratios as follows:

	Product A	*Product B*
Unit selling price	₹10	₹20
Variable costs	4	16
Marginal contribution	6	4
P/V ratio	60%	20%

With comparatively low variable costs, product A has a relatively high P/V ratio; each unit of product A sold contributes ₹6 to fixed costs recovery and profit. Product B, with comparatively high variable costs, has a low P/V ratio; each unit sold contributes only ₹4 to fixed costs recovery and profit. Other things being equal, the sale of product A is more profitable than that of product B, despite the fact that the selling price of product B is twice that of product A. It is correct to say that profits will decline as the sales mix shifts from product A to product B. This also implies, however, that new analyses of profit volume relationship must be made as the product-mix changes.

Different combinations of sales-mix (based on the above-figure) will result in different net income. For example, if the total sales volume is ₹1,00,000 equally divided between the two products, the net income would be ₹15,000.

	Product A	*Product B*	*Total*
Per cent of sales revenue	50%	50%	100%
Sales revenue	₹50,000	50,000	1,00,000
P/V ratio	60%	20%	40%
Marginal contribution	30,000	10,000	40,000
Fixed costs			25,000
Net income			₹15,000

$$\text{Break-even point} = \frac{\text{Fixed cost}}{\text{P/V ratio}}$$

$$= \frac{25{,}000}{40\%} = ₹62{,}500$$

If the sales mix is changed so that product A has 60% of the sales revenue, the profit on sales of ₹1,00,000 would increase to ₹19,000.

	Product A	*Product B*	*Total*
Per cent of sales revenue	60%	40%	100%
Sales revenue	₹60,000	40,000	1,00,000
P/V ratio	60%	20%	44%
Marginal contribution	36,000	8,000	44,000
Fixed cost			25,000
Net income			₹19,000

$$\text{BEP} = \frac{25{,}000}{40\%} = ₹56{,}818$$

SALES MIX AND BREAK-EVEN POINT

Sales mix is the relative proportion of each product line to the total sales of various products sold by an enterprise. As stated earlier, if there are no constraints or limitations, management should try to maximise the sales of the product(s) with higher P/V ratio. However, a sales mix results because there are limits to the quantities of any given product that can be produced and there may also be certain market limitations on how much can be sold.

When different products have their own different production facilities, selling prices, variables costs and fixed costs separately, cost-volume-profit analysis can be done for each product separately. But, in many situations, this is not found and different products share common facilities and have common fixed costs. In such a situation, CVP analysis is performed by averaging the data using the sales mix as weights. The break-even point is computed for a specified sales mix and break-even chart and P/V graph are constructed for any specified sales mix. But, any one break-even chart or P/V graph will show a constant sales mix for the total sales of different products, covering the cost and revenue lines as well. The sales necessary to achieve desired or target level of operating profit can be computed on the basis of specified sales mix. If the sales mix changes, CVP analysis, break-even point, desired sales for target profit, costs and revenue lines will also change accordingly.

To illustrate the computation of break-even point in a sales mix situation, an example is given here. Assume, for a company, the fixed costs are ₹6,75,000. Further, assume that the unit sales volume, units selling prices, unit variable costs, unit contribution margins for products A, B and C are as follows:

Products	*Sales Volume (Units)*	*Unit Selling (Price) (₹)*	*Unit Variable Cost (₹)*	*Contribution Per Unit (₹)*	*Margin % (P/V Ratio) (₹)*
A	20,000	50	20	30	60
B	10,000	50	30	20	40
C	10,000	50	40	10	20
	40,000				

Break-even points (in units) will be computed using a weighted average contribution margin as follows:

Products	*Sales Mix (%)*		*Contribution Margin Per Unit (₹)*	*Weighted Contribution Margin (₹)*
A	50%	×	30	15
B	25%	×	20	5
C	25%	×	20	2 .50
Total weighted contribution margin				₹22.50

$$\text{BEP (Units)} = \frac{\text{Fixed cost}}{\text{Weight contribution margin}}$$

$$= \frac{₹\,6,75,000}{₹22.50} = 30,000 \text{ units}$$

The detailed composition of sales and contribution margins at this level (30,000 units) are as follows:

Products	*Sales Mix*		*Total Units*		*Units of Products*		*Contribution Margin Per Unit (₹)*	*Total Contribution (₹)*
A	50%	×	30,000	=	15,000	×	30	4,50,000
B	25%	×	30,000	=	7,500	×	20	1,50,000
C	25%	×	30,000	=	7,500	×	10	75,000
Break-even contribution margin.								₹6,75,000

Break-even point (sales in rupees) can also be calculated. For this, first, total P/V ratio is required, and then, divide the fixed costs by total P/V ratio. Using the above information, calculation is shown below:

	Products			
	A	*B*	*C*	*Total*
Sales (units)	20,000	10,000	10,000	40,000
Selling price (₹) per unit	50	50	50	
Sales (₹)	10,00,000	5,00,000	5,00,000	20,00,000
Less: Variable costs (₹)	4,00,000	3,00,000	4,00,000	11,00,000
Contribution margin	6,00,000	2,00,000	1,00,000	9,00,000
Less: Fixed costs				6,75,000
Profit before tax				2,25,000

$$\text{Total P/V ratio} = \frac{\text{Total contribution}}{\text{Total sales}}$$

$$= \frac{₹9,00,000}{₹20,00,000}$$

$$= 45\%$$

$$\text{Break-even sales (₹)} = \frac{\text{Fixed cost}}{\text{Total P / V ratio}}$$

$$= \frac{₹6,75,000}{45\%}$$

$$= ₹15,00,000$$

₹15,00,000 as break-even sales can be verified by computing break-even sales of individual products as follows:

Product	*Break-even Units*	*Selling Price (₹)*	*Break-even Sales (₹)*
A	15,000	50	7,50,000
B	7,500	50	3,75,000
C	7,500	50	3,75,000
Total break-even sales:			15,00,000

If there is any change in the above sales mix, the break-even point, P/V ratio, amount of profit before tax may change. For instance, assume that the quantities sold of products *A*, *B* and *C* are 5,000 units, 20,000 units and 15,000 units, respectively. Further, assume that there are no changes with regard to fixed costs, variable cost per unit and selling price per unit. The change in the sales mix will influence the factors of CVP analysis as shown below:

Products	*Sales Volume (Units)*	*Sales Mix %*	*Contribution Margin Per (Units) (₹)*	*Total Contribution (₹)*	*Sales Revenue (₹)*
A	5,000	12.50%	30	1,50,000	2,50,000
B	20,000	50%	20	4,00,000	10,00,000
C	15,000	37.5%	10	1,50,000	7,50,000
Total contribution margin				7,00,000	
Less: Fixed costs				6,75,000	
Profit before tax				25,000	

$$\text{Total P/V ratio} = \frac{\text{Total contribution}}{\text{Total sales}}$$

$$= \frac{₹7,00,000}{₹20,00,000}$$

$$= 35\%$$

$$\text{Break-even sales} = \frac{\text{Fixed costs}}{\text{Total P / V ratio}}$$

$$\text{Break-even sales} = \frac{₹\,6,75,000}{₹17.50}$$

$$= ₹19,28,571$$

Break-even point in units will be computed using a weighted average contribution margin, as stated earlier.

The calculation is shown below:

Products	*Sales Mix (%)*		*Contribution Margin Per Unit (₹)*	*Weighted Contribution Margin (₹)*
A	12.50%	×	30	3.75
B	50%	×	20	10.00
C	37.50%	×	10	3.75
Total weighted contribution margin				17.50%

$$\text{BEP (units)} = \frac{\text{Fixed cost}}{\text{Weight contribution margin}}$$

$$= \frac{₹\,6,75,000}{17.50}$$

$$= 38,571 \text{ units}$$

It can be observed that due to change in sales mix profit before tax is considerably lower (₹25,000) although the amount of sales revenue is the same. The total contribution is less than the earlier ones. P/V ratio has decreased (35%) and break-even-point in units has increased to 38,571 units. These differences are due to changes in sales mix. On the need of promoting products having different P/V ratios, Anderson and Sollenberger advise:

> "One way to encourage the sales force to sell more of the high contribution margin lines is to compute sales commissions on the contribution margin and not on sales revenue. If sales commissions are based on sales revenue, a sales force may have a high volume of sales of less profitable product lines and still earn a satisfactory commission. But, if sales commission are related to contribution margin, the sales force is encouraged to strive for greater sales of more profitable products, and, in doing so, will help to improve total company profits."[1]

DESIRED PROFIT AND TAX

The amount of desired profit before income tax is treated as if it were additional fixed costs in finding out the sales units or sales revenue required to give the amount of desired profit. The usual formula is:

$$\text{Desired sales units} = \frac{\text{Fixed cost + Profit before tax}}{\text{Contribution margin per unit}}$$

$$\text{Desired sales revenue} = \frac{\text{Fixed cost + Profit before tax}}{\text{P/V ratio}}$$

The amount of desired profit can be mentioned as a profit after income taxes. In such a case, the profit before tax is calculated by the following formula:

$$\text{Profit before tax} = \frac{\text{Profit after tax}}{(1 - \text{Tax rate})}$$

For instance, if profit after tax is ₹1,20,000 and tax rate is 40%, profit before tax will be ₹2,00,000 as calculated below:

$$\text{Profit before tax} = \frac{1{,}20{,}000}{(1 - .40)}$$
$$= ₹2{,}00{,}000$$

Sometimes, management is interested in knowing the sales units required to give a specified amount of profit on per-unit basis. The formula for computing such number of sales units to give desired profit per unit is as follows:

$$\text{Sales unit for desired profit per unit} = \frac{\text{Fixed cost}}{(\text{Contribution margin per unit} - \text{Desired profit per unit})}$$

Say, if fixed costs are ₹1,00,000, contribution margin per unit is ₹10 and the desired profit per unit is ₹2, then the sales units required to give this profit will be 12,500 units, as calculated below:

$$\text{Sales units for desired profit per unit} = \frac{₹1{,}00{,}000}{(₹10 - ₹2)}$$

$$= \frac{₹1{,}00{,}000}{₹8}$$

$$= 12{,}500 \text{ units}$$

1 Lane K. Anderson and Harold M. Sollenberger, *Managerial Accounting*. South Western Publishing Co., pp. 156–157.

Similarly, if the desired profit is stated not on a per-unit basis, but as a percentage of sales, the relevant formula for calculating the required sales volume is:

$$\text{Sales volume for desired profit (as percentage of sales)} = \frac{\text{Fixed cost}}{(\text{P/V ratio} - \text{Profit margin})}$$

Say, if fixed costs are ₹1,00,000, P/V ratio 40% and profit margin (percentage of sales) 20%, the required sales revenue will be ₹5,00,000 as calculated below:

$$\text{Sales volume (for desired profit margin)} = \frac{₹1,00,000}{(40\% - 20\%)} = ₹5,00,000$$

IMPROVING PROFIT-VOLUME RATIO

P/V ratio can be improved by the following possible courses of action:

(i) Increase the unit selling price of product.
(ii) Reducing the product unit variable/marginal cost.
(iii) Increasing the share of high contribution margin products in a multiproduct company.
(iv) Reducing the share of low contribution margin products in the total sales.

COST INDIFFERENCE POINT

A cost indifference point is that point at which total costs (fixed cost and variable cost) associated with the two alternatives are equal. There may be two methods or two alternatives of doing a thing, say two methods of production. It is also possible at a particular level of activity, one production method or method of doing a thing is superior to another, and vice versa. Accordingly there is a need to know at which level of production, it will be preferable to shift from one production method to another production method. This level or point is known as cost indifference point and at this point total cost of two production methods are the same.

Cost indifference point is useful in many decision situations, such as quality improvement schemes, different marketing plans, production plans or methods etc.

Cost indifference point should be distinguished from break-even point. Break-even point compares total sales and total cost of a product. Also, at break-even point, total cost line intersects total sales line. As stated above, cost indifference signifies equality of total costs of two alternatives or two methods of doing the same thing. At cost indifference point, total cost lines of two alternatives intersect each other.

EXAMPLE 16.2

A factory is thinking whether to hire a machine at an annual charge of ₹12,00,000 to increase the production of a product from current level of 6,000 units. It is expected that hiring of new machine will reduce the variable cost per unit by ₹100 due to savings in labour cost. Fixed costs of the factory will remain the same, except the hiring charges of ₹12,00,000. The selling price of the product is ₹1,200 per unit. The present cost breakup of the product is as follows:
Variable cost ₹900 per unit
Fixed cost ₹100 per unit.

Required: Calculate cost indifference point for the new machine (that is, additional units which must be produced and sold to justify hiring the machine).

☞ **Solution**

Contribution Per Unit

	Existing	*New*
Selling price per unit (₹)	1,200	1,200
Variable cost per unit (₹)	900	800
Contribution per unit	300	400

Total contribution required:

Existing contribution = 6,000 units × ₹300	= ₹18,00,000
Hiring charges of the machine	= ₹12,00,000
Total contribution required	30,00,000

$$\text{Number of units to be sold} = \frac{\text{Total contribution required}}{\text{Proposed contribution per unit}}$$

$$= \frac{₹30{,}00{,}000}{₹400}$$

$$= 7{,}500 \text{ units}$$

Additional number of units to be sold = 7,500 – 6,000 = 1,500 units

Thus, 1,500 additional units need to be produced and sold to justify hiring of the machine.

Notes:

For the new machine, indifference point is the point indicating the extra units to be manufactured and sold to achieve the existing level of profit. Production and sale of 7,500 units with hiring the new machine will give total contribution of ₹30,00,000 and after deducting hiring charges of ₹12,00,000, remaining contribution ₹18,00,000 will help in maintaining the current level of profit which is also ₹18,00,000.

LIMITATIONS OF CVP ANALYSIS

CVP analysis is a useful planning and control device, usually in the form of a chart, showing how revenue, costs, and profit fluctuate with volume. The CVP technique is useful to management in areas of budgeting, cost control and decision-making. In spite of CVP being a useful technique, it suffers from some limitations.

Some limitations of CVP are as follows:

1. It is difficult to classify exactly all the expenses into fixed and variable category. In fact, most of the expenses are neither totally variable nor wholly fixed in a realistic situation.
2. Contribution itself is not a guide if there is some key or limiting factor. Therefore, contribution needs to be linked with key or limiting factor.
3. Sales staff and marketing personnel may give undue importance to marginal cost as compared to total cost and decide to sell at a price based on marginal cost, which will result in low profits or loss.

4. Fixed overheads cannot altogether be excluded particularly in large contracts while valuing work-in-progress. In other situations or business decisions as well, consideration of fixed overheads becomes necessary to judge the performance and profitability.
5. In a multiproduct situation, different products typically yield different contribution margins and are produced in various volumes with differing costs. As a result, neither the revenue curve nor the cost curve is necessarily straight and the break-even point is difficult to find.

Because of the many assumptions, CVP is only an approximation at best. If prices, unit costs, sales mix, operating efficiency, or other relevant factors change, then the overall CVP analysis and relationships also must be modified. Because of these assumptions, cost data are of limited significance.

Therefore, while preparing or interpreting cost-volume profit analysis, all assumptions and limitations should be carefully considered. A series of CVP analysis based on different sets of assumptions and circumstances may be prepared to reflect situations prevailing in different business enterprises. When circumstances change, CVP analysis should also be revised to reflect the changing situations. It is also necessary to have up-to-date analysis so that it can act as a useful device in profit forecast, budgeting, cost control and managerial decision-making.

EXAMPLE 16.3

Prepare income statements under marginal costing and absorption costing from the following information for the year 2019–20:

Opening stock : 500 units valued at ₹35,000 including variable cost of ₹50 per unit.
Fixed cost : ₹1,00,000
Output : 5,000 units, variable cost: ₹60 per unit
Sales : 3,000 units @ ₹100 per unit

Closing stock is valued on the basis of FIFO. Also explain the reason for difference in profits in both the cases.

Solution

Income Statement

Particulars	*Absorption Costing System*	*Marginal Costing System*
Sales (3000 × ₹100)	3,00,000	3,00,000
Less: Cost of manufactured and sold:		
Variable cost	3,00,000	3,00,000
Fixed cost	1,00,000	–
Add: Opening inventory		
Variable cost	25,000	25,000
Fixed cost	10,000	–
Cost of goods available for sales	4,35,000	3,25,000
Less: Closing inventory:		
Variable cost (for 2,500 units)	(1,50,000)	(1,50,000)
Fixed cost	(50,000)	–

(Contd.)

Particulars	*Absorption Costing System*	*Marginal Costing System*
Cost of manufactured and sold	2,35,000	1,75,000
Gross margin/contribution	65,000	1,25,000
Less: Fixed cost	–	1,00,000
Profit	65,000	25,000

The difference between two profits under two systems is because of fixed cost charged on opening inventory and closing inventory. Under absorption system, fixed cost included in opening stock (relating to previous year) is charged to this year sales. While under the marginal cost system, the fixed cost of the whole output is charged to the current sales. Difference in net income in absorption costing and marginal costing is simply due to difference in inventory values in the two costing techniques. This is clear from the following analysis.

Absorption costing profit	=	₹65,000
Marginal costing profit	=	₹25,000
Difference in net income	=	₹40,000
Inventory values		
Absorption costing:		
Opening inventory		₹35,000
Closing inventory		2,00,000
Difference		1,65,000
Marginal costing:		
Opening inventory		25,000
Closing inventory		1,50,000
Difference		1,25,000
Net difference in inventory values		₹40,000

Notes: (i) Variable cost has been assumed as variable production cost.
(ii) Fixed cost has been treated as fixed production cost.

EXAMPLE 16.4

You are given the following information relating to the year 2019–20 and 2020–21:

	2019–20	*2020–21*
Opening stock (units)	–	300
Production (units)	1200	1400
Fixed cost	₹2,00,000	₹2,10,000
Variable cost	₹1,50,000	₹2,80,000
Sales (units)	900	1100
Selling price (₹/per unit)	400	500
Closing stock (units)	300	600

Prepare profit and loss account using FIFO under marginal costing and under absorption costing.

☞ **Solution**

Profit and Loss Account (Absorption Costing)

	2019–20	2020–21
Sales (₹)	3,60,000	5,50,000
Less: Cost of goods sold:		
Opening stock	–	87,500
Variable cost	1,50,000	2,80,000
Fixed cost	2,00,000	2,10,000
Cost of goods available for sales	3,50,000	5,77,500
Less: Closing inventory	87,500	2,10,000
Cost of goods sold	2,62,500	3,67,500
Net profit	97,500	1,82,500

Valuation of Closing Stock (Based on FIFO)

$$2019\text{–}20 = \text{Fixed cost}\left(₹2{,}00{,}000\times\frac{300\text{ units}}{1{,}200\text{ units}}\right)+\text{Variable cost}\left(₹1{,}50{,}000\times\frac{300}{1{,}200}\right)$$

$$= ₹87{,}500$$

$$2020\text{–}21 = \text{Fixed cost}\left(₹2{,}10{,}000\times\frac{600}{1{,}400}\right)+\text{Variable cost}\left(₹2{,}80{,}000\times\frac{600}{1{,}400}\right)$$

$$= ₹2{,}10{,}000$$

Profit and Loss Account (Marginal Costing) FIFO

	2019–20	2020–21
Sales	3,60,000	5,50,000
Less: Cost of goods sold:		
Opening stock	–	37,500
Variable cost	1,50,000	2,80,000
Cost of goods available for sales	1,50,000	3,17,500
Less: Closing stock	37,500	1,20,000
Cost of goods sold	1,12,500	1,97,500
Margin	2,47,500	3,52,500
Less: Fixed cost	2,00,000	2,10,000
Net profit	47,500	1,42,500

Valuation of Closing Stock (FIFO)

$$2019\text{–}20 = ₹1{,}50{,}000 \times \frac{300}{1{,}200} = ₹37{,}500$$

$$2020\text{–}2 = ₹2{,}80{,}000 \times \frac{600}{1{,}400} = ₹1{,}20{,}000$$

Notes:

For preparing Profit and Loss Account, variable cost has been assumed as variable production cost. Further, fixed cost has been assumed as fixed production cost.

EXAMPLE 16.5

The data given below relate to Modern Garments which produced and sold T-shirts during 2019–20:
Opening stock of 500 T-shirts valued at ₹1,00,000 including variable cost of ₹80 per T-shirt:

Production	5,000 T-shirts
Sales @ ₹300 per T-shirt	4,000 T-shirts
Direct material cost	₹2,00,000
Direct labour cost	₹1,00,000
Factory overheads:	
Variable	₹1,00,000
Fixed	₹6,00,000
Selling and distribution overheads:	
Variable	₹20,000
Fixed	₹30,000

Closing stock is valued at current cost.

Prepare income statements under (a) absorption costing, (b) marginal costing, and (c) explain the reasons for the difference in profit under the two systems.

Solution

(a) **Income Statement under Absorption Costing System**

		(₹)
Sales (4,000 × 300)		12,00,000
Less: Cost of production and sold		
Variable production cost:		
Direct material	2,00,000	
Direct labour	1,00,000	
Factory overhead	1,00,000	
Fixed:		
Factory overheads	6,00,000	
Cost of production	10,00,000	

(Contd.)

		(₹)
Add: Opening inventory:		
Variable and fixed cost	1,00,000	
	11,00,000	
Less: Closing inventory:		
$\left(\frac{10,00,000}{5,000} \times 1,500\right)$	3,00,000	
	8,00,000	8,00,000
Gross margin		4,00,000
Less: Selling and distribution cost:		
Variable	20,000	
Fixed	30,000	50,000
Profit		3,50,000

✍ **NOTE:**

Closing inventory (1500 T-shirts) have been costed in terms of only current production cost that is, ₹10,00,000 based on FIFO assumption.

(b) **Income Statement (Marginal Costing)**

			₹
	Sales (4000 × 300)		12,00,000
Less :	Variable production cost of goods sold:		
	Direct material	₹2,00,000	
	Direct labour	1,00,000	
	Factory overheads	1,00,000	
		4,00,000	
Add :	Opening inventory (500 × 80)	40,000	
		4,40,000	
Less :	Closing inventory (1500 × 80)	1,20,000	
	Variable cost of production of goods sold		3,20,000
	Contribution		8,80,000
Less :	(i) Fixed factory overheads		(6,00,000)
	(ii) Variable selling and distribution overheads		(20,000)
	(iii) Fixed selling and distribution overheads		(30,000)
	Net income		2,30,000

(c) The reasons for difference in profit in the two costing techniques are due to differences in inventory values in absorption costing and marginal costing. In absorption costing fixed factory overheads is considered in the valuation of closing stock. But in marginal costing, fixed factory overheads are not charged to inventory but simply written off in the profit and loss account.

EXAMPLE 16.6

Your company has a production capacity of 12,500 units and normal capacity utilisation is 80%.Opening inventory of finished goods on 1-1-2019 was 1,000 units. During the year ending 31-12-2019, it produced 11,000 units while it sold only 10,000 units.

Standard variable cost per unit is ₹6.50 and standard fixed factory cost per unit ₹1.50. Total fixed selling and administration overhead amounted to ₹10,000. The company sells its product at ₹10 per unit.

Prepare Income Statements under Absorption Costing and Marginal Costing. Explain the reasons for difference in profit, if any.

Solution

Income Statement for the Year Ended 31st Dec., 2019
(Under Absorption Costing Method)

	₹	₹
Sales: 10,000 units @ ₹10 per unit		1,00,000
Less: Cost of goods sold		
Variable production costs:		
11,000 units @ ₹6.50 per unit	71,500	
Fixed factory cost @ ₹1.50 per unit		
11,000 × 1.50 =	16,500	
	88,000	
Add: Opening stock: 1,000 units		
@ ₹8 per unit (that is, ₹6.50 + ₹1.50)	8,000	
Costs of goods available for sales	96,000	
Less: Closing stock: 2000 units valued at current cost.		
$\frac{96{,}000 \times 2{,}000}{12{,}000}$	16,000	80,000
Gross Profit		20,000
Less: Fixed selling and administrative overhead.		10,000
Net Profit		10,000

Income Statement for the Year Ended 31st December, 2019
(Under Marginal Costing Method)

	₹	₹
Sales: 10,000 units @ ₹10 per unit		1,00,000
Less: Marginal cost:		
Variable production cost:		
11,000 units @ ₹6.50 per unit	71,500	
Variable cost of opening stock of finished stock		
(1,000 units @ ₹6.50 per unit)	6,500	
Cost of goods available for sales	78,000	

(Contd.)

		₹	₹
Less:	Closing stock of finished stock:		
	2,000 units @ ₹6.50 per unit	13,000	
		65,000	65,000
	Contribution		35,000
Less:	Fixed selling and administrative overhead	10,000	
	Fixed factory cost @ ₹1.50 per unit	16,500	26,500
	Net profit		8,500

Reason for difference The difference in profits, ₹1,500 (that is ₹10,000 – ₹8,500), as arrived at under absorption and marginal costing methods is due to the element of fixed cost included in the valuation of opening and closing stock under the absorption costing method.

✍ EXAMPLE 16.7

Sunita Enterprises released the figures given below from its records for Year I and Year 2:

	Year 1	*Year 2*
Sales units	2,40,000	2,40,000
Production units	2,40,000	4,00,000
Selling price per unit (₹)	20	20
Variable manufacturing cost per unit (₹)	12	12
Annual fixed manufacturing cost (₹)	12,00,000	12,00,000
Variable marketing and administrative costs per unit (₹)	1.25	1.25
Fixed marketing and administrative costs (₹)	4,20,000	4,20,000

(i) Prepare income statements for both years, using full-absorption costing.
(ii) Prepare income statements for both years, using variable costing.
(iii) Comment on the different operating profit figures.

☞ Solution

Income Statement (Absorption Costing)

	Year 1 (₹)	*Year 2 (₹)*
Soles @ ₹20 p.u.	48,00,000	48,00,000
Less: Variable manufacturing cost	28,80,000	48,00,000
Fixed manufacturing cost	12,00,000	12,00,000
Factory cost	40,80,000	60,00,000
Add: Opening stock	Nil	Nil
Less: Closing stock @ ₹15 p.u.	Nil	24,00,000
Cost of goods sold	40,80,000	36,00,000
Gross profit	7,20,000	12,00,000

(Contd.)

	Year 1 (₹)	Year 2 (₹)
Less: Variable mkt. & admn. overheads @ ₹1.25 p.u.	3,00,000	3,00,000
Fixed mkt. & admn. overheads	4,20,000	4,20,000
Net profit	Nil	4,80,000

Income Statement (Variable Costing)

	Year 1 (₹)	Year 2 (₹)
Sales @ ₹20 p.u.	48,00,000	48,00,000
Variable mfg, cost @ 12 p.u.	28,80,000	48,00,000
Add: Opening stock	Nil	Nil
Less: Closing stock @ ₹12 p.u.	Nil	19,20,000
Variable cost of production of goods sold	28,80,000	28,80,000
Margin	19,20,000	19,20,000
Less: Variable marketing and administration overheads @ ₹1.25	3,00,000	3,00,000
Fixed manufacturing cost	12,00,000	12,00,000
Fixed marketing & administration	4,20,000	4,20,000
Net profit	Nil	Nil

Comments: In year 1, profit under Absorption Costing and Marginal (Variable Costing) are equal to nil because units produced are equal to units sold. In year 2, production is more than sales, profit under Absorption Costing is higher than Marginal (Variable) Costing. The profit is ₹4,80,000 which is just equal to the difference in the value of Closing Stock, *i.e.* ₹24,00,000 – ₹19,20,000 = ₹4,80,000.

EXAMPLE 16.8

Rivilin is a uni-product firm with the following budgeted amounts:

	₹
Unit selling price	60
Unit variable cost	20
Fixed production overhead per month	9,600

Rivilin's planned level of production is 800 units a month. However, actual activity was as follows:

	April	May	June
Units produced	800	750	820
Units sold	800	700	850

There was no opening stock at 1st April.
The actual fixed production overhead incurred was accurately predicted at ₹9,600 a month.
The non-production fixed overheads are ₹10,000 a month.

Required:

1 A variable costing profit statement for each month.
2 An absorption costing profit statement for each month.
3 An explanation of the difference in profits between the two statements.

☞ Solution

Workings:

	₹/unit
Variable production cost	20 – variable costing production and stock value
Fixed production cost	12 – ₹9,600/800 units – planned absorption rate
Absorption production cost	32 – absorption costing production and stock value

Stock Movements (Units)

	April	May	June
Opening stock	–	–	50
Production	800	750	820
Sales	(800)	(700)	(850)
Closing stock	–	50	20
Change in level	–	+50	–30

1 Variable Costing Profit Statement (₹)

	April	May	June
Opening stock	–	–	1,000
Production (@ ₹20)	16,000	15,000	16,400
Less: Closing stock	–	1,000	400
Cost of sales	16,000	14,000	17,000
Sales (@ ₹60)	48,000	42,000	51,000
Gross profit	32,000	28,000	34,000
Less: Production overheads	9,600	9,600	9,600
Less: Non-production overheads	10,000	10,000	10,000
Net profit	12,400	8,400	14,400

2 Absorption Costing Profit Statement (₹)

	April		May		June
Opening stock	–		–		1,600
Production (@ ₹32)	25,600		24,000		26,240
Less: Closing stock	–		1,600		640
Cost of sales	25,600		22,400		27,200
Under/(over)recovery of fixed production overheads	–	(50 × ₹12)	600	(20 × ₹12)	(240)
Adjusted cost of sales	25,600		23,000		26,960
Sales (@ ₹60)	48,000		42,000		51,000
Gross profit	22,400		19,000		24,040
Less: Non-production overheads	10,000		10,000		10,000
Net profit	12,400		9,000		14,040

3 Explanation of Profit Differences

April – no stock movement – identical profits
May – stock increase – absorption profits higher by ₹600 (50 × ₹12)
June – stock decrease – absorption profits lower by ₹360 (30 × ₹12)

EXAMPLE 16.9

ABC Motors assembles and sells motor vehicles. It uses an actual costing system, in which unit costs are calculated on a monthly basis. Data relating to March and April, 2020 are:

	March	*April*
Unit data:		
Beginning inventory	0	150
Production	500	400
Sales	350	520
Variable-cost data:		
Manufacturing costs per unit produced	₹10,000	₹10,000
Distribution costs per unit sold	3,000	3,000
Fixed-cost data:		
Manufacturing costs	₹20,00,000	₹20,00,000
Marketing costs	6,00,000	6,00,000
The selling price per motor vehicle is ₹24,000		

Required:

(i) Present income statements for *ABC* Motors in March and April of 2020 under (a) variable costing, and (b) absorption costing.
(ii) Explain the differences between (a) and (b) for March and April.

Solution

(i) Income Statement (Variable Costing)

	March (₹)	*April (₹)*
Sales	84,00,000	1,24,80,000
Less: Variable cost of goods sold:		
Opening stock	Nil	15,00,000
Variable manufacturing cost	50,00,000	40,00,000
Cost of goods available for sales	50,00,000	55,00,000
Less: Closing stock	15,00,000	3,00,000
Cost of goods sold	35,00,000	52,00,000
Contribution margin	49,00,000	72,80,000
Less: Other costs:		
Fixed manufacturing	(20,00,000)	(20,00,000)
Fixed marketing	(6,00,000)	(6,00,000)
Variable distribution	(10,50,000)	(15,60,000)
Net Income	12,50,000	31,20,000

Income Statement (Absorption Costing)

		March (₹)	April (₹)
Sales		84,00,000	1,24,80,000
Less:	Cost of goods sold:		
	Opening stock	Nil	21,00,000
	Variable manufacturing cost	50,00,000	40,00,000
	Fixed manufacturing cost	20,00,000	20,00,000
	Cost of goods available for sales	70,00,000	81,00,000
Less:	Closing stock	21,00,000	4,50,000
	Cost of goods sold	49,00,000	76,50,000
	Gross profit	35,00,000	48,30,000
Less:	Distribution cost	(10,50,000)	(15,60,000)
	Fixed marketing	(6,00,000)	(6,00,000)
	Net Income	18,50,000	(26,70,000)

Note:

The company follows actual costing system and calculates unit costs on monthly basis. Therefore, in absorption costing, for April month, inventory of 30 units has been valued as follows:

Variable manufacturing cost 30 × ₹10,000	=	3,00,000
Fixed manufacturing cost @ ₹5,000 × 30	=	1,50,000
(₹20,00,000, Current production 400 units)		
That is, inventory at ₹15,000 per unit	=	4,50,000

For March month, inventory of 150 units has been calculated as follows:

Variable manufacturing ₹10,000 × 150	=	₹15,00,000
Fixed manufacturing ₹4,000 × 150	=	₹ 6,00,000
That is, inventory at ₹14,000 per unit	=	₹21,00,000

(ii) Difference in Profit

	March	April
Absorption costing profit	₹ 18,50,000	₹ 26,70,000
Variable costing profit	↑ 12,50,000	↓ 31,20,000
	6,00,000	4,50,000

Difference in profit is due to difference in inventory values in the two costing techniques.

	March (₹)	*April (₹)*
Absorption costing:		
Opening stock	Nil	21,00,000
Closing stock	21,00,000	4,50,000
Difference	21,00,000	16,50,000

(Contd.)

Variable costing:		
Opening stock	Nil	15,00,000
Closing stock	15,00,000	3,00,000
Difference	15,00,000	12,00,000
Net difference (effect)	6,00,000	4,50,000

EXAMPLE 16.10

ABC Ltd. can produce 4,00,000 units of a product per annum at 100% capacity. The variable production costs are ₹40 per unit and the variable selling expenses are ₹12 per sold unit. The budgeted fixed production expenses were ₹24,00,000 per annum and the fixed selling expenses were ₹16,00,000. During the year ended 31st March, 2020, the company worked at 80% of its capacity. The operating data for the year are as follows:

Production	3,20,000 units
Sales @ ₹80 per unit	3,10,000 units
Opening stock of finished goods	40,000 units

Fixed production expenses are absorbed on the basis of capacity and fixed selling expenses are recovered on the basis of period.

You are required to prepare the statements of cost and profit for the year ending 31st March, 2020:

(i) On the basis of marginal costing

(ii) On the basis of absorption costing

Solution

(i)

Statement of Cost and Profit under Marginal Costing for the Year Ending 31st March, 2020 Output = 3,20,000 units

Particulars	*Amount* (₹)	*Amount* (₹)
Sales: 3,10,000 units @ ₹80		2,48,00,000
Less: Cost of goods sold.		
Variable cost of production (3,20,000 × ₹40)	1,28,00,000	
Add: Opening stock 40,000 units @ ₹40	16,00,000	
	1,44,00,000	
Less : Closing stock [(3,20,000 + 40,000 – 3,10,000) @ ₹40 = 50,000 units @ ₹40]	20,00,000	
Variable cost of production of 3,10,000 units		1,24,00,000
Margin		1,24,00,000
Less: Fixed production cost		24,00,000
Variable selling expenses @ ₹12 per unit		37,20,000
Fixed selling expenses		16,00,000
Net profit		46,80,000

(ii) **Statement of Cost and Profit under Absorption Costing for the Year Ending 31st March, 2020**
Output = 3,20,000 units

Particulars	*Amount* (₹)	*Amount* (₹)
Sales: 3,10,000 units @ ₹80		2,48,00,000
Less: Cost of goods sold:		
Variable cost of production (3,20,000 @ ₹40)	1,28,00,000	
Add: Fixed cost of production absorbed 3,20,000 units @ ₹6[(1)]	19,20,000	
	1,47,20,000	
Add: Opening Stock: 40,000 × ₹46 per unit	18,40,000	
Cost of goods available for sales	1,65,60,000	
Less: Closing stock: 50,000 × ₹46 per unit	23,00,000	
Unadjusted cost of goods sold	1,42,60,000	
Add: Amount of under-absorption	4,80,000	
Actual cost of goods sold		1,47,40,000
Gross profit		1,00,60,000
Less: Variable selling expenses		37,20,000
Fixed selling expenses		16,00,000
Net profit		47,40,000

Workings:

1. Absorption rate for fixed cost of production $= \dfrac{₹24,00,000}{4,00,000 \text{ units}} = ₹6$ per unit.
2. Fixed production overhead under absorbed – ₹(24,00,000 – 19,20,000) = ₹4,80,000.
3. Total manufacturing cost per unit ₹40 + ₹6 = ₹46

✍ EXAMPLE 16.11

Clamco makes car clamps. The following information is from January's budget, which is based on a production volume of 6,000 clamps:

	₹
Opening stock of clamps	0
Fixed manufacturing overhead	72,000
Variable manufacturing overhead	18,000
Selling and administrative expenses (all fixed)	25,000
Direct labour	1,20,000
Direct materials used	90,000
Selling price (per unit)	64

The actual production and sales volumes for the first three months of the year were as follows:

Number of clamps:	January	February	March	Quarter
Production level	6,000	5,000	7,000	18,000
Sales	4,000	6,000	7,000	17,000

Actual variable costs per unit and total fixed overheads incurred were exactly as forecast.

Required:

1 Calculate the profit for each month and for the quarter

a) using absorption costing;

b) using variable costing.

2 Reconcile the profits for each month and for the quarter. Explain why they differ.

Solution

Workings:

January:

Direct labour	1,20,000
Direct materials	90,000
Variable production overhead	18,000
Variable cost	2,28,000
Fixed production overhead	72,000
Absorption cost	3,00,000

Variable cost/unit = ₹2,28,000/6,000 units = ₹38/unit

Absorption cost/unit = ₹3,00,000/6,000 units = ₹50/unit

Fixed production overhead/unit = ₹72,000/6,000 units = ₹12/unit

Physical Stock Changes (Number of Units)

	Jan	Feb	Mar	Qtr
Opening stock	0	2,000	1,000	0
Actual production	6,000	5,000	7,000	18,000
Actual sales	4,000	6,000	7,000	17,000
Closing stock	2,000	1,000	1,000	1,000

1 a) Absorption Costing (₹000) (Abs. Prod. Cost = ₹50/unit)

	Jan	Feb	Mar	Qtr
Opening stock	0	100	50	0
Add: Production cost	300	250	350	900
Less: Closing stock	100	50	50	50
Under/(over)absorption	0	12	(12)	0
Cost of sales	200	312	338	850
Sales revenue	256	384	448	1,088
Gross profit	56	72	110	238
Non-production overhead	25	25	25	75
Net profit	**31**	**47**	**85**	**163**

b) Variable Costing (₹000) (Var. Prod. Cost = ₹38/unit)

	Jan	Feb	Mar	Qtr
Opening stock	0	76	38	0
Add: Production cost	228	190	266	684
Less: Closing stock	76	38	38	38
Cost of sales	152	228	266	646
Sales revenue	256	384	448	1,088
Gross profit	104	156	182	442
Production overheads	72	72	72	216
Non-production overhead	25	25	25	75
Total fixed overheads	97	97	97	291
Net profit	**7**	**59**	**85**	**151**

2 Reconciliation of Profits (₹000)

	Jan	Feb	Mar	Qtr
Absorption net profit	31	47	85	163
Variable net profit	7	59	85	151
Difference	**24**	**(12)**	–	**12**
Increase in stock (units)	2,000	(1,000)	–	1,000
Production overheads in stock increase (@ ₹12 a unit)	**24**	**(12)**	–	12

EXAMPLE 16.12

Margin of safety ₹64,000, Break-even sales 1,600 units, Total cost ₹41,600, Margin of safety 6,400 units. Calculate the Fixed costs.

Solution

(i) $\text{Margin of safety (\%)} = \dfrac{\text{Margin of safety (units)}}{\text{Actual sales (units)}} \times 100 = \dfrac{6,400}{6,400 + 1,600} \times 100 = 80\%$

(ii) $\text{Total sales} = \dfrac{\text{Margin of safety (₹)}}{\text{Margin safety (\%)}} = \dfrac{₹64,000}{80\%} = ₹80,000$

(iii) Profit = Total sales – Total cost = ₹80,000 –₹41,600 = ₹38,400

(iv) $\text{P/V ratio} = \dfrac{\text{Profit}}{\text{Margin of safety}} \times 100 = \dfrac{₹38,400}{₹64,000} \times 100 = 60\%$

(v) Break-even sales = Total sales × (100 – Margin of safety %) = ₹80,000 × 20% = ₹16,000

(vi) Fixed costs = BEP × P/V ratio = ₹16,000 × 60% = ₹9,600.

EXAMPLE 16.13

MNP Ltd sold 2,75,000 units of its product at ₹37.50 per unit. Variable costs are ₹17.50 per unit (manufacturing costs of ₹14 and selling cost ₹3.50 per unit). Fixed costs are incurred uniformly throughout the year and amount to ₹35,00,000 (including depreciation of ₹15,00,000). There is no beginning or ending inventories.

for excel template, scan

Required:

(i) Estimate break-even sales level quantity and cast break-even sales level quantity.

(ii) Estimate the P/V ratio.

(iii) Estimate the number of units that must be sold to earn an income (EBIT) of ₹2,50,000.

(iv) Estimate the sales level achieve an after-tax income (PAT) of ₹2,50,000. Assume 40% corporate income tax rate.

Solution

(i) $$\text{Break-even sales quantity} = \frac{\text{Fixed cost}}{\text{Contribution margin per unit}} = \frac{₹35,00,000}{₹20} = 1,75,000 \text{ units}$$

$$\text{Cash Break-even sales qty} = \frac{\text{Cash fixed cost}}{\text{Contribution margin per unit}} = \frac{₹20,00,000}{₹20} = 1,00,000 \text{ units.}$$

(ii) $$\text{P/V ratio} = \frac{\text{Contribution / unit}}{\text{Selling price / unit}} \times 100 = \frac{20}{37.50} \times 100 = 53.33\%$$

(iii) No. of units that must be sold to earn an income (EBIT) of ₹2,50,000

$$\frac{\text{Fixed cost + Desired EBIT level}}{\text{Contribution margin per unit}} = \frac{35,00,000 + 2,50,000}{20} = 1,87,500 \text{ units}$$

(iv) After Tax Income (PAT) = ₹2,50,000

Tax rate = 40%

Desired level of profit before tax

$$\frac{₹2,50,000}{60} \times 100$$

= ₹4,16,667/-

$$\text{Estimated sales level} = \frac{\text{Fixed cost + Desired profit}}{\text{P/V ratio}}$$

$$\frac{₹35,00,000 + ₹4,16,667}{53.33\%} = ₹73,43,750/-$$

EXAMPLE 16.14

A company sells two products, *J* and *K*. The sales mix is 4 units of *J* and 3 units of *K*. The contribution margins per unit are ₹40 for *J* and ₹20 for *K*. Fixed costs are ₹6,16,000 per month. Compute the break-even point.

Solution

Let $4x$ = No. of units of *J*

Then $3x$ = No. of units of *K*

$$\text{BEP in } x \text{ units} = \left(\frac{\text{Fixed cost}}{\text{Contribution}}\right) = \frac{₹6,16,000}{4(40) + 3(20)}$$

Or $$\frac{6,16,000}{220} = 2,800 \text{ units}$$

Break-even point of product $J = 4 \times 2,800 = 11,200$ units
Break-even point of product $K = 3 \times 2,800 = 8,400$ units

EXAMPLE 16.15

A company produces single product which sells for ₹20 per unit. Variable cost is ₹15 per unit and fixed overhead for the year is ₹6,30,000.

Required:

(a) Calculate sales value needed to earn a profit of 10% on sales.
(b) Calculate sales price per unit to bring BEP down to 1,20,000 units.
(c) Calculate margin of safety sales if profit is ₹60,000.

Solution

(a) Suppose sales units are x then

S = V + F + P
S = Sales
V = Variable cost
F = Fixed cost
P = Profit

$20x = 15x + 6,30,000 + 2x$

$20x - 17x = 6,30,000$

$$\therefore \quad x = \frac{6,30,000}{3} = 2,10,000 \text{ units}$$

Sales value = 2,10,000 × 20= ₹42,00,000

(b) Sales price to down BEP 1,20,000 units

$$S = V + \frac{F}{\text{New BEP}} \quad \therefore S = 15 + \frac{6,30,000}{1,20,000} \quad \therefore ₹20.25.$$

$$\text{(c) MS Sales} = \frac{\text{Profit}}{\text{P/V ratio}} \quad \therefore \quad \frac{60,000}{\text{P/V}} \text{ where P/V} = \frac{C}{S} \times 100.$$

$$\frac{60,000}{25} \times 100 = 2,40,000 \quad \text{Or} \quad \frac{5}{20} \times 100 = 25\%.$$

EXAMPLE 16.16

A company has fixed cost of ₹90,000, sales ₹3,00,000 and profit of ₹60,000.

Required:

(i) Sales volume if in the next period, the company suffered a loss of ₹30,000.
(ii) What is the margin of safety for a profit of ₹90,000?

Solution

$$\text{P/V ratio} = \frac{\text{Contribution}}{\text{Sales}} \times 100$$

$$= \left(\frac{1,50,000}{3,00,000} \times 100\right) = 50\%$$

(i) If in the next period company suffered a loss of ₹30,000, then
Contribution = Fixed Cost ± Profit
= ₹90,000 – ₹30,000 (as it is a loss)
= ₹60,000.

Then, Sales = $\frac{\text{Contribution}}{\text{P/V ratio}}$ or $\frac{60,000}{.50}$ = ₹1,20,000.

So, there will be loss of ₹30,000 at sales of ₹1,20,000.

(ii) Margin of safety = $\frac{\text{Profit}}{\text{P/V ratio}}$ or $\frac{90,000}{.50}$ = ₹1,80,000.

Alternative solution of this part:

Break-even sales = $\frac{\text{Fixed cost}}{\text{P/V ratio}} = \frac{90,000}{.5}$ = ₹1,80,000

Sales at profit of ₹90,000 = $\frac{\text{Fixed cost} + \text{Profit}}{\text{P/V ratio}}$

$= \frac{90,000 + 90,000}{.5}$

$\frac{1,80,000}{.5}$

= ₹3,60,000.

Margin of safety = Sales – Break-even sales
= 3,60,000 – 1,80,000
= ₹1,80,000.

✍ EXAMPLE 16.17

Following information are available for the year 2019 and 2020 of PIX Limited:

Year	2019	2020
Sales	₹32,00,000	₹57,00,000
Profit/(Loss)	(₹3,00,000)	₹7,00,000

Calculate – (a) P/V ratio, (b) Total fixed cost, and (c) Sales required to earn a profit of ₹12,00,000.

☞ ***Solution***

(a) P/V ratio = $\frac{\text{Change in profit}}{\text{Change in sales}} \times 100$

$= \frac{7,00,000 + 3,00,000}{(57,00,000 - 32,00,000)} \times 100$

$= \frac{10,00,000}{25,00,000} \times 100$

= 40%

(b) Total fixed cost = Total contribution – Profit
= (Sales × P/V ratio) – Profit

$= (₹57,00,000 \times \frac{40}{100}) - ₹7,00,000$

= ₹22,80,000 – ₹7,00,000
= ₹15,80,000

(c) Contribution required to earn a profit of ₹12,00,000 = Total fixed cost + Profit required
= ₹15,80,000 + 12,00,000 = ₹27,80,000

$\text{Required sales} = \frac{27,80,000}{\text{P/V ratio}} = \frac{27,80,000}{40\%} = ₹69,50,000$

EXAMPLE 16.18

Following information is available for the first and second quarter of the year 2019–20 of ABC Limited:

	Production (In Units)	*Semi-Variable Cost* (₹)
Quarter I	36,000	2,80,000
Quarter II	42,000	3,10,000

You are required to segregate the semi-variable cost and calculate:

(a) Variable cost per unit; and
(b) Total fixed cost.

Solution

	Production (Units)	*Semi Variable Cost (₹)*
Quarter I	36,000	2,80,000
Quarter II	42,000	3,10,000
Difference	6,000	30,000

$\text{Variable cost per unit} = \frac{\text{Change in semi variable cost}}{\text{Change in production}}$

$= \frac{₹30,000}{6,000 \text{ units}}$

= ₹5 per unit

Total fixed cost = Semi variable cost – (Production × Variable cost per unit)

Total fixed cost in Quarter I :
= 2,80,000 – (36,000 × 5)
= 2,80,000 – 1,80,000
= 1,00,000

Total fixed cost in Quarter II:
= 3,10,000 – (42,000 × 5)
= 3,10,000 – 2,10,000
= 1,00,000

EXAMPLE 16.19

PQ Ltd. reports the following cost structure at two capacity levels:

	(100% capacity) *2,000 units*	*1,500 units*
Production overhead I	₹3 per unit	₹4 per unit
Production overhead II	₹2 per unit	₹2 per unit

If the selling price reduced by direct material and labour is ₹8 per unit, what would be its break-even point?

Solution

Computation of break-even point in units:

	2,000 units	1,500 units
Production overhead I: Fixed cost (₹)	6,000 (2,000 units × ₹3 per unit)	6,000 (1,500 units × ₹4 per unit)
Selling price – Material and labour (₹) (A)	8	8
Production overhead II (Variable Overhead) (B)	2	2
Contribution per unit (A) – (B)	6	6

$$\text{Break-even point} = \frac{\text{Fixed cost}}{\text{Contribution per unit}} = \frac{6,000}{6} = 1,000 \text{ units}$$

EXAMPLE 16.20

WSM Enterprises introduced the Wizkid in 2019 to compete with Action Man. Although the peak demand for these products occurred several years ago, sales have stabilised and WSM sells 15,000 Wizkids a year.

The recommended retail price is ₹24.99 and the current wholesale price is ₹10.00. However, the managing director wishes to increase the return on this product and has proposed a 100% mark-up on total variable costs.

WSM has an annual output of 15,000 Wizkids. The fixed costs related to this product are ₹40,000 and the variable (or marginal) costs are ₹6.00 per unit.

Required:

1 What is the breakeven volume of this product if a selling price of ₹10.00 is charged? What is the profit at this price?
2 What price would the MD like to charge? What would the resulting net profit be if there was no change in demand?
3 The marketing director has forecast a 10% drop in orders if the price is raised as suggested. What would WSM's profit be if this were to happen?
4 Discuss the other factors the MD should take into account when deciding on the selling price of Wizkids.

☞ *Solution*

	₹
Selling price	10.00
Variable cost	6.00
Unit contribution	4.00

1 At BEP (say, at N units)

Total contribution = Total fixed costs

N × 4.00 = 40,000

N = 10,000

Thus, BEP is 10,000 units

Total contribution = 15,000 × 4.00	= 60,000
Total fixed costs	= 40,000
Profit	= 20,000

2

	₹
Variable cost	6.00
100% mark-up	6.00
Selling price	12.00

	₹
Total contribution (15,000 × 6.00)	90,000
Less: Total fixed costs	40,000
Net profit	**50,000**

3

	₹
(15,000 – 10%) × unit contribution	
13,500 × 6.00	= 81,000
Less: Total fixed costs	= 40,000
Net profit	**= 41,000**

4 Other factors to be taken into account include:

- competitors' prices;
- corporate objectives;
- pricing strategy;
- product life cycle stage; and
- effect on profit of lowering prices and increasing demand.

✍ EXAMPLE 16.21

Your company manufactures three products, Alpha, Beta and Gamma. The following information refers to next month:

	Alpha	**Beta**	**Gamma**
Sales demand (units)	50	150	200
Raw materials/unit	₹100	₹150	₹80
Direct labour hours/unit	5	10	2
Fixed overheads/unit	₹30	₹60	₹12

Direct labour is paid at ₹3.00 per hour. Variable overhead is equal to 10% of the cost of materials. Fixed overheads are attached to the products at the rate of 200% of the total direct labour cost. The selling price is calculated by doubling the prime cost (= total direct cost).

Required:

1 Calculate the contribution per unit for each product and rank them.
2 Using the ranking from the previous answer, prepare a forecast of the profit for each product and in total for next month if only 1,650 direct labour hours are available.
3 Calculate the contribution per direct labour hour for each product and rank them.
4 Using the ranking from the previous answer, prepare a forecast of the profit for each product and in total for next month if only 1,650 direct labour hours are available.
5 Quantify the difference between the answers to 2. & 4. and comment on your findings.

Solution

		Alpha	Beta	Gamma	Total
Direct costs:					
Raw materials		100	150	80	
Direct labour		15	30	6	
Prime cost		115	180	86	
Variable overhead		10	15	8	
Variable cost		125	195	94	
Fixed overhead		30	60	12	
Total cost/unit		155	255	106	
Fixed overhead/unit		30	60	12	
Sales demand (units)		50	150	200	
Total fixed overhead		1,500	9,000	2,400	12,900
1	Selling price	230	360	172	(200% of prime cost)
	Variable cost	125	195	94	
	Contribution/unit	105	165	78	
	Ranking	2	1	3	
2		**Alpha**	**Beta**	**Gamma**	**Total**
	Labour hours/unit	5	10	2	
	No. of labour hours	150	1,500	–	1,650
	No. of units sold	30	150	–	
	Contribution/unit	105	165	78	
	Total contribution	3,150	24,750	–	27,900
	Less: Fixed costs				12,900
	Net profit				**₹15,000**
3	Contribution/unit	105	165	78	
	Labour hours/unit	5	10	2	
	Contribution/labour hour	**21.0**	**16.5**	**39.0**	
	Ranking	**2**	**3**	**1**	

4

				Total
Labour hours/unit	5	10	2	
No. of labour hours	250	1,000	400	1,650
No. of units sold	50	100	200	
Contribution/unit	105	165	78	
Total contribution	5,250	16,500	15,600	37,350
Less: Fixed costs				12,900
Net profit				₹24,450

5 Using the contribution per direct labour hour ranking gives ₹9,450 more profit than the contribution per unit ranking. So, using the contribution per unit of scarce resource does give the highest profit.

EXAMPLE 16.22

A company producing a single product sells it at ₹50 per unit. The unit variable cost is ₹35 and fixed cost amounts to ₹12 lakh per annum. With this data, you are required to calculate the following, treating each as independent of the other:

(i) P/V ratios and break-even sales
(ii) New break-even sales if the variable cost increases by ₹3 per unit, without any increase in the selling price.
(iii) Increase in the sales required if profits are to be increased by ₹2,40,000
(iv) Percentage increase/decrease in the sales-volume units to offset:
  (a) An increase of ₹3 in the variable cost per unit.
  (b) A 10% increase in the selling price without affecting the existing profit quantum.
(v) Quantum of advertisement expenditure permissible to increase the sales by ₹1,20,000, without affecting the existing profit quantum.

Solution

(a) $\text{P/V ratio} = \dfrac{\text{Contribution per unit}}{\text{Selling price per unit}}$

$= \dfrac{50-35}{50} = 30\%$

$\text{Break-even sales} = \dfrac{\text{Fixed cost}}{\text{P/V ratio}}$

$= \dfrac{₹12 \text{ lakhs}}{30\%} = ₹40 \text{ lakhs}$

(b) Revised P/V ratio

$= \dfrac{\text{Existing contribution per unit}}{\text{Selling price per unit}}$

$= \dfrac{15-3}{50} = \dfrac{12}{50} = 24\%$

Revised break-even sales = $\dfrac{12}{24\%}$ = ₹50 lakhs

(c) Increase in sales required

$$= \frac{\text{Increase in contribution}}{\text{P/V ratio}}$$

$$= \frac{24}{30\%} = ₹8 \text{ lakhs}$$

(d) (i) Percentage in sales volume (units)

$$= \frac{\text{Reduction in contribution}}{\text{New contribution per unit}}$$

$$= \frac{3}{12} \times 100 = 25\%$$

(ii) Percentage decrease in sales volume (units)

$$= \frac{\text{Increase in contribution per unit}}{\text{New contribution per unit}}$$

$$= \frac{5\,(i.e.\,10\% \text{ of } ₹50)}{20\ i.e.\,(55-35)}$$

$$= 25\%$$

(e) The contribution by sales arising out of advertisement expenses should be equal to amount of ₹1.2 lakhs the sale increase to avoid profit or loss. Hence, 30% of 1.2 lakhs or ₹36,000 should be the maximum permissible advertisement expenditure for being incurred to get an increase of sale of ₹1.2 lakhs without affecting existing profits.

for excel template, scan

✍ EXAMPLE 16.23

There are two factories under the same management. The management desires to merge these two plants. The following particulars are available:

	Factory I	*Factory II*
Capacity operation	100 per cent	60 per cent
Sales	₹300 lakhs	₹120 lakhs
Variable costs	₹220 lakhs	₹ 90 lakhs
Fixed costs	₹ 40 lakhs	₹ 20 lakhs

You are required to calculate:

(i) What would be the capacity of the merged plant to be operated for the purpose of breaking even?

(ii) What would be the capacity of the merged plant to earn a profit of ₹60 lakhs?

(iii) What would be the profit on working at 80 per cent of the merged capacity?

Solution

Statement of Cost and Contribution at 100%

₹ *Lakhs*

	Factory I *100%*	*Factory II* *100%*	*Merged plant* *100%*
Sales	300	200	500
Less: Variable cost	220	150	370
Contribution	80	50	130
Fixed cost	40	20	60

(i) P/V ratio of the merged plant $= \dfrac{\text{Contribution of merged plant}}{\text{Total sales}} \times 100$

$$= \frac{130}{500} \times 100 = 26\%$$

Break-even point $= \dfrac{\text{F.C.}}{\text{P/V ratio}} = \dfrac{60}{26\%} =$ **₹230.77 lakhs**

Capacity at B.E. point $= \dfrac{230.77}{500} \times 100 =$ **46.15%**

(ii) Sales to earn ₹60 lakhs as profit $= \dfrac{\text{F.C.} + \text{Profit}}{\text{P/V ratio}}$

$$= \frac{60+60}{20\%} = \frac{120 \times 100}{26} = \textbf{₹461.54 lakhs}$$

Capacity $= \dfrac{461.54}{500} \times 100 =$ **92.31%**

(iii) Sales at 80% capacity = 500 × 80% = ₹400 lakhs

Profit = (Sales × P/V ratio) – F.C.

= (400 × 26%) – 60 = **₹44 lakhs**

EXAMPLE 16.24

A Japanese soft-drink company is planning to establish a subsidiary company in India to produce mineral water.

Based on the estimated annual sales of 40,000 bottles of mineral water cost studies produced the following estimates for Indian subsidiary:

	Total Annual Costs (₹)	*Variable Cost as % of Total Annual Cost (%)*
Material	2,10,000	100
Labour	1,50,000	80
Factory overheads	92,000	60
Admn. overheads	40,000	35

The Indian production will be sold by manufacturer's representatives who will receive a commission of 8% of the sale price. No portion of the Japanese office expenses is to be allocated to the Indian subsidiary.

You are required to:

(i) Compute the sale price per bottle to enable the management to realise an estimated 10% profit on sale proceeds in India.

(ii) Calculate the break-even point in rupee sales on the assumption that the sale price per bottle is ₹14.

☞ **Solution**

(i) **Price to earn a profit of 10% on sales:**

Suppose selling price = ₹x per bottle

Less: Commission @ 8%	= 0.08x
Less: Profit @ 10%	= 0.10x
Total cost	= 0.82x

Total cost of 40,000 bottles = 40,000 × 0.82x = 32,800x

Variance Cost:	₹
Material	2,10,000
Labour (1,50,000 × 80%)	1,20,000
Factory overheads (92,000 × 60%)	55,200
Admn. overheads (40,000 × 35%)	14,000
Total variable cost	3,99,200

Fixed Cost:	₹
Labour	30,000
Factory overheads	36,800
Admn. overheads	26,000
Total fixed cost	92,800

Therefore, total cost = ₹3,99,200 + ₹92,800 = ₹4,92,000

Thus, 32,800x = ₹4,92,000 $\quad \therefore x = \dfrac{4,92,000}{32,800} = ₹15$

Thus selling price = **₹15 per bottle**

(ii) Break-even point = $\dfrac{\text{Fixed cost}}{\text{Contribution}} \times \text{Sales}$

Sales (40,000 × ₹14)	₹5,60,000
Less: Variable cost	₹3,99,200
	₹1,60,800
Less: Commission (5,60,000 × 8%)	₹ 44,800
Contribution	₹1,16,000

$$\text{Break-even point} = \frac{92,800}{1,16,000} \times 5,60,000 = ₹4,48,000$$

$$\text{No. of bottles to break-even} = \frac{4,48,000}{14} = 32,000 \text{ bottles}$$

✍ EXAMPLE 16.25

A company is deciding which of two new thermostat systems to produce and sell. The Basic System has variable costs of ₹8.00 per unit, excluding sales commissions, and annual fixed costs of ₹520.000; the Deluxe System has variable costs of ₹6.40, excluding sales commissions, and fixed costs of ₹6,72,000. The company's selling price is ₹32 per unit for the Basic Model and ₹38 for the Deluxe Model. The company pays a 10 percent sales commission.

(a) Which of the two systems will be more profitable for the firm if sales for either system are expected to average 1,50,000 units per year?

(b) How many units must the company sell to break even if it selects the Deluxe System?

(c) Suppose, the Basic System requires the purchase of additional equipment that is not reflected in the preceding figures. The equipment will cost ₹2,24,000 and will be depreciated over a 10-year life by the straight-line method. How many units must the company sell to earn ₹40,000 of income, after considering depreciation, if the Basic System is selected?

(d) Now, ignore the information presented in part (c). Write a report that explains to management the level of volume at which it should be indifferent between the Basic System and the Deluxe System.

☞ *Solution*

(a) The Deluxe System would be more profitable, as shown below.

	Basic	Deluxe
Sales	₹48,00,000	₹57,00,000
Less Variable costs:		
1,50,000 units × ₹8.00	₹12,00,000	
1,50,000 units × ₹6.40		₹ 9,60,000
Commissions	4,80,000	5,70,000
Total variable cost	₹16,80,000	₹15,30,000
Contribution margin	₹31,20,000	₹41,70,000
Less fixed costs	5,20,000	6,72,000
Net income	₹26,00,000	₹34,98,000

(b) Break-even point in units = $\frac{\text{Fixed cost}}{\text{Unit contribution margin}}$

= ₹6,72,000/[₹38–(₹6.40 + {₹38 × 0.10})]

= 24,173 units.

(c) Straight-line depreciation associated with the new equipment would increase fixed costs by ₹22,400 (= ₹224,000/10 years). Thus,

Number of units = $\frac{\text{Fixed costs + Target profit}}{\text{Unit contribution margin}}$

= (₹5,20,000 + ₹22,400 + ₹40,000)/ {₹32 – [₹8 + (₹32 × .10)]}

= ₹5,82,400/ (₹32 – ₹11.20)

= 28,000 units.

(d) The point of indifference will produce equal levels of profitability. On the basis of the information presented in part (*a*), the Basic System has a unit contribution margin of ₹20.80 (= ₹31,20,000/1,50,000 units), and the Deluxe System has a unit contribution margin of ₹27.80 (= ₹41,70,000/1,50,000 units). Thus, if X = the required quantity at which you are indifferent:

₹20.80X – ₹5,20,000 = ₹27.80X – ₹6,72,000

₹7.00X = ₹1,52,000

X = 21,714 units.

EXAMPLE 16.26

Bodgit Ltd makes 200 wooden kitchen chairs every month and sells them for ₹50 each. Fixed monthly overheads are ₹3,000 and the standard cost of one chair is as follows:

	₹
Materials	15
Direct labour	8
Variable overheads	7

Required:

1 Calculate for one month:
 a) the variable cost of one chair;
 b) the breakeven point;
 c) the profit if 200 chairs are sold; and
 d) the number of chairs sold to give a profit of ₹4,000.

2 In an attempt to boost sales, Bodgit plans to reduce the selling price to ₹48, improve the quality by spending 20% more on materials and increase its advertising by ₹1,000 a month.

Calculate:
 a) the new breakeven point;
 b) the profit if 350 chairs are sold;
 c) the margin of safety (expressed as a % of sales) if 350 chairs are sold; and
 d) the number of chairs sold to give a profit of ₹4,000.

3 Explain why your answers to the above questions should be seen as estimates rather than exact answers.

☞ ***Solution***

		₹	**Workings**	₹
1 a)	Materials	15	Sales price	50
	Direct labour	8	Less: Variable cost	30
	Variable overheads	7	Unit contribution	20
	Variable cost	**30**		

b) BEP = Fixed costs/Unit contribution = 3,000/20 = 150 chairs

c) Total contribution = Fixed costs + Profit

200 × 20 = 3,000 + Profit

Profit = ₹1,000

d) Total contribution = Fixed costs + Profit

N × 20 = 3,000 + 4,000

N = 7,000/20

= **350 chairs**

2 a) BEP = Fixed costs/unit contribution

= (3,000 + 1,000)/15

= **267 chairs**

Workings	₹
Materials	18 (15 × 1.20)
Direct labour	8
Variable overheads	7
Variable cost	33
Sales price	48
Unit contribution	15

b) Total contribution = Fixed costs + Profit

350 × 15 = 4,000 + Profit

Profit = 5,250 – 4,000

Profit = ₹1,250

c) Margin of safety = (Actual – BEP)/Actual

= (350 – 267)/350

= 83/350

= **24% of sales**

d) Total contribution = Fixed costs + Profit

N × 15 = 4,000 + 4,000

N = 8,000/15

N = **533 chairs**

3 The answers to these questions should be viewed as estimates because the variable costing financial model is based on several assumptions and approximations. For example, total revenue and total cost are shown as straight lines on the breakeven chart. In reality, they are curved as the selling price and total cost per unit tend to decrease as the volume of activity increases.

Also, breakeven charts are applicable only to single products (or constant sales mixes of several products). In reality, almost all manufacturers make more than one product. For breakeven purposes, this necessitates a theoretical apportionment of the firm's fixed assets between different products. Some degree of approximation and subjectivity is unavoidable in this process.

EXAMPLE 16.27

(a) Flex Ltd. has been offered a choice to buy Machine *A* or Machine *B*. The relevant data are given below:

	Machine *A*	Machine *B*
Annual output (in units)	10,000	10,000
Fixed cost	₹30,000	₹16,000
Profit at the above level of production	₹30,000	₹24,000

Market price of the product is expected to be ₹10 per unit.
You are required to compute:

(i) Break-even point for each of the two machines.
(ii) Level of sales at which both the machines earn equal profit.
(iii) Range of sales at which Machine *B* is more profitable.
(iv) The level of sales above which Machine *A* is more profitable.

(b) Work Well Ltd. is a single product producer with P/V ratio of 40% for the product during the current year. Due to increasing competition, it is believed that the price will have to be reduced by 10% in the next year. By what percentage sales value and sales quantity should increase so that Work Well Ltd. earns same profit in the next year also.

Solution

(a) Contribution = Fixed cost + Profit
$A = 30{,}000 + 30{,}000 = ₹60{,}000$
$B = 16{,}000 + 24{,}000 = ₹40{,}000$
Contribution per unit $A = ₹60{,}000 \div 10{,}000$ units = ₹6
$B = ₹40{,}000 \div 10{,}000$ units = ₹4

(i) $\text{Break-even point} = \dfrac{\text{Fixed cost}}{\text{Contribution per unit}}$

$\text{A} = \dfrac{30{,}000}{6} = \textbf{5,000 units}\text{B} = \dfrac{16{,}000}{4} = \textbf{4,000 units}$

(ii) Sales at which both the machines earn equal profit

$= \dfrac{\text{Difference in fixed cost}}{\text{Difference in contribution}}$

$= \dfrac{30{,}000 - 16{,}000}{6-4} = \dfrac{14{,}000}{2} = \textbf{7,000 units}$

(iii) B is more profitable between 4,000 and 7,000 units.
(iv) A is more profitable when sales are above 7,000 units.

(b) Suppose price = ₹100, Contribution = ₹40, and variable cost = ₹60.
When price is reduced by 10% the new price is ₹90 and new contribution is ₹30.

$\text{New P/V ratio} = \dfrac{\text{C}}{\text{S}} = \dfrac{30}{90} = \dfrac{1}{3}$

$\text{New sales to earn profit} = \dfrac{\text{Old contribution}}{\text{New P/V ratio}} = \dfrac{40}{1/3} = ₹120$

$$\text{New quantity of sales} = 120 \times \frac{100}{90} = 133$$

Thus 20% increase in sales value and 33% increase in sales quantity is required.

EXAMPLE 16.28

ABC Ltd. manufactures three products—*P*, *Q* and *R*. The unit selling prices of these products are ₹100, ₹80 and ₹50 respectively. The corresponding unit variable costs are ₹50, ₹40 and ₹20. The proportions (quantity-wise) in which these products are manufactured and sold are 20%, 30% and 50% respectively. The total fixed costs are ₹14,80,000.

Given the above information, you are required to work out the overall break-even quantity and the product-wise break-up of such quantity.

Solution

Product	*Sales Price Per Unit*	*Variable Cost Per Unit*	*Contribution Per Unit*	*Ratio of Contribution Per Unit*	*Ratio of Sales*	*Ratio of Contribution*
P	100	50	50	5	2	10
Q	80	40	40	4	3	12
R	50	20	30	3	5	15
					Total	37

$$\text{Composite B.E.P. (in units)} = \frac{\text{Fixed cost}}{\text{Ratio of contribution per unit}}$$

$$= \frac{14,80,000}{37} = 40,000 \text{ units}$$

Product mix break up

$$P = 40,000 \times \frac{2}{10} = 8,000 \text{ units}$$

$$Q = 40,000 \times \frac{3}{10} = 12,000 \text{ units}$$

$$R = 40,000 \times \frac{5}{10} = 20,000 \text{ units}$$

Verification

Product	*Unit*	*Sales Price Per Unit*	*Sales Value*	*Variable Cost Per Unit*	*Variable Cost*	*Contribution*
P	8,000	100	8,00,000	50	4,00,000	4,00,000
Q	12,000	80	9,60,000	40	4,80,000	4,80,000
R	20,000	50	10,00,000	20	4,00,000	6,00,000
Total	40,000		27,60,000		12,80,000	14,80,000

As we know that at BEP

Sales – Variable costs = Fixed costs

₹27,60,000 – ₹12,80,000 = ₹14,80,000

Fixed cost is ₹14,80,000 (given in the question).

EXAMPLE 16.29

The following is cost data relating to two alternative machines:

	Inferior Machines	*Superior Machines*
Fixed cost	₹ 5,00,000	₹ 8,00,000
Variable cost per unit	₹ 30	₹ 25
Selling price	₹ 50	₹ 55

Calculate the level of output at which you are indifferent about the two machines and beyond which the superior machine should be preferred.

Solution

To calculate the level of output at which we are indifferent about the two machines, computation of contribution per unit is as follows:

	Inferior Machine	*Superior Machine*
Sales price	50	55
Less: Variable cost	30	25
Contribution	20	30
Fixed cost	5,00,000	8,00,000

Let the amount of profit at which we will be indifferent to both of the machines = ₹x

$$\frac{5,00,000 + x}{20} = \frac{8,00,000 + x}{30}$$

$$15,00,000 + 3x = 16,00,000 + 2x$$

$$x = 1,00,000$$

Hence, the level of output for indifference at a profit of ₹1,00,000 will be:

$$\text{Inferior machine} = \frac{\text{FC} + \text{Des. Profit}}{\text{Contribution per unit}} = \frac{5,00,000 + 1,00,000}{20}$$

$$= 30,000 \text{ units}$$

$$\text{Superior machine} = \frac{₹8,00,000 + ₹1,00,000}{30}$$

$$= 30,000 \text{ units}$$

EXAMPLE 16.30

Calculate break-even for a train journey between Delhi–Bangalore where cost of an engine is ₹1,00,000 and of a bogie ₹20,000. Capacity of a bogie is 80 passengers and each ticket for the journey is ₹600. There is no variable cost per passenger.

Solution

Calculation of contribution per bogie:

Sales of tickets (600 × 80)	48,000
Less: Cost of bogie	20,000
Contribution per bogie	28,000

Calculation of break-even for one train journey

$$= \frac{\text{Cost of engine (as fixed)}}{\text{Contribution ratio}}$$

$$= \frac{1,00,000}{\frac{28,000}{48,000}} = 1,00,000 \times \frac{48,000}{28,000}$$

$$= ₹\frac{12,00,000}{7} = ₹1,71,429 \text{ approximately}$$

EXAMPLE 16.31

M/s Natraj Stationers manufactures plastic files for office use. The break-up of its cost and sales is as follows:

Variable cost per file	:	₹40
Fixed cost	:	₹60,000 per year
Production capacity	:	3,000 files per year
Selling price	:	₹100 per file.

You are required to compute the following:

(i) Break-even point;
(ii) Number of files to be sold to earn a net profit of ₹30,000.
(iii) If the firm manufactures and sells 500 files more per year with an additional fixed cost of ₹2,000, what should be the selling price to earn the same amount of profit per file as in (ii) above?

Solution

(1) Calculation of cost per unit and P/V ratio

	₹
(a) Sales per unit	100
Less: Variable cost	40
Contribution	60

(b) Calculation of P/V ratio

$$= \frac{\text{Contribution}}{\text{Sales}} = \frac{60}{100} \times 100 = 60\%$$

(2) Calculation of BEP

$$= \frac{FC}{\text{P/V ratio}} = \frac{60,000}{60\%} = ₹1,00,000$$

(3) No. of files to be sold to earn a net profit of ₹30,000

$$= \frac{\text{FC} + \text{Des. profit}}{\text{Contribution per file}} = \frac{60,000 + 30,000}{60}$$

$$= \frac{90,000}{60} = 1,500.$$

Profit per file = ₹30,000 ÷ 1500 files = ₹20

(4) Selling price to earn the same amount profit per file as in (2) above

Desired profit (2,000 × 20)	40,000
Fixed cost (60,000 + 2,000)	62,000
Cost	102,000
Variable cost (2,000 × 40)	80,000
Sales desired	1,82,000

$$\text{Sales price per file} = \frac{1,82,000}{2,000} = ₹91$$

EXAMPLE 16.32

A producer installed a machine which can produce product *A* as well product *B*. Annual maximum machine running capacity is 4,000 hours. Cost details about the products are as follows:

	Product A	*Product B*
Selling price per unit	₹50	₹20
Variable cost per unit	₹30	₹12
Machine hours required per unit of product	10 hrs.	2 hrs.
Annual demand	300 units	1,600 units
Annual fixed cost: ₹10,000.		

Calculate optimum product-mix showing annual contribution and profit. Give necessary explanation. Also show that a product-mix other than that suggested by you will affect the profits.

Solution

Calculation of Contribution Per Hour

	A	*B*
Sales	50	20
Less: Variable cost	30	12
Contribution	20	8
Machine hours.	10	2
Contribution per machine hour $\left(\frac{\text{Contribution}}{\text{Machine hour}}\right)$	2	4

Since the contribution per machine hour is more in case of product *B*. Hence, product *B* should be produced in maximum.

Calculation of No. of Units to be Produced (Optimum Product Mix)

Total machine hours	4,000
Less: Machine hours for *B* (1600 × 2)	3,200
Machine hours for *A*	800

$\therefore$ No. of units of *A* should be $= \dfrac{800}{10}$

$= 80$ units

No. of units of *B* should be = 1,600 units

Calculation of Annual Contribution and Profit

	A	*B*	*Total*
Sales (*A* = 80 × 50)	4,000	32,000	36,000
(*B* = 1,600 × 20)			
Less: Variable cost			
A 80 × 30	2,400	19,200	21,600
B 1,600 × 120			
Contribution	1,600	12,800	14,400
Less: Fixed cost			10,000
Profit			4,400

Any product mix other than suggested above will reduce the profits as is clear from the following example:

	A	*B*	*Total*
Sales units	100	1,500	1,600
Sales	5,000	30,000	35,000
Less: Variable cost	3,000	18,000	21,000
Contribution	2,000	12,000	14,000
Less: Fixed cost profit			10,000
Profit			4,000

EXAMPLE 16.33

An exporter of garments is earning a profit of ₹1,00,000 on a sale of ₹12,00,000. Selling price is ₹40 per garment and variable cost is ₹30 per garment. The exporter incurs an additional fixed cost of ₹3,00,000 on product improvement which also enables him to economise ₹5 in per garment variable cost. As per trade agreements, the sale of his garments is restricted to the old value of ₹12,00,000. What should be the selling price per garment so that the exporter earns the same profit at the same sales value?

Solution

$$\text{Units sold} = \frac{\text{Sales}}{\text{Selling price per unit}} = \frac{₹12,00,000}{₹40}$$

$$= 30,000 \text{ units}$$

Computation of Fixed Cost before Incurring Additional Fixed Cost

	Sales	40	12,00,000
Less:	Variable cost	30	9,00,000
	Contribution	10	3,00,000
Less:	Profits		1,00,000
	Fixed cost		2,00,000

Hence, total fixed cost in the new case

= ₹2,00,000 + ₹3,00,000 = ₹5,00,000

Contribution in the new case = New fixed cost + Profits

= 5,00,000 + 1,00,000 = ₹6,00,000

Since as per agreement the sale value is restricted to the old value that is ₹12,00,000. Hence P/V ratio will be:

$$= \frac{6,00,000}{12,00,000} \times 100 = 50\%$$

The variable cost in the new case = ₹30 – 5 = ₹25

Variable cost ratio = 100 – P/V ratio = 100 – 50 = 50%

Computation of New Selling Price:

If VC is 50, then SP = ₹100

$$\text{If VC is 1, then SP} = \frac{100}{50}$$

$$\text{If VC is 25, then SP} = \frac{100}{50} \times 25 = ₹50 \text{ per unit}$$

EXAMPLE 16.34

(a) A company has a project to install a new machine exclusively for the manufacture of a new product which is expected to have good demand and reasonably high margin. Maximum possible annual sales may not exceed ₹50 lakhs and if there is competition it may fall considerably. The company has obtained quotations and short listed two offers for the new machine. Details in respect of the two models are given below:

	Machine Models	
Maximum possible sales per year	₹50 lakhs	₹50 lakhs
Fixed costs per year	5 lakhs	8 lakhs
Estimated profit for maximum sales	15 lakhs	17 lakhs

You are required to calculate:

(i) Break-even sales of each machine.

(ii) Sales at which both models will give the same profit;

(iii) Range of sales over which one model is better than the other.

(b) For the final assembly of a product in an engineering company, a certain component is required. The company has the options either to produce the component itself or purchase it from the market. The production department which can make the component is currently working to full capacity and earning a contribution of ₹10 per hour on an order which will last for another ten months. Repeat orders are very likely. Variable cost of making the component is ₹42 and it takes one hour per unit. Market price of the component is ₹45 per unit.

What advice will you give to the management of the company?

☞ Solution

(a) Statement Showing Parameters of Two Machines

(₹ *in lakhs*)

	Type of Machines	*Model M1*	*Model M2*
1.	Maximum possible sales per year	50	50
2.	Fixed costs per year	5	8
3.	Estimated profit for maximum sales	15	17
4.	Total contribution based on max. sales (2 + 3)	20	25
5.	P/V ratio (Contribution/Sales) (4/1).	0.40	0.50
	(i) Break-even sales FC ÷ P/V	12.50	16.00
	(ii) Sales at which both models will give the same profit *[Ref. Working Note 1]*	30.00	30.00
	Profit	7.00	7.00

Working Note 1:

Let S be the sales at which profit will be the same for both models.

	M1	*M2*
Sales = $[F + P] \div C/S$	$[5 + P]/0.40$	$[8 + P]/0.50$

where, F = fixed costs; P = Profit; C = Contribution; S = Sales.

Accordingly to given expression,

$$\frac{5+P}{0.40} \quad \frac{8+P}{0.50} = 2.5 + 0.50P = 3.20 + 0.40P = 0.10P = 0.70 = P = 7$$

Substituting,

$$S = \frac{5+7}{0.4} \Rightarrow \frac{8+7}{0.50} ₹30 \text{ lakhs}$$

(iii) *Range of sales over which one model is better than the other:*

In the light of supra-comparative parameters, up to ₹30 lakhs annual sales Model $M1$ will be more profitable than Model $M2$, since it ($M1$) has lower fixed cost and a lower break-even point and, at an annual sale of ₹30 lakhs both will have the same profit of ₹7 lakhs.

Model $M2$ having higher fixed cost and a higher break-even point will be more profitable than Model $M1$ when the annual sale for the product exceeds ₹30 lakhs.

(b) If the company makes the component now, the effective cost would be ₹52 per unit that is, variable cost of ₹42 plus contribution of ₹10 foregone for the one hour diverted from current production.

Since it is available at ₹45 in the market, purchase from the market may be made. Since repeat orders are very likely, purchase from the market may continue.

If the capacity becomes available in the factory and the market price and variable cost of making continue to be ₹45 and ₹42 respectively, the component may be made in the company since it is cheaper to make. Similarly, if the market price rises above ₹52, then also it is cheaper to make the component curtailing current production.

EXAMPLE 16.35

The comparative profit statement of two quarters of a firm is as under:

	Quarter I	*Quarter II*
Units sold	2,500	3,750
	₹	₹
Direct materials	87,500	?
Direct wages	62,500	?
Fixed and variable factory overheads	75,000	95,000
Sales	2,75,000	?
Profit	50,000	66,250

In the second quarter, the direct material price has increased by 20%. There was a saving of ₹5,000 in fixed overheads in the second quarter. The other costs and selling price remained the same. Determine the quantity that should have been sold in the second quarter to maintain the same amount of profit per unit as in the first quarter.

Solution

Working Notes:

1. *Direct Material, Direct Wages, Selling Price and Profit Per Unit*

$$\text{Direct material (p.u)} = \frac{₹87{,}500}{2{,}500 \text{ units}} = ₹35$$

$$\text{Direct wages (p.u)} = \frac{₹62{,}500}{2{,}500 \text{ units}} = ₹25$$

$$\text{Selling price (p.u)} = \frac{₹2{,}75{,}000}{2{,}500 \text{ units}} = ₹110$$

$$\text{Profit (p.u)} = \frac{₹50{,}000}{2{,}500 \text{ units}} = ₹20$$

2. *Variable Factory Overhead Per Unit and Fixed Factory Overheads for II Quarter*

$$\text{Variable factory overhead (p u)} = \frac{\text{Changes in semi-variable overheads}}{\text{Changes in production volume}}$$

$$= \frac{₹1,00,000^{**} - ₹75,000}{3,750 \text{ units} - 2,500 \text{ units}}$$

$$= \frac{₹25,000}{1,250 \text{ units}} = ₹20/-$$

Fixed Factory Overheads for II Quarter

	₹
Total factory overheads of II quarter	1,00,000
Less: Variable factory overheads (3,750 units × ₹20)	75,000
Total fixed factory overheads for II quarter	25,000
Less: Saving of fixed factory overheads	5,000
Net fixed factory overheads for II quarter	20,000

Statement of Quantity of Units To Be Sold in Second Quarter to Maintain Same Amount of Profit Per Unit as in the First Quarter

	₹	₹
Selling price per unit: (A) *(Refer to Working Note 1)*		110
Variable costs: (per unit):		
Direct materials $\left(₹35 \times \frac{120}{100}\right)$	42	
Direct wages	25	
Variable factory overheads *(Refer to Working Note 2)*	20	
Total variable cost: (B)		87
Contribution per unit: {(A – D)}		23
Less: Profit per unit *(Refer to Working Note 1)*		20
Balance for fixed cost per unit		3
Total fixed cost		20,000

** In fact the fixed and variable factory overheads during the quarter (II) were ₹1,00,000 but due to saving of ₹5,000 the balance amount of ₹95,000 was paid.

Hence, the number of units to be sold in the second quarter to maintain the same amount of profit p.u. as in the first quarter

$$= \frac{\text{Total fixed cost}}{\text{Balance for fixed cost p.u.}}$$

$$= \frac{₹20,000}{₹3 \text{ per unit}} = 6,667 \text{ units (Approx.)}$$

EXAMPLE 16.36

A company manufactures a product, currently utilising 80% capacity with a turnover of ₹8,00,000 at ₹25 per unit. The cost data are as under:

Material cost ₹7.50 per unit, Labour cost ₹6.25 per unit.

Semi-variable cost (including variable cost of ₹3.75 per unit) ₹1,80,000.

Fixed cost ₹90,000 upto 80% level of output, beyond this an additional ₹20,000 will be incurred.

Calculate:

(i) Activity level at break-even-point

(ii) Number of units to be sold to earn a net income of 8% of sales

(iii) Activity level needed to earn a profit of ₹95,000

(iv) What should be the selling price per unit, if break-even-point is to be brought down to 40% activity level?

Solution

Working Notes:

1. (i) *Number of Units Sold at 80% Capacity*

$$= \frac{\text{Turnover}}{\text{Selling price p.u}} = \frac{₹8,00,000}{₹25} = ₹32,000 \text{ units}$$

(ii) *Number of Units Sold at 100% Capacity*

$$= \frac{32,000 \text{ units}}{80} \times 100 = 40,000 \text{ units}$$

2. *Component of Fixed Cost included in Semi-Variable Cost of 32,000 units*

Fixed cost = {Total semi-variable cost – Total variable cost}

= ₹1,80,000 – 32,000 units × ₹3.75

= ₹1,80,000 – ₹1,20,000

= ₹60,000

3. (i) *Total Fixed Cost beyond 80% Capacity*

= Fixed cost + Component of fixed cost included in semi-variable cost

(Refer to Working Note 2)

= ₹90,000 + ₹60,000 = ₹1,50,000

(ii) *Total Fixed Cost beyond 80% Capacity*

= Total fixed cost at 80% capacity + Additional fixed cost to be incurred

= ₹1,50,000 + ₹20,000 = ₹1,70,000

4. *Variable Cost and Contribution Per Unit*

Variable cost per unit = Material cost + Labour cost + Variable cost component in semi-variable cost

= ₹7.50 + ₹6.25 + ₹3.75 = ₹17.50

Contribution per unit = Selling price per unit – Variable cost per unit

= ₹25 – ₹17.50 = ₹7.50

5. *Profit at 80% Capacity Level*

= Sales revenue – Variable cost – Fixed cost

= ₹8,00,000 – ₹5,60,000 (32,000 units × ₹17.50) – ₹1,50,000 = ₹90,000

(i) *Activity Level at Break-even Point*

$$\text{Break-even point (units)} = \frac{\text{Fixed cost}}{\text{Contribution per unit}} = \frac{₹1,50,000}{₹7.50} = 20,000 \text{ units}$$

(Refer to Working Notes 3 & 4)

$$\text{Activity level at Break-even point} = \frac{\text{Break-even point (units)}}{\text{No. of units at 100\% capcity level}} \times 100$$

(Refer to Working Note 1(ii))

$$= \frac{20,000 \text{ units}}{40,000 \text{ units}} \times 100 = 50\%$$

(ii) *Number of Units to be Sold to Earn a Net Income of 8% of Sales*

Let x be the number of units sold to earn a net income of 8% of sales.

Mathematically, it means that:

(Sales revenue of x units)= Variable cost of x units + Fixed cost + Net income

or $₹25x = ₹17.5x + ₹1,50,000 + \frac{8}{100} \times (₹25x)$

or $₹25x = ₹17.5x + ₹1,50,000 + ₹2x$

or x = (₹1,50,000/ ₹5.5) units

or x = 27,273 units.

(iii) *Activity Level Needed to Earn a Profit of ₹95,000*

The profit at 80% capacity level is ₹90,000 which is less than the desired profit of₹95,000. Therefore, the needed activity level would be more than 80%. Thus, the fixed cost to be taken to determine the activity level needed should be ₹1,70,000 *(Refer to Working Note 3(ii))*

$$\text{Units to be sold to earn a profit of ₹95,000} = \frac{\text{Fixed cost + Desired profit}}{\text{Contribution per unit}}$$

$$= \frac{₹1,70,000 + ₹95,000}{₹7.5}$$

= 35,333.33 units

$$\text{Activity level needed to earn a profit of ₹95,000} = \frac{35,333.33}{40,000 \text{ units}} \times 100$$

= 88.33%

(iv) ***Selling Price Per Unit, if Break-even-Point is to be Brought Down to 40% (16,000 units) Activity Level***

Let x be the selling price per unit

$$\text{Units at break-even-point} = 16{,}000 \text{ units}$$

$$\text{Break-even-point} = \frac{\text{Fixed cost}}{\text{Contribution per unit}}$$

$$\text{At } 16{,}000 \text{ units} = \frac{₹1{,}50{,}000}{(x - ₹17.50)}$$

or $$(x - ₹17.50) = \frac{₹1{,}50{,}000}{16{,}000 \text{ units}}$$

or $$(x - ₹17.50) = \frac{₹75}{8 \text{ units}}$$

or $$8x - 8 \times ₹17.50 = ₹75$$

or $$8x - ₹140 = ₹75$$

or $$8x = ₹215$$

or $$x = ₹26.875$$

Hence, selling price (per unit) = ₹26.875

EXAMPLE 16.37

ABC Ltd. which produces three products furnishes the following data for the year 2020.

	Products		
	Alfa	*Beta*	*Gamma*
Selling price per unit	₹100	75	50
Profit/Volume ratio	10%	20%	40%
Maximum sales potential (units)	40,000	25,000	10,000
Raw material as % of variable cost	50%	50%	50%

The company uses the same raw material for all the three products. Raw material is in short supply and the company has a quota for supply of raw material of the value of ₹18,00,000 for the year 2020 for manufacture of its products to meet its sales. Total fixed cost is ₹6,80,000.

You are required to:

(a) Determine a sales mix which will give the maximum overall profit keeping in view the short supply of raw material.

(b) Compute the maximum profit.

Solution

Particulars		Products		
		Alfa	*Beta*	*Gamma*
Selling price per unit	₹	100	75	50
Profit volume ratio		10%	20%	40%

Particulars		Products		
		Alfa	*Beta*	*Gamma*
Contribution per unit	₹	10	15	20
Variable cost per unit	₹	90	60	30
Raw material per unit	₹	45	30	15
Contribution per rupee of raw material	=	10/45	15/30	20/15
	=	2/9	1/2	4/3
Ranking		3	2	1

(a) Computation of Sales Mix

Product	*Units* ₹	*Sales* ₹	*Raw Material Used*
Gamma	10,000	5,00,000	1,50,000
Beta	25,000	18,75,000	7,50,000
Alfa	20,000	20,00,000	9,00,000
Balance	55,000	43,75,000	18,00,000

(b) Computation of Profit

Product	*Sales* ₹	*P/V Ratio*	*Contribution*
Gamma	5,00,000	40	2,00,000
Beta	18,75,000	20	3,75,000
Alfa	20,00,000	10	2,00,000
			7,75,000
	Less: Fixed cost		6,80,000
	Net profit		95,000

✍ EXAMPLE 16.38

Starlight Co. Ltd. and Jupiter Co. Ltd. sell the same type of product. Budgeted Profit & Loss Account of these companies for the year ended 31st March 2020 given below:

	Starlight Co. (₹'000)		Jupiter Co. (₹'000)	
Sales		300		300
Less : Variable cost :				
Material	100		80	
Labour	110		100	
Overhead	30	240	20	200
Fixed cost		30		70
Budgeted profit		30		30

You are required to find out the break-even point of each company. Also state clearly which company is likely to earn greater profit if there is (i) heavy demand; and (ii) poor demand for its product.

Solution

	Starlight Co. (₹'000)	Jupiter Co. (₹'000)
Sales	300	300
Variable cost	240	200
Contribution	60	100
Fixed cost	30	70
Budgeted profit	30	30
P/V ratio × 100	$\frac{60}{300}$	$\frac{100}{300}$
	= 20%	$= 33\frac{1}{3}\%$
$BEP = \frac{F}{P/V \text{ ratio}}$	$\frac{30{,}000}{20\%}$	$\frac{70{,}000}{33\frac{1}{3}\%}$
	₹1,50,000	₹2,10,000
Margin of safety	₹3,00,000 – 1,50,000	3,00,000 – 2,10,000
(Sales– BE = P)	₹1,50,000	90,000

(i) In case of high demand, Jupiter Co. is more profitable as its PV ratio is higher at $33\frac{1}{3}\%$. After meeting its fixed cost of ₹70,000 the profit in Jupiter Co. will be $33\frac{1}{3}\%$. of sales, whereas, it will be 20% of sales in case of Starlight Co. after meeting its fixed cost of ₹30,000.

(ii) In case of low demand, Starlight Co. is more profitable as its fixed cost and BEP are very low. After meeting fixed cost of ₹30,000, it will earn profit: Margin of safety is also higher in case of Starlight Co. Even if the sale is reduced to 50% due to low demand, it will touch BEP and the Co. will not incur any loss.

EXAMPLE 16.39

A company makes 1,500 units of a product for which the profitability statement is given below:

		₹
Sales		1,20,000
Direct materials	30,000	
Direct labour	36,000	
Variable OH	15,000	

	₹	
Subtotal variable cost	81,000	
Fixed cost	16,800	
Total cost		97,800
Profit		22,200

After the first 500 units of production, the company has to pay a premium of ₹6 per unit towards overtime labour. The premium so paid has been included in the direct labour cost of ₹36,000 given above. You are required to compute the break-even point.

☞ *Solution*

Data/Unit	1–500	501–1,500
	₹	₹
Sales (1,20,000 / 1,500)	80	80
Direct material (20,000 / 1,000)	20	20
Direct labour	20	26
Variable overheads 15,000 / 1,500	10	10
Contribution	30	24
No. of units	500	
Total contribution	15,000	
Fixed costs	16,800	
Shortfall	1,800	

No. of units required above 500 to recover shortfall 1,800 / 24 = 75

Break-even point (500 + 75) = 575 units

Let X be the Direct Labour per unit upto 500 units.

Total Direct Labour 500X + 1,000 (X + 6) = 36,000

$$1{,}500X + 6{,}000 = 36{,}000$$

$$X = 20.$$

Therefore, up to 500 units the Direct Labour is ₹20. After 500 units it is ₹26.

✍ EXAMPLE 16.40

Shri Rani Sati Ltd. provides you the following information:

Year 2019		Year 2020	
Sales	₹15,00,000	Sales	₹5,00,000
Total profit	₹3,60,000	Total cost	₹5,40,000

During the next year 2021, the selling price and variable cost are expected to be reduced by 20% and $33\frac{1}{3}$ respectively and fixed costs are expected to increase by 25%.

Required:

(i) Estimate the profit if sales units are expected to increase by 100%.
(ii) Estimate the sales in order to increase profit by ₹2,40,000 per year.
(iii) Estimate the sales so as to earn a return of 25% on sales.
(iv) Estimate the sales so as to earn a return of 30% on capital employed. Working capital is 25% of sales and 20% of capital employed.
(v) Estimate the BEP for the next year 2021.

☞ ***Solution***

(a)

	₹	
A. Sales	8,00,000	(₹5,00,000 × 200% × 80%)
B. *Less:* Variable cost	4,00,000	(₹3,00,000 × 200% × 66-2/3%)
C. Contribution (A – B)	4,00,000	
D. *Less:* Fixed Cost	3,00,000	(2,40,000 × 125%)
E. Profit (C – D)	1,00,000	

(b) **Desired Sales** = $\dfrac{\text{New fixed costs} + \text{Expected profit}}{\text{New P / V ratio}}$

Desired Sales = $\dfrac{₹3,00,000 + ₹2,00,000\ (\text{i.e. } ₹2,40,000 - ₹40,000)}{50\%} = ₹10,00,000$

(c) **Desired Sales** = $\dfrac{\text{New fixed costs} + \text{Expected profit}}{\text{New P / V ratio}}$

Let Sales be x, = $x = \dfrac{₹3,00,000 + 0.25x}{50\%} = ₹12,00,000$

(d) **Desired Sales** = $\dfrac{\text{New fixed costs + Expected profit}}{\text{New P/V ratio}}$

Let Sales be x, Working capital = $0.25x$, Capital employed = $0.25x/20\% = 1.25x$
Desired return on capital employed = 30% or $1.25x = 0.375x$

$= \dfrac{₹3,00,000 + 0.375x}{50\%} = ₹24,00,000$

(e) New BEP = $\dfrac{\text{New fixed cost}}{\text{New P / V ratio}} = \dfrac{(₹2,40,000 \times 125\%)}{50\%} = ₹6,00,000$

Working Notes:

(i) Profit volume ratio = $\dfrac{\text{Change in profit}}{\text{Change in sales}} \times 100 = \dfrac{₹4,00,000 - ₹3,60,000}{₹5,00,000 - ₹15,00,000} \times 100 = 40\%$

(ii) Fixed costs = Contribution – Profit = 40% of ₹15,00,000 – ₹3,60,000 = ₹2,40,000

(iii) New P/V ratio = $\dfrac{\text{New selling price} - \text{New variable cost}}{\text{New selling price}} \times 100$

$$= \frac{[(₹10 - 20\% \text{ of } ₹10) - (₹6 - 331/3\% \text{ of } ₹6)]}{(₹10 - 20\% \text{ of } ₹10)} \times 100 = 50\%$$

(iv) New fixed costs = ₹2,40,000 + 25% of ₹2,40,000 = ₹3,00,000

EXAMPLE 16.41

A company manufactures a single product with a capacity of 1,50,000 units per annum. The summarised profitability statement for the year is as under:

	₹	₹
Sales: 1,00,000 units @ ₹15 per unit		15,00,000
Cost of sales:		
Direct materials	3,00,000	
Direct labour	2,00,000	
Production overhead: Variable	60,000	
Fixed	3,00,000	
Administration overheads (Fixed)	1,50,000	
Selling and Distribution overheads: Variable	90,000	
Fixed	1,50,000	12,50,000
Profit		2,50,000

You are required to evaluate the following options:

(i) What will be the amount of sales required to earn a target profit of 25% on sales, if the packing is improved at a cost of ₹1 per unit?

(ii) There is an offer from a large retailer for purchasing 30,000 units per annum, subject to providing a packing with a different brand name at a cost of ₹2 per unit. However, in this case there will be no selling and distribution expenses. Also, this will not, in any way, affect the company's existing business. What will be the break-even price for this additional offer?

(iii) If an expenditure of ₹3,00,000 is made on advertising, the sales would increase from the present level of 1,00,000 units to 1,20,000 units at a price of ₹18 per unit. Will that expenditure be justified?

(iv) If the selling price is reduced by ₹2 per unit, there will be 100% capacity utilisation. Will the reduction in selling price be justified?

Solution

Working Notes:

	₹
(1) *Contribution Per Unit:*	
Selling price per unit: (A)	15.00
Variable cost per unit:	
Direct materials (₹3,00,000/1,00,000 units)	3.00

Direct labour (₹2,00,000/1,00,000 units)	2.00
Variable production overheads (₹60,000/1,00,000 units)	0.60
Variable selling and distribution overheads (₹90,000/1,00,000 units)	0.90
Total variable cost per unit: (B)	6.50
Contribution per unit: {(A) – (B)} (₹15 – ₹6.50)	8.50

(2) *Total Fixed Cost:*

Production overheads	3,00,000
Administration overheads	1,50,000
Selling and distribution overheads	1,50,000
Total fixed cost	6,00,000

(i) Amount of sales required to earn a target profit of 25% on sales after improving the packing

	₹
Present variable cost per unit *(Refer to Working Note 1)*	6.50
Improved packing cost per unit	1.00
Revised variable cost per unit	7.50

$$\text{P/V ratio} = \frac{\text{Contribution}}{\text{Sales}} \times 100 \left\{ \frac{₹15 - ₹7.50}{₹15} \times 100 \right\} = 50\%$$

Let x is the desired sales revenue to earn a target profit of 25% on sales; then the desired contribution would be: Total fixed cost + 25% × x

$$\text{Since P/V ratio} = \frac{\text{C}}{\text{S}} \times 100 = \frac{\text{Fixed cost} + \text{Profit}}{x} \times 100$$

$$\therefore \qquad x = \frac{₹6,00,000 + 25\%\ x}{50\%} \quad \textit{(Refer to Working Note 2)}$$

or $\quad x \times 50\% = ₹6,00,000 + 25\%\ x$

or $\quad \left[\frac{x}{2} - \frac{x}{4}\right] = ₹6,00,000$

or $\quad x = ₹24,00,000$

Hence, the desired amount of sales required to earn a target profit of 25% on sales is ₹24,00,000. On the sale of ₹24,00,000, the desired contribution is 50% of sales that is ₹12,00,000 and profit is 25% of sales that is ₹6,00,000.

(ii) Evaluation of an offer of purchasing 30,000 units per annum (subject to providing a packing with a different brand name at a cost of ₹2 per unit) from a large retailer. Determine also the break-even price for this additional offer.

	₹
Present variable cost per unit	6.50
Less: Variable selling and distribution overheads per unit	0.90
	5.60
Add: Special packing cost per unit	2.00
Revised variable cost per unit	7.60

The break-even price per unit for this additional offer of 30,000 units would be ₹7.60 per unit. In other words, the break-even price for this additional offer here means the price per unit at which 30,000 units offer can be accepted without earning any profit on it.

Note: The existing business will bear the impact of fixed cost. Fixed costs will not affect this additional offer of 30,000 units.

(iii) Justification of incurring advertisement expenses of ₹3,00,000 for increasing the sale from 1,00,000 units to 1,20,000 units.

	₹
New selling price per unit	18.00
Less: Variable cost per unit *(Refer to Working Note 1)*	6.50
Contribution per unit	11.50
Total contribution *(1,20,000 units ×₹11.50)*	13,80,000
Less: Present fixed cost	(6,00,000)
Less: Additional expenditure on advertising	(3,00,000)
Profit	4,80,000

Justification: The amount of profit on the sale of 1,00,000 units was ₹2,50,000 *(Refer to the statement of the question)*. On increasing the sale of product units from 1,00,000 to 1,20,000 the profit of the concern increased from ₹2,50,000 to ₹4,80,000. Therefore, the expenditure on advertisement is justifiable and the proposal under consideration is viable.

(iv) Justification of reduction in selling price to increase capacity utilisation to 100%

	₹
Revised selling price per unit	13.00
Less: Variable cost per unit *(Refer to Working Note 1)*	6.50
Contribution per unit	6.50
Total contribution at 100% capacity utilisation *(1,50,000 units ×₹6.50)*	9,75,000
Less: Fixed cost	6,00,000
Profit	3,75,000

Justification: A reduction in selling price by ₹2 per unit for 100% capacity utilisation, increases the present profit of ₹2,50,000 to ₹3,75,000. Hence, the reduction in selling price is justified.

Theory Questions

1. What do you mean by marginal costing? Discuss its usefulness and limitations.
2. Write a lucid note on marginal costing indicating its effect on profit computations.
3. What are the most important areas of management decisions opened up by the application of the marginal (direct) costing method?
4. Marginal costs reveal the lowest price at which a product can be sold during a trade depression, but they also reveal to management the most profitable lines during the period of intense trade activity. Explain with examples, the second part of this statement.
5. Discuss the following terms in relation to marginal costing.
   (a) Key factor, (b) P/V ratio, and (c) Margin of safety.
6. (a) What do you understand by the term "margin of safety" with reference to volume of production?
   (b) How do the following reflect on a break-even volume and on a P/V ratio; (i) increase in total fixed cost; (ii) increase in total physical sales; (iii) decrease in variable costs per unit.
7. What do you understand by the term "break-even analysis"? Enumerate its uses.
8. How do income statements prepared under the absorption costing and marginal costing concepts differ?
9. Compared with absorption costing when will variable costing report lower profits, higher profits, and the same profits?
10. In what ways is variable costing better adapted to managerial use in profit planning, decision-making and control?
11. Why do the supporters of marginal costing state that fixed costs are not to be included in inventories?
12. Discuss the uses of CVP analysis and its significance to management.
13. "In classifying a particular cost as fixed or variable, the volume or activity level is extremely important." Discuss and illustrate this statement.
14. "The contribution approach is the foundation of CVP logic and related techniques." Discuss.
15. Discuss the role of contribution in marginal costing in decisions relating to fixation of selling price.
16. State with reasons whether the following propositions are correct.
    (a) In an undertaking with a high fixed cost, break-even point can be attained at a lower level of activity.
    (b) Profit is represented by the product of the margin of safety and the P/V ratio.
    (c) In relation to normal sales, a low margin of safety along with a high P/V ratio is generally an indication of high fixed costs.
17. Distinguish between absorption costing and variable costing.
18. Enumerate the factors which can change the break-even point.
19. "Marginal costing rewards sales whereas absorption costing rewards production. Comment.
20. "Absorption costing obscures the total amount of fixed costs whereas variable costing highlights it" Comment.
21. Mention some possible courses of action to improve profit-volume ratio.
22. What is meant by cost-volume-profit analysis? How CVP analysis is useful for the management?
23. Mention the basic assumption made for "Break-even Analysis" and examine how far they are valid.
24. What is profit-volume graph? Explain how it is drawn? What are its important limitations?
25. What are the limitations of break-even analysis?
26. "The techniques of variable costing are more used to provide a reasonable and sound basis for managerial decisions than to arrive at product cost." Explain this statement with reference to the various types of decisions in which variable costing is useful.
27. Discuss the importance of fixed and variable costs for decision making at project stage and at operations stage.
28. Distinguish between "marginal costing" and "absorption costing".
29. "The effect of a price reduction is always to reduce the P/V ratio, to raise the break-even point, and to shorten the margin of safety." Explain with a suitable illustration.

30. Define break-even point. How can the break-even point be computed?
31. How is a break-even chart prepared? What information does the break-even chart give?
32. What are the basic assumptions in cost-volume-profit analysis under (a) absorption costing, and (b) variable costing?
33. Describe how a P/V chart is drawn. How does the P/V chart differ from a break-even chart?
34. For product-mix decisions, what criteria can be used to select products that will maximise net income?
35. Break-even analysis assumes that variable costs and revenues are linear and that fixed costs are fixed. Briefly explain why these assumptions may not be realistic.
36. "Marginal costs reveal the lowest price at which a product can be sold during a trade depression, but they also reveal to management the most profitable lines during a period of intense trade activity." Explain with examples the second part of this statement.
37. Can there be two break-even points? Show with the help of a graph.
38. Distinguish between contribution and profit.
39. What do you mean by cost volume profit analysis? What are its assumptions?
40. What is meant by margin of safety and angle of incidence? Show these on a break-even chart.
41. Compared with absorption costing, when variable costing report will lower profits, higher profits and equal profits?
42. Define margin costing and explain its main characteristics.
43. Write notes on cost volume profit analysis.
44. Write notes on assumptions of break-even chart.
45. Distinguish between absorption costing and marginal costing.
46. What is margin of safety? How can an unsatisfactory margin of safety ratio be improved?
47. What are the limitations of break-even analysis?
48. Explain the term "break-even point" and give its uses.
49. What are the assumptions on which marginal costing technique is based?
50. What is P/V ratio? Explain its uses.
51. Write note on key factor and its significance.
52. What is meant by break-even analysis? What are its assumptions?

Self-Evaluation Questions

I. Choose the correct answer for the following multiple choice questions:

(i) To obtain the break-even point in rupee sales value, total fixed costs are divided by:
   (a) Variable cost per unit;
   (b) Contribution margin per unit;
   (c) Fixed cost per unit; and
   (d) Profit/volume ratio.

(ii) The break-even point is the point at which:
   (a) There is no profit, no loss;
   (b) Contribution margin is equal to total fixed cost;
   (c) Total revenue is equal to total cost;
   (d) All of the above.

(iii) The primary difference between a fixed budget and a variable (flexible) budget is that a fixed budget:
   (a) includes only fixed costs, while a variable budget includes only variable costs.
   (b) is concerned with only further acquisitions of fixed costs, while a variable budget is concerned with expenses which vary with sales.
   (c) cannot be changed after the period begins, while a variable budget can be changed after the period begins.

(d) is a plan for a single level of sales (or other measure of activity), while a variable budget consists of several plans, one for each of several levels of sales (or other measures of activity).

(iv) Margin of safety is referred to as:
(a) Excess of actual sales over fixed expenses;
(b) Excess of actual sales over variable expenses;
(c) Excess of actual sales over break-even sales;
(d) Excess of budgeted sales over fixed costs.

Ans: (i) d (ii) a (iii) d (iv) c

II. Attempt the following (working notes should form part of the answer):

(i) Total fixed cost ₹12,000; Contribution ₹20,000, No. of units sold 10,000; Variable cost is 60% of sales. Determine selling price per unit and also the total profit/loss.
(ii) Total fixed cost ₹12,000, Actual sales ₹48,000, Margin of safety ₹8,000. Determine the P/V ratio.
(iii) When output is 3,000 units, the average cost per unit is ₹4. When output is increased to 4,000 units, the average cost is ₹3.50 per unit. The break-even point is 5,000 units. Find the P/V ratio.

Ans: (i) ₹5 (ii) 30% (iii) 37.5%

III. Choose the correct answer for the following multiple choice questions:

(i) Contribution margin is known as
(a) Marginal income (b) Gross profit
(c) Net income (d) Net profit

(ii) The break-even analysis may be described as
(a) Comparison between production and sales
(b) Comparison to make out capacity utilisation
(c) Comparison between target set and actual achievement
(d) Comparison between sales and costs

(iii) An increase in sales price
(a) Does not affect the break-even point
(b) Lowers the net profit
(c) Increases the break-even point
(d) Lowers the break-even point

(iv) Profit under traditional costing and marginal costing system will be the same if
(a) There are no opening and closing stocks
(b) There is opening stock and no closing stock
(c) There is closing stock and no opening stock
(d) There are opening and closing stocks

(v) A decrease in sales price
(a) Does not affect the break-even point
(b) Lowers the net profit
(c) Increases the break-even point
(d) Lowers the break-even point

(vi) Fixed cost per unit decrease when
(a) Production volume increases
(b) Production volume decreases
(c) Variable costs per unit decreases
(d) Prime costs per unit decreases

(vii) Within a relevant range, the amount of variable costs per unit
(a) Differs at each production level
(b) Remains constant at each production level
(c) Increases as production increases
(d) Decreases as production increases

(viii) Margin of safety is referred to as
- (a) Excess of budgeted or actual sales over the variable expenses and fixed expense at break-even.
- (b) Excess of budgeted or actual sales revenue over the fixed expenses.
- (c) Excess of actual sales over budgeted sales.
- (d) Excess of sales revenue over the variable expenses.

(ix) The most useful information derived from a break-even chart is the
- (a) Amount of sales revenue needed to cover variable costs.
- (b) Amount of sales revenue needed to cover fixed costs.
- (c) Relationship among revenues, variable costs and fixed costs at various levels of activity.
- (d) Volume or output level at which the enterprise break-even.

(x) Each of the following would affect the break-even point except a change in the
- (a) Number of units sold
- (b) Variable cost per unit
- (c) Total fixed costs
- (d) Sales price per unit

(xi) Under marginal costing system, the contribution margin discloses the excess of
- (a) Revenue over fixed costs
- (b) Projected revenues over the break-even point
- (c) Revenues over variable costs
- (d) Variable costs over fixed costs

(xii) The method of cost accounting that lends itself to break-even analysis is
- (a) Variable (Marginal) (b) Standard
- (c) Absolute (d) Absorption

(xiii) Cost volume profit analysis allows management to determine relative profitability of a product by
- (a) Highlighting potential bottlenecks in the production process.
- (b) Keeping fixed costs to an absolute minimum.
- (c) Determining contribution margin per unit and projected profits at various levels of production.
- (d) Assigning costs to a product in a manner that maximises the contribution margin.

(xiv) To obtain the break-even point in rupees, total fixed costs are divided by which of the following:
- (a) Variable cost per unit
- (b) Fixed cost per unit
- (c) Variable cost per unit, Sales price per unit
- (d) (Sales price per unit – Variable cost per unit), Sales price per unit.

(xv) Given the following notations, what is the break-even sale in rupees?
- (a) $\frac{SP}{FC \div VC}$ (b) $\frac{VC}{SP - FC}$
- (c) $\frac{FC}{VC \div SP}$ (d) $\frac{FC}{(SP - VC) \div SP}$

(xvi) What is the term that means all manufacturing costs (direct and indirect, variable and fixed) which contribute to the production of the product and are traced to output and inventories?
- (a) Job-order costing
- (b) Process costing
- (c) Full or absorption costing
- (d) Variable or marginal or direct costing

(xvii) What costs are treated as product costs under variable (marginal) costing?
- (a) Only direct costs
- (b) Only variable production costs
- (c) All variable costs
- (d) All variable and fixed manufacturing costs

Problems

1. Hind General Corporation produces only one product which had the following costs.

Variable manufacturing costs	₹4 per unit
Fixed manufacturing costs	₹2,00,000 per year

The normal capacity is set at 2,00,000 units. There are no work-in-progress inventories.
In 2019, the company produced 2,00,000 units and sold 90 per cent of them at a price of ₹7 per unit. In 2020, the company produced 2,10,000 units and sold 2,15,000 units at the same price.
You are required to prepare income statements for 2019 and 2020 based on absorption costing and marginal costing.

Ans:	*2019*	*2020*
	(₹)	(₹)
Profit (marginal costing)	3,40,000	4,45,000
Profit (Absorption costing)	3,60,000	4,40,000

2. The following cost information relates to factory for two years.

	2019	*2020*
Installed capacity (units)	10,000	10,000
Opening stock (units)	Nil	1,000
Closing stock (units)	1,000	Nil
Output (units)	10,000	9,000
Selling price per unit	14	14
Fixed costs for the year	85,000	85,000
Variable cost per unit	2.90	2.90

Work out the profit under absorption costing and marginal costing for the two years. Also state any abnormality in the results disclosed by absorption costing. Assume FIFO basis.

Ans:	2019	2020
Profit (Absorption)	₹23,400	17,500
Profit (Marginal)	₹14,900	26,000

3. Using the information below, prepare profit statements for the months of June and July using (i) marginal costing (ii) full absorption costing. Also, explain why the two methods disclose different amounts of profit for June and July.

Data Per Unit:	₹
Selling price	50
Direct material cost	18
Direct labour cost	4
Variable production overheads	3
Monthly Costs:	
Fixed production overheads	99,000
Fixed selling expenses	15,000
Fixed administration expenses	25,000

Variable selling costs are 10% of sales revenue and normal production capacity is 11,000 units per month.

	Sales (units)	Production (units)
June	10,000	12,000
July	12,000	10,000

Ans:

	June	*July*
Profit (Marginal costing)	₹61,000	1,01,000
Profit (Absorption costing)	₹79,000	83,000

4. Stock, production and sales data for Industrial Detergents Ltd. are given below:

		Period 1	*Period 2*	*Period 3*	*Period 4*
Production	(litres)	60,000	70,000	55,000	65,000
Sales	(litres)	60,000	55,000	65,000	70,000
Opening stock	(litres)	–	–	15,000	5,000
Closing stock	(litres)	–	15,000	5,000	–

The company has a single product, for which the financial data, based on an activity level of 60,000 litres per period, are as follows:

	Cost per litre ₹
Direct material	2.50
Direct labour	3.00
Production overheads	
= 200% of direct labour	6.00
= Total cost/litre	₹11.50
Selling price per litre	₹18.00

Administrative overheads are fixed at ₹1,00,000 per period and half of the production overheads are fixed.
From the above information, prepare operating statements on marginal and absorption costing principles.

Ans:

	Period (1)	(2)	(3)	(4)
Marginal costing profit (₹)	2,90,000	2,42,500	3,37,500	3,85,000
Absorption costing profit	2,90,000	2,57,500	3,22,500	3,55,000

5. The directors of a company have been studying the following condensed profit reports for the years 2019 and 2020:

	2019	*2020*
Sales (₹)	3,00,000	4,50,000
Profit (or loss) (₹)	55,000	35,000

The directors are perturbed over the trend, for a 50% increase in sales resulted in a decrease in profit in 2020. The chief cost accountant explains that unabsorbed overhead was charged to 2020 operations. His statement was based on the following data:

Data	*2019*	*2020*
Sales (units)	20,000	30,000
Production (units)	30,000	20,000
Sales price per unit (₹)	15	15
Variable cost per unit (₹)	5	5
Fixed factory overhead (₹)	1,80,000	1,80,000
Fixed factory overhead per unit (standard)	6	6
Fixed selling and administrative expenses	25,000	25,000

Prepare:

(a) Income statement by the conventional method to which the chief cost accountant referred;

(b) Income statements by variable costing method.

Ans:	2019	2020
Absorption costing profit	₹55,000	₹35,000
Variable costing profit	(5,000)	95,000

6. Using the information given below, calculate the net income for the months of October, November and December and the value of finished goods on hand at the end of period using absorption costing and marginal costing. Also, comment on the differences in profits under these two methods.

	October	November	December
Production units	45,000	36,000	45,000
Sales units	36,000	42,000	48,000
Opening stock	–	9,000	3,000
Closing stock	9,000	3,000	–

Additional information:

Selling price per unit	₹50
Variable production cost per unit	₹30
Fixed production cost per unit	₹10
Total fixed production costs per month	₹3,90,000
Normal output per month	39,000 units

Ans:	October	November	December
Absorption costing profit	₹4,20,000	3,90,000	5,40,000
Marginal costing profit	3,30,000	4,50,000	5,70,000

7. The ratio of variable cost to sales is 70%. The break-even point occurs at 60% of the capacity sales. Find the capacity sales when fixed costs are ₹90,000. Also compute profit at 75% of the capacity sales.

Ans: Capacity sales ₹5,00,000

Profit at 75% capacity ₹22,500

8. Profit/Volume ratio of a company is 50%, while its margin of safety is 40%. If sales volume of the company is ₹50 lakhs, find out its break-even point and net profit.

Ans: Break-even-sales ₹30 lakhs
Net profit ₹10 lakhs

9. *X* Ltd. has earned contribution of ₹2,00,000 and net profit of ₹1,50,000 on sales ₹8,00,000. What is its margin of safety?

Ans: ₹6,00,000

10. If margin of safety is ₹2,40,000 (40% of sales) and P/V ratio is 30% of *AB* Ltd. Calculate its (1) Break-even sales and (2) Amount of profit on sales of ₹9,00,000.

Ans: Break-even sales ₹3,60,000
Profit ₹1,62,000

for excel template, scan

11. (i) Ascertain profit, when sales = ₹ 2,00,000
Fixed cost = ₹ 40,000
BEP = ₹ 1,60,000
(ii) Ascertain sales, when fixed cost = ₹ 20,000
Profit = ₹ 10,000
BEP = ₹ 40,000

Ans: (i) ₹10,000 (ii) ₹60,000

12. The profit volume ratio of *X* Ltd. is 50% and the margin of safety is 40%. You are required to calculate the net profit if the sales volume is ₹1,00,000.

13. B & Co. has recorded the following data in the two most recent periods:

Total Cost of Production (₹)	*Volume of Production (Units)*
14,600	800
19,400	1,200

What is the best estimate of the firm's fixed costs per period?

Ans: ₹5,000

14. *XYZ* Ltd. furnishes you the following income information:

Particulars	*Year 2020*	
	First-half (₹)	*Second-half (₹)*
Sales	8,10,000	10,26,000
Profit earned	21,600	64,800

From the above, you are required to compute the following assuming that the fixed cost remains the same in both the periods:

(i) P/V ratio
(ii) Fixed costs
(iii) The amount of profit or loss where sales are ₹6,48,000.
(iv) The amount of sales required to earn a profit of ₹1,08,000.

Ans: (i) 20% (ii) ₹1,40,400 (iii) ₹10,800 (iv) ₹12,42,000

15. Two firms A & Co. and B & Co. sell the same type of product in the same market. Their budgeted Profit & Loss Account for the year ending 31st March, 2020 are as follows:

Particulars	*A & Co.*		*B & Co*	
	₹	₹	₹	₹
Sales		5,00,000		6,00,000
Variable costs	4,00,000		4,00,000	
Fixed costs	30,000	4,30,000	70,000	4,70,000
Net profit		70,000		1,30,000

Required:

1. Calculate at which sales volume of both the firms will earn equal profit.
2. State which firm is likely to earn greater profits in condition of:

(i) Heavy demand for the product,; and

(ii) Low demand for the product

Give reasons. *Ans:* (i) ₹3,00,000

(ii) B & Co. is likely to earn higher profits under conditions of heavy demand, higher profits under conditions of low demand A & Co. is likely to earn

16. Indian Plastics make plastic buckets. An analysis of their accounting reveals:

Variable cost per bucket	₹20
Fixed cost	₹50,000 for the year
Capacity	2,000 buckets per year
Selling price per bucket	₹70

Required:

(i) Find the break-even point.

(ii) Find the number of buckets to be sold to get a profit of ₹30,000.

(iii) If the company can manufacture 600 buckets more per year with an additional fixed cost of ₹2,000, what should be the selling price to maintain the profit per bucket as at (ii) above?

Ans: (i) 1000 buckets (ii) 1600 buckets (iii) ₹62.39 per bucket

17. A retail dealer in garments is currently selling 24,000 shirts annually. He supplies the following details for the year ended 31st December, 2020

	₹
Selling price per shirt	40
Variable cost per shirt	25
Fixed cost: Staff salaries for the year	1,20,000
General office costs for the year	80,000
Advertising costs for the year	40,000

As a cost accountant of the firm, you are required to answer the following each part independently:

(i) Calculate the break-even point and margin of safety in sales revenue and number of shirts sold.

(ii) Assume that 20,000 shirts were sold in a year. Find out the net profit of the firm.

(iii) If it is decided to introduce selling commission of ₹3 per shirt, how many shirts would require to be sold in a year to earn a net income of ₹15,000.

(iv) Assuming that for the year 2016 an additional staff salary of ₹33,000 is anticipated, and price of a shirt is likely to be increased by 15% what should be the break-even point in number of shirts and sales revenue?

Ans: (i) BEP ₹6,40,000; Margin of safety ₹3,20,000
(ii) ₹60,000
(iii)21,250 shirts
(iv) BEP 13000 shirts, ₹5,98,000

18. Cadbury Schweppes Limited, a British chocolate and soft drink company, is planning to establish a subsidiary company in India to produce Schweppes Mineral Water.

Based on the estimated annual sales of 40,000 bottles of the mineral water, cost studies produced the following estimates for the Indian subsidiary:

	Total Annual Costs	*Per cent of Total Annual Cost That is Variable*
Material	₹1,93,600	100%
Labour	90,000	70%

Overhead	80,000	64%
Administration	30,000	30%

The Indian production will be sold by manufacturer's representatives who will receive a commission of 8 per cent of the sale price. No portion of the British office expenses is to be allocated to the Indian subsidiary.

It is required to:

(i) Compute the sale price per bottle to enable management to realise an estimated 10 per cent profit on sale proceeds in India; and

(ii) Calculate the break-even point in rupee sales for the Indian subsidiary on the assumption that the sale price is ₹11 per bottle.

Ans: (i) ₹12 (ii) ₹3,84,000

19. Triple *X* company produces these products with the following characteristics:

	Product I	*Product II*	*Product III*
Price per unit	₹5	₹6	₹7
Variable cost per unit	3	2	4
Expected sales (units)	1,00,000	1,50,000	2,50,000

Total fixed costs for the company are ₹12,40,000.

Assuming that the product mix would be the same at the break-even point, compute the break-even point in:

(a) Unit (total and by product line)

(b) Sales rupees (total and by product line)

Ans: (a) 4,00,000 units
(b) ₹25,20,000 approx.

20. The following figures are available from the records of Venus Enterprises as at 31st March:

	2019	*2020*
	₹ lakhs	₹ lakhs
Sales	150	200
Profit	30	50

Calculate:

(a) The P/V ratio and total fixed expenses;

(b) The break-even level of sales;

(c) Sales required to earn a profit of ₹90 lakhs; and

(d) Profit or loss that would arise if the sales were ₹280 lakhs.

Ans: (a) 40% 130 lakhs (b) ₹75 lakhs
(c) ₹300 lakhs (d) ₹82 lakhs

21. Two manufacturing companies which have the following operating details decide to merge.

	Company No. 1	*Company No. 2*
Capacity utilisation %	90	60
Sales (₹ lakhs)	540	300
Variable cost (₹ lakhs)	396	225
Fixed costs (₹ lakhs)	80	50

Assuming that the proposal is implemented, calculate:

(i) Break-even sales of the merged plant and the capacity utilisation at that stage.

(ii) Profitability of the merged plant at 80% capacity utilisation.

(iii) Sales turnover of the merged plant to earn a profit of ₹75 lakhs.
(iv) When the merged plant is working at a capacity to earn a profit of ₹75 lakhs, what percentage increase in selling price is required to sustain an increase of 5% of fixed overheads.

Ans: (i) 25.909% P/V ratio, ₹501.67 lakhs, 45.6%
(ii) ₹98 lakhs (iii) ₹791.23 lakhs (iv) 0.8215%

22. Company *A* and Company *B*, both under the same management, make and sell the same type of product. Their budgeted profit and loss accounts for January–June 2020 are as under:

		Company A		*Company B*	
		₹	₹	₹	₹
Sales			3,00,000		3,00,000
Less:	Variable cost	2,40,000		2,00,000	
	Fixed costs	30,000	2,70,000	70,000	2,70,000
			30,000		30,000

You are required to
(i) Calculate the break-even point for each company.
(ii) Calculate the sales volume at which each of the two companies will make a profit of ₹10,000.
(iii) Assess how their profitability will change with decrease or increase in volume.

Ans: (i) *A* ₹1,50,000 *B* ₹2,10,000
(ii) *A* ₹2,00,000 *B* ₹2,40,000

23. Delhi Equipments Ltd. manufactures four components, the cost particulars of which are given below:

	Components			
	A	*B*	*C*	*D*
Elements of cost:				
Direct material	₹80	100	100	120
Direct labour	20	25	25	30
Variable overhead	10	12	15	10
Fixed overhead	15	23	20	20
	125	160	160	180
Output per machine hour (units)	4	2	3	3

The key factor is shortage of machine capacity.
You are required to advise management as to whether they should continue to produce all or some of these components (which are used in its main product) or they should buy them from a supplier who has quoted the following prices:
A = ₹115; *B* = ₹175; *C* = ₹135; *D* = ₹185.

Ans: Component *C* should be purchased from outside. continue the production of *A*, *B* and *D*.

24. A company having annual sales of ₹10 crores is earning 12% profit before charging interest and depreciation. Interest and depreciation amount to ₹60 lakhs and ₹100 lakhs respectively. If the contribution/sales ratio of the company is 0.4, calculate its break-even sales.

Ans: ₹11,00,00,000

25. In a purely competitive market, 10,000 units of a product can be manufactured and sold and a certain amount of profit is generated. It is estimated that 2,000 units of that product need to be manufactured and sold in a monopoly market to earn the same amount of profit. Profit under both the market conditions is targeted at ₹2,00,000. The variable cost per unit is ₹100 and the total fixed cost is ₹60,000. You are requited to determine the selling prices under both monopoly and competitive conditions.

Ans: Monopoly ₹236 Competitive conditions ₹126.

26. A company has a fixed cost of ₹20,000. It sells two products *A* and *B*, in the ratio of 2 units of *A* and 1 unit of *B*. Contribution is ₹1 per unit of *A* and ₹2 per unit of *B*. How many units of *A* and *B* would be sold at break-even point?

Ans: A 10,000 units, *B* 5,000 units

27. *ZED* Ltd. produces two products, *P* and *Q*. The budgeted selling price per unit for *P* and *Q* are ₹3,600 and ₹4,320 respectively. Variable costs of production and sales for *P* and *Q* are ₹1,800 and 3,600 respectively. Annual fixed costs of the company amounts to ₹1,76,000. The company has two different production/sales options as under:
Option 1—A mix of 2 units of *P* for every 3 units of *Q*
Option 2—A mix of 1 unit of *P* for every 2 units of *Q*
Find out the combined break-even point under each option and the optimal mix that the company should adopt.

Ans: Option 1, BEP. ₹6,16,000; Option 2 BEP ₹6,64,889

28. *A* Ltd. has been offered a choice to buy a machine between *M*1 and *M*2. The following data are provided:

	*M*1	*M*2
Annual output in units	10,000	10,000
Fixed cost	₹60,000	₹32,000
Profit at above level	₹60,000	₹48,000

The market price of the product is expected to be ₹20 per unit.
You are required to compute:
(i) Break-even point of each machine
(ii) The level of sales at which both the machines earn equal profit
(iii) The range of sales at which one is more profitable from the other.

Ans: (i) M1, 5,000 units, M2, 4,000 units (ii) 7,000 units

29. A company sells its product at ₹15 per unit. In a period, if it produces and sells 8,000 units, it incurs a loss of ₹5 per unit. If the volume is raised to 20,000 units, it earns a profit of ₹4 per unit.
Calculate break-even point in terms of rupees as well as in units.

Ans: 12,000 units; ₹1,80,000

30. A company manufactures radios, which are sold at ₹1,600 per unit. The total cost is composed of 30% for direct materials, 40% for direct wages and 30% for overheads. An increase in material price by 30% and in wage rates by 10% is expected in the forthcoming year, as a result of which the profit at current selling price may decrease by 40% of the present profit per unit. You are required to prepare a statement showing current and future profit at present selling price.
How much selling price should be increased to maintain the present rate of profit?

Ans: Revised selling price ₹1808.00

31. Raj Ltd. manufactures three products—*X*, *Y* and *Z*. The unit selling prices of these products are ₹100, ₹160 and ₹75 respectively. The corresponding unit variable costs are ₹50, ₹80 and ₹30. The proportions (quantity-wise) in which these products are manufactured and sold are 20%, 30% and 50% respectively. The total fixed costs are ₹14,80,000.
Calculate overall break-even quantity and the product-wise break up of such quantity.

Ans: Composite BEP 26,195 units

32. Calculate the effect on profit of a proposed change in "Sales Mix" from the following data:

Existing Sales Mix	*M*	*N*	*O*	*P*	*Total*
Sales (in ₹)	80,000	1,00,000	40,000	20,000	2,40,000
Variable cost (in ₹)	48,000	68,000	32,000	8,000	1,56,000
Fixed cost (in ₹)	–	–	–	–	58,800
Proposed sales mix	₹60,000	88,000	80,000	12,000	2,40,000

Ans: Proposed sales mix is less profitable as profit will decline by ₹8,640

33. *SV* Ltd., a multi-product company furnishes you the following data relating to the year 2020:

	First Half of the Year	Second Half of the Year
	₹	₹
Sales	45,000	50,000
Total cost	40,000	43,000

Assuming that there is no change in prices and variable cost and that the fixed expenses are incurred equally in the two half year periods, calculate for the year 2020:

(i) The P/V ratio
(ii) Fixed expenses
(iii) Break-even sales
(iv) Percentage of margin of safety

Ans: (i) 40% (ii) 26,000; (iii) 65,000 (iv) 31.58%

34. The Chief Cost Accountant of Vikas Limited found to his surprise that the actual profit for the period ending 30th June 2020 was the same as budgeted in spite of realising 10% more than the budgeted selling prices. The following were the results:

Particulars	*Budget*	*Actuals*
	₹	₹
Sales	5,00,000	8,25,000
Variable costs of sales	3,00,000	5,75,000
Fixed costs	1,00,000	1,50,000
Profit	1,00,000	1,00,000

You are required to assist the Chief Cost Accountant in preparing the necessary explanations as to why the profit remained the same despite an increase in sales.)

Ans: Increase in profit equals to the increase in cost. Therefore, profit of the firm has remained the same.

35. Taurus Ltd. produces three products—*A*, *B* and *C*, from the same manufacturing facilities. The cost and other details of the three products are as follows:

	A	*B*	*C*
Selling price/unit (₹)	200	160	100
Variable cost/unit (₹)	120	120	40
Fixed expenses/month (₹)			2,76,000
Maximum production per month (units)	5,000	8,000	6,000
Total hours available for the month	200 hours		
Maximum demand per month (units)	2,000	4,000	2,400

The processing hours cannot be increased beyond 200 hours per month.

You are required to:

(a) Compute the most profitable product-mix:
(b) Compute the overall break-even sales of the company for the month based on the mix calculated in (a) above.

Ans: (a) *A* 2000 units, *B* 1600 units, *C* 2,400 units
(b) ₹6,72,000

36. The budgeted income statement by product lines of Multiproducts Ltd. for 2020 is as follows:

	Product A	*Product B*	*Product C*
	₹	₹	₹
Sales	2,00,000	5,00,000	3,00,000
Variable expenses:			
Cost of goods sold	90,000	2,70,000	1,50,000
Selling	30,000	90,000	45,000
Fixed expenses:			
Overhead	36,000	90,000	54,000
Administrative	16,000	40,000	24,000
Income before tax	28,000	10,000	27,000
Income tax @ 40%	11,200	4,000	10,800
Net income	16,800	6,000	16,200

All products are manufactured in the same facilities under common administrative control. Fixed expenses are allocated among the products in proportion of their budgeted sales volume:

(a) Compute the budgeted break-even point of the company as a whole, from the data provided.

(b) What would be the effect on Budgeted Income, if half of the budgeted sales volume of product *B* were shifted to product *A* and *C* in equal rupee amounts so that the total budgeted sales in rupees remain the same.

(c) What would be the effect of the shift in the product mix suggested in (b) above on the budgeted break-even point of the whole company?

Ans: (a) ₹8,00,000
(b) Total income will increase by ₹14,250
(c) BEP will reduce to sales of ₹7,45,520 from ₹8,00,000.

37. Mr. *X* has ₹2,00,000 investments in his business firm. He wants a 15% return on his money. From the analysis of recent cost figures, he finds that his variable operating cost is 60% of sales and his fixed costs are ₹80,000 per year. Show computations to answer the following questions:

(a) What sales volume must be obtained to break-even?

(b) What sales volume must be obtained to get 15 per cent return on investment?

(c) Mr. *X* estimates that even if he closed the doors of his business, he would incur ₹25,000 as expenses per year. At what sales would he be better off by locking his business up?

Ans: (a) ₹2,00,000
(b) ₹2,75,000
(c) Mr. *X* will be better off by locking his business, if sales falls below ₹1,37,500.

38. A company seeking to improve its competitive position has launched a cost-reduction programme in its existing plants, apart from trying to increase output.

The present profit before tax comes to 15% of turnover and 30% of capital employed. Other relevant working ratios are:

Gross margin	35%
Margin of safety	43%
Capital turnover ratio	2

The operating figures for the last year were as follows:

Total sales value	₹12,00,000
Variable costs	7,80,000
Fixed costs	2,40,000
Capital employed	6,00,000
Break-even sales	6,84,000

It has been proposed to reduce the sale price by 10% and increase the output by 20%. No change in fixed costs is expected. The estimated cost reduction amounts to ₹42,000.

You are required to work out the relevant figures and ratio based on the proposal, and present those along with the existing ones in a meaningful manner and offer your comments.

Ans:		*Existing*	*Proposed*
	Profit	₹180	162
	Return on capital	30%	27%

The proposal should not be accepted as it will adversely affect the overall profitability of the company.

39. The following data are available from the budget records of Fitwell Shoe Company for the forthcoming budget period

	₹
Selling price	100.00
Variable cost:	
Cost of shoes	75.00
Sales commission	5.00
Total	80.00
Annual fixed expenses:	
Rent	80,000
Salaries	2,20,000
Other fixed expenses	60,000
	₹3,60,000

Although the firm manufactures shoes with different styles, they have identical purchase costs and selling price.

You are required to consider the following questions. Each question is to be treated independently.

(a) What is the annual break-even point both in terms of units and value?

(b) If the store manager is paid 0.3 per cent commission on sales, what would be the annual break-even point both in terms of units and value?

(c) If the firm decides to pay a fixed salary of ₹1,00,000 in lieu of sales commission, what would be the annual break-even point in terms of units and value. Compute the point of indifference.

(d) If the stores manager is paid 0.3 per cent commission on each paid sold in excess of the break-even point, what would be the profit if 30,000 pairs were sold?

Ans: (a) BEP units 18000; BEP ₹18,00,000
(b) BEP units 18274, BEP ₹18,27,411
(c) BEP units 18400; BEP ₹18,40,000
Indifference point 20,000 units
(d) Profit ₹2,36,400

40. An automobile manufacturing company produces different models of cars .The budget in respect of model 118 for the month of September, 2020 is as under:

Budgeted Output		40,000 units
	(₹ in lakhs)	*(₹ in lakhs)*
Net realisation		700
Variable costs:		
Materials	264	
Labour	52	440
Direct expenses	124	

Specific fixed costs	90	
Allocated fixed costs	112.50	202.50
Total costs		642.50
Profit		57.50
Sales		700.00

Calculate:

(i) Profit with 10 per cent increase in selling price with a 10 per cent reduction in sales volume.

(ii) Volume to be achieved to maintain the original profit after a 10 per cent rise in material costs, at the originally budgeted selling price per unit.

Ans: (i) ₹94.5 lakhs (ii) sale of 44,521 cars

41. A company has annual fixed costs of ₹14,00,000. In 2020, sales amounted to ₹60,00,000 as compared with ₹45,00,000 in 2019 and profit in 2020 was ₹4,20,000 higher than in 2019.

(i) At what level of sales does the company break-even?

(ii) Determine profit or loss on a forecast sales volume of ₹80,00,000.

(iii) If there is a reduction in selling price in 2021 by 10% and the company desires to earn the same profit as in 2020, what would be the required sales volume?

Ans: (i) ₹50,00,000 (ii) ₹8,40,000 (iii) ₹84,00,000

42. A company has three factories situated in North, East and South with its head office in Mumbai. The management has received the following summary report on the operations of each factory for a period:

(₹ in '000)

Particulars	*Sales*		*Profit*	
	Actual	*Over/(Under) Budget*	*Actual*	*Over/(Under) Budget*
North	1,100	(400)	135	(180)
East	1,450	150	210	90
South	1,200	(200)	330	(110)

Calculate for each factory and for the company as a whole for the period:

(i) Fixed Costs.

(ii) Break-even Sales

Ans: (i) ₹13,50,000 (ii) ₹25,00,000

43. The variable cost structure of a product manufactured by a company during the current year is as under:

	₹ Per Unit
Material	120
Labour	30
Overheads	12

The selling price per unit is ₹270 and the fixed cost and sales during the current year are ₹14 lakhs and ₹40.5 lakhs respectively.

During the forthcoming year, the direct workers will be entitled to a wage increase of 10% from the beginning of the year and the material cost, variable overhead and fixed overhead are expected toincrease by 7.5%, 5% and 3% respectively.

The following are required to be computed:

(a) New sale price in the forthcoming year if the current P/V ratio is to be maintained.

(b) Number of units that would require to be sold during the forthcoming year so as to yield the same amount of profit in the current year, assuming that selling price per unit will not be increased.

Ans: (a) ₹291.00 (b) 17,422 units

CASE STUDY

1. Marginal Costing: Cost Volume Profit Analysis: Case of Apex Homesets Pvt Ltd

Apex Homesets Pvt Ltd was the manufacturer of kitchen appliances producing and selling appliances like chimneys, mixer grinders, juicers, gas stoves and rice cookers etc. Nikumbh Pawar was heading the rice cooker division. The price of the best-selling 5-litre rice cooker was ₹2,500. The variable cost for the same was ₹1,500 and the fixed cost for the current sales of ₹10,00,000 per month was ₹3,50,000.

Although the rice cooker division was making profit, Nikumbh was concerned about the margin of safety. He thought that it was time to make serious efforts towards increasing sales and capturing better market share. He called his sales managers and asked them to brainstorm over this and get back to him within a week with individual solutions to improve sales.

After a week, he got the following proposals from his managers:

- *Manager 1:* An increase in sales budget by ₹1,00,000 will provide ₹3,00,000 increase in sales.
- *Manager 2:* Increasing quality of rice cooker at an additional cost of ₹100 per unit would improve the sales by 80 more units.
- *Manager 3:* If selling price is dropped by ₹200 per rice cooker and advertising budget is increased by ₹1,50,000 per month, the sales would increase by 50%.
- *Manager 4:* If there is a switch for salespeople from flat salary of ₹60,000 per month to a sales commission of ₹150 per rice cooker sold, the sales would increase by 15%.

Nikumbh called his cost accountant Rajiv to analyse all these proposals and find out if these proposals were indeed helpful in increasing sales as well as profit. He decided to reward the manager whose idea generated maximum profit.

QUESTIONS FOR DISCUSSION:

1. What was the current margin of safety (MoS) for rice cooker sales? Was Nikumbh's fear of low MoS reasonable?
2. If you are in place of Rajiv, whose idea you would determine as the best?
3. There was a proposal from one of the distributors who was willing to buy 200 rice cookers if the company gave him a discount off the price of ₹2,500. The sale would not disturb regular sales and since there was available capacity, it would not change the fixed costs. Nikumbh wanted to make ₹80,000 on this sale. What price should he quote?

2. A Case of 'Coppice Garden'

Coppice Garden in Kullu Valley, Himachal Pradesh was a fruit orchard, growing apples, plums, cherries, and peaches. It was managed by a couple Mr. and Mrs. Prem Singh. The total cultivable area with Coppice Garden was 450 acres which was divided between these four fruits with sufficient supply of manpower for cultivation.

So far, the decisions like which fruit to grow, in what quantity and in how many acres etc., were taken on the basis of availability of seeds and their market price. The allocation of land among last year has been 60 acres, 190 acres, 110 acres and 90 acres for apple, cherry, peaches and plums respectively. However, this time Prem Singh's son Shivam who had joined his parents and was looking after the family business had different plans. Shivam wanted to finalise the allotment of the area for the cultivation with respect to the four different fruits based on cost benefit analysis so as to achieve maximum profit.

In order to determine the most profitable fruit-acre mix, Shivam called his friend Hely Upadhyay and gave her all the details related to his orchard and the fruits grown therein. The detailed statement was as follows:

Particulars	*Apple*	*Cherry*	*Peaches*	*Plum*
Yield per acre (in no. of boxes)	500	100	150	200
Selling price per box (₹)	300	600	300	900
Material required per acre (₹)	5,400	1,800	2,100	3,000
Labour charges (₹):				
Sowing & tending per acre	6,000	3,000	4,500	3,900
Picking & packing per box	30	60	30	90
Transport per box	60	30	60	90

In addition to the variable costs like material and labour, there were some fixed charges as well. The total fixed cost for cultivation and irrigation was ₹1,12,500. Fixed cost for picking the fruits was ₹84,000. Charges for administration, transportation and taxes were fixed at ₹1,67,500, ₹22,000 and ₹34,000.

All of his 450 acres were used for growing fruits; however due to varying soil condition of his land, 300 acres were not suitable for cultivating apples and plums. Only cherry and peaches could be grown there. Remaining 150 acres could be used for growing any or all of the four fruits. So, Shivam asked Hely to select the fruit yielding maximum revenue for these 150 acres.

Mr. and Mrs Prem Singh were not very impressed with all these plans of Shivam. Although, they allowed him to do the land allotment on the basis of expected profit, they put certain conditions before him. These conditions were:

(a) Coppice Garden was known for its fruit variety and catering to different tastes and preferences of the customers. Therefore, Prem Singh asked Shivam to produce all four varieties of fruits. In addition, he wanted Shivam to ensure that no fruit variety should be produced in quantity less than 18,000 boxes.

(b) The second condition was more to do with bank requirements. As the produce sometimes were hypothecated to banks, it was required to allot the area in complete acres and not in fractions of an acre.

Shivam appraised Hely about these conditions and requested her to calculate the estimated total profit of the best fruit-acre mix. He also wanted to know the amount of increase in overall profitability as a result of land allocation on the basis of cost benefit analysis. His objective was to buy another tractor for his farm if the profit increased by ₹8,00,000 or more.

QUESTIONS FOR DISCUSSION:

1. Imagine that you are Hely Upadhyay and determine the most profitable fruit-acre mix. Also calculate the total profit incurred out of that fruit-acre mix.
2. Compare this year's profit with the previous year profit. Can Shivam buy a tractor now?

3. Wood-Art Furniture Company: A Case of Cost Volume Profit Analysis

Wood-Art Furniture Company, registered and headquartered in Bangalore, produced high-end office furniture and supplied to all the upcoming as well as established companies in and around the city. In Bangalore being hub of start-ups, there was lot of demand for office furniture.

The company manufactured only three types of products—revolving chairs, office desks and filing cabinets in standardised form. The standard variable costs and standard selling prices for these per unit were as follows:

Particulars	*Chairs (₹)*	*Desks (₹)*	*Cabinets (₹)*
Direct material	1,500	3,000	4,000
Direct wages	2,000	2,000	5,000
Variable overheads	1,500	2,500	3,500
Selling price	9,000	12,500	24,000

The selling price that the company charged was quite competitive in the high-end segment compared to its competitors, and therefore, the company was able to capture significant portion of the demand in the market. The company took pride in conveying that their customers got great quality product at a price which could be compared to economical segment market.

Ashish Kapur, the Sales Head of Wood-Art, however, was worried. His counterpart in the Finance Department—Riya Ranjan—had told him that the overall profit in the month of July has fallen down compared to that of the previous month. Ashish was surprised. He was thinking of opposite. His team had worked very hard this time to improve sales and that had happened too. The chairs and desk sales had improved significantly. Cabinet sales had fallen down but compared to the increase in the sale of other two items, the fall was less. He showed the same in the form of statement to Riya which was as follows:

Sales for the Months of June and July 2019

Particulars	*Chairs (units)*	*Desks (units)*	*Cabinets (units)*
June	2,00,000	2,00,000	2,00,000
July	4,00,000	2,60,000	1,00,000
Increase/decrease	2,00,000	60,000	(1,00,000)

Riya had asked her team for some more details to analyse the reason for fall in the overall profit. She also got the details about the budgeted monthly fixed overheads which amounted to the following for each month without any increase:

Lease rent—₹1,50,00,000
Salaries—₹4,50,00,000
Fixed administrative charges—₹4,00,00,000
Distribution expenses (fixed)—₹ 3,50,00,000

Looking at all the details, it seemed that in spite of the increased sales and no change in costs, whether variable or fixed, the profit for the month of July had fallen below that of the previous month. What could be the reason?

QUESTION FOR DISCUSSION:

You are required to present the figures for consideration of the top management and explain why this fall in profit has occurred.

Chapter 17

Alternative Choices Decisions

Learning Objectives

After reading this chapter, you should be able to:

1. understand concept of decision-making and importance of qualitative factors in managerial decision-making;
2. explain relevant information, relevant revenues, relevant costs; and
3. discuss different choices decisions such as make or buy, add or drop products sell or process further, operate or shutdown, special orders, replace or retain.

DECISION-MAKING

Decision-making, also known as decision model, is the process of evaluating two or more alternatives leading to a final choice, known as Alternative Choices Decisions. It is a formal method for making a choice, frequently involving both, quantitative and qualitative analyses. Decision-making is closely associated with planning for the future and is directed towards a specific objective or goal. The care put into each decision often determines the level of outcome. Still the best process and even the best decision do not guarantee a successful outcome. The future determines its own fate, but the best prepared decision is more likely to produce the desired result than any other selection.[1] The overall decision process (also referred to as decision model) contains the following decision-making steps or elements:

1. Identify and define the problem.
2. Identify alternatives as possible solutions to the problem.
3. Eliminate alternatives that are clearly not feasible.
4. Collect relevant data (costs and benefits) associated with each feasible alternative.
5. Identify costs and benefits (revenues) as relevant or irrelevant and eliminate irrelevant costs and benefits (revenues) from consideration.
6. Identify, to the extent possible, non-financial advantages and disadvantages (also known as qualitative factors) about each feasible alternative.

1. Lane K. Anderson and Harold M. Sollenberger, *Managerial Accounting,* South Western Publishing Co., 1992, p. 548.

7. Total the relevant costs and benefits (revenue) for each alternative.
8. Select the alternative with the greatest overall benefit, that is, make the decision.
9. Implement or execute the decision.
10. Evaluate the results of the decision made.

RELEVANT INFORMATION

Managerial decision-making is a process of making choices. If a choice is to be made among alternatives, there must be differences among the alternatives. Relevant information should be used by the decision maker in evaluating the alternatives and in making decisions. Relevant information implies relevant costs and relevant revenues (benefits) which are useful to evaluate alternatives, to ascertain the effect of various alternatives on profit and to finally select the alternative with the greatest benefit.

Relevant revenues and relevant costs are defined as the current and the future values that differ among the alternatives under consideration. They are the differences between the alternatives under consideration. The amount of such differences is called differentials and the (accounting) analysis concerned with the effect of alternatives on revenues and costs is called differential analysis. Relevant revenues and costs are also known as differential revenues and differential costs. Horngreen, Foster and Datar[2] have summarised the key features of relevant information as follows:

Key Features of Relevant Information

(i) Pat (historical) costs may be helpful as a basis for making *predictions*. However, past cost themselves are always irrelevant when making *decisions*.

(ii) Different alternatives can be compared by examining differences in expected total future revenues and costs.

(iii) Not all expected future revenues and costs are relevant. Expected future revenues and costs that do not differ across alternatives are irrelevant and hence can be eliminated from the analysis.

(iv) Due weight must be given to qualitative factors and quantitative nonfinancial factors.

Relevant (differential) analysis focuses on the future because every decision deals with selecting courses of action for the future. Nothing can be done to alter the past. This analysis provides a decision rule to managers in decision-making which is "the alternative that gives the greatest incremental profit should be selected". Incremental profit is the difference between the relevant revenues and relevant costs of each alternative.

RELEVANT REVENUES

Relevant (differential) revenue is the amount of increase or decrease in revenue expected from a particular course of action as compared with an alternative. For instance, assume that a plant is being used to manufacture product *A*, which gives revenue of ₹3,00,000. If the plant could be used to make product *B*, which will provide revenue of ₹3,50,000, the differential revenue from making and selling product *B* will be ₹50,000.

---

2. Charles T. Horngreen, George Foster and Srikant M. Datar, Cost Accounting, A Managerial Emphasis, Prentice Hall of India, New Delhi, 2000, p. 380.

Relevant revenues have two features:

(i) They are expected future revenues.
(ii) They differ between different alternatives.

Relevant revenues are like cash inflows. If the amount of accrual profit and cash flow differs, the manager should give importance to cash flow. For short-run managerial decisions, timing of cash flow, that is, when the cash flows are received, is not so important. However, for long-run decisions where the time span is usually for more than one year, the timing of cash flows is important in the evaluation of alternatives and in making decisions.

RELEVANT COSTS

Relevant costs are also known as differential costs, decision-making costs. Relevant or differential cost is the difference in the total costs between alternative choices. When a decision results in an increased cost, the differential cost may be referred to as an incremental cost. If the cost decreases, the differential cost may be referred to as a decremental cost. The incremental cost includes the change in fixed component as well as the variable component. Assume that a company has physical facilities to manufacture 20,000 units of a product; production beyond that point would require the installation of additional equipment, that is, fixed costs as well as variable costs will have to be incurred if management desires to produce more than 20,000 units.

Relevant costs vary with the type of decision. However, the following are the common characteristics of relevant costs:

1. Relevant costs are expected future costs.
2. They differ between different alternatives.

Expected future costs imply that the costs are expected to occur during the time period covered by the decision. For example, new product will need the incurrence of direct material, direct labour and other costs.

QUALITATIVE FACTORS

Although relevant costing is a numerical or quantitative analysis technique, only a poor manager would ignore the non-numerical or qualitative factors involved in a decision. These are just as important, if not more so, and should be given serious consideration before the decision is made.

Differential analysis or relevant cost analysis should be considered as only one input for the final decision to be made by the managers. In fact, a number of qualitative factors may have vital impact on managerial decisions. Qualitative factors are those elements relating to a decision which cannot be expressed in monetary terms or can be expressed in monetary terms with great difficulty or inaccuracy. Managers should consider qualitative factors also while making decisions otherwise it is likely that a wrong decision will be made.

For example, in a make or buy decision, decision-makers should consider many qualitative factors such as quality of items being purchased from outside, reliability of supply sources, expected stability of prices over the next several years, service quality, labour relations in the supplier's company etc. It may also be found that decision to purchase from outside could result in closing down of the company's facilities for manufacturing the component. Such a decision will influence adversely the morale of company's employees which may, in turn, affect future production and plans of the company. Dependence on an outside supplier is also risky as the suppliers sometimes may not supply the components on time. In such a case, the buyer-company will not be in a position to fulfil customers' orders and thus the company may lose its goodwill in the market resulting, further, in poor future sales.

Qualitative factors are difficult to quantify in monetary terms. However, the decision-maker should try to have as much quantifiable information as possible in these situations. For instance, the effect on customer goodwill due to delay on the part of supplier in meeting orders can be estimated. If there are many suppliers available in the market for the components, this qualitative factor can be ignored as components can be purchased from any supplier in case of delay. However, if the components can be purchased from a single supplier, these qualitative factors will be of great importance. In this situation, the decision-maker should compare the cost savings due to purchasing the component from outside (rather than manufacturing within the company) with the risk associated with the supplier delaying the fulfilment of orders. If cost savings are more than the (quantifiable) risk, the company may continue to purchase from outside; if cost savings are insufficient to cover the risk related with this qualitative aspect, probably it may not be advisable to purchase the component from outside.

Other qualitative factors besides cost should also be given proper attention. The pressure of competition, the maintenance of source of supply and of certain marketing outlets, and the maintenance of the existing personnel organisation and morale, opportunity to balance risk, benefit of providing complete product line to attract new customers may often be the real determinants of business decisions. The quantitative information alone does not provide a solution to all business problems. Sometimes, other factors are more important than cost factors.

TYPES OF CHOICES DECISIONS

Most management decisions may be referred to as alternative choice decisions. Alternative choice decisions cover situations with two or more alternative courses of action from which the manager (decision-maker) must select the best alternative. A decision involving more than two alternatives is called a multiple alternative choice decision. Some examples of alternative choice decisions are: make or buy, own or lease, retain or replace, repair or renovate, now or later, change versus *status quo*, slower or faster, export versus local sales, shutdown or continue, expand or contract, change the produce-mix, take or refuse orders, place special orders, select sales territories, replace present equipment with new machinery, sell at split-up point or process further, etc.

Some of the above alternative choices decisions and the information relevant to the decisions are discussed below.

MAKE OR BUY (OUTSOURCING DECISION)

Make or buy decision is also referred to as outsourcing decision. Nowadays, there is a growing trend toward outsourcing (buying) a large part of materials, components and services required by an enterprise.

Make or buy decisions arise when a company with unused production capacity consider the following alternatives:

(a) To buy certain raw materials or subassemblies from outside suppliers.
(b) To use available capacity to produce the items within the company.

A make or buy decision is basically one of determining which alternative is economically most desirable and most effectively utilises the firm's resources. These decisions can affect the firm's production methods and capacities, available working capital, cost of borrowing funds, and competitive position. Costs that will be incurred under both alternatives are not relevant to the analysis. The firm should make an analysis of the cost, quality, and quantity considerations of the individual make or buy decisions. Differential cost analysis is especially useful if the company has idle capacity and idle workers that can be used to make the tools or parts. Other potential use of available capacity should also be considered; and qualitative factors must be evaluated in the decision process. These considerations include price stability from suppliers, reliability of delivery and quality of the material or component involved. Qualitative factors are not included in differential cost analyses, but they should be used to test the reasonableness of any decision based purely on quantitative cost studies. Figure. 17.1 presents the factors that should be considered in the outsourcing decision.

Relevant Quantitative Factors:
Incremental production costs for each unit
Unit cost of purchasing from outside supplier (price less any discounts available plus shipping, etc.)
Number of available suppliers
Production capacity available to manufacture components
Opportunity costs of using facilities for production rather than for other purposes
  Amount of space available for storage
  Costs associated with carrying inventory
  Increase in throughput generated by buying components
Relevant Qualitative Factors:
Reliability of supply sources
Ability to control quality of inputs purchased from outside
Nature of the work to be subcontracted (such as the importance of the part to the whole)
Impact on customers and markets
Future bargaining position with supplier(s)
Perceptions regarding possible future price changes
Perceptions about current product prices (are the prices appropriate or, in some cases with international suppliers, is product dumping involved?)

Fig. 17.1 Outsource Decisions Considerations

Source: Jesset T. Barfield, Cecily A. Raiborn and Michael R. Kinney, *Cost Accounting: Traditions and Innovations*, 5th Ed., Thomson, 2003, p. 505.

For example, assume that a company can make a part that it has been purchasing at a unit cost of ₹30. The company has been operating at 75% of normal capacities and in the foreseeable future no use for the excess capacity is contemplated except for the possible production of the part. Fixed manufacturing cost amounts to ₹17,00,000 a year whether the plant operates at 75% or 100% of capacity. The cost to manufacture 50,000 units of the part that will be needed has been estimated as follows:

	Units Cost	*Total Cost*
Direct materials	12.5	6,25,000
Direct labour	8.0	4,00,000
Variable manufacturing overhead	5.0	2,50,000
Total incremental cost	25.5	12,75,000
Cost to purchase part	30.0	15,00,000
Net advantage in parts production	4.5	2,25,000

In the above analysis, the fixed manufacturing overhead has not been considered because it has to be incurred under both alternatives. Logically, the costs that will be increased or decreased as a result of making the part should be considered. In some cases, both the variable and fixed costs will be affected.

Add or Drop Products

The decision to eliminate an unprofitable product is a special case of product profitability evaluation. To evaluate the financial consequences of eliminating a product, it is necessary to concentrate on the differential or incremental profit effect of the decision. An important factor in the decision to add or drop a product is whether it will increase or decrease the future income of the business. Appropriate cost and profit measures must be developed for each alternative.

Assume that a company is considering dropping product *B* from its line because the accounting statements show that product *B* is being sold at a loss.

Income Statement

	Product A	*Product B*	*Product C*	*Total*
Sales revenue	50,000	7,500	12,500	70,000
Cost of sales:				
Direct material	7,500	1,000	1,500	10,000
Direct labour	15,000	2,000	2,500	19,500
Indirect manufacturing cost (50% of direct labour)	7,500	1,000	1,250	9,750
	30,000	4,000	5,250	39,250
Gross margin on sales	20,000	3,500	7,250	30,750
Selling and administrative expenses	12,500	4,500	4,000	21,000
(allocation on arbitrary basis)	–	–	–	–
Net income (loss)	7,500	(1,000)	3,250	9,750

Additional Information

(i) Factory overhead costs are made up of fixed costs of ₹5,850 and variable costs of ₹3,900. Variable costs by products are: product *A* ₹3,000, product *B* ₹400, and product *C* ₹500.

(ii) Fixed costs and expenses will not be changed if product *B* is eliminated.

(iii) Variable selling and administrative expenses to the extent of ₹11,000 can be traced to the product as follows: *A*, ₹7,500; *B*, ₹1,500; *C*, ₹2,000.

(iv) Fixed selling and administrative expenses are ₹10,000.

The decision to drop product *B* cannot be reasonably made from the above data prepared under a conventional income statement. This information together with the following statement may be helpful to management.

	Product A	Product B	Product C	Total
	₹	₹	₹	₹
Sales revenue	50,000	7,500	12,500	70,000
Less: Variable production costs:				
Direct material	7,500	1,000	1,500	10,000
Direct labour	15,000	2,000	2,500	19,500
Factory overhead	3,000	400	500	3,900
Selling and administrative expenses	7,500	1,500	2,000	11,000
	33,000	4,900	6,500	44,400
Contribution margin	17,000	2,600	6,000	25,600
Less: Fixed costs:				
Factory overhead				5,850
Selling and administrative expenses				10,000
Total fixed costs				15,850
Net income				9,750

This statement shows that product *B* exceeds its variable costs by ₹2,600. If the sale of product *B* were discontinued, this marginal contribution would be lost and the net income of the firm would be reduced by ₹2,600. That is, net income will be ₹7,150 (₹9,750 – ₹2,600). In this illustration, it has been assumed that sales of products *A* and *C* will not be increased after product *B* is dropped. Further, it has been assumed that dropping product *B* will not change the fixed costs and expense. If these assumptions are not true, new analysis must be made. Assume, for example, that after dropping product *B*, the sales of product *A* increase by 10%. The total profit of the firm will not increase by this sales increase. Product *A* makes only a marginal contribution of 34%.

Sales revenue	₹50,000	100%
Variable costs	33,000	66%
Marginal contribution	17,000	34%

On additional sales of ₹5,000, the marginal contribution would be ₹1,700;

Sales revenue	₹5,000
Variable costs (66%)	3,300
Marginal contribution (34%)	1,700

This contribution is less than ₹2,600 now being realised on the sales of product *B*. It would take additional sales of product *A* of approximately ₹7,647 to equal the marginal contribution of ₹2,600 now being made by product *B*:

$$\frac{\text{Marginal contribution of product } B}{\text{Marginal contribution of product } A} = \frac{2,600}{34\%} = ₹7,647$$

It is possible that dropping product *B* may result in reduction in some of the fixed costs..Product *B* now contributes ₹2,600 towards recovery of fixed costs and expenses. Only if the fixed costs and expenses can be reduced by more than this amount will it be advisable to drop product *B*.

Sell or Process Further

The decision whether a product should be sold at the split-off point or processed further is faced by many manufacturers. The choice between selling a product at split-off or processing it further is a short-run operating decision. Additional processing adds value to a product and increases its selling price above the amount for which it could be sold at split-off. The decision to process further depends upon whether the increase in total revenues exceeds the additional costs incurred for processing beyond split-off. Generally speaking, there are two general conditions under which a sell or process further decision could occur.

1. The company is evaluating the possibility of processing beyond split-off and must incur certain equipment costs and other fixed costs if additional processing is to occur.
2. The company already processes a product beyond split-off and has invested in the equipment and required manpower.

The first situation is really a capital budgeting problem and here it is not sufficient to determine whether incremental revenues exceed incremental costs. Since new investments in machinery and building are involved, the rate of return on this investment must also be considered.

In the second situation, the relevant costs are only those costs which relate to the additional processing of each product beyond the split-off point. The joint costs are relevant to the further processing decisions. Certain fixed costs such as supervisory salaries are related to additional processing. If these costs are eliminated by selling products at split-off, they are incremental and should be included in the decision analysis. If salaried personnel are assigned other duties in the company when additional processing is discontinued, the salary costs are not incremental since they are incurred under either decision alternative. If the equipment used for additional processing sits idle or can be used in other processes, it should be ignored in the decision analysis. Depreciation expense is never relevant in short-run operating decisions, since depreciation is an allocation of costs incurred in a past period.

In deciding upon which course of action to follow, the company compares the contribution margin from the sale of the partially processed product with the contribution margin from the sale of the completely processed product. The revenue to be derived from the sale of the partially processed product is the opportunity cost attached to the decision of further processing. Assume, for example, a partially processed product can be sold for ₹90 per unit which is manufactured at a cost of ₹60. Further processing can be done at an additional cost of ₹30 per unit and the final product can be sold at ₹150 per unit. The firm can produce 10,000 units. The analysis is shown below:

	Sell	*Process and Sell*
Sales revenue	₹ 9,00,000	₹15,00,000
(10,000 units)		
Less: Manufacturing costs	6,00,000	9,00,000
	3,00,000	6,00,000

Net advantage in further processing ₹6,00,000 – 3,00,000 = ₹3,00,000

Thus, there is a net advantage of ₹3,00,000 in processing the product further. The market value of the partially processed product (₹9,00,000) is considered to be the opportunity cost of further processing.

The figure of net advantage of ₹3,00,000 can be arrived at in the following manner also:

Revenue from sale of final product (10,000 × 150)	₹15,00,000	
Less: Additional processing cost (10,000 × 30)	3,00,000	
Revenue from sale of intermediate product	9,00,000	12,00,000
Net advantage in further processing		3,00,000

Operate or Shutdown

Differential cost analysis is also used when a business is confronted with the possibility of a temporary shutdown. This type of analysis has to determine whether in the short-run a firm is better off operating than not operating. As long as the products sold recover their variable costs and make a contribution towards the recovery of fixed costs, it may be preferable to operate and not to shutdown. Also management should consider the investment in the training of its employees which would be lost in the event of a temporary shutdown. Recruiting and training new workers would add to present costs. Another factor is the loss of established markets. Also, a temporary shutdown does not eliminate all costs. Depreciation, taxes, interest, and insurance costs are incurred during shutdown also. The other points (benefits) which should be considered are the following: avoiding operating losses, savings in maintenance and repair costs, savings in indirect labour costs and savings in fixed costs.

A company operating below 50% of its capacity expects that the volume of sales will drop below the present level of 10,000 units per month. Management is concerned that a further drop in sales volume will create a loss and has under consideration a recommendation of operations be suspended until better market conditions prevail and also a better selling price. The present operating income statement is as follows:

Sales revenue (10000 units @ ₹3.00)		₹ 30,000
Less: Variable costs @ ₹2.00 per unit	20,000	
Fixed costs	10,000	30,000
Net income		0

The following income statements have been prepared for sales at different capacities:

Units Produced

	Shutdown	2,000	4,000	6,000	8,000	10,000
Sales revenue @ ₹3	0	6,000	12,000	18,000	24,000	30,000
Variable costs @ ₹2	0	4,000	8,000	12,000	16,000	20,000
Contribution	0	2,000	4,000	6,000	8,000	10,000
Fixed costs	4,000	10,000	10,000	10,000	10,000	10,000
Loss	(4,000)	(8,000)	(6,000)	(4,000)	(2,000)	0

It would appear that shutdown is desirable when the sales volume drops below 6,000 units per month, the point at which operating losses exceed the shutdown cost. This volume of 6,000 units could be arrived at without an income statement as follows:

Fixed costs if plant operates	₹10,000
Fixed costs if plant shutdown	4,000
Additional cost to be recovered when operating	6,000

Each unit of product sold contributes ₹1.00 to fixed costs recovery:

Selling price per unit	₹3.00
Variable cost per unit	₹2.00
Contribution	₹1.00

Sale of 6000 units is necessary to recover ₹6,000 of fixed costs.

$$\frac{₹6,000}{₹1.00} = 6,000 \text{ units}$$

If the selling price is cut to ₹2.80, then the contribution margin will be ₹0.80 per unit. Required sale to recover an additional ₹6,000 of fixed costs:

$$\frac{₹6,000}{₹0.80} = 7500 \text{ units}$$

That is, sales of 7500 units would be necessary to recover an additional ₹6,000 of fixed costs.

Special Orders

The question of special orders or one-time orders arises when a company has excess or idle production capacity and management considers the possibility of selling additional products at less than normal selling prices, provided that such a special order will not affect the regular sales of the same product.

The basic problem is to determine an acceptable price for the special order units. Cost analysis using the contribution approach is a useful technique to determine the short-run profit effects of special order transactions. In deciding the pricing of special orders where normal operations are not disturbed and where unused production capacity exists, it is not advisable to attach fixed costs to products. Price determination should take into account the recovery of incremental (variable) costs caused by accepting the special order. If the normal fixed costs are included in the price of the special order, the price may be too high and the business firm could lose the entire order and the contribution margin to be earned on the special order. Only the relevant (variable) costs should be used in the decision analysis to arrive at an appropriate price. Fixed costs are relevant only if incurred to facilitate the special order.

The following example illustrates the special order decisions.

A manufacturing company produces 20,000 units by operating at 60% of the capacity and sells at a price of ₹30 per unit. The budgeted figures for the year 2020 are as follows:

	Production
	(20,000 units)
Raw material @ ₹4.25	₹85,000
Direct labour @ ₹5.75	1,15,000
Variable factory overhead @ 7.75	1,55,000
Fixed factory overhead	1,25,000
Variable selling costs 2.75% of selling price	
Fixed selling and administrative costs	72,500

The company receives a special order for 10,000 units from a firm. The company desires to earn a profit of ₹1.00 per unit and no selling expenses are to be incurred for the special order. The minimum price on the special order and income statements are as follows:

Pricing of Special Order

	(10,000 units)
Variable costs to be incurred:	(₹)
Raw materials	4.25
Direct labour	5.75
Variable overhead	7.75
Variable cost per unit (no selling expenses)	17.75
Desired profit	1.00
Minimum price	18.75

Increase in sales = 10,000 units × ₹18.75 = ₹1,87,500

Income Statement

	Without Special Order	*Special Order*	*With Special Order*
	(₹)	(₹)	(₹)
Sales	6,00,000	1,87,500	7,87,500
Less: Variable costs:			
Raw materials	85,000	42,500	1,27,500
Direct labour	1,15,000	57,500	1,72,500
Variable factory overhead	1,55,000	77,500	2,32,500
Variable selling costs (2.75% of selling price)	16,500	–	16,500
Total variable costs	3,71,500	1,77,500	5,49,000
Less: Fixed costs:			
Fixed factory overhead	1,25,000	–	1,25,000
Fixed selling and administrative cost	72,500	–	72,500
Total fixed costs	1,97,500	–	1,97,500
Total costs	5,69,000	1,77,500	7,46,500
Net income before taxes	31,000	10,000	41,000

From the above analysis, it is clear that the acceptance of the special order will increase the profit by ₹10,000. Also the bid price (₹18.75) is significantly less than the normal price of ₹30. However, before arriving at a proper decision, management should consider some qualitative factors other than just the immediate impact on income. An important point is the effect on regular customers. If regular customers are paying more for the products, they may demand price reduction or quit buying from the firm and seek another source of supply. Another consideration is the possibility of special order customers being the regular customers.

Replace or Retain

The decision to replace or retain plant and equipment is also an important decision and should be taken very carefully. The differential costs which are important in retain or replace decisions are the following: change in fixed overhead costs, loss on sale of old equipment, capital investment and related costs such as rate of return and interest. Management should also consider differential benefits likely to be derived such as higher production and increased sales, realisable value of old machine, savings in operating costs, tax advantages, if any. Suppose, a company has purchased a plant for ₹1,00,000 five years ago which has a life of 10 years with no salvage value. The present book value is ₹50,000. Management is considering the replacement of this plant with a new plant costing ₹80,000 having a life of five years with no scrap value at the end of its life. The costs of operating present plant and the proposed plant are as follows:

	Present Plant (₹)	*Proposed Plant* (₹)
Variable costs:		
Labour, supplies, power, etc.	80,000	48,000
Fixed costs: Insurance, taxes, etc.	10,000	12,000
Depreciation	10,000	16,000
	1,00,000	76,000

It appears that the proposed plant would result into cost savings of ₹24,000 (₹1,00,000 – 76,000). However, the book value of the present equipment is a sunk cost and not relevant in the decision. The following table helps in making a better analysis of the data:

	Present Plant (₹)	*Proposed Plant* (₹)
Variable costs:		
Labour, supplies, power, etc.	80,000	48,000
Fixed costs: Insurance, taxes, etc.	10,000	12,000
Depreciation	0	16,000
	90,000	76,000

The purchase of the new plant results in a saving of ₹14,000 (₹90,000 – 76,000). Management has to consider whether this benefit is enough to justify the investment of ₹80,000 in new machinery.

✎ EXAMPLE 17.1 (PRODUCT MIX DECISION)

A manufacturer is producing a standard mix of 35,000 units. Detail is as follows:

	A	B	C
Unit produced	15,000	10,000	10,000
Variable cost (₹)	44	66	72
Selling price (₹)	62.5	75	105

He desires to change the mix as follows:

	Mix. 1	Mix. 2	Mix. 3
	Units	Units	Units
A	18,000	15,000	22,000
B	12,000	6,000	8,000
C	7,000	13,000	8,000
Total units	37,000	34,000	38,000

Total fixed cost is ₹7,00,000.

Required:

(i) Comparative profitability statement of three products.

(ii) Recommendation for most profitable product mix.

☞ ***Solution***

Statement Showing Marginal Cost and Contribution Per Unit

	Product A	*Product B*	*Product C*
Selling price (₹)	62.5	75	105
Less: Variable cost	44	66	72
Contribution per unit	18.5	9	33

Comparative Contribution and Profit from Product Mixes

Product	*Contribution*	*Mix 1*		*Mix 2*		*Mix 3*	
	Per Unit	*Qty*	*Amt.*	*Qty*	*Amt.*	*Qty*	*Amt.*
A	18.5	18,000	333,000	15,000	277,500	22,000	407,000
B	9	12,000	108,000	6,000	54,000	8,000	72,000
C	33	7,000	231,000	13,000	429,000	8,000	264,000
Total contribution			672,000		760,500		743,000
Less: Fixed cost			700,000		700,000		700,000
Profit (Loss)			(28,000)		60,500		43,000

Product Mix (2) which yield highest total contribution of ₹7,60,500 and maximum profit of ₹60,500 is the best.

EXAMPLE 17.2 (ADD/DROP PRODUCTION)

The V&A Group is made up of four operating subsidiaries: *A*, *B*, *C* and *D*. Its corporate accounting system has produced the following figures which show that the group has made a loss of ₹1,000. Analyse them and state which operations (if any) you would recommend for closure in order to return the group to profitability.

Summarised profit and loss accounts for last year (₹ '000):

	A	B	C	D	Group
Sales	180	420	500	900	2,000
Raw materials	41	95	202	370	708
Direct labour	62	89	37	105	293
Direct cost	103	184	239	475	1,001
Gross profit	62	236	261	425	999
Total overheads	90	210	250	450	1,000
Net profit	(13)	26	11	(25)	(1)

Note: Fixed overheads have been apportioned according to the amount of sales revenue from each operation. Overheads are considered to be 90% variable and 10% fixed.

Required:

(a) State which operations you would recommend closing and why.
(b) What would the group's profit be if your recommendations were actioned?
(c) What would the group's profit be if *A* and *D* were closed?

Solution

	A	B	C	D	Group
Total overheads	90	210	250	450	1,000
Variable overheads (90%)	81	189	225	405	900
Fixed overheads (10%)	9	21	25	45	100
Variable costs					
Raw materials + direct labour	103	184	239	475	1,001
Add: Variable overheads	81	189	225	405	900
Variable costs	184	373	464	880	1,901
Sales income	180	420	500	900	2,000
Contribution	(4)	47	36	20	99

(a) Close factory *A* only

If *A* is closed

	A	B	C	D	Group
Contribution	–	47	36	20	103
Less: Fixed costs					100
(b) Net profit					3

If *A* and *D* are closed

	A	B	C	D	Group
Contribution	–	47	36	–	83
Less: Fixed costs					100
(c) Net loss					**(17)**

EXAMPLE 17.3 (MINIMUM PRICE DECISION)

ABC Limited has been working below normal capacity due to recession. The directors of this company have been approached by a customer with an enquiry for a special purpose job. The costing department estimated the following in respect of the job:
Direct materials ₹60,000.
Direct labour hours 800 @ ₹25 per hour;
Overhead costs (normal rates of recovery variable ₹10 per hour and fixed ₹15 per hour)
The directors of the company seek your advice on the minimum price to be charged. Assume that there are no production difficulties regarding the job.

Solution

Costs Estimate for the Job

	₹
Direct materials	60,000
Direct labour cost (800 hrs @ ₹25)	20,000
Variable overheads (800 hrs @ ₹10)	8,000
Minimum price to be charged for the job	88,000

Fixed overheads are not to be considered since ABC Ltd. is working below normal capacity. These fixed overheads will be incurred whether this special purpose job is accepted or not. Therefore, the fixed overheads are not relevant costs to be considered in this decision situation.

EXAMPLE 17.4 (MAKE/BUY DECISION)

PSL Co. Ltd. produces a variety of products each having a number of component parts. It is producing product *Z* which takes 5 hours to produce on machine A23. *Z* has a selling price of ₹100 and a variable cost of ₹60 per unit. Component part *XT* could be made on the same machine A23 in two hours at a variable cost of ₹10 per unit. The supplier's price of the component is ₹24 per unit.

Advise whether the company should make or buy component part *XT* from the market under both the situations:

(i) when machine A23 is working at full capacity; and
(ii) when machine A23 has idle capacity.

Give reasons.

Solution

Contribution per unit of $Z = S - V$

$= ₹100 - ₹60 = ₹40$

$$\text{Contribution per hour} = \frac{₹40}{5 \text{ hours}} = ₹8$$

Variable cost of *XT* = ₹10

Loss of contribution, if made = ₹8 × 2 hours = ₹16

Cost to make = ₹16 + ₹10 = ₹26

Cost if it is purchased from the supplier = ₹24

Therefore difference = ₹26 – ₹24 = ₹2

ADVICE:

(i) When machine A23 is working at full capacity, the component *XT* should be bought and not made because total cost to make it is ₹26 which is more than the supplier's price of ₹24. If XT is made, it will result in a loss of ₹2 per unit.

(ii) When machine A23 has idle capacity then the component *XT* should be made because there will be no loss of contribution of ₹16 and it would be utilising the idle capacity. Making of *XT* would then be cheaper than buying it.

EXAMPLE 17.5 (SALES MIX DECISION)

Allied Manufacturing Company gives you the following information:

	Product A	*Product B*
	₹	₹
Fixed overheads ₹10,000 p.a.		
Direct materials per unit	20	25
Direct labour per unit	10	15
Variable overheads (100% of direct labour)		
Selling price per unit	60	100

You are required to present a statement showing the marginal cost of each product and recommend which of the following sales mixes should be adopted:

(a) 900 units of *A* and 600 units of *B*;
(b) 1,800 units of *A* only;
(c) 1,200 units of *B* only;
(d) 1,200 units of *A* and 400 units of *B*.

Solution

Statement of Marginal Cost

	Product A	*Product B*
	₹	₹
Materials cost per unit	20	25
Direct labour per unit	10	15
Variable overheads	10	15
	40	55
Selling price	60	100
Contribution	20	45

Profitability:

		₹
Sales mix (a) Contribution-	*A* 900 × ₹20	= 18,000
	B 600 × ₹45	= 27,000
Total		= 45,000
Less: Fixed cost		= 10,000
Profit		= **35,000**
Sales mix (b) Contribution-	*A* 1800 × ₹20	= 36,000
	B	= Nil
Total		= 36,000
Less: Fixed cost		= 10,000
Profit		= **26,000**
Sales mix (c) Contribution -	*A*	= Nil
	B 1200 × ₹45	= 54,000
Total		= 54,000
Less: Fixed cost		= 10,000
Profit		= **44,000**
Sales mix (d) Contribution -	*A* 1200 × ₹20	= 24,000
	B 400 × ₹45	= 18,000
Total		= 42,000
Less: Fixed cost		= 10,000
Profit		= **32,000**

Recommendation. Sales mix (c) gives the highest amount of profit at ₹44,000. So this sales mix should be adopted.

✍ EXAMPLE 17.6 (SELLING PRICE DECISION)

A manufacturing company has an installed capacity of 1,20,000 units per annum. The cost structure of the product is given below:

Variable cost (per unit)	₹
Material	8
Labour (subject to a minimum of ₹56,000 per month)	8
Overheads	3

Fixed overheads	: ₹1,68,750 per annum.
Semi-variable overheads	: ₹48,000 per annum at 60% capacity, which increase by ₹6,000 per annum for every 10% increase in the capacity utilisation or any part thereof for the year as a whole.

The capacity utilisation for next year is estimated at 60% for first 2 months; 75% for next 6 months and 80% for the remaining part of the year. If the company is planning to have a profit of 25% on the selling price, then calculate the selling price per unit for the year under consideration.

Assume that there is no opening or closing stock.

Solution

(A) Variable Cost of Production for Next Year

		Amount (₹)
A-1	First two months 60% capacity	
	Production = 6,000 × 2 = 12,000 units	
	Direct material @ ₹8	96,000
	Direct wages	1,12,000
	Overhead cost = 12,000 × ₹3	36,000
		2,44,000
A-2	Next six months : 75% capacity	
	Production = 7,500 × 6 = 45,000 units	
	Variable cost = (8 + 8 + 3) = 19 = 45,000 × 19	**8,55,000**
A-3	Next four months : 80% capacity	
	Production = 8000 × 4 = 32,000 units	
	Variable cost = (8 + 8 + 3) 19 = 32,000 × 19	**6,08,000**
A = [(A–1) + (A–2) + (A–3) = 89,000 units		
	Total variable cost (89,000 units)	17,07,000
	Add: Semi-variable cost	58,000
	Add: Fixed overheads	1,68,750
	Total cost	**19,33,750**
	Add: Profit 1/3rd of total cost or 1/4th of sales	6,44,583
	Sales for 89,000 units	**25,78,333**
	S.P./unit (₹25,78,333/89,000)	**₹28.97**

WORKING NOTES:

1. Monthly production: $\frac{1,20,000}{12}$ = 10,000 units p.m. at 100% capacity
2. Direct wages @ ₹56,000 per month (minimum) ₹1,12,000
   [even though it comes to 6,000 × ₹8 = ₹48,000 per month]
3. Semi-variable overheads:

		₹
First two months = $\frac{48,000}{12}$	= ₹4,000 × 2	8,000
Next ten months = $\frac{60,000}{12}$	= ₹5,000 × 10	50,000
		58,000

EXAMPLE 17.7 (DIFFERENTIAL COST ANALYSIS)

A company has a capacity of producing 50,000 units of a product in a month. The sales department reports that the following schedule of selling prices is possible:

Volume of Sales (% Capacity)	*Selling Price Per Unit*
50%	2.00
60%	1.90
70%	1.85
80%	1.80
90%	1.70
100%	1.60

Total fixed cost at 100% capacity is ₹20,000 per month and variable cost per unit is ₹1 per unit.

Prepare a statement showing total and differential costs and incremental revenue at each of the above levels of production and sales. At which level the profit will be maximum? Give reasons.

Solution

Calculation of Differential Cost and Incremental Revenue

Capacity	*Output Units*	*V.C.* ₹	*F.C.* ₹	*T.C.* ₹	*D.C.* ₹	*Sales* ₹	*I.R.* ₹
50%	25,000	25,000	20,000	45,000	–	50,000	–
60%	30,000	30,000	20,000	50,000	5,000	57,000	7,000
70%	35,000	35,000	20,000	55,000	5,000	64,750	7,750
80%	40,000	40,000	20,000	60,000	5,000	72,000	7,250
90%	45,000	45,000	20,000	65,000	5,000	76,500	4,500
100%	50,000	50,000	20,000	70,000	5,000	80,000	3,500

V.C. = Variable cost @ ₹1 per unit
F.C. = Fixed cost
T.C. = Total cost
D.C. = Differential cost
I.R. = Incremental revenue

Profit will be maximum at 80% because up to this level incremental revenue is more than differential cost. After 80%, differential cost is more than incremental revenue.

EXAMPLE 17.8 (FOREIGN MARKET DECISION)

Xpro & Co. Ltd. annually manufactures 10,000 units of a product at a cost of ₹4 per unit and sells these in the home market at a selling price of ₹4.25 per unit. In the next year, there is a fall in demand in home market which can absorb 10,000 units only at a price of ₹3.72 per unit. The total cost of 10,000 units is made up as follows:

Materials	₹15,000
Wages	₹11,000
Fixed overhead	₹8,000
Variable overhead	₹6000

The foreign market is explored and it is found that this market can consume 20,000 units of the product at a price of ₹3.55 per unit. (Assume that Co. has sufficient plant capacity to produce additional output.) It is also discovered that fixed overheads will increase by 10% for additional output above initial output of 10,000 units. Is it worth-while to try to capture the foreign market? Give reasons.

☞ Solution

	Current	*Next Year*	
Sales (units)	10,000 (*Home*)	10,000 (*Home*)	20,000 (*Export*)
	₹	₹	₹
Material cost	15,000	15,000	30,000
Wages	11,000	11,000	22,000
Variable overhead	6,000	6,000	12,000
Fixed overhead	8,000	8,000	800
Total cost	40,000	40,000	64,800
Sales	42,500	37,200	71,000
Profit/Loss	(+) 2,500	(–) 2,800	(+) 6,200

In the current year, the company is earning a profit of ₹2,500. Next year, the company will incur a loss of ₹2,800 in the home market, but will earn a profit of ₹6,200 from exports. Net profit in the next year will be 6,200 – 2,800 = ₹3,400. Hence, it is worth-while to capture the foreign market.

✍ EXAMPLE 17.9 (PRODUCT MIX DECISION)

Super India Ltd. is producing three products *X*, *Y* and *Z*. The data for the three products is given below:

	X	*Y*	*Z*
Maximum capacity	5,000 units	2,000 units	3,000 units
Direct material @ Ps. 10 per kg	₹40	₹10	₹30
Other variable costs	₹36	₹25	₹10
Selling price	₹100	₹50	₹60
Fixed cost (unavoidable)	₹20,000	₹15,000	₹10,000

Calculate the best product-mix in each of the following three independent cases:

(i) Total availability of raw materials is limited to 18,000 kg.

(ii) Under a trade agreement, the firm cannot produce more than 7,500 units of the three products taken together.

(iii) Total sales value of the three products cannot exceed ₹6,50,000.

Give complete workings showing contribution and total profit.

☞ **Solution**

Marginal Cost Statement

	X	Y	Z
Capacity in units	5,000	2,000	3,000
	₹	₹	₹
Selling price	100	50	60
Material	40	10	30
Other variable costs	36	25	10
Total variable cost	76	35	40
Contribution (Sales – VC)	24	15	20
Material used in kg	4	1	3
Contribution per kg (₹)	6	15	6.67
P/V ratio (C ÷ S)	24%	30%	33.33%

(i) Total raw material available is 18,000 kg ranking on the basis of contribution per kg of material is *Y*, *Z*, *X*. Thus, on this basis

2,000 units of *Y* @ 1 kg per unit =	2,000 kg
3,000 units of *Z* @ 3 kg per unit =	9,000 kg
1,750 units of *X* @ 4 kg per unit =	7,000 kg (balance)
	18,000

Profit Computation

	₹
Contribution of *Y* = 2,000 units × ₹15 =	30,000
Contribution of *Z* = 3,000 units × ₹20 =	60,000
Contribution of *X* = 1,750 units × ₹24 =	42,000
Total	1,32,000
Less: Fixed cost (20,000 + 15,000 + 10,000)	45,000
Profit	**87,000**

(ii) Output 7,500 units. Ranking on the basis of contribution per unit is *X*, *Z* and *Y*.

		₹
Contribution of X—5,000 units × ₹24		1,20,000
Contribution of Z–2,500 units × ₹20		50,000
7,500	Total	1,70,000
	Less: fixed cost	45,000
	Profit	**1,25,000**

(iii) Total sales limited to ₹6,50,000. Ranking on the basis of P/V ratio is *Z*, *Y*, *X*.

	₹	
Sale of 3,000 units of *Z* @ ₹60	1,80,000	
Sale of 2,000 units of *Y* @ ₹50	1,00,000	
Sale of 3,700 units of *X* @ ₹100	3,70,000	(balance)
	6,50,000	

Contribution and Profit

		₹
Contribution — Z 1,80,000 × $33\frac{1}{3}$%		60,000
Y 1,00,000 × 30%		30,000
X 3,70,000 × 24%		88,800
	Total	1,78,800
	Less: Fixed cost	45,000
	Profit	**1,33,800**

✍ EXAMPLE 17.10 (RELEVANT COST ANALYSIS)

X Ltd. has been approached by a customer who would like a special job to be done for him and is willing to pay ₹22,000 for it. The job would require the following materials:

Materials	*Total Units Required*	*Units Already in Stock*	*Book Value of Units in Stock (₹/Unit)*	*Realisable Value (₹/Unit)*	*Replacement Cost (₹/Unit)*
A	1,000	0	–	–	6
B	1,000	600	2	2.5	5
C	1,000	700	3	2.5	4
D	200	200	4	6	9

(i) Material *B* is used regularly by X Ltd., and if stocks were required for this job, they would need to be replaced to meet other production demand.

(ii) Materials *C* and *D* are in stock as the result of previous excess purchase and they have a restricted use. No other use could be found for material *C* but material *D* could be used in another job as substitute for 300 units of material, which currently cost ₹5 per unit (of which the company has no units in stock at the moment).

What are the relevant costs of material, in deciding whether or not to accept the contract? Assume all other expenses on this contract are to be specially incurred besides the relevant cost of material is ₹550.

Solution

Computation of relevant cost of the job:

A	(1,000 × 6)	6,000.00
B	(1,000 × 5)	5,000.00
C	[(700 × 2.5) + (300 × 4)]	2,950.00
D	(300 × 5)	1,500.00
		15,450.00
Add other expenses		550.00
		16,000.00

Conclusion: As the revenue from the order, which is more than the relevant cost of ₹16,000, the order should be accepted.

for excel template, scan

EXAMPLE 17.11 (SELL OR PROCESS FURTHER DECISION)

In a factory, three products *A*, *B* and *C* are produced from a single process. Each product can be sold at the end of each process or can be further processed independently to produce separate products, which are marketed under different names *X*, *Y*, *Z* respectively. Details for a period are given below:

Product	*Initial Output (Units)*	*Sales Price (₹)*	*Further Processing Cost (₹)*	*Rejection Rate*
A	5,000	24 per unit	14 per unit	–
B	8,000	10 per unit	6 per unit	–
C	10,000	30 per unit	16 per unit	–
X		44 per unit	–	5%
Y		18 per unit	–	10%
Z		48 per unit	–	8%

Initial total process cost ₹4 lakhs.
Further processing costs are incurred at the commencement of the second stage of operations.

You are required to:

(i) Calculate the apportionment of total cost to products *A*, *B* and *C* using sales value,
(ii) State whether further process should be undertaken for each product or not.

Solution

(i) Initial process cost is ₹4,00,000 to be apportioned on the basis of sales value.

Product	*Sale Value* ₹	%	*Apportioned Cost* ₹
A	1,20,000	24	96,000
B	80,000	16	64,000
C	3,00,000	60	2,40,000

Total sale value of ₹5 lakh exceeds the apportioned cost of ₹4 lakh. Therefore, initial process is beneficial.

(ii)

Product	Final Output (Units)	Revenue (₹)	Original Revenue (₹)	Incremental Revenue (₹)	Incremental Cost (₹)	Profit/Loss (₹)
X	4,750	2,09,000	1,20,000	89,000	70,000	19,000
Y	7,200	1,29,600	80,000	49,600	48,000	1,600
Z	9,200	4,41,600	3,00,000	1,41,600	1,60,000	(18,400)

Products *A* and *B* shall be processed further, product *C* shall be sold without further processing.

EXAMPLE 17.12 (SELLING PRICE DECISION)

A company produces a single product which is sold presently in the market at ₹75 per unit. The present production and sales are 40,000 units per month representing 50% of the capacity available. The cost data of the product is as under:

	₹
Variable cost per unit	50
Fixed cost per month	10 lakh

To utilise the idle capacity and improve profitability, the management has two proposals on hand as under:

(i) To increase sales by selling to a chain store 30,000 units at ₹55 per unit, retaining existing sales at the existing price.

(ii) To reduce selling price as advised by the sales department as under:

Reduced Selling Price Per Unit by	Expected Increase in Sale
₹5	10,000 units
₹8	30,000 units
₹11	35,000 units

Prepare a table to present the results of the above proposals and give your comments.

Solution

The problem is solved by incremental and differential cost analysis. The present capacity utilisation is only 50% and as such there is a scope to increase sales up to another 40,000 units. Fixed cost is not affected up to full utilisation.

Computation of Contribution at Various Price Level

Particulars	Present Level	Proposal (i)	Proposal (ii)		
			(a)	(b)	(c)
Quantities in units	40,000	70,000	50,000	70,000	75,000
Selling price per unit (₹)	75	40,000 @ ₹75	70	67	64

(contd.)

Particulars	Present Level	Proposal (i)	Proposal (ii)		
			(a)	(b)	(c)
		30,000 units @ ₹55			
Variable cost per unit (₹)	50	50	50	50	50
Total contribution (₹ in lakhs)	10	10.00 + 1.50 = 11.50	10.00	11.90	10.50

Purely on cost consideration, proposal to reduce selling price by ₹8 (proposal (ii)(b) to get total sales of 70,000 units is most profitable, since it yields a total contribution of ₹11.90 lakhs.

Comments: Proposal (i) selling to a chain store at a reduced price of ₹55 per unit is not desirable, though it increases contribution by ₹1.50 lakh (11.50 – 10). There may be a possibility that 30,000 units sold to a chain store may be competitor against own production at higher prices.

Proposal (ii)(b) is preferable because it gives a higher contribution of ₹1.90 lakh (11.90 – 10) which is more than proposal (i).

EXAMPLE 17.13 (LABOUR TURNOVER IMPACT DECISION)

The management of Zenith Co. Ltd. are worried about their increasing labour turnover in the factory and before analysing the causes, they want to have an idea of the profit foregone as result of labour turnover in the last year.

Last year, sales amounted to ₹83,03,300/- and the P/V ratio was 1/5. The total number of actual hours worked by the direct labour force was 4.45 lakhs. As a result of delays by personnel department in filling up the vacancies due to labour turnover, 60,000 potentially productive hours were not worked. The actual direct labour hours included 30,000 hours attributable to training new recruits, out of which half of the hours were unproductive. The costs consequent on labour turnover revealed on analysis the following:

	₹
Settlement costs due to leaving	43,250
Recruitment costs	34,520
Selection and placement costs	42,610
Training costs	69,270
Total	1,89,650

Assuming that the potential production lost as a consequence of labour turnover could have been sold at the prevailing prices, find out the profit foregone last year as a result of labour turnover.

Solution

Background data:

(i) P/V ratio or contribution @ 20% on sales ₹83,03,300 = ₹16,60,660

(ii) Actual direct labour hours worked
= 4,45,000 – (1/2 of 30,000 hours which were ineffective due to training)
= 4,45,000 – 15,000 = 4,30,000 productive hours.

(iii) Contribution per direct labour hour = $\frac{₹16,60,660}{4,30,000}$ = 3.862.

Contribution foregone —

1. Potential Productive hours lost due to delays in filling vacancies		60,000 hrs
2. Unproductive labour hours due to training new recruits		15,000 hrs
Total 75,000 hours @ ₹3.862		2,89,650
Costs consequent on labour turnover —		
1. Recruitment costs	₹34,520	
2. Selection & Placement costs	₹42,610	
3. Training costs	₹69,270	1,46,400
Total profit foregone due to labour turnover		4,36,050

Note: Settlement costs are not considered since these were legitimate dues to the workers who left the organisation. Labour turnover in general also affected working capital management because of unplanned costs as stated above.

✍ EXAMPLE 17.14 (PROFITABILITY DECISION)

A company manufactures a standard component. The details of current operations of the company are as follows:

Number of workers employed	100
Weekly working hours	48
Average number of hours lost due to idle time per employee per week	8
Standard time required per unit	2 hours
Hourly wage rate	₹15
Current level of efficiency	80%

For every unit sold, the company is getting a cash profit of ₹120 before charging labour cost. In view of the increased demand for the product, the company has come to an agreement with the labour union to raise the wage rate by ₹3 per hour in return for the workers reducing the idle time by 4 hours and raising the operational efficiency to 90%.

Required:

To calculate

(i) Net profit at current operations;
(ii) Net profit after the agreement; and
(iii) Increase/decrease in net profit.

☞ *Solution*

Cash profit earned by the company at present and anticipated profit after implementation of the agreement and worked out as follows:

Current Operation		*Operation after the Agreement*	
Total hours available per week 48 × 100	4,800	Total hours available per week 48 × 100	4,800
Hours actually worked 40 × 100	4,000	Hours actually worked per week 44 × 100	4,400
Production possible at 100% efficiency 4,000 hrs. ÷ 2	2,000	Production at 100% efficiency 4400 ÷ 2 hrs.	2,200
Production at current level of efficiency 80% : 80% of 2000	1,600	Production at 90% efficiency 90% of 2,200	1,980
Cash profit earned before charging labour cost 1600 hrs. × ₹120	1,92,000	Cash profit earned before charging labour cost 1980 hrs. × ₹120	2,37,600
Labour cost @ ₹15 × 4800 hours	72,000	Labour cost @ ₹15 × 4800 hours	86,400
Profit	**1,20,000**	**Profit**	**1,51,200**

In spite of an increase in wage rate by 20%, overall profit has increased by ₹1,51,200 – 1,20,000 = ₹31,200.

✎ EXAMPLE 17.15 (LIMITING FACTOR DECISION)

ABC Ltd. is manufacturing three products *X*, *Y* and *Z*. All the products use the same raw material which is scarce and available to the extent of 61,000 kg. only. The following information is available from records of the company:

Particulars	*Product X*	*Product Y*	*Product Z*
Selling price per unit (₹)	100	140	90
Variable cost per unit (₹)	75	110	65
Raw material requirement per unit (kg)	5	8	6
Market demand (units)	5,000	3,000	4,000

Fixed costs are ₹1,50,000.

Advise the company about the most profitable product mix. Compute the amount of profit resulting from such product mix.

☞ Solution

It is given that availability of raw material is limited to the extent of 61,000 kg only. It can be noticed that if the products are produced to the maximum possible extent according to the market demand, the resultant profit will be highest. However, it is not possible as the raw material is not available to that extent. Therefore, it is necessary to find out priority of the product by ranking them on the basis of contribution per kg. of raw material.

	Product X	*Product Y*	*Product Z*
Selling price per unit	₹100	₹140	₹90
Less: Variable cost/unit	75	110	65
Contribution per unit	₹25	30	25
Contribution per constraint (raw material)	25/5	30/8	25/6
i.e., kg. of raw materials	= 5	= 3.75	= 4.16
Priority ranking	I	III	II

It is evident that product *X* will be produced first to meet total market demand of 5000 units.

Product	*No. of Units*	*Raw Material Consumed*	*Contribution*
X	5,000	25,000 kg.	₹1,25,000
Z	4,000	24,000 kg.	1,00,000
Y	1,500	12,000 kg.*	45,000
		* (Balance to go up to 61,000 kg.)	
		61,000 kg.	₹2,70,000

Amount of profit = ₹2,70,000 *Less* ₹1,50,000 (Fixed cost) = ₹1,20,000
This will be the highest profit in the given situation by producing 5,000 units of *X*, 1,,500 units of *Y* and 4000 units of *Z*

EXAMPLE 17.16 (SELLING PRICE DECISION)

Maximum production capacity of JK Ltd. is 5,20,000 units per annum. Details of estimated cost of production are as follows:

- Direct material ₹15 per unit.
- Direct wages ₹9 per unit (subject to a minimum of ₹2,50,000 per month).
- Fixed overheads ₹9,60,000 per annum.
- Variable overheads ₹8 per unit.
- Semi-variable overheads are ₹5,60,000 per annum up to 50 per cent capacity and additional ₹1,50,000 per annum for every 25 per cent increase in capacity or a part of it.

JK Ltd. worked at 60 per cent capacity for the first three months during the year 2020, but it is expected to work at 90 per cent capacity for the remaining nine months.

The selling price per unit was ₹44 during the first three months.

You are required, what selling price per unit should be fixed for the remaining nine months to yield a total profit of ₹15,62,500 for the whole year.

Solution

Statement of Cost and Sales for the Year 2020

Maximum Production Capacity = 5,20,000 Units Per Annum

Particulars	*First 3 Months*	*Next 9 Months*	*Total*
Capacity utilised	60%	90%	
Production	$\frac{5,20,000 \times 3 \times 60\%}{12}$	$\frac{5,20,000 \times 9 \times 90\%}{12}$	
	= 78,000 units	= 3,51,000 units	4,29,000 units
	₹	₹	₹
Direct materials @ ₹15 per unit	11,70,000	52,65,000	64,35,000
Direct wages @ 9 per unit or ₹2,50,000 per month whichever is higher	7,50,000	31,59,000	39,09,000
Prime cost *(A)*	19,20,000	84,24,000	1,03,44,000

(contd.)

Particulars	*First 3 Months*	*Next 9 Months*	*Total*
Overheads			
Fixed	2,40,000	7,20,000	9,60,000
Variable @ ₹8 per unit	6,24,000	28,08,000	34,32,000
Semi variable	1,77,500	6,45,000	8,22,500
Total overheads (*B*)	10,41,500	41,73,000	52,14,500
Total cost (*C*) [(*A* + *B*)]	29,61,500	1,25,97,000	1,55,58,500
Profit during first 3 months	4,70,500		
Sales @ ₹44 per unit	34,32,000		
Desired profit during next 9 months (₹15,62,500 – ₹4,70,500) (D)		10,92,000	
Sales required for next 9 months (E) [(C + D)]		1,36,89,000	
Total profit			15,62,500
Total sales			1,71,21,000

$$\text{Required selling price per unit for last 9 months} = \frac{\text{Total sales required for last 9 months}}{\text{Units produced during last 9 months}}$$

$$= ₹\ \frac{1,36,89,000}{35,10,000} = ₹39 \text{ per unit.}$$

✍ WORKINGS:

(1) Semi-variable overheads:

(a) For first 3 months at 60% capacity = ₹(5,60,000 + ₹1,50,000) × 3/12
= ₹7,10,000 × 3/12
= ₹1,77,500.

(b) For remaining 9 months at 90% capacity = ₹(5,60,000 + ₹3,00,000) × 9/12
= ₹8,60,000 × 9/12
= ₹6,45,000

✍ EXAMPLE 17.17 (SELL OR PROCESS FURTHER DECISION)

A firm manufactures three joint products *A*, *B*, *C* and a by-product *X* by processing a common stock of material, which cost ₹8 per kg. The details of output, market price and the initial processing cost for an input of 10,000 kg. of raw material is as follows:

Product	*Output/kg.*	*Current Market Price/kg.–₹*	*Initial Processing Cost*
A	5,000	18	Direct labour 1,000 hours @ ₹20
B	2,500	20	Variable overheads: 80% of direct labour
C	1,500	24	Fixed overheads: ₹21,000
X	500	4	

The company apportions common cost among joint products on physical unit basis.
All the by-products can be further processed and sold at a higher market price, with some sales promotion efforts. The estimated processing cost, marketing cost and the final selling price are given below:

Product	*Further Processing Cost Per Kg. – ₹*	*Further Marketing Cost Per.Kg. – ₹*	*Final Price Per Kg. – ₹*
A	4	2	28
B	5	2	26
C	6	2	34
X	2	1	6

You are required to compute:

(i) Cost of joint products at the point of separation after initial processing.
(ii) Profit or loss if the products are sold without further processing.
(iii) Which of the products have to be processed further for maximising profits? Show working.

☞ **Solution**

(i) Statement Showing Cost of Joint Products at the Point of Separation.

Particulars	*Amount (₹)*
Raw material: 10,000 kg @ ₹8 per kg	80,000
Direct labour: 1,000 hours @ ₹20 per hour	20,000
Variable overheads : 80% of direct labour	16,000
Fixed overheads	21,000
Total cost	1,37,000
Less : Sales value of by-product	2,000
Cost of joint product at the separation point	1,35,000

(ii) Statement of Profit or Loss If the Products are Sold without Further Processing

Product	*Quantity Kg*	*Proportion %*	*Joint Cost Allocation*	*Sales Per Kg*	*Sales ₹*	*Profit ₹*
A	5,000	55.55	75,000	18	90,000	15,000
B	2,500	27.78	37,500	20	50,000	12,500
C	1,500	16.67	22,500	24	36,000	13,500
Total	9,000	100.00	1,35,000		1,76,000	41,000

(iii) Evaluation of Products to be Processed Further for Maximising Profits

Product	*Further Processing Cost ₹*	*Further Marketing Cost ₹*	*Total Cost ₹*	*Sales Value at Split Off ₹*	*Sales Value after Further Processing ₹*	*Incremental Revenue ₹*	*Incremental Profit/Loss ₹*
(a)	(b)	(c)	(d) = (b) + (c)	(e)	(f)	(g) = (f) – (e)	(h) = (g) – (d)
A	4	2	6	18	28	10	4
B	5	2	7	20	26	6	(1)
C	6	2	8	24	34	10	2
X	2	1	3	4	6	2	(1)

Products *A* and *C* are giving incremental profit of ₹4 and ₹2 respectively if they are further processed and hence they can be processed further. Products *B* and *X* have loss if they are processed further. In this situation, they can be sold at split off point instead of further processing.

Example 17.18 (Limiting Factor Decision)

The following particulars are extracted from the records of a company

	Product A	*Product B*
Sales (per unit)	₹100	₹120
Consumption of material	2 kg	3 kg
Material cost	₹10	₹15
Direct wages cost	₹15	₹10
Direct expenses	₹5	₹6
Machine hours used	3	2
Overhead expenses:		
Fixed	₹5	₹10
Variable	₹15	₹20

Direct wage per hour is ₹5. Comment on the profitability of each product (both use the same raw material) when

(a) (i) total sales potential in units is limited;
(ii) total sales potential in value is limited;
(iii) raw material is in short supply;
(iv) production capacity (in terms of machine hours) is the limiting factor.

(b) Assuming raw material is the key factor, availability of which is 10,000 kg and maximum sales potential of each product being 3,500 units, find the product-mix which will yield the maximum profit.

Solution

(Per Unit Costs)

	Product A	*Product B*
(a) Sales	₹100	₹120
(b) Variable cost:		
Direct material	10	15
Direct wages	15	10
Direct expenses	5	6
Variable overheads	15	20
Total variable cost	₹45	₹51
(c) Contribution per unit (a – b)	₹55	₹69

(a) Ranking of products in terms of profitability

(i) *Total sales potential in units is limited.*

Basis: Contribution per unit: Product *A* ₹55

Product *B* ₹69

Ranking: 1st Product *B*

2nd Product *A*

(ii) *Total sales potential in value is limited.*

Basis: Contribution per rupee of sales value, that is,

$$\frac{\text{Contribution per unit}}{\text{Selling price per unit}}$$

Product *A* = ₹55/₹100 = ₹0.55

Product *B* = ₹69/₹120 = ₹0.575

Ranking: 1st Product *B*

2nd Product *A*

(iii) *Raw material is in short supply.*

Basis: Contribution per unit of raw material consumption, that is,

$$\frac{\text{Contribution per unit}}{\text{Material consumption (in quantity) per unit}}$$

Product *A* = ₹55/2 kg = ₹27.50 per kg.

Product *B* = ₹69/3 kg = ₹23.00 per kg.

Ranking: 1st Product *A*

2nd Product *B*

(iv) *Production capacity (in terms of machine hours) is the limiting factor.*

Basis: Contribution per unit of machine hour, that is

$$\frac{\text{Contribution per unit}}{\text{Machine hours used per unit}}$$

Product *A* = ₹55/3 hrs. = ₹18.33 per hour

Product *B* = ₹69/2 hrs. = ₹34.50 per hour

Ranking: 1st Product *B*

2nd Product *A*

(b) When raw material is the key factor, our ranking is Product *A*—1st, and Product *B*—2nd. Therefore, the firm would like to produce only Product *A*, which best utilises the available raw material. However, there is another limiting factor in operation, that is, the maximum sales potential. This factor will set the limit for production of the Product *A*. The following will be the allotment of available raw material between Product *A* and Product *B*:

Available raw material	10,000 kg
Maximum sales potential for Product *A* (ranked 1st) 3500 units	
Raw material required for Product *A* 3,500 × 2 kg =	(7,000 kg)
Balance available for Product *B*	3,000 kg

Maximum number of Product *B* that can be produced with available raw material is = 3,000/3 kg, that is 1,000 units.

Product-mix which will yield the maximum profit:

Product *A*	3,500 units	
Product *B*	1,000 units	
Total contribution:		
Product *A*	3,500 × ₹55	₹1,92,500
Product *B*	1,000 × ₹69	₹69,000
	Total:	₹2,61,500
Total fixed cost:		
Product *A*	3,500 × ₹5	₹17,500
Product *B*	1,000 × ₹10	₹10,000
	Total:	₹27,500

Total profit = Total contribution – Total fixed cost
= ₹2,61,600 – ₹27,500
= ₹2,34,000

NOTES:

(i) Fixed cost per unit reflects only the allocated cost and is irrelevant for decision-making.

(ii) In estimating the total fixed cost, it is assumed that the total fixed cost is equal to the fixed cost absorbed by Product *A* and Product *B*. This is a simplistic assumption and not likely to hold good in most of the situations.

EXAMPLE 17.19 (MAKE OR BUY)

Auto Parts Ltd. has an annual production of 90,000 units for a motor component. The component's cost structure is as below:

	₹
Materials	270 per unit
Labour (25% fixed)	180 per unit
Expenses:	
Variable	90 per unit
Fixed	135 per unit
Total	675 per unit

(a) The purchase manager has an offer from a supplier who is willing to supply the component at ₹5.40. Should the component be purchased and production stopped?

(b) Assume the resources now used for this component's manufacture are to be used to produce another new product for which the selling price is 485.

In the latter case, the material price will be ₹200 per unit. 90,000 units of this product can be produced on the same cost basis as above for labour and expenses. Discuss whether it would be advisable to divert the resources to manufacture the new products, on the footing that the component presently being produced would, instead of being produced, be purchased from the market.

☞ Solution

(a)

Statement Showing the Variable Cost and Purchase Cost of Component... Used by Auto Parts Ltd.

Variable Cost	*Per Unit*	*Total for 90,000 Units*
	₹	₹
Materials	270	2,43,00,000
Labour	135	1,21,50,000
Expenses	90	81,00,000
Total variable cost (when component is produced)	495	4,45,50,000
Cost of purchase (when component is purchased)	540	4,86,00,000
Difference, excess of purchase price over variable cost	45	40,50,000

Fixed expenses not being affected, it is evident from the above statement that if the component is purchased from the outside supplier, the company will have to spend ₹45 per unit more and on 90,000 units the company will have to spend ₹40,50,000 more. Therefore, the company should not stop the production of the component.

(b) The following statement shows the cost implications of the proposal to divert the available facilities for a new product.

Statement Showing the Contribution per Unit if the Existing Resources are Used for the Production of Another New Product

	₹	₹
Selling price of the new product per unit		485
Less: Materials cost	200	
Labour (variable)	135	
Expenses (variable)	90	425
Contribution per unit		60
Loss per unit if the present component is purchased:		
Purchase price of the existing product		540
Less: Total variable cost of producing the existing component		495
Excess cost		45

Thus, if the company diverts its resources for the production of another new product, it will benefit by ₹15 per unit that is ₹60 – 45 per unit. On 90,000 units the company will save ₹13,50,000. Therefore, it is advisable to divert the resources to manufacture the new product and the component presently being produced should be purchased from the market. This is also brought out by the following figures:

	₹
Total cost producing the component (90,000 × 675) (A)	6,07,50,000
Cost of purchasing the component (90,000 × 540)	4,86,00,000
Fixed expenses, not having been saved (90,000 × 180, that is, 675 – 495)	1,62,00,000
	6,48,00,000

Less: Contribution from the new product (90,000 × 60)	54,00,000
Total cost if component is purchased and new product is made (*B*)	5,94,00,000
Savings (*A* – *B*)	13,50,000

EXAMPLE 17.20 (PRODUCT MIX DECISION)

From the following particulars, find the most profitable product mix and prepare a statement of profitability of that product-mix:

	Product A	*Product B*	*Product C*
Units budgeted to be produced and sold	1,800	3,000	1,200
Selling price per unit (₹)	60	55	50
Direct material required per unit (kg)	5	3	4
Direct labour per unit (hrs.)	4	3	2
Variable overheads (₹)	7	13	8
Fixed overheads (₹)	10	10	10
Cost of direct material per kg (₹)	4	4	4
Direct labour hour rate (₹)	2	2	2
Maximum possible units of sale	4,000	5,000	1,500

All the three products are produced from the same direct material using the same type of machines and labour. Direct labour which is the key factor is limited to 18,600 hours.

Solution

Statement Showing the Budgeted Profitability

	Per Unit		
	Product A	*Product B*	*Product C*
	₹	₹	₹
Selling price per unit	60	55	50
Direct material @ ₹4 per kg	20	12	16
Direct labour @ ₹2 per hour	8	6	4
Variable overheads	7	13	8
Marginal cost	35	31	28
Contribution per unit	25	24	22
Budgeted production in units	1,800	3,000	1,200
Total contribution	1,800 × 25 = 45,000	3,000 × 24 = 72,000	1,200 × 22 = 26,400
Fixed cost @ ₹10 per unit	18,000	30,000	12,000
Profit	27,000	42,000	14,400

Optimal Product Mix and Profit

	Per Unit		
	A	*B*	*C*
	₹	₹	₹
Sales per unit	60	55	50
Material @ ₹4 per kg	20	12	16
Labour @ ₹2 per hour	8	6	4
Variable overhead	7	13	8
Marginal cost	35	31	28
Contribution per unit	25	24	22
Contribution per ₹ of sales $\left(\frac{C}{S.P}\right)$	$\frac{25}{60}$ = ₹0.417	$\frac{24}{55}$ = ₹0.436	$\frac{22}{50}$ = ₹0.44
Labour required per unit	4 hours	3 hours	2 hours
Contribution per hour of labour	$\frac{25}{4}$ = ₹6.25	$\frac{24}{3}$ = ₹8	$\frac{22}{2}$ ₹11
Ranking	III	II	I

Product	*Maximum No.*	*Labour Hour Per Unit*	*Labour Hours Used*	*Contribution*	*Total* (₹)
C	1,500	2	3,000	22	33,000
B	5,000	3	15,000	24	1,20,000
A	1,500	4	600	25	3,750
			18,600		1,56,750
Less: Fixed cost *C* 1,200 × 10			12,000		
B 3,000 × 10			30,000		
A 1,800 × 10			18,000		60,000
Profit					**96,750**

EXAMPLE 17.21 (LIMITING FACTOR DECISION)

A company manufactures three products—the budgeted quantity, selling prices and unit costs are as under:

	A	*B*	*C*
	₹	₹	₹
Raw materials (@ ₹20 per kg)	80	40	20
Direct wages (@ ₹5 per hour)	5	15	10

(contd.)

	A	B	C
	₹	₹	₹
Variable overheads	10	30	20
Fixed overheads	9	22	18
Budgeted production (in units)	6,400	3,200	2,400
Selling price per unit (in ₹)	140	120	90

Required:

(i) Present a statement of budgeted profit.

(ii) Set optimal product-mix and determine the profit if the supply of raw materials is restricted to 18,400 kg.

☞ Solution

(i)

Statement Showing the Budgeted Profitability

(₹)

	Per Unit		
Selling Price Per Unit	*Product A*	*Product B*	*Product C*
	140	*120*	*90*
Raw materials (@ ₹20 per kg)	80	40	20
Direct wages (@ ₹5 per hour)	5	15	10
Variable overheads	10	30	20
Marginal cost	95	85	50
Contribution per unit	45	35	40
Budgeted production (in units)	6,400	3,200	2,400
Total contribution	6,400 × 45	3,200 × 35	2,400 × 40
	= 2,88,000	= 1,12,000	= 96,000
Fixed cost	6,400 × 9	3,200 × 22	2,400 × 18
	= 57,600	= 70,400	= 43,200
Profit	2,30,400	41,600	= 52,800

(ii) **Optimal Product Mix and Profit**

	Per Unit		
	A	*B*	*C*
	₹	₹	₹
Sales	140	120	90
Materials (@ ₹20 per kg)	80	40	20
Direct wages (@ ₹5 per hour)	5	15	10
Variable overhead	10	30	20
Marginal cost	95	85	50
Contribution per unit	45	35	40
Contribution per ₹ of sale $\left(\frac{C}{S}\right)$	$\frac{45}{140}$ = ₹0.321	$\frac{35}{120}$ = ₹0.29	$\frac{40}{90}$ = ₹044
Material required per unit	$\frac{80}{20}$ = 4 kg	$\frac{40}{20}$ = 2 kg	$\frac{20}{20}$ = 1 kg
Contribution per kg. of material	$\frac{45}{4}$ = ₹11.25	$\frac{35}{2}$ = ₹17.5	$\frac{40}{1}$ = ₹40
Ranking	III	II	I

Product	Maximum No.	Consumption Per Unit (kg)	Material Used (kg) Per Unit	Contribution	Total
C	6,400	1	6,400	40	25,600
B	3,200	2	6,400	35	1,12,000
A	1,400	4	5,600	45	63,000
			18,400		4,31,000

Less: Fixed cost

C	6,400 × 18	=	1,15,200
B	3,200 × 22	=	70,400
A	2,400 × 9	=	21,600
		=	1,98,200

	1,98,200
Profit =	2,32,800

Thus, product mix of 6,400 units of *C*, 3,200 units of *B* and 1,400 units of *A* will give maximum profit of ₹2,32,800.

EXAMPLE 17.22 (DIFFERENTIAL COST ANALYSIS)

Pioneer Manufacturing Company, makers of a specialised line of toys, received an order for 2,000 units of toy battle tank from a large mail-order house at a price of ₹3 per unit. The company sells this type of toy to its other customers at ₹5 each but it has surplus capacity and can take the special order without adversely affecting its regular operations for coming month.
The income statement of the company for the preceding year is as follows:

	₹
Net sales—10,000 units @ ₹5 each	50,000
Costs:	
Direct material—₹1.50 per unit	15,000
Direct labour—₹1 per unit	10,000
Factory overhead	10,000
Selling and administrative overheads	10,000
Total costs	45,000
Net profit	5,000

Direct material and direct labour costs to be incurred on the special order are estimated to be of the same amount per unit as for the regular business. Special tools costing ₹500 would be required to meet the specifications of the mail-order house.

You are required to prepare a differential costs statement for deciding about the acceptance of the order.

Solution

Differential Cost Analysis

Output (In Units)	*Selling Price Per Unit*	*Sales Value*	*Incremental Revenue*	*Variable Cost*	*Fixed Cost*	*Total Cost (V + F)*	*Differential Cost*
	₹	₹	₹	₹	₹	₹	₹
10,000	5	50,000	–	25,000	20,000	45,000	–
10,000	5	50,000	6,000	30,500	20,000	50,500	5,500
2,000 } 2,000	3	6,000 } 56,000	(56,000–50,000)	(12,000 @ 2.50 + ₹500 special tool cost)			(50,500 – 45,000)

From the above statement, it is clear that incremental revenue of ₹6,000 is more than the differential cost of ₹5,500, so order of 2,000 units at a price of ₹3 per unit from a large mail-order house should be accepted. The acceptance of the order will increase profit by ₹500.

EXAMPLE 17.23 (DIFFERENTIAL COST ANALYSIS)

P Ltd. is at present operating at 80% capacity level, the production being 15,000 units per annum. The company operates a flexible budgetary control system. The following relevant cost data are obtained from the company's budget at different capacity utilisation levels:

Capacity Utilisation Level

	80%	100%
Sales	₹20,00,000	₹25,00,000
Variable overheads	₹ 2,25,000	₹ 2,50,000
Semi-variable overheads	₹ 1,05,000	₹ 1,11,000
Fixed overheads	₹ 4,00,000	₹ 4,70,000
Output (in units)	15,000	18,750

Material and labour cost per unit are constant under present conditions. The management expects a profit margin of 10% on sales.

You are required to compute the differential cost of producing the additional 3,750 units by increasing the capacity utilisation level to 100 per cent and the minimum price per unit at 10% profit on cost.

☞ Solution

	₹	₹
Sales at 80% capacity		20,00,000
Less: Profit 10% $\left(\frac{20,00,000 \times 100}{80}\right)$		2,00,000
Cost of goods sold:		18,00,000
Less: Expenses:		
Variable overheads	2,25,000	
Semi-variable overheads	1,05,000	
Fixed overheads	4,00,000	7,30,000
Cost of material and labour at 80% capacity		10,70,000

Therefore, material and labour cost at 100% capacity

$$\frac{10,70,000 \times 100}{80} = ₹13,37,500$$

Differential cost analysis is as follows:

	80% Capacity 15000 Units	*100% Capacity 18750 Units*	*Differential Cost*
	₹	₹	₹
Material and labour	10,70,000	13,37,500	2,67,500
Variable expenses	2,25,000	2,50,000	25,000
Semi-variable exp.	1,05,000	1,11,000	6,000
Fixed expenses	4,00,000	4,70,000	70,000
Total cost	18,00,000	21,68,500	3,68,500

(a) Differential cost for 3750 units = ₹3,68,500

(b) Minimum price = $\frac{₹3,68,500}{3750 \text{ units}}$ ₹98.266

Add: 10% profit on cost 9.826

108.092

EXAMPLE 17.24 (DIFFERENTIAL COST COMPUTATION)

A company has an installed production capacity of 1,00,000 units and presently it is working at 70% capacity utilisation. As production capacity utilisation increases, cost per unit decreases as follows:

Capacity Utilisation	*Cost Per Unit*
70%	₹97
80%	₹92
90%	₹87
100%	₹82

The company has received three export orders from different sources as under:
Source *A*–5,000 units at ₹55 per unit
Source *B*–10,000 units at ₹52 per unit
Source *C*–10,000 units at ₹51 per unit
Advise the company whether any or all the export orders should be accepted or not.

Solution

Statement Showing Differential Costs at Different Capacity Utilisation Levels (Installed Capacity 100,000 Units)

Capacity Utilisation (Percent)	*Production at Different Levels Capacity Utilisation (Units)*	*Unit Cost* ₹	*Total Cost* ₹	*Differential Cost* ₹	*Differential Cost Per Unit* ₹
70	70,000 $\left(1,00,000 \times \frac{70}{100}\right)$	97	67,90,000	–	–
80	80,000 $\left(1,00,000 \times \frac{80}{100}\right)$	92	73,60,000	5,70,000	57 $\left[\frac{5,70,000}{10,000}\right]$
90	90,000 $\left(1,00,000 \times \frac{90}{100}\right)$	87	78,30,000	4,70,000	47 $\left[\frac{4,70,000}{10,000}\right]$
100	1,00,000	82	82,00,000	3,70,000	37 $\left[\frac{3,70,000}{10,000}\right]$

Statement Showing Profit or Loss Accepting the Various Export Orders

Export Order Source	*Export Order Unit*	*Capacity Utilisation Percent*	*Differential Costs* Per Unit ₹	*Differential Costs* Total ₹	*Price Per Unit* ₹	*Sales Reverse from the Order Export* ₹	*Profit or Loss* ₹
A	5,000	75	57	2,85,000	55	2,75,000	(10,000)
B	10,000	85	First 5,000 units being Up to 80% @ ₹57 Next 5,000 units ₹@ ₹47		52	5,20,000	Nil
C	10,000	95	First 5,000 units being Up to 90% @ ₹47 Next 5,000 units @ ₹37	4,20,000	51	5,10,000	90,000
Total	25,000	95%		12,25,000		13,05,000	80,000

It is clear from the above statement that it is advantageous for the company only when it accepts all the export orders. If the company accepts export orders only for one or two of three sources, it will suffer a loss. Therefore, the company should accept export orders from all the three sources to earn additional profits.

✎ EXAMPLE 17.25 (MATERIAL PROCUREMENT DECISION)

A company has the option to procure a particular material from two sources:

Source I assures that defectives will not be more than 2% of supplied quantity.

Source II does not give any assurance, but on the basis of past experience of supplies received from it, it is observed that defective percentage is 2.8%.

The material is supplied in lots of 1,000 units. Source II supplies the lot at a price, which is lower by ₹100 as compared to Source I. The defective units of material can be rectified for use at a cost of ₹5 per unit.

You are required to find out which of the two sources is more economical.

Solution

Comparative Statement of Procuring Material from Two Sources

	Material Source I	*Material Source II*
Defectives (in %)	2 *(Future estimate)*	2.8 *(Past experience)*
Units supplied *(in one lot)*	1,000	1,000
Total defective units in a lot	20 *(1,000 units × 2%)*	28 *(1,000 units × 2.8%)*
Additional price paid per lot (₹): (A)	100	–
Rectification cost of defect (₹) (B)	100 *(20 units × ₹5)*	140 *(28 units × ₹5)*
Total additional cost per lot (₹): {(A) + (B)}	200	140

Decision: On comparing the total additional cost incurred per lot of 1,000 units, we observe that it is more economical, if the required material units are procured from material source II.

EXAMPLE 17.26 (SELLING PRICE DECISION)

The accounts of a company are expected to reveal a profit of ₹14,00,000 after charging fixed costs of ₹10,00,000 for the year ended 31st March, 2020. The selling price of the product is ₹50 per unit and variable cost per unit is ₹20.

Market investigations suggest the following responses to the price changes:

Alternatives	*Selling Price Reduced by*	*Quantity Sold Increased by*
I	5%	10%
II	7%	20%
III	10%	25%

Evaluate these alternatives and state which of the alternatives, on profitability consideration, should be adopted for the forthcoming year.

Solution

Statement for Evaluating Three Alternatives on Profitability Consideration

	Alternatives		
	I	*II*	*III*
Selling price per unit (₹)	47.50 (₹50 – 5% of ₹50)	46.50 (₹50 – 7% of ₹50)	45.00 (₹50 – 10% of ₹50)
Less: Variable cost per unit (₹)	20.00	20.00	20.00
Contribution per unit (₹)	27.50	26.50	25.00
Revised quantity of units to be sold *(Refer to working note-3)*	88000	96000	100,000
Total contribution (₹)	24,20,000 (88000 units × ₹27.50)	25,44,000 (96000 units × ₹26.50)	25,00,000 (100,000 units × ₹25)

Recommendation: An evaluation of the above three alternatives on profitability consideration clearly shows that alternative II is the best as it gives maximum contribution and hence profitability. Therefore, this alternative should be adopted.

WORKING NOTES:

1. *Contribution per unit*

= Selling price per unit – Variable cost per unit

= ₹50 – ₹20 = ₹30

2. *Expected quantity of units to be sold*

	(₹)
Profit	14,00,000
Add: Fixed costs	10,00,000
Total contribution	24,00,000

$$\text{Quantity of units sold} = \frac{\text{Total contribution}}{\text{Contribution per unit}} = \frac{₹24,00,000}{₹30} = 80,000 \text{ units}$$

3. *Revised quantity of units to be sold*

Alternatives	*Units to be Sold*
I	80,000 units + 10% of 80,000 units = 88,000 units
II	80,000 units + 20% of 80,000 units = 96,000 units
III	80,000 units + 25% of 80,000 units = 100,000 units

EXAMPLE 17.27 (COST INDIFFERENCE POINT)

XYZ Company is considering hiring a machine at an annual charge of ₹12,000 to increase the output of a product from its present level of 6,000 units. It is anticipated that with the introduction of the machine the variable cost per unit will be reduced by ₹1.00 due to savings in labour cost. The new machine will not affect fixed cost in total, except for the hiring charges. The selling price of the product is ₹12 per unit. The present cost structure of the product is—variable cost ₹9 per unit and fixed cost ₹1.00 unit.

You are required to calculate the number of extra units, which must be produced and sold to justify hiring the machine, (that is the cost indifference point for the new machine).

Solution

Contribution Per Unit:

	Current	*Proposed*
Selling price per unit	₹12.00	₹12.00
Variable cost per unit	(₹9.00)	(₹8.00)
Contribution per unit	₹3.00	₹4.00
Total Contribution Required:		
Current contribution	6,000 × ₹3.00	₹18,000.00
Hiring charges of the machine		12,000.00
Total		₹30,000.00

Number of units to be sold: $\frac{\text{Total contribution required}}{\text{Proposed contribution per unit}} = \frac{₹30{,}000}{₹4.00} = 7{,}500$

Additional number of units to be sold: (7,500 – 6,000) units = 1,500 units

Thus, 1,500 extra units to be manufactured and sold to justify hiring the machine.

NOTES:

(i) Indifference point for the new machine refers to the extra units to be produced and sold to maintain the current level of profit. Additional contribution from extra units should equal the hiring charges, the incremental fixed cost.

(ii) Fixed cost per unit is irrelevant because that represents average fixed cost. Incremental fixed cost is relevant for decision-making.

EXAMPLE 17.28 (EXPORT ORDER, OUTSOURCING)

Novina Industries Ltd. has received an export order for its only product that would require the use of half of the factory's present capacity of 4,00,000 units per annum. The factory is currently operating at 60% level to meet the demand of its domestic market.

As against current price of ₹6.00 per unit, the export order offers @ ₹4.50 per unit, which is less than the cost of production, the details of which are given below:

Direct materials	₹2.50 per unit
Direct labour	₹1.00 per unit
Direct expenses	₹0.50 per unit
Fixed overheads	₹1.00 per unit

The condition of the export is that it has either to be accepted in full or totally rejected.

The company is considering the following alternatives:

(a) Accept the order and keep domestic sales unfulfilled to the excess demand for the same.

(b) Increase factory capacity by installing a few balancing machinery and equipments and also by working extra time to meet the balance of the required capacity. This will increase fixed overheads by ₹20,000 annually and the additional cost of overtime will work out to ₹40,000 per annum.

(c) Outsource the production of additional requirements by supplying direct materials and paying conversion charges of ₹1.75 per unit to a small converter, and engaging one supervisor at a cost of ₹3,000 per month to look after quality, packing and despatch.

(d) Reject export order and continue with domestic market.

As a Management Accountant, you are required to make comparative analysis of various proposals and suggest which of the alternative proposals is the most attractive to Novina Industries Ltd.

Solution

Novina Industries Ltd
Analysis of Four Alternative Proposals

	₹
Proposal-A: (Accept export order and domestic sale of 20,000 units)	
Export sales – 2,00,000 units @ ₹4.50 per unit.	9,00,000

(Contd.)

		₹
Domestic sales – 2,00,000 units @ ₹6.00 per unit.		12,00,000
Total 4,00,000 units		21,00,000
Less: Direct cost of sales (variable) @ ₹4		16,00,000
Contribution		5,00,000
Less: Fixed costs (60% level that is 2,40,000 units × 1)		2,40,000
Profit		2,60,000

Proposal-B

			₹
Export sales	2,00,000 units @ ₹4.50 per unit		9,00,000
Domestic sales	2,40,000 units @ ₹6.00 per unit.		14,40,000
	4,40,000 units	Total	23,40,000
Variable cost of sales @ ₹4	= ₹17,60,000		
Additional cost of overtime	₹ 40,000		18,00,000
	Contribution		5,40,000
Less: Fixed overheads (2,40,000 + Additional 20,000)			2,60,000
	Profit		2,80,000

Proposal-C

			₹
Export sales	2,00,000 units @ ₹4.50 per unit.		9,00,000
Domestic sales	2,40,000 units @ ₹6.00 per unit		14,40,000
	4,40,000 units	Total	23,40,000
Less: Direct cost of sales (Variable) 4,00,000 × 4 =		₹16,00,000	
Direct material cost of 40,000 units × 2.50		= ₹ 1,00,000	
Conversion charges of 40,000 units × 1.75		= ₹ 70,000	
Supervision charges @ 3,000 × 12		= ₹ 36,000	
Total		18,06,000	18,06,000
Contribution			5,36,000
Less: Fixed overheads			2,40,000
Profit			2,94,000

Proposal-D: (Rejecting export order and remaining with domestic market)

	₹
Domestic sales 2,40,000 units @ ₹6.00 per unit.	14,40,000
Less: Direct cost of sales (2,40,000 × 4)	9,60,000
Contribution	4,80,000
Less: Fixed overheads	2,40,000
Profit	2,40,000

Decision: On making comparative analysis of four alternative proposals (A, B, C and D), it is revealed that for accepting export order proposal-C is most profitable and should be accepted by Novina Industries Ltd.

EXAMPLE 17.29 (SHUT DOWN DECISION)

The annual flexible budget of TBA Ltd. is as follows:

Production capacity	40%	60%	80%	100%
Costs:	₹	₹	₹	₹
Direct wages	20,000	30,000	40,000	50,000
Direct material	16,000	24,000	32,000	40,000
Production overheads (fixed and variable)	11,400	12,600	13,800	15,000
Administrative overheads (fixed and variable)	5,800	6,200	6,600	7,000
Selling and distribution overheads (Fixed and variable)	6,200	6,800	7,400	8,000
Total	59,400	79,600	99,800	1,20,000

The company is presently passing through a period of very lean market demand and operating at 50% capacity and have also selling its product at a discounted price generating a sales revenue of ₹60,000 at that level.

It is expected that the market scenario will improve in the next year and, on a conservative rate, the company is likely to operate at 70% capacity level with increased sales revenue of ₹20,000.

As an option, the management is considering to close down the operation for one year and start operation after one year when the market conditions are likely to improve. If closed down for one year it is estimated that

(i) the present fixed costs will reduce by 60%;
(ii) there will be a cost of ₹10,000 towards closing down operations;
(iii) to maintain a skeleton maintenance service for which ₹24,000 to be incurred;
(iv) an initial cost of re-opening of ₹20,000 to be incurred.

The other option is to keep the factory operational for one year and wait for better time next year. You are required to work out the profitability under the two options and give your comment.

Solution

TBA Ltd.

Cost Structure

	Total Cost at 100%	*Variable Cost at 100%*	*Fixed Cost*
	(₹)	(₹)	(₹)
Direct wages	50,000	50,000	Nil
Direct material	40,000	40,000	Nil
Production overhead	15,000	6,000	9,000
Admn. overhead	7,000	2,000	5,000
Selling and Distribution overhead	8,000	3,000	5,000
	1,20,000	1,01,000	19,000

Comparative Profitability of two Options

	Current Operation 50% Level (₹)	*Closure for One Year* (₹)	*Operation after One Year 70% Level* (₹)
Revenue	60,000	Nil	1,20,000
Variable costs:			
Direct materials	20,000		28,000
Direct wages	25,000		35,000
Production overhead	3,000		4,200
Admn. overhead	1,000		1,400
Selling and distribution overhead	1,500		2,100
	50,500	Nil	70,700
Fixed costs	19,000	7,600 (40%)	19,000
Closing down costs	–	10,000	–
Maintenance cost	–	24,000	–
Re-opening cost	–	20,000	–
Total cost	69,500	61,600	89,700
Profit/loss	(9,500)	(61,600)	30,300

Comment: In the light of assessment of comparative profitability, it is better to continue with operation in current year and wait for the next year.

EXAMPLE 17.30 (MODE OF CONVEYANCE DECISION)

ACME Company is considering three proposals for conveyance facilities for its sales staff, who normally travels on an average 20,000 kilometres per annum locally. The proposals are as follows:

I. Purchase and maintain own fleet of cars. Average cost of a car is ₹2.50 lakhs. Petrol consumption is @ 12 km/litre. Each has a resale value of ₹50,000 at the end of five years.
II. Allow the executive to use their own car and reimburse expenses @ ₹5 per km and insurance premium.
III. Hire cars from outside agency for ₹30,000 per year per car, the company shall also bear the cost of petrol (₹3.75 per km), taxes and tyres etc.

Following cost data are available for consideration

(i) Petrol—₹45 per litre
(ii) Repairs and maintenance—@ 50 paise per km
(iii) Insurance—₹4,800 per year per car
(iv) Taxes—₹2,400 per year per car
(v) Tyres—@ 40 paise km
(vi) Driver's wages and bonus ₹30,000 per annum per car

Which of the proposals is acceptable?

☞ Solution

Acme Company

Statement Showing Comparative Cost of Operation Per Car Per Annum and Per Km. (20,000 Kilometres p.a)

Particulars of Expenses	*Company's Purchased and Own Car (I)* ₹	*Executive Car (II)* ₹	*Hire Car (III)* ₹
Petrol @ ₹45 per litre/12 km per litre	75,000.00	–	75,000.00
Repairs and maintenance @ 50 p/km	10,000.00	–	–
Tyre @ 40 paise/km	8,000.00	–	8,000.00
Insurance ₹4,800 per year/car	4,800.00	4,800.00	–
Taxes @ ₹2,400 p.a. per car	2,400.00	–	2,400.00
Depreciation ₹(2,50,000 – 50,000)/5	40,000.00	–	–
Re-imbursement of expenses @ ₹5 per km	–	1,00,000.00	–
Driver's wages and bonus @ ₹30,000 p.a	30,000.00	–	–
Hire charges	–	–	30,000.00
Total cost: (A)	1,70,200.00*	1,04,800.00	1,15,400.00
Cost per kilometre (A/20,000 km)	8.51	5.24	5.77

*This cost will go up, because company would have earned interest, if it invested ₹2.50 lakhs elsewhere.

Comment: In consideration of the comparative analysis as stated in the tabulated statement, second proposal (allow executives to use their own cars) is most economic and recommended to accept.

✎ EXAMPLE 17.31 (SELL OR PROCESS FURTHER)

Modern Mills Ltd. manufactures certain grades of products known as M, B_1 and B_2. In course of manufacture of product M (main product), by products B_1 and B_2 emerge. The joint expenses of manufacture amount to ₹2,37,600.

All the three products are processed further after separation and sold as per details given below:

	Product M	*(By-products)*	
		Product B_1	*Product B_2*
Sales	₹2,00,000	1,20,000	80,000
Cost incurred after separation	₹20,000	15,000	10,000
Profit as percentage on sales	25	20	15

Total fixed selling expenses are 10% of total cost of sales which are apportioned to the three products in the ratio of 20 : 40 : 40.

Required:

(i) Prepare a statement showing the apportionment of joint costs to the products (M, B_1 and B_2).

(ii) If the Product B_1 (by-product) is not subject to further processing and is sold at the point of separation, for which there is a market at ₹1,00,440 without incurring any selling expenses. Would you advise its disposal at this stage? Show the workings.

Solution

Modern Mills Ltd.

Statement of Apportionment of Joint Cost

(Fig. in ₹)

	Total	*Product M*	*(By-products) Product B_1*	*Product B_2*
Sales	4,00,000	2,00,000	1,20,000	80,000
Less: Profit	86,000	50,000	24,000	12,000
Cost of sales	3,14,000	1,50,000	96,000	68,000
Less: Selling and distribution expenses (10 % of ₹3,14,000) apportioned in the ratio of 20 : 40 : 40	31,400	6,280	12,560	12,560
Cost of production	2,82,600	1,43,720	83,440	55,440
Less: After split-off cost (Separation cost)	45,000	20,000	15,000	10,000
Joint cost apportioned	2,37,600	1,23,720	68,440	45,440

(iii) If product B_1 (by-product) is sold after further processing, a profit of ₹24,000 is earned on this product as shown in the statement above. However if it is sold at the point of separation, its profit will be as follows:

Sales of product B_1	₹1,00,440
Less: Share in joint cost	₹ 68,440
Profit	32,000

Recommendation: It reveals from the comparative assessment of profitability as stated above that when product B_1 is sold at the point of separation, profit to the tune of ₹32,000 is earned resulting in enhancement of profit by ₹8,000 (that is, ₹32,000 – ₹24,000). Hence, it is advisable to sell the product B_1 at the point of separation instead of selling after further processing.

EXAMPLE 17.32 (LIMITING FACTOR DECISION)

A company has plans to manufacture five different types of product using a common raw material which is locally available according to requirement at ₹16 per kg. However, skilled labour required for manufacture is in short supply and current availability is only 30,000 hours per month @ ₹20 per hour.

Variable production overheads amounts to ₹10 per labour hour and variable selling and distribution cost is 10% of sales value.

Total fixed costs of selling, distribution and administration is estimated to be ₹3,00,000 per month. Further details relating to the products are given below:

Product	Current Demand (Units)	Selling Price Per Unit (₹)	Raw Material Required (Kg/Unit)	Direct Labour Required (Hrs/Unit)
A	8,000	100	2	1
B	6,000	120	2.5	1.2
C	5,000	160	3	2
D	3,000	220	4	3
E	2,000	300	5	4

Required:

(a) Contribution analysis statement showing the relative profitability of the products under:
   (i) Normal conditions without any constrains on resources.
   (ii) When skilled labour hours are in short supply.

(b) Production plan for optimum profit when available labour hours are only 30,000. What is the expected profit?

(c) If the company decides to produce and sell even relatively less profitable products to meet at least 10% of the current demand, what revised plan will you suggest? What is the anticipated profit?

☞ Solution

(a) Contribution Analysis Statement

(i) Under normal condition and (ii) Under the condition when skilled labour hours is in short supply

	Products				
	A	B	C	D	E
Raw material required (kg/unit)	2	2.5	3	4	5
Direct labour required (hrs./unit)	1	1.2	2	3	4
Variable cost per unit (₹):					
Raw materials @ ₹16 per kg.	32	40	48	64	80
Direct labour @ ₹20 per hr.	20	24	40	60	80
Production overhead @ ₹10 per hr.	10	12	20	30	40
Selling and Distribution cost	10	12	16	22	30
Total (*A*)	72	88	124	176	230
Selling price per unit ₹(*B*)	100	120	160	220	300
Contribution per unit (₹) (*B* – *A*):	28	32	36	44	70
P/V ratio (contribution/sales)	28%	26.7%	22.5%	20%	23.3%
(i) Profitability ranking	I	II	IV	V	III
Contribution per labour hour (₹)					
(Contribution/labour hour per unit)	28.00	26.67	18.00	14.67	17.50
(ii) Ranking	I	II	III	V	IV

(b) Expected Profit (Under Production Plan for Optimum Profit)

	Products					Total
	A	*B*	*C*	*D*	*E*	
Total labour hours available						30000
Contribution per labour hr. (₹)	28	26.67	18.00	14.67	17.50	
Ranking	I	II	III	V	IV	
Allocation of labour hours	8,000	7,200	10,000		4,800	
No. of units to be produced (Maximum)	8,000	6,000	5,000		1,200	
Total contribution (₹)	2,24,000	1,92,000	1,80,000		84,000	6,80,000
Less: Fixed cost (₹)						3,00,000
Expected profit (₹)						3,80,000

(c) Profitability Statement

(When at least 10% of current demand of product *D* is to be maintained)

Total labour hours available: 30,000 hrs.

Products	*Rank of Contribution Per Hr.*	*No. of Units to be Produced*	*Labour Hrs Required*	*Contribution Per Unit* (₹)	*Total Contribution* (₹)
A	I	8,000 (max)	8,000	28	2,24,000
B	II	6,000 (max)	7,200	32	1,92,000
C	III	5,000 (max)	10,000	36	1,80,000
D	V	300 (10%)	900	44	13,200
E	IV	975	3,900	70	68,250
Total			30,000		6,77,450
Less:	Fixed cost				3,00,000
Anticipated	Profit				3,77,450

Comments: Since total profit is declined by ₹2,550, this revised plan cannot be recommended.

✍ EXAMPLE 17.33 (SELL OR PROCESS FURTHER DECISION)

A certain raw material on undergoing a chemical process yield three products *A*, *B* and *C* and a by-product *X*. The relevant particulars of the process for a month are given below:

Joint processing cost:

Raw materials input	: 20,000 kg @ ₹15
Other materials	: ₹30,600
Direct labour	: 4000 hours @ ₹20
Production overheads	: ₹1,00,000

Output, selling price and other particulars:

Product	*Output (Kg)*	*Selling Price/Kg if Sold without Further Processing*	*Further Processing Cost*	*Selling Price/Kg after Further Processing*
A	8,000	₹28	₹56,000	₹38
B	6,000	30	60,000	42
C	5,000	32	60,000	43
X	500	6	1,500	8

Required:

(a) If the company apportions the joint cost after taking credit for the sale value of the by-product, in proportion to the sale value of the three main products at the point of separation, what is the cost per kg of each production at that stage?

(b) Which of the products should be processed further? Show workings.

(c) What is the profit earned if all the main products are sold without further processing? Give product-wise details.

(d) If further processing is done as suggested in (b), what is the total profit earned? Give product-wise details.

☞ ***Solution***

(a) Joint Processing Cost.

	₹
Raw materials input: 200,000 kg @ ₹15	3,00,000
Other materials	30,600
Direct labour: 4000 hrs. @ ₹20	80,000
Production overheads	1,00,000
	5,10,600
Less: Sale value of by-product X (500 kg @ ₹6)	3,000
Total (Net)	5,07,600

Apportionment of joint cost among main products and determination of cost per kg:

Product	*Output/Sales*	*Sale Value (₹)*		*Apportionment of Joint Cost of ₹5,07,600*	*Cost/Kg*
	(Kg)	*Per Kg*	*Total*	*(₹)*	*(₹)*
A	8,000	28	2,24,000	2,01,600	25.2000
B	6,000	30	1,80,000	1,62,000	27.0000
C	5,000	32	1,60,000	1,44,000	28.8000
	19,000		5,64,000	5,07,600	26.7158

(b) Incremental sale value and additional cost, if processed further.

Product	Output/Sales	Incremental Sale Value (₹)		Further Processing Cost	Net Gain/(Loss)
	(Kg.)	Per Kg.	Total	(₹)	(₹)
A	8,000	10	80,000	56,000	24,000
B	6,000	12	72,000	60,000	12,000
C	5,000	11	55,000	60,000	(5,000)
X	500	2	1,000	1,500	(500)

In the light of above statement, only Product *A* and Product *B* should be processed further.

(c) Determination of profit earned if all products sold without further processing.

Product	Quantity	Share of Joint Cost	Sale Value (₹)		Profit/(Loss)
	(Kg)	(₹)	Per Kg	Total	(₹)
A	8,000	2,01,600	28	2,24,000	22,400
B	6,000	1,62,000	30	1,80,000	18,000
C	5,000	1,44,000	32	1,60,000	16,000
Total		5,07,600		5,64,000	56,400

(d) Determination of total profit earned if sold after further processing as suggested in (b).

Product	Quantity	Share of Joint Cost	Further Processing Cost	Total Cost	Sale Value (₹)	Total	Profit/(Loss)
	(Kg)	(₹)	(₹)	(₹)	Per Kg	(₹)	(₹)
A	8.000	2,01,600	56,000	2,57,600	38	3,04,000	46,400
B	6.000	1,62,000	60,000	2,22,000	42	2,52,000	30,000
C	5.000	1,44,000		1,44,000	32	1,60,000	16,000
Total		5,07,600	1,16,000	6,23,600		7,16,000	92,400

EXAMPLE 17.34 (ALTERNATIVE PLAN DECISIONS)

A company manufactures and sells two standards products *X* and *Y* using the same raw material, labour and identical machines. Further particulars are given below:

	X		Y	
Selling price/unit	₹	80	₹	100
		Per unit		
Direct materials @ ₹20/kg	₹	20	₹	30
Direct labour @ ₹15/hr	₹	15	₹	15
Variable overheads	₹	15	₹	15
Machine hours required		1/2 hr		3/4 hr
Fixed overheads (allocated)	₹	12	₹	18
		Per annum		
Maximum demand (units)		18,000		15,000
Current production (units)		15,000		12,000

Labour and materials are available according to requirements. But machine capacity cannot be increased immediately and the available capacity has been fully utilised by the current production plan.

Required:

(i) Current contribution analysis.
(ii) Profit currently earned by the company.
(iii) Alternative production plan, if any, more profitable to the company.
(iv) Profit expected to be earned under the suggested plan.

Solution

(i) Analysis of Current Contribution of Two Products

Products		*X*		*Y*
		₹		₹
Selling price unit (S)		80.00		100.00
Less: Variable costs:				
Direct materials	20.00		30.00	
Direct labour	15.00		15.00	
Direct overheads	15.00	50.00	15.00	60.00
Contribution per unit (C)		30.00		40.00
P/V ratio = C/S × 100		37.50%		40.00%
Machine hours required per unit (hrs.)		1/2		3/4
Contribution per machine hour (limiting factor) (₹)		60.00		53.33

(ii) Profitability Statement for Current Year

Products	*X*	*Y*	*Total*
Production (current) in units	15,000	12,000	
Contribution/unit (₹) as above	30	40	
Total contribution (₹)	4,50,00	4,80,000	9,30,000
Less: Fixed overheads (₹)			(3,96,000)
15,000 × 12 = 1,80,000			
12,000 × 18 = 2,16,000			
Profit (earned)			5,34,000

(iii) Alternative Production Plan Since machine hour is the limiting factor, maximum demand and contribution per machine hour for products *X* and *Y* are to be given weightage for preparation of production plan more profitable to the company.

Production Plan

Products	X	Y	*Total*
Maximum demand (units)	18,000	15,000	
Available machine hours:			
(15,000 × 0.5 + 12,000 × 0.75)			16,500
Optimum Product Mix			
Production (units)	18,000	10,000	28,000
Allocation of M/c hours	9,000	(bal.) 7,500	16,500

(iv) Profit Expected to be Earned Under the Suggested Plan

Products	X	Y	*Total*
Production (suggested) in units vide Ref. (iii)	18,000	10,000	28,000
Contribution/unit (₹)	30	40	
Total contribution (₹)	5,40,000	4,00,000	9,40,000
Less: Fixed overhead cost (₹)			(3,96,000)
Profit (expected)			5,44,000

EXAMPLE 17.35 (ALTERNATIVE PROPOSALS)

A review, made by the top management of M/s. Sweat and Struggle Ltd., which makes only one product, of the result of first quarter of the year revealed the following:

Sales in units	10,000
Loss in ₹	10,000
Fixed cost (for the year ₹1,20,000) in ₹	30,000
Variable cost per unit in ₹	8

The Finance Manager who feels perturbed suggests that the company should at least break-even in the second quarter with a drive for increased sales. Towards this, the company should introduce a better packing which will increase the cost by ₹0.50 per unit.

The Sales Manager has an alternate proposal. For the second quarter additional sales promotion expenses can be increased to the extent of ₹5,000 and a profit of ₹5,000 can be aimed at for the period with increased sales.

The Production Manager feels otherwise. To improve the demand, the selling price per unit has to be reduced by 3 percent. As a result, the sales volume can be increased to attain a profit level of ₹4,000 for the quarter.

The Managing Director asks you as a Cost Accountant to evaluate these three proposals and calculate the additional sales volume that would be required in each case, in order to help him take a decision.

☞ Solution

Results of the First Quarter: Sales 10,000 units

Particulars	*Per Unit* (₹)	*Amount* (₹)
Variable cost (V)	8	80,000
Fixed cost	3	30,000
Total cost	11	1,10,000
Loss	1	10,000
Sales (S)	10	1,00,000
Contribution (S – V) =	2	20,000

Comparative Statement of Three Proposals

Particulars	*Proposal of* Finance Manager (₹)	Sales Manager (₹)	Production Manager (₹)
Selling price per unit	10.00	10.00	9.70
Variable cost per unit (8.00 + 0.50)	8.50	8.00	8.00
Contribution per unit	1.50	2.00	1.70
Fixed cost	30,000	35,000	30,000
Profit required	Nil	5,000	4,000
B.E.P. (unit) = $\frac{\text{F.C.}}{\text{Contribution}}$	= 30,000/1.50 = 20,000		
Sales (unit) = (F + P)/C per unit		(35,000 + 5,000)/2.00 = 20,000	(30,000 + 4,000)/1.70 = 20,000
Additional sales volume required In second quarter as compared to first quarter	10,000	10,000	10,000

Theory Questions

1. What is meant by the term "differential costing"? Does differential cost mean the same thing as variable cost?
2. What is incremental cost? Does incremental cost mean the same thing as variable cost?
3. Give examples of how incremental costs are used in decision-making.
4. A departmental store is thinking of eliminating one of its departments because the accountant, using the total cost basis to profitability analysis, says the department is operating at a loss. What should be investigated before the final decision is made?
5. Explain the meaning and features of relevant costs. Give suitable examples to support your explanation.

6. Ventilators Ltd. wants to stabilise its production through the year. The approaches recommended are:
   (a) Maintain production at an even pace throughout the year, and get the off-season production stored on the premises.
   (b) Maintain production at an even pace, but offer dealers a special discount for off-season purchases.
   (c) Extend special terms to dealers, but maintain prices at a level that will enable regular movement of goods throughout the year.

   Discuss the relative merits and demerits of the above proposals.
7. What do you mean by "make or buy" decision? State the quantitative as well as qualitative considerations in influencing a make or buy decision.
8. Cost-benefit analysis is needed for resolving many managerial problems. List the various items of cost and benefits that you will quantify in respect of managerial decisions:
   (a) Add or drop a product
   (b) Retain or replace
   (c) Operate or shutdown
9. Explain the basic characteristics of costs involved in decision-making.
10. State the costing data required for (i) determining the priority of products, and (ii) make or buy decisions.)
11. How would you go about determining the point at which a manufacturing company that is facing a period of operating losses should shut assuming that profitability of operations is the only point to be considered?
12. Why is the contribution that a product makes towards the recovery of non-escapable costs a better measure of its profitability than the profit or loss reported on its sale after it has been charged with its fair share of all costs?
13. What are the cost and non-cost factors in accepting export orders? What do you mean by relevant costs and irrelevant costs in decision-making? Give examples.
14. Write note on make or buy decisions.
15. Write notes on relevant costs.

Self-Evaluation Questions

Choose the correct answer for the following multiple-choice questions:

(i) The type of costs presented to management for a non-routine decision should be limited to
   (a) Relevant costs (b) Standard costs
   (c) Controllable costs (d) Conversion costs

(ii) Other things remaining the same, ideal product mix is determined in terms of
   (a) Sales (b) Variable costs
   (c) Total costs (d) Contribution margin

(iii) In a make or buy decision
   (a) Only variable costs are relevant.
   (b) Fixed costs that can be avoided in the future are relevant.
   (c) Fixed costs that will continue regardless of the decision are relevant.
   (d) (a) and (b)

(iv) Relevant costs are
   (a) Future costs (b) Standard costs
   (c) Controllable costs (d) Historical costs

(v) The decision maker should consider in case of limiting factor(s) to maximise the profit
   (a) Sales (b) Contribution margin
   (c) Variable costs (d) Fixed costs

(vi) The measurable value of an alternative use of resources is referred to as a(an)
(a) Opportunity cost (b) Imputed cost
(c) Differential cost (d) Sunk cost

(vii) A manager of a company reported the total additional cost required for the proposed increased production level. The increase in total cost is known as
(a) Controllable cost (b) Incremental cost
(c) Opportunity cost (d) Out-of-pocket cost

(viii) Which of the following is usually an incremental cost?
(a) Conversion cost (b) Period cost
(c) Manufacturing overhead cost (d) Direct product cost

(ix) A cost incurred in the past and hence irrelevant for current decision-making is a
(a) Fixed cost (b) Discretionary cost
(c) Sunk cost (d) Direct cost

(x) A cost that cannot be changed by any decision made now or in the future is a (an)
(a) Indirect cost (b) Uncontrollable cost
(c) Opportunity cost (d) Sunk cost

Problems

1. Dropping a product

The costs per unit of three products *X*, *Y* and *Z* are given below:

Products	*X*	*Y*	*Z*
Direct material (₹)	20	16	18
Direct labour (₹)	12	14	12
Variable overheads (₹)	8	10	6
Fixed expenses (₹)	6	6	4
	₹46	46	40
Profit	18	14	12
Selling price (₹)	64	60	52
No. of units produced	10,000	5,000	8,000

Production arrangements are such that if one product is given up the production of the others can be raised by 50%. The directors propose that product *Z* should be given up because the contribution from the product is the lowest. Present suitable analysis of the data indicating whether the proposal should be accepted.

Ans: The profit under proposed situation will increase by ₹42,000. Hence, the proposal for discontinuance of product *Z* should be accepted.

2. Revised selling price

Merry-make Cassettes Co. is expecting a profit of ₹2,50,000 for the current year. The following further information is available from records.

Selling price per unit	₹20
Variable cost per unit	₹10
Fixed cost for the year	₹1,00,000

The company's production capacity is not fully utilised and market research suggests following alternative strategies for the forthcoming year.

Strategy 1: Reduction in selling price by 5%. Expected increase in sales volume 10%.

Strategy 2: Reduction in selling price by 7%. Expected increase in sales volume 20%.
Strategy 3: Reduction in selling price by 10%. Expected increase in sales volume 25%.

Required:

(a) Evaluate the alternative strategies and state which is the most profitable. Assume the same cost structure as in the current year.

(b) Suggest other factors, which must be considered by management before taking a decision.

Ans: Strategy 2 is most profitable.

3. Profitability of two orders

X Limited has been offered an order from A Ltd. for 10,000 units of output @ ₹100 each which has a variable cost of ₹60 and will involve an outlay of ₹60,000 to set-up jigs and dies. At the same time, there is another offer of B Ltd., for 8,000 units of output at ₹110 each. Variable costs are estimated at ₹68 each and involve an outlay of ₹50,000 to set-up jigs and dies. Which offer should the company accept?

Ans: A Ltd. offer should be accepted.

4. Decision to increase sales

Quality Product Limited has drawn up the following budget for the year 2019–20:

	₹
Raw materials	20,00,000
Labour, stores, power and other variable costs	6,00,000
Fixed manufacturing overheads	7,00,000
Packing and variable distribution cost	4,00,000
Fixed general overheads including selling	3,00,000
	40,00,000
Sales revenue @ ₹50 per unit	50,00,000
Budgeted profit	₹ 10,00,000

The General Manager suggests to reduce the selling prices by 5%, and expects to achieve an additional volume of 5%. The more intensive manufacturing programme will involve additional costs of ₹15,000 for production planning. It will also be necessary to open an additional sales office at the cost of ₹1,00,000 per annum.

The Sales Manager, on the other hand, suggests to increase selling price by 10% which it is estimated will reduce sales volume by 10%. At the same time, a saving in manufacturing overheads and general overheads of ₹50,000 and ₹1,00,000 per annum respectively is expected on this reduced volume.

Which of these two proposals would you accept and why? Show complete working.

Ans: The proposal of sales manager should be accepted.

5. Minimum Price Decision

An umbrella manufacturer makes an average profit of ₹2.50 per unit on a selling price of ₹14.30 by producing and selling 60,000 units at 60 per cent of potential capacity.

His cost of sales per unit is as follows:

Direct materials	₹3.50
Direct wages	₹1.25
Factory overhead	₹6.25 (50% fixed)
Sales overhead	₹0.80 (25% variable)

During the current year, he intends to produce the same number but estimates that his fixed costs would go up by 10 per cent while the rates of direct wages and direct materials will increase by 8% and 6% respectively. However, the selling price cannot be changed.

Under this situation, he obtains an offer for a future 20% of his potential capacity.
What minimum price would you recommend for acceptance of the offer to ensure the manufacturer an overall profit of ₹1,67,300?

Ans: ₹11.30

6. Dropping a Product

A company manufactures three products *A*, *B* and *C*. There are no common processes and the sale of one product does not affect price or volume of sales of any other.
The company's budgeted profit/loss for 2020 has been abstracted as follows:

	Total	*A*	*B*	*C*
Sales	₹ 3,00,000	₹ 45,000	₹ 2,25,000	₹ 30,000
Production cost: Variable	1,80,000	24,000	1,44,000	12,000
Fixed	60,000	3,000	48,000	9,000
Factory cost	2,40,000	27,000	1,92,000	21,000
Selling and administration costs: Variable	24,000	8,100	8,100	7,800
Fixed	6,000	2,100	1,800	2,100
Total cost	2,70,000	37,200	2,01,900	30,900
Profit	30,000	7,800	23,100	(–) 900

On the basis of the above, the Board had almost decided to eliminate product *C*, on which a loss was budgeted. Meanwhile, they have sought your opinion. As the company's Cost Accountant, what would you advice? Give reasons for your answer.

Ans: P/V ratio, *A* 28.7%, *B* 32.4%, *C* 34%

It is found that product *C*, though has the highest P/V ratio, yet seems to be non-profitable because it has to bear a higher percentage of fixed cost as compared to its total cost. The percentage comes to about 36 $\left(\text{that is, } \frac{11,100}{39,900} \times 100\right)$ which in case of other products is too less. Since the surplus capacity generated by one product cannot be used for other products, there seems to be no justification for discontinuing product *C* till some new product is developed which will have a higher P/V ratio than product *C*. In the present circumstances, since *C* has a higher P/V ratio, and if the sales continue to rise, *C* may start giving profit too.

7. Foreign Market Sales Decision

A factory produces 24,000 units. The cost sheet gives the following information:

Direct material	₹1,20,000
Direct wages	84,000
Variable overheads	48,000
Semi-variable overheads	28,000
Fixed overheads	80,000
Total cost	3,60,000

The product is sold at ₹20 per unit. The management proposed to increase the production by 3,000 units for sales in the foreign market. It is estimated that semi-variable overheads will increase by ₹1,000. But the product will be sold at ₹14 per unit in the foreign market. However, no additional capital expenditure will be incurred. The management seeks your advice as cost accountant. What will you advise them?

Ans: Sales of additional units 3,000 in the foreign market will give a profit of ₹9,500. Hence, the proposal should be accepted

8. Export Order

A machine tool manufacturing company sells its lathes at ₹36,500 each made up as follows:

Direct materials	₹16,000	
Direct labour	2,000	
Variable factory overheads	5,000	
Fixed factory overheads	3,000	
Variable selling overheads	500	
Royalty	1,000	
Profit	5,000	32,500
Central excise duty		1,000
Sales tax		3,000
		36,500

There is enough idle capacity.

(a) A firm in Arabia has offered to buy 10 company's lathes at ₹28,500 each. Should the company be interested in the business?

(b) It has been decided to sell 5 such lathes to an engineering company under the same management at bare cost. What price should you charge?

Ans:

(a) Contribution	₹4,000
Less: Sales tax	2,340
Savings	₹1,660

Company may accept the export order.

(b) The company may charge ₹31,000 (₹36,000 – ₹5,500) (profit and selling overheads)

9. Changing Product Mix Decision

The budgeted results for X Co. include the following:

	₹ in Lakhs	*Variable Cost as % of Sales Value*
Sales: Product A	60	50%
Product B	50	60%
Product C	80	65%
Product D	40	80%
Product E	30	70%
	260	

Fixed overheads for the period are ₹100.00 lakhs.

You are required to

(a) Prepare a statement showing the amount of loss expected;

(b) Assuming that the sale of only one product can be increased at a time, recommend a change in the sales volume of each product which will eliminate the expected loss.

Ans: (a) Total loss ₹5,00,000.

10. Alternative Proposals Decision

Quality Products. Ltd. manufactures and markets a single product. The following data are available:

	Per Unit		Per Unit
Materials	₹16	Dealer's margin	₹4
Conversion costs (Variable)	12	Selling price	40

Fixed cost: ₹5 lakhs
Present sales: 90,000 units
Capacity utilisation: 60 per cent
There is acute competition. Extra efforts are necessary to sell. Suggestions have been made for increasing sales:

(a) By reducing sales price by 5 per cent.
(b) By increasing dealer's margin by 25 per cent over the existing rate.
Which of these two suggestions you would recommend, if the company desires to maintain the present profit? (Give reasons)

Ans: Present profit ₹2,20,000

(a) Units required to maintain the same profit 1,16,111 units
(b) Units required to maintain the same profit 1,02,857 units. Second proposal is recommended.

11. Product Profitability

The following particulars are taken from the records of a company engaged in manufacturing two products, *A* and *B*, from a certain material:

Particulars	*Product A (Per Unit)* ₹	*Product B (Per Unit)* ₹
Sales	2,500	5,000
Material cost (₹50 per kg)	500	1,250
Direct labour (₹30 per hour)	750	1,500
Variable overhead	250	500
Total fixed overheads: ₹10,00,000		

Comment on the profitability of each product when:

(i) Total sales in value are limited.
(ii) Raw materials are in short supply.
(iii) Production capacity is the limiting factor.
(iv) Total availability of raw materials is 20,000 kg and maximum sales potential of each product is 1,000 units, find the product mix to yield maximum profits.

Ans. (i) Product *A* is more profitable. (ii) Product *A* is more Profitable. (iii) Product A is more Profitable. (iv) Product *A* 1,000 unit, *B* 400 units.

12. Capacity Decision

A factory is currently working at 50% capacity and produces 5,000 units at a cost of ₹90 per unit as per details given below:

Materials	₹50
Labour	₹15
Factory overhead	₹15 (₹6 fixed)
Administration overhead	₹10 (₹5 fixed)

The current selling price is ₹100 per unit.
At 60% working, material cost per unit increases by 2% and selling price per unit falls by 2%.

At 80% working, material cost per unit increases by 5% and selling price per unit falls by 5%. Calculate the current profit at 50% working. Estimate profits of the factory at 60% and 80% working. Which capacity of production would you recommend?

Ans: 50%, 60%, 80%
Profit ₹50,000, 53,000, 53,000
60% capacity is recommended.

13. Minimum Price Decision

S. Ltd is engaged in manufacturing activities. It has received a request from one of its important customers to supply a product which will require conversion of Material M, which is a non-moving item.

The following details are available:

Book value of Material M	₹60
Realizable value of Material M	₹80
Replacement cost of Material M	₹100

It is estimated that conversion of one unit of M into one unit of finished product will require one unit of labour hour. At present labour is paid @ ₹20 per hour.

Other costs are as follows:

Out of pocket expenses	₹30 per unit.
Allocated overheads	₹10 per unit.

The labour will be re-deployed from other activities. It is estimated that the temporary redeployment will not result in loss of contribution. The employees to be redeployed are permanent employees of the company.

Estimate the minimum price to be charged from the customer so that the company is not worse-off by executing the order.

Ans: ₹110.

14. Export Decision

Due to industrial depression, a plant is running, at present, at 50% of its capacity. The following details are available.

	Cost of Production Per Unit
Direct material	₹200
Direct labour	100
	₹
Variable overhead	300
Fixed overhead	200
	800
Production per month	20,000 units
Total cost of production	₹1,60,00,000
Sale price	1,40,00,000
Loss	₹20,00,000

An exporter offers to buy 5,000 units per month at the rate of ₹650 per unit and the company hesitates to accept the offer for fear of increasing its already large operating losses.

Advise whether the company should accept or decline this offer.

Ans: The company should accept the offer.

15. Decision about Mechanisation

Management of a manufacturing unit is considering extensive modernisation of the factory through progressive mechanisation which would result in improved productivity and reduced strength. Through negotiations with the union, it was agreed that for every 1% increase in productivity, workers would be paid 0.5% incentive wages. It was also agreed that through voluntary retirement the staff strength would be reduced to 300 from the present level of 400. The following further comparative data are available before and after the proposed mechanisation:

	Before Mechanisation	*After Mechanisation*
No. of articles produced per month	50,000	48,000
Fringe benefits	50% of wages	
Wages paid per month	₹4,00,000	
Sales per month (value)	₹24,00,000	
P/V ratio	25%	

Based on the above data, you are required to work out the annual financial implication of the proposal.

Ans: There will be increase in annual contribution due to mechanisation.

16. Special Order

Nubo Manufacturing Company is presently operating at 50% of practical capacity producing about 50,000 units annually of a patented electronic component. Nubo recently received an offer from an overseas market to sell 30,000 components at ₹6.00 per unit FOB Nubo's Plant. Nubo has not previously sold components in the market. Budgeted production costs for 50,000 and 80,000 units of output are as follows:

Units	50,000	80,000
Costs:	₹	₹
Direct material	75,000	1,20,000
Direct labour	75,000	1,20,000
Factory overheads	2,00,000	2,60,000
	3,50,000	5,00,000
Cost per unit	₹7.00	₹6.25

The sales manager thinks the order should be accepted, even if it results in a loss of ₹1.00 per unit, because he feels the sales may build up future markets. The production manager does not wish to have the order accepted primarily because the order would show a loss of ₹0.25 per unit when computed on the new average unit cost. The cost accountant has made a quick computation indicating that accepting the order will actually increase profit.

You are required to:

(a) Explain what apparently caused the drop in cost from ₹7.00 per unit to ₹6.25 per unit when budgeted production increased from 50,000 to 80,000 units. Show supporting computations.

(b) Should the order be accepted?

Ans: The order of overseas market be accepted.

17. Profitable Product Mix

A manufacturing company produces and sells three products *P*, *Q* and *R*. It has an available machine hour capacity of one lakh hours, interchangeable among the three products. Presently, the company produces and sells 20,000 units of *P* and 15,000 units each of *Q* and *R*. The unit selling price of the three products are ₹25, ₹32 and ₹42 for *P*, *Q* and R respectively. With this price structure and the aforesaid sales-mix, the company is incurring loss. The total expenditure, exclusive of fixed charges (presently ₹5 per unit), is ₹13.75

lakhs. The unit cost ratio among the products *P*, *Q* and *R* is 4 : 6 : 7. Since the company desires to improve its profitability without changing its cost and price structures, it has been considering the following three mixes so as to be within its total available capacity.

Products	*Mix I* (*In Units*)	*Mix II* (*In Units*)	*Mix III* (*In Units*)
P	25,000	20,000	30,000
Q	15,000	12,000	5,000
R	10,000	18,000	15,000

You are required to compute the quantum of loss now incurred and to advise the most profitable mix which could be considered by the company.

Ans: Loss ₹15,000. Mix III gives the highest contribution and is therefore, recommended.

18. Production Decision

A Ltd. Co. has capacity to produce 1,00,000 units of a product every month. It works cost at varying levels of production is as under:

Level	*Works Cost Per Unit* ₹
10%	400
20%	390
30%	380
40%	370
50%	360
60%	350
70%	340
80%	330
90%	320
100%	310

Its fixed administration expenses amount to ₹1,50,000 and fixed marketing expenses amount to ₹2,50,000 per month respectively. The variable distribution cost amount to ₹30 per unit.

It can market 100% of its output at ₹500 per unit provided it incurs the following further expenditure:

(a) It gives gift items costing ₹30 per unit of sale;

(b) It has lucky draws every month giving the first prize of ₹50,000; 2nd prize of ₹25,000, 3rd prize of ₹10,000 and three consolation prizes of ₹5,000 each to customers buying the product.

(c) It spends ₹1,00,000 on refreshments served every month to its customers; and

(d) It sponsors a television programme every week at a cost of ₹20,00,000 per month.

It can market 30% of its output at ₹550 per unit without incurring any of the expense referred to in (a) to (d) above.

Advise the company on its course of action. Show the supporting cost sheets.

Ans: The company should produce 1,00,000 units.

19. Product Mix Decision

A company produces three products. The cost data are as under:

		A	*B*	C
Direct materials	₹	64	152	117
Direct labour:				
Deptt.	Rate per hour	hrs.	hrs.	hrs.
	₹			
1	5	18	10	20
2	6	5	4	7
3	4	10	5	20
Variable overheads		₹16	9	21
Fixed overheads		₹4,00,000 per month		

The budget was prepared at a time, when the market was sluggish. The budgeted quantities and selling prices are as under:

Product	*Budgeted Quantity*	*Selling Price (₹)/Unit*
A	9,750	270
B	7,800	280
C	7,800	400

Later the market improved and the sales quantities could be increased by 20% for product *A* and 25% each for products *B* and *C*. The sales manager confirmed that the increased quantities could be achieved at the prices originally budgeted. The production manager stated that the output cannot be increased beyond the budgeted level due to limitation of direct labour hours in Department 2.

Required:

(i) Present a statement of budgeted profitability.
(ii) Set optimal product mix and calculate the optimal profit.

Ans: (i) Profit ₹3,99,500
Optimal Product mix,
A—11700 units, *B*—9,750 units, *C*—5,292 units.
Profit – ₹4,06,430

20. Make/Buy Decision

Stirling Industries Ltd. manufactures a product *Z* by making and assembling three components *A*, *B* and *C*. The components are made in a machine shop using three identical machines each of which can make any of the three components. However, the total capacity of the three machines is only 12,000 machine-hours per month and is just sufficient to meet the current demand. Labour for assembling is available according to requirements. Further details are given below:

Components	*Machine-Hours Required Per Unit*	*Variable Cost Per Unit*	*Market Price At Which the Component can be Purchased If Required*
A	4	₹48	₹64
B	5	60	75
C	6	80	110
	15		
Assembling (per unit of *Z*)		30	-
		218	

Fixed costs per month amount to ₹50,000. Product *Z* is sold at ₹300 per unit. From next month, the company expects the demand for *Z* to rise by 25%. As the machine capacity is limited, the company wants to meet the increase in demand by buying such numbers of *A*, *B* or *C* which is most profitable.

You are asked to find out the following:

(a) Current demand and profit made by the company.

(b) Which component and how many units of the same should be bought from the market to meet the increase in demand?

(c) Profit made by the company if suggestion in (b) is accepted.

Ans: Profit if suggestion (b) is accepted ₹23,000.

21. Product Mix Decision

A multi-product company has the following costs and output data for the last year.

	Product		
	X	*Y*	*Z*
Sales mix	40%	35%	25%
	₹	₹	₹
Selling price	20	25	30
Variable cost per unit	10	15	18
Total fixed cost			1,50,000
Total sales			5,00,000

The company proposes to replace product *Z* by product *S*. Estimated cost and output data are:

Sales mix	50%	30%	20%
Selling price	20	25	28
Variable cost per unit	10	15	14
Total fixed costs			1,50,000
Total sales			5,00,000

Analyse the proposed change and suggest what decision the company should take.

Ans: Profit would increase by ₹15,000.

22. Product Mix Decision

Vinak Ltd. which produces three products furnishes you the following data for 2019–20.

	Products		
	A	*B*	*C*
Selling price per unit (₹)	100	75	50
Profit/Volume ratio (%)	10	20	40
Maximum sales potential (units)	40,000	25,000	10000
Raw material content as percentage of variable costs (%)	50	50	50

The fixed expenses are estimated at ₹6,80,000. The company uses a single raw material in all the three products. Raw material is in short supply and the company has a quota for the supply of raw materials of the value of ₹18,00,000 for the year 2019–20 for the manufacture of its products to meet its sales demand.

You are required to:

(i) Set a product mix which will give the maximum overall profit keeping the short supply of raw material in view.

(ii) Compute that maximum profit.

Ans: (i) *A*—20,000 units, *B*—25,000 units, *C*—10,000 units. (ii) Profit ₹95,000.

CASE STUDY

1. Make or Buy: A Case of Weldmach Ltd

Weldmach Ltd was an engineering unit in Bommasandra, Bangalore that produced radiators for cars. Though the company had an installed capacity to produce 1,60,000 pieces of radiator annually, the present production level was 1,40,000 per annum owing to the demand in the market. Because of its sophisticated technology, all the intermediate parts and components like reserve tank, heater core and hoses, pressure cap, thermostat, fan etc were produced internally except the "transmission Cooler". The cooler was purchased from the vendor Cohent Pvt. Ltd. at ₹95 each (excluding the transportation cost amounting to ₹5 per unit).

For the financial year 2018–19, Coherent Ltd. informed Weldmach about increase in the price of its transmission coolers from ₹95 per unit to ₹105 per unit owing to increase in the cost of raw materials for the same. Wedmach was already operating on a lesser profit margin and this increase could have brought them nearer to the breakeven. Therefore, the MD Yeshwanth Reddy consulted his Plant Manager—Praveen about this issue. Praveen, who was responsible for the resource utilisation, suggested that they should manufacture the transmission cooler instead of buying from Coherent Ltd. One more benefit of producing the cooler internally was saving the transportation cost besides avoiding the dependence on the supplier for timely delivery.

Yeshwanth was not so sure so he asked Praveen to give him estimates related to the cost of production. Praveen, after 2–3 days of estimating and calculating the costs related to manufacturing of the coolers, submitted the following details:

Material parts for producing coolers per unit – 80
Labour rate per hour for operating the machine – ₹60 per hour
Machine hours required per 100 units – 30 minutes
Additional overhead cost – ₹20 per cooler

Weldmach had two of such machines (costing ₹5,00,000 each) which could also be used in the production of transmission coolers, having spare capacity of one hour each per day out of 8 working hours per day for 350 working day in the year. The depreciation on these machines was calculated at ₹10 per machine hour. The other machine related costs like fuel, power, repairs etc. amounted to ₹30 per hour. In case, a greater number of machines hours were required, they could go for buying another machine. However, the additional fixed cost related to increase in the capacity would be ₹12 per unit.

Looking at the details submitted, Yeshwanth wanted to know the following:

a. What would be the required total number of extra hours run by the machines to produce the transmission coolers internally? Would the spare time available be sufficient or they would be required to buy a new machine?
b. Should Yeshwanth go for making the coolers internally or continue buying it from Cohent Ltd. even at higher cost?
c. In case, there is more demand for radiators in the market and Weldmach has to produce 1,60,000 radiators, would it be able to continue its production at the existing capacity without buying the coolers from outside vendor?

2. Adonex India: A Case of Alternative Choices and Decision-Making

Adonex India Engineering Company was into manufacturing of auto parts—'axle shafts'—for automotive industries since 2003. The company was an emerging one concerning manufacturers and exporters. Adonex had been gaining acclamation across the globe because of its quality manufacturing process. Further, the company's products were highly acclaimed in UK, Germany, France and Italy. The price charged for domestic as well as export market has been same so far albeit in the relevant currency.

With an ever-growing demand for its product and the company's export percentage being 30%, Adonex India Engineering Company had national and international projects contributing to the integrated and technically important projects. In the year 2019, it was operating at 80%-capacity level catering to both domestic and foreign market.

The company CEO, Raghavendra had just received an export order from a new market—USA—which he did not want to miss. The order required a capacity utilisation of 40% of the plant capacity. There was no scope for splitting the order; it had to be executed in one lot and that too, as quickly as possible. The price offered after a lot of negotiation was still 10% less than the current price being charged.

He called his Production Manager—Sathya Sathwik, and the Finance Manager—Prabhat Kumar, who were looking after the costing and budgeting of the project; and asked them to submit the details related to the current production and possibility of additional capacity utilisation. He was given the following statement with respect to sales and costs:

Particulars (For a Pack of 10 units)	*₹ in lakhs*
Sales	2,400
Direct material	1,120
Direct labour	480
Factory overheads (20% variable)	360
Selling, distribution & administrative overheads (40% fixed)	200

Sathwik told him that variable cost—part of selling, distribution & administrative overheads—will increase by 10% because of the special type of packaging required for exports to the USA. He was of the opinion that the company should reject the export order from the customer from USA as it would result in unnecessary increase in the cost where as revenue from the order would be less thereby impacting the profits significantly.

Prabhat, on the other hand, wanted the company to accept the offer because this would have meant exposure to a new market and possibility of more clients and better pricing in future. For this, he said that the company should be ready to let the domestic sales to fall to the extent required.

There was another view proposed by the Marketing Manager—Prakash Sinha. He thought that it was not wise to let go off the domestic market share. Instead the company should create additional plant capacity by installing new machinery. Prakash checked with some suppliers of the machines as well as the finance team and reported that the additional capacity because of new machinery will increase the fixed cost by ₹20,00,000 per annum.

Raghavendra was now in dilemma as to go for which of these proposals given by Sathwik, Prabhat and Prakash.

✍ QUESTIONS FOR DISCUSSION:

1. Evaluate each of the options given and suggest the best course of action for Raghavendra.
2. Discuss various other factors which have to be considered before taking the decision.

Chapter 18

Pricing Decisions

Learning Objectives

After reading this chapter, you should be able to:

1. describe factors influencing pricing decisions;
2. discuss different methods of pricing;
3. understand circumstances when a business firm can sell a product below the variable cost; and
4. explain the concept of target pricing and prices indifference point.

The chapter on "Alternative Choices Decisions" has discussed how cost and revenue analysis and relevant information help management in making various alternative choices decisions such as make or buy, add or drop product, product mix, sell or process further, operate or shutdown, replace or retain, buy or lease, special order, export proposals, etc. The present chapter discusses "pricing decisions" which is one of the most crucial and difficult decisions which a business firm has to make, and determine how cost information can be useful to management in framing suitable pricing policy.

FACTORS INFLUENCING PRICING DECISIONS

Pricing of a product or service refers to the assignment of a selling price to a product or service provided by a firm. The pricing decisions are influenced by internal and external factors both. Some such factors (determinants) are as follows:

1. Cost data of the product which may be actual, replacement, standard or any other cost base.
2. Firm's profit and other objectives.
3. Demand for the product or service and its elasticity.
4. Nature of product and its life expectancy.
5. Pricing decision as a long-run decision or short-term decision or a one-time spare capacity decision.
6. Type of competition for the product or service and availability of close substitutes.
7. Number of suppliers in the market.
8. Economic and political climate and trends and likely changes in them in future.

9. Type of industry to which the product belongs and future outlook of the industry.
10. Government guidelines, if any.

DIFFERENT METHODS OF PRICING

The different methods of pricing are generally the following:

1. Total Cost-plus or Full Cost-plus Pricing

Total cost-plus or full cost-plus pricing involves all costs plus a profit margin. It includes not only the product's direct costs but also the indirect costs incurred by the overall company which have to be allocated to different products in case different products are manufactured. An example of price calculation using full cost-plus method is as follows:

	(₹)	(₹)
Direct material		10
Direct labour		20
Factory overheads:		
Fixed	15	
Variable	5	20
Total manufacturing cost		50
Non-manufacturing overheads:		
Fixed	10	
Variable	0	10
Total cost		60
Add: Profit margin (25% on total cost)		15
Selling price		75

Full cost-plus method has the following advantages:

1. It is simple to operate if cost structures of products are known.
2. The pricing decision under full cost approach becomes standardised and such decisions can easily be delegated to lower management.
3. It ensures recovery of total costs and also provides a reasonable rate of returns to the firm.
4. It helps a business firm to predict the selling prices of other competitive firms, specially of those firms who are having similar cost structures.
5. This pricing method is important in contracting industries where price of the contracts needs to be determined considering fixed costs also.
6. This brings stability in the pricing policy and selling price can be justified to customers.
7. Full cost pricing is consistent with absorption costing system.

Full cost-plus method has the following disadvantages too:

1. It ignores demand and competition and may result into underpricing or overpricing of products.
2. Fixed costs are likely to be distributed on some arbitrary basis as there are different methods of apportionment and thus total costs of different products will be different depending on which apportionment method is used.

3. In full cost-plus pricing, the choices of volume or capacity base is very important. Different unit products costs will emerge under different concepts of capacity.
4. This method does not distinguish between relevant costs (for example, variable costs and incremental fixed costs) and irrelevant costs (fixed costs).
5. This method cannot always shield the firm from a loss. If sales demand falls below the volume level used to calculate the fixed cost per unit, the total sales revenue will be inadequate to cover the total costs.

Within full cost-plus method, some other cost bases can be used for determining the selling price such as manufacturing cost plus or conversion cost plus.

Manufacturing cost (or product cost) plus pricing includes cost incurred specifically for manufacturing the product plus a profit margin. The profit margin added to this cost must cover all operating expenses and generate a satisfactory level of profit. Using the information given in the earlier example, a cost of ₹50 will be used. To this cost, a higher profit margin needs to be added to cover non-manufacturing overheads as well as to provide a satisfactory level of profit to the firm. For example, selling price calculation may be as follows:

	Total manufacturing costs	₹50
Add:	Profit margin (50% on manufacturing cost)	₹25
	Selling price	₹75

Conversion cost plus pricing uses conversion cost for determining the selling price and to this cost a profit margin is added. This pricing method is generally followed when the customer provides the materials. This method depends on the assumption that greater profits can be realised if efforts are directed to products requiring less labour and overhead because more units can be produced and sold.

2. Marginal Cost-plus Pricing

This method, also known as contribution approach, uses only variable costs as the basis for pricing. Fixed costs are not added to the product, service or contract. However, fixed costs should be taken into account in determining the profit margin to be added to variable costs to arrive at the selling price.

Marginal cost approach helps a business firm to enter into new markets easily, to increase its competitive position in the existing markets, to survive during trade depressions, to utilise spare available capacity, to dispose of surplus or obsolete stock.

Marginal cost-plus pricing brings some disadvantages to the firm as well. For instance, recovery of fixed costs may be doubted. There is likely to be undesirable competition for cutting prices to a lower level. In case, management decides to increase lower marginal cost pricing, it may face dissatisfaction from the consumers.

Using the information given in the earlier example, marginal costs of ₹35 can be used to set the selling price. Obviously, it indicates the cost below which the price should not fall otherwise the company would have losses. Also, a higher profit margin can be added to marginal cost which may work as a long-term selling price even for normal sales. For instance, if the profit margin of 100% is added to marginal costs of ₹35, the selling price will be ₹70.

3. Differential Cost-plus Pricing

This method involves adding a mark up on differential cost which is the increase in total cost resulting from the production of additional units. Differential cost pricing differs from variable cost pricing in which a mark up on variable cost is added, whereas both variable costs and fixed costs are included in the differential costs on which a mark up is determined. This method can be applied where some revenue above differential cost may be received rather than no revenue at all. Such additional revenue makes some contribution towards the recovery of fixed costs which are already incurred.

4. Standard Costs

Standard costs represent the costs that should be attained under efficient operating conditions at a normal capacity. The cost-based methods discussed above have some adverse implications and include costs due to inefficient manufacturing, wasteful operations, etc. That is, it is likely that unnecessary costs may be assigned to the product. On the other hand, standard costs use costs from efficient operations plus the agreed profit. Also, pricing can be done more quickly.

FIXING SELLING PRICE BELOW VARIABLE COST

The situations where a business firm is justified to sell its products at a price below the variable cost are as follows:

(i) When a new product is introduced in the market or to popularise a new product.
(ii) When a weaker competitor is to be driven out of market.
(iii) When it is feared that future market will go out of hand.
(iv) When there is acute competition in the market
(v) When products are of perishable nature.
(vi) When there is a need to earn foreign exchange, goods may be exported at less than the variable cost.
(vii) When workers are to be kept engaged and production is to be maintained.
(viii) When a company does not want to lose business connections and market prices have fallen drastically.

TARGET PRICING

A target price is the estimated price for a product or service that potential customers will be willing to pay. This estimate is based on an understanding of customers' perceived value for a product and competitors' responses. The target price forms the basis for calculating target costs. A target cost is the estimated long-run cost of a product or service that when sold enables the company to achieve targeted profit. It is derived by subtracting the target profit from the target price. Developing target prices and target costs requires the following four steps:

Step 1 – Develop a product that satisfies the needs of potential customers.

Step 2 – Choose a target price based on customers' perceived value for the product and the prices competitors charge.

Step 3 – Derive a target cost by subtracting the desired profit margin from the target price.

Step 4 – Estimate the actual cost of the product.

Step 5 – If estimated actual cost exceeds the target cost, investigate ways of driving down the actual cost to the target cost.

PRICES INDIFFERENCE POINT

A price indifference point is the sales level at which a firm's net income is same between two pricing alternatives. The price indifference point indicates the volume of sales at which the new price gives a profit equal to the profit of old sales volume and price. In case, sales volume at new price is lower than sales volume at old price (when there is price indifference point), firm should reject the price increase since firm's profit will decrease. In contrary to this, if expected sales volume with price increase is greater than the price indifference point, profit will increase. Price indifference point's concept is very useful in short-term decision-making situations.

EXAMPLE 18.1 (*Computing New Price*)

Suman Ltd. manufactured and sold 1000 electric irons last year at a price of ₹800 each. The cost structure of electric irons is as follows:

Materials	200
Labour	100
Variable cost	50
Marginal cost	350
Factory overhead (fixed)	200
Total cost	550
Profit	250
Sale price	800

Due to heavy competition, price has to be reduced to ₹750 for the coming year. Assuming no change in costs, state the number of electric irons that would have to be sold at the new price to ensure the same amount of total profits as that of the last year.

Solution

Profit on sale of 1000 electric irons = ₹250 × 1000 = ₹2,50,000

Reduced sales price		₹750
Less: Material	₹200	
Labour	₹100	
Variable cost	₹50	350
Contribution per unit		400

No. of units to be sold to earn ₹2,50,000

$$= \frac{\text{Fixed cost + Required profit}}{\text{Contribution per unit}}$$

$$= \frac{₹2,00,000 + ₹2,50,000}{400}$$

$$= \frac{₹4,50,000}{400} = 1125 \text{ units to be sold}$$

Verification:

Sales – VC – Fixed cost
(1125 × 750) – (350 × 1125) – 2,00,000
₹8,43,750 – ₹3,93,750 – 2,00,000
₹8,43,750 – ₹5,93,750 = ₹2,50,000

for excel template, scan

EXAMPLE 18.2 (*Using Price Elasticity of Demand in Selling Price*)

A company decides to manufacture 100,000 units of its product. The variable cost per unit is ₹10 and fixed costs amount to ₹600,000. In board meeting, the finance manager suggests that the full-cost method should be used in fixing selling price for the company's product. He has also suggested a profit margin of 25% on total costs. The marketing manager while disagreeing with the finance manager's proposal presents the following information regarding possible demand of product at different prices:

Price Per Unit (₹)	*Demand (Units)*
18	84,000
20	76,000
22	70,000
24	64,000
26	54,000

Which proposal (Finance Manager's or Marketing Manager's) will be useful for the company?

Solution

(A) *Finance manager's proposal*

	(₹)
Variable cost	10
Fixed cost	6
Total cost	16
Profit margin (25%)	4
Selling price	20

No. of units to be sold at a price of ₹20 per unit (as given in the question)
= 76000 units

Total contribution = 76000 units × ₹10 =	₹7,60,000
Less: Fixed costs	6,00,000
Net profit	₹1,60,000

(B) Before evaluating marketing manager's proposal, a profitability statement at different selling prices needs to be prepared.

Profitability Statement

Selling Price Per Unit (₹)	*Units Demanded*	*Contribution Per Unit* (₹)	*Total Contribution* (₹)	*Fixed Cost* (₹)	*Net Profit* (₹)
18	84,000	8	6,72,000	(6,00,000)	72,000
20	76,000	10	7,60,000	(6,00,000)	1,60,000
22	70,000	12	8,40,000	(6,00,000)	2,40,000
24	64,000	14	8,96,000	(6,00,000)	2,96,000
26	54,000	16	8,64,000	(6,00,000)	2,64,000

It can be found that at a selling price of ₹20 (finance manager's proposal), the net profit is ₹1,60,000. But if the company fixes a selling price of ₹24 per unit, the maximum profit of ₹2,96,000 will be earned. Therefore, the finance manager's proposal is rejected and marketing manager's proposal is recommended. In fact, while making the proposal the finance manager has not considered the price elasticity of demand of company product which can be an important factor in fixing the selling price.

✍ EXAMPLE 18.3 *(Considering Opportunity Costs in Selling Price)*

V Ltd. manufactures small chairs for children. The following information is provided:

	Per Unit (₹)
Material (3 kg @ ₹2 per kg)	6
Labour	5
Variable overheads	4
Allocated fixed overheads	2

Material is currently used to make desks which provide contribution of ₹5 per unit and 2 kg of material are required for each desk. What is the minimum price per chair if

(i) material is plentiful
(ii) material is scarce

☞ *Solution*

The minimum price of product is determined in different manners depending on different situations as listed below:

(i) *When the product has been made*—The minimum price will be whatever is recoverable subject to recovering any disposal costs. All costs incurred in manufacturing the product are sunk costs, and therefore, not relevant in pricing decisions.

(ii) *When the product is to be made and there are no scarce resources*—In this case, the minimum price will be equal to incremental costs of making the product.

(iii) *When the product is to be made and there are scarce resources*—In this case, the minimum price is calculated as follows:

Minimum price = Incremental costs of making (external opportunity costs) + Opportunity costs of scarce product resources (internal opportunity cost)

Using the above guidelines, the minimum price per chair will be as follows:

(i) *Material is plentiful*

Minimum price = Incremental cost of making chairs

= 6 + 5 + 4 = ₹15 per chair.

(iii) *Material is scarce*

Minimum price = Incremental costs + Internal opportunity costs of scarce resources

$$= 15 + \left(\frac{\text{Contribution}}{\text{Kg of material}} = \frac{₹5}{2\text{ kg}} \times 3\text{ kg}\right)$$

= 15 + 7.50

= ₹22.50 per chair

EXAMPLE 18.4 (*Minimum Price*)

ACE Ltd. has an inventory of 5,000 units of a product left over from last year's production. This model is no longer in demand. It is possible to sell these at reduced prices through the normal distribution channels. The other alternative is to ask someone to take them on "as is where is" basis. The latter alternative will cost the company ₹5,000.

The company produced 240,000 units of the product, last year, when the unit costs were as under:

	₹	₹
Manufacturing costs		
Variable	6.00	
Fixed	1.00	7.00
Selling and distribution cost:		
Variable	3.00	
Fixed	1.50	4.50
Total cost		11.50
Selling price per unit		14.00

Required:

Should the company scrap the items or sell them at a reduced price? If you suggest the latter, what minimum price would you recommend?

Solution

Minimum recommended price per unit of 5,000 units of a product (obsolete model) of ACE Ltd.

(i) Historical cost of ₹11.50 per unit of 5,000 units of a product is irrelevant (as it is a sunk cost) for determining the recommended price per unit.

(ii) If, at all, this model is sold in the market through normal distribution channels, it will entail a variable selling and distribution cost of ₹3 per unit.

(iii) If the stock is disposed of by asking someone to take them on "as is where is basis", the company would have to spend ₹5,000 over 5,000 units that is ₹1/- per unit.

(iv) In view of (ii) and (iii), the option of selling 5,000 obsolete units of model using regular channels will have a differential cost of ₹2 (₹3 – ₹1) per unit.

Recommendation

Hence, if the company can get anything more than ₹2/- per unit, then it is worthwhile to sell the stock of 5,000 units and earn an additional contribution.

✍ EXAMPLE 18.5 (*Export Order Price*)

Somesh of Agra presently operates its plant at 80% of the normal capacity to manufacture a product only to meet the demand of Government of Tamil Nadu under a rate contract.

He supplies the product for ₹4,00,000 and earns a profit margin of 20% on sales realisations. Direct cost per unit is constant.

The indirect costs as per his budget projections are:

Indirect costs	20,000 units (80% capacity)	22,500 units (90% capacity)	25,000 units (100% capacity)
	₹	₹	₹
Variable	80,000	90,000	1,00,000
Semi-variable	40,000	42,500	45,000
Fixed	80,000	80,000	80,000

He has received an export order for the product equal to 20% of its present operations. Additional packing charges on this order will be ₹1,000.

Arrive at the price to be quoted for the export order to give him a profit margin of 10% on the export price.

☞ *Solution*

Working Notes:

1. Direct cost per unit

	₹
Selling price per unit (₹400,000/20000 units)	20
Less: Profit margin (20% × ₹20)	4
Total cost	16
Less: Indirect costs (₹2,00,000 / 20000 units)	10
Direct cost per unit	6

2. Statement of differential cost for 4,000 units (20% of 20,000 units)

	Present Production 20,000 Units	*Proposed Production 24,000 Units*	*Differential for 4,000 Units*
Direct cost @ ₹6/- p.u.	₹1,20,000	₹1,44,000	₹24,000
Indirect cost:			
Variable @ ₹4 p.u.	80,000	96,000	16,000
Semi-variable	40,000	44,000	4,000
Fixed	80,000	81,000	1,000
Total	3,20,000	3,65,000	45,000

Computation of the price to be quoted for the export order of 4,000 units

	₹
Differential cost *(Refer to working note-2)*	45,000
Add: Profit (10% of export price or 1/9th cost)	5,000
Price to be quoted	50,000
Export price per unit ₹12.50 (₹50000/4000 units)	

EXAMPLE 18.6

Demarco makes miniature mobile generators and has a standard profit margin of 20% for all its products. Its annual budget includes marketing, administration and production overhead allowances of ₹60,000, ₹20,000 and ₹50,000 respectively. It also shows that the company intends to use ₹18,000 of materials and pay direct wages of ₹32,000. Marketing and administration overheads are all fixed but 10% of production overheads are considered to be variable. Demarco uses the cost-plus method of setting its selling price.

Required:
Calculate the cost-plus percentage if the base was:

(a) variable cost;
(b) production cost; and
(c) full cost.

Solution

	₹000
Direct materials	18
Direct labour	32
Variable production overheads	5
Variable cost	**55**

	₹000
Fixed production overheads	45
Production cost	**100**
Administration overheads	20
Marketing overheads	60
Full cost	**180**
Margin @ 20%	45
Sales revenue	**225**

(a) Variable cost = 55:

$$\frac{225-55}{55}\times 100=\frac{170}{55}\times 100=309\%$$

Variable cost plus 309%

(b) Production cost = 100:

$$\frac{225-100}{100}\times 100=\frac{125}{100}\times 100=125\%$$

Production cost plus 125%

(c) Full cost = 180:

$$\frac{225-180}{180}\times 100=\frac{45}{180}\times 100=25\%$$

Full cost plus 25%

Theory Questions

1. "In the long run, selling price will tend to equal costs plus reasonable profits." Discuss.
2. List the factors taken into consideration in fixing the selling price by a business firm.
3. Discuss full cost-plus and marginal cost-plus methods of pricing. Which pricing method can be useful to a firm and under what situations?
4. Product pricing is an important area for management decision-making. State briefly the broad objectives of pricing policy. Mention specifically situations where prices are fixed below the variable cost.

Problems

1. An Electronics Company has the following cost structure for an electronic product.

	₹
Direct material	50
Direct labour	75
Variable overheads	30
Fixed overheads	45
Total unit cost	200

Fixed selling and administrative costs ₹6,00,000.

for excel template, scan

→ Additional information:

(i) Budgeted production and sale for the next year is 20,000 units.

(ii) The management feels that a minimum return of 20% is required on equity investments of ₹20,00,000. What price should it charge for one unit of its output?

Ans. ₹250

2. MPC Ltd. of Mumbai presently sells as equipment for ₹42,000. Increase in prices of material and labour cost is anticipated to the extent of 10% and 20% respectively in the coming year. Material cost represents 40% of cost of sales and labour cost 30% of cost of sales. The remaining relate to overheads.

If the existing selling price is retained, despite the increase in labour and material prices, the company would face a 25% decrease in the existing amount of profit on the equipment.

Required:

(i) Calculate a selling price so as to give the same percentage of profit on increased cost of sales, as before.

(ii) Prepare a statement of profit/loss per unit showing the new selling price and cost per unit in support of your answer.

Ans. (i) ₹46,200

(ii) Percentage of profit on sales, Existing 40%, New 40%.

3. A company presently sells an equipment for ₹35,000. Increase in prices of labour and material costs is anticipated to the extent of 15% and 10% respectively in the coming year. At present, material cost represents 40% of cost of sales and labour cost 30% of the cost of sales. The remaining relate to overheads. If the existing selling price is retained, despite the increase in labour and material prices, the company would face 20% decrease in the existing amount of profit on the equipment.

You are required to arrive at a selling price so as to give the same percentage of profit on increased cost of sales, as before. Prepare a statement of profit/loss per unit, showing the new selling price and cost per unit in support of your answer.

Ans: Revised selling price ₹37,975

Percentage of profit on cost of sales 42.5%.

CASE STUDY

Pricing Decision: A case of Atlantis Vending Machine

Atlantis VendMach Ltd manufactured and sold wall mounted automatic vending machines to beverages companies like Coca Cola, Pepsi, Amul, etc. The machine had a currency selection option of ₹10, ₹20, ₹50 and ₹100. Atlantis' factory had a capacity of producing 18,000 vending machines per month. However, due to presence of other competitors, the company was able to produce and sell 10,000 machines per month at a sale price of ₹8,000 per machine. The company was performing satisfactorily with all cost control measures in place. The data related to the cost of producing the vending machines for the month of May 2019 was as follows:

Raw material consumed—₹360 lakh
Wages and salaries—₹76 lakh
Manufacturing expenses—₹76 lakh
Office and administrative overheads—₹40 lakh
Selling and distribution overheads—₹60 lakh

During the second last week of May, in the monthly-budget meeting, the various department managers discussed about how the prices were kept under control until now due to the election. The managers talked about the expected increase in prices after the election results. The Purchase Manager estimated that the raw material price would go up by 10% on an average in June. The HR Manager also predicted the increase in the labour rate by 5% owing to the much talked about wage revision by the government. The operations head, although did not specify any increase but informed that the manufacturing costs always varied in proportion to the labour costs. The administrative head, however, was confident of maintaining his office expenses to the same level like previous month. The Sales and Distribution Manager showed a positive indication by talking about the good effect of the new advertisement that they launched at the beginning of that month. According to him, sales were expected to pick up the momentum in June and he was confident that his team would be able to sell 12,000 vending machines in June 2019.

The managing director, after listening to all of them informed the managers that the company in that case would also revise (increase) the price of the vending machine. This decision was based on the assumption that the increase in price and wage revision by the government would impact all the market players (competitors) alike. The MD desired that the company should get as much profit as previous month. However, he also wanted to know that if the selling price was kept constant, would it affect the profit margin significantly? The Cost & Finance Manager of Atlantis Vendmach was given a day to work out the new price for the Vending Machine.

Accordingly, the Finance Manager submitted two proposed prices the next day i.e ₹8,122.60 per vending machine and ₹8,436 per machine. However, the marketing team was of the opinion that it would be difficult to maintain the promise of selling 12,000 vending machines at the second price proposed as the competitors were not expected to increase their selling price by more than 5%. The MD was in dilemma as to what should be the right price.

Questions for Discussion:

1. What is the present cost and profit structure?
2. After the expected changes in various cost of production what would be the impact on profit if the same sales price is maintained?
3. How did the finance manager arrive at these two prices?
4. If the apprehensions of the marketing team are well-founded, what should be the right selling price?

Chapter 19

Standard Costing

Learning Objectives

After reading this chapter, you should be able to:

1. explain historical costing and its limitations;
2. define standard costs and its differences with estimated cost, standard costing and its advantages and limitations;
3. understand different types of standards and explain how tight should standards be;
4. describe developing or setting standards; revision of standards;
5. explain the procedure of computing material cost variances, labour cost variances, overhead cost variances and sales variances;
6. discuss disposition of variance, managerial uses of variances, and
7. understand different types of control ratios.

Control of cost is one of the most important objectives of cost accounting and cannot be achieved without some standard against which actual can be compared. This chapter introduces the concepts and basic procedures of standard costing and also explains the techniques used in standard cost variance analysis. However, before discussing standard costing it will be appropriate to evaluate briefly historical cost accounting and its limitations.

HISTORICAL COSTING AND ITS LIMITATIONS

Historical cost systems are principally associated with recording of historical, or as they are commonly called, actual cost. Historical costing is the ascertainment of costs after they have been incurred. Historical costs have the following limitations:

1. Historical costs are collected after they have been incurred and therefore are ineffective in cost control. The costs have been incurred, they cannot be undone and no steps can be taken to correct inefficiencies.
2. Historical costs are not helpful in cost reduction since they contain no standards or goals towards which employees can work.

3. Historical costs do not provide reliable guides to management in the tasks of budgeting, planning, and decision-making because they reflect a situation in a previous period. But the enterprise, in fact, may be working under conditions different from those prevailing during that previous period.

DEFINITIONS OF STANDARD COST AND STANDARD COSTING

A standard cost is a planned cost for a unit of product or service rendered. Standard costs represent excellent target costs that should be obtained. The Institute of Cost and Management Accountants (UK) defines standard cost as "a pre-determined cost which is calculated from management's standards of efficient operation and the relevant necessary expenditure. It may be used as a basis for price-fixing and for cost control through variance analysis." Standard cost expresses what costs should be under attainable good performance.

Standard costing is the setting of pre-determined cost estimates in order to provide a basis for comparison with actual costs. The Institute of Cost and Management Accountants (UK) defines standard costing as "the preparation and use of standard costs, their comparison with actual costs, and the analysis of variances to their causes and points of incidence."

STANDARD COSTS AND ESTIMATED COSTS

The term "standard costs" should not be confused with "estimated costs". Standard cost and estimated costs differ in the following respects:

First, estimated costs are frequently less accurately determined. Estimated costs are developed from projections using averages of past data regarding performance. Standard costs are pre-determined realistically and much more scientifically through the use of time and motion studies, engineering estimates and specifications, selected measures of plant capacity, cost behaviour patterns.

Second, estimated costs are not helpful to management in accomplishing managerial functions as they are not scientifically pre-determined costs. But, standard costs involve more sophistication, operation analysis and evaluation and comprehensive review of internal and external factors and provide reliable measures for product costing, product pricing, planning, coordination and cost control purposes.

Third, estimated cost emphasises on actual cost with which it is compared at the end of the accounting period. If the estimated costs are found higher or lower than actual costs they are revised for use in the next accounting period. In standard costing, the emphasis is on standard costs, that is, what costs of material, labour and overhead should be incurred if the factory is to be operated as a highly-efficient unit with each manager, foreman, worker, plant and machine functioning as an efficient part of the production process. Under standard costing, actual costs are ascertained only to facilitate their comparison with standard costs.

ADVANTAGES OF STANDARD COSTING

Among the many advantages generally attributed to standard costing, the most important may be listed as follows:

1. *Managerial planning* Planning is a process of using all resources in such a manner that maximises business profits. Standard costs are more convenient than actual costs for budget

preparation because the standard costs at different production levels and for different product-mixes are readily built up into total costs as called for by the budget. On the other hand, using actual costs requires a great deal of analysis and adjustment when extensive changes in product volume or product-mixes take place.

2. *Coordination* The establishment of standards coordinates all functions—manufacturing, marketing engineering, research, and accounting towards the achievement of a common goal. Setting standards involves defining and communicating targets so that they can work towards the attainment of the goal.
3. *Cost control* Cost control and cost reduction are probably the most important aims of any costing system; and standard costing gives due recognition to this fact. Cost control has the objective of production of the required quality at the lowest cost attainable under existing conditions. Standards enable management to make periodic comparison of actual costs with standard costs in order to measure performance and to take action to maintain control over costs.
4. *Economical means of costing and record-keeping* The use of standard costs can reduce clerical labour and expense by avoiding the detailed record-keeping which is necessary when actual costs alone are used.
5. *Formulating price and production policies* Standard costs as compared to actual costs can be used for estimating selling prices. When standard unit costs are available, expected costs and sales prices can be computed on the basis of standard costs. Standards already established can easily be modified to reflect current conditions and changes in material prices or labour rates and the price of the product can be determined on a realistic basis.

   Actual costs, on the other hand, may reflect excessive usage of material, abnormal labour times or an inequitable charge for overhead. Actual overhead cost per unit at any given time may be so influenced by temporary fluctuations in production levels as to make actual cost entirely unusable for pricing.
6. *Standards as incentives to employees* If standards are reasonable and attainable they act as incentives to employees to improve their performances and to maintain the quality of the product. Standards motivate workers, supervisors and foremen to work more efficiently in the accomplishment of their respective standards.

DIFFERENT TYPES OF STANDARDS

The two principal considerations affecting the classification of standards are: (i) attainability of standards, that is, the ease with which it is possible to achieve the standards, and (ii) frequency with which the standards are revised. On the basis of these two factors, it is possible to classify standards as ideal, normal, basic, current or expected actual standards.

Ideal, Perfect, Maximum Efficiency or Theoretic Standards

Ideal standards (costs) are the standards which can be attained under the most favourable conditions possible. The level of performance under ideal standards would be achieved through the best possible combination of factors—the most favourable prices for materials and labour, highest output with best equipment and layout, and maximum efficiency in the utilisation of the production resources—in other words, maximum output at minimum cost. Such standards reflect only goals or targets without any hope of performance being currently achieved. These standards are extremely tight and do not provide for waste and inefficiency in any form; no material is wasted; no units are spoiled; there are no idle hours; operators work at pre-determined speed; the available capacity is fully utilised.

Normal Standards

Normal standards are the average standards which (it is anticipated) can be attained during a future period of time, preferably long enough to cover one business cycle. These standards are not revised until the cycle has run its full course. This generally results in an incorrect valuation of inventories and consequent errors in the profit disclosed, as the inventories are understated in periods of high prices, and over-stated when prices are low. Normal standards are mainly used as a device to solve the problem of absorbing fixed overhead rather than in connection with material cost and wages. Since these standards do not reflect the goals to be attained, they are not often used.

Basic Standards

The Institute of Cost and Management Accountants (UK) defines a basic standard as the standard which is established for use unaltered for an indefinite period which may be a long period of time. Basic standards are seldom revised or updated to reflect current operating costs and price level changes.

Currently Attainable or Expected Actual Standards

Current standards are standards which are established for use over a short period of time, and are related to current conditions. They represent current costs to be expected from efficient operations. Currently, attainable standards are formulated after making allowance for the cost of normal spoilage, cost of idle time due to machine breakdowns, and the cost of other events which are unavoidable in normal efficient operations. They take the place of actual cost and are recorded in account books and financial statements. Any deviation from these standards reflect inefficiencies in the production activities, unless the variances have occurred due to uncontrollable factors. These standards are most accurate and very useful to management in product costing, inventory valuations; estimates, analyses, performance evaluation, planning, employee motivation, and for managerial decision-making and external financial reporting.

HOW TIGHT SHOULD STANDARDS BE?

It can be rightly said that a single standard may not be suitable for all purposes. For the purposes of cost control, tight standards need to be established. The attainable (good) performance standards are useful for purposes of inventory valuation, product costing and income determination.

High Standards

A high standard helps in cost reduction and motivating employees to try to reach the targets established. High standards represent the best possible performance and, if achieved, raise the levels of performance and efficiency as compared to poor or loose standards. High standards being unattainable in practice may not be good for the employees. Employees may not seriously accept them because they know that they are unattainable and impossible to achieve. High standards are also not realistic and therefore cannot be used in product costing, inventory valuation, financial statement, planning, and capital investment decisions.

Low (Loose) Standards

A standard which is low or loose can be attained by poor performance. However, it defeats the purpose of standard costing and fails to disclose inefficiencies. Such standards do not help management in cost control as they are not accurate measures to compare actual results.

In conclusion, it can be said that accountants generally seem to favour currently attainable standards which are most appropriate for performance appraisal, accounting purposes, cost control and decision-making. Such standards produce good performance, promote employee motivation and include unavoidable elements, such as spoilage, lost time, capacity not utilised in setting standards.

DEVELOPING OR SETTING STANDARD

All factors related with standards-setting should be considered in the establishment of standards. Whatever method is used, standards must be established for a definite period of time so that they can be effective in performance evaluation, control and analysis of costs. Standards are usually set for a six- or twelve-month period. Sometimes, a longer period is used but rarely a shorter period. Standards are developed for:

1. Materials.
2. Labour, and
3. Overhead.

Materials Standards

Two standards must be developed for materials:

1. Materials quantity (usage) standard
2. Materials price standard

Labour Standards

As in the case of direct materials, labour standards are also established for both cost and quantity (efficiency). For standard cost purposes, direct labour is treated separately from indirect labour, which is included in the factory overhead. Two standards are usually developed for labour costs;

1. Labour usage (or efficiency) standard
2. Labour cost (or rate) standard

Factory Overhead Cost Standards

Setting Overhead Standards

Setting standard overhead cost requires the determination of: (1) standard capacity and (2) standard overhead costs for this capacity. The standard overhead costs can be computed using normal capacity. The normal or expected actual capacity aims at a production level according to an existing set of conditions. This capacity does not require complete utilisation of all available facilities but is based on the efficient utilisation of resources and operations.

After standard capacity is determined, overhead—variable and fixed—to be incurred at that capacity is prepared. The standard overhead rate is found by dividing the standard or budgeted overhead at standard capacity by the volume selected to represent standard capacity. Volume may be measured in units of product, standard productive hour (labour or machine) or some standard cost, such as direct labour.

$$\text{Standard overhead rate} = \frac{\text{Standard overhead}}{\text{Standard production}}$$

REVISION OF STANDARDS

Standard costs require continuous review and, at times, frequent change. Changing prices, technological advances, new personnel, new machinery, changing quality of materials and new labour negotiations, all influence standards and make them obsolete resulting in unrealistic budgets, poor cost control, and unreasonable unit cost for inventory valuation and income determination.

A company should establish a programme to revise standards whenever required so that standards can be set at a currently attainable level. Labour rate standards should be revised for any change in labour rates; material quantity standards for any change in type, quality of material or method of production. If a new machine is purchased to replace an old machine, labour time standards and material quantity standards should be updated. In addition to these obvious revisions, in every business firm there should be a system for revising standards for adequacy and suitability at least once a year. A periodic review of standards is desirable to accomplish the objectives of standard costing.

VARIANCE ANALYSIS

The function of standards in cost accounting is to indicate variances between standard costs which are allowed and actual costs which have been recorded. The Institute of Cost and Management Accountants (UK) defines variance as the difference between a standard cost and the comparable actual cost incurred during a period. Variance analysis can be defined as the process of computing the amount of, and isolating the cause of variances between actual costs and standard costs. Variance analysis involves two phases:

1. Computation of individual variances, and
2. Determination of the cause(s) of each variance

First, we concentrate on the computation of material, labour and factory overhead variances. Analysis of causes, reporting variances to managers, and accounting disposition of variances conclude the study of standard costing in this chapter.

MATERIALS VARIANCE

Variances as given in Fig. 19.1 constitute materials variances:

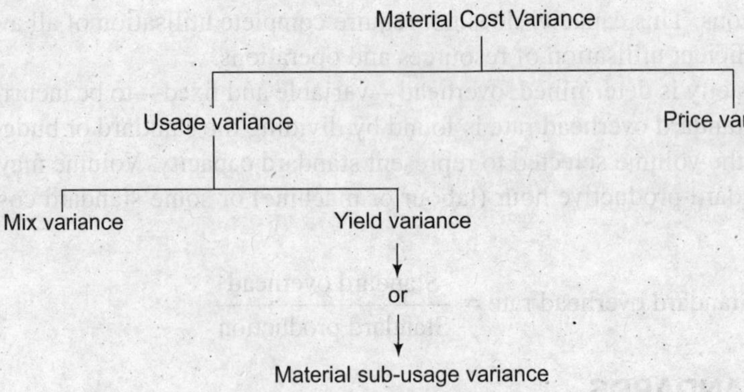

Fig. 19.1 Types of Materials Variances

Material Cost Variance

Material cost variance is the difference between the actual cost of direct materials used and standard cost of direct materials specified for the output achieved. This variance results from differences between quantities consumed and quantities of materials allowed for production and from differences between prices paid and prices pre-determined. This can be computed by using the following formula.

Material cost variance = $(AQ \times AP) - (SQ \times SP)$

where AQ = Actual quantity
AP = Actual price
SQ = Standard quantity for the actual output
SP = Standard price

Materials Usage Variance

The material quantity or usage variance results when actual quantities of raw materials used in production differ from standard quantities that should have been used to produce the output achieved. It is that portion of the direct materials cost variance which is due to the difference between the actual quantity used and standard quantity specified. As a formula this variance is shown as:

Materials quantity variance = (Actual quantity – Standard quantity) × Standard price

A material usage variance is favourable when the total actual quantity of direct materials used is less than the total standard quantity allowed for the actual output.

EXAMPLE

Compute the materials usage variance from the following information:

Standard material cost per unit		Materials issued
Material *A* 2 pieces @ ₹1.00	= 2.00	Material *A* 2,050 pieces
Material *B* 3 pieces @ ₹2.00	= 6.00	Material *B* 2,980 pieces.
	₹ 8.00	
Units completed 1,000		

☞ ***Solution***

Materials usage variance = (Actual quantity – Standard quantity) × Standard price

Material A = (2,050 – 2,000) × ₹1.00 = ₹50 (Adverse or Unfavourable)

Material B = (2,980 – 3,000) × ₹2.00 = ₹40 (Favourable)

Total = ₹10 (Unfavourable)

It should be noted that the standard rather than the actual price is used in computing the usage variance. Use of actual price would have introduced a price factor into a quantity variance. Because different departments are responsible, these two factors must be kept separate.

As a general principle, actuals (cost, quantity, price, output, etc.) are compared with respective standard data to compute variances. Therefore, any formula to calculate, mathematically, any variance would be as follows:

(Actual — Standard)

However, one may use variance formula as "Standard — Actual" as it does not influence in any way the variance figure calculated by using the formula "Actual — Standard".

Materials Price Variance

A materials price variance occurs when raw materials are purchased at a price different from standard price. It is that portion of the direct materials which is due to the difference between actual price paid and standard price specified and cost variance multiplied by the actual quantity. Expressed as a formula,

Materials price variance (Actual price – Standard price) × Actual quantity

Materials price variance is unfavourable when the actual price paid exceeds the pre-determined standard price. It is advisable that materials price variance should be calculated at the time of materials purchase rather than when materials are used. Purchase of materials is an earlier event than the use of materials. Therefore, a variance based on quantity purchased is basically an earlier report than a variance based on quantity actually used. This is quite beneficial from the viewpoint of performance measurement and corrective action.

EXAMPLE

Assuming in above example that material A was purchased at the rate of ₹1.00 and material B was purchased at the rate of ₹2.10 the material price variance will be as follows:

Materials price variance = (Actual price – Standard price) × Actual quantity

Material A = (1.00 – 1.00) × 2,050 = Zero

Material B = (2.10 – 2.00) × 2,980 = ₹298 (Unfavourable)

The total of materials usage variance and price variance is equal to materials cost variance.

Materials Mix Variance

The materials usage or quantity variance can be separated into mix variance and yield variance.

A mix variance will result when materials are not actually placed into production in the same ratio as the standard formula. For instance, if a product is produced by adding 100 kg of raw material A and

200 kg of raw material *B*, the standard material mix ratio is 1 : 2. Actual raw materials used must be in this 1 : 2 ratio, otherwise a materials mix variance will be found.

Materials mix variance is that portion of the materials quantity variance which is due to the difference between the actual composition of a mixture and the standard mixture. It can be computed by using the following formula:

Materials mix variance = (Standard cost of actual quantity of the actual mixture – Standard cost of actual quantity of the standard mixture)

or

Materials mix variance = (Actual mix – Revised standard mix of actual input) × Standard price

Revised standard proportion is calculated as follows:

$$\frac{\text{Standard mix of a particular material}}{\text{Total standard quantity}} \times \text{Actual input}$$

EXAMPLE

A product is made from two raw materials, material *A* and material *B*. One unit of finished product requires 10 kg of material. The following is standard mix:

Material *A*	20%–	2 kg @	₹2.00	=	₹4.00
Material *B*	80%–	8 kg @	₹1.00	=	₹8.00
	100%–	10 kg	₹1.20		₹12.00

During a period, one unit of product was produced at the following costs:

Material *A*	8 kg @	₹2.00	=	₹16.00
Material *B*	4 kg @	₹1.25	=	₹15.00
	12 kg	₹1.75		₹21.00

Compute the materials mix variance.

Solution

Materials mix variance = (Actual proportion – Revised standard proportion of actual input) × Standard price

Revised standard proportion:

$$\frac{\text{Standard proportion of a particular mix}}{\text{Total standard quantity}} \times \text{Actual input}$$

Revised standard proportion:

$$\text{Material } A = \frac{2}{10} \times 12 = 2.40 \text{ kg}$$

$$\text{Material } B = \frac{8}{10} \times 12 = 9.60 \text{ kg}$$

Materials mix variance:

Material A = (8 kg – 2.40 kg) × 2.00

= 5.60 × 2.00 = ₹11.20 (Unfavourable)

Material B = (4 kg – 9.60) × 1.00

= 5.60 × 1.00 = ₹5.60 (Favourable)

Total mix variance = ₹5.60 (Unfavourable)

Materials Yield Variance

Materials yield variance explains the remaining portion of the total materials quantity variance. It is that portion of materials usage variance which is due to the difference between the actual yield obtained and standard yield specified (in terms of actual inputs). In other words, yield variance occurs when the output of the final product does not correspond with the output that could have been obtained by using the actual inputs.

The total of materials-mix variance and materials-yield variance equals materials quantity or usage variance. When there is no materials-mix variance, the materials-yield variance equals the total materials quantity variance.

The formula for computing yield variance is as follows:

Yield variance = (Actual yield – Standard yield specified) × Standard cost per unit

or

Yield variance = (Actual loss – Standard loss on actual input) × Standard cost per unit

Example

Standard input = 100 kg, standard yield = 90 kg, standard cost per kg of output = ₹20. Actual input 200 kg, actual yield 182 kg Compute the yield variance.

Solution

$$\text{Standard yield for the actual input} = \frac{90}{100} \times 200 = 180 \text{ kg}$$

Yield variance = (Actual yield – Standard yield for the actual input) × Standard cost per unit.

= (182 – 180) × ₹20

= 2 × 20 = 40 (Favourable)

The above yield variance can be computed by using another formula also, for example,

Yield variance = (Actual loss – Standard loss on actual input) × Standard cost per unit

= (18 kg – 20 kg) × ₹20

= ₹40 (Favourable)

In this example, there is no mix variance and therefore, the materials-usage variance will be equal to the materials-yield variance.

The above formula uses output or loss as the basis of computing the yield variance. Yield variance can also be computed on the basis of input factors only. The fact is that loss in inputs equals loss in output. A lower yield simply means that a higher quantity of inputs has been used and the anticipated or standard output (based on actual inputs) has not been achieved. Yield, in such a case, is known as sub-usage variance (or revised usage variance) which can be computed by using the following formula:

Sub-usage or revised-usage variance = (Revised standard proportion of actual input –Standard quantity) × Standard cost per unit of input

Important Note

Variances, generally, can be computed by using two approaches namely by comparing the actuals with standards or comparing standard with actuals as displayed below.

Actual — Standard

or

Standard — Actual

A survey of relevant literature, books and publications on cost and management accounting in India and abroad reveals that both the above approaches have been recognised by the authors. In this text, both the methods have been followed in calculating variances to avoid any confusion among the students and readers. The use of only one of the above two approaches may create some doubt among the students.

EXAMPLE 19.1

Following details relating to product *X* during the month of April, 2020 are available:
Standard cost per unit of *X*:

Materials	:	50 kg @ ₹4 0/kg
Actual production	:	100 units
Actual material cost	:	₹42/kg
Material price variance	:	₹9,800 (Adverse)
Material usage variance	:	₹4,000 (Favourable)

Calculate the actual quantity of material used during the month of April, 2020.

Solution

		₹
Standard cost of materials for actual output		
[(100 units × 50 kg) × ₹40 per kg]	=	2,00,000
Material usage variance		4,000 (F)
		1, 96, 000
Material price variance		9,800 (A)
Actual cost of materials used		2,05,800
Actual material cost = ₹42 per kg		

∴ Actual quantity of materials used during the month = $\frac{₹2,05,800}{42}$ = 4,900 kg

Alternative solution

Material price variance = ₹9,800 (A)
Actual price per kg = ₹42
Actual quantity of material used = ₹9,800/(42 – 40) = 4,900 kg

EXAMPLE 19.2

UV Ltd. presents the following information for November, 2020:

Budgeted production of product P = 200 units.
Standard consumption of raw materials = 2 kg per unit of P.
Standard price of material A = ₹6 per kg.
Actually, 250 units of P were produced and material A was purchased at ₹8 per kg and consumed at 1.8 kg per unit of P. Calculate the material cost variances.

Solution

Actual production of P	= 250 units
Standard quantity of A for actual production = 2 × 250	= 500 kg (SQ)
Actual quantity of A for actual production = 1.8 × 250	= 450 kg (AQ)
Standard price/kg of A	= ₹6 (SP)
Actual price/kg of A	= ₹8 (AP)

(1) Total material cost variance = (Standard price × Standard quantity) – (Actual price × Actual quantity)
= (6 × 500) – (8 × 450)
= 3,000 – 3,600 = 600 (A)

(2) Material price variance = (Standard price – Actual price) × Actual quantity
= (6 – 8) × 450 = 900 (A)

(3) Material usage variance = (Standard quantity – Actual quantity) × Standard price
= (500 – 450) × 6 = 300 (F)

EXAMPLE 19.3

Standard material cost for manufacturing 1,000 units of output is 400 kg of material at ₹2.50 per kg When 2,000 units are produced, it is found that actual cost is 825 kg of material at ₹2.70 per kg. Calculate material cost variance, material price variance and material usage variance.

Solution

(i) Material cost variance = (Standard cost – Actual cost)
= (800 × 2.50) – (825 × 2.70)
= 2,000 – 2,227.50 = **₹227.50 (A)**

(ii) Material price variance = (Standard price – Actual price) × Actual quantity
= (2.50 – 2.70) × 825 = **₹165 (A)**

(iii) Material usage variance = (Standard quantity – Actual quantity) × Standard price
= (800 – 825) × 2.50 = **₹62.50 (A)**

EXAMPLE 19.4

Modern Tiles Ltd. makes plastic tiles of standard size of 6″ × 6″ × 1/8″. From the information given ahead you are required to calculate:

(i) Total material cost variance;
(ii) Material price variance;
(iii) Material usage variance;

(iv) Material mix variance; and
(v) Material yield variance.

A standard mix of the compound required to produce an output of 20,000 sq. ft. of tiles of 1/8″ thickness is as follows:

Direct Material	*Quantity* *kg*	*Price Per kg* ₹
A	600	9.00
B	400	6.50
C	500	4.00

For the month of March 2020, actual production of plastic tiles was 6,20,000 units. The actual data for direct material consumed was as under:

Direct Material	*Quantity Consumed* *kg*	*Price Per kg* ₹
A	5,000	8.50
B	2,900	6.00
C	4,400	4.50

☞ ***Solution***

Working Notes:

1. One mix of 20,000 sq. ft of titles would produce = $\dfrac{20{,}000 \times 12 \times 12}{6 \times 6}$ = 80,000 tiles
2. To produce 6,20,000 tiles, Standard quantity required = $\dfrac{6{,}20{,}000}{80{,}000} \times 1{,}500 = 11{,}625$ kg.
3. Total standard quantity is apportioned in the ratio of standard quantity of direct material *i.e.* 6 : 4 : 5

   $\text{SQ (A)} = 11{,}625 \times \dfrac{6}{15} = 4{,}650 \text{ kg}$

   $\text{SQ (B)} = 11{,}625 \times \dfrac{4}{15} = 3{,}100 \text{ kg}$

   $\text{SQ (C)} = 11{,}625 \times \dfrac{5}{15} = 3{,}875 \text{ kg}$

4. Revised standard quantity
   Total actual quantity = 5,000 + 2,900 + 4,400 = 12,300 kg

   RSQ = Total actual quantity × Standard proportion

   $\text{RSQ (A)} = 12{,}300 \times \dfrac{6}{15} = 4{,}920 \text{ kg}$

   $\text{RSQ (B)} = 12{,}300 \times \dfrac{5}{15} = 3{,}280 \text{ kg}$

$$RSQ (C) = 12{,}300 \times \frac{5}{15} = 4{,}100 \text{ kg}$$

5. Total standard cost

$$= [600 \times 9] + [400 \times 6.50] + [500 \times 4] = ₹10{,}000$$

$$RSQ (B) = 12{,}300 \times \frac{4}{15} = 3{,}280 \text{ kg}$$

6. Standard cost per unit of standard output

$$= \frac{\text{Total standard cost}}{\text{Total standard output}} = \frac{10{,}000}{80{,}000} = 0.125$$

$$\text{or} \quad \frac{77{,}500}{6{,}20{,}000} = 0.125$$

7. Standard yield for actual input

$$= \frac{80{,}000}{1{,}500} \times 12{,}300 = 6{,}56{,}000 \text{ tiles}$$

Basic Calculation Table

Direct Material	*Standard*			*Actual*		
	Quantity (kg)	*Rate (₹)*	*Amount (₹)*	*Quantity (kg)*	*Rate (kg)*	*Amount (₹)*
A	4,650	9.00	41,850	5,000	8.50	42,500
B	3,100	6.50	20,150	2,900	6.00	17,400
C	3,875	4.00	15,500	4,400	4.50	19,800
Total	11,625		77,500	12,300		79,700

Computation of Variances:

(i) Total Material Cost Variance:

= Standard cost for actual output – Actual cost

= 77,500 – 79,700 = **₹2200 (A)**

(ii) Material Price Variance:

= Actual quantity (Standard price – Actual price)

= AQ (SP – AP)

A = 5,000(9.0 – 8.50) = ₹2,500 (F)

B = 2,900(6.50 – 6.00) = ₹1,450 (F)

C = 4,400(4.00 – 4.50) = ₹2,200 (A)

₹1,750 (F)

(iii) Material Usage Variance:

= Standard price (Standard quantity – Actual quantity)

= SP (SQ – AQ)

A = 9.00 (4,650 – 5,000) = ₹3,150 (A)

B = 6.50 (3,100 – 2,900) = ₹1,300 (F)

C = 4.00 (3,875 – 4,400) = ₹2,100 (A)

₹3,950 (A)

(iv) Material Mix Variance:

= Standard price (Revised standard quantity – Actual quantity)

= SP(RSQ – AQ)

A = 9.00(4,920 – 5,000) = ₹ 720 (A)

B = 6.50(3,280 – 2,900) = ₹2,470 (F)

C = 4.00(4,100 – 4,400) = ₹1,200 (A)

₹ 550 (F)

(v) Material Yield Variance:

= Standard cost per unit of output (Actual yield – Standard yield for actual input)

= 0.125(6,20,000 – 6,56,000)

= 0.125 × 36,000 = **₹4,500 (A)**

for excel template, scan

EXAMPLE 19.5

The standard material cost for 100 kg of chemical D is made up of:

Chemical A—30 kg @ ₹4 per kg
Chemical B—40 kg @ ₹5 per kg
Chemical C—80 kg @ ₹6 per kg

In a batch, 500 kg of chemical D were produced from a mix of

Chemical A — 140 kg @ cost of ₹588
Chemical B — 220 kg @ cost of ₹1,056
Chemical C — 440 kg @ cost of ₹2,860

How do the yield, mix and the price factor contribute to the variance in the actual per 100 kg of chemical D over the standard cost?

Solution

	Standard for 100 kg			*Actual for 100 kg*		
	Quantity (kg)	*Rate (₹)*	*Amount (₹)*	*Quantity (kg)*	*Rate (₹)*	*Amount (₹)*
A	30	4	120	28	4.20	117.60
B	40	5	200	44	4.80	211.20
C	80	6	480	88	6.50	572.00
	150		800	160		900.80

1. Material cost variance = SC – AC
= 800 – 900.80
= **₹100.80 (A)**

2. Material price variance = (SP – AP) × AQ

A = (4 – 4.20) × 28 = ₹ 5.60 (A)

B = (5 – 4.80) × 44 = ₹ 8.80 (F)

C = (6 – 6.50) × 88 = ₹44.00 (A)

Total = **₹40.80 (A)**

3. Material usage variance = (SQ – AQ) × SP

A = (30 – 28) × 4 = ₹ 8 (F)

B = (40 – 44) × 5 = ₹20 (A)

C = (80 – 88) × 6 = ₹48 (A)

Total = **₹60 (A)**

4. Material mix variance = (RSQ – AQ) × SP

$$A = \left[\left(\frac{160}{150} \times 30\right) - 28\right] \times 4 = ₹16.00\ (F)$$

$$B = \left[\left(\frac{160}{150} \times 40\right) - 44\right] \times 5 = ₹\ 6.67\ (A)$$

$$C = \left[\left(\frac{160}{150} \times 80\right) - 88\right] \times 6 = ₹16.00\ (A)$$

Total = **₹6.67 (A)**

5. Material yield variance

(Actual yield – Standard yield) × Standard output price

$$= \left[\left(100 - \frac{160}{150} \times 100\right)\right] \times 8 = \left(100 - \frac{320}{3}\right) \times 8\ = \mathbf{₹53.33\ (A)}$$

✍ EXAMPLE 19.6

Finolex Co. uses a standard cost system and manufactures product Z. Standard cost per 1,000 kg of output is as under:

Material	*Quantity (in kg)*	*Price (in ₹)*
A	800	2.50
B	200	4.00
C	200	1.00

In March 2020, the company produced 2,00,000 kg of output. Actual consumption was:

Material:

A—1,57,000 kg @ ₹2.40

B—38,000 kg @ ₹4.20
C—36,000 kg @ ₹1.10

Calculate material variances.

Solution

Standards Material Cost of 2,00,000 kg of Output

		Standard Quantity (kg)	*Standard Price (₹)*	*SQ × SP (₹)*
A	800 × 200 =	1,60,000	2.50	4,00,000
B	200 × 200 =	40,000	4.00	1,60,000
C	200 × 200 =	40,000	1.00	40,000
		2,40,000		6,00,000

Actual Material Cost of 2,00,000 kg of Output

	AQ (kg)	*AP (₹)*	*AQ × AP (₹)*
A	1,57,000	2.40	3,76,800
B	38,000	4.20	1,59,600
C	36,000	1.10	39,600
	2,31,000		5,76,000

(i) Material cost variance = (SQ × SP) – (AQ × AP) = 6,00,000 – 5,76,000 = ₹24,000 (F)

(ii) Material price variance = AQ(SP – AP)

A	=	1,57,000 (2.50 – 2.40)	=	15,700 (F)
B	=	38,000 (4.00 – 4.20)	=	7,600 (A)
C	=	36,000 (1.00 – 1.10)	=	3,600 (A)
MPV	=			₹4,500 (F)

(iii) Material usage variance = SP(SQ – AQ)

A	=	2.50 (1,60,000 – 1,57,000)	=	7,500 (F)
B	=	4.00 (40,000 – 38,000)	=	8,000 (F)
C	=	1.00 (40,000 – 36,000)	=	4,000 (F)
MUV	=			₹19,500 (F)

MCV = MPV + MUV = 4,500 (F) + 19,500 (F) = ₹24,000 (F)

(iv) Material mix variance

MMV = SP (AQ in std. prop – AQ)

A	=	2.50 (1,54,000 – 1,57,000)	=	7,500 (A)
B	=	4.00 (38,500 – 38,000)	=	2,000 (F)
C	=	1.00 (38,500 – 36,000)	=	2,500 (F)
				₹3,000 (A)

(v) Material yield variance $= \dfrac{SQ \times SQP}{\text{Output}} \times$ (Expected output from AQ – Actual output)

$$= \frac{6,00,000}{2,00,000} \times \left(\frac{2,00,000}{2,40,000} \times 2,31,000\right) - 2,00,000$$

= 3 (1,92,500 – 2,00,000) = ₹22,500 (F)

MUV = MMV + MYV = 3,000 (A) + 22,500 (F) = ₹19,500 (F)

AQ in Std. Proportion = A = 2,31,000 × 16/24 = 1,54,000;

B = 2,31,000 × 4/24 = 38,500; C = 2,31,000 × 4/24 = 38,500

EXAMPLE 19.7

From the following data, calculate the following variances:

(i) Material cost variance;
(ii) Material price variance;
(iii) Material quantity variance;
(iv) Material mix variance; and
(v) Material yield variance.

Material	*Standard*		*Actual*	
	Qty.	*Unit Price*	*Qty.*	*Unit Price*
A	60%	₹20	88	₹30
B	40%	₹10	132	₹10

Standard loss: 10%
Actual output: 180 units

Solution

Comparative Statement of Costs

Article	*Standard*			*Actual*		
	Qty.	*Price ₹*	*Cost ₹*	*Qty.*	*Price ₹*	*Cost.₹*
A	120	20	2,400	88	30	2,640
B	80	10	800	132	10	1,320
	200		3,200	220		3,960
Less: Std. Loss	20			40		–
	180		3,200	180		3,960

Material cost variance = Std. cost – Actual cost

= 3,200 – 3,960 = ₹760 (A)

Material quantity variance = (SQ – AQ) SP

A = (120 – 88) 20 = 640 (F)

$$B = (80 - 132)\ 10 = 520\ (A)$$

$$\overline{₹120\ (F)}$$

Material price variance $= (SP - AP) \times AQ$

$$A = (20 - 30)\ 88 = 880\ (A)$$

$$B = (10 - 10)\ 132 = \text{Nil}$$

$$\overline{₹880\ A}$$

Material mix variance $A = \left(\frac{120}{200} \times 220 - 88\right) 20 = 880\ (F)$

$$B = \left(\frac{80}{200} \times 220 - 132\right) 10 = 440\ A$$

$$\overline{₹440\ (F)}$$

Material yield variance $= \left(\frac{180}{200} \times 220 - 180\right) \frac{3,200}{180}$

$$= (198 - 180)\ \frac{3,200}{180}$$

$$= ₹320\ (A)$$

Working Notes

(i) *Standard quantity of materials A and B*

Standard quantity	= 60 + 40 = 100
Less: Standard loss	10
Standard output	90

When standard output is 90, quantity of material *A* is 60

When output is 180, material *A* quantity will be $\frac{180 \times 60}{90} = 120$

Similarly quantity of material *B* will be $\frac{180 \times 40}{90} = 80$

(ii) *Standard output for the actual input*

Actual input = 88 + 132 = 220

When standard input is 100, standard output is 90

When actual input is 220, standard output will be $\frac{220 \times 90}{100} = 198$

(iii) *Revised standard quantity for actual input*

Material $A = \frac{120}{200} \times 220$

Material $B = \frac{80}{200} \times 220$

EXAMPLE 19.8

Pragati Company manufactures a product *P* by mixing three raw materials. For every 100 kg of output 125 kg of raw material input are used. In April 2020, there was an output of 5,600 kg of product *P*. The standard and actual particulars of April, 2020 are as follows:

Raw Material	Standard		Actual	
	Mix	Price Per kg	Mix	Price Per kg
I	50%	₹40	60%	₹42
II	30%	₹20	20%	₹16
III	20%	₹10	20%	₹12

Calculate all material variances. The actual quantity of material used was 7,000 kg.

☞ **Solution**

Raw Material	Standard for Output of 5,600 kg			Actual for Output of 5,600 kg		
	Qty	Rate	Amt.	Qty	Rate	Amt.
	kg	₹	₹	kg	₹	₹
I	3,500	40	1,40,000	4,200	42	1,76,400
II	2,100	20	42,000	1,400	16	22,400
III	1,400	10	14,000	1,400	12	16,800
Total	7,000*		1,96,000	7,000		2,15,600

$$\frac{*5{,}600}{100} \times 125$$

DMCV = Std. cost for actual output – Actual cost

= 1,96,000 – 2,15,600 = ₹19,600 (A)

DMPV = Actual qty. × (SR – AR)

I = 4,200 × (40 – 42) = 8,400 (A)

II = 1,400 × (20 – 16) = 5,600 (F)

III = 1,400 × (10 – 12) = 2,800 (A)

5,600 (A)

DMUV = SR × (Std. qty. for actual output – Actual qty.)

I = 40 × (3,500 – 4,200) = 28,000 (A)

II = 20 × (2,100 – 1,400) = 14,000 (F)

III = 10 × (1,400 – 1,400) = Nil

14,000 (A)

DMMV = SR × (SRQ – AQ)

Since total standard mix and actual mix are the same, the RSQ will be the same as standard quantity.

I = 40 × (3,500 – 4,200) = 28,000 (A)

II = 20 × (2,100 – 1,400) = 14,000 (F)

$$III = 10 \times (1{,}400 - 1{,}400) = 0$$

$$\underline{14{,}000\ (A)}$$

The direct material yield variance will be *nil.*

EXAMPLE 19.9

A company is manufacturing a chemical product making use of four different types of raw materials as follows:

Raw Material	*Share of Total Input (%)*	*Cost of Raw Materials (₹/kg)*
A	40	50
B	30	80
C	20	90
D	10	100

There is an inevitable normal loss of 10% during the processing.
For April 2020, the management furnished the following information:

Raw Material Consumed	*Quantity Consumed (kg)*	*Cost of Material (₹/kg)*
A	42,000	48
B	31,000	80
C	18,000	92
D	9,000	110

Output obtained for the month was 92,000 kg.

Calculate:

(a) Material cost variance,
(b) Material price variance,
(c) Material mix variance,
(d) Material yield variance, and
(e) Material usage variance.

Solution

Standard cost of the finished product is worked out as follows:

Input	*Quantity (kg)*	*Standard Price/kg (₹)*	*Standard Cost (₹)*
A	40	50	2,000
B	30	80	2,400
C	20	90	1,800

(Contd.)

Input	Quantity (kg)	Standard Price/kg (₹)	Standard Cost (₹)
D	10	100	1,000
	100	7,200	7,200
Processing loss	10	–	–
Output	90		7,200
Standard cost per unit (7,200 ÷ 90)			₹80

Computation of variances:

(a) *Material cost variance* = Standard cost of actual finished output – Actual cost of output

$$= 92{,}000 \times 80 - \begin{bmatrix} A = 42{,}000 \times 48 = 20{,}16{,}000 \\ B = 31{,}000 \times 80 = 24{,}80{,}000 \\ C = 18{,}000 \times 92 = 16{,}56{,}000 \\ D = 9{,}000 \times 110 = 9{,}90{,}000 \end{bmatrix}$$

$$71{,}42{,}000$$

= 73,60,000 – 71,42,000 = ₹2,18,000 (F)

(b) *Material price variance* = (Standard price – Actual price) Actual quantity consumed

A = (50 – 48) 42,000 = ₹84,000 (F)

B = (80 – 80) 31,000 = –

C = (90 – 92) 18,000 = ₹36,000 (A)

D = (100 – 110) 9,000 = ₹90,000 (A)

₹42,000 (A)

(c) *Material mix variance* = (Actual input in standard proportion – Actual input) × Standard price

A = (40,000 – 42,000) ₹50 = ₹ 1,00,000 (A)

B = (30,000 – 31,000) ₹80 = ₹ 80,000 (A)

C = (20,000 – 18,000) ₹90 = ₹ 1,80,000 (F)

D = (10,000 – 9,000) ₹100 = ₹ 1,00,000 (F)

₹ 1,00,000 (F)

(d) *Material yield variance* = (Standard yield of actual input – Actual yield) × Standard rate of finished product

= (1,00,000 × 90 – 92,000) × ₹80

= ₹1,60,000 (F)

(e) *Material usage variance* = Standard cost of actual finished output – Stand cost (input) of actual input.

$$₹73{,}60{,}000 - \begin{bmatrix} A = 42{,}000 \times 50 = 20{,}00{,}000 \\ B = 31{,}000 \times 80 = 24{,}80{,}000 \\ C = 18{,}000 \times 90 = 16{,}20{,}000 \\ D = 9{,}000 \times 110 = 9{,}00{,}000 \end{bmatrix} \quad \underline{71{,}00{,}000}$$

= 73,60,000 – 71,00,000

= ₹2,60,000 (F)

(i) Check: Material usage variance = (Mix variance + Yield variance)

= (1,00,000 (F) + 1,60,000 (F)) = ₹2,60,000 (F)

(ii) Material cost variance = Material price variance + Material usage variance

2,18,000 (F) = 42,000 (A) + 2,60,000 (F)

EXAMPLE 19.10

In a manufacturing process, the following standards apply:
Standard prices : Raw material A ₹10 per kg, B ₹50 per kg.
Standard mix : 75% A and 25% B (by weight)
Standard output (weight of product as a percentage of weight of raw material) – 90%
In a particular period, actual costs, usages and output were as follows:
4,400 kg of A costing ₹46,500
1,600 kg of B costing ₹78,500
Output 5,670 kg of product.
The budgeted output for the period was 7,200 kg.
Compute the material cost variances.

Solution

Standard yield from 6,000 kg (4,400 kg + 1,600 kg) of input is

			₹
Material A (75%) 4,500 kg @ ₹10		=	45,000
Material B (25%) 1,500 kg @ ₹50		=	75,000
6,000 kg			1,20,000
Less:			
Normal loss @ 10%	600 kg		
Std. Output	5,400 kg		
Std. cost of actual output of 5,670 kg		=	$\frac{1{,}20{,}000}{5{,}400} \times 5{,}670$
		=	₹1,26,000

(Contd.)

Actual cost of actual output of 5,670 kg

			₹
	4,400 kg × ₹10.568	=	46,500
	1,600 kg × ₹49.063	=	78,500
	6,000 kg		1,25,000
Less actual loss	330 kg		
Actual output	5,670 kg		

(i) Material cost variance = 1,26,000 – 1,25,000 = ₹1,000 (F)

(ii) Material price variance:

A (10 – 10.568) × 4,400 = 2,499.20 (A)

B (50 – 49.063) × 1,600 = 1,499.20 (F)

1,000.00 (A)

(iii) Material usage variance:

₹

$$A \left(\frac{4,500}{5,400} \times 5,670 - 4,400\right) \times 10 = 3,250\ (F)$$

$$B \left(\frac{1,500}{5,400} \times 5,670 - 1,600\right) \times 50 = \frac{1,250\ (A)}{2,000\ (F)}$$

(iv) Material mix variance:

A (4,500 – 4,400) × 10 = 1,000 (F)

B (1,500 – 1,600) × 50 = 5,000 (A)

4,000 (A)

(v) Yield variance $= (5,400 - 5,670) \times \frac{12,00,000}{5,400} = 6,000\ (F)$

✍ EXAMPLE 19.11

A factory manufactures a chemical product with three ingredient chemicals A, B and C as per standard data given below:

Chemical	*Percentage of Total Input*	*Standard Cost Per kg (₹)*
A	50%	40
B	30%	60
C	20%	95

There is a process loss of 5% during the course of manufacture.

The management gives the following details for a certain week:

Chemical Consumed	*Quantity Purchased and Issued*	*Actual Cost (₹)*
A	5,200 kg	2,34,000
B	3,600 kg	2,19,600
C	1,700 kg	1,58,100

Output of finished product: 10,200 kg.
Calculate all the relevant variances.

Solution

Standard Cost of a Chemical Product

Chemical	Percentage of Input	Quantity (kg)	Standard Cost Per kg (₹)	Total Cost ₹
A	50%	0.50	40	20
B	30%	0.30	60	18
C	20%	0.20	95	19
Total input		1.00		57
Less: Loss on processing (5%)		0.05		57
Output		0.95		

Standard cost of a chemical product = $\frac{₹57}{0.95}$ = ₹60

Computation of variances:

(1) *Total Material Cost Variances:*
Standard cost of actual production (output) – Actual material cost for production
= 10,200 × ₹60 – ₹(2,34,000 + 2,19,600 + 1,58,100)
= ₹6,12,000 – ₹6,11,700 = ₹300 (FAV).

(2) *Material Price Variance:*
(Standard price – Actual price) × Actual quantity consumed.

A: [40 – (2,34,000 / 5,200)] × 5,200	₹ 26,000 (A)
B: [60 – (2,19,600 / 3,600)] × 3,600	₹ 3,600 (A)
C: [95 – (1,58,100 / 1,700)] × 1,700	₹ 3,400 (F)
	₹ 26,200 (A)

(3) *Material Mix Variance:*
= (Actual input in standard proportion – Actual input) × Standard cost of input/kg.

A: (0.50 × 10,500 – 5,200) × ₹40	₹ 2,000 (F)
B: (0.30 × 10,500 – 3,600) × ₹60	₹ 27,000 (A)
C: (0.20 × 10,500 – 1,700) × ₹95	₹ 38,000 (F)
	₹ 13,000 (F)

(4) *Yield Variance*
(Standard yield from actual input – Actual output) × Standard cost of finished product
= (10,500 × 0.95 – 10,200) × ₹60 = ₹13,500 (F)

(5) *Usage Variance:*
Standard cost (output) of actual output – Standard cost of actual quantity consumed.

$$= 10{,}200 \times ₹60 - \begin{bmatrix} 5{,}200 \times ₹40 \\ 3{,}600 \times ₹60 \\ 1{,}700 \times ₹95 \end{bmatrix} - ₹6{,}12{,}000 - ₹5{,}85{,}500$$

= ₹26,500 (F)
Usage variance: Mix variance + Yield variance
= ₹13,000 (FAV) + ₹13,500 (FAV) = ₹26,500 (F)
Total material cost variance:
Material price variance + Material usage variance
= ₹26,200 (ADV) + ₹26,500 (F)
= ₹300 (F)

LABOUR VARIANCES

Direct labour variances arise when actual labour costs are different from standard labour costs. Labour variances constitute the following:

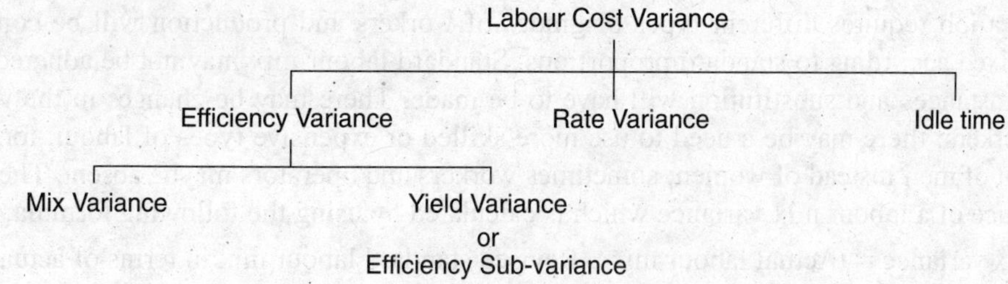

Labour Cost Variance

Labour cost variance denotes the difference between the actual direct wages paid and the standard direct wages specified for the output achieved. This variance is calculated by using the following formula:
Labour cost variance = (AH × AR – SH × SR)

where AH = Actual hours
AR = Actual rate
SH = Standard hours
SR = Standard rate

Labour Efficiency Variance

The calculation of labour efficiency or usage variance follows the same pattern as the computation of materials usage variance. If actual direct labour hours required to complete a job differ from the number of standard hours specified, a labour efficiency variance results; it is the difference between actual hours expended and standard labour hours specified multiplied by the standard labour rate per hour. The formula is:

Labour efficiency variance = (Actual hours – Standard hours for the actual output) × Std. rate per hour.

It may be noted that the standard labour hour rate and not the actual rate is used in computing labour efficiency variance. If quantity variances are calculated, changes in prices/rates are excluded, and when price variances are calculated, standard quantities are ignored.

Labour Rate Variance

Labour rate variance is computed in the same manner as materials price variance. When actual direct labour hour rates differ from standard rates, the result is a labour rate variance. It is that portion of the direct wages variance which is due to the difference between the actual rate paid and standard rate of pay specified. The formula for its calculation is:

Labour rate variance = (Actual rate – Standard rate) × Actual hours

Favourable rate variance arises whenever actual rates are less than standard rates; unfavourable variances occur when actual rates exceed standard rates.

Labour Mix Variance

Labour mix variance is computed in the same manner as materials mix variance. Manufacturing or completing a job requires different types or grades of workers and production will be completed if labour is mixed according to standard proportions. Standard labour mix may not be adhered to under some circumstances and substitution will have to be made. There may be changes in the wage rates of some workers; there may be a need to use more skilled or expensive types of labour, for example, employment of men instead of women; sometimes workers and operators maybe absent. These lead to the emergence of a labour mix variance which is calculated by using the following formula:

Labour mix variance = (Actual labour mix – Revised standard labour mix in terms of actual total hours) × Standard rate per hour

To take an example, suppose the following were the standard labour cost data per unit in a factory:

Class	*Proportion*			*Cost*
	%			₹
A	50	3 hours @	₹4.00	12
B	50	3 hours @	₹2.00	6
	100	6 hours	₹3.00	18

In a period, many class *B* workers were absent and it was necessary to substitute class *B* workers. Since the class *A* workers were less experienced with the job, more labour hours were used. The recorded costs of a unit were:

Class	*Proportions*		*Cost*	
	%		₹	
A	75	6 hours @	₹4.00	24.00
B	25	2 hours @	₹2.00	4.00
	100	8 hours	₹3.50	28.00

Labour mix variance will be calculated as follows:

Labour mix variance = (Actual proportion – Revised standard proportion of actual total hours) × Standard rate per hour

Revised standard proportion:

$$\text{Class } A = \frac{3}{6} \times 8 = 4 \text{ hours}$$

$$\text{Class } B = \frac{3}{6} \times 8 = 4 \text{ hours}$$

Applying the formula:

Class A = (6 – 4) × ₹4 = 8 (Unfavourable)

Class B = (2 – 4) × ₹2 = 4 (Favourable)

Total labour mix variance = ₹4 (Unfavourable)

Labour Yield Variance

The final product cost contains not only material cost but also labour cost. Therefore, higher or lower output than the standard output should take into account of labour yield variance also. A lower output simply means that final output does not correspond with the production units that should have been produced from the hours expended on the inputs. It can be computed by applying the following formula:

Labour yield variance = (Actual output – Standard output based on actual hours) × Average standard labour rate per unit of output

or

Labour yield variance = (Actual loss – Standard loss on actual hours) × Average standard labour rate per unit of output

Labour yield variance is also known as labour efficiency sub-variance which is computed in terms of inputs, i.e. standard labour hours and revised labour hours mix (in terms of actual hours). Labour efficiency sub-variance is computed by using the following formula:

Labour efficiency sub-variance = (Revised standard mix – Standard mix) × Standard labour rate

Substitution Variance This type of variance arises in the case of labour, due to the substitution of labour, that is, when one grade of labour is substituted by another. This variance in fact represents the difference between the actual hours at standard rate of standard worker and the actual hours at standard rate of actual worker.

The formula for computation is:

Substitution variance = (Standard hours × Standard rate for standard worker) – (Standard hours × Standard rate of actual worker)

Idle Time Variance

Idle time variance occurs when workers are not able to do the work due to some reason during the hours for which they are paid. Idle time can be divided according to causes responsible for creating idle time, for example, idle time due to breakdown, lack of materials or power failures. Idle time variance will be equivalent to the standard labour cost of the hours during which no work has been done, but for which workers have been paid for unproductive time. Suppose, in a factory 2,000 workers were idle because of a power failure. As a result of this, a loss of production of 4,000 units of product *A* and 8,000 units of product *B* occurred. Each employee was paid his normal wage (a rate of ₹20 per hour). A single standard hour is needed to manufacture four units of product *A* and eight units of product *B*. Idle time variance will be computed in the following manner:

Standard hours lost:

$$\text{Product } A = \frac{4{,}000}{4} = 1{,}000 \text{ hr}$$

$$\text{Product } B = \frac{8{,}000}{8} = 1{,}000 \text{ hr}$$

$$\text{Total hours lost} = 2{,}000 \text{ hr}$$

Idle time variance (power failure)

2,000 hours @ ₹20 per hour = ₹40,000 (Adverse)

EXAMPLE 19.12

Calculate labour variances from the following information:

Actual hours	5,800
Actual direct wages	₹1,800
Standard rate per hour	₹ 0.35
Standard hours	6,000

Solution

$$\text{Actual Rate (AR)} = \frac{₹1{,}800}{5{,}800} = ₹0.3103448$$

Total standard wage	=	6,000 × 0.35 =	₹2,100
Labour cost variances	=	Std. wage – Actual wage =	2,100 – 1,800 = ₹300 (F)
Labour rate variance	=	AH (SR – AR) =	5,800 (0.35 – 0.3103448) = ₹230 (F)
Labour efficiency variance	=	SR (SH – AH) =	0.35 (6,000 – 5,800) = ₹70 (F)
Labour cost variance	=	LRV + LEV =	230(F) + 70(F) = ₹300 (F)

EXAMPLE 19.13

The standard labour cost for producing 200 metres of cloth was pre-determined as 20 skilled labour hours @ ₹15 per hour and 30 unskilled labour hours @ ₹10 per hour. 300 metres of cloth was produced with the help of 30 skilled labour hours paid @ ₹17 per hour and 30 unskilled labour hours paid @ ₹12 per hour.

Calculate:

(i) Labour mix variance; and
(ii) Labour yield variance.

☞ **Solution**

Labour Mix Variance:

$$A = \left(\frac{30}{75} \times 60 - 30\right) 15 = 90 \text{ (A)}$$

$$B = \left(\frac{45}{75} \times 60 - 30\right) 10 = 60 \text{ (F)}$$

$$₹30 \text{ (A)}$$

Labour Yield Variance

$$A = \left(\frac{300}{75} \times 60 - 300\right) \frac{900}{300} = ₹180 \text{ (F)}$$

✍ EXAMPLE 19.14

The following standard and actual data in respect of Chemical X is made available to you from the records of Naulakha Chemicals Ltd.

		Total
Standard Data:		
Materials:	₹	₹
450 kg of material *A*		
@ ₹20 per kg	9,000	
360 kg of material *B*		
@ ₹10 per kg	3,600	12,600
810		
Labour: @ per hour	₹	
2,400 skilled hours ₹2		4,800
1,200 unskilled hours ₹1		1,200
90 kg Normal loss		–
720 kg		18,600
Actual Data:		Total
Materials:	₹	₹
450 kg of material *A*		
@ ₹19 per kg	8,550	
360 kg of material *B*		
@ ₹11 per kg	3,960	12,510
810		
Labour: @ per hour		
2,400 skilled hours ₹2.25		5,400
1,200 unskilled hours ₹1.25		1,500
50 kg Actual loss		19,410
760		

You are required to compute:

(a) Material cost variance;
(b) Material price variance;
(c) Material yield variance;
(d) Labour cost variance;
(e) Labour rate variance; and
(f) Labour yield variance.

☞ Solution

(a) Material Cost Variance:

$$(RSQ \times SP) - (AQ \times AP)$$

RSQ of Material *A* $= \frac{760}{720} \times 450 = 475$ kg

RSQ of Material *B* $= \frac{760}{720} \times 360 = 380$ kg

Material *A* $= (475 \times 20) - (450 \times 19)$

$= 9{,}500 - 8{,}550 = 950$ (F)

Material *B* $= (380 \times 10) - (360 \times 11)$

$= 3{,}800 - 3{,}960 = \frac{160 \text{ (A)}}{790 \text{ (F)}}$

(b) Material Price Variance:

(SP – AP) AQ		₹
Material A = (20 – 19) × 450 kg		450 (F)
Material B = (10 – 11) × 360 kg		360 (A)
	Total	90 (F)

(c) Material Yield Variance:

Std. price (Std. loss – Actual loss)

$₹\frac{12{,}600}{720}$ (90 kg – 50 kg)

$= \frac{12{,}600}{720} \times 40 = ₹700$ (F)

(d) Labour Cost Variance:

(SH × SR) – (AH × AR)		
Skilled (2,400 × 2) – (2,400 × 2.25)		
4.800 – 5.400 =		₹600 (A)
Unskilled = (1,200 × 1) – (1,200 × 1.25)		
1,200 – 1,500 =		₹300 (A)
	Total	900 (A)

(e) Rate Variance:

(SR – AR) AH

Skilled (₹2 – ₹2.25) × 2,400 = ₹600 (A)
Unskilled (₹1 – ₹1.25) × 1,200 = ₹300 (A)
Total 900 (A)

(f) Labour Yield Variance – NIL

Example 19.15

In a factory, 100 workers are employed and standard average wage rate is ₹50 per hour. Standard working hours per week are 40 and the standard performance is 10 units per hour. During a week, wages paid for 50 workers are at the rate of ₹50 per hour, 10 workers at ₹70 per hour and 40 workers at ₹40 per hour. Actual output was 380 units. The factory did not work for 5 hours due to breakdown of machinery. Calculate labour variances.

Solution

Standard cost = 100 workers × ₹50 × 40 hours	=	₹2,00,000
Standard cost of actual output = ₹2,00,000 × $\frac{380}{400}$	=	₹1,90,000
Actual cost of 50 workers = 50 × ₹50 × 40 hours	=	₹1,00,000
Actual cost of 10 workers = 10 × ₹70 × 40 hours	=	₹ 28,000
Actual cost of 40 workers = 40 × ₹40 × 40 hours	=	₹ 64,000
Total actual cost	=	₹1,92,000

1. *Labour Cost Variance* = Standard cost of actual output – Actual cost
   = ₹1,90,000 – ₹1,92,000 = ₹2,000 (A)
2. *Labour Rate Variance* = This variance is calculated in three parts as follows:
   (Standard rate – Actual rate) × Actual hours

   (i) (₹50 – ₹50) × 50 workers × 40 hours = Nil
   (ii) (₹50 – ₹70) × 10 workers × 40 hours = ₹ 8,000 (A)
   (iii) (₹50 – ₹40) × 40 workers × 40 hours = ₹16,000 (F)
   Total labour rate variance = ₹ 8,000 (F)
3. *Labour Efficiency Variance* = (SH – AH) × Standard rate
   $= \frac{380 \text{ units}}{10 \text{ units}} \times 100 \text{ workers} - [(40 \text{ hrs} - 50 \text{ hrs}) \times 100 \text{ workers}] \times ₹50$
   = (3,800 – 3,500) × ₹50 = ₹15,000 (F)
4. *Idle Time Variance* = Idle hours × Standard rate
   = 5 hrs. × 100 workers × ₹50 = ₹25,000 (A)

Example 19.16

The standard labour employment and the actual labour engaged in a week for a job are as under:

	Skilled Workers	*Semi-skilled Workers*	*Unskilled Workers*
Standard no. of workers in the gang	32	12	6
Actual no. of workers employed	28	18	4
Standard wage rate per hour (₹)	3	2	1
Actual wage rate per hour (₹)	4	3	2

for excel template, scan

→ During the 40 hours working week, the gang produced 1,800 standard labour hours of work. Calculate:

(a) Labour cost variance;
(b) Labour rate variance;
(c) Labour efficiency variance;
(d) Labour mix variance;
(e) Labour yield variance.

☞ ***Solution***

	Standard			*Actual*		
	Hours	*Rate*	*Amount*	*Hours*	*Rate*	*Amount*
Skilled	1,280	3	3,840	1,120	4	4,480
Semi-skilled	480	2	960	720	3	2,160
Unskilled	240	1	240	160	2	320
	2,000		5,040	2,000		6,960

Labour Cost Variance = SC – AC

$$= \left(\frac{5,040}{2,000} \times 1,800\right) - 6,960 = \text{₹}\mathbf{2,424\ (A)}$$

Labour Rate Variance = (SR – AR) × AH

Skilled	(3 – 4) × 1,120	=	1,120 (A)
Semi-skilled	(2 – 3) × 720	=	720 (A)
Unskilled	(1 – 2) × 160	=	160 (A)
		=	**₹2,000 (A)**

Labour Efficiency Variance = (ST* – AT) × SR

Skilled	(1,152 – 1,120) × 3	=	96 (F)
Semi-skilled	(432 – 720) × 2	=	576 (A)
Unskilled	(216 – 160) × 1	=	56 (F)
		=	**424 (A)**

Labour Mix Variance = (RST – AT) × SR

Skilled	(1,280 – 1,120) × 3	=	480 (F)
Semi-skilled	(480 – 720) × 2	=	480 (A)
Unskilled	(240 – 160) × 1	=	80 (F)
		=	**80 (F)**

Labour Revised Efficiency Variance = (ST* – RST) × SR

Skilled	(1,152 – 1,280) × 3	=	384 (A)
Semi-skilled	(432 – 480) × 2	=	96 (A)
Unskilled	(216 – 240) × 1	=	24 (A)
		=	**504 (A)**

Verification:

Labour cost variance	= Labour rate variance	+ Labour efficiency variance
2,424 (A)	= 2,000 (A)	+ 424 (A)

Labour efficiency variance = Labour mix variance + Labour revised efficiency variance
424 (A) = 80 (F) + 504 (A)

EXAMPLE 19.17

The following standards have been set to manufacture a product by a company:

	₹
Direct Material:	
2 units of "*A*" @ ₹4 per unit	8.00
3 units of "*B*" @ ₹3 per unit	9.00
15 units of "*C*" @ ₹1 per unit	15.00
Direct Labour:	
3 lab. hrs. @ ₹8 per lab. hr.	24.00
Total standard prime cost	56.00

The company had manufactured and sold 6,000 units of the product during the year. Direct material costs incurred were as follows:

12,500 units of "*A*" @ ₹4.40 per unit
18,000 units of "*B*" @ ₹2.80 per unit
88,500 units of "*C*" @ ₹1.20 per unit

The company worked for 17,500 direct labour hours during the year. For 2,500 of these labour hours, the company paid @ ₹12 per labour hr., while for the remaining labour hrs,. it paid at the standard rate. You are required to calculate:

(i) Material price, usage, mixture and yield variances;
(ii) Labour rate and efficiency variances.

Solution

	Standard for 6,000 units			*Actual*		
	Qty.	*Rate (₹)*	*Amt (₹)*	*Qty.*	*Rate (₹)*	*Amt (₹)*
A	12,000	4	48,000	12,500	4.40	55,000
B	18,000	3	54,000	18,000	2.80	50,400
C	90,000	1	90,000	88,500	1.20	1,06,200
Total	1,20,000		1,92,000	1,19,000		2,11,600

(i) 1. *Material Price Variance* = (SP – AP) × AQ

A = (4 – 4.40) × 12,500 = ₹ 5,000 (A)
B = (3 – 2.80) × 18,000 = ₹ 3,600 (F)
C = (1 – 1.20) × 88,500 = ₹17,700 (A)
MPV = ₹19,100 (A)

2. *Material Usage Variance* = (SQ – AQ) × SP

A = (12,000 – 12,500) × 4 = ₹2,000 (A)
B = (18,000 – 18,000) × 3 = ₹ Nil
C = (90,000 – 88,500) × 1 = ₹1,500 (F)
MUV = ₹ 500 (A)

3. *Material Mix Variance* = (RSQ – AQ) × SP

$$A = \left(1{,}19{,}000 \times \frac{12{,}000}{1{,}20{,}000} - 12{,}500\right) \times 4 = ₹2{,}400\ (A)$$

$$B = \left(1{,}19{,}000 \times \frac{18{,}000}{1{,}20{,}000} - 18{,}000\right) \times 3 = ₹450\ (A)$$

$$C = \left(1{,}19{,}000 \times \frac{90{,}000}{1{,}20{,}000} - 88{,}500\right) \times 1 = ₹750\ (F)$$

MMV = **₹2,100 (A)**

4. *Material Yield Variance* = (Actual yield – Standard yield) × SP

MYV $= (6{,}000 - 5{,}950^*) \times \frac{₹1{,}92{,}000}{6{,}000 \text{ units}} = ₹1{,}600\ (F)$

*Standard yield $= 6{,}000 \text{ units} \times \frac{1{,}19{,}000}{1{,}20{,}000} = 5{,}950$ units

(ii) *Labour Variance:*

Standard labour cost = 18,000 hrs. × ₹8 = ₹1,44,000

Actual cost = (2,500 × ₹12) + (15,000 × ₹8) = ₹1,50,000

Labour rate variance = (SR – AR) × AH
= (8 – 12) × 2,500 + (8 – 8) × 1,500 = ₹10,000 (A)

Labour efficiency variance = (SH – AH) × SR
= (18,000 – 17,500) × 8 = ₹4,000 (F)

EXAMPLE 19.18

Standard hours for producing two products *A* and *B* are 15 hours and 20 hours per unit respectively. Both products require identical type of labour and the standard wage rate is ₹5 per hour. In a year 10,000 units of *A* and 15,000 units of *B* were produced. The total labour hours actually worked were 4,50,500 and actual wage bill came to ₹23,00,000. This included 12,000 hours paid for at ₹7 per hour and 9,400 hours paid for @ ₹7.50 per hour, the balance having been paid at ₹5 per hour.

You are required to compute labour cost variance, labour rate variance and labour efficiency variance.

Solution

Standard Cost = 10,000 units × 15 hours × ₹5 = ₹ 7,50,000
+ 15,000 units × 20 hours × ₹5 = ₹15,00,000
Total = ₹22,50,000

Labour Cost Variance = Standard cost – Actual cost
= 22,50,000 – 23,00,000 = **₹50,000 (A)**

Labour Rate Variance = (Standard rate – Actual rate) × Actual hours
= (5 – 7) × 12,000 + (5 – 7.50) × 9,400 + (5 – 5) × 4,29,100
= 24,000 (A) + 23,500 (A) + Nil = **₹47,500 (A)**

Labour Efficiency Variance = (Standard hours – Actual hours) × Standard rate
= (4,50,000 – 4,50,500) × 5 = **₹2,500 (A)**

EXAMPLE 19.19

Standard labour cost of producing 40 units of a product is 30 hours work by skilled workers at a standard rate of ₹60 per hour and 90 hours work by unskilled workers at the standard rate of ₹20 per hour. 40 units of the product were produced for which skilled workers were paid for 20 hours at ₹55 per hour and unskilled workers were paid for 130 hours at ₹24 per hour. Due to a machine breakdown, both skilled and unskilled workers lost 9 hours each. They were paid even for this time.

Calculate:

(i) Labour cost variance;
(ii) Labour rate variance;
(iii) Labour efficiency variance unadjusted;
(iv) Labour mix variance;
(v) Labour yield variance; and
(vi) Idle time variance.

Solution

Standard Cost for 40 units

	Hours	*Rate* ₹	*Amount* ₹
Skilled	30	60	1,800
Unskilled	90	20	1,800
	120		3,600

Actual Cost

	Hours	*Rate* ₹	*Amount* ₹
Skilled	20	55	1,100
Unskilled	130	24	3,120
	150		4,220

(i) Labour cost variance = Standard cost – Actual cost
= 3,600 – 4,220 = **₹620 (A)**

(ii) Labour rate variance = (Standard rate – Actual rate) × Actual hrs.

Skilled	= (60 – 55) × 20	= ₹100 (F)
Unskilled	= (20 – 24) × 130	= ₹520 (A)
	Total	**420 (A)**

(iii) Labour efficiency variance = (Standard hrs. – Actual hrs.) × Standard rate

Skilled	= (30 – 20) × 60	= ₹600 (F)
Unskilled	= (90 – 130) × 20	= ₹800 (A)
	Total	**200 (A)**

(iv) For calculating labour mix variance and labour yield variance, idle hours are excluded from actual hours, *i.e.*

Skilled	= 20 hrs. – 9 hrs	=	11 hrs.
Unskilled	= 130 hrs. – 9 hrs.	=	121 hrs
	Total		**132 hrs.**

Revised standard hours (RSH) are calculated as follows:

Skilled	= 132 × 30/120	= 33
Unskilled	= 132 × 90/120	= 99
	Total	**132**

Labour mix variance = (RSH – Actual hrs,) × Standard rate

Skilled	= (33 – 11) × 60	= ₹1,320 (F)
Unskilled	= (99 – 121) × 20	= ₹ 440 (A)
	Total	**₹ 880 (F)**

(v) Labour yield variance = (Actual yield – Standard yield) × Standard output rate

$$= (40 \text{ units} - 132 \times \frac{40}{120} \text{ units}) \times \frac{3{,}600\ (₹)}{40 \text{ units}}$$

$= (40 - 44) \times 90 =$ **₹360 (A)**

(vi) Idle time variance = Idle hrs. × Standard rate

Skilled	= 9 × 60	= ₹540 (A)
Unskilled	= 9 × 20	= ₹180 (A)
	Total	**₹720 (A)**

✍ EXAMPLE 19.20

The following information is available from the cost records of Vatika & Co. for the month of August, 2020:

Material purchased 24,000 kg ₹1,05,600

Material consumed 22,800 kg

Actual wages paid for 5,940 hours ₹29,700

Unit produced 2,160 units.

Standard rates and prices are:

Direct material rate is ₹4.00 per unit

Direct labour rate is ₹4.00 per hour

Standard input is 10 kg for one unit

Standard requirement is 2.5 hours per unit.

Calculate all material and labour variances for the month of August, 2020.

☞ Solution

Material Variances:

(i) Material cost variance
= (SQ × SP) – (AQ × AP)
= (2,160 × 4 × 10) – (22,800 × 4.40)
= ₹86,400 – ₹1,00,320 = 13,920 (A)

(ii) Material price variance
= AQ (SP – AP)
= 22,800 kg (4 – 4.40) = 9,120 (A)

(iii) Material usage variance
= SP (SQ – AQ)
= 4 (21,600 – 22,800) = 4,800 (A)

Verification:
MCV = MPV + MUV
13,920 (A) = 9,120 (A) + 4,800 (A)

Labour Variances:

(i) Labour cost variance
= (SH × SR) – (AH × AR)
= (2,160 × 2.50 × 4) – (29,700)
= 21,600 – 29,700 = 8,100 A

(ii) Labour rate variance
= AH (SR – AR)
= 5,940 (4 – 5) = 5,940 (A)

(iii) Labour efficiency variance
= SR (SH – AH)
= 4 (5,400 – 5,940) = 2,160 (A)

Verification:
LCV = LRV + LEV
8,100 (A) = 5,940 (A) + 2,160 (A)
SH = 2,160 units × 2.50 hours = 5,400 hrs.

EXAMPLE 19.21

A building can be constructed by engaging a gang of workers as per details given below, for 100 working days of eight hours each.

Standard Data:

	Skilled	*Semi-skilled*	*Unskilled*
No. of workers in the gang	6	8	6
Standard rate of wages/hr	₹25	₹20	₹16

Actual completion of the work, however, took 104 days of eight hours each. This includes 16 hours of stoppages due to heavy rains. The actual number of workers engaged and the actual rates paid are given below:

	Skilled	*Semi-skilled*	*Unskilled*
Number engaged	8	6	6
Actual rate/hr.	₹30	₹24	₹16

Calculate the following variances:

(a) Labour cost variances
(b) Labour rate variance
(c) Labour efficiency variance

(d) Labour mix variance
(e) Idle time variance

(i) Standard Labour Cost:

			Days' hrs.		
Skilled workers	=	6 Nos. @ ₹25 for	100 × 8	=	₹1,20,000
Semi-skilled workers	=	8 Nos. @ ₹20 for	100 × 8	=	₹ 1,28,000
Unskilled workers	=	6 Nos. @ ₹16 for	100 × 8	=	₹ 76,800
					₹3,24,800

Standard gang time	=	800 hours.		
Standard gang rate/hr.	=	₹3,24,800 ÷ 800	=	₹406/hr.

(ii) Actual Labour Cost:

		No.		Days		Hr. day		Rate	=	₹
Skilled workers	=	8	×	104	×	8	×	₹30	=	₹1,99,680
Semi-skilled workers	=	6	×	104	×	8	×	₹24	=	₹1,19,808
Unskilled workers	=	6	×	104	×	8	×	₹16	=	₹ 79,872
										₹3,99,360

(iii) Standard Labour Cost for Actual Hours of Actual Gang:

			Days' hrs.		
Skilled workers	=	8 Nos. @ ₹25 for	104 × 8	=	₹ 1,66,400
Semi-skilled workers	=	6 Nos. @ ₹20 for	104 × 8	=	₹ 99,840
Unskilled workers	=	6 Nos. @ ₹16 for	104 × 8	=	₹ 79,872
					₹ 3,46,112

(iv) Standard Labour Cost for Actual Hours of Standard Gang:

			Days' hrs.		
Skilled workers	=	6 Nos. @ ₹25 for	104 × 8	=	₹1,24,800
Semi-skilled workers	=	8 Nos. @ ₹20 for	104 × 8	=	₹1,33,120
Unskilled workers	=	6 Nos. @ ₹16 for	104 × 8	=	₹ 79,872
					₹3,37,792

(v) Standard Labour Cost for Actual Hours Utilised for Completion of the Work.

(104 × 8 – 16) × ₹406 = ₹3,31,296

Calculation of Variances:

(a) Labour Cost Variance:

(Actual labour cost – Std cost of actual hours utilised for completion of the work):
(3,99,360 – 3,31,296) = ₹68,064 (Adv.)

(*b*) *Labour Rate Variance:*
(Actual labour cost – Std labour cost for actual hours of actual gang):
(3,99,360 – 3,46,112) = ₹53,248 (Adv.)

(*c*) *Labour Efficiency Variance:* (Std labour cost of actual hrs – Std. labour cost of actual hrs. utilised for completion of the work):
= (3,46,112 – 3,31,269) = ₹14,816 (Adv.)

(*d*) *Labour Mix Variance:* (Std labour cost of actual hours – Std labour cost of actual hrs in Std mix)
= (3,46,112 – 3,37,792) = ₹8,320 (Adv.)

(*e*) *Idle Time Variance* = Idle time × Std rate = 16 × 406 = ₹6,496 (Adv)
Alternatively: Labour cost variance: (Labour rate variance + Labour efficiency variance)
= [53,248 (A) + 14,816 (A)]
= ₹68,064 (Adv.)
Labour efficiency variance = (Labour mix var. + Idle time var.)
= [8,320 (A) + 6,496 (A)]
= ₹14,816 (Adv.)

EXAMPLE 19.22

The following cost data are available for the year 2020:

	Budgeted		*Actual*
Fixed overhead	96,000	(yearly)	8,500 (monthly)
Working days	300	(yearly)	–
Production (units)	24,000	(yearly)	2,100 (monthly)
Working hours in a day	8		–
Idle time (hrs.)	–		4

Find out idle time variance.

Solution

Let FO_2 stand for budgeted fixed overhead for one month = ₹96,000/12 = ₹8,000
Let FO_3 stand for standard fixed overhead for hours available during the period at standard rate.

$$= \frac{\text{Fixed overhead for one month}}{\text{Budgeted hours} \times \text{Hours available in a month}}$$

$$= \frac{₹8{,}000}{\dfrac{\text{Budgeted hours available in a year}}{12}} \times \text{Hours available in a year}$$

$$= \frac{₹8{,}000}{\dfrac{300 \text{ days} \times 8 \text{ hours}}{12}} \text{(Budgeted hrs. for a month – Idle hrs)}$$

$$= \frac{₹8{,}000}{200 \text{ hrs}} (200 \text{ hrs} - 4) = \frac{₹8{,}000}{200}\ 196 \text{ or } ₹7{,}840$$

Idle time variance = $FO_2 - FO_3$
= ₹8,000 – ₹7,840 = ₹160 (A)

EXAMPLE 19.23

Stanley & Co. manufactures door frames from a bought-in wooden moulding. The budget for one door frame has costs of ₹20 for materials and ₹6 for labour. Each frame has a standard usage of 5 metres of wooden moulding at a standard cost of ₹4.00 per metre. Each frame has a standard time of 0.50 hours and the standard rate of pay is ₹12.00 per hour.

The budget for April was for 2,200 frames with a material cost of ₹44,000 and a labour cost of ₹13,200.

However, 2,100 frames were actually produced in April, taking 1,000 hours to make at a total labour cost of ₹13,000. Also, 11,550 metres of wooden moulding were used at a total cost of ₹43,890.

Required:

1. Calculate the cost, quantity and price variances of materials and labour in April.
2. Suggest possible reasons for these variances.
3. If 50 of the 1,000 hours paid were during a power cut which prevented work continuing, what changes would you make to your answers to parts 1 and 2?

Solution

Workings:

Flexed Budget (For 2,100 Frames)

			₹
Materials:	2,100 × 5.0 m × ₹4.00/m	= 10,500 m × ₹4.00/m	= 42,000
Labour:	2,100 × 0.50 h × ₹12.00/h	= 1,050 h × ₹12.00/h	= 12,600
		Total	= 54,600

Actual Performance (For 2,100 Frames)

Materials:	11,550 m × ₹3.80/m	= 43,890
Labour:	1,000 h × ₹13.00/h	=13,000
	Total	= 56,890

1. Variance Calculations

Materials usage:	(BQ – AQ)BP	
	(10,500 – 11,550)4.00	**= (4,200) A**
Materials price:	(BP – AP)AQ	
	(4.00 – 3.80)11,550	**= 2,310 F**
Materials cost:	Budgeted cost – actual cost	
	42,000 – 43,890	**= (1,890) A**
Labour efficiency:	(BQ – AQ)BP	
	(1,050 – 1,000)12.00	**= 600 F**

Labour rate:	(BP – AP)AQ	
	(12.00 – 13.00)1,000	= (1,000) A
Labour cost:	Budgeted cost – actual cost	
	12,600 – 13,000	= (400) A

2. Possible Explanations for Variances

Materials usage = (4,200)A	– wastage from poorer-quality materials
	– wastage due to demotivated workforce
	– out-of-date standards
Materials price = 2,310 F	– lower-priced substitute material used
	– unexpected discounts achieved
	– lower prices from new supplier
	– out-of-date standards
Labour efficiency = 600 F	– motivated workforce due to pay rise
	– more highly skilled type of labour used
	– out-of-date standards
Labour rate = (1,000) A	– recent pay rise
	– some overtime at premium rates may have occurred
	– out-of-date standards

3. Amendments

The payment of "idle time" during the power cut affects the labour efficiency variance only.

Labour efficiency:	(BQ – AQ ***worked***)BP	
	(1,050 – 950)12.00	= 1,200 F
Idle time:	Idle hours × budgeted rate	
	–50 × 12.00	= (600) A
	Combined (as previous)	= 600 F

It was originally thought that the operatives had worked efficiently by saving 50 hours at ₹12 = ₹600 (50/1,050 = 4.8% improvement on standard). It is now clear that they were twice as efficient as originally thought as they saved 100 hours at ₹12 = ₹1,200 (100/1,050 = 9.5% improvement on standard).

OVERHEAD VARIANCES

The analysis of factory overhead variances is more complex than variance analysis for direct materials and direct labour. Generally, overhead variances constitute the following variances:

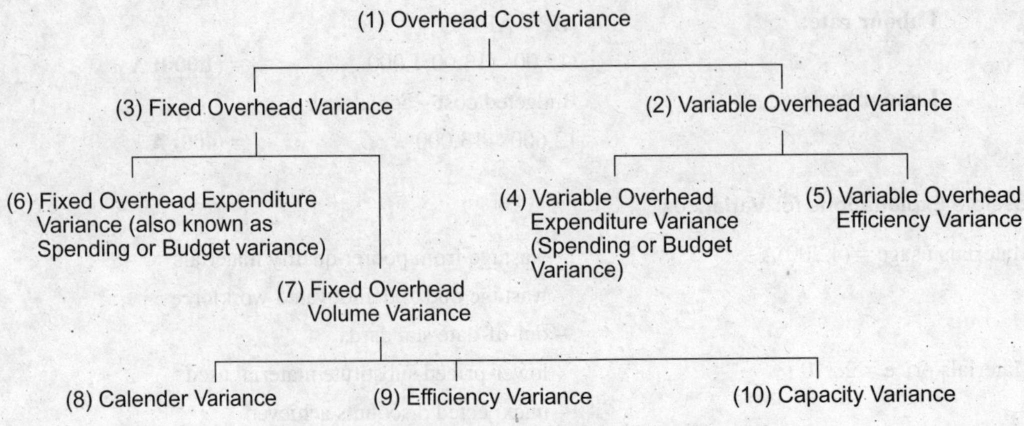

Fig. 19.2 Types of Overhead Cost Variances

Total Overhead Cost Variance

This overall overhead variance is the difference between the actual overhead cost incurred and the standard cost of overhead for the output achieved. This can be computed by applying the following formula:

(Actual overhead incurred – Standard hours for the actual output × Standard overhead rate per hour)

or

Actual overhead incurred – (Actual output × Standard overhead rate per unit)

To illustrate the overall overhead variance, assume that the actual overhead for a department amounts to ₹10,00,000 for the month of January, 2020 and standard (or allowed) hours for work performed total 4,500 hours, while actual hours used are 5,000. If overhead rate is ₹200 per hour, the overall overhead variance will be the following:

Actual department overhead	₹10,00,000
Overhead charged to production	
(4,500 hr × ₹200)	₹ 9,00,000
Overall or net overhead variance	
(Unfavourable)	₹1,00,000

Variable Overhead Variance

It is the difference between actual variable overhead cost and standard variable overhead allowed for the actual output achieved. The formula for computing this variance is as follows:

Actual overhead cost – (Actual output × Variable overhead rate per unit)

or

Actual overhead cost – (Standard hours for actual output × Standard variable overhead rate per hour)

Fixed Overhead Variance

This variance indicates the difference between the actual fixed overhead cost and standard fixed overhead cost allowed for the actual output. This variance is found by using the following formula.

Fixed overhead variance = Actual overhead cost – Fixed overhead absorbed

or

Actual overhead cost – (Standard hours for actual output × Standard fixed overhead rate per hour).

Variable Overhead Expenditure (Spending or Budget) Variance

This variance indicates the difference between actual variable overhead and budgeted variable overhead based on actual hours worked. This variance is found by using the following formula:

(Actual variable overhead – Budgeted variable overhead)

Variable Overhead Efficiency Variance

This variance is like labour efficiency variance and arises when actual hours worked differ from standard hours required for good units produced. The actual quantity produced and standard quantity fixed might be different because of higher or lower efficiency of workers employed in the manufacturing of goods. This variance is found by using the following formula:

(Actual hours – Standard hours for actual output) × Standard variable overhead rate per hour

Fixed Overhead Expenditure (Spending or Budget) Variance

This variance indicates the difference between actual fixed overhead and budgeted fixed overhead. The formula for computing this variance is as follows:

(Actual fixed overhead – Budgeted fixed overhead)

If actual fixed overhead costs are greater than budgeted fixed costs, an unfavourable variance results because actual costs exceed the budget. Actual overhead costs seldom equal budgeted costs because property tax rates may change, insurance premiums may increase or equipment charges may affect depreciation rates. As an illustration, assume that a company completed 36,000 units (equal to 18,000 standard productive hours) in 18,500 hours at the recorded fixed cost of ₹75,100. The standard fixed cost rate per hour is ₹4. Therefore,

Expenditure variance = (Actual overhead costs – Budgeted overhead costs)

That is = (75,100 – 18,500 × 4)

= (75,100 – 74,000)

= ₹1,100 (unfavourable)

The expenditure or budget variance provides management with information which helps in controlling costs. The budget variance is usually prepared on a departmental basis and the factors that cause the budget variance are, therefore, controllable by departmental managers.

Fixed Overhead Volume Variance

Volume variance relates to only fixed overhead. This variance arises due to the difference between the standard fixed overhead cost allowed (absorbed) for the actual output and the budgeted fixed overhead based on standard hours allowed for actual output achieved during the period. The variance shows the over- or under-absorption of fixed overheads during a particular period. If the actual output is more than the standard output, there is over-absorption and variance is favourable. If actual output is less than the standard output, the volume variance is unfavourable. The formula for computing this variance is as follows:

(Budgeted overhead applied to actual output – Budgeted fixed overhead based on standard hours allowed for actual output)

or

(Actual production – Budgeted production) × Standard fixed overhead rate per unit

Volume variance is further sub-divided into three variances.

Fixed Overhead Calendar Variance

It is that portion of volume variance which is due to the difference between the number of actual working days in the period to which the budget is applicable and budgeted number of days in the budget period.

If actual working days is more than the budgeted working days, the variance is favourable as work has been done on days more than budgeted or allowed and vice versa. The formula is as follows:

(No. of actual working days – No. of budgeted working days) × Standard fixed overhead rate per day

Calendar variance can be computed based on hours or output. Then the formulae are:

Hours Basis

Calendar variance = (Revised budget capacity hours – Budgeted hours) × Standard fixed overhead rate per hour

If revised budgeted capacity hours are more than the budgeted hours, the variance will be favourable. In the reverse situation, the variance will be unfavourable.

Output Basis

Calendar variance = (Revised budgeted quantity in terms of actual number of days worked – Budgeted quantity) × Standard fixed overhead rate per unit

If revised budgeted quantity is more than the budgeted quantity, the variance is favourable; if revised budgeted quantity is less, the variance will be unfavourable.

Fixed Overhead Efficiency Variance

It is that portion of volume variance which arises when actual hours of production used for actual output differ from the standard hours specified for that output. If actual hours worked are less than the standard hours, the variance is favourable and when actual hours are more than the standard hours, the variance is unfavourable. The formula is:

Fixed overhead efficiency variance = (Actual hours – Standard hours for actual production)× Standard fixed overhead rate per hour

or

Fixed overhead efficiency variance = (Actual production – Standard production as per actual time available) × Standard fixed overhead rate per unit

Fixed Overhead Capacity Variance

It is that part of fixed overhead volume variance which is due to the difference between the actual capacity (in hours) worked during a given period and the budgeted capacity (expressed in hours). The formula is:

Capacity variance = (Actual capacity hours – Budgeted capacity hours)
× Standard fixed overhead rate per hour

This variance represents idle time also. If actual capacity hours are more than the budgeted capacity hours, the variance is favourable and if actual capacity hours are less than the budgeted capacity hours, the variance will be unfavourable.

In case actual number of days and budgeted number of days are also given, then budgeted capacity hours will be calculated in terms of actual number of days and it will be known as revised budgeted capacity hours, that is, budgeted hours for actual days worked. In this situation, the formula for calculating capacity variance will be as follows:

Capacity variance = (Actual capacity hours – Revised budgeted capacity hours)
× Standard fixed overhead rate per hour

In the above formula, the variance will be favourable if actual capacity hours are more than the revised budgeted hours. However, if actual capacity hours are lesser than the revised budgeted hours, the variance will be adverse as lesser hours means that lesser actual hours have been worked taking the actual days utilised into account.

Two-way, Three-way and Four-way Variance Analysis

The above overhead variances are also classified as Two-way, Three-way and Four-way variance. The different variances under these categories are listed below. The formulae for computing these variances are similar to as explained in the preceding section.

A. Two-way Variance Analysis

1. Controllable variance (Budget variance)
2. Volume variance (Uncontrollable variance)

B. Three-way Variance Analysis

1. Expenditure variance (Spending variance)
2. Capacity variance
3. Efficiency variance

C. Four-way Variance Analysis

1. Expenditure variance (Spending variance)
2. Variable overhead efficiency variance
3. Fixed overhead efficiency variance
4. Capacity variance

EXAMPLE 19.24

From the following data, calculate fixed overhead variances:

Hours, when working at normal capacity	2,000
Fixed overhead hourly rate	₹2
Hours allowed for actual production	1,600
Actual details: Hours	1,550
Overheads	₹3,750

Solution

(1) *Overhead Cost Variance:*

= Absorbed overheads – Actual overheads

= (1,600 hours × ₹2) – ₹3,750 = ₹550(A)

(2) *Overhead Budget Variance:*

= Budgeted overheads – Actual overheads

= (2,000 hours × ₹2) – ₹3,750 = ₹250(F)

(3) *Overhead Volume Variance:*

= Absorbed overheads – Budgeted overheads

= (1,600 hours × ₹2) – (2,000 hours × ₹2) = ₹800(A)

(4) *Overhead Efficiency Variance:*

= Absorbed overheads – Standard overheads

= (1,600 hours × ₹2) – (1,550 hours × ₹2) = ₹100(F)

(5) *Overhead Capacity Variance:*

= Standard overheads – Budgeted overheads

= (1,550 hours × ₹2) – (2,000 hours × ₹2) = ₹900(A)

EXAMPLE 19.25

A company has a normal capacity of 120 machines working 8 hours per day for 25 days in a month. The fixed overheads are budgeted at ₹1,44,000 per month. The standard time required to manufacture one unit of product is 4 hours.

In November 2020, the company worked for 24 days utilising 840 machine hours per day and produced 5,305 units of output. The actual fixed overheads were ₹1,42,000.

You are required to calculate:

(i) Total Fixed Overhead Cost Variance;
(ii) Fixed Overheads Budget/Expenditure Variance;
(iii) Fixed Overheads Volume Variance;
(iv) Fixed Overheads Capacity Variance;
(v) Fixed Overheads Efficiency Variance; and
(vi) Fixed Overheads Calendar Variance.

Solution

$$\text{Budgeted overhead rate} = \frac{₹1{,}44{,}000}{\text{120 machines 8 hours 25 days}} = ₹6 \text{ per unit}$$

(i) *Total Fixed Overheads Cost Variance:*

= Absorbed overheads – Actual overheads

= [5,305 units × 4 hrs. × ₹6] – ₹1,42,000

= ₹1,27,320 – ₹1,42,000 = **₹14,680 (A)**

(ii) *Fixed Overheads Budget/Expenditure Variance:*

= Budgeted overheads – Actual overheads

= ₹1,44,000 – ₹1,42,000

= **₹2,000 (F)**

(iii) *Fixed Overheads Volume Variance:*

= Absorbed overheads – Budgeted overheads

= (5,305 units × 4 hrs. × ₹6) – ₹1,44,000

= ₹1,27,320 – ₹1,44,000 = **₹16,680 (A)**

(iv) *Fixed Overheads Capacity Variance:*

= Standard overheads – Revised budgeted overheads

$$= (₹20,160 \times ₹6) - \left(1,44,000 \times \frac{24 \text{ days}}{25 \text{ days}}\right)$$

= ₹1,20,960 – ₹1,38,240 = **₹17,280 (A)**

(v) *Fixed Overheads Efficiency Variance:*

= Absorbed overheads – Standard overheads

= (5,305 units × 4 hrs. × ₹6) – (₹20,160 × ₹6)

= ₹1,27,320 – ₹1,20,960 = **₹6,360 (F)**

(vi) *Fixed Overheads Calendar Variance:*

= (Actual days – Standard days) × St. rate per day

$$= (24 - 25) \times \frac{₹1,44,000}{25 \text{ days}} = \textbf{₹5,760 (A)}$$

Verification:

Total F.O. cost variance = Budget variance + Volume variance

₹14,680 (A) = ₹2,000 (F) + ₹16,680 (A)

Volume variance = Capacity variance + Efficiency variance + Calendar variance

₹16,680 (A) = ₹17,280 (A) + ₹6,360 (F) + ₹5,760 (A)

EXAMPLE 19.26

A company using standard costing system has the following information for the budget period:

Budgeted variable overheads = ₹8,00,000

Budgeted fixed overheads = ₹5,00,000

Overheads are recovered on the basis of standard machine hours. The company had budgeted for 100,000 machine hours for the year.

During the budge period the company used 1,10,000 machine hours while it should have used 95,000 machine hours for actual output.

Actual variable overheads ₹8,00,000

Actual fixed overheads ₹4,70,000

Calculate the following variances:

(i) Variable Overhead Cost Variance;
(ii) Variable Overhead Spending Variance;
(iii) Variable Overhead Efficiency Variance;
(iv) Fixed Overhead Cost Variance;
(v) Fixed Overhead Expenditure Variance;
(vi) Fixed Overhead Volume Variance;
(vii) Fixed Overhead Efficiency Variance; and
(viii) Fixed Overhead Capacity Variance.

☞ **Solution**

$$\text{Budgeted fixed overheads per standard hour} = \frac{\text{Budgeted fixed overheads}}{\text{Budgeted std. hours}} = \frac{₹5,00,000}{100,000} = ₹5$$

$$\text{Budgeted variable overheads per standard hour} = \frac{\text{Budgeted variable overheads}}{\text{Budgeted std. hours}}$$

$$= \frac{₹8,00,000}{1,00,000} = ₹8$$

(i) $\text{Variable overhead cost variance} = \begin{array}{c}\text{Budgeted variable overhead}\\ \text{for actual output}\end{array} - \begin{array}{c}\text{Actual variable overheads}\\ \text{for actual output}\end{array}$

= (Budgeted variable overheads per standard hour × Actual output in Std. hrs) – Actual variable overheads

= (8 × 95,000) – ₹8,00,000 = ₹7,60,000 – ₹8,00,000 = ₹40,000 (A)

(ii) Variable overhead spending variance = Budgeted variable overheads – Actual variable overheads

= ₹8,00,000 – ₹8,00,000 = Nil

(iii) $\begin{array}{c}\text{Variable overheads}\\ \text{efficiency variance}\end{array} = \begin{array}{c}\text{Budgeted variable overheads}\\ \text{per standard hour}\end{array}\left(\begin{array}{c}\text{Budgeted output in}\\ \text{standard hours}\end{array} - \begin{array}{c}\text{Actual output in}\\ \text{standard hours}\end{array}\right)$

= 8(1,00,000 – 95,000) = ₹40,000 (A)

$\text{Variable overhead cost variance} = ₹40,000\ (A) = \left(\begin{array}{c}\text{Variable overheads}\\ \text{spanding variance}\end{array} - \begin{array}{c}\text{Variable overhead}\\ \text{efficiency variance}\end{array}\right)$

= Nil + ₹40,000 (A) = ₹40,000 (A)

(iv) $\text{Fixed overheads cost variance} = \begin{array}{c}\text{Budgeted fixed overheads}\\ \text{for actual output}\end{array} - \begin{array}{c}\text{Actual fixed overheads}\\ \text{for actual output}\end{array}$

= (Budgeted fixed overheads per standard hour × Actual output in standard hours) – Actual fixed overheads

= ₹5 × 95,000 – ₹4,70,000 = ₹4,75,000 – ₹4,70,000 = ₹5,000 (F)

(v) Fixed overheads expenditure variance = Budgeted fixed overheads – Actual fixed overhead

= ₹5,00,000 – ₹4,70,000 = ₹30,000 (F)

(vi) $\text{Fixed overheads volume variance} = \text{Budgeted fixed overheads per standard hour}\left(\text{Budgeted output in standard hours} - \text{Actual output in standard hours}\right)$

$= 5(1{,}00{,}000 - 95{,}000) = ₹25{,}000\ (A)$

Fixed overhead variance = ₹5,000 (F) = Fixed overheads expenditure variance + Fixed overheads volume variance

$= ₹30{,}000\ (F) + ₹25{,}000\ (A) = ₹5{,}000\ (F)$

(vii) $\text{Fixed overheads efficiency variance} = \text{Budgeted fixed overheads per standard hour}\left(\text{Budgeted hours for actual output} \quad \text{Actual hours worked for actual output}\right)$

$= ₹5\ (95{,}000 - 1{,}10{,}000) = ₹75{,}000\ (A)$

(viii) $\text{Fixed overheads capacity variance} = \text{Budgeted fixed overheads per standard hour}\ (\text{Budgeted hours} - \text{Actual hours woked})$

$= ₹5\ (1{,}00{,}000 - 1{,}10{,}000) = ₹50{,}000\ (F)$

Fixed overhead volume var. = ₹25,000 (A) = Fixed overhead efficiency variance + Fixed overhead capacity variance

$= ₹75{,}000\ (A) + ₹50{,}000\ (F) = ₹25{,}000\ (A).$

✍ EXAMPLE 19.27

Details of fixed overheads, production hours and production for a period are:

Budgeted hours	10,000 hours
Standard fixed overheads per hour	₹10
Standard hours per unit of output	5 hours
Actual production	1,920 units
Actual fixed overheads	₹94,000

Calculate:

(i) Fixed overhead cost variance;
(ii) Fixed overhead expenditure variance; and
(iii) Fixed overhead volume variance.

☞ ***Solution***

FOCV = Std. F/O for actual output – Actual F/O for actual output

$= 1{,}920 \times 50 - 94{,}000 = 2{,}000\ (F)$

FO. expenditure variance = Budgeted exp. – Actual exp

$= 1{,}00{,}000 - 94{,}000 = 6{,}000\ (F)$

$\text{Fixed overhead volume variance} = \left(\text{Budgeted overhead} - \text{Actual overhead}\right) \times \text{Budgeted rate}$

$= (2{,}000 - 1{,}920)\ 50 = 4{,}000\ (A)$

Workings:

$$\text{Budgeted output} = \frac{\text{Budgeted hours}}{\text{Budgeted rate}} = \frac{10,000}{5} = 2,000 \text{ units}$$

Budgeted expenditure = Budgeted hours × Std. F/O per hour.
= 10,000 × ₹10 = ₹1,00,000

Budgeted rate per unit of output.

$$₹= \frac{1,00,000}{2,000} = ₹50 \text{ per unit}$$

EXAMPLE 19.28

The following information is available from the cost records of a company for December, 2020:

	₹
Materials purchased 20,000 pieces	88,000
Materials consumed 19,000 pieces	
Actual wages paid for 4,950 hours	24,750
Fixed factory overheads budgeted	40,000
Fixed factory overheads incurred	44,000
Units produced – 1,800	
Standard rates and prices are:	
Direct material rate – ₹4 per piece.	
Standard output – 10 pieces per unit	
Direct labour rate – ₹4 per hour	
Standard hours required to produce a unit – 2.5 hours	
Overheads – ₹8 per labour hour	

Compute the following variances:

(a) Material price and usage;
(b) Labour rate and efficiency;
(c) Fixed overheads expenditure variance; and
(d) Fixed overheads volume variance.

Solution

Standard Cost Card (Per Unit)

Element of Cost	*Quantity of Hour*	*Rate* ₹	*Standard Cost*
Direct material	10 pieces	4	40
Direct labour	2.5 hours	4	10
Overheads	2.5 hours	8	20
Total standard cost			70

Calculation of Variance

(a) *Material Price Variance:*
= Actual usage (Standard price – Actual price)
= 19,000 pieces (₹4 – ₹4.40) = ₹7,600 Adverse

$$\text{(Actual price} = \frac{₹88,000}{20,000} = ₹4.40)$$

Material Usage Variance

= Standard price (Standard usage – Actual usage)

= ₹4 (18,000 pieces – 19,000 pieces) = ₹4,000 (Adverse)

(Standard usage = For 1,800 units @ 10 pieces = 18,000 pieces.

(*b*) *Labour Rate and Efficiency Variance:*

Labour rate variance = Actual time (Standard rate – Actual rate)

= 4,950 hrs. (₹4 – ₹5) = ₹4,950 (Adverse)

$$\text{Actual rate} = \frac{\text{Actual labour cost}}{\text{Actual time}} = ₹5$$

Labour Efficiency Variance:

Standard rate (Standard time – Actual time)

= ₹4 (4,500 hours – 4,950 hours) = ₹1,800 (Adverse)

(*c*) *Fixed Overhead Expenditure Variance:*

Budgeted overheads – Actual overheads

₹40,000 – ₹44,000 = ₹4,000 (Adverse)

(*d*) *Fixed Overhead Volume Variance:*

= Standard fixed overhead rate per unit (Actual output – Budgeted output)

= 2.5 hrs. × ₹8 (1,800 units – 2,000 units)

= ₹4,000 (Adverse)

$$\text{Budgeted output} = \frac{\text{Budgeted overheads}}{\text{Standard overhead per unit}}$$

$$= \frac{₹40,000}{₹20} = 2,000 \text{ units.}$$

EXAMPLE 19.29

From the following data, calculate:

(1) Fixed overhead expenditure variance;
(2) Fixed overhead volume variance; and
(3) Fixed overhead cost variance.

	Budgeted	*Actual*
Fixed overheads for July	₹10,000	₹10,200
Units of production in July	5,000	5,200
Standard time for one unit	4 hours	–
Actual hours worked		20,100 hrs

Solution

(1) *Fixed Overhead Expenditure Variance:*

Budgeted overhead – Actual overhead

₹10,000 – ₹10,200 = ₹200 (A)

(2) *Fixed Overhead Volume Variance:*

(i) Where std. rate per unit is given,

(Actual production – Budgeted production) × Std. rate per unit,

$$\text{Standard fixed overhead rate per unit} = \frac{10{,}000}{5{,}000} = ₹2$$

(5,200 – 5,000) × ₹2 = 400 (F)

(ii) When std. rate per hour is given,

(Std. hours for actual production – Budgeted hours) × Std. rate per hour

$$\text{Standard fixed overhead rate per hour} = \frac{₹2}{4 \text{ hours}} = ₹0.50$$

(5,200 × 4 – 5,000 × 4) × ₹0.50

(20,800 – 20,000) × ₹0.50

800 × ₹0.50 = 400 (F)

(3) *Fixed Overhead Cost Variance:*

(Standard overhead cost of actual output – Actual overhead costs)

(5,200 × ₹2) – 10,200

₹10,400 – 10,200 = ₹200 (F)

EXAMPLE 19.30

Kolkata Furniture manufactures modular tables, chairs and office desks. The standard labour times required per unit of table, chair and desk are 4 hours, 2 hours and 8 hours respectively. The budgeted production per week is 140 standard hours and budgeted fixed overheads per week are ₹70,000. During a particular week, the firm achieved the following output:

Tables	8 nos.
Chairs	8 nos.
Desks	9 nos.

The actual fixed production overhead amounted to ₹75,000.

Calculate:

(i) Fixed overhead variance;
(ii) Expenditure variance; and
(iii) Volume variance.

Solution

Standard FOH rate per hour = ₹70,000 ÷ 140 hrs. = ₹500

Standard hours of actual production: 120 hours

Tables = 8 × 4 = 32 hours
Chairs = 8 × 2 = 16 hours
Desks = 9 × 8 = 72 hours

Actual fixed production overhead: ₹75,000

(i) Fixed Production OH: Total variance:

(Standard FOH of actual production – Actual FOH)

= ₹(120 × 500) – ₹75,000 = ₹60,000 – ₹75,000 = ₹15,000 (Adv.)

(ii) Fixed Production OH: Expenditure variance:

(Budgeted FOH – Actual FOH) = ₹70,000 – ₹75,000 = ₹5,000 (Adv.)

(iii) Fixed Production OH: Volume variance:
(Budgeted FOH – Std. FOH of actual production)
= ₹70,000 – ₹120 × 500 = ₹70,000 – ₹60,000 = ₹10,000 (Adv.)

	₹	₹
Reconciliation		
Standard FOH of actual production: (120 × 500)		60,000
Add: Adverse variances –		
Expenditure variance	5,000	
Volume variance	10,000	15,000
Actual fixed overhead		75,000

EXAMPLE 19.31

The following information was obtained from the records of a manufacturing unit using Standard Costing System:

	Standard	*Actual*
Production	4,000 units	3,800 units
Working days	20	21
Fixed overhead (₹)	40,000	39,000
Variable overhead (₹)	12,000	12,000

You are required to calculate the following overhead variances:

(a) Variable overhead variance
(b) Fixcd overhead variance
  (i) Expenditure variance
  (ii) Volume variance
  (iii) Efficiency variance
  (iv) Calendar variance
(c) Also, prepare a reconciliation statement for the standard fixed expenses worked out at standard fixed overhead rate and the actual fixed overhead.

Solution

Basic Calculations	*Budgeted Data*	*Actual Data*
Variable overhead (₹)	12,000	12,000
Fixed overhead (₹)	40,000	39,000
Production (units)	4,000	3,800
Working (days)	21	20

Standard variable overhead rate per unit = $\frac{12,000}{4,000 \text{ units}}$ = ₹3

Standard production per day = $\frac{4,000 \text{ units}}{20 \text{ days}}$ = 200 units

Standard fixed overhead per day = 200 × ₹10 = ₹2,000

(a) Variable overhead cost variance = Actual variable overhead – Recovered variable overhead
= 12,000 – 3,800 × 3
= 12,000 – 11,400 = ₹600 (A)

(b) Fixed overhead variance = (Actual fixed overheads – Recovered fixed overheads)
= 39,000 – 3,800 × 10
= 39,000 – 38,000 = ₹1,000 (A)

(i) Fixed overhead expenditure variance = Actual overheads – Budgeted overheads
= 39,000 – 40,000 = ₹1,000 (F)

(ii) Fixed overhead volume variance = Recovered overheads – Budgeted overheads
= 38,000 – 40,000 = ₹2,000 (A)

(iii) Fixed overhead efficiency variance = Standard fixed overhead rate per day × (Actual time – Standard time for actual output)
= 2,000 × (21 – 3,800/200)
= 2,000 (21 – 19) = 4,000 (A)

(iv) Fixed overhead calendar variance = Standard fixed overhead rate per day × (Actual days – Budgeted days)
= 2,000 × (21 – 20)
= ₹2,000 (F)
or
Standard fixed overhead rate per day × Extra days/Deficit worked
= 2,000 × 1 = 2,000 (F)

(c) Reconciliation statement

Standard fixed overheads 3,800 × 100		₹38,000
Less: Fixed overhead expenditure variance	1,000 (F)	
Less: Fixed overhead calendar variance	2,000 (F)	3,000 (F)
		35,000
Add: Fixed overhead efficiency variance (A)		4,000
Actual Fixed overheads		39,000

EXAMPLE 19.32

The following data is given:

	Budget	*Actuals*
Production (in units)	400	360
Man-hours to produce above	8,000	7,000
Variable overheads (₹)	10,000	9,150

The standard time to produce one unit of the product is 20 hours.
Calculate variable overhead variances and give necessary journal entries to record the transactions.

☞ Solution

Basic Calculations

1. *Standard Variable Overhead per unit:*
   ₹10,000/400 units = ₹25 per unit
2. *Standard Variable Overhead per hour:*
   ₹10,000/8,000 hrs. = ₹1.25 per hour
3. *Recovered Variable Overhead:*
   = Actual output × Standard variable overhead per hour
   = 360 units × ₹25 = ₹9,000
4. *Budgeted Variable Overhead (based on actual hours worked):*
   = Actual hours worked × Standard variable overhead per hour
   = 7,000 hrs. × ₹1.25 = ₹8,750
5. *Standard Hours for Actual Output:*
   = Actual output × Standard hours per unit
   = 360 units × 20 hours = 7,200 hours

Computation of Variances:

(i) *Variable Overhead Cost Variance:*
   = Recovered variable overhead – Actual variable overheads
   = ₹9,000 – ₹9,150 = ₹150 (A)

(ii) *Variable Overhead Budget or Expenditure Variance:*
   = Budgeted variable overheads – Actual variable overheads
   = ₹8,750 – ₹9,150 = ₹400 (A)

(iii) *Variable Overhead Efficiency Variance:*
   = Standard variable overhead per hour (Standard hours for actual output – Actual hours)
   = Recovered variable overheads – Budgeted variable overheads
   = ₹9,000 – ₹8,750
   = ₹250 (F)

Verification:

Variable overhead cost variance = Variable overhead budgets variance
+ Variable overhead efficiency variance

₹150 (A) = ₹400 (A) + ₹250 (F)

Journal Entries

			Dr.	Cr.
			₹	₹
1.	Variable Overheads Control A/c	Dr.	8,750	
	Variable Overheads Expenditure Variance A/c	Dr.	400	
	To Bank/Creditors			9,150

(Contd.)

			Dr.	Cr.
			₹	₹
2.	Work-in-Progress Control A/c	Dr.	9,000	
	To Variable Overheads Control A/c			8,750
	To Variable Overheads Efficiency Variance A/c			250

SALES VARIANCES

Sales variance is the difference between the actual value of sales achieved in a given period and budgeted value of sales. There are many reasons for the difference in actual sales and budgeted sales such as selling price, sales volume, sales mix. Sales variances can be calculated by using any one of the following two methods.

A. *Sales variance based on turnover*
B. *Sales variances based on margin (i.e. contribution margin or profit)*

The first approach, that is sales variance based on turnover, accounts for difference in actual sales and budgeted sales. The sales variances using margin approach accounts for differences in actual profit and budgeted profit. In the margin method, it is assumed that cost of production is constant, that is no difference is assumed between actual cost of production and standard cost of production. The reason for this assumption is that cost variances are calculated separately to analyse the difference between actual cost and standard cost of production. Therefore, cost side of the sales variance is assumed constant under the margin method. Sales variances computed under these two methods show different amounts of variance.

The different sales variances under these two approaches and their formulae are given below:

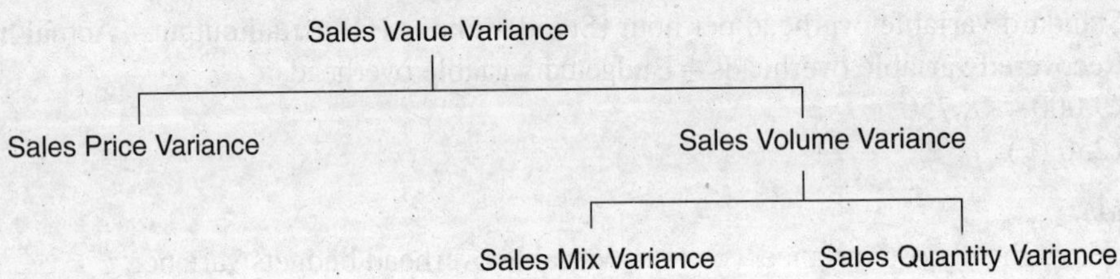

Sales Variances Based on Turnover

(i) *Sales Value Variance* Also known as sales variance, this variance shows the difference between actual sales value and budgeted sales value. The formula is

Sales value variance = (Actual value of sales – Budgeted value of sales)
Actual sales = Actual quantity sold × Actual selling price
Budgeted sales = Standard quantity × Standard selling price

or

Sales value variance = (Actual quantity × Actual selling price)
– (Standard quantity × Standard selling price)

If actual sales are more than the budgeted sales, there is favourable variance and if actual sales less than the budgeted sales, unfavourable variance arises.

(ii) *Sales Price Variances* This variance is due to the difference between actual selling price and standard or budgeted selling price. The formula is:

Sales price variance = (Actual selling price – Budgeted selling price) × Actual quantity

If actual selling price is less than the budgeted selling price, variance is unfavourable and if actual selling price is more than the budgeted selling price, there will be favourable sales price variance.

(iii) *Sales Volume Variance* Sales volume variance arises when the actual quantity sold is different from the budgeted quantity. If actual sales quantity exceeds the budgeted sales quantity, there is a favourable sales volume variance and if actual quantity sold is less than the budgeted quantity, the variance is unfavourable. The formula is:

Sales volume variance = (Actual quantity – Budgeted quantity) × Budgeted selling price

Sales volume variance is divided into two variances:

(a) Sales mix variance (b) Sales quantity variance.

(a) *Sales Mix Variance* Sales mix variance is one part of overall sales volume variance. This variance shows the difference between actual mix of goods sold and budgeted mix of goods sold. The formula is:

Sales mix variance = (Actual mix of quantity sold – Actual quantity in standard proportion) × Standard selling price

Sales mix variance = (Budgeted price per unit of actual mix – Budgeted price per unit of budgeted mix) × Total actual quantity

If actual mix of sales are more than the actual mix sales in standard or budgeted proportion, the variance is favourable and if actual mix sales are less than the standard mix (of actual sales), the variance is unfavourable. Similarly, if budgeted price per unit of actual mix is more than the budgeted price per unit of budgeted mix, favourable variance will arise. In the reverse situation, variance will be unfavourable.

(b) *Sales Quantity Variance* This variance is also a part of overall volume variance. This variance shows the difference between total actual sales quantity and total budgeted sales quantity. If total actual quantity is more than the total budgeted quantity, variance will be favourable and if total actual quantity less than the total budgeted quantity, there will be unfavourable sales quantity variance. The formula is

Sales quantity variance = (Total actual quantity – Total budgeted quantity) × Budgeted price per unit of budgeted mix

The total of sales mix variance and sales quantity variance will be equal to sales volume variance.

Sales Variance based on Margin (that is, Contribution Margin or Profit)

As stated earlier, the sales variances using margin approach show the difference in actual profit and budgeted profit only, whereas sales variances based on turnover show the difference between total actual sales and total budgeted sales.

The following sales variances are calculated if margin or profit is the basis of calculation:

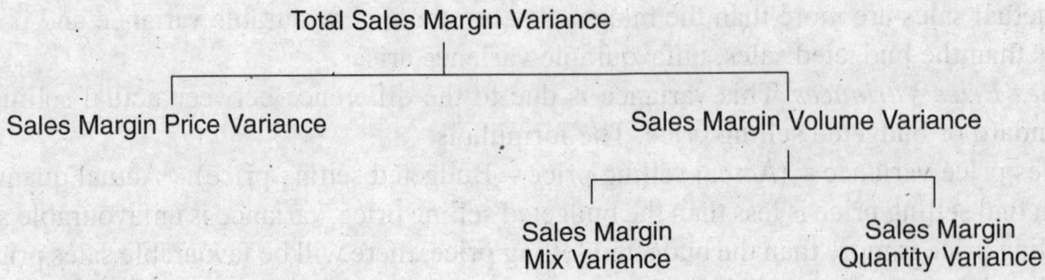

(i) *Total Sales Margin Variance*—This variance indicates the aggregate or total variance under the margin method. This variance shows the difference between actual profit and budgeted profit. The formula is:

Total sales margin variance = Actual profit – Budgeted profit

If actual profit is more than the budgeted profit, variance will be favourable and if actual profit less than the budgeted profit, unfavourable variance will arise.

(ii) *Sales Margin Price Variance*—This variance is one part of total sales margin variance and arises due to the difference between actual margin per unit and budgeted margin per unit. It is significant to note that assuming cost of production being constant, the difference in the actual margin and budgeted margin will be only because of the difference between actual selling price and budgeted selling price. The formula for calculating sales margin price variance is:

Sales margin price variance = (Actual margin per unit – Budgeted margin per unit) × Actual quantity

If actual margin per unit is more than the budgeted margin per unit, favourable variance will be found and if actual margin less than the budgeted margin, variance will be unfavourable.

(iii) *Sales Margin Volume Variance*—This variance shows the difference between actual sales units and budgeted sales unit. The formula is:

Sales margin volume variance = (Actual quantity – Budgeted quantity) × Budgeted margin per unit

If actual sales units are more than budgeted sales units, variance will be favourable and if actual sales units less than the budgeted sales unit, unfavourable variance will arise.

Sales margin volume variance can be calculated using another formula which is:

Sales margin volume variance = (Standard profit on actual quantity of sales – Budgeted profit)

If standard profit exceeds budgeted profit, variance will be favourable and if standard profit is less than the budgeted profit, unfavourable variance will emerge.

Sales margin volume variance consists of (a) sales margin mix variance and (b) sales margin quantity variance.

(a) Sales Margin Mix Variance This variance shows the difference between actual mix of goods sold and budgeted (standard) mix of goods sold. The formula is

Sales margin mix variance = (Actual sales mix – Standard proportion of actual sales mix) × Budgeted margin per unit

If budgeted margin per unit on actual sales mix is more than the budgeted margin per unit on budgeted mix, variance will be favourable. In the reverse situation, unfavourable variance will arise.

(b) Sales Margin Quantity Variance This variance will be found when the total actual sales quantity in standard proportion is different from the total budgeted sales quantity. The formula is:

Sales margin quantity variance = (Actual sales in standard proportion – Budgeted sales) × Budgeted margin per unit on budgeted mix

If actual sales (in standard proportion) are more than the budgeted sales, variance will be favourable and if actual sales are less than the budgeted sales, unfavourable variance will arise.

EXAMPLE 19.33

Greenfield Co. provides the following data for the month of March 2020:

Budget:

Product	*Budgeted Sales (in units)*	*Budgeted Selling Price Per Unit (₹)*
A	2,160	12
B	1,440	5

Actual:

Product	*Budgeted Sales (in units)*	*Budgeted Selling Price Per Unit (₹)*
A	2,240	11
B	960	6

You are required to compute:

(i) Sales value variance;
(ii) Salcs volume variance;
(iii) Sales price variance; and
(iv) Mix variance

Solution

	Budgeted Sales				*Actual Sales*		
	BQ (units)	*BP (₹)*	*BQ × BP*		*AQ (units)*	*AP (₹)*	*AQ × AP*
A	2,160	12	25,920	A	2,240	11	24,640
B	1,440	5	7,200	B	960	6	5,760
	3,600		₹33,120		3,200		₹30,400

Sales value variance = (BQ × BP) – (AQ × AP) = 33,120 – 30,400 = ₹2,720 (A)

Sales volume variance = BP(BQ – AQ)

A = 12 (2,160 – 2,240) = 960 (F)

B = 5 (1,440 – 960) = 2,400 (A)

Sales volume variance ₹1,440 (A)

Sales price variance = AQ (BP – AP)

A = 2,240 (12 – 11) = 2,240 (A)

B = 960 (5 – 6) = 960 (F)

Sales price variance = ₹1,280 (A)

Sales value variance = Volume var + Price var = 1,440 (A) + 1,280 (A) = ₹2,720 (A)

Sales mix variance = SP (AQ in Std. Proportion – AQS)

AQ in std. prop = A $3,200 \times \frac{2,160}{3,000} = 1,920$; B $3,200 \times \frac{1,440}{3,600}$ = 1,280

Sales mix variance = BP (AQS in std. prop – AQ)

A = 12 (1,920 – 2,240) = 3,840 (F)

B = 5 (1,280 – 960) = 1,600 (A)

Sales mix variance ₹ 2,240 (F)

EXAMPLE 19.34

H Ltd. furnishes the following information relating to budgeting sales and actual sales for the month of March, 2020:

	Product	*Sales Quantity Units*	*Sale Price Per Unit ₹*
Budget Sales:			
	A	1,200	15
	B	800	20
	C	2,000	40
Actual Sales:			
	A	880	18
	B	880	20
	C	2,640	38

You are required to calculate:

(i) Sales price variance;
(ii) Sales volume variance;
(iii) Sales mix variance; and
(iv) Total sales value variance.

Assume products to be homogeneous.

☞ **Solution**

Table of Basic Calculations

Product	*Standard*			*Actual*		
	Quantity (Units)	*Rate (₹)*	*Amount (₹)*	*Quantity (Units)*	*Rate (₹)*	*Amount (₹)*
A	1,200	15	18,000	880	18	15,840
B	800	20	16,000	880	20	17,600
C	2,000	40	80,000	2,640	38	1,00,320
Total	**4,000**		**1,14,000**	**4,400**		**1,33,760**

Calculation of Standard Sales

Product	*Actual Quantity (Units)*	*Budgeted Price (₹)*	*Standard Sales (₹)*
A	880	15	13,200
B	880	20	17,600
C	2,640	40	1,05,600
	4,400		**1,36,400**

Calculation of Revised Standard Quantity (RSQ)

RSQ = Total actual quantity × Standard proportion

$$\text{RSQ (A)} = 4{,}400 \times \frac{1{,}200}{4{,}000} = 1{,}320$$

$$\text{RSQ (B)} = 4{,}400 \times \frac{800}{4{,}000} = 880$$

$$\text{RSQ (C)} = 4{,}400 \times \frac{2{,}000}{4{,}000} = 2{,}200$$

Computation of Variances

(i) **Sales Price Variance**

= Actual quantity (Actual price – Budgeted price)

= AQ (AP – BP)

A = 880 (18 – 15) = ₹ 2,640 (F)

B = 880 (20 – 20) = ₹ NIL

C = 2,640 (38 – 40) = ₹5,280 (A)

Total sales price variance = **₹2,640 (A)**

Alternatively: Sales price variance

= Actual sales – Standard sales

= ₹1,33,760 – ₹1,36,400

= **₹2,640 (A)**

(ii) **Sales Volume Variance**

= Budgeted price (Actual quantity – Budgeted quantity)

= BP (AQ – BQ)

A = 15(880 – 1,200) = ₹4,800 (A)

B = 20(880 – 800) = ₹1,600 (F)

C = 40(2,640 – 2,000) = ₹25,600 (F)

Total sales volume variance = **₹22,400 (F)**

Alternatively: Sales volume variance = Standard sales – Budgeted sales

= ₹1,36,400 – ₹1,14,000

= **₹22,400 (F)**

(iii) **Sales Mix Variance**

= Budgeted price (Actual quantity – Revised standard quantity)

= BP(AQ – RSQ)

A = 15(880 – 1,320) = ₹6,600 (A)

B = 20(880 – 880) = ₹ NIL

C = 40(2,640 – 2,200) = ₹17,600 (F)

Total sales mix variance = **₹11,000 (F)**

(iv) **Total Sales Value Variance**

= Actual sales – Budgeted sales

= ₹1,33,760 – ₹1,14,000 = **₹19,760 (F)**

EXAMPLE 19.35

From the following information about sales, calculate:

(i) Total sales variance;
(ii) Sales price variance;
(iii) Sales volume variance;
(iv) Sales mix variance; and
(v) Sales quantity variance.

	Standard		*Actual*	
	Units	*Rate* ₹	*Units*	*Rate* ₹
Product A	5,000	5	6,000	6
B	4,000	6	5,000	5
C	3,000	7	4,000	8

☞ Solution

(i) **Total Sales Variance** = Actual sales – Standard sales

A	(6,000 × 6) – (5,000 × 5)	= ₹11,000 (F)
B	(5,000 × 5) – (4,000 × 6)	= ₹ 1,000 (F)
C	(4,000 × 8) – (3,000 × 7)	= ₹11,000 (F)
	Total	**₹23,000 (F)**

(ii) **Sales Price Variance** = (Actual price – Standard price) × Actual quantity

A	(6 – 5) × 6,000	= ₹6,000 (F)
B	(5 – 6) × 5,000	= ₹5,000 (A)
C	(8 – 7) × 4,000	= ₹4,000 (F)
	Total	**₹5,000 (F)**

(iii) **Sales Volume Variance** = (Actual quantity – Standard quantity) × Standard price

A =	(6,000 – 5,000) × 5	= ₹5,000 (F)
B =	(5,000 – 4,000) × 6	= ₹6,000 (F)
C =	(4,000 – 3,000) × 7	= ₹7,000 (F)
	Total	**₹18,000 (F)**

(iv) **Sales Mix Variance** = (Actual quantity – Revised standard quantity) × Standard price

A =	(6,000 – 6,250) × 5	=	₹1,250 (A)
B =	(5,000 – 5,000) × 6	=	₹ Nil
C =	(4,000 – 3,750) × 7	=	₹1,750 (F)
	Total		**₹500 (F)**

RSQ (Revised Standard Quantity) is calculated as follows:

$$\text{RSQ} = \frac{\text{Standard quantity}}{\text{Total standard quantity}} \times \text{Total actual quantity}$$

$$A = \frac{5,000}{12,000} \times 15,000 = 6,250 \text{ units}$$

$$B = \frac{4,000}{12,000} \times 15,000 = 5,000 \text{ units}$$

$$C = \frac{3,000}{12,000} \times 15,000 = 3,750 \text{ units}$$

(v) **Sales Quantity Variance** = (Revised standard quantity – Standard quantity) × Standard price

A = (6,250 – 5,000) × 5	= ₹6,250 (F)
B = (5,000 – 4,000) × 6	= ₹6,000 (F)

C = (3,750 – 3,000) × 7 = ₹5,250 (F)

Total **₹17,500 (F)**

EXAMPLE 19.36

Compute the sales variances (total, price and volume) from the following figures:

Product	*Budgeted Quantity*	*Budgeted Price Per Unit (₹)*	*Actual Quantity*	*Actual Price Per Unit (₹)*
P	4,000	25	4,800	30
Q	3,000	50	2,800	45
R	2,000	75	2,400	70
S	1,000	100	800	105

Solution

Working:

Product	*Budgeted Price (₹)*	*Actual Price (₹)*	*Budgeted Qty.*	*Actual Qty.*	*Budgeted Sales (₹)*	*Standard Sales (Actual Sales at Budgeted Price ₹)*	*Actual Sales (₹)*
	a	*b*	*c*	*d*	*e = a × c*	*f = a × d*	*g = b × d*
P	25	30	4,000	4,800	1,00,000	1,20,000	1,44,000
Q	50	45	3,000	2,800	1,50,000	1,40,000	1,26,000
R	75	70	2,000	2,400	1,50,000	1,80,000	1,68,000
S	100	105	1,000	800	1,00,000	80,000	84,000
					5,00,000	5,20,000	5,22,000

Calculation of Variances:

Sale price variance = Actual quantity (Actual price – Budgeted price)
= Actual sales – Standard sales
= 5,22,000 – 5,20,000 = ₹2,000 (Favourable)

Sales volume variance = Budgeted price (Actual quantity – Budgeted quantity)
= Standard sales (Actual sale at standard price) – Budgeted sales
= 5,20,000 – 5,00,000 = ₹20,000 (Favourable)

Total sales variance = Actual sales – Budgeted sales
= 5,22,000 – 5,00,000 = ₹22,000 (Favourable)

Verification: Total Sales Variance (₹20,000/- Favourable) = Sales Price Variance (₹2,000/- Favourable) + Sales Volume Variance (₹20,000 Favourable)

EXAMPLE 19.37

The summarised budget and actual working results of GEMCO LTD. for the year 2019–20 are given below:

Details	Budget Products			Actual Products		
	A	B	C	A	B	C
	₹	₹	₹	₹	₹	₹
Selling price per unit	12	16	25	13	16	27
Cost per unit	9	11	20	10	12	21
Sales (units)	40,000	32,000	24,000	42,000	40,000	22,000

Analyse the results and calculate the following:

(i) Budgeted profit, actual profit and variance in profit.

(ii) Analysis of the variance in profit in the following:

(1) Price variance

(2) Cost variance

(3) Sales margin volume variance

(4) Sales margin mix variance

(5) Sales margin quantity variance

Solution

GEMCO Ltd.

	₹
(i) *Budgeted Profit*	4,00,000
(40,000 × 3 + 32,000 × 5 + 24,000 × 5)	
Actual profit	4,18,000
(42,000 × 3 + 40,000 × 4 + 22,000 × 6)	
Variance in profit:	18,000 (FAV)

(ii) *Analysis of Variance in Profit:*

(a) Cost variance = (Standard cost – Actual cost) × Actual no. of units

	₹	
A: (9 – 10) × 42,000	= 42,000 (Adv)	
B: (11 – 12) × 40,000	= 40,000 (Adv)	
C: (20 – 21) × 22,000	= 22,000 (Adv)	₹1,04,000 (Adv)

(b) Price variance = (Std price – Actual price) × Actual no. of units

	₹	
A: (12 – 13) × 42,000	= 42,000 (Fav)	
B: (16 – 16) × 40,000	= 0	
C: (25 – 27) × 22,000	= 44,000 (Fav)	₹86,000 (Fav)

(c) Sales margin volume variance:

= (Budgeted vol. – Actual vol) × Standard profit

A: (40,000 – 42,000) × 3 = 6,000 (Fav)
B: (32,000 – 40,000) × 5 = 40,000 (Fav)
C: (24,000 – 22,000) × 5 = 10,000 (Adv) ₹36,000 (Fav)

Reconciliation:

Variance in profit = Cost variance + Price variance + Volume variance

= 1,04,000 (Adv) + 86,000 (Fav) + 36,000 (Fav)

= ₹18,000 (Fav)

(d) Sales margin mix variance:
(Revised standard qty – Actual qty.) × Standard profit

		₹	
A: (40/96 × 1,04,000 – 42,000) × 3	=	4,000 (Adv)	
B: (32/96 × 1,04,000 – 40,000) × 5	=	26,667 (Fav)	
C: (24/96 × 1,04,000 – 22,000) × 5	=	20,000 (Adv)	₹2,667 (Fav)

(e) Sales margin quantity variance

		₹	
A: (40/96 × 1,04,000 – 40,000) × 3	=	10,000 (Fav)	
B: (32/96 × 1,04,000 – 32,000) × 5	=	13,333 (Fav)	
C: (24/96 × 1,04,000 – 24,000) × 5	=	10,000 (Fav)	₹33,333 (Fav)

Reconciliation:

		₹
Sales margin mix variance	:	2,667 (Fav)
Sales margin qty. variance	:	33,333 (Fav)
Sales margin volume variance	:	36,000 (Fav)

EXAMPLE 19.38

The budgeted and the actual sales for a period in respect of three products are given below:

Budgeted Figures

Product	*Quantity*	*Price* ₹	*Value* ₹
A	1,000	5	5,000
B	750	10	7,500
C	500	15	7,500
	2,250		20,000

Actuals

Product	*Quantity*	*Price* ₹	*Value* ₹
A	1,200	6	7,200
B	700	9	6,300
C	600	14	8,400
	2,500		21,900

Calculate sales variances.

Solution

Basic Calculations

Products	Budgeted Qty.	Budgeted Price	Budgeted Value	Actual Qty.	Actual Price	Actual Value	Standard Sales (Actual Qty. × Budgeted Price)
		₹	₹	₹	₹	₹	
A	1,000	5	5,000	1,200	6	7,200	6,000
B	750	10	7,500	700	9	6,300	7,000
C	500	15	7,500	600	14	8,400	9,000
	2,250		20,000	2,500		21,900	22,000

Computation of Sales Variances

1. *Sales value variance* = Budgeted sales – Actual sales
   = ₹20,000 – 21,900
   = ₹1,900 (F)

2. *Sales price pariance* = Actual Quantity × (Std. price – Actual price)
   A = 1,200 × (5 – 6) = ₹1,200 (F)
   B = 700 × (10 – 9) = ₹ 700 (A)
   C = 600 × (15 – 14) = ₹ 600 (A)
   ₹ 100 (A)

3. *Sales volume variance* = Std. selling price × (Budgeted qty. – Actual qty.)
   A = 5 × (1,000 – 1,200) = ₹1,000 (F)
   B = 10 × (750 – 700) = ₹ 500 (A)
   C = 15 × (500 – 600) = ₹1,500 (F)
   ₹2,000 (F)

4. *Sales mix variance* = Std. price × (Revised std. qty. – Actual qty.)

$$A = 5 \times \left(\frac{2,500}{2,250} \times 1,000 - 1,200\right)$$

$$= 5 \times \left(\frac{10}{9} \times 1,000 - 1,200\right) = ₹444 \text{ (F)}$$

$$B = 10 \times \left(\frac{2,500}{2,250} \times 750 - 700\right)$$

$$= 10 \times \left(\frac{7,500}{9} - 700\right) = ₹1,333 \text{ (A)}$$

$$C = 15 \times \left(\frac{2,500}{2,250}\right) \times 500 - 600$$

$$= 15 \times \left(\frac{5,000}{9} - 600\right) = ₹667 \text{ (F)}$$

222 (A)

5. *Sales quantity Variance* = Std. rate × (Budgeted qty. – Revised std. qty.)

$$A = 5 \times \left(1{,}000 - \frac{10{,}000}{9}\right) = ₹556\ (F)$$

$$B = 10 \times \left(750 - \frac{7{,}500}{9}\right) = ₹833\ (F)$$

$$C = 15 \times \left(500 - \frac{5{,}000}{9}\right) = ₹833\ (F)$$

₹2,222 (F)

Revision Variance

When a budget is revised, but where as a matter of policy, the change is not incorporated in the standard cost rate, a variance will arise termed as a "revision variance". Revision variance is the difference between the basic standard cost and the revised standard cost.

DISPOSITION OF VARIANCE

Variance may be disposed of in either of the following ways:

1. Inventories and the cost of goods sold may be adjusted to reflect the actual costs.
2. Variances may be transferred to the profit and loss account.

Under the first method, all variances are allocated between the inventory accounts and cost of goods sold account. This method, in fact, converts the accounts balances from standard costs to actual historical costs.

The following arguments are given in support of this method:

1. Only actual costs should be recorded in the cost of goods sold account and inventory accounts. The supporters of this method do not favour standard costs as true costs or costs suitable for use in the profit and loss account but as merely guides in factory management.
2. Variances from the standard are costs and not losses and therefore should be reflected in the inventory valuations and cost of goods sold.
3. If the variances are large, standard costs do not represent the actual costs and therefore are not good measures to determine the costs of goods sold and inventory.

Under the second method, the variances are considered as profit or loss items in the period in which they occurred. The work-in-process, finished goods inventory, and cost of goods sold are stated at standard costs. Unfavourable cost variances are deducted from the gross profit at standard costs. Favourable cost variances are added to the gross profit calculated at standard cost. The treatment of the cost variances under this method is shown on the income statement given below.

ABC Company
Income Statement for the Year Ending December 31, 2020

	₹	₹
Sales revenue		5,00,000
Cost of sales (standard)	3,00,000	

(Contd.)

	₹	₹
Selling and administrative expenses		
(standard)	1,50,000	4,50,000
Net income (standard)		50,000
Deduct unfavourable variance from net income:		
Material price	200	
Material usage	800	
Labour efficiency	900	
Overhead:		
Volume	2,000	
Budget	1,100	5,000
Net income (actual)		45,000

The second method has the following arguments in its favour:

1. Standard costs help in the preparation of statements at the early date; actual cost delays the determination of inventory costs and cost of goods sold.
2. Standard costs avoid the inclusion of costs due to wastage, losses, inefficiencies, excessive overheads from low-production volume. Standard cost represent normal costs and therefore inventory figures are conservative and acceptable for income determination and other purposes.
3. In a multi-product company, it may be difficult to determine accurately how much variance should be distributed to each product.
4. In taking corrective action, managers may find it more useful when variances are depicted in the profit and loss account. Managerial attention is usually hampered when variances are combined with cost of goods manufactured.

It is difficult to suggest which method should be followed in accounting for variances. If the variances are large and significant, the first method, that is, distribution of variances to the respective accounts appears to be appropriate for financial reporting, tax and job and contract pricing purposes. The second method may be preferable when the variances are insignificant. Thus, the treatment of variances depends on many factors such as (i) size of variance, (ii) accuracy of standard costs, (iii) cause of variances such as incorrect standard costs, (iv) timing of variances, for example, caused by seasonal fluctuation, (v) type of variance–material, labour, and overhead.

MANAGERIAL USES OF VARIANCES

Determination of variances is only the first step in the process of standard cost variance analysis. Mere computation of material, labour and overhead variances is useless for cost control and performance evaluation. The final objective of variance analysis is to determine the person(s) responsible for each variance and to pinpoint the cause(s) for incurrence of these variances. That is, before management can take effective action for improving control over costs, it needs to know not only the amount of variances, but also where the variances originated, who was responsible for them, and what caused them to arise.

Analysis of Variances by Responsibilities

Variances must be identified with the manager responsible for the costs incurred who should be held responsible for that cost. The cost factors which are directly controllable by operating supervision must be separated from those costs factors from which executive management is responsible.

Specific titles of individuals who are responsible for each type of variance differ among business enterprises. Generally speaking, the following personnel are held accountable for variances noted against them:

Responsibility for Cost Variances

Variance	*Personnel Responsible*
(i) Materials price variance	Purchasing agent or purchasing manager.
(ii) Materials quantity variance	Plant superintendent, departmental supervisors, machine operators, quality control department and material handlers.
(iii) Labour rate standard	Personnel (employment) department manager, departmental supervisor and plant superintendent.
(iv) Labour efficiency variance	Plant superintendent, departmental supervisors, production scheduling department, quality control department, material handlers and machine operators.
(v) Overhead expenditure variance	Variable portion is the responsibility of the individual foreman or supervisor; they are expected to keep actual expenses within the budget. Fixed portion is the responsibility of top management.
(vi) Overhead efficiency variance	Same personnel who are responsible for labour efficiency variance.
(vii) Overhead volume variance	Top management and production schedulers.

Analysis of Variances by Causes

Reasons for the variance should be determined and plans for necessary corrective action made either by discussing possible causes with the supervisors or by examining underlying data and records. The analysis of variances by causes is therefore an important aspect of the use of standard costs to attain effective cost control. For any standard cost variance, there are many possible causes. The following list is not all inclusive but does indicate causes responsible for variances.

Possible Causes of Standard Cost Variances

Materials Price Variance

1. Recent changes in purchase price of materials.
2. Failure to purchase anticipated quantities when standards were established resulting in higher prices owing to non-availability of quantity purchase discounts.
3. Not taking cash discounts anticipated at the time of setting standards resulting in higher prices.
4. Substituting raw material differing from original materials specifications.
5. Freight cost changes and changes in purchasing and storekeeping costs if these are debited to the materials cost.

Materials Quantity Variance

1. Poor materials handling.
2. Inferior workmanship by machine operator.
3. Faulty equipment.
4. Cheaper, defective raw material causing excessive scrap.
5. Inferior quantity control inspection.
6. Pilferage.
7. Wastage due to inefficient production method.

Labour Rate Variance

1. Recent labour rate changes within industry.
2. Employing a man of a grade different from the one laid down in the standard.
3. Labour strike leading to utilisation of unskilled help.
4. Labour layoff causing skilled labour to be retained at higher rates, so as to prevent resignations and job switching.
5. Employee sickness and vacation time.
6. Paying a higher-overtime allowance than provided for in the standard.

Labour Efficiency Variance

1. Machine breakdown, use of defective machinery and equipment.
2. Inferior raw materials.
3. Poor supervision.
4. Lack of timely material handling.
5. Poor employee performance.
6. Inefficient production scheduling—delays in routing work, materials, tools and instructions.
7. Inferior engineering specifications.
8. New inexperienced employees.
9. Insufficient training of workers.
10. Poor working conditions—inadequate or excessive heating, lighting, ventilation, etc.

Overhead Volume Variance

(Factors causing either idle time or overtime of plant and facilities)

1. Failure to utilise normal capacity.
2. Lack of sales order.
3. Too much idle capacity.
4. Inefficient or efficient utilisation of existing capacity.
5. Machine breakdown.
6. Defective materials.
7. Labour troubles.
8. Power failures.

Overhead Efficiency Variance

These included all causes which are listed under labour efficiency variance.

Analysis of Variances by Products

Since management usually wants current true costs when decisions are to be made with respect to pricing and related questions, variances are often analysed by products in order to arrive at current product costs. Companies producing non-standard goods according to customer's specifications may also help analyse variances by job orders. The analysis of variances by causes is useful in deciding whether or not cost variances should be allocated to products in arriving at product costs for pricing. Standard product costs should be reviewed periodically and revised when it is found that the standard product costs in use are no longer useful for the purpose.

Variance Reports to Management

Variance reports basically aim to inform managers responsible for the operation when actual performance differs from the standards. To be effective, the report must be timely, accurate and clearly understood by the recipients.

Control of production and costs is a matter of timing; the effectiveness of the control is often in direct proportion to the speed with which variances are reported. Timely reporting often requires daily and weekly reporting of performance information. Therefore, it is important to focus managerial attention on off-standard conditions immediately following each shift, day or week, rather than to accumulate and summarise variances from standards each month. A month, and generally even a week, is too long a period for many off-standard conditions to remain unchecked and uncorrected, because the time interval may prevent positive identification of employees who are responsible for the unsatisfactory work.

Variance analysis reports are primarily control reports. In developing and reporting the variances, it should be remembered that the variance data must (i) deal with relevant distinctions, (ii) be understandable, (iii) measure with reasonable accuracy what they are supposed to measure, (iv) be presented and explained concisely, (v) be timely, and (vi) provide the amount of detáils needed by different persons at each level of management.

LIMITATIONS OF STANDARD COSTING

Standard costs are not without their shortcomings. The first limitation is regarding the pre-determined nature of standard costs. The accuracy of standard costs is limited by the knowledge and skill of the people who created them and they contain the prejudices of their makers. Such badly conceived standard costs do not enjoy the confidence of the users of the system.

Secondly, it is difficult to select a type of standard (ideal, currently attainable, normal, etc.) which can help in cost control and achieve other managerial purposes. If standards are too low, they defeat the objective of standard costing and bring the operating efficiency down. If they are too high, they can create ill-will and encourage employees to beat the system by fair means or foul.

Thirdly, a good programme of standard costing requires that both management and operating personnel should have full confidence in it and standards should be fair and workable. Educating employees is necessary in this regard. However, lack of acceptability, education and communication is a major difficulty in operating a standard costing system.

In spite of the above limitations, standard costing has developed into an extraordinary and very useful tool and has contributed much in providing different kinds of cost data for so many different purposes.

CONTROL RATIOS

Control ratios are useful to management to know whether the deviations of actuals from budgeted results are favourable or unfavourable. These control ratios are expressed in percentage. The ratio is taken as favourable if it is 100% or more. In case it is less than 100%, the ratio is considered as unfavourable.

Control ratios are as follows:

1. *Activity Ratio* Activity ratio is used to measure the level of activity achieved over a period. It is obtained when the number of standard hours equivalent to the output produced, are expressed at a percentage of the budgeted hours

$$\text{Activity ratio} = \frac{\text{Standard hours for actual production}}{\text{Budgeted hours}} \times 100$$

2. *Capacity Ratio* This ratio points out to what extent budgeted hours have been utilised. This ratio shows the relationship between actual working hours and budgeted working hours.
3. *Efficiency Ratio* Efficiency ratio shows the degree of efficiency achieved in production. It is derived when the standard hours equivalent to the output produced, are expressed as a percentage of the actual hours spent in producing the output.

$$\text{Efficiency ratio} = \frac{\text{Standard hours for actual production}}{\text{Actual hours worked}} \times 100$$

✍ EXAMPLE 19.39

Based on the data given below show the calculation of:

(i) Efficiency ratio;
(ii) Production volume ratio; and
(iii) Idle capacity ratio.

Data	*Standard Hour of Output*	*Hours of Actual Operations*
Theoretical capacity	100	100
Theoretical capacity less Unavoidable loss time	95	95
Planned activity for period	81	90
Actual activity for period	68	85

☞ Solution

(i) Efficiency ratio: $\frac{\text{Output expressed in standard hour}}{\text{Actual hours spent}} \times 100$

$$= \frac{68}{85} \times 100 \text{ or } 80\%$$

(ii) Production volume ratio: $\frac{\text{Actual output in standard hour}}{\text{Budgeted output in standard hours}} \times 100$

$$= \frac{68}{81} \times 100 \text{ or } 84\%$$

(iii) Idle capacity ratio: $\dfrac{\text{Practical capacity in standard hour} - \text{Budgeted capacity}}{\text{Practical capacity in standard hours}} \times 100$

$$= \frac{95 - 81}{95} \times 100 \text{ or } 14.7\%$$

EXAMPLE 19.40

In a day of 8 hours, a direct worker is expected to produce 12 units of product *P* or 16 units of product *Q* or 10 units of product *R*. The budgeted production of a month is 225 units of *P*, 180 units of *Q* and 300 units of *R*. During the month of November 2020, 450 direct labour hours were worked and the actual production was 240 units of *P*, 400 units of *Q* and 250 units of *R*.

Calculate the efficiency and capacity ratios.

Solution

	Standard Time		
P	8/12	=	0.6667 per unit
Q	8/16	=	0.5 per unit
R	8/10	=	0.8 per unit

Budgeted Hours: *(Hours)*

P	225 units × 0.6667	150
Q	180 units × 0.5	90
R	300 units × 0.8	240
		480

Standard Hours Produced: *(Hours)*

P	240 × 0.667	160
Q	400 × 0.50	200
R	250 × 0.8	200
		560
Actual hours:		450

Capacity utilisation ratio	450/480 ×100	= 93.75%
Efficiency ratio	560/450 × 100	= 124.44%

EXAMPLE 19.41

Calculate from the following figures:

(i) Efficiency ratio
(ii) Activity ratio and
(iii) Capacity ratio

Budgeted production	880 units
Standard hours per unit	10
Actual production	750 units
Actual working hours	6,000

Solution

(i) Efficiency ratio $= \dfrac{\text{Standard hours for actual production}}{\text{Actual hours worked}} \times 100$

$= \dfrac{750 \text{ units} \quad 10 \text{ hours}}{6{,}000} \times 100 = 125\%$

(ii) Activity ratio $= \dfrac{\text{Standard hours for actual production}}{\text{Budgeted hours}} \times 100$

$= \dfrac{750 \text{ units} \times 10 \text{ hours}}{880 \text{ units} \times 10 \text{ hours}} \times 100 = 85.23\%$

(iii) Capacity ratio $= \dfrac{\text{Actual hours worked}}{\text{Budgeted hours}} \times 100$

$= \dfrac{6{,}000 \text{ hours}}{880 \text{ units} \times 10 \text{ hours}} \times 100 = 68.18\%$

EXAMPLE 19.42

In a manufacturing shop, product *X* requires 2.5 man-hours and product *Y* requires 6 man-hours. In a month of 25 working days of 8 hours a day, 2,000 units of *X* and 1,000 units of *Y* were produced. The company employs 50 workers in the shop and the budgeted man-hours are 1,08,000 for the year. You are required to work out the capacity ratio, activity ratio and efficiency ratio.

Solution

Standard Man-hours Produced:

Product *X*: 2,000 units @	2.5 man-hours	= 5,000 man-hours
Product *Y*: 1,000 units @	6 man-hours	= 6,000 man-hours
	Total	= 11,000 man-hours

Budgeted man-hours per month = 108,000/12 = 9,000

Actual man-hours worked = 50 workers × 25 days × 8 hours = 10,000 man-hours

Ratios:

Activity ratio $= \dfrac{\text{Standard man-hours produced}}{\text{Budgeted man-hours}} \times 100$

$= \dfrac{10{,}000}{9{,}000} \times 100 = 122.22\%$

Efficiency ratio $= \dfrac{\text{Standard man-hours produced}}{\text{Actual man-hours worked}} \times 100$

$= \dfrac{11{,}000}{10{,}000} \times 100 = 111.00\%$

EXAMPLE 19.43

A factory produces two products *P* and *Q*. *P* takes 10 hours to produce and *Q* requires 16 hours as per the budget. A month has 25 budgeted days of 8 hours each. During the month, 500 units of *P* and

400 units of Q were produced. The factory employs 50 workers. They actually worked for 9 hours daily for 24 days. Calculate;

(i) Efficiency ratio;
(ii) Capacity ratio; and
(iii) Calender ratio.

Solution

(i) Efficiency ratio $= \dfrac{\text{Budgeted hours for actual output}}{\text{Actual hours worked}} \times 100 = \dfrac{11,400}{10,800} \times 100 = 105.5\%$

(ii) Capacity ratio $= \dfrac{\text{Actual hours worked}}{\text{Budgeted hours}} \times 100 = \dfrac{10,800}{10,000} \times 100 = 108\%$

(iii) Calender ratio $= \dfrac{\text{Actual days worked in the month}}{\text{Budgeted days in the month}} \times 100 = \dfrac{24}{25} \times 100 = 96\%$

Activity ratio has not been asked in the question. However, it will be calculated as follows:

Activity ratio $= \dfrac{\text{Budgeted hours for actual output}}{\text{Budgeted hours}} \times 100 = \dfrac{11,400}{10,000} \times 100 = 114\%$

EXAMPLE 19.44

Calculate efficiency and activity ratio from the following data:

Capacity ratio	=	75 %
Budgeted output	=	6,000 units
Actual output	=	5,000 units
Standard time per unit	=	4 hours

Solution

Capacity ratio $= \dfrac{\text{Actual hours}}{\text{Budgeted hours}} \times 100$

75% $= \dfrac{\text{AH}}{6,000 \text{ units} \times 4 \text{ hour per unit}}$

.75 $= \dfrac{\text{AH}}{24,000 \text{ hours}}$

AH $= 18,000$ hours

Efficiency ratio $= \dfrac{\text{Actual output in term of standard hours}}{\text{Actual working hours}} \times 100$

$= \dfrac{5,000 \text{ units} \times 4 \text{ hours per unit}}{18,000 \text{ hours}} \times 100$

$= \dfrac{20,000 \text{ hours}}{18,000 \text{ hours}} \times 100 = 111.11\%$

$$\text{Activity ratio} = \frac{\text{Actual output in term of standard hours}}{\text{Budgeted output in term of standard hours}} \times 100$$

$$= \frac{20{,}000 \text{ units}}{6{,}000 \text{ units} \times 4 \text{ hour per unit}} \times 100$$

$$= \frac{20{,}000 \text{ units}}{24{,}000 \text{ units}} \times 100 = 83.33\%$$

EXAMPLE 19.45

Calculate efficiency and capacity ratio from the following figures:

Budgeted production	80 units
Actual production	60 units
Standard time per unit	8 hours
Actual hours worked	500

Solution

$$\text{Efficiency ratio} = \frac{\text{Actual output in terms of standard hours}}{\text{Actual hour worked}} \times 100$$

$$\text{Or} \quad \frac{480}{500} \times 100 = 96\%$$

$$\text{Capacity ratio} = \frac{\text{Actual hours worked}}{\text{Budgeted hours}} \times 100$$

$$\text{Or} \quad \frac{500}{640} \times 100 = 78.12\%$$

Theory Questions

1. Define and explain the concepts of standard cost and standard costing.
2. Discuss briefly the use of standard costs in the following management activities: cost reductions, operating performance, evaluation, product pricing decisions and providing incentives.
3. Compare and contrast the usefulness of ideal standards, basic standards, and currently attainable standards.
4. "Standard costs are bases for a proper managerial control of manufacturing operation." Define standard cost and explain the above statement.
5. What is standard costing and how would you distinguish it from budgetary control?
6. What are the points of similarity and difference between budgeted and standard costs.
7. "Variance analysis is an integral part of standard cost accounting." Explain this statement.
8. By purchasing low-grade materials, a company reports favourable material price variance, but it consistently experiences unfavourable material quantity variances. What relationship may exist between these conditions? Ares the price variances really favourable?
9. What are the shortcomings of historical costs for managerial uses?
10. What is the difference between an estimated cost and a standard cost?
11. Describe briefly how standard costs are set for (a) material (b) labour.
12. Briefly explain the meaning of each of the following variances: material prices, material usage, labour efficiency, and labour rate.

13. Discuss some of the problems that might be created by standards which are set too high and by standards which are too loose.
14. What are the advantages and limitations of standard costing?
15. Discuss briefly shortcomings of standard cost system.
16. Explain why overhead variances are generally treated as period costs.
17. Discuss the information which a well-designed cost report should give to management from the point of view of production and control. How should such information be given?
18. What is a "two variance analysis" of factory overheads? Give a brief description.
19. Explain the term "variance" and distinguish between controllable and uncontrollable variances.
20. Describe briefly the managerial use of variances.
21. Point out the difference between historical costing and standard costing.
22. Briefly distinguish between the two cost-control techniques—"Budgetary Control" and "Standard Costing".
23. In analysing variance, it is found frequently that an adverse variance from one standard is related directly to a favourable variance from another. Give two examples of such a situation and comment briefly on each.
24. Distinguish between standard costs and budgeted costs.
25. What is sales value volume variance?
26. Define variance analysis. What are the ways of disposing cost variances?
27. What is fixed-production overhead variance? Explain how this is calculated and further analysed.
28. Distinguish between budgetary control and standard costing.
29. Explain fixed overhead cost variance.
30. Briefly describe the following control ratios:
    (i) Activity ratio
    (ii) Capacity ratio
    (iii) Efficiency ratio
31. Distinguish between standard costing and budgetary control.
32. Proper interpretation of variances from standard is very important for the success of standard costing system as a tool for cost control. Mention some important factors that must be born in mind while interpreting variances from standard.
33. In analysing variance, it is found frequently that an adverse variance from one standard is related directly to a favourable variance from another.
    Give two examples of such a situation and comment briefly on each.

    Ans: Two examples where adverse variance may be off-set by a favourable variance are as under:

    (i) **Direct Materials:** A favourable price variance may arise when material is purchased at cheaper price. But the quality may be poor and this may result in inefficient usage causing an adverse usage variance.

    (ii) **Direct Wages:** Employing workers of higher grade may lead to adverse wage-rate variance. But this may be offset by favourable efficiency variance because more skilled workers do the work in less time than allowed.

Self-Evaluation Questions

Choose the correct answer for the following multiple-choice questions.

1. The difference between the standard hours for the actual output and actual hours is
   (a) Labour rate variance. (b) Overhead cost variance.
   (c) Labour efficiency variance. (d) Overhead volume variance.
2. Cost variance includes all but one of the following
   (a) Direct material variance. (b) Direct labour variance.
   (c) Variable overhead variance. (d) Sales variance.

3. A standard cost system may be used in
   (a) Either job order costing or process costing.
   (b) Job order costing but not process costing.
   (c) Process costing but not job order costing.
   (d) Neither process costing nor job costing.
4. If actual hours worked exceed the standard hours allowed what type of variance will occur
   (a) Favourable labour usage (efficiency) variance.
   (b) Favourable labour rate variance.
   (c) Unfavourable labour usage (efficiency) variance.
   (d) Unfavourable labour rate variance.
5. An unfavourable materials price variances occurs because of
   (a) Price increases in raw materials.
   (b) Price decreases in raw materials.
   (c) Less than anticipated normal wastage in the manufacturing process.
   (d) More than anticipated normal wastage in the manufacturing process.
6. Which of the following is a purpose of standard costing?
   (a) Determine a break even production level.
   (b) Control costs.
   (c) Allocate cost with more accuracy.
   (d) Eliminate the need for subjective decisions by management.
7. When calculating variances from standard costs, the difference between actual and standard price multiplied by actual quantity gives a
   (a) Total price and quantity variance.
   (b) Price variance.
   (c) Volume variance.
   (d) Mix variance.
8. If a company follows a practice of isolating variances at the earliest point in time, what would be the appropriate time to isolate and calculate a material price variance?
   (a) When material is issued.
   (b) When material is purchased.
   (c) When material is used in production.
   (d) When purchased order is originated.
9. In a standard cost system, the materials price variance is obtained by multiplying the
   (a) Actual price by the difference between actual quantity purchased and standard quantity used.
   (b) Actual quantity purchased by the difference between actual price and standard price.
   (c) Standard price by the difference between standard quantity purchased and standard quantity used.
   (d) Standard quantity purchased by the difference between actual price and standard price.
10. How is a labour rate variance computed?
    (a) Difference between standard and actual rate multiplied by standard hours.
    (b) Difference between standard and actual hours multiplied by actual rate.
    (c) Difference between standard and actual rate multiplied by actual hours.
    (d) Difference between standard and actual hours multiplied by the difference between standard and actual rate.
11. Materials usage variances are normally chargeable to which department?
    (a) Production (b) Purchasing
    (c) Finished goods (d) Materials storage

Problems

Material Cost Variances

1. The standard set for material consumption was 100 kg @ ₹2.25 per kg

In a cost period:	Opening stocks was	100 kg @ ₹2.25 per kg
	Purchase made	500 kg @ ₹2.15 per kg
	Consumption	110 kg

Calculate:

(a) Usage variance.

(b) Price variance: (i) when variance is calculated at point of purchase; (ii) when variance is calculated at point of issue on FIFO basis; (iii) when variance is calculated at point of issue on LIFO basis.

(c) What is the effect on closing stock valuation when materials are charged out to cost on basis (ii) and (iii) above?

Ans: (a) Usage variance ₹22.50 (A) (b) (i) ₹50 (F) (ii) ₹1 (F) (iii) ₹11 (F)

2. Standard material and standard price for manufacturing one unit of a product is given below:

	Standard Material	*Standard Price*
Material *A*	5 kg	@ ₹4
Material *B*	3 kg	@ ₹6

The actual production of the product is 400 units.

The actual material *A* 2500 kg @ ₹3.90
B 1000 kg @ ₹6.25

Calculate the materials sub-usage variance. *Ans*: ₹1425 (unfavourable)

3. From the following particulars, compute: (a) materials cost variance; (b) materials price variance; (c) materials usage variance:

Quantity of materials purchased	3,000 units
Value of materials purchased	₹9,000
Standard quantity of materials required per kg of output	30 units
Standard rate of material	₹2.50 per unit
Opening stock of materials	Nil
Closing stock of materials	500 units
Output during the period	80 kg

Ans: (a) MCV ₹1,500 (A), (b) Material Price Variance ₹1,250 (A) (C) Material Usage Variance ₹250 (A)

4. The standard materials cost to produce a tonne of chemical *X* is:

300 kg of material *A* @ ₹10 per kg
400 kg of material *B* @ ₹5 per kg
500 kg of material *C* @ ₹6 per kg

During a period, 100 tonnes of mixture *X* was produced from the usage of:

35 tonnes of material *A* at a cost of ₹9,000 per tonne
42 tonnes of material *B* at a cost of ₹6,000 per tonne
53 tonnes of material *C* at a cost of ₹7,000 per tonne

Calculate the price, usage and mix variances.

Ans: MPV ₹60,000 (A),Usage Variance ₹78,000 (A) Mix Variance ₹11,333 (A)

5. A company manufacturing "distempers" operates a costing system. The standard cost of one of the products of the company shows the following standards:

Materials	*Quantity*	*Standard Price Per kg (₹)*	*Total* ₹
A	40 kg	75	3,000
B	10 kg	50	50
C	50 kg	20	1,000
Material cost per unit (Total)			4,500

The standard input mix is 100 kg and the standard output of the finished product is 90 kg.
The actual results for period are:
Materials used

A	=	2,40,000 kg	@ ₹80/kg
B	=	40,000 kg	@ ₹52/kg
C	=	2,20,000 kg	@ ₹21/kg

Actual output of the finished product = 4,20,000 kg
You are required to calculate the material price, mix and yield variances.

Ans: Materials price ₹15,00,000 (A), Material mix ₹19,00,000 (A), Material yield ₹15,00,000 (A)

6. S.V. Ltd. manufacturers a single product, the standard mix of which is:
Material A 60% at ₹20 per kg
Material B 40 % at ₹10 per kg
Normal loss in production is 20% of input. Due to shortage of Material A, the standard mix was changed. Actual results for March 2020 were;

Material *A*	105 kg at ₹20 per kg
Material *B*	95 kg at ₹9 per kg
Input	200 kg
Loss	35 kg
Output	165 kg

Calculate:
(i) Material Price Variance
(ii) Material Usage Variance
(iii) Material Mix Variance
(iv) Material Yield Variance

Ans: (i) ₹95 (F) (ii) ₹250 (F) (iii) ₹150 (F) (iv) ₹100 (F)

7. The standard cost of a certain chemical mixture is:
35% Material A at ₹25 per kg
65% Material B at ₹36 per kg
A standard loss of 5% is expected in production
During a period there is used:
125 kg of Material A at ₹27 per kg and
275 kg of Material B at ₹34 per kg
The actual output was 365 kg

Calculate:

(a) Material Cost Variance
(b) Material Price Variance
(c) Material Mix Variance
(d) Material Yield Variance

Ans: (a) ₹373 (A) (b) ₹300 (F) (c) ₹165 (A)(d) ₹508 (A)

8. Mixers Ltd. is engaged in producing a "standard mix" using 60 kg of chemical *x* and 40 kg of chemical *y*. The standard loss of production is 30%. The standard price of *x* is ₹5 per kg and of *y* ₹10 per kg. The actual mix and yield were as follows:

x 80 kg @ ₹4.50 per kg
y 70 kg @ ₹8.00 per kg

Actual yield 115 kg

Calculate Direct Material Cost, Price, Usage, Mix and Yield variances.

Ans: Material cost ₹230 (F), Price ₹180 (F), Usage ₹50 (F), Mix ₹50 (A), Yield ₹100 (F)

9. One kilogram of product *K* requires two chemicals *A* and *B*. The following were the details of product *K* for the month of June 2020.

(a) Standard mix: Chemical *A* 50% and chemical *B* 50%
(b) Standard price per kilogram of chemical *A* ₹12 and chemical *B* ₹15.
(c) Actual input of chemical *B* 70 kilogram.
(d) Actual price per kilogram of chemical *A* ₹15.
(e) Standard normal loss 10% of total input.
(f) Material cost variance total ₹650 adverse.
(g) Material yield variance total ₹135 adverse.

You are required to calculate:

(i) Material mix variance.
(ii) Material usage variance.
(iii) Material price variance.
(iv) Actual loss of actual input.
(v) Actual input of chemical *A*.
(vi) Actual price per kilogram of chemical *B*.

Ans: (i) ₹45 (F) (ii) ₹180 (A) (iii) ₹470 (A) (iv) 20 kg (v) 40 kg (vi) ₹20

10. S.V. Ltd. manufactures BXE-mixing three raw materials. For every batch of 100 kg of BXE, 125 kg of raw materials are used. In April 2020, 60 batches were prepared to produce an output of 5,600 kg of BXE. The standard and actual particulars from April 2020 are as follows:

	Standard		*Actual Raw Material*		
Raw Material	*Mix %*	*Price Per kg (₹)*	*Mix %*	*Price Per kg (₹)*	*Purchased kg*
A	50	10	60	21	5,000
B	30	10	20	8	2,000
C	20	5	20	6	1,200

Calculate all variances.

Ans: Material cost variance ₹17,500 (A); Material price variance ₹300 (A); Material usage variance ₹14,500 (A); Material mix variance ₹7500 (A); Material yield variance ₹7000 (A)

11. The standard material inputs required for 1,000 kg of a finished product are given below:

Material	*Quantity (in kg)*	*Standard Rate Per kg (in ₹)*
P	450	20
Q	400	40
R	250	60
	1,100	
Standard loss	100	
Standard output	1,000	

Actual production in a period was 20,000 kg of the finished product for which the actual quantities of material used and the prices paid therefore are as under:

Material	*Quantity Used (in kg)*	*Purchased Price Per kg (in ₹)*
P	10,000	19
Q	8,500	42
R	4,500	65

Calculate:

(i) Material Cost Variance (MCV)
(ii) Material Price Variance (MPV)
(iii) Material Usage Variance (MUV)
(iv) Material Mix Variance (MMV)
(v) Material Yield Variance (MYV)

Present a reconciliation among the variances.

Ans: (i) ₹39,500 (A); (ii) ₹29,500 (A); (iii) ₹10,000(A); (iv) ₹26,360 (F); (v) ₹36,360 (A)

Labour Cost Variances

12. From the data given below, calculate labour variances for the two departments:

	Deptt. A	*Deptt. B*
Actual gross wages (Direct)	₹2,00,000	₹1,80,000
Standard hours produced	8,000	6,000
Standard rate per hour	₹30	₹35
Actual hours worked	8,200	5,800

Ans:	*Deptt. A*	*Deptt. B*
Labour cost variance	₹40,000 (F)	₹30,000 (F)
Labour rate variance	46,000 (F)	23,000 (F)
Labour efficiency	6,000 (A)	₹7,000 (F)

13. The details regarding composition and the weekly wage rates of labour force engaged on a job scheduled to be completed in 30 hours are as follows:

Category of Workers	*No. of Labourers*	*Standard Hourly Wage Rate*	*Actual No .of Labourers*	*Hourly Wage Rate*
Skilled	75	60	70	70
Semi-skilled	45	40	30	50
Unskilled	60	30	80	20

The work is actually completed in 32 hours. Calculate the various labour variances.

Ans: Labour cost variance, ₹13,000 (A), Rate variance ₹6,400 (A), Labour efficiency 6,600 (A), Mix variance ₹9,600 (F), Labour sub-efficiency ₹16,200 (A).

14. Standard hours for manufacturing two products *M* and *N* are 15 hours per unit and 20 hours per unit respectively. Both products require identical kind of labour and the standard wages rates per hour is ₹5. In the year 2020, 10,000 units of *M* and 15,000 units of *N* were manufactured. The total of labour hours actually worked were 4,50,000 and the actual wage bill came to ₹23,00,000. This includes 12,000 hours paid for @ ₹7 per hour and 9,400 hours paid for @ ₹7.50 per hour, the balance having been paid at ₹5 per hour. You are required to compute the labour variances.

Ans: Labour cost variance ₹50,000 (A); Labour rate variance ₹47,500 (A); Labour efficiency variance ₹2,500 (A)

15. The following standards have been set to manufacture a product:

Direct materials:

2 units of A at ₹4 per unit	8.00
3 units of B at ₹3 per unit	9.00
15 units of C at ₹1 per unit	15.00
	32.00
Direct labour 3 hrs @ ₹8 per hour	24.00
Total standard prime cost	56.00

The company manufactured and sold 6,000 units of the product during the year. Direct material costs were as follows:

12,500 units of A at ₹4.40 per unit.
18,000 units of B at ₹2.80 per unit.
88,500 units of C at ₹1.20 per unit.

The company worked 17,500 direct labour hours during the year. For 2,500 of these hours the company paid at ₹12 per hour while for the remaining the wages were paid at the standard rate. Calculate materials price and usage variances and labour rate and efficiency variances.

Ans: Material price variance ₹19,100 (A) Material usage variance ₹500 (A) Labour rate variance ₹10,000 (A) Labour efficiency variance ₹4,000 (F)

16. From the following data of A and Co. Ltd. relating to budgeted and actual performance for the month of March, 2020, compute the Direct Material and Direct Labour Cost Variances.

Budgeted data for March:

Units to be manufactured	1,50,000
Units of direct material required (based on standard rates)	4,95,000
Planned purchase of raw materials (units)	5,40,000

Average unit cost of direct material	₹8
Direct labour hours per unit of finished goods	3/4 hr
Direct labour cost (Total)	₹29,92,500
Actual data at the end of March:	
Units actually manufactured	1,60,000
Direct material cost (Purchase cost based on units actually issued)	₹43,41,900
Direct material cost (Purchase cost based on units actually purchased)	₹45,10,000
Average units cost of direct material	₹8.20
Total direct labour hours for March	1,25,000
Total direct labour cost for March	₹33,75,000

Ans: MCV ₹1,17,900 (A), MPV ₹1,05,900 (A), MUV ₹12,000 (A), LCV ₹1,83,000 (A), LRV ₹50,000 (A), LEV ₹1,33,000 (A)

17. The standard labour component and the actual labour complement engaged during the month are given as follows:

	Skilled	*Semi-skilled*	*Unskilled*
(a) Standard number of workers in a group	30	10	10
(b) Standard wage rate (rupee per hour)	5	3	2
(c) Actual number of workers employed during the month in the group	24	15	12
(d) Actual wage rate per hour (₹)	6	2.5	2

During the month of 200 working hours, the group produced 9,600 standard hours of work.

Required:

Calculations showing wage rate variance, labour efficiency variance, labour mix variance and total labour cost variance.

Ans: Labour cost variance ₹2,700 (A); Labour rate variance ₹3,300 (A); Labour efficiency variance ₹2,400 (A); Labour mix variance ₹3,000 (F)

18. The following was the composition of a group of workers in a factory during a particular month, in one of the production departments. The standard composition of workers and wage rate per hour were as below:

Skilled	:	Two workers at a standard rate of ₹20 per hour each
Semi-skilled	:	Four workers at a standard rate of ₹12 per hour each
Unskilled	:	Four workers at a standard rate of ₹8 per hour each

The standard output of the group was four units per hour, of the product. During the month in question, however, the actual composition of the group and hourly rates paid were as under:

Nature of Workers	*No. of Workers*	*Wage Rate Per Worker Per Hour*
Skilled	2	₹20
Semi-skilled	3	₹14
Unskilled	5	₹10

The group was engaged for 200 hours during the month, which included 12 hours when no production was possible due to machine break down. 810 units of the product were recorded as output of the group during the month.

You are required:

(a) to compute the standard unit labour cost of the product;

(b) to compute the total variance in labour cost during the month;

(c) analyse the variances in (b) above into sub-variances and reconcile.

Ans: Standard unit labour cost ₹30 per unit Labour cost variance ₹2,100 (A); Labour rate variance ₹3,200 (A); Labour efficiency variance ₹1,740 (F); Labour idle time variance ₹1,440 (A); Labour mix variance ₹800 (F)

19. The standard output of production "EXE" is 25 units per hour in manufacturing department of a company employing 100 workers. The standard wage rate per labour hour is ₹6.

In a 42 hour week, the department produced 1,040 units of "EXE", despite 5% of the time paid was lost due to an abnormal reason. The hourly wage-rates actually paid were ₹6.20, ₹6 and ₹5.70 respectively to 10, 30 and 60 of the workers.

Compute relevant variances.

20. From the following records of Apollo Bolt Nut Manufacturing Company, you are required to compute material and labour variances:

An input of 100 kg of material yields to standard output of 10,000 units.
Standard price per kg of material = ₹20
Actual quantity of material issued and used by production department 10,000 kg
Actual price per kg of material = ₹21 per kg
Actual output = 9,00,000 units
Number of employees = 200
Standard wage rate per employee per day = ₹40
Standard daily output per employee = 100 units
Total number of days worked = 50 days
(Idle time paid for and included in the above half day for each employee)
Actual wage rate per day = ₹45

Overhead Cost Variance

21. Vinak Ltd. has furnished you the following information for the month of August, 2020:

	Budget	Actual
Output (units)	30,000	32,500
Hours	30,000	33,000
Fixed overhead	₹45,000	50,000
Variable overhead	₹60,000	68,000
Working days	25	26

Calculate the variances on the basis of output.

Ans: Total overhead cost variance ₹4,250 (A)
Variable overhead cost variance ₹3,000 (A)
Variable overhead expenditure variances ₹2000 (A)
Variable overhead efficiency variance ₹1000 (A)
Fixed overhead cost variance ₹1,250 (A)
F. Expenditure variance ₹5000 (A)
F. Volume variance ₹3,750 (F)
F. Efficiency variance ₹750 (A)
F. Capacity variance ₹2700 (F)
F. Calender variance ₹1,800 (F)

22. A cost accountant of a company was given the following information regarding the overhead for February 2020:
    (a) Overhead cost variance ₹1,400 adverse
    (b) Overhead volume variance ₹1,000 adverse
    (c) Budgeted hours of February 2020, ₹1,200 hours
    (d) Budgeted overheads for February 2020, ₹6,000
    (e) Actual rate of recovery of overhead = ₹8 per hour

    You are required to assist him in computing the following for February 2020:
    (a) Overhead expenditure variance
    (b) Actual overheads incurred
    (c) Actual hours for actual production
    (d) Overheads capacity variance
    (e) Overhead efficiency variance
    (f) Standard hours for actual production

Ans: (a) ₹400 (A), (b) ₹6,400, (c) 800 hrs, (d) ₹2,000 (A), (e) ₹1,000 (F), (f)1,000 hrs

23. The standard cost card for product "SIMCO" reveals:

	₹
Standard materials	
2 kg of A ₹2 per kg	4.00
1 kg of B ₹6 per kg	6.00
Direct labour (3 hours @ ₹6 per hour)	18.00
Variable overheads (3 hours @ ₹4 per direct labour hour)	12.00
Total standard cost per unit	40.00

It is proposed to produce 10,000 units of SIMCO in the month of March and budgeted cost based on the information contained in the standard cost card are as follows:

Direct Materials	
A 20,000 kg @ ₹2 per kg	40,000
B 10,000 kg @ ₹6 per kg	60,000
Direct labour (30,000 hours @ ₹6 per hour)	1,80,000
Variable overhead (30,000 hours @ ₹4 per direct labour)	1,20,000
	4,00,000

The actual results are:

	₹
Direct Materials	
A 19,000 kg @ ₹2.20 per kg	41,800
B 10,000 kg @ ₹5.60 per kg	56,560
Direct labour (28,500 hours @ ₹6.40 per hour)	1,82,400
Variable overheads	1,04,000
	3,84,760

Actual production was 9,000 units

From the above, calculate the following variances:
(a) Materials: Price and usage
(b) Labour: Wages rate and labour efficiency
(c) Variable overhead total and overhead expenditure variance

Ans: MPV ₹240 (F), MUV ₹8,600 (A), LRV ₹11,400 (A), LEV ₹9,000 (A), Total variable overhead variance ₹4,000 (F), Variable overhead expenditure variance ₹10,000 (F)

24. Compute the missing data indicated by the question marks from the following:

Particulars	*A*	*B*
Standard price per unit	₹12	₹15
Actual price per unit	₹15	₹20
Standard input (kg)	50	?
Actual input (kg)	?	70
Material price variance	?	?
Material usage variance	?	₹300 Adverse
Material cost variance	?	?

Material mix variance for both products together was ₹45 Adverse.

Ans: Standard input (B) 50 kg Actual input (A) 40 kg Material price variance A, ₹120 (A), B ₹350 (A), Material usage variance A, ₹120 (F) Material cost variance A ₹NIL, Material cost variance B ₹650 (A)

25. From the following data, calculate overhead variances:

	Budget	*Actual*
Output	15,000 units	16,000 units
No. of working days	25	27
Fixed overheads	₹30,000	₹30,500
Variable overheads	₹45,000	₹47,000

There was an increase of 5% in capacity.

Sales Variances

26. Pioneer Plastics Limited operates a budgetary control and standard costing system. From the following data calculate:

(i) Sales variance
(ii) Sales volume variance
(iii) Sales price variance

Product	*Budget*				*Actual*	
	Std. Selling Price Per Unit	*Std. Cost Price Per Unit*	*Units to be Sold*	*Sales Value*	*Units Sold*	*Sales Volume*
A	10.00	12.00	100	₹1,200	100	1,100
B	9.40	12.00	50	600	50	600
C	7.50	9.00	100	900	200	1,700
D	4.00	6.00	75	450	50	300
Total	—	—	325	3,150	400	3,700

Ans: Sales value variance ₹550 (F), Sales price variance ₹200 (A), Sales volume variance ₹750 (F).

27. PH Ltd. furnishes the following information relating to budgeted sales and actual sales for April 2020.

	Product	*Sales Quantity (Units)*	*Selling Price Per Unit (₹)*
Budgeted sales	*A*	1,200	15
	B	800	20
	C	2,000	40
Actual sales	*A*	880	18
	B	880	20
	C	2,640	38

Calculate the following variances:

(i) Sales quantity variance
(ii) Sales mix variance
(iii) Sales price variance
(iv) Total sales variances

Ans: ₹22,400 (F); ₹11,000 (F); (₹2640 (A), ₹19,760 (F)

28. Compute the following variance from the data given below:

(i) Total sales margin variance
(ii) Sales margin volume variance
(iii) Sales margin price variance
(iv) Sales margin quantity (sub-volume) variance.

	Budgeted Quantity Units	*Actual Qty Units*	*Budgeted Sale Price Per Unit ₹*	*Actual Sale Price Per Unit ₹*	*Standard Cost Per Unit ₹*
X	240	400	50	45	30
Y	160	200	25	20	15

Ans: (i) ₹600 (F), (ii) ₹3,600 (F), (iii) ₹3,000 (A), (iv) ₹3,200 (F)

29. From the following information about sales, calculate:

(a) Total Sales Variance
(b) Sales Price Variance
(c) Sales Volume Variance
(d) Sales Mix Variance
(e) Sales Quantity Variance

	Product Nos.	*Standard Rate in ₹ Per Unit*	₹	*Product*	*Actual Rate in ₹ Per Unit*	₹
A	5,000	5	25,000	6,000	6	36,000
B	4,000	6	24,000	5,000	5	25,000
C	3,000	7	21,000	4,000	8	32,000
	12,000		70,000	15,000		93,000

Ans: (a) ₹23,000 (F), (b) ₹5,000 (F), (c) ₹18,000 (F), (d) ₹500 (F), (e) ₹17,500 (F)

Control Ratios

30. Narang Ltd. produces two commodities—Good and Better—in one of its departments. Each unit takes 5 hrs and 10 hrs as production time, respectively. 1,000 units of Good and 600 units of Better were produced during March 2020. Actual man-hours spent in this production were 10,000. Yearly budgeted hours are 96,000. Compute the various control ratios.

Ans:	Capacity ratio	1.25
	Efficiency ratio	1.10
	Activity ratio	1.8

31. ABC Ltd. manufactures two products *A* and *B*. Product *A* takes 6 hours to make while product *B* takes 12 hours. In a month of 25 days of 8 hours each, 1,200 units of *A* and 750 units of *B* were produced. The firm employs 75 men in the department responsible for producing these two products. The budgeted hours are 1,86,000 per annum. You are required to calculate activity ratio, capacity ratio and efficiency ratio.

Ans:	Activity ratio	104.5%
	Capacity utilisation ratio	96.8%
	Efficiency ratio	108%

32. From the following data, calculate activity ratio. A factory manufactures two products *A* and *B*. Standard time to manufacture product *A* is 2 hours and product *B* 10 hours. The budgeted and actual production in December 2020 was as follows:

	Budgeted Production	*Actual Production*
Product *A*	125 units	100 units
Product *B*	30 units	24 units

Total hours worked were 660

Ans: Activity ratio 80%

33. If the "activity ratio" and "capacity ratio" of a company is 104% and 96% respectively, find out its "efficiency ratio".

Ans: Efficiency ratio 108.33%

CASE STUDY

1. Art-Wood Enterprise's Cost Control Dilemma

Art-Wood Enterprise produced office desks in its manufacturing unit at Peeniya, Bangalore (Karnataka). Since 2015, Art-Wood Enterprises was successfully selling the office desks in the market of Karnataka and nearby states. Its production capacity and average demand in the market were 1,300 and 1,100 office desks per month respectively. Although the MRP of the desk was ₹3,400 per unit, Art-Wood Enterprise delivered the finished goods to dealers on Landed Cost at their warehouse at ₹2,800 per desk unit.

The total standard hours to produce the office desk were 8 hours which included 5 hours in the workshop for plywood cutting, setting, and fitting with nuts & bolts; and 3 hours for varnishing, polishing and packing for keeping as inventory in the store or sending for delivery. Standard rate for payment to the labour of workshop division (process one labour—P1) was ₹50 per hour and the same for varnishing division (process two labour—P2) was ₹40 per hour.

The total direct material requirement for making one unit of office desk was 20 cubic foot of plywood. The standard price determined for plywood for the financial year 2018–19 was ₹50 per cubic foot. The variable overheads and fixed over-heads were budgeted at ₹12 per hour and ₹20.5 per hour respectively.

Although, the budgeted production for March 2019 was reported to be 1,250 units, 1,200 units were produced and all units produced were delivered to the dealers in the same month without any closing stock left. The actual labour costs incurred on production were as follows:

Department	*Actual Time*	*Actual Rate*	*Actual Cost*
Workshop	6,100 Hours	₹52 p.hr	₹2,92,800
Varnishing & finishing	3,550 Hours	₹48 p.hr	₹1,84,600

The Production Manager had reported that in total 25,500 cubic foot of plywood at ₹48 per cubic foot had been purchased and utilised in March. He also reported that variable overheads were ₹12.5 per hour. Art-Wood Enterprise had to hire labour at ₹52 per hour for workshop work (P1) and at ₹48 per hour for varnishing and finishing work (P2). The fixed overheads incurred was ₹2,20,000.

The owner Ganesh Satyapathi was satisfied with the overall performance of his team and the profit incurred, but was in dilemma as to how much credit should be given to which of his departments for their performance.

Manager of each department—production, purchase etc. were claiming for the success of their teams. Art-Wood Accounts Officer had submitted the following summary of records & profit calculation. Ganesh Satyapathi asked his Finance Consultant—Vivek Panigrahi to help him in the analysis of various Variances and determine the efficiency/inefficiency of various departments based on the following summary of records prepared by accounts department.

Summary of Data & Profit Calculation by the Accounts Officer:

Production Costs	*Rate for One Desk*	*Standard Costs (₹)*
Material cost	20 cubic foot @ ₹50 per cubic foot	1,000
Labour costs	P1—5hrs @ ₹50 + —3 hrs @ ₹40	370
Variable overhead	8 hrs @ ₹12 per hour	96
Fixed overhead	8 hrs @ ₹20.5	164
Total standard cost per unit		**1,630**
Selling price per unit		**2,800**
Profit per unit		**1,170**

Budgeted sales per month—1,250 units @ ₹2,800 = ₹35,00,000

Production Costs	*Rates for 1,200 Desks*	*Actual Costs Incurred (₹)*
Material cost	25,500 cubic foot @ ₹48 per cubic foot	12,24,000
Labour costs	P1—6,100 hrs @ ₹52 per hr + P2—3,550 hrs @ ₹48 per hr	4,87,600
Variable overhead	9 650 hrs @ ₹12.5 per hr	1,20,625
Fixed overhead		2,20,000
Total cost of production of 1,200 units		**20,52,225**
Sales revenue (1,200 units × ₹2,800)		**33,60,000**
Actual profit		**13,07,775**

Mr Alok Kumar, Financial Consultant has submitted the followings with various variances & recommendations—credit should be given only to the purchase manager, other departments have been inefficient in performing their responsibilities. Ganesh Satyapathi, after reading the recommendation, was in dilemma. How did Vivek Panigrahi reach this conclusion?

QUESTIONS FOR DISCUSSION:

1. Calculate all the material, labour, overheads, sales and capacity variances to determine the efficiency or otherwise of various departments.
2. Do you agree with the recommendation of Vivek Panigrahi? What steps the owner— Ganesh Satyapathi should take based on these recommendations?

ANSWER: HINT

Calculation of Total Profit Variance:

Total profit variance = (Total actual profit – Total budgeted profit)

Total Actual Profit

Particulars		*Amount (₹)*
Sales revenue	(1,200 units × Rs. 2,800)	33,60,000
Less: Total actual cost		
Material cost	12,24,000	
Labor costs	4,87,600	
Variable overhead	1,20,625	
Fixed overhead	2,20,000	20,52,225
Actual profit		13,07,775
Total budgeted profit (1,200 units × ₹1,170 per unit)		14,04,000

Total profit variance = Total actual profit – Total budgeted profit

= ₹14,04,000 – ₹13,07,775 = ₹96,225 (unfavourable)

Calculation of Sales Profit, Sales Quantity and Total Cost Variances

1. Sales Price Variance (SPV) = (ASP – BSP) × TAQ sold
   = (₹2,800 – ₹2,800) × 1,200 units = Nil
2. Sales Quantity Variance (SQV) = (AQ – BQ) SP per unit (as part of profit)
   (1,200 units – 1,250 units) × ₹1,170 per unit = ₹63,500 (unfavourable)
3. Total Cost Variance (TCV): (TAC – TSC)
   ₹20,52,225 – (₹1,630 per unit × 1,200 units i.e. ₹19,56,000) = ₹96,225 (unfavourable)

(a) Material Cost Variance (MCV) = (TAMC – TSMC)
(25,500 cubic foot @ ₹48 per cubic foot i.e., ₹12,24,000) – (₹50 per cubic foot × 20 per cubic foot × 1,200 units i.e. ₹12,00,000) = ₹24,000 (Unfavourable)

i) Material Price Variance (MPV) = (AP – SP) × TAQ
= (₹48 per hr – ₹50 per hr) × 25,500 hrs = ₹51,000 (favourable)

ii) Material Quantity Variance(MQV): (TAQ – TSQ) × SP per cubic foot
= (25,500 cf – 24,000 cf) × ₹50 per cf = ₹75,000 (unfavourable)

(b) Labour Cost Variance(LCV) = TALC – TSLC
= ₹4, 87,600 – (6,000 hrs × ₹50 + 3,600 hrs × ₹40) i.e. ₹4,44,000 = ₹43,600 (unfavourable)

i) Labour Rate Variance (LRV) = (AR – SR) × TAH
(₹52 per hr – ₹50 per hr) × 6,100 hrs + (₹48 per hr – ₹40 per hr) × 3,550 hrs
= ₹40,600 (unfavorable)

ii) Labour Efficiency Variance = (TAH – TSH) × SR per hr
(6,100 hrs – 6,000 hrs) × ₹50 per hr + (3,550 hrs – 3,600 hrs) × ₹40 per hr
= ₹3,000 (unfavourable)

(c) Variable Overhead Cost Variance = TAVOC – TSVOC
= (9,650 hrs @ ₹12.5 per hr i.e., ₹1,20,625) – (₹96 per unit × 1,200 units i.e. ₹1,15,200) = ₹5,425 (unfavourable)

i) Variable Overhead Spending Variance: (AR – SR) × TAH
= (₹12.5 per hr – ₹12 per hr) × 9,650 hrs = ₹4,825 (unfavourable)

ii) Variable Overhead Efficiency Variance: (TAH – TSH) × SVOR per hr
= (9,650 hrs – 9,600 hrs) × ₹12 per hr = ₹600 (unfavourable)

(d) Fixed Overhead Cost Variance: TAFOC – TSFOC
= ₹2,20,000 – (₹164 per unit × 1,200 units i.e. ₹1,96,800) = ₹23,200 (unfavourable)

i) Fixed Overhead Spending Variance: TAFOC – TBFOC
= ₹2,20,000 – (₹164 per unit × 1,300 units i.e. ₹2,13,200) = ₹6,800 (unfavourable)

ii) Fixed Overhead Efficiency Variance: (TAH – TSH) × SFOR per hr
= (9,650 hrs – 9,600 hrs) × ₹20.5 per hr = ₹1,025 (unfavourable)

iii) Capacity Variance: (Actual Hours – Normal Capacity) × SFOR per hr
= (9,650 hrs – 10,400 hrs) × ₹20.5 per hr = ₹15,375 (unfavourable)

Summary of All the Variances

Sales price variance	Nil	
Sales quantity variance	63,500	Unfavourable
Total cost variance	96,225	Unfavourable
(a) Material cost variance	24,000	Unfavourable
(b) Labour cost variance	43,600	Unfavourable
(c) Variable overhead cost variance	5,425	Unfavourable
(d) Fixed overhead cost variance	23,200	Unfavourable
(a) (i) Material price variance	51,000	Favourable
(iii) Material quantity variance	75,000	Unfavourable

(b) (i)	Labour rate variance	40,600	Unfavourable
(ii)	Labour efficiency variance	3,000	Unfavourable
(c) (i)	Variable overhead spending variance	4,825	Unfavourable
(ii)	Variable overhead efficiency variance	600	Unfavourable
(d) (i)	Fixed overhead spending variance	6,800	Unfavourable
(ii)	Fixed overhead efficiency variance	1,025	Unfavourable
(iii)	Capacity variance	15,375	Unfavourable

2. A Case of Epoxy Chemical Pvt. Ltd.

Anil Kumar was the Production Manager in Epoxy Chemicals Pvt. Ltd. which was in the business of manufacturing and sale of industrial glue. There were three different departments under production catering to different type of glue being produced i.e., *Acrylic*, *Cyanoacrylate* and *Epoxy Resin* adhesives. Anil was in charge of department P3 responsible for the production of epoxy resin adhesive.

For the production process, Anil used to send his raw material requirements to the Purchase Manager—Rommel Pandey who in turn issued the required quantity to the shop floor of that department.

For producing the epoxy resin glue, raw materials required were epichlorohydrin (ECH), bisphenol-A (BPA), and caustic soda (CS) & methylisobutylketone (MIBK). For producing 100 kg of epoxy resin, these raw materials were required in the following standard quantity and composition at the following standard price:

Raw Material	*Quantity*	*Rate/Price*
ECH	45 kg	₹20 per kg
BPA	40 kg	₹40 per kg
CS & MIBK	25 kg	₹60 per kg

During the production process, ECH and BPA were charged into a reactor. Then, a CS-solution was mixed to the solution which was brought to the boiling point. After the evaporation of un-reacted ECH, the two phases were separated by adding an inert solvent such as methylisobutylketone (MIBK). The resin was then washed with water and the solvent was removed by vacuum distillation to get Epoxy[1]. In this process, about 10 kg of the mixture was normally lost through evaporation.

It was the end of the month of July 2019, a particularly difficult month in terms of labour attrition. Anil had lot of difficulty in managing different set of labourers every week. He felt that a lot of time was wasted in training the new joinees and also the cases of wastage got increased because of inexperienced handling of material. He, in fact, had complained to HR Manager—Prakruti Shukla, a lot of times about this and requested for permanent workers in his departments.

Anil was going through the production sheet of July 2019. During the month, 2,000 kg of epoxy resin were produced and the actual status of raw material used by Anil's team was as follows:

[1] https://guichon-valves.com/faqs/epoxy-resins-manufacturing-process-of-epoxy-resins/

Raw Material	*Quantity*	*Rate/Price*
ECH	1,000 kg	₹19 per kg
BPA	850 kg	₹42 per kg
CS & MIBK	450 kg	₹65 per kg

Looking at the material-usage statement, Anil was worried that his team has consumed more than the standard quantity but was not able to determine the extent of overconsumption and its impact on profit. Looking at the purchase prices, he also had a doubt that his counterpart in purchase department—Rommel too was equally guilty of not being able to put cost under control.

Although, the appraisal time was two months away, he did not want to take any chance and wanted to ascertain the causes of exceeding cost (if any) and take corrective measures.

QUESTIONS FOR DISCUSSION:

1. Calculate all the material variances—(a) Total Material Cost Variance, (b) Material Quantity/ Usage Variance, (c) Material Price Variance, (d) Material Mix Variance, and (e) Material Yield Variance.
2. Was Anil right in thinking that his production team has over-stepped on the cost part?
3. How would you rate the performance of Rommel, the Purchase Manager?
4. In case the appraisal was to be done on the basis of the variance analysis of the month of July, who among Anil and Rommel would be in a better position?
5. Was Prakruti, the HR Manager, responsible for adverse variance in cost in any way?

Chapter 20

Budgeting

Learning Objectives

After reading this chapter, you should be able to:

1. explain concept of budgeting, its objectives and functions, advantages and limitations;
2. understand budgeting process, organisation for budgeting, budget manual, budget period, budget centres, principal budget factor;
3. explain elements of a successful budgeting plan;
4. distinguish between budgets and standard costs;
5. importance and differences between fixed and flexible budgeting;
6. discuss the procedure of preparing different types of functional and financial budgets; and
7. explain the concept of Zero Base Budgeting (ZBB), Planning, Programming and Budgeting System (PPBS), Performance Budgeting.

CONCEPT OF BUDGETING

One of the primary objectives of cost accounting is to provide information to business managements for planning and control. Budgeting acts as tool of both planning and control. Budgeting is a formal process of financial planning using estimated financial and accounting data. The Institute of Cost and Management. Accountants (UK) defines a budget as "a financial and/or quantitative statement, prepared and approved prior to a defined period of time, of the policy to be pursued during that period for the purpose of attaining a given objective. It may include income, expenditure and the employment of capital".

Budgeting and Forecasting

Sometimes, the terms "budgeting" and "forecasting" are used interchangeably. Both terms have some similarities, for example, both relate to future events and involve prediction of something. The basic difference between budgeting and forecasting lies in degree of sophistication involved in the predictions used by them. According to the National Association of Accountants (USA), "forecasting is a process of predicting or estimating a future happening". Forecasting is an essential part of the budgeting process. Forecasting is estimating future events and their effects on the budget. Forecasting comes to an end after mere estimating. Budgeting is a process of preparing budgets and further control aspects are involved in its procedure. Besides, forecasting can be made by a firm for purposes other than budgeting, such as a forecast of general business conditions. Such forecasts are sometimes not used in budgeting.

Thus, budgeting is not merely forecasting of a particular event. It is not simply an estimation or prediction; it is a plan. In simple terms, budgeting is an attempt, at the beginning of the year (or at any other period), to plan the profit and loss account for the year and to aim for a definite balance sheet at its end, instead of relying upon chance.

CONCEPT OF BUDGETARY CONTROL

Budgetary control is a means of control in which the actual state of affairs is compared with the budget so that appropriate action may be taken with regard to any deviations before it is too late. Briefly, the use of a budget to control a firm's activities is known as budgeting control. Budgetary control has the following main objectives:

1. To provide an organised procedure for planning. It provides a detailed plan of action for a business over a definite period of time.
2. To coordinate all the activities of various departments of a business firm in such a manner that the maximum profit will be achieved for the minimum use of resources.
3. To provide a means of determining the responsibility for all deviations from the plan (budget), and to supply information on the basis of which necessary corrective action may be taken. Thus, budgetary control has the objective of controlling cost.

OBJECTIVES AND FUNCTIONS OF BUDGETING

An effective budgeting system is vital to the success of a business firm. Budgeting is needed in organisations to perform the following functions: (i) Planning, (ii) coordination, (iii) communication, and (iv) control and performance evaluation.

Planning

Almost all business activities require some planning to ensure efficient and maximum use of scarce resources. The budget is a formal planning framework that provides specific deadlines to achieve departmental objectives and contributes towards the overall objectives of an organisation. A budget incorporates expected performance and present managerial targets. These targets guide the business operations and help in overcoming problems and analysing the future. Budgeting influences the formulation of all business strategies and subsequently assists business managers in executing such strategies.

Coordination

Coordination is a managerial function under which all factors of production and all departmental activities are balanced and integrated to achieve the objectives of the organisation. The budgeting process provides the basis for individuals in all parts of the organisation to exchange ideas on how best to achieve these objectives. According to Horngreen*, budgets help management to coordinate in the following ways:

1. The existence of a well-laid plan is the major step towards achieving coordination. Executives are forced to think of the relationships among individual operations, and the company as a whole.
2. Budgets help to restrain the empire-building efforts of executives. Budgets broaden individual thinking by helping to remove unconscious biases on the part of engineers, sales and production officers.
3. Budgets help to search out weaknesses in the organisational structure. The formulation and administration of budgets isolate problems of communication, of fixed responsibility, and of working relationships.

Communication

It is necessary in an efficient organisation that all people be informed about the objectives, policies, programmes and performances. This is made possible through their participation in the budgeting process. Budgets inform each manager of what others have agreed to do. They also inform managers of the resources available to achieve objectives and targets.

Control and Performance Evaluation

Budgeting enters into control at three points:

1. When a budget is being formulated, departments analyse their plans for the future and submit estimates as per their requirements, justifying each of their demands by demonstrating a need.
2. After budgets of different departments have been reviewed and approved they become targets that set desirable limits on spending.
3. At the end of the budget period, a comparison of actual expenditures with budget expenditure is made as a means of judging performance and fixing responsibility for deviations.

Budgets are the basis of performance evaluation in an organisation as they reflect realistic estimates of acceptable and expected performance. It is more accurate, reliable and reasonable to measure current performance against a budget rather than against a vague expectation or against results of previous year when conditions might have changed.

ADVANTAGES OF BUDGETING

Budgeting plays an important role in the effective use of resources and achieving overall organisational goals. It has the following advantages:

1. Budgeting compels and motivates management to make an early and timely study of its problems. It generates a sense of caution and care, and adequate study among managers before decisions are made by them.
2. Budgeting provides a valuable means of controlling income and expenditure of a business as it is a "plan for spending".
3. Budgeting provides a tool through which managerial policies and goals are periodically evaluated, tested and established as guidelines for the entire organisation.

* Charles T. Horngreen, *Cost Accounting, A Managerial Emphasis,* Prentice-Hall of India, New Delhi, p. 123.

4. Budgeting helps in directing capital and other resources into the most profitable channels.
5. Budgeting coordinates and correlates all business activities. It enables management to decentralise responsibility without losing control of the business. It reveals weaknesses, inefficiencies, deviations in the organisation very promptly which can be checked immediately to achieve a desired goal.
6. The use of budgeting in an organisation develops an attitude of "cost consciousness," stimulates the effective use of resources, and creates an environment of profit-mindedness throughout the organisation.
7. It provides a norm, basis or yardstick for measuring performance of departments and individuals working in organisations.
8. Budgeting encourages productive competition, provides incentive to perform efficiently and gives a sense of purpose to each individual in the organisation.
9. Budgeting provides a systematic and disciplined approach to the solution of problems in the organisation. Horngreen observes: "The uppermost point is that budgets provide a discipline that brings planning to the forefront as a key managerial responsibility."
10. Budgeting, if executed in nearly every enterprise, helps the total national economy by providing stability of employment, economic use of resources and effective prevention of waste.

LIMITATIONS OF BUDGETING

While budgeting has many advantages that are vital to an organisation, it has certain limitations which require careful consideration:

1. Planning, budgeting or forecasting is not an exact science; it uses approximations and judgement which may not be cent-per-cent accurate. At best, a budget is an estimate; no one knows precisely what will happen in the future.
2. The success and utility of budgeting depends on the cooperation and participation of all members of management. Many a time, budgeting has failed because executive management has paid only lip service to its execution.
3. A budget is only a tool and does not eliminate nor take over the place of management. Executives generally feel "circled in" by a budget and its related figures. They fail to understand that budget is meant to provide detailed information, goals and targets which may help them in achieving the company objectives.
4. The establishment of a budgeting process takes time. Also, sometimes too much is expected from a budget and in case expectations are not fulfilled, the blame is put on the budget.
5. Excessive emphasis on budgeting may result in attempts by lower level management and employees to buck the system by providing inaccurate estimates of future costs and revenues. As the end of budget period approaches and employees realise that actual expenses have not been as great as allowed by the budget, there may be a temptation to spend excessive amounts in order to "use up" the budget allowance. Such activities result in sub-optimal profits for the company.

BUDGETING PROCESS

The budgeting process or programme varies widely from one organisation to another. Differences in management style, organisation objectives, structure of competition and similar factors affect the procedures companies adopt in budget preparations. However, there are a set of guidelines (procedures) which are used in the budgeting process by a large number of organisations. These common steps can be listed as follows:

1. *Obtaining estimates of sales, production levels, expected costs, and availability of resources from each sub-unit/division/department* The departmental heads or managers are required to provide estimates of future conditions and activities that will have an impact on the company.
2. *Coordinating estimates* In many organisations, the budget committee evaluates the different plans submitted by the various organisational units to determine the potentiality of plans in the overall interest of the company and to estimate what resources are available and can be fairly allocated among the various units of the organisation.
3. *Communicating the budget to responsible managers and the concerned departments* After individual budget plans have been approved in the light of organisational goals and availability of resources, the budgets should be communicated to departments and responsible managers. Changes and modifications incorporated in the final budget should be made known to managers to obtain their cooperation and support for the budgets.
4. *Implementing the budget plan* The final budget is presented to the managers concerned and adopted as the plan of operation for the coming budget period.
5. *Reporting interim progress towards budgeted objectives* As a feedback in the budgeting process, performance reports are prepared to inform departmental managers and top management about the performances achieved in terms of budgeted figures. Such an investigation may call for a need to revise the budget during the year. This feedback of information can also be used as a basis for preparing the next year's budget.

ORGANISATION FOR BUDGETING (THE BUDGET COMMITTEE)

Responsibility for budget direction and execution is usually placed in the hands of a Budget Committee which reports directly to top management. In large companies, the budget committee is composed of Executives Incharge of major functions of the business and includes the sales manager, HRD manager, finance manager, the production manager, the chief engineer, the treasurer and the chief accounts officer.

The principal functions of the budget committee are to:

1. Decide the company's general policies and objectives.
2. Receive and review individual budget estimates concerting different departments/divisions.
3. Suggest changes, modifications in accordance with organisational objectives.
4. Approve budgets which act as an authority/target for departmental action.
5. Receive and analyse performance reports regarding the implementation of budgets.
6. Suggest corrective action to improve efficiency and achieve budgetary goals.

BUDGET MANUAL

A budget manual is a document which defines the responsibilities of persons engaged in a budgetary programme and sets out the routine, the forms and records required under budgeting. Budget manuals specify the procedures to be followed in developing the budget. Since organisations differ in terms of structure, method of production, and operating requirements, it is difficult to prepare a budget manual suitable for use in all business enterprises.

THE BUDGET PERIOD

The budget period is an important factor in developing a comprehensive budgeting programme. The length of the budget period depends on the type of business, the length of the manufacturing cycle from raw material to finished product, the ease of difficulty of forecasting future market conditions and other factors. However, a business enterprise generally prepares a short-range budget, and a long-range budget.

Short-range Budget

Short-range budgets may cover periods of three, six or twelve months depending upon the nature of the business. Most manufacturing firms use one year as the planning period. Wholesale and retail firms usually employ a six-month budget which is related to their selling seasons. In determining the period of the short-range budget, the following factors should be considered:

1. The budget period should be long enough to cover complete production of various products.
2. For business of a seasonal nature, the budget period should cover at least one entire seasonal cycle.
3. The budget period should be long enough to allow for the financing of production well in advance of actual needs.
4. The budget period should coincide with the financial accounting period to compare actual results with budget estimates and thus to facilitate better interpretation of the performance.

Long-range Budget

A long-range budget or planning is defined as a systematic and formalised process for directing and controlling future operations towards a desired objective for periods extending beyond one year. Such budgets cover specific areas, such as future sales, future production, long-term capital expenditures, extensive research and development programmes, financial requirements, profit forecast. They evaluate the future implications associated with present decisions and help management in making present decisions and select the most profitable alternative.

There are many factors which are duly considered while preparing long-term budgets, such as market trends, economic factors, growth of population, consumption pattern, industrial production, national income, government economic and industrial policy. Quantitative sales can be budgeted for a three- to five-years period. After forecasting sales, a budgeted profit and loss account can be prepared relating anticipated sales to corresponding cost and thus net operating profit can be forecasted. Likewise, a balance sheet for many years can be prepared to forecast cash, inventory levels, accounts receivable, accounts payable, liabilities, etc. The forecasted profit and loss account and balance sheet for a long range is a very useful tool in accomplishing the objectives of the organisation as a whole.

ELEMENTS OF A SUCCESSFUL BUDGETING PLAN

The success of the budgeting process in an organisation depends on the following essential elements:

1. *Accurate forecasting of business activities* Forecasting is a prerequisite in a budgeting process. It is not only the starting point, but is also critical to the development of an accurate budget.
2. *Coordinating business activities* Budgeting needs to coordinate all the individual budgets into an integrated plan as each budget has certain implications for the other budgets. There must be coordination between sales, production, purchasing, personnel budgets etc.

3. *Communicating the budgets* The success of a comprehensive budgeting programme depends on communication of individual budgets to the different units in the organisation. Managers are not responsible for budget unless the budget is communicated clearly, concisely and in an authoritative manner to them.
4. *Acceptance and cooperation* Successful budgeting also requires that budgets should be accepted by the people who must execute them. Budgeting should have the active cooperation of the entire organisation from the top to the bottom.
5. *Reasonable flexibility* The budgeting programme should contain reasonable flexibility if the situation so demands. However, it should be noted that too much flexibility and too much tightness are both undesirable. Too much flexibility will weaken the cost control and the budget will become inoperative. Similarly, too much rigidity not permitting reasonable deviations will create problems and restrictions in the implementation of the budget.
6. *Providing a framework for evaluation* Budgeting provides a basis to evaluate the performance of different departments.

BUDGET CENTRES

An organisation is usually broken down into different budget centres for administrative and control purposes. A budget centre is the lowest level in an organisation for which detailed costs are budgeted, separately from those of other budget centres. The main factor in setting up budget centres is one of the fixing responsibilities for action and inaction. To ensure adequate cost control, the budget centres should fulfil the following conditions:

1. The budget of a particular budget centre should specify precisely the costs controllable by the person responsible for that centre.
2. Costs for which responsibility is joint, for example, work carried out by a maintenance department, should be kept separate from costs which can be controlled by one manager.
3. Costs that are apportioned between two or more budget centres should also be controlled and for such costs one person should be made responsible.

LIMITING OR PRINCIPAL BUDGET FACTOR

When budgets are made, there is invariably some factor which governs or sets a limit to the quantity which can be made or sold. This is known as the limiting or principal budget factor. The Institute of Cost and Management Accountant (UK) defines a principal budget factor as "the factor the extent of whose influence must first be assessed in order to ensure that the functional budgets are reasonably capable of fulfilment". In the field of sales, the limiting factor is customer's demand which is influenced by many factors, such as price and quality of the product, competition, the general purchasing power of the public, advertising, etc. In the field of production, the principal budget factor may be plant capacity, the supply of labour of the right quality, or the availability of scarce materials.

Some examples of key factors are:

(a) Shortage of raw material
(b) Shortage of labour
(c) Plant capacity availability

(d) Sales capacity availability
(e) Cash availability

BUDGETS AND STANDARD COSTS

Standard costs and budgets are both vital tools in planning, operation and control of a business enterprise. Both differ in the following respects:

1. A standard costing system can operate without any comprehensive budgeting system.

   But budgets in absence of standard costs will only be fair estimates and cannot provide a reasonable base against which the actual results can be compared.
2. The objectives of budgeting are different from standard costing. A budget is a profit plan reflecting anticipated financial inflows and outflows. Budgets include both income and expenditure, but standards are set usually for expenses only.

   Standard costs are developed only for the production and related manufacturing cost.
3. Budgets project the volume of business and levels of costs which should be maintained. That is, they reflect cost ceilings which should not be exceeded if the budgeted profit is to be attained. Budgeted costs are expected costs.

   Standard costs emphasise the cost levels to which cost should be reduced. If costs reach this level, profit will be increased. Standards are minimum targets which are to be attained by actual performance at specific efficiency. Standard costs aims at what the costs should be.
4. Budgets covering the entire business present the forecasted profit and loss account and sometimes balance sheet also. Therefore, budgets act as guides for operating the business on a definite course of action.

   Standards are frequently used only in labour operation and do not represent expected costs but the cost that should be in a certain assumed conditions of performance. Horngreen* observes that the term "standard" is a unit concept and the term budgeted cost is a total concept. It may be helpful to think of a standard as a budget for the production of a single unit of output.
5. Budgets if achieved by the organisation do not usually involve much variance analysis. Under standard costing detailed variance analysis is carried out to find out deviations so that corrective action may be taken.
6. Review and revision of budgets is more frequently based on the changing circumstances than those of standard costs.

   Standard costs are more static and subject to less change.
7. Budgets are equally important for planning, organisation, coordination, and control functions of management.

   Standard costs contribute relatively more to the control function than other managerial functions although standards are used for all business functions.
8. Budgets are the maximum limits of expenses above which expenditure should not be incurred. Budgets are projects of financial accounts.

   Standards are minimum targets which are to be attained.
9. In budgeting, no further analysis is required if costs are within the budgets.

   Detailed analysis is needed in case of variances whether they are favourable or unfavourable.

*Charles T. Horngreen, *Cost Accounting, A Managerial Emphasis,* Prentice-Hall of India, New Delhi, p. 73.

In spite of the above differences, there are some similarities between standard costing and budgeting. Both have, in common, the establishment of pre-determined measures of performance and the comparison of actual and planned performance so as to disclose deviations which are used for the purpose of cost control. Both help in the preparation of reports which compare actual costs and pre-determined costs for management planning and control. Standards are almost indispensable to the work of establishing and operating a budget. A study made by the National Association of Accounts (USA) concludes that standard costs are especially valuable in developing the cost side of the budget because they provide a reliable and convenient source of data for converting the budgeted production schedule into requirements for raw materials, labour and services.

FIXED AND FLEXIBLE BUDGETING

Fixed Budgeting

The Institute of Costs and Management Accounts (UK) defines a fixed budget as the budget which is designed to remain unchanged irrespective of the level of activity actually attained. It is based on a single level of activity. A fixed budget performance report compares data from actual operations with the single level of activity reflected in the budget. Fixed budgets do not change when production level changes.

However, in practice, fixed budgeting is rarely used. The main reason is that actual output is often significantly different from the budgeted output. In such a case, the budget cannot be used for the purpose of cost control. The performance report may be misleading and will not contain very useful information. For example, if actual production is 12,000 units in place of the budgeted 10,000 units, the costs incurred cannot be compared with the budget which relates to different levels of activity. Since, in fixed budgeting, units are overlooked, a cost to cost comparison without considering the units may give misleading results. The performance report prepared under fixed budgeting merely discloses whether actual costs were higher or lower than budgeted costs. Therefore, the fixed budget is unable to provide useful information when actual output differs significantly from expected or budgeted output. The fact the costs and expenses are affected by fluctuations in volume limits the use of the fixed budget. Clearly, the idea of comparing performance at one activity level with a plan that was developed at some other activity level is nonsense from the viewpoint of judging how efficiently the manager has produced any given output.

A fixed budget can be usefully employed when budgeted output is close enough to the actual output. If output can be estimated within close limits, the fixed budget can be a good basis for performance measurement. Maximum managerial control may be exercised by making comparisons with actual operating figures.

Flexible Budgeting

A flexible budget is a budget that is prepared for a range, that is, for more than one level of activity. It is a set of alternative budgets to different expected levels of activity. The flexible budget is also known by other names, such as variable budget, dynamic budget, sliding scale budget, step budget, expenses formula budget and expenses control budget. The underlying principle of a flexible budget is that every business is dynamic, ever-changing, and never static. Thus, a flexible budget might be developed that would apply to a "relevant range" of production, say 8,000 to 12,000 units. Under this approach, if actual production slips to 9,000 units from a projected 10,000 units, the manager has a specific tool (that is., the flexible budget) that can be used to determine budgeted cost at 9,000 units of output. The flexible budget provides a reliable basis for comparisons because it is automatically geared to changes in production activity. A flexible budget has the following important features:

1. It covers a range of activity (output).
2. It is flexible, that is, easy to change with variation in production levels.
3. It facilitates performance measurement and evaluation.

Planning or budgeting for a range of activity rather than for a single level of activity is always preferable due to the uncertainty about the changes in activity levels. In flexible budgeting, that range of activity is selected which is likely to occur. Most often, one activity level at each extreme of the activity range is selected, with one or more in between. Among different activity levels the most likely activity level is made the basis for planning business operations. Flexible budgeting makes it easy to adjust plans to changing production levels without any delay. The flexibility involved in this budget makes a very useful decision-making tool for management.

Steps in Flexible Budgeting

The following steps (stages) are involved in developing a flexible budget:

1. Deciding the range of activity to which the budget is to be prepared.
2. Determining the cost behaviour patterns (fixed, variable, semi-variable) for each element of cost to be included in the budget.
3. Selecting the activity levels (generally in terms of production) to prepare budgets at those levels.
4. Preparing the budget at each activity level selected by associating the activity level with corresponding costs. The corresponding costs to be attached with each activity level are determined in terms of their behaviour, that is, fixed, variable or semi-variable.

Advantages of Flexible Budgeting

Flexible budgeting is budgeting that is automatically tailored to any level of activity. Although it is most often associated with the control of overhead, a flexible budget may also include direct materials and direct labour. Welsch* has listed three specific uses of the flexible budget.

1. To facilitate development of the departmental expense budgets for inclusion in the profit plans.
2. To provide expense goals for the managers of responsibility centres during the period covered by the profit plan.
3. To provide adjusted budget allowances for comparison purposes (against actual expenses) in the monthly performance reports.

In general, flexible budgeting has the following important advantages:

1. *Accurate budgeting* The use of flexible budgets may result in the preparation of more accurate budgets. Flexible budgeting techniques require that consideration is to be given to the output factor in budget preparation. Since all costs do not behave in the same manner (as some costs rise faster than others when production increases) a budget giving consideration to the volume (output) factor is bound to be more accurate than one where volume is not considered.
2. *Accurate performance measurement* The flexible budgeting technique incorporates changes in activity level and compares actual results with the budget in terms of output achieved. This

*Glenn A,Welsch, *Budgeting, Profit Planning and Control,* P.22

facilitates more meaningful comparison and evaluation between actual and budgeted data as comparable data are compared.

3. *Coordination* Flexible budgeting results in coordination between all activities/departments of a business. Production is planned in relation to expected sales; materials and labour are acquired to meet expected production requirements. Facilities are provided to achieve budgetary goals, and funds are made available for the investments necessary to have higher output.
4. *Control tool* Flexible budgeting is an effective management control tool. Comparisons between the budgeted costs (at the actual production level) and actual costs form the basis for analysing cost variances and fixing responsibility for the same. In fact, managers themselves feel motivated in controlling costs for which they are responsible. This contributes to cost control throughout the organisation.

EXAMPLE 20.1

The following are the budget estimates of plant servicing department in a manufacturing company:

Items of Cost	*Planned at 6,000 Service Hour (₹)*	*Planned at 9,000 Service Hour (₹)*
Salaries	28,000	28,000
Indirect materials	42,000	63,000
Miscellaneous costs	16,000	20,500

Required:
Prepare a flexible budget for the department for 7,000, 8,000 and 9,500 service hours.

Solution

Flexible Budget of the Department

	7,000 Service Hrs (₹)	*8,000 Service Hrs (₹)*	*9,500 Service Hrs (₹)*
Salaries (fixed)	28,000	28,000	28,000
Indirect materials (Variable @ ₹7 per hour)	49,000	56,000	66,500
Miscellaneous costs:			
Variable @ ₹1.5 per hour	10,500	12,000	14,250
Fixed	7,000	7,000	7,000
	94,500	1,03,000	1,15,750

Working Notes:

(i) *Salaries* are fixed as they are constant at both 6,000 service hours and 9,000 service hours.

(ii) *Indirect materials*

Increase in cost = ₹63,000 – ₹42,000

= ₹21,000

Increase in service hours = 9,000 – 6,000

= 3,000 hours

(Contd.)

Variable portion of indirect material

= ₹21,000 ÷ 3000 hrs

= ₹7 per hour

Indirect material at 6,000 hrs = 6,000 × ₹7 = ₹42,000

Indirect material at 9,000 hrs = 9,000 × ₹7 = ₹63,000

Thus, indirect materials in total are variable cost

(iii) *Miscellaneous costs*

Increase in cost = ₹20,500 – 16,000

= 4,500

Increase in hrs = 9,000 – 6,000 = 3,000

Variable portion = ₹4,500 ÷ 3,000 hrs

= ₹1.5 per hour

Miscellaneous cost at any level, say 6,000 hrs

Variable portion = 6,000 hrs × 1.5 = ₹9,000

Remaining fixed miscellaneous cost = ₹16,000 – 9,000 = ₹7,000

EXAMPLE 20.2

The following are the estimated sales of Philips Company for eight months ending 30-10-2020:

April 2020	—	12,000 units
May 2020	—	13,000 units
June 2020	—	9,000 units
July 2020	—	8,000 units
August 2020	—	10,000 units
September 2020	—	12,000 units
October 2020	—	14,000 units
November 2020	—	12,000 units

for excel template, scan

As a matter of policy, the company maintains the closing balance of finished goods and raw materials as follows:

(i) Finished goods—closing stock of a month will be 50% of the estimated sales for the next months.

(ii) Raw material—closing stock of a month will be equal to estimated consumption for the next month.

Each unit of production consumes 2 kg of raw material costing ₹6 per kg.

Prepare the following budgets for the half year ending 30-9-2020:

(i) Production budget (month-wise in units)

(ii) Raw material purchase budget (month-wise in units and cost).

Solution

Production Budget for the Half Year Ending 30-09-2020

	April	May	June	July	Aug.	Sep.	Total
Sales (units)	12,000	13,000	9,000	8,000	10,000	12,000	
Add: Closing stock	6,500	4,500	4,000	5,000	6,000	7,000	
Less: Opening stock	(6,000)	(6,500)	(4,500)	(4,000)	(5,000)	(6,000)	
Estimated production	12,500	11,000	8,500	9,000	11,000	13,000	

Raw Material Purchase Budget for Half Year Ending 30-09-2020

	April	May	June	July	Aug.	Sep.	Total
Material @ 2 kg per unit of production (kg.)	25,000	22,000	17,000	18,000	22,000	26,000	
Add: Closing stock	22,000	17,000	18,000	22,000	26,000	26,000	
Less: Opening stock	(25,000)	(22,000)	(17,000)	(18,000)	(22,000)	(26,000)	
Purchases	22,000	17,000	18,000	22,000	26,000	26,000	
Cost @ ₹6 per kg	1,32,000	1,02,000	1,08,000	1,32,000	1,56,000	1,56,000	7,86,000

EXAMPLE 20.3

Appex Co. can produce 4,000 units of a product at 100% capacity. The following information is available from its records:

	April	May
Units produced	2,800	3,600
	₹	₹
Power	1,800	2,000
Repair and maintenance	500	560
Indirect labour	700	900
Consumable stores	1,400	1,800
Inspection	200	240
Depreciation	1,400	1,400
Salaries	1,000	1,000

Direct material cost per unit is ₹1 and direct wages per hour is ₹4. Rate of production per hour is 10 units.

You are required to:

(i) Compute the cost of production at 100%, 80% and 60% capacity levels showing variable, fixed and semi-variable items under the flexible budget.

(ii) Compute overhead absorption rate at 80% capacity.

☞ Solution

Flexible Budget

	60%	80%	100%
Units of production	2,400	3,200	4,000
Variable Costs	₹	₹	₹
Direct materials	2,400	3,200	4,000
Direct wages	960	1,280	1,600
Indirect labour	600	800	1,000
Consumable stores	1,200	1,600	2,000
Semi-Variable Costs			
Power	1,700	1,900	2,100
Inspection	180	220	260
Repairs and maintenance	470	530	590
Fixed Costs			
Depreciation	1,400	1,400	1,400
Salaries	1,000	1,000	1,000
Total Cost	9,910	11,930	13,950

(ii) *Overhead absorption rate at 80% capacity*

			₹
	Total cost at 80%		11,930
Less:	Direct materials	3,200	
	Direct labour	1,280	4,480
	Overhead cost		7,450

$$\text{Overhead rate per unit} = \frac{₹7,450}{3,200\text{ units}} = \mathbf{₹2.33}$$

✍ EXAMPLE 20.4

The monthly budgets for factory overheads for two levels of activity were as follows:

Budgeted production (units)	60%	100%
	600	1,000
	₹	₹
Wages	1,200	2,000
Consumable stores	900	1,500
Maintenance	1,100	1,500
Power and fuel	1,600	2,000
Depreciation	4,000	4,000

(Contd.)

Budgeted production (units)	60%	100%
Insurance	1,000	1,000
Total	9,800	12,000

You are required to prepare a budget for 80% capacity.

Solution

Classification of cost according to the variability:

(a) *Wages:* ₹2 per unit (Variable cost)

(b) *Consumable Stores:* ₹1.50 per unit (Variable cost)

(c) *Maintenance Cost*

Variable cost per unit = Change in cost/Change in output

= ₹400/400 = ₹1 per unit

At 600 units variable maintenance cost are = 600 × ₹1 = ₹600

At 600 units maintenance fixed costs are = ₹1,100 – ₹600 = ₹500

At 100 units the fixed maintenance costs are = ₹1,500 – ₹1,000

= ₹500

Thus, maintenance cost is a semi-variable cost.

(d) *Power and Fuel Cost Per Unit*

Variable cost per unit = Change in cost/Change in output

= 400/400 = ₹1

At 600 units fixed power & fuel costs are = ₹1,600 – ₹600 = ₹1,000

At 1,000 units fixed powers & fuel costs are = ₹2,000 – ₹1,000 = ₹1,000

Thus, power and fuel is a semi-variable cost

(e) Depreciation remains constant at both levels of activity and therefore, it is fixed cost.

(f) Insurance remains constant at both levels of activity and, therefore, it is fixed cost.

Budget for 80% Capacity

Item		*Nature*	*Costs*
Wages		Variable	1,600
Consumable stores		Variable	1,200
Maintenance		Semi-variable	
Variable	800		
Fixed	500		1,300
Power & Fuel		Semi-variable	
Variable	800		
Fixed	1,000		1,800
Depreciation		Fixed	4,000
Insurance		Fixed	1,000
		Total	10,900

EXAMPLE 20.5

A factory is currently running at 50% capacity and produces 5,000 units at a cost of ₹90 per unit as per details given below:

Material	50
Labour	15
Factory overheads	15 (₹6 fixed)
Administrative overheads	10 (₹5 fixed)

The current selling price is ₹100 per unit. At 60% working, material cost per unit increases by 2% and selling price per unit falls by 2%. At 80% working, material cost per unit increases by 5% and selling price per unit falls by 2.5%. Prepare a flexible budget showing profits of the factory at 60% and 80% working and offer your comments.

for excel template, scan

Solution

Flexible Budget
Present Capacity 50% (5,000 Unit)

	Nature of Cost	50% Capacity 5,000 Units		60% Capacity 6,000 Units		80% Capacity 8,000 Units	
		Per Unit ₹	Total ₹ (Lakhs)	Per Unit ₹	Total ₹Lakhs	Per Unit ₹	Total ₹Lakhs
Raw materials	V	50	2.50	51	3.06	52.50	4.20
Labour	V	15	0.75	15	0.90	15.00	1.20
Factory overhead (₹9)	V	09	0.45	09	0.54	09.00	0.72
Adm. overheads (₹5)	V	05	0.25	05	0.30	05.00	0.40
(1) Total variable cost		79	3.95	80	4.80	81.50	6.52
Factory overhead (₹6 fixed)	F	06	0.30	–	0.30	–	0.30
Adm. overheads (₹5 fixed)	F	05	0.25	–	0.25	–	0.25
(2) Total fixed cost		11	0.55	09	0.55	07.00	0.55
(3) Total cost (1 + 2)		90	4.50	89	5.35	88.50	7.07
(4) Profit		10	0.50	09	0.53	09.00	0.73
(5) Sales		100	5.00	98	5.88	97.50	7.80

EXAMPLE 20.6

G.S. Ltd. manufactures a single product for which market demand exists for additional quantity. Present sales of ₹60,000 per month utilises only 60% capacity of the plant. Marketing manager assures that with the reduction of 10% in the price he would be in a position to increase the sale by about 25% to 30%.

The following data are available:

(i) Selling price	₹10 per unit
(ii) Variable cost	₹3 per unit
(iii) Semi-variable cost	₹6,000 fixed + 50 paise per unit
(iv) Fixed cost	₹20,000 at present level estimated to be ₹24,000 at 80% output.

You are required to prepare the following statements:

(i) The operating profits at 60%, 70% and 80% levels at current selling price; and
(ii) The operating profits at proposed selling price at the above levels.

Solution

Statement of Cost and Profit (at Current Prices)

	60% Capacity 6,000 Units	*70% Capacity 7,000 Units*	*80% Capacity 8,000 Units*
	₹	₹	₹
Fixed cost	20,000	20,000	20,000
Semi-variable cost: Fixed	6,000	6,000	6,000
Variable @ 50 paise per unit	3,000	3,500	4,000
Variable costs @ ₹3 per unit	18,000	21,000	24,000
Total cost	47,000	50,500	54,000
Sales	60,000	70,000	80,000
Profit	13,000	19,500	26,000

Statement of Cost and Profit (at Proposed Price)

	60% Capacity 6,000 Units	*70% Capacity 7,000 Units*	*80% Capacity 8,000 Units*
	₹	₹	₹
Total cost	47,000	50,500	54,000
Sales @ ₹9 per unit	54,000	63,000	72,000
Profit	7,000	12,500	18,000

EXAMPLE 20.7

Figures regarding sales, cost and profit at 50% capacity are given below:

	₹
Sales	20,00,000
Direct cost	8,00,000
Factory overheads	4,00,000

Office overheads	2,00,000
Selling overheads	3,00,000
Profit	3,00,000

Every 10% increase in sale beyond 50% capacity is possible only after reducing the price by 1% on the base level of 50% capacity. Direct material cost is 25% of the total direct cost at 50% capacity. With every 10% increase in capacity above this level, the price of direct material comes down by 2%. 50% of the factory overheads are fixed and the rest are full variable. Office overheads are of step character. Every 10% increase in output results in 2% increase in office overheads over 50% capacity. Selling overheads increase in proportion of sales value.

Prepare a flexible budget at 80% capacity level.

Solution

Flexible Budget

Particulars	*At 50% of Capacity* ₹	*At 80% Capacity* ₹
Direct cost	8,00,000	12,60,800
Factory overheads		
Variable	2,00,000	3,20,000
Fixed	2,00,000	2,00,000
Factory cost	12,00,000	17,80,800
Office overheads	2,00,000	3,39,587
Cost of production	14,00,000	21,20,387
Selling overheads	3,00,000	4,65,600
Cost of sales	17,00,000	25,85,987
Profit	3,00,000	5,18,013
Sales	20,00,000	31,04,000

Working Notes:

(i) At 50% capacity direct material is 25% of direct cost that is $8,00,000 \times \frac{25}{100} = ₹2,00,000$

At 80% capacity $= \frac{2,00,000}{50} \times 80 = ₹3,20,000$

Less 2% decrease with every 10%

Remaining direct cost at 50% capacity

₹8,00,000 – ₹2,00,000 = ₹6,00,000

Increase in capacity $= \frac{3,20,000 \times 6}{100} = \frac{19,200}{3,00,800}$

$$\text{At 80\% capacity} = \frac{6,00,000 \times 80}{50} = \frac{9,60,000}{12,60,800}$$

(ii) Factory overhead = ₹2,00,000 (Fixed)

$$\text{Variable at 80\% capacity} = \frac{2,00,000 \times 80}{50} = ₹3,20,000$$

(iii) Office overheads

At 50% capacity = ₹2,00,000

$\text{At 60\% capacity} = \frac{2,00,000}{50} \times 60$ ₹2,40,000

Add: 2% increase 4800

2,44,800

$\text{At 70\% capacity} = \frac{2,44,800}{60} \times 70$ ₹2,85,600

Add: 2% increase 5,712

2,91,312

$\text{At 80\% capacity} = \frac{2,91,312}{70} \times 80$ ₹3,32,928

Add: 2% increase 6,659

(iv) Selling overhead: proportionate to sale value

$$₹\ \frac{3,00,000}{20,00,000} \times 31,04,000 = ₹4,65,600$$

(v) Sales at 80%

$\frac{20,00,000}{50} \times 80$ ₹32,00,000

Less: 1% decrease with every 10% increase in sale that is, 3% of ₹32,00,000 96,000

₹31,04,000

✍ EXAMPLE 20.8

G. Ltd. is currently operating at 75% of its capacity. In the past two years, the levels of operations were 55% and 65% respectively. Presently, the production is 75,000 units. The company is planning for 85% capacity level during 2019–20.

The cost details are as follow:

Particulars	55% ₹	65% ₹	75% ₹
Direct materials	11,00,000	13,00,000	15,00,000
Direct labour	5,50,000	6,50,000	7,50,000
Factory overheads	3,10,000	3,30,000	3,50,000
Selling overheads	3,20,000	3,60,000	4,00,000

(Contd.)

Administrative overheads	1,60,000	1,60,000	1,60,000
	24,40,000	28,00,000	31,60,000

Profit is estimated @ 20% on sales. The following increases in costs are expected during the year:

	In Percentage
Direct materials	8
Direct labour	5
Variable factory overheads	5
Variable selling overheads	8
Fixed factory overheads	10
Fixed selling overheads	15
Administrative overheads	10

Prepare a flexible budget for the period 2019–20 at 85% level of capacity and ascertain the profit on sales.

☞ ***Solution***

Statement showing the flexible budget at 85% capacity level during 2019–20.

	Working Notes	*85% Capacity Level*
		₹
Sales	1	47,31,500
Variable Costs:		
Direct material	2	18,36,000
Direct labour	3	8,92,500
Variable factory	4	1,78,500
Variable selling overhead	5	3,67,200
Total Variable cost		32,74,200
Contribution		14,57,300
Fixed Cost:		
Factory overhead	6	2,20,000
Selling overhead	7	1,15,000
Administrative overhead	8	1,76,000
Total Fixed Cost		5,11,000
Total Cost of Sales		37,85,200
Profit (I–IV)		9,46,300

WORKING NOTES:

1. It is given that budgeted profit is 20% of sales equal to 25% of cost of sales. Total cost of sales at 85% capacity level is as follows:

   $$\text{Sales} = ₹37{,}85{,}200 \times \frac{125}{100} = ₹47{,}31{,}500.$$

2. Raw material is variable in nature. The raw material cost at 75% level

	₹
material cost at 75% level	= 15,00,000
At 65% level	= 13,00,000
At 10% level	= 2,00,000

   At 85% level material cost = ₹15,00,000 + ₹2,00,000 = ₹17,00,000 with 8% increase, the budgeted raw material cost will be:

   $$₹\frac{17{,}00{,}000 \times 108}{100} = ₹18{,}36{,}000$$

3. Direct wages is also variable in nature

Direct labour at 75% level	= 7,50,000
Direct labour at 65% level	= 6,50,000
Direct labour at 10% level	= 1,00,000

   Direct labour at 85% level = ₹7,50,000 + ₹1,00,000 = ₹8,50,000

   $$\text{With 5\% increase} = ₹\frac{8{,}50{,}000 \times 105}{100} = ₹8{,}92{,}500$$

4. Factory overhead is semi-variable in nature. Therefore, the same has to be segregated into variable portion and fixed portion.

   $$= \frac{₹3{,}50{,}000 - ₹3{,}30{,}000}{75 - 65} = \frac{20{,}000}{10} = ₹2{,}000$$

   Variable factory overhead at 85% = ₹2,000 × 85 = ₹1,70,000.

   $$\text{With 5\% increase} = \frac{₹1{,}70{,}000 \times 105}{100} = ₹1{,}78{,}500$$

5. Variable selling overhead

   $$= \frac{₹4{,}00{,}000 - ₹3{,}60{,}000}{75 - 65}$$

   $$= \frac{40{,}000}{10} = ₹4{,}000$$

   At 85% level ₹4,000 × 85 = 3,40,000

   $$\text{With 8\% increase } \frac{₹3{,}40{,}000 \times 108}{100} = ₹3{,}67{,}200$$

6. Total factory overhead (55% level) = 3,10,000

   Less: Variable portion $₹2{,}00{,}000 \times \frac{55}{10}$ = 1,10,000

   Fixed portion 2,00,000

With 10% increase = ₹20,000 × $\frac{110}{100}$ = 2,20,000

7. Total selling overhead (55% level) = 3,20,000

Less: Variable portion = 40,000 × $\frac{55}{10}$ = 2,20,000

Fixed portion 1,00,000

With 15% increase = $\frac{₹1,00,000 \times 115}{100}$ = ₹1,15,000

8. Administration overhead.

= ₹1,60,000 × $\frac{110}{100}$ = ₹1,76,000

EXAMPLE 20.9

From the following data, prepare a flexible budget for production of 40,000 units and 75,000 units, distinctly showing variable cost and fixed cost as well as total cost. Also indicate element-wise cost per unit. Budgeted output is 100,000 units and budgeted cost per unit is as follows:

Direct material	95
Direct labour	50
Production overhead (variable)	40
Production overhead (fixed)	5
Administration overhead (fixed)	5
Selling overhead (10% fixed)	10
Distribution overhead (20% fixed)	15

Solution

Flexible Budget

	1,00,000 Units		*40,000 Units*		*75,000 Units*	
	Per Unit	*Total*	*Per Unit*	*Total*	*Per Unit*	*Total*
Variable Cost:	₹	₹	₹	₹	₹	₹
Direct material	95	95,00,000	95	38,00,000	95	71,25,000
Direct labour	50	50,00,000	50	20,00,000	50	37,50,000
Production overhead	40	40,00,000	40	16,00,000	40	30,00,000
Selling overhead = $\frac{10 \times 90}{100}$	9	9,00,000	9	3,60,000	9	6,75,000
Distribution overhead = $\frac{15 \times 80}{100}$	12	12,00,000	12	4,80,000	12	9,00,000
Total variable cost	206	20,600,000	206	82,40,000	206	1,54,50,000

(Contd.)

	1,00,000 Units		40,000 Units		75,000 Units	
	Per Unit	Total	Per Unit	Total	Per Unit	Total
Fixed Cost:						
Production overhead	5	5,00,000	12.50	5,00,000	6.67	5,00,000
Administrative overhead	5	5,00,000	12.50	5,00,000	6.67	5,00,000
Selling overhead	1	1,00,000	2.50	10,00,000	1.33	1,00,000
Distribution overhead	3	3,00,000	7.50	30,00,000	3.00	3,00,000
Total fixed cost	14	14,00,000	35.00	14,00,000	17.67	14,00,000
Total cost	260	2,20,00,000	231.00	96,40,000	223.67	1,68,50,000

EXAMPLE 20.10

Brilliant Ltd. is engaged in production of certain products, 100% capacity being 10,000 units per month. Given below is the information for the just concluded previous two months:

	Month 1	Month 2
Unit produced	6,000	9,000
Costs (other than direct material and labour)		
	₹	₹
Salaries	30,000	30,000
Power	30,000	39,000
Consumable stores	30,000	45,000
Repair	40,000	46,000
Indirect shop labour	15,000	22,500
Depreciation	25,000	25,000
Inspection	10,000	13,000

Rate of production per hour is 10 units. Direct material costs are ₹20 per unit and direct labour hour costs per hour are ₹80. You are required to compute cost of production segregating fixed, semi-variable and variable costs separately at 100%, 80% and 50% capacity utilisation levels respectively. Also work out the overhead absorption rate per hour at 100% capacity utilisation level. (Show your workings as part of the answer).

Solution

Workings

As a first step, the semi-variable expenses to be identified by seeing which of the expenses do not vary directly in proportion to the activity levels.

	Diff. in Capacity	Diff. in Overhead	Variable	Fixed	Total
		₹	₹	₹	₹
Power	30%	9,000			
	1%	300			
at capacity level	60%	18,000	18,000	12,000	30,000
	90%	27,000	27,000	12,000	39,000
	100%	30,000	30,000	12,000	42,000
	80%	24,000	24,000	12,000	36,000
	50%	15,000	15,000	12,000	27,000

Similarly repairs and inspection costs are to be calculated.

Brilliant Ltd.
Cost of Production at Various Capacity Levels

Capacity	100%	80%	50%
Units	10,000	8,000	5,000
Production hours	1000	800	500
	₹	₹	₹
Element of cost:			
Direct material	2,00,000	1,60,000	1,00,000
Direct labour	80,000	64,000	40,000
Prime cost	2,80,000	2,24,000	1,40,000
Factory Overheads:			
Variable:			
Consumables	50,000	40,000	25,000
Ind. shop labour	25,000	20,000	11,500
Semi variable:			
Power	42,000	36,000	27,000
Repairs	48,000	44,000	38,000
Inspection	14,000	12,000	9,000
Fixed:			
Salaries	30,000	30,000	30,000
Depreciation	25,000	25,000	25,000
	2,34,000	2,07,000	1,65,500
Total cost of production	5,14,000	4,31,000	3,05,500

Overhead absorption rate at 100% capacity = ₹2,34,000/1,000 = ₹234

for excel template, scan

EXAMPLE 20.11

The cost of an article at a capacity level of 5,000 units is given in the table below under column *A*. For a variation of 25% in capacity above or below this level, the individual expenses vary, as indicated in column *B*.

	A (₹)	*B* (₹)
Material cost	25,000	100% variable
Labour cost	15,000	100% variable
Power	1,250	80% semi-variable
Repairs and maintenance	2,000	75% semi-variable
Stores	1,000	100% variable
Inspection	500	20% semi-variable
Administrative overheads	5,000	25% semi-variable
Selling overheads	3,000	50% semi-variable
Depreciation	10,000	100% fixed
Total	62,750	
Cost per unit	12.55	

You are required to prepare the production cost budget (flexible) at 4,000 units and 6,000 units.

Solution

Production Cost (Flexible) Budget

(Figures are in ₹)

	4,000 Units	6,000 Units
Material cost (variable)	20,000	30,000
Labour cost (variable)	12,000	18,000
Stores (variable)	800	1,200
Power (semi-variable)	1,050	1,450
Repairs and maintenance (semi-variable)	1,700	2,300
Inspection (semi-variable)	480	520
Administrative overheads (semi-variable)	4,750	5,250
Selling overhead (semi-variable)	2,700	3,300
Depreciation (fixed)	10,000	10,000
Total	53,480	72,020
	13.37	12.00

EXAMPLE 20.12

A newly established manufactured company has an installed capacity to produce 1,00,000 units of a consumer product annually. However, its practical capacity is only 90%. The actual capacity utilisation may be substantially lower, as the firm is new to the market and demand is uncertain. The following budget has been prepared for 90% capacity utilisation:

	Cost Per Unit	
	₹	
Direct materials	12	
Direct labour	8	
Direct expense	5	
Production overheads	10	(40% variable)
Administration overheads	5	(100% fixed)
Selling and distribution	6	(50% variable)

You are required to prepare budgets at 60%, 70% and 80% levels of capacity utilisation giving clearly the unit variable cost, the unit fixed cost, and the total costs under various heads at all the above levels.

☞ ***Solution***

Flexible Budget of a Consumer Product

Capacity	*60%*		*70%*		*80%*	
Production (Units)	*60,000*		*70,000*		*80,000*	
	Total Cost (₹in Lakhs)	*Cost Per Unit (₹)*	*Total Cost (₹in Lakhs)*	*Cost Per. Unit (₹)*	*Total Cost (₹in Lakhs)*	*Cost Per Unit (₹)*
Direct Costs:						
Direct materials	7.20	12.00	8.40	12.00	9.60	12.00
Direct labour	4.80	8.00	5.60	8.00	6.40	8.00
Direct expenses	3.00	5.00	3.50	5.00	4.00	5.00
Variable Overheads:						
Production overhead	2.40	4.00	2.80	4.00	3.20	4.00
Selling and Distribution Overhead: *(Ref. W.N.1)*	1.80	3.00	2.10	3.00	2.40	3.00
Total variable cost (A)	19.20	32.00	22.40	32.00	25.60	32.00
Fixed Overheads:						
Production overhead	5.40	9.00	5.40	7.71	5.40	6.75
Administration overhead	4.50	7.50	4.50	6.43	4.50	5.62
Selling and Distribution Overhead. *(Ref. W.N.2)*	2.70	4.50	2.70	3.86	2.70	3.38
Total fixed cost (B)	12.60	21.00	12.60	18.00	12.60	15.75
Total cost (A + B)	31.80		35.00		38.20	

(Contd.)

Capacity	*60%*		*70%*		*80%*	
Production (Units)	*60,000*		*70,000*		*80,000*	
	Total Cost (₹in Lakhs)	*Cost Per Unit (₹)*	*Total Cost (₹in Lakhs)*	*Cost Per. Unit (₹)*	*Total Cost (₹in Lakhs)*	*Cost Per Unit (₹)*
Cost per unit (₹)		53.00		50.00		47.75

Working Notes:

1. Variable Overheads:
   Production overhead: 40% of ₹10 = ₹4.00
   Selling and Distribution overhead: 50% of ₹6 = ₹3.00
2. Fixed Overheads:
   Practical capacity is 90% that is, of 100.000 = 90,000 units

Production overhead: (60% of ₹10 = ₹6) = 90,000 × ₹6 = ₹5,40,000
Administration overhead: 9,00,000 × 5 = ₹4,50,000
Selling and Distribution overhead (50% of ₹6 = 3): 90,000 × 3 = ₹2,70,000

TYPES OF BUDGETS

Budgets are the end product of the budgeting process. The numbers and types of budgets in a business enterprise depend on the size and nature of the business. However, in a manufacturing concern, the following budgets are generally prepared:

(A) Operating and functional budgets:
1. Sales budget
2. Production budget
3. Production cost budget
   (i) Direct materials budget
   (ii) Direct labour budget
   (iii) Factory overhead budget
4. Ending inventories budget
5. Cost of goods sold budget
6. Selling expense budget
7. Administrative expense budget
8. Budgeted income statement

(B) Financial budgets:
1. Capital expenditure budget
2. Research and development budget
3. Cash budget
4. Budgeted balance sheet
5. Budgeted statement of changes in financial position.

Sales Budget

The most important budget, which all other budgets are contingent upon, is the sales budget. All budgets, such as production budget, selling and distribution budget and others are all affected by the sales budget and are dependent upon the revenue derived from sales.

A specimen of sales budget is given in Fig. 20.1.

ABC Company Ltd.
Sales Budget for the Year Ending December 31, 2020

Products	*Budgeted Sales Units*	*Budgeted Sales Price* (₹)	*Total*
A	70,000	80,000	56,00,000
B	80,000	1,20,000	96,00,000
Total	1,50,000		1,52,00,000

Fig. 20.1 Sales Budget

Forecasting Sales

Developing a sales budget requires forecasting future sales levels. The three main factors that should be considered by management in forecasting sales are: (a) information concerning past performance, (b) information about present conditions within the individual company and in each sales territory, and (c) data concerning the industry and general business conditions.

The information about past performance is the starting point for sales forecasting. The sales record for past years, and particularly for the year just ending should be available to management in minute detail.

The second essential step in forecasting sales is the accumulation of data regarding conditions within the company and in each sales territory. The management can obtain a good picture of sales prospects through information sent to the head office by salesmen, dealers, and sales officers of different territories.

Information about general business conditions is known as "business barometers" and they should be considered in preparing a sales forecast. The following are important business indicators:

1. Gross national product, which is the total market value of output of goods and services produced in the entire economy.
2. Personal income and purchasing power of the population.
3. Unemployment conditions.
4. Government crop reports.
5. Steel, coal and oil production.
6. Wholesale price indices.
7. Business failures.
8. Industrial production index.
9. Governmental policies.
10. Cyclical phases of the country's economy.

Sales Analysis

After collecting all relevant information for a sales forecast, a sales analysis or budget is prepared. The sales budget is usually prepared on the lines of (i) product, (ii) territory, and (iii) customer.

Production Budget

After preparing the sales budget, the production budget is prepared. A production budget is stated in physical units. It specifies the number of units of each product that must be produced to satisfy the sales forecasts and to achieve the desired level of closing finished goods inventory. Essentially, the production budget is the sales budget adjusted for inventory changes as follows:

Units to produce = Budgeted sales + Desired closing inventory of finished goods – Beginning inventory of finished goods

A specimen production budget is given is Fig. 20.2.

ABC Company
Total Production Budget for the Month of December, 2020

	Products	
	A	*B*
Budgeted sales (units)	70,000	80,000
Add: Desired closing finished goods inventory	20,000	30,000
	90,000	1,10,000
Less: Beginning finished goods inventory	40,000	50,000
Units to be produced	50,000	60,000

Fig. 20.2 Production Budget

The production budget, like other budgets, is detailed by months or quarters along with a tentative annual budget. Further, budgets are prepared for every production centre for comparison with actual production.

Production Cost Budget

A production cost budget summarises the materials budget, labour budget, the factory overhead budget, and may be expressed and analysed by departments and or products. A production cost budget, also known as a manufacturing budget is made up of three budgets: (i) materials, (ii) labour, and (iii) factory overhead.

Direct Materials Budget

This budget specifies the cost of direct materials used and the cost of the direct materials purchased. Figure 20.3 explains the calculation of the direct materials budget. The usage part of the direct materials budget determines the cost of purchases of direct materials.

ABC Company
Direct Materials Budget for the Year Ending December 2020

A. Usage Budget

	Products		
	A	*B*	*Total*
Budgeted production in units	50000	60000	
Direct materials requirements			
Product A 5 kg per unit	× 5		
Product B 8 kg per unit		× 8	
Direct materials usage (kg)	2,50,000	4,80,000	
Cost per kg	₹1.00	₹1.50	
Cost of direct materials used	₹2,50,000	₹7,20,000	₹9,70,000

B. Purchase Budget

	Direct material (in kg)		
	A	*B*	*Total*
Direct materials usage	2,50,000	4,80,000	
Budgeted closing direct materials inventory	+ 50,000	+ 75,000	
Total requirements	3,00,000	5,55,000	
Beginning direct materials inventory	70,000	1,00,000	
Purchase of direct materials	2,30,000	4,55,000	
Cost per kg	× ₹1.00	× ₹1.50	
Cost of purchase	₹2,30,000	₹6,82,500	₹9,12,500

Fig. 20.3 Direct Materials Budget

The direct materials budget is useful in the following ways:

1. It helps the purchasing department to prepare a schedule to ensure delivery of materials when needed.
2. It helps in fixing minimum and maximum levels of inventories in the stores department.
3. It helps the finance manager to determine the financial requirements to meet production targets.

The materials budget usually deals with direct materials only. Supplies and indirect materials are generally included in the factory overhead budget.

Direct Labour Budget

The labour budget estimates the labour, adequate in number and grades, to enable the production budget to be achieved. It is generally preferable to prepare a separate direct labour budget and to include indirect labour in the factory overhead budget. The labour budget prepared must disclose the following information: (i) the number of each type or grade of worker required in each period to achieve the budgeted output; (ii) budgeted cost of such labour in each period; and (iii) period of training necessary for different types of workers.

Figure 20.4 illustrates the preparation of a direct labour budget.

ABC Company
Direct Labour Budget for the Year Ending December 2020

	Products		
	A	*B*	*Total*
Budgeted production requirements	50,000	60,000	
Direct labour hours per unit	3	2	
Total direct labour hours	1,50,000	1,20,000	2,70,000
Direct labour cost per hour	₹5.00	₹5.00	₹5.00
Total direct labour cost (₹)	₹7,50,000	₹6,00,000	₹13,50,000

Fig. 20.4 Direct Labour Budget

Factory Overhead Budget

The factory overhead budget is prepared on the basis of the chart of accounts which reflects different expense accounts and which properly classifies expenses accounts and details the cost centres or departments. Although expenses can be classified in different manners such as natural classification, variability, the preparation of the factory overhead budget requires that expenses should be classified by departments since expenses are incurred by various departments. In this way, departmental heads should be held accountable for expenses incurred by their departments.

Figure 20.5 depicts the factory overhead budget where in overhead costs have been classified into fixed and variable components.

ABC Company
Factory Overhead Budget for the Year Ending December 2020
(Based on Budgeted Capacity of 2,70,000 Direct Labour Hours)

Items	*Direct Labour*	*Rate Per Direct Hour* ₹	*Total Cost* ₹
A. *Variable Factory Overhead:*			
(i) Supplies	2,70,000	1.00	2,70,000
(ii) Repairs	2,70,000	0.50	1,35.000
(iii) Indirect labour	2,70,000	1.00	2,70,000
(iv) Others	2,70,000	0.40	1,08,000

(Contd.)

Items	Direct Labour	Rate Per Direct Hour ₹	Total Cost ₹
Total variable factory overhead cost			7,83,000
B. *Fixed Factory Overhead cost:*			
(i) Supervision		₹4,00,000	
(ii) Depreciation		5,50,000	
(iii) Property tax		2,50,000	
(iv) Others		1,77,000	
Total fixed factory overhead cost			13,77,000
Total factory overheads cost			21,60,000

Pre-determined overhead rate $= ₹\frac{21,60,000}{2,70,000}$ hours

= ₹8.00 per direct labour hour

Fig. 20.5 Factory Overhead Budget

Ending Inventories Budget

An inventory budget can be prepared to find out the values of direct materials and finished goods inventory as shown in Fig. 20.6.

ABC Company
Ending Inventory Budget for the Year Ending December 2020

Direct Materials Inventory		₹
Product A	5,000 kg × ₹1.00 per kg	50,000
Product B	75,000 kg × ₹1.50 per kg	1,12,500
		1,62,500
Finished Goods Inventory		
Product A	20,000 units × ₹25.00	5,00,000
Product B	30,000 units × ₹30.00	9,00,000
		14,00,000

Fig. 20.6 Ending Inventories Budget

Cost of Goods Sold Budget

After preparing direct materials, direct labour, factory overhead, and ending inventory budgets, the cost of goods sold budget can be prepared. The cost of goods sold budget summarises all the above budgets as shown in Fig. 20.7.

ABC Company
Cost of Goods Sold Budget for the Year Ending Dec. 31, 2020

Direct Materials:	₹	₹
Beginning inventory	2,00,000	
Purchases	9,12,500	
	11,12,500	
Less: Closing inventory	1,62,500	
Cost of direct materials used		9,50,000
Direct labour		13,50,000
Factory overhead		21,60,000
Total factory cost		44,60,000
Beginning finished goods inventory		25,00,000
Total goods available for sale		69,60,000
Closing finished goods inventory		14,00,000
Cost of goods sold		55,60,000

Fig. 20.7 Cost of Goods Sold Budget

Selling Expenses Budget

Closely related with the sales budget is the selling and distribution cost budget which shows the budgeted costs of promoting sales for the budget period. It is also known as the marketing expense budget. The selling cost budget is made up of a number of cost items, some of which are fixed and some variable. The principal fixed expenses are salaries and depreciation; the principal variable expenses are commissions, travel advertising and bad debts.

Figure 20.8 exhibits an annual selling expenses budget classified according to fixed and variable expenses. Separate budgets for each of these expenses may be prepared especially in the case of a large company.

ABC Company
Selling Expense Budget for the Year Ending December 31, 2020

Items	*Costs (₹)*	*Total Costs ₹*
(A) ***Variable Selling Expenses:***		
(i) Sales commission	**35,000**	
(ii) Salary and wages	**40,000**	
(iii) Advertising	**15,000**	
(iv) Travelling	**22,000**	**1,12,000**
(B) ***Fixed Selling Expenses:***		
(i) Warehousing	**60,000**	
(ii) Advertising	**30,000**	
(iii) Marketing manager's salary	**60,000**	
(iv) Depreciation	**27,000**	

(Contd.)

Items	Costs (₹)	Total Costs ₹
		1,77,000
Total selling expenses		**2,89,000**

Fig. 20.8 Selling Expenses Budget

Administrative Expenses Budget

The administrative expenses budget covers the administrative costs for non-manufacturing business activities. The administrative expense budget contains expenses like directors' remuneration, legal charges, audit fees, salaries, rent, office expenses, interest, property taxes, postage, telephone, telegraph, etc. These expenses should be properly classified under different headings to determine the responsibility of cost incurrence and control. For example, these expenses can be classified into different categories such as company administration, general accounting, general office, etc. Figure 20.9 presents an administrative expense budget.

ABC Company
Administrative Expenses Budget for the Year Ending December 31, 2020

Items	*Amount* ₹	*Amount* ₹
(A) *Variable Administrative Expenses:*		
(i) Supplies	35,000	
(ii) Clerical wages	60,000	
Total variable administrative expenses		95,000
Fixed Administrative Expenses:		
(i) Director's remuneration	1,20,000	
(ii) Legal charges	20,000	
(iii) Depreciation	25,000	
(iv) Salaries	30,000	
(v) Rent	60,000	
(vi) Postage, telephone, etc.	32,000	
Total fixed administrative expenses		2,87,000
Total administrative expenses		3,82,000

Fig. 20.9 Administrative Expense Budget

Budgeted Income Statement

A budgeted income statement summarises all the individual budgets, that is, sales budget, cost of goods sold budget, selling budget, and administrative expense budget. No new estimates are made; figures are taken from budgets previously prepared. This budget determines income before taxes. If the tax rate is available, net income after taxes can also be computed. Figure 20.10 exhibits a budgeted or projected income statement.

ABC Company
Budgeted Income Statement for the Year Ending December, 2020

		₹
Sales		1,52,00,000
Cost of goods sold		55,60,000
Gross margin		96,40,000
Selling expenses	2,89,000	
Administrative expenses	3,82,000	6,71,000
Income before taxes		89,69,000
Income taxes (assuming 50%)		44,84,500
Net Income		44,84,500

Fig. 20.10 Budgeted Income Statement

Capital Expenditure Budget

The budgeting of capital expenditure is one of the most important areas of managerial decisions. Capital expenditures represent long-term commitments. Also, the benefits of capital expenditure spread over a long period of time. Capital expenditure budgets are prepared for both short- and long-range projects depending on the requirements of the business firm. Short-range projects are implemented during the current accounting period. Long-range projects are not executed in the current period; they are expressed only in general terms. They become budget commitments only when the time for their implementation approaches.

Research and Development Budget

The research and development budget is the most important tool for planning and controlling research and development costs. It compels management to think in advance about the fairness of these expenses both in total amounts and in each field of a research programme. It helps in coordination with the company's other plans and projects. Since the research and development programmes compete with other desirable activities in allocation of funds, coordination is needed to balance financially immediate and long-term company plans. Also, this budget guides the research and development department to plan correctly the staff and equipment requirements and special facilities needed for the work.

Cash Budget

A cash budget contains detailed estimates of cash receipts (cash inflows) and disbursements (cash outflows) for the budget period or some other specific period. The preparation of a cash budget has the following objectives:

1. It indicates the effect on the cash position of seasonal requirements, large inventories, unusual receipts, and slowness in collecting receivables.
2. It indicates the cash requirements needed for a plant or equipment expansion programme.
3. It points up to the need for additional funds from sources such as bank loans or sales of securities and the time factors involved.
4. It indicates the availability of cash for taking advantage of discounts.

5. It assists in planning the financial requirements of bond redemption, income tax instalments, and payments to pensions and retirement funds.
6. It shows the availability of excess funds for short-term investments.

Period of Cash Budget

The period of time covered by a cash budget depends on the type of business, management planning needs, and cash position. A cash budget may generally be related to the following time periods:

1. *Operational cash planning* Cash budgets may be prepared monthly, weekly or even daily to meet informational requirements of management.
2. *Short-range* Short-range cash budgeting is prepared annually and is in correspondence with the annual profit plan. It indicates cash inflows and outflows as generated by the annual profit plan.
3. *Long-range* Long-range budgeting does not disclose detailed estimates of revenue and expenses. The effects of business expansion and long-term trends are incorporated in long-range cash budgeting. Long-range cash projection is in accord with (i) the timing of the capital expenditure projects, and (ii) the timing of the long-range profit plan (usually five years).

Preparation of a Cash Budget

A cash budget may be prepared by either of the following three generally accepted procedures:

1. The receipts and disbursements method.
2. The adjusted profit and loss or adjusted net income method.
3. Balance sheet method.

In the first method, all anticipated cash receipts are carefully forecasted such as cash sales, cash collections from debtors, dividends, interest on investments, proceeds from sale of assets, royalties, bank loans, etc. Likewise, cash disbursements for materials purchases, supplies, salaries, repayment of loans, dividends, taxes, expenses, and purchases of plant or equipment are also determined. This method is useful for short-range cash projection but is not appropriate for long-term cash budgeting. This method is in accordance with the annual profit plan.

The second approach is the profit and loss or adjusted net income method. The starting point in this approach is budgeted profit reflected in the income statement. Basically, projected profit is converted from an accrual basis to a cash basis. That is, the budgeted profit of a period is adjusted for non-cash transactions and expected cash-oriented changes in asset and liability accounts not affected by profit calculations. Using the budgeted profit for a period as a starting point, various non-cash transactions are added back to net profit for the period. Non-cash items are depreciation, bad and doubtful accounts, expired insurance premiums, and income tax accruals. After this, anticipated decreases in assets or increase in liabilities are further added and anticipated increases in assets or decreases in liabilities are deducted. The budgeted cash at the end of a period is the cash balance at the beginning of the period plus the net cash increase (or minus the net cash decrease) as indicated in the analysis of the adjusted profit method.

The third approach is the balance sheet method. In this approach, closing balances of all (budgeted) balance sheet items except cash and bank balances are found and put in a budgeted balance sheet. If the total of liabilities side items is more than the total of asset side items, the balancing figure will be cash/bank balance. On the contrary if the total of assets side items is more than the total of liabilities side items, the balancing figure will be bank overdraft or shortage in cash. Budgeted figures of closing balance sheet items can be found after adjusting the opening balance sheet items with the transactions anticipated for the year.

Budgeted or Projected Balance Sheet

A projected balance sheet represents the expected financial position at a particular date. The projected balance sheet is prepared from the budgeted balance sheet at the beginning of the budget period and the expected changes in the account balances reflected in the operating budgets, capital expenditure budgets, and cash budget. The projected balance sheet also automatically determines the arithmetical accuracy of other budgets since they are used in preparing the forecasted balance sheet.

Budgeted Statement of Changes in Financial Position

The projected statement of changes in financial position is usually prepared from data in the budgeted income statement and changes between the projected balance sheet at the beginning of the budget period and projected balance sheet at the end of the budget period. This projected statement is very useful to management in the financial planning process.

Master Budget

A master budget, sometimes called a comprehensive budget, is the summary or total budget package for a business firm. It is the end product of the budget-making process. It shows the budgeted profit and loss account for the budget period and the budgeted balance sheet at the end of the period. It reveals the top management's goals of revenues, expenses, net income, cash flows, and financial position. The other budgets prepared by a business firm are specific, that is, they deal with separate distinct activities of the organisation such as sales, production, selling and distribution and administrative activities. They incorporate plans and budgetary goals for a small segment of a business enterprise. However, to achieve business objectives, it is necessary to have coordination among different budgets reflecting diverse activities of a business firm. For example, there should be coordination between sales and production departments and the goals of the production department should match the goals of the sales department. In the absence of coordination among the budgets, a business firm may have problems, such as surplus inventory, shortage of stock, non-availability of raw materials and other resources, employees' dissatisfaction, etc. A master budget takes the macro (aggregate) view of the business enterprise and coordinates sales with production, raw materials, manpower, machinery and other resources with production targets, and the like. The master budget is an integrative tool that cuts across divisional boundaries in order to coordinate the firms' diverse activities. While master budgets provide plans for an entire system, operating budgets provide plans for the organisation's sub-system, that is, operating budgets constitute the building blocks used to complete the master budget.

REVISION OF BUDGETS

As stated earlier in the chapter, successful budgets should have adequate flexibility to meet changing business conditions. Since budgets are used for planning, operation, coordination and control, they should be revised if changes occur in the environment. Revision of budgets may be necessary due to the following factors some of which might have been considered earlier in the development of budgets:

1. Errors committed in preparing the budgets which may subsequently be known.
2. Emergence of unforeseen and unanticipated situations which may cause the budget to be revised.
3. Changes in internal factors, for example, production, forecast, capacity utilisation, etc.
4. Changes in external factors, for example, market trends, nature of the economy, prices of inputs and resources, consumers' tastes and fashions.

Changes in the above factors do not affect a firm's budgets if they are of minor significance. Some changes, however, considerably affect budgets and in this situation management is faced with two problems:

1. Whether only individual budgets should be changed; and
2. Whether the master budget be changed.

Regarding the first question, most business firms are in agreement and suggest that specific individual budgets should be changed. For instance, if there is likely to be a significant change in expected sales (increase or decrease), production and purchasing departments should be informed about this to avoid over-stocking or under-stocking.

A revision of the master budget is debatable and sometimes is opposed mainly on two counts: (i) the master budget process is highly complex and expensive; (ii) the evaluation process may take care of these changes if the changes take place. The second argument is more or less on middle ground. While it argues for revision when changes do occur, it focuses on actual effects rather than projected changes. It is felt that this avoids making small changes in the plan that are of little consequence. Those who support the revision of the master budget argue that the revised budget is a better and more effective basis for performance evaluation and control. By revising budget, all members of the organisation come to know of the expectations and standards for which they will be accountable.

EXAMPLE 20.13

You are producing an alloy. Production of one ton of alloy requires 1.5 tons iron and 0.5 ton of zinc. The producer plans to sell 50,000 tons of alloy during the year 2020. Prepare Materials Procurement Budget for the year 2020 from the following:

Balances as on Jan. 1, 2020:	
Stock of alloy	6,000 tonnes
Stock of iron ore	12,000 tonnes
Stock of zinc	4,000 tonnes
Iron ore on order	5,000 tonnes
Zinc on order	3,000 tonnes
Balances as desired on Dec. 31, 2020:	
Stock of alloy	5,000 tonnes
Stock of iron ore	8,000 tonnes
Stock of zinc	3,000 tonnes
Iron ore on order	7,000 tonnes
Zinc on order	2,000 tonnes

Solution

Computation of quantity of production of alloy:

= Sales + closing stock – opening stock

= 50,000 + 5000 – 6,000 = 49,000 tonnes.

Procurement Budget for the Year 2020

Particulars	*Iron*	*Zinc*
(1) Quantity of product of alloy (tonnes)	49,000	49,000
(2) Quantity of R.M. required for 1 tonne of alloy (tonnes)	1.5	0.5
(3) Raw material consumption (1) × (2)	73,500	24,500
Add: Closing stock (tonnes)	15,000	5,000
Total requirements (tonnes)	88,500	29,500
less: Outstanding (tonnes)	17,000	7,000
Procurement of RM (tonnes)	71,500	22,500

EXAMPLE 20.14

The following are the details of the budgeted and the actual cost of *X* Production Ltd. for six months from January to June, 2019. From the figures given below, you are required to prepare the production cost budget from January to June, 2020.

January–June 2019

	Budget	*Actual*
Material cost	₹40,00,000	₹39,90,000
	(2000 MT @ ₹2,000)	(@ ₹2,100)
Labour cost	₹8,00,000	₹7,99,920
	(₹20 per hour)	(@ ₹22 per hour)
Variable overheads	₹2,40,000	₹2,16,000
Fixed overheads	₹4,00,000	₹4,20,000

The budgeted production for first half of 2019 was 20,000 units, whereas the company produced only 18,000 units during the period. In first half of 2020, production is budgeted for 25,000 units. Material cost per tonne will increase from last year's actual by ₹100 but it is proposed to maintain the consumption efficiency of 2019 as budgeted. Labour efficiency will be lower by another 1% and labour rates will be ₹22 per hour. Variable and fixed overheads will go up by 20% over 2019 actual.

Solution

Production Cost Budget for the Six Months Ending 30th June, 2020

	25,000 Units	
	Total Cost	*Unit Cost*
Material cost *(see note-1)*	₹55,00,000	₹220.00
Labour cost *(see note-2)*	11,22,000	44.88
Variable overheads *(see note-3)*	3,60,000	14.40
Fixed overheads *(see note-4)*	5,04,000	20.16
Total	74,86,000	299.44

WORKING NOTES:

1. Materials cost:

   Consumption per unit = $\frac{2{,}000}{20{,}000}$ = 0.10 unit

   Consumption for 25,000 units = 2,500 mt.

   Cost of 2.500 mt @ ₹2.200 per mt = 55,00,000

2. Labour cost

	Hr.
2011: Total budgeted labour hours $\frac{8{,}00{,}000}{20}$	40,000
Labour hour budget for each unit $\frac{40{,}000}{20{,}000}$	2
Actual time paid for $\frac{7{,}99{,}920}{22}$	36,360 hrs
Less: Standard labour hours for 18,000 units	36,000 hrs
Extra time taken (i.e., 1% extra) in 2011 $\left(\frac{360}{36{,}000}\times 100\right)$	360 hrs
For 2012:	
Time required for 25,000 units	50,000
Add: 2% for lower efficiency	1,000
[In 2020, labour efficiency will be lower by another 1%. That is, total efficiency will be lower by 2% (1% lower of 2019 and 1% of 2020 as given in the question).]	51,000
51,000 hr at ₹22 per hour	₹11,22,000

3. Variable overheads:

   Rate per unit in 2019 = $\frac{2{,}40{,}000}{20{,}000}$ = ₹12

Cost for 25,000 @ 2019 rates	3,00,000
Add: 20%	60,000
	3,60,000

4. Fixed overheads:

Actual in 2019	4,20,000
Add: 20%	84,000
	5,04,000

EXAMPLE 20.15

The following data pertains to Mr. Y for the month budget for November 2020:

	₹
Direct materials used	847
Beginning finished goods inventory	?
Ending finished goods inventory	94
Direct manufacturing labour	389
Manufacturing overhead	?
Cost of goods manufactured	1,878
Cost of goods sold	?
Cost of goods available for sale	1,949

Prepare the cost of goods sold budget for the month of Nov. 2020 by filling the missing figures.

Solution

	₹
Direct material used	847
Beginning finished goods inventory	71
Ending finished goods inventory	94
Direct manufacturing labour	389
Manufacturing overhead	642
Cost of goods manufactured	1,878
Cost of goods sold	1,855
Cost of goods available for sale	1,949

As, we know that cost of goods manufactured is the aggregate of direct material, direct manufacturing labour and manufacturing overhead.

∴ ₹1,878 = ₹847 + 389 + Manufacturing overhead

∴ ₹1,878 – 847 – 389 = Manufacturing overhead

∴ ₹642 = Manufacturing overhead

Cost of goods available for sale = Cost of goods manufactured + Opening balance of finished goods.

₹1,949 = ₹1,878 + Opening balance of finished goods

₹1,949 – ₹1,878 = Opening balance of finished goods

₹71 = Opening balance of finished goods.

Cost of goods sold = Cost of goods manufactured + Opening balance of finished goods – Closing balance of finished goods

Cost of goods sold + ₹1,878 + ₹71 – ₹94

Cost of goods sold = ₹1,855

Cost of Goods Sold Budget for the Month of November, 2020

		₹
Direct material used		847
Direct manufacturing labour		389
Manufacturing overhead		642
	Cost of goods manufactured	1,878
Add:	Opening balance of finished goods	71
	Cost of goods available for sale	1,949
Less:	Closing stock of finished goods	94
	Cost of goods sold	1,855

✍ EXAMPLE 20.16

Nestley Ltd. has prepared the following sales budget for the first five months of 2020:

	Sales Budget (Units)
January	10,800
February	15,600
March	12,200
April	10,400
May	9,800

Inventory of finished goods at the end of every month is to be equal to 25% of sales estimate for the next month. On 1st Jan., 2020, there were 2,700 units of product on hand. There is no work-in-progress at the end of any month.

Every unit of product requires two types of materials in the following quantities:

Material A—4 kg

Material B—5 kg.

Materials equal to one half of the requirement of next month's production are to be in hand at the end of every month. This requirement was met on 1st Jan., 2020.

Prepare the following budgets for the quarter ending 31st March, 2020:

(a) Production Budget (Quantitative)

(b) Material Purchase Budget (Quantitative).

☞ Solution

Nestley Ltd.
Production Budget (in Units)

For Quarter Ending 31st March, 2020

Particulars	*Jan.*	*Feb.*	*March*
Sales	10,800	15,600	12,200
Add: Closing stock	3,900	3,050	2,600
	14,700	18,650	14,800
Less: Opening stock	2,700	3,900	3,050
	12,000	14,750	11,750

Materials Requirement Budget
For the Quarter Ending 31st March, 2020

Particulars	*Jan.*	*Feb.*	*March*
Production (units)	12,000	14,750	11,750
Material A	*kg*	*kg*	*kg*
Required for Production	48,000	59,000	47,000
Add: Desired Closing Stock	28,500	23,500	20,500
	76,500	82,500	67,500
Less: Opening stock	24,000	28,500	23,500
	52,500	54,000	44,000
Material B			
Required for production	60,000	73,750	58,750
Add: Desired closing stock	36,875	29,375	25,625
	96,875	1,03,125	84,375
Less: Opening stock	30,000	36,875	29,375
	66,875	66,250	55,000

WORKING NOTES:

1. Production for April in Units

Sales	10,400
Add: Closing Stock	2,450
	12,850
Less: Opening Stock	2,600
	10,250

2. Material required for production in April
   A $10,250 \times 4 = 41,000$ kg
   B $10,250 \times 5 = 51,250$ kg

EXAMPLE 20.17

A company manufactures two products *X* and *Y*. A forecast of unit to be sold in the first 4 months of the year is given below:

Months	*Product X*	*Product Y*
January	1,000	2,800
February	1,200	2,800
March	1,600	2,400
April	2,000	2,000
May	2,400	1,600

Other information is as follows:

Cost Per Unit (₹)	*Product X*	*Product Y*
Direct material	12.50	19.00
Direct labour	4.50	7.00
Factory overhead/unit	3.00	4.00

There will be no opening and closing work-in-progress (WIP) at the end of any month and finished product (in units) is equal to half of the budgeted sale of the next month should be in stock at the end of each month (including previous year—December).

You are required to prepare:

(i) Production Budget for the period January to April, and

(ii) Summarised Production Cost Budget.

☞ Solution

Production budget of *X* and *Y* for the period January to April.

Budgeted production = Budgeted sales + Desired Closing inventory – Opening inventory.

Month	*Projected Sales (Units)*		*Planned Inventory level (Units)*				*Budgeted Production (Units)*	
			Closing		*Opening*			
	X	*Y*	*X*	*Y*	*X*	*Y*	*X*	*Y*
January	1,000	2,800	600	1,400	500	1,400	1,100	2,800
February	1,200	2,800	800	1,200	600	1,400	1,400	2,600
March	1,600	2,400	1,000	1,000	800	1,200	1,800	2,200
April	2,000	2,000	1,200	800	1,000	1,000	2,200	1,800
Total Budgeted production in units							6,500	9,400

Production Cost Budget of X and Y for the Period January to April

	Product X			*Product Y*			*Total Cost*
	Cost/Unit (₹)	*Budgeted Production*	*Total Cost (₹)*	*Cost/Unit (₹)*	*Budgeted Production*	*Total Cost (₹)*	*X and Y (₹)*
Direct material	12.50	6,500	81,250	19.00	9,400	1,78,600	2,59,850
Direct labour	4.50		29,250	7.00		65,800	95,050
Factory O/H	3.00		19,500	4.00		37,600	57,100
Total	20.00		1,30,000	30.00		2,82,000	4,12,000

EXAMPLE 20.18

The following information relating to the third and last quarter of 2019–20 is furnished by a company which manufactures and sells a single product:

		Third Quarter (Actual)	Last Quarter (Estimate)
Sales		₹6,24,000	₹6,60,000
Inventory of raw material and finished goods:	*Opening Balance*	*Closing Balance*	*Closing Balance*
Raw material *A* (kg)	25,000	23,500	25,000
Raw material *B* (kg)	12,650	13,400	15,000
Finished goods (units)	670	700	1,000

Unit cost data:

Raw material *A* : 10 kg @ ₹3 = ₹30

Raw material *B* : 5 kg @ ₹2 = ₹10

Direct labour (Machine time 5 hrs @ ₹4): Machine shop = ₹20

Assembly 2 hrs. @ ₹5 (labour time) = ₹10

Production overheads:

Machine shop @ ₹12 per machine hr.

Assembly @ ₹10 per labour hr.

Selling and Administration O.H. : 20% of production cost

Profit margin : 10% on selling price

Production and sales occur evenly during the budget period. You are required to prepare for the last quarter of the year.

(a) Production budget (in units)
(b) Purchase budget (quantity and value)
(c) Production cost budget.

Solution

Cost of Production and Selling Price Per Unit.

	₹	₹
Direct material.		
A = 10 kg @ ₹3	30.00	
B = 5 kg @ ₹2	10.00	40.00
Direct labour:		
Machine shop = 5 hrs. @ ₹4	20.00	
Assembly = 2 hrs. @ ₹5	10.00	30.00
Production overheads:		
Machine shop = 5 hrs @ ₹12	60.00	
Assembly = 2 hrs. @ ₹10	20.00	80.00

Production cost	150.00
Selling and administration overheads @ 20%	30.00
Cost of sales	80.00
Profit margin 10% on S.P. (or 10/90 on cost)	20.00
Selling price	200.00

(a) Production Budget for last Quarter of 2019–20

	Units
Sales in last quarter (4th quarter) 660,000/200	3,300
Add: Closing balance at end of 1st qtr.	1,000
Less: Opening balance	(700)
Production for last quarter	3,600

(b) Purchase Budget for Last Quarter of 2019–20

	Material A		*Material B*		*Total*
	Qty. (kg)	*Amt. (₹)*	*Qty.(Kg)*	*Amt.(₹)*	*Value(₹)*
Consumption (Prodn. × Qty./unit) $A = 3600 \times 10$ kg $B = 3600 \times 5$ kg	36,000		18,000		
Add: Closing balance	25,000		15,000		
Less: Opening balance	(23,500)		(13,400)		
Purchase to be made	37,500		19,600		
Price per kg.		3		2	
Total value		1,12,500		39,200	1,51,700

(c) Production cost Budget for Last Quarter of 2019–20

Particulars	*Cost (₹)*	*Total (₹)*
Direct material:		
A: 36,000 @ ₹3	1,08,000	
B: 18,000 @ ₹2	36,000	1,44,000
Direct labour:		
Machine shop: 18,000 hrs. @ ₹4	72,000	
Assembly: 7,200 hrs. @ ₹5	36,000	1,08,000
Production overheads:		
Machine shop: 18,000 @ ₹12	2,16,000	
Assembly shop: 7,200 @ ₹10	72,000	2,88,000
Total		5,40,000

EXAMPLE 20.19 (SALES OVERHEAD BUDGET)

You are requested to prepare a sales overhead budget from the estimates given below:

Advertisement	₹2,500
Sales of the sales department	5,000
Expenses of sales department	1,500
Counter salesmen's salaries and dearness allowance	6,000
Commission to counter salesmen at 1% on their sales	

Travelling salesmen's commission is at 10% on their sales and expenses are at 5% on their sales. The sales during the period were estimated as follows:

Counter Sales	*Travelling Salesmen*
₹80,000	₹10,000
1,20,000	15,000
1,40,000	20,000

Solution

Sales Overhead Budget for the Period Ending

	Estimated Sales		
	₹90,000	*₹1,35,000*	*₹1,60,000*
Fixed overheads:			
Advertisement	2,500	2,500	2,500
Salaries of sales department	5,000	5,000	2,500
Expenses of sales department	1,500	1,500	1,500
Counter salesmen's salaries and DA	6,000	6,000	6,000
	15,000	15,000	15,000
Variable overheads:			
Counter salesmen's commission @ 1% on sales	800	1,200	1,400
Travelling salesmen's commission @ 10%	1,000	1,500	2,000
Expenses @ 5%	500	750	1,000
	2,300	3,450	4,400
Total sales overheads	17,300	18,450	19,400

EXAMPLE 20.20 (CASH RECEIPTS BUDGET)

A company normally collects cash from credit customers as follows: 50 per cent in the month of sale, 30 per cent in the first month after sale, 18 per cent in the second month after sale, and 2 per cent are never collected. Sales, all on credit, are expected to be as follows:

	₹
January	5,00,000
February	6,00,000
March	4,00,000
April	5,00,000

(a) Calculate the amount of cash expected to be received from customers during March.
(b) Calculate the amount of cash expected to be received from customers during April.

Solution

	₹
(a) Budgeted cash collection in March:	
From January sales (.18 × 500,000)	90,000
From February sales (.30 × 600,000)	1,80,000
From March sales (.50 × 400,000)	2,00,000
Total budgeted collections in March	4,70,000
(b) Budgeted cash collections in April:	
From February sales (.18 × 600,000)	1,08,000
From March sales (.30 × 400,000)	1,20,000
From April sales (.50 × 500,000)	2,50,000
Total budgeted collections in April	4,78,000

EXAMPLE 20.21

From the following forecast of income and expenditure prepare a "Cash Budget" for the three months ending on June, 2020:

Month	*Sales* (₹)	*Purchase* (₹)	*Wages* (₹)	*Misc.* (₹)
2020, February	1,20,000	84,000	10,000	7,000
March	1,30,000	1,00,000	12,000	8,000
April	80,000	1,04,000	8,000	6,000
May	1,16,000	1,06,000	10,000	12,000
June	88,000	80,000	8,000	6,000

Additional Information:

(i) Sales: 20% realised in the month of sales, discount allowed 2%, balance realised equally in two subsequent months.
(ii) Purchases: These are paid in the month following the month of supply.
(iii) Wages: 25% paid in arrears following month.
(iv) Misc. Expenses: Paid a month in arrears.

(v) Rent: ₹1,000 per month paid quarterly in advance due, in April.
(vi) Income Tax: First instalment of advance tax ₹25,000 due on or before 15th June to be paid within the month.
(vii) Income from Investment: ₹5,000 received quarterly in April, July etc.
(viii) Cash in hand ₹5,000 in April 1, 2020.

Solution

Cash Budget for the Month of April, May and June 2020

	April ₹	May ₹	June ₹
Opening Balance	5,000	5,680	(–) 7,084
Cash Receipt:			
Collection for debtors	1,15,680	1,06,736	95,648
Income from investment	5,000	—	—
	1,25,680	1,12,416	88,564
Cash Payment:			
Payment to supplier	1,00,000	1,04,000	1,06,000
Wages	9,000	9,500	8,500
Rent	3,000	—	—
Misc. expenses	8,000	6,000	12,000
Advance Income Tax	—	—	25,000
	1,20,000	1,19,500	1,51,500
Closing balance (minus balance indicate bank overdraft)	5,680	(–) 7,084	(–) 62,936
	1,25,680	1,12,416	88,564

Working Notes

1. Collection for Debtors

	April ₹	May ₹	June ₹
Collection in the month of sale (20% of total less 2% discount)	15,680	22,736	17,248
Collection in the next month (50% of 80% of total sales in the previous month)	52,000	32,000	46,400
Collection after two months (50% of 80% of total sales in the month preceding two months of sale)	48,000	52,000	32,000
	1,15,680	1,06,736	95,648

2. Payments of Wages

	April ₹	May ₹	June ₹
75% of current months wages	6,000	7,500	6,000
25% of wages of the previous month	3,000	2,000	2,500
	9,000	9,500	8,500

EXAMPLE 20.22 (CASH BUDGET)

The January 1 cash balance of the Jay Company is ₹5,000. Sales for the first four months of the year are expected to be as follows: January, ₹65,000; February, ₹54,000; March, ₹66,000; and April, ₹63,000. On January 1, uncollected amounts for November and December of the previous year are ₹13,500 and ₹39,150, respectively. Collections from customers follow this pattern; 55% in the month of sale, 30% in the month following the sale, 13% in the second month following the sale, and 2% uncollectable.

Materials purchases for December were ₹10,000. Forecast purchases for the coming year are: ₹12,500; February, ₹16,500; March, ₹13,000; and April, ₹14,000. Purchases are usually paid by the 10th of the month following the month of purchase. Other cash expenditures of ₹41,000 are forecasted for each month.

Calculate:

(i) Expected cash collection during February
(ii) Expected cash balance, February 1
(iii) Expected cash balance, February 29.

Solution

Cash Budget of Jay Company for Months of January and February

		January (₹)	February (₹)
Opening balance		5,000	27,550
Receipts—From customers		73,550	60,510
	(A)	78,550	88,060
Payments:			
For purchases		10,000	12,500
Other expenditures		41,000	41,000
	Total payments (B)	51,000	53,500
Closing balance (A) – (B)		37,550	34,560

Thus

(i) Expected cash collections during February	= ₹60,510
(ii) Expected cash balance–February 1	= ₹27,550
(iii) Expected cash balance–February 29	= ₹34,560

WORKING NOTE:

Collections on account of sales

January

For November arrears 13,500 × 13/15	=	₹11,700
For December arrears $\frac{39,150}{45} \times 30$	=	26,100
For January sales 65,000 × 55/100	=	35,750
		73,550

February

For December arrears $\frac{39,150}{45} \times 13$	=	₹11,310
For January sales 65,000 × 30/100	=	₹19,500
For February sales 54,000 × 55/100	=	29,700
		60,510

EXAMPLE 20.23

Based on the following information, prepare a Cash Budget for ABC Ltd:

	1st Quarter (₹)	*2nd Quarter* (₹)	*3rd Quarter* (₹)	*4th Quarter* (₹)
Opening cash balance	10,000	–	–	–
Collection from customers	1,25,000	1,50,000	1,60,000	2,21,000
Payments:				
Purchase of material	20,000	35,000	35,000	17,000
Other expenses	25,000	20,000	20,000	17,000
Salary and wages	90,000	95,000	95,000	1,09,200
Income tax	5,000	–	–	–
Purchase for machinery	–	–	–	20,000

The company desires to maintain a cash balance of ₹15,000 at the end of each quarter. Cash can be borrowed or repaid in multiple of ₹500 at an interest of 10% per annum. Management does not want to borrow cash more than what is necessary and wants to repay as early as possible. In any event, loans cannot be extended beyond four quarters. Interests is computed and paid when the principal is repaid. Assume that borrowings take place at the beginning and repayments are made at the end of the quarters.

☞ **Solution**

Cash Budget for ABC Ltd.

Particulars	*1st Quarter* (₹)	*2nd Quarter* (₹)	*3rd Quarter* (₹)	*4th Quarter* (₹)
Opening cash balance	10,000	15,000	15,000	15,325
Add: Collection from customers	1,25,000	1,50,000	1,60,000	2,21,000
(A) Total cash available	1,35,000	1,65,000	1,75,000	2,36,325
Payments:				
Purchase of materials	20,000	35,000	35,000	17,000
Other expenses	25,000	20,000	20,000	17,000
Salary and wages	90,000	95,000	95,000	1,09,200
Income tax	5,000	–	–	–
Purchase of machinery	–	–	–	20,000
(B) Total cash payment	1,40,000	1,50,000	1,50,000	1,63,200
Minimum cash balance reqd.	15,000	15,000	15,000	15,000
(C) Total cash required	1,55,000	1,65,000	1,65,000	1,78,200
Excess (Deficit) A – C	(20,000)	–	10,000	58125
Financing:				
Borrowing	20,000	–	–	–
Repayment	–	–	(9000)	(11000)
Interest Payment	–	–	(675)*	(1,100)*
(D) Total effect of financing	20,000	–	(9,675)	(12,100)
Cash balance at the end of quarters (A + D – B)	15,000	15,000	15,325	61025

*9,000 × 0.10 × 9/12 = ₹675. Similarly interest has been calculated for one year @ 10% per annum on ₹11,000.

ZERO BASE BUDGETING (ZBB)

Zero Base Budgeting (ZBB) is a method of budgeting whereby all activities are revaluated, each time budget is formulated and every item of expenditure in the budget is fully justified. That is, ZBB involves starting from scratch or zero.

In traditional budgeting, departmental managers need to justify only increases over the prior year's budget known as incremental budgeting. This implies that what is already being spent is automatically sanctioned. Under the ZBB concept, each department's functions are reviewed completely and all expenditures, rather than only the increases, must be approved.

Also in some departments, ascertainment of budgeted costs is easier than other departments. For example, in production departments, it is easier to determine costs of inputs to achieve a level of budgeted output. But in other departments, such as accounts, personnel, research and development, it is difficult to even identify the output, and therefore, it is greater difficult to determine the cost of input to sustain (unidentifiable) output. Consequently, the budgets of previous year tend to be subjectively increased as the next year's budgeted expenditure. However, the previous year's budgets may be inefficient, and adjusting merely new year's budgets to the previous year's budget may result in wastage. ZBB overcomes this problem, and to a certain extent, ZBB rejects the traditional view of annual budgeting as an incremental process which takes into account current expenditure plus an estimate of next year's expenditure to arrive at the next budget. Instead the projected expenditure for existing programmes should start from base zero with each year's budgets being compiled as if the programmes were being launched for the first time.

Application of ZBB

ZBB involves the following stages (steps):

1. Each separate activity of the organisation is identified and called a decision package. A decision package is a document that identifies and describes a specific activity in such a manner that management can (i) evaluate it and rank it against other activities competing for limited resources, and (ii) decide whether to approve or disapprove it.
2. Each decision package must be justified, that is, it should be enquired into whether a decision package promotes the goals of an enterprise.
3. If justified, then the cost of minimum efforts needed to sustain that each decision package is determined.
4. Alternatives for each decision package are considered in order to select better and cheaper options for the package.
5. Incremental decision packages are also justified and costed in the above manner. These incremental packages describe the costs and benefits of additional work that would be done above that required by the base package for the minimum amount of work needed to carry out the activity.
6. Managers rank their decision packages in order of priority for resource allocation.
7. Resources are allocated to the packages.

Advantages of ZBB

1. It represents a move towards allocation of resources by need and benefit and thus results in more efficient allocation of resources.
2. It identifies and eliminates wastage and obsolete operations.
3. It ensures that the best possible methods of performing jobs are used and that new ideas emerge.
4. It creates a questioning attitude rather than one which accepts that current practices represent value for money.
5. It leads to increased staff involvement which may lead to improved motivation and greater interest in the job.
6. It increases communication and coordination within the organisation.
7. Managers become more aware of the costs of inputs which help them to identify priorities.
8. The documentation of decision packages provides management with a deep, coordinated knowledge of all the organisation's activities.
9. It is useful especially for service departments where it can be difficult to identify output.

Disadvantages of ZBB

1. The cross involved in preparing a vast number of decision packages in a large firm is very high.
2. It is very time-consuming and a large amount of additional paper work is involved.
3. Managers develop fear and feel threatened by ZBB and therefore may oppose new ideas and changes.
4. The ranking of decision packages and allocation of resources is subjective to a certain degree, which can result in departmental conflict.
5. Administration and communication of ZBB process may become critical problems because more managers become involved in this process than in most budgeting and planning procedures and these problems are further compounded in large organisations.

PLANNING, PROGRAMMING AND BUDGETING SYSTEM (PPBS)

Planning, Programming and Budgeting System (PPBS) is used in non-profit or non-commercial organisations to enable them to make more informed decisions about resources allocation. PPBS differs from traditional non-profit and non-manufacturing budgets in the sense that the latter are prepared as line item budgets whereas the former (PPBS) are prepared on the basis of programmes, that is, planned activities that have specified objectives. In PPBS, budgets for line/functional items for whole department are not presented. Instead, the expenses associated with specific programmes are detailed. For instance, a railway authority may have the programmes of total computerisation of its booking system, and a municipal authority may have programmes of providing drinking water or providing health facilities in the city. Such programmes require greater coordination among several departments to make a specific programme successful.

PPBS is taken by extending the planning period beyond the one-year budget period. PPBS is the counterpart of the long-term planning process which is operated in profit-oriented organisations. PPBS is based on a rational model of decision-making and involves the following stages:

1. Identify and define the objectives of programme.
2. Select performance or output measures to assess the effectiveness of the programme.
3. Identify and evaluate alternative methods of achieving the objectives laid down for each specific programme. For this, costs and benefits associated with each alternative course of action should be detailed.
4. Select the appropriate programmes on the basis of cost benefit analysis as done in (3).
5. Implement the selected alternative and monitor its performance to ensure that the objectives of the programmes are achieved given the resources allocated to those programmes.

PPBS has certain advantages compared to traditional department/functional budgets:

1. PPBS leads to a more effective allocation of resources by cutting across departmental barriers, providing to managers specific information related to the activities and by coordinating scarce resources and skilled personnel located in different departments on a particular programme or project.
2. PPBS compels management to identify and evaluate the activities, functions or programmes which are carried out in terms of their objectives, efficiency and effectiveness.
3. Programme budgeting provides adequate information which will enable management to assess the effectiveness of its plans and to focus on the organisation's outputs (the objectives to be achieved).

4. PPBS enables management to have long-term perspective and commitments in certain programmes while preparing the annual budget. For instance, an education programme may involve capital expenditure for a ten-year period. In this situation, the decision-makers will have to keep in mind future commitments and resources availability while constructing the annual programme budget. In this way, the annual budget is placed in the long-term context and becomes a part of long-term programme.

PERFORMANCE BUDGETING

The concept of performance budgeting is used extensively in the government and public sector undertakings. A performance budget is essentially a projection of the government activities and expenditure thereon for the budget period. It shows budgeted expenses classified by functions and activities and wherever practical, units cost also. In comparison to other budget forms, the objectives of performance budgeting are to provide a closer linkage between planning and action and to provide a more common basis for review, control and reporting.

The basic issues involved in the preparation of performance budgets are that of developing work programmes and performance expectations by assigning responsibilities necessary for the attainment of the goals of objectives of the enterprise. It also involves establishment of well-defined centres of responsibility, establishment of targets for each responsibility centre in terms of physical units so that actual performance can be measured against the same, forecasting the amount of expenditure required to meet physical plan laid down and evaluation of actual performance with both physical targets and monetary targets performance.

Theory Questions

1. Define "budget" and "budgetary control". Give a description of two important budgets.
2. (a) Define budgetary control and explain its objectives.
   (b) Define how functional budgets are built up, taking any one specific example.
3. Explain the meaning of a business budget. How does it serve as an instrument of control?
4. Discuss the mode of operation of systems of budgets and budgetary control.
5. What do you understand by budgetary control? Explain the mechanism that would lead to effective control.
6. What are the advantages arising out of the budgetary control system? What do you think are the essentials of an effective budgetary control system?
7. Discuss the objectives and limitations of budgetary control.
8. Define budgetary control and discuss the objectives of introducing a budgetary control system in an organisation.
9. Discuss the cardinal features and objectives of budgetary control.
10. Explain the difference between a forecast and a budget. Give examples to illustrate the differences between:
    (a) Fixed budget,
    (b) Flexible budget, and
    (c) Functional budget.
11. What are functional budgets? Which functional budgets are most commonly used by management?
12. Define budgetary control and distinguish it from standard costing. Discuss the inter-relationship between budgetary control and the standard costing system.

13. Discuss briefly the procedure for the preparation of a sales budget.
14. What do you understand by a "flexible budget"?
15. What is a sales budget? How is it prepared?
16. Describe briefly the fundamental functions of business budgets.
17. Explain the concept of a flexible budget. How is it prepared?
18. What is flexible budget? How does the sales forecast differ from the sales budget?
19. What do you understand by "Flexible Budget"? How is it prepared? Distinguish between fixed budgeting and flexible budgeting.
20. Explain the following:
(a) Zero Base Budgeting (b) Master Budget
21. List the important functional budgets prepared by a business.
22. Distinguish between budget and forecast. What is a cash budget? What are its uses?
23. Explain three control ratios used for performance evaluation.
24. State the important features of Zero Base Budgeting.
25. Distinguish between fixed and flexible budget.
26. Write short notes on the following:
(a) Flexible budget
(b) Principal budget factor
27. Discuss the necessary steps for the success of budgetary control system in an organisation.
28. What purpose is served by instituting a budgetary control system in an organisation having both manufacturing and selling activities?
29. Distinguish between the following:
(i) Zero base budget and conventional budget
(ii) Cost control and cost reduction
30. ''Budget is an aid to management, not a substitute for management." Comment.
31. "Standard costing and budgeting control are inter-related but not inter-dependent". Comment.
32. Distinguish between standard costing and budgetary control.
33. What are the main objectives of a system of budgetary control? Do you think budgetary control is subjected to certain limitations?
34. Define flexible budget and explain its importance as a budgeting technique and tool of control.
35. Distinguish between "standard costing" and "budgeting control". What are the essential requirements for installing an efficient system of budgetary control?
36. Distinguish between conventional budgeting and zero base budgeting.
37. Briefly explain the essentials of an effective budgetary control system.
38. "Flexible budgets are more realistic and useful than fixed budgets". Do you agree? Explain.
39. Explain zero base budget.
40. Distinguish between budgetary control and standard costing.
41. Write notes on zero base budgeting.
42. Define the terms "budget" and "budgetary control". List down the objectives of budgetary control.
43. What do you mean by fixed budget and flexible budget? Is flexible budget useful to the management?
44. (a) What is budgeting? Explain its advantages and limitations.
(b) Distinguish between fixed and flexible budgets.
45. Distinguish between budgeting control and standard costing as measures of cost control.
46. Write short notes on:
(i) Zero base budgeting;
(ii) Master budget.
(iii) Flexible budget.
47. Explain the meaning and uses of cash budget.

48. What is a budgetary control system? State the advantages of budgetary control system in an organisation.
49. Discuss the limitation of budgetary control.
50. Briefly describe any five objectives of budgetary control.
51. Define budgetary control and state its advantages and disadvantages.
52. What is meant by zero based budgeting? What are the essentials of introducing a system of zero based budgeting? Explain in brief the drawbacks of this system.

Self-Evaluation Questions

Choose the correct answer for the following multiple choice questions:

1. Information to prepare a flexible budget includes
   (a) Total fixed costs, total variable cost
   (b) Total fixed costs, total variable costs and capacity base
   (c) Unit fixed costs and unit variable costs
   (d) Total fixed costs, variable costs per unit, and several levels of activity.
2. The scarce factor of production is known as
   (a) Key factor (b) Limiting factor
   (c) Critical factor (d) All of the above
3. Which of the following is a budget designated to furnish budgeted costs for any level of activity actually attained.
   (a) Fixed budget (b) Flexible budget
   (c) Master budget (d) Production budget
4. Flexible budgets are useful for
   (a) Planning purposes only
   (b) Planning, performance evaluation and feedback control
   (c) Control of performance only
   (d) Nothing at all

Problems

1. The budgeted cost of a factory specialising in the production of a single product at the optimum capacity of 6,400 units per annum amounts ₹1,76,048 as detailed below:

Fixed cost		₹20,688
Variable costs:		
Power	₹1,440	
Repairs etc.	1,700	
Miscellaneous	540	
Direct material	49,280	
Direct labour	1,02,400	1,55,360
		1,76,048

Having regard to possible impact on sales turnover by market trends, the company decided to have a flexible budget with a production target of 3,200 and 4,800 units (the actual quantity proposed to be produced being left to a later date before commencement of the budget period). Prepare a flexible budget for production levels at 50% and 75% capacity.

Assume that selling price per unit is maintained at ₹40 at present, and indicate the effect on net profit. Administration, selling and distribution expenses continue at ₹3,600.

Ans: Net profit
(a) 100%, ₹75,352
(b) 75% ₹51,192
(c) 50% ₹26,032

2. Goldman Company Limited operates on a system of Flexible Budgets. With the aid of the following information, you are required to prepare Flexible Budget at 80%, 90% and 100% level of activity showing the profits that would result at these levels:
   (i) The present sale of 8,00,000 units at ₹10 each is at the normal level of 80%. If the output is increased to 90%, the selling price will be reduced by 2.5% and if the output reached 100%, the original selling price will be reduced by 5% in order to reach a wider market.
   (ii) The prime cost per unit is ₹5 made up of direct materials ₹3.50, direct labour ₹1.25 and direct expenses ₹0.25. If output reaches 90% level of activity and above, a saving of 5% can be affected in the purchase price of raw materials.
   (iii) Variable overhead—Salesmen's commission will be 5% of the sales value.
   (iv) Semi-variable overhead at normal level of activity are:

	₹
Supervision	80,000
Power	70,000
Heat and light	40,000
Maintenance	50,000
Salesmen expenses	60,000
Indirect labour	1,00,000
Transport costs	2,00,000

These are expected to increase by 5% if output reaches 90% level and by a further 10% if it reaches the 100% level.
   (v) Fixed overheads are:

	₹
Rent and rates	1,00,000
Depreciation	4,00,000
Advertisement	5,00,000
Administration	7,50,000
Sales department	2,00,000
General	50,000

Ans:

	Capacity levels		
	80%	*90%*	*100%*
Profit (₹)	10,00,000	13,63,750	15,40,000

3. For production of 10,000 electrical automatic irons, the following are the budgeted expenses:

	Per Unit
Direct materials	₹60
Direct labour	30
Variable overheads	25
Fixed overheads (₹1,50,000)	15
Variable expenses (direct)	5

	Per Unit
Selling expenses (10% fixed)	15
Administration expenses (₹50,000 fixed for all levels of production)	5
Distribution expenses (20% fixed)	5
Total cost of sale per unit	160

Prepare a budget for production of 6,000; 7,000; and 8,000 irons, showing distinctly marginal cost and total cost.

Ans:	6000 units	7000 units	8000 units
Total cost (₹)	2,25,000	11,87,500	13,25,000

4. The following data are available in a manufacturing company for a yearly period.

	₹(Lakhs)
Fixed expenses:	
Wages and salaries	9.5
Rent, rates and taxes	6.6
Depreciation	7.4
Sundry administrative expenses	6.5
Semi-variable expenses at 50% of capacity:	
Maintenance and repairs	3.5
Indirect labour	7.9
Sales department salaries, etc.	3.8
Sundry administrative salaries	2.8
Variable expenses (at 50% of capacity):	
Materials	21.7
Labour	20.4
Other expenses	7.9
Total cost	98.0

Assume that the fixed expenses remain constant for all levels of production: semi-variable expenses remain constant between 45% and 65% of capacity, increasing by 10% between 65% and 80% capacity and by 20% between 80% and 100% capacity.

Sales at Various Levels are:	₹(Lakhs)
50% capacity	100
60% capacity	120
75% capacity	150
90% capacity	180
100% capacity	200

Prepare a flexible budget for the year and forecast the profit at 60%, 75%, 90% and 100% capacity.

Ans:	60%	75%	90%	100%
Profit (₹in lakhs)	12.0	25.2	38.4	48.4

5. A department of Company X attains sale of ₹6,00,000 at 80% of the normal capacity and its expenses are given below:

	₹
Office salaries	90,000
General expenses	2% of the sales
Depreciation	7,500
Rates and taxes	8,750
Selling costs:	
Salaries	8% of the sales
Travelling expenses	2% of the sales
Sales office	1% of the sales
General expenses	1% of the sales
Distribution costs:	
Wages	15,000
Rent	1% of the sales
Other expenses	4% of the sales

Draw up a flexible administration, selling and distribution costs budget, operating at 90%, 100% and 110% of normal capacity.

Ans:	90%	100%	110%
Total cost (₹)	2,49,500	2,63,750	2,78,000

6. The budget manager of Jaypee Electricals Ltd. is preparing a flexible budget for the accounting year commencing from 1st April 2020. The company produces one product, component—Peekay. Direct material costs ₹7 per unit. Direct labour averages ₹2.50 per hour and requires 1.60 hours to produce one unit of Peekay.

Salesmen are paid a commission of ₹1 per unit sold. Fixed selling and administration expenses amount to ₹85,000 per year.

Manufacturing overhead has been estimated in the following amounts under specified conditions of volume:

Volume of production (in units)	120,000	150,000
Expenses:	(₹)	(₹)
Indirect material	2,64,000	3,30,000
Indirect labour	1,50,000	1,87,500
Inspection	90,000	1,12,500
Maintenance	84,000	1,02,000
Supervision	1,98,000	2,34,000
Depreciation—Plant and equipment	90,000	90,000
Engineering services	94,000	94,000
Total manufacturing overhead	9,70,000	11,50,000

Normal capacity of production of the company is 1,25,000 units.
Prepare a budget of total cost at 1,40,000 units of output.

Ans: Total cost ₹28,55,000

7. The profitability statement of Gourmet Co. Ltd. has been summarised as follows:

	₹	₹
Sales		15,00,000
Direct materials	4,50,000	
Direct wages	3,00,000	
Variable overheads	1,20,000	
Fixed overheads	4,40,000	13,10,000
Profit		1,90,000

The budgeted capacity of the company is ₹20,00,000 but the key factor is sales demand. It is proposed that in order to utilise the existing capacity the selling price of this only product manufactured by the company should be reduced by 5%.

You are required to prepare a forecast statement which should show the effect of the proposed reduction in selling price and include any changes in costs expected during the coming year. The following additional information is given:

(i) Sales forecast ₹19,00,000 (after reduction).
(ii) Direct material prices are expected to increase by 2%.
(iii) Direct wage rates are expected to increase by 5% per unit.
(iv) Variable overheads are expected to increase by 5% per unit.
(v) Fixed overheads will increase by ₹20,000.

Ans: Profit ₹2,40,000

8. Paints Private Ltd. Company, manufacturing a single product, is facing severe competition in selling it at ₹50 per unit. The company is operating at 60% level of capacity at which level the sales are ₹12,00,000 and variable costs are ₹30 per unit. Semi-variable costs may be considered as fixed at ₹90,000 when output is nil and the variable elements is ₹250 for each additional 1% level of activity. Fixed costs are ₹1,50,000 at the present level of activity. But at 80% level of activity or above, these costs are expected to increase by ₹50,000.

To cope with the competition, the management of the company is considering a proposal to reduce the selling price by 5%. You are required to prepare a statement showing the operating profit at levels of activity of 60%, 70%, 80%, 90% assuming that:

(a) The selling price remains at ₹50
(b) The selling price is reduced by 5%

Ans:	60%	70%	80%	90%
Profit (₹)	1,65,000	2,32,500	2,50,000	3,17,500

9. Viveka Elementary School has a total of 150 students consisting of 5 sections with 30 students per section. The school plans for a picnic around the city during the weekend to places such as the zoo, the amusement park, the planetarium, etc. A private transport operator has come forward to lease out the buses for taking the students. Each bus will have a maximum capacity of 50 (excluding 2 seats reserved for the teachers accompanying the students). The school will employ two teachers for each bus, paying them an allowance of ₹50 per teacher. It will also lease out the required number of buses. The following are the other cost estimates:

	Cost Per Student (₹)
Breakfast	5
Lunch	10
Tea	3
Entrance fee at zoo	2

Rent ₹650 per bus

Special permit fee ₹50 per bus.

Block entrance fee at the planetarium ₹250.

Prizes to students for games ₹250.

No costs are incurred in respect of the accompanying teachers (except the allowance of ₹50 per teacher).
You are required to prepare;

(a) A flexible budget estimating the total cost for the levels of 30, 60, 90, 120 and 150 students. Each item of cost is to be indicated separately.

(b) Compare the average cost per student at these levels.

(c) What will be your conclusions regarding the break-even level of students if the school proposes to collect ₹45 per student?

Ans:

	Students				
	30	60	90	120	150
(a) Total cost (₹)	1,900	3,300	3,900	5,300	5,900
(b) Average cost per student (₹)	66.63	55	43.33	44.17	39.33

	Levels		
	Up to 50	51 to 100	101 to 150
(c) Break-even point (No. of students)	52	82	116

10. Bala Company expects to sell 84,000 units of finished goods over the next 3-months period. The company currently has 44,000 units of finished goods on hand and wishes to have an inventory of 48,000 units at end of the 3-months period. To produce 1 unit of finished goods requires 4 units of raw materials. The company currently has 2,00,000 units of raw materials on hand and wishes to have an inventory of 2,20,000 units of raw materials on hand at the end of the 3-months period. How many units of raw materials must the Bala Company purchase during the 3-months period?

Ans: 3,72,000 units

11. Draw a material procurement budget (quantitative) from the following information:
Estimated sales of a product are 40,000 units. Each unit of the product requires 3 units of material *A* and 5 units of material *B*.

Estimated opening balances at the commencement of the next year:

Finished product	5,000 units
Material *A*	12,000 units
Material *B*	20,000 units
Materials on order:	
Material *A*	7,000 units
Material *B*	11,000 units

The desirable closing balances at the end of the next year:

Finished product	7,000 units
Material *A*	15,000 units
Material *B*	25,000 units
Material on order:	
Material *A*	8,000 units
Material *B*	10,000 units

Ans: Units to be procured *A* 1,30,000, *B* 2,14,000

12. A company is drawing its production plan for the year ending 2020 in respect of two of its products: "Gamma" and "Delta". The company's policy is not to carry any closing WIP at the end of any month. However, its policy is to hold a closing stock of finished goods at 50% of the anticipated quantity of sales of the succeeding month. For the year 2020 the company's budgeted production is 20,000 units of "Gamma" and 25,000 units of "Delta". The following is the estimated cost data:

Particulars	*Gamma* ₹	*Delta* ₹
Direct materials per unit	50	80
Direct labour per unit	20	30
Other manufacturing expenses apportionable to each type of product based on production	2,00,000	3,75,000

The estimated units to be sold in the first seven months of the year 2020 are as under:

Particulars	*April*	*May*	*June*	*July*	*Aug.*	*Sept.*	*Oct.*
Gamma	900	1,100	1,400	1,800	2,200	2,200	1,800
Delta	2,900	2,900	2,500	2,100	1,700	1,700	1,900

You are required to:

(a) Prepare a production budget showing month-wise number of units to be manufactured:

(b) Present a summarised production cost budget for the half-year ending 30.9.2020.

Ans: Budgeted production Gamma total 10,050 units
Delta total 13,300 units, total production cost
Gamma ₹8,04,000 Delta ₹16,62,500

13. Gama Engineering Company Limited manufactures two products *X* and *Y*. An estimate of the number of units expected to be sold in the first seven months of 2020 is given below:

	Product X	*Product Y*
January 2020	500	1,400
February	600	1,400
March	800	1,200
April	1,000	1,000
May	1,200	800
June	1,200	800
July	1,000	900

It is anticipated that:

1. There will be no work-in-progress at the end of any month; and
2. Finished units equal to half and anticipated sales for the next month will be in stock at the end of each month (including December 2019).

The budgeted production and production costs for the year ending 31st December, 2020 are as follows:

	Product X	*Product Y*
Production (units)	11,000	12,000
Direct materials per unit (₹)	12	19
Direct wages per unit (₹)	5	7
Direct manufacturing charges apportionable to each type of product (₹)	33,000	48,000

You are required to prepare:

(a) A production budget showing the number of units to be manufactured each month.

(b) A summarised production cost budget for the six-month period January to June 2020.

Ans:	*X*	*Y*
Total production units	5,550	6,350
Total cost	1,11,000	1,90,500

14. The following are the estimated sales of a company for eight months ending 30.11.2020:

Months		*Estimated Sales (Units)*
April	2020	12,000
May	2020	13,000
June	2020	9,000
July	2020	8,000
August	2020	10,000
September	2020	12,000
October	2020	14,000
November	2020	12,000

As a matter of policy, the company maintains the closing balance of finished goods and raw materials as follows:

Stock item	Closing balance of a month
Finished goods	50% of the estimated sales for the next month
Raw materials	Estimated consumption for the next month.

Every unit of production requires 2 kg of raw material costing ₹5 per kg.

Prepare production budget (in units) and raw material purchase budget (in units and cost) of the company for the half year ending 30 September, 2020.

Ans: Production budget units 65,000

Raw material purchase budget Rate ₹5, Cost ₹6,55,000

15. ABC Co. wished to arrange overdraft facilities with its bankers during the period April to June 2020 when it will be manufacturing mostly for stock. Prepare a cash budget for the above period from the following data, indicating the extent of the bank facilities the company will require at the end of the each month:

(a)

	Sales	*Purchases*	*Wages*
	₹	₹	₹
February	1,80,000	1,24,800	12,000
March	1,92,000	1,44,000	14,000
April	1,08,000	2,43,000	11,000
May	1,74,000	2,46,000	10,000
June	1,26,000	2,68,000	15,000

(b) 50 per cent of the credit sales are realised in the month following the sales and the remaining 50 per cent in the second month following. Creditors are paid in the month of purchase.

(c) Cash at bank on 1.4.2020 (estimated) ₹25,000.

Ans:	April	May	June
Closing balance	56,000	–	–
overdraft	–	47,000	1,67,000

16. From the following budget data, forecast the cash position at the end of April, May and June 2020:

Month	*Sales*	*Purchase*	*Wages*	*Miscellaneous Expenses*
	₹	₹	₹	₹
February	1,20,000	84,000	10,000	7,000
March	1,30,000	1,00,000	12,000	8,000
April	80,000	1,04,000	8,000	6,000
May	1,16,000	1,06,000	10,000	12,000
June	88,000	80,000	8,000	6,000

Additional information:

Sales: 20% realised in the month of sales, discount allowed 2%. Balance realised equally in two subsequent months.

Purchase: These are paid for in the month following the months of supply.

Wages: 25% paid in arrears following month.

Miscellaneous expenses: paid a month in arrears.

Rent: ₹1,000 per month paid quarterly in advance due in April.

Income tax: First instalment of advance tax ₹25,000 due on or before 15th June.

Income from investments: ₹5,000 received quarterly, in April, July etc.

Cash in hand: ₹5,000 on 1st April 2002.

Ans:	April	May	June
Closing balance	5680	(–) 7,084	(–) 62,936

CASE STUDY

1. Sales & Cash Budget: A Case of Gift-Wrapper Company

The Gift-Wrapper Company manufactured corporate gifts for various companies and supplied them to retailers in spread across the state of Maharashtra and Karnataka. It had recently (2017) signed agreements with a few event management companies hosting corporate events, Conferences or workshops to push their sales by offering them 20% discounts on gift items. For retailers, the margin was 15%.

The sales showed seasonal trend with maximum revenue generated in January through sales of New Year's diaries, calendars and other gift items. The next best season was during Diwali when sales picked up significantly—specially in North India. However, with these tie ups with event planners as well as the business going online, there has been a change in their seasonal sales patterns in since 2017 with all the months faring similarly well.

One of its best-selling items was card-holder with an MRP of ₹200. They procured these card-holders from Kanpur, Uttar Pradesh at ₹100 each including transportation, customised it and then supplied it at ₹170 to the retailers. This was available at the same price on their online portal. For the year 2018–19, the sales of card-holder had shown a growth of 20% compared to the previous year in which they could sell 90,000 card holders. For the year 2019–20, the company had forecasted an increase of 18% over the sales of 2018–19 taking into account good reviews of its products on its online portal.

The estimated sales quantity forecasted for the year 2019–20 classified on the basis of mode of sales month-wise was given as below:

	Sales in Number of Units		
Month	*Retail Sales*	*Online Sales*	*Sales through Event Management Companies*
April	3,150	2,600	3,200
May	4,500	3,200	3,000
June	3,900	3,100	2,600
July	4,000	3,050	2,400
August	4,500	4,000	3,000
September	4,200	3,300	2,800
October	4,800	4,100	3,800
November	4,700	3,000	2,500
December	6,500	2,500	3,500
January	5,100	3,800	4,000
February	4,000	3,300	2,500
March	3,540	2,800	2,500.

Customers (retailers) used to pay for the goods, on average, two months after the sales were made, whereas Event Management Companies took on an average, one month to pay back. Online sales generated revenue in the same month. The materials (10% over the estimate for the month) were bought and customised in the month before sales took place; customisation charges were treated as an expense in the month that the card-holders were sold and they were paid for one month after the purchase (i.e. in the month in which sales took place). Creditors for purchase were paid two months after the purchases were made. The cost of customisation made to card-holders was estimated at ₹15 per unit.

There was a basic labour force costing ₹1,50,000 each month except in the months where units to be customised were more than 10,000. For those months, wages were ₹2,50,000.

The only other expense was depreciation that amounted to ₹30,000 a month. One of the machines (depreciation—₹3000 p.m.) was getting towards the end of its useful life and was needed to be replaced by a new one, costing ₹6,00,000, which was to be paid for in October 2019. Depreciation on the new machine was to be charged at 10% per annum on a straight-line basis. The old machine was to be sold in the same month and expected to fetch ₹95,000 (its net book value) at the end of the year (in March 2020). The other fixed costs were ₹2,40,000 per month.

Taxation of ₹50,000 was payable in March 2020, and dividends of ₹2,80,000 was to be paid in May 2019. Purchase for the month of March 2020 was expected to be 8,000 units. Creditors to be paid in April and May 2019 amounted to ₹10,15,000 and ₹9,65,000 respectively. Collection from the debtors (retailers or event management companies) for the sales made before April 2019 were ₹12,35,000 and ₹11,10,500 for the month of April and May 2019 respectively.

The owner wanted to know if there would be enough cash available in the month of October 2019 so that the new machine could be purchased. Or should he postpone the purchase for the future? There was ₹50,000 in the company's bank account as on April 1, 2019.

QUESTIONS FOR DISCUSSION:

1. Prepare monthly sales budget for the year 2019–20.
2. Prepare the cash budget for the coming year 2019–20, showing receipts and payments for each month; the net cash surplus or deficit for the month; and the bank balance at the end of each month.
3. Prepare the income statement for the coming year 2019–20, showing sales, expenses and profit in total.
4. After examining the cash budget, what changes in plan would you suggest to the owner about the purchase of machinery?

2. A Case of Epoxy Chemicals

Epoxy Chemicals Ltd., a mid-sized firm based in Peeniya, Bangalore, was engaged in the production and selling of industrial glue. The company manufactured three varieties of glue i.e., **Resin, Acrylic** and **Epoxy adhesives** in its plant in Peeniya and marketed and distributed the same across the country. For convenience, they divided their market into three regions—Zone 1, Zone 2 and Zone 3. Zone 1 catered to north and eastern region of India; Zone 2 related to western zone; and Zone 3 represented the southern regions of India.

The company followed the budgetary control systems for their cost planning. For the year 2019–20 too, it was in the process of preparing the budget and, as desired by the CEO—Ramanujam, the Cost Accountant—Shruthi Madavaran had submitted the previous year's sales data as given below:

Sales in Units (2018–19)

Glue Type	*Zone 1*	*Zone 2*	*Zone 3*	*Total*
Resin Adhesive	2,000	3,000	3,000	8,000
Acrylic Adhesive	1,500	4,000	2,000	7,500
Epoxy Adhesive	1,000	6,000	2,500	9,500
Total	**4,500**	**13,000**	**7,500**	**25,000**

As a strategic plan and also as a matter of policy, the prices of these adhesives were kept fixed by the company. Resin was priced at ₹200, Acrylic at ₹300 and Epoxy at ₹800 per pack of 1 kg.

Ramanujam had asked his Sales Managers for different zone to submit the expected demand for these adhesives for their respective regions. He was particularly worried about Zone 1 covering north and eastern part of India where the sales over the years has been disappointing. The company had increased the advertisement budget for that region the previous year and therefore were expecting some improvement in the demand. There was prediction of a general increase in costs this time too where wages and salaries were expected to be up by 10%.

The Zonal Sales Managers in consultation with their sales team submitted the projections for their region. The Zonal Sales Manager 1 forecasted that the demand for resin adhesive was expected to increase by 30% whereas the demands for the other two adhesives were showing a decline of 5%. However, the forecast by Zonal Sales Manager 2 was little more optimistic. He predicted increase in demand for resin by 40%, for acrylic increase by 30% but decrease in demand for epoxy by 10%. Zonal Sales Manager 3 estimated 20% and 30% increase in demand of resin and acrylic respectively and a decrease of 10% in epoxy's demand.

The decrease of demand for epoxy was common across the zones and therefore Ramanujam asked his Sales Managers to propose ways to increase the sales of the same. The managers put forward the proposal of an intensive sales campaign which could increase the sale of epoxy by 20%, 30% and 30% for Zones 1, 2 and 3 respectively. However, the campaign was supposed to increase the costs in the following manner:

a. Hiring of two additional salesmen for Zones 2 and 3 at a salary of ₹5,000 per month each.
b. Increase in the cost of travelling i.e., vehicle expenses by 5%.
c. Advertisement on television & print media to be increased by 20%.
d. Display and promotion cost to go up by ₹40,000.
e. Additional marketing person to be hired to monitor the epoxy sales performance at a salary of ₹5,000 per month.
f. Increasing the sales commission of epoxy to 10% over and above the existing 5% commission for all (on turnover).

Ramanujam asked his accountant to submit the data related to last year's sales and distribution expenses which he promptly submitted. The sales and distribution expenses of last year amounted to ₹34,24,600 as given below:

Salaries of Sales Managers—₹2,14,000
Salaries of the other sales and marketing staff—₹5,32,500
Commission on sales—₹5,72,500
Store/warehouse staff salaries—₹1,89,000

Drivers' salaries—₹1,82,500
Vehicle expenses—₹2,52,000
Advertisement on TV & print media—₹5,90,000
Sales promotion expenses—₹4,86,400
Shop window display cost—₹1,00,000
Rent—₹92,000
Lighting—₹33,700
Miscellaneous expenses—₹15,500
Internet charges—₹2,500
Depreciation—₹94,000
Entertainment—₹68,000

Ramanujam was yet to take a decision about approval or non-approval of the proposal submitted by the Sales Managers. He wanted to know about the impact of this proposal on costs and profit. So, he referred the details to Shruthi (Cost Accountant) and waited for her recommendations.

QUESTIONS FOR DISCUSSION:

1. Calculate previous year's (2018–19) sales and distribution expenses as percentage of sales and compare with the budgeted sales and distribution expenses as percentage of budgeted sales of 2019–20.
2. Should Ramanujam accept the proposal given by Sales Managers? Would it be worth—both in the short run as well as in the long run? Discuss.

Chapter 21

Responsibility Accounting and Divisional Performance Measurement

Learning Objectives

After reading this chapter, you should be able to:

1. explain the need of divisionalisation;
2. discuss different types of responsibility centres;
3. explain the meaning of responsibility accounting;
4. explain different techniques of measuring divisional performance; and
5. understand transfer pricing, its different methods and the objectives in sound transferring pricing system.

NEED OF DECENTRALISATION/DIVISIONALISATION

In small organisations, decision-making and management of the business are often done by a single individual. However, in large organisations, especially organisations engaged in manufacturing/undertaking multiple products and activities, successful management of it by the top management becomes more difficult. In order to overcome this difficulty, the large organisation may be decentralised or divisionalised, that is, different responsibility centres may be created where individual managers have the authority over a given area of operation and freedom to make their own decisions. The process of delegating decision authority and responsibility in an organisation is known as decentralisation. Also, the term decentralisation or divisionalisation refers to those situations where individual managers of decentralised subunits are given responsibility for profit and not just costs or revenues.

TYPES OF RESPONSIBILITY CENTRES

A responsibility centre may be defined as an area of responsibility which is controlled by an individual. Generally, the following types of responsibility centres are found:

Cost Centre

A cost or expense centre is a segment of an organisation in which the managers are held responsible for the costs incurred in that segment. Responsibility in a cost centre is restricted to cost. Performance evaluation of a cost centre is guided by a cost variance equal to the difference between the actual and budgeted costs for a given period. Cost centre managers have control over some or all of the costs in their segment of business, but not over revenues. Cost centres are widely-used forms of responsibility centres. In manufacturing organisations, the production and service departments are classified as cost centres. Also, a marketing department, a sales region or a single sales representative can be defined as a cost centre. Cost centre managers are responsible for the costs that are controllable by them and their subordinates. However, the question "Which costs should be charged to cost centres?" is an important question in evaluating cost centre managers.

Revenue Centre

A revenue centre is a segment of the organisation which is primarily responsible for generating sales revenue. A revenue centre manager does not possess control over cost, investment in assets, but usually has control over some of the expenses of the marketing department. The performance of a revenue centre is evaluated by comparing the actual revenue with budgeted revenue. The Marketing Manager of a product line or an individual sales representative are examples of revenue centres.

Profit Centre

A profit centre is a segment of organisation for which both revenue and costs are accumulated. The main purpose of profit centre is to earn profit. Profit centre managers aim at both the production and marketing of a product. The performance of the profit centre is evaluated in terms of whether the centre has achieved its budgeted profit. A division of the company which produces and markets the products may be called a profit centre. Such a divisional manager determines the selling price, marketing programmes and production policies. Profit centres make managers more concerned with finding ways to increase the centre's revenue by increasing production or improving distribution methods.

Investment Centre

As investment centre is responsible for both profits and investments. The investment centre manager has control over revenues, expenses and the amounts invested in the centre's assets. He also formulates the credit policy which has a direct influence on debt collection, and the inventory policy which determines the investment in inventory.

MEANING OF RESPONSIBILITY ACCOUNTING

The term "responsibility accounting" refers to the accounting process that reports how well managers (of responsibility centres) have fulfilled their responsibility. Also known as activity or profitability accounting, it is an information system that personalises control reports by accumulating and reporting cost and revenue information according to defined responsibility areas within a company. According to Horngreen[1], the responsibility accounting system recognises various division centres throughout an organisation and traces costs (as well as revenue, assets, and liabilities, where relevant) to the individual managers who are primarily responsible for making decisions about these variables. The responsibility accounting system makes the following important assumptions:

1. The areas of responsibility are defined for which managers should be held responsible.
2. Managers are only charged with the items and responsibility over which they can exercise a significant degree of direct control.
3. Managers should actively participate in establishing the goals or budgets against which their performance is measured.
4. Goals defined for each area of responsibility should be attainable with efficient and effective performance.
5. Control (performance) reports should contain significant information related to each area of responsibility.
6. Responsibility centre managers should try to accomplish the budgets and objectives established for their respective areas of responsibility.

The above are also considered as pre-requisites of responsibility accounting.

MEASURING DIVISIONAL PERFORMANCE

Performance measurement is aimed in respect of all responsibility divisions. The following techniques can be used to measure the performance of a division.

1. Variance Analysis In this technique, standard costs and budgets are set in order to provide a basis for comparison with actual performance. Any variance between the two requires that corrective actions should be taken. The performance of cost centre and revenue centre is measured in terms of standard costs and budgets determined for the respective centres. On measuring the performance, attempts are made to minimise the costs of cost centre and increase the revenue of the revenue centre.

2. Profit This measure can be used to judge the performance of a profit centre. Besides, budgetary control and contribution to sales (c/s ratio) can be applied for measuring profit centre's performance. However, there is difficulty in measuring profit of a division as net profit is equal to divisional revenue minus total costs. Total costs include direct divisional costs plus allocated fixed-costs and this raises the question of finding a suitable cost allocation method. Hence, the determination of divisional profit, that is, its performance, can itself be unreliable if it includes a part of indirect cost.

It is suggested that while measuring the performance of a profit division, it is better to use a measure of divisional revenue less divisional costs and a divisional revenue less divisional controllable costs should be used to measure the performance of divisional manager. Controllable profit (divisional revenue – divisional controllable costs) is a much better measure of divisional manager's performance as it considers all costs—fixed or variable—which are within his control. The full cost can be suitable to measure a division's performance but not the performance of a divisional manager because then he is held responsible for some costs (allocated fixed costs) which is not controllable by him and which he cannot influence directly or indirectly.

[1] Charles T. Horngreen, *Cost Accounting: A Managerial Emphasis*, Prentice Hall of India.

3. Return on Investment (ROI) This measure expresses divisional profit as a percentage of the firm's investment in the division and is similar to widely accepted "return on capital employed" method. This is calculated as:

$$\text{ROI} = \frac{\text{Divisional Profit}}{\text{Divisional Investment}}$$

The ROI ratio can be divided into other ratios such as net profit margin and the asset turnover. The net profit margin is the result of firm's pricing policy and its cost control. The asset turnover shows the amount of sales generated by the capital available and whether a firm has over- or under-utilised its assets.

$$\text{ROI} = \underset{\text{(Net profit margin)}}{\frac{\text{Net profit}}{\text{Sales}} \times 100} \times \underset{\text{(Asset turnover)}}{\frac{\text{Sales}}{\text{Capital employed}} \times 100}$$

The ROI formula recognises that the absolute size of divisional operating profit alone does not provide a basis for measuring its performance, but rather the relation between the division's net income and the assets used in the generation of that income. For example, the fact that division *A* has net income of ₹50,000 does not necessarily mean that it was more successful than division *B* which has profit of ₹40,000. The difference between these profit levels could be attributable entirely to a difference in the investment size of divisions. In such a situation, ROI proves to be a good measure of performance of a division. For example, assuming that the investments in division *A* and *B* are ₹2,00,000 and ₹1,00,000 respectively, the ROI can better indicate their comparative performances.

$$\text{ROI} = \frac{\text{Divisional Profit}}{\text{Divisional Investment}}$$

$$\text{Division } A = \frac{₹50{,}000}{2{,}00{,}000} = 25\%$$

$$\text{Division } B = \frac{₹40{,}000}{1{,}00{,}000} = 40\%$$

Thus, using ROI, it is proved that division *B* is more efficient and has made more profit than division *A*. ROI can be increased by any of the following actions, all other factors remaining constant.

1. An increase in sales price or sales volume.
2. A decrease in operating costs (fixed or variable).
3. A reduction in divisional investment.

ROI has the following advantages:

1. It relates net income to investments made in a division giving a better measure of divisional profitability.
2. It can be used as a basis for other ratios which are useful for analytical purposes.
3. It is easy to understand as it is based on financial accounting measurements.
4. It may be used for inter-firm comparisons, provided that the firms whose results are being compared are of comparable size and of the same industry.

ROI has the following limitations:

1. Satisfactory definition of profit and investment are difficult to find. Profit has many concepts such as profit before interest and tax, profit after interest and tax, controllable profit, profit after deducting all allocated fixed costs. Similarly, the term investment may have many connotations

such as gross book value, net book value, historical cost of assets, current cost of assets, and assets including or excluding intangible assets.

2. While comparing ROI of different companies, it is necessary that the companies use similar accounting policies and methods in respect of valuation of stocks, valuation of fixed assets; apportionment of overheads, treatment of research and development expenditure etc.
3. ROI may influence a divisional manager to select investments with high rates of return (that is rates which are in line or above his target ROI). Other investments that would reduce the division's ROI but could increase the value of the business may be rejected by the divisional manager. These types of decision are sub-optimal and can distort an enterprise's overall allocation of resources and may motivate a manager for underinvesting in order to preserve his ROI. Suppose, a division's ROI is 25% as shown below.

$$\text{ROI} = \frac{\text{Profit ₹1,00,000}}{\text{Investment ₹4,00,000}} \times 100 = 25\%$$

Suppose, there is an opportunity to make additional investment of ₹2,00,000 which will give 20% ROI. This investment is acceptable to the company because the company requires a minimum 15% ROI for this type of investment. This investment lowers the division's ROI to 23.3% calculated as follows:

Old investment + New investment

$$\text{New ROI} = \frac{₹1,00,000 + ₹40,000}{₹4,00,000 + ₹2,00,000} \times 100 = 23.3\%$$

A comparison of old ROI (25%) with the new ROI (23.3%) would imply that performance has declined. Consequently, a divisional manager might decide not to make such an investment.

4. *Residual income (RI)* can be defined as the net income of a division, less the "imputed" capital charge on the assets used by the division. The capital charge is the minimum acceptable rate of return and is calculated by applying this required (or target) rate of return to the division's investment base. Theoretically, rate of return should be the division's cost of capital, in most cases, however, it is a cut-off rate based on the firm's objectives and strategies. RI is calculated as:

$$\text{RI} = \text{Divisional profit} - (\text{Percent capital charge} \times \text{Divisional investment})$$

The "divisional profit" and "divisional investment" are as they are defined in ROI. Using the data given in the above example, that is, divisional profit ₹1,00,000, investment ₹4,00,000 and further assuming capital charge of 15%, the RI will be ₹40,000, calculated as follows:

$$\begin{aligned} \text{RI} &= ₹1,00,000 - (15\% \times ₹4,00,000) \\ &= 1,00,000 - 60,000 \\ &= ₹40,000 \end{aligned}$$

Residual income from the additional investment of ₹2,00,000 will be

$$\begin{aligned} \text{RI} &= ₹40,000 - (15\% \times ₹2,00,000) \\ &= ₹10,000 \end{aligned}$$

Therefore, after making additional investment, the total residual income of the division will be ₹50,000, that is,

$$\begin{aligned} \text{RI} &= \text{Profits } 1,00,000 + 40,000 - (15\% \times ₹4,00,000 + 2,00,000) \\ &= 1,40,000 - 90,000 \\ &= ₹50,000 \end{aligned}$$

Thus, the additional investment increases residual income, appropriately improving the measure of performance, whereas the use of ROI has worsened the measure of performance as it gives an overall lower ROI.

RI has following advantages:

1. It avoids sub-optimal decisions as investments are not rejected merely because they lower the divisional manager's ROI.
2. It maximises growth of the company and increases shareholders' wealth by accepting opportunities which earn a rate of return in excess of the cost of capital.
3. The cost of capital charge on divisional investments ensures that divisional managers are aware of the opportunity cost of funds.
4. Charging each division with the company's cost of capital ensures that decisions taken by different divisions are compatible with the interests of organisation as a whole.

The following are the weaknesses of RI:

1. Like ROI, it is difficult to have satisfactory definition of "divisional profit" and "divisional investment".
2. It may be difficult to calculate an accurate cost of capital.
3. Identifying controllable and uncontrollable factors at divisional level may be difficult.

EXAMPLE 21.1

M/s Moonlight Co. Ltd. fixes the inter-divisional transfer prices for its products on the basis of cost plus an estimated return on investment in its divisions. The relevant particulars of the budget for the Division "X" for the year 2019–20 are given below:

Particulars	*Amount* (₹)
Fixed assets	6,00,000
Current assets (other than cash at bank)	3,00,000
Cash at bank	1,00,000
Yearly fixed cost for the division	9,00,000
Variable cost per unit	10
Budgeted volume of production per year (in units)	5,00,000
Desired return on investment	30%

You are required to determine the transfer price for Division "X".

SOLUTION

Note 1: Investment in division *A* = (Fixed asset + Current asset)
= ₹(6,00,000 + 3,00,000 + 1,00,000)
= ₹10,00,000

Note 2: Return on investment
Desired return 30% ₹10,00,000 = ₹3,00,000

Budgeted volume of production per year = 5,00,000 units
Profit margin per unit = 3,00,000 /5,00,000 = ₹0.60
Transfer price for division *A*

		₹
Variable cost per unit		10.00
Fixed cost per unit ₹9,00,000/₹5,00,000	1.80	
Profit margin per unit 3,00,000 /5,00,000		0.60
Transfer price per unit		12.40

EXAMPLE 21.2

Divisions A and B both are considering an outlay on new investment projects.

	Division A	*Division B*
Investment outlay	₹1,00,000	₹1,00,000
Net return on the new investment	₹16,000	₹11,000
Current ROI	18%	11%

The company's cost of capital is 13%. Should the project be accepted or rejected?

Solution

(i) Using ROI

$$\text{ROI on new investment} = \frac{\text{Net return}}{\text{New investment}}$$

$$\text{Division } A = \frac{₹16{,}000}{₹1{,}00{,}000} \times 100 = 16\%$$

$$\text{Division } B = \frac{₹11{,}000}{₹1{,}00{,}000} \times 100 = 11\%$$

Division A should reject the new investment as its ROI is 16% which is less than the current ROI of 18%. Division B can accept the investment as its current ROI of 11% is equal to new ROI on new investments.

(ii) Using RI

	Division A	*Division B*
Investment	₹1,00,000	₹1,00,000
Net income on new investment	16,000	11,000
Less: Imputed cost of capital 13%	13,000	13,000
Residual income	3,000	(2,000)

Division A should accept the investment as it will make RI of ₹3,000 and Division B should reject it because it will give a loss of ₹2,000.

EXAMPLE 21.3

The following information relates to budgeted operations of division X of a manufacturing company.

	(₹)
Sales (50,000 units at ₹8)	4,00,000
Less: Variable costs @ ₹6 per unit	3,00,000
Contribution margin	1,00,000
Less: Fixed costs	75,000
Divisional profit	25,000

The amount of divisional investment is ₹1,50,000 and the minimum desired rate of return on the investment is the cost of capital of 20%.

Required:

(i) Calculate divisional expected ROI
(ii) Calculate divisional expected RI
(iii) Comment on the result of (i) and (ii)
(iv) The divisional manager has the opportunity to sell 10,000 units at ₹7.50 per unit. Variable cost per unit would be the same as budgeted, but fixed costs would increase by ₹5,000. Additional investment of ₹20,000 would also be required. If the manager accepts the special order, by how much and in what direction would his residual income change?

Solution

(i) $\text{ROI} = \dfrac{₹25{,}000}{₹1{,}50{,}000} \times 100 = 16.7\%$

(ii) RI = Divisional profit – Minimum desired rate of return
= ₹25,000 – (20% × ₹1,50,000)
= 25,000 – 30,000
RI = (₹5,000)

(iii) The desired rate of return is 20% but the division *X* is expecting to achieve an ROI of 16.7%. The expected profit of ₹25,000 is less than the minimum return of ₹30,000 required resulting in the negative of ₹5,000 residual income.

(iv) Opportunity to sell additional 10,000 units

	Original Budget (₹)	*Additional Budget* (₹)	*Total* (₹)
Sales	4,00,000	75,000	4,75,000
Less: Variable costs	3,00,000	60,000	3,60,000
Contribution	1,00,000	15,000	1,15,000
Less: Fixed costs	75,000	5,000	80,000
Divisional profit	25,000	10,000	35,000
Less: Cost of capital (20%)	30,000	4,000	34,000
Residual income	(5,000)	6,000	1,000

The target residual income changes from a negative balance of ₹5,000 to a positive one of ₹1,000 as a result of the new opportunity to sell 10,000 units. This is due to the fact that ₹10,000 expected profit from additional order is offset by a further ₹4,000 cost of capital, thereby increasing residual income by ₹6,000.

EXAMPLE 21.4

XYZ company has three divisions whose income statements and balance sheets are summarised below:

	Division X	Division Y	Division Z
Sales (₹)	5,00,000	(d)	(g)
Operating income (₹)	25,000	30,000	(h)
Operating assets (₹)	1,00,000	(e)	2,50,000
Turnover	(a)	(f)	0.4
Margin	(b)	0.4%	5%
ROI	(c)	2%	(i)

Required:

(i) Supply the missing data in the table above and summarise the results.

(ii) Comment on the relative performance of each division. What questions can be raised as a result of their performance?

Solution

(i) Return of Investment (ROI) is

$$= \frac{\text{Operating income}}{\text{Operating assets}} = \frac{\text{Operating income}}{\text{Sales}} \times \frac{\text{Sales}}{\text{Operating assets}}$$

$$= \text{Margin} \times \text{Turnover}$$

(a) Division × Turnover $= \frac{5,00,000}{1,00,000} = 5$ times

(b) Division × Margin $= \frac{25,000}{5,00,000} = 5\%$

(c) Division × ROI = Turnover × Margin

= 5 times × 5%

= 25%

(d) Division *Y* sales

$$\text{Margin} = 0.4\% \quad = 0.004 = \frac{30,000}{\text{Sales } d}$$

$$d = \frac{30,000}{.004} = ₹75,00,000$$

(e) Division *Y* operating assets

$$\text{ROI} = \frac{\text{Operating income}}{\text{Operating assets}}$$

$$2\% = \frac{30,000}{\text{Operating assets}}$$

$$e = \frac{30,000}{.02} = ₹15,00,000$$

(f) Division Y turnover

$$= \frac{\text{Sales}}{\text{Operating assets}}$$

$$= \frac{75,00,000}{15,00,000} = 5 \text{ times}$$

(g) Division Z sales

$$\text{Turnover} = \frac{\text{Sales}}{\text{Operating assets}}$$

$$0.4 = \frac{\text{Sales g}}{2,50,000}$$

$$g = .4 \times 2,50,000 = ₹1,00,000$$

(h) Division Z operating income

$$\text{Margin} = \frac{\text{Operating income}}{\text{Sales}}$$

$$5\% = \frac{h}{10,00,000}$$

$$h = 1,00,000 \times 5\% = ₹5,000$$

(i) ROI Division Z

$$= \text{Turnover} \times \text{Margin}$$

$$= 0.4 \times 5\%$$

$$= 2\% \text{ or } \frac{5,000}{2,50,000} = 2\%$$

Summarising the Results:

	Div. X	*Div. Y*	*Div. Z*
Turnover	5 times	5 times	0.4 times
Margin	5%	0.4%	5%
ROI	25%	2%	2%

(ii) Division X performed best. It appears that divisions Y and Z are in trouble. Division Y turns over its assets as often as division X, but Y's margin on sales is much lower. Thus, division Y must work on improving its margin. The following questions are raised about division Y. Is the low margin due to inefficiency? Is it due to excessive material, labour and/or overhead costs?

Division Z, on the other hand, does just as well as division X in terms of profit margin—both divisions earn 5% on sales. But, division Z has a much lower turnover of capital than division X. Therefore, division Z should take a close look at its investments. Is it too much tied up in inventories and receivables? Are there unused fixed assets? Is there idle cash sitting around?

EXAMPLE 21.5

The table below shows the annual results for the four divisions of a group company.

Division	A	B	C	D
		₹000		
Sales revenue	156	445	3,014	2,036
Variable costs	134	400	2,642	1,781
Contribution	**22**	**45**	**372**	**255**
Controllable fixed costs	14	35	298	211
Controllable profit	**8**	**10**	**74**	**44**
Non-controllable fixed costs	6	7	50	30
Profit before head office charges	**2**	**3**	**24**	**14**
Head office charges	1	1	6	4
Divisional pre-tax profit	**1**	**2**	**18**	**10**
Capital employed	**30**	**60**	**450**	**240**

Required:

1 Calculate the return on capital employed for each of the four divisions and rank them accordingly.

2 Calculate the residual income for each of the four divisions using an interest rate of 5% and rank them accordingly.

3 Comment on your findings.

Solution

Division	A	B	C	D
Profit before head office charges	2	3	24	14
Capital employed	30	60	450	240
ROCE	6.7%	5.0%	5.3%	5.8%
ROCE preferences	**1**	**4**	**3**	**2**
Notional interest @ 5%	1.5	3.0	22.5	12.0
RI (profit before HO charges – interest)	0.5	0.0	1.5	2.0
RI preferences	**3**	**4**	**2**	**1**

Comment: "Profit before head office charges" has been used to calculate ROCE as this is the most appropriate measure of divisional performance. Note that the two sets of rankings give different answers as to which divisions have performed better than others. Both answers are correct; which one is used depends entirely on head office.

EXAMPLE 21.6

ABC is a diversified company producing and distributing different products. Product-*X* division within the company handles a specific product and would like to earn a long-run rate of return of 20%. Product *X* division will charge its unit selling price as necessary to provide this return. The following data are available on the division and its products:

Variable cost per unit	₹200
Total annual fixed costs	₹12,20,000
Long-run normal demand	10,000 units each year
Average operating assets owned by the division	₹14,00,000

Required:

(i) Compute the per-unit selling price that will provide the desired rate of return.

(ii) Assume that actual sales fluctuate from 8,500 units to 11,500 units. Compute the margin, turnover and ROI that would be realised on sales at 8,500 units, 10,000 units and 11,500 units level of activity (use the selling price computed in part 1 for your computations).

Solution

$$\text{ROI} = \underset{\text{Margin}}{\underbrace{\frac{\text{Operating income}}{\text{Sales}}}} \times \underset{\text{Turnover}}{\underbrace{\frac{\text{Sales}}{\text{Assets}}}}$$

(i) *Total Sales Value of 10,000 units*

Variable cost (₹200 × 10,000)	=	₹20,00,000
Fixed cost	=	12,20,000
Return @ 20% $\left(14{,}00{,}000 \times \frac{20}{10}\right)$	=	2,80,000
Total sales value		35,00,000

$$\text{Selling price per unit} = \frac{35{,}00{,}000}{10{,}000 \text{ units}} = ₹350$$

(ii) *Calculation of Margin, Turnover and ROI at 8,500 units*

Operating income = (8,500 units × ₹350) – (8,500 × ₹200) – ₹12,20,000

= 29,75,000 – 17,00,000 – 12,20,000

= ₹55,000

$$\text{Margin} = \frac{55{,}000}{29{,}75{,}000} \times 100 = 1.85\%$$

$$\text{Turnover} = \frac{29{,}75{,}000}{14{,}00{,}000} = 2.125$$

ROI = Margin × Turnover

ROI = 1.85% × 2.125 = 3.93%

or

$$\frac{55{,}000}{14{,}00{,}000} \times 100 = 3.93\%$$

At 10,000 units level

Operating income $= (10{,}000 \times 350) - (10{,}000 \times 200) - 12{,}20{,}000$

$= 35{,}00{,}000 \quad 20{,}00{,}000 \quad 12{,}20{,}000$

$= ₹2{,}80{,}000$

Margin $= \dfrac{2{,}80{,}000}{35{,}00{,}000} \times 100 = 8\%$

Turnover $= \dfrac{35{,}00{,}000}{14{,}00{,}000} = 2.5$

ROI = 8% × 2.5 = 20%

At 11,500 units

Operating income $= (11{,}500 \times 350) - (11{,}500 \times 200) - 12{,}20{,}000$

$= 40{,}25{,}000 - 23{,}00{,}000 - 12{,}20{,}000$

$= 5{,}05{,}000$

Margin $= \dfrac{5{,}05{,}000}{40{,}25{,}000} \times 100 = 12.25\%$

Turnover $= \dfrac{40{,}25{,}000}{14{,}00{,}000} = 2.875$

ROI = 12.55 × 2.875 = 36.08%

Summary of Calculations

Sales in Units	*Margin*	*Capital Turnover*	*ROI*
8,500	1.85%	2.125	3.93%
10,000	8%	2.5	20%
11,500	12.55%	2.875	36.08%

EXAMPLE 21.7

Compro Electronics is facing stiff competition from imported goods. Its operating income margin has been declining steadily for the past several years; the company has been forced to lower prices so that it can maintain its market share. The operating results for the past three years as follows:

	Year 1	*Year 2*	*Year 3*
Sales	₹1,00,00,000	₹95,00,000	₹90,00,000
Net operating income	12,00,000	10,45,000	9,45,000
Average assets	1,50,00,000	1,50,00,000	1,50,00,000

For the coming year, Compro's CEO plans to install a JIT purchasing and manufacturing system. He estimates that inventories will be reduced by 70 per cent during the first year of operations, producing a 20 per cent reduction in the average operating assets of the company, which would remain unchanged without the JIT system. He also estimates that sales and operating income will be restored to year-1 levels because of simultaneous reductions in operating expenses and selling prices. Lower selling prices will allow Compro to expand its market share.

Required:

(i) Compute the ROI, margin, and turnover for years 1, 2 and 3.

(ii) Suppose that the sales and operating income in year 4 were achieved as expected but inventories remained at the same level as in year 3. Compute the expected ROI, margin and turnover. Explain why the ROI increased over the year-3 level.

(iii) Suppose that the sales and net operating income for year 4 remained the same as in year 3 but inventory reductions were achieved as projected. Compute the ROI, margin and turnover. Explain why the ROI exceeded the year-3 level.

(iv) Assume that all expectations for year 4 were realised. Compute the expected ROI, margin and turnover. Explain why the ROI increased over the year-3 level.

☞ ***Solution***

	Year 1	*Year 2*	*Year 3*
(i) ROI	$= \frac{₹12,00,000}{₹1,50,00,000} \times 100$	$\frac{₹10,45,000}{₹1,50,00,000} \times 100$	$\frac{₹9,45,000}{₹1,50,00,000} \times 100$
	= 8.00%	= 6.97%	= 6.30%
Margin	$= \frac{₹12,00,000}{₹1,00,00,000} \times 100$	$\frac{₹10,45,000}{₹95,00,000} \times 100$	$\frac{₹9,45,000}{₹90,00,000} \times 100$
	= 12.00%	= 11.00%	= 10.50%
Turnover	$= \frac{₹1,00,000}{₹1,50,00,000} \times 100$	$\frac{₹95,00,000}{₹1,50,00,000} \times 100$	$\frac{₹90,00,000}{₹1,50,00,000} \times 100$
	= 0.67	= 0.63	= 0.60

(ii)

$$\text{ROI} = \frac{₹12,00,000}{₹1,50,00,000} \times 100 = 8\%$$

$$\text{Margin} = \frac{₹12,00,000}{₹1,00,00,000} \times 100 = 12\%$$

$$\text{Turnover} = \frac{₹1,00,00,000}{₹1,50,00,000} \times 100 = 0.67$$

The ROI increased because expenses decreased and assets turned over at a higher rate (sales increased).

(iii)

$$\text{Operating assets} = ₹1,50,00,000 \times 80\% = ₹1,20,00,000$$

$$\text{ROI} = ₹9,45,000/₹1,20,00,000 = ₹7.88\%$$

$$\text{Margin} = ₹9,45,000/₹90,00,000 = 10.5\%$$

$$\text{Turnover} = ₹90,00,000/₹1,20,00,000 = 0.75$$

The ROI increased because assets decreased.

(iv)

$$\text{ROI} = ₹12,00,000/₹1,20,00,000 = 10\%$$

$$\text{Margin} = ₹12,00,000/₹1,00,00,000 = 12\%$$

$$\text{Turnover} = ₹1,00,00,000/₹1,20,00,000 = 0.83$$

The ROI increased because expenses decreased and assets turned over at a higher rate (sales increased and the amount of assets decreased). Both margin and turnover increased.

TRANSFER PRICING

In divisionalised companies, where profit or investment centres are created, there is likely to be inter-divisional transfer of goods or services and this internal transfer create the problem of transfer pricing. A transfer price is that notional value at which goods and services are transferred between divisions in a decentralised organisation. Transfer prices are normally set for intermediate products which are goods and services that are supplied by the selling division to the buying division. The goods that are produced by the buying division and sold to the outside world are known as final products.

A question arises as to how the transfer of goods and services between divisions should be priced. The transfer prices can have impact on the evaluation of each division's performance and measures applied for such measurements of performance.

Objectives in Sound Transfer Pricing System

A question arises as to how the transfer of goods and services between divisions should be priced. The price charged to the interdivisional transfer of goods and services is revenues to the selling division and cost to the buying division. Therefore, the price charged will affect the profit of both divisions; benefit (revenue) to one division can be created only at the expense of the other division. For example, the selling division will benefit from charging higher prices for such transfers of goods and services. However, for the buying division, this will result into higher costs. While determining transfer prices, a number of criteria (objectives) should be fulfilled.

(i) Transfer prices should help in the accurate measurement of divisional performance (profitability) measurement.

(ii) Transfer prices should motivate the divisional managers into maximising the profitability of their divisions and making decisions that are in the best interests of the organisations as a whole.

(iii) Transfer prices should ensure that divisional autonomy and authority is preserved. The main purpose of decentralisation is to enable divisional managers to exercise greater autonomy and to measure the overall results achieved on a profit centre or investment centre. It is, therefore, not proper to give divisional managers authority by one hand by placing them in charge of divisional operations and to remove that authority by dictating transfer prices that affect the performance of the division.

(iv) Transfer prices should allow goal congruence to take place, which in effect means that the objectives of divisional managers are compatible with the objectives of overall company.

(v) A transfer pricing system, if properly established, can check multinational companies and international groups which may try to manipulate transfer prices between countries in order to minimise the overall tax burden.

Methods of Transfer Pricing

Broadly, there are four bases available for determining transfer prices, but many options are also available within each base. These methods are:

(1) Market-based prices

(2) Cost-based prices

(a) Variable cost
(b) Actual full cost
(c) Full cost plus profit margin
(d) Standard full cost

(3) Negotiated prices
(4) Dual prices

(1) Market-based Prices

Market price refers to a price in an intermediate market between independent buyers and sellers. When there is a competitive external market for the transferred product, market prices work well as transfer prices. When transferred goods are recorded at market prices, divisional performance is more likely to represent the real economic contribution of the division to total company profit. If the goods cannot be bought from a division within the company, the intermediate product would have to be purchased at the current market price from the outside market. Divisional profits are therefore likely to be similar to the profits that would be calculated if the divisions were separate organisations. Consequently, divisional profitability can be compared directly with the profitability of similar companies operating in the same type of business. In the market price situation, top management will not be tempted to intervene.

Market-based prices are based on opportunity costs concepts. The opportunity cost approach signals that the correct transfer price is the market price. Since the selling division can sell all that it produces at the market price, transferring internally at a lower price would make the division worse off. Similarly the buying division can always acquire the intermediate goods at the market price, so it would be unwilling to pay more for an internally transferred good. Since the minimum transfer price for the selling division is the market price and the maximum price for the buying division is also the market price, the only possible transfer price is the market price.[2]

However, there are some problems using the market price approach.

Firstly, finding a competitive market price may be difficult if such a market does not exist. Catalogue price may only vaguely relate to actual sales prices. Market prices may change often.

Secondly, another problem with market prices can occur when a selling division is not operating at full capacity and cannot sell all its products. To illustrate this point, assume that materials used by division *A* in a company are being purchased from outside market at ₹20 per unit. The same materials are produced by division *B*. If division *B* is operating is full capacity, say of 50,000 units and can sell all its products to either division *A* or to outside buyers, then the use of transfer price of ₹20 per unit (market price) has no effect on division *B*'s income or total company profit. Division *B* will earn revenue of ₹20 per unit on all its production and sales, regardless of who buys its product and division *A* will pay ₹20 per unit, regardless of whether it purchases the materials from division *B* or from an outside supplier. In this situation, the use of market price as the transfer price is appropriate.

However, if division *B* is not operating at full capacity and unused capacity exists in that division, the use of market price may not lead to maximisation of total company profit. To illustrate this point, assume that division *B* has additional unused capacity of 30,000 units and it can continue to sell only 50,000 units to outside buyers. In this situation, the transfer price should be set to motivate the manager of division *A* to purchase from division *B* if the variable cost per unit of product of division *B* is less than the market price. If the variable costs are less than ₹20 per unit but the transfer price is set equal

2. Don R. Hanen and Maryamne M. Mowen, *Management Accounting*, South Western Publishing Co. 1992, p. 871.

to the market price of ₹20, then the manager of division *A* is indifferent as to whether materials are purchased from division *B* or from outside suppliers, since the cost per unit to division *B* would be the same, i.e. ₹20. In fact, there is no gain for division *A* to buy materials at ₹20 from division *B* when same materials is available in the market for ₹20 per unit. However, division *A*'s purchase of 20,000 units of materials from outside suppliers at a cost of ₹20 per unit would not maximise overall company profit, since this market price per unit is greater than the unit variable cost of division *B*, say ₹10. Hence, the intra-company transfer could save the company the difference between the market price per unit and division *B*'s unit variable expenses that is ₹10 (₹20 – ₹10). This savings of ₹10 per unit would add ₹2,00,000 (20,000 units × ₹10) to overall company profit.

(2) Cost-based Prices

When external markets do not exist or are not available to the company or when information about external market prices is not readily available, companies may decide to use some forms of cost-based transfer pricing system.

As stated earlier, cost-based transfer prices may be in different forms such as variable cost, actual full cost, full cost plus profit margin, standard full cost, opportunity cost.

(a) Variable Cost: Variable cost-based pricing approach is useful when the selling division is operating below capacity. The manager of the selling division will generally not like this transfer price because it yields no profit to that division. In this pricing system, only variable production costs are transferred. These costs are direct materials, direct labour and variable factory overhead. Variable cost has the major advantage of encouraging maximum profits for the entire firm. By passing only variable costs alone to the next division, production and pricing decisions are based on cost-volume-profit relationships for the firm as a whole. The obvious problem is that selling division is left holding all its fixed costs and operating expenses. That division is now a loss division, nowhere near a profit centre.[3]

(b) Actual Full Cost: In actual full cost approach, transfer price is based on the total product cost per unit which will include direct materials, direct labour and factory overhead. When full cost is used for transfer pricing, the selling division cannot realise a profit on the goods transferred. This may be disincentive to the selling division. Further, full cost transfer pricing can provide perverse incentives and distort performance measures. A full cost transfer price would have shutdown the chances of any negotiation between divisions about selling at transfer prices.

(c) Full Cost Plus Profit Margin: Full cost plus mark-up (or profit margin) overcomes the weaknesses of full-cost basis transfer pricing system. The full cost plus transfer price include the allowed cost of the item plus a mark-up or other profit allowance. With such a system, the selling division obtains a profit contribution on units transferred and hence, benefits if performance is measured on the basis of divisional operating profits. However, the manager of the buying division would naturally object that his costs (and hence reported performance) are adversely affected.

The basic question in full cost plus mark up is "What should be the percentage of mark?" It can be suggested that the mark-up percentage should cover operating expenses and provide a target return on sales or assets.

(d) Standard Costs: In actual cost approaches, there is a problem of measuring cost. Actual cost does not provide any incentive to the selling division to control cost. All product costs are transferred to the

3. Lane K. Anderson and Harold M Sollenberger, *Management Accounting*. South-Western Publishing Co. 1992, p.174.

buying division. While transferring actual costs any variances or inefficiencies in the selling division are passed along to the buying division. The problem of isolating the variances that have been transferred to subsequent buyer division becomes extremely complex. To promote responsibility in the selling division and to isolate variances within divisions, standard costs are usually used as a basis for transfer pricing in cost-based systems.

Whether transferring at differential costs or full costs, standard costs, where available, are often used as the basis for the transfer. This encourages efficiency in the selling division because inefficiencies are not passed onto the buying division. Otherwise, the selling division can transfer cost inefficiencies to the buying division. Use of standard cost reduces risk to the buyer. The buyer knows that standard costs will be transferred and avoids being charged with suppliers' cost overruns.[4]

(3) Negotiated Prices

Negotiated prices are generally preferred as a middle solution between market prices and cost-based prices. Under negotiated prices, the managers involved act much the same as the managers of independent companies. Negotiation strategies may be similar to those employed when trading with outside markets. If both divisions are free to deal either with each other or in the external market, the negotiated price will likely be close to the external market price. If all of a selling division's output cannot be sold in the external market (that is, a portion must be sold to the buying division), the negotiated price will likely be less than the market price and the total margin will be shared by the divisions.

Negotiated prices avoid mistrusts, bad feelings and undesirable bargaining interests among divisional managers. Also, it provides an opportunity to achiever the objectives of goal congruence, autonomy and accurate performance evaluation. The overall company is beneficiary if selling and buying divisions can agree upon some mutually transfer prices. Negotiated transfer price is considered as a vital integrating tool among divisions of a company which is necessary to achieve goal congruence. If negotiations help ensure goal congruence, top management has little temptation to intervene between divisions. The agreed prices can also be used for performance measurement without creating any friction. The use of negotiated prices is consistent with the concept of decentralised decision-making in the divisionalised firms.

However, negotiated prices have the following disadvantages:

(1) A great deal of management effort, time and resources can be consumed in the negotiating process.

(2) The final emerging negotiated price may depend more on the divisional manager's ability and skill to negotiate than on the other factors. Thus, performance measures will be distorted leading to incorrect evaluation of divisional performance.

(3) One divisional manager having some private information may take advantage of another divisional manager.

(4) Dual Prices

Under dual prices of transfer pricing, selling division sells the transferred goods at a profit using full cost plus profit margin. But the transfer price for the buying division is the market price. The difference in transfer prices for the two divisions could be accounted for by a special centralised account. This system would preserve cost data for subsequent buyer departments, and would encourage internal transfers by providing a profit on such transfers for the selling divisions.

---

[4] Sidney Davidson et al., *Managerial Accounting,* The Dryden Press 1988. p. 683.

Dual prices give motivation and incentive to selling divisions as goods are transferred at a profit or mark-up. Market price can be considered as the most appropriate base for the buying division. Thus, dual pricing system has the function of motivating both the selling division and buying division to make decisions that are consistent with the overall goals of decentralisation—goal congruence, accurate performance measurement, autonomy, adequate motivation to divisional manager.

EXAMPLE 21.8

Division *S* sells one of its products, an electric motor, to division *B* in the same group. One motor costs ₹36 in materials, ₹9 in direct labour, ₹5 in variable overhead and is assigned ₹15 of fixed overhead. The division sets its profit margin equal to 40% of its variable cost.

What is the ideal transfer price if the division is operating at (a) full capacity and (b) less than full capacity? Suggest practical transfer prices if the division is operating at (a) full capacity and (b) less than full capacity.

Solution

	₹
Materials	36
Direct labour	9
Variable overhead	5
Variable cost	50
Fixed overhead	15
Full cost	65
Profit margin	20
Sales price	85

If operating at full capacity, the *ideal transfer price* is ₹85.
If operating at less than full capacity, the *ideal transfer price* is ₹50.
If operating at full capacity, the profit margin may be shared between supplying and buying divisions, so the *practical transfer price* may be ₹75 [65 + (50% × 20)].
If operating at less than full capacity, full cost may be used, giving the supplying division a contribution to its fixed overheads. The *practical transfer price* would be ₹65 giving a positive contribution of ₹15.

EXAMPLE 21.9

A company has two divisions—*A* and *B*. Division *A* manufactures a component which is used by division *B* to produce a finished product. For the next period, output and costs have been budgeted as follows:

	Division *A*	Division *B*
Component units	50,000	
Finished units	—	50,000
Total variable costs	₹2,50,000	6,00,000
Fixed costs	₹1,50,000	2,00,000

The fixed costs are separable for each division. You are required to advise on the transfer price to be fixed for division *A*'s component under the following circumstances.

(i) Division *A* can sell the component in a competitive market for ₹10 per unit. Division *B* can also purchase the component from the open market at that price.

(ii) As per the situation described in (i) above, and further assume that division *B* currently buys the component from an external supplier at the market price of ₹10 and there is reciprocal agreement between the external supplier and another division *C*, within the group. Under this agreement, the external supplier agrees to buy one product unit from division *C*, at a profit of ₹4 per unit to that division, for every component which division *B* buys from the supplier.

Solution

(i) Transfer Price = Incremental (marginal) cost + Opportunity costs of the company due to not being able to use the components in the next most profitable way.

= ₹5 + ₹5 (Contribution foregone by transferring internally as opposed to selling in the open market)

= ₹10

The transfer price of ₹10 is equal to the market price of the component which is also ₹10.

(ii) Transfer Price = Marginal cost + Contribution + Profit foregone by division *C* as division *B* will acquire its units from division *A* in place of external supplier.

= ₹5 + ₹5 + 4

= ₹5 + ₹9 (₹9 is the opportunity cost to the whole company)

= ₹14

The transfer price of ₹14 should result in the Manager of division *B* continuing to buy from the external supplier at the market price of ₹10. However, the transfer price of ₹14 is appropriate from the viewpoint of the organisation as a whole, since, if the component is transferred internally not only will division *A* forgo an external profit of ₹5, but division *C* will also forego an external profit of ₹4. It is assumed that division *C* could not achieve the same profit by selling elsewhere.

EXAMPLE 21.10

A company fixes the inter-divisional transfer prices for its products on the basis of cost plus an estimated return on investment in its divisions. The relevant portion of the budget for the division *A* for the year 2019–20 is given below:

Fixed assets	₹5,00,000
Current assets (other than debtors)	3,00,000
Debtors	2,00,000
Annual fixed cost of the division	8,00,000
Variable cost per unit of product	10
Budgeted volume of production per year (units)	4,00,000
Desired return on investment	28%

You are required to determine the transfer price for the division *A*.

Solution

Basic Calculations:

(i) Computation of investment in division *A*.

Fixed assets	₹5,00,000
Current assets (Debtors + Other current assets)	5,00,000
	₹10,00,000

(ii) Return on investment

Desired return 28% on ₹10,00,000	₹2,80,000
Budgeted volume of production p.a.	4,00,000 units
Profit margin per unit $\frac{2,80,000}{4,00,000}$ =	₹0.70

Computation of Transfer Price for Division *A*

Variable cost per unit	₹10.00
Fixed cost per unit 8,00,000/4,00,000	2.00
Profit margin per unit	.70
Transfer price per unit	₹12.70

EXAMPLE 21.11

A company has two divisions—*A* and *B*. Division *A* normally purchase its parts from division *B* of the same company. Division *A* has learned that division *B* is increasing its price to ₹110 per unit. As a result, division *A* manager has decided to purchase the parts from an outside supplier at a unit cost of ₹100, ₹10 less than it would cost to purchase the same part from division *B*. The Division *B* manager has explained that inflation is the cause of the price-increase and that the loss of parts normally transferred to division *A* will hurt the division as well as the company profits. The division *B* manager feels that the company as a whole would benefit from the sale of parts of division *A*. The following costs and unit purchases represent the normal annual transaction.

for excel template, scan

	₹
Units purchased	1,000
Division *B*'s variable cost per unit	95
Division *B*'s fixed cost per unit	10

Required:

(i) Will the company as a whole benefit if division *A* purchases the unit from the outside supplier for ₹100 per unit? Assume that there are no alternative uses for division *B*'s facilities.

(ii) What would be the effect if the outside selling price decreases by ₹8 per unit, assuming that division *B* remains idle?

(iii) If division *B*'s facilities could be put into production for other sales at an annual cost saving of ₹14,500, should division *A* still purchase from the outside?

☞ Solution

The straightforward comparative income statement approach has been used to solve the questions:

(i) Division *A*'s action to purchase at ₹100

	Buy Outside	Buy Inside
	₹	₹
Total purchase costs	1,00,000	
Total outlay costs	–	95,000
Net cash outflow to the company as a whole.	1,00,000	95,000

The company as a whole will benefit if division *A* buys inside.

	Buy Outside	Buy Inside
	₹	₹
(ii) Total purchase costs	92,000	–
Total outlay costs	–	95,000
Net cash outflow to the company as a whole.	92,000	95,000

The company as a whole will benefit if division *A* buys from the outside supplier at ₹92 per unit.

	Buy Outside	Buy Inside
	₹	
(iii) Total purchase costs	1,00,000	–
Total outlay costs	–	95,000
Revenue (or cost savings) from using division *B*'s facilities	(14,500)	
Net cash outflow to the company as a whole	85,500	95,000

In this case, the company as a whole will be better off if division *A* buys outside and division *B*'s facilities are utilised elsewhere.

Alternative Solution

Using opportunity cost concept, the question can be analysed as follows:

	1	*2*	*3*
(a) Total purchase costs	1,00,000	92,000	1,00,000
Total outlay costs if purchase inside	95,000	95,000	95,000
Total opportunity costs if purchased inside		—	14,500
(b) Total relevant costs	95,000	95,000	1,09,500
Net advantage (disadvantage) to company as a whole (a – b)	5,000	(3000)	(9,500)

Theory Questions

1. Explain the concept of responsibility accounting. What are the different types of responsibility centres?
2. Discuss the essential of responsibility performance reporting.
3. How will you measure the performance of cost and revenue division?
4. Distinguish between cost centre and profit centre.
5. Discuss responsibility accounting in brief.
6. What is responsibility centre? Discuss briefly the nature of various types of responsibility centres.
7. Write short notes on the following:
   Responsibility centres—cost centre and profit centre.
8. Describe and compare the main performance measures that have been suggested to measure the divisional performance.
9. Profit, return on investment and residual income have stood the test of time and are widely used for measuring the performance of a division. Describe the strengths and weaknesses of these measures of performance.
10. Outline problem in defining and measuring capital employed in a division.
11. Explain the rationale of using an interest charge while measuring the performance of a division.
12. "In ROI, there is lack of consensus on the definition of numerator and denominator both." Explain the statement.
13. Explain the essential ingredients of a system of "Responsibility Accounting".
14. Outline the basic principles of "Responsibility Accounting".
15. What are the financial and non-financial methods of performance measurement? Explain with examples, wherever, feasible.
16. What is meant by divisional performance measurement? Describe any two techniques used for this purpose.
17. Discuss the important of market prices in transferring pricing system.
18. What do you mean by responsibility accounting?
19. Discuss the merits and demerits of ROI and RI for divisional performance measurement.
20. What are the objectives of transfer pricing system?
21. Explain the utility of cost-based prices under transfer pricing.
22. Write notes on (i) Negotiated prices and (ii) Dual prices.
23. What are the different methods of measurement of divisional performance?
24. Explain the concept of responsibility accounting. What are the prerequisites of responsibility accounting? Also explain the various responsibility centres in this regard.
25. Explain the essential ingredients of the system of responsibility accounting.
26. (a) What are the criteria for evaluating the performance of a division?
    (b) Write notes on the following as used in "Responsibility Accounting".
    (i) Cost centre (ii) Revenue centre (iii) Profit centre.
27. Discuss any two financial measures of divisional performance measurement.
28. Define responsibility accounting. Explain various responsibility centres that are necessary ingredients for the success of the system of responsibility accounting.
29. Define and explain responsibility accounting. What are the prerequisites for introducing responsibility accounting in a company?
30. The aim of responsibility accounting is not to place blame. Instead, it is to evaluate performance and provide feedback so that future operations can be improved. Discuss.
31. What is responsibility centre? Discuss briefly the nature of various types of responsibility centres.

Problems

1. Yonex India Ltd. is segmented into three divisions—*A*, *B* and *C*. All were formed in the same year and now all assets have left exactly one-half of their expected life. Top management is attempting to determine which of the division is the most profitable. The following data have been prepared for your analysis:

	Division		
	A (₹)	*B* (₹)	*C* (₹)
Net income before taxes	78,000	90,000	96,000
Investment base-gross book value	3,90,000	5,00,000	6,00,000
Investment base-net book value	1,95,000	2,50,000	3,00,000

Prepare rankings of the three divisions using ROI and RI with a capital charge of 12.5% that each division manager might use to assert that this is the most profitable division.

Ans:

Ranking		
ROI	RI (Gross Value)	RI (Net Value)
A	A	B
B	B	C
C	C	A

2. The operating performance of the three divisions of ABC company for 2020 is as follows:

	Division A (₹)	*Division B* (₹)	*Division C* (₹)
Sales	38,00,000	1,70,00,000	2,00,00,000
Operating profit	2,00,000	5,00,000	10,00,000
Investment	20,00,000	62,50,000	80,00,000

(a) Using the operating profit margin percentage as the criterion, which is the most profitable division?
(b) Using the rate of return on investment as the criterion, which is the most profitable division?
(c) Which of the two measures do you think gives the better indication of overall operating performance? Explain your reasoning.

Ans: (a) Ranking Division *A*, Division *C*, Division *B*
(b) Ranking Division *C*, Division *A* and Division *B*
(c) ROI is better than operating profit margin

3. The components division produces a part that is used by the Goods Division. The cost of manufacturing the part is given below:

	₹
Direct materials	10
Direct labour	2
Variable overhead	3
Fixed overhead	5
Total cost	20

Fixed overhead is based on a practical volume at 2,00,000 parts
Other costs incurred by the Components Division are as follows:

	₹
Fixed selling and administrative	5,00,000
Variable selling	₹1/unit

The part usually sells for between ₹28 and ₹30 in the external market. Currently, the Components Division is selling it to external customers for ₹29. The division is capable of producing 2,00,000 units of the part per year; however, because of a weak economy, only 1,50,000 parts are expected to be sold during the coming year. The variable selling expenses are avoidable if the part is sold internally.

The Goods Division has been buying the same part from an external supplier for ₹28. It expects to use 50,000 units of the part during the coming year. The manager of the Goods Division has offered to buy 50,000 units from the Components Division for ₹18 per unit.

Required:

(i) Determine the minimum transfer price that the Components Division would accept.
(ii) Determine the maximum transfer price that the manager of the goods division would pay.
(iii) Should an internal transfer take place? Why? If you were the manager of the Components Division, would you sell the 50,000 components for ₹18 each? Explain.
(iv) Suppose that the average operating assets of the Components Division total ₹100 lakhs. Compute the ROI for the coming year, assuming that the 50,000 units are transferred to the Goods Division for ₹21 each.

Ans. (i) ₹15, (ii) ₹28, (iii) Yes, because the opportunity cost of the transferring division is less than the opportunity cost of the buying division, (iv) 0.075 or 7.5%

4. Green World Company is a nursery products firm. It has three divisions that grow and sell plants: Western Division, Southern Division and Northern Division. Recently, the Southern Division of the company acquired a plastics factory that manufactures green plastic pots. These pots can be sold both externally and internally. Company policy permits each manager to decide whether to buy or sell internally. Each divisional manager is evaluated on the basis of return on investment.

The Western Division has bought its plastic pots in lots of 100 from a variety of vendors. The average price paid was ₹750 per box of 100 pots. However, the acquisition made Rohan, manager of the Western Division, wonder whether or not a more favourable price could be arranged. He decided to approach John Mathew, manager of the Southern Division, to see it he wanted to offer a better price for an internal transfer. Rohan suggested a transfer of 3,500 boxes at ₹700 per box.

John Mathew gathered the following information regarding the cost of a box of 100 pots:

	₹
Direct materials	350
Direct labour	80
Variable overhead	100
Fixed overhead (based on ₹20,00,000/20,000 boxes)	100
Total unit cost	630
Selling price	750
Production capacity	20,000 boxes.

Required:

(i) Suppose that the plastics factory is producing at capacity and can sell all that it produces to outside customers. How should John Mathew respond to Rohan's request for a lower transfer price?
(ii) Now, assume that the plastics factory is currently selling 16,000 boxes. What are the minimum and maximum transfer prices? Should John Mathew consider the transfer at ₹700 per box?
(iii) Suppose that Green World's policy is that all transfer prices be set at full cost plus 20 percent. Would the transfer take place? Why? Or why not?

Ans: (i) John Mathew should not reduce the price charged to Rohan if he can sell all the produces.

(ii) Minimum transfer price ₹530.
Maximum transfer price ₹750

(iii) The transfer price will be ₹756. No, the transfer will not take place.

PART 5

Specialised Topics

Part 5 discusses a few specialised topics which are broadly covered in cost accounting and about which managers and cost accounting practitioners should be fully aware. Uniform costing and Inter-firm comparison, cost audit are such useful areas and have been discussed in this part.

- *Uniform Costing and Inter-firm Comparison*
- *Cost Audit*

Chapter 22

Uniform Costing and Inter-Firm Comparison

Learning Objectives

After reading this chapter, you should be able to:

1. explain uniform costing, its advantages, factors for establishing a uniform costing system, its areas of uniformity;
2. describe the contents of uniform cost manual; and
3. explain the important requirements of inter-firm comparison, its benefits and limitations.

UNIFORM COSTING

Uniform costing is defined as the use by several undertakings of the same costing principles and/or practices. Uniform or identical methods may be applied by various members of a group of similar companies under common control. Sometimes, trade and business associations bring uniformity in costing principles and practices among all industries. Uniform costing is not a separate method of cost accounting like process or job costing, standard or marginal costing. It only points to a situation where a number of business firms are applying similar costing principles and practices.

Features of Uniform Costing

The following are the features of uniform costing:

(i) Common basis for the apportionment and allocation of overhead are followed by all units in the same industry.

(ii) The departments, sections or production centres to be used for analysis and comparison of costs are determined.

(iii) What items shall be regarded as factory and are distinct from administration expenses are clearly indicated

(iv) Common basis for recovery of overheads are adopted.

(v) Common rates of depreciation should be applied to plant and machinery.

(vi) There should be uniform method of arriving at service departments cost.

(vii) An organisation should be setup to prepare comparative statistics for the use of those adopting the uniform system.

(viii) Privacy of individual data and confidence in the co-ordinating office are essential factors.

Advantages of Uniform Costing

The advantages of uniform costing may be listed as follows:

1. Small business firms are not able to maintain a full costing system as it is costly and complicated. If the business associations and federations develop some costing principles for the benefit of all business concerns, much cost likely to be incurred on designing and establishing a costing system is likely to be saved.
2. It is always possible for management to be able to compare the cost of its own business with the average costs in the industry. Comparison helps to minimise areas of inefficiencies and weaknesses.
3. Some business associations use the costs provided by the members to prepare a standard price list, the existence of which tends to reduce destructive competition and help all members to obtain at least a fair price for their goods or services. It prevents unhealthy price cutting.
4. The applications of uniform costing in an industry provide the means whereby relevant information can be obtained to help in negotiations with government departments, trade unions, etc.
5. It promotes a sense of cost consciousness among member units and helps to improve their efficiency.
6. When customers find that quotations are based on sound costing principles, they accept them more readily, and the relationship of business enterprises with their customers is thus improved.
7. Uniform cost accounting facilitates the work of wage boards set up to fix minimum wages and fair wages for industry.
8. The benefits of research and development carried out by big firms may be made available to smaller firms also through uniform costing.
9. Uniform costing makes available cost data which are vital to government and regulatory authorities. In many areas, such as price control, protection or subsidy to industry, import licenses, quota for scarce materials, uniform costing provides suitable and important statistics.
10. Uniform costing is helpful in comparing the production efficiency of two units at the time of an amalgamation and merger.

Disadvantages

1. Business firms differ in nature of work, conditions and organisational characteristics. It becomes difficult to suggest a uniform costing for all business firms which widely differ from each other.
2. Uniform costing requires utmost cooperation, openness and confidence among members of the business and industry groups.
3. Uniform costing tends to suggest a single price within the industry which may create monopolistic tendencies.

ESTABLISHING A UNIFORM COSTING SYSTEM

Uniform costing may be useful to those business firms which are in the same industry, within a single management and also to industries of a similar nature, big or small. The success of uniform costing depends on the following factors:

1. Free exchange of ideas, information practices and techniques;
2. Mutual trust, cooperation, confidence and a desire to share with each other;
3. Bigger enterprises should lend more cooperation and help to smaller enterprises;
4. No concealment of any information; and
5. Absence of competition and hatred among participating members.

In uniform costing, the purpose is to establish uniformity in cost accounting principles and practices, and therefore, an attempt should be made to locate differences and remove the causes creating such differences. The differences in cost accounting practices of different firms may be due to the following reasons:

(i) *Difference in nature, size and organisational set-up of business enterprises*—Managing personnel, division of labour, division of work, number and size of department, services provided, smaller firms, larger firms, salary and wage structure.

(ii) *Methods of production*—Use of plant and equipment, degree of mechanisation, manufacturing process or operation, sequence in processing.

(iii) *Use of cost accounting principles and procedures*—Different methods of pricing materials issues, methods of wage payment, classifications, apportionment and absorption of overheads, methods of depreciation, treatment of administrative and selling and distribution overheads.

AREAS OF UNIFORMITY

Uniform costing requires uniformity in cost accounting principles and procedures especially in the following areas:

1. *General classifications of accounts* Uniformity in classification and codification of accounts should be maintained.
2. *Method of overhead allotment* The basis on which the various overheads should be allotted to producing and servicing departments should be followed by all members of the industry groups using uniform costing.
3. *Method of overhead absorption* Uniformity in the method of overhead absorption is most important.
4. *Scrap and losses* The general method of treatment to be accorded to scrap and losses should be specified. The method of dealing with income from the sale of waste products should also be specified.
5. *Joint costs* The treatment of joint costs is also very important and a uniform method should be followed. It should also be decided as to which costs should or should not be included in cost.

UNIFORM COST MANUAL

The designing and applications of uniform costing require that a uniform cost manual containing instructions, clarifications, rules and guidelines about cost determination, cost analysis and cost control, should be developed and circulated among the business enterprises that have decided to use uniform costing. A uniform cost manual usually contains the following materials:

1. *Introduction* The introduction of the manual describes the statement of objectives of the system, scope of the system, advantages to be achieved and its basic features.
2. *Accounting organisation* It contains a scheme of organisation for designing and operating the cost accounting system.
3. *Accounting system* It contains general principles of accounting, a coding system, terminology, classification and description of accounts.
4. *Cost accounting system* It describes methods of costing (job, process, standard costing, etc.), system of integration in accounts, relation between cost and financial accounts, items to be included or excluded in stocks, classification of departments into producing and servicing, treatment of materials cost and materials losses, pricing of materials issues, classification of materials into direct and indirect, classification of labour cost and treatment of labour related costs such as idle time, overtime, holidays and shift allowances, etc., classification, collection, apportionment and absorption of overhead, calculation of depreciation, treatment of under- and over-absorption.
5. *Presentation of information* This section clearly describes how the cost information should be presented. It contains forms and contents of statements to be prepared, forms of reports to management, forms of report to shareholders, detailed operation and production costs, cost ratios, financial ratios and other supplementary information.

INTER-FIRM COMPARISON

Inter-firm comparison is the technique of evaluating the performance efficiencies, costs and profits of firms in an industry. Inter-firm comparison is greatly facilitated if uniform costing has been used. Inter-firm comparison requires exchanges of information relating to costs, profits, prices, efficiency on a voluntary basis among participating firms. Trade and commerce associations usually employ accountants to collect cost information about business firms and make inter-firm comparisons.

ESSENTIALS OF INTER-FIRM COMPARISON

Inter-firm comparison can succeed when uniform costing principles and procedures have been used among member business firms. The following are the important requirements of inter-firm comparison:

1. *Nature and extent of information to be accumulated* Inter-firm comparison requires that all relevant and detailed cost information should be collected regarding business firms. No definite list of information can be suggested for collection. However, the following are the usual information which are applicable to all industries and therefore can be collected for inter-firm comparison:
   - (i) Information regarding cost and cost structure.
   - (ii) Labour efficiency and labour utilisation.
   - (iii) Machine efficiency and machine utilisation.
   - (iv) Raw materials consumed, wastage and stores-keeping.
   - (v) Return on capital employed.
   - (vi) Liquidity and liquid resources.
   - (vii) Reserve and appropriation of profits.

(viii) Debtors and creditors.
(ix) Methods of production and technical aspects.
(x) Inventory and inventory systems.

2. *Responsibility for collection, coordination and presentation of information* In some countries, separate organisations have been established for collecting and presenting information. In India, inter-firm comparison information is collected by various trade associations, chambers of commerce, the National Productivity Council, research and statistics divisions of several commerce and trade journals and periodicals and newspapers.
3. *Method of collection and presentation of information* Information for the purpose of inter-firm comparison is usually supplied by business enterprises to organisation(s) regularly. Information can be collected by field workers also. After the information is collected, it is properly compiled and arranged and finally a consolidated report is prepared for the benefit of business firms. For the information to be purposeful, it is essential that participating firms should agree about the meaning of various terms used in ratios and accounting information.

BENEFITS OF INTER-FIRM COMPARISON

Inter-firm comparison has the following advantages:

1. It makes a business firm aware of its limitations as compared to other in the industry.
2. It eliminates confusion and uncertainty and encourages business firms to take some positive steps to improve performance and increase efficiency.
3. Information about the industry and business is available which is useful to present and prospective business entrepreneurs.
4. Reporting of data on business firms is generally treated free from bias.
5. Useful data about business enterprises becomes available to government for formulating economic, commercial and other policies for the well-being of the nation.

LIMITATIONS OF INTER-FIRM COMPARISON

1. Business firms may be afraid that disclosure of information may help competitors, and may thus be reluctant to part with facts which are detrimental to their interests.
2. Some management are not convinced about the utility of inter-firm comparison.
3. If business firms have not established suitable cost accounting systems, the information supplied by them may not be usable for inter-firm comparison.
4. Business firms usually do not agree about a common suitable basis for comparison.

However, the above limitations are basically due to differences in the nature of participating business firms and use of accounting methods. Therefore, a uniform cost accounting system should be established in every participating firm and business firms should be educated about the advantages and uses of inter-firm comparison.

Theory Questions

1. Explain the concept of "uniform costing". What is a uniform costing manual?
2. What principal factors should be considered in introducing a system of uniform costing in an industry?

3. What is a uniform cost accounting system? What are the items on which you would seek uniformity so far as overheads are concerned in a uniform cost accounting system?
4. "A scheme of inter-firm comparison combines the advantages of a uniform costing system and the benefits arising out of the use of ratios." Discuss.
5. Discuss the scope and applications of uniform costing methods and their usefulness especially in the context of the economy of our country. Assume that you are advising a trade association in this regard in the interest of its member firms and outline your views and suggestions.
6. Why is inter-firm comparison desirable? What are the essential points that should be considered in inter-firm comparison? What are its advantages?
7. What are the purposes of uniform costing when it is introduced in an industry under a federation? What are the basic requirements of uniform costing?
8. Explain in brief, the advantages and limitations of uniform costing.
9. State the essential requirements for the installation of uniform costing system in an industry.

Chapter 23

Cost Audit

Learning Objectives

After reading this chapter, you should be able to:

1. discuss meaning,objectives and advantages of cost audit, its preparation and scope;
2. distinguish between financial and cost audit, efficiency and cost audit;
3. explain concept and scope of management audit;
4. list some important areas requiring cost reduction within the management audit;
5. describe areas of activity for which accounting records are to be maintained under Cost Accounting Record Rules; and
6. explain the concept, advantages and procedure of value analysis.

MEANING OF COST AUDIT

The Institute of Cost and Management Accountants (UK) defines cost audit "as the verification of cost accounts and a check on the adherence to the cost accounting plan". Cost audit is verifying the correctness of cost accounts, cost reports, cost data and costing methods.

OBJECTIVES OF COST AUDIT

In the beginning years, cost audit was taken merely as a tool for "price control mechanism" for consumer and infrastructure industries in India. The main objective of cost audit in the Companies Act, 2013 is to meet the government requirements for regulating the price mechanism in core industries. The objective is to provide an authentic data to the government to regulate the demand and supply in the country through a price control mechanism. The liberalisation of the economy and consequential globalisation has further enhanced the need for authentic and correct data.

Cost audit has both general and social objectives. The *general objectives* of cost audit are as follows:

- Verification of cost accounts with a view to ascertaining that these have been properly maintained and compiled according to the cost accounting system followed by the enterprise.
- Ensuring that the prescribed procedures of cost accounting records rules are duly adhered to for detection of errors and frauds.

- Verification of the cost of each "cost unit" and "cost centre" to ensure that these have been properly ascertained.
- Determination of inventory valuation.
- Facilitating the fixation of prices of goods and services.
- Periodical reconciliation between cost accounts and financial accounts.
- Ensuring optimum utilisation of human, physical and financial resources of the enterprise.
- Detection and correction of abnormal loss of material and time.
- Inculcation of cost consciousness.
- Advising management, on the basis of inter-firm comparison of cost records, in the areas where performance calls for improvement.
- Promoting corporate governance through various operational disclosures to the directors.

The *social objectives* of cost audit are as follows:

- Assisting in fixation of reasonable prices of goods and services produced by the enterprise.
- Improvement in productivity of human, physical and financial resources of the enterprise.
- Channelising of enterprise resources to most optimum, productive and profitable areas.
- Availability of audited cost data as regards contracts containing escalation clauses.
- Facilitation in settlement of bills in the case of cost-plus contracts entered into by the Government.
- Highlighting areas of inefficiency and mismanagement, if any for the benefit of shareholders, consumers, etc., so that necessary corrective actions could be taken in time.

Central Government to Specify Audit of Items of Cost in respect of Certain Companies [Section 148]

(1) The Central Government may, by order, in respect of such class of companies engaged in the production of such goods or providing such services as may be prescribed, direct that particulars relating to the utilisation of material or labour or to other items of cost as may be prescribed shall also be included in the books of account kept by that class of companies.
Provide that the Central Government shall, before issuing such order in respect of any class of companies regulated under a special Act, consult the regulatory body constituted or established under special Act.

(2) If the Central Government is of the opinion, that it is necessary to do so, it may, by order, direct that the audit of cost records of class of companies, which are covered under sub-section (1) and which have a net worth of such amount as may be prescribed or a turnover of such amount as may be prescribed, shall be conducted in the manner specified in the order.

(3) The audit under sub-section (2) shall be conducted by a Cost Accountant in practice who shall be appointed by the Board on such remuneration as may be determined by the members in such manner as may be prescribed.
Provided that no person appointed under section 139 as an auditor of the company shall be appointed for conducting the audit of cost records.
Provided further that the auditor conducting the cost audit shall comply with the cost auditing standards.
Explanation: For the purpose of this sub-section, the expression "cost auditing standards" mean such standards as are issued by the Institute of Cost and Works Accountants of India, constituted under the Cost and Works Accountants Act, 1959, with the approval of the Central Government.

(4) An audit conducted under this section shall be in addition to the audit conducted under Section 143.

(5) The qualifications, disqualifications, rights, duties and obligations applicable to auditors under this Chapter shall, so far as may be applicable, apply to a cost auditor appointed under this section and it shall be the duty of the company to give all assistance and facilities to the cost auditor appointed under this section for auditing the cost records of the company.
Provided that the report on the audit of cost records shall be submitted by the cost accountant in practice to the Board of Directors of the company.

(6) A company shall within thirty days from the date of receipt of a copy of the cost audit report prepared in pursuance of a direction under sub-section (2) furnish the Central Government with such report along with full information and explanation on every reservation or qualification contained therein.

(7) If, after considering the cost audit report referred to under this section and the information and explanation furnished by the company under sub-section (6), the Central Government is of the opinion that any further information or explanation is necessary, it may call for such further information and explanation and the company shall furnish the same within such time as may be specified by that Government.

(8) If any default is made in complying with the provisions of this section,—
  (a) the company and every officer of the company who is in default shall be punishable in the manner as provided in sub-section (1) of section 147;
  (b) the cost auditor of the company who is in default shall be punishable in the manner as provided in sub-sections (2) to (4) of section 147.

ADVANTAGES OF COST AUDIT

Cost audit is useful to many parties such as (i) management, (ii) shareholder, (iii) statutory auditor, and (iv) government and consumers.

(i) *Management* Cost audit adds reliability to cost statements and cost data. It helps in detection of errors, frauds and irregularities. Management can make sound decisions on the basis of correct and reliable cost data.

(ii) *Shareholders* Cost audit increases the reliability of many cost data which are used by shareholders to analyse the financial position of a business firm.

(iii) *Statutory Auditor* Statutory auditor is also benefitted if cost system has been set up in an organisation. The statutory auditor can determine scope of his audit and make audit programme after evaluating cost accounting system used in organisation.

(iv) *Government and Consumers* Government needs cost data for many purposes such as fixation of prices, cost plus contract, productivity measurement, evaluation of management efficiency, week points of management and organisation. All these activities require that cost data should be correct and reliable which is possible if a good costing system has been followed in an organisation.

FINANCIAL AUDIT AND COST AUDIT

Financial audit is the audit of financial accounts whereas cost audit is the audit of cost accounts. Financial audit aims to know whether the financial statements, namely, profit and loss account and balance sheet present a true and fair view of the business result and state of affairs of a business enterprise or not. On the other hand, cost audit aims to determine the correctness of cost figures of each activity after proper analysis. Cost audit focuses on propriety of expenditure and efficiency of performance.

Financial audit is related with only historical figures and data after the expenditures have been incurred and accounts have been prepared. Cost audit is performed with the help of budgets and therefore has a futuristic focus.

EFFICIENCY AUDIT AND COST AUDIT

Efficiency audit ensures that the resources flow into the most remunerative channels, namely. (a) every rupee invested in capital or in other fields gives optimum return; and (b) the planning of investment between the different functions and aspects is designed to give optimum results. The financial auditor does not comment on the performance efficiency of the company.

Since an appraisal of the extent of efficiency of utilisation of factors of production is done in cost audit, it is rightly called "efficiency audit".

The following are the evidences to prove that cost audit is efficiency audit:

(i) The Cost Auditor has to report in para (3) of the annexure*, the financial position of the company, giving *inter alia*—financial ratios like profit as % of capital, profit as % of net sales, current assets expressed as % of current liabilities, cost of production as % of capital employed, and working capital as % of cost of production. These ratios are useful for assessment of operational efficiency and comparing the financial health of one undertaking with another as well as for measurement of internal efficiency.

(ii) The Cost Audit Report under Para 4 of the annexure reflects the installed capacity and actual capacity utilised as well as analysis of the reasons for shortfall in actual capacity utilised as compared to installed capacity.

(iii) Under Para 6 of the annexure to Cost Audit Report, an analytical study of the consumption of raw materials per unit of production both in quantity and in value is made.

(iv) Under Para 7, the cost auditor is expected to comment on the consumption of power and fuel in total as well as per unit of output.

(v) The Cost Auditor has to report on the direct labour cost per unit of output of the product under cost audit alongwith brief explanation for variation in the cost, as compared to two preceding years.

(vi) The details of expenditure under overheads, with reasons for significant variation in expenditure as compared to preceding two years, particularly increase in overhead expenditure without corresponding increase in turnover or output of the product under cost audit has to be commented upon in Para 11 of annexure to Cost Audit Report.

(vii) The Cost Audit Report, under Para 9, contains information regarding consumption of stores and spare parts per unit of output which serves as a good indicator of upkeep of machines.

(viii) The Cost Audit Report contains information regarding the extent of non-moving items of stores as compared to the total inventory (vide Para 9 of Annexure to the report).

---

* The Department of Company Affairs, Government of India has framed Cost Accounting Record Rules which contains format of Cost Audit Report and an Annexure containing the guidelines for preparing Cost Audit Report by the cost auditor.

(ix) In Para 13 of Annexure to the Cost Audit Report, the profitability of other exports from the company has to be commented upon.

(x) A cost auditor is expected to offer comments on various matters like rectification of imbalances in production facilities, fuller utilisation of installed capacities, increased productivity, limiting factors causing production bottlenecks and improved inventory policies.

(xi) A cost auditor is also expected to offer comments on the budgetary control systems and internal audit systems, prevailing in the organisation.

Thus, it can be established that no other audit except cost audit is so well-designed to bring about the efficiency aspect of operations of a manufacturing unit in such elaborate detail.

MANAGEMENT AUDIT

Management audit is a detailed and critical review of all aspects of the management. Management audit encompasses all facets of managerial operations, including internal controls, and ascertaining the extent of compliance with established policies, plans and procedures within an organisation. Management audit is sometimes known as operational audit. The basic objectives of a management audit are to:

(i) help management to manage better;
(ii) improve organisational profitability; and
(iii) ensure that management objectives are being met.

The management audit covers a very vast and broad scope and extends beyond the scrutiny of books of accounts to areas such as production, maintenance, materials management, consumption of inputs, marketing, personnel matters, etc. Technical aspects are also involved.

Scope of Management Audit

Some important areas which management audit should probe to evaluate the performance efficiency to ascertain the drawbacks in the systems and procedures and to make suggestions to the management for remedial action and better control, could be the following:

(i) Production performance; (ii) sales performance; (iii) capacity utilisation; (iv) inventory holdings; (v) liquidity position; (vi) consumption efficiencies; (vii) costs of production; (viii) preventive maintenance; (ix) idle capacity; (x) purchases; (xi) receivables; (xii) overtime; and (xiii) controllable expenses.

Potent Tool for Managerial Control

Management audit as the eyes and ears of the management can bring to focus the weak areas of the operation and bring the improvement in the operational efficiency by interaction with the functionaries and highlighting these areas to the top management for improvement in the systems, procedures and methods of internal control. It is, thus a potent tool for managerial control.

Cost Reduction through Improvement in the Performance Efficiency

Cost of production is directly related with the operational efficiency and continuous efforts to improve operational efficiency. It will result in the reduction of costs and increase in the profitability. Some important areas needing a probe and suggestions towards reduction of costs by management audit could be:

(i) Input mix and cheaper substitutes; (ii) consumption efficiencies; (iii) preventive maintenance to reduce idle capacity; (iv) utilisation and performance of plant and machinery; (v) control in inventory holdings; (vi) economic purchases; (vii) improvement of sales turnover of products having high P/V ratio; (viii) control over recoverable; (ix) control over overtime; (x) improvement of industrial relations.

PREPARATION OF COST AUDIT

Before starting the cost audit, an auditor should acquaint himself with several factors such as the following:

1. Cost accounting system used in organisation.
2. Production methods and manufacturing processes.
3. Information about raw materials and components used in production.
4. Concessions received from government, if any.
5. Memorandum and Articles of Association and important point mentioned therein about the costing requirements.
6. Information about cost records and documents.
7. Cost Accounting Rules or Cost Accounting Manual used in the organisation.

SCOPE OF THE COST AUDIT

Cost audit covers the following important areas:

1. *Materials:* The cost auditor generally verifies the following items relating to materials:
   (i) Goods inward procedure
   (ii) Store-keeping arrangement.
   (iii) Accounting for scrap, wastage, materials transfers.
   (iv) Perpetual inventory system.
   (v) Materials pricing methods used.
   (vi) Adequacy of stock checking methods.
2. *Wages:*
   (i) Documents used in preparation of payroll.
   (ii) Wage rate changes authorisation for wage payments and overtime payments.
   (iii) Time recording.
   (iv) Internal check system.
3. *Overhead:*
   (i) Classification of overhead.
   (ii) Overhead budgets.
   (iii) Apportionment and allocation of overhead.
   (iv) Methods of absorption.
   (v) Policy regarding inclusion of overhead in work-in-progress.
   (vi) Accounting treatment of under- or over-absorption.
4. *General:*
   (i) Methods of establishing standards, revision of standards.
   (ii) Methods of calculating standards cost variances.
   (iii) Accounting codes and instructions.

COST AUDIT REPORT RULES

In exercise of the powers conferred by sub-section (4) of section 233 B, read with sub-section (1) of section 227 and clause (b) of sub-section (1) of section 642, of the Companies Act, 1956 (1 of 1956), and in supersession of the Cost Audit (Report) Rules, 1996, except as things done or omitted to be done, before such supersession, the Central Government hereby makes the following rules, namely:

1. Short title and commencement —

(1) These rules may be called the Cost Audit Report Rules, 2001;

(2) They shall come into force on the date of their publication in the Official Gazette.

2. Definitions — In these rules, unless the context otherwise requires —

(a) "Act means the Companies Act, 1956 (1 of 1956);

(b) "Cost Auditor" means an auditor directed to conduct an audit under sub-section (1) of section 233B of the Act;

(c) "Form" means the Form of the Cost Audit Report and includes auditor's observations and suggestions, Annexure and Proforma to the Cost Audit Report;

(d) "Report" means Cost Audit Report duly audited and signed by the Cost Auditor in the prescribed form of Cost Audit Report;

(e) "Product under reference" means the product or activity to which the report relates;

(f) All other words and expressions used in these rules but not defined, and defined in the Act and rules made under clause (d) of sub-section (1) of section 209 of the Act shall have the same meanings as assigned to them in the Act or rules, as the case may be.

3. Application — These rules shall apply to every company in respect of which an audit of the cost accounting records has been ordered by the Central Government under sub-section (1) of section 233B of the Act. The Cost Audit Report submitted on or after 1st October, 2002, irrespective of the financial year of the company to which it relates, shall be in the form prescribed under these rules.

4. Form of the Report — (1) Every Cost Auditor, who conducts an audit of the cost accounting records of the company shall submit the report (a hard copy and a soft copy) along with auditor's observations and suggestions, Annexure and Proforma to the Central Government in the prescribed form and at the same time forward a copy of the report to the company.

(2) Every Cost Auditor, who submits a report under sub-rule (1), shall also give clarifications, if any, required by the Central Government on the Cost Audit Report submitted by him, within thirty days of the receipt of the communication addressed to him calling for such clarifications.

(3) The forms prescribed in these rules may be filed through electronic media or through any other computer readable media as referred under section 610A of the Companies Act, 1956 (1 of 1956).

(4) The electronic form shall be authenticated by the authorised signatories using digital signatures, as defined under the Information Technology Act, 2000 (21 of 2000).

(5) The forms prescribed in these rules, when filed in physical form, may be authenticated by authorised signatory by affixing his signature manually.*

5. Time limit for submission of Report — The Cost Auditor shall forward his report referred to in sub-rule (1) of rule 4 to the Central Government and to the concerned company within one hundred and eighty days from the close of the company's financial year to which the report relates.

* Inserted by Notification No. GSR 148 (E) dated 8th March 2006.

6. Cost Auditor to be furnished with the cost accounting records etc. — Without prejudice to the powers and duties the Cost Auditor shall have under sub-section (4) of section 233B of the Act, the company and every officer thereof, including the persons referred to in sub-section (6) of section 209 of the Act, shall make available to the Cost Auditor within one hundred and thirty five days from the close of the financial year of the company, such cost accounting records, cost statements, other books and documents, Annexure and Proforma to the Report, duly completed, as would be required for conducting the cost audit, and shall render necessary assistance to the Cost Auditor so as to enable him to complete the cost audit and submit his report within the time limit specified in rule 5.

7. Authentication of Annexure to the Cost Audit Report — The Annexure and Proforma prescribed with the Cost Audit Report shall be approved by the Board of Directors before submitting the same to the Central Government by the Cost Auditor. The Annexure and Proforma, duly audited by the Cost Auditor, shall also be signed by the Company Secretary and at least one Director on behalf of the company. In the absence of Company Secretary in the company, the same shall be signed by at least two Directors.

8. Penalties — (1) If default is made by the Cost Auditor in complying with the provisions of rule 4 or rule 5, he shall he punishable with fine, which may extend to five thousand rupees.

(2) If the company contravenes the provisions of rule 6 or 7, the company and every officer thereof who is in default, including the persons referred to in sub-rule (6) of section 209 of the Act, shall subject to the provisions of section 233B of the Act, be punishable with fine which may extend to five thousand rupees and where the contravention is a continuing one, with a further fine which may extend to five hundred rupees for every day after the first day during which such contravention continues.

9. Saving of action taken or that may be taken for contravention of Cost Audit (Report) Rules, 1996 — It is hereby clarified that the supersession of tile Cost Audit (Report) Rules, 1996, shall not in any way affect—

(i) any right, obligation or liability acquired, accrued or incurred thereunder;
(ii) any penalty forfeiture of punishment incurred in respect of any contravention committed thereunder;
(iii) any investigation, legal proceeding or remedy in respect of any such right, privilege, obligation, liability, penalty, forfeiture or punishment as aforesaid, and any such investigation, legal proceeding or remedy may be instituted, continued or enforced and any such penalty, forfeiture or punishment may be imposed as if those rules had not been superseded.

SPECIMEN OF COST AUDIT REPORT

[See rule 2(c) and rule 4]

I/We, ... having been appointed a Cost Auditor(s) under section 233B of the Companies Act, 1956 (1 of 1956) of .... (mention name of the company) having its registered office at .... (mention registered office address of the company) (hereinafter referred to as the company), have examined the books of account prescribed under clause (d) of sub-section (1) of section 209 of the said Act, and other relevant records in respect of the unit .... (mention name and location of the unit) for the period/year .... (mention the financial year) relating to .... (mention name of the product or activity) maintained by the company and report, in addition to my/our comments in para 3 relating to auditor's observations and suggestions, that —

1. (i) I/We have/have not obtained all the information and explanations, which to the best of my/our knowledge and belief were necessary for the purpose of this audit,

   (ii) proper cost accounting records, as prescribed under clause (d) of sub-section (1) of section 209 of the Companies Act, 1956, have/have not been kept by the company;

   (iii) proper returns adequate for the purpose of my/our Cost Audit have/have not been received from the branches not visited by me/us.

   (iv) the said books and records give/do not give the information required by the Companies Act, 1956 in the manner so required.

   (v) the cost statements in respect of product or activity under reference as specified in the Annexures/Performance of Schedule I, Schedule II or Schedule III of the concerned Cost Accounting Records (** ....) Rules duly audited by me/us are kept in the company.

2. In my/our opinion, the company's cost accounting records have/have not been properly kept so as to give a true and fair view of the cost of production, cost of sales and margin of the product under reference as prescribed under the rules.

3. Based on my/our examination of the records of the company subject to aforesaid qualifications, if any, I/We give my/our observations and suggestions on the following—

   (a) the adequacy or otherwise of the cost accounting system including inventory valuation in vogue in the company and suggestions for the improvement thereof. The Cost Auditor shall also indicate the persistent deficiencies in the system, pointed out in earlier reports but not rectified;

   (b) the adequacy or otherwise of the budgetary control system, if any, in vogue in the company;

   (c) matters which appear to him to be clearly wrong in principle or apparently unjustifiable;

   (d) cases, where price charged for related party transactions as defined in the respective Cost Accounting Records Rules is different from normal price, impact of such lower/higher price on margin of the product under reference shall be specified;

   (e) areas where the company is incurring losses or where there is considerable decline in profitability, the cost auditor should comment on the reasons thereof including indicative break-even point. The Cost Auditor shall also comment on the default, if any on the payments due to the Government, financial institutions and banks, penal interest levied thereon and its impact on the cost of sales and profitability;

   (f) steps required to strengthen the company under the competitive environment especially with regard to need for protection from cheaper imports, if any;

   (g) export commitments of the company vís-a-vís actual exports for the year under review. Also comment on comparative profitability and pricing policy of the company for domestic and export sales. Give impact of exports benefits/incentives offered by the Government on export profitability;

   (h) the scope and performance of internal audit of cost records, if any, and comment on its adequacy or otherwise.

4. The Cost Auditor shall suggest measures for making further improvements in the performance in respect of cost control and cost reduction.

5. The Cost Auditor may also give his other observations and suggestions, if any, relevant in the cost audit.

Dated: this .... date of .... 200...
at .... (mention name of place of signing this report)

Signature & Seal of the Cost Auditor (s)
Membership Number

Notes:

1. Delete words not applicable.
2. **Specify the title of the concerned Cost Accounting Records Rules made under clause (d) of sub-section (1) of section 209 of the Companies Act, 1956 which are applicable to the product or activity of the company.
3. If, as a result of the examination of the books of account, the Cost Auditor desires to point out any material deficiency or give a qualified report, he shall indicate the same against the relevant paras (i) to (vi) only in the prescribed form of the Cost Audit Report giving details of discrepancies he has come across.
4. The report, suggestions, observations and conclusions given by the Cost Auditor under this paragraph shall be based on verified data, reference to which shall be made here and shall, wherever practicable be included after the company has been afforded an opportunity to comment on them.

ANNEXURE TO THE COST AUDIT REPORT

The following Annexures are required to be attached alongwith the Cost Audit Report.

1. General.
2. Cost Accounting System.
3. Process of Manufacture.
4. Quantitative Details.

5(A) Major Input Materials/Components consumed.
5(B) Standard/Actual Consumption of Input Materials per unit.
6. Break-up of Cost of Input Materials imported during the year.
7(A) Power, Fuel and Utilities.
7(B) Standard/Actual Consumption of Power, Fuel and Utilities in Terms of Quantity Per Unit of Production.
8. Salaries and Wages.
9. Repairs and Maintenance.
10. Fixed Assets Register and Depreciation.
11. Gross Block, Depreciation and Lease Rent.
12. Overheads.
13. Research and Development Expenses.
14. Royalty and Technical Knowhow Charges.
15. Quality Control Expenses.
16. Pollution Control Expenses.
17. Abnormal Non-recurring Costs.
18(A) Non-moving Stock (at the end of the year).
18(B) Written off stock (during the year).
19(A) Inventory Valuation (at the end of the year).
19(B) Physical Verification of Inventory.

20. Sales of the Product under Reference.
21. Margin per unit of Output.
22. Competitive Margin Against Imports.
23. Value Addition and Distribution of Earnings.
24. Financial Position and Ratio Analysis.
25. Capitalisation of Revenue Expenditure.
26. Related Party Transactions.
27. Central Excise Reconciliation for the Product under Reference.
28. Profit Reconciliation.

VALUE ANALYSIS

Value analysis or value engineering is a technique applied to analyse all aspects of an existing product or component to determine the minimum cost necessary for specific function requirements. This may result in various alterations being made to the product with object of reducing costs.

Advantages of Value Analysis

The primary advantage of value analysis is reduction in product cost. Some other advantages are the following:

1. Value analysis improves sale and customer satisfaction since it determines the exact requirements of customers and product designing is done accordingly.
2. The quality of the product is improved.
3. The latest methods of production and technology are used in product manufacture.
4. By simplification and standardisation of design and method, problems and complexities in production methods are eliminated.
5. It coordinates all managerial functions and builds up a spirit of cooperation and team work.
6. It helps in accomplishing effective utilisation of production resources like capital, employees, materials, time, etc.

Procedure of Value Analysis

Value analysis basically consists of determining the essential characteristics of a product that the customer requires and determining the most economical method of producing it by balancing cost with the utility of the product. The following are the steps involved in value analysis:

1. *Collecting relevant information* All necessary information about a product is first gathered, such as physical characteristics, materials specification, product costs like materials, labour and overhead, market, competitive products, production methods, etc.
2. *Deciding alternatives* All alternatives are to be developed and the most appropriate alternative is to be decided upon in terms of suitability of method and costs involved. That alternative is considered best which gives the best satisfaction to customers and reduces the cost.
3. *Approval for the accepted alternative* Management should approve the best alternative and give authority for the development of the modified or revised product.
4. *Execution* Production drawings and models are developed and production is done accordingly.
5. *Follow-up* Finally, the extent of cost reduction that has been achieved should be investigated.

Theory Questions

1. What are the areas of activity which a cost audit programme is expected to cover?
2. "The statutory cost audit under the provisions of the Indian Companies Act is also intended to sub-serve social interests." Comment.
3. Distinguish between:
   (i) Cost audit and financial audit
   (ii) Cost audit and management audit.
4. "Cost audit is a necessity and not a luxury and is viewed as a barometer to measure the operational performance, the effectiveness of utilisation and working results." Illustrate.
5. Explain the advantages of cost audit.
6. Is it correct to say that cost audit is efficiency audit? Give arguments.
7. Discuss the aspects usually covered in management audit.
8. What areas are covered in cost audit?
9. Explain the concept of value analysis as a technique of cost reduction.
10. Discuss the purpose of cost audit and circumstances under which a cost audit is desirable.
11. What as a cost auditor will you verify in the area of work-in-progress?
12. Define cost audit. How is it useful to the following?
    (i) Management (ii) Society
    (iii) Share holders (iv) Government?
13. What are the areas of activity which a cost audit programme is expected to cover?

CASE STUDY

Value-Chain Analysis – A Case of Spectron Dilemma

Spectron Ltd., based in Bangalore, was dealing in assembling and trading of computers. It purchased computer parts from various suppliers and sold them to its distributors across south India region. The company assembled computers based on demand and followed JIT for most of its parts. Lately, because of most of the established companies reducing the prices for their computers, Spectron was facing major competition and reduction in the demand for its product.

To tackle the situation, Spectron MD, R. Raghavan hired a consultant Mr. Krishnan to analyse the situation and suggest changes in the cost and pricing of the products. Krishnan, after a week of studying the various costs related to assembling of the computers couldn't find any way of cost reduction. He then proceeded to look at the vendors for various parts. He started with the Fan (heat sink) and Sound cards and identified the vendors for it. Spectron submitted to him the following details related to the two vendors Norton Electronics and Sintara Electronics supplying these parts:

	Norton Electronics		*Sintara Electronics*	
	Fan	*Sound card*	*Fan*	*Sound card*
Purchase price per unit (₹)	11	26	12	28
No. of units purchased	40,000	20,000	5,000	5,000

Krishnan realised that Spectron used to purchase these parts majorly from Norton Electronics for the obvious reasons of lesser price. At the same time, the company did not want to depend on a single vendor and therefore also procured these parts in small numbers from Sintara Electronics.

Upon further analysis, Krishnan could also identify some more costs related to these parts. They were costs related to repair of defective pieces of these fans and sound cards which amounted to ₹2,00,000 and also overtime paid to compensate for late delivery amounting to ₹50,000. He found that fan and sound cards, although brought at a cheaper price, were not always 100% defect-free. Krishnan got hold of the detail that out of 40,000 fans purchased from Norton, 800 were defective and also that out of 20,000 sound cards purchased, 190 needed repairs. The number of defective fans and sound cards from Sintara out of 5,000 pieces purchased each were 6 and 4 respectively.

Krishnan discovered that Sintara Electronics followed the JIT policy religiously and not once did it delivered the consignment late. Norton, on the other hand, delayed the delivery of fans to Spectron 30 times in the year and 20 times was responsible for the late shipment of sound cards.

Based on his discovery and analysis thereon, Krishnan submitted his report to Spectron Computers. The report suggested that the company should change its policy of buying majorly from Norton and instead purchase maximum number of parts from Sintara. Spectron MD—Raghavan was surprised to read the report as he could not understand the basis of this suggestion.

✎ QUESTION FOR DISCUSSION:

Why do you think Krishnan gave the suggestion to purchase the computer parts—fan and sound cards from Sintara instead of Norton? Show your answer through calculating the costs related to purchase of fan and sound cards from both the suppliers.

Index

P

Q

R

S

T